# › accounting ›› ‹‹ INFORMATION systems ››››››

*understanding business processes* ››

3rd edition

# › accounting ››
# ‹‹ INFORMATION
# systems ››››››

## *understanding business processes* ››

### 3rd edition

brett considine ‹‹ alison parkes
karin olesen ‹‹ derek speer ‹‹ michael lee

**WILEY**

John Wiley & Sons Australia, Ltd

Third edition published in 2010 by
John Wiley & Sons Australia, Ltd
42 McDougall Street, Milton, Qld 4064

Second edition published 2008 by
© Brett Considine, Abdul Razeed, Michael Lee, Derek Speer, Philip Collier 2008

First edition published 2005
© Brett Considine, Abdul Razeed, Michael Lee, Philip Collier 2005

Typeset in 9.5/12 pt ITC Giovanni LT

The moral rights of the authors have been asserted.

National Library of Australia
Cataloguing-in-Publication entry

| | |
|---|---|
| Title: | Accounting information systems: understanding business processes / Brett Considine ... [et al.]. |
| Edition: | 3rd ed. |
| ISBN: | 9781742165554 (pbk.) |
| Target Audience: | For tertiary students. |
| Subjects: | Accounting—Data processing—Textbooks. Information storage and retrieval systems— Accounting Textbooks. |
| Other Authors/ Contributors: | Considine, Brett. |
| Dewey Number: | 657.0285 |

Typeset in India by diacriTech

Printed in China by
1010 Printing International Limited

10 9 8 7 6 5 4 3 2 1

## Brett Considine

Brett Considine is a lecturer in the Department of Accounting and Finance at Macquarie University. He completed a Bachelor of Commerce degree (with Honours) at Melbourne University in 1999, with a specialisation in accounting and accounting information systems. He has taught at Macquarie University in the areas of introductory accounting, auditing and accounting information systems, as well as at The University of Melbourne in the areas of accounting information systems and introductory accounting. Brett has also taught across a number of the residential colleges affiliated with The University of Melbourne, including Trinity, Ormond, Queen's, Newman and International House. Additionally, Brett has completed a Graduate Diploma in Education (Secondary) at Australian Catholic University and has some secondary school teaching experience.

## Alison Parkes

Alison Parkes is a senior lecturer in the Department of Accounting and Business Information Systems at The University of Melbourne. She spent the first decade of her career as a CPA, and then moved to more systems-focused areas, ultimately spending seven years as a senior project manager leading multidisciplinary teams implementing large-scale financial systems. Alison holds a Bachelor of Commerce (Accounting) from the University of Wollongong; a Masters (Honours) in Business Systems from Massey University, New Zealand; and a PhD in Business Information Systems from The University Of Melbourne. She teaches accounting information systems in the graduate school of the Business and Economics faculty at The University of Melbourne, and has twice been awarded a dean's certificate of teaching excellence. Her research, which has been published in numerous conferences and journals, explores various forms of human–computer interactions with a particular focus in the performance implications and behavioural consequences of technology design choices.

## Karin Olesen

Karin Olesen is a lecturer in the Department of Accounting at AUT University. She holds a Bachelor of Commerce in Accounting & Finance, a Masters (with First Class Honours) and a PhD in Information Systems. She has 18 years' experience in teaching at AUT and The University of Auckland in the Information Systems and Operations Management Department across diverse subject areas, including accounting information systems, introductory accounting, advanced financial reporting, financial modelling, knowledge management systems, and digital media production at undergraduate and postgraduate levels. The first part of Karin's career was spent in company and chartered accounting as a financial accountant involved in business planning, budgeting, financial reporting, implementation of accounting systems and taxation preparation for multiple organisations.

## Derek Speer

Derek Speer holds both a Bachelor of Commerce and a Master of Commerce in Accounting with equivalent First Class Honours from The University of Auckland. He is a lecturer in the Department of Accounting and Finance at The University of

Auckland focusing principally on accounting information systems and management accounting. Prior to commencing his academic career 24 years ago he held a number of positions in industry. His research interests include public sector reform, accounting information systems, accounting education and the history of accounting information systems.

## Michael Lee

Michael Lee is an assistant professor in the W.P. Carey School of Business at Arizona State University in the United States. He teaches in the MBA program. Prior to Arizona State University, Michael completed his PhD at The University of Melbourne in accounting and business information systems and has 15 years' experience in management consulting and investment banking. Building on this experience, Michael's research activities centre on enterprise information systems and their application to management control systems strategy and design. His research draws upon organisational cases and considers the implications of business information systems on company performance. He has also written and contributed numerous finance and accounting articles. Michael was awarded a senior fellowship for his contributions and work with the Financial Services Institute of Australasia in 2002, and a certificate for teaching excellence in 2003, 2004 and 2005 at The University of Melbourne.

# ›› CONTENTS ›››

The third edition of *Accounting Information Systems* offers a uniquely Australian and New Zealand perspective of the business processes that are central to many organisations, and contains additional material and improved chapter content from the second edition. In order to maximise the benefit of its Australian context, this text uses, wherever possible, contemporary Australian and New Zealand examples and issues as a basis for explaining and exploring the many issues associated with accounting information systems (AIS).

## For students

This text offers you an Australian and New Zealand perspective of the AIS discipline. Written by a team of authors from Australia and New Zealand for an Australian and New Zealand tertiary audience, this text guides you through your studies in the AIS area. The area of accounting information systems is one to be familiar with because it presents issues that are relevant to practitioners in a range of disciplines, from auditing to accounting to general trade and commerce. In recent years the need to be abreast the areas covered in the text have been emphasised by corporate failures and the global financial crisis, both of which saw attention placed on the way organisations operate and the control structures they employ. This book will help you complete your studies in the AIS area and, while on this journey, you will gain a core set of essential skills and analytical approaches that will reap benefits for you both now and well into the future.

## For lecturers

The structure of the text allows teaching in several different ways, depending on the pedagogy of the instructor and the desired epistemological outcomes. The partitioning of the book into four sections provides flexibility of material delivery that makes sense in most sequence structures. Educationally, the text provides a range of learning and assessment material and additional end-of-chapter questions and problems. Further, each chapter employs a range of small case vignettes to illustrate, using Australian and New Zealand examples, the main ideas being conveyed in the chapter. Learning objectives relate to the major issues and themes of the chapter and are outlined at the commencement of the chapter and then emphasised in the relevant place as the chapter proceeds. The end-of-chapter review material also links to the learning objectives. This linkage allows for the setting of targeted questions based on the emphasis adopted when delivering the material to students. From a student's perspective, this structure has definite benefits, providing a clear link between the requirements of the question material and the theoretical concepts discussed throughout the chapter.

Central to the discussion throughout the book is the notion of the business process. As business processes become increasingly important to the organisation, impacting on organisational design and operation, the perspective adopted by the text makes it contemporary and relevant. The third edition sees a revamped business process section, with chapters on the revenue process (chapter 9), expenditure process (chapter 10), production process (chapter 11), human resources management and payroll process (chapter 12) and the general ledger and financial reporting process (chapter 13). The scope of these processes offers a complete and comprehensive coverage of the typical business processes within the organisation. In addition, the range of processes included means that the instructor has flexibility in which processes are covered and the extent of emphasis within their specific AIS course design.

Linked closely to the business processes is the in-depth discussion of issues in business process design and re-engineering, and how this relates to enterprise resource planning (ERP) systems. The text offers a discussion of ERP systems and also covers systems alternatives for organisations, acknowledging that the ERP approach is not a universal panacea. ERP systems for both medium and large organisations are ever evolving in the business environment and is therefore an area where this book makes a solid contribution.

Overall, content has been enhanced in the third edition, with the revision of chapters on auditing of accounting information systems; ethics, fraud and computer crime; and systems development. Two chapters have been allocated to internal controls material in the third edition — the first chapter (chapter 7) covering the general concept of internal control and its relationship to corporate governance and the second chapter (chapter 8) addressing specific control issues within the organisation. This revised structure includes greater discussion on corporate and IT governance and the COSO and COBIT frameworks for control, and includes discussion of controls within the context of the corporate governance principles put in place by the Australian Securities Exchange.

In covering this material, the link has also been made to the financial reporting process, thus providing an introduction to some of the issues considered in auditing subjects in other parts of the typical undergraduate accounting degree. This link across the various areas of the undergraduate degree is also borne out in other topics in the text; for example, the chapter on systems documentation. The intent is to reinforce the fact that the area of AIS is not standalone — it has direct relevance to the various areas of the professional accountant's roles and responsibilities. This perspective means that a comprehensive coverage of AIS issues is offered by the text, while also offering greater flexibility in the selection and sequencing of topics over the course of the semester.

Much of the other material in the text has also been revised and updated, including the business processes chapter (chapter 2), which offers introductory examples of how technology can influence the design and operation of business processes while also stressing the link between business process problems and IT-based solutions. It also reinforces the link between the overall objectives of the business, as represented by strategy, and how this flows down to the choices in the activities to be performed within the individual business processes.

Additionally, at the end of each chapter this text offers discussion questions, self-test activities in the form of multiple-choice questions, and problems. Developed in relation to the material covered throughout the chapter, these questions guide students through the various levels of understanding and application of the key concepts in the chapter, from a basic understanding of the core concepts and ideas through to the analysis and synthesis of material and application to new scenarios.

This text represents a significant effort by each of the authors in terms of meeting the deadlines to publish this edition in time for the second half of the 2010 academic year. The authors are grateful for the contributions and feedback provided by the various reviewers, who took the time to review and comment on the various chapter drafts. In particular, we extend a special thanks to the following academics who reviewed the developing manuscript providing insightful guidance and directions on improving the textbook you are about to read: Carolyn Cordery, Victoria University of Wellington; Neelam Goela, Notre Dame University; Gerard Illott, Central Queensland University;

Maria Italia, Victoria University; Cathy Michael, Victoria University; Cherry Randolph, The University of Western Australia; Alastair Robb, The University of Queensland; Pat Thomspon, The University of  Ballarat; Trevor Tonkin, The University of Melbourne; Jayantha Wickramasinghe, Massey University; Kent Wilson, University of South Australia; and Zheng Zhong, Australian National University.

In receiving this constructive feedback, the authors have attempted to accommodate the helpful suggestions received. Each of the authors would welcome any comments or suggestions about the content of the text and any suggested changes or improvements for future editions of the text.

*Brett Considine*
*Alison Parkes*
*Karin Olesen*
*Derek Speer*
*Michael Lee*
*March 2010*

## ›› ACKNOWLEDGEMENTS ›››

*The authors and publisher would like to thank the following copyright holders, organisations and individuals for their permission to reproduce copyright material in this book.*

### Images

• **p. 14:** © Virgin Blue Airlines • **p. 16:** © American Accounting Association • **p. 51:** © Sandoe et al. 'Enterprise Integration' (2001). Reprinted with permission of John Wiley & Sons, Inc. • **p. 251:** Julie Smith David, William E. McCarthy & Brian Sommer © ACM, Inc. Reprinted by permission • **p. 258:** © Julie Smith David • **p. 300:** Reproduced with permission from SAI Global under licence l00l–c010 • **p. 311:** Copyright 2001 by AICPA, reproduced with permission • **pp. 349, 350:** Copyright © 2010 Intuit lnc. All rights reserved • **pp. 397, 465:** © John Wiley & Sons, Australia • **pp. 406, 413, 418, 419, 429, 447, 457, 458, 462, 468, 470, 472, 474, 497, 511, 512, 513, 514, 517, 518, 519:** © Copyright SAP AG 2008 • **p. 466:** © Albert Lozano. Used under licence from Shutterstock • **pp. 507, 510, 513:** © IT3. www.it3inc.com • **p. 510:** Infor ERP Visual • **pp. 597, 600:** Sage Business Solutions. www.sagebusiness.com.au.

### Text

• **pp. 6–7:** Mark Jones, *The Australian Financial Review*, 19 March 2007 • **p. 7:** Copyright 2004. Reproduced with the permission of CPA Australia • **p. 8:** Copyright 2004. Reproduced with the permission of CPA Australia • **pp. 10–11:** Sue Mitchell, *The Australian Financial Review*, 12 April 2007 • **pp. 24–5:** 'Cyber criminals targeting small businesses', by Lolita C. Baldor, *AP*, 15 September 2009 • **pp. 25–6:** 'Fast Track to Recovery', by Julia Talevski, *Sydney Morning Herald*, 30 June 2009 • **pp. 31–2:** Helene Zampetakis, *The Australian Financial Review*, 30 March • **pp. 33–4:** Emma Connors, *The Australian Financial Review*, 28 March 2007 • **p. 46:** © Dick Smith Foods • **p. 56:** © Sandoe et al. 'Enterprise Integration' (2001). Reprinted with permission of John Wiley & Sons, Inc. • **pp. 58–60:** Renee Switzer, *The Age*, 20 March 2006 • **pp. 70–2:** Case study taken from 'Reengineering the corporation: a manifesto for business revolution' Michael Hammer & James Champy (Nicholas Breasley Publishing, London 2001) **pp. 39–42** • **pp. 85, 88–9, 90, 91:** © Australian Bureau of Statistics Cat. No. 8129.0 • **p. 96:** This material has been produced from the Proceedings of the Institution of Mechanical Engineers', Part B, *Journal of Engineering Manufacture*, 2003, Vol. 217 (B1), p. 2, Table l, from *Total quality management versus business process re-engineering: a question of degree*. Authors: Williams, Davidson, Waterworth, Partington. © Professional Engineering Publishing. ISSN: 0954-4054 (Print) 2041-2975 (Online). Issue: Vol. 217, No. l/2003, pp. 1–10 • **pp. 293–4:** Jim Dickins, *The Sunday Telegraph*, 1 October 2006 • **p. 294:** 'Cap Salaries of chief executives: unions', by Mark Davis, *Sydney Morning Herald*, 1 June 2009 • **p. 32l:** © Sam Varghese • **pp. 381–2:** 'Make no mistake, this will save money', by Fiona Smith, *The Australian Financial Review*, 3 April 2007 • **p. 398:** © Possum IT • **p. 448:** © City of Armadale • **p. 445:** © The ARA Retailer/©Australian Retailers Association www.retail.org.au • **p. 496:** © Sun Microsystems • **pp. 498–9:** © Vinidex www.vinidex.com.au • **pp. 575–7:** © NASSCOM EMERGE http://blog.nasscom.in • **pp. 579–80:** blueStar Business Solutions: 'blueStar's expertise with Greentree, instils confidence in a dynamic long-term partnership'. Michael O'Conner (CFO) The Davey Group www.bluestar.net.au or phone 1300 653 011 • **pp. 601, 602–3:** Reproduced with the permission of BHP Billiton • **pp. 635, 638–9:** Kasavana & David, *Cornell Hotel and Restaurant Administration Quarterly*, June 1992, pp. 75–83, copyright 2005 by Sage Publications Inc. Reprinted by permission • **p. 672:** © PCAOB www.pcaobus.org • **pp. 711–2:** © Graham Phillips • **p. 726:** © Steven Deare, 2 February 2007, from www.silicon.com.

Every effort has been made to trace the ownership of copyright material. Information that will enable the publisher to rectify any error or omission in subsequent editions will be welcome. In such cases, please contact the Permissions Section of John Wiley & Sons Australia, Ltd.

# PART 1

# Systems fundamentals

**In part 1** of the text we introduce some of the fundamental ideas and principles that underlie the operation of systems within organisations. Systems are an integral part of any operation, providing a way of structuring and organising. The accounting information system is no different, providing a way of capturing the inputs that enter an organisation and converting them into useful information for decision makers both inside and outside the organisation. In this section we explore these ideas in more detail, providing illustrations of the concept of a system, the historical development of the accounting information systems function, and a discussion of some of the issues that arise at various stages in a system.

Familiarisation with the systems concepts discussed in part 1 provides the foundation for subsequent chapters, which cover the types of processes that exist in an organisation and how these are designed and documented. Relevance to subsequent parts is also discussed, and an overview and roadmap for the rest of the text and brief chapter descriptions are provided.

# Introduction

## Learning objectives

After studying this chapter, you should be able to:

**1** define and describe accounting and explain how information systems have altered the role of accounting and the job of the accountant

**2** define and describe information

**3** define and describe a system, using examples

**4** define 'accounting information systems' and discuss their evolution

**5** discuss and provide examples of the role of accounting information.

# Introduction

Welcome to the study of accounting information systems! You are embarking on the study of an area that has far-reaching impacts on your daily life — often without your even thinking so. Accounting information systems is a field that offers exciting career opportunities and increases the value of any business degree. In recent times the accounting profession has been confronted by the ubiquitous nature of information systems and information technology in general. Audit professionals have been forced to re-evaluate the approaches employed in a financial statement audit, with the traditional means fast becoming irrelevant and ineffective as computers and the automation of information systems emerge in business designs. This has led to an increased need to understand the business processes and information systems used by the organisation.[1] Similarly, those working in consulting and traditional accounting services have been confronted by the emergence of information systems in their daily jobs, which brings a need to be aware of information systems and their impact on accounting.

Dare we say it: you have most probably encountered an accounting information system in one form or another several times today without even realising it! For example, if you travelled to university on public transport, then you probably had to validate your travel ticket when you boarded the vehicle. This act of validating your ticket captured data in an accounting information system, which is then used by public transport companies for revenue allocation and information on patronage on different routes. Alternatively, if you paid for a purchase using EFTPOS, you engaged with the information system of the store and the bank to transfer funds from your account to the store's. Accounting information systems, and information systems in general, are omnipresent.

This chapter introduces you to the concept of an accounting information system, as well as some general principles relevant to the study of accounting information systems. This chapter forms a foundation for working through subsequent chapters.

## WHAT IS AN ACCOUNTING INFORMATION SYSTEM?

What accounting information systems *are* has been an ongoing issue in much of the research that has tried to define the discipline. One of the constant challenges confronting the field of accounting information systems is the need to carve out its own little area distinct from other disciplines. This section introduces you to some ideas about what accounting information systems actually are, leading to the formation of a definition of an accounting information system that serves as the basis for the remainder of the text.

The search for the meaning of accounting information systems is begun by going back to first principles, and looking at the three words on their own: 'accounting', 'information' and 'system'.

**LEARNING OBJECTIVE** **1**

*Define and describe accounting and explain how information systems have altered the role of accounting and the job of the accountant.*

## ACCOUNTING

No doubt you will have some concept of what accounting is and what it involves. The traditional role of accounting and accountants is seen as recording the details of transactions that occur within an organisation, starting with the general journal through to the preparation of the financial statements. Recall the traditional accounting cycle, which has typically included the following steps:

1. transaction occurs
2. analyse transaction
3. journalise transaction
4. post journal to ledger
5. prepare trial balance
6. adjust entries
7. adjust trial balance
8. close entries
9. prepare financial statements.

When first developed, the aim of this cycle was to capture data about an organisation's financial activities and convert that data into a meaningful set of reports that could be used for decision making. The accounting process, and the accountants who were part of that process, acted as a data storage and classification system, with transactions classified by the accounts they affected (e.g. by determining which account to debit and credit when entering a transaction into the general journal), with these accounts detailed in the general journal and then the amounts posted to the respective accounts that appeared in the general ledger.

As computers have become more popular and present in both the private and business worlds, these steps of the accounting system are increasingly handled by computers. So the once mundane and often frustrating task of journalising and posting transactions, as well as preparing trial balances and financial reports, can now be performed highly efficiently by computer programs. These programs range in scope and complexity, from a relatively simple small business package like MYOB to the organisation-wide enterprise resource planning (ERP) systems of PeopleSoft and SAP.

Traditionally the domain of larger organisations, enterprise systems (which are discussed in chapter 6) have increasingly become the focus of small and medium-sized entities (SMEs), with a concerted move by both IBM and SAP (see figure 1.1) to make enterprise software accessible to a broader spectrum of the business marketplace, particularly those who do not have the funding to support the traditional costs associated with large enterprise systems.

**FIGURE 1.1** Enterprise systems available to all businesses

### IBM and SAP come up with package deal

IBM and SAP, two of the technology industry's target companies, have formed a pact in Australia to deliver medium-sized companies a prepackaged version of SAP's enterprise software.

The deal will blend IBM's services and channel distribution network with a customised version of SAP business software to address a gap in the two companies' offerings for firms with revenue between $50 million and $500 million.

Known as SAP All-In-One, the software is designed to address a key weakness in SAP's enterprise resource planning platform: its installation requires that engineers and consultants embark on a complex, costly and lengthy integration project.

Large SAP implementations have a reputation for being associated with overbudget or failed technology projects.

'It's really about making an SAP product far more accessible to organisations that have a smaller wallet,' said IBM Australia and New Zealand's Global Business Services commercial leader, Sarah Adam-Gedge.

**FIGURE 1.1** *(continued)*

Another IBM spokesman said the cost of the IBM–SAP system would vary depending on how many end users a customer wanted to support. 'A small to medium business could expect to pay $500 000,' he said.

The two companies have pitched the product as 'fixed-scope bundled solutions for specific industries with predictable deployment time of eight to 16 weeks.'

It will also come embedded with Australian business requirements including GST, business activity statement and payroll functions.

SAP has traditionally focused its financial and enterprise software at the largest companies, but has been forced to wade into the SME sector to sustain growth.

IBM does not develop enterprise resource planning software but has one of Australia's strongest distribution networks.

The company, which employs more than 10 000 people in Australia, also views the SAP deal as a way to reach new customers for its services, hardware and technology integration tools.

'Unlike our competitors, we are able to provide to a client not only a [software] licence but the services that go with that,' Ms Adam-Gedge said.

Ms Adam-Gedge spearheaded the partnership, which will be adopted in Australia before it is rolled out in other Asia–Pacific countries, including India, China and Korea.

IBM aims to sign 20 to 30 new clients a year using the deal. Financial details of the partnership and the product were not released.

IBM said it was also considering a similar partnership with Oracle, SAP's main competitor.[2]

Enterprise systems are one example of the way that the traditional accounting information system has been revolutionised and broadened in scope to encompass tasks beyond the traditional accounting functions. Enterprise systems also emphasise the role that technology has played in changing the perception and functioning of accounting information systems in the organisation.

As computer systems have been developed to perform the recording and classification tasks associated with business activities, the nature of accounting and the work of the accountant have also been pushed in a new direction. Increasingly, the role of the accountant is seen to be to add value and provide and interpret information for an organisation. As an example, look at the following two quotes from the two major professional accounting bodies in Australia, CPA Australia (certified practising accountants) and the Institute of Chartered Accountants in Australia (ICAA).

Under the heading of 'Why accounting?', CPA Australia provides the following argument:[3]

Accounting studies give you the tools to understand how and why key business decisions are made, and how to have input into those decisions. Having a qualification in accounting will open doors to career opportunities within: finance and accounting, information technology, marketing, human resource management, e-commerce, international business, economics, running your own business, management, strategy and business development.

Similarly, the ICAA defines a chartered accountant (CA) as someone who:[4]

bring[s] their analytic expertise to fields as diverse as strategic planning, market analysis, compliance, change management and the use of information technology.

The CPA Australia website also lists some of the potential career paths associated with accounting, which are reproduced in figure 1.2.

The main sectors you can choose from as an accountant are:
- *Corporates:* private enterprise, ranging from large multinationals, the finance sector (such as NAB or ANZ) and the mining/resources and manufacturing sector.
- *Small to medium enterprises (SMEs):* private enterprise with less than 200 employees, SMEs include the recording industry, wineries, sporting clubs and fashion.
- *Public sector:* organisations including commonwealth, state and local government departments.
- *Public practice:* firms offering services to clients for a fee, these range from large multinationals (such as the big 4) through to medium and small firms, as well as public practitioners who advise small business and individuals.

Specific jobs an accounting degree can lead you to include:
- *Audit:* Check accounting ledgers and financial statements.
- *Budget analysis:* Responsible for developing and managing an organisation's financial plans.
- *Financial:* Prepare financial statements based on general ledgers and participate in important financial decisions involving mergers and acquisitions.
- *Management accounting:* Analysis of the structure of organisations.
- *Tax:* Prepare corporate and personal income tax statements and formulate tax strategies.
- *Business risk:* Identify strategic and operational business risks, provide assessments of the effectiveness of business controls and develop business risk solutions.
- *Environmental accountant:* Address issues of how companies can be both environmentally responsible and profitable.
- *Forensic accountant:* Identifying and tracking fraud, particularly in the realm of e-commerce — may be called to give testimony in legal cases.
- *International accounting specialist:* Handles cross-border transactions, overseas trade agreements and other activities related to international business.[5]

**FIGURE 1.2** Careers in accounting

As shown in figure 1.2, the accountant's role has extended beyond the task of capturing and recording financial information about an organisation to being more of a knowledge worker: someone who provides information and solves problems for an organisation. The days of the accountant only being the one who maintains the books are long gone. The career paths mentioned in figure 1.2, however, still rely on a knowledge of accounting. Accounting is still an important skill to possess — it is just that what those with accounting skills do with them has changed.

The category of information systems is also notable. Accountants are increasingly exposed to and working with technology and information systems; indeed, this is the major theme of this text. Accountants of the twenty-first century must be comfortable with information systems concepts because computer systems are playing an increasing part in the management and functioning of the organisation, as well as how it manages knowledge and its data resources.

This shift in definition of accounting and accountants towards this role in information technology as a knowledge worker leads to the second component of the subject area: information.

*Data* Raw facts relating to or describing an event.

# INFORMATION

The traditional accounting process described in learning objective 1 is established with the aim of capturing data about the organisation's financial activities. For example, every time a sale is completed, the details of the sale will be recorded in the sales journal. The details of the sale are the data. **Data** are the raw facts relating to or describing an event. For example, the data relating to a sale could include the sale date, salesperson, customer involved, items purchased, sale price and so on. Every time a sale occurs, this data will be gathered and recorded in the accounting system. The main details will be captured in the journals and subsidiary ledgers. On its own, however, this mass of data is of very little use. Consider as an example of this principle the data shown in figure 1.3, extracted from an organisation's sales journal.

| Date | Customer | Invoice # | Post Reference | Debit | | Credit | | |
| --- | --- | --- | --- | --- | --- | --- | --- | --- |
| | | | | Accts Rec. | COGS | GST Payable | Sales | Inventory |
| 02-6-10 | A Bligh | 1001 | | 350 | 180 | 31.82 | 318.18 | 180 |
| 04-6-10 | A Phillip | 1002 | | 121 | 65 | 11.00 | 110.00 | 65 |
| 05-6-10 | G Macquarie | 1003 | | 143 | 80 | 13.00 | 130.00 | 80 |
| 07-6-10 | P Lap | 1004 | | 400 | 200 | 36.36 | 363.64 | 200 |
| 08-6-10 | B Tulloch | 1005 | | 650 | 400 | 59.09 | 590.91 | 400 |
| 09-6-10 | S Line | 1006 | | 500 | 300 | 45.45 | 454.55 | 300 |
| 10-6-10 | K Town | 1007 | | 423 | 290 | 38.45 | 384.55 | 290 |
| 11-6-10 | M Power | 1008 | | 644 | 500 | 58.55 | 585.55 | 500 |
| 12-6-10 | D Vechio | 1009 | | 1110 | 670 | 100.91 | 1009.09 | 670 |
| 12-6-10 | O Star | 1010 | | 225 | 100 | 20.45 | 204.55 | 100 |
| 13-6-10 | F Omagh | 1011 | | 75 | 39 | 6.82 | 68.18 | 39 |
| 14-6-10 | P Lap | 1012 | | 685 | 400 | 62.27 | 622.73 | 400 |
| 15-6-10 | K Town | 1013 | | 590 | 300 | 53.64 | 536.36 | 300 |
| 16-6-10 | M Blue | 1014 | | 170 | 80 | 15.45 | 154.55 | 80 |
| 17-6-10 | M Diva | 1015 | | 367 | 200 | 33.36 | 333.64 | 200 |

**FIGURE 1.3** Sales journal

The sales journal in figure 1.3 contains a collection of data relating to the business event of making credit sales to customers. As a basis for decision making, however, this mass of data is not very useful. To understand why, consider a real-world business that might engage in hundreds of transactions every day. This would mean hundreds of individual entries would be made into the sales journal in a day. How useful is that for those who have to make decisions? Probably not very useful at all. Imagine the task of analysing sales or trying to identify trends in sales and customer sales levels if all you had were the raw data in figure 1.3. It would be very time-consuming, difficult and potentially inaccurate. So a way is needed to make the data useful.

Data become useful when they are subject to the application of rules or knowledge, which enables us to convert data into information. Information is used in decision making and can prompt action, as well as be a guiding tool for decision making. The sales data contained in the sales journal in figure 1.3 can be made useful by summarising them in some meaningful way. Examples of this could include weekly sales summaries, sales by customer reports, profit margins per customer and so on.

Alternatively, the data could be summarised on a basis of customer by customer, sales by geographic region (assuming geographic region data are available), sales by product type and so on. When this is done, the data become more meaningful and easier to work with. Summarising the data converts them into a useful tool to assist decision making. That is, they have been turned into information. The concept of data and their storage is returned to later in examining databases and enterprise information systems.

Of course, there can be too much information. This is described as information overload, which happens when an individual has more information than he or she needs and can process meaningfully when working through a decision. This is obviously undesirable. Consequently, organisations need to be conscious of what information they produce (whether reports or some other type of information) and make sure that it is relevant to the people who need it. Commonly in large organisations, people will request reports for a specific problem. Over time that problem may disappear, yet the reports are still produced. In many cases these reports will then just be filed away because 'that's what has always been done'. So resources are wasted in generating the reports and potentially, for the person receiving the irrelevant information, there is a risk of **information overload**.

As an example of some of the different ways that organisations today are looking to go beyond their conventional accounting systems for information, read the article by Sue Mitchell from *The Australian Financial Review* in AIS focus 1.1. This article reports on an initiative from Australian retail giant Woolworths designed to gain a better understanding of its customers, restoring traditional customer intimacy. This was done by pooling data from various avenues of the business' operations — transaction data, credit and EFT data — in a bid to better understand customer purchasing habits and offer customisation on a mass scale to its large customer base. The Woolworths project involved both conventional accounting data and other data combined, and introduced systems capability to produce valuable information about customer spending habits.

## AIS FOCUS 1.1

## Woolworths' pursuit of customer intimacy

The chief executive of Australia's largest retailer has fond memories of how retailing used to be.

When Woolworths' Michael Luscombe was a boy living in Melbourne, the grocer, the greengrocer, the butcher and the baker would all ring his mother for her weekly shopping list.

They already knew her standard order — with three sons and six daughters Mrs Luscombe had many mouths to feed.

But by knowing the cuts and quantities of meat she favoured and the fruit and vegetables she preferred, the shopkeepers were able to offer other products that might be available or special deals that had come their way.

'We have moved from a position where the shopkeeper had intimate knowledge of the customer to mass market retailing where we've been able to deliver greater efficiency and lower prices,' Luscombe says. 'But we've lost that intimacy and ability to know what the customer wants.'

In a major data-mining project now under way, Woolworths hopes to regain that knowledge of consumer buying habits, so it can better tailor its product range, pricing and promotions.

It has collected the information over the past two years from a number of sources, including credit card data from its Ezy Banking alliance with Commonwealth Bank of Australia.

But Woolworths has only recently gained the capacity to analyse the data in a meaningful way and formulate plans to put it to use.

Unlike Woolworths' business transformation project, Refresh, or its supply chain overhaul, dubbed Mercury, the customer relationship management project has not been given a fancy name.

'It's called good shopkeeping' says Luscombe, who took over as chief executive from Roger Corbett last October.

'It's all about understanding and listening to our customers.

'We buy and sell for a profit, and we can only sell for a profit if people are interested in buying what we have for sale at the appropriate value and in the appropriate time.'

The project, while embryonic, has received increased resources, including a dedicated team led by former supermarket buying and marketing general manager Richard Umbers, who has recently been appointed to the new role of general manager customer engagement.

Luscombe, who was head of supermarkets before taking the top job, says Woolworths' renewed focus on customer needs has already delivered results.

But he expects more benefits to flow as the information collected and analysed is exploited.

Industry sources say the information will eventually enable Woolworths, for example, to promote nappies and other baby products to new mothers and tailor special pet food offers to pet owners.

'There's no doubt that customer relationship management is going to be a significant weapon in a retailer's armoury going forward,' one source says.

The customer relationship management project is one of several initiatives, in varying stages of development, aimed at reducing costs and driving further sales and margin growth, enabling Woolworths to maintain its seven-year record of double-digit profit growth.

Another is the development of a switch that will allow the company to sort credit and debit card transactions and send them directly to card issuers, cutting processing costs.

The system — now on trial and expected to be fully operational by Christmas — also creates a platform from which Woolworths can launch its own credit and transaction cards as part of a broader financial services strategy. This could eventually include offering personal loans, insurance and mortgages.

'There's a whole range of opportunities that we are considering at the moment,' Luscombe says.

'At the appropriate time, we'll talk about which of those products we'll move into.'[6]

**System** *Something that takes inputs, applies a set of rules or processes to the inputs and generates outputs.*

**Inputs** *Data and other resources that are the starting point for a system.*

# SYSTEM

A **system** can be defined as something that takes inputs, applies a set of rules or processes to the inputs and generates outputs.

**Inputs** can include data, as well as other resources, that are the starting point for a system. As an example, a list of inputs into an accounting system could include the data relating to the transactions that occur, with this data coming from the various source documents that an organisation generates and receives in its normal business operations. There are several alternatives available for an organisation to choose from when determining how the inputs to a system are going to be captured. These can include:

- *Manual keying.* As the name suggests, manual keying requires a person to enter data into a system via a keyboard. This could introduce errors in the data if items such as names and amounts are incorrectly keyed.
- *Scanning through barcode technology.* This involves scanning a barcode with a laser device. The barcode number is then searched for on a database and appropriate details returned to the system. Examples of this include scanners at a supermarket, where universal product codes are used.
- *Scanning through image scanners.* Image scanners are a useful input approach where the input is in the form of a diagram or graphic image. Scanners are used to capture the image, which is then stored electronically.
- *Magnetic ink character recognition (MICR).* This technology is used on bank cheques. A special ink and character set is used, with computers able to read the ink due to its magnetic properties. MICR offers a security control for banks and provides a quick method for scanning information into a system.[7]
- *Voice recognition.* Using voice recognition technology allows a computer to convert spoken words and commands into data inputs. Issues with voice recognition technology can include training the system to recognise words and deal with accents and different voice intonations.
- *Optical mark readers.* You have most probably used this technology when completing multiple-choice exams at university. Alternatively, if you have ever placed a bet at the TAB you will have used this technology as well. Data inputs are coded onto a sheet by colouring in the appropriate space, and the sheet is then fed through a machine that identifies where the dots are and, based on their location, converts them into data that can be stored electronically.

**Processes** *The sets of activities that are performed on the inputs into the system.*

The **processes** are the sets of activities that are performed on the inputs into the system. Again using the sales system as an example, once sales data are entered into the system, various processes are performed on them, including checks on their format and validity, manipulations of inputs and finally storage. Examples of some of these checks are discussed in the chapters on the different transaction cycles, as well as the internal controls chapter, but the basic aim of initial data processes is ensuring that data are correct and in a valid format for future storage and processing. Manipulations refer to the act of performing calculations and adjusting the data inputs. As an example, if a sales order is entered and the unit prices and the quantity of units sold are keyed in, the system can then manipulate these two figures to generate the total price (sales price × units sold). Other checks and manipulations performed on the data can be hash checks, to ensure that inputs like credit card numbers and customer numbers are valid. These are discussed in more detail in later chapters.

**Outputs** *What is obtained from a system, or the result of what the system does.*

**Outputs** refer to what is obtained from a system, or the result of what the system does. In the sales system outputs will typically include reports for decision making. Some examples of outputs from the sales system could be receipts and invoices that are given to customers when a sale is executed, sales summary reports used by management to assess performance and other such reports. When designing a system, it is a sound practice to consider what outputs are required as a starting point. After all, if it is not known what outputs are required from a system, then it can hardly be ensured that those outputs can be generated from the inputs that are being gathered. If, for example, customer details were not gathered when sales data were being input into the sales system, then it would be impossible to generate a sales report that breaks sales down by customer.

**Feedback** *The method using alerts to ensure that the system is running as normal and that there are no problems or exceptional circumstances.*

Interacting with the inputs, processes and output will be the provision of **feedback**, which is the method for ensuring that the system is running as normal and that there are no problems or exceptional circumstances. For example, when a datum about a customer, such as a customer number, is entered into a system, the system will take the datum and check that it is in the required format and is a valid number. If the system finds an error in the customer number (e.g. it has been entered as alphanumeric when it should be numeric), then it will alert the data entry person responsible and prompt them to re-enter the customer number in the correct format.

Another example of feedback is when you book a flight online through Virgin Blue. If you try to enter a departure date later than the return date, you will get an error message alerting you to an incorrect sequence of dates. An example of this is contained in figure 1.4 overleaf, where the departure date was entered as 11 November 2009 and the return date was entered as 9 November 2009. Obviously this sequence of dates does not make sense. To help ensure that only accurate and reliable data enter the system, the feedback mechanism is in place. Feedback can also operate at the processing and output stages, bringing to notice problems in handling a transaction processing event and generating reports that summarise a system's performance, which can then be used for management review and action.

A system will also have a defined task or domain to which it is applied — one system cannot do everything. This is the idea of **system scope**: the domain that a system addresses. Systems also operate within a particular **external environment** or context, which will affect the operation of the system. As an example, an accounting system within an organisation has the scope of preparing the financial statements that the organisation provides to its shareholders and other dependent users of the financial information. The financial reporting system operates within the environment of the relevant accounting rules, regulations, generally accepted accounting principles (GAAP) and standards that govern accounting practice. These rules and regulations are established externally through bodies such as the federal and state governments and the Australian Accounting Standards Board (AASB), yet they have a definite impact on the way that the accounting system is designed and operates within an organisation.

**System scope** *The domain or problem that a system addresses.*

**External environment** *The factors or pressures outside a system that influence its design and operation.*

The idea of a system is an important one for the remainder of this text. Throughout the text, a range of different systems and processes that operate throughout an organisation will be examined. As you will see, each of these systems can be broken down and analysed in terms of their inputs, processes and outputs. The systems analysed include the sales, payments and purchases systems. These three systems form the spine of most organisations and an understanding of the inputs, processes and outputs within them is essential. They are three different examples of the more generic transaction processing system (TPS), which is a system designed to capture and record events that occur in a business's operations. They can be customised to different types of transactions, including a purchasing TPS to handle purchases, a human resources TPS to handle payroll and associated human resources transactions, a sales TPS to handle sales activities and so on. Other system types that you may come across in organisations include decision support systems and expert systems.

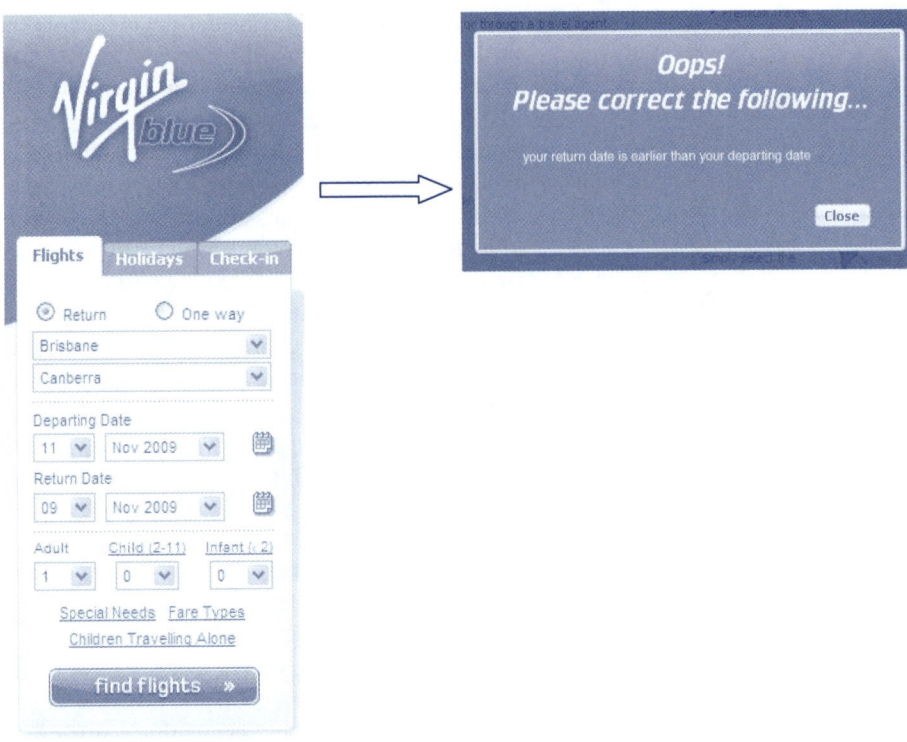

**FIGURE 1.4** Feedback in the Virgin Blue online booking system
*Source:* Virgin Blue 2009, www.virginblue.com.au.

**LEARNING OBJECTIVE 4**
*Define 'accounting information systems' and discuss their evolution.*

**Accounting information system** *The application of technology to the capturing, verifying, storing, sorting and reporting of data relating to an organisation's activities.*

# DEFINITION AND EVOLUTION OF ACCOUNTING INFORMATION SYSTEMS

From the above discussion, an **accounting information system** can be defined as the application of technology to the capturing, verifying, storing, sorting and reporting of data relating to an organisation's activities. This encompasses the definitions of accounting, information and systems that were discussed above. Bear in mind that the definition of an accounting information system includes technology that currently would mean computer technology. However, as was discussed in the introduction to systems, a system does not have to be computerised. An accounting information system, indeed any system, can operate manually. Given the reality for organisations today, however, it is likely that part if not all of the accounting system will be computerised.

## A brief history of accounting information systems

Perspectives on accounting information systems, as well as their role within the organisation, have changed over the years. It is fairly uncontroversial to say that nowadays 'accounting is a data management function dependent upon information technology'.[8] While accounting as a bookkeeping function can be performed manually, most organisations have computerised their accounting process to some extent, ranging from a standalone PC with a package such as MYOB running on it to the large organisation that implements an ERP system throughout the organisation to manage all the business processes. This section presents an historical perspective on the development of the accounting information systems function and draws on Kee (1993).[9]

Record keeping and systems have always been present in organisations. From the clay tablets used by the Sumerians to the paper ledger books maintained before the introduction of computers and today's computerised records, history is riddled with record keeping relating to commerce. (If you are interested in a discussion on ancient history and the evidence of recording systems, then Kee's 1993 article in *The Accounting Historians Journal* is a useful initial reference.) The essential functions of any accounting system have always been the organisation, storage, retrieval and processing of details pertaining to economic activity.

Pacioli's development of the double-entry accounting system was the first real step towards a classification scheme and framework for converting data about economic events into useful information about business performance. Before the emergence of double-entry accounting techniques, record keeping was based mainly around recording economic activity — that is, gathering data. These data were seldom summarised or converted into information.

The first double-entry accounting systems were operated manually, which created a great potential for errors and inaccuracies during the capturing, transcription and classification of data, as well as during the reporting of information. By the late 1800s firms began to create less labour-intensive methods for operating their accounting information systems, including adding machines and cash registers. These developments allowed for data to be more efficiently captured and provided for the use of batch totals within the organisation. This emergence of batch totals is significant in terms of the controls that operate in the organisation, evidenced in chapters 7 and 8 on internal controls.

Punch cards were soon developed as a means of data entry and storage, and IBM emerged in the marketplace with several developments in machines that were able to verify, sort and total data, handling debits and credits. Punch cards introduced flexibility into a firm's accounting information system, because the individual cards could be sorted and processed in a variety of ways to attain different results — for example, sales by product, region and so on — that the traditional sales journal struggled with. Thus emerging in the accounting information system is the ability to apply different perspectives to data to convert them into information.

This historical perspective is much more than just a fascinating narrative. What it represents is the development of the accounting information system. Up until the development of machines, the system operated manually and those who performed the accounting process knew the system and its technicalities — for example, the role of the journals, ledgers, chart of accounts and so on. (Note that an accounting information system does not have to be computerised or automated. Modern thinking assumes that such a system is computerised but this is not necessarily so.) This changed with the introduction of machine technology into the accounting information system. Suddenly it required two domains of experience: a technical aspect to run the machines and an accounting aspect to do the accounting for the organisation. This is the early origin of the accounting and information system subgroups. Data management and technical requirements were the domain of what may now be called the information systems group, while the rules of accounting were the domain of the accounting group. Within an organisation the relative balance between these two groups has changed over time, as reflected in figure 1.5.

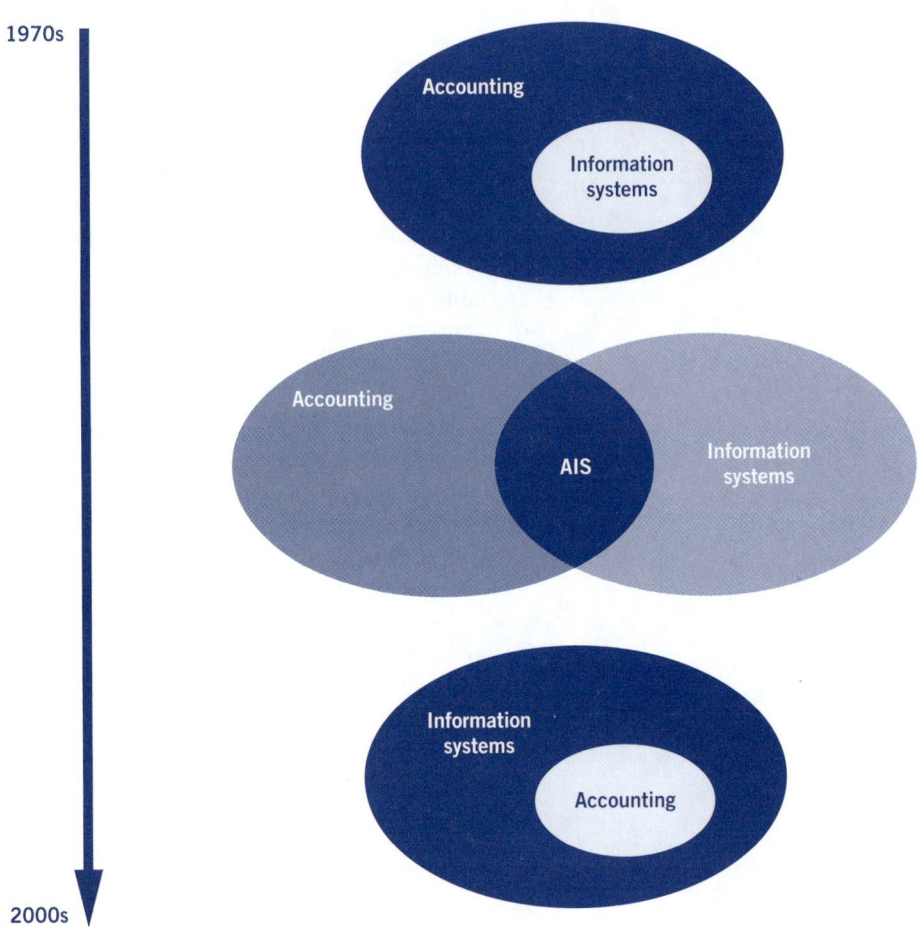

**FIGURE 1.5** Accounting and information systems — a changing relationship
*Source:* Sutton & Arnold 2002.[10]

Until the 1970s, information systems were seen as a support tool for the accounting function: the technology was provided to enable accounting to be done better. Information systems were almost a subset of the accounting function, acting in support of the accounting requirements.

As technology continued to develop, including management information systems, database technology and electronic data processing technologies, and with the emergence of the microcomputer, organisations began to see that the technology of the computer could be applied beyond the domain of the accounting function. The effect of this realisation was that the information systems function began to develop an identity of its own, becoming more distinct from the accounting function, which had previously subsumed it. This is shown in figure 1.5 by the two intersecting circles. Accounting was still an important function, but information systems had grown in prominence. Information systems were still used in accounting, as represented by the intersection of the circles, labelled 'AIS' in the figure.

As these new techniques emerged, the accounting function's reliance on the information systems function increased. As Kee observes, 'The cumulative effect of computer technology has been further absorption of much of accounting's traditional data management function by EDP [electronic data processing] professionals. Thus, accounting has become increasing[ly] separate from the technology and data used to implement its function.'[11]

The reliance on the information services function has extended beyond just the accounting function, with multipurpose applications and technologies and developments emerging. Examples include ideas such as end-user computing and shared databases as well as the integration of organisations through technologies such as electronic data interchange.

Such developments meant that information systems technologies were being incorporated into other functional areas of the organisation apart from accounting. From the organisation's perspective this increases the role of information systems within the organisation and makes the other functional areas dependent on the information systems function. It also means that more information flows occur than previously and these might involve external parties.[12]

The traditional function of accounting as a provider of financial reports can also be affected by technology. As questions are raised about the timeliness of annual reports and their usefulness to decision making by shareholders and other like parties, there is increased discussion about the prospect of real-time reporting of financial information.[13] Again, this would place the accounting function in a position where it depended on the communication and storage technologies of the information systems division. This final shift of power from accounting is represented in the bottom part of figure 1.5, with the accounting function a subset or part of the information systems function.

Thus what can be seen is the gradual change in the relationship between accounting, information systems and the rest of the organisation. This has developed from the days before computer technology where record keeping was the primary focus, to the emergence of double-entry recording, which enabled classification of data to generate accounting information, to the stage where computer technology now pervades the whole organisation and accounting is just one of the functions that depend on the technologies of information systems.

**LEARNING OBJECTIVE 5**

*Discuss and provide examples of the role of accounting information.*

# THE ROLE OF ACCOUNTING AND ACCOUNTING INFORMATION

Accounting information is central to many different activities within and beyond an organisation. As is evident from the definition and discussion of accounting in the earlier part of this chapter, accounting's role is to gather data about a business's activities, provide a means for the data's storage and processing, and then convert those data into useful information. The information that can be generated by an accounting information system is diverse. No doubt you are familiar with the typical accounting statements that are produced by the accounting process, including the income statement (or statement of comprehensive income), the statement of financial position (or balance sheet) and the statement of cash flows. These reports represent information generated by the accounting system to support decision making by providers of scarce economic resources. Such information is used by providers of economic resources in making decisions about whether to invest in a company, as well as for evaluating company performance at the end of the financial year.

The statements of accounting concepts issued by the Australian Accounting Research Foundation provide particular guidance on the role accounting information plays in everyday society. Some of the purposes of accounting information mentioned in 'Statement of Accounting Concepts 2: Objective of General Purpose Financial Reporting'[14] are assessing whether a business is operating profitably and making sufficient cash flows, assessing the ability of a supplier to continue operating into the future and providing goods or services, and generally assessing whether the business is achieving its aims and objectives.

However, the traditional financial statements are by no means the only source of information available through the accounting information system. The general purpose financial statements are used by shareholders and potential shareholders, creditors and debtors alike to assess the above dimensions. Accounting information that typically extends further is also available for decision makers within an organisation. Within an organisation, employees will have access to the data that are stored and can query and manipulate them in various ways to answer questions that may arise in the day-to-day running of the organisation. It is not practical for employees to rely solely on the general purpose financial statements, since they are produced once a year (twice if mid-year reports are produced) and very quickly lose their time relevance.

What sort of decisions need to be made within a firm that require accounting information? Consider the following hypothetical examples:

1. A customer wants to make a purchase on his or her store credit card.
2. The business needs to decide how much inventory to order for the coming month.
3. The organisation needs to assess the bad debts amount at the end of the financial year.
4. Managers need to evaluate the performance of the factory staff and how well resources have been used in production.

How can accounting information be used in each of these scenarios? How can accounting information other than that contained in the traditional financial statements be used?

1. *A customer wants to make a purchase on his or her store credit card.* In this situation accounting information can be used as a tool for deciding whether to approve the credit sale. The store may check the customer's credit history, including any past defaults on payment, to determine his or her creditworthiness. Additionally, the account balance already owed by this customer may be compared to the customer's individual credit limit, to assess whether there is sufficient space on the customer's account for the transaction to proceed. In this example can be seen the use of accounting information as a part of the authorisation process: if the customer's credit history is satisfactory, then the credit sale will be authorised to proceed. Many organisations have developed expert systems and neural networks to aid the credit rating and approval decision. These examples of artificial intelligence draw upon the accounting data that are gathered by the accounting information system and automate the credit approval decision.

2. *The business needs to decide how much inventory to order for the coming month.* When deciding how much to purchase from suppliers, an organisation needs to have an

estimate for its expected sales in the coming month, because it does not want to purchase too much or too little stock. Estimates of sales and demand from the product can be gained in a variety of ways, one of which is to forecast based on past sales figures and trends. Underlying this are the accounting data on sales that are used to form the forecasts. In this example, accounting information is being used as a planning tool within the organisation.

3. *The organisation needs to assess the bad debts amount at the end of the financial year.* When companies prepare their financial statements at the end of the financial year they are required to assess the value of their accounts receivable account, assessing whether it represents a true and fair value. This task is performed to avoid any potential misstatement and overvaluation of the assets in their statement of financial position. If they suspect that not all the accounts receivable will actually be received from customers, then they estimate the amount that will not be collected and place it in a provision for bad and doubtful debts. How do they estimate the value of this provision? There are several techniques available including an ageing analysis of accounts receivable and a percentage of credit sales technique. Both of these techniques rely on accounting data: the ageing analysis uses accounting data on amounts owed to the organisation classified by the age of the debt to produce information about the age breakdowns of accounts receivable. Past sales, ageing information and bad debts information stored in the accounting information system can also be used to estimate probabilities of a debt in an age group going bad. Thus the accounting data and information they are used to generate are essential parts of the organisation's decision making and reporting. The information being used in this example is not restricted to financial statement information — information about the age of accounts receivable and the probability of debtor default is not generally made public. However, it would usually be available to those within the organisation, through the accounting information system, for decision-making purposes such as valuing bad debts.

4. *Managers need to evaluate the performance of the factory staff and how well resources have been used in production.* Organisational performance depends on many factors and can be assessed in many different ways. One area that a manufacturing organisation will be concerned about is how well its production process is converting raw materials into finished goods for resale to customers. Accounting information plays a role in evaluating this aspect of business performance, with budgets and variance reports key assessment tools. At the commencement of the accounting period organisations will have a budget for manufacturing levels, which will forecast materials usage, based on expected production levels. At the end of the period management will rescale the budget, based on actual levels of production, and compare this rescaled budget to actual costs and material usage. Any significant differences between actual and budgeted outcome will be followed up and investigated by management. This is an example of accounting information being used as a control tool within the organisation.

AIS focus 1.2 overleaf discusses some of the many different ways that data is used within an organisation. In particular, it focuses on data mining. The earlier example of Woolworths and its intention to analyse data from various sources (AIS focus 1.1, page 10) is another example of the application of data within the organisation to assist in improving business performance and solving business problems. In the case of Woolworths, the identified issue was that of better knowing the customer.

## Using data in the organisation

As would have become evident in the discussion earlier in the chapter on data collection techniques and different input methods into a system, there can be several methods for an organisation to gather data. As a consequence, data can be gathered from a range of sources and, in some cases, in a relatively unobtrusive manner. An organisation today will gather and store more voluminous data than organisations of a bygone era. This raises the organisational problem of having more data than can possibly be used. As Braue observes, 'although many companies have successfully implemented data warehouses ... many more have struggled to do more with that data than run basic reports using simple tools'.[15] The consequence of this is evident in a survey cited by Braue, which found that more than half the 50 Australian executives surveyed felt as though 'they don't have enough information to make intelligent business decisions'.

One solution that has emerged to help make the data more useful for the organisation is data mining. This is a technology that analyses large pools of data and identifies patterns in them that can then be used by organisations for decision making. Some examples of data mining are listed in table 1.1.

**TABLE 1.1** Examples of data mining

| Business | Application of data mining |
|---|---|
| Tax office | Analysing tax returns |
| Banks | Identifying credit card fraud<br>Customer profiling |
| Law enforcement | Identifying money laundering activities |
| Retail stores | Analysing sales patterns and levels |
| Australian Securities and Investments Commission | Detecting insider trading activities |
| AC Milan soccer club | Analysing players' injury patterns |

*Source:* Based on Braue 2003.[16]

A related issue for an organisation is being clear on how the data that are being gathered and stored relate to the business processes within it. This broader issue of data management is a very real problem for organisations, with one of the major problems being that organisations are simply unaware of what data are being gathered. This makes the role of understanding what data are being gathered critical, because if it is not known what is being gathered, then how can it possibly be used? One approach that is an important early step for an organisation is data classification, which is 'a fundamental process that drives value throughout an organisation by enabling the alignment of information to best address business needs'.[17] Data classification involves understanding the organisation, its processes and the data necessary to support those processes. This helps ensure that the right data can be converted into useful information for those who need it, thus helping the organisation realise the full value potential of the data it is gathering.

## WHERE NEXT?

The chapters of this text can be conceptually grouped into four sections. Their relationship is illustrated in figure 1.6 overleaf. Part 1 introduces you to the role of accounting information systems, providing the background for the environment in which the AIS operates. This material is contained in this chapter. In part 2 we explore the characteristics and operational issues associated with systems within the organisation. This discussion includes an overview of what a business process is, how business processes are documented, issues in capturing data within a business process, and steps that can be put in place to monitor process operations. The evolution of systems to typologies that encompass the entire organisation is also included in this section. With this conceptual background in hand we then progress to examine five specific examples of common business processes or transaction cycles. These include the revenue, payment or expenditure, production, human resource management and payroll, and the general ledger and financial reporting processes or transaction cycles. Each of these are described in a way that highlights the major design issues and control considerations, in order to crystallise the application of the concepts discussed in part two and to highlight the importance of business process operation to the success of the organisation. In part 4 we consider some of the overarching issues relating to the operation and design of the spectrum of systems and processes within the organisation, including systems development, auditing of systems and ethical issues related to systems. As a result, the issues and concepts discussed in this section can be seen as the macro issues confronting systems within the organisation. A brief explanation of the content and type of issues addressed in each of the following chapters is outlined below, as a way of setting the scene for the remainder of the text.

## Part 2: Systems characteristics and considerations

In this second section we look at some of the issues to consider when designing the operation of systems within the organisation, including the way systems will fit within the structure of the organisation and its business processes, the way data is gathered and managed within the processes and systems, the records of how the systems operate, and the structures put in place to facilitate the smooth running of systems. These topics are addressed in chapters 2 through to 8, briefly introduced below.

### *Business processes (chapter 2)*

Business processes are a key part of how an organisation attains its objectives. They represent the series of activities that, when combined, deliver something of value to the customer, whether internal or external. The discussion commences with a look at the broader issues of organisational mission and strategy. These involve the organisation setting its broad objectives and thinking about how such objectives will be achieved. The attainment of objectives requires a set of activities to be put in place and this is where business processes are important. Business processes represent the engine room of the organisation — the means by which the goals of the organisation are translated into specific activities that need to be carried out to achieve its goals.

This makes business processes increasingly relevant to organisations as the push for value-added organisational designs gains prominence. Further, the idea of a business process fundamentally underpins an ERP system. Therefore, organisations have started to ask how they can redesign their business processes to maximise the contribution they make to the organisation. This business process focus has led to the adoption of organisational change techniques such as continuous improvement and business process re-engineering. The consideration of how organisations use information technology within their business processes is also covered in the concluding stages of the chapter, highlighting how technology that is consistent with the organisation's mission, strategy and business process design can be of benefit.

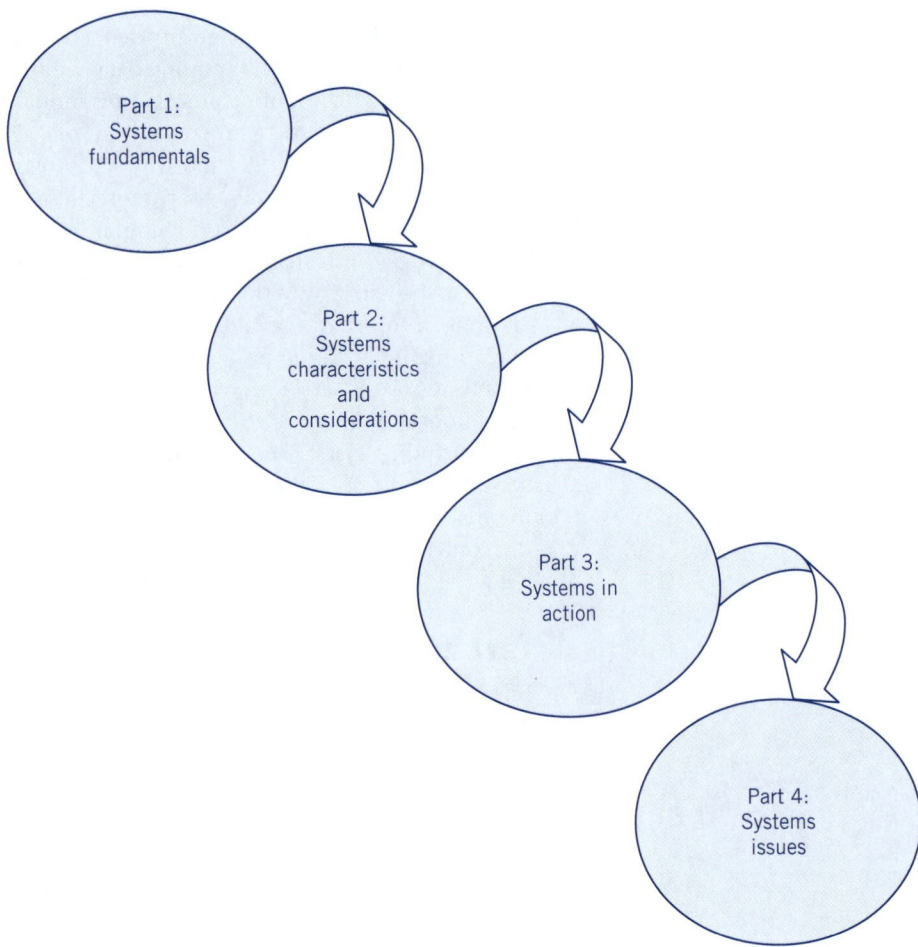

**FIGURE 1.6** Structure of topics in the text

## *Database concepts (chapters 3 and 4)*

Recall from earlier in this chapter that data represent the raw facts about an event or activity. There are several options the organisation can pursue when making decisions about the storage of data, with different database design alternatives providing an example of this choice. In chapter 3 you will be introduced to the process that an organisation will follow in determining what data to store and the structures put in place for managing such storage. The key issue in making these determinations is the accuracy, reliability and timeliness of the data. You will note that these themes recur in much of the discussion in the remainder of the text. One of the commonly employed approaches is the relational database approach, which looks for relationships between different pieces of data as a means of logically connecting the different pieces of data. You will see that the relational approach offers several advantages for organisations in managing and using the tremendous amounts of data that move through an organisation. In the past, many organisations have found themselves in a position where data was duplicated across the organisation (i.e. the same data being stored in numerous locations). We will see a link between the material discussed in chapter 2, where the evolution of the business process is discussed, and the emergence of the relational database as an organisation-wide tool, potentially leading to ERP systems, which are discussed later in the text.

Any database, however, is more than just computer software. Rather, a database represents the culmination of people, procedures, hardware, software and data. These elements combine to assist the organisation in managing its data resources. A key aspect of the operation of a database system is the associated documentation that captures the underlying design and structure of the database. To support this function we are introduced to the entity-relationship diagram technique as a way of showing the logical design of the database from a top-down perspective. This is a technique that is used to show the relationships between different pieces of data — a key to the relational database model.

In chapter 4, the database design concepts are taken a step further as we look at normalisation and the process of arriving at appropriate data models for a database within an organisation. Normalisation is an important process in database design, since it works to minimise potential anomalies that can emerge in a data management system. Normalisation ensures all the lower-level operational aspects are also included, as normalisation starts with the tables, forms and data of the organisation. Once both the top-down entity-relationship diagram technique and bottom-up normalisation process are applied, they are reconciled to ensure that an organisation-wide database model, or enterprise model, is created that includes the upper level view as well as the operational data.

## System mapping and documentation (chapter 5)

The role of systems documentation is crucial for an organisation, serving a purpose in systems development and systems review, and in recording a process's operation for new staff and external auditors. Systems documentation also serves as an important memory device for the organisation, recording how business processes are designed, the data that moves through the processes and the activities that occur within the processes. Several techniques are available to document a business process, including process maps, data flow diagrams and systems flowcharts. In this chapter we introduce each of these documentation techniques and show how to read and prepare such documentation. This knowledge is extremely useful for all accounting graduates, with accounting firms valuing an information systems perspective in conjunction with traditional accounting skills.

## Enterprise information systems (chapter 6)

Organisations looking for technology to support their accounting operations face choices, which, depending on the size and needs of the organisation, range from a small desktop application such as Microsoft Money, to medium-sized applications such as MYOB, to an enterprise system such as PeopleSoft or SAP. In making the choice about which technology to adopt, an organisation must understand its own needs and the future direction that the organisation will take. In chapter 6, you are introduced to a framework for making these decisions within the organisation. If the organisation is heavily geared around business processes, discussed generally in chapter 2, an ERP system may be a viable option. These organisation-wide systems offer several advantages to an organisation and have increased in prominence in recent times.

However, ERP systems also bring with them a range of very real organisational issues, ranging from the technology infrastructure required to support them to how they will interact with existing systems and how they may operate in an inter-organisational environment.

Chapter 6 links ERP systems to business processes, data management and database design discussed in earlier chapters. Further, enterprise resource systems represent an example of the application of relational database concepts to a system that spans the organisation and integrates different processes. In chapters 9 to 11, you are taken through some examples of organisation-wide business processes, which are often captured in an ERP system.

## Internal controls (chapters 7 and 8)

Having gained a familiarity with the concept of business processes, databases, and how enterprise systems can be used to facilitate the operation of these concepts, the issue we are confronted with is that of execution. Essentially, even with the best designed processes and systems in place, structures, policies and procedures need to be in place in the organisation to manage risks that have the potential to interfere with an organisation achieving its goals. The organisational response to risks commences with a sound policy of corporate governance and extends to the management and use of technology and the implementation of procedures at the operational level of the organisation to mitigate risk exposure.

Internal controls are instigated across the organisation to manage financial risk exposures (e.g. the possibility that financial reports could be materially misstated as a result of an error or irregularity such as a transaction being entered incorrectly or classified incorrectly) as well as other exposures that do not necessarily have a direct consequence for the financial statements (e.g. being subject to specific legislative requirements relating to pollution discharge or noise levels). Recent threats against organisations' information technology resources have also meant that appropriate controls to protect technology resources need to be given serious consideration. As the article in AIS focus 1.3 indicates, businesses of all sizes need to be aware of the risks that confront their resources, including information-based resources.

## AIS FOCUS 1.3

## Cyber criminals targeting small businesses

Cyber criminals are increasingly targeting small and medium-sized businesses that don't have the resources to keep updating their computer security, according to federal authorities.

Many of the attacks are being waged by organized cyber groups that are based abroad, and they are able to steal not only credit card numbers, but personal information, including social security numbers, of the card holders, said Michael Merritt, assistant director of the US Secret Service's office of investigations.

Merritt, in testimony prepared for the Senate Homeland Security and Governmental Affairs, said that as larger companies have taken on more sophisticated computer network protections, cyber criminals have adapted and gone after the smaller businesses who do not have such high-level security.

Phil Reitinger, the deputy under secretary at the Department of Homeland Security said there are many simple steps that businesses can take to protect themselves.

'Securing the entrances of one's factory or store is second nature to any business owner and so cyber security protections must become,' he said in his testimony to the panel. He added that a recent study suggested that as many as 87 per cent of data breaches could be avoided by installing simple to intermediate preventative measures.

Reitinger and Merritt said government agencies are working to coordinate more both with each other and with the private sector to improve cyber security. But law makers working on cyber security legislation in several committees across Capitol Hill are pressing for the administration to do more.

'Security cannot be achieved by the government alone,' said Sen. Joseph I. Lieberman, I-Conn. and chairman of the homeland security panel. 'Public-private partnership is essential. Together, business, government, law enforcement, and our foreign allies must partner to mitigate these attacks and bring these criminals to justice.'[18]

Internal controls are an important part of any system, representing a way of providing a degree of assurance that the organisation and its systems are running normally, and preventing, detecting and correcting anomalous and undesirable occurrences, such as fraud, theft and errors in data. They also encompass methods that the organisation may employ to help guarantee its ability to operate in the event of natural disasters and other catastrophic disruptions. The area of disaster recovery is one that is often ignored by businesses since the perceived threat of a disaster is remote at best. This issue is discussed in AIS focus 1.4.

## AIS FOCUS 1.4

## Fast track to recovery

In recent times we've witnessed the full range of natural disasters in Australia, from flash flooding to bushfires. Man-made disasters such as virus attacks, accidentally wiping data and power outages can also affect businesses.

Having a disaster recovery plan in place is one thing small business owners should consider. What would happen if everything that relied on IT suddenly vanished? Would you have the ability to continue running the business? How long could you do it without IT before it begins to affect performance?

*continued*

It is almost impossible to prepare for the worst but planning is critical to ensure your business has the ability to get through in the worst-case scenario.

A Telstra-commissioned survey revealed more than half of all Australian small businesses don't have a disaster recovery plan in place. It indicates about 52 per cent of businesses have not thought ahead and given more consideration towards a disaster recovery plan.

When a storm struck the call centre of national delivery company Couriers Please in Homebush, it had no communication links for up to eight days. The storm struck during the Christmas period, one of the busiest times of the year for most businesses. Without any solid indication on when its systems would be back in full swing, the company had to think quickly of how it was going to keep its call centre operations running without affecting customers.

'The downpour flooded the exchange pit that holds all of our telecoms,' says the chief information officer of Couriers Please, Alistair Alderson. 'At the time we thought it was going to be a one- or two-hour outage, nothing to the point of what we were going to be out for. It was hard to make calls on how we would deal with it.'

'We had to make a call on how we would deal with the NSW area and luckily we had a network connection in our head office and we were able to move hardware and staff there. It kind of saved our bacon a bit. It's hard to gauge the damage on the business but overall it was a successful disaster recovery plan.'

The flooding experience gave the company the ability to deal with more disasters as they occur. And the flooding hasn't been the last disaster, either. Alderson says there was another situation where head office burnt down and there have been other communication outages since. 'We knew exactly how to deal with it,' Alderson says. 'What you think won't happen, will.'

It can often be difficult for a small business to justify funding towards a disaster recovery plan versus other areas of investment. 'For SMBs [small to medium businesses], the issues they face in terms of resilience to disaster recovery, they're no different to what enterprises face,' says IBM's business continuity and disaster recovery services executive, Andrew Fry. 'It's fair to say that SMBs may have a greater impact from a disaster.'

A disaster recovery plan isn't something most business owners consider until disaster strikes or they have a close call with losing their most precious assets, says the chief technologist at Hitachi Data Systems, Simon Elisha. 'Solutions can be as simple as having back-ups that work and replications in place, along with a whole raft of technology solutions. The first step is the strategic decision to ensure the longevity of the company,' Elisha says.

'If you fail to plan, you plan to fail.'[19]

As shown in figure 1.7, by the end of part 2 of the text, the linkages between concepts begin to emerge. In pursuing its strategy, an organisation designs its business processes in a particular way. As part of designing business processes, there is a need to consider what data will be generated and required. This leads to the design of databases within the organisation in order to capture and disseminate the data upon which the organisation relies (flow 1 in figure 1.7). The organisation also requires a record of the business process, including the activities that occur, the people involved and the data and paperwork that move through the process. This leads to the preparation of systems documentation and is reflected by flows 2 and 4 in figure 1.7. As mid- to large-sized businesses have embarked on integration of processes across their organisations, enterprise information systems have risen in prominence as a way of facilitating a common database for the organisation and a business-process driven approach to the organisation. In shifting to enterprise approaches, organisations will typically reconsider process design, the information architecture of the organisation and refer to documentation of existing and planned designs for the business. This is represented by flows 3, 5 and 7 in figure 1.7, with the enterprise approach reliant on database technology for its ability to integrate business processes. Finally, internal controls are built into the design of the business process to facilitate the attainment of organisational goals. These controls need to be documented by the organisation and impact on the way that data is gathered, stored and accessed in the organisation. This is reflected in flows 6, 8 and 9 in figure 1.7.

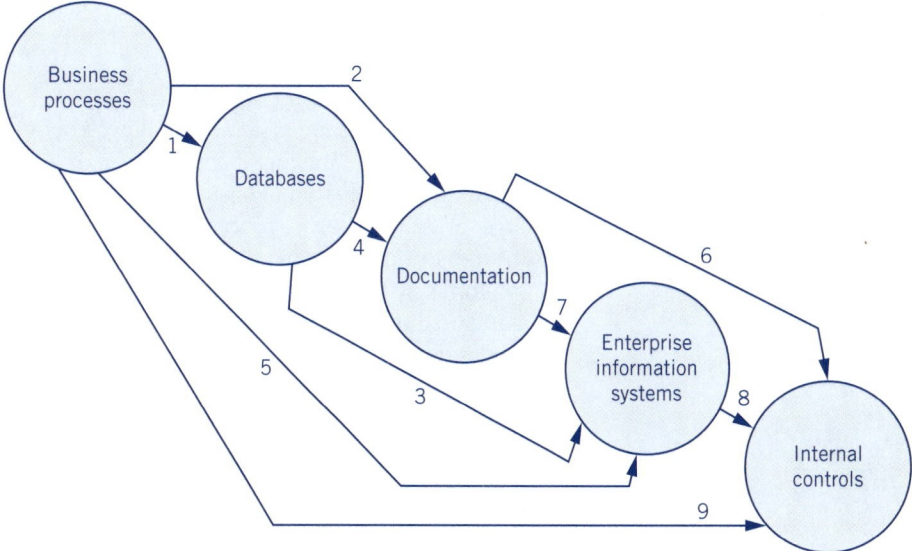

**FIGURE 1.7** Linkages between part 2 concepts

# Part 3: Systems in action

In this section of the text you will examine the application of the concepts introduced in part 2 to specific examples of business processes that operate within a wide range of businesses. These examples of transaction cycles that occur within a business are central to the business being able to attain its objectives. Each cycle operates through a series of activities aimed at achieving a particular goal or solving a particular problem within the organisation. Each chapter outlines the particular business process and the appropriate systems documentation.

## Revenue cycle (chapter 9)

The revenue cycle is central to an organisation's ability to generate cash. It covers selling goods to customers and turning these sales into cash receipts as soon as possible. Typical activities that form a part of the revenue cycle include receiving customer orders, checking a customer's credit history, approving a sale, packing and shipping the goods for delivery to the customer, sending an invoice to the customer and receiving the cash from the customer. From an organisation's cash management perspective, the time it takes to convert sales into cash will ideally be shorter than the time it takes to pay accounts payable. If this is not the case, then the business can run in to cash flow problems. Therefore, the efficient operation of the revenue cycle is important to a business's liquidity.

## Expenditure cycle (chapter 10)

The expenditure cycle is an example of a business process. It is centred on the organisation's purchasing activities, and aims to acquire goods from suppliers to meet customer demand. It will also handle the payment for those purchases as and when they are due. As for the revenue cycle, the functioning of the expenditure cycle is important for an organisation and its operation is closely linked to a business's liquidity. Typical activities in the expenditure cycle include receiving invoices from suppliers, confirming that goods have been received in a suitable condition, preparing a cheque requisition, authorising the cheque, sending the cheque, updating the organisation's records with the details of the payment, and ensuring relevant details are recorded in the general ledger.

## Production cycle (chapter 11)

The production cycle is an essential cycle within a manufacturing organisation. It is responsible for managing the raw materials associated with producing finished goods, scheduling production to ensure sufficient stock is available and making sure that costings for manufacturing processes are performed. There is a critical role for accounting information systems in this process: The costing system within the accounting information system allocates costs to goods manufactured and handles variances for standard and actual costs. Sales information, another form of accounting information, guides decisions within the production process. As an example, decisions about how much to produce for a particular period may be made based on seasonally adjusted sales data or the sales volume for the equivalent time period last financial year. This process can also have accounting consequences — producing too much stock can lead to obsolescence and the need for inventory write-downs, while insufficient stock leads to missed sales and disgruntled customers. The data generated in this process also has an impact on the financial statements — particularly the calculation of cost of goods manufactured and cost of sales on the income statement and inventory on the statement of financial position. Consequently, data generated in this process will be used by the financial reporting process.

## HR management and payroll cycle (chapter 12)

The human resources (HR) management and payroll cycle is responsible for acquiring the services of employees, managing employees and paying wages, as well as dealing with situations where employees leave the organisation. Like the other transaction cycles, the HR management and payroll cycle is linked to the accounting information system and will also impact on other processes in the organisation. Decisions about who to hire will impact upon the way the other processes are executed (e.g. the competence and experience sales employees have will directly impact the number of customer orders received in the revenue cycle). From an accounting perspective, the HR cycle impacts the general ledger in numerous ways. For example, employee hours worked are used to calculate payroll expense, estimate annual and long service leave provisions and apportion wages between accrued and paid components. These data are primarily quantitative and flow from various element of the HR process to payroll and then to the general ledger. The HR management and payroll cycle can also generate and handle non-quantitative data about employees. As a result, the security and confidentiality of the data the cycle uses are particularly important. This gives rise to an important role for internal controls within this process.

## *General ledger and financial reporting cycle (chapter 13)*

The general ledger and financial reporting cycle is, in effect, the culmination of other cycles within the organisation, and covers maintenance of the organisation's accounting records. This cycle receives a great deal of data from the payment and revenue cycles, which is used to prepare and update journals and ledger accounts. Periodically, this cycle will prepare end-of-period adjusting entries and close the temporary accounts to profit and loss. Trial balances will also be prepared, with a set of financial statements to provide to shareholders being the main output from this process. Budgeting and forecasting activities can also be aided by the general ledger and financial reporting cycle.

In summary, part 3 looks at how the concepts from part 2 are applied to the typical business processes in an organisation. As you progress through chapters 9 to 13 you will notice some linkages between the processes, which reinforces the concept discussed in chapter 6 on enterprise information systems — that data needs to be shared across the organisation and between the various business processes. To illustrate this, figure 1.8 gives examples of the interrelationships between business processes.

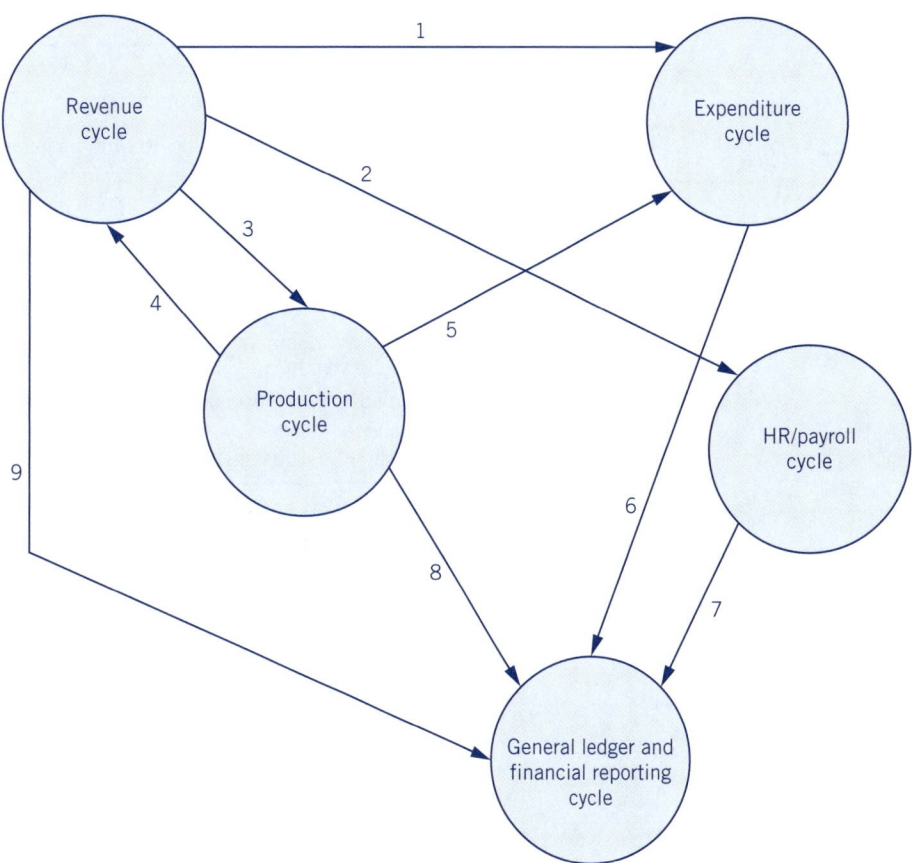

**FIGURE 1.8** Linkages between business processes

| Flow | Explanation |
|---|---|
| 1 | The sales department will send data about sales forecasts or order levels to the expenditure process so that appropriate levels of goods can be ordered to meet customer demand. |
| 2 | The revenue process will forward data to the HR process so sales staff can be paid (e.g. based on hours worked or commissions based on sales levels). Details about staff sales levels may also be used for performance review purposes. |
| 3, 4 | The revenue process will communicate with the production process in the case of a manufacturing organisation, with sales forecasts determining planned production levels and raw material acquisition. Similarly, manufacturing would inform sales staff about finished goods or goods approaching completion. |
| 5 | Manufacturing will communicate with the expenditure process to ensure the necessary raw materials and resources are acquired for production. |
| 6 | The expenditure cycle will communicate with the general ledger and financial reporting cycle so that details about expenditure are appropriately included in the accounting records. This will include updating ledger accounts and including the data in the financial statements. |
| 7 | HR will communicate with the general ledger and financial reporting process so that details about payroll-related items, including leave and other entitlements claimed by employees, are incorporated into the accounts. Provisions for annual leave, long service leave, income tax payable and sick leave are then updated. The details will also impact on the profit and loss through line items such as salaries expenses and annual leave expenses. |
| 8 | Production will communicate with the general ledger and financial reporting process to update the ledger accounts for the details of goods produced or in the process of being produced. This will impact on statement of financial position accounts such as finished goods, work in process and raw materials. Profit and loss will also be impacted by the allocation of direct costs used in manufacturing and the overhead costs accumulated as goods move through the production process. |
| 9 | Sales will communicate with the general ledger and financial reporting process so that details about sales and revenue related activities can be appropriately included in the accounting records; for example, revenue in the income statement, the balance of accounts receivable on the statement of financial position and the cash receipts from customers on the statement of cash flows. |

# Part 4: Systems issues

The issues considered in the final section of chapters are the macro type issues that apply across the organisation and its collection of business processes. These include system development, ethics and auditing. In this final section, with the knowledge that you will have acquired about systems concepts and process examples, you are able to take a step back and place the operation of the processes in the broader context of the organisation. Issues that emerge as part of doing this include questions about how the organisation can manage change within its business process. The reality is that the environment and the needs of the organisation will change over time, necessitating systems development. In addition, issues of how the technology is used and the risk of inappropriate use of technology emerge, raising ethical considerations in the operation of our processes. The role of monitoring process operation also becomes important, with internal audit filling this capacity.

## Systems development (chapter 14)

Regardless of whether you intend to work strictly in the accounting domain or extend beyond accounting, the reality is that, as a working professional, you will encounter some form of systems development. Whether it be providing input into the design and implementation of a new accounting system or the impact a new system has on the way you carry out your day-to-day roles and responsibilities, systems development will be a part of your professional career. The systems development chapter introduces you to some principles and concepts about how an accounting information system, indeed systems in general, can be developed and managed within an organisation. The systems development area is unique in that it often requires the organisation to broach both technical (i.e. hardware, programming) and non-technical issues (professional requirements, user thoughts, impact on people, strategy). This has the potential to make systems development a contentious issue.

As an example of a system that will potentially have a large impact on users, refer to figure 1.9, which describes how the Institute of Internal Auditors Australia (IIA) intends trialling a new online testing facility for its members to use as part of their professional examinations. This approach will change the way the members sit their professional exams, and the time required for getting results to members, as well as the security required for conducting exams. It also highlights some of the people issues; in this case, getting members to switch from paper-based to electronic exams. A big part of systems development can be that of changing user behaviour to suit the new system.

**FIGURE 1.9** Computer-based testing for internal auditors

**Of mice and matriculation, auditors click for exams**

Internal auditors will be throwing away pencils and paper and picking up the mouse from 2008 when they switch to writing exams on computer.

The global peak body for the industry, the Institute of Internal Auditors, will be introducing computer-based testing in order to improve the examination system.

In the past, those seeking certification as internal auditors could take $3\frac{1}{2}$-hour multiple choice exams twice a year, but with about 50000 candidates around the world and 400 in Australia, the process was becoming cumbersome.

'The numbers keep growing,' said Julie Young, manager of member services at IIA Australia.

'That means a lot of paper travelling around the world from the time the earliest candidate sits the exam in Fiji to when the papers are collated in the US and sent out for marking. We have wanted to move to a computer-based system for some time.'

The IIA will trial the computer-based exam system from next year using Pearson VUE, a provider of electronic services for certification programs, to iron out glitches.

Between 20 and 30 candidates from Australia will be invited to participate in the trial.

'The assumption is that candidates will be computer literate,' Ms Young said.

'There may be a concern that computer literacy may not be as high in some regions'.

While the new system is designed to alleviate complex administrative challenges to the Board of Regents, which maintains the security and rigour of the exams, candidates will see some benefits too. For a start, the electronic system will ensure that testing is more consistent.

*(continued)*

**FIGURE 1.9** *(continued)*

As well, exam results will be available immediately instead of weeks later.

And candidates will be able to sit exams at more than 400 centres worldwide, choosing from four sessions a year instead of the current two in May and November.

However, the new system will require increased security measures.

'There will be a much more rigorous checking of people's identity using biometrics and other measures,' Ms Young said.

The IIA will introduce fingerprint scanning to check candidates' identity when they register for the exam, along with photo ID and a letter of registration.

Candidates will also pay more to sit an exam.

The IIA has been raising the charge progressively to adjust expectations to the new level.[20]

Systems development can be driven by many different factors, one of which is a change in the regulatory and business environment. An example of this type of change is reported in the article about the Royal Australian Mint (see AIS focus 1.5). The large second-hand store franchise announced an upgrade to the financial reporting system that it uses. This upgrade came about as a response to federal legislation, and the organisation was also trying to promote consistency across its many franchise stores. Figure 1.10 contains an article about the introduction of a new passport checking system introduced at Brisbane International Airport. The process being followed in the introduction of the new technology highlights the importance of adequate testing and ensuring the functionality of the system is as expected before a new system goes live.

## AIS FOCUS 1.5

## The Royal Australian Mint's system upgrade

The Royal Australian Mint has the responsibility of producing currency for use in Australia. It has undergone an updating of its manufacturing processes, including the incorporation of The Titan (a robot that lifts more than 700 kilograms as part of the coin manufacturing process) to increase automation. Manufacturing aside, attention was also directed towards other business processes and the systems to support their operation. Part of the upgrade saw a $3.6 million dollar contract awarded to a provider of ERP knowledge management and quality management software. The aim of the project was to integrate various business information systems in use across the organisation.

While the mint had previously been using an ERP system, it found that, over time, additional programs and report requests had been added on to the system to meet the changing information needs of management. The system, with all of its add-ons, had become problematic to support, especially as staff employed when the add-ons were designed had left the organisation.

Recognising the need for a new integrated system, the Royal Australian Mint had each of its business areas map out their major process activities. The aim was to understand how the current way of doing things worked, as well as look for ways that processes could be improved.

It is expected that the new system will offer improvements across the organisation, including the way annual leave applications are processed. Instead of relying on paper forms, the new system will allow staff to enter their leave requests directly into the system. The process of authorising leave will be significantly faster, since authorisation can be made electronically rather than waiting on a trail of paper documents. There will also be better recording and monitoring of the hours employees work through tracking the times that employees clock on and clock off at work each day. The other benefit expected is in the area of planning, since the fully integrated system will encompass the entire organisation and reduce the need for people to design their own systems (e.g. spreadsheets) to handle problems outside the scope of the system. The organisation hopes that the changes will add up to a more productive and efficient workplace in the future.[21]

**FIGURE 1.10** New passport technology for customs

**Customs stalled at SmartGate**

Customs is still waiting on clearance for a new passport-checking system using biometric technology that was due to begin processing passengers last month.

The long-awaited SmartGate system is installed at Brisbane International Airport but is not yet working.

A Customs spokeswoman said it was not possible to say when testing would be complete, but the technology should be operating before the middle of the year.

'Testing has identified a number of issues that need to be addressed prior to moving to a public trial,' she said.

'Our desire is to make sure SmartGate is fully operational before opening it up to Australian travellers, even if this means a delay in implementation.'

The technology would be introduced at other Australian international airports once it had been evaluated at Brisbane.

SmartGate is designed to provide an alternative to lengthy passport-processing queues by using biometric technology to verify identity. It draws on biometric data stored on a computer chip in new passports that began to be phased in from October 2005.

At the beginning of this year, 1.4 million Australians had the new ePassports, and Customs expects 1.2 million more documents will be issued this year. The matching scanning technology is due to begin operating this year at airports around Australia, beginning with Brisbane.

Once the new system is running, ePassport holders will place their passports on a reader to record the passport image. They will then go to a gate where a video image of their face is captured and compared with the recorded passport photo using facial recognition software.

If the images match, the gate will open. If not, the traveller will be referred to a Customs officer for further checks.

Customs has said the new system should be faster than manual processing, which takes about 45 seconds.

The SmartGate technology has been in the works for four years. Early trials revealed the system was not as accurate as it needed to be. Problems with the facial recognition software contributed to false rejection rates of between 6 per cent and 8 per cent.

*(continued)*

**FIGURE 1.10** *(continued)*

> The system now installed at Brisbane is a new version that reduces rejection rates and uses more robust software to capture video images.
>
> The technology previously ran into difficulties if people spoke or moved in front of the scanner, or wore hats or glasses.
>
> Customs says the biometric technology is crucial for dealing with increasing passenger numbers.
>
> The service will be available to Australian e-Passport holders and will progressively be made available to people with eligible passports from other countries.
>
> The federal government has committed $61.7 million to the new technology.[22]

Systems development is inherently linked to the concepts covered in parts 2 and 3 of the text. In carrying out systems development, many of the issues raised in earlier chapters (e.g. business process design, systems documentation, data requirements, enterprise information systems and internal controls) will need to be considered. This makes systems development an organisation-wide task involving people from a cross-section of the business. Systems design will also impact on the operation of traditional business processes, potentially changing the types of activities performed and the means by which these activities are executed. The practical reality for any business process is that it will undergo change as new technologies emerge or the competitive environment evolves. This change in process operation can be facilitated and managed through the application of systems development techniques.

## Auditing of accounting information systems (chapter 15)

The requirement for companies to undergo financial statement audits has been long-standing. In recent times, as organisations have become increasingly computerised, the approach used by auditors for financial statement audits has been modified to take into account the increased reliance on computerised information systems in capturing financial data and using this data to prepare financial statements. The new emphasis includes increased attention to how computerised systems are designed, implemented, operated and controlled within the day-to-day operations of the organisations. There are many factors that will impact on the way an auditor goes about the audit of an information system, with these including legislative requirements (e.g. the impact of Sarbanes–Oxley in the United States), professional requirements, prescriptions of the various auditing standards and the unique characteristics of the individual client. In chapter 15 we consider these aspects in more detail and examine the responsibilities of the audit function in relation to accounting information systems, as well as the stages involved in performing an AIS audit.

Chapter 15 is strongly linked to the concepts discussed in chapter 2 on business processes and chapters 7 and 8 on internal controls. That is, much of the focus, for both internal and external auditors, is about assessing the risks within a business process and evaluating the extent to which internal controls have been put in place and how well these controls operate.

## Ethics, fraud and computer crime (chapter 16)

Ethics is concerned with how we act and how we make decisions. In recent years, the corporate world has been plagued by cases where employees and management have made unethical decisions, with the consequences, in many cases, being extreme. For the accountant, ethics is an important part of everyday professional life. The professional bodies have ethical standards that members must follow and engagement with clients needs to be carried out in an ethical manner. This extends to the accounting information system, and the need to be aware of the potential for fraudulent and unethical behaviour that could be perpetrated. The ethics chapter introduces you to some of the different perspectives of ethical behaviour, as well as describing some of the ethical issues associated with the accounting information system. It also provides you with some background and statistics relating to the Australian and New Zealand business environment and the incidence of fraud, computer crime and technology usage in organisations.

## ›› SUMMARY ›› ›

LEARNING OBJECTIVE **1** *What is accounting and how have information systems altered the role of accounting and the job of the accountant?*

The traditional role of accounting and accountants was recording the details of an organisation's transactions. The accounting process, and the accountants who were part of that process, acted as a data storage and classification system, with transactions classified based on the accounts they affected, with these accounts detailed in the general journal and then the amounts posted to the respective accounts that appeared in the general ledger. Journalising and posting transactions, as well as preparing trial balances and financial statements, can now be performed in a highly efficient manner by computerised information systems. Increasingly, the role of the accountant is being seen as to add value and provide and interpret information for an organisation. The role of the accountant has changed from a recorder of data to a user of information.

LEARNING OBJECTIVE **2** *What is information?*

Data are raw facts relating to or describing an event. Information is the product of applying rules to data to make them meaningful. This task of converting data to information is part of the role of a system.

LEARNING OBJECTIVE **3** *What is a system?*

A system takes inputs captured through various means, processes these inputs and generates useful outputs for decision makers and users of information.

LEARNING OBJECTIVE **4** *What are 'accounting information systems' and how have they evolved?*

The history of accounting information systems involved information processing long before the dawn of computer technology. However, with the advent of computers came the decline in the power of accounting divisions in organisations. Once having a powerful influence over an organisation, since it captured, recorded and stored data, as well as produced the information from that data, accounting has seen its position eroded by the birth of what is now referred to as information systems. With the emergence of information systems came new storage technologies that accountants did not have control over, so the two functions were forced to work together. As technology continued to develop, accounting became increasingly dependent on information systems, to the point where it is now viewed as a subset of information systems.

LEARNING OBJECTIVE **5** *What are some examples of the role of accounting information?*

Accounting information is central to many different activities inside and outside an organisation. The information that can be generated by an accounting information system is diverse and informs the decisions of internal and external stakeholders.

## DISCUSSION QUESTIONS

1.1 Describe some inputs, processes and outputs of an accounting information system. (LO1, LO2, LO3)

1.2 What is the difference between data and information? (LO2)

1.3 What is information overload? What are its consequences? (LO2)

1.4 Briefly summarise the changing relationship between accounting and information systems. (LO4)

1.5 Compare the role of the accountant today to his or her role before the introduction of computer technology. How have the responsibilities and duties changed over time? (LO4)

1.6 What are some of the uses of accounting information? Provide five examples of how accounting information may be used and who it would be used by. (LO5)

## SELF-TEST ACTIVITIES

1.1 Information is:
   (a) a collection of raw facts about an organisation's activities.
   (b) prepared from data through the application of rules and procedures.
   (c) always useful for those who receive it.
   (d) always in scarce supply for decision makers.

1.2 A system:
   (a) is the combination of inputs, processes, outputs and feedback.
   (b) can be influenced by external factors.
   (c) will address a specific function or purpose.
   (d) all of the above.

1.3 Data is:
   (a) useful for decision making.
   (b) increasingly captured as new input technologies emerge.
   (c) best used by an organisation when linked to the processes that generate or require them.
   (d) managed by data-mining technology.

1.4 An example of an external factor affecting the operation of an organisation's payroll system is:
   (a) how many employees the organisation has working for it.
   (b) the government's requirement to prepare payment summaries for all employees.
   (c) the request by the human resources director for a new report to be added to the system.
   (d) an employee requesting information about his or her current pay level.

1.5 MICR technology offers benefits to organisations that:
   (a) want to ensure no fraudulent transactions occur.
   (b) need security in data processing, such as devices for banks.

(c) are unable to process cheques manually.

(d) are looking for an efficient means of processing data.

1.6 Which are correct? An accounting information system must (i) capture inputs, (ii) process data, (iii) prepare report outputs, (iv) be computerised, (v) store data, (vi) verify data inputs are correct.

(a) i, ii, iii, iv

(b) ii, iii, iv, v

(c) i, ii, iv, vi

(d) i, ii, v, vi

1.7 Which of the following could be examples of feedback in an airline's online reservation system? (i) A message asking for confirmation of chosen flight dates, (ii) a link to a web page of an affiliated car rental company, (iii) a page seeking confirmation of payment details, (iv) a message informing the buyer that no flights are available at the chosen time, (v) a pop-up screen, which appears once the transaction is completed, containing the buyer's updated frequent flyer points balance.

(a) i, ii, iii, iv

(b) ii, iii, iv, v

(c) i, ii, iii, v

(d) i, iii, iv, v

1.8 The accounting function within the organisation has:

(a) over time increased in power and presence throughout the organisation.

(b) typically been merged with data management divisions, such as the information systems department.

(c) become less prominent and increasingly dependent on data storage and processing technologies, thus increasing its reliance on the information systems function.

(d) typically been well preserved within the organisation.

## PROBLEMS

1.1 Conduct a web search and find an example of each of the following data input techniques: manual keying via a keyboard, MICR, barcode scanning, image scanning, voice recognition, and optical mark readers. Construct a table describing for each technique how the technology can be used in an organisation, and its advantages and disadvantages.

1.2 You are responsible for advising a new grocery store on appropriate data capture techniques that can be used in its sales system. Using the table you completed in problem 1.1 as a guide, select an appropriate input technique and advise management on its strengths and weaknesses and why it is the best option for the organisation. Conduct a brief web search for your chosen input technique and see whether you can find some cost estimates.

1.3 The chapter discussed the idea of a system and its components. Construct a table listing the objective, inputs, processes, outputs and the external environment that affects the operation of each of the following systems:

(a) University enrolment system

(b) Public transport ticketing system

(c) Citilink road tolling system

(d) Myercard charge card system

1.4 Describe some of the external influences that affect an accounting information system. To what extent do you think these influences dictate the design of an accounting system?

1.5 Based on the historical perspective of accounting information systems presented earlier in this chapter, consider the following questions.

(a) Do you think that the accounting function will be totally engulfed by the information systems function?

(b) What are the implications of the shifts in emphasis described for potential graduates?

(c) What sort of skills do you think an accounting graduate would require as a result of these changes over time?

Conduct a web search of the big accounting firms and identify some of the skills they are typically looking for in graduates. Do they seem to be emphasising accounting skills or information skills? Why do you think this is so?

1.6 Read the article in figure 1.1 'IBM and SAP come up with package deal', and answer the following:

(a) What is viewed by the author as one of the key weaknesses of SAP's existing ERP platform?

(b) What are the expected benefits of the alliance between SAP and IBM?

(c) What are the motivations for SAP to undergo this new packaging of its product?

1.7 A computer science student says to you, 'Any information system purporting to be useful to an organisation *must* be computerised, otherwise we are just wasting our time developing new technologies like storage devices, processors and so on.' How would you respond to such a statement? Do you think the computer science student is correct? Why?

1.8 Read the article in AIS focus 1.1 'Woolworths' pursuit of customer intimacy', and answer the following:

(a) Why has Woolworths moved towards the data-mining project?

(b) What are the different data sources that will be used in the project?

(c) What would be some of the expected benefits of this project?

(d) How has the retail environment changed over the years and how can technology attempt to reverse those changes?

1.9 Using the data in figure 1.3 as a basis, describe how data are converted into information. In doing so, you should describe what differentiates data from information and provide at least three examples of the different types of information that could be generated from the data in figure 1.3.

1.10 Read the article in figure 1.9 'Of mice and matriculation, auditors click for exams', and answer the following:

(a) Why is the IIA switching to computer based exams?

(b) What are some of the people-based issues that may be confronted in making the switch from paper to computer-based exams?

(c) What are some of the technology-based issues that could be confronted in making the switch from paper to computer-based exams?

(d) Why do you think that small group testing is important before the IIA implements the new system?

(e) What has the IIA done (or what could it do) to encourage acceptance of the new system?

1.11 Read AIS focus 1.5, 'Royal Australian Mint's system upgrade', and answer the following.
   (a) What benefits do you think the Royal Australian Mint would expect from the new system?
   (b) Based on your understanding of the article, what problems did the Royal Australian Mint have with its previous system?
   (c) Why do you think the Royal Australian Mint had each business area map out their process as a part of adopting the new system?
   (d) What issues may the Royal Australian Mint face in implementing the new system throughout the organisation?
1.12 Read the article 'Customs stalled at SmartGate' in figure 1.10, and answer the following:
   (a) Why do you think it is important to do adequate testing before implementing a new system?
   (b) What benefits could come from the new Customs technology?
   (c) What different types of technology are necessary for this system to work?
   (d) What are some of the technical problems that earlier versions of the technology have faced?
   (e) How could this system impact on the users of the system? (This could include people employed by Customs as well as travellers.)

## FURTHER READING

Waring, A 1989, 'Chapter 1: Systems ideas', in *Systems methods for managers: a practical guide*, Blackwell Scientific, London, pp. 2–17.

## SELF-TEST ANSWERS

1.1 b, 1.2 d, 1.3 b, 1.4 b, 1.5 b, 1.6 d, 1.7 b, 1.8 c

## END NOTES

1. Sutton, SG 2000, 'The changing face of accounting in an information technology dominated world', *International Journal of Accounting Information Systems*, vol. 1, no. 1, pp. 1–8; Jeppesen, KK 1998, 'Reinventing auditing, redefining consulting and independence', *The European Accounting Review*, vol. 7, no. 3, pp. 517–39; Elliot, RK 1994, 'Confronting the future: choices for the attest function', *Accounting Horizons*, vol. 8, no. 3, pp. 106–24.
2. Jones, M 2007, 'IBM and SAP come up with package deal', *The Australian Financial Review*, 19 March 2007, p. 47.
3. CPA Australia 2009, 'Why accounting?', www.cpacareers.com.au.
4. The Institute of Chartered Accountants in Australia 2009, 'About chartered accountants?', www.charteredaccountants.com.au.
5. CPA Australia 2009, 'Where will I end up?', www.cpacareers.com.au.
6. Mitchell, S 2007, 'Retailer pursues lost intimacy', *The Australian Financial Review*, 12 April 2007, p. 16.
7. Webopedia 2001, 'What is MICR?', www.webopedia.com.
8. Kee, R 1993, 'Data processing technology and accounting: a historical perspective', *The Accounting Historians Journal*, vol. 20, no. 2, p. 187.
9. Kee 1993, p. 187.
10. Sutton, S & Arnold, V 2002, 'Foundations and frameworks for AIS research', in V Arnold & S Sutton (eds), *Researching Accounting as an Information Systems Discipline*, American Accounting Association, Florida, USA, p. 5.
11. Kee, p. 187.
12. Elliot 1994.

13. Elliot 1994.
14. Australian Accounting Research Foundation 2004, 'Statement of accounting concepts 2: objective of general purpose financial reporting', in J Knapp & S Kemp, *Accounting handbook 2003*, vol. 1, Prentice Hall, Sydney.
15. Braue, D 2003, 'There's gold in them thar databases', ZDNet Australia, www.zdnet.com.au.
16. Braue, 2003.
17. Heers, M 2004, 'Data classification can make or break your business', ZDNet Australia, www.zdnet.com.au.
18. Baldor, LC 2009, 'Cyber criminals targeting small business', *The Sydney Morning Herald*, 30 June, www.smh.com.au.
19. Talevski, J 2009, 'Fast track to recovery', *The Sydney Morning Herald*, 30 June, www.smh.com.au.
20. Zampetakis, H 2007, 'Of mice and matriculation, auditors click for exams', *The Australian Financial Review*, 30 March 2007, p. 68.
21. Australian Government, Royal Australian Mint 2009, 'Governor-general opens new mint in Canberra', 9 September, www.ramint.gov.au; McConnachie, D 2009, 'Australian Mint invests in technology', 26 August, www.techworld.com.au.
22. Connors, E 2007, 'Customs stalled at SmartGate', *The Australian Financial Review*, 28 March 2007, p. 55.

**40** ‹‹‹‹‹ **PART 1** ‹‹‹ SYSTEMS FUNDAMENTALS ‹‹‹

# PART  2 ›››››

# Systems characteristics and considerations

**In part 2** of the text we look at some of the issues to consider when designing the operation of systems within the organisation, including the way systems will fit within the structure of the organisation and its business processes, the way data is gathered and managed within the processes and systems, the records of how the systems operate, and the structures put in place to facilitate the smooth running of systems.

# 2
# Business processes

## Learning objectives

After studying this chapter, you should be able to:

**1** describe the components of organisational strategy and mission

**2** describe alternative organisational structures and their strengths, weaknesses and implications for organisational operations

**3** define and give examples of a business process

**4** discuss the benefits of organisations adopting a business process perspective

**5** explain the role enterprise resource planning (ERP) systems play in business process design

**6** consider some of the issues for organisations changing to a process-based focus

**7** describe and evaluate approaches to changing business processes, in particular business process re-engineering (BPR)

**8** critically evaluate BPR

**9** evaluate the application of information technology (IT) to business processes by Australian firms.

# Introduction

Do you remember what happened when you first enrolled as a new student on campus? Think back to some of the different steps that were involved and the different tasks that had to be performed for you to become a fully fledged student of the university. Initially, you probably received an offer letter in the mail that asked you to turn up at a set date and time for commencement of the enrolment process. Upon arrival at campus you may have been issued with forms for HECS and university records. Your HECS forms may have then been given to a university official for entry into the system. At the next stage you would have been photographed for your student ID card and then forwarded on to another data entry point for receipt of a concession card. Then it would have been off to the faculty, for a meeting with a course adviser, to discuss your subject enrolments for the year and where you want to take your degree. Finally, your subject choices would have been entered into the system, your student loading calculated, and then you would probably have been sent off to the bank to pay your student amenities fee. Upon completion of this you would be a fully fledged student ready to commence your studies.

This is an example of a business process in action. The business process of enrolments within the university environment is designed with the aim of enrolling new students as quickly and efficiently as possible. It has a specific objective. What you may also note from this example is that there are several different tasks that relate to different areas of the university involved in the completion of this process.

For a commercial enterprise the reality is no different. While the business processes that occur in the commercial world may be different from enrolment, the underlying philosophy is the same. Business processes lie at the heart of the modern-day organisation. As they have faced changing competitive environments over recent years, many organisations have been forced to examine their business processes and consider the assumptions and philosophies that embody their design. This chapter explores some of these ideas in further detail. We begin with a description of how an organisation determines its objectives, which stem from its mission and strategy and drive the establishment of business processes. We then look at the traditional hierarchical organisation, describing the advantages and disadvantages that a hierarchical structure provides. This organisational structure is then compared to the leaner model of the organisation, referred to as the process-based model. From this model is derived a definition of a business process. We then explore the benefits of adopting a business process perspective and explain how business processes are central to the design of the modern organisation.

Organisations changing from the hierarchical model to the process-based model, however, must undergo organisational change. One approach for implementing such organisational change is by adopting a process-based system, which leads to a discussion of enterprise resource planning (ERP) systems and how they support the process perspective of the organisation, potentially contributing to the attainment of a competitive advantage. From there, the discussion progresses to the concept of business process re-engineering (BPR) as an approach for organisational change, and looks at some of BPRs advantages and disadvantages.

**LEARNING OBJECTIVE 1**

*Describe the components of organisational strategy and mission.*

# ORGANISATIONAL STRATEGY AND MISSION

When organisations are created they will typically have a mission statement. The mission statement typically contains an expression of the organisation's vision, business domain, competencies and values.[1] The vision makes a clear statement about what the organisation wants to be in the future, the business domain is the area in which the business will operate, competencies express the business's unique strengths to be applied in the chosen domain, and values are the principles upon which the business will operate.[2] Two examples of mission statements are contained in figures 2.1[3] and 2.2.[4]

> **Wiley mission**
>
> Wiley's mission is to provide must-have content and services to professionals, scientists, educators, students, lifelong learners, and consumers worldwide. Wiley is dedicated to serving our customers' needs, while generating attractive intellectual and financial rewards for all of our stakeholders — authors, colleagues, partners, and stockholders.

**FIGURE 2.1** Wiley mission statement

> **AUSTRALIAN MADE and AUSTRALIAN OWNED**
>
> Dick Smith Foods are made in Australia by Australian owned companies. We believe this is important because it provides employment for Australians and all the profits remain here, helping the future of our country.
>
> Dick Smith Foods supports products which are produced by Australian owned businesses, which are Australian grown and made, and those Australian owned companies which operate in a highly ethical manner.
>
> Since the beginning of Dick Smith Foods we have donated over $3.50 million to a large number of charitable organisations

**FIGURE 2.2** Dick Smith Foods mission statement

You have probably heard the term 'strategy' used in a wide range of contexts. For example, sports commentators and coaches will often talk about particular defensive or attacking strategies that allow them to overcome their opposition in a game. The essence of these sentiments reflects what strategy is all about — a choice about a course of action, a means of putting a mission statement into practice. Strategy can be seen to operate at three levels: (1) internal, (2) competitive and (3) business portfolio. Internal strategy relates to the decisions that are made within the organisation; for example, organisational design and activities that are performed (this will be discussed in more detail later in the chapter). Competitive strategy is concerned with understanding the industry within which the organisation operates and distinguishing the organisation within an industry. Business portfolio strategy operates at a broader level, looking at the decision of which industry an organisation should compete within and how organisations can compete in new industries. Information technology and the application of information systems can impact each of these strategy levels, which makes their discussion in an accounting information systems text extremely relevant.[5]

Strategy determines how an organisation deals with its competitors and what products is sells in what markets and through what delivery method.[6] Michael Porter, a well-known writer on strategy, sees a business as having two options when deciding on a strategy: (1) cost leadership or (2) differentiation.[7] A cost leadership strategy sees organisations able to carry out their activities cheaper than their competitors, through economies of scale, technology, low overhead costs or efficient links with suppliers.

The alternative, the differentiation strategy, involves a business adding that little bit extra for customers, offering unique products and services targeted to the customer's needs. This higher degree of customer attention and personalisation to meet customer demands allows the organisation to charge a higher price. A contrast, albeit extreme, would be to compare a fast food restaurant to a five star restaurant. Both offer meals but there are obvious differences between the two when it comes to the personalisation of the provision of the meal, the service offered while dining and the overall ambience of the dining experience.

Essentially, Porter sees the implementation and attainment of these alternative strategies as consisting of five steps:[8]

1. *Operational effectiveness* or being able to do things better than your competitors.
2. *Uniqueness.* A business needs to choose activities different to the rest of the market to distinguish itself from its rivals and gain a strategic advantage.
3. *Trade-offs.* The set of activities chosen by an organisation means it needs to make conscious choices about the market it wishes to serve, the product or service it wishes to provide, or the particular means of delivery of its product or service.[9]
4. *Fit* or how the different activities performed by an organisation combine to achieve a common objective. The more that the activities complement each other, the stronger the fit will be and the more difficult it will be for a competitor to replicate.
5. *Sustainability.* The more activities there are within a business and the greater the unity in objective and execution between these activities, the more difficult it will be for others to copy.

The perspective on strategy we have just discussed focuses on the organisation's choice of activities. This raises the question of how to go about this process. Once again, Porter has a model to help in analysing the structure of an industry and identifying areas where an organisation business can gain an advantage. Porter argues that for an organisation to distinguish itself from its competitors and succeed in its industry it needs to look beyond its internal functions to understand the five forces that shape the industry in which it operates. These five forces are briefly described below:[10]

1. *Rivalry among existing competitors.* Refers to the current status within the market that a business operates within. Competition between participants in the market can be intense, due to competitors developing new products, using marketing strategies and techniques, offering different levels of customer service or offering lower prices.
2. *Threat of substitute products or services.* Substitute products or services are those that can be used as an alternative to what the industry currently produces. As an example, shredded paper may be seen as a substitute for polystyrene foam when packing goods in boxes.
3. *Bargaining power of suppliers.* A supplier of inputs to an organisation's manufacturing or service provision can find itself in a strong bargaining position if it is the only business able to provide a particular product or service.
4. *Bargaining power of buyers.* This refers to the relative positioning of customers in their relationship with the organisation. An organisation that provides to a small number of specialist customers can ill afford to lose them; hence, the customer is in a position of relative strength.
5. *Threat of new entrants.* New organisations entering an industry alter the competitive dynamics of the marketplace and create increased competition for the existing participants.

Using the five forces as a guide, an organisation can analyse its industry to identify particular opportunities or threats, and then develop tactics for these situations. For example, an organisation may identify that the industry is made up of a large number of customers who are not particularly loyal to one organisation. This may prompt the organisation to reconsider the activities it performs and the means of interaction it has with customers in the hope that customers will develop an allegiance or loyalty to their business. This could be done by introducing loyalty schemes or reward programs to encourage return patronage and add a cost for the customer who decides to shop elsewhere.

An organisation's choice about the set of activities to perform has been influenced in recent times by the advent of the internet and the emergence of e-commerce. In addition, the internet has led to new industries and new opportunities, for example, online auctions, digital markets for music and movies, and organisations that acquire and compile data and customise it for user needs (aggregators), such as wotif.com for hotel accommodation (the aggregator example is discussed later in the chapter).

The internet has also enabled organisations to reach a wider audience. However, that audience is potentially better informed, since the internet provides a wide array of product information and buying alternatives, which can lead to price pressure. Through the internet, businesses are also able to reconsider their choice of activities, better manage outsourcing and form partnerships more readily[11] since the internet is the 'ideal tool for distributing and providing access to information'.[12] Further, the integration of activities within an organisation and between organisations is potentially more readily achieved through the internet, due to its speed and its ability to link geographically remote places to make them virtual neighbours.

As an example, consider a traditional book publisher. Its conventional activities are that books are written, printed, warehoused and sold to customers through retail outlets. If we think about the impact of the internet on these activities, stores like Amazon have potentially eliminated the need for retail stores by having warehouses ready to send goods directly to the customer. An extension of this could be the elimination of the printing process through the delivery of books electronically. For publishers, this would see a new set of activities in book production and distribution.

 **AIS FOCUS 2.1**

## ALDI in the Australian supermarket industry

The Australian supermarket industry is dominated by Coles and Woolworths, which between them hold around 75 per cent of the national grocery market.[13] In 2001, the supermarket industry was affected by the entry of the German-based supermarket chain ALDI. From initially having only one store in Australia, over the space of eight years, ALDI has expanded to having more than 200 stores along Australia's east coast[14] and expanding distribution centres in Melbourne and Sydney.[15] ALDI sees itself as a discount supermarket chain, with the equivalent of its mission statement stating that 'Our philosophy still stands. All people, wherever they live, should have the opportunity to buy everyday groceries of the highest quality at the lowest possible price'.[16]

ALDI has established itself in the supermarket industry and now attracts more than 1 million customers each week. Sales revenue estimates are around $2 billion.[17] This raises the question about how ALDI has been able to survive and thrive in the Australian supermarket industry, given the domination by the two existing participants, Coles and Woolworths.

An application of some of Porter's five forces to ALDI could yield the following observations:

- *Position of suppliers.* The shortage of shelf space available in the large supermarket chains could mean that ALDI creates opportunities for suppliers to get their product on shelves.[18] This would be seen as a strength in negotiating with suppliers and provide ALDI with a potential means of locking in suppliers.
- *Position of customers.* ALDI is a substitute for consumers for their staple products. The cheaper, smaller shopping experience may be a way of attracting customers. The quality of products at a cheaper price (as a result of the no brand-name effect) could also be a way of attracting customers. Some customers may also be looking for a change from the traditional supermarket duopoly.[19]
- *Threat of new entrants.* With the supermarket industry dominated by two main chains that have existing relationships with suppliers and customers, ALDI's entry could be seen as a challenge. However, ALDI's simple model has seen it establish a presence and operate as a viable competitor. New entrants to the industry face the challenges of building supplier and customer relations as well as acquiring the necessary space to establish a store.[20]
- *Threat of substitutes.* ALDI is a substitute for the larger stores, just as convenience stores could be seen as a substitute. Convenience stores are probably not a long-term threat, due to their tendency to carry brand-name products and charge higher prices.[21]
- *Overall industry position.* The supermarket industry has traditionally been dominated by the two large chains that have well established technology, physical infrastructure and relationships with suppliers. ALDI has established a viable presence in this duopoly.

ALDI has operationalised its strategy through:

1. Smaller number of staff — multi-skilled staff that can complete the range of responsibilities in-store which keeps overhead costs down.
2. Smaller number of suppliers and range of products — ALDI has made a conscious choice about its suppliers, typically choosing non-branded or private labels, which allows it to offer the products at 30 to 40 per cent cheaper than branded products.[22] On average, ALDI carries 900 different products in its stores, in contrast o what is reported as the 'tens of thousands'[23] carried by Coles and Woolworths.
3. Smaller shopping premises — the smaller range of products enables costs to be kept down; for instance, the size of ALDI's stores are somewhere around one-fifth of the size of the typical Woolworths or Coles store. The activities have also been customised to support the adopted strategy, with 'no marketing department, no advertising department, no legal department and no human resources department'.[24]
4. Simple in-store processes with a no add-ons approach — even the customer experience in the store reminds us that this is a store operating leanly;

*continued*

customers need to buy their shopping bags and pack their shopping after making a purchase.

5. Quality products at cheap prices — allows for built-in features, such as being able to go to the ALDI website and see the price for all items they sell (this is seen as prohibitive as the product range increases to the level of the larger retailers).[25]

The processes and activities — from a smaller number of suppliers and products, smaller premises and smaller overhead costs — mean that ALDI has been able to build a tight fit in its activities that allow it to fulfil its chosen strategy.

# ORGANISATIONAL DESIGN

An organisation is an organised body or system. In a commerce context, an organisation is the business enterprise, for example, Qantas, Telstra or Ernst & Young. These enterprises have mission statements and adopted strategies, with the challenge being the implementation of these in practice. In order to successfully implement their chosen strategy, organisations will consider the issues of organisational design. In this section, we discuss and compare different types of organisational design.

Business enterprises organise themselves in different ways — that is, by adopting different methods to provide a structure for their operations and coordinate the efforts of their employees so that they work towards a common purpose. This common purpose should be reflected in the organisation's mission statement. As discussed above, the mission statement outlines the reasons for the company's existence, where it sees itself as making a contribution, and what its aims and objectives are.

One technique to organise a business enterprise is through its internal **organisational design** (also called organisational structure or hierarchy) — the structure of the relationships, interactions and reporting responsibilities among staff. Over the years, organisations have adopted a range of organisational designs. We will discuss two approaches: the functional perspective and the business process perspective. Both have advantages and disadvantages for the organisation, and the different contexts in which a business may operate will dictate a different structure. This text focuses on the business process perspective, but you should also be familiar with the more historical functional perspective, from which the business process perspective emerged.

*Organisational design* (also called organisational structure or hierarchy) The organisation of a business enterprise through the structure of the relationships, interactions and reporting responsibilities among staff.

## The functional perspective of the organisation

Analysis of well established organisations often reveals a very hierarchical design. A hierarchically designed organisation or the **functional perspective** of the organisation is one with clear organisational structures in place, including functional divisions and reporting responsibilities within and among these functions clearly defined.

An early management writer, Frederick Taylor, developed a management philosophy that was referred to as **scientific management**.[26] Typical of the hierarchical, manual labour and control-based environment of the time, Taylor proposed that employee tasks and responsibilities should be clearly specified, with each employee having a defined role. A range of employees would collectively perform a range of

*Functional perspective* A view of organisational design that emphasises hierarchical reporting roles, narrowly specified worker roles and an emphasis on departments.

*Scientific management* An approach to job design that sees workers repeatedly perform narrowly defined tasks.

tasks, but each individual employee would perform only a small variety of tasks. Thus, employees would develop a specific skill-set and become specialists in this narrow area. The implementation of Taylor's ideas within the organisation led to the creation of hierarchies, with employees supervised by middle management, who reported to top management. Because of the nature of each employee's role — clearly defined, highly specific and structured — each employee was largely unaware of what others did.

This management philosophy, primarily geared at the individual level of work design, also infiltrated the organisational level, with organisations frequently designed and departmentalised based on the different functions performed. A **business function** or department is a specific subset of the organisation that performs a particular role that contributes to the organisation achieving its objectives. Examples of business functions or departments include the sales department, responsible for selling products or services, the manufacturing department, responsible for making goods, the accounting department, responsible for keeping records of the organisation's financial activities, and so on. Notice how the function of each department is specifically defined, with minimal overlaps to other functions.

This structure is represented in figure 2.3, which contains a hierarchy for a typical functionally based organisation.

**Business function** *A specific subset of the organisation that is designed to perform a particular task that contributes to the organisation achieving its objectives.*

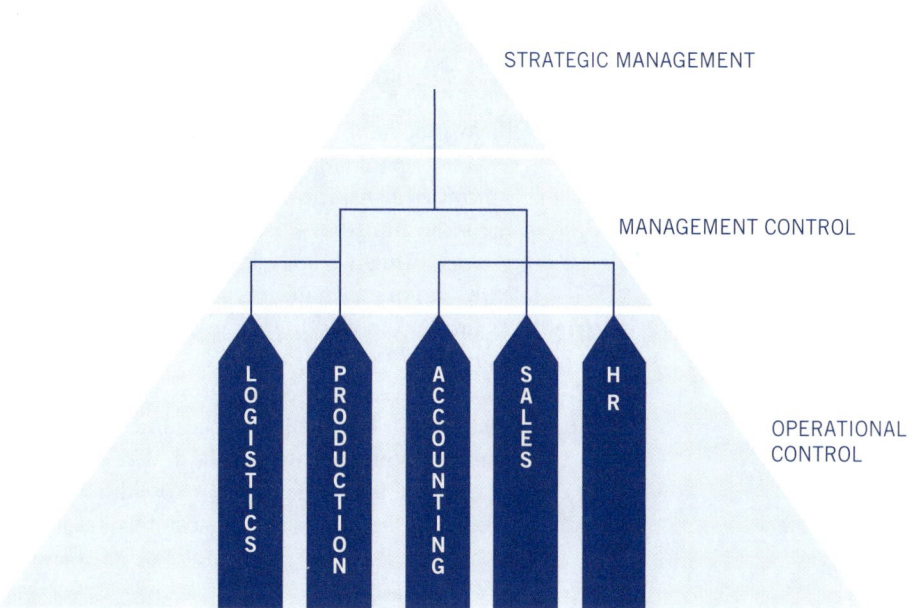

**FIGURE 2.3** A functionally based organisation
*Source:* Based on Sandoe, Corbitt & Boykin 2001.[27]

In the organisation depicted in figure 2.3 there are five functional areas or departments: logistics, production, accounting, sales and human resources. Each performs a specific function within the organisation. Notice how the organisation is divided into three levels: strategic, management control and operational control. This division, developed by Anthony, is a way of classifying the different nature of tasks in different levels of the organisation.[28] At the operational level, the concern is to complete the tasks in the functional areas or departments in a proper manner. This will include those actually performing the tasks and those who supervise the performance of the tasks. Above this is the management control level, responsible for monitoring the performance of the different functional areas. In this case, two of the departments (logistics and production) report to one manager, while the remaining three departments (accounting, sales and human resources) report to a second manager. These managers will synthesise information about the performance of the departments under their control and forward this to a higher level of management, labelled the strategic level. The strategic level is concerned with developing strategies for business success and coming up with an appropriate mission for the organisation. Such tasks are completed based on an analysis of the performance information that filters up from the management control level, as well as through the strategic management's analysis of the external environment.

It is notable that communication across the departments does not occur below a high level in the organisation. To share information throughout the organisation it must first be sent up and then across the hierarchy, before it filters down to lower levels. The practical reality for many organisations today is that this is an unworkable business model. Some have chosen to flatten their organisation by removing some layers within a department. In the process of flattening the organisation, some have adopted a business process perspective. Business processes are discussed in the following section.

## Benefits

There were, and still are, many arguments for pursuing a functionally based organisational design. These include strong control and coordination, stability, and task specificity that can be built into the organisation.

- *Control and coordination.* One strong benefit of the functional perspective is that it provides a great deal of organisational control. Due to the high volume of reporting relationships that exist — for example, operational staff in each department report to department managers, who report to managers at the management control level, who report to managers at the strategic level — there is a strong monitoring network. Of course, the disadvantage is the bureaucracy required to support such a structure. This is discussed later in the chapter.
- *Specificity.* As we mentioned previously, tasks within the functionally based organisation will be highly defined and specified. This means employees and managers are clear on what their tasks and responsibilities are. The functional structure provides a delineation of tasks across different departments of the organisation, as well as within departments. This can be a useful tool for an organisation wishing to gain clarity and specificity of employee roles and responsibilities.

## Problems and limitations

For each of these advantages, there are disadvantages or limitations to the functional perspective. It does not necessarily reflect the reality of today, can lead to information and communication problems or a focus on the wrong things, and can result in the organisation lagging behind when reacting to the environment.[29]

- *Not reflective of the reality of today.* Businesses today need to be driven by customer needs, rather than by the best way to control operations within the organisation. It is often difficult to provide customer service through a hierarchically and departmentally based organisational design that suffers from poor communication across the organisation where it possibly matters most.

- *Information and communication problems.* The functional perspective can create an overly hierarchical and bureaucratic organisation. A common consequence of this is the perception that 'staff create overheads and bureaucracies that far exceed their value'.[30] Take, for example, a loans consultant working on loan applications in a bank. The consultant may process a particular part of the loan application, for example, the credit check. In an extremely hierarchical organisation, the consultant would conduct the credit check and forward the result to a supervisor, who would then make a decision on the creditworthiness of the applicant and send this back to the consultant, who would then pass on the decision to the next person involved in handling the application.
- *Slow to react to the environment.* The hierarchical and bureaucratic nature of the functional organisation means it can be slow to react to changes in both the internal organisational environment and the external operating environment. It takes time for information to filter up and down in the organisation. That is, if strategic management decides upon a new strategy, it must be communicated to the management control level. These middle managers then need to communicate the strategy to the operational managers, who then need to communicate it to the operational staff performing tasks in the different department. This makes the organisation extremely slow and clumsy in responding to change. Similarly, in the reverse, it takes time for information to flow up the organisation, meaning there will be delays between when something is reported at the operational level and when it can be addressed at the strategic level.
- *Focuses on the wrong things.* As Byrne so eloquently states, functionally based organisations are built around the idea that staff should 'look up to bosses instead of out to customers'.[31] The managers and employees scattered throughout the organisational hierarchy in figure 2.3 will be solely concerned with pleasing their immediate supervisor. This comes about due to the precisely defined task specifications and the hierarchy and monitoring network that is superimposed on this type of organisation. However, as can be seen in the following sections, focusing on reporting hierarchies can be dangerous for an organisation because it can lead to an ignorance of customer requirements.

These disadvantages led to an alternative organisational design: the business process perspective.

# WHAT IS A BUSINESS PROCESS?

A **business process** is a series of *interlocking activities* that work together, *across the organisation*, to achieve some *predetermined organisational goal*. This predetermined goal is typically defined around satisfying *customer needs*. Look at the definition of a business process presented above. You should note that four key aspects of this definition have been italicised: 'interlocking activities', 'across the organisation', 'predetermined organisational goal', and 'customer needs'. Each of these aspects will now be discussed in more detail, enabling you to gain a comprehensive understanding of what a business process is.

## Interlocking activities

A business function was defined above as a specific subset of the organisation that is designed to perform a particular task that contributes to the organisation achieving its objectives. In a business process, various business functions are involved in a series of interactions with one another to provide a good or service for the end customer. Thus, the nature of a business process is such that business functions are integrated and work together.

## Across the organisation (the horizontal perspective)

In the hierarchical structure in the functional perspective, information flows are vertical. However, the practical reality is that flows occur across an organisation. These horizontal flows are representative of business processes and reflect that different departments and functional areas need to communicate with each other to provide the good or service a customer may require. As a practical example, consider what may happen in a retail organisation when it makes a sale to a customer. The sales staff will process the customer's order and enter it into their sales system. Once the order is captured they check for availability of the goods, since any stock that is unavailable may need to be placed on back-order. If items that are out of stock, this out-of-stock notification may be sent to the manufacturing division, so that more units can be produced. After collection from the warehouse, the goods will be forwarded to the shipping department for distribution to the customer. In the process of making the sale to the customer there has been a role for the sales department and several other functional areas in the organisation. This is the true nature of a business process, with flows occurring across the organisation.

## Predetermined goal

Business processes are designed to achieve some predetermined goal or objective of the organisation. Thinking of some typical business processes, you can intuitively identify the predetermined goal they are designed to achieve. For example, the sales process aims to make and capture sales from customers, and the purchasing process aims to acquire goods from suppliers, and keep order costs and inventory carrying costs to a minimum.

## Customer needs

The objective of a business process is to achieve an organisational goal, which is typically geared to the needs of a customer.

Figure 2.4 illustrates an example of the process perspective for a sales process. A quick explanation may help in understanding the definition of a business process. A sales process is designed with the aim of selling goods and delivering them to customers. Assume that a mobile salesperson visits customer sites and canvasses products that customers may require. If a customer wishes to make a purchase, the sales representative remotely logs on to the office network and accesses inventory information to check that the goods are in stock and ready to be delivered. Before approving a sale, the sales representative will also want to confirm that the customer does not have a history of bad debts. So he or she might check with the accounts receivable department for a quick credit rating. Once inventory availability and creditworthiness are confirmed, the sales representative will approve the sale and send details to the logistics department. The logistics department will arrange for delivery of the goods to the customer. Finally, since the sales representative is paid on commission, details of the sale will be sent to human resources so that the commission attached to the sale can be calculated.

Notice how, in carrying out the sales process, information was required from across the organisation. The process perspective designs organisations around this principle, making sure that interaction and coordination are present so that information is readily accessible. Also notice how much of the customer's interaction with the organisation is through the sales representative. The reduced hierarchy in the process organisation, with flows across the organisation at lower levels, allows the process to be completed quickly and efficiently.

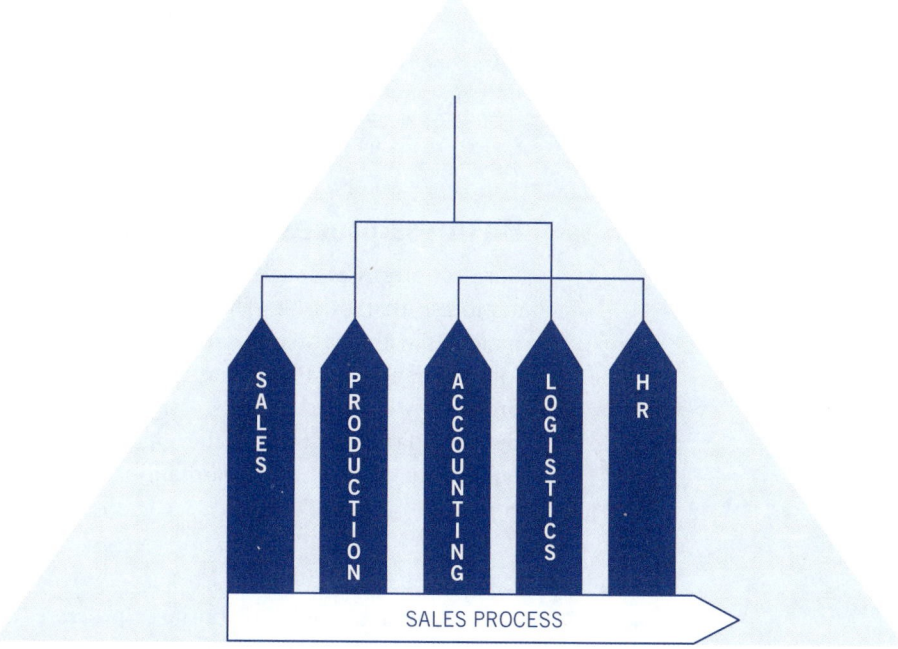

**FIGURE 2.4** A process-based organisation

## What is a business process compared with a business function?

To appreciate the remainder of this chapter, you should be clear on the distinction between a business process and a business function. Recall that a business process was defined as a series of interlocking activities that work together across the organisation to achieve some predetermined organisational goal that is typically defined around satisfying customer needs. A business function was defined as a specific subset of the organisation that performs a particular role that contributes to the organisation achieving its objectives. Notice the differences in these definitions. A business function is a specific task or role that is performed, for example, accounting, sales or marketing. Moving from business function to business process shifts the frame of reference from looking at specific individual functions to how these functions interact with one another to deliver a good or service to the customer. So, the business process is a combination of business functions operating together to achieve a goal.

A summary of the distinctions between the process and functional perspective is contained in table 2.1 overleaf.

**TABLE 2.1** Functional versus process perspective

| | Functional perspective | Process perspective |
|---|---|---|
| Focus | What is done — e.g. accounting, sales, logistics | How is it done |
| Orientation | Vertical, hierarchical | Horizontal, across the organisation |
| Objective | Task driven | Customer driven |
| Personnel | Specialists perform highly defined tasks | Generalists perform tasks across the process |

*Source:* Based on Sandoe, Corbitt & Boykin 2001.[32]

## Business processes within the organisation

Business processes are the key to any organisation. Businesses do not operate without a process that can be followed, with examples including processes to order raw materials within a manufacturing firm, manufacture products, sell products to customers, handle customer enquiries and hire new employees. Each of these broad processes will be an integral part of an organisation, because, for example, without the manufacturing process the organisation has no goods to sell and without the purchasing process, the organisation has no raw materials to convert into finished goods.

### *Examples*

Some typical examples of business processes are the sales process, the purchasing process and the manufacturing process. A brief discussion of their operation is now provided, including their general aims, the participants involved and their inputs and outputs. For a more detailed discussion, refer to chapters 9 to 11.

**Sales**
Aim: To sell goods to the customer and collect cash from sales.
Participants: Sales staff, customer, billing staff, warehouse.
Inputs: Sales order.
Outputs: Invoice, receipt, shipping document.

**Purchasing**
Aim: To acquire goods from suppliers and manage stock in order to sell to customers and avoid stock-outs.
Participants: Warehouse staff, purchasing staff, sales staff, vendor.
Inputs: Purchase requisition, back-order.
Outputs: Purchase order.

**Manufacturing**
Aim: To convert raw materials into finished goods.
Participants: Manufacturing staff, sales staff.
Inputs: Back-order, manufacturing notice, raw materials.
Outputs: Finished goods.

# WHY BUSINESS PROCESSES?

There are several reasons for adopting a business process perspective within the organisation, one of which is the resource benefits that flow from having a process emphasis. This comes about because the process perspective offers an organisation a more coordinated and integrated approach, reducing wasted time due to rework, bureaucracy and administration. This becomes evident in exploring the IBM Credit discussion later in the chapter, seeing some of the benefits that were realised by shifting from a functional to a process-based design. Toyota is another example of a company that was able to realise significant benefits by introducing a process focus into its vehicle manufacturing operations.[33]

The business process perspective can yield benefits for an organisation through improved customer service and customer relations, a value-adding emphasis and, potentially, a competitive advantage. Business processes are typically built around the desired product or result that is to be achieved. More often than not this will be based around the customer, whether inside or outside the organisation. As a result, customer satisfaction, attention and service are potentially higher in a process-focused organisation.

The process perspective can also lead to the better use of resources. As is discussed in the section that examines ERP systems and business processes, business processes can eliminate duplication of data and wastage in storage and can also restructure ineffective interdepartmental communication networks. This can lead to better information flows through the organisation, potentially leading to more effective decision making by management.

In the functional perspective of the organisation, the complex and well-developed hierarchies introduce bureaucracy and can lead to the creation of jobs and functions that do not add any value to the goods or services provided by the organisation but are necessary to support the bureaucracy. In the process prospective, a flattened organisational design can reduce bureaucracy and create a more flexible organisation. Part of this flattening will involve identifying tasks and functions that do not add value and eliminating them — after all, if they cost resources to perform but do not give anything in return, why bother doing them in the first place? A well-structured business process will have minimal non-value-adding activities included in its design.

Business processes can also provide an organisation with a competitive advantage, with organisations increasingly looking towards the design of their business processes as a means of distinguishing themselves from the host of competitors they may face in their industry.[34] This competitive advantage comes from the design of business processes that are unique or offer something different. For example, a company may design its manufacturing process to enable it to offer a high degree of customisation in the products that consumers purchase, or build in added customer service features, which could distinguish the company from its competitors. The issue of the design of business processes, ERP systems and competitive advantage is further discussed later in the chapter.

It was mentioned earlier (refer to learning objective 3, page 53) that a business process consists of a series of interlocking activities that work together to achieve an organisational goal. We also mentioned that business processes can be outsourced. The outsourcing of components of a business process is something that has increased in prevalence as the impact of technology is progressively felt across the world.

In his book *The World is Flat*, Thomas Friedman[35] describes a series of events that he sees as having flattened the world, reducing international boundaries for commercial communication and collaboration. The common theme in Friedman's discussion is that technology has had a significant role in 'flattening' the world, allowing the distribution of activities across the globe with this distribution appearing seamless to the end customer. For businesses this is significant, since it allows them to outsource offshore parts of their business process with relative ease, with the realisation of benefits such as potential cost savings and better performing processes. Martin Conboy, the president of a company that provides outsourcing connections for businesses, is well aware of the motivations businesses have for outsourcing part of their business processes, as well as the technology that has made it possible. Conboy, in an interview with *The Age*, was quoted as saying that 'This is all because of the internet because basically any particular business process that can be done more efficiently by computer ... or more cost-effectively by cheaper Asian labour, that can be shoved down a wire, that doesn't add value to your company, will be outsourced.'[36] The increased role of technology in business processes has made outsourcing beyond our shores a reality for many organisations, with the worldwide outsourcing market estimated to be worth around US$130 billion.[37]

Common examples of outsourcing of parts of business processes include the operation of a call centre for customer enquiries, and the maintenance of IT requirements — including software design and development — in remote locations. Friedman[38] estimates that approximately 245 000 Indians work in call centres in India, receiving enquiries from customers worldwide. This is reflective, in part, of the modular nature of a business process, and also the role that information technology is playing within the design of business processes. Friedman's notion of a flattened world is evident in the higher levels of technology integration that have enabled global communication to occur in a seamless manner. Such technological integration enables a customer to seamlessly deal with a call centre operating from India without even being aware of the thousands of kilometres between them and the assistant on the other end of the line. To further enhance the seamless nature of this process, many call centres will train their employees in the accent and phonetics of the customers they will be dealing with, to the extent that they even adopt anglicised names when dealing with customers![39]

One benefit derived from outsourcing part of a business process is cost savings, with many international destinations offering equivalent services for less cost, particularly in labour, than that in Australia. Of course, this approach can also create social and ethical issues that need to be considered when making the outsourcing decision, particularly the nature of the conditions that overseas workers encounter. More generally, outsourcing part or all of a business process also allows a company to 'take layers of cost out of its operating structure in order to return more profits to shareholders.'[40]

AIS focus 2.2 describes the rationale and also some of the issues for businesses that are looking to outsource some or all of their business process.

## AIS FOCUS 2.2

## Outsourcing opens doors in global village

The offshore outsourcing train has left the station and Australia doesn't even have a ticket, according to FoobooOnline.com president Martin Conboy.

Mr Conboy is in the business of match-making.

His newly launched FooBooOnline.com (Front Office Outsourcing Back Office Outsourcing) business offers a website portal as a single point of contact between buyers and suppliers of outsourcing services in the Asia–Pacific marketplace.

He believes businesses that do not assess their outsourcing or offshoring opportunities will be left behind.

'If we don't get on to this train then overseas organisations will come over here and where (companies) have got comfortable ... will eat their lunch,' Mr Conboy said.

'Unless they've got something so fantastically special that people are prepared to pay a premium for it, they'll go out of business. Outsourcing is not a blip on the economic radar. It's a growing and accelerating trend. Currently the market is worth about $US130 billion ($A180 billion).'

Many Australian businesses are now choosing to outsource their services overseas to where there is cheap labour.

'There isn't a company in the country that hasn't been trying to take layers of cost out of its operating structure in order to return more profits to shareholders,' Mr Conboy says.

But unions argue the practice is sending Australian jobs overseas and hurting the country's skills base.

Mr Conboy disagrees. 'Australia is facing a massive skills shortage,' he said, and employers were forced to look overseas.

But Austrade chief economist Tim Harcourt said some companies were also outsourcing to other Australian companies because of the country's high-quality skilled labour.

Mr Harcourt said there were some skill shortages but said they needed to be dealt with by investing in education and training.

He believes companies are outsourcing their services overseas to secure a foothold in the global market rather than just to reduce costs.

'There's one argument to say companies that stay domestic lose out on international trends and innovation ... to those that go global and lift their technology and are more productive.'

These globalised companies were more likely to win in the competitive business world.

And while Mr Harcourt believes the trend to outsource services is increasing 'a little bit', he said it made up a very small proportion of companies conducting business overseas.

FooBooOnline.com's vice-president of operations and information technology, James Haensly, believes Australian companies need to actively participate in the global village, which has emerged since the advent of the internet.

'Right now Australia's primary export is commodities but there's a whole range of goods and services that can be offered into these markets of Asia with these huge populations,' he said.

With the increasing trend towards outsourcing, there were many business process outsourcing companies springing up that were of varying quality, he said.

'For a business to even consider (offshoring), for them to get in a plane and land in Delhi or Mumbai and try to figure out how to do this is next to impossible, and that's where FooBoo comes in because we know this market.'

*continued*

Mr Conboy said business were looking to outsource front-office voice services such as customer service usually delivered by call centres, and back-office services such as payroll, cheque and claims processing, software development and human resources.

Businesses could save 30–40 per cent by outsourcing these sorts of services.

'It's economics 101,' he said. 'This is all because of the internet because basically any particular business process that can be done more efficiently by computer ... or more cost-effectively by cheaper Asian labour, that can be shoved down a wire, that doesn't add value to your company, will be outsourced.'

Mr Conboy said companies were being driven to outsource services because shareholders were demanding increasing dividends.

'Boards of directors who for the last five years have spent an inordinate amount of time looking to take costs out of their business have reached their credential limit,' he said.

FooBooOnline.com, after being launched last week, has already had an 'enormous amount of interest' from companies looking to outsource services. However, 50 per cent of this interest has come from the United States.

In Australia the interest has come from a number of sectors, including pharmaceutical, manufacturing, telecommunications, finance and retail.[41]

---

The selection of processes to outsource is critical, because an organisation would obviously be reluctant to outsource a process that provided it with a competitive advantage. Outsourcing can also create social, political and ethical issues for an organisation. A recent example of business process outsourcing is Telstra's decision to outsource part of its software development process. This is discussed further in AIS focus 2.3.

## AIS FOCUS 2.3

### Telstra's outsourcing

Businesses have long sought to outsource activities and processes that they perform. Typically, organisations will outsource activities or processes that add little value to their primary activities, or activities for which they do not have the expertise and technology and it would be too costly to acquire them. Examples of such activities could be the outsourcing of the IT function to a computer specialist or the outsourcing of the payroll function.

An organisation's business process can be designed to include activities of outsourced service providers, and many organisations are doing this. For example, Company A may outsource its call centre operations to Company B. The call centre is the number that the customer calls if he or she has enquiries, complaints and so forth. From the customer's perspective it will appear as though they are interacting with Company A, but the reality is that they are actually interacting with Company B, which is providing the service for Company A. The service provided by Company B is then integrated into the processes of Company A, so that any data gathered from customers is available to Company A.

In January 2004, a fiery debate about the outsourcing of business processes hit the Australian press, driving home some of the ethical and social issues associated with outsourcing. Telstra, Australia's large telecommunications provider, was placed under pressure because of a planned outsourcing arrangement it had with IBM. The controversy emerged because Telstra was in the process of implementing a significant cost-saving plan that would reduce its spending by about $957 million. IBM was an outsourced service provider for Telstra, responsible for the management and execution of the software development process. The cost savings were to be achieved by IBM giving some 1500 jobs to overseas providers.[42]

The decision by Telstra and IBM led to several prominent politicians, including the federal treasurer, Peter Costello, and union representatives'[43] condemning the move, fearful of the impact on Australian workers and the development of skills in Australia.[44] This raises some interesting issues for companies looking to outsource some or all of their business processes. In this case, Telstra outsourced to IBM and IBM was looking to go offshore. The argument from Telstra was that the decision was IBM's, the outsource provider, and as such it should not be blamed.[45]

## End–user perspective

Business processes are typically geared around the needs of the customer, inside or outside the organisation. A common example of an external customer could be a client who purchases a product or service from the organisation, while an example of an internal customer could be someone within the organisation who uses the output of a particular process to perform his or her own task. An example of this latter type of customer could be a purchasing manager who uses the outcome of the sales budgeting and manufacturing scheduling process to determine what type and quantity of raw materials need to be ordered.

**LEARNING OBJECTIVE 5**

*Explain the role enterprise resource planning (ERP) systems play in business process design.*

# ERP SYSTEMS, BUSINESS PROCESSES AND BEST PRACTICE

An ERP system is a complex set of computer program modules that integrate the different functional areas of the organisation. The hierarchical structure of organisations designed around business functions created problems in that they tended to be inadvertently developed around an information silo principle.

This leads each functional area of the organisation to develop its own information system to solve its own function-based problems. For example, sales will develop its own systems to handle sales records and customer sales orders, the warehouse division will develop its own systems for inventory management and marketing will develop unique systems for marketing products and services. More often than not, these systems are developed in isolation, and each function will fail to consider how it fits in with other departments. This can lead to duplication of data across the organisation, which creates its own problems. The systems become like silos within the organisation — operating on their own with little interaction.

While the idea of functionally based systems may seem logical — after all, one would assume that those within a function know what they require a system to do, and are consequently best equipped to develop their own systems — it fails to recognise the realities that confront the modern organisation. As organisations adopt the business process perspective, they also require information systems that recognise and are designed around these realities.

ERP systems are a way for organisations to implement a system to overcome the information silos of the functional approach and put into practice the philosophy of a process perspective. ERP systems accomplish this by having a series of modules related to the different functional areas of an organisation — for example, typical modules include sales, accounts receivable, inventory and purchasing. However, unlike in the information silo approach, in an ERP system these modules are all part of one package. As a result, the modules are integrated and able to operate efficiently. For example, when a sale is entered into the sales module, the inventory data will be updated to record the commitment of goods, and accounts receivable will be updated to reflect the new outstanding balance of the customer. This integration more accurately reflects the reality of a process-driven organisation. Additionally, all modules will operate from a single shared database central to the ERP system. As a result, the problems of data duplication and redundancy are resolved. A more detailed discussion of ERP systems is contained in chapter 6.

Additionally, the design philosophy of ERP systems is centered on the idea of **best practice**. The business processes supported by an ERP system have been designed and programmed into the system based on what is deemed to be, following research and investigation, the best way to perform them. These standards of best practice are one of the compelling reasons for organisations to adopt ERP systems as they are and not change the software. After all, why would you change something that is the best design? However, this necessitates thinking about some of the situations in which a business may want to adopt a business process but not how it is configured in an ERP system.

Davenport describes some of the scenarios where businesses are better off changing an ERP package rather than changing their existing business processes.[46] Conventional wisdom says that an organisation is best to adopt an ERP system as is, rather than change it, for two reasons. The first is that the system represents best practice for a process. The second is that the cost of an ERP system, without modifying it, can be enormous (maybe millions of dollars). Once you start altering and modifying the design of the system, these costs rise rather rapidly. Altering an ERP system can be a very costly process for an organisation. On their own, these two arguments are reasonably compelling reasons for changing the organisation and its processes to suit the system. However, there is one critical factor to understand before doing so: competitive advantage.

The aim of any organisation is to gain some form of competitive advantage over its competitors. A competitive advantage is something unique that a business does that is not offered by its competitors and thus represents a way for the organisation to distinguish itself from the rest of the field. One way for an organisation to do this can be through the configuration of its business processes. As an example, a retail company may configure its sales and support process to offer total customer service and support that none of its competitors are able to match, allowing it to keep existing customers and attract new ones. The retail firm would most probably be extremely unwilling to adjust this process, as long as it remained unique, since it would be one of the ways it distinguishes itself from its competitors. So for it to adopt an ERP system, with its standardised business processes, would not make sense. This is because the processes embodied in the way the organisation currently operates would most probably not be embodied in the design of the ERP system and adopting the ERP system would mean giving up its uniqueness in the marketplace.

So organisations designing business processes and considering the adoption of ERP systems need to carefully consider their existing business practices, how they provide a competitive advantage, and how the business processes represented in an ERP system will fit or conflict with them. The aspect of homogeneity can also be a reason not to configure a business process around an ERP system; after all, the ERP system and its processes are available to every organisation willing to pay for it. If all organisations adopt the software and have the same underlying processes, how can they distinguish themselves and gain a competitive advantage?

Volkoff describes the example of a photographic company that was adopting an ERP package throughout its organisation.[47] Having adapted to some of the modules already, the time came to apply the sales and marketing module within the organisation. What the organisation found was that by adopting the module, thus changing the organisation to suit the design of the system, it would lose some of its uniqueness. This was because up until the adoption of the ERP system, the company's sales and marketing process had been designed to allow a great deal of flexibility and customisation in the sales representatives' duties. As a consequence, the representatives were able to tailor prices and packages to individual customers, as well as handle back orders and delivery of goods. The organisation found that by blindly adopting the ERP package a lot of these 'customer friendly' aspects would be lost as they were replaced by the generic processes designed into the software. Alternatively, because of the vast array of options that were used by sales representatives when dealing with customers, the prospect of configuring the ERP system to accommodate these was a daunting, if not unrealistic, task.

Porter alludes to this idea when he mentions that strategy and competitive advantage are all about choosing to do the activities in a business process differently from competitors. If all your competitors are adopting ERP systems, then perhaps keeping your existing business processes can be a way for you to distinguish your organisation. At the very least, in the short term, it might be possible to provide processes at a lower cost than competitors, because you do not have the large overhead associated with the acquisition and installation of an ERP system.[48]

On the other hand, those adopting ERP systems may be able to design faster, more efficient business processes, benefiting from the centralised database, lack of duplication, integration and business process perspective that an ERP system provides. One benefit that could be available from an ERP system, particularly through integration, is that the performance of customer service-based processes could improve.

Think about how many times you have rung a business, asked a question, received an answer, asked a second question and been told, 'I'm sorry, I can't answer that question, I will need to transfer you through to John in the accounts department.' This is symptomatic of a functional organisation with its information silo design. The integration of functions through ERP systems means that, potentially, one person, a customer service representative for example, can handle all customer enquiries, from sales orders to order status, to accounts owing details, to returns and complaints. The integration of data in ERP systems allows organisations to build the information into the business processes, with the benefit flowing on to the customers of that process.

# ISSUES IN MOVING TO A BUSINESS PROCESS–BASED ENVIRONMENT

There are often many issues that need to be addressed and managed for organisations that shift from the functional information silo approach to the business process approach. These include changes in the role of management and in the design of employee tasks and responsibilities.

## Management change

The first stage in adopting a business process perspective is that it must be represented in the design of the organisation. There is little point to an organisation saying 'we are committed to a business process perspective' and then in the same breath saying 'we are maintaining our functionally based structure'. The result would be that the organisation's purported commitment to processes will probably fade away as just another management fad and the status quo of the functional approach will quickly be restored.

How the organisation is managed must change if the change in perspective is to be taken seriously. As with most things associated with change, support needs to come from the top down. But the reality for some organisations can be that the change at the top is difficult. As Hammer and Stanton observe:[49]

> [T]he power in most companies still resides in vertical units — sometimes focused on regions, sometimes on products, sometimes on functions — and those fiefdoms still jealously guard their turf, their people and their resources ... the horizontal processes pull people in one direction; the traditional vertical [functional] management systems pull them in another.

Why does management act like this? The answer lies in the effect of a business process perspective on roles and responsibilities within the organisation. Shifting to a process-based organisation can mean significant changes in the way people perform their duties. What was once a traditional, narrowly defined specialist job can become a generalist and diverse role. This pushes the rights to decision making further down in the organisation's hierarchy. As a result there can be a power shift in the organisation, with the middle layers of management resisting such changes to their responsibilities.

Hammer and Stanton[50] describe the example of Texas Instruments, a manufacturer of calculators and electronic products, and some of the management issues it had in shifting to a process-based perspective for its product development. Those who were entrenched in the functional perspective of the organisation refused to cooperate with the process-based push, with the resistance resulting in some functional managers refusing to release staff, resources and authority to those on the new process teams. This can be seen as reflective of management's resistance to the change, as well as the process focuses being implemented within what was ostensibly still a functional firm: the power and authority for the running of the organisation still rested with the functional departments.

## People change

A shift to a process perspective has the effect of breaking down functional barriers and divisions that previously existed. The person in the accounts department is no longer concerned solely with doing the accounting job, but rather doing it so that it integrates with the rest of the business process. The focus shifts beyond the traditional and narrowly defined duties associated with the functional perspective of the organisation. This can lead to increased authority for those lower in the organisation, as well as a more stimulating work environment. Instead of turning up to work knowing that all they will be doing is one specific, narrowly defined task, as is generally the case in the functional environment, employees become involved in a range of tasks across the process and see how the tasks integrate with each other. This creates a much more stimulating environment for the employees.

Pursuing a process focus can often mean shedding a layer of middle management, as the organisation looks for value-adding activities and the removal of non-value-adding activities and functions. As you would logically expect, this can create a degree of resistance among those threatened by the change for two reasons. First, the manager may face redundancy, which is not an enticing prospect. Second, the manager may face a change in roles and responsibilities and, possibly, the loss of some authority.

# CHANGING BUSINESS PROCESSES

Business processes are not static and concrete. Indeed, they should be viewed as being in a constant state of flux, as the impacts of new technologies, competition and general changes in the business environment all have an impact on how organisations choose to design their business processes. The means of changing processes is referred to as **business process design**, with several variants available to an organisation undergoing change. One approach is what is referred to as *Total Quality Management (TQM)*, the second alternative is *business process re-engineering*, and the third approach is a combination of these approaches, otherwise known as an eclectic approach.[51]

## Total Quality Management (TQM)

**Total Quality Management (TQM)** is a progressive approach to organisational change that works on the principle that a series of small progressive steps is the best way to improve operations. The philosophy of TQM is geared around four main concepts: quality, people, organisations and the role of management.[52] These are described briefly below.

### Quality

The assumption relating to quality is that the costs of poor quality, as represented through the costs involved with rework and product returns, are greater than the costs associated with developing and refining business processes to generate high-quality output. This idea makes sense if one adopts a long-term perspective for the organisation. While in the short term it may be possible to cut corners and not worry about quality in processes, in the long term this will generate faulty or defective outputs that will ultimately be rejected by customers. If customers leave the organisation, then ultimately the organisation will go out of business.

### People

The people aspect of TQM refers to how people within the organisation are valued for both their contributions towards the process and their ideas about how the process can be improved. People within the organisation need to be encouraged to provide feedback about the design of a process — particularly at the lower levels of the organisation — since it is often these people who have the best understanding of how the process really operates, because they work as a part of it every day. There are many examples where this inclusive approach towards the thoughts and ideas of lower-level employees has reaped numerous benefits for an organisation when redesigning its processes. An example of this is the Toyota motor company, which designed its own processes rather than adopting American techniques, and in the process built in employee creativity and innovation, which led to higher output and productivity levels.[53]

## Organisations

The organisational aspect of TQM essentially refers back to the earlier discussion of business processes and the process-based organisation. It emphasises that the organisation does not operate as a series of independent departments but that functions interact to provide a good or deliver a service. This presents some issues for the organisation that is looking to improve its processes, because it requires representatives from all the functions involved in a process to be involved. There is little point having only the sales department involved in improving the sales process, because this ignores the reality that the accounts receivable, warehouse, manufacturing and marketing departments are also potentially involved in the process of selling goods.

## Management

Finally, TQM asserts that change and improvement can only occur if they have the support and endorsement of top management. After all, it is the top management of an organisation that designs the structure of the business and the processes that occur. So TQM requires management to focus on processes, rather than individual functions, and provide strong guidance and support for change efforts. A big part of providing this guidance and support is nurturing an environment where employees are encouraged to comment and provide feedback on the performance of existing processes, as well as on how they can be improved. Management does not perform the process in a hands-on way — the employees who do so are the best source of ideas about improvements. Additionally, involving employees in the generation of ideas for process improvement can help to increase the acceptance of the change when it is actually implemented.

Another critical aspect of the TQM process is that, potentially, ideas for change and improvements to a process can be driven through the organisation from the bottom up. That is, ideas from the factory floor can be filtered up to top management for official approval, and then put into place within the organisation. The impetus for change and improvement comes from the initial ideas of the lower-level employees in the organisation. By comparison, as is seen in the following section, BPR is more of a top-down approach to process improvement.

## Business process re-engineering

**Business process re-engineering (BPR)** The fundamental rethinking and radical redesign of business processes to achieve dramatic improvements in critical contemporary measures of performance, such as cost, quality, service and speed.

Many of the large organisations in operation today were first designed decades ago. As a result, they will typically have a very hierarchical structure, remnants of an era when organisational control and reporting hierarchies were the priority, instead of business processes and customer services. Increasingly, they are being confronted with the need to redesign their operations, shifting from processes built around the organisational hierarchy to a newer process-based organisation. **Business process re-engineering (BPR)** is one approach to this redesign.

Hammer and Champy, in one of the key reference texts on the topic of BPR, define it as 'the *fundamental* rethinking and *radical* redesign of business *processes* to achieve *dramatic* improvements in critical contemporary measures of performance, such as cost, quality, service, and speed'.[54] They then go on to emphasise four key components of this definition, these being *fundamental*, *radical*, *dramatic* and *process*. These four components will now be discussed, including aspects of their importance to BPR and their practical relevance to organisations.

- The *fundamental* aspect of the BPR definition forces an organisation to question what activities it performs as a part of its current process. It is aimed at looking at what takes place in the current system and questioning whether it is really needed.

- The *radical* component of the definition essentially compels organisations to start again, discard what already exists and redesign from scratch. Also known as the clean slate approach, its objective is to encourage thoughts about new ways that a process could be performed, rather than just tinkering at the edges of existing approaches.

- If an organisation undergoes a BPR effort, it is looking for a *dramatic* return or improvement, especially when the risk and cost of a BPR project are considered. Therefore, BPR is aimed at achieving large improvements in the key performance indicators that an organisation uses.

- The *process* aspect, reflected by its appearing in the name of the concept, is central to BPR. The thrust is that organisations must forget about functional perspectives, as well as the associated hierarchies and bureaucracies, and place the emphasis on the processes that are actually performed. Business processes, as previously discussed, comprise the mechanism for provision of value to the customer, and BPR is about improving processes to provide more value to the customer.

The philosophy and approach of BPR should not be confused with alternative approaches to organisational change, such as continuous improvement, TQM, right-sizing, restructuring, cultural change and turnaround. Certainly, a BPR effort may contain elements of these change approaches within its general philosophy and aims; however, BPR as a concept is far broader than any of these individual concepts.

## *Principles and approaches*

Given the extent of the BPR effort there are several key steps that should be followed within an organisation to successfully manage the change. Kotter identifies eight steps that should be followed to manage the transformation of an organisation successfully: establish a sense of urgency, form a leadership team, create a vision, communicate the vision, empower others to meet the vision, plan for and create short-term wins, consolidate improvements and encourage further change, and institutionalise the new approaches.[55] Each of these steps is further explained in the following sections.

### Establish a sense of urgency

The first step in a BPR project is to convince others within the organisation that it is actually required. While the term 'establish a sense of urgency' may seem a little drastic, the challenge is to convince those who decide whether the project goes ahead that the re-engineering effort is actually required. Since BPR is such a drastic, organisation-wide approach to redesigning business processes, the people that will most likely need to be convinced are the top-level management. Managers who have been within the organisation for a long time may not respond to the call because they do not see the problem or it challenges their position and sense of security. Therefore, organisational change in the league of BPR often gets past this first hurdle when a new manager starts work in the organisation, since he or she does not have the organisational blinkers of a tenured staff member.

### Form a leadership team

BPR is not something that can be accomplished overnight. It is a time-consuming and challenging process that must involve representatives from across the organisation. It is important, from very early on, that a leadership team is established to guide the project. This team should be representative of the entire organisation, and not be made up of representatives from one division within the organisation. The team may also include some influential external stakeholders, depending on the nature of the changes to be made.

Those on the team should also be of authority sufficient that when they say something needs to be done it will not be questioned or challenged. A common mistake, according to Kotter, is for companies to underestimate how difficult it can be to produce change.[56] Caron et al. quote a senior manager at a corporation involved in re-engineering as saying, 'Everyone knew this was my project. I was the chief cheerleader, but I also carried a big stick when necessary. I made it clear that this was a project that required everyone's commitment and cooperation.'[57]

### Create and communicate a vision

Just as you need a road map to find your way through new cities and towns, so too do organisations need a map of where they are heading. This business map is described as a vision, outlining where the business will be after the change takes place, how things will be better, the effect it will have on the key stakeholders, both internal and external, as well as some outline of how the vision can be achieved. Communication of the vision throughout the organisation is also a key factor. Akin to giving the Sermon on the Mount, the preacher of the vision should be able clearly to explain what is happening, why it is happening and how everyone will be better off as a result. More importantly, it should be in terms that people can understand. A vision based around technical jargon of a specific discipline is of little use because it will prove difficult to communicate to the rest of the organisation. So, as an example, a change geared around IT should steer away from framing the vision in terms of the technical jargon that often accompanies the technology discipline. Rather, it should be framed in terms that non-IT people can relate to, which might include the impact on working roles, work environment and so on.

However, for the people communicating the vision, there can be an added challenge of negative attitudes from the receiver — particularly when visions involving re-engineering are mentioned. In recent times the term 're-engineering' has become synonymous with corporate downsizing: an excuse to get rid of some staff. Perhaps one of the causes for this impression was the oft-cited case noted by Hammer and Champy involving Ford's re-engineering of its accounts payable department.[58] Ford was able to reduce the staff in its accounts payable from 500 people to about 120 people through a total overhaul of the process in place. With cases such as this it is little wonder that re-engineering and overhaul have become interchangeable terms. From an employee's perspective this can lead to fear and insecurity about future employment within the organisation. The team entrusted with the task of communicating the re-engineering vision should be aware of this. Kotter suggests that each negative should be accompanied by a positive.[59] For example, a company may foresee the elimination of 100 staff members in the manufacturing floor as a result of re-engineering, but it also foresees room for growth in the management of supplier accounts, necessitating new employees in that area. When framed this way, there is the possibility that the re-engineering may bring about a new job within the firm and not total job loss.

### Empower others to meet the vision

Those within the organisation need to be encouraged to try the new way of doing things. Quite often this can involve more than just employee retraining. While there may be an element of new skills and training that is required for the employee in the re-engineered environment, organisations should also consider other factors that influence employee behaviour in the workplace. For example, the type of bonus schemes and incentive schemes that are used in the functional environment may not be appropriate in the process-oriented re-engineered environment.

People do things that get measured, so if performance measures that were appropriate for the old way of doing things are maintained, then people will still do those things. As an example, looking at the inventory management of a manufacturing company, if the previous performance criterion had been that inventory stock-outs should be minimised, then the natural response of the manager would be to purchase inventory and store it on-site, thus avoiding the chance of significant disruption caused by stock-outs. If this inventory management process is re-engineered, and as a result adopts a just-in-time inventory management system, but still pays the manager based on the number of stock-outs that occur, there will be a problem. The performance system does not match the policy. As long as the manager's bonus depends on avoiding stock-outs, that is what he or she will do — through the purchase of inventory and storing it on-site. It would be better to change the performance criterion at the same time to one compatible with just-in-time.

The same principle applies to things such as job descriptions and organisational hierarchies. These should be adjusted so that they can efficiently operate with the re-engineered process.

### Plan for and create short-term wins

Any long-term project requires positive feedback for the impetus to remain. Without it, motivation and drive for the re-engineering effort will wane and people who originally supported the concept may drop off the idea. To avoid this possibility, landmark events or deliverables should be built into the re-engineering effort, and acknowledged or celebrated when they are achieved. Even though their attainment does not represent the completion of the re-engineering effort, it does signal to employees that the project is progressing. Psychologically, having to meet short-term deadlines on the way to meeting long-term goals can also help maintain the urgency and commitment to the project.[60]

### Consolidate improvements and encourage further change

One big risk faced by an organisation is that once the re-engineering effort is complete, the employees will adopt the new process for a short time but gradually revert back to the 'old way of doing things', rendering the re-engineering effort unsuccessful. Re-engineering is not only about changing a process within an organisation; it can also be about changing the culture and attitude that pervade that process. This is no easy task and can take several years.[61]

### Institutionalise the new approaches

Linked to the previous point, the challenge for the organisation is to make the re-engineered process the second nature of employees — that is, change their behaviour so that the new way of doing things fast becomes the usual way of doing things. This has a lot to do with the culture of the organisation. The ingraining of the process can be supported through the careful selection of staff when hiring, ensuring that they display a degree of fit with the process in place. This is particularly important because a manager, having completed his or her time with the organisation, could leave and all his or her work in re-engineering and changing the process could be undone by a new appointment.

As an example of BPR, consider the following discussion of IBM Credit, based on Hammer and Champy.[62] IBM Credit is a subsidiary of IBM. Its primary operations are to provide credit and financing arrangements for those purchasing new computers through retail chains that are supplied with computers and parts by IBM. Its process was originally designed around specialists and specialist knowledge, with individuals performing specific tasks and forwarding their output on to the next person in the process. The process began when a store dealer would call the IBM office with details of an application for finance. This request would be logged by the staff at the IBM office and the details recorded on a document. The document would be sent to the credit department, where a specialist credit evaluator would enter the details of the application on to the computer and make a decision on the creditworthiness of the customer. The decision on creditworthiness would be documented, and this document forwarded to the business practices department. The business practices department staff would draw up loan details, customising the terms and conditions to meet the requirements of the individual applicant. Any special terms would be added to the application form and these documents were sent to a specialist loan pricer, who would determine a suitable interest rate for the loan. The loan pricer used a separate computer system, based around a customised spreadsheet, to determine an interest rate. The interest rate and other documentation were then forwarded to the clerical group. An administrator within the clerical group is responsible for drawing up the loan document, along with a quote letter. The quote letter was couriered to the sales representative who lodged the initial enquiry.

This process is illustrated in figure 2.5. The shaded box represents what happens within IBM Credit, and the rectangles within the shaded box represent the different divisions or departments that are involved in the handling of a loan application. The arrows connecting the departments are labelled with the documentation that the process generates and passes through the different departments.

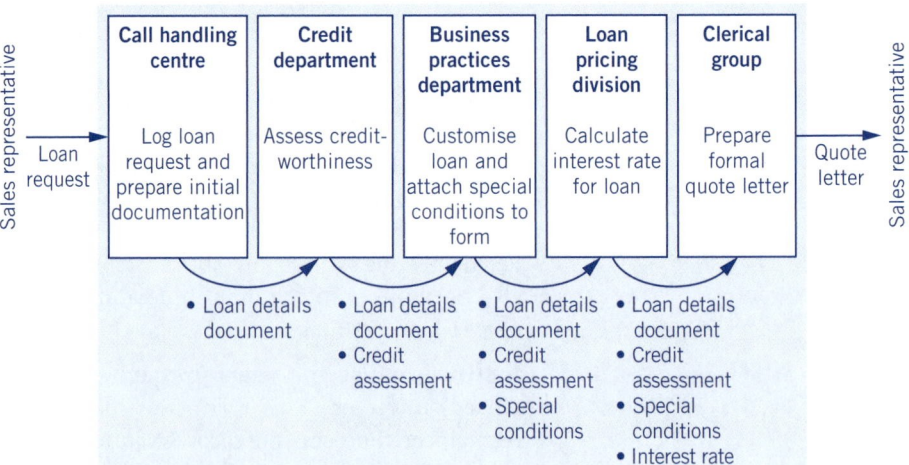

**FIGURE 2.5** IBM Credit's pre-BPR loan application procedure

Having read the description and examined the illustration of the business process in figure 2.5, can you identify problems with the design of the loan application process at IBM Credit? Consider some of the discussion presented earlier in the chapter about what a business process is and some of the benefits of a business process. Does IBM Credit's procedure before BPR represent more of a business process-based perspective or a functional perspective of the organisation?

Arguably, the IBM process represents a very traditional, functional perspective of organisational design. Notice how the individuals within each department perform a specific function. For example, the loan pricer's sole responsibility is to calculate interest rates for loans. He or she has no role in customising the terms and conditions of the loan or determining the creditworthiness of the applicants. The demarcation of responsibilities in the different functional areas of IBM Credit is very strong, with each department having clearly defined duties based around their functional role. This is an attribute of the functional organisation.

This process design led to some severe problems for IBM, similar to those identified earlier in looking at the limitations of the functional perspective of the organisation. The primary limitation of this design was the time that it took to go from the initial request received by the call centre to sending out the actual loan document to the sales representative. In the process illustrated above, it took anywhere between six days and two weeks to go from start to finish. That is a long time, especially if you are the customer waiting for the approval for your purchase to go ahead. This is also undesirable for the sales representatives, because it risks customers going elsewhere for their purchases because of the lag in the loan process.

However, an examination of the process revealed that there was not two weeks actual processing time involved in handling a loan request. A walkthrough of an application through the system found that actual processing time was about 90 minutes. Why then was it taking two weeks to complete? A disadvantage of the functional perspective is that there can be bottlenecks in a process. A bottleneck is a backing up or stoppage that delays the normal operation of a process. In the case of IBM, individuals within the departments would finish their specific task and forward the documents on to the next division. However, once the documents got to the next stage and division they would often spend considerable time waiting in the 'in tray' of the person responsible for the task. This occurred because the design of the process required a lot of hand-offs from one department to another. Sending documents from one person to another was essential for the operation of the process within IBM, but it did not really add any value to the loan application procedure and created bottlenecks and delays.

What also emerges in the IBM case is the high reliance on specialist knowledge. A specialist is defined as someone who is recognised as particularly competent in a certain task or procedure. Specialists were used in assessing the creditworthiness of the customers as well as in determining the loan interest rates that were to be applied to the approved loan applications. This approach makes sense where specialist knowledge is a scarce resource that is needed for abnormal applications. However, it was possible to re-engineer the process without relying on the use of specialist knowledge for all loan applications.

Because of these problems, IBM underwent a BPR effort to produce the following process. In the re-engineered process IBM focused on removing the passing of paper between the different specialists involved in the original process. The result was that one person handled a loan application from start to finish and was involved in the entire process. In this way IBM was able to use generalists and move away from the use of specialist staff. Instead of having specialists to calculate an interest rate, customise loan terms and so on, these tasks were given to all staff involved in the process. Conceptually, this may sound like a strange solution, because it would seem certain that these tasks require a degree of knowledge and expertise to be performed competently. This is indeed true. The approach of IBM was not so much to make everyone an expert in all stages of the process, but rather to make the knowledge that is required to complete the process available to all staff. How did the company do this?

IT played a large role in the new loan process, developing computer programs that would support staff through it. The knowledge of the various specialists was encoded into the program and made accessible to all staff. As a result, all staff gained the ability to handle a claim from start to finish. How might this benefit the organisation? For starters, it meant that the large amount of paper shuffling back and forth between the different specialists involved in the task was eliminated, since one person was able to handle a loan application from start to finish, and the consequent bottlenecks were removed.

Obviously, such a radical organisational change risks delegating tasks to employees who are not sufficiently skilled to perform them. IBM recognised this by designing the computer application to support the loan process, and keeping a few specialists in each area within the organisation, so that employees handling loan applications could consult them for advice should any irregular loan applications enter the system. An examination of the process, however, found that the vast majority of the cases entering the system were within the realms of a normal application and could be competently handled by a deal structurer. So the specialists passed from an integral role in the original process to a support role in the re-engineered process.

In the end, IBM effectively developed three different processes to handle loan applications. Simple cases were handled entirely by the computer system, slightly complex cases were handled by the deal structurer, while the irregular and extremely complex cases were handled by the deal structurer with the assistance of the specialists in the different areas of the loan application process.

The benefits for IBM were tangible, with a 90 per cent drop in the time it took to process a normal loan application to about four hours. Additionally, IBM's loan application handling ability was increased by a factor of 100.

## Some BPR principles in practice

From the foregoing, some principles of a BPR effort become clear. Hammer and Champy[63] identify some aspects to consider. These include combine jobs, have workers make decisions, perform process steps in a natural order, allow processes to vary, perform tasks at their logical location, reduce the impediment of controls, reduce the need for reconciliations, and create a single reference point for customers.

### Combine jobs and let workers make decisions

In a functional perspective, the precisely defined duties of employees cause bottlenecks and delays in the process. On top of this, should a person need to consult a superior for a decision, the process can stop until the decision output from that superior is obtained. One way BPR overcomes this is by changing the role of the worker. Instead of just performing a particular function, workers have their duties broadened to include a range of tasks involved in the process. This removes the flow between parties in the process and can reduce the delays and bottlenecks. Giving the employee the power to make decisions removes the emphasis on specialists and specialist knowledge that was present in the traditional structure. In the IBM case this can be seen in the consolidation of tasks and the use of generalists: now a loan application is handled by one person, instead of being passed through the organisation.

### Create a single reference point for customers

The principle here is that customers should not be passed from one person to another as they search for answers to questions they have. You have probably experienced this frustrating process, when you call an organisation, are put on hold, are forwarded on to another staff member, who cannot answer your question and forwards you on to someone else and so on, and so on. This approach sends the wrong signal to the customers. It most definitely does not convey the message that the process is geared around serving its customer. Rather, it suggests that the organisation sees customers' time as of little value. Giving this impression to customers is a surefire way of losing them!

IBM considered this issue at two different stages of its re-engineering. One idea originally proposed was to create a central desk that all customers would repeatedly pass through as the different stages of the application process were completed. The overriding theme was that IBM wanted only one point of contact for the customer. If a customer had a query they could call the central desk and get an answer without being passed around in a game of 'phone tag' from one person to the next. The actual implementation of the single reference point for customers is arguably evident in the creation of the position of 'deal structurers', who process applications from start to finish. Customers only need contact their deal structurer with a query and he or she should be able to answer it, because the continuity in handling the application allows them to answer any questions that the customer may have about it, such as about the application's status in the system.

### Perform process steps in a natural order and at their logical location

The idea behind this principle is that if a process consists of several different activities that can be performed simultaneously, then they should be. Traditionally, the functional perspective and its design of a business process saw clearly defined tasks that were to be performed in a set order. There was little deviation in the sequencing of activities. In some situations this made little sense, because activities could be done concurrently. The benefit of doing things concurrently is that it can allow for a quicker process time, benefiting the customer.

In addition to this, work should be performed at its logical location. While this may seem like an obvious statement, it is not uncommon for work to be passed around from location to location for different tasks to be performed. Elements of this can be seen in the IBM case, with the applications moving from department to department when, in reality, as is evident in the re-engineered process, all the work could actually be performed in one place by one person. The benefit of this design is that the process can be completed quicker with less reliance on specialists.

### Allow processes to vary

A process is not necessarily a homogeneous structure that can be applied to all cases. In the IBM case this can be seen in the role of the specialists in assisting with the more complex loan application cases. As a result, organisations may need to have slight variations of their process to cater for the different cases they will encounter. In IBM this occurred at three levels, with a process for simple, slightly complex, and complex loan applications. Most cases fell into the first two categories. Importantly, there was not one generic process designed to handle the most complex of cases and through which all applications were sent. This was the mistake in the original design: all cases were treated as though they required the knowledge of the specialist when, in reality, they did not. There is a need to recognise that variations in process design might be needed to handle different degrees of complexity once a process is operating.

### Reduce the impediment of controls and reconciliations

Traditional process design for the functionally based organisation will typically contain a series of inbuilt controls. Examples of this can include approval of a superior before an event can occur, reporting structures, and frequent reconciliations. Quite often these controls and reconciliations add little value to the process that is being performed. Alternatively, the controls may be important but could potentially be improved by combining them with technology. BPR calls for an examination of controls embedded within a process and a questioning of their value in the process's operation.

While the theory of BPR is that a clean-slate approach is necessary, as will be discussed later in this chapter, this approach is not necessarily optimal. Organisations would seldom start from scratch — the risks would be immense! However, the principles of BPR can be applied when reviewing and redesigning processes, even if not to the extent of the clean-slate approach advocated under a traditional BPR perspective.

## Technology–driven process improvements

One of the principles for business process re-engineering is that technology should be used as an enabler — the re-engineering process should be geared towards the recognition of the ways that technology can be applied to improve the operation and functionality of business processes. As is noted by Gregor et al,[64] 'Organisations that achieve the most significant benefits from IT exploit these new capabilities to reform business processes and create new business opportunities'. Businesses will benefit most from the application of **information technology (IT)** when the use of IT is driven by the need to solve business problems — the use of IT is driven by business needs and opportunities. IT is not incorporated into a business process just because it is there — there must be an underlying activity or problem that can benefit from the application of IT. The extent of IT adoption in business processes can start with the integration of the technology into existing processes, which allows for potentially better process performance and ultimately, in the future, the ability to build new capabilities into the process.[65] Further down the line, IT can be used to redesign business processes and alter the way that they are executed.

If we refer back to our process definition we note that it is customer based. As such, the improvements that are derived from the technology application should also be driven by the needs of the end customer, since business processes should be customer driven and designed to meet customer needs. But remember also that the customers of a business process can be both internal and external to a business.

The benefits of re-engineering that can be enjoyed by a customer can include more efficient service provision, better information availability or a more convenient means of participating in a process. This is not to say that the business will not benefit from the application of technology within its business processes as well. Some of the benefits a business can get from the application of technology within a process can include a more efficient process, with benefits in quantitative performance indicators such as turnover rates, as well as more satisfied customer and lower administrative/processing costs. More generally, a study by Gregor et al[66] lists four main areas in which an organisation can benefit from the application of technology to its business processes. These areas are summarised below:

1. *Information based* — refers to the higher level of information that can be made available and the potentially higher quality of that information.
2. *Strategy based* — the application of technology that allows a business to create or extend its competitive advantage.
3. *Transaction based* — the benefit of being able to execute transactions in a more efficient manner and realise associated cost savings.
4. *Change based* — the benefits that come from the positive organisational change that can result from the application of technology within a business process, including new ways of doing business, new business models, new business plans.

With this in mind, this section provides a brief discussion of some of the different ways in which technology can be incorporated into a business process. The process examples that are referred to are very much generic — you will encounter a more detailed discussion of the individual processes in subsequent chapters. As you read the subsequent process based chapters you may find it useful to refer back to some of the concepts discussed in this section. The intent in this chapter is more to familiarise you with the ways in which technology can be applied to solve business problems and how it can be incorporated as part of a redesign of a business process, while also keeping in mind the benefits that can be accrued to both the customer and the provider of goods and services.

The examples that will be discussed in this section are:

- vendor-managed inventory
- evaluated receipts settlement
- electronic bill payment
- electronic bill presentation and payment
- RFID or barcoding.

## *Vendor-managed inventory*

**Vendor-managed inventory** A system that involves the buyer transferring to the seller the responsibility for determining what, when and how much is purchased.

**Vendor-managed inventory** involves the buyer transferring the responsibility for determining what, when and how much is purchased. The purchasing decision is effectively shifted from the buyer to the seller. For example, a bicycle company purchases its gear assemblies from Gears Plus. Under a vendor-managed inventory system, the systems of the bicycle company and Gears Plus would be integrated, allowing Gears Plus to see how many gear sets the bicycle company has in stock, current bicycle order levels and expected future bicycle production levels. Based on this data, Gears Plus can determine how many gear assemblies will be required by the bicycle company. It can then ensure that this amount is delivered to the bicycle company in time, minimising disruption and delays in production.

Electronic notification of forthcoming deliveries from Gears Plus will be received by the bicycle company prior to the arrival of the products, which facilitates a more efficient inventory receipt process.

Visy Industries, a large Australian company that manufactures packaging products, such as boxes and cans, embarked on such a system with Berri Limited, Unilever and Masterfoods — three of its major customers. The results included better data sharing, a better supplier–buyer understanding of processes and more efficient handling of accounts payable.[67] These systems can also lead to less duplication in processes — for example, the buyer entering details for a purchase order and sending that to a vendor who then re-enters the same data into its sales system. This elimination of duplicated processes has been found to be a factor in whether or not trading partners engaged in the integration of e-commerce technology in their respective business processes.[68]

## Evaluated receipts settlement

During the course of business process re-engineering, it is often possible for businesses to completely overhaul generally accepted procedures; for example, a business might successfully remove the invoice from its accounts payable process. Such a system is described as an evaluated receipt settlement (ERS) system. The idea behind the ERS system is that there is little value added by waiting for an invoice to arrive before paying accounts payable. From an accounting perspective, if we have received the goods then a liability is able to be recognised in our accounting system. Waiting for the invoice prior to confirming and recording the payable merely slows the process and adds delays to our accounts payable turnover.

A critical issue for a business in the purchasing process (which is discussed in more detail in subsequent chapters) is that the goods ordered (as detailed on the purchase order) match the goods received (detailed on the shipping notice and receiving report) and that the goods received were actually ordered in the first place (evidenced by the purchase order). If a business is able to confirm that the delivery is for a valid order and items received match the requested items then there is little point in delaying recognition and settlement until the invoice is received.

The only requirement for such a system to work is that the transaction must be conducted at a pre-approved price, and transaction costs need to be foreseeable at the time the purchase order is generated. This approach allows for agreed prices, freight and any taxes or duties to be included in the purchase order, allowing the vendor to pay earlier since it is able to accurately determine how much it owes its supplier.

The benefit of an ERS system is that it potentially speeds up the accounts payable process by the elimination of the invoice from the cash payments process. Such a system allows for expedited payments to suppliers, which can be beneficial for the supplier's accounts receivable turnover and liquidity.

In Australia, as a consequence of the GST legislation and the requirements for tax invoices, the ERS based system has led to the introduction of a Recipient Created Tax Invoice. Under a conventional system where the supplier prepares the invoice and sends it to the customer, this invoice would serve as a tax invoice for GST purposes. Since the ERS removes the invoice from the system, the preparation of the invoice for tax purposes is made the responsibility of the purchaser. Legally, this requires a set of agreements to be in place between the buyer and the supplier and for both parties to be registered with the Australian Taxation Office with an Australian Business Number.[69]

## Electronic bill payment

Electronic bill payment (EBP) systems allow the customer to pay its bills via the internet or telephone. This saves the customer the time of having to write a cheque or go to its financial institution to make a payment. Several well-known examples of electronic payment systems are in operation within Australia, including BPAY and Australia Post's POSTbillpay (see table 2.2).[70]

The advantages of electronic payment systems are that the payment is executed in a more timely manner and the cost of a transaction is reduced due to the elimination of time and money spent on matters like clearing cheques. Additionally, removing cheques from the receipts process reduces the risks for a business or service provider from bounced cheques.

**TABLE 2.2** EBP providers in Australia and services provided

| EBP provider | Web address | Services |
| --- | --- | --- |
| BPAY View | www.bpay.com.au | Bill presentation<br>Bill payment |
| Australia Post | www.postbillpay.com.au | Bill presentation<br>Bill payment<br>Bill management |

As an example of the use of electronic bill payment technology, the operation of BPAY is discussed in the following paragraphs. POSTbillpay payments can be made over the counter at post offices or through the telephone and internet, and BPAY payments are made over the phone or through the internet.

### EBP example: BPAY

BPAY[71] is a technology motivated by a need for a more efficient means of enabling a customer to pay its bills and a business to receive its funds. The initial BPAY system was introduced in Australia in 1997, when nine financial institutions signed up for the technology, and was built around telephone banking. Since then the adoption rate has rapidly grown, to see more than 18 million bills per month paid through BPAY and more than 17 000 vendors registered in the BPAY system.[72] BPAY provides a means for customers to pay its bills electronically at any time they choose. For a business it has the key advantage of eliminating the timely process of waiting for cheques to arrive from customers, and then having to go through the process of depositing cheques and waiting for them to clear. The system can also potentially lead to a reduction in bad debts. These benefits alone can have considerable positive impacts in the area of liquidity. From a customer's perspective BPAY offers the convenience of being able to pay bills in a convenient manner, without having to write a cheque or go into a bank in order to make a payment.

BPAY is made possible through a unique biller code and reference number that can be found on the documents of participating institutions. Customers who need to pay a bill simply access their bank account through either a telephone or an internet banking service. They then enter the biller code and reference number. The biller code identifies who the payment is going to be received by, while the reference number identifies the customer and the transaction being paid for. These details are sent through BPAY to the recipient financial institution, while also letting the recipient know that funds have been transferred into their account. The customer will receive a transaction number that enables the transaction to be identified and followed up if required.

To explain the operation of BPAY, let us assume that a student has received a re-enrolment notice from their university advising them that they may pay the annual re-enrolment fee of $250 and that this can be paid through BPAY. The steps involved would be as follows (follow along in figure 2.6 overleaf for reference):

1. The university sends the invoice for re-enrolment to the customer. This will have information about how much the student must pay as well as a biller code and a reference number.
2. When the customer receives the bill they can pay using BPAY. In order to do this they will access their own banking facilities by phone or through the internet. The internet has become a preferred option for many. As for back as 2005, 40 per cent of internet users were paying bills online, up from 25 per cent in 2001.[73] By 2009,

the percentage of BPAY payments made through the internet had increased to 84 per cent, with 17 000 vendors offering BPAY services. The growth in BPAY vendors has been around 4.5 per cent per annum.[74] The student will then enter details that include the account the funds are coming from, the biller code and reference number from the invoice and the amount to be paid. The student's bank account will be updated at this time, with the money being debited.

3. The details of the transaction (the biller code, reference number, amount and a unique transaction number allocated by BPAY) are then sent through BPAY to the university's nominated bank. This does not have to be the same bank as that used by the student.

4. The university's bank account will then have the amount paid by the student credited to its balance.

5. The details of the transaction will be electronically sent to the university to inform them of the receipt and provide them with a record of the transaction.

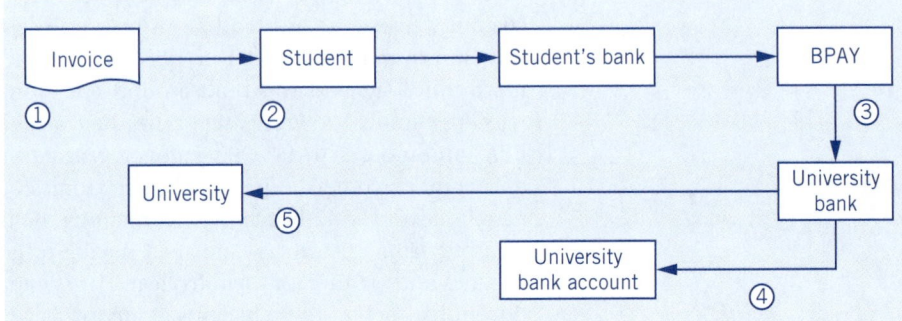

**FIGURE 2.6** The BPAY process

The advantages of the BPAY system for a business process (e.g. billing and accounts receivable, which is discussed later in the text) are several, including a reduced turnaround time between sending out the invoice and receiving payment from the customer. This benefit is possible because BPAY eliminates the need for the billing organisation to process receipts and wait for customer payments (perhaps by cheque) to be cleared. From an accounting perspective, this can have benefits in areas such as accounts receivable turnover, cash flow performance and overall liquidity.

Additionally, BPAY can allow the business to focus on its core processes and leave the administration and processing associated with cash receipts to the BPAY system. For its record keeping, the business still receives a summary of all payments received from customers through BPAY. This is made available in an electronic format that can be uploaded into existing electronic accounts receivable records. Potentially, this facilitates more efficient accounts receivable record keeping.

## Electronic bill presentment and payment

Electronic bill presentment and payment (EBPP) is a technology that uses the internet to deliver bills to customers and then allows customers to electronically make payments on those bills.[75] Several examples of electronic bill presentment and payment systems are in operation within Australia, including BPAY View and POSTbillpay. As at 2009, 1081 registered billers were a part of Australia Post's Billmanager POSTbillpay system, with 688 offering electronic billing and payment on the internet.[76]

### EBPP Example: BPAY View

An example of electronic bill presentment and payment in Australia is BPAY View, which can be seen as an extension of BPAY. While BPAY and similar EBP developments reduced the time required to process payments from customers, they still relied on the business sending out a paper invoice to the customer. This use of conventional mail can be slow and faces a potential risk of the invoice not reaching the customer due to, for example, the customer changing address or the mail getting lost in the postal system. In order to enhance the benefits of the existing BPAY system, BPAY View was devised removing the need for a paper invoice. Using what is referred to as electronic bill presentation and payment, BPAY view operates as follows:

1. The business prepares billing information in an electronic format, usually through a bill service provider. The service provider then forwards this information to BPAY View, who forwards it on to the banking institution of the customers concerned. A notification is sent by the customer's bank to the customer about the arrival of an electronic bill.
2. The customer then logs on to their internet banking site to view a summary of the bill. They can also follow direct links to the bill service provider, where more information about the bill can be obtained.
3. The customer is then able to pay the bill. Payment is able to take place when viewing the account or at a later date.

Advantages of the BPAY View system (and similar EBPP technologies) are that, like BPAY, they offer an organisation the potential to redesign a billing or cash receipts process. While BPAY and EBP in general provided benefits in the cash receipts process, as described above, BPAY View and EBPP go one step further and introduce the application of technology within the billing process. Potentially, this means that organisations will no longer need to prepare and mail out invoices to their customers alerting them of amounts owing. The benefits of this for an organisation can be cost savings associated with no longer having to prepare and mail out the invoices, as well as cash flow benefits, since the invoice reaches the customer sooner, enhancing the prospect of prompter payment from the customer. Furthermore, in times of increased environmental awareness, it could be seen as advantageous to eliminate the production of paper-based invoices.

From a customer's perspective EBPP offers the advantage of a centralised bill management function that can be accessed from anywhere in the world. This means customers no longer have to manage a collection of paper documents, wait for invoices to arrive, or run the risk of losing an invoice. The electronic delivery and access of invoices makes them available to the customer anywhere that internet access is available. EBPP provides a summary of all invoices due for payment and the date when they are due, as an organisation tool for the customer, reducing the risk of lost invoices going unpaid.

These systems have been expanded to include further bill management facilities as well as EBPP, with Australia Post offering Billmanager.[77] While incorporating EBPP, the management facilities go a step further and offer the ability for customers to schedule their bill payments, or plan for fixed regular payments to meet their bills, and thus maintain smooth, regular payments to meet their payables. For the seller, this can facilitate on-time payments from customers and lower accounts receivable handling costs. Providers of goods and services need to register with a provider, as they would with EBP or EBPP, for bill management services to be available to their customers. Once this is complete their system will be integrated with the EBPP system in order to facilitate the electronic process.

## RFID or barcoding

Barcode technology can offer a quick and convenient way to capture data within an accounting information system. Barcodes can be incorporated into a business process in a seemingly endless range of ways. Examples could include the following:

- *Barcode on turnaround documents (e.g. remittance advice slips) to save re-keying as the document moves through different processes.* This can help with the speed at which data is captured, as well as the accuracy of data entering a system.
- *Barcode inventory.* This helps with quick capture of data about inventory receipts and dispatches, as well as inventory picked, although a direct line of sight is required (i.e. the scanner has to have a clear line to the barcode in order to read it). For bulky or irregular shaped items this can present a restriction on the usefulness of barcodes.
- *Barcode for customer and shipping details.* These are referred to as serial shipping container codes (SSCCs) and allow for the tracking of parcels as they move through a logistics process. A barcode is allocated to each package and it contains details of the supplier, the order details and links back to data about the contents of the package. The buyer receives electronic notice of the delivery, which can be incorporated into the buyer's system so the barcode is recognisable when the goods are received. This allows the buyer to use SSCC to identify goods as they arrive in the warehouse. Use of an international standard for barcoding is important for inter-company operability, for example the GS1 System standards.[78]

Radio frequency identification tags (RFID tags) are tags that contain a small micro-chip. As the microchip comes within range, a transceiver detects a small radio signal from the chip which contains information about the item or package to which the tag is attached. RFID tags do not require a person to scan the items as they pass through a reader and do not need a direct line of sight for the tags to be read. Additionally, data can be stored in the tags and several tags can be read at once by an RFID transceiver.[79] This makes capturing data from tags easier and more efficient than barcode based systems. An example of the application of RFID technology that exhibits some of these features and resulted in an improved business process is described in AIS focus 2.4.

Table 2.3 lists the technologies that could be used within a business process to help redesign and improve the business processes. Keep this table in mind as you read through the subsequent chapters which describe the operation of the different business processes, and consider how these technologies could be implemented to improve process design for the business and its customers.

**TABLE 2.3** Examples of the business processes where the technologies could be applied

| Technology example | Business process where it could be used |
| --- | --- |
| Vendor-managed inventory | Purchasing process (for buyer) |
| Evaluated receipts settlement | Purchasing and expenditure process (for buyer) Billing and cash receipts (for seller of goods) |
| Electronic bill payment | Purchasing and payment (for buyer of goods) Billing and cash receipts (for provider) |
| Electronic bill presentation and payment | Purchasing and payment (for buyer of goods) Billing and cash receipts (for provider) |
| RFID or barcoding | Receiving goods (for buyer) Packing or shipping goods (for seller of goods) |

## AIS FOCUS 2.4

### Moraitis lengths ahead

Nick Moraitis is known to many as the main owner of Might and Power, the gelding crowned 1997 Caulfield and Melbourne Cup champion and 1998 Cox Plate king. (The Caulfield and Melbourne Cups and the Cox Plate are three of the largest annual horse races in Australia.) Indeed, while Nick is known as a successful racehorse owner, he is also a successful businessman, having started up his own fruit and vegetable delivery business, Moraitis Fresh, in Sydney.

The Moraitis business has grown rapidly, and with the growth has come the need for better methods of tracking the produce moving through the company's distribution system. Moraitis Fresh has always prided itself on being 'an industry leader boasting a professional operation and state-of-the-art management systems and technology'.[80] As such, the old system of inventory tracking, which relied on markings on boxes, pieces of paper and standard barcodes to identify boxes, was in need of vast improvement — it was not as efficient or effective as desired.

In response to this, Moraitis Fresh incorporated RFID technology within its business processes. This allowed for greater levels of precision when tracking items throughout the business process, with information now available about the date a package was packed, where it came from, and the contents and quality of a package. This allows for better supply chain management and the ability to better monitor the quality of different suppliers.

The initial setup costs were estimated to be around $100 000, but Moraitis Fresh is confident of quickly recovering that amount. Moraitis Fresh has also been driven by the needs of the business processes it operates, rather than just adopting technology for technology's sake. As the Department of Communications, Information Technology and the Arts states, 'As with any technology, its theoretical capability is only half the story. Its real worth is in how it is put to work. It is the improvements to *business processes* made possible by RFID — or the *business problems that it solves* — that will yield the real value.'[81] Moraitis Fresh has evidently thought about how to put RFID to work within its business processes, envisaging that using RFID will allow it to significantly improve its processes and reinvigorate its supply chain. This should ultimately deliver a competitive advantage and ensure Moraitis Fresh is just like Nick's beloved Might and Power — lengths ahead of the next best in the field.[82]

**LEARNING OBJECTIVE 8**

*Critically evaluate BPR.*

## BPR EVALUATED

Hammer and Champy discuss some of the characteristics present in successfully re-engineered business processes.[83] These characteristics (work units change from functional to process, and jobs change and people are empowered), as well as the benefits they present for an organisation, are discussed in the following paragraphs.

The big benefit for the organisation undergoing BPR, particularly if it is one that was originally designed around functional principles, is the opportunity to embrace the business process based design, with the advantages discussed.

Employees within the organisation undergoing BPR can experience a big change in the nature of the work that they will perform. We saw this in the IBM case, where employees suddenly had a role in all of the tasks involved in the loan approval process, rather than just one small segment of it. For an employee this will arguably increase the diversity of the job and make it more interesting. It also gives employees a greater sense of involvement and control over the process because, in some cases, the restructuring of responsibilities can lead to decision rights being pushed further down in the organisation.

## Risks and criticisms of BPR

When BPR first emerged as an approach to organisational change there were several high-profile companies that experienced dramatic benefits from its application, including IBM, Ford and Mutual Benefit Life. While it worked well for these organisations, a large practical problem ensued. Given the high profile of the successful companies using BPR, and the nature of the improvements that they experienced, many organisations reading or hearing about it thought 'this is something we can use as well' without giving adequate consideration to all that must go into a re-engineering effort. As a result, many efforts failed or organisations were left disappointed with worse-than-expected results from BPR.[84]

Strassman describes how re-engineering emerged from a heritage of industrial engineering principles, 'except that it has none of its analytic rigour'.[85] Quite often it will involve a management that 'dictates change primarily from the top of the organization' and often reflects an approach to organisational change that considers the reason a particular process design was adopted. Additionally, it should be remembered that the reality of re-engineering is that it concerns people. Certain ethical and social issues emerge when we start to glibly refer to people as things that can be moved around, retrained or 're-engineered', much as we would describe a part of a machine.

People are not machine parts that can be 're-engineered'.[86] Further, given that re-engineering is often perceived as nothing more than an attempt at 'downsizing', employees will be extremely wary when the word is mentioned. As Strassman states:[87]

> The anxiety of the survivors of reengineering is perhaps the principal reason why companies do not realize the gains for which they originally planned. Employees who pull through endless waves of cuts become so distrustful, overworked, insecure and traumatized that their productivity drops and morale is permanently injured.

One of the major thrusts of BPR is the idea of IT as an enabler of organisational change. This was evident in the IBM case, with the development of the computer package to handle loan applications, thus allowing it to create what were effectively case managers while shifting away from the emphasis on employee specialisation. However, IT is not necessarily the great panacea that Hammer and Champy make it out to be.[88] There is a range of existing research literature that suggests that investments in IT do not necessarily lead to increases in performance and productivity,[89] a phenomenon referred to as the productivity paradox. Reasons for this include the reality that investing in a new IT infrastructure to support a BPR effort will typically bring with it a large range of costs, from hardware through to support. Any benefits gained through improved resource efficiency in the process perspective could potentially be negated by the increased resources required to support the new IT within the organisation.

Many organisations are also very wary about the extremity of the clean slate approach that is endorsed by Hammer and Champy for fear that they will throw the baby out with the bathwater.[90] The risks involved in the clean slate approach are obviously great because with the organisation essentially starting from scratch, if the newly designed and re-engineered process fails, then there may be nothing left to fall back on. Davenport provides an example of such concerns at Owens Corning, where, in preference to a clean slate approach, it adopted a philosophy of '"good enough" re-engineering',[91] while Garvin, in an interview with a CEO of a large American company, found that, 'process improvement isn't limited to large scale reengineering... [r]eal power comes from working with small processes — that's where the inefficiencies are'.[92] As Strassman observes, '[r]adical engineering may apply... under emergency conditions of imminent danger as long as someone remembers this may leave an enterprise in a crippled condition'.[93] Davenport and Stoddard observe that although designing from a dirty slate (by considering existing structures and processes within the organisation) can be 'a less exciting and more difficult design method, [it] will normally lead to a more implementable process'.[94]

In parable-like terms, the fisher who throws back the small fish in the hope of catching the big fish runs the risk of getting no fish at all, and so going hungry. However, the fisher who keeps the little fish will eat at night. Many little fish or one big fish — they all taste just as good when they are frying in the pan. For the organisation, the choice becomes one of waiting for the big fish or being happy to fry lots of little fish.

**LEARNING OBJECTIVE 9**

*Evaluate the application of information technology (IT) to business processes by Australian firms.*

# WHAT ARE AUSTRALIAN ORGANISATIONS DOING WITH INFORMATION TECHNOLOGY AND PROCESSES?

The preceding discussion of business processes and the use of technology emphasised the way many people believe organisations should use IT and map their processes. In this section of the chapter we look at some Australian statistics on technology usage by organisations. These statistics will be linked back to some of the ideas that we have discussed throughout the chapter as a way of illustrating the different issues and concepts of how IT can be incorporated into organisational design and business processes.

## How are businesses using IT?

As discussed previously, the central tenet of business process re-engineering, and indeed any form of organisational redesign or improvement, is to look for ways technology can potentially be applied to solve a business problem or create a unique strategic position for an organisation. While the theoretical perspective presented thus far makes sense on paper, the questions you are hopefully asking are 'To what extent does this actually apply in the real world?' and 'How are businesses actually using information technology within their organisational and process design?'

One of the obvious means for organisations to use technology is to establish a website to promote the organisation and potentially provide links forward and backward in the value chain by linking suppliers and customers to the organisation. As shown in table 2.4 overleaf, in 2007–08, more than 86 per cent of Australian organisations reported using the internet, with 42.7 per cent having placed orders through the internet. The amount of internet-based income has also risen steadily.

**TABLE 2.4** Australian business use of the internet

|  | 2003–04 | 2005–06 | 2007–08 |
|---|---|---|---|
| Internet use (per cent) | 74.2 | 81.3 | 86.8 |
| Web presence (per cent) | 25.1 | 29.8 | 36.3 |
| Placed orders using internet or web (per cent) | 31.3 | 37.3 | 42.7 |
| Received orders using internet or web (per cent) | 12 | 20.9 | 23.7 |
| Internet income ($b) | 33.3 | 56.7 | |

*Source:* Australian Bureau of Statistics[95]

Referring to table 2.5, it is evident that the vast majority of businesses are using the internet as a way of promoting their business activities in the electronic world, with 94.2 per cent of Australian businesses surveyed reporting the use of a website for the presentation of information about their business. However, this presence could simply be a home page with pictures and little else. The more interesting question, in terms of how the internet is being used, is what are business websites able to do? In other words, how well do websites link to business processes. For example, if a website is integrated with systems in other parts of the organisation, sales received over the internet can be sent to the sales process and trigger the shipping of goods and the management of accounts receivable and billing.

The data in table 2.5 tell us that while most businesses are using the internet (94.2 per cent) and most websites have some form of customer contact facility (88.4 per cent), the extent to which the internet has been incorporated into processes is questionable. While the data is aggregated, the table highlights a number of points as we think about the role of IT as an enabler in improving the design and operation of a business process. Firstly, the concept that IT is a tool that is relevant for all organisations. Secondly, a look at the table clearly highlights how web-based technology for selling goods and services or managing customer transactions is relevant to specific types of businesses. For example, the use of online ordering and shopping cart facilities appear particularly well suited to industries we would typically think of when referring to buying and selling, for example, retail and wholesale transactions. Thirdly, we also notice that there are several industries, for example, the construction industry, that do not use such technologies. Thinking about the nature of these industries makes this fact understandable. For example, when engaging in a construction transaction (e.g. building a house) the business processes followed by the construction company will probably be relatively hands on and face-to-face (e.g. discussing and drafting plans, selecting materials, and so on). As such, the applicability of technology to the 'ordering' part of the process is probably limited (although the company may use it to order raw materials and supplies from its suppliers). However, the ordering of more standardised retail products, such as CDs or books, are well suited to the use of internet technology, since the types of goods are generally common and standard.

It was mentioned earlier in the chapter that one way that technology is impacting on processes is in the execution of transactions; for example, the use of BPAY. If BPAY is extended and carried out over the internet, as outlined above, it would fall into the category of online payment facilities.

**TABLE 2.5** How businesses are using IT

| Industry | Info about business | Inquiry/ contact facility | Online ordering | Shopping carts | Online payment facilities | Secure access or transactions | Account info | Able to track orders | Personalised page | Automated link with back end systems |
|---|---|---|---|---|---|---|---|---|---|---|
| Mining | 97.5 | 81.9 | 7.5 | | 1.6 | 3.2 | 3.5 | | | 0.5 |
| Manufacturing | 96.5 | 90.4 | 23.7 | 9.8 | 10.7 | 8.8 | 6.9 | 4.3 | 3.5 | 2.5 |
| Electricity, Gas, Water and Waste Services | 95.5 | 82.8 | 17.5 | 2.8 | 11.4 | 14.3 | 12.8 | 7.7 | 7.1 | 3.3 |
| Construction | 95.2 | 91.8 | 7.3 | 3.5 | 10.2 | 4.4 | 8.5 | 0.7 | | 3.6 |
| Wholesale Trade | 97.9 | 94.2 | 26.9 | 19.3 | 18.0 | 12.8 | 8.4 | 8.0 | 4.9 | 3.3 |
| Retail Trade | 92.1 | 86.8 | 33.0 | 22.2 | 23.0 | 20.9 | 11.6 | 12.8 | 5.8 | 6.6 |
| Accommodation and Food Services | 96.5 | 87.7 | 19.3 | 0.6 | 10.3 | 10.2 | 8.1 | 1.7 | 3.7 | 5.0 |
| Transport, Postal and Warehousing | 90.8 | 91.5 | 20.1 | 3.2 | 16.7 | 9.3 | 15.2 | 17.9 | 6.3 | 5.6 |
| Information Media and Telecommunications | 96.2 | 91.1 | 27.3 | 6.4 | 17.2 | 17.8 | 10.5 | 4.6 | 5.0 | 9.1 |
| Financial and Insurance Services | 94.7 | 86.8 | 13.6 | 1.3 | 9.7 | 13.8 | 17.8 | 2.7 | 4.1 | 10.8 |
| Rental, Hiring and Real Estate Services | 97.4 | 91.0 | 16.0 | 4.1 | 8.9 | 5.5 | 7.0 | 5.8 | 7.5 | 6.2 |
| Professional, Scientific and Technical Services | 92.0 | 87.3 | 12.0 | 8.5 | 9.0 | 11.3 | 9.5 | 7.4 | 5.7 | 6.5 |
| Administrative and Support Services | 89.5 | 90.1 | 17.2 | 6.4 | 12.9 | 6.7 | 6.0 | 4.2 | 4.0 | 7.5 |
| Health Care and Social Assistance | 94.9 | 82.2 | 10.2 | 2.6 | 7.7 | 7.7 | 5.2 | | 7.6 | 2.7 |
| Arts and Recreation Services | 94.1 | 88.9 | 21.6 | 5.9 | 14.5 | 9.4 | 8.5 | 1.5 | 1.4 | 4.7 |
| Other Services | 93.5 | 82.1 | 22.5 | 10.6 | 10.5 | 6.2 | 5.1 | 3.3 | 2.4 | 1.0 |
| **Total** | **94.2** | **88.4** | **18.9** | **9.1** | **12.5** | **10.8** | **8.9** | **5.9** | **4.6** | **5.2** |

*Source:* Australian Bureau of Statistics 2009.[96]

The ability to track items was also mentioned earlier, with the example of the use of RFID tags. Table 2.5 indicates that the use of technology to track orders is particularly common in the transport industry. An example of this is the ability for a customer to log on to a courier company's website and see exactly where their order is while it is in transit from the company's warehouse. Several online retail sites also offer this tracking facility. This is an example of being able to use data (in this case, the movement of the parcel from origin to destination) to add value or build information into the process. A famous example of this, referred to by Davenport and Brooks,[97] is that of Federal Express, the international shipping and logistics company. Federal Express was a pioneer in providing customers with the ability to log on to a website to gain information about the process of their shipment in real time. The system worked based on data gathered as packages passed through various checkpoints on their journey, with the data able to be converted into information that added value for the customer. Following Federal Express' success, other courier services developed similar services. The customer satisfaction benefits of this technology are obvious. In addition, using internet technology instead of customers phoning an operator to track their packages meant the business was able to reduce the overall delivery cost to the customer and provide to the customer a more convenient process.[98]

## What parts of the business are using IT?

Table 2.6 (page 88) shows how technology impacts the way people work, and use and share information in organisations.

Reinforcing the idea of IT enabling the re-engineering of business processes, table 2.6 provides an insight into the ways that processes and operations within organisations are being altered by information technology. Notice from the table how traditional banking and payment functions have been impacted by IT, with 82.3 per cent of businesses reporting the use of technology in this area. Additionally, we can also see that technology has been applied to allow people flexibility in where work is performed, with employees able to work from home and other locations and still have access to the organisation by virtue of IT. We can also see that organisations are increasingly using IT as a way of integrating the organisation with customers, suppliers and other organisations. This would appear consistent with the concepts of business-to-business e-commerce and integrating systems across the organisation — an emerging idea within the realm of enterprise resource planning systems (discussed in chapter 6).

## Is IT really improving processes?

The concept of IT as an enabler is fundamental to business process re-engineering as discussed above. Indeed, whether talking in terms of business process re-engineering or process change in general, there is little argument against the fact that IT can play a role for an organisation, whether through the use of the internet or moving towards an enterprise resource planning system. The Australian evidence on business use of IT provides some interesting insights into how IT is being applied.

A look at table 2.7 (page 90) tells us that most organisations have an email facility as a means of receiving orders. In simple terms, this would appear to be a positive step, since it removes the need for a paper document to be sent by the customer to the organisation. However, the question that we should then consider is how the email facility links to the rest of the organisation. An email facility in isolation would suggest that orders are sent by email and then printed out or re-entered into the organisation's other systems (e.g. the sales system). While this would increase the speed at which the order is received by the organisation, bottlenecks could still exist in the re-entry of the order into other systems. Essentially, a paper document has been made electronic (the email) but all other processes remain as per the old way of doing things.[99] The other point to notice is that larger organisations tend to be more sophisticated users of IT when it comes to receiving orders, with almost 20 per cent of businesses with more than 200 staff using websites with shopping cart features for taking orders. In contrast, 10.9 per cent of small (0–4 people) businesses use shopping carts on their websites, with most small organisations opting instead for an independent email system for receiving orders.

The issue of integrating processes and data flows across processes, highlighted as missing in the discussion above about re-entering orders from emails, is brought to the surface in table 2.8 (page 91), with 78 per cent of businesses having no integration between their automated order receipt system and other processes. In situations where systems are integrated, the typical target system is the invoicing and payment system, suggesting sales data automatically flows through to the invoicing and payment system to facilitate prompt billing of customers and the better management of receipts from customers.

What the above statistics suggest is that while IT has been recognised by organisations as a resource that can assist in building their wider presence (e.g. promoting the organisation through the establishment of a website) as well as improving the operations of the organisation and the workings of business processes, many organisations attribute the uptake of the technology to several factors, including government support, customer pressure for e-commerce development and the ability to access technological support for e-commerce adoption.[100] Overall, however, the extent to which technology has been adopted and embraced in line with the tenets of BPR seems to be limited. The integration of processes, as well as integration with customer and supplier systems, also appears to be restricted to larger organisations. One could speculate the causes of this discrepancy between the degree of integration for small and large businesses as including different levels in the need for integration and the availability of technology and financial resources to support such integration. In its extreme, integration could be attained through an enterprise system, discussed in chapter 6. However, ERP systems have traditionally been seen as costly and prohibitive for smaller organisations.

## Information as a business

Another aspect to consider is the way in which technology is building an entirely new dimension for business processes — the information dimension. As mentioned above in the package tracking example, the ability to gather and process data quickly and efficiently using IT has created a means for organisations to add value in their processes and provide added information for customers. In addition, increasingly, technology-based processes have created opportunities for third party organisations to thrive and offer services based solely on the data available to them. Examples of such a business model include well-known websites such as wotif.com and Need It Now. These sites provide a resource for those looking to book accommodation by offering a tool that provides the customer with information in one place about available rooms and their prices. These sites do not provide accommodation. They do not run hotels. Their business is built solely around being able to synthesise and present data in a way that adds value to the customer. This business model is referred to as an aggregator — the business operates by sourcing data from various sources and compiling or aggregating it in a way that adds value for the end customer.[101]

**TABLE 2.6** How people in businesses are using IT

| Industry | Financial including online banking, invoicing, making payments | Enabling persons working for this business to: | | Information gathering or researching for: | | | | | Information sharing or data exchange (eg. EDI, FTP) with: | |
|---|---|---|---|---|---|---|---|---|---|---|
| | | work from home | work from other locations | assessing or modifying this business's range of products, services, processes or methods | development of new or improved products, services, processes or methods | monitoring competitors | identifying future market trends | Online training/ learning | customers or clients | other businesses or organisations |
| Mining | 86.3 | 48.6 | 44.9 | 26.3 | 20.5 | 26.5 | 21.7 | 26.0 | 21.5 | 21.0 |
| Manufacturing | 82.9 | 32.3 | 20.9 | 38.1 | 27.8 | 28.9 | 20.0 | 18.4 | 21.1 | 10.8 |
| Electricity, Gas, Water and Waste Services | 87.2 | 40.4 | 25.1 | 31.0 | 20.7 | 24.6 | 14.5 | 19.2 | 18.8 | 12.5 |
| Construction | 85.2 | 32.8 | 14.2 | 26.7 | 13.4 | 14.4 | 8.1 | 20.1 | 17.5 | 9.4 |
| Wholesale Trade | 83.3 | 38.9 | 30.4 | 44.6 | 29.4 | 36.4 | 28.9 | 25.5 | 27.5 | 17.9 |
| Retail Trade | 82.8 | 36.0 | 21.9 | 45.0 | 23.1 | 31.0 | 24.4 | 20.5 | 15.0 | 14.8 |
| Accommodation and Food Services | 81.4 | 18.8 | 15.6 | 34.0 | 21.7 | 24.4 | 14.8 | 21.9 | 8.4 | 10.7 |
| Transport, Postal and Warehousing | 82.3 | 26.6 | 14.6 | 23.5 | 13.8 | 14.6 | 8.9 | 15.9 | 15.3 | 10.2 |
| Information Media and Telecommunications | 87.0 | 55.3 | 46.1 | 45.4 | 42.7 | 40.5 | 32.0 | 29.1 | 37.4 | 21.2 |
| Financial and Insurance Services | 87.7 | 56.4 | 38.4 | 44.0 | 21.5 | 32.5 | 31.1 | 53.8 | 27.3 | 20.2 |
| Rental, Hiring and Real Estate Services | 84.5 | 40.2 | 21.9 | 40.0 | 21.5 | 35.7 | 25.9 | 22.8 | 24.8 | 16.2 |

| Industry | Financial including online banking, invoicing, making payments | Enabling persons working for this business to: | | Information gathering or researching for: | | | | | Information sharing or data exchange (eg. EDI, FTP) with: | |
| | | work from home | work from other locations | assessing or modifying this business's range of products, services, processes or methods | development of new or improved products, services, processes or methods | monitoring competitors | identifying future market trends | Online training/ learning | customers or clients | other businesses or organisations |
|---|---|---|---|---|---|---|---|---|---|---|
| Professional, Scientific and Technical Services | 85.2 | 61.9 | 46.6 | 43.6 | 31.8 | 28.8 | 21.2 | 39.0 | 31.8 | 22.3 |
| Administrative and Support Services | 78.9 | 38.5 | 26.7 | 31.2 | 25.1 | 22.2 | 16.8 | 24.7 | 21.6 | 11.6 |
| Health Care and Social Assistance | 69.7 | 32.0 | 15.5 | 28.8 | 22.0 | 13.6 | 7.7 | 38.1 | 20.4 | 18.1 |
| Arts and Recreation Services | 78.8 | 34.5 | 21.8 | 35.5 | 27.1 | 37.7 | 23.5 | 25.1 | 25.8 | 12.1 |
| Other Services | 77.1 | 26.4 | 8.4 | 36.6 | 22.0 | 25.3 | 14.7 | 19.4 | 14.5 | 11.1 |
| **Total** | **82.3** | **38.8** | **24.6** | **36.3** | **23.3** | **25.1** | **17.8** | **26.6** | **21.3** | **14.7** |

*Source:* Australian Bureau of Statistics 2009.[102]

**TABLE 2.7** How orders are received over the internet

| | Email not linked to website | Website with linked email facility | Website with online order form | Website with shopping cart | Other methods |
|---|---|---|---|---|---|
| | per cent | per cent | per cent | per cent | per cent |
| **Employment size** | | | | | |
| 0–4 persons | 68.1 | 28.8 | 14.1 | 10.9 | 1.8 |
| 5–19 persons | 63.2 | 38.6 | 19.7 | 14.6 | 0.8 |
| 20–199 persons | 60.6 | 37.2 | 24.2 | 10.8 | 2.0 |
| 200 or more persons | 48.1 | 44.7 | 55.7 | 19.9 | 5.0 |
| **Industry** | | | | | |
| Mining | 86.3 | 18.7 | | 0.0 | 0.0 |
| Manufacturing | 73.8 | 32.0 | 11.2 | 7.7 | 0.8 |
| Electricity, Gas, Water and Waste Services | 72.2 | 33.8 | 12.2 | 3.8 | |
| Construction | 76.7 | 14.2 | 11.9 | 5.3 | |
| Wholesale Trade | 62.5 | 30.3 | 22.3 | 19.0 | 2.0 |
| Retail Trade | 62.6 | 30.0 | 19.2 | 25.3 | 1.0 |
| Accommodation and Food Services | 48.0 | 69.2 | 26.9 | 2.7 | 2.7 |
| Transport, Postal and Warehousing | 76.4 | 26.8 | 18.7 | 3.6 | |
| Information Media and Telecommunications | 66.9 | 31.4 | 22.5 | 10.4 | |
| Financial and Insurance Services | 53.0 | 30.0 | 23.8 | 3.3 | 3.4 |
| Rental, Hiring and Real Estate Services | 52.4 | 53.3 | 19.8 | 9.6 | |
| Professional, Scientific and Technical Services | 66.9 | 34.5 | 17.4 | 16.8 | |
| Administrative and Support Services | 62.7 | 38.2 | 16.5 | 6.1 | 0.1 |
| Health Care and Social Assistance | 64.2 | 35.6 | 11.7 | 6.0 | |
| Arts and Recreation Services | 54.9 | 46.5 | 38.6 | 8.9 | 6.4 |
| Other Services | 53.2 | 45.9 | 11.8 | 10.5 | |
| **Total** | **65.5** | **33.1** | **17.3** | **12.2** | **1.5** |

*Source:* Australian Bureau of Statistics 2009.[103]

**TABLE 2.8** Automated links between systems used to receive orders and other business systems

| | Business's systems for: | | | | | | | |
|---|---|---|---|---|---|---|---|---|
| | Suppliers' business systems | Customers' business systems | Reordering replacement supplies | Invoicing and payment | Production or service operations | Logistics, including e-delivery | Marketing operations | No automatic system links |
| | per cent | per cent | per cent | per cent | per cent | per cent | per cent | per cent |
| **Employment size** | | | | | | | | |
| 0–4 persons | 8.2 | 4.9 | 2.6 | 9.7 | 2.1 | 3.8 | 3.3 | 82.0 |
| 5–19 persons | 9.8 | 8.8 | 3.3 | 15.1 | 4.4 | 4.9 | 6.5 | 73.6 |
| 20–199 persons | 9.4 | 6.5 | 4.6 | 14.8 | 4.6 | 3.0 | 6.7 | 73.8 |
| 200 or more persons | 25.5 | 27.7 | 23.6 | 37.6 | 13.1 | 16.5 | 13.8 | 42.2 |
| **Industry** | | | | | | | | |
| Mining | | 12.6 | | 11.2 | 0.0 | | 0.0 | 83.2 |
| Manufacturing | 6.4 | 7.5 | 3.6 | 9.2 | 2.9 | 1.7 | 3.3 | 83.8 |
| Electricity, Gas, Water and Waste Services | 0.6 | | 4.3 | 4.7 | 0.8 | 0.6 | | 94.7 |
| Construction | 8.4 | 6.6 | 6.9 | 12.3 | | 3.2 | 2.6 | 83.4 |
| Wholesale Trade | 4.8 | 7.1 | 4.9 | 13.7 | 3.4 | 1.2 | 3.1 | 79.5 |
| Retail Trade | 7.3 | 3.7 | 3.9 | 12.2 | 2.7 | 5.1 | 0.4 | 75.9 |
| Accommodation and Food Services | 9.0 | 10.6 | 2.0 | 8.7 | 1.8 | 2.1 | 2.4 | 78.2 |
| Transport, Postal and Warehousing | 16.5 | 7.8 | 1.3 | 15.0 | 4.1 | 12.0 | 5.0 | 63.0 |
| Information Media and Telecommunications | 7.3 | 8.1 | 0.6 | 10.7 | 8.8 | 4.0 | 5.6 | 76.8 |
| Financial and Insurance Services | 26.0 | 4.6 | | 17.8 | 8.9 | 4.5 | 8.7 | 51.9 |
| Rental, Hiring and Real Estate Services | 10.2 | 8.9 | | 14.1 | 0.3 | 3.6 | 12.3 | 71.1 |
| Professional, Scientific and Technical Services | 6.7 | 6.4 | 0.8 | 14.7 | 7.4 | 6.5 | 9.5 | 81.8 |
| Administrative and Support Services | 11.9 | 12.0 | 5.5 | 7.9 | 1.0 | 5.0 | 6.6 | 78.4 |
| Health Care and Social Assistance | 18.9 | | | 6.4 | 0.1 | | 6.4 | 74.6 |
| Arts and Recreation Services | 7.6 | 6.4 | 3.3 | 8.9 | 0.8 | 7.3 | 4.2 | 76.9 |
| Other Services | 14.6 | 5.6 | 2.9 | 15.3 | 1.1 | 4.9 | 7.5 | 72.2 |
| **Total** | **9.0** | **6.5** | **3.2** | **12.2** | **3.2** | **4.1** | **4.8** | **78.0** |

*Source:* Australian Bureau of Statistics 2009.[104]

How do such sites add value to the customer? In the accommodation example, the benefit for the customer comes from the fact that they are able to see all rooms available and their prices in one place, reducing their search costs (the time and effort required to find accommodation). The website provider's entire business exists due to the availability of data from the various hotels about what rooms are available and when. It earns income through commissions received from hotels for bookings.

This idea can be applied to any information-based process, including airline bookings and car hire. Indeed, the potential exists for these services to be combined. For example, after booking a flight, some sites present accommodation options at the chosen destination. In this manner, organisations are able to link their business processes and build strategic links with other businesses, for example, airlines with car hire companies or hotel chains. These links rely on the data about the primary business process (e.g. airline booking) being available, and the technology to share and manipulate the data so it can be used in a way that adds value for the customer.

An example is Lufthansa. The company made an early move towards understanding its customers through capturing booking data and other details and using this data to regularly email customers about travel options, accommodation availability and online booking facilities. This innovation saw Lufthansa generate more than £17 million in revenue.[105] Australian airlines carry out similar procedures through their frequent flyer programs, which allow them to gather data about passengers, their travel preferences and patterns. In turn, this allows the airlines to send customised emails to customers detailing the latest flight discounts and destinations. As another example, Marriot had a database of customer bookings and details that allowed it to 'create products and services that manifest superior value to the customer, thus gaining [for Marriot the] ultimate advantage in the marketplace'.[106] This would not have been possible if the data had not been available. As technology continues to proliferate, businesses will increasingly look to the ability to leverage process data to create avenues for new services, particularly in service industries where information is the basis of business processes.

## ››› SUMMARY ›››

LEARNING OBJECTIVE

*What are the components of organisational strategy and mission?*
The process of forming a strategy is based on the overarching mission statement. The mission statement essentially expresses the organisation's reason for existence and what it aims to do. The operationalisation of the mission commences with the decisions on strategy, which requires the business to distinguish itself from its competitors and develop a set of activities that best deliver its product or service to its target group. A business needs to be clear on a strategy and cannot afford to try and be everything to everyone.

LEARNING OBJECTIVE

*What are the alternative organisational structures, their strengths, weaknesses and implications for organisational operations?*
Two typical organisational structures are the functional and the business process perspectives. In the functional perspective a highly structured, rigid organisation is observed that has specifically defined tasks for employees, with these tasks centred on the various departments of the organisation. In contrast, the business process perspective recognises the interaction that occurs among departments to accomplish organisational goals. As a result, the business process-based design for an organisation will produce an organisation that is leaner, uses its resources better and is more driven by customer needs, since satisfying these is the aim of the business process.

LEARNING
OBJECTIVE  **What is a business process and what are some examples of business processes?**

A business process is a series of interlocking activities that work together across the organisation to achieve some predetermined organisational goal. This predetermined goal is typically defined around satisfying customer needs. A business process is a combination of business functions. Business processes can include processes to order raw materials within a manufacturing firm, to manufacture products, to sell products to customers, to handle customer enquiries or to hire new employees.

LEARNING
OBJECTIVE  **What are the benefits of organisations adopting a business process perspective?**

Resource benefits flow from having a process emphasis. These emerge due to the more highly coordinated and integrated approach that the process perspective offers an organisation, reducing wasted time due to rework, bureaucracy and administration. The business process perspective can yield benefits through improved customer service and customer relations, a value-adding emphasis and, potentially, a competitive advantage. Because processes are usually based around the product and therefore the customer, customer satisfaction, attention and service are potentially higher in a process-focused organisation.

LEARNING
OBJECTIVE  **What role do enterprise resource planning (ERP) systems play in business process design?**

An ERP system is a complex set of computer program modules that attempts to integrate the different functional areas of the organisation. Because an ERP system is built around the notion of best practice, it provides a way for businesses to adopt it. These systems can provide several advantages for the organisation; however, when adopting them those in charge should be aware of the risks, including the strategy of the organisation being different from that embodied in the design of the ERP system.

LEARNING
OBJECTIVE  **What are some of the issues for organisations changing to a process-based focus?**

Issues that need to be addressed and managed include changes in the role of management and changes in the design of employee tasks and responsibilities. Changing to a process perspective can mean significant changes in the way people perform their duties and as a result decision making occurs further down an organisation's hierarchy. Middle managers can see this as a loss of power and offer resistance. In some cases a layer of managers can become redundant. Workers tend to move from doing one narrowly defined task to a range of tasks, which can create a more stimulating environment.

LEARNING
OBJECTIVE **What are some approaches to changing business processes, in particular business process re-engineering (BPR)?**

Business processes need to change as the life of the business extends. There are several approaches to business process change, for example, TQM and BPR. Compared with BPR, TQM is a more conservative approach to change, working from the bottom up and using several small improvements to a process as the means of improving it, rather than a total overhaul. In contrast, BPR is a radical approach to change that can sometimes necessitate starting from a clean slate and totally redesigning the way the process is performed in the organisation. Eight steps to managing BPR are to: establish a sense of urgency, form a leadership team, create a vision, communicate the vision, empower others to meet the vision, plan for and create short-term wins, consolidate improvements and encourage further change, and institutionalise the new approaches.

Information technology (IT) can be implemented as part of a BPR strategy. Vendor-managed inventory, evaluated receipts settlement, electronic bill payment, presentation and management and RFID or barcode technology can all achieve significant results in a BPR implementation.

LEARNING OBJECTIVE

### *What are the strengths and weaknesses of BPR?*

BPR can achieve dramatic improvements by overhauling or replacing an outdated organisational design, but it carries with it a higher degree of risk than other change approaches and involves more of a top-down approach. BPR is not without its critics, who often claim it ignores that organisations primarily consist of people, who are not something that can be re-engineered, as a machine can.

Further, critics often say that to throw out everything and start from scratch is an extreme measure that introduces unnecessary risk. Many would advocate a much more conservative, small-step approach to change, rather than the all-encompassing approach that is inherent in BPR.

LEARNING OBJECTIVE

### *What trends can be observed in the application of IT to business processes by Australian firms?*

The data available indicates that the adoption by IT is on the rise, with increased volume of e-commerce sales and the use of technology to integrate systems within and across organisations. The data also points to the industry specific nature of technology application — some industries are well suited to the application of technology by virtue of their chosen activities or product and service choices, whereas others are not so suited.

## KEY TERMS

best practice, p. 62
business function, p. 51
business process, p. 53
business process design, p. 65
business process re-engineering (BPR), p. 66

functional perspective, p. 50
information technology, p. 74
organisational design, p. 50
scientific management, p. 50
Total Quality Management (TQM), p. 65
vendor-managed inventory, p. 75

## DISCUSSION QUESTIONS

2.1 Explain why Porter argues that it is not possible for a business to adopt more than one strategy at a time. (LO1)

2.2 What is meant by the term 'operational effectiveness'? (LO1)

2.3 Summarise the components of organisational strategy. (LO1)

2.4 Describe the relationship between the mission statement, strategy and business processes. (LO1)

2.5 Explain what it means for a business if it is considered an aggregator. What is unique about such a business's operations? (LO1)

2.6 Explain the difference between a strategy of cost leadership and differentiation. (LO1)

2.7 Describe the differences between the functionally based and process-based organisation. How do these differences affect how the organisation operates? (LO2)

2.8 What are the organisational advantages and disadvantages of the functionally based and process-based organisational designs? (LO2)

2.9 What is the relationship between business processes and ERP systems? (LO5)

2.10 How do ERP systems promote better-designed processes within the organisation? (LO5)

2.11 Describe briefly two of the methods of making changes to a business process, namely TQM and BPR. (LO7)

2.12 What are some of the advantages and disadvantages of BPR? (LO7)

2.13 Explain what is meant by the term 'clean slate approach' in the discussion of BPR. (LO7)

2.14 List and describe, through the use of examples, the principles of BPR. (LO7)

2.15 Identify some of the organisational issues that may emerge from BPR. Discuss their cause, likely consequences and how the organisation may manage these issues effectively. (LO7, LO8)

## SELF-TEST ACTIVITIES

2.1 The focus of the functional perspective of the organisation is on:
   (a) controlling the organisation so customers are satisfied.
   (b) ensuring the organisation can promptly respond to its operating environment.
   (c) controlling staff through specifically defined duties.
   (d) integrating the functional areas for efficient operations.

2.2 The benefits of a business process perspective include:
   (a) a well-defined hierarchy for organisational control.
   (b) an integrated horizontal organisation.
   (c) delegated power to employees through less reliance on specialists.
   (d) specialists doing a large amount of work to ensure its proper completion.

2.3 ERP systems will help an organisation improve its process design when:
   (a) the existing process is flawed and the strategy of the organisation is consistent with the ERP approach.
   (b) the existing process is flawed and strategies are different to the ERP approach but the organisation can change to the ERP-defined process.
   (c) the existing process is old, having been in place for several years.
   (d) the process in the ERP system is different from the existing process used by the organisation.

2.4 In managing changes in a business process, organisations will often consult lower-level staff for ideas about improvements. This is done because:
   (a) lower-level employees need to have the perception they are involved in the change.
   (b) lower-level employees perform most of the process and possess valuable knowledge about its operation.
   (c) top-level management fears union reprisals if it does not consult lower-level staff.
   (d) lower-level employees can be useful in managing the change process.

2.5 IT as an enabler of BPR means that:
   (a) all jobs should be performed by computers.
   (b) existing processes should be automated using the latest technology.
   (c) IT can enable people to better enjoy their work roles.
   (d) IT should be used in newly designed processes where possible.

2.6 TQM is designed for (i)_____, (ii)_____ change, while BPR is more of a (iii)_____, (iv)_____ approach to change.
   (a) (i) incremental, (ii) top-down, (iii) moderate risk, (iv) clean slate
   (b) (i) incremental, (ii) bottom-up, (iii) radical, (iv) top-down
   (c) (i) top-down, (ii) quick, (iii) long-term, (iv) incremental
   (d) (i) narrow, (ii) within function, (iii) narrow, (iv) across function

# PROBLEMS

2.1 Compare and contrast the functional perspective and the business process perspective of the organisation. In particular, comment on the different abilities of the structures to (1) delegate work to employees, (2) respond to change and (3) service the customer.

2.2 James McFarlane is the manager of a medium-sized manufacturing company. His company is looking at improving the design of its sales and manufacturing processes and one employee has suggested that it considers adopting an ERP system. The employee said something about the benefit of best practice in ERP systems. James is not sure which way to go. He believes that the organisation's current practices are basically sound, unique in the industry and that, with a little modification, they could be even more of a distinguishing factor for the business. He has reservations about ERP systems and was contemplating TQM and BPR as other alternatives for the existing process.

Advise James on the risks and benefits an organisation faces in adopting the processes in an ERP system. Should his company go ahead with the ERP system?

Do you think, based on the few facts available, that James should be considering BPR and TQM? If so, which do you think is appropriate for his business? Explain your reasoning.

2.3 Table 2.9 compares TQM and BPR as ways of improving business processes.

**TABLE 2.9** Comparing TQM and BPR

| Primary criteria | TQM (process improvement) | BPR (process innovation) |
|---|---|---|
| Level of change | Incremental | Radical |
| Starting point | Existing process | Clean slate |
| Frequency of change | One-time/continuous | One-time |
| Time required | Short | Long |
| Participation | Bottom-up | Top-down |
| Typical scope | Narrow, within functions | Broad, cross-functional |
| Risk | Moderate | High |
| Primary enabler | Statistical control | IT |
| Type of change | Cultural | Cultural/structural |

*Source:* Williams et al., 2003, p. 2.[107]

Describe each of the primary criteria used for comparing the two approaches and highlight the important distinctions between the two approaches for each criterion.

2.4 Review the before and after re-engineering process descriptions for IBM Credit in the chapter.
(a) Explain how this case demonstrates the four elements of re-engineering that were described in the chapter (fundamental, radical, dramatic, process).
(b) Draw a diagram of the operation of the re-engineered IBM loan application process. Compare this diagram with that of the original process in figure 2.5. What are the major differences in the way the process is performed?
(c) One of the solutions for IBM's process design that was tried was to establish a central desk and integrate that into the original process. As each person completed their individual task he or she would return the loan application to the central desk where it would await collection by the next person in the

process. What do you think would be some of the possible advantages of such an approach?

(d) Do you think that there could be any disadvantages to implementing the central desk approach described in part (c)? Explain why.

(e) Why do you think IBM did not pursue this option, instead opting for the re-engineered approach described in the case contained in the chapter?

(f) What could be some of the issues (ethical, technical, legal or otherwise) that IBM would have to address in implementing the loan application computer support program in the re-engineered organisation?

2.5 Publications by Hammer and Champy[108] and Hammer[109] advocate a clean slate approach to BPR.

(a) Why do you think they encourage this clean slate approach?

(b) Can you think of any problems that might arise if an organisation simply automates an existing process, in preference to redesigning it? Explain some of these problems.

(c) Critically evaluate the clean slate approach to BPR. Do you think it is a suitable approach for all organisations in the midst of process redesign? Why? What could be an alternative to the clean slate approach?

2.6 Describe the operation of electronic payment systems, for example BPAY.

2.7 Describe and evaluate the advantages of electronic payment systems for the:

(a) provider of goods and services.

(b) buyer of goods and services.

2.8 Compare the operation of electronic bill payment (EBP) systems and electronic bill presentation and payment (EBPP) systems. Describe the differences between the two systems.

2.9 Assess the relative benefits for a business of adopting EBP and EBPP. Which do you think would offer the greater benefits when re-engineering a business process? Explain the reasoning behind your conclusion.

2.10 Describe the operation of evaluated receipt payment systems. What advantages would this system present for buyers of goods and services? How would it improve the operation of a business process that is undergoing re-engineering?

2.11 List some of the potential ways that a business could apply the following technologies within its business processes:

(a) barcode scanning

(b) radio frequency identification tags.

2.12 Read AIS focus 2.4 that describes how Moraitis Fresh has employed RFID in its business processes. Answer the following questions based on the AIS focus material.

(a) What were the weaknesses of the original processes used by Moraitis Fresh?

(b) Describe how RFID may have potentially improved the operation of the business processes at Moraitis Fresh.

(c) How may the quality of information available within the business processes at Moraitis Fresh improve as a result of the re-engineered processes that include RFID?

(d) What factors would Moraitis Fresh have considered when deciding to re-engineer its process and include RFID tags?

(e) What obstacles might have been faced as part of the re-engineering effort?

2.13 Two EBP providers in Australia include BPAYView and Australia Post. For each provider:

(a) View its website.

(b) List the services offered by each organisation.

(c) Based on the information on the website, describe the differences between bill presentation, bill payment and bill management services.

(d) How might the customers of a business process benefit from each of these services (bill presentation, bill payment and bill management)? Which do you think would best benefit a business that is considering reengineering its business processes?

2.14 Strides for Strides manufactures and sells athletic wear to retail stores, who then stock the goods and sell them to customers. Its range of products includes warm-up tracksuits, body suits and running shoes and spikes. The business process followed by Strides for Strides in supplying retail stores is as follows:

- The retail store will send an order to Strides for Strides, where it will be received by the customer service representative. Orders are generated by and originate from the retail stores and can arrive on an ad hoc and irregular basis. Retail stores, while all being long-standing and regular customers, have typically ordered at the last minute, resulting in irregular demand levels across the year. Two copies of the order form are made, with one being sent to the warehouse assistant, who checks that all goods are available for dispatch to the retail store. The second copy goes to the accounts receivable office.

- Once confirmed as available, the goods are packed, manually recorded on the goods release form (two copies are prepared) and sent to the shipping department for dispatch. A courier collects goods and a goods release form every morning and afternoon and delivers these to the retail store. Once delivery details are confirmed, an invoice is prepared by accounts payable, based on the details in the customer order and the goods release form. Paper invoices are sent out at the end of each week. Retail stores currently have standard payment terms of 2/15, n/35. Payment is made in the form of a cheque, which is sent back to the customer service representative who forwards it on to the accounts receivable office.

Strides for Strides has recently noticed that it is having inventory management problems due to the spasmodic and irregular nature of orders. This has impacted on its own ability to meet customer demands. It is also concerned that incorrect quantities of goods may be packed and shipped, and not detected until the goods reach the retail stores. This introduces extra costs of handling returns and allowances. Strides for Strides has also noticed that its accounts receivable turnover has dropped from 11.7 times per year to 9.5 times per year over the last 12 months.

An independent consultant has suggested that by re-engineering the process these problems could be addressed.

**Required**

(a) For the business process described above, identify:
  (i) the participants.
  (ii) the inputs.
  (iii) the outputs.

(b) Identify and describe any inefficiencies that are present in the current system.

(c) Suggest ways that the business process inefficiencies could be corrected through business process re-engineering.

(d) Prepare a brief narrative that describes how your newly re-engineered system would operate.

(e) Identify and describe the role that technology would play in implementing your proposed changes.

(f) Describe some of the issues that may be faced by Strides for Strides in re-engineering processes. Propose some strategies for dealing with these issues.

2.15 Describe the differences between RFID and barcodes as a means of capturing data in a process. In what situations may RFID be preferable to barcodes?

2.16 Damocles' Kitchenware sells cutlery and dinnerware to customers through a small retail outlet located in downtown Brisbane. All of Damocles' sales are to customers who purchase on credit. Since the existing process for receiving payments from customers is not technology based, all receipts from customers are either received through the mail or in person from the customer. Over the past few years, sales for Damocles' Kitchenware have steadily increased. So too have accounts receivable levels. A summary of the details is shown below:

| Year | 2007 | 2008 | 2009 | 2010 |
|---|---|---|---|---|
| Sales for year ending 30 June (all on credit) | 125450 | 157993 | 188014 | 212331 |
| Net profit after tax for year ending 30 June | 35014 | 44761 | 48536 | 51664 |
| Accounts receivable at 30 June | 12500 | 29746 | 55484 | 72467 |

Concerned about its liquidity, Damocles is investigating the introduction of electronic bill presentation and payment (EBPP), and EBPP combined with bill management systems (EBPP/BMS).

**Required**

Prepare a memo that advises the management of Damocles about the difference in the services offered through EBPP versus EBPP or BMS. The memo should address the following:

(a) A description of what EBPP and EBPP/BMS are and how they operate.

(b) The advantages of each option for the business and for its customers.

(c) The impacts of the technology on the current operation of the process.

(d) The impact of both systems on process performance and key financial statement ratios.

(e) A conclusion as to which (if any) technology option Damocles should select.

2.17 Describe the operation of an ERS system.

2.18 Describe how the use of barcode systems could improve the operation of a business process.

2.19 What are some of the potentially negative consequences of integrating technology into a re-engineered business process?

2.20 Describe the usage of an SSCC. How does an SSCC help a seller and a buyer improve the operation of its business processes? Why is it important to have standards when using barcodes between different organisations?

2.21 List, describe and provide a potential example of each of the four benefits that businesses can enjoy from applying technology to their business processes.

2.22 Refer to figures 2.1 and 2.2 in the chapter. For each mission statement, provide a breakdown of how it addresses the four components of mission statements mentioned in the chapter.

2.23 Use Porter's five forces model to analyse the Australian university sector. (*Hint:* You may need to consult university websites and newspapers to complete this)

(a) How many universities are there in Australia?

(b) How does each of the five forces apply to universities?

(c) Do you think all universities are affected equally by the same forces? Why?

2.24 The strategy discussion in the chapter mentions the need to have activities that are interconnected and built towards the target goal. Select a business that you know and describe the following:

(a) The target of the business's strategy (i.e. customers, product, delivery).

(b) The activities the business engages in to deliver its product or service.

(c) The extent to which you think there is a fit between the chosen strategy and the activities in the business process.

2.25 Explain, using examples, how businesses can operate on data alone, without providing a physical product.

2.26 Describe the ways in which you think the business processes of a manufacturing organisation would be different to those of an aggregator.

## FURTHER READING

Davenport, TH 1993, *Process innovation: reengineering work through information technology*, Harvard Business School Press, Boston.

Davenport, TH 1998, 'Putting the enterprise into the enterprise system', *Harvard Business Review*, July–August, pp. 121–31.

Hammer, M 1990, 'Reengineering work: don't automate, obliterate', *Harvard Business Review*, July–August, pp. 104–12.

## SELF-TEST ANSWERS

2.1 c, 2.2 c, 2.3 a, 2.4 b, 2.5 d, 2.6 b

## END NOTES

1. Sidhu, J 2003, 'Mission statements: is it time to shelve them?', *European Management Journal*, vol. 21, no. 4, pp. 439–46.

2. Sidhu, J 2003.

3. Wiley 2009, 'Mission', www.wiley.com.

4. Dick Smith Foods 2009, 'Mission statement', www.dicksmithfoods.com.au.

5. Bakos, JY & Treacy, ME 1986, 'Information technology and corporate strategy: a research perspective', *Management Information Systems Quarterly,* vol. 10, no. 2, pp. 107–19; Simons, R 2000, *Performance measurement and control systems for implementing strategy*, Prentice Hall, United States, pp. 16–37.

6. Porter, M 2008, 'The five competitive forces that shape strategy', *Harvard Business Review*, January, pp. 78–93; Edwards, C & Peppard, J 1994, '*Forging a link between business strategy and business reengineering*', Cranfield School of Management, SWP 15/94.

7. Porter, M 1985, *Competitive advantage — creating and sustaining superior performance*, Free Press, New York, as cited in Morschett, D, Swoboda, B & Schramm-Klein, H 2006, 'Competitive strategies in retailing – an investigation of the applicability of Porter's framework for food retailers', *Journal of Retailing and Consumer Services*, vol. 13, pp. 275–87; Porter, M 1980, *Competitive strategy: techniques for analyzing industries and competitors*, Free Press, New York, as cited in Morschett, D. Swoboda, B & Schramm-Klein, H 2006, 'Competitive strategies in retailing – an investigation of the applicability of Porter's framework for food retailers', *Journal of Retailing and Consumer Services*, vol. 13, pp. 275–87.

8. Based on Porter 1996, 'What is strategy?', *Harvard Business Review*, November–December, pp. 61–78.

9. Based on Porter 1996; Markides, C 2004, 'What is strategy and how do you know if you have one?', *Business Strategy Review*, vol. 15, no. 2, pp. 5–12.

10. Based on Porter 2008.
11. Based on Porter, M 2001, 'Strategy and the internet', *Harvard Business Review*, March, pp. 62–78.
12. Davenport, T 2000, 'Mission critical: realizing the promise of enterprise systems', Harvard College, p. 3, www.harvardbusiness.org/products/9067/9067p4.pdf.
13. Jacenko, A & Gunasekera D 2005, 'Australia's retail food sector: some preliminary observations', *ABARE conference paper 05.11, the pacific food system outlook 2005–06*, Kunming, China, 11–13 May.
14. ALDI Australia 2009, 'About ALDI Australia', www.aldi.com.au.
15. Speedy, B 2009 '"Frantic" ALDI planners seeing double', *The Australian*, 21 January, www.theaustralian.news.com.au.
16. ALDI Australia 2009.
17. Webb, C 2008, 'ALDI's simple recipe for success', *The Age*, 26 July, www.theage.com.au.
18. Round, DK 2006, 'The power of two: squaring off with Australia's large supermarket chains', *The Australian Journal of Agricultural and Resource Economics*, vol. 50, pp. 51–64.
19. Burke, K 2009, 'Supermarket giants checked out, found wanting', *The Sydney Morning Herald*, 9 July, www.smh.com.au.
20. Speedy, B 2009; Griffith, GR 2004, 'Policy forum: competition issues in the Australian grocery industry', *The Australian Economic Review*, vol. 37, no. 3, pp. 329–336.
21. Griffith, GR 2004.
22. Merrilees, B & Miller, D 2001, 'Innovation and strategy in the Australian supermarket industry', *Journal of Food Products Marketing*, vol. 7, no. 4, pp. 3–18.
23. Webb, C 2008.
24. Webb, C 2008.
25. Hintz, P 2009, 'Now I get it mum', Paddy Hintz shopsmart blog, *The Courier-Mail*, 12 June, www.couriermail.com.au.
26. Sofer, C 1972, *Organisations in theory and practice*, Heinemann, London.
27. Based on Sandoe, K, Corbitt, G & Boykin, R 2001, *Enterprise Integration*, John Wiley & Sons, Inc., New York, figure 2.2, p. 18; figure 2.4, p. 20; figure 2.10, p. 31.
28. Anthony, RN 1965, *Planning and control systems: a framework for analysis*, Harvard University Graduate School of Business Administration, Boston.
29. Powell, L 2002, 'Shedding a tier: flattening organizational structures and employee empowerment', *The International Journal of Educational Management*, vol. 16, no. 1, pp. 54–9; Stoner, JAF, Yetton, PW, Craig, JF & Johnston, KD 1994, *Management*, 2nd edn, Prentice Hall, Sydney.
30. Powell 2002, p. 58.
31. Byrne, JA 1993, 'The horizontal corporation', *Business Week*, vol. 20, December, p. 44.
32. Based on Sandoe, Corbitt & Boykin 2001, table 4.1, p. 55.
33. Cusumano, MA 1988, 'Manufacturing innovation: lessons from the Japanese auto industry', *Sloan Management Review*, vol. 30, Fall, pp. 29–39.
34. Sussan, AP & Johnson, WC 2003, 'Strategic capabilities of business process: looking for competitive advantage', *Competitive Review*, vol. 13, no. 2, pp. 46–52.
35. Friedman, TL 2006, *The World Is Flat: A Brief History of the Twenty-first Century*, Penguin Group Australia, Camberwell.
36. Switzer, R 2006, 'Outsourcing opens doors in global village', *The Age*, 19 March www.theage.com.au.
37. Switzer 2006.
38. Friedman 2006, p. 24.
39. Friedman 2006, pp. 24–28.
40. Switzer 2006.
41. Switzer 2006.

42. AAP 2004a, 'Lees concerned at Telstra outsourcing', *Australian IT*, www.australianit.news.com.au.

43. AAP 2004b, 'Unions to campaign against Telstra outsourcing', *Sydney Morning Herald Online*, smh.com.au.

44. Balogh, S & DiGirolamo, R 2004, 'Costello warns on Telstra jobs', *Australian IT*.

45. Balogh & DiGirolamo 2004.

46. Davenport, TH 1998, 'Putting the enterprise into the enterprise system', *Harvard Business Review*, July–August, pp. 121–31.

47. Volkoff, O 2003, 'Configuring an ERP system: introducing best practices or hampering flexibility?', *Journal of Information Systems Education*, vol. 14, no. 3, pp. 319–24.

48. Porter, ME 1996, 'What is strategy?', *Harvard Business Review*, November–December, pp. 61–78.

49. Hammer, MJ & Stanton, S 1999, 'How process enterprises really work', *Harvard Business Review*, September–October, p. 109.

50. Hammer & Stanton 1999, pp. 109–10.

51. Smith, M 2003, 'Business process design: correlates of success and failure', *The Quality Management Journal*, vol. 10, no. 2, pp. 38–49.

52. Hackman, JR & Wageman, R 1995, 'Total Quality Management: empirical, conceptual and practical issues', *Administrative Science Quarterly*, vol. 40, 1995, pp. 309–42.

53. Cusumano 1988.

54. Hammer, M & Champy, J 1994, *Reengineering the corporation: a manifesto for business revolution*, Allen & Unwin, Sydney, p. 32.

55. Kotter, JP 1995, 'Why transformation efforts fail', *Harvard Business Review*, March–April, pp. 59–67.

56. Kotter 1995, pp. 59–67.

57. Caron, JR, Jarvenpaa, SL & Stoddard, DB 1994, 'Business reengineering at CIGNA Corporation: experiences and lessons learned from the first five years', *MIS Quarterly*, September, p. 237.

58. Hammer & Champy 1994.

59. Kotter 1995.

60. Kotter 1995, p. 66.

61. Kotter 1995, p. 66.

62. Hammer & Champy 1994.

63. Hammer & Champy 1994, pp. 50–64.

64. Gregor, S et al. 2004, *Achieving Value from ICT: key management strategies*, Department of Communications, Information Technology and the Arts, ICT Research Study, Canberra, p. 12.

65. Gregor et al. 2004, pp. 81–84.

66. Gregor et al. 2004, p. 11.

67. National Office for the Information Economy 2006a, 'Advancing with e-business: Supply chain case studies: Visy Industries', www.dcita.gov.au; National Office for the Information Economy 2006b, 'Advancing with e-business: Supply chain case studies: Berri Limited', www.dcita.gov.au.

68. Department of Communications, Information Technology and the Arts 2006a, *Engaging Trading Partners in e-business*, Commonwealth of Australia, Canberra, p. 29.

69. Australian Taxation Office 2006, 'Grants and GST: Recipient created tax invoices', www.ato.gov.au.

70. Reserve Bank of Australia 2006, 'Payment Systems Developments and Architecture: Some Background', www.rba.gov.au, p. 4.

71. BPAY and BPAY View are registered trademarks of BPAY Pty Ltd. POSTBillPay and Billmanager are registered trademarks of the Australian Postal Corporation. Use here is purely for educational and demonstrative purposes.

72. BPAY 2009, 'About BPAY — The BPAY story', www.bpay.com.au.

73. Centre for International Economics and Edgar, Dunn & Company 2006, *Exploration of Future Electronic Payments Markets*, Australian Government Department of Communications, Information Technology and the Arts (DCITA), Canberra, p. 49.
74. BPAY 2009, 'BPAY today', www.bpay.com.au.
75. Reserve Bank of Australia 2006.
76. Australia Post 2009, www.postbillpay.com.au.
77. Australia Post 2003, 'Billmanager — A new convenient way for your customers to manage household bills', www.auspost.com.au.
78. GS1 2007, 'GS1 BarCodes: Implementation', www.gs1.org.
79. Department of Communications, Information Technology and the Arts 2006, 'Getting the most out of RFID', Commonwealth of Australia, Department of Communications, Information Technology and the Arts, www.dcita.gov.au, pp. 1–5.
80. Moraitis Wholesale 2006, www.moraitis.com.au.
81. Department of Communications, Information Technology and the Arts 2006, p. 2.
82. IBM Corporation 2005, 'Moraitis Fresh can deliver improved customer relationships with an IBM RFID solution', *On Demand Business*, IBM Corporation, NY, USA, www-935.ibm.com.
83. Hammer & Champy 1994, pp. 65–82.
84. Davenport, TH & Stoddard, DB 1994, 'Reengineering: business change of mythic proportions?', *MIS Quarterly*, June, pp. 121–7.
85. Strassman, PA 1995, *The politics of information management: policy guidelines*, The Information Economics Press, New Canaan, Connecticut, p. 226.
86. Strassman 1995, p. 226.
87. Strassman 1995, p. 234.
88. Hammer & Champy 1994.
89. Davenport, TH 1993, *Process innovation: reengineering work through information technology*, Harvard Business School Press, Boston.
90. Hammer & Champy 1994.
91. Davenport, TH 1999, 'Enterprise systems and process change: still no quick fix', *Financial Times*, London, 22 February, p. 6.
92. Garvin, DA 1995, 'Leveraging processes for strategic advantage', *Harvard Business Review*, September–October, p. 82.
93. Strassman 1995, p. 230.
94. Davenport & Stoddard 1994, p. 123.
95. Australian Bureau of Statistics 2005, 2007, 2009, cat. no. 8129.0 *Business use of information technology*, www.abs.gov.au.
96. Australian Bureau of Statistics 2009, 'Characteristics of internet and web use, 2007–08, Table 6 Selected web features, by employment size, by industry, 2007–08', cat. no. 8129.0 *Business use of information technology*, www.abs.gov.au.
97. Davenport, TH & Brooks, JD 2004, 'Enterprise systems and the supply chain', *Journal of Enterprise Information Management*, vol. 17, no. 1, pp. 8–19.
98. Brynjolfsson, E & Hitt, LM 2000, 'Beyond computation: information technology, organizational transformation and business performance', *The Journal of Economic Perspectives*, vol. 14, no. 4. pp. 23–48.
99. Kandampully, J 2002, 'Innovation as the core competency of a service organisation: the role of technology, knowledge and networks', *European Journal of Innovation Management*, vol. 5, no. 1, pp. 18–26.
100. Scupola, A 2009, 'SME's e-commerce adoption: perspectives from Denmark and Australia', *Journal of Enterprise Information Management*, vol. 22, no. 1/2, pp. 152–66.
101. Madnick, S & Siegel, M 2001, 'Seizing the opportunity : exploiting web aggregation', Paper 144, December, Centre for ebusiness at MIT, www.digitalmit.edu.
102. Australian Bureau of Statistics 2009, 'Characteristics of internet and web use, 2007–08, Table 8 Selected business internet activities, by employment size, by industry, 2007–08'.

103. Australian Bureau of Statistics 2009, 'Internet commerce, 2007–08, Table 4 Methods of receiving orders via the internet or web, by employment size, by industry, 2007–08'.

104. Australian Bureau of Statistics 2009, 'Internet commerce, 2007–08, Table 6 Automated links between systems used to receive orders and other business systems, by employment size, by industry, 2007–08'.

105. Willocks, LP & Plant, R 2001, 'Pathways to e-business leadership: getting from bricks to clicks', *MIT Sloan Management Review*, Spring, pp. 50–9.

106. Kandampully, J 2002.

107. Williams, A, et al. 2003, 'Total quality management versus business process re-engineering: a question of degree', *Proceedings of the Institution of Mechanical Engineers*, vol. 217, no. 1, p. 2.

108. Hammer & Champy 1994.

109. Hammer, M 1990, 'Reengineering work: don't automate, obliterate', *Harvard Business Review*, July–August, pp. 104–12.

# 3

# Database concepts I

## Learning objectives

After studying this chapter, you should be able to:

**(1)** explain the role of databases in decision making and reporting systems

**(2)** define the function of a database and the concept of database systems

**(3)** discuss the concept of data redundancy and the advantages of databases

**(4)** discuss database models focusing on the relational database

**(5)** discuss database modelling and develop database models using entity-relationship diagrams

**(6)** understand how relationships in a database model reflect how an organisation works.

# Introduction

In any organisation, accurate, relevant and timely information is crucial for good decision making and reporting. In modern organisations, databases are the foundation of high-quality data capture, storage and management for decision making and reporting. This chapter firstly discusses basic database concepts. Next we examine poor data system characteristics to gain an insight into the main anomalies that can occur in poorly designed systems and the benefits that databases can provide if properly designed. This discussion provides a useful perspective for accountants, and database users, designers, developers and implementers. Thirdly, we look at the operation of database systems, including the role of database management systems (DBMS). Examples of how to develop relational databases based on business relationships is examined in some detail. This is because relational databases are the most common in business organisations.

To maximise the benefits offered by relational databases, careful database modelling, data relationship design and systems implementation are crucial. The final section of the chapter looks at how to construct database models of an organisation and its interactions with suppliers and customers. These constructs are called entity-relationship diagrams (shortened to E-R diagrams). E-R diagrams consist of entities (the 'E' in E-R diagrams). Entities are anything about which an organisation may want to store information. Examples of entities for Bart Industries (described in AIS focus 3.1 below) include inventory supplies, suppliers, customers and houses. The 'R' in E-R diagrams stands for relationships. This looks at the relationships between entities, for example, the relationship between customers and houses or the relationship between inventory and suppliers. As the name suggests, E-R diagrams model the entities an organisation wants to record information about and the relationships between those entities. Once the entities and relationships in an organisation have been modelled, the E-R diagram can be used as a basis for implementing a physical database in a database product such as Microsoft Access. E-R diagrams can also be used in the opposite way: they can help users, designers and developers of databases to understand the relationships that already exist in an operating organisation's database. The good design of databases is essential for the efficient, fast, error- and duplication-free flow of information in a database system. A discussion of top down modelling (E-R diagrams) and bottom up modelling (normalisation) concludes the chapter. In chapter 4, the normalisation process for efficient database design from the bottom up is examined. This process overcomes the problems of repeating groups, data anomalies and data redundancies.

## AIS FOCUS 3.1

### Bart Construction Industries

Aaron Hardjo is the financial accountant for Bart Construction Industries. He wants to purchase a new accounting system database for his organisation. In doing this, he wants to know if all databases are the same; that is, how he can evaluate a database to find out how suitable it is to how his organisation operates. He is concerned that if he buys a certain database package he may need to change how his organisation works to fit with the new system. Aaron needs to know the specific decision-making aspects he wants included in the system, and evaluate potential systems against these aspects. He also needs to ensure that the system stores data in the most efficient and effective manner. Katrin, a friend of Aaron, has suggested that she design a database system to fit his organisation. Aaron likes this idea as a potential alternative to buying an existing database system. Katrin has suggested that Aaron, as an accountant, needs to understand database concepts to ensure that the database he chooses or has designed will fit his organisation. This will also allow him to make informed user contributions to the design of the system and communicate with systems analysts and programmers, an equally important requirement for small databases an organisation constructs and large-scale information system implementations.

**LEARNING OBJECTIVE**

Explain the role of databases in decision making and reporting systems.

**Data** Raw facts relating to or describing an event.

**Information** Data or facts that are processed in a meaningful form.

## THE ROLE OF DATABASES IN DECISION MAKING AND REPORTING SYSTEMS

One of the advantages of a database is that all the **data** for the whole of the organisation is contained within the database system. For example, in the absence of a database, an employee in one department such as sales wanting to check on inventory levels would have to contact the inventory department and enquire about inventory balances. This is because each department in an organisation would have its own information system. A database system enables all the data of the organisation to be contained within the one system. In a database system, data such as inventory levels can be updated in the system by the inventory department and accessible to any staff members across all departments in the organisation that need the information. The same information may be needed for a variety of purposes. For instance, an employee in sales may want to know how much inventory is available for immediate delivery to customers, while an employee in accounts receivable may want to know how much inventory customers have purchased on credit. Using the database system, both employees could access the information for their own purposes.

Managers require accurate, relevant and timely **information** to make strategic and operational decisions for their organisations. Examples of such decisions would be whether to continue manufacturing and selling an existing product (generally a strategic decision), to invest in new plant and equipment (generally a strategic decision) or to stop production and service machinery because reports show an increasing number of defects from production (generally an operating decision). Decisions involve the formulation of different scenarios and making a choice between the alternatives. A database system allows managers to access and evaluate the data they require to make such decisions. For example, given the database will contain all sales orders, a manager could access the sales orders for the day and match them to the goods that have been delivered during that day. At the end of the day, they could see the number of orders that were made during the day and not dispatched. This information could be kept in the database system and if the percentage of undelivered orders rose above the previous week, the dispatch or general manager could be advised that there may be an issue with deliveries. The manager could then investigate the number of orders outstanding and make a decision about what action to take, for example, increase the level of inventory for a particular item of stock if a majority of the orders relate to that item. This decision-making example illustrates the importance of timely and accurate information, in this case, so that decisions can be made on whether or not there is an issue with dispatching goods.

Information is derived from facts or data that are processed in a meaningful form. The form of the information must suit the objective of the information. For example, an item of data could be the expenditure of each customer in the current month. To determine the total sales for the month, you would sum the sales amount for each customer. But this is not the only question you might ask of the data. What if you want to know how much each customer spent in the month? Or which customers spent more than a particular amount? Or who were the first-time customers for a promotion? These questions can be answered if the data are captured and stored at their most basic level, and then aggregated at a level that will answer each question.

To ensure meaningful information can be derived, it is important to capture, store and manage data as efficiently and effectively as possible. Data is not information; rather, data is stored in databases and information is derived from this data by retrieving it in a meaningful manner. Storing data is best achieved in a database. A **database** (or database system) is a computerised software program that enables data in an organisation to be captured and stored. A relational database stores data in tables, which form the entities in an E-R diagram. Entities are the items you want to collect data about such as customers, suppliers and inventory. The relationships between entities are also captured in a relational database. A database management system within a database contains programs that enable adding data to entities, manipulating existing data and producing reports.

It is important that database entities and relationships be designed to eliminate repetition and inconsistent data. Such a well designed data structure allows for efficient and effective data sharing across an organisation. In addition, with all data in a central place, data privacy, security and backup are essential to ensure data are protected. After studying this chapter, you should fully understand the advantages of databases. For now, some key points that underpin the importance of database concepts in information systems used by modern organisations can be stated.

- Correct decision making and reporting are vital for organisational performance.
- Correct decision making and reporting require accurate, relevant and timely information.
- Accurate, relevant and timely information comes from quality data capture, storage and management.
- Data are the building blocks of information.

The next section will begin to discuss the concepts of databases and, in particular, the relational database, as this is the most widely used database model used in business.

> **Database** A shared computerised structure that captures, stores and relates data.

**LEARNING OBJECTIVE 2**

*Define the function of a database and the concept of database systems.*

> **Relational database** A database that stores data in a number of tables.

> **Table** A collection of columns (attributes) and rows (objects) that describe an entity.

# DATABASE CONCEPTS

There are various types of databases available. The most commonly used in business is the relational database. As a result, this discussion of database concepts concentrates on the relational database. This type of database is based on the entities in the database and the relationships between them. **Relational databases** typically store data in a number of tables. The way the relational database system stores things is very similar to how the E-R diagram depicts them. So, it is very easy to go from an E-R diagram (a diagram with entities and relationships) to a relational database. The relational database uses entities, which it calls tables, and shows the relationships between the tables.

Therefore, a relational database is a collection of carefully defined tables. A **table** is a collection of columns or attributes that describe an entity (or something you wish to record data about in a database). A **record** consists of a set of fields, which characterises a person, place or thing within the business or linked to the business. **Fields** describe a particular characteristic of each record, such as name, address or phone number. Fields are derived from data or facts.

Consider the example of a retail store that sells shoes. The store keeps a customer **file** containing a record for each customer. Each customer record contains fields that include customer number, customer name, customer phone number and customer address. Each of the fields contains data. The computerised customer table shown in figure 3.1 is recorded in much the same way as a record would be made in an old-fashioned, paper-based filing system. As in a paper-based filing system, each customer has his or her own file and every time he or she buys shoes from the retail store, the store updates the information in the file with a new record.

As shown in figure 3.1, a table can also be called an entity or an entity occurrence. A field can also be referred to as a column or attribute. Individual objects are stored as records within the table. A record can also be called a tuple or row. These words are used interchangeably to describe databases so familiarity with all the terms is important.

Field, column, attribute

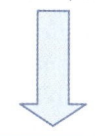

| Customer_number | Customer_name | Customer_address | Customer_phone |
|---|---|---|---|
| 1 | Andrew Johns | 6 Glenelg Street, Melbourne, VIC | 03 1234 5678 |
| 2 | George Brown | 36 Bourke Street, Melbourne, VIC | 03 9876 4321 |
| 3 | Britney Considine | 12 Jones Street, Melbourne, VIC | 03 5678 3456 |
| 4 | Michelle Lee | 4 Lonsdale Street, Melbourne, VIC | 03 2376 1048 |

Record, tuple, row

Table, entity, entity occurrence

**FIGURE 3.1** Example of a file — 'Customer file'

Before computers, many organisations kept separate files for each administrative function, such as sales orders or entry processing, accounts receivable, inventory and invoicing. For example, when a sales order or entry was taken, organisations would process the order by updating three files: a sales file, inventory file and customer file. In addition, in accounts receivable, staff would update a similar sales file, inventory file and customer file. Staff in the warehouse would also update their inventory file and customer file. In other words, the one transaction required changes to two sales files, three inventory files and three customer files! Databases enable all departments to access a single view of the sales, inventory and customer data.

The table in figure 3.1 could represent the entity 'customer' for an organisation. This is because there is a customer number (Customer_number) that represents a customer name (Customer_name), which is one instance of a customer that is stored in the customer table. A number is used to represent a customer as customer names are not unique. You might think your name, for example, John White, is unique. But my university had six John Whites enrolled at the same time. Five were students and one was a teaching staff member. If we only used 'John White' to identify the record (row/tuple) when we wanted to retrieve the data about the student John White we would retrieve one of the records but lose five. Therefore, it is important to have a unique identifier for each instance in a table, such as each student in a student table. Since names are not unique, we generally assign a number (e.g. a student number or customer number). Assigning a name a unique number is important — just think of all the numbers you have, for example, student numbers, customer numbers, library numbers, etc.

Every table in a relational database must have a **primary key**, which is an attribute (or column) that uniquely identifies a particular object (or row) in the table. Suppose figure 3.2 is a project table with project number (Proj_num), project name (Proj_name), project start (Proj_start) and project budget (Proj_budget) as attributes. Either Proj_num or Proj_name could be used to find a particular project entry, but Proj_num is a better primary key because it is likely to be unique, whereas a project name can be duplicated. The uniqueness of the number relies on the organisation assigning a unique number to each project — it could do the same with the name, but it would become difficult over time to come up with different names. A combination of unique alpha-numeric codes may be suitable. Therefore, the most important issue with a primary key is that it is unique and can never point to more than one object (or row) in the table. The primary key is also shown by a bold underline as shown for project number (Proj_num) in figure 3.2.

| Proj_num | Proj_name | Proj_start | Proj_budget |
|----------|-----------|------------|-------------|
| 1 | Rain | 01/01/2009 | $10 000 |
| 2 | Hail | 01/04/2009 | $30 000 |
| 3 | Flood | 01/12/2008 | $50 000 |

**FIGURE 3.2** Project table

The table in figure 3.3 shows the case of employees assigned to work on projects. In this case, the table will use more than one column as part of the primary key. These are called **composite keys**.

| Proj_num | Proj_name | Emp_num | Emp_name | Time_charged |
|----------|-----------|---------|----------|--------------|
| 1 | Rain | 101 | Michael Lee | 12 |
| 1 | Rain | 105 | Brett Considine | 2 |
| 1 | Rain | 110 | Phil Collier | 3 |
| 2 | Hail | 101 | Michael Lee | 4 |
| 2 | Hail | 108 | David Smith | 5 |
| 3 | Flood | 110 | Phil Collier | 6 |
| 3 | Flood | 105 | Brett Considine | 5 |
| 3 | Flood | 123 | Michael Davern | 5 |
| 3 | Flood | 112 | Anne Wyatt | 8 |

**FIGURE 3.3** Project employee table showing data redundancy and anomalies

Take a look at figures 3.2 and 3.3. These two tables are common in consultancy businesses, which have projects and employees who charge time to the different projects that they work on. We have a table in figure 3.2 that contains the project details that relate the project name with its unique project number. The primary key is the project number. The table in figure 3.3 is the project employee table, which shows the projects and which employees are engaged on each project. This table has two primary keys: Proj_num and Emp_num, because the table is designed to show which employees are engaged on a project and how much time they charge to that project. Each employee (Emp_num) can be engaged on many projects (Proj_num). For instance, Emp_num 101 appears against project numbers 1 and 2. Because each employee can be engaged on many projects, Proj_num must be part of the primary key. Similarly, each project can engage many employees (e.g. Proj_num 1 has three employees). Since each project can engage many employees, Emp_num must be part of the primary key. The combination of Proj_num and Emp_num as primary keys is known as a composite key. This is because we need both attributes, Proj_num and Emp_num, to define each line uniquely. A composite key can also be called a concatenated key as the composite key is comprised of two or more attributes together (the word concatenate means to put together).

Some examples will illustrate the application of the primary key. Note that in the Proj_num, Emp_num example, although two attributes are used to determine the primary key, the primary key is still a singular. That is, there is one primary key made up of two attributes. A primary key (a singular) can be made up of more than two attributes. Three or four attributes could be used to determine a primary key. The number of attributes used is the minimum number of attributes required to uniquely identify each line in the table. For example, in the above case you would not use the project name as it is not needed; project number and employee number are the minimum sufficient number of attributes required for the primary key to uniquely identify one line in the table.

To show that you need both attributes, Proj_num and Emp_num to define one line uniquely, consider Proj_num = 1, Emp_num = 105. This will return the row shown in figure 3.4 from figure 3.3.

| Proj_num | Proj_name | Emp_num | Emp_name | Time_charged |
|----------|-----------|---------|----------------|--------------|
| 1 | Rain | 105 | Brett Considine | 2 |

**FIGURE 3.4** Selected rows in project employee table Proj_num = 1, Emp_num = 105

Another example would be Proj_num = 3, Emp_num = 105, which returns the row from figure 3.3 shown in figure 3.5.

| Proj_num | Proj_name | Emp_num | Emp_name | Time_charged |
|----------|-----------|---------|----------------|--------------|
| 3 | Flood | 105 | Brett Considine | 5 |

**FIGURE 3.5** Selected rows in project employee table Proj_num = 3, Emp_num = 105

A secondary key is also possible. Traditionally, the secondary key was a key you wanted to search the table on after the primary key. For example, with an employee table you may want to search on the primary key, employee number. You could also search on a secondary key, employee name. However, given that in relational databases all attributes become items we can search and create queries on (i.e. they are automatically secondary keys), it is not necessary to indicate a secondary key in a relational database and the concept of a secondary key is not that important.

An important aspect of a relational database is that the tables must be carefully defined to provide flexibility with minimum issues. The issues that may result from an inflexible file structure will be illustrated in the next section on data redundancy.

# DATA REDUNDANCY

Well designed databases contain all the information an organisation needs in one place. Because data is updated immediately, any information extracted from the database is accurate and up-to-date. This is important for the managers of an organisation in making decisions.

**Data redundancy** occurs when the same information is stored in multiple locations in an organisation. For example, an accounts receivable department has a customer table with each customer's primary key, and their address and phone number. The marketing department has a customer table containing the customers they send brochures to. This table also has the customer's primary key, and their name, address and phone number. This is an example of data redundancy, as the same information is stored twice for one customer in a database. If a customer's details change, there is a risk that the changes are only made in one place, which will result in inconsistent as well as repeated data in the organisation.

Good database design can eliminate problems of repetition, inconsistent data and data errors (that could result from inconsistent data). That is, data in databases are recorded in files that are shared across functions and departments, rather than having the same data stored in different places and by different functions across the business (as occurred before the advent of databases). Early information systems, sometimes referred to as functional or silo systems, serviced independent departments. In contrast, more modern, cross-functional systems share data in order to leverage a competitive advantage. However, if data are to be stored only once and only in one place, the data structure needs to flexible. For example, assume the customer file in figure 3.6 is stored in a database. This table includes the customer details and inventory sold to them. This means that if Michael Lee's address changes it needs to change in two places: line 2 and line 5. If there were thousands of purchases by Michael Lee, the address would need to be updated correctly on every line. If not, it would cause an update inconsistency.

| | Customer_name | Customer_address | Customer_phone | Salesperson | Bicycle_model | Bicycle_amount | Date |
|---|---|---|---|---|---|---|---|
| 1 | Britney Considine | 55 Apple Street, Melbourne, VIC | 03 1234 5678 | TLM | VZ4717 | $1229.90 | 20-Jul-08 |
| 2 | Michael Lee | 4 Banana Street, Melbourne, VIC | 03 9876 4321 | CBD | DF3966 | $2379.50 | 30-Jul-08 |
| 3 | Phillipa Collier | 8 Carrot Street, Melbourne, VIC | 03 5678 3456 | MTL | WE9447 | $1050.30 | 4-Aug-08 |
| 4 | Devine Smith | 3 Orange Street, Melbourne, VIC | 03 2376 1048 | JFK | XC8187 | $845.50 | 6-Oct-08 |
| 5 | Michael Lee | 4 Banana Street, Melbourne, VIC | 03 9876 4321 | CBD | BF7266 | $1790.50 | 30-Sep-08 |
| 6 | Britney Considine | 55 Apple Street, Melbourne, VIC | 03 1234 5678 | TLM | XV2397 | $825.90 | 20-Aug-08 |

**FIGURE 3.6** A customer file showing the importance of flexible data structure

In summary, only one correct record of the customer details is required in the organisation. Having the details occur in more than one place produces data redundancy. The first implication of data redundancy is data inconsistency, where there are different and conflicting versions of the same data in different places. For instance, if a customer's address is changed in most of the lines but not all, the sales reports will yield inconsistent and incorrect results. In this way, the inconsistent data lead to a lack of **data integrity**.

The second implication of data redundancy is that it can lead to a number of **data anomalies**. These anomalies occur because changes need to be made in several places rather than in just one. More specifically, these anomalies can be classified into different types: modification, insertion and deletion. Figure 3.6 of the customer file of a bicycle retailer has already shown a modification anomaly.

## Modification anomalies

**Modification anomalies** can occur when a field value is changed. For example, the new address for a customer (such as Michael Lee above) requires changes to be made to all the customer file records that relate to Michael Lee in the system. Depending on the size of the file system, this could number hundreds or even thousands of records. Inconsistencies and a breakdown in integrity are likely. For example, the allocation of a new salesperson to specific customers that is not correctly updated in all files would result in a different salesperson recorded for the same customer in different places in the organisation.

## Insertion anomalies

**Insertion anomalies** can occur when new customers are entered into the customer file. Businesses can often acquire many new customers in a single day. If this occurs, customers must be matched with a particular salesperson and their details. Such a situation may occur in a construction business such as Bart Industries in AIS focus 3.1. Customers that begin with certain letters of the alphabet may be assigned a certain salesperson. As the details of the salespeople must be entered as many times as there are new customers, errors are likely to occur. Similarly, if the organisation employs a new salesperson, their details would have to be filed together with the customers they will look after.

Look again at the project employee table in figure 3.3 (page 110). This table is a good example of an insertion anomaly. As we discussed earlier, the project employee table has a composite primary key: the primary key is composed of two attributes, Proj_num and Emp_num. We wouldn't be able to add a new project with no employee assigned to it. This is because both attributes that constitute the primary key are required. Therefore, we couldn't insert a project until an employee is assigned. Or we couldn't enter an employee until they are assigned to a project.

## Deletion anomalies

**Deletion anomalies** can occur when a salesperson decides to resign from the organisation or the organisation terminates the employee's employment. As illustrated in figure 3.6, when this occurs, customer records have to be modified to reflect the lack of a salesperson or with the details of a newly assigned salesperson. Another example is shown in figure 3.3: if we decide to delete project 3 we would lose all the information about Anne Wyatt (employee number 112), as this is the only project she is assigned to.

As a result, when we design database systems, we need to ensure their structure is flexible and won't result in modification, insertion and deletion anomalies. The technique called normalisation, covered in chapter 4, is a process we can perform to ensure we do not encounter anomalies in our database structures.

LEARNING OBJECTIVE  4

Discuss database models focusing on the relational database.

# DATABASE MODELS

This part of the chapter explains database systems and database management system (DBMS) functions. Currently, most businesses use relational databases, so this chapter concentrates on this model. Older database models, including hierarchical and network models, are not discussed in depth. These older database models were built around separate files while modern information systems collect, store and retrieve data from a database shared with other departments. Object-oriented databases are discussed briefly.

## Database systems

**Database system** A system of hardware, software, people, procedures and data that allow the capture, storage, management and use of data within a database environment.

**Hardware** Physical devices including the computer and network.

**Client** A computer that requests services from a server.

**Server** A computer that has special processing functions that provide requests for clients.

**Software** Computer programs that are written in programming languages or code and instruct the operations of a computer.

**Operating system** Computer programs that control hardware to interface with software application programs.

**Database management system (DBMS)** A group of programs that manipulate the database and provide the interface between the database and the user as well as other application programs.

A **database system** (another term for a database) is a collection of elements that allow the capture, storage, management and use of data within a database environment. These elements include hardware, software, people, procedures and data.

**Hardware** refers to the system's physical devices, which include the computer and computer peripherals. The computer may be a microcomputer, minicomputer or mainframe computer. It may even be part of a **client–server** network. Peripherals include items such as keyboards, mice, modems and printers. The **software** is the collection of programs used by the computers to function and includes **operating system** software, **database management system (DBMS)** software, application programs and utilities. Operating system software makes it possible to run all other software on the computer. Microsoft Windows is an example of operating system software. The DBMS software allows the database within the database system to be managed. The DBMS is in effect an operating system exclusively for the database. Some examples of DBMS software include Microsoft Access and SQL Server. Application programs and utility software are used to access and manipulate the data for generating reports and any other information for decision making. Utilities also help to manage the different components of the database system.

There are likely to be several *people* involved in a database system. System administrators manage and supervise the database system's general operations. There are also database administrators, who manage the use of the database and ensure that all the functions are working properly. Since a database serves cross-functional information systems and also exists independent of the separate information systems, it requires a technical specialist such as database administrators to monitor performance, deal with changes to the structure and carry out backup procedures. Ensuring that data has privacy controls, security and backup are extremely important tasks of a database administrator. They also give access to staff to different areas of the database depending on the level of access approved for each staff member. Database designers develop structures and designs that capture data for storage and manipulation. As shown by the discussion on data redundancy above, data structures and designs play a critical role in overcoming some of the limitations that can be inherent in some systems. Systems analysts and programmers create the screens, reports and procedures by which end users can access and manipulate the data in a database system.

**Procedures** are the rules that govern the design and use of the database system for the organisation. They often reflect the processes by which a business deals with its customers, updates its records and reports to its shareholders. They ensure that the data and information maintain quality and are meaningful and consistent.

The determination of which data are entered into the database and how they are organised is the role of the people within the database system, especially the database designer. The database designer often analyses the decision-making and reporting requirements of the business before defining what data is required and how it should be defined and captured in the database. Figure 3.7 shows the elements of the database system: the DBMS, data, application programs, hardware, people (in particular, the database administrator, database designers, analyst and programmers) and procedures.

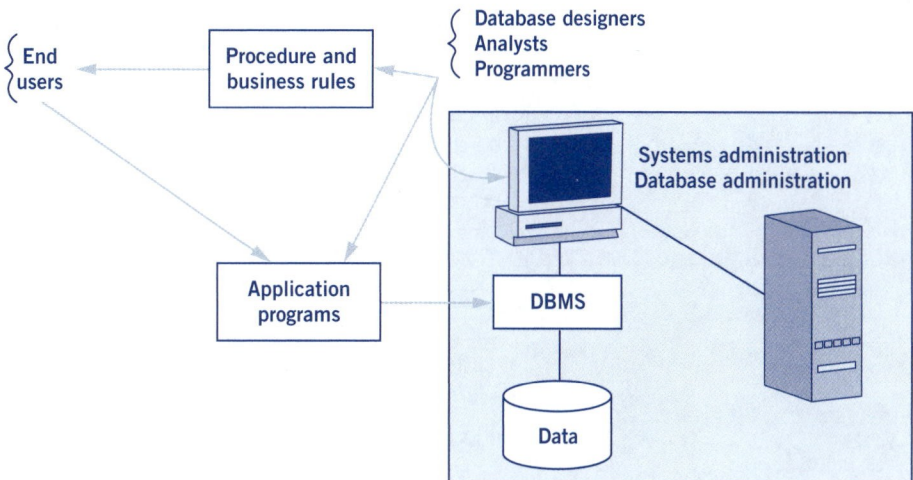

**FIGURE 3.7** The database system

## Advantages of database systems

Database systems are designed to eliminate the repetition of data and the incidence of inconsistent data by ensuring data is structured so that it is stored in only one location. This structure allows for data sharing across the organisation and provides the foundation on which any database can be developed. The incidence of errors is reduced considerably by independent data structures, with only one location for entering and manipulating data. Program maintenance is also reduced because there is only one centrally located point, the database management system (DBMS), that requires reprogramming for all data (this will be covered in the next section). This increases the speed and flexibility with which the organisation can prepare information that is crucial to decision making. The centralisation of data and the DBMS enforces consistent standards for data structures and storage across the organisation. It also aids data and system security by having only one access point into the database to control. Given this, and as indicated above, privacy, security and adequate backups to the system are important.

To maximise the advantages offered by the database system, careful database modelling, data relationship design and systems implementation are essential. Details on these issues are provided in the next part of this chapter, which deals with the principles behind each of the database system aspects of development, design and implementation.

## DBMS functions

Figure 3.8 shows the data flow for a typical database system.

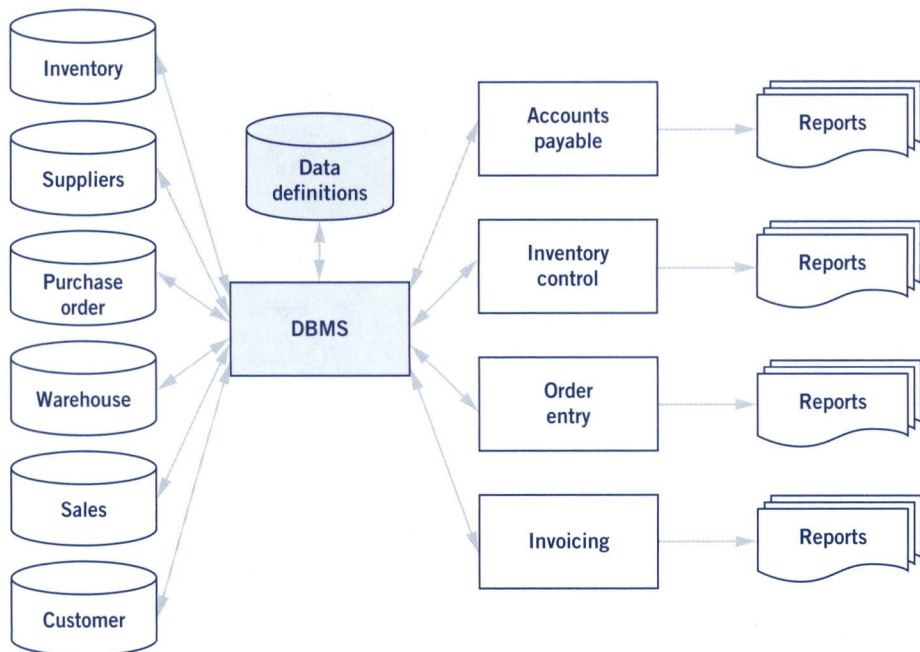

**FIGURE 3.8** The DBMS function in a typical database system

Data are stored in a central location such as a specific database storage device in the IT department of an organisation, and managed by a DBMS. Data definitions are required in the DBMS before programming, and the DBMS is used to define and specify the business rules and corresponding data requirements and calculations for the organisation's business processes. Reports as required by the organisation can be produced from these business processes.

The DBMS contains a number of useful functions. They include:

- a data dictionary
- data storage management
- data transformation and presentation
- security management
- multiuser access control
- backup and recovery management
- data integrity management
- access language and application programming interfaces
- communication interfaces.

The *data dictionary* contains a definition of the data elements and their relationships with one another, such as the relationship between a supplier number and an inventory number, or between a customer number and an invoice number. For example, the definition of 'purchase date' and the way it is to be coded (e.g. 'Purchase_date') are used consistently for that attribute throughout the database. Also, if the attribute is a date, the day, month and year order will be provided to show how it should be formatted throughout the database (e.g. 'dd/mm/yy'). *Data storage management* helps to manage the capture of input, and the application of business rules, codes and structures to those inputs so that the inputs can be transformed and stored in the database structure. Behind data storage management lies entry forms, screen definitions, data validation rules, procedural code and structures to handle video, pictures and the like. *Data transformation and presentation* allows the entered data to conform to the existing data structure. It translates requests into commands that store, locate and retrieve the requested data. The *security management* of the database enforces user security and data privacy within the database by scrutinising access and data operations, while *multi-user access controls* provide data integrity and consistency to many users simultaneously without compromising the integrity of the database. The DBMS also provides for *backup and recovery management*, which contains procedures that perform routine and special backup and restorations in the event of database failure caused by, for example, bad sectors on a disk or power failure. *Access language and application programming interfaces* allow the database to be queried using an appropriate query language such as **structured query language (SQL)**, while *communication interfaces* such as Internet Explorer allow the database to accept end-user requests within the computer network environment. SQL, for example, is a language that allows the user to specify what must be done without having to specify how it is to be done. Many of the tasks of a DBMS are administered by a **database administrator** whose job it is to control access by users to the database, maintain the data dictionary and oversee backup and recovery in the DBMS. The database administer is very important from the internal control perspective as they plan, design and give access to the database and ensure the ongoing operation and maintenance of the database. For example, if a request for a report is made, the database administrator must ensure that the user requesting that data view should have access to the information in the tables they have requested.

## Types of database models

**Database models** are a collection of logical constructs used to represent the data structure and the data relationships found within the database. These database models can be grouped into two categories: conceptual models and implementation models. **Conceptual models** focus on a *logical* view of what is represented in the database. The conceptual model covered in this chapter is the entity-relationship model, which is explained for database modelling and design in the next part of this chapter through the E-R diagram. The conceptual model's **logical representation** or view as shown in this chapter shows what is represented in the database independent of hardware and software. **Implementation models** show how data are represented in a database product such as Microsoft Access, including the structures implemented. Implementation models are not covered in detail in this book.

This book discusses predominantly the logical view of conceptual models. The **physical representation** of the client–server model, which shows all the specifications of hardware and software, is not considered until the final section in the next chapter on database implementation.

### *Older database models*

Two older database models are the hierarchical database model and the network database model. These are discussed next.

### Hierarchical database model

The *hierarchical database model*'s logical structure is best understood by relating it to a manufacturing or assembly process. The structure dates back to the 1970s and early 1980s when manufacturing companies wanted to handle the management of a large number of parts without the data redundancy and anomalies of file systems. In short, the main advantage of the hierarchical database model was its ability to access data, as long as it was from the top of the hierarchical database structure. However, there were some fundamental limitations with data storage. This was because there were difficulties searching for items in the bottom or middle layers of the hierarchy. For example, in figure 3.9 below, to access the data in node 7 you would need to search node 1, then 2, then 4, then 5, then move to node 3, then search 6, then 7. Therefore you had to search all the nodes before node 7 up and down the tree until you found the data you wanted.

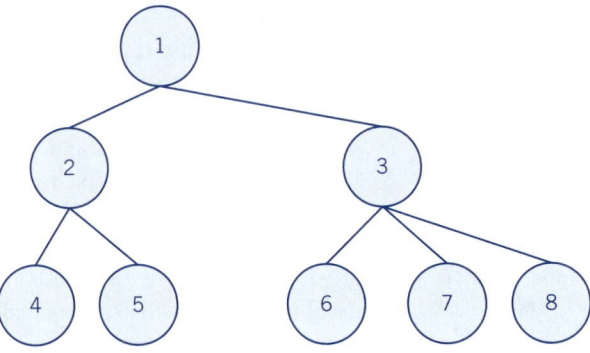

**FIGURE 3.9** Hierarchical database structure

### Network database model

The main goal of the *network database model*, which dominated during the 1980s, was to solve the inefficient methods with which the hierarchical database model stored and searched for data. The major advantage of the network model is that it solves the search problem. It is easier to view the database conceptually and the design process is simpler and more flexible than hierarchical designs. The indexes and pointers allow for flexibility because the DBMS can be programmed to access the database at pre-determined points within the database to obtain data to answer questions and aid in decision making. Indexes record where data is stored in the system much like an index to a book tells us which page a particular concept is on. Much like chapter tabs that sometimes appear at the side of a book, pointers in the system enable data to be accessed directly, rather than having to search each node from the top of the database. However, the cost to implement a network model is high. This is because indexes and pointers that will answer the types of queries that may be asked of the system have to be built into the database when it is developed; however, developers are often not aware of these types of queries, or the types of queries may change as the organisation changes over time. Developers must therefore try to anticipate every possible question that users may ask of the data. Further, building and maintaining indexes and pointers can require large amounts of processing time and storage space. Therefore, the relational database superseded the network model.

## *Relational databases*

The relational database was first conceived in the 1970s by E.F. Codd. The relational database operates through a sophisticated relational database management system

(RDBMS). The RDBMS performs the functions of the hierarchical and network models but adds other functions that make the relational database more flexible and easier to understand, implement and manipulate. The relational database records data at the lowest level of data possible; for example, rather than recording a customer name and address together, it separates them in a table. Similarly, an address may be broken up by house number, street name, suburb and so on.

The key is in the tables (also called relations by Codd), which store sets of data. Figure 3.10 shows two tables: customer and salesperson.

#### Table: Customer

| Customer_code | Customer_name | Customer_address | Customer_phone | Salesperson_code |
|---------------|---------------|------------------|----------------|------------------|
| 1000 | Andrew Johns | 2 Apple Street, Melbourne, VIC | 03 1234 5678 | 9001 |
| 1001 | David Smith | 6 Banana Street, Melbourne, VIC | 03 9876 4321 | 9002 |
| 1002 | John Brown | 9 Carrot Street, Melbourne, VIC | 03 5678 3456 | 9003 |
| 1003 | Mary Jones | 3 Durian Street, Melbourne, VIC | 03 2376 1048 | 9001 |
| 1004 | Michael Lee | 5 Enchilada Lane, Melbourne, VIC | 03 9386 9191 | 9002 |

#### Table: Salesperson

| Salesperson_code | Salesperson_name | Salesperson_initials | Salesperson_phone |
|------------------|------------------|----------------------|-------------------|
| 9000 | Andrew Fred Davis | AFD | 03 8344 3677 |
| 9001 | Ashley Smith Brown | ASB | 03 8344 3678 |
| 9002 | Peter Thomas Burkitt | PTB | 03 8344 3679 |
| 9003 | William Edward Chong | WEC | 03 8344 3680 |

**FIGURE 3.10** A simple relational database linking customer and salesperson tables

The tables are not physically connected; instead, the connections exist through matching data stored in each table. In the example in figure 3.10, the customer is linked to the salesperson through the field 'Salesperson_code'. This connection allows users to match customers to salespersons through the customer data stored in one table or the salesperson data stored in another table. For instance, you can easily determine that Andrew Johns's salesperson is Ashley Smith Brown because the 'Salesperson_ code' in the customer table is '9001', which references Ashley Smith Brown in the salesperson table. Similarly, you can determine that Peter Thomas Burkitt, salesperson 9002, has two customers — David Smith and Michael Lee — and so on. The point is that although the tables are independent, it is easy to connect data between the tables and answer different questions that might be asked of the data. For example, we can find out the name and phone number of Michael Lee's salesperson, even though that information is not contained in the customer table.

The strength of the relational approach is that the designer does not need to know which questions may be asked of the data. If the data are specified and defined carefully, the database can answer virtually any question efficiently. The efficiency and flexibility of a relational database is the main reason for its dominance today.

These strengths come from the **structural independence** of the data. That is, it is possible to make changes to the database structure without affecting the ability of the DBMS to access data. This is because every table is independent, and, because

*Structural independence* A data attribute that exists when changes in the database structure do not affect access.

relationships can be constructed just by linking key fields in tables. There are other strengths of a relational database. Conceptually, users can easily comprehend the logical view of the database as the tables of data are easy to understand. The structural independence of the data makes it easier to design, implement, manage and use. There are also some very powerful and flexible query languages that users can easily learn (as they do not require programming skills) that can be used to manipulate the data for answering their own questions. For most relational databases, the query language is SQL. The SQL engine does all the tough jobs in the database, such as creating table structures and maintaining the data dictionary, system catalogue and table access, and translating user requests into a format that the computer can handle.

While the relational database has significant benefits over hierarchical and network databases, there are still some disadvantages. However, the benefits over the hierarchical and network models outweigh these disadvantages, and the relational database has become the dominant database model for everyday use in organisations. While the basic concepts provided superior efficiency for manipulation and storage, it was the lack of suitably powerful hardware, operating systems and computing power for manipulation that restricted growth originally of relational databases. However, today, relatively small **client–server systems** such as an SQL server can run relational database software such as Oracle or DB2. Fast processing power and powerful operating systems are available to facilitate the structural independence of the data and SQL provides flexibility in fulfilling users' data query requests.

However, the conceptual simplicity of the relational database makes it easy for poor design and implementation to creep in. Users can find it easy to generate reports and queries without much thought about database design.

It is also easy for organisations to have databases within databases because users may start creating their own databases and applications for their specific use. As the database grows, a lack of proper design slows the system down and produces the types of repetition, data anomalies and data redundancies found in other database systems. That is why well designed database systems are essential, as is a knowledge of the basics of database design for a business accountant.

Most small business systems software, such as MYOB and QuickBooks, uses relational database structures. To maximise the advantages offered by the relational database system, careful database modelling, data relationship design and systems implementation are critical. These factors are explained in the next section.

## *Object-relational and object-oriented databases*

Object-relational databases and object-oriented databases are other database models, which, as the names suggest, are object relational and object oriented. Object-relational databases have the advantage of being able to use the relational tools of structured query language (SQL) and tables to be able to interrogate the database. Object-oriented databases are based on the concept of objects, which, in turn, are based on object-oriented programming principles. Object-oriented databases are a good model if the database is required to store a lot of sounds, pictures or video (e.g. films, medical or scientific images). The concepts of classes, inheritance, extensibility and encapsulation from object-oriented programming are applied to object-relational and object-oriented databases. Data is stored as objects; an example of an object would be a customer. A customer object would store data and programs that would act on that data in the same object. Many customer objects would be stored as class of objects. Classes of objects such as customers can be stored in a hierarchy. Customer objects at the bottom of a hierarchy (such as a retail customer) can inherit data attributes such as customer payment terms from above them in the hierarchy (such as a wholesale customer). Objects are encapsulated, meaning that objects cannot see all the data and programs of other objects.

Object-oriented databases also have the advantage of data types. Accounting systems have, for example, dollars, dates and whole numbers as data types. In object-oriented databases, new data types can be created; however, given dollars terms are generally used in accounting systems, we generally don't need this ability to create new data types, which is called extensibility. An item of data stored as an object in an object-oriented or object-relational database has data and methods that can be performed on the data. So, the data and the programs that operate on the data are not separate as they are in a relational database. This fact introduces more complexity into the database design process.

For financial accounting systems that focus on monetary values, usually a relational database is sufficient, and this is why we study the relational database in this book.

**LEARNING OBJECTIVE (5)**

Discuss database modelling and develop database models using entity-relationship diagrams.

# DATABASE MODELLING, DESIGN AND IMPLEMENTATION OF RELATIONAL DATABASES

Database modelling and design are the first two steps in describing complex real-world activities in such a way that they can be captured by and represented in a database system. Database modelling and design as discussed in this section utilise a *conceptual* view with *logical* representations of database structures.

## Database modelling

Database models are used to describe and represent complex real-world data structures. These conceptual models provide a logical representation, in graphical form, of the complexities of real-world data entities and their relationships with one another. At the same time, a database designer can depict the data structures, relations, characteristics and constraints on their design using a database model. Consequently, it is a communication tool that can provide the blueprint for developing new database structures or create improved understanding of an organisation's database.

There are important reasons for database modelling. First, a good database design is the foundation of good applications. It provides a blueprint to build the tables and relationships that are required in a database application. Second, different people — managers, administration staff and programmers — view data differently. Managers see database applications from a decision-making perspective, while administration staff are more concerned about its ease of use. Programmers often think about design simplicity without considering decision making and ease of use capabilities. If there is a good database model, it does not matter that people have different views, because these views will all be encapsulated in the database model.

Database modelling often starts with a conceptual model that provides a global view of the data. This is usually an organisation-wide view of the data from the perspective of senior managers, and will be referred to later in the chapter as the concept of a top-down view. The most widely used database model is the **entity-relationship model**. The entity-relationship model is a database model that logically and graphically depicts relationships between entities and attributes, and between entities and entities. Database modelling is the first step in developing a database, before designing and implementing. It uses E-R diagrams to develop the blueprint for the design.

*Entity-relationship model* A data model that graphically depicts relationships between entities and attributes.

## Entity-relationship models

Entity-relationship models are depicted by entity-relationship diagrams (E-R diagrams) and provide a conceptual view that incorporates:

- entities
- attributes
- relationships.

**Entities** in an E-R diagram represent real-world things or objects such as employees, types of employees, customers, types of customers, suppliers and types of suppliers. Entities usually correspond to an entire table rather than a row in a table of a relational database. They are usually represented by rectangles. Each entity will have attributes.

**Attributes** are the characteristics of entities. For example, a customer may have attributes including first name, last name, address, telephone number and email. Figure 3.11 shows the attributes of the customer entity using two representations: *Chen's model* and the *crow's foot model*. Some conceptual material is best explained through Chen's model, while the crow's foot model is more useful for implementations. These models are discussed in greater detail later in the chapter.

**Entities** *Representations of real-world things or objects that are involved in a process and correspond to a table in a relational database.*

**Attributes** *Characteristics of entities.*

Chen's model

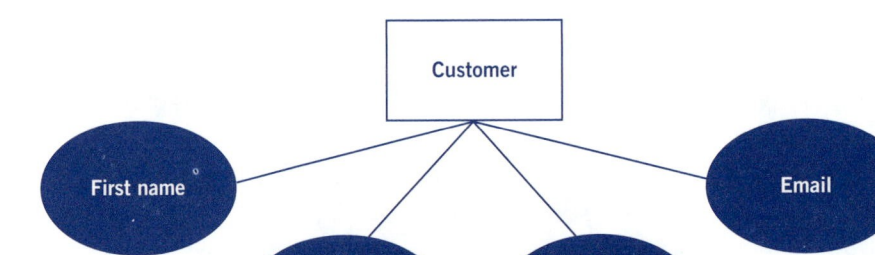

The crow's foot model

**FIGURE 3.11** Entities in Chen's model and the crow's foot model

**Cardinality** *The specific number of allowed entity occurrences associated with a single occurrence of the related entity by assigning a specific value to connectivity.*

Relationships are associations between entities. **Cardinality** among the entities describes the relationship as 1:1 (one-to-one), 1:M (one-to-many) or M:N (many-to-many). M:N is used to indicate many-to-many as convention. While cardinality describes the relationship between entities, business rules express the number of entity occurrences associated with one occurrence of a related entity. A business rule assigns a specific value to the cardinality.

For instance, the entity-relationship diagram in figure 3.12 depicts the relationship between a salesperson and a customer of a particular organisation. The cardinality shows that in this organisation each salesperson has many customers but each customer has only one salesperson. The business rules represent the number of occurrences in the related entity. In figure 3.12, each salesperson can have up to and no more than 10 customers. Similarly the business rule of (1,1) written next to the customer indicates that each customer must have one and only one salesperson. The business rules show the minimum and maximum number of entities that can be involved in a relationship. An example illustrating this is the relationship between the entities manager and company car. This may be written as (0,1): many managers may not be given a company car so 0 is the minimum, and 1 is the maximum as a manager will only be assigned one company car at a time. So, the minimum and maximum of this relationship is 0 and 1 respectively.

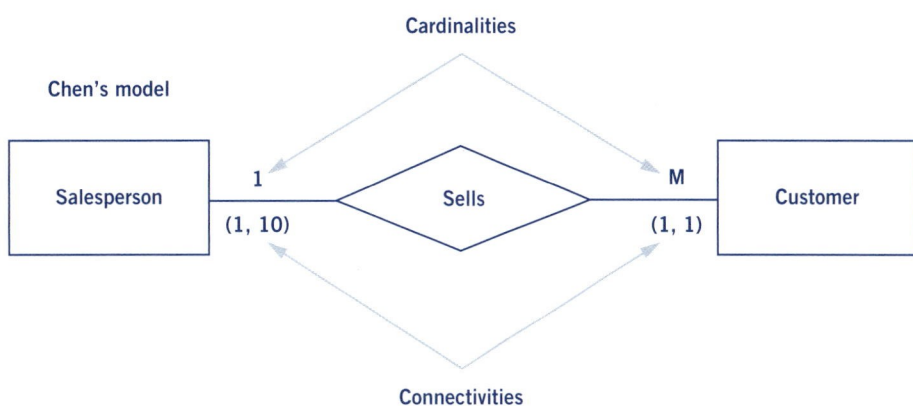

**FIGURE 3.12** An entity-relationship model

To illustrate how this E-R diagram can be applied to relational databases, consider the table structure of the E-R diagram in figure 3.13. It puts the operationalisation of Chen's model in figure 3.11 into a relational database context. The attributes in figure 3.13 have been assumed for the purposes of illustrating the link between the salesperson and customer. Organisations are likely to have their own attributes that may not be the same as those in figure 3.11.

| Table: Salesperson | | | | |
|---|---|---|---|---|
| Salesperson_ID | Last Name | First Name | Address | Email |
| | | | | |

| Table: Customer | | | | |
|---|---|---|---|---|
| Customer_ID | Last Name | First Name | Email | Salesperson_ID |
| | | | | |

**FIGURE 3.13** Table structure related to an entity-relationship model

These diagrams show how a database designer can use the E-R diagram representation of a specific relationship between real-world entities and apply it to an implementable database model, which in this case is the relational database. The operationalisation of an E-R diagram is the concern of database design. This is outlined in the next section on database design.

Now, suppose an organisation had the table structure shown in figure 3.13 in its database. If you work the other way, you could take the table structure in figure 3.13 and develop the E-R diagram shown in figure 3.12 to represent the organisation-wide activities of the employees of the organisation.

Chen's model uses rectangles to depict entities, diamonds to depict relationships and circles (see figure 3.11) to depict attributes. Cardinalities are written next to the entities. The other established version of the E-R diagram is the crow's foot model, in which rectangles represent the entities, which are related by lines with single and multiple prongs to show the cardinalities. Figure 3.14 summarises the shapes used for each of the simple Chen's model and crow's foot model.

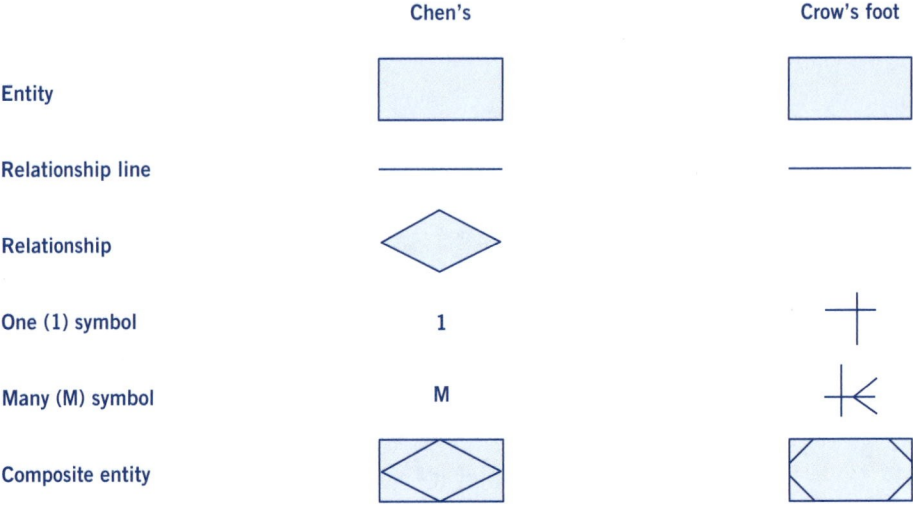

**FIGURE 3.14** Entity-relationship model shapes

In summary, E-R diagrams provide a logical and graphical representation of the entities within an organisation and the relationships among those entities. They serve as database models that can be used to construct databases that adhere to the organisation's business rules and record the transactions among the entities.

## Developing entity-relationship diagrams (E-R diagrams)

The development of an E-R diagram is an iterative process involving four steps.

1. Develop a general narrative of the organisation's operations including the business process, policies and business rules.
2. Construct the E-R diagram by identifying the internal and external entities and the relationships among them from the narrative in step 1. Cardinalities and business rules can also be assigned based on the narrative.
3. Have the E-R diagram reviewed by each area of the organisation with ownership of the operations, policies and processes.
4. Make the necessary modifications to incorporate any newly discovered entity relationship components.

This four-step process should be repeated until the designers and users agree that the E-R diagram is complete and represents the relationships and the rules that govern the organisation's entities.

These steps are performed by systems analysts and database designers; however, it is important for an accountant to be involved in reviewing the E-R diagram to ensure that the business rules reflect how the organisation works. Therefore, understanding how to read and interpret E-R diagrams is critical for accountants.

The four-step process will be demonstrated in the section on database design using an example of employees that charge their time to projects.

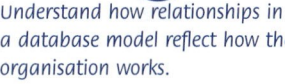
# DATABASE DESIGN

The table is the basic building block in database design. Table structures must be efficient to allow fast and error- and duplication-free flow of information.

In database design, tables are created to represent every internal and external entity and their attributes. As stated earlier, examples of entities are the salesperson, manager, supervisor, customer, type of customers, supplier and type of suppliers to the organisation. Projects are also entities; in the example looking at employees charging time to projects, employees and projects are the entities we need in our database design, as these are the entities about which we want to record information. We use the singular for the names of the entities such as customer or project not customers or projects. We also name the association between them in the diamond as 'charges time to'. Try to name the association (the words in the diamond) from left to right so that it makes grammatical sense.

Using the example of employees that charge their time to projects on consulting jobs, we can construct a table structure. Both employees and the projects they work on are entities that we wish to record information about. This is shown in figure 3.15.

**FIGURE 3.15** Employee project E-R diagram

The E-R diagram shows that the employee charges time to different projects. The employee and the project are entities and the relationship between them is the charging of the time. Attributes have not been given to the entities yet; this can be done later. This relationship can be implemented differently depending on the business rules in the organisation. As shown in figure 3.16, the relationship can be implemented in four different ways.

Each of these relationships means different things with regards to the organisation's operations.

Take the first line as shown in figure 3.17. The relationship can be read from both sides of the diagram. Reading the relationship from left to right, as the arrow in figure 3.17 indicates, take one of the first entity and relate it to the number of the second entity. Therefore:

**ONE Employee can charge time to ONE Project.**

You must always consider one (singular) of the first entity and then look at how many of the second entity that relates to. The ONE next to the second entity means that an employee can only charge time to (or work on) ONE project.

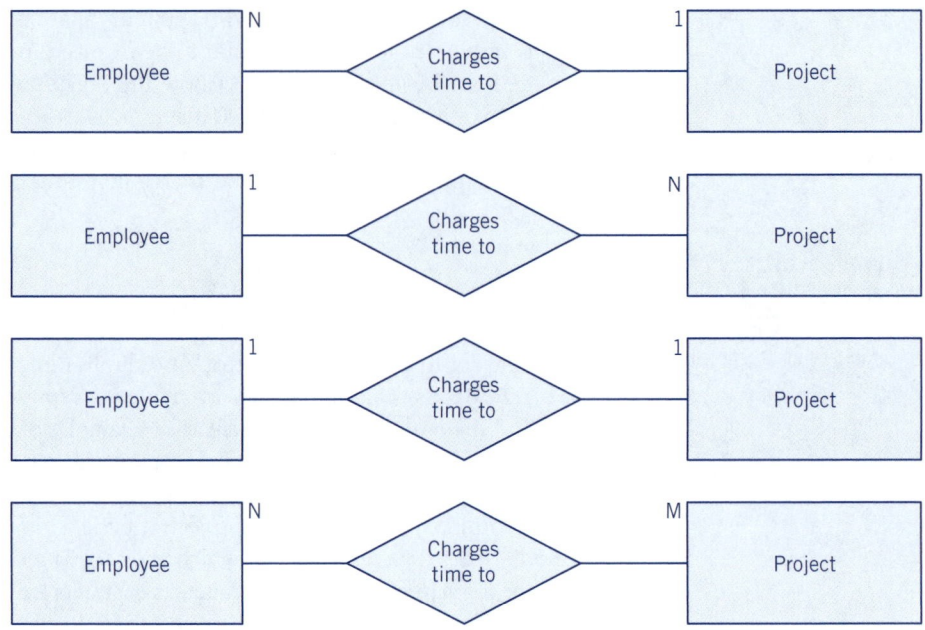

**FIGURE 3.16** Employee project E-R diagram with different organisational business rules

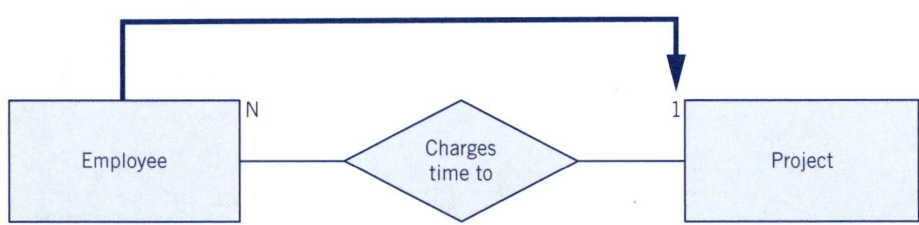

**FIGURE 3.17** Employee project E-R diagram with N:1

Reading this relationship from the other direction (see figure 3.18), take one of the first entity, which is project this time as we are reading the relationship from right to left. Then relate this one project to how many occurrences of employee. Therefore:

**ONE Project can have MANY Employees working on it.**

Figure 3.18 shows taking one of the first entity, project, and relating it to the N on the other side of the diagram, which is written next to the employee entity.

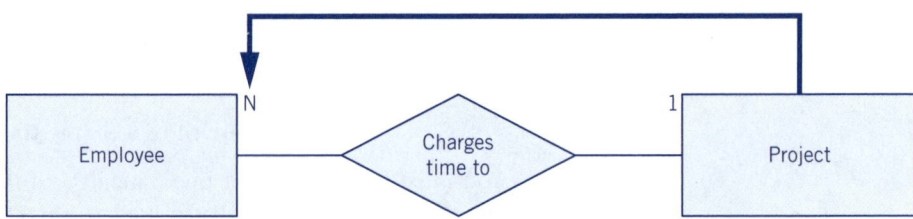

**FIGURE 3.18** Employee project E-R diagram with 1:N (on different entities)

Overall, the relationship in figures 3.17 and 3.18 is shown in figure 3.19

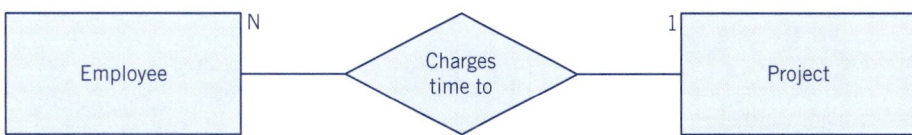

**FIGURE 3.19** Employee project E-R diagram with 1:N (no arrows)

The relationships in this diagram are read as:

ONE Employee can charge time to ONE Project.

ONE Project can have MANY Employees working on it.

The business logic underlying this relationship is that an employee can only work on one project at a time, yet a project can have many employees working on it at any one time. If the organisation wants an employee to be able to work on more than one project, this database model is not suitable. This is an example of a **one-to-many relationship (1:N)**.

The next model with different business rules from figure 3.16 is shown below as figure 3.20. Notice that the one and the many are on different sides of the entities than in figure 3.17. The different placement of the one-to-many (1:N) means that the relationship between the two entities will be different.

*One-to-many relationship (1:N) A relationship between two entities in which the cardinality of one entity in the relationship is one and the other entity's cardinality is many.*

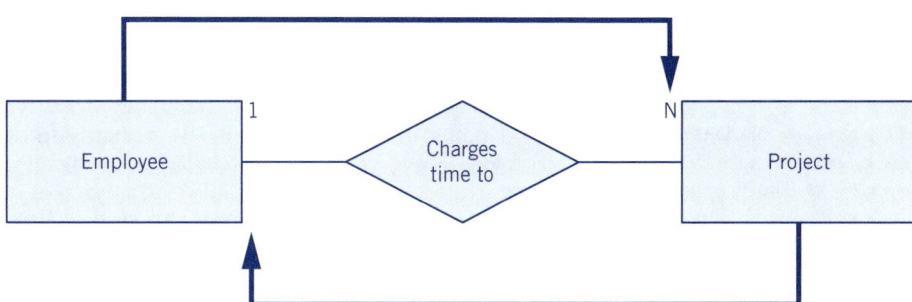

**FIGURE 3.20** Employee project E-R diagram with 1:N (project side)

Reading figure 3.20 from left to right, take one employee and relate it the number of occurrences of projects:

ONE Employee can charge time to MANY Projects.

Reading figure 3.20 from right to left, the bottom arrow on the figure:

ONE Project can only have ONE Employee working on it.

So, the logic underlying this relationship is that an employee can work on many projects but a project can only have one employee working on it at a time. If this does not match how the organisation works, this is not a suitable model of the data relationships.

The third relationship in figure 3.16 is shown as figure 3.21 overleaf.

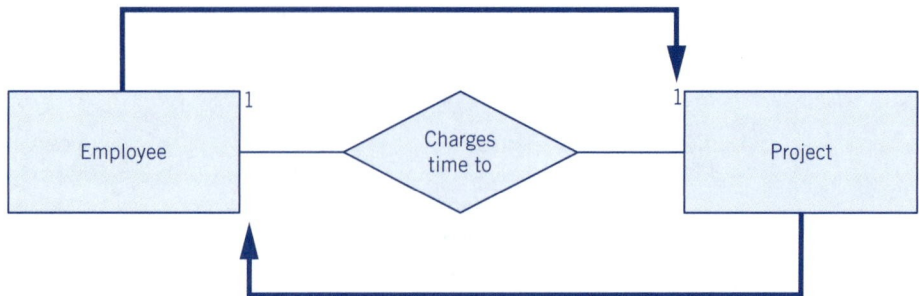

**FIGURE 3.21** Employee project E-R diagram with 1:1 relationship

**One-to-one relationship (1:1)** *A relationship between two entities in which the cardinality for each entity is one.*

This is a **one-to-one relationship (1:1)** as there is one beside both entities. The relationship reads from left to right:

**One Employee can charge time to ONE Project.**

Reading the relationship from right to left:

**ONE Project can only have ONE Employee working on it.**

So, figure 3.21 shows quite a restrictive relationship in that an employee can only work on one project and a project can only have one employee working on it at any time. One-to-one (1:1) relationships are reasonably rare. However, if the organisation is taking over a database from another organisation it needs to ensure that the relationships between the entities match how the organisation works. Accepting a 1:1 relationship between the employee and the project entity in a database but allowing multiple employees to work on one project in practice means the database would be unable to record data in the way the organisation works. This highlights the importance of the relationships between entities, and of not implementing any database design before determining if it matches how the organisation operates.

**Many-to-many relationships (N:M)** *A relationship between two entities in which the cardinality of both entities in the relationship is many.*

Finally, in figure 3.22 we have a **many-to-many relationship (N:M)**, which is shown as a N:M. To read this relationship from the left to the right:

**ONE Employee can charge time to MANY Projects.**

Reading the relationship sentence from right to left:

**ONE Project can have MANY Employees working on it.**

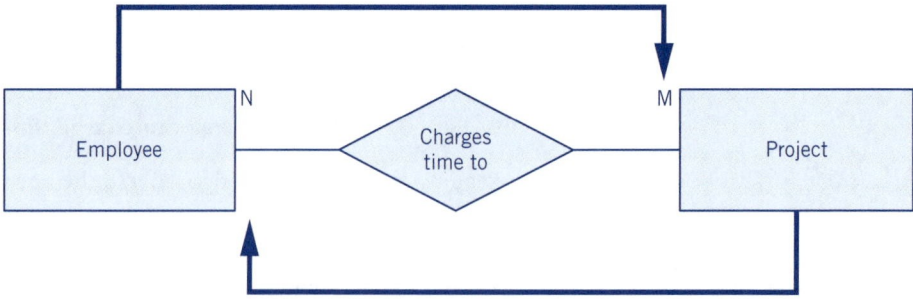

**FIGURE 3.22** Employee project E-R diagram with N:M relationship

This process of identifying the entities and the relationships between the entities continues until all entities and relationships are identified. This process would normally be undertaken by systems analysts and database designers in conjunction with a team of users of the system. After the identification process is complete, the relationships between the entities should be verified with a range of employees in the organisation. This ensures that the identified relationships are correct for the organisation. One such employee involved in verifying the relationships is the accountant, and hence the importance of accountants understanding what these relationships mean.

After the relationships have been identified and verified, they can be logically implemented in a database system. Figure 3.23 summarises the different relationships that can be implemented between two entities, depending on how the business operates.

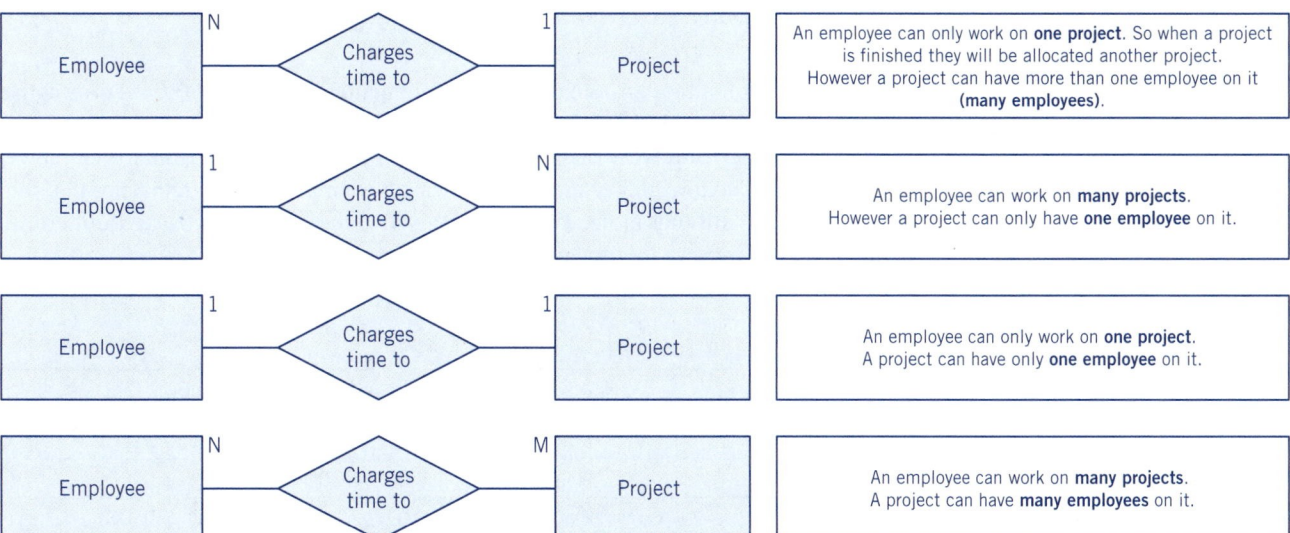

**FIGURE 3.23** Summary of employee project E-R diagram with different organisational business rules

The next section discusses how 1:1 (one-to-one), 1:N (one-to-many) and N:M (many-to-many) relationships need to be implemented in computer database packages. This is moving from the conceptual view to the logical representation of the implementation view.

## Implementing relationships

Figures 3.24, 3.25, 3.28 and 3.29 show the relationships between the project table and employee table from figures 3.2 and 3.3 on page 110. Note that the project number has been chosen as the primary key (unique identifier) in the project table and the employee number has been chosen as the primary key in the employee table. Each of the tables includes attributes as illustrated in figure 3.2 (page 110).

### *Implementing one-to-many (1:N) relationships*

To implement the 1:N (one-to-many) relationship as shown in figure 3.24 and figure 3.25 the general rule is the primary key of the one becomes the foreign key of the many. A **Foreign key** is an attribute whose values must match the primary key in another table. Therefore, for figure 3.24 the primary key of the one is the primary key of the project table (Proj_num) and would become the foreign key of the many (the employee table).

**Foreign key** *An attribute whose values must match the primary key in another table.*

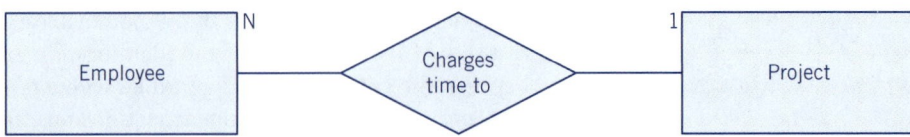

**FIGURE 3.24** Employee project E-R diagram with 1:N

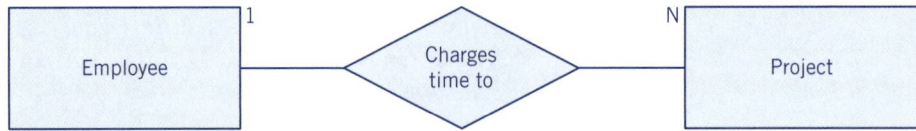

**FIGURE 3.25** Employee project E-R diagram with 1:N (project side)

This results in figure 3.26, the database implementation of figure 3.24. From figure 3.26 we can see that project number now becomes the foreign key of the employee table. As an employee can only work on one project, having the project number in the employee table is correct. The foreign key project number in the employee table indicates that it is a primary key in another table. A foreign key is also indicated by a dashed underline. Remember primary keys are shown using a bold underline.

| Project table | | | |
|---|---|---|---|
| **Proj_num** | **Proj_name** | **Proj_start** | **Proj_budget** |
| 1 | Rain | 01/01/2009 | $10000 |
| 2 | Hail | 01/04/2009 | $30000 |
| 3 | Flood | 01/12/2008 | $50000 |

| Employee table | | |
|---|---|---|
| **Emp_num** | **Emp_name** | **Proj_num** |
| 101 | Michael Lee | 1 |
| 105 | Brett Considine | 1 |
| 110 | Phil Collier | 2 |

**FIGURE 3.26** Database implementation of employee project E-R diagram with 1:N

For figure 3.25, to implement the database, we need the primary key of the one (which is the primary key of the employee table, Emp_num) to become the foreign key of the many (the project table) in figure 3.27. This makes sense as a project can only have one employee working on it, and the employee can be indicated in the project table against the project. The details of the employee are not transferred to the project table, as, if they are working on multiple projects, their name and other details would be duplicated, potentially causing update and modification data anomalies and data integrity issues as discussed earlier in the chapter (i.e. all instances of an employee's details would need to be updated if any changes were made to those details). As the structure stands, employee details are contained in the employee table.

Any updates would need to be made once and once only in the employee table. This means that data redundancy and anomalies are avoided.

| Project table | | | | |
|---|---|---|---|---|
| Proj_num | Proj_name | Proj_start | Proj_budget | Emp_num |
| 1 | Rain | 01/01/2009 | $10 000 | 101 |
| 2 | Hail | 01/04/2009 | $30 000 | 101 |
| 3 | Flood | 01/12/2008 | $50 000 | 105 |

| Employee table | |
|---|---|
| Emp_num | Emp_name |
| 101 | Michael Lee |
| 105 | Brett Considine |
| 110 | Phil Collier |

FIGURE 3.27 Database implementation of employee project E-R diagram with 1:N (project side)

## Implementing 1:1 (one-to-one) relationships

In implementing a one-to-one relationship (1:1) as shown in figure 3.28, the general rule is to anticipate which side is most likely to become many in the future and implement as though it was a one-to-many (1:M) relationship now. So, the database for the 1:1 relationship would be implemented as shown in figure 3.26 if you thought that a project could have multiple employees working on it in the future. Or, you could implement it as shown in figure 3.27 if you thought that employees would be more likely to work on multiple projects in the future.

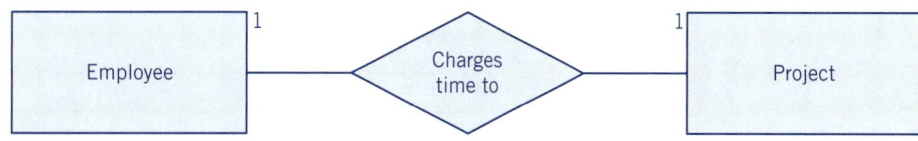

FIGURE 3.28 Employee project E-R diagram with 1:1 relationship

## Implementing N:M (many-to-many) relationships

The implementation of a many-to-many (N:M) relationship as shown in figure 3.29 is probably the most complex but by far the most common in organisations. This relationship is shown as N:M not as N:N.

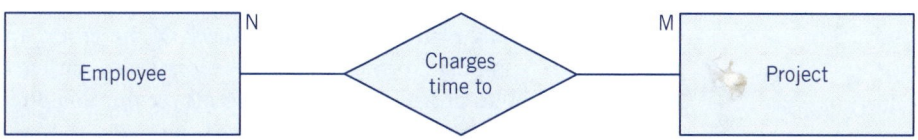

FIGURE 3.29 Employee project E-R diagram with N:M relationship

The relationship diamond between the two entities needs to be converted to a composite entity holding the primary keys of each of the entities as shown in figure 3.30. A composite entity is shown as a rectangle with a diamond inside it. That is, the relationship (diamond) becomes an entity (rectangle).

**Project table**

| Proj_num | Proj_name | Proj_start | Proj_budget |
|---|---|---|---|
| 1 | Rain | 01/01/2009 | $10 000 |
| 2 | Hail | 01/04/2009 | $30 000 |
| 3 | Flood | 01/12/2008 | $50 000 |

**Employee table**

| Emp_num | Emp_name |
|---|---|
| 101 | Michael Lee |
| 105 | Brett Considine |
| 108 | David Smith |
| 110 | Phil Collier |
| 112 | Anne Wyatt |

**Employee project table**

| Proj_num | Emp_num |
|---|---|
| 1 | 101 |
| 1 | 105 |
| 1 | 110 |
| 2 | 101 |
| 2 | 108 |
| 3 | 105 |
| 3 | 110 |
| 3 | 112 |

**FIGURE 3.30** Database implementation of employee project E-R diagram with N:M relationship

This linking entity (the employee project table) has the primary keys of both the tables attached to it (shown by the bold underlines), to enable the implementation of the relationship of employees being able to charge time to many projects and projects being able to have many employees work on them. The primary key of this linking entity is the primary key of each of the tables attached to it. So, the primary key, is a composite primary key, as we discussed earlier in the chapter, made up of the attributes project number and employee number, Proj_num, Emp_num. This new composite entity and the breaking of the many-to-many relationship into two one-to-many relationships is shown in figure 3.31.

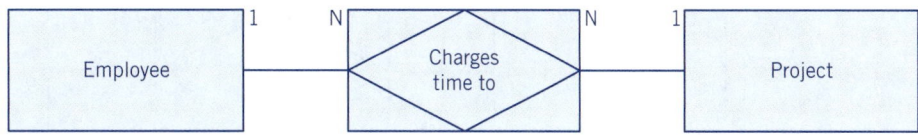

**FIGURE 3.31** Employee project E-R diagram with N:M relationship broken into two 1:N relationships

This splitting of the many-to-many relationship into two one-to-many relationships needs to occur so that the relationships can be implemented in a computerised database package.

To show that a many-to-many relationship has been broken down into two one-to-many relationships we can use the example of projects and employees. In the format of the many-to-many relationship shown in figure 3.29, if we trace onto this relationship the data from figure 3.30 we get the situation shown in figure 3.32.

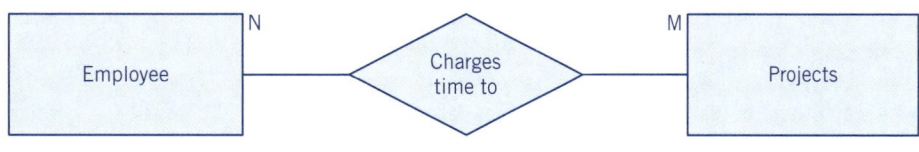

| Employee table | |
|---|---|
| **Emp_num** | **Emp_name** |
| 101 | Michael Lee |
| 105 | Brett Considine |
| 108 | David Smith |
| 110 | Phil Collier |
| 112 | Anne Wyatt |

| Project table | | | |
|---|---|---|---|
| **Proj_num** | **Proj_name** | **Proj_start** | **Proj_budget** |
| 1 | Rain | 01/01/2009 | $10 000 |
| 2 | Hail | 01/04/2009 | $30 000 |
| 3 | Flood | 01/12/2008 | $50 000 |

**FIGURE 3.32** Project employee data

Figure 3.32 shows the project employee assignments in a many-to-many relationship. The assignments come from the employee project table in figure 3.30. The many-to-many relationship in figure 3.32 has not been implemented as yet. We can see, given figure 3.30, that project number 1 has an arrow to employee number 101 the first row in the employee project table in figure 3.30. Project number 1 also has a line to employee number 105, the second row in figure 3.30, and also to employee number 110. Project 2 has an arrow to employee number 101 (fourth line in figure 3.30) and also to employee number 108.

So, we can see that project 1 has multiple employees charging time to it, in particular, employee numbers 101, 105 and 110. Also, employee number 101 works on both project 1 and project 2.

The semantics or logic in figure 3.32 is impossible to implement in a database structure so the many-to-many relationship is broken down into two one-to-many relationships as shown in figure 3.33 overleaf.

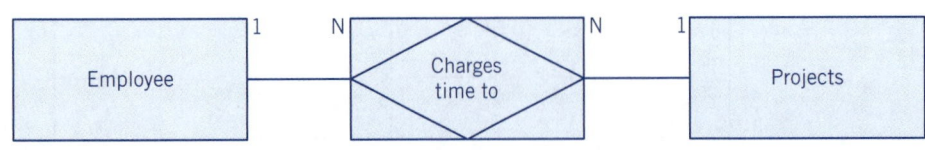

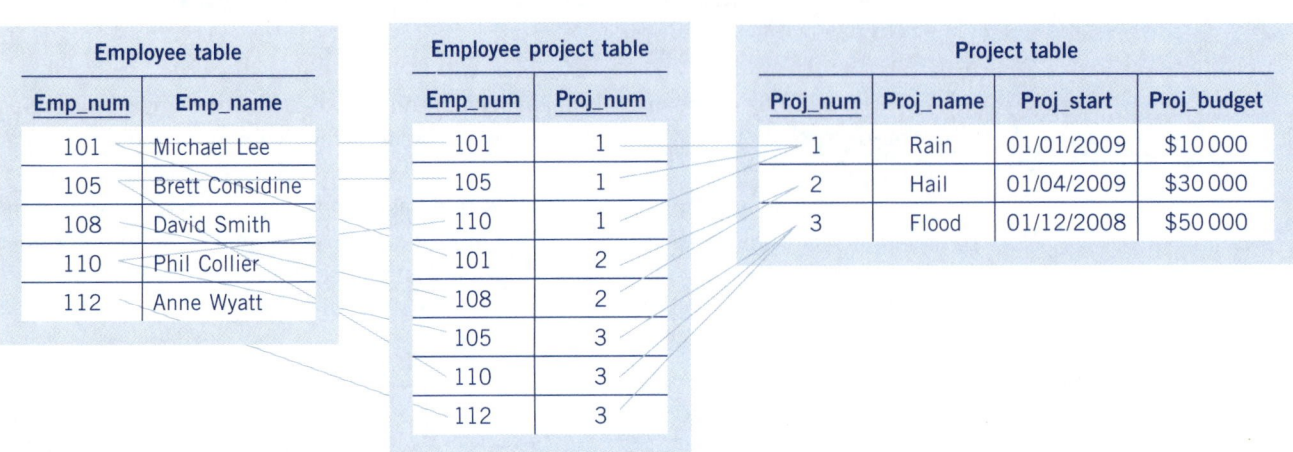

**FIGURE 3.33** Employee project and employee project mappings table

Figure 3.33 shows that the many-to-many relationship can now be implemented as two one-to-many relationships. So, we know there are four relationships in the logical model as shown in figure 3.34.

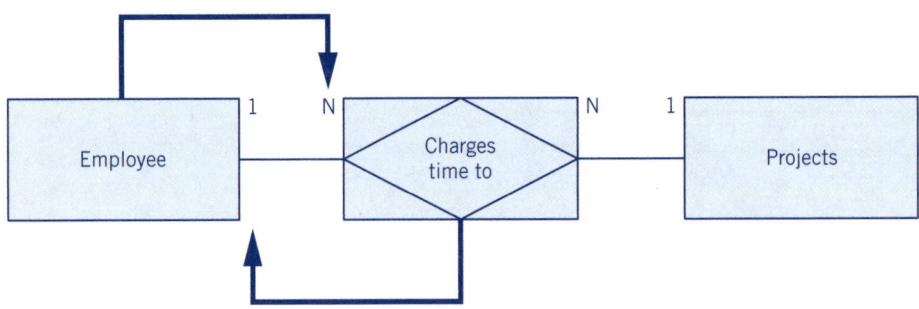

**FIGURE 3.34** Employee to project/employee (left-hand side) and project/employee to project (right-hand side)

Reading the relationships marked by arrows in figure 3.34 from the left:

**ONE Employee can have MANY Employee/Project charges.**

And from the right:

**ONE Employee/Project charge can only belong to ONE Employee.**

Therefore, the relationship goes from the employee entity to the employee/project entity and shows the allocation of employees to projects. It shows that an employee can work on many employee/projects (e.g. employee 101 works on employee/projects 1 and 2). But any employee/project charges, for example, the first one in the employee/project table of employee number 101 and project number 1, must go back to only one row in the employee table, in this case to employee number 101.

Likewise, the second half of the relationship between project and employee/project can be read from left to right:

**ONE Employee/Project relates to only ONE Project.**

And from right to left:

**ONE Project relates to MANY Employee/Project allocations.**

This exhibits the one-to-many status of this relationship.

Overall, we need to build database models that are conceptual and that provide a logical representation, in graphical form, of the complexities of real-world data structures. These database models show us how an organisation works (i.e. the business rules that apply to the organisation). It is very important to understand what the database model means in terms of how the business works. If we implement the database using relationships other than how the organisation works, the organisation's transactions cannot be recorded.

A database designer can also depict the data structures, relations, characteristics and constraints of the database design in a database model. Hence, a database model is a communication tool that creates improved understanding of an organisation's existing database, or provides the blueprint for developing new database structures.

As outlined above, the relationships that exist in an E-R diagram are a function of how the business works. Choosing a database design that does not allow for many-to-many relationships when the business uses them will have far reaching implications for the information systems built to use the database. Figure 3.35 summarises the four ways a relationship can be implemented, the corresponding database design and what each implies for business rules.

## AIS FOCUS 3.2

## Aquaplan Limited

The accountant at Aquaplan a horticultural business wanted to create a mini information systems using desktop software Microsoft Access. By using the techniques outlined in this chapter on database concepts they will save themselves many false starts if they have some basic understanding of database design.

Even though they may have a database professional creating the database, the accountant at Aquaplan Limited will need to understand that the database professional will be using using the top-approach described in this chapter. The database professional will first create a data model using an entity-relationship diagram. To do this, they will need to consider the important entities required to record data on the business. Then they need to consider how these entities are related using relationships.

The database professional will ask questions of the accountant about how entities within the Aquaplan Limited business are related. At times, the database professional may seem to ask certain questions twice, but the accountant will realise that the database professional is looking at the relationships between entities from both directions.

*continued*

This knowledge of what the database professional is asking ensures that the accountant can consider and answer the questions carefully and fully. Then, when the data model (entity-relationship diagram) is complete, the accountant can evaluate it to ensure that it accurately represents how Aquaplan Limited's business works before the relationships are created in the software program and the organisation's valuable data is loaded into the system.

**FIGURE 3.35** Summary of database models, design and business rules

| Model | Database design | Business rules |
|---|---|---|
| Employee–Project N:1 <br><br> Employee —N— Charges time to —1— Project | **Project table** <br> Proj_num  Proj_name  Proj_start  Proj_budget <br><br> **Employee table** <br> Emp_num  Emp_name  Proj_num | An employee can only work on one project. A project can have more than one employee working on it. |
| Employee–Project 1:N <br><br> Employee —1— Charges time to —N— Project | **Project table** <br> Proj_num  Proj_name  Proj_start  Proj_budget Emp_num <br><br> **Employee table** <br> Emp_num  Emp_name | An employee can work on many projects. A project can only have one employee working on it. |
| Employee–Project 1:1 <br><br> Employee —1— Charges time to —1— Project | As either model above, depending on which side is more likely to become many in the future. | An employee can only work on one project. A project can only have one employee working on it. |
| Employee–Project N:M <br><br> Employee —1 N— Charges time to —N 1— Project | **Project table** <br> Proj_num  Proj_name  Proj_start  Proj_budget <br><br> **Employee table** <br> Emp_num  Emp_name <br><br> **Project/Employee table** <br> Proj_num  Emp_num | An employee can work on many project/employee assignments. A project/employee assignment can relate to one employee only. A project can have many project/employee assignments. A project/employee assignment can only relate to one project. |

## Top-down versus bottom-up database design

The entity-relationship diagram looks at entities and their relationships from an overall perspective. So it is a strategic or top-down way of viewing the organisation and developing a database model. Normalisation, the technique detailed in chapter 4, is the bottom-up view of designing a database. In reality, when designing databases, both techniques will be used. The entity-relationship diagrams ensure that upper-level strategic objectives of the organisation are included in the database model. So the materials in this chapter are valuable in their own right, even without normalisation. However, normalisation ensures that the lower-level operational aspects are included in the database model as the normalisation process starts with the tables, forms and data of the organisation. Once each technique is applied, they are reconciled to ensure an organisation-wide database model is created that includes strategic objectives as well as operational data.

Once the table structure is defined, normalisation is used to assign attributes to entities. **Normalisation** is the process of assigning attributes to entities to eliminate repeating groups and data redundancies. The goal is to form tables representing entities that promote structural and data independence. Therefore, normalisation maximises the efficiency of the structure. Given that many table structures will provide the information required by the organisation's E-R diagrams, normalisation maximises the efficiency of the structure by reducing data redundancies, eliminating data anomalies and producing a set of **controlled redundancies** to link tables that provide the most flexible system for the organisation.

Chapter 4 will take a table and illustrate both the need for normalisation and the normalisation process. Following discussion on the data redundancy problems of the table, normalisation will be applied to come up with a solution that resolves those problems. Note that there are a number of forms of normalisation from first normal form (1NF) to fifth normal form (5NF), with a special case of 3NF, so six normal forms altogether. However, we will only concentrate up to third normal form (3NF) as this is all that business applications require. Each of the first three forms of normalisation is explained in the next chapter.

*Normalisation* A set of rules and a process of assigning attributes to entities to eliminate repeating groups and data redundancies, and form tables representing entities that promote structural and data independence.

*Controlled redundancies* Redundancies that are allowed for the convenience of structuring data, data manipulation or reporting.

## ›› SUMMARY ›››

**What is the role of databases in decision making and reporting systems?**
Company managers and employees require good information to make strategic and operational decisions. Information is only accurate, timely and relevant if data are captured, stored and managed efficiently and effectively in a database. Database concepts such as database modelling, design and implementation help to capture, store, manage and manipulate data efficiently and effectively.

LEARNING OBJECTIVE **2**

**What is the function of a database and the concept of database systems?**
A relational database is a collection of tables and each table describes an entity about which you want to record data. A table is a collection of columns or attributes that describe an entity. A record is a row in a table that describes one occurrence of an entity. Every table in a database must have a unique primary key, which is an attribute that uniquely identifies a particular row in a table.

LEARNING OBJECTIVE **3**

**What is the concept of data redundancy and the advantage of a database?**
When data such as the address of a customer is repeated in a database, database redundancy has occurred. This means that the address of the customer needs to be updated in multiple locations. The advantage of a database is that data can be structured in such a way that the customer address appears only once in the database. It therefore needs to be updated only once in the database should it change and so is always up to date.

LEARNING OBJECTIVE **4**

**What are database models, and, in particular, what is the relational database?**
A database system is a collection of elements that allow the capture, storage, management and use of data within a database environment. These elements include hardware, software,

people, procedures and data. In general, data are stored in a central location in computer and storage hardware that is managed by software that incorporates a DBMS. Database administrators and programmers establish procedures or business rules for the organisation to collect, store, manage and use the data for decision making and reporting.

LEARNING OBJECTIVE  **What is database modelling and how are models developed using entity-relationship diagrams?**
Database modelling involves developing conceptual models that provide a logical representation, in graphical form, of the complexities of real-world data structures. A database designer can also depict the data structures, relations, characteristics and constraints of the database designs. A database model is a communication tool that creates improved understanding of an organisation's database, or provides the blueprint for developing new database structures. Database modelling is the first step before designing and implementing a database and uses E-R diagrams to develop the blueprint.

LEARNING OBJECTIVE  **How do the relationships in a database model reflect how an organisation works?**
The conceptual database models or E-R diagrams can be read from left to right and vice versa to find out how the relationships in the database work. This understanding can be compared to how the organisation works to ensure a match.

## KEY TERMS

attributes, p. 122
cardinality, p. 122
client, p. 114
client–server system, p. 120
composite key, p. 110
conceptual models, p. 117
controlled redundancies, p. 137
data, p. 107
data anomalies, p. 113
data integrity, p. 113
data redundancy, p. 112
database, p. 108
database administrator, p. 117
database models, p. 117
database management system (DBMS), p. 114
database system, p. 114
deletion anomalies, p. 113
entities, p. 122
entity-relationship model, p. 121
field, p. 109
file, p. 109

foreign key, p. 129
hardware, p. 114
implementation models, p. 117
information, p. 107
insertion anomalies, p. 113
logical representation, p. 117
many-to-many relationships (N:M), p. 128
modification anomalies, p. 113
normalisation, p. 137
one-to-many relationships (1:N), p. 127
one-to-one relationship (1:1), p. 128
operating system, p. 114
physical representation, p. 117
primary key, p. 110
procedures, p. 115
relational database, p. 108
record, p. 109
server, p. 114
software, p. 114
structural independence, p. 119
structured query language (SQL), p. 117
table, p. 108

## DISCUSSION QUESTIONS

3.1 What advantages do databases offer for decision-making and reporting processes? (LO1)

3.2 Define the operation of a relational database. Why has it taken over as the optimal structure to implement in organisations? (LO2, LO4)

3.3 How do the characteristics of poor file system design limit their usefulness for decision making and reporting? (LO3)

3.4 Describe the elements of a database system, including the DBMS. (LO4)

3.5 Explain why database modelling is performed. How is it performed? (LO5)

## SELF-TEST ACTIVITIES

3.1 Which of the following statements is false?
- (a) Good decision making and reporting are vital for organisational performance.
- (b) Good decision making and reporting require accurate information.
- (c) Accurate information comes from quality data capture, storage and use.
- (d) None of the above.

3.2 The limitations of poor file systems come from:
- (a) data management.
- (b) structural independence.
- (c) database redundancy.
- (d) all of the above.

3.3 Which of the following statements is true?
- (a) Implementation models show how the data are represented in the database.
- (b) Conceptual models focus on what is represented in the database.
- (c) Implementation and conceptual models can be either logical or physical.
- (d) All of the above.

3.4 The advantage of a relational database is:
- (a) structural dependence.
- (b) its powerful and flexible query language.
- (c) a data dictionary.
- (d) all of the above.

3.5 Database modelling is used for:
- (a) describing and representing complex real-world data structures.
- (b) improving understanding of an organisation's existing database.
- (c) providing a blueprint for developing new database structures.
- (d) all of the above.

3.6 Which of the following is a step to developing an E-R diagram?
- (a) Develop a general narrative of a business's operations.
- (b) Construct a working version of the E-R diagram for review by the business.
- (c) Make the necessary modifications for newly discovered entities or relationships.
- (d) All of the above.

3.7 Which of the following statements is true?
- (a) Normalisation should eliminate all redundancies every time.
- (b) Controlled redundancies should not be allowed in database design.
- (c) Data anomalies cause data integrity problems.
- (d) All of the above.

## PROBLEMS

3.1 'My manager wants to make important strategic and operational decisions for the company, but complains about the quality of information from the files. I tell him or her that he or she needs to understand some database concepts and invest in a database.' Do you agree? Provide reasons.

3.2 No More Smelly Shoes is a large manufacturer of children's school and sports shoes. The organisation runs a file system. The following is an extract of its sales file.
- (a) Discuss the limitations of this file.
- (b) Explain how a database would overcome these limitations.
- (c) Illustrate your explanation by developing a database design.

| Customer_name | Customer_address | Customer_phone | Salesperson | Shoe_model | Shoe_amount | Date |
|---|---|---|---|---|---|---|
| Britney Considine | 2 Apple Street, Melbourne, VIC | 03 1234 5678 | TLM | VZ4717 | $29.90 | 20-Jul-08 |
| Michelle Lee | 6 Organic Street, Melbourne, VIC | 03 9876 4321 | CBD | DF3966 | $79.50 | 30-Jul-08 |
| Phillipa Collier | 8 Grapefruit Street, Melbourne, VIC | 03 5678 3456 | MTL | WE9447 | $50.30 | 4-Aug-08 |
| Devine Smith | 3 Echo Street, Melbourne, VIC | 03 2376 1048 | JFK | XC8187 | $45.50 | 6-Oct-08 |

3.3 Best Bikes is a large bicycle retailer that also manufactures its own brand, assembles made-to-order bicycles from purchased components and sells fully assembled branded names. You have been employed as a consultant to Best Bikes. Answer the following three questions.
  (a) What databases are available to help Best Bikes capture, store, manage and manipulate data for decision making and reporting?
  (b) How do these databases operate?
  (c) What are their advantages and disadvantages?

3.4 Beautiful Flowers Company has been running an outdated file system for many years. It has just employed you as a consultant to advise it on updating its file system to a database. It knows that the initial stages before implementation involve database modelling and database design but does not understand their implications.
  (a) Explain to Beautiful Flowers Company the objectives of database modelling in its situation.
  (b) Discuss the role and development of E-R diagrams in database modelling.
  (c) Explain to the company how database design will be conducted including the function of normalisation.

3.5 Using the tables provided below relating to customer and salespersons:
  (a) Prepare entity-relationship diagrams to model the relationships between sales person and customer as one-to-one (1:1), one-to-many (1:N) and many-to-many (N:M).
  (b) Discuss and provide relationship sentences for each of the models.
  (c) Implement the relationships on the entity-relationship diagram with primary and foreign keys.
  (d) Which relationship between salesperson and customer do you think would be the most common for a business to have? Give reasons why.

| Table: Salesperson | | | | |
|---|---|---|---|---|
| Salesperson_ID | Last Name | First Name | Address | Telephone |
| | | | | |

| Table: Customer | | | |
|---|---|---|---|
| Customer_ID | Last Name | First Name | Telephone |
| | | | |

3.6 Using the following entity-relationship diagram for the partial order entry system.
   (a) Write relationship sentences for all of the relationships.
   (b) Discuss what each of the relationships mean in terms of how the business works.
   (c) Does the business allow partial picks (i.e. only part of the goods on the sales order to be picked)?
   (d) Does the business allow partial shipments (i.e. only part of the goods that have been picked to be shipped)?
   (e) Are all shipments invoiced in full or partially (i.e. does the business allow partial invoices)?

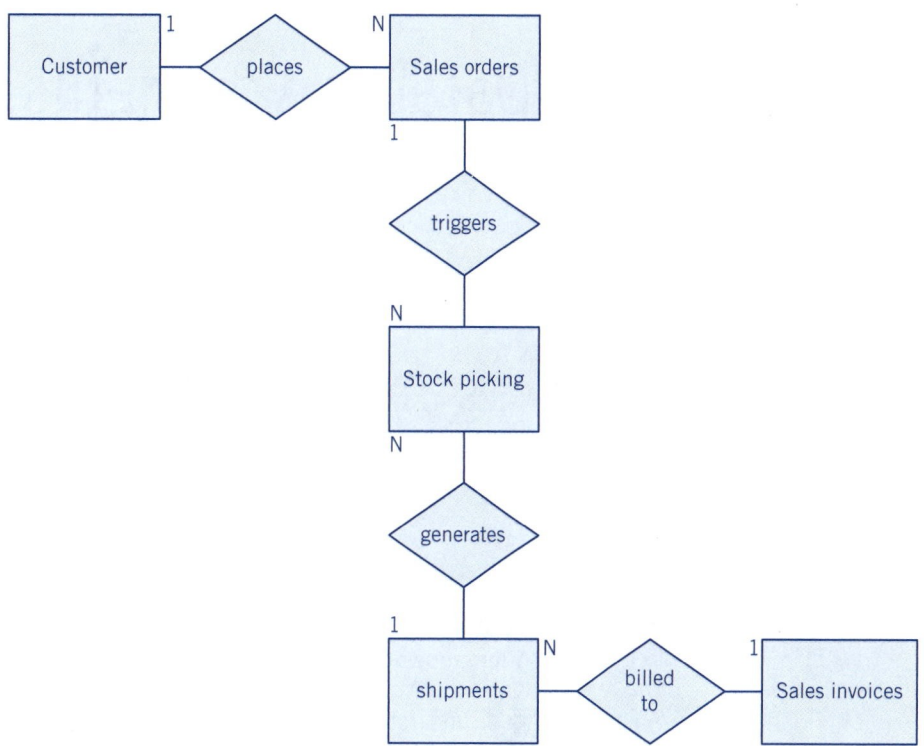

## FURTHER READING

Chen, PPS 1976, 'The entity-relationship model: toward a unified view of data', *ACM Transactions on Database Systems*, vol. 1, no. 1, pp. 9–36.

Codd, EF 1990, *The relational database for database management*, Addison-Wesley, Reading, Massachusetts.

Post, GV 2002, Database management systems: designing and building business applications, 2nd edn, McGraw-Hill, New York.

Rob, P & Coronel, C 2002, *Database systems: design, implementation, and management*, 5th edn, Course Technology, Thomson Learning, Cambridge, Massachusetts.

## SELF–TEST ANSWERS

3.1 d, 3.2 a, 3.3 d, 3.4 b, 3.5 d, 3.6 d, 3.7 c.

# 4

# Database concepts II

## Learning objectives

After studying this chapter, you should be able to:

**1** understand and apply the process of normalisation to achieve efficient database designs

**2** understand the different ways a business works and how this reflects in different data structures

**3** construct an enterprise model of a business using entity-relationship modelling and normalisation

**4** discuss the REA (resources–events–agents) Accounting Model as a template for modelling accounting systems

**5** understand the differences between REA and entity-relationship modelling

**6** discuss the technologies relating to database implementation.

# Introduction

Chapter 3 discussed the concept, importance and benefits of databases. To achieve these benefits, databases need to be designed to reflect how an organisation works. Database design for corporate activities is a highly technical activity performed by information systems experts. As an accountant, however, you need to be aware of the process these experts perform and how to check that the outcomes reflect how your organisation works. For a small system, you will need to ensure that the database structures correctly remove insertion, deletion and addition anomalies.

One way of designing databases is from the top down using entity-relationship or E-R modelling. This was illustrated in chapter 3. A second way of designing databases is from the bottom up using normalisation. In designing databases, organisations generally use both methods. This chapter covers the bottom-up method using the technique of normalisation. Normalisation, much like E-R modelling, only occurs in conjunction with the relational database. When we turn to the enterprise view in this chapter we will see how the output of both methods (E-R modelling and normalisation) is combined and reconciled to form an enterprise model.

Overall, we need to build database models that are conceptual and provide a logical representation, in graphical form, of the complexities of real-world data structures. Database models show us how an organisation works, that is, the business rules that apply to the organisation. A database designer also depicts the data structures, relationships, characteristics and constraints of their own database designs. A database model is a communication tool that promotes improved understanding of an organisation's database, or provides the blueprint for developing new database structures. Database modelling is the first step before designing and implementing a database, and uses entity-relationship diagrams (E-R diagrams).

Designing a database requires taking the database model and creating tables to represent every entity that is important to the processes of the organisation, including all internal and external entities. Once the table structure is defined, normalisation is used.

Normalisation is the process of assigning attributes to entities. The goal is to form tables that promote structural and data independence. In this way, normalisation enables us to create tables that are free from data anomalies and redundancies. Therefore, normalisation maximises the efficiency of the structure. There are a number of forms of normalisation from first normal form (1NF) to fifth normal form (5NF). However, we will only continue to third normal form, which is sufficient for most business applications.

The normalisation examples follow much the same format as in chapter 3. The first table to normalise is called example A; it has data attributes that reflect how the business works. The underlying data is then changed several times to become the normalised examples B, C and D. These examples can be compared, as the attributes in each of the tables is the same, but the normalisation process produces very different results.

After the normalisation process is covered, a full implementation model for an enterprise will be developed. Also discussed in this chapter is the REA (resources–events–agents) Accounting Model as a template for developing database models that can be used for an accounting information system. The chapter concludes with a discussion of the technologies relating to database implementation.

## TOP-DOWN VERSUS BOTTOM–UP DATABASE DESIGN

As discussed in chapter 3, an E-R diagram presents the top-down view of an organisation from the manager's overall perspective. The technique for normalisation looks at the bottom-up view of designing a database. It is important to note, however, that in reality when designing databases both techniques will be used. Entity-relationship diagrams ensure that the upper-level view of the organisation is included in the database model. Normalisation ensures all of the lower-level operational aspects are also included, as normalisation starts with the tables, forms and data of the organisation. Once each technique is applied, they are reconciled to ensure that an organisation-wide database model is created that includes the upper level view as well as the operational data.

Once the table structure is defined, normalisation is used. **Normalisation** is the process of assigning attributes to entities to eliminate repeating groups and data redundancies. The goal is to form tables that promote structural and data independence. Given that many table structures will provide the data required by the organisation's E-R diagrams, normalisation maximises the efficiency of the structure by reducing data redundancies, eliminating data anomalies and producing a set of **controlled redundancies** to link tables that provide the most flexible system for the organisation.

In this chapter, we will take a table and illustrate both the need for normalisation and the normalisation process. Note that in our illustration we will address a number of forms of normalisation, from first normal form (1NF) to third normal form (3NF).

**LEARNING OBJECTIVE 1**

*Understand and apply the process of normalisation to achieve efficient database designs.*

## NORMALISATION AND DATABASE DESIGN

The process of normalisation has three outcomes and three actions or steps to achieve those outcomes.

1. First normal form
   *Outcome:* A table has no repeating groups.[1]
   *Action:* Select a primary key that uniquely identifies each line in the table.
2. Second normal form
   *Outcome:* A table is in first normal form and has no partial dependencies. A partial dependency is where the attribute is not wholly dependent on the primary key but on part of it.
   *Action:* Draw dependency arrows. Remove partial dependencies and make the attributes fully dependent on their primary keys.
3. Third normal form
   *Outcome:* A table is in second normal form and has no transitive dependencies. A transitive dependency is where an attribute is dependent on the primary key but via a non-key attribute.
   *Action:* Remove transitive dependencies by making the non-key attribute that an attribute is dependent on a primary key in a new table with the attribute. Also leave the non-key attribute as a foreign key in the existing table so the attribute is dependent on the primary key but via a non-key attribute.

To illustrate these steps and the benefits of normalisation, table 4.1 has been created to represent the worst way of recording data. That is, entities and their attributes have been combined without regard for relationships.

Figure 4.1 is an example of a table that was constructed by a consulting organisation to track its client projects. The consulting organisation's employees are attached to one or more client projects, their charge-out rate, the number of hours they have spent on each of the projects and their phone number. The organisation's objective is to be able to cost each client project for billing purposes.

Although it may be possible to calculate the charges associated with each project, extracting information from the table is difficult. For example, calculating the charge for each project is a matter of inserting another column and multiplying Job_chg_hr by Proj_hrs. What if you want to work out the billings of each of the organisation's employees (e.g. Michael Lee, Brett Considine and Phil Collier)? What if you want to reassign an employee to a different project but retain the hours that the person has already billed, even after the reassignment (e.g. Michael Lee to Project 3)? What if you want to change the contact details for an employee (e.g. Michael Lee)? The lack of flexibility in this table makes it difficult to answer any of these questions because the table was designed primarily with one question in mind. That is, how long each employee has worked on a project. The difficulties with this table are similar to those that plagued older file systems, namely, data management issues, structural and data dependence, and data redundancies.

| Proj_num | Proj_name | Emp_num | Emp_name | Job_code | Job_chg_hr | Proj_hrs | Emp_phone |
|---|---|---|---|---|---|---|---|
| 1 | Rain | 101 | Michael Lee | EE | $170 | 13.3 | 03 1234 5678 |
| 1 | Rain | 105 | Brett Considine | CT | $120 | 16.2 | 03 2345 6789 |
| 1 | Rain | 110 | Phil Collier | CT | $120 | 14.3 | 03 4321 0987 |
| 2 | Hail | 101 | Michael Lee | EE | $170 | 19.8 | 03 1234 5678 |
| 2 | Hail | 108 | David Smith | EE | $170 | 17.5 | 03 3456 7890 |
| 3 | Flood | 110 | Phil Collier | CT | $120 | 11.6 | 03 4321 0987 |
| 3 | Flood | 105 | Brett Considine | CT | $120 | 23.4 | 03 2345 6789 |
| 3 | Flood | 123 | Michael Davern | EE | $170 | 19.1 | 03 4567 1234 |
| 3 | Flood | 112 | Anne Wyatt | BE | $170 | 20.7 | 03 3456 4567 |

**FIGURE 4.1** A table used by a consulting organisation to track client projects

More formally, the redundancies can be described as follows:
- There are repeating groups in the table. That is, when an employee is assigned to a project, there is unnecessary repetition. The repeating groups are Proj_name, Proj_num, Emp_num, Emp_name, Job_code, and Emp_phone. This redundancy causes addition, update and deletion anomalies as described in the following three points.
- There are addition anomalies. When you want to add a new employee's details, their Emp_num, Emp_name, Job_code and Emp_phone need to be entered. You cannot add these details without having an employee assigned to a project; therefore, you must have a Proj_name and Proj_num before you can enter the employee into the table.
- There are update anomalies. For example, modifying Emp_name requires many alterations. If Michael Lee wanted to change his name to Michael Lee Majors, this would require alterations to all the projects that Michael has worked on. Aside from the unproductive consequences of repetition, there are increased chances of errors.

- There are deletion anomalies. For example, if Emp_num 101 decides to resign from the consulting organisation, vital data are lost. This is because Emp_num 101 has worked on Job_code EE, and deleting the employee from the table will prevent his hours from being charged to the project. This will understate the consultancy's total costs and lead to undercharging the client.
- There are data integrity problems. The table allows for spelling and typographical errors. For example, Michael Lee may be spelt Michelle Lee on a different row in the table.

These items of data redundancy were described in chapter 3. The process of normalisation can be applied to the table to eliminate data redundancies as shown in the following section.

## Database tables and normalisation

Normalisation involves several objectives as follows that together produce a set of related database tables:

1. Reduce or eliminate repeating groups.
2. Reduce or eliminate data anomalies.
3. Reduce or eliminate data redundancies.
4. Form or organise entities and tables that have structural and data independence.

The normalisation process to achieve these objectives is about defining and reorganising the data so that each entity (table) contains only the attributes of that entity. For example, the employee table would contain only details of the employees, and not the details of the projects the employees work on. Different forms of normalisation can be applied to data. Lower normal forms *reduce* repeating groups, data anomalies and data redundancies, while higher normal forms *eliminate* these groups, anomalies and redundancies. It should be noted that the highest form of normalisation is not always the best table structure. Sometimes controlled redundancies via lower forms of normalisation allow for more convenient and quicker structuring, manipulating or reporting.

The first three normal forms will be explained and applied to the table in figure 4.1. The normal forms beyond these three will be briefly mentioned. The essence of normalisation is to split the data into several tables, which are connected to one another based on the data within them. This saves space; minimises duplication, anomalies and redundancies; protects the data to ensure consistency; and provides faster transactions because there are fewer data items. For example, an employee's details are only recorded once in a database, not in each row of each project they work on. Before illustrating the normalisation process, some definitions need to be recapped.

## Definitions

As discussed in chapter 3, a **relational database** is a collection of carefully defined tables. A **table** is a collection of columns or **attributes** or **fields** that describe an **entity** (or something you wish to record data about in a database). Individual objects are stored as rows or **records** within the table. The table in figure 4.1 (page 145) could represent the entity 'client projects' for a consulting company. An important aspect of the relational database is that the tables must be carefully defined to provide flexibility with minimum problems. A list of synonyms is included in table 4.1 to remind you of the differing terms used interchangeably in database discussions.

**Relational database** *A database that stores data in a number of tables.*

**Table** *A collection of columns (attributes) and rows (objects) that describe an entity.*

**Attributes** *Characteristics of entities.*

**Field** *A characteristic of a record that contains data that have a specific meaning.*

**Entities** *Representations of real-world things or objects that correspond to a table in a relational database.*

**Record** *A connected set of fields that describes a person, place or thing.*

**TABLE 4.1** Synonyms used in database discussions

| Name | Synonym |
| --- | --- |
| Table | Entity, entity occurrence |
| Row | Record, tuple |
| Attribute | Field, column |

**Primary key** *An attribute (or column) that uniquely identifies a particular object (or row).*

Every table must have a **primary key**, which is an attribute (or column) that uniquely identifies a particular object (or row) in the table. Also remember that it is better that primary keys are numeric because they are likely to be unique, short and unchanging, whereas a project name, for example, can be duplicated. The uniqueness of the number relies on the organisation assigning a unique number to each project — it could do the same with the name, but it could become difficult over time to come up with different names. However, alphanumeric combinations — letters in combination with numbers, such as passport numbers — have many more possible combinations and are therefore appropriate primary keys. The relationship between the primary key and the rest of the data will be one-to-one; that is, each entry for a primary key points to exactly one project row. Therefore, the most important issue with a primary key is that it is unique and can never point to more than one object (or row) in a table.

**Composite key** *A combination of more than one primary key. It indicates an M:N (many-to-many) relationship between the columns.*

In many cases a table will use more than one column as part of the primary key. These are called **composite keys**. In such cases, one primary key is composed of multiple attributes; a sufficient number of attributes to uniquely identify each line in the table.

## First normal form

Figure 4.1 (page 145) will be used as the starting point to illustrate the first normal form of normalisation. This table shows the projects that employees work on. With no primary keys chosen, figure 4.1 is in 0 normal form (0NF). From zero normal form we need to move to first normal form. The *first normal form* (1NF) outcome states that we need the table to have no repeating items. That is, for each cell in a table (the intersection of one row and one column), there can only be one value. This value should not be able to be decomposed into smaller pieces. Therefore, to achieve no repeating groups we need to choose a primary key that uniquely identifies each line in the table.

Take a look at figure 4.1. If we consider using a project number that relates to a project name as the primary key, we can see that project number 1 will not uniquely identify one line in the table. Rather, it will identify three lines. So it is not a satisfactory primary key. If we consider using an employee number as a primary key, for employee number 101 we will have two rows. However, the primary key of project number and employee number combined is sufficient, as with each project number, employee number combination only one line on the table is returned. For example, project number 1, employee number 101 returns only one line; project number 2, employee number 101 returns only one different line. In summary, this table should have two attributes as a primary key: Proj_num and Emp_num, as the table is designed to show which employees are engaged on each project. Each employee (Emp_num) can be engaged on many projects (Proj_num). For instance, Emp_num 101 appears on project numbers 1 and 2. Because each employee can appear on many different projects, Proj_num must be part of the primary key. Similarly, each project can engage many employees (e.g. Proj_num 1 has three employees). Since each project can have many employees, Emp_num must also be part of the primary key. Whenever there is an M:N (many-to-many) relationship, a composite key is required. The combination of Proj_num and Emp_num as primary key is known as a composite key. As discussed in chapter 3, a composite key can also be called a concatenated key as the composite key is comprised of two or more attributes together (the word concatenate means to put together).

Primary and composite keys must be properly defined for the normalisation process. The choice of primary key depends on the 1:M and M:N relationships within the organisation. Figure 4.2 shows the table from figure 4.1 in first normal form (1NF). Figure 4.2 differs from figure 4.1 by the underlining of Proj_num and Emp_num, the primary key.

| Proj_num | Proj_name | Emp_num | Emp_name | Job_code | Job_chg_hr | Proj_hrs | Emp_phone |
|---|---|---|---|---|---|---|---|
| 1 | Rain | 101 | Michael Lee | EE | $170 | 13.3 | 03 1234 5678 |
| 1 | Rain | 105 | Brett Considine | CT | $120 | 16.2 | 03 2345 6789 |
| 1 | Rain | 110 | Phil Collier | CT | $120 | 14.3 | 03 4321 0987 |
| 2 | Hail | 101 | Michael Lee | EE | $170 | 19.8 | 03 1234 5678 |
| 2 | Hail | 108 | David Smith | EE | $170 | 17.5 | 03 3456 7890 |
| 3 | Flood | 110 | Phil Collier | CT | $120 | 11.6 | 03 4321 0987 |
| 3 | Flood | 105 | Brett Considine | CT | $120 | 23.4 | 03 2345 6789 |
| 3 | Flood | 123 | Michael Davern | EE | $170 | 19.1 | 03 4567 1234 |
| 3 | Flood | 112 | Anne Wyatt | BE | $170 | 20.7 | 03 3456 4567 |

**FIGURE 4.2** A table used by a consulting organisation to track client projects in first normal form (1NF)

We could also display the table, as in figure 4.3 below, showing only the attributes and the primary key (i.e. the table header row), but excluding the data. The data is useful in that you can see how attributes within the table are related. The primary key is underlined as previously discussed. The second part of the figure shows a different format.

| Proj_num | Proj_name | Emp_num | Emp_name | Job_code | Job_chg_hr | Proj_hrs | Emp_phone |
|---|---|---|---|---|---|---|---|

OR

**First normal form (1NF)**

Proj_num, Proj_name, Emp_num, Emp_name, Job_code, Job_chg_hr, Proj_hrs, Emp_phone

**FIGURE 4.3** A table used by a consulting organisation to track client projects in first normal form (1NF)

## Second normal form

A table is in *second normal form* (2NF) if it is in 1NF and does not contain any partial dependencies. To convert figure 4.2 to 2NF we need to remove the partial dependencies. To do this we need to first determine the dependencies. Figure 4.4 shows the table from figure 4.2 with the first dependency arrow drawn on it. The process of identifying dependencies looks at each non-key attribute and what it is dependent on. Since Proj_num and Emp_num are both a part of the primary key they are not considered when we are looking at dependency on the primary key (as they are the primary key). Therefore, the first attribute we consider is Proj_name. Proj_name is the project name and we need to consider what this is dependent on. For example, if I had the Proj_num, could you give me the project name? The answer is yes: Proj_num 1 would give us Proj_name Rain; Proj_num 2 would give us Proj_name Hail and so on. Therefore, the project name is dependent on the project number, as one project number gives us one project name. This is shown in figure 4.4 with the arrow pointing from the Proj_name column to the part of the primary key it is dependent on: Proj_num. So, Proj_name is a partial dependency: it is only dependent on Proj_num, which is part of the primary key. (Remember, the primary key in this case is a composite key consisting of both Proj_num and Emp_num.) We will refer to figure 4.4 as Example A. Example A will relate to the data from figure 4.2. Later in the discussion, we will change the data and illustrate the normalisation process for examples B, C and D. This will enable us to understand how different data can result in different database structures.

| Proj_num | Proj_name | Emp_num | Emp_name | Job_code | Job_chg_hr | Proj_hrs | Emp_phone |
|----------|-----------|---------|----------------|----------|------------|----------|--------------|
| 1 | Rain | 101 | Michael Lee | EE | $170 | 13.3 | 03 1234 5678 |
| 1 | Rain | 105 | Brett Considine | CT | $120 | 16.2 | 03 2345 6789 |
| 1 | Rain | 110 | Phil Collier | CT | $120 | 14.3 | 03 4321 0987 |
| 2 | Hail | 101 | Michael Lee | EE | $170 | 19.8 | 03 1234 5678 |
| 2 | Hail | 108 | David Smith | EE | $170 | 17.5 | 03 3456 7890 |
| 3 | Flood | 110 | Phil Collier | CT | $120 | 11.6 | 03 4321 0987 |
| 3 | Flood | 105 | Brett Considine | CT | $120 | 23.4 | 03 2345 6789 |
| 3 | Flood | 123 | Michael Davern | EE | $170 | 19.1 | 03 4567 1234 |
| 3 | Flood | 112 | Anne Wyatt | BE | $170 | 20.7 | 03 3456 4567 |

**FIGURE 4.4** Example A — table used by a consulting organisation to track client projects in first normal form (1NF) with first dependency arrow

Continuing the process, we can see that Emp_name is dependent on Emp_num: one Emp_num can identify one employee name. For example, Emp_num 110 gives us the Emp_name Phil Collier. Next is the attribute Job_code, which is dependent on the employee number. That is, each Emp_num has only one Job_code. For example, Emp_num 101 returns Job_code EE. Next, Job_chg_hr depends on Job_code: all Job_code = EE are charged out at Job_chg_hr = $170. The next attribute is Proj_hrs, which depends on the employee and the time they have spent on the project, which depends on Proj_num and Emp_num. So, Proj_hours is actually dependent on the whole of the primary key. Lastly, the attribute Emp_phone is dependent on Emp_num, a part of the primary key. Figure 4.5 overleaf shows all of the dependencies discussed above.

| Proj_num | Proj_name | Emp_num | Emp_name | Job_code | Job_chg_hr | Proj_hrs | Emp_phone |
|---|---|---|---|---|---|---|---|
| 1 | Rain | 101 | Michael Lee | EE | $170 | 13.3 | 03 1234 5678 |
| 1 | Rain | 105 | Brett Considine | CT | $120 | 16.2 | 03 2345 6789 |
| 1 | Rain | 110 | Phil Collier | CT | $120 | 14.3 | 03 4321 0987 |
| 2 | Hail | 101 | Michael Lee | EE | $170 | 19.8 | 03 1234 5678 |
| 2 | Hail | 108 | David Smith | EE | $170 | 17.5 | 03 3456 7890 |
| 3 | Flood | 110 | Phil Collier | CT | $120 | 11.6 | 03 4321 0987 |
| 3 | Flood | 105 | Brett Considine | CT | $120 | 23.4 | 03 2345 6789 |
| 3 | Flood | 123 | Michael Davern | EE | $170 | 19.1 | 03 4567 1234 |
| 3 | Flood | 112 | Anne Wyatt | BE | $170 | 20.7 | 03 3456 4567 |

**FIGURE 4.5** Example A — table used by a consulting organisation to track client projects in first normal form (1NF) with dependency arrows

To convert figure 4.5 to second normal form (2NF), we need to remove the partial dependencies. To do this we list the primary key attributes severally and together as the primary key. We do not worry about whether the keys will have any attributes; they are required to join the tables together so cannot be eliminated. Listing the primary keys severally and together gives us three tables as shown in figure 4.6.

1. Project table:

   Proj_num

2. Employee table:

   Emp_num

3. Charge table:

   Proj_num, Emp_num

**FIGURE 4.6** Primary keys listed for consulting organisation

Each key will define a new table. The final step in 2NF is to link the dependent attributes to each of the keys as they are defined in the table. The example in the original table in figure 4.2 (page 148) will now be divided into three tables: project, employee and charge. This is shown in figure 4.7 overleaf.

1. Project table:
    <u>Proj_num</u>, Proj_name

2. Employee table:
    <u>Emp_num</u>, Emp_name, Emp_phone, Job_code, Job_chg_hr

3. Charge table:
    <u>Proj_num</u>, <u>Emp_num</u>, Proj_hrs

**FIGURE 4.7** Converting to second normal form (2NF)

Notice from the bottom of the table that finding the project charge is simply a matter of constructing a relevant composite entity with composite keys that include the Proj_hrs attribute of each Emp_num.

Therefore, project name (Proj_name) is now an attribute in the project table as it is dependent on project number. Employee name (Emp_name) and employee telephone number (Emp_phone) are now attributes of the employee table. As mentioned above, project hours (Proj_hrs), which relates to the amount of time the employee spends on a project, becomes the attribute of the table with the composite primary key of Proj_num, Emp_num. Finally, the job code (Job_code) is dependent on the employee number. Therefore, job code is shown as an attribute of employee number. The job charge hour (Job_chg_hr) in this case is dependent on the job code (Job_code) so we put it behind job code (Job_code) in the employee table.

Converting to 2NF adds further manipulation flexibility to the structure by allowing a project to involve a group of employees and their recorded hours. The second normal form solves several basic problems. It reduces duplication because there is no need to enter the employee data every time a new project is initiated. This also saves storage space because employee details no longer need to be allocated to every project. In second normal form, partial dependencies have now been removed. As the project name is now dependent on the project number primary key in the project table, project name is now fully dependent on its primary key. It is no longer partially dependent. When project name was in first normal form it had **partial dependency**, as it was dependent on part of a composite primary key (Proj_num, Emp_num). In figure 4.7, only Proj_num is needed to determine Proj_name. Similarly, in the employee table, only Emp_num is needed to find Emp_name, Job_code and Job_chg_hr. The charge table and both Proj_num and Emp_num are needed to see which employee numbers (Emp_num) are engaged on which projects (Proj_num).

**Partial dependency** *A dependency based on only part of a composite primary key.*

## Third normal form

A table is said to be in *third normal form* (3NF) if it is in 2NF and it contains no transitive dependencies. Figure 4.8 contains the original dependency from job charge hour to job code from figure 4.5. A **transitive dependency** occurs where one attribute is dependent on another, but neither is part of the primary key. Therefore, an attribute is dependent on the primary key but via a non-key attribute. These dependencies can contain further anomalies. In figure 4.8 overleaf, Job_chg_hr is dependent on Job_code

**Transitive dependency** *A dependency that occurs when one attribute is dependent on another, but neither is part of a primary key.*

and Job_code is dependent on Emp_num. Therefore, we can see there is a transitive dependency: Job_chg_hr is dependent on Emp_num but via a non-key attribute, Job_code. To transform it into third normal form we need to remove the transitive dependency.

**FIGURE 4.8** Example A — second normal form (2NF) with dependency arrows

Figure 4.9 shows the tables in third normal form. The project table and charge table from figure 4.8 have remained the same. The employee table, however, has been changed to remove the transitive dependency.

In particular, Job_code has now become a **foreign key** in the employee table. A foreign key requires a primary key elsewhere in the design. Job_code is also a primary key in its own table with an attribute Job_chg_hr. Job_chg_hr is completely dependent on its primary key, Job_code. Remember that primary keys are underlined with a hard line. Foreign keys are underlined with a dashed line.

**Foreign key** *An attribute whose values must match the primary key in another table.*

**FIGURE 4.9** Example A — converting to third normal form (3NF)

By creating a fourth table, job code, and assigning Job_code as a primary key, we have made a fully flexible database that can capture almost all of the business structures and rules of the organisation, as well as answer almost any question that can be asked of the data.

Not only can we have many projects and employees, we can update the charge code for any job code in one place, and we can record the time spent by employees on each of the projects they work on. Note that the charge table will always have a composite key signifying the M:N relationship among projects and employees. If the business wanted to create a new charge-out rate, it would simply create a new Job_code, enter the new Job_chg_hr, and apply it to the project and employee in the project charge table. Changes to employee phone numbers can be made in one location on the employee table; project names can also be changed in one location on the project table.

What is more, finding out which projects each employee is working on and how many hours they spend on each is simply a matter of making small changes to the database structure. For example, a table could be constructed to show each employee's total billings.

The normalised structure removes update, deletion and modification anomalies. Further, the normalised structure, as a bottom-up approach, can be used to generate an E-R diagram. This is illustrated in the next section and is a similar process to the top-down approach outlined in chapter 3.

## Relating the normalised tables

Converting from a normalised structure to an E-R diagram is done using the following process. The structure from figure 4.9 shows a project table with Proj_num and Proj_name, and a charge table with Proj_num, Emp_num and Proj_hrs. The relationship between the project table and the charge table is that Proj_num in the project table can relate to many occurrences of Proj_num, Emp_num in the charge table. However, one occurrence in the charge table, Proj_num, Emp_num, relates to one line in the project table. Therefore, the relationship between the project table and the charge table is a **one-to-many relationship**. As discussed in chapter 3, the tables are not physically connected; instead, the connections exist through the matching of data stored in each table.

*One-to-many relationship (1:N)* A relationship between two entities in which the cardinality of one entity in the relationship is one and the other entity's cardinality is many.

Likewise, the employee table from figure 4.9 contains Emp_num, Emp_name, Emp_phone and Job_code, and the charge table contains Proj_num, Emp_num and Proj_hrs. The relationship between the employee table and the charge table is that Emp_num in the employee table can relate to many occurrences of Proj_num, Emp_num in the charge table. However, one occurrence in the charge table, Proj_num, Emp_num, relates to one line in the employee table. Therefore, the relationship between the employee table and the charge table is one-to-many.

The job code table contains Job_code and Job_chg_hr, which can relate to many occurrences of Job_code in the employee table. However, one Job_code in the employee table relates to only one Job_code in the employee table. Therefore, this relationship is also one-to-many.

The E-R diagram for figure 4.9 is shown in figure 4.10.

In short, normalisation of the consulting organisation's table involved organising a number of tables that reflect each entity, with each table containing only the dependent attributes of those entities.

The process has reduced, and in some cases eliminated, the data redundancy problems of the original table (figure 4.1 on page 145). Further, it has introduced a level of flexibility to meet the information needs of the organisation that were not available in the original table structure. These design principles are critical for an efficient and fast-processing database.

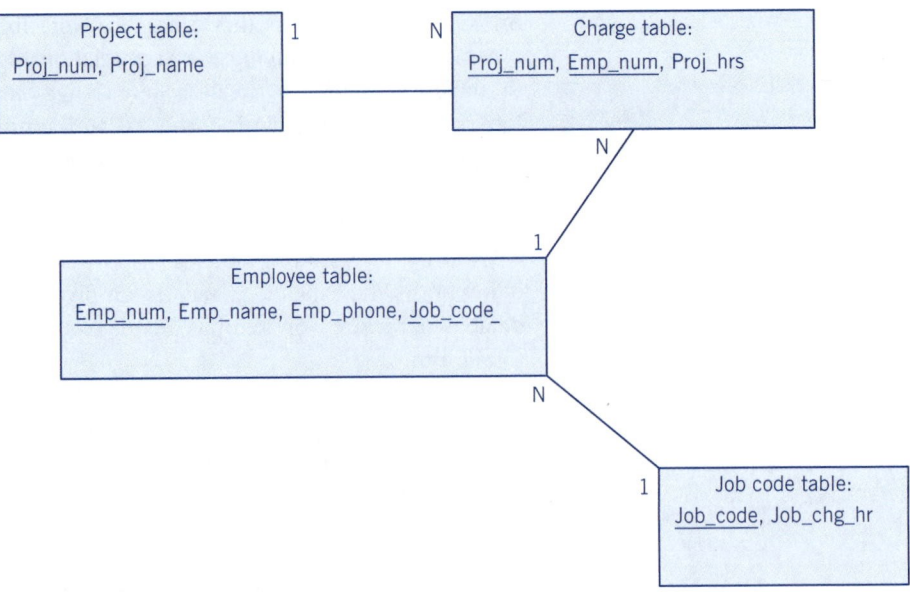

**FIGURE 4.10** Example A — E-R diagram used by a consulting organisation to track client projects in third normal form (3NF)

## Beyond 3NF

There are normalisation processes beyond 3NF. A special type of third normal form, Boyce-Codd normal form (BCNF), fourth normal form (4NF) and fifth normal form (5NF) are often not performed because the process usually requires artificial assumptions that rarely hold in the business environment. These assumptions may not be true all of the time and conducting this further normalisation, ironically, can reduce the flexibility that the first three normal forms are intended to achieve. As a result, explanation of the normalisation process beyond 3NF is omitted from this book.

## Further examples of normalisation

In figure 4.9 for Example A, we saw that the semantics (underlying logic) of the operation of the organisation is that each employee can only have one job code, and one job code relates to one charge-out rate. To illustrate a change of semantics, suppose you were to asked to design a database where each employee has different roles in the business, each of which is linked to a different charge-out rate. The current database design does not allow this. One change will be implemented at a time to illustrate the effect on how the business works. Firstly, we will look at the situation where many employees have the same job code at different charge-out rates. We will refer to this situation as Example B. Figure 4.11 shows this, highlighting employee numbers 101, 108 and 123 which all have job code EE with a charge-out rate of $170, $150 and $70 respectively. Since no primary keys have been chosen, figure 4.11 is in 0 normal form (0NF).

As discussed, the process of normalisation has three steps.

1. First normal form: select a primary key that uniquely identifies each line in the table.
2. Second normal form: first normal form and remove partial dependencies.
3. Third normal form: second normal form and remove transitive dependencies.

| Proj_num | Proj_name | Emp_num | Emp_name | Job_code | Job_chg_hr | Proj_hrs | Emp_phone |
|---|---|---|---|---|---|---|---|
| 1 | Rain | **101** | **Michael Lee** | **EE** | **$170** | 13.3 | 03 1234 5678 |
| 1 | Rain | 105 | Brett Considine | CT | $120 | 16.2 | 03 2345 6789 |
| 1 | Rain | 110 | Phil Collier | CT | $130 | 14.3 | 03 4321 0987 |
| 2 | Hail | **101** | **Michael Lee** | **EE** | **$170** | 19.8 | 03 1234 5678 |
| 2 | Hail | **108** | **David Smith** | **EE** | **$150** | 17.5 | 03 3456 7890 |
| 3 | Flood | 110 | Phil Collier | CT | $130 | 11.6 | 03 4321 0987 |
| 3 | Flood | 105 | Brett Considine | CT | $120 | 23.4 | 03 2345 6789 |
| 3 | Flood | **123** | **Michael Davern** | **EE** | **$70** | 19.1 | 03 4567 1234 |
| 3 | Flood | 112 | Anne Wyatt | BE | $170 | 20.7 | 03 3456 4567 |

**FIGURE 4.11** Example B — table used by a consulting organisation to track client projects in 0 normal form (ONF)

## First normal form

In selecting a primary key, we consider the minimum number of attributes needed to uniquely identify one record in the table. Proj_num and Emp_num are sufficient as a composite primary key to uniquely identify each line. The choice of primary key has not changed from the original case. The first normal form is shown in figure 4.12, with the primary key of Proj_num and Emp_num underlined.

| Proj_num | Proj_name | Emp_num | Emp_name | Job_code | Job_chg_hr | Proj_hrs | Emp_phone |
|---|---|---|---|---|---|---|---|
| 1 | Rain | **101** | **Michael Lee** | **EE** | **$170** | 13.3 | 03 1234 5678 |
| 1 | Rain | 105 | Brett Considine | CT | $120 | 16.2 | 03 2345 6789 |
| 1 | Rain | 110 | Phil Collier | CT | $130 | 14.3 | 03 4321 0987 |
| 2 | Hail | **101** | **Michael Lee** | **EE** | **$170** | 19.8 | 03 1234 5678 |
| 2 | Hail | **108** | **David Smith** | **EE** | **$150** | 17.5 | 03 3456 7890 |
| 3 | Flood | 110 | Phil Collier | CT | $130 | 11.6 | 03 4321 0987 |
| 3 | Flood | 105 | Brett Considine | CT | $120 | 23.4 | 03 2345 6789 |
| 3 | Flood | **123** | **Michael Davern** | **EE** | **$70** | 19.1 | 03 4567 1234 |
| 3 | Flood | 112 | Anne Wyatt | BE | $170 | 20.7 | 03 3456 4567 |

**FIGURE 4.12** Example B — table used by a consulting organisation to track client projects in first normal form (1NF)

## Second normal form

To convert the table to second normal form we need to remove the partial dependencies. To do this we first identify the dependencies, as shown in figure 4.13 overleaf. Note the differences from the dependencies illustrated in figure 4.5 (page 150), our original case. In particular, note the difference in the job charge hour. In figure 4.5 this was dependent on the job code as all job code EE were charged out at the same rate, $170. In this case, Job_chg_hr is $170 for Emp_num 101 on Job_code EE; whereas, Job_chg_hr is $150 for Emp_num 108 on Job_code EE. The job charge hour now is not dependent on the job code but on the level of expertise of the individual employee, so Job_chg_hr is now dependent on Emp_num.

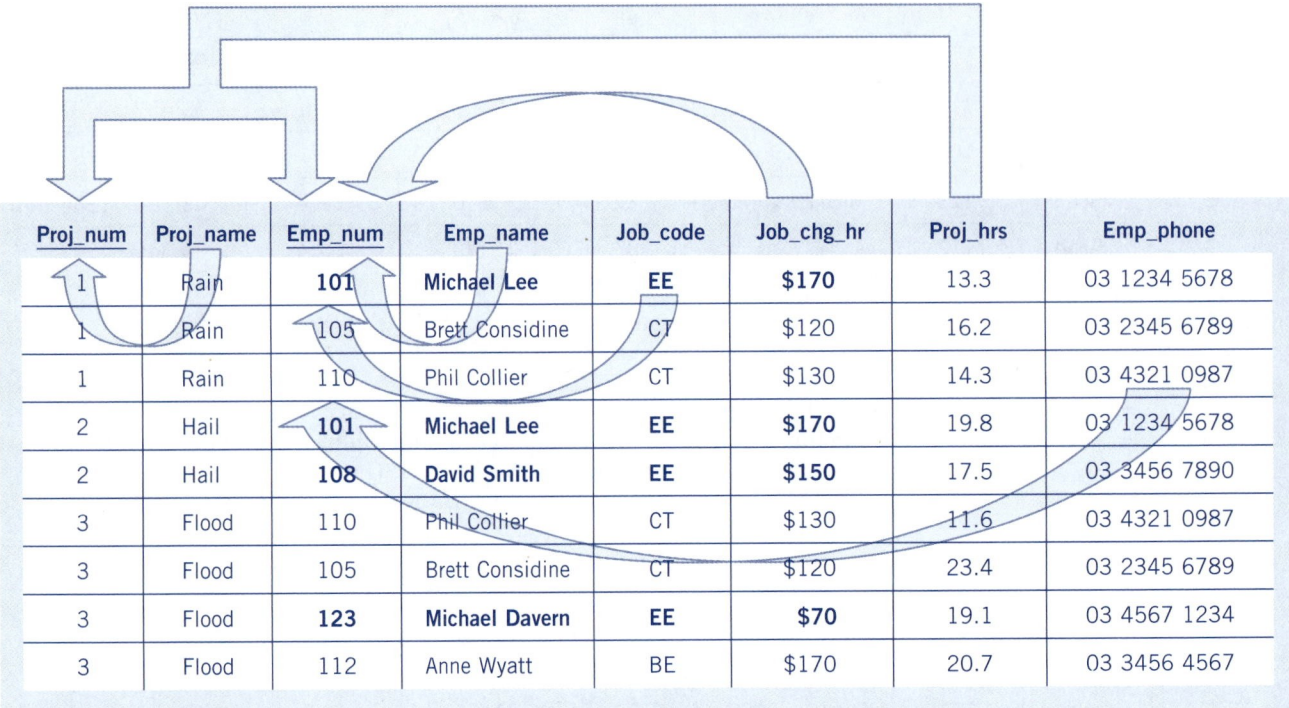

| Proj_num | Proj_name | Emp_num | Emp_name | Job_code | Job_chg_hr | Proj_hrs | Emp_phone |
|---|---|---|---|---|---|---|---|
| 1 | Rain | **101** | **Michael Lee** | **EE** | **$170** | 13.3 | 03 1234 5678 |
| 1 | Rain | 105 | Brett Considine | CT | $120 | 16.2 | 03 2345 6789 |
| 1 | Rain | 110 | Phil Collier | CT | $130 | 14.3 | 03 4321 0987 |
| 2 | Hail | **101** | **Michael Lee** | **EE** | **$170** | 19.8 | 03 1234 5678 |
| 2 | Hail | **108** | **David Smith** | **EE** | **$150** | 17.5 | 03 3456 7890 |
| 3 | Flood | 110 | Phil Collier | CT | $130 | 11.6 | 03 4321 0987 |
| 3 | Flood | 105 | Brett Considine | CT | $120 | 23.4 | 03 2345 6789 |
| 3 | Flood | **123** | **Michael Davern** | **EE** | **$70** | 19.1 | 03 4567 1234 |
| 3 | Flood | 112 | Anne Wyatt | BE | $170 | 20.7 | 03 3456 4567 |

**FIGURE 4.13** Example B — table used by a consulting organisation to track client projects in first normal form (1NF) with dependency arrows marked

We convert this table into second normal form in figure 4.14 by writing down the primary key for each table with each attribute that is part of the primary key severally and together. Then we write down the attributes that are wholly dependent on part of the primary key behind the key they are dependent on. These attributes are then only partially dependent on the composite primary key.

1. Project table:
   Proj_num, Proj_name

2. Charge table:
   Proj_num, Emp_num, Proj_hrs

3. Employee table:
   Emp_num, Emp_name, Emp_phone, Job_code, Job_chg_hr

**FIGURE 4.14** Example B — converting to second normal form (2NF)

## Third normal form

Given there are no transitive dependencies in this case, second normal form is third normal. Figure 4.15 shows the E-R diagram for the situation in Example B.

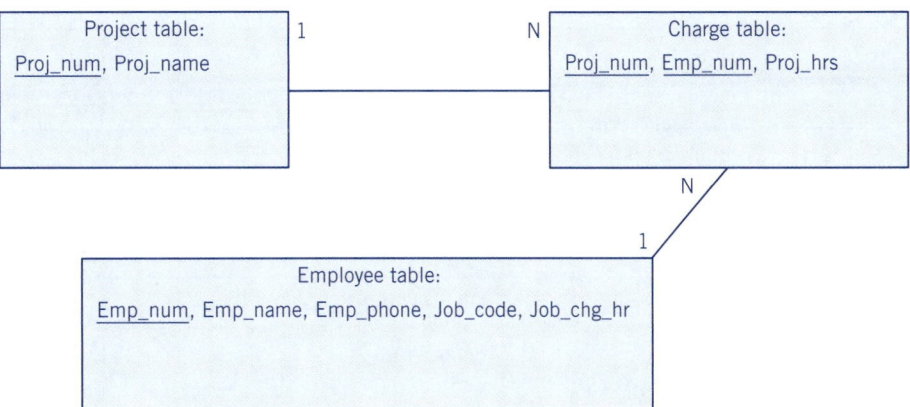

**FIGURE 4.15** Example B — E-R diagram used by a consulting organisation to track client projects in third normal form (3NF)

## Relating the normalised tables

Converting from a normalised structure to an E-R diagram is done using the following process. Figure 4.14 shows a project table with Proj_num and Proj_name and a charge table with Proj_num, Emp_num and Proj_hrs. The relationship between the project table and the charge table is that Proj_num in the project table can relate to many occurrences of Proj_num, Emp_num in the charge table. However, one occurrence in the charge table, Proj_num, Emp_num, relates to one line in the project table. Therefore, the relationship between the project table and charge table is one-to-many. Similarly for the employee table containing Emp_num, Emp_name, Emp_phone, Job_code and Job_chg_hr, a line in the charge table containing Emp_num and Proj_num relates to one line in the employee table, as one charge out rate relates to one Emp_num. However, an employee in the employee table can have multiple project-employee assignments. Therefore, there is also a one-to-many relationship between the employee table and the charge table. This is shown graphically in the E-R diagram for the business in figure 4.15. Compare this to figure 4.10 (page 154), which displayed the business logic of the original example. Notice that the E-R diagram for Example A shown in figure 4.10 has four tables, but Example B, with a change of semantics (underlying logic) of how the business works, has three tables.

A future change could be that the charge-out rate depends on the employee and which project they are working on. The data for this new example (Example C) is shown in figure 4.16 overleaf. Depending on whether Emp_num 101 is working on Proj_num 1 or 2, they would be charged out at $170 or $52 respectively.

As outlined above, the process of normalisation has three steps that need to be performed to move from first normal form to third normal form.

1. First normal form: select a primary key that uniquely identifies each line in the table.
2. Second normal form: first normal form and remove partial dependencies.
3. Third normal form: second normal form and remove transitive dependencies.

| Proj_num | Proj_name | Emp_num | Emp_name | Job_code | Job_chg_hr | Proj_hrs | Emp_phone |
|---|---|---|---|---|---|---|---|
| 1 | Rain | **101** | **Michael Lee** | **EE** | **$170** | 13.3 | 03 1234 5678 |
| 1 | Rain | 105 | Brett Considine | CT | $120 | 16.2 | 03 2345 6789 |
| 1 | Rain | 110 | Phil Collier | CT | $130 | 14.3 | 03 4321 0987 |
| 2 | Hail | **101** | **Michael Lee** | **EE** | **$52** | 19.8 | 03 1234 5678 |
| 2 | Hail | 108 | David Smith | EE | $150 | 17.5 | 03 3456 7890 |
| 3 | Flood | 110 | Phil Collier | CT | $130 | 11.6 | 03 4321 0987 |
| 3 | Flood | 105 | Brett Considine | CT | $120 | 23.4 | 03 2345 6789 |
| 3 | Flood | 123 | Michael Davern | EE | $70 | 19.1 | 03 4567 1234 |
| 3 | Flood | 112 | Anne Wyatt | BE | $170 | 20.7 | 03 3456 4567 |

FIGURE 4.16 Example C — table used by a consulting organisation to track client projects in 0 normal form (ONF)

## First normal form

In first normal form we need to identify the primary key that uniquely identifies each line of the table. As above, Proj_num and Emp_num are sufficient to do this so we have a primary composite key consisting of Proj_num and Emp_num. This is shown in figure 4.17.

| Proj_num | Proj_name | Emp_num | Emp_name | Job_code | Job_chg_hr | Proj_hrs | Emp_phone |
|---|---|---|---|---|---|---|---|
| 1 | Rain | **101** | **Michael Lee** | **EE** | **$170** | 13.3 | 03 1234 5678 |
| 1 | Rain | 105 | Brett Considine | CT | $120 | 16.2 | 03 2345 6789 |
| 1 | Rain | 110 | Phil Collier | CT | $130 | 14.3 | 03 4321 0987 |
| 2 | Hail | **101** | **Michael Lee** | **EE** | **$52** | 19.8 | 03 1234 5678 |
| 2 | Hail | 108 | David Smith | EE | $150 | 17.5 | 03 3456 7890 |
| 3 | Flood | 110 | Phil Collier | CT | $130 | 11.6 | 03 4321 0987 |
| 3 | Flood | 105 | Brett Considine | CT | $120 | 23.4 | 03 2345 6789 |
| 3 | Flood | 123 | Michael Davern | EE | $70 | 19.1 | 03 4567 1234 |
| 3 | Flood | 112 | Anne Wyatt | BE | $170 | 20.7 | 03 3456 4567 |

FIGURE 4.17 Example C — table used by a consulting organisation to track client projects in first normal form (1NF) with dependency arrows

## Second normal form

In removing the partial dependencies we examine the table and look at what each non-key attribute is dependent on. Figure 4.17 shows the dependencies, which are the same as the prior cases except for Job_chg_hr. In this case, Job_chg_hr depends on Emp_num and Proj_num. We can see in the table that Emp_num 101 with Job_code = EE is charged out at $170 and $52, depending on which project he is working on. Therefore, Job_chg_hr now becomes an attribute of the Proj_num and Emp_num table as shown in second normal form in figure 4.18.

1. Project table:
   Proj_num, Proj_name

2. Charge table:
   Proj_num, Emp_num, Proj_hrs, Job_chg_hr

3. Employee table:
   Emp_num, Emp_name, Emp_phone, Job_code

**FIGURE 4.18** Example C — converting to second normal form (2NF)

## Third normal form

Second normal form is also third normal form as we have no transitive dependencies. Everything is dependent on the primary key. See figure 4.18.

## Relating the normalised tables

The linking for the normalised tables occurs the same way as discussed above. There is a one-to-many relationship between the project table and the charge table. Proj_num from the project table can occur in multiple occurrences in the charge table, but any row in which Proj_num, Emp_num occurs in the charge table relates to only one line in the project table. This is the same with the employee table. There is therefore a one-to-many relationship between the employee table and the charge table. This is illustrated in figure 4.19 overleaf.

Lastly, what about the semantics when an employee can have multiple job codes? In practice, an employee may be able to perform more than one skill. For example, EE could stand for electrical engineer and CT for structural engineer. As another example, an individual may be able to perform more than one type of job, for instance, accountant and information technology expert. The base table has been changed (in bold) to reflect these semantics in figure 4.20 overleaf. This is Example D. Emp_num 101 can charge out as Job_code CT or EE, and even work as both a CT and an EE on the same project (Proj_num = 1).

## First normal form

To convert the table into first normal form we need to choose the primary key that will uniquely identify each line in the table. This time the primary key is different from the previous examples: we need Proj_num, Emp_num and Job_code to identify a unique line, as there may be one employee (e.g. Emp_num = 101) working on one project (e.g. Proj_num = 1) but in multiple capacities (e.g. Job_code = CT and Job_code = EE).

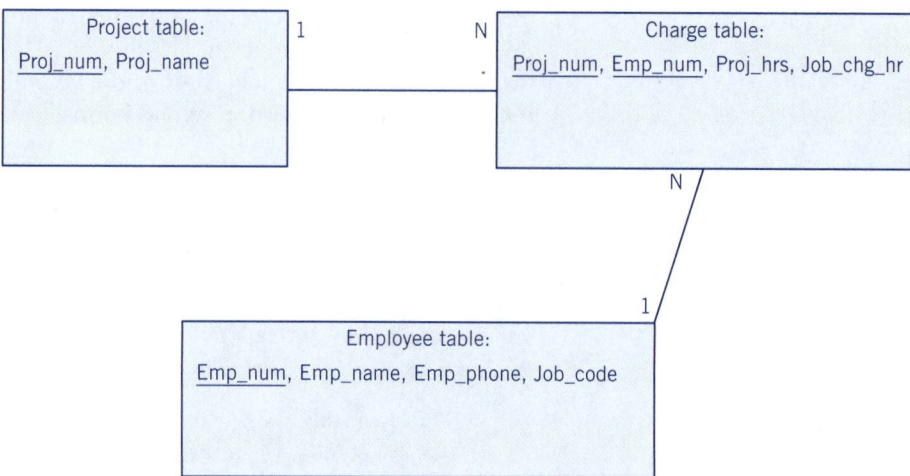

**FIGURE 4.19** Example C — E-R diagram used by a consulting organisation to track client projects in third normal form (3NF)

| Proj_num | Proj_name | Emp_num | Emp_name | Job_code | Job_chg_hr | Proj_hrs | Emp_phone |
|----------|-----------|---------|----------|----------|------------|----------|-----------|
| 1 | Rain | **101** | **Michael Lee** | **CT** | **$120** | 13.3 | 03 1234 5678 |
| 1 | Rain | **101** | **Michael Lee** | **EE** | **$52** | 16.2 | 03 2345 6789 |
| 1 | Rain | 110 | Phil Collier | CT | $120 | 14.3 | 03 4321 0987 |
| 2 | Hail | **101** | **Michael Lee** | **EE** | **$52** | 19.8 | 03 1234 5678 |
| 2 | Hail | 108 | David Smith | EE | $52 | 17.5 | 03 3456 7890 |
| 3 | Flood | 110 | Phil Collier | CT | $120 | 11.6 | 03 4321 0987 |
| 3 | Flood | 105 | Brett Considine | CT | $120 | 23.4 | 03 2345 6789 |
| 3 | Flood | 123 | Michael Davern | EE | $52 | 19.1 | 03 4567 1234 |
| 3 | Flood | 112 | Anne Wyatt | BE | $170 | 20.7 | 03 3456 4567 |

**FIGURE 4.20** Example D — table used by a consulting organisation to track client projects in O Normal Form (ONF)

## Second normal form

To convert the table to second normal form we need to remove the partial dependencies. The dependency arrows are shown in figure 4.21.

The dependencies shown in figure 4.21 are similar to those shown previously for project name, employee name, project hours and employee phone. Job_code is now part of the primary key so it is no longer considered in regards to dependency. Job_chg_hr in this case is dependent on Job_code as all employees with the same job code are charged out at the same rate. Figure 4.22 shows the tables in second normal form. Note that the primary key consists of three attributes written severally and together. Also, Proj_hrs are dependent on the employee number (Emp_num), the project the employee worked on (Proj_num) and in what capacity the employee worked (Job_code).

| Proj_num | Proj_name | Emp_num | Emp_name | Job_code | Job_chg_hr | Proj_hrs | Emp_phone |
|----------|-----------|---------|----------|----------|------------|----------|-----------|
| 1 | Rain | 101 | Michael Lee | CT | $120 | 13.3 | 03 1234 5678 |
| 1 | Rain | 101 | Michael Lee | EE | $52 | 16.2 | 03 2345 6789 |
| 1 | Rain | 110 | Phil Collier | CT | $120 | 14.3 | 03 4321 0987 |
| 2 | Hail | 101 | Michael Lee | EE | $52 | 19.8 | 03 1234 5678 |
| 2 | Hail | 108 | David Smith | EE | $52 | 17.5 | 03 3456 7890 |
| 3 | Flood | 110 | Phil Collier | CT | $120 | 11.6 | 03 4321 0987 |
| 3 | Flood | 105 | Brett Considine | CT | $120 | 23.4 | 03 2345 6789 |
| 3 | Flood | 123 | Michael Davern | EE | $52 | 19.1 | 03 4567 1234 |
| 3 | Flood | 112 | Anne Wyatt | BE | $170 | 20.7 | 03 3456 4567 |

**FIGURE 4.21** Example D — table used by a consulting organisation to track client projects in first normal form (1NF)

1. Project table:

   Proj_num, Proj_name

2. Charge table:

   Proj_num, Emp_num, Job_code, Proj_hrs

3. Employee table:

   Emp_num, Emp_name, Emp_phone

4. Job code table:

   Job_code, Job_chg_hr

**FIGURE 4.22** Example D — converting to second normal form (2NF)

## Third normal form

Since there are no transitive dependencies, second normal form is third normal form. Also note that in the tables some primary keys may not have attributes. This is not a concern as the normalisation process in an organisation addresses every document, report and table and then reconciles the results. Normalising a large volume of elements and reconciling them with the primary key will often result in attributes.

Even if a primary key does not have attributes it cannot be deleted as it is needed for linking between tables.

## Relating the normalised tables

Figure 4.23 shows the E-R diagram for Example D. Linking the normalised tables is done in the same way as for the previous examples.

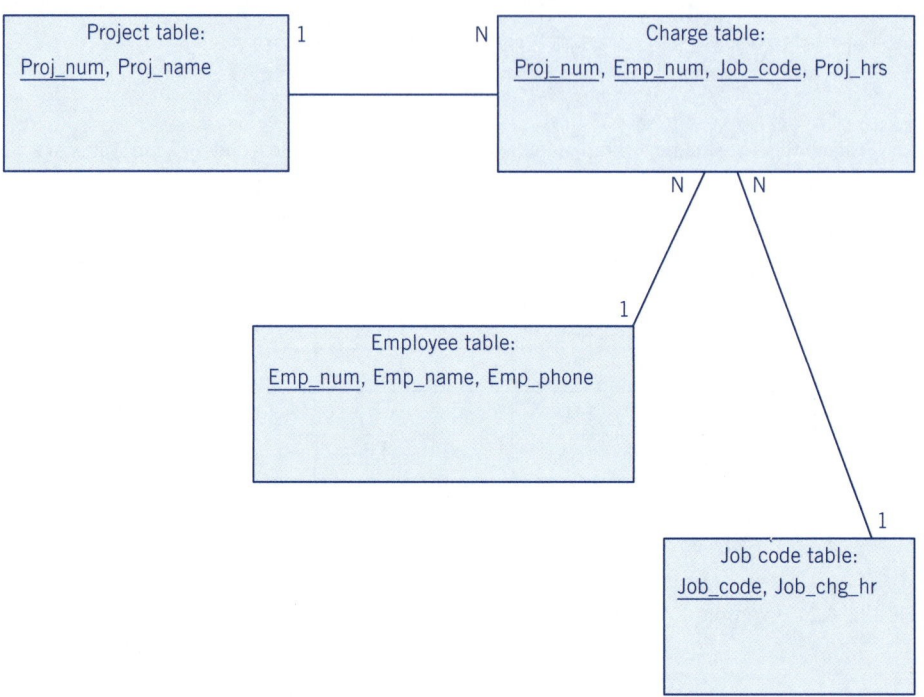

**FIGURE 4.23** Example D — E-R diagram used by a consulting organisation to track client projects in third normal form (3NF)

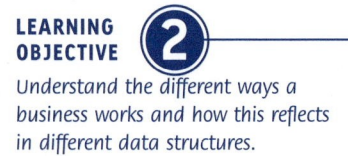

# DIFFERENT WAYS A BUSINESS WORKS = DIFFERENT DATA STRUCTURES

Figure 4.24 shows the E-R diagrams from the above examples following the normalisation process. Remember, the examples used different underlying logic about how the organisation works, but the same attributes, which resulted in different database structures. Compare the diagrams, noting the number of tables and how Job_code and Job_chg_hr have been treated. In Example A, an employee had one job code and was charged out according to that job code. In Example B, different employees could be charged out at different rates, even employees with the same job code. In Example C, the job charge-out rate depended on the employee and the project they are working on. Example D allowed an employee to have multiple job codes and work in multiple capacities on the same project. Changing the semantics (underlying logic of the data) again would result in further differences in the database structure.

**FIGURE 4.24** Examples A–D — E-R diagrams used by a consulting organisation to track client projects in third normal form (3NF)

### E-R Diagram — Example A

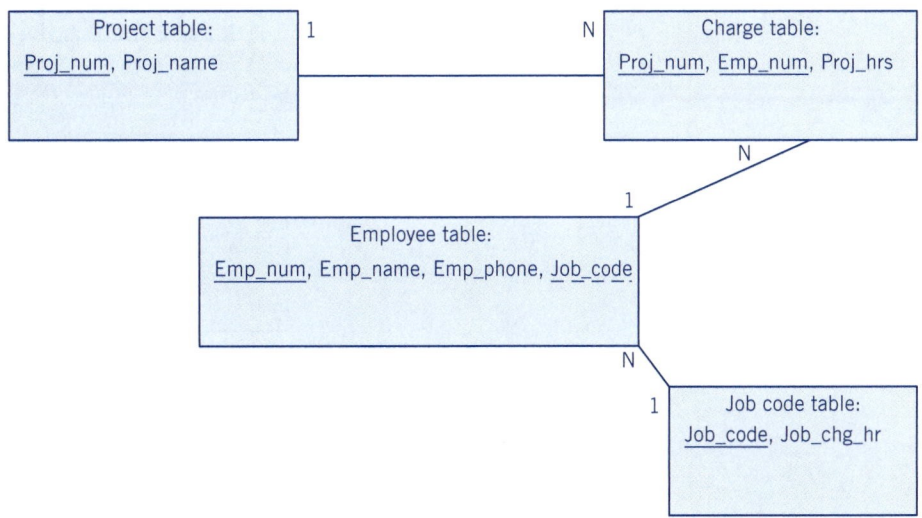

### E-R Diagram — Example B

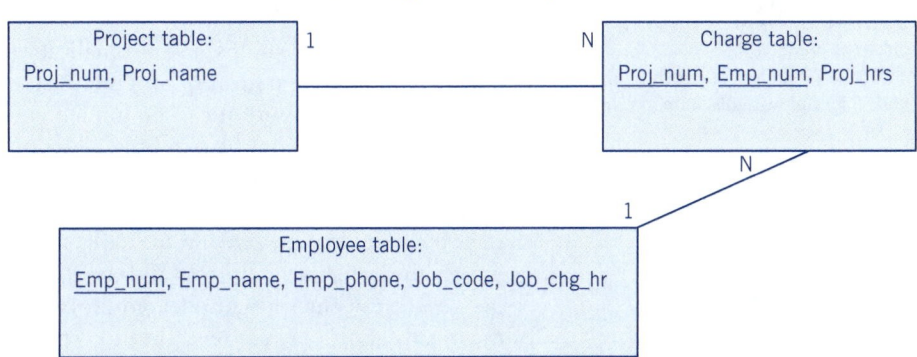

### E-R Diagram — Example C

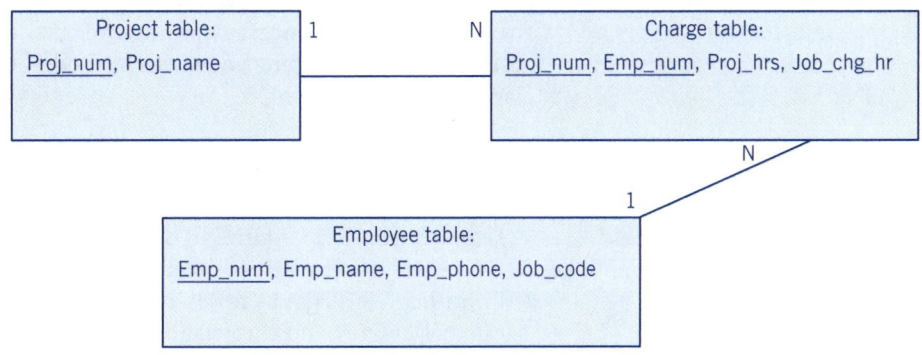

*(continued)*

**FIGURE 4.24** *(continued)*

**E-R Diagram — Example D**

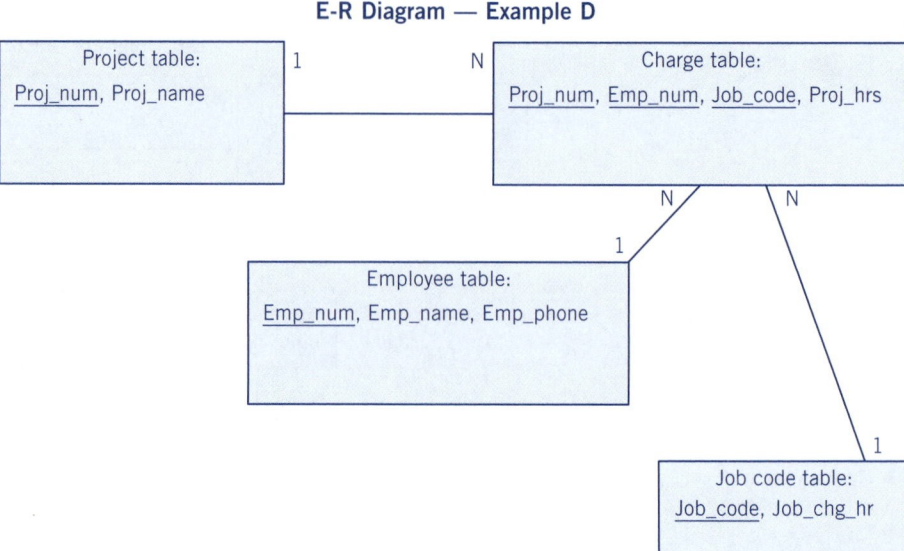

**LEARNING OBJECTIVE 3**

*Construct an enterprise model of data using entity-relationship modelling and normalisation.*

# ENTERPRISE MODELS

Combining the E-R diagrams and normalisation results for each part of the organisation allows the preparation of an enterprise model. From the enterprise model, a database for the organisation can be implemented. In practice, the task of preparing the enterprise model would be completed by technical database designers. However, the steps in the development of an enterprise model (outlined below) require the input of users and accountants as to how the business operates. This section of the chapter does not aim to provide the skills to develop an enterprise model; rather, it overviews the steps in the process and the input required in each step.

Developing the enterprise model requires taking the E-R diagrams for different parts of the organisation (e.g. the revenue and expenditure parts of the business) and combining them with any normalisation of the forms and reports within the organisation. This model can then be implemented in a database that could be called the enterprise database, as it will contain all the entities and relationships in the organisation. The E-R diagrams use the top-down method and normalisation uses bottom-up techniques. Therefore, top-level strategic views are covered as well as lower operational level input.

The steps for developing an enterprise model start with the steps for developing E-R diagrams given in chapter 3.

## Developing an enterprise model

The development of an enterprise model is an iterative process involving six steps.

1. Develop a general narrative of the organisation's operations including the business processes, policies and business rules.
2. Construct E-R diagrams for each area of operations by identifying the internal and external entities and the relationships among them from the narrative in step 1. Assign connectivities and cardinalities based on the narrative.
3. Have the E-R diagrams reviewed by the areas of the organisation with ownership of the operations, policies and processes.

4. Make necessary modifications to incorporate any newly discovered entity-relationship components.
5. Normalise the entities to ensure well structured data and no data anomalies or data redundancy.
6. Consolidate the E-R diagrams.

Repeat this process until the designers and users agree that the enterprise model (which consists of all the E-R diagrams and normalisations combined and reconciled) is complete and represents the relationships and rules that govern the organisation's entities. Then the organisation can implement the enterprise model as a database.

The following example illustrates a simplistic revenue and expenditure cycle in an organisation. For the purposes of this example, some elements such as stock picking and sales returns have been omitted. The connectivities and cardinalities have been assumed in this simple example; in a real organisation, each area would need to identify these on the basis of how the business works. The example shows the combination of separate revenue and expenditure E-R diagrams and normalisations to form an enterprise model that can be implemented as a database for the organisation.

## *Developing an enterprise model — steps 1 and 2*
Figure 4.25 shows the unnormalised E-R diagram for a simple revenue cycle. Figure 4.26 shows the unnormalised E-R diagram for a simple expenditure cycle. (Note that there would be many more entities (tables) if we were looking at a real organisation's revenue and expenditure cycles.) Figures 4.25 and 4.26 overleaf would be the result of steps 1 and 2 above.

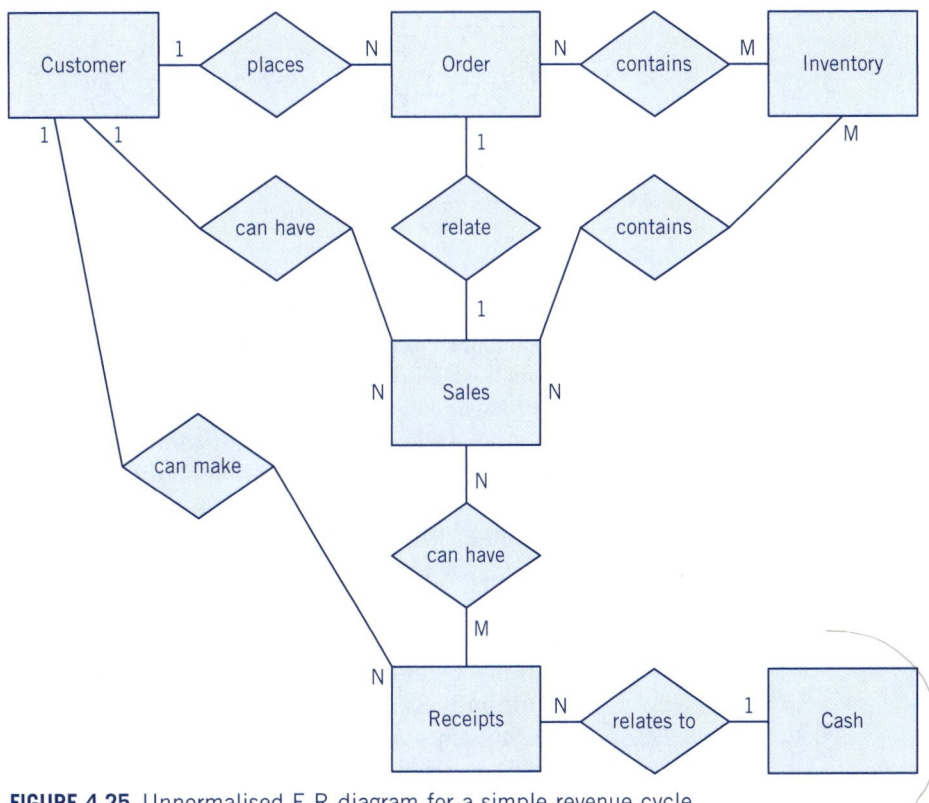

**FIGURE 4.25** Unnormalised E-R diagram for a simple revenue cycle

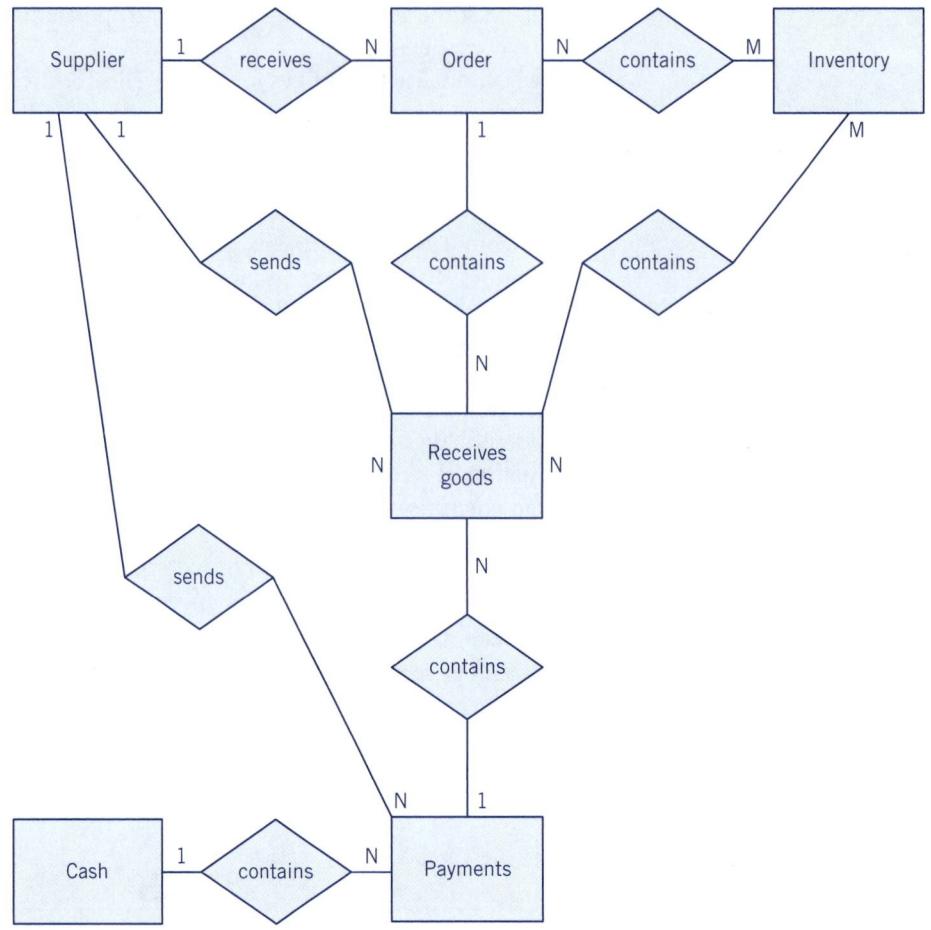

**FIGURE 4.26** Unnormalised E-R diagram for a simple expenditure cycle

We can see that figures 4.25 and 4.26 are unnormalised E-R diagrams as they contain **many-to-many relationships**. To normalise, we need to resolve these many-to-many relationships. Figure 4.25, the unnormalised E-R diagram for the revenue cycle, contains customer, sales order, inventory, sales, receipts and cash entities. The unnormalised E-R diagram for the expenditure cycle in figure 4.26 contains supplier, purchase order, inventory, receives goods, payments and cash entities. The two cycles have cash and inventory entities in common. When combined into a single E-R diagram, the separate diagrams will join on these common entities.

## Developing an enterprise model — steps 3 and 4

In step 3, each area of the organisation would review the E-R diagrams in figures 4.25 and 4.26 to ensure the diagrams reflect the business rules by which the organisation works. As discussed in chapter 3, as an accountant, your input into this area, in particular by looking at each of the depicted relationships and ensuring they reflect how the business operates, is critical.

In step 4, modifications to the E-R diagrams will be made should any area of the business find discrepancies between how the relationships are represented in the diagrams and how they actually work.

## Developing an enterprise model — steps 5

Step 5 involves normalising the entities to ensure good structure and no data anomalies or data redundancy. The normalised tables are represented in the E-R diagram in figure 4.27 for the revenue cycle and figure 4.28 for the expenditure cycle. Moving the E-R diagrams to the normalised format involves resolving the many-to-many relationships by creating two one-to-many relationships with a new bridging entity in the middle.

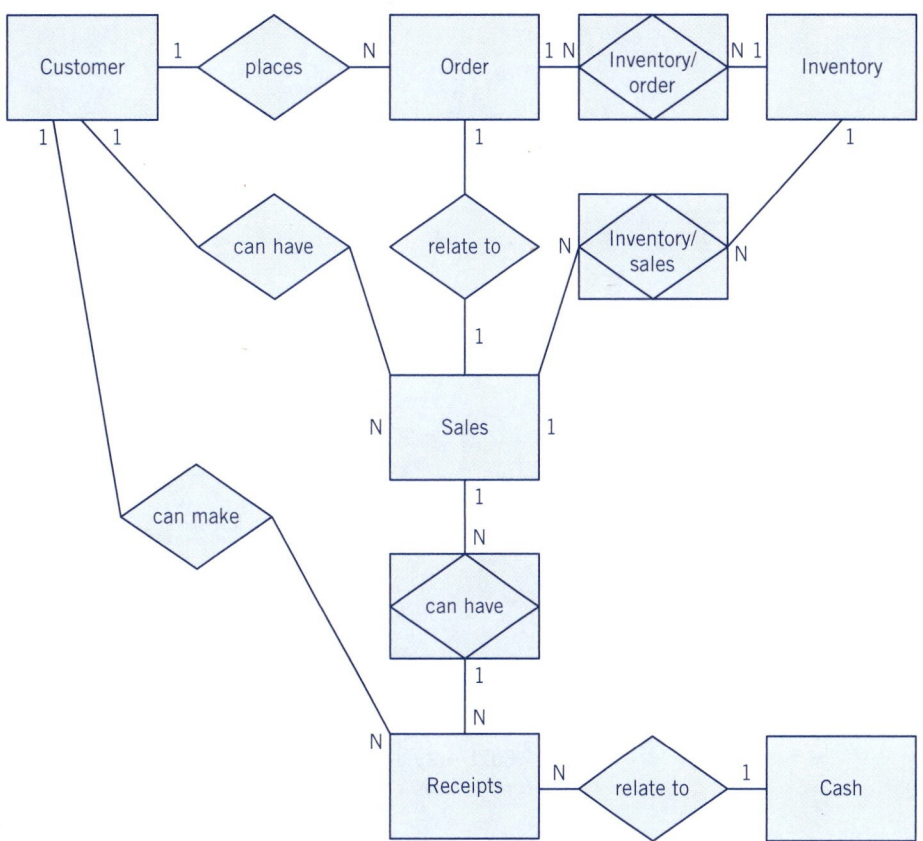

**FIGURE 4.27** Normalised E-R diagram for a simple revenue cycle

In moving to the normalised diagram for the revenue cycle, the first many-to-many relationship in figure 4.25 is the relationship between order and inventory. To move to the normalised model in figure 4.27, place an entity between the order table and the inventory table called inventory/order. The relationship between order to inventory/order now becomes a one-to-many; likewise, the relationship between inventory and inventory/order becomes a one-to-many. The same process is applied to the relationship between inventory and sales, and between sales and receipts.

Similarly, in figure 4.28 overleaf, the many-to-many relationships between the entities order and inventory and inventory and receives goods in figure 4.26 have been resolved by inserting the new entities order/inventory and inventory/receipt.

In the normalised E-R diagram for the revenue cycle in figure 4.27 you can see the primary and foreign keys for the entities (tables) within this diagram. For example, for the customer table a primary key of customer number; for the sales order table a primary key of sales order number, and a foreign key of customer number. The primary and foreign keys are shown in figure 4.29.

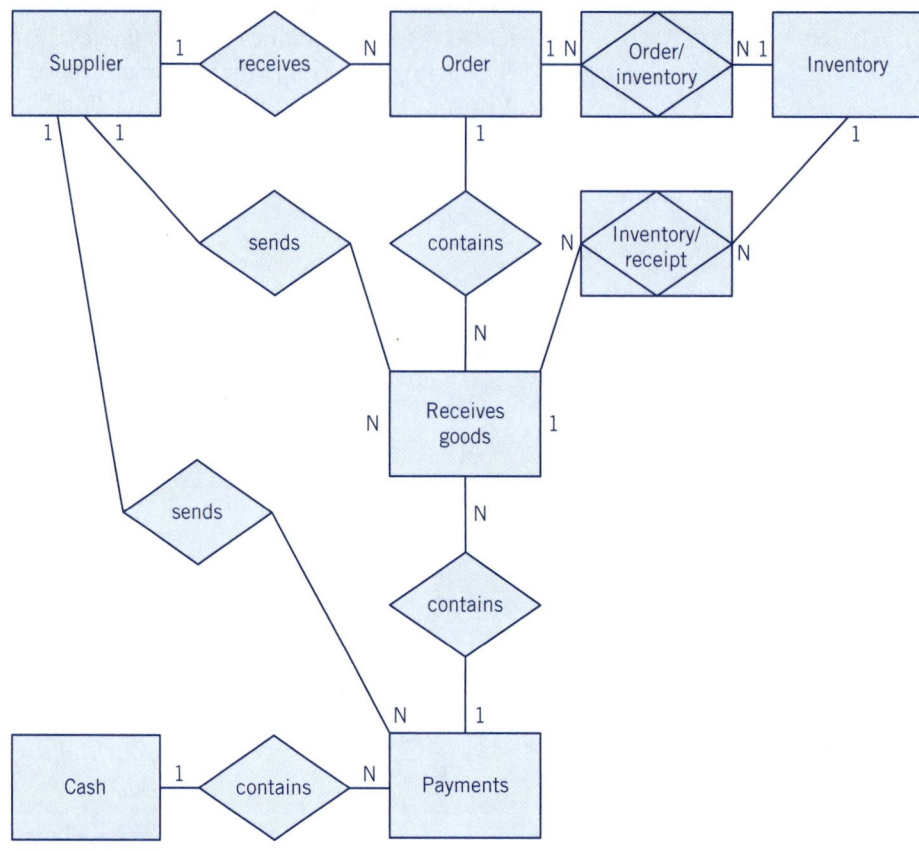

**FIGURE 4.28** Normalised E-R diagram for a simple expenditure cycle

**FIGURE 4.29** Normalised database tables for simple revenue cycle showing primary and foreign keys

| Table: Customer | | |
|---|---|---|
| Customer no. | | |

| Table: Sales | | |
|---|---|---|
| Sales order no. | Customer no. | |

| Table: Inventory | | |
|---|---|---|
| Inventory no. | | |

| Table: Sales order/inventory | | |
|---|---|---|
| Sales order no. | Inventory no. | |

**FIGURE 4.29** *(continued)*

**Table: Sales/inventory**

| Sales invoice no. | Inventory no. | |
|---|---|---|

**Table: Sales**

| Sales invoice no. | Customer no. | |
|---|---|---|

**Table: Receipts**

| Cash receipt no. | Customer no. | |
|---|---|---|

**Table: Sales invoice/cash receipts**

| Sales invoice no. | Cash receipt no. | |
|---|---|---|

**Table: Cash**

| Account no. | | |
|---|---|---|

The primary and foreign keys for the expenditure cycle are shown in figure 4.30.

Once the tables are normalised, additional attributes are generated. Take, for example, the sales order form shown in figure 4.31 overleaf. When the sales order form is normalised to third normal form it will generate the tables as shown in figure 4.32 (page 171). These can be added to figure 4.29 (the basic tables for the revenue cycle) to give figure 4.33 (page 171), which now shows the complete attributes for the revenue cycle.

**FIGURE 4.30** Normalised database tables for simple expenditure cycle showing primary and foreign keys

**Table: Supplier**

| Supplier no. | | |
|---|---|---|

**Table: Order**

| Purchase order no. | Supplier no. | |
|---|---|---|

**Table: Inventory**

| Inventory no. | | |
|---|---|---|

*(continued)*

**FIGURE 4.30** *(continued)*

| Table: Sales order/inventory | | |
|---|---|---|
| Purchase order no. | Inventory no. | |
| | | |

| Table: Receives goods — inventory/receipt | | |
|---|---|---|
| Receipt invoice no. | Inventory no. | |
| | | |

| Table: Receives goods | | |
|---|---|---|
| Invoice no. | Supplier no. | |
| | | |

| Table: Payments | | |
|---|---|---|
| Cash payment no. | Supplier no. | |
| | | |

| Table: Cash | | |
|---|---|---|
| Account no. | | |

Simple company
Level 9, 1 Governor Fitzroy Place
Auckland, 1002

| Sales order form | No: So-1245 | Date: 16 September 2009 |
|---|---|---|

TO: Ms Henriette Videbaek (Customer no: 444545)
46 Mount Wellington Road
Mount Wellington          Ph. 455 3523

| Item no. | Description | Price | Quantity | Total | |
|---|---|---|---|---|---|
| | | | | | |
| | | | | | |
| | | | | | |
| | | | | | |
| | | | | | |

**FIGURE 4.31** Sales order form

**Table: Customer**

| Customer no. | Customer name | Customer address | Customer phone |
|---|---|---|---|
| | | | |

**Table: Sales**

| Sales order no. | Sales order date | Customer no. | |
|---|---|---|---|
| | | | |

**Table: Inventory**

| Inventory no. | Inventory description | Inventory price | |
|---|---|---|---|
| | | | |

**Table: Sales order/inventory**

| Sales order no. | Inventory no. | Qty | |
|---|---|---|---|
| | | | |

**FIGURE 4.32** Sales order form tables and attributes

**FIGURE 4.33** Normalised database tables for simple revenue cycle

**Table: Customer**

| Customer no. | Customer name | Customer address | Customer phone | Customer credit limit |
|---|---|---|---|---|
| | | | | |

**Table: Sales**

| Sales order no. | Sales order date | Customer no. |
|---|---|---|
| | | |

**Table: Inventory**

| Inventory no. | Inventory description | Inventory price |
|---|---|---|
| | | |

**Table: Sales order/inventory**

| Sales order no. | Inventory no. | Qty |
|---|---|---|
| | | |

**Table: Sales/inventory**

| Sales invoice no. | Inventory no. | Qty |
|---|---|---|
| | | |

**Table: Sales**

| Sales invoice no. | Sales invoice date | Customer no. | Sales invoice date |
|---|---|---|---|
| | | | |

*(continued)*

**FIGURE 4.33** *(continued)*

**Table: Receipts**

| Cash receipt no. | Customer no. | Total amount | Cash receipts date |
|---|---|---|---|
| | | | |

**Table: Sales invoice/cash receipts**

| Sales invoice no. | Cash receipt no. | Amount |
|---|---|---|
| | | |

**Table: Cash**

| Account no | Balance | |
|---|---|---|

Figure 4.34 shows the attributes for the expenditure cycle.

**Table: Supplier**

| Supplier no. | Supplier name | Supplier address | Supplier phone |
|---|---|---|---|

**Table: Order**

| Purchase order no. | Purchase order date | Supplier no. |
|---|---|---|

**Table: Inventory**

| Inventory no. | Inventory description | Inventory price |
|---|---|---|

**Table: Sales order/inventory**

| Purchase order no. | Inventory no. | Qty |
|---|---|---|

**Table: Receive goods — inventory/receipt**

| Receipt invoice no. | Inventory no. | Qty |
|---|---|---|

**Table: Receive goods**

| Invoice no. | Invoice date | Supplier no. | Supplier invoice date |
|---|---|---|---|

**Table: Payments**

| Cash payments no. | Supplier no. | Total amount | Cash payments date |
|---|---|---|---|

**Table: Cash**

| Account no. | Balance | |
|---|---|---|

**FIGURE 4.34** Normalised database tables for simple expenditure cycle

## Developing an enterprise model — step 6

Notice that the cash and the inventory entities are common between the revenue and expenditure E-R diagrams. Therefore, these tables can be consolidated across the entities. If the cash entity and the inventory entity had different attributes, they would be combined and normalised. The tables and attributes for the enterprise model are a combination of the tables and attributes from figure 4.33 (tables and attributes for the revenue cycle) and figure 4.34 (tables and attributes for the expenditure cycle), joined via the inventory and cash tables. Since both figures 4.33 and 4.34 have cash and inventory tables, the final model will have only one table for inventory and one for cash. The enterprise model (which is an E-R diagram for the whole of the organisation) is shown in figure 4.35.

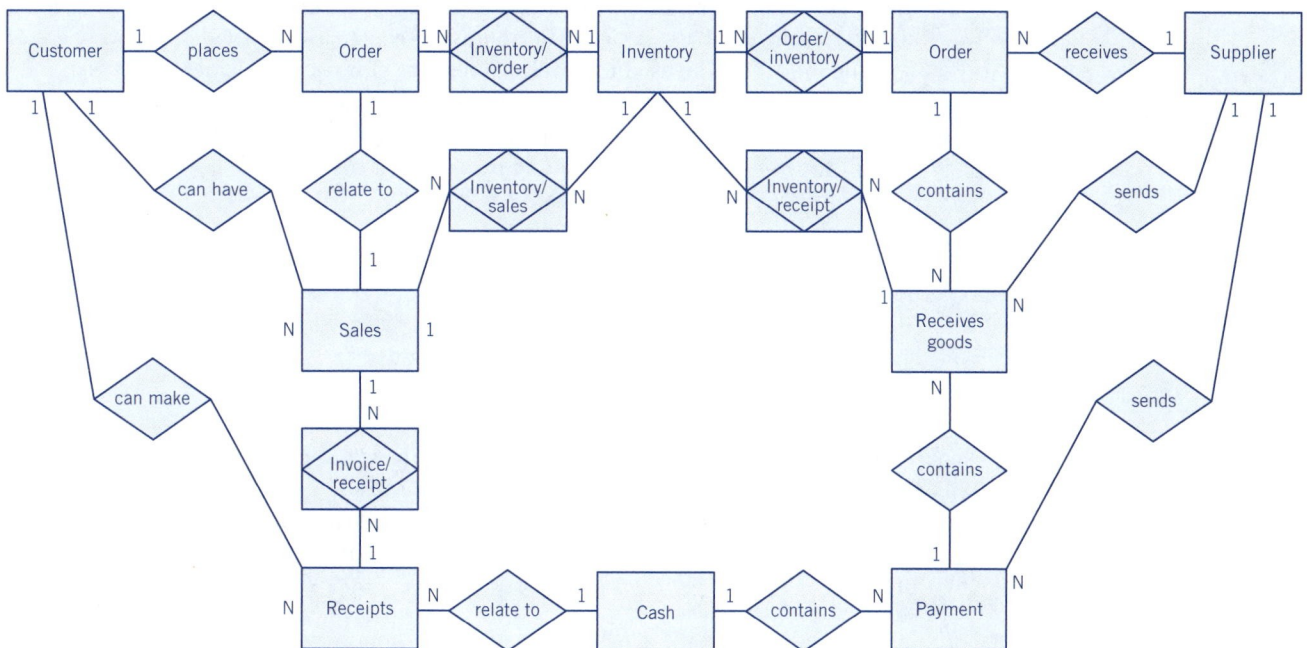

**FIGURE 4.35** Enterprise model for the organisation

After consolidating the diagrams into a single enterprise model, users and other members of the organisation need to agree that the model represents the relationships in the organisation and that the table designs in figure 4.33 and 4.34 represent all the data that needs to be collected in the database.

Note that the above example only includes a few entities and attributes, and minimal interaction between them. The number would increase for a real-world organisation, in particular, if other transaction cycles such as human resources, payroll, finance, general ledger and goods returns were included.

**LEARNING OBJECTIVE 4**

*Discuss the REA (resources-events-agents) Accounting Model as a template for modelling accounting systems.*

# THE REA ACCOUNTING MODEL

Another way to model data is to use the REA (resources-events-agents) Accounting Model. Database designers have used the REA Accounting Model as a template for developing database models that can be used for accounting information systems.

The REA Accounting Model was developed by William McCarthy in 1982[2] and since expanded in a series of papers. McCarthy suggested that an enterprise information system should be a representation of the actual activities or events that occur in the organisation rather than a particular view of the data such as a debit or credit or a journal entry. He used the enterprise information system to show the information system for the whole of the business. (In learning objective 3 above we used the term enterprise model (or enterprise database) instead of enterprise information system to indicate the system for the whole of the business.) The REA Accounting Model defines common patterns in entities, and activities or events that are found in all organisations. It is based on a thorough understanding of an organisation's context, entities, business processes, risks and information needs through systems mapping and documentation. The REA Accounting Model is beyond the scope of this book. However, there are books and courses that explain in great depth the model and its use in database design. The following explanation provides an overview of how the model can be used to develop a database for a sales business process.

REA models the exchanges in the various processes in an organisation and brings these exchanges together to form an enterprise system. Consider the simple sales process shown in figure 4.36 where a sale is made to a customer.

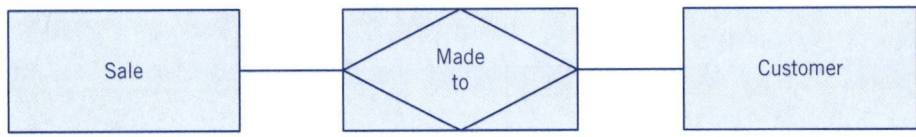

**FIGURE 4.36** Sales process

The process can be described as a customer sale of a product. The diagram in figure 4.36 can be expanded to the E-R diagram in figure 4.37 to show the entities that are recorded as a result of the sales process: customer, cash and product. Tables in the database must be able to capture the interactions between the customer and the cash, and the cash and the product.

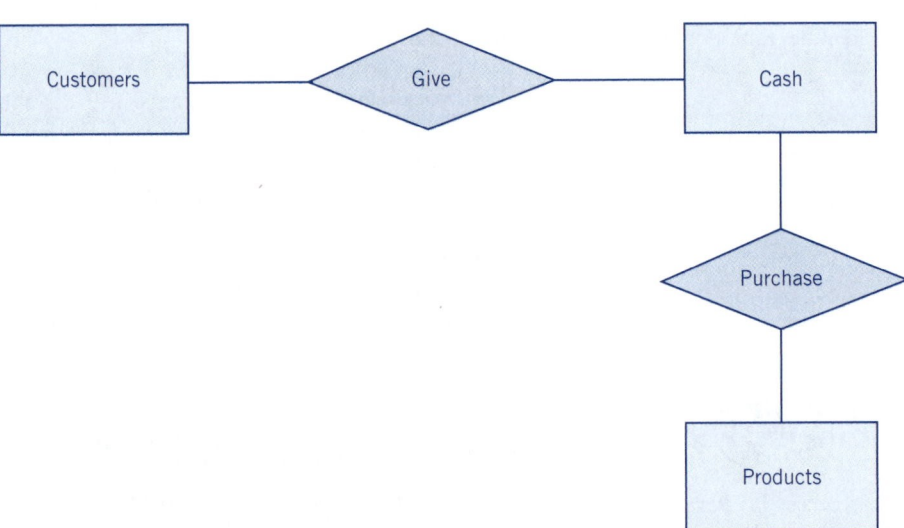

**FIGURE 4.37** Expanded E-R diagram showing entities and exchanges between them

How did we come up with the elements of the E-R diagram? How did we know how to define the entities and the interactions between the entities? The answer is based on understanding and experience of the business and the relationships within it.

REA database modelling provides a more structured approach to developing a database model and database structure for a business process such as the sales process. REA is based on the premise that in every exchange in a process there is a resource, event and agent involved. A resource is an item that is anything but an agent. In our sales process example, it could be the product or the cash. Hence, an agent is the human that is involved in the exchange. In our sales process example, the agent could be the customer, cashier or salesperson. The event is the occurrence between the resources and the agents. William McCarthy proposed that in every exchange, such as the sales process, there are common patterns of inflows and outflows. He presented the concept of 'duality', and concluded that all exchanges could be represented by the general REA pattern in figure 4.38.

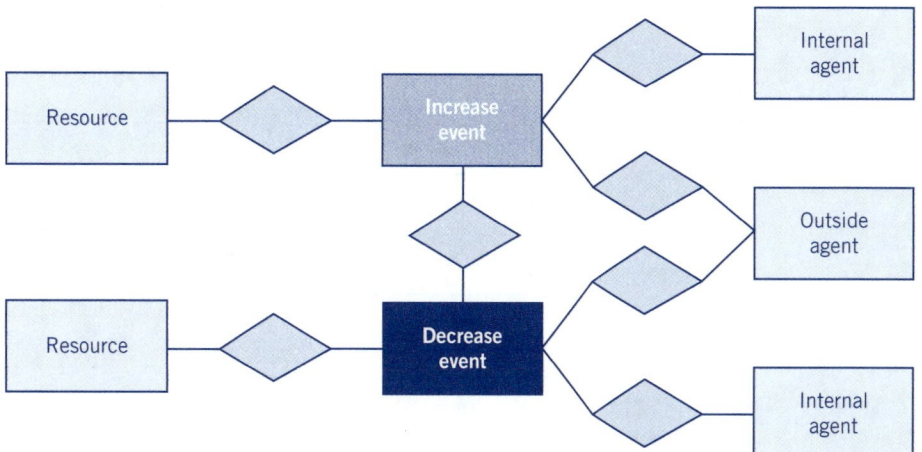

**FIGURE 4.38** General REA pattern

Our simple sales process can therefore be translated into the REA pattern shown in figure 4.39.

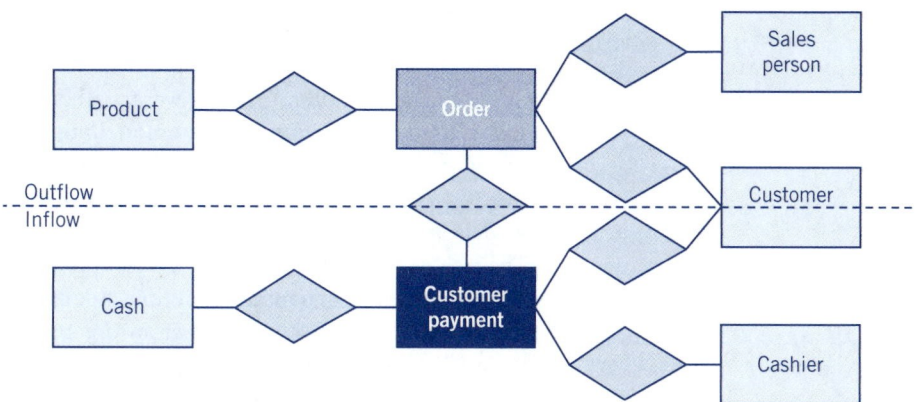

**FIGURE 4.39** Sales process REA pattern

The resources, events and agents represent the key tables and the relationships that have to exist in a database in order to capture the details underlying that exchange, as shown in the database structure in figure 4.40.

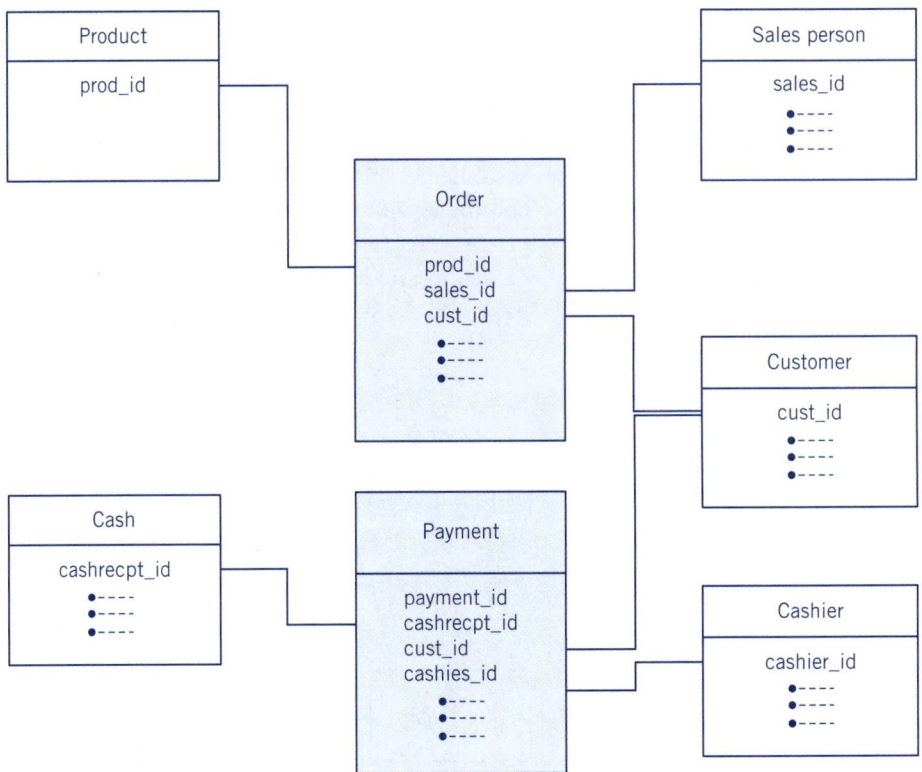

**FIGURE 4.40** Database structure

In summary, the REA Accounting Model, which involves defining the exchanges and developing the dualities between resources, events and agents, assists the development of database structures that can be used to capture the details of a business process.

## REA Accounting Model example

The REA model has not been implemented in an actual accounting system in practice, as it concentrates on economic events rather than debit/credit transactions. However, REA is used for accounting system modelling. Resources, events and agents are depicted when an economic event occurs such as a sale. The resulting model does not contain debits and credits, journals or ledgers, or other items of accounting convention such as debtors, creditors or capital as accounts with balances in an event-driven model. The lack of these elements may explain the reluctance of or resistance by accountants to implementing this model as it does not reconcile with the debit/credit systems that they would be used to. Further, if an organisation has an existing legacy system that uses debit and credits, it is not possible to amend it to add new functionality using the REA model. Still, REA is useful for modelling business events. In addition, developments are continually being made to the REA model.

The following example illustrates the REA model and how it is different from the relational database that we have been using up to this point by showing the same transactions using a traditional debit and credit system (a non-REA model) and an REA model. The transactions are an example of a sale and a cash receipt.

> **Transaction 1:**
> 1 March 2009, 10 units of Product A is sold for $10 per unit to Customer B. Product A cost $500 per unit.
>
> **Transaction 2:**
> 10 March 2009, $50 is received from Customer B.

## Traditional relational database accounting system (non-REA model)

Figure 4.41 illustrates the entries under a traditional, non-REA accounting system.

**FIGURE 4.41** Traditional accounting system (non-REA) — journal entries and subsequent ledger balances

| Journal entries | | | |
|---|---|---|---|
| **2009** | | **Debit** | **Credit** |
| Mar. 1 | Debit – Debtor B | 100 | |
| | Credit – Sales | | 100 |
| | Debit – Cost of Goods Sold | 50 | |
| | Credit – Inventory | | 50 |
| Mar. 10 | Debit – Cash | 50 | |
| | Credit – Debtor B | | 50 |

| Ledger balances | | | |
|---|---|---|---|
| **Debtor B** | | **Debit** | **Credit** |
| 2009 | | | |
| | Opening Balance | 0 | |
| Mar. 1 | Credit Sales | 100 | |
| 10 | Cash | | 50 |
| | Closing Balance | 50 | |

| Sales | | | |
|---|---|---|---|
| **Sales** | | **Debit** | **Credit** |
| 2009 | | | |
| | Opening Balance | 0 | |
| Mar. 1 | Debtors | | 100 |

*(continued)*

**FIGURE 4.41** *(continued)*

| Cost of Goods | | Debit | Credit |
|---|---|---|---|
| 2009 | | | |
| Mar. 1 | Opening Balance<br>Inventory | 0<br>50 | |

| Inventory | | Debit | Credit |
|---|---|---|---|
| 2009 | | | |
| Mar. 1 | Opening Balance<br>Cost of Goods Sold | 0 | 50 |

| Cash | | Debit | Credit |
|---|---|---|---|
| 2009 | | | |
| Mar. 10 | Opening Balance<br>Debtors<br>Closing Balance | 0<br><u>50</u><br>50 | —<br> |

We can see from the traditional accounting system (the non-REA model) that we have a balance of $50 in debtors using journals and ledgers.

## REA model

Figure 4.42 illustrates the entries under an REA Accounting Model. Attributes have been chosen to illustrate the system (more attributes could be used in reality).

**FIGURE 4.42** REA model tables

**Table: Customer**

| Customer no. | Customer name | Customer address | Customer credit limit |
|---|---|---|---|
| 101 | Customer B | | |

**Table: Invoice**

| Invoice no. | Invoice date | Customer no | |
|---|---|---|---|
| 1 | 1 March 2009 | 101 | |

**Table: Sales**

| Invoice no. | Product no. | Qty | |
|---|---|---|---|
| 1 | 201 | 10 | |

**FIGURE 4.42** *(continued)*

**Table: Product**

| Product no. | Product description | Price | Cost |
|---|---|---|---|
| 201 | Product A | 10 | 5 |

**Table: Cash receipts**

| Cash receipts no. | Date | Customer no. | Amount |
|---|---|---|---|
| 301 | 10 March 2009 | 101 | 50 |

**LEARNING OBJECTIVE**  **5**

*Understand the differences between REA and entity-relationship modelling.*

# DIFFERENCES BETWEEN REA AND E–R MODELLING

In the REA model, in the absence of a debtors account to work out the debtors balance, look at the sales table, link it to the price in the product table less what is in the cash receipts table relating to that customer. Using normal database conventions, primary keys are shown with the attribute underlined and foreign keys are shown with the attribute having a dashed underline. Therefore, we can see from the invoice table that customer 101 bought goods on 1 March 2009. The invoice table is linked to the customer table via the foreign key of customer no. via the invoice number, we can link the invoice table to the sales table in which we can see customer 101 bought 10 of product 201. We can then link the product no. in the sales table to the product table to see that product number 201 is Product A and it sells for $10. So, we can calculate a sale of $100 to customer 101. Next, we can see from the cash receipts table that we have $50 received from customer number 101, which is Customer B. This is done via the link in the cash receipts table to the foreign key customer no. which in turn links to the customer table that has customer no. as its primary key. If we take the $100 sale from Customer B and take away the $50 cash receipt from Customer B, we have a balance of $50 owing from Customer B. This is quite a different process than for the traditional accounting model (non-REA model) where we can easily see the balance of Customer B (Debtor B).

Despite the reluctance of businesses to use REA to implement accounting systems, one of the REA model's greatest advantages is that it can store non-financial data as well as financial data. And it is possible for organisations to use REA to model their business processes, but then implement the relationships via a traditional accounting system (i.e. that uses debits and credits). In this way, REA is implemented as a relational database.

**LEARNING OBJECTIVE**  **6**

*Discuss the technologies relating to database implementation.*

# DATABASE IMPLEMENTATION

Relational databases need to be centralised within the organisation, but still allow organisation-wide access. Hardware and networks provide the critical platforms to achieve this. Only relatively recently have computer power, operating systems and data communications reached a level that makes it possible to operationalise the use, manipulation and storage of relational databases.

This final section of this chapter briefly explains how client–server systems and e-commerce have affected the design, implementation and management of relational database systems and business information systems in general. In particular, this section overviews how client–server systems have provided opportunities for organisations to use developments in logically designed relational database implementation models. While logical views of database implementation models such as relational databases have been used in the discussion up to this point, the next section explains the client–server implementation model using a physical perspective.

## Client–server systems

A **client–server system** distributes computing functions between two types of independent and autonomous processes: servers and clients. A **client** is any process that requests specific services from server. A **server** is a process that provides requested services for clients. Client and server processes commonly exist on different computers connected by a network. For example, many workplaces have individual PCs (clients), which contain the individual email accounts of users. These individual PCs are likely to be connected through a network to an email server, which receives and sends email into and out of the organisation.

When client and server processes reside on two or more computers on a network, the server can provide services for more than one client. A client can also request services from several servers on a network without regard to the location of the computer on which the server process resides. Figure 4.43 shows three of many possibleclient–server configurations. Panel A illustrates a single computer as client and server. A small business using a database may employ such a configuration. The PC processes every request within itself. In panel B, a server is shown with a number of clients. Small to medium businesses with a number of employees running a database may require employees to have access at the same time. The server houses the centralised database, which can be accessed by employees using their client. Panel C shows a single client with more than one server. This configuration may be used by an organisation that requires servers for specialised functions such as databases, email, applications and so on. Clients may access each of these servers depending on the functionality that they require in conducting business. This configuration is normally used in large organisations that have multiple locations.

The technical details behind client–server systems relate to how far processing is shared, the tiers of client–servers, and the architecture including components and middleware.

A server or client can be described as fat or thin depending on how far the processing is shared between the client and the server. A *thin client* conducts minimal processing and is normally used in conjunction with a *fat server*, which conducts most of the processing. Conversely, a *fat client* takes on a relatively large processing load and is usually used in combination with a *thin server*, which carries relatively lower processing load. Thin clients are frequently implemented for users that perform basic administration and operational functions in the database such as the bank teller's computer in a bank. The fat client is typically given to database managers, administrators or programmers who need the processing power to make significant changes or maintain a relational database.

Client–server systems can also be classified as two-tier or three-tier. A client requesting services directly from a server is known as a two-tier client–server system. Where the client's request is handled by intermediate servers (which coordinate the execution of the client requests with other servers), this is known as a three-tier client–server system.

Panel A

Panel C

Panel B

**Hardware** *Physical devices including the computer and network.*

**Software** *Computer programs that are written in programming languages or code that instruct the operations of a computer.*

**Front-end application software** *Software that is usually loaded onto the client computers as the means for the users to interact with the server as part of the client process.*

**Back-end application software** *Software that is usually loaded onto the server to provide essential background services to clients.*

**Communications middleware** *Software that holds different types of software that aid the transmission of data and control of information between the client and server.*

**FIGURE 4.43** Client–server models

Client–server architecture is based on three major components: hardware, software and communications middleware. The **hardware** is made up of the physical computers and physical servers that represent the client and the server. **Front-end application software** is **software** that is usually loaded onto the client computers as the means for the user to interact with the server as part of the client process. **Back-end application software** is usually loaded onto the server to provide essential background services to the clients. **Communications middleware** is the software by which clients and servers communicate. The communications middleware or communication layer holds different types of software that aid the transmission of data and control of information between the client and server. The middleware sits partly on the client and partly on the server and allows the two to communicate and interact.

Figure 4.44 shows how client and server components interact through communications middleware. A client computer sends the request in SQL through the middleware on its computer, which routes the SQL request through the network to the middleware sitting in the database server process. The database server processes the request, validates it and executes it, sending the data back to the client via the middleware layer.

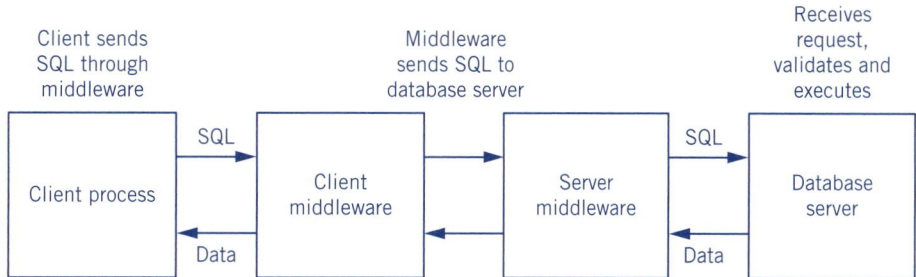

**FIGURE 4.44** The interaction of client–server components

The ability to allocate processing between clients and servers in a network allows:

- organisations to centralise information that can be accessed by everyone through client PCs
- flexibility, adaptability and scalability for the organisation to add and subtract users and capacity to a growing or changing organisation
- the above to be accomplished without the costs of purchasing and developing new systems each time.

This discussion on the client–server environment also shows how the system architecture permits these advantages because the system can:

- be built on independent hardware and software platforms
- optimise the distribution of processing activities using the comparative advantages of each of the platforms
- use a variety of techniques, methodologies and specialised tools to develop systems that are user-friendly, cost-effective and communicative across all boundaries.

The implementation of truly flexible relational database systems could only have been brought about with client–server architecture. This architecture has reduced the development and implementation costs in constructing a system to capture complex and diverse business activities. This architecture manifests itself in the myriad enterprise information systems in use today. Small business systems such as MYOB, and large ERP systems such as SAP and Oracle use these relational databases as a basis to capture, store and manage data and information for decision making and reporting. Chapter 6 on enterprise information systems discusses these database applications in detail.

## Databases in e–commerce

The internet has changed the way organisations of all types operate. Buying and selling goods and services between businesses, suppliers and customers have become commonplace, and this interaction, known as e-commerce, is the topic of chapter 6.

E-commerce and the internet have also affected database systems. Organisations with relational database systems, for example, are now allowing their staff to access the system externally through the internet. In addition, the internet is allowing organisations to give their suppliers and customers access to their internally focused relational database. A wide range of supply chain and customer relationship management software has been developed that can be linked with database systems, to permit communication and commerce between organisations. There are other relational databases with structures that are specifically constructed for supply chain and customer relationship purposes. Chapter 6 describes the application of relational databases to enterprise information systems and discusses these links with supply chain and customer relationship management software.

LEARNING OBJECTIVE

*How does the process of normalisation result in efficient database design?*
Designing a database requires taking the database model and creating tables to represent every internal and external entity that is important to the business. Once the table structure is defined, normalisation is used. Normalisation is the process of assigning attributes to entities to eliminate the repetition of groups and data redundancies in order to form tables that promote structural and data independence. Therefore, normalisation maximises the

efficiency of the structure of data. There are a number of forms of normalisation from 1NF to 5NF; however, for financial systems we stop at 3NF.

LEARNING OBJECTIVE

### How are the different ways a business works reflected in different data structures?

Different underlying logic in the data will result in different data structures even though the business's attributes may be the same as those of another business. Therefore, given the same attributes of two organisations, one business's database is unable to be used in the other business.

LEARNING OBJECTIVE

### What is an enterprise model of a business and how is it created?

An enterprise model of a business is the complete model of the business that can be implemented in an enterprise database. An enterprise model of a business is created by combining the E-R diagrams of different parts of the business along with the normalisation of different forms and reports in the organisation. By combining and reconciling the tables and attributes a model of the whole enterprise can be created. Consultation with the users in the organisation is required to ensure the enterprise model reflects how the organisation works.

LEARNING OBJECTIVE

### What is the REA Accounting Model?

The REA (resources-events-agents) Accounting Model is a way of modelling data for accounting information systems. REA is based on the premise that in every exchange in a process there is a resource, event and agent involved. A resource is an item that is anything but an agent. In our sales process example, it could be the product or the cash. Hence, an agent is the human that is involved in the exchange. In a sales process example, the agent could be the customer, cashier or salesperson. The event is the occurrence between the resources and the agents. It is proposed that in every exchange, such as the sales process, there are common patterns of inflows and outflows, and all exchanges can be represented by the general REA pattern.

LEARNING OBJECTIVE

### What are the differences between REA and E-R modelling?

REA uses events modelling rather than the traditional accounting system, which uses journal entries, ledgers and debits and credits. Balances for debtors, creditors, bank and capital need to be calculated from the events that occur in the business. For example, the debtors balance must be calculated from the sales to the customer, minus the payments from the customer and any returns. The balance needs to be calculated because it is not available as it would be in a traditional relational database accounting system. However, REA has the capability of storing non-financial data, while a traditional relational database accounting system does not.

LEARNING OBJECTIVE

### What technologies relate to database implementations?

Client–server computing is a physical implementation model that is based on distributing functions between the two types of independent and autonomous processes: servers and clients. Servers have special processing functions that provide requests for clients. Clients request services from a server. This functionality allows organisations to run networks with centralised information in a relational database that is accessible by everyone through client PCs. It also permits flexibility, adaptability and scalability for databases. Employees can configure databases to best suit their output needs, which improves workflow and hence productivity. This is because the system is built on independent hardware and software platforms, which can be optimised for distribution of processing activities.

## DISCUSSION QUESTIONS

4.1 Describe the process of normalisation for database design. (LO1)

4.2 How does normalisation enhance decision making and reporting? (LO1)

4.3 How do normalised structures change depending on different relationships in the data? (LO2)

4.4 Discuss the steps required to construct an enterprise model of a business. (LO3)

4.5 Discuss the REA model. (LO4)

4.6 Discuss the differences between an REA model and E-R modelling. (LO5)

4.7 Discuss the implications of client–server computing for implementing relational databases. (LO6)

4.8 How have e-commerce and the internet affected the accessibility of database applications? (LO6)

## SELF-TEST ACTIVITIES

4.1 A table to be normalised starts at what normal form?
   (a) 0NF
   (b) 1NF
   (c) 2NF
   (d) 3NF

4.2 Can a table which is in 2NF also be in 3NF?
   (a) Yes when there are no partial dependencies.
   (b) Yes when there are no transitive dependencies
   (c) Yes when there are no functional dependencies.
   (d) None of the above.

4.3 A composite primary key can also be called a:
   (a) concatenated primary key.
   (b) foreign key.
   (c) primary key.
   (d) none of the above.

4.4 A partial dependency is when:
   (a) an attribute is dependent on the primary key wholly.
   (b) an attribute is dependent on the primary key but via a non-key attribute.

(c) an attribute is only dependent on part of the primary key.

(d) none of the above.

4.5 A transitive dependency is when:

(a) an attribute is dependent on the primary key wholly.

(b) an attribute is dependent on the primary key but via a non-key attribute.

(c) an attribute is only dependent on part of the primary key.

(d) none of the above.

4.6 Client–server architecture is based on:

(a) hardware, software and communications middleware.

(b) mainframes and terminals.

(c) databases, tables and keys.

(d) none of the above.

## PROBLEMS

4.1 No More Smelly Shoes is a large manufacturer of children's school and sports shoes. The organisation runs a file system. The following is an extract of its sales file.

| Customer_name | Customer_address | Customer_phone | Salesperson | Shoe_model | Shoe_amount | Date |
|---|---|---|---|---|---|---|
| Britney Considine | 2 Apple Street, Melbourne, VIC | 03 1234 5678 | TLM | VZ4717 | $29.90 | 20-Jul-08 |
| Michelle Lee | 6 Organic Street, Melbourne, VIC | 03 9876 4321 | CBD | DF3966 | $79.50 | 30-Jul-08 |
| Phillipa Collier | 8 Grapefruit Street, Melbourne, VIC | 03 5678 3456 | MTL | WE9447 | $50.30 | 4-Aug-08 |
| Devine Smith | 3 Echo Street, Melbourne, VIC | 03 2376 1048 | JFK | XC8187 | $45.50 | 6-Oct-08 |

**Required**

(a) Normalise this table to third normal form. Show all forms.

(b) Discuss any assumptions you have made in normalising the table.

(c) Illustrate your normalisation by providing an entity-relationship (E-R) diagram.

4.2 Magnificent Music started in Melbourne and is expanding by setting up stores in every other capital city in Australia. It will be selling CDs and DVDs of all varieties in every store. Magnificent Music has decided that it wants a centralised database that can be accessed by every store in Australia. To operate efficiently and effectively, it requires a client–server system.

**Required**

(a) Explain the importance of client–server computing for database access in each of its stores.

(b) How does the client–server architecture extract the best from the database?

**4.3 Part A:** Below is a table for a university database.

## ONF

| Student number | Course number | Course title | Instructor number | Instructor name | Instructor location | Grade |
|---|---|---|---|---|---|---|
| 38214 | FM6000 | Financial Modelling | 1 | AARON | 927 | A |
| 38214 | AIS7909 | Accounting Information Systems | 2 | KARIN | 947 | C |
| 69173 | AIS7909 | Accounting Information Systems | 2 | KARIN | 947 | A |
| 69173 | FR8204 | Environmental Accounting | 3 | HELEN | 935 | B |
| 69173 | RM7000 | Research Methods | 4 | KEN | 327 | C |

## First normal form

| Student number | Course number | Course title | Instructor number | Instructor name | Instructor location | Grade |
|---|---|---|---|---|---|---|
| 38214 | FM6000 | Financial Modelling | 1 | AARON | 927 | A |
| 38214 | AIS7909 | Accounting Information Systems | 2 | KARIN | 947 | C |
| 69173 | AIS7909 | Accounting Information Systems | 2 | KARIN | 947 | A |
| 69173 | FR8204 | Environmental Accounting | 3 | HELEN | 935 | B |
| 69173 | RM7000 | Research Methods | 4 | KEN | 327 | C |

## First normal form with dependency arrows

| Student number | Course number | Course title | Instructor number | Instructor name | Instructor location | Grade |
|---|---|---|---|---|---|---|
| 38214 | FM6000 | Financial Modelling | 1 | AARON | 927 | A |
| 38214 | AIS7909 | Accounting Information Systems | 2 | KARIN | 947 | C |
| 69173 | AIS7909 | Accounting Information Systems | 2 | KARIN | 905 | A |
| 69173 | FR8204 | Environmental Accounting | 3 | HELEN | 935 | B |
| 69173 | RM7000 | Research Methods | 4 | KEN | 327 | C |

In first normal form, student number and course number have been chosen as a primary key to uniquely identify each line in the table.

### Second normal form

Student table:
Student number

Course table:
Course number, Course title, Instructor number, Instructor name, Instructor location

Student course (enrolment table):
Student number, Course number, Grade

Note that the student table has no attributes in this problem. However, as discussed in the chapter, when forming the enterprise model for the business it is likely that in combining tables the student table will have attributes such as student name, student phone number and student address. Even though the student table does not have attributes in this problem it is important and should not be deleted. Remember that when the full enterprise model is formed it is likely that this table will have attributes.

There is a dependency arrow from instructor name to instructor number and from instructor location to instructor number. Therefore, we have a transitive dependency: instructor name is dependent on the primary key, course number, via the non-key attribute instructor number. The same situation arises with instructor location. To remove the transitive dependencies we need to move to third normal form.

### Third normal form

Student table:
Student number

Course table:
Course number, Course title, Instructor number

Instructor table:
Instructor number, Instructor name, Instructor location

Student course (enrolment table):
Student number, Course number, Grade

Note that to remove the transitive dependency, instructor number becomes a foreign key in the course number table (shown by a dashed line underneath the instructor number in the course table). Then instructor number becomes a primary key in its own table. The attributes instructor name and instructor location are now attributes of the instructor table.

## E-R diagram

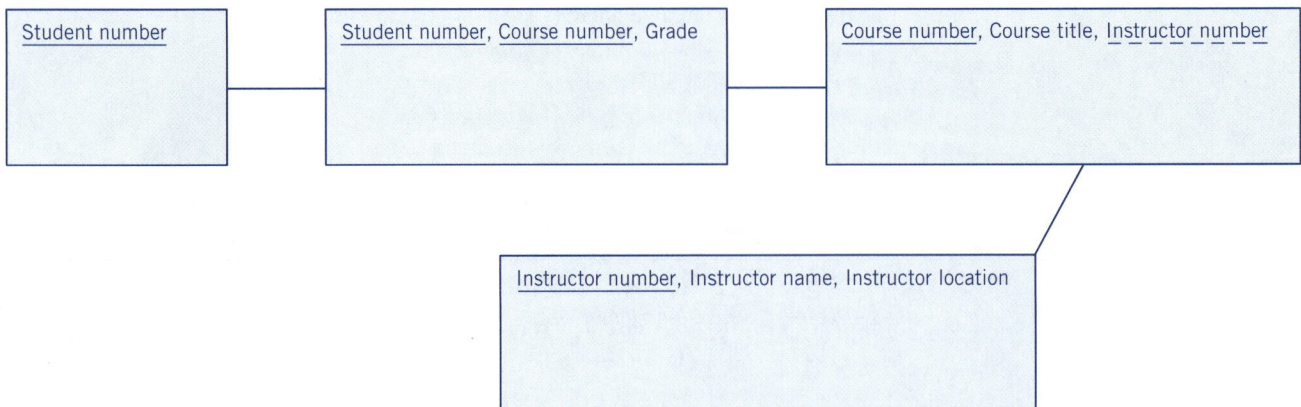

**Required**

(a) The table has been normalised to third normal form. Explain the logic underlying the table; that is, how the university works. Comment on the entity-relationship diagram.

**Part B:** The university table has been amended as shown in bold below. Paul is now
also an instructor for Accounting Information Systems. This table has again been
normalised to third normal form.

**ONF**

| Student number | Course number | Course title | Instructor number | Instructor name | Instructor location | Grade |
|---|---|---|---|---|---|---|
| 38214 | FM6000 | Financial Modelling | 1 | AARON | 927 | A |
| 38214 | AIS7909 | Accounting Information Systems | 2 | KARIN | 947 | C |
| 69173 | AIS7909 | Accounting Information Systems | 5 | **PAUL** | **944** | A |
| 69173 | FR8204 | Environmental Accounting | 3 | HELEN | 935 | B |
| 69173 | RM7000 | Research Methods | 4 | KEN | 327 | C |

**First normal form**

| Student number | Course number | Course title | Instructor number | Instructor name | Instructor location | Grade |
|---|---|---|---|---|---|---|
| 38214 | FM6000 | Financial Modelling | 1 | AARON | 927 | A |
| 38214 | AIS7909 | Accounting Information Systems | 2 | KARIN | 947 | C |
| 69173 | AIS7909 | Accounting Information Systems | 5 | **PAUL** | **944** | A |
| 69173 | FR8204 | Environmental Accounting | 3 | HELEN | 935 | B |
| 69173 | RM7000 | Research Methods | 4 | KEN | 327 | C |

Note that a primary key consisting of the attributes student number and course number is a sufficient composite primary key to identify each line in the table.

**First normal form with dependency arrows**

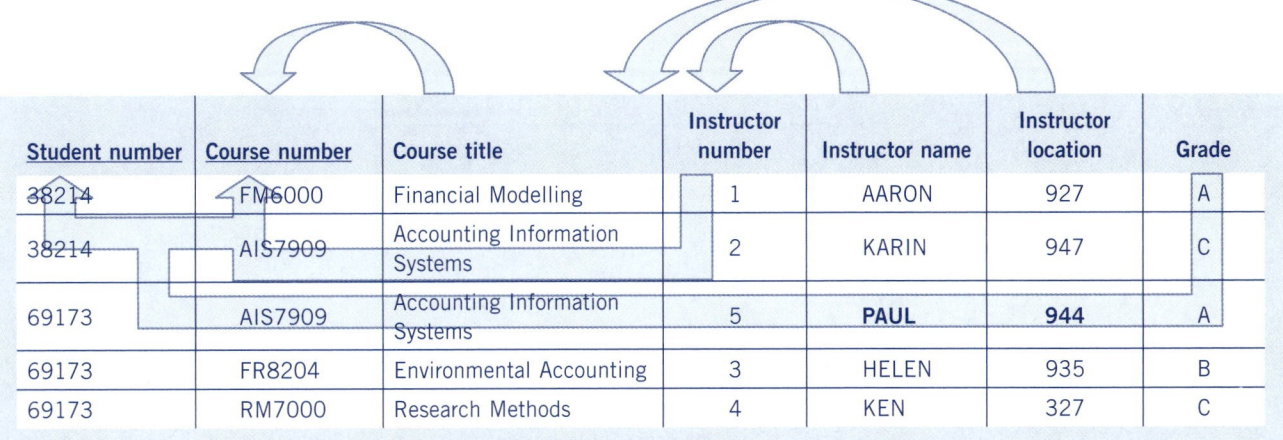

| Student number | Course number | Course title | Instructor number | Instructor name | Instructor location | Grade |
|---|---|---|---|---|---|---|
| 38214 | FM6000 | Financial Modelling | 1 | AARON | 927 | A |
| 38214 | AIS7909 | Accounting Information Systems | 2 | KARIN | 947 | C |
| 69173 | AIS7909 | Accounting Information Systems | 5 | **PAUL** | **944** | A |
| 69173 | FR8204 | Environmental Accounting | 3 | HELEN | 935 | B |
| 69173 | RM7000 | Research Methods | 4 | KEN | 327 | C |

**Second normal form**

Student table:
Student number

Course table:
Course number, Course title

Student course (enrolment table):
Student number, Course number, Instructor number, Instructor name, Instructor location, Grade

Note that both instructor name and instructor location are dependent on instructor number. Therefore, instructor name and instructor location are dependent on the primary key of the student course (enrolment table) but via the non-key attribute of instructor number. Therefore, the transitive dependency needs to be removed before the third normal form is achieved.

**Third normal form**

Student table:
Student number

Course table:
Course number, Course title

Student course (enrolment table):
Student number, Course number, Instructor number, Grade

Instructor table:
Instructor number, Instructor name, Instructor location

**E-R diagram**

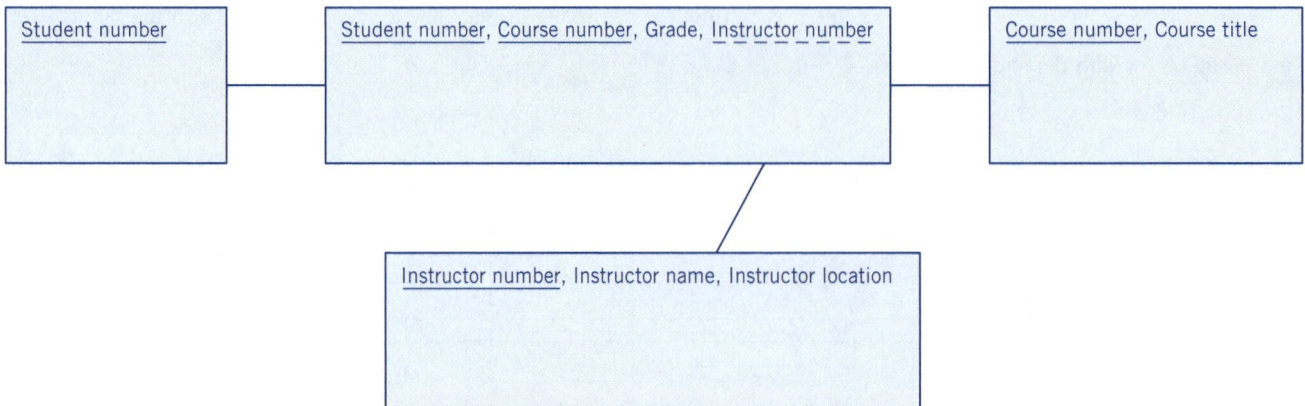

| Student number | Student number, Course number, Grade, Instructor number | Course number, Course title |

Instructor number, Instructor name, Instructor location

**Required**

(b) Explain the logic underlying the table; that is, how the university works given the above change. Comment on the E-R diagram.

**Part C:** The university table below has again been amended as shown in bold. Karin is now the lecturer for Research Methods. This table has again been normalised to third normal form.

**ONF**

| Student number | Course number | Course title | Instructor number | Instructor name | Instructor location | Grade |
|---|---|---|---|---|---|---|
| 38214 | FM6000 | Financial Modelling | 1 | AARON | 927 | A |
| 38214 | AIS7909 | Accounting Information Systems | 2 | KARIN | 947 | C |
| 69173 | AIS7909 | Accounting Information Systems | 5 | **PAUL** | **944** | A |
| 69173 | FR8204 | Environmental Accounting | 3 | HELEN | 935 | B |
| 69173 | RM7000 | Research Methods | 4 | KEN | 327 | C |
| 09667 | RM7000 | Research Methods | 2 | **KARIN** | **925** | C |

**First normal form**

| Student number | Course number | Course title | Instructor number | Instructor name | Instructor location | Grade |
|---|---|---|---|---|---|---|
| 38214 | FM6000 | Financial Modelling | 1 | AARON | 927 | A |
| 38214 | AIS7909 | Accounting Information Systems | 2 | KARIN | 947 | C |
| 69173 | AIS7909 | Accounting Information Systems | 5 | **PAUL** | **944** | A |
| 69173 | FR8204 | Environmental Accounting | 3 | HELEN | 935 | B |
| 69173 | RM7000 | Research Methods | 4 | KEN | 327 | C |
| 09667 | RM7000 | Research Methods | 2 | **KARIN** | **925** | C |

**First normal form with dependency arrows**

| Student number | Course number | Course title | Instructor number | Instructor name | Instructor location | Grade |
|---|---|---|---|---|---|---|
| 38214 | FM6000 | Financial Modelling | 1 | AARON | 927 | A |
| 38214 | AIS7909 | Accounting Information Systems | 2 | KARIN | 947 | C |
| 69173 | AIS7909 | Accounting Information Systems | 5 | **PAUL** | **944** | A |
| 69173 | FR8204 | Environmental Accounting | 3 | HELEN | 935 | B |
| 69173 | RM7000 | Research Methods | 4 | KEN | 327 | C |
| 09667 | RM7000 | Research Methods | 2 | **KARIN** | **925** | C |

**Second normal form**

Student table:
Student number

Course table:
Course number, Course title

Student course (enrolment table):
Student number, Course number, Instructor number, Instructor name, Instructor location, Grade

Note that instructor name is dependent on the primary key of the student course (enrolment table) via the non-key attribute of instructor number. Instructor location is dependent on part of the primary key (the course number attribute) and instructor number (a non-key attribute). Therefore, we need to remove these transitive dependencies to achieve third normal form.

**Third normal form**

Student table:
Student number

Course table:
Course number, Course title

Student course (enrolment table):
Student number, Course number, Instructor number, Grade

Instructor table:
Instructor number, Instructor name

Course room allocation table:
Course number, Instructor number, Instructor location

**Entity-relationship diagram**

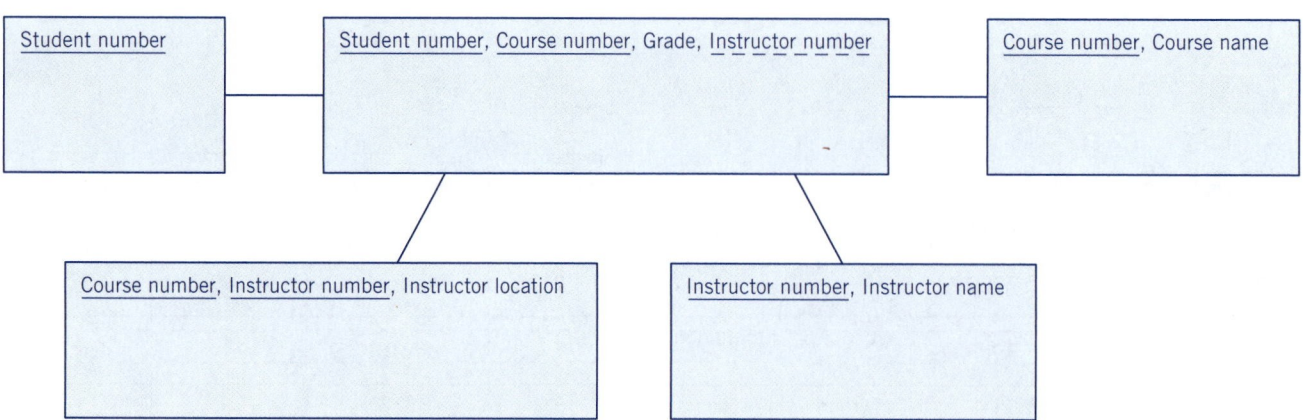

**Required**

(c) Explain the logic underlying the table; that is, how the university works given the above change. Comment on the E-R diagram.

## FURTHER READING

Hoffer, JA, Prescott, MB & McFadden, FR 2001, *Modern database management*, 6th edn, Prentice Hall, New Jersey.

McCarthy, WE 2003, 'The REA modelling approach to teaching accounting information systems', *Issues in Accounting Education,* iss. 18, no. 4, pp. 427–41.

Robb, P & Coronel C 2002, *Database systems: design, implementation, and management*, 5th edn, Course Technology, Thomson Learning, Cambridge, Massachusetts.

Satzinger, JW, Jackson, RB & Burd, SD 2009, *Systems analysis and design in a changing world*, 5th edn, Cengage Learning, United States.

Shelly, GB & Rosenblatt, HJ 2010, *Systems analysis and design*, 8th edn, Cengage Learning, United States.

## SELF-TEST ANSWERS

4.1 a, 4.2 b, 4.3 a, 4.4 c, 4.5 b, 4.6 a

## END NOTES

1. Hoffer, JA, Prescott, MB & McFadden, FR 2001, *Modern database management*, 6th edn, Prentice Hall, New Jersey.
2. McCarthy, WE 1982, 'The REA Accounting Model: a generalized framework for accounting systems in a shared data environment', *The Accounting Review*, July, pp. 554–77.

# 5

# Systems documentation

## Learning objectives

After studying this chapter, you should be able to:

**(1)** explain why systems documentation is important to the organisation and the accounting function

**(2)** describe how systems documentation can be used as a part of business process redesign and re-engineering

**(3)** describe how the accountant and auditor can be exposed to systems documentation

**(4)** identify legislative reform that has impacted on systems documentation

**(5)** read and interpret different forms of systems documentation

**(6)** explain the concept of a balanced set of systems documentation

**(7)** prepare different forms of systems documentation

**(8)** compare and contrast different forms of systems documentation.

# Introduction

Have you ever travelled to a new city or country and arrived in the middle of a thriving metropolis only to discover you do not know where you are or in which direction you should be heading? Alternatively, recall your first few days on campus, as you tried to find your way around the layout of the buildings and the location of key lecture theatres, coffee shops and libraries. The navigation process can be tough ... especially if you have no assistance and are in a totally new environment. However, with a map, or some reference material, finding your way around suddenly becomes a whole lot easier.

It is the same with information systems. A system without any 'maps' to explain how the system works is a potential problem ... just like arriving at Victoria Station in London without knowing where you are, or in which direction you need to head to find your already booked accommodation. Instead of looking for coffee shops and accommodation, as an accountant, you will be looking for the operation of business processes, internal controls and data flows. With the appropriate systems documentation, which is the road map for understanding and navigating the business, navigating a system becomes a lot easier. This makes other tasks, like redesigning and auditing a system, easier to accomplish and ensures they are done with the full scope of the information system's operations in mind.

This chapter will introduce you to some different techniques for mapping a business process,[#] beginning with the process map, or 'swim lanes' approach. The discussion will then move on to data flow diagrams (DFDs) — including the context diagram, logical DFD and physical DFD. Following this, the systems flowchart will be introduced. The aim in going through each of these documentation forms is to enable you to (1) understand some of the different ways that a system can be diagrammatically represented, (2) prepare your own set of systems documentation, and (3) see the relationships among some of the different forms of systems documentation.

**LEARNING OBJECTIVE**  1

*Explain why systems documentation is important to the organisation and the accounting function.*

## THE PURPOSE AND ROLE OF SYSTEMS DOCUMENTATION

Systems documentation, as mentioned in the introduction, is a way of visually depicting the operations of a system. The documentation can come in a variety of forms, depending on the perspective of the system that needs to be represented. Essentially, when we prepare systems documentation we are preparing a document that will answer one or more of the following questions.

- Who is involved?
- What activities occur?
- Where do the activities occur?
- Why do the activities occur?
- Where do the activities fit within the rest of the organisation?

When we look at the three types of documentation in the following sections — process maps, DFDs and systems flowcharts, we will see that each addresses at least

---

\# A business process is defined as the activities that work together to achieve business objectives. An information system — the collection of data, processing, storage and generation of outputs, supported by people, processes, technology, hardware and software — is a support for the business process. A business process may involve various information systems interacting with each other, for example, sales, marketing and finance. The emphasis in this chapter is being able to depict the systems and their interaction across the business process, with an emphasis on being aware of data flows and how the data moves through a business process. As such, when we talk about documenting a business process we are showing the interaction of information systems within that process.

one of the above questions. In fact, some of the documentation types address several of the questions. However, what we will also notice is that each of the documentation types addresses the questions in a different manner. As a result, it is not possible to say which form of documentation is better or which one is more important — it all depends on what we want to know about the system.

**Process maps** provide a simple graphical representation of a business process, detailing the activities that occur, the areas of the business responsible for completing the activities, and any decisions that need to be made as part of the process.

**Data flow diagrams (DFDs)** are graphical representations of where data flows within a system and can have three forms: the context diagram, physical DFD and logical DFD. The **context diagram** provides a representation of the system of interest and the entities that provide inputs to, or receive outputs from, the system of interest. The **system of interest** is the system or process that is the focus of the documentation. It will have a clear boundary or scope. The **physical data flow diagram** provides details of the *entities* involved in a process and the flows among those entities, as well as their interaction with external entities. The **logical data flow diagram** illustrates the *processes* that take place within a system, the flows between these processes, and how these processes interact with the external entities that provide inputs to, or receive outputs from, the system of interest. There is no need to be too concerned about the distinction between internal and external entities and the finer points that differentiate the types of DFDs at this point: these concepts will be explained in more detail further on in the chapter.

**Systems flowcharts** illustrate a system and its inputs, processes and outputs in more detail than a process map or DFD. They provide information about the documents and processes performed within a system, as well as who is involved in the system. You will be introduced to the different symbols and notations, and how to read and draw a flowchart later in the chapter.

Many accounting students ask why they need to know about systems documentation, since a considerable amount of their accounting studies involves executing debits and credits. Such a view of accounting ignores the important role of the accounting profession in relation to information systems and the broader business environment. Accordingly, we will now spend some time answering the question, 'Why is it important that accountants know about the various forms of systems documentation?' As you will find out in the next section, there are many reasons why you, as an accountant, need to be able to prepare and understand systems documentation. Whether you end up in a career as an accountant, consultant, auditor, programmer ... or follow just about any other business-related career path, you will be involved in a system at some stage. Whether that involvement is through you being a user of a system, or a designer or a manager overseeing the use and design of a system, it is imperative that you understand how the system is set up and operates. Increasingly, there are also compelling legal reasons for preparing systems documentation, as we will explore.

**LEARNING OBJECTIVE**

Describe how systems documentation can be used as a part of business process redesign and re-engineering.

# PROCESS REDESIGN AND RE-ENGINEERING, AND SYSTEMS DOCUMENTATION

In chapter 2 we discussed the concept of the business process and how it is central to the operation of the organisation. We also mentioned the idea of business process re-engineering (BPR) — the procedure undertaken by an organisation looking to significantly restructure the operation of a business process and improve the process's

---

**Process map** *A simple graphical representation of a business process, detailing the activities that occur, the areas of the business responsible for completing the activities, and any decisions that need to be made as part of the process.*

**Data flow diagrams (DFDs)** *Graphical representations of the data flows that occur within a system.*

**Context diagram** *A representation of the system of interest and the entities that provide inputs to, or receive outputs from, the system of interest.*

**System of interest** *The system or process that is the focus of the documentation; it will have a clear boundary or scope.*

**Physical data flow diagram** *A diagram that provides details of the entities involved in a process and the flows between those entities, as well as their interaction with external entities.*

**Logical data flow diagram** *A diagram that illustrates the processes that take place within a system, the flows among these processes, and how these processes interact with the external entities that provide inputs to, or receive outputs from, the system of interest.*

**Systems flowchart** *A flowchart that illustrates a system and its inputs, processes and outputs in more detail than a process map or DFD, providing information about the documents and processes performed within the system, as well as who is involved in the system.*

performance. There are several reasons business process re-engineering may be required, including the potential for the business to gain a competitive advantage.

How is redesign and re-engineering done? The first essential step is to understand how the existing process operates, identifying the activities that occur, the people involved, the parts of the organisation that interact with the process and the trail of data that moves through the process, to name just a few aspects. This extensive analysis requires an ability to get inside the business process. One way that this can be achieved is by understanding and reviewing the systems documentation for the process. The systems documentation provides an overview of the sequence of activities in the business process; for example, the logical DFD will show the key process activities that occur and the data that is needed and generated within each process; the physical DFD will provide a perspective on who is involved in the process (i.e. the people and their respective functional areas). Similarly, a flowchart will show the movement of data and documents between functional areas and personnel and allow the analysis of what occurs and who is involved. Such a perspective is a useful starting point for any re-engineering or systems redesign project. Booth (1995) points out that an analysis of process documentation as part of process redesign can allow for the identification of such aspects as where activities can run in parallel, where paper items can be eliminated, where unnecessary data collection can be removed and where the same activity is performed multiple times. Each of these represents potential ways of 'trimming the fat' from a business process, but are possible only through a thorough understanding of process operation, and thus a thorough understanding of the associated systems documentation.

**LEARNING OBJECTIVE** ③

*Describe how the accountant and auditor can be exposed to systems documentation.*

# ORGANISATIONAL MEMORY AND CHANGE

As mentioned above, chapter 2 discussed the process perspective and how an organisation's design might be changed in a BPR effort. It showed how enterprise resource planning (ERP) systems (covered in more detail in chapter 6) can have a part to play in this effort. For the adoption of an ERP system to be successful, or for BPR to yield benefits, an organisation must first understand its existing business processes. One way it can do this is through systems documentation. For consultants coming into an organisation and assisting in implementing an ERP system, or managing a re-engineering effort, systems documentation will be one of the first ports of call to understand how the business operates. Accountants also play a role in systems documentation. That is, the key piece of knowledge the accountant can offer the organisation in situations of implementing new systems, designing new systems or adopting new modifications to a system concerns the need for well designed internal controls. The means through which this information can be communicated in system development is through systems documentation. When systems development is undertaken, the accountant (and the auditor) will be interested in reviewing the documentation that shows how the new system will operate, paying particular attention to the design and functioning of the internal controls.

Alternatively, in starting a new organisation and building new business processes, there is a need to record their design. The original designers of the business process will not always be with the organisation — people leave, get fired, die — making it important that all the knowledge of a process's operations is captured before it is too late. Systems documentation is important in preserving this knowledge of the process.

# AUDITING AND SYSTEMS DOCUMENTATION

Closer to the accounting front, systems documentation plays a key role in the execution of an external financial statement audit. According to Australian Auditing Standard ASA 200 *Overall Objectives of the Independent Auditor and the Conduct of an Audit in Accordance with Australian Auditing Standards*, 'the purpose of an audit is to enhance the degree of confidence of intended users in the financial report. This is achieved by the expression of an opinion by the auditor on whether the financial report is prepared, in all material respects, in accordance with an applicable financial reporting framework'.[1] This means that a financial statement auditor will need to understand the processes that are used in handling the various transactions in which an entity engages. Paragraph 95 of ASA 315 requires the following:

> The auditor shall obtain an understanding of the information system, including the related business processes, relevant to financial reporting, including the following areas:
> (a) The classes of transactions in the entity's operations that are significant to the financial report;
> (b) The procedures, within both information technology (IT) and manual systems, by which those transactions are initiated, recorded, processed, corrected as necessary, transferred to the general ledger and reported in the financial report;
> (c) The related accounting records, supporting information and specific accounts in the financial report that are used to initiate, record, process and report transactions; this includes the correction of incorrect information and how information is transferred to the general ledger. The records may be in either manual or electronic form;
> (d) How the information system captures events and conditions, other than transactions, that are significant to the financial report;
> (e) The financial reporting process used to prepare the entity's financial report, including significant accounting estimates and disclosures; and
> (f) Controls surrounding journal entries, including non-standard journal entries used to record non-recurring, unusual transactions or adjustments.[2]

The requirements of ASA 315, paragraph 18(a) are such that the major groups of transactions that an entity participates in must be understood by the auditor. This translates to, amongst other things, knowledge and awareness of the business processes and transaction cycles that are a part of the organisation's activities. We discussed the generic concept of a business process in chapter 2. In future chapters we will examine specific examples of business processes. For now, the key point for you to be aware of is the need to understand how a business process works and the fact that systems documentation is one way of gaining and recording that understanding. The understanding of processes includes, as is mentioned in paragraph 18(b) of ASA 315, the commencement of transactions, the steps followed in processing the transaction and how the transaction impacts on the financial reports. This requires the auditor to obtain and document evidence about the operation of the business processes. The requirement to document the understanding of a business process and its internal controls is left up to the auditor's professional judgement under the revised ASA 315; however, the previous version of the standard did specify that documentation includes techniques such as 'narrative descriptions, questionnaires, check lists and flow charts'.[3] As is noted by Booth, 'Only by describing the operation of a process can areas of poor understanding be highlighted'.[4] In other words, the best way to ensure that you know how a process works is to try to explain it to someone else, that is, prepare systems documentation.

In gaining this understanding of a business process, the auditor will be concerned with how data is handled, the steps that are followed, the internal controls that are built into the process and the potential for errors to occur that could result in the financial statements being materially misstated. One of the ways the auditor can do this is through the observation and inspection of documents within the organisation, with both the Australian[5] and New Zealand[6] (in New Zealand, AS-302 and its replacement ISA (NZ) 315, which came into effect in 2008 following international harmonisation of auditing standards) auditing standards mentioning that this can include such documentation sources as organisation charts, procedures manuals and, potentially, systems documentation. Research also supports the importance of systems documentation to the auditor, with Bradford et al[7] finding that 41 per cent of respondents surveyed (who were all members of the Institute of Management Accountants and had roles including auditing, accounting and financial controlling) used flowcharts to assess internal controls, while 58 per cent used flowcharts to evaluate the current system within an organisation.

**LEARNING OBJECTIVE** **4**
*Identify legislative reform that has impacted on systems documentation.*

# THE LAW AND SYSTEMS DOCUMENTATION

Auditors are also facing legislative pressure to use systems documentation. In Australia, the auditing standards referred to above now have the force of law. As such, auditors now must comply with the prescribed standards when carrying out an audit, including using and preparing appropriate documentation. In addition, as a result of the introduction of the Sarbanes–Oxley Act in the United States, organisations are now facing legal pressures to ensure that adequate systems documentation exists within the organisation. Sarbanes–Oxley was brought into existence with the purpose of protecting investors 'by improving the accuracy and reliability of corporate disclosures made pursuant to the securities laws, and for other purposes'.[8] While Sarbanes–Oxley is a piece of US legislation, it has implications beyond the shores of the United States since some of its provisions will apply to foreign companies that are listed on US stock markets. As such, some Australian and New Zealand firms listed on US stock markets have had to confront the requirements of Sarbanes–Oxley and work towards being Sarbanes–Oxley compliant, since its provisions became binding on Australian firms trading on US stock exchanges from 15 July 2006.

Section 404 of the Sarbanes–Oxley legislation impacts documentation. This section requires organisations to put in place, review and have procedures for the management of internal controls. In addition, these controls and management techniques are subject to an audit by an external auditor as part of the annual financial report audit. The management and recording of internal controls includes the preparation of documentation on how the controls work.[9] Accordingly, it is now imperative that those within the organisation, as well as those auditing the organisation, are familiar with systems documentation techniques.

A publication by PricewaterhouseCoopers,[10] which aimed to provide advice for companies faced with the prospect of Sarbanes–Oxley compliance, makes abundantly clear the increased role of systems documentation for those within the organisation and for the external auditors. PricewaterhouseCoopers comment that 'The effect of section 404, and related regulations, is that companies and their auditors put a much greater emphasis on documentation than in the past. This applies at two levels. First, the controls must be documented so that management can assess their design and test them. Second, in the testing, the execution of the controls should have been evidenced in some way. One US company representative said that 'good documentation early on was crucial. We had always done it at a desk level but this was raising it up a level to have top-level flow charts'.[11]

As a result of the requirements of auditing standards, most of the large international accounting and consulting firms now use and rely increasingly on systems documentation, whether as part of providing a routine audit or providing consulting advice to reconfigure a business process.[12]

Systems documentation also serves a very important role within an organisation. That is, it provides a record of how the organisation's systems are set up and supposed to operate. When problems arise in a process, changes need to be made to a process, or internal controls need to be designed, the systems documentation will invariably be a point of reference.

**LEARNING OBJECTIVE 5**
*Read and interpret different forms of systems documentation.*

# READING SYSTEMS DOCUMENTATION

Having established the importance of systems documentation to the accountant and the need to visualise the functioning of the accounting information system, we will now examine some of the different types of systems documentation. In particular, we will examine process maps, DFDs and systems flowcharts. In this section, we will look at how to read and interpret different types of systems documentation, while in the next section we will go through the steps in preparing systems documentation.

While we will examine process maps, DFDs (including context diagrams, and logical and physical DFDs) and systems flowcharts, it should be noted that there are many other forms of systems documentation available, including entity-relationship diagrams (which you saw in chapter 3), resources–events–agents diagrams and UML diagrams. Discussion of these other forms is beyond the scope of this chapter. The documentation techniques we will cover in this chapter are typically the forms of documentation used by accounting professionals in recording the operation of a business process, gaining an understanding of a process, evaluating controls in a process and designing or changing a process.[13] The use of the various types of documentation is summarised in table 5.1.[14] As is evident from the results in the table, accounting professionals use a range of systems documentation formats in their day-to-day duties, and most accountants will use more than one form of systems documentation. Also, AIS focus 5.1 overleaf discusses some documentation issues for the accounting professional.

**TABLE 5.1** Frequency and purpose of usage of systems documentation method

| Documentation method | Overall usage of documentation | | How the specific documentation is used | | | |
|---|---|---|---|---|---|---|
| | Number using | Percent using | Evaluate current system % | Design or change system % | Assess internal controls % | Describe business process % |
| System flowcharts | 187 | 46 | 58 | 45 | 47 | 79 |
| DFDs | 85 | 21 | 51 | 47 | 35 | 68 |
| E-R diagrams | 56 | 14 | 36 | 25 | 36 | 61 |
| REA diagrams | 81 | 20 | 49 | 30 | 49 | 65 |
| Process maps | 115 | 29 | 47 | 23 | 38 | 76 |
| UML | 24 | 6 | 46 | 33 | 42 | 38 |
| No technique | 164 | 41 | n/a | n/a | n/a | n/a |

## AIS FOCUS 5.1

### The role of software in systems documentation

With the recent run of corporate collapses and the global financial crisis prompting questions to be levelled at the management of organisations, as well as those responsible for auditing and reviewing the processes of organisations, pressure has emerged for professionals to be literate in the different documentation techniques available to them. One area where this pressure has been felt is in the auditing profession, with independent auditors now required to document their understanding of the processes in an organisation and the basis for any risk assessments that they may make in the conduct of the audit. In order to handle these requirements, auditors are increasingly turning to software to help them manage the different forms of documentation and ensure it is linked correctly into the audit process. Typically, the auditor would look towards electronic working paper tools as a way of automating the audit process. Increasingly, they will also be required to understand business processes and the sources of risk within these processes, with this also needing to be documented. This has made systems documentation like process maps and systems flowcharts an important tool in the auditor's array of skills.[15]

## Entities

Before we begin the process of reading systems documentation, it is important that you are familiar with the conventions for identifying who and what is included in systems documentation. The central technique for answering this question is to focus on the entities that are part of the business process or system. Entities refer to the people and things that are a part of the process. An **entity** is any person or thing involved in the activities of a business process. Entities can be further classified as being either internal or external. The distinction between internal and external is dependent on (a) the process that is being documented and (b) the functions and tasks that are carried out by the entity.

In chapter 2, it was mentioned that a business process is set up to achieve a specific purpose or objective within the organisation. The logical extension of this idea is that a process will have a defined starting point and finishing point — a clear boundary that specifies the business process's scope and operation. Firstly, when we are preparing systems documentation, it is important to be clear about the process being documented and to clearly focus on that process. If you are documenting the sales process, for example, then focus on the sales process. What happens in other processes or other parts of the organisation is not relevant to the documentation being prepared for the sales process. Being clear on the scope or domain covered by the process being documented is the first step to being clear about the entities within the process.

The second step is to be clear about what each entity does within a process. When we look at a written description of a process, such as in figure 5.1 (which we look at in further detail shortly), we notice that there are several different people and things mentioned as being involved in the process. However, what should also be clear is

> **Entity** Representations of real-world things or objects that are involved in a process and correspond to a table in a relational database.

that each entity performs a different function within the process. This is the important distinction when classifying entities as either internal or external.

**External entity** *Any entity that provides inputs into a process or receives outputs from a process.*

An **external entity** is any entity that provides inputs into a process or receives outputs from a process. An external entity to the process does not use the data. This is where clarity about the process being documented is important; that is, an entity may be an external entity for one process but an internal entity of a different process. This will become apparent as we look at specific business processes (or transaction cycles) in later chapters.

**Internal entity** *An entity that processes or transforms the data within the business process of interest.*

In contrast to external entities, an **internal entity** is defined as an entity that processes or transforms the data within the business process of interest (the one that is being documented). When we refer to data being processed or transformed, we are referring to activities in which the data is used. Transforming or processing data is more than just sending or receiving data — it is about applying the data to the specific tasks and requirements within the business process being documented. Some key words to look for that indicate that data is being transformed or processed within a process include reviews, confirms, reconciles, data entry, approves, batches, calculates, authorises, compares, annotates, prepares, records, sorts and matches.

As examples of some of the typical activities that suggest data is being processed or transformed, read the following explanations.

- *Comparison of data* — the data from one source is reconciled to data from another source.
- *Entry of data* — data is converted from one format (i.e. paper document) to another format (i.e. computer data) or vice versa.
- *Reports are reviewed* — the information in the report is processed (whether manually or by a computer) in order to reach some sort of decision or conclusion.
- *Approval of documents or events* — details about an event are considered and authorisation is provided. In order to provide the approval the details need to be processed and evaluated against a set of criteria. In other words, the person who must provide the approval does so after processing the details they have available to them.

In summary, the key in determining whether an entity is internal or external is the activities that the entity performs. If the entity's sole activities involve sending or receiving data, they are considered external. In contrast, if the entity performs data processing or transformation, it is considered internal. Remember also that this classification depends on the process (i.e. an entity can be external to one process but internal to another), so make sure you are clear on the process being documented.

## The narration

**Structured narration** *A written description of how a process operates.*

The starting point for systems documentation is the structured narration. The structured narration is a written description of how the process operates. Typically, the **structured narration** will be prepared after observing a process in operation and interviewing the key participants in the process. Having observed the process and carried out the interviews, the accountant will prepare a written description of the operation of the process. The advantage of the structured narration is that it is readily accessible to anyone who can read. This can make it a popular form for documenting a process. However, for a deeper analysis and a better understanding of the process, the structured narration can be subject to limitations. One of the limitations inherent in the structured narration is that its preparation and readability are contingent on the writer's writing style. Some people may write in a wordy, verbose manner, while others may be extremely brief in their preparation of the narrative. Additionally, written work can be subject to different interpretations and may lead to two people interpreting the process in different ways. Consequently, you would seldom expect the structured narrative to be the sole source of systems documentation. However, this is not to say that it is without a purpose, for it provides the basis of the documentation we are about to explore. Shown in figure 5.1 is an example of a structured narration. We will refer to this case in working through the reading of systems documentation, so take time to familiarise yourself with its contents.

As you read through the narration pay particular attention to the people, places and things that are involved in the process — as we mentioned earlier, these are referred to as entities. Also focus on what each entity is doing. Remember back to chapter 2 on business processes and chapter 1 where the concept of inputs–processes–outputs was referred to, and apply these ideas to the case in figure 5.1. For example, consider what inputs are being used? What processes/activities are being carried out using the inputs? What outputs are generated as a result? We will return to this emphasis when we look at preparing the system documentation in the next section.

The requesting department sends a purchase requisition to the purchasing officer. When the purchasing officer receives the purchase requisition they enter the details into the computer, which stores the data in the purchase requisitions received data store. The computer then displays a list of suppliers, which are stored in the supplier master file, and the purchasing officer selects a supplier for the goods that have been requested. The details of the products are extracted from the purchase requisition data and used to fill in the purchase order on the computer screen. The purchasing officer will review the details on the screen and make sure they match the purchase requisition and then click on the 'Confirm' button, which prompts the computer to save the purchase order in the purchase orders pending file. The purchase requisition is then stamped as 'Entered' and filed in the purchase requisitions file.

Each Wednesday, the purchasing supervisor logs into the computer and reviews the pending purchase orders. Once the supervisor has reviewed an order they click on the 'Confirm and print' button and three copies of the purchase order are printed and signed by the supervisor. The computer saves the details in the confirmed purchase orders file. One copy is sent to the supplier, a second copy is sent to the requesting department, while the third copy is given to the purchasing officer who matches it with the purchase requisition and files it in the orders sent file.

**FIGURE 5.1** Reading documentation case example

## Structured narrative table

The structured narrative table is a means of summarising the narrative in a systematic way to emphasise who is involved in the process, what is being used in the process (e.g. what data and documents are moving through the process), what activities are occurring in the process and the destination for the outputs generated at the various stages of the process. The structure of the table is shown in table 5.2, which has been completed for the example narrative shown in figure 5.1.

**TABLE 5.2** Structured narrative table

| No. | Entity | Input | Process/activity | Output |
|---|---|---|---|---|
| 1 | Requesting department | | | Purchase requisition |
| 2 | Purchasing officer | Purchase requisition | Enter details into computer | Purchase requisition data |
| 3 | Computer | Purchase requisition data | Capture purchase requisition data | Saved in purchase requisitions received data store |
| 4 | Computer | Supplier master data list | Display list on screen | Supplier list on computer screen |
| 5 | Purchasing officer | Supplier list on screen | Selects supplier from list | Selected supplier |
| 6 | Computer | Selected supplier and purchase requisition data from purchase requisition received data store data | Prepares purchase order | Completed purchase order on screen |
| 7 | Purchasing officer | Completed purchase order | Reviews order details | |
| 8 | Purchasing officer | | Confirms order details | Enters confirmation |
| 9 | Computer | Confirmation from Purchasing officer | Saves purchase order | Data stored in purchase order pending file |
| 10 | Purchasing officer | | Stamps purchase requisition | |
| 11 | Purchasing officer | | Files purchase requisition | Requisition filed in purchase requisition file |
| 12 | Computer | Purchase order data from purchase order pending file | Displays purchase orders | Purchase order details on computer screen |
| 13 | Purchasing supervisor | Purchase order details on screen | Reviews purchase order details | |
| 14 | Purchasing supervisor | | Confirms purchase order details | Keyed confirmation |
| 15 | Computer | Keyed confirmation | Prints purchase orders | Three copies of purchase orders |
| 16 | Computer | | Saves purchase orders | Confirmed purchase orders data file updates |
| 17 | Purchasing supervisor | Printed purchase orders | Signs purchase orders | Signed purchase orders |
| 18 | Purchasing supervisor | | | Purchase order to supplier |
| 19 | Purchasing supervisor | | | Purchase order to requesting department |
| 20 | Purchasing supervisor | | | Purchase order to purchasing officer |
| 21 | Purchasing officer | Purchase orders | Retrieves purchase Requisition | |
| 22 | Purchasing officer | | Matches purchase order and requisition | |
| 23 | Purchasing officer | | Files matched documents | Matched documents in orders sent file |

There are a few things that you should notice about the structured narrative table as follows.

1. The entities are listed in the order in which they are involved in the process. Their order in the process is indicated in the first column, titled 'No.'
2. An entity can appear more than once in the table. For example, it may perform more than one activity. Examples here include the purchasing officer and the computer, which perform several activities.
3. The inputs column refers to the inputs that are used or received by an entity to carry out an activity. For example, in activity 2, the purchasing officer is not able to enter the details of what is being purchased unless they have the purchase requisition.
4. The process column refers to the activity that is being performed. This will be the specific action or specific task that is being carried out by the entity. This column represents the 'what is being done' aspect of the process. It tells us how the entity is using the inputs it has received.
5. The output column refers to the destination for the product of the process. For example, if a paper document is prepared, what document is it and where does it end up? For example, in activities 15 to 17, the computer prints three copies of the purchase order (an output of activity 15), saves the data on a disk (the data is an output of the saving process; in other words, the data is placed in the data store) and the purchase orders go to the purchasing supervisor (an input into the purchasing officer's activity listed in activity 17 in the table).
6. The rows of the structured narrative table should be read in conjunction with each other. Taking a row on its own may not make total sense, but, when a specific activity is considered in relation to the antecedent and subsequent activities, the rows provide a more meaningful and clearer perspective.

You may also notice that some of the input and output cells in the table are blank. Examples are activities 10 and 11. In activity 10, the purchasing officer is stamping the purchase requisition and in activity 11 they are filing the requisition. Both of these activities use the same input — the purchase requisition that the purchase officer obtained in activity 2. Listing the purchase requisition again in activities 10 and 11 has been omitted to avoid redundancy and duplication. However, adding the document in to those cells would also be acceptable. Similarly, in activities 7 and 8, we see only one output for the two activities. In this case, we have two consecutive activities that are performed together and the output is not generated until the second of these activities is complete. Also notice how the requesting department sends a document but does not perform data processing. In the case we are told that it sends a purchase requisition but has no details of the activities it performs in preparing the document. As such, we can only document what is included in the narrative, so all we can show is what is included in activity 1 — the act of sending the purchase requisition to the purchasing officer. These points highlight, as was mentioned earlier, the need to consider the contents of each row in relation to its antecedent and subsequent rows.

## Process maps

A process map is a simple graphical representation of a business process, detailing the activities that occur, the areas of the business responsible for completing the activities, the links between the different areas of the business, and any decisions that need to be made as part of the process. Process mapping is an important technique for documenting a system and represents an extremely useful tool that is regularly employed by both consultants and auditors to understand a process and its operations.[16] Jones and Lancaster note that as a result of this widespread usage, process mapping 'has become a necessary element in the accountant's skill set and that accounting students would benefit by learning how to map a business process'.[17] It is also noted by Burns (2007, p. 16) that with process improvement as the new mantra of business, process maps are a key component of process improvement as they are easy to understand and apply.

## Reading a process map

A process map is much simpler than a DFD or systems flowchart. It has a limited set of symbols and an easy-to-read format. The body of the process map consists of rectangles, which represent the processes or activities that take place, and arrows connecting the processes, which typically represent flows of documents or information among activities. These activities and flows are placed in the map according to the division or functional area that performs the task. The different organisational divisions or functional areas are represented by the horizontal rows that run across the diagram. You may draw a comparison between the appearance of the map with the divisions and that of lanes in a swimming pool.

Some rules to keep in mind when reading a process map[18] are listed below and discussed in detail with reference to figure 5.2 overleaf, a process map drawn for the case in figure 5.1.

1. The functional areas appear down the left-hand side of the diagram.
2. The functional areas are separated with a solid line.
3. The subfunctions are separated with a dashed line.
4. The standard symbol is a rectangle for a process or activity.
5. Lines that connect processes are labelled with documents.
6. Process rectangles describe processes *not* documents.
7. The process map reads left to right and top to bottom.

From the narrative in figure 5.1 we note that there are five different entities involved — the requesting department, purchasing officer, purchasing supervisor, computer and supplier. In our process map, each entity has its own lane. Also notice that the line separating the purchasing officer and the purchasing supervisor is a dashed line — this tells us that both of these entities are from the same division of the organisation, in this case, the purchasing department.

The arrows in the process map represent the movement of data or documents. From the process map we can clearly see the movement of the paper documents (purchase requisition and purchase order) and the electronic data (requisition data and the confirmation from the supervisor).

Each rectangle in the process map gives an indication of the activities or stages that are occurring within our process. You should be able to map the stages in the process map back to the different parts of the structured narrative table and the original narrative in figure 5.1.

From the process map, we gain a good idea of who is involved in the process (i.e. the entities) and some idea of what activities they perform (from the rectangles). However, we have very little indication of how the activities are performed (e.g. Are the activities manual or computerised? Where does the data come from when preparing a purchase order?).

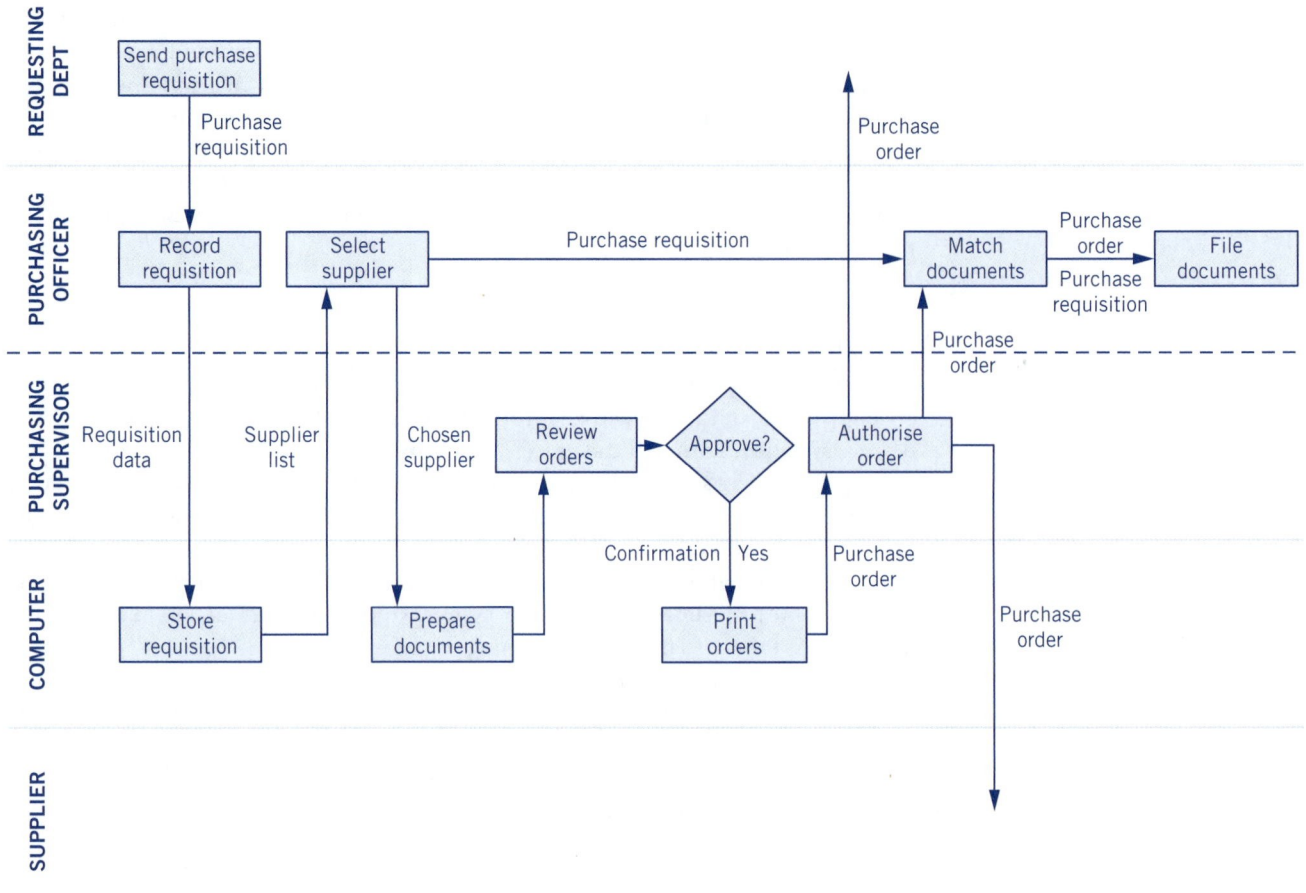

**FIGURE 5.2** Process map — reading a map

## Data flow diagrams

A data flow diagram or DFD is a form of systems documentation that illustrates a system and the components that make up the system, as well as the flows between these components. It allows the user of the documentation to identify the entities involved in a system, the processes that take place within the system and the flows of data that occur between these entities and processes. There are three types of DFDs: a context diagram, a physical data flow diagram, and a logical data flow diagram.

The context diagram is the simplest of the three, describing only what the system or process of interest is and how it interacts with external entities (where the system gets its data from and where the data ends up). A physical DFD identifies the people, places and things that perform the process (the internal *entities*), thus showing who is involved in the system and the physical flows among these entities and the external *entities*. The focus in the physical DFD, as the name would suggest, is very much on who or what is involved: the physical reality of the system. A logical DFD conveys the *processes* that are performed within a system. Instead of identifying who is involved in the system, the logical DFD shows what takes place inside the system, with descriptions of the major processes that occur. Remember, the focus in the physical DFD is on the *entities* that perform the activities. The focus in the logical DFD is on the *logical activities* and *processes* that occur.

The remainder of this section takes you through the process of reading and preparing a context diagram, logical DFD and physical DFD. Prior to the reading and preparation process, it is necessary to understand the symbols used in DFDs.

## Symbols

There are relatively few symbols used in preparing a DFD. These symbols are shown in figure 5.3. You will notice that, in comparison to the systems flowchart, which will be discussed later, the symbols are far less descriptive. This relative simplicity of DFDs is seen as one of their strengths, since it can facilitate communication between users and designers of a system, particularly when undertaking systems development activities.[19] The emphasis of the DFD is to show how data moves through a process and how the data is used, provided and distributed by a system.[20] Take some time now to familiarise yourself with the DFD symbols.

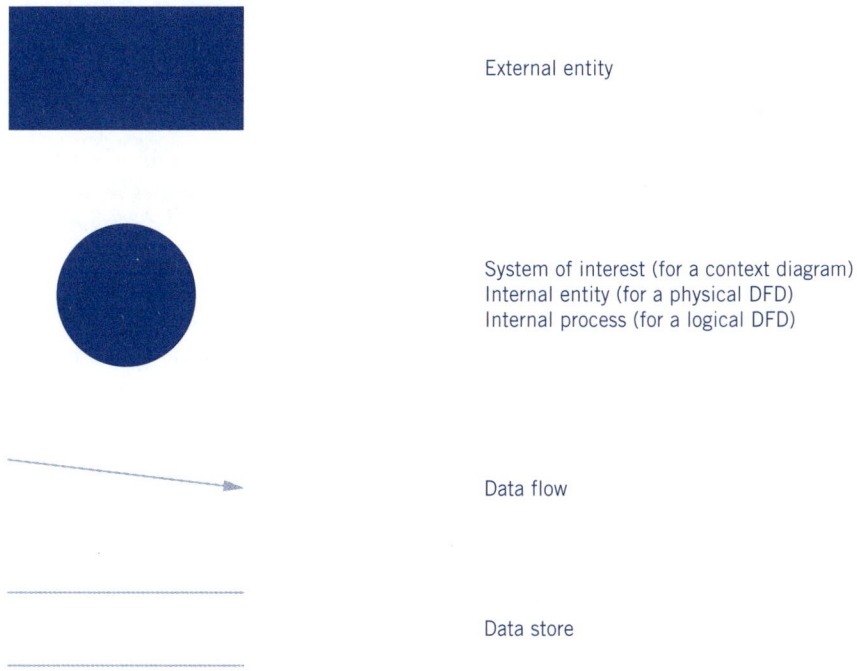

External entity

System of interest (for a context diagram)
Internal entity (for a physical DFD)
Internal process (for a logical DFD)

Data flow

Data store

**FIGURE 5.3** Data flow diagram symbols

## Context diagram

The context diagram provides a representation of the system of interest and the entities that provide inputs to, or receive outputs from, the system of interest. It is an *overview* of the data flow and says nothing about what actually happens within the process. An example of a context diagram can be found in figure 5.4 overleaf, which describes a very simple ordering process for an organisation.

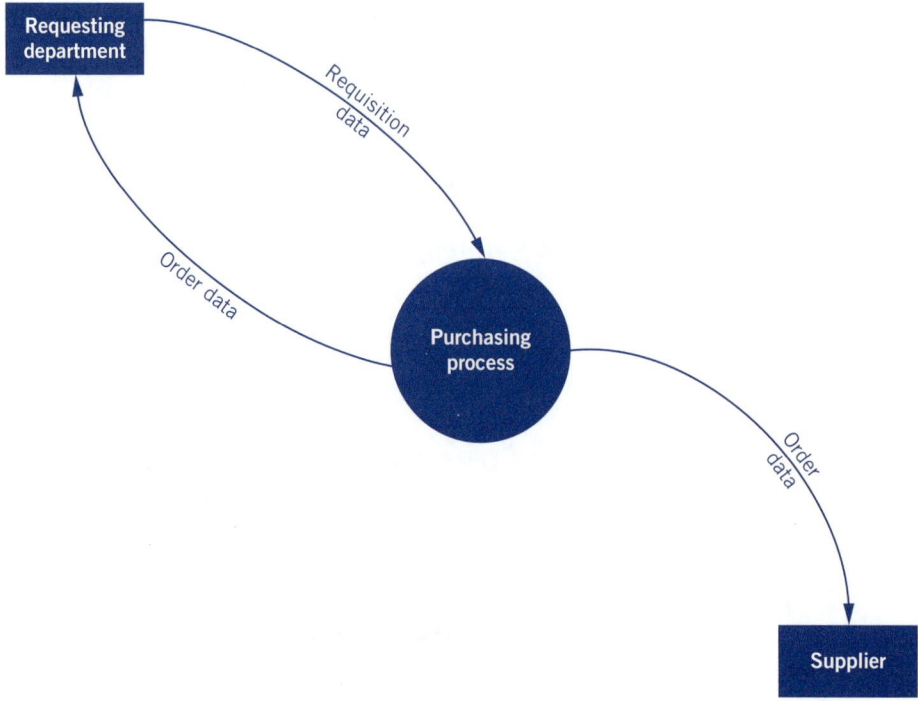

**FIGURE 5.4** Context diagram — reading a DFD

The main features to observe in this diagram are described below.

1. *External entities.* The two rectangles represent the two external entities. The external entities provide the inputs to the system or receive outputs from the system. They are not involved in the actual information-processing activities of the system. External entities will only send or receive information to or from a system, represented by the flows to and from the bubble, or system of interest.

   For example, the requesting department sends the purchase requisition and receives the purchase order, but we do not know how the department actually uses (processes) these documents. Similarly, the order is sent to the supplier but we do not know how the supplier processes the document. Linking back to our structured narrative table in figure 5.2 (page 206), those entities involved in ONLY sending or receiving data will be those that appear in the context diagram. Note that even though the requesting department is within the organisation, it is still an external entity. This is because it does not perform any information-processing activities. All it does is provide an input to the system.

2. *System of interest.* The bubble represents the *system of interest*. Anything that happens outside the system of interest is *not* relevant to the DFDs. This reinforces the point made above about needing to be clear on the boundaries of the system being documented. As a result, in the context diagrams, as well as in the physical and logical DFDs, there *cannot* be flows between external entities. By definition, external entities are not involved in the data processing of the system of interest and, therefore, any flows between them are irrelevant.

3. *Level of detail.* In the context diagram there is no detail about what actually occurs when preparing the purchase order. This detail is essentially what happens within the bubble of the context diagram. For example, it can be seen from the context diagram that the requesting department sends requisition data and the system

generates order data that goes to the supplier and the requesting department, but it cannot be seen who it is within the system that prepares the order, or what steps are involved in preparing the order before it is sent to the supplier. To find out who performs the activities in the process and what these activities are we need to look at the physical (who or what entities are involved) and logical (what processes are involved) DFDs. These are discussed later in this chapter.

This process of progressing from a higher level document to lower levels, thus extracting more detail about who is involved and what gets done, is referred to as **decomposing** (from the noun decomposition) or **stepwise refinement**,[21] and is an example of the ability of DFDs to be layered. This is a strength of DFDs as it enables detail to be shown in successive diagrams, rather than cluttering or over-detailing a single diagram.

## Physical data flow diagram

The physical DFD shows the people, places and things involved in a system. Taking the context diagram illustrated in figure 5.4, the question 'Who is involved in the information-processing activities of this purchasing process?' can be answered by reference to the physical DFD in figure 5.5 (overleaf). Moving from the context diagram to the physical DFD is an example of decomposing, or stepwise refinement. In this case, we are expanding the bubble in 5.4 to obtain details about the internal entities within the process.

In contrast to the context diagram, the bubbles in figure 5.5 now represent the people, places and things involved in data processing within the system of interest. This makes them internal entities. So the physical DFD can contain many more bubbles than just the bubble for the system of interest shown in the context diagram. In this case, the physical DFD contains three bubbles: purchasing officer, computer and purchasing supervisor. The numbering of the internal entities indicates the order in which they take part in the process. The parallel lines indicate data stores or files. We can see that two files are used by the purchasing officer, and the computer accesses four different data files.

From the physical DFD, we can see, for example, that the purchase requisition is sent to the purchasing officer, who then keys the details into the computer and files the requisition in a paper file. Do not be too concerned about the specific documents and file labels; they will become clearer in looking at the different processes in later chapters. For now, you should be able to recognise that the purchasing process, which was the bubble in the context diagram, has been 'exploded' in the physical DFD to represent the different entities that are involved in the process. The flows within the physical DFD refer to the document or data that is moving between entities. The number in brackets on each flow also links each data flow back to the structured narrative table we looked at in table 5.2.

## Logical data flow diagram

The logical DFD uses the same symbols as the physical DFD and context diagram. However, there is one important distinction to make. Where the bubble in the physical DFD represents an entity that is involved in the information-processing activities of the system, in a logical DFD, the bubble represents the processes that occur within the system. Referring to figure 5.5 overleaf as a basis for comparison bears out this distinction. An example of a logical DFD for our purchasing process is contained in figure 5.6 (p. 211).

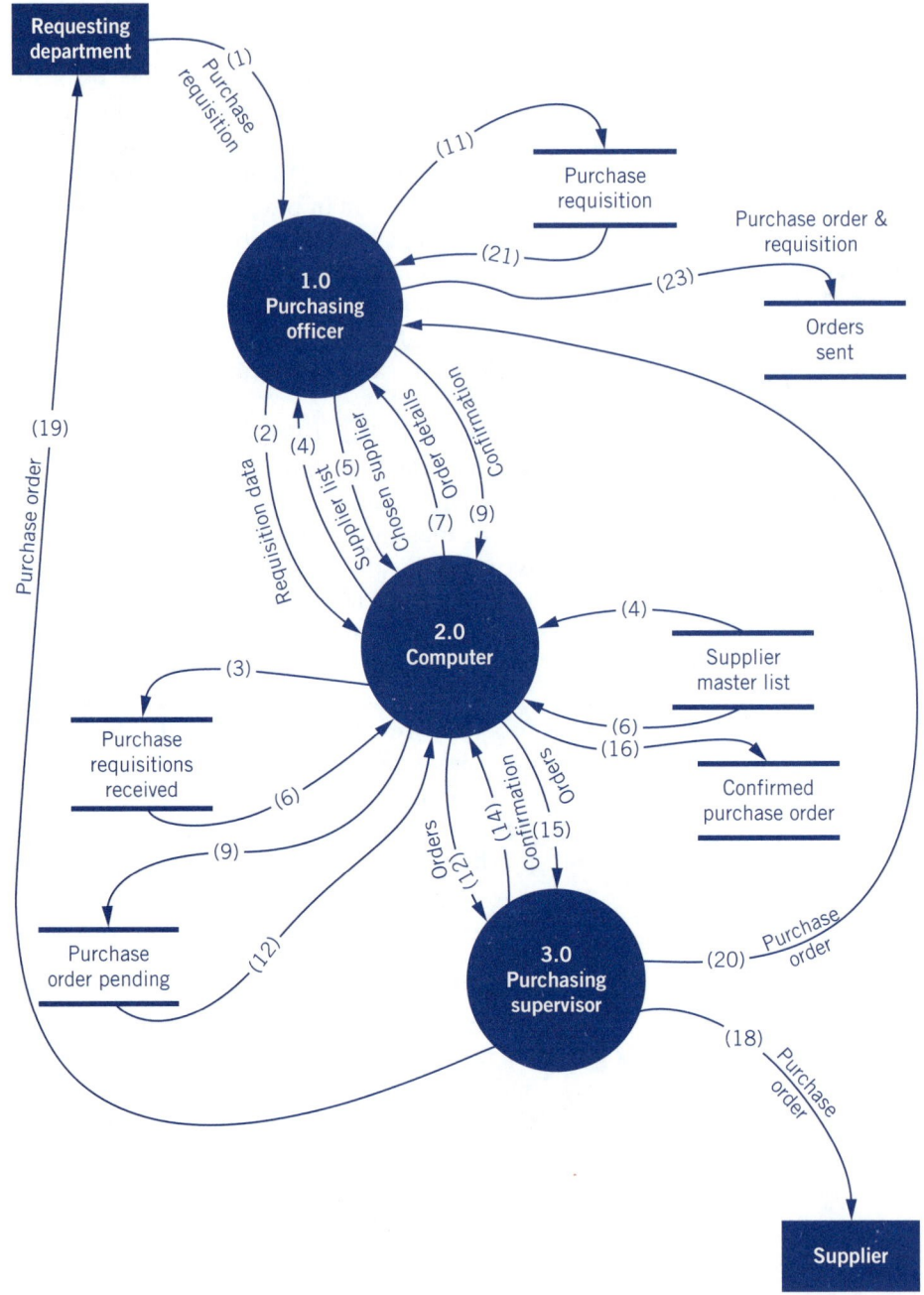

**FIGURE 5.5** Physical data flow diagram — reading a DFD

Compare the physical DFD in figure 5.5, to the logical DFD for the same system in figure 5.6. The first difference you should have detected was that the bubbles contain different labels. This is because the logical DFD is concerned with the activities that take place. As a result, the bubbles now depict the major stages or activities that constitute the purchasing process.

Take a moment to recall the definition of a logical DFD provided at the start of the chapter. The definition refers to illustrating the processes that take place within

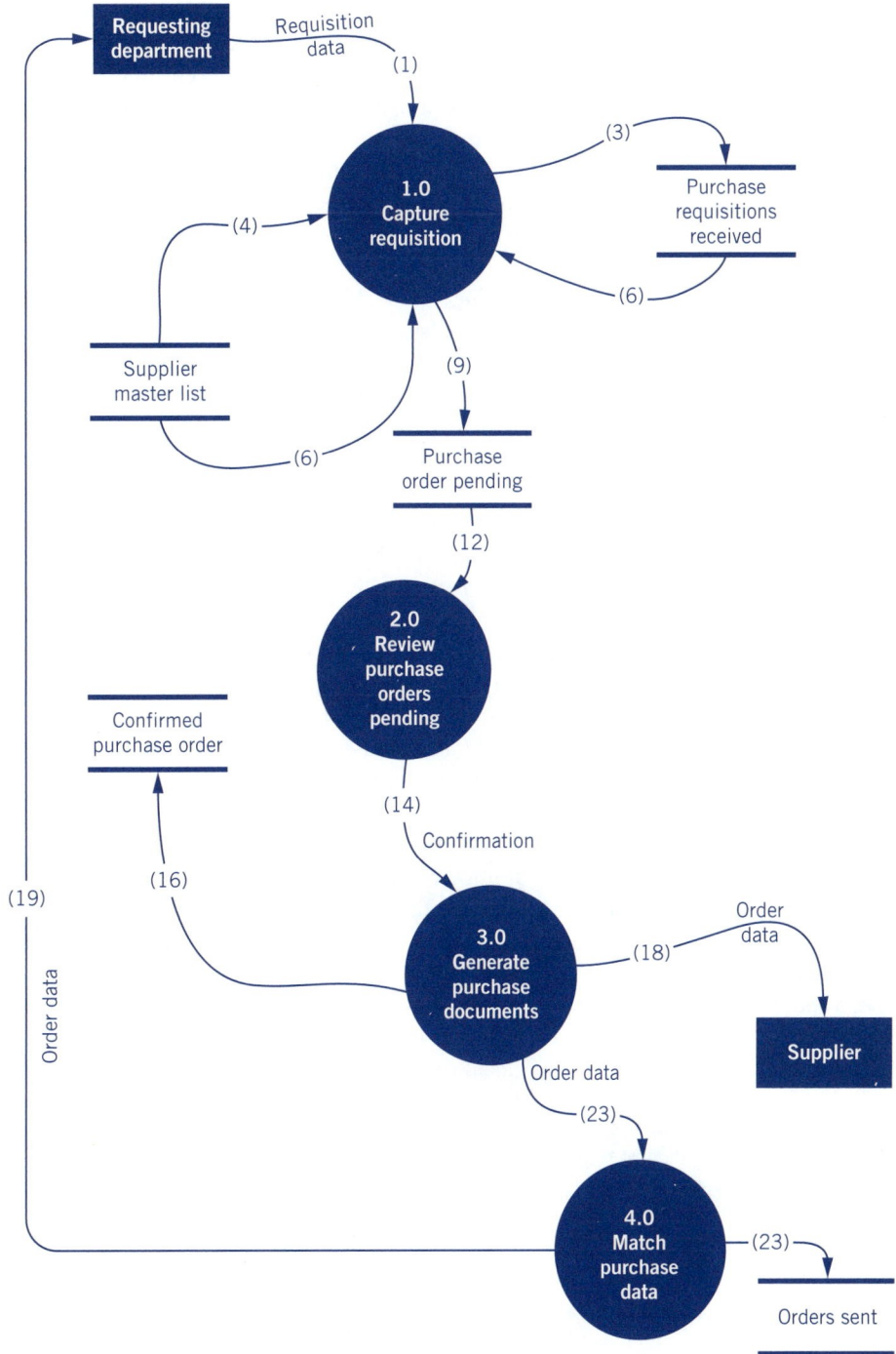

**FIGURE 5.6** Logical data flow diagram — reading a DFD

a system, the flows between these processes and how these processes interact with the external entities that provide inputs to, or receive outputs from, the system of interest. Notice the difference in this definition to that provided for the physical DFD, which is more concerned with the people, places and things involved in the system. This difference is why we have the different labels in the two diagrams, since the logical DFD is concerned with the processes that make up a system, whereas the physical DFD is focused on the entities that perform these processes. So the bubbles in the logical DFD describe the processes and activities that occur within a system, while the bubbles in the physical DFD detail the entities involved in the system. This is an important distinction that you should understand before progressing, as it highlights the different perspectives of the diagrams. The physical is concerned with the 'Who is involved?' perspective while the logical is concerned with the 'What is happening?' question.

The steps in drawing the logical DFD will be discussed later in the chapter, including how to develop the process bubbles. At this point, however, you should be comfortable with the idea that the logical DFD describes the processes that happen within a system.

Another difference to note between the logical and physical DFDs is the nature of the labels on the data flow arrows. *In the physical DFD, these labels all referred to documents or physical items that flowed through the system. In the logical DFD, the flows tell us the type of information being sent.* For example, the flow from the requesting department to the first process contains data relating to what needs to be ordered (the purchase requisition would be the physical document in the physical DFD). The logical DFD is not concerned with the physical form of the data, be it paper or electronic, rather it emphasises what type of data is used in the process.

As a general guide, where the same data store is accessed in different stages and it cannot be linked to both stages without complicating the flows, the data store may be repeated and shown as a three-sided rectangle. This presentation format is used where the same data store appears more than once in the diagram. This will happen where it is easier to depict the data store twice than have data flows crossing all over the page.

Also observe that, as in the physical DFD, the bubbles in the logical DFD are numbered. These numbers represent the order in which the processes occur. Notice how all the numbers in the processes in figure 5.6 end in zero; for example, process 1.0 is 'Capture requisition', process 2.0 is 'Create purchase order' and so on. This numbering provides an indication of the level of the diagram. The diagram in figure 5.6 is a **level 0 data flow diagram**, which is an overarching view of the processes that occur. For each of the processes that appear in figure 5.6 you could go into more detail, just as we did when we went from the context diagram to the logical DFD. For example, expanding process 1.0 can be done through the preparation of a **level 1 data flow diagram**, which would take the bubble for process 1.0 and expand it to illustrate the activities that are part of the level 0 process labelled 'Capture requisition'. This example is shown in figure 5.7.

Take a few moments to compare the level 0 (figure 5.6) and level 1 (figure 5.7) logical DFDs. All that the level 1 diagram has done is to take the bubble labelled '1.0 Capture requisition' and open it up to show the activities that comprise this first process, 1.0. It should become apparent that the inputs and outputs from process 1.0 must also appear in the level 1 diagram. Thus, we have two inputs (the requisition data and the supplier list), two data stores (purchase requisitions received and supplier master list) and one outflow (the confirmation of the requisition provided by the officer before the system moves on to process 2.0 and creates the purchase order). The confirmation flow from bubble 1.3 is the same as the flow from process 1.0 in the level 0 DFD that is labelled 'Payment details', except that in the level 1 diagram it can be seen where in the procedure of processing invoice details this flow occurs.

**Level 0 data flow diagram** *The highest level logical DFD providing an overarching view of the processes that occur.*

**Level 1 data flow diagram** *The second level logical DFD that takes one of the process bubbles from the level 0 diagram and expands it to provide detail about the activities that occur within the process.*

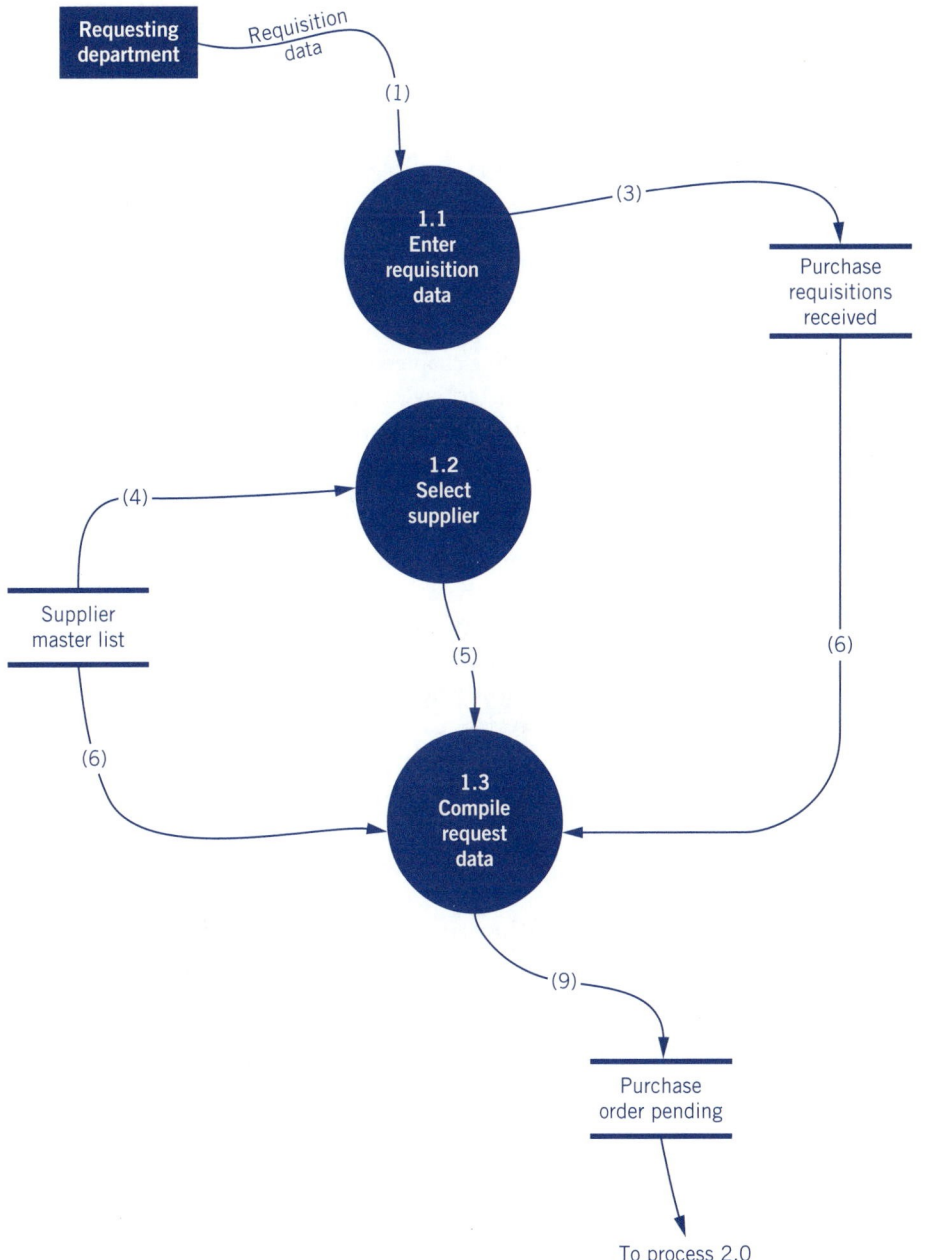

**FIGURE 5.7** Level 1 logical DFD decomposition

A final point to remember about the process of exploding the DFD is how the bubbles should be numbered. For the level 0 diagram, the process numbers will always end in 0, so in figure 5.6 there are processes 1.0, 2.0, 3.0 and 4.0. The numbering changes for a level 1 diagram, as shown in figure 5.7, and can be explained as follows: The number before the decimal point indicates the level 0 process and the number after the decimal point refers to the sequence of steps within the process. Should more detailed descriptions of activities within a process be required, the level 1 diagram can be further expanded into a level 2, level 3 or level 4 diagram. There is no limit to the level, beyond the practicality of describing the minute details of the system as the level becomes lower and lower.

## Systems flowcharts

Conceptually, a systems flowchart represents a combination of the logical and physical DFDs, because it provides details of the processes that are performed (logical perspective) as well as the physical resources that are used to perform them (physical perspective). However, the systems flowchart does not show only what the processes are, as does the logical DFD, or who is involved, as does the physical DFD. Rather, it provides much more detail about what actually happens within the system. Instead of just showing that incoming requisitions are recorded, as the level 0 logical DFD does, the systems flowchart shows what is actually involved in recording the incoming receipts. The systems flowchart is also analogous to the process map, discussed earlier in the chapter. It will provide more detail of what actually happens within each process (or rectangle) that appears in the process map. However, in contrast to the process map, where entities are listed down the left-hand margin, the systems flowchart lists the entities across the top of the document.

The other point to note is that, in comparison with the process map and the DFDs, systems flowcharts have a much wider range of symbols that can be used, thus allowing more detail and insight for the user of the documentation. Given this, it is crucial that, before proceeding too far in to this section, you spend a moment familiarising yourself with the different symbols used in a systems flowchart.

Accountants will be exposed to systems flowcharts and need to read and prepare them when confronted with the task of having to describe the computerised processes, manual operations, and inputs and outputs of an application system. Auditors use system flowcharts to identify key control points in an accounting system's internal control structure'.[22] As technology becomes an ever increasing reality in the day-to-day activities of the accountant and auditor, so too does exposure to systems documentation like the systems flowchart.

### *Systems flowchart symbols*

Table 5.3 contains some of the symbols typically used in drawing a systems flowchart, with a brief description of the symbols. Take some time now to learn these symbols, since the remainder of the chapter will draw upon these in taking you through how to read and draw a systems flowchart.

**TABLE 5.3** Flowchart symbols

| Symbol | Description |
| --- | --- |
| | Start or stop, or an external entity. Indicates the beginning and end of a process and is used whenever something enters or exits the system of interest. |
| | Document — one single document. |
| | Multiple (three) documents. Can be three copies of the same document or three different documents batched together. |

| Symbol | Description |
|---|---|
| | Magnetic disk storage. |
| | Tape drive or magnetic tape storage. |
| | Manual input — data input manually into a computer through, for example, the keying in of details on a keyboard. |
| | Manual process — a process performed manually. For example, manually counting how many invoices are in a batch prior to processing them. |
| | Computer process — a process performed by a computer. For example, sales entered into the system are used to update the accounts receivable file. |
| | Offline process. For example, data gathered in a handheld barcode reader that are later uploaded into the central computer. |
| (A) | On-page connector — joins two different locations on the same page of the flowchart. In this case joining the two points labelled 'A'. |
| | Off-page connector — joins two different locations on separate pages of the flowchart. |
| | Punch card. |
| | Temporary paper data store. Data in the store can be filed numerically, alphabetically or chronologically. This is indicated by an 'N', 'A' or 'C' inside the data store symbol. |
| | Permanent paper data store. Data in the store can be filed numerically, alphabetically or chronologically. This is indicated by an 'N', 'A' or 'C' inside the data store symbol. |

*(continued)*

**TABLE 5.3** *(continued)*

| Symbol | Description |
| --- | --- |
| | On-screen display — data displayed on a computer display or monitor. |
| | General journal or general ledger. |
| | Flow of a document or process. |
| | Flow of data or information. |
| | Sending of data between two different places via a telecommunications link. |
| | Batch total. |
| | Annotation — used to provide descriptions or explanations within the flowchart. |
| | Physical goods or object moving through a process (e.g. goods delivered by a supplier or goods to be sent to a customer). |

## Reading a flowchart

There are two main features that you should be familiar with to be able to understand and read a systems flowchart: the organisational division and the flowchart symbols. When reading flowcharts you will typically start at the top left-hand corner of the document and progress to the bottom right-hand corner. The start of the flowchart is typically indicated by the use of a start/stop symbol or the presence of an external entity symbol containing the name of the external entity.

You will also notice that a flowchart has several columns. Each column is allocated to an internal entity that is a part of the process being documented. You will recall from our earlier discussion the concept of an internal entity. Accordingly, one of the things that you should notice when you read a systems flowchart and compare it with the physical data flow diagram is that the number of columns in the flowchart and the labelling of the columns in the flowchart is identical to the number of internal entities and the labelling of internal entities in the physical DFD.

Each internal entity in the flowchart is separated by a solid line and the name of the entity can be found across the top of the page. Everything that appears within the column for an internal entity is a graphical representation of the entity's activities and how the entity carries out its activities within the system.

The flowchart symbols appear within the columns, and show what is happening within a division. Each symbol conveys a different meaning, as shown in table 5.3. Not only do the symbols tell us what data is used or what task is being performed, they also convey to us how a task is performed. For example, the difference between a computer process and a manual process — an activity performed by a person versus an activity performed by a computer — is evident through the different symbol for each. These add to the semantic appeal of the flowchart, since they convey an added depth that was not present in the DFDs. Now we become privy to not only what is done but also how it is done.

Refer back to table 5.3 for an explanation of the different symbols used in preparing a systems flowchart. After familiarising yourself with the symbols, examine figure 5.8 to help understand how to read a flowchart. In figure 5.8, person A manually keys a document into the computer. The computer performs a process on the data and saves the result on disk. The document is then filed in alphabetical order.

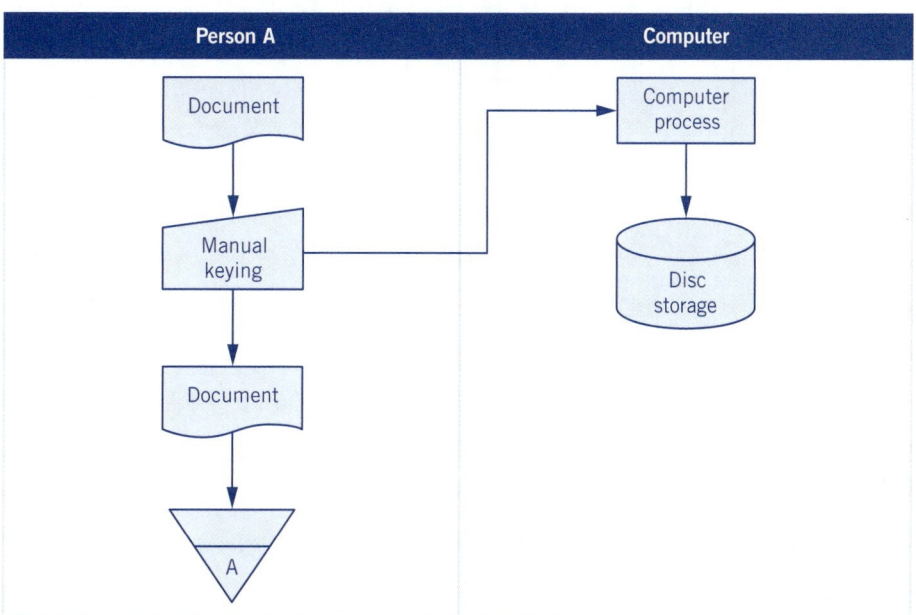

**FIGURE 5.8** A simple flowchart

Now look at figure 5.9 overleaf. In figure 5.9, department A sends two copies of document A to person A. The details of document A are manually keyed in to the computer, which stores the results on disk. One copy of document A is then filed away in alphabetical order, while the second copy is forwarded to person B. Person B receives a document B from the customer, with document B then manually matched up with document A. The details of document B are manually keyed in to the computer. The computer processes the input, saves the details and displays a confirmation on the screen used by person B. Person B then files both documents away in chronological order.

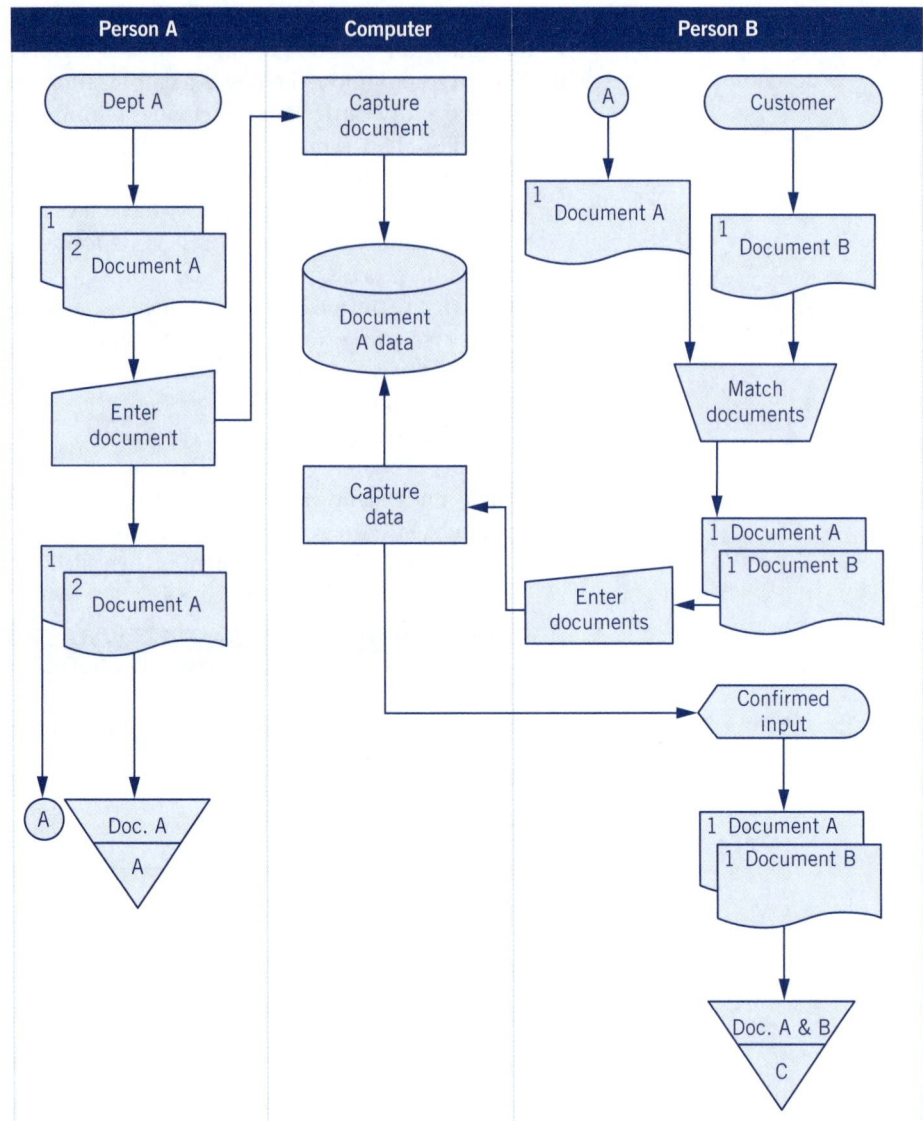

**FIGURE 5.9** A more complex flowchart

You should notice the use of on-page connectors in figure 5.9 (refer back to table 5.3). The connectors have been used to show the movement of document A from person A to person B. Why use connectors and not a line to connect person A and person B? Using connectors avoids the problem of lines going all over the place, avoiding confusion and clutter in the diagram. As a general rule, if a flow goes to a non-adjacent column then on-page connectors should be used. Off-page connectors, which also appear in the table of flowchart symbols, are used for a similar purpose.

To test your understanding of flowcharting symbols, take a few moments to read over figure 5.10 and then write a narrative describing what is happening in the flowchart.

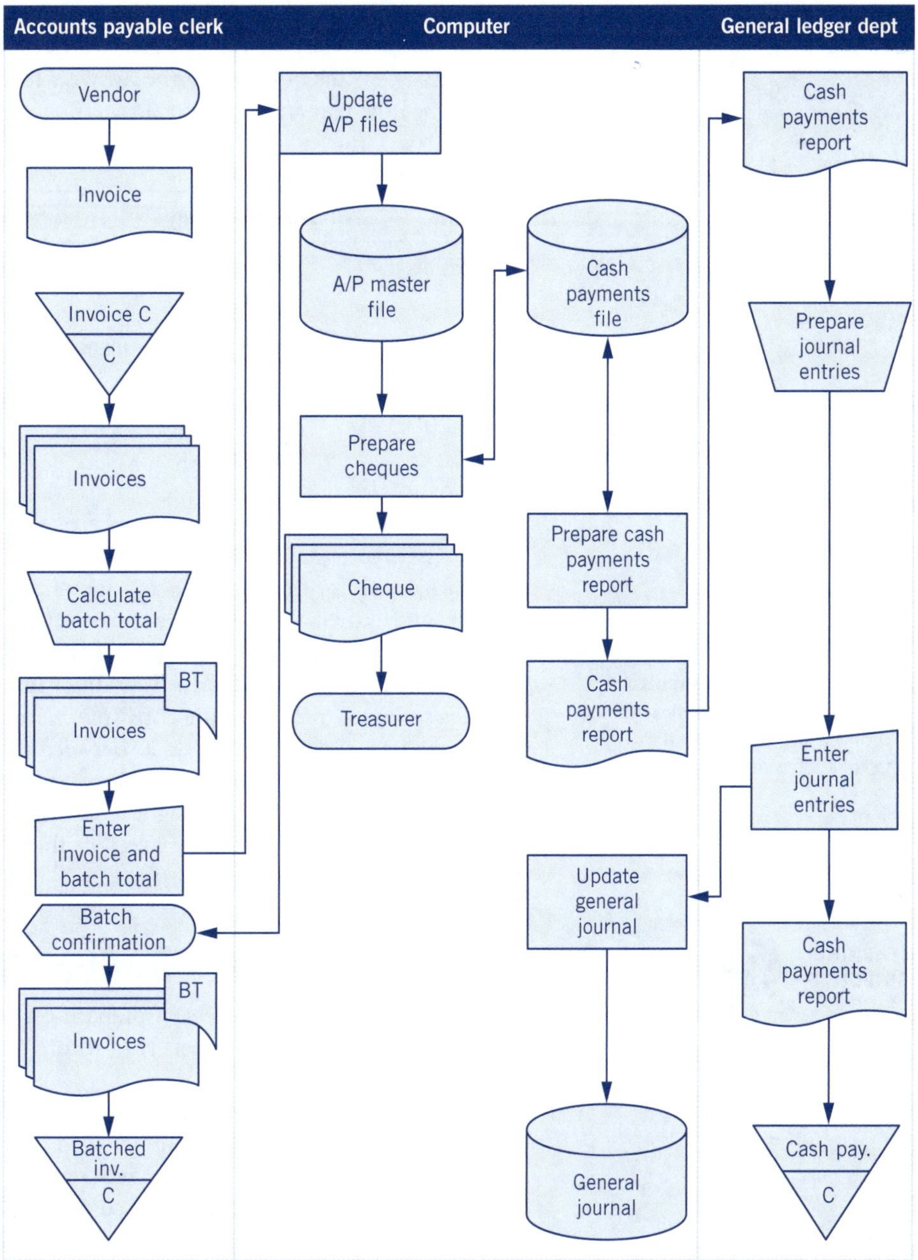

| Accounts payable clerk | Computer | General ledger dept |
|---|---|---|

Flowchart diagram:

**Accounts payable clerk column:**
Vendor → Invoice → Invoice C (C) → Invoices → Calculate batch total → Invoices (BT) → Enter invoice and batch total → Batch confirmation → Invoices (BT) → Batched inv. (C)

**Computer column:**
Update A/P files → A/P master file → Prepare cheques → Cheque → Treasurer

Cash payments file → Prepare cash payments report → Cash payments report → Update general journal → General journal

**General ledger dept column:**
Cash payments report → Prepare journal entries → Enter journal entries → Cash payments report → Cash pay. (C)

**FIGURE 5.10** Flowchart reading self test

LEARNING
OBJECTIVE **6**

*Explain the concept of a balanced set of systems documentation.*

# BALANCING A DATA FLOW DIAGRAM

An essential criterion for a set of systems documentation is consistency. Each of the context diagram, physical DFD or logical DFD must provide us with a consistent representation of the external entities involved in a system. As an example of this point, refer back to figure 5.4, the sample context diagram. How many external entities appear in figure 5.4? How many flows from external entities appear in figure 5.4? How many data flows to external entities appear in figure 5.4?

Now refer to figures 5.5 and 5.6, the sample physical DFD and logical DFD for the process, and ask yourself the same set of questions. If the set of systems documentation has been drawn correctly the answers to the above questions should be identical. Hopefully, you arrived at the answers shown in table 5.4.

**TABLE 5.4** Balancing DFDs example

| Diagram | External entity | Data sent | Data received |
| --- | --- | --- | --- |
| Context diagram | Requesting department<br>Supplier | Purchase requisition<br>— | Purchase order<br>Purchase order |
| Physical DFD | Requesting department<br>Supplier | Purchase requisition<br>— | Purchase order<br>Purchase order |
| Logical DFD | Requesting department<br>Supplier | Requisition data<br>— | Order data<br>Order data |

Do not underestimate the importance of the results in table 5.4. If the diagrams do not agree, your systems documentation is incorrect. That is, because the three diagrams are drawn for the same system, they should have the same external entities and flows in and out of the external entities. Diagrams (context diagram, physical DFD and logical DFD) with the same external entities and flows to and from these external entities are called **balanced data flow diagrams**.

Take a moment to observe the consistency, in terms of external entities and flows to and from external entities, that exists between the context diagram, physical DFD and logical DFD in table 5.4. For the diagrams to be balanced, we would expect to see the same external entities in each diagram and the same number of inflows/outflows for each external entity (note that the label for the flows will change as we move from the physical to the logical perspective).

**Balanced data flow diagrams**
*Diagrams (context diagram, physical DFD and logical DFD) with the same external entities and flows.*

**LEARNING OBJECTIVE**  **7**
*Prepare different forms of systems documentation.*

# DRAWING SYSTEMS DOCUMENTATION

As we work through the process of preparing systems documentation we will use the case shown in figure 5.11. As you read through the narration, pay attention to three things:

1. Who are the people and things that perform activities? Focusing on this question will help identify the entities that are involved in the process. In identifying entities, you should be looking for the mention of specific people or things that are involved in the process. Examples could include the customer, suppliers and specific people within the organisation (e.g. across the different functional areas). However, entities do not have to be restricted to people — items like a computer can also be included as they will typically be involved in the sending, receiving and processing of data within a process.

2. What activities are being performed by each entity? Focusing on this question will help identify the activities that are part of the process. In identifying the activities, you should pay particular attention to what the entities are doing. As a tip, pay attention to the verbs in the process narrative. Examples of typical activities performed by entities include:
   - preparing a document
   - entering data
   - reconciling data or documents
   - approving a transaction or event

- sorting documents
- confirming details
- filing documents
- sending documents
- receiving documents.

This list is by no means exhaustive, but it should give you an idea of what to look for as you read through a narrative for a process.

3. What are the inputs and outputs for each activity? In the previous step we identified the activities; we now need to further decompose these activities to be aware of the inputs used and the outputs generated by the entity. For example, the activity 'Prepare customer order form' — in other words prepare a record of what a customer wants to purchase — cannot be performed without data about what the customer is purchasing. So our interest would be where this data comes from. Does it come from a document? Does it come from a computer file? We identify these inputs to be clear about where the data comes from within the process to ensure we are clear about what data is necessary for a particular activity to properly function.

Also, pay attention to what outputs are generated by an activity. For example, if someone enters data into the computer and the computer processes and saves it, where is the data saved to? What documents are generated, by a computer or a person, as part of an activity? Be clear about these outputs and their destination.

The clearer you are about the answers to these three questions, the easier it is for you to prepare the systems documentation. It is probably worthwhile, as a starting point, to highlight each of the entities, activities, inputs and outputs as you read through the process narrative in figure 5.11.

Once the sales order is sent by the sales office to the warehouse clerk, the warehouse clerk manually prepares a picking slip. This is then used to pick the goods the customer has ordered and pack the goods in a box. As the goods are packed, the items on the picking slip are initialled to indicate the correct quantities have been taken from the shelves. The goods, sales order and picking slip are then forwarded to the dispatch administrator who compares the details of the picking slip to the items in the box. If there is any discrepancy between the packed goods and the documentation, the warehouse manager resolves the difference.

Once the goods and the documentation are matched, the dispatch administrator keys the details of the order into the computer; the details are stored in the 'goods packed' file. The computer then displays a list of approved couriers. The list of approved couriers is stored by the computer in the 'authorised carrier' file. The administrator selects a supplier from the list and clicks on 'Confirm'. The computer then retrieves the details from the goods packed file, adds the courier details, saves the updated data in the goods packed file and displays the full details on the computer screen. The dispatch officer reviews the details on the screen and then clicks 'Accept details'. The computer then creates a shipping notice, which is stored in the 'shipping notice' file, and a bill of lading, which is stored in the 'bill of lading' file.

Two copies of the shipping notice and one copy of the bill of lading are printed. The bill of lading and one copy of the shipping notice are attached to the goods and placed in the shipping area, where the courier collects them and delivers them to the customer. The sales order and picking slip are matched to the shipping notice and sent to accounts receivable. Once received by accounts receivable, the sales order, packing slip and shipping notice are matched with the purchase order (stored in the 'orders awaiting delivery' file) and filed by shipment date in the 'orders to be invoiced' file.

**FIGURE 5.11** Narrative for drawing systems documentation

Once you are familiar with the case narrative and have considered the three questions of who/what is involved, what activities occur and what inputs and outputs are involved, you are ready to complete the first step in the systems documentation process — the structured narrative table.

## Analysing the case

The first step in preparing the systems documentation is to complete the structured narrative table.

As a starting point for preparing the structured narrative table, make a list of the entities that are involved in the case in figure 5.11. If you have read through the case you should have identified the following entities:

- sales office
- warehouse clerk
- dispatch administrator
- computer
- customer
- accounts receivable.

By using these entities in preparing our structured narrative table we will become clear in classifying them as either internal or external, since the table will make it readily apparent whether the entity is only engaged in sending and receiving data or whether it also performs information-processing activities. Note that the courier is not included as an entity in our diagrams. The courier is merely a form of sending or receiving data. Our concern is where the courier gets its data (the dispatching officer) and where the data ends up (the customer).

Having identified the entities, the next step is to place them in the structured narrative table, adding in the specification of the inputs, process and outputs associated with each entity. It is useful to complete the table based on the order in which the entries are mentioned in the case narration. This process will also be useful when preparing other forms of systems documentation, particularly the logical DFD and the systems flowchart. The structured narrative table for the case in figure 5.11 is shown in table 5.5.

**TABLE 5.5** Completed structured narrative table

| No. | Entity | Input | Process/activity | Output |
|-----|--------|-------|------------------|--------|
| 1 | Sales office | | | Sales order |
| 2 | Warehouse clerk | Sales order | Prepares packing slip | Picking slip |
| 3 | Warehouse clerk | Picking slip | Packs goods ordered | |
| 4 | Warehouse clerk | Picking slip | Initials packing slip items | Initialled packing notice, sales order, packed goods |
| 5 | Dispatch officer | Initialled picking slip, sales order, packed goods | Compares packed goods to picking slip | Initialled packing notice, sales order, confirmed packed goods |
| 6 | Dispatch officer | Sales order, initialled picking slip | Enters order details into computer | |
| 7 | Computer | Order details | Saves order details | Data saved to goods packed file |

| No. | Entity | Input | Process/activity | Output |
|---|---|---|---|---|
| 8 | Computer | Authorised carriers file | Retrieves list of approved couriers | List of approved couriers on computer screen |
| 9 | Dispatch officer | List of approved couriers on computer screen | Selects a supplier | Selected supplier |
| 10 | Computer | Selected courier data from goods packed file | Adds courier details to order details | Details of goods and courier displayed on screen |
| 11 | Computer | | Updates goods packed file for courier selection | Goods packed file |
| 12 | Dispatch officer | Details of goods and courier | Reviews details | Click on 'Accept details' |
| 13 | Computer | Acceptance | Updates goods packed file | |
| 14 | Computer | Goods packed data, acceptance from officer | Prepares shipping notice | |
| 15 | Computer | Goods packed data, acceptance from officer | Prepares bill of lading | |
| 16 | Computer | | Saves shipping notice | Data saved to shipping notice file |
| 17 | Computer | | Saves bill of lading | Data saved to bill of lading file |
| 18 | Computer | | Prints documents | Two copies of shipping notice, bill of lading |
| 19 | Dispatch officer | Bill of lading, shipping notice | Attaches to goods | Matched documents on goods |
| 20 | Dispatch officer | Shipping notice, sales order, packing slip | Matches documents | Matched shipping notice, sales order and packing slip |
| 21 | Customer | Shipping notice, bill of lading, goods | | |
| 22 | Accounts receivable | | Retrieves purchase order | Purchase order from orders awaiting delivery |
| 23 | Accounts receivable | Purchase order, shipping notice, sales order, packing slip | Matches documents | |
| 24 | Accounts receivable | | Files documents by shipment date | Purchase order, shipping notice, sales order and packing slip filed in orders to be invoiced file |

In preparing the table you should pay particular to the specific activities that occur and the order in which they occur. The more precise you can be about the activities at this stage, the clearer your systems documentation.

You will notice in table 5.5 that some cells are blank. This is because the activity either uses an input already acquired (e.g. the accounts receivable department already has the source documents that are necessary in activity 24, having acquired and matched them in activity 23) or because an activity only generates an output (e.g. the sales office sending the sales order in activity 1). Also note that inputs and outputs are specified in relation to the specific activity that is being documented in each row of the table. As a result, where an input or output is used by different entities it may appear more than once in the table. An example of this is the sales order which is an output from the sales office, and an input and output from the dispatch officer, warehouse clerk and accounts receivable department.

Another aspect to notice is the specification of computer activities. For example, look at the choice of the supplier by the dispatch officer. Once the details of the shipment have been entered, the computer retrieves a list of suppliers from an electronic data file. In order for the dispatch officer to be able to select a supplier from the list, the computer must first retrieve the data and display it on the screen. This is evident in activities 8, 9 and 10, where the list is displayed, a supplier is selected and data is subsequently updated. In some cases this will be made explicit in the narrative. In other cases it should be something to pay attention to. If the computer displays something on the screen, or if a person selects something from a list displayed on the screen, always look for an indication of where the computer got the underlying data from.

## Preparing a process map

Preparing a process map is relatively simple. You need to be familiar with the case or process that you are mapping. The shipping of goods process described in figure 5.11 will again be used. You should also refer back to the structured narrative table that was prepared in table 5.5. For the exercises in this chapter you will be provided with a narrative for a system and will draw the process map based on the narrative. The task of data gathering has essentially been performed for you and is represented in the narrative. In a real-world organisation, the task of gaining an understanding of the business process could be far more complex and time consuming and involve activities that include data gathering, data structuring, mapping documentation and feedback interaction.[23] These four stages are discussed briefly in figure 5.12.

1. Data gathering
   Data gathering involves the map preparer gaining an understanding and knowledge of the process from any existing documentation that may exist. Once familiar with the process, the map preparer will then interview 'experts' in the process and process their comments and observations.
2. Map structuring
   An early draft of the process map will then be prepared, based on the interviews with the process experts. This is a preliminary diagram that assimilates the information gathered from the different process experts during the interview stage.
3. Map documentation
   A written description of the process's operation will be prepared, along with a final version of the process map.
4. Feedback interaction
   The process maps will then be distributed to different participants for comment. Any comments can be taken from readers of the documentation and can, in some instances, lead to further interviews and group meetings to discuss the process maps.[24]

**FIGURE 5.12** Process mapping stages

## *Step 1: Identify entities and divisions*

Once you understand the process and how it operates (in the case of the material in this chapter that means once you have read and understood the narrative), you are ready to commence preparing the process map. The first step is to compile a chronological list of the entities and their respective activities in the process. As described above, an entity can be any person, place or thing involved, including people and computers. Remember, data processing means using or transforming information in some way. Sending and receiving documents does not constitute an information-processing activity.

Reviewing the structured narrative table in figure 5.5, which breaks down the shipping goods process by entity, activity, input and output, provides us with the entities and their order of appearance within the process. As a result we are now ready to prepare the lanes for each entity.

## Step 2: Draw the lanes for each division

Based on the identified entities, you are now ready to commence drawing the diagram. Start by drawing a large rectangle. Divide this rectangle up, using solid horizontal lines. If you have four entities identified in the previous step, then the rectangle will need to be divided up into four parts; five entities will require five parts, and so on. Once the 'swim lanes' have been created, label them down the left-hand side with the entity name. Note that the courier is not included as an entity in the diagram. The courier is merely a form of sending or receiving data. In such a case our concern is with where the courier gets its data (the dispatching officer) and where the data ends up (the customer).

## Step 3: Indicate any subfunctions

Next, if you have two different entities working in the same division involved in the process, you need to represent this in the process map. Do you remember that rule 3 mentioned that a dashed line is used to separate two different people from the same division? Based on this rule, where you have a division with more than one entity involved, break the division up using a broken horizontal line, so that there is a swim lane for each person. In this case both the warehouse clerk and dispatch officer could be viewed as being in the same division (inventory control) and as a result they are separated by a dashed line.

Having progressed this far, you should now have something representing a swimming pool with the lane ropes in place, and each lane should bear the name of the entity involved. An example of the process map up to this point is contained in figure 5.13 overleaf.

## Step 4: Illustrate the activities of each entity

In this step, the task is to fill in the lanes for each person involved: that is, provide a representation of the tasks performed, how the tasks link up with one another, and the documents and information that flow among the entities.

Completing this task requires a synthesis of the details in our structured narrative. The aim is to provide an overview of the major steps that occur but to not put too much detail in the document that it becomes unreadable. Essentially, you are trying to summarise the process into the major stages that it follows.

If we were to review the structured narrative table in table 5.5 we can deduce that the following major stages occur, with the predominant entity in the stage shown in brackets:
1. sales order sent to warehouse (sales office)
2. goods packed (warehouse clerk)
3. packed goods inspected (dispatch officer)
4. shipping documentation prepared (computer)
5. matching of shipping details to customer purchase order (accounts receivable).

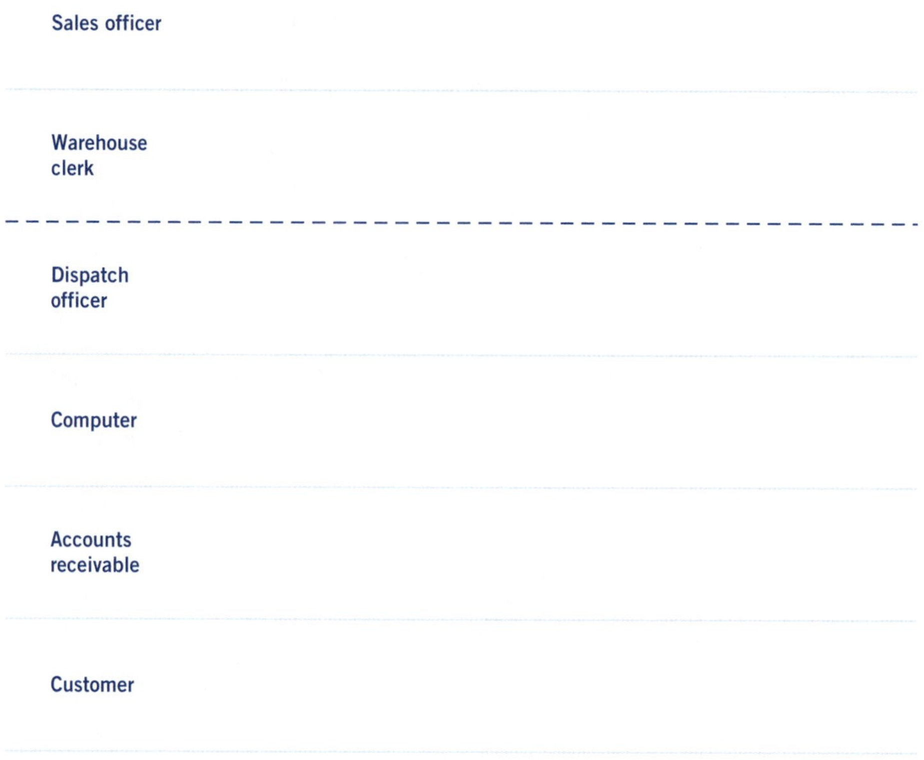

| Sales officer | |
| --- | --- |
| Warehouse clerk | |
| Dispatch officer | |
| Computer | |
| Accounts receivable | |
| Customer | |

**FIGURE 5.13** The empty swim lanes

Note that this is a very high level summary of what happens in the process. Effectively we are summarising the structured narrative table into the major stages that are followed in the shipping goods process. Each of these processes will be represented by a rectangle. In some instances, we note that decisions need to be made. For example, the dispatch officer must compare whether the goods in the box match the goods listed on the picking slip. If they do agree, the process can continue. If they do not agree, the normal operations of the process must be stopped in order that the discrepancy can be resolved. This decision point is represented by a diamond in our process map. The flows between the stages, be they documents or data, are shown by the arrows that connect each stage.

If we were to summarise the major stages in the process and the inputs and outputs for our process we would have something similar to table 5.6.

The final stage is to integrate table 5.6 with the empty swim lanes. Remember, rule 4 describes two symbols used in drawing a process map. A rectangle represents a process and a diamond represents a decision. These decisions and processes are connected by flows, which are the sending and receiving of data.

It should be apparent, at this point, that the completion of the structured narrative table was a significant step towards completing the process map, since it details who the entities are that are involved in the process and the processes that each performs, as well as what each sends and receives. In addition, the summary table we created above further provides a structure for putting the process map together since it clarifies the major stages and their inputs and outputs. So it is now possible to fill in

**TABLE 5.6** Major stages in process for inclusion in the process map

| Stage | Input | Output |
|---|---|---|
| Sales order sent to warehouse (sales office) | | Completed sales order |
| Goods packed (warehouse clerk) | Completed sales order | Packed goods<br>Sales order<br>Initialled packing slip |
| Packed goods inspected (dispatch officer) | Packed goods<br>Sales order<br>Initialled picking slip | Packed goods<br>Sales order<br>Initialled picking slip |
| Shipping documentation prepared (computer) | Packed goods<br>Sales order<br>Initialled picking slip | Packed goods<br>Sales order<br>Initialled picking slip<br>Bill of lading<br>Shipping notice |
| Matching of shipping details to customer purchase order (accounts receivable). | Sales order<br>Initialled picking slip<br>Shipping notice | Sales order<br>Initialled picking slip<br>Shipping notice<br>Purchase order |

the empty swim lanes by drawing a rectangle for each process and an arrow labelled with the appropriate data flows. Attempt to complete the swim lanes in figure 5.13 before looking at the completed process map in figure 5.14 overleaf. If you have any differences or discrepancies between your version and the version in figure 5.14, you may wish to first go back and check your completed table against the structured narrative table. How you have described and how detailed you have been in describing processes to produce the table will have an effect on the contents of your process map. However, also keep in mind that the description of the major stages is somewhat subjective — so your answer may be just as correct as the one we present, with the difference being the way you have broken up and described the major stages. As Burns notes, 'There is no such thing as a perfect swim lane. If you described a business process to 100 people all trained in swim lane you would get 100 different flowcharts. You're only looking for a reasonable approximation'[25] of the process being mapped.

## Preparing data flow diagrams

We will now work through the process of preparing the DFDs. Again the reference will be our narrative and our structured narrative table in figure 5.11 and table 5.5 respectively.

### *Drawing a context diagram*

Drawing the context diagram requires you to be clear on two main aspects of the system. Firstly, what system or process you are documenting. The following refers to the shipping of goods process. The narrative for this process was illustrated in figure 5.11, and was used in the preparation of the process map. Clearly defining the system of interest is crucial for correct documentation because it sets the scope for what the logical and

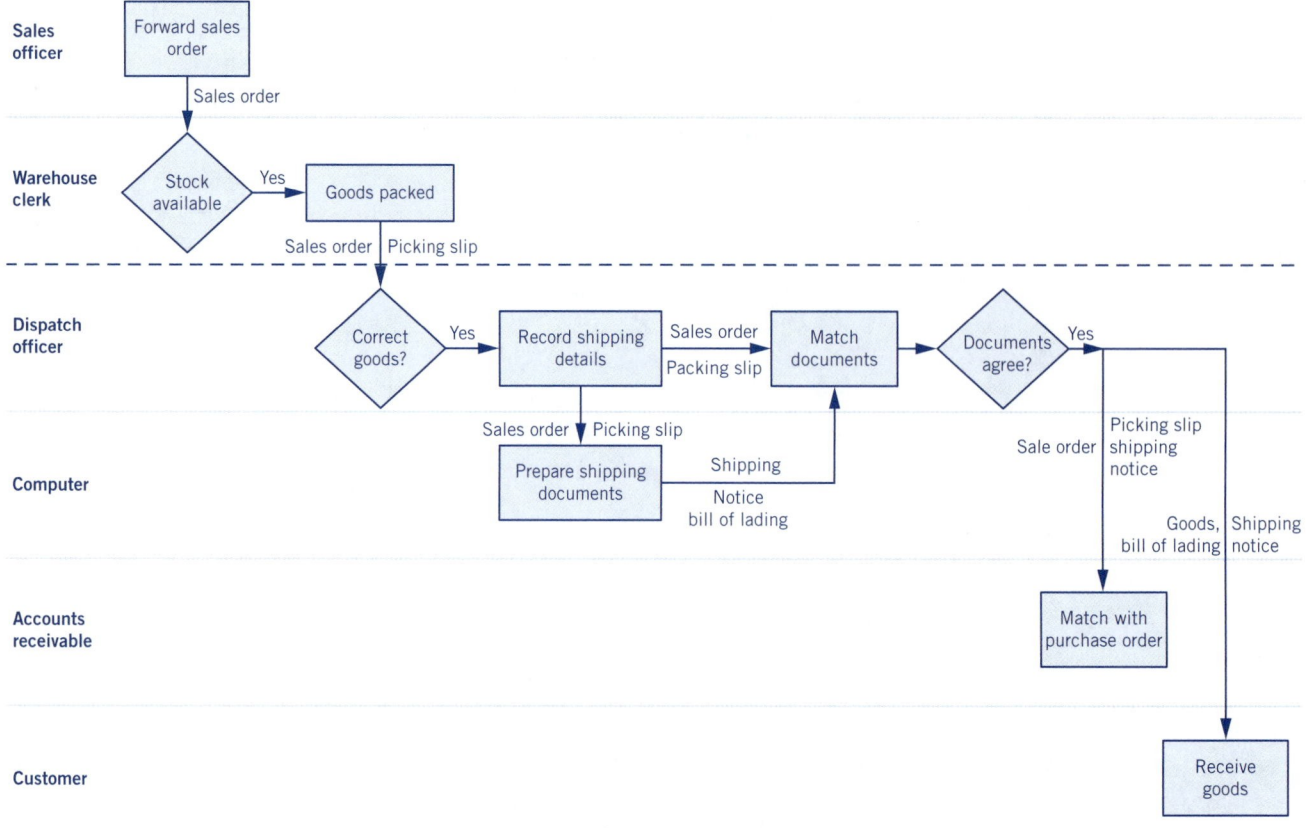

**FIGURE 5.14** Completed process map

physical DFD will cover. If you think you need to include more than one bubble in a context diagram, then you are not totally clear on what the system of interest is. Once you have decided what process or system is being documented, you have the bubble for your context diagram.

The next step is to work out what the external entities are that receive outputs from or provide inputs into the system of interest. If you have completed the structured narrative table from the preparation of the process map, this is a relatively simple exercise. One of the critical things to remember when classifying entities is that external entities are *not* involved in the actual information-processing activities of the system — they simply send inputs or receive outputs. A quick way to determine which entities are external entities is to have a look at the input and output columns of table 5.5 prepared for the process map. If these are the only columns that are filled for an entity, the entity performs no processing and is therefore an external entity. Based on this criterion, re-examine table 5.5 and prepare a list of the external entities.

Once you have defined your system of interest as well as your external entities, the final stage is to identify the data flows that originate from or end at the external entity. Again, depending on how much detail you used in completing the structured narrative table, you should be able to identify these flows from your table. These flows are then drawn in as data flow arrows that connect the external entity and the system of interest.

Before looking at figure 5.16, make an attempt at drawing the context diagram on your own. Remember the symbols used in the context diagram — a bubble for the system of interest, a rectangle for the external entities and arrows for the inputs and outputs relating to the system of interest. A summary of the main steps in preparing the context diagram is contained in figure 5.15. Compare your result to that in figure 5.16 and reconcile any differences. Be sure to consult your lecturer or tutor if you are not sure of anything.

1. Identify the system of interest. Draw a bubble and label it to represent the system of interest.
2. Identify the external entities (those that do not perform information-processing activities). Draw and label a rectangle for each external entity.
3. Identify any data flows between the external entities and the system of interest.
4. Draw in the data flows connecting the external entities and system of interest and label them accordingly.

**FIGURE 5.15** Summary of steps in drawing a context diagram

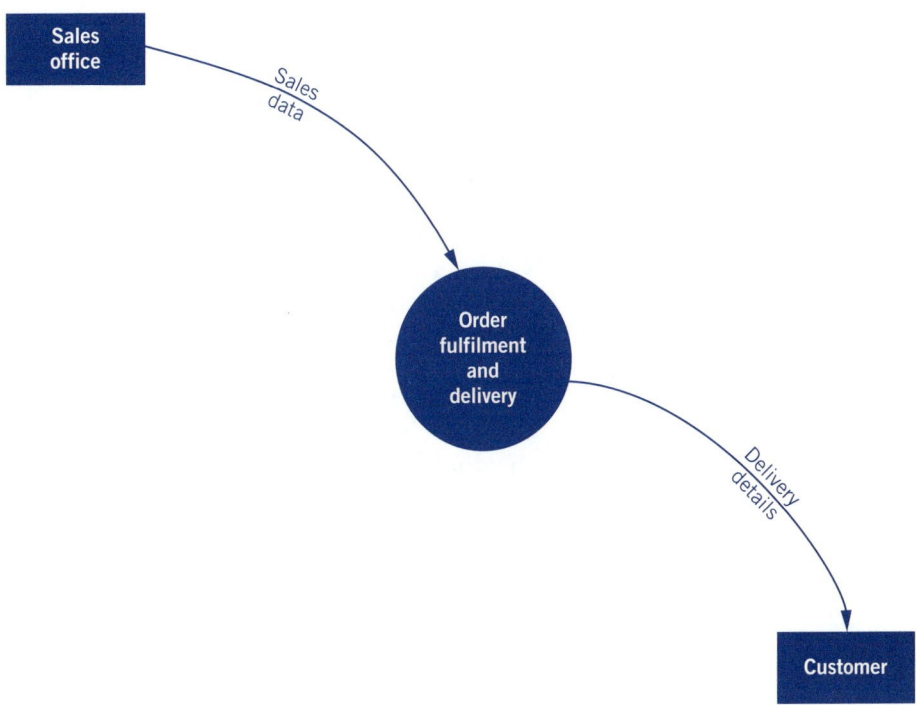

**FIGURE 5.16** Completed context diagram

## Drawing a physical data flow diagram

The definition of a physical DFD is a graphical representation of the people, places and things involved in a system. The preparation of the DFD builds from where the context diagram left off. Indeed, having the context diagram prepared is a good starting point for the physical DFD, because the context diagram contains the external entities. All that is needed when preparing the physical DFD is to expand the process bubble of the context diagram, adding more detail to it, so that it shows who the people, places and things are that perform information-processing activities within the system of interest. These will be the internal entities.

Again, a good starting point for determining who the internal entities are for the system is to refer back to the structured narrative table. In the case in table 5.5, the external entities are the customer and the sales office, since all they do is send or receive data. The remaining entities are those that perform at least one information-processing activity. These entities will all appear in the physical data flow diagram, represented by bubbles, and labelled with their name and a number, to represent the order in which they appear in the process.

To draw these entities into the physical data flow diagram you should initially work out the order in which they appear in the system. This allows the entities in the diagram to be numbered. For example, the sales office sends the sales order to the warehouse clerk. Therefore, the warehouse clerk is the first of the internal entities to be involved in the process and would therefore be numbered 1.0. The process is repeated for all the entities. You should have as many numbers as there are internal entities. For this system there are four internal entities — can you list them?

Once you have numbered the internal entities, you can then place them on the data flow diagram. As mentioned above, keep in mind that documentation conventions suggest that your diagram should commence in the top left-hand corner and progress left to right and top to bottom, thus ending in approximately the bottom right corner of the page. However, this is a guideline that, while encouraged for ease of reading the diagram, should not be seen as an unbreakable law.

With your external entities already identified from the context diagram and your internal entities drawn in, the next step is to identify the data flows between the entities. This information is readily available from the structured narrative table. Data stores also need to be drawn in, for example, when a document gets filed away. One thing to note when preparing the diagram is that in the table both sending and receiving were listed. For example, the table notes that the sales office sends the sales order and the warehouse clerk receives the sales order. This was done to clearly identify the flows each entity is involved in. When drawing the diagram only one of these flows needs to be included, because they are the same data flow. Be careful to avoid drawing in duplicate flows. As the flows are drawn in they will be labelled with the line number from the structured narrative and a description of the data that is being sent or received. This description will typically be the document type for paper documents and the data type for electronic data.

Care must also be taken where there are many people performing the same role. For example, it may be the case that there are five warehouse clerks all performing the same function. Does this mean that five bubbles are needed in the physical data flow diagram? No. In this case you only need to draw the entity once and will only need one bubble to represent the five clerks.

A summary of the steps in preparing a physical DFD is contained in figure 5.17. A physical DFD for the sample process is contained in figure 5.18 on page 232. You should be able to obtain a similar diagram by following the steps in figure 5.17 and the previous discussion.

## Drawing a logical data flow diagram

The example logical DFD uses the same shipping goods case as the other diagrams. Having seen how to read a logical DFD, you should be reasonably comfortable with the idea that the logical diagram tells us the activities that occur within a system or process. Therefore, in preparing a logical DFD the different activities that occur within the system need to be determined? Once again, a good starting point for this is the structured narrative table in table 5.5 prepared for the process diagram.

1. Identify the external entities (those that do not perform information-processing activities). Draw and label a rectangle for each external entity.
2. Identify the internal entities and list them in the order they appear in the system's operation.
3. Draw in a bubble for each internal entity and label and number the bubbles accordingly.
4. Identify any data flows between the external entities and internal entities. Draw in these flows and label the data flow arrows.
5. Identify the data flows between the internal entities. Draw in these data flows between internal entities and label the arrows with the physical document/information that is being sent or received.
6. Identify any data stores that are accessed to get data or to store data as part of the process. These may be paper-based or electronic. Draw these data stores in and link them to the entity that accesses them by including data flow arrows.

**FIGURE 5.17** Drawing a physical DFD

### Determine information-processing activities

Look at table 5.5 once again. In preparing the logical DFD the major concern is with the processing activities that are listed in the 'Process/activity' column. The external entities, along with the inputs they provide and the outputs they receive, were defined in preparing the context diagram. The challenge when preparing the logical DFD is to show how these inputs and outputs fit into the activities performed within the system.

As a starting point, from the list of activities that are presented in table 5.5, identify those entities that perform information-processing. Next, highlight the information-processing activities. Note in table 5.5 that the sales office in activity 1 and the customer in activity 21 are only involved in sending and receiving activities (i.e. they are external entities). Any activities performed by internal entities that are just sending or receiving should also be noted. This is because when creating the logical DFD there is only a need to focus on the information-processing activities that are performed by the internal entities.

### Group activities logically

The information-processing activities that remain in table 5.5 need to be grouped so that they are logically representative of the system of interest. This grouping process can be subjective, with the groupings arrived at by one person potentially different from the groupings of another. Thus, while there is only one correct diagram for a physical DFD, there can be many correct solutions for a logical DFD. However, this is subject to the overriding disclaimer that the grouping of your activities must make sense — activities cannot just be grouped at random!

This raises the question of how to go about grouping the information-processing activities. A common approach is to group activities that take place at the same time. With the time-based approach, it may be a useful exercise to make sure that your structured narrative table is sequenced chronologically, because this makes it much easier to group activities based on order of performance within the process. This is also where it is important to fully understand the details of the system or the system narrative that you are working on. Hopefully, you are starting to see the benefit of preparing the structured narrative table as part of the documentation process, because it allows

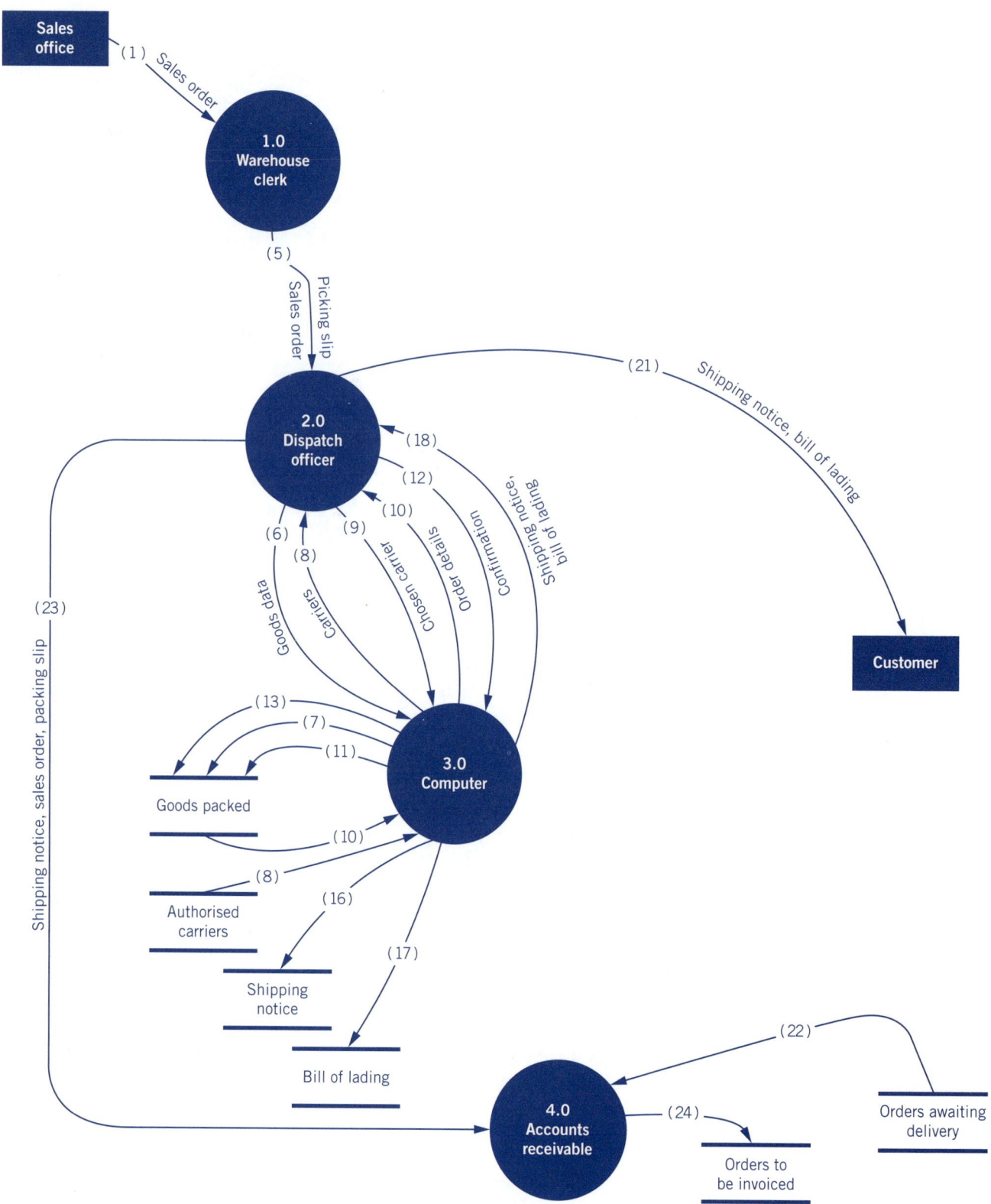

**FIGURE 5.18** Completed physical data flow diagram

the case to be broken down into a chronological series of events. Narratives for systems do not always do this; so, as system documentation preparers, you should take some time to fully understand a narrative and the sequence of events before putting pen to paper. This approach will make the whole process easier in the long run.

To group the activities in table 5.5 means looking for activities that occur at the same time and contribute towards the same general aim or underlying objective. Cast your eye over the list of information-processing activities shown in table 5.5 and see whether you can group them in some logical manner. Are there some activities that logically go together? Are there activities that occur at the same time and contribute to the same underlying goal of a particular stage of a process? If so, group them together. A suggested template for doing this is shown below. The first column refers to the position of the stage in the process, the second is a brief description of what happens at that stage and the third column is for the activities from the structured narrative table that are part of the stage.

| Stage | Description | Related activities |
| --- | --- | --- |
|  |  |  |

A suggested table for the shipping goods process is shown in table 5.7.

**TABLE 5.7** Grouping of information-processing activities

| Stage | Description | Related activities |
| --- | --- | --- |
| 1.0 | Pack goods | 2, 3, 4 |
| 2.0 | Check packed goods | 5, 6, 7, 8 |
| 3.0 | Select supplier | 9, 10, 11 |
| 4.0 | Prepare shipping documentation | 12, 13, 14, 15, 16, 17, 18, 19, 20 |
| 5.0 | Confirm shipment with purchase order | 21, 22, 23 |

The information-processing activities identified in table 5.5 have been grouped into five processes/stages. Note that each process is numbered and, because a level 0 DFD is being prepared, all the process numbers end in 0. The numbering of the processes indicates the order they are performed in.

A brief explanation of these five process groupings follows.

1. *Process 1.0 Pack goods.* This is the stage where the sales order is received and the goods are retrieved from the shelf and packed, with the picking slip being prepared, annotated and matched to the sales order. Activities 2, 3 and 4 all relate to this process of packing the goods the customer has ordered.

2. *Process 2.0 Check packed goods.* Using the data about the packed goods, the dispatch officer will ensure that what is in the box matches what is on the documentation. To do this, the goods need to have been packed (process 1.0) and data is required (from the documentation).

3. *Process 3.0 Select supplier.* Once confident that the right goods have been packed, shipment is arranged. The first part of this activity is to enter the details of the goods to be sent and then select an approved courier to deliver the goods to the customer.

4. *Process 4.0 Prepare shipping documentation.* Once the goods are packed and a supplier is selected, the documentation that relates to the sending of the goods can be prepared — the bill of lading and the shipping notice. This stage requires all of the

preceding stages to have been completed (i.e. know what is being sent and who the courier is). It involves the creation of source documents and several computer actions to save data and print reports.

5. *Process 5.0 Confirm shipment with purchase order.* Before accounts receivable is able to arrange for an invoice to be prepared and for the ledgers to be updated to reflect the goods sold, what was sent needs to be matched with what the customer ordered. Accounts receivable therefore needs data about the goods sent (from process 4.0) to reconcile against the purchase order received from the customer at a different time (outside this process of shipping goods).

You should notice from these groupings that the emphasis is on activities that occur at roughly the same time and contribute to a specific goal or stage of the process, be it packing the goods, checking the goods or recording data about shipments. There is a clear chronology from process 1.0 to 5.0 as well as necessary data flows from process 1.0 to subsequent processes.

Having identified the processes that will appear in the logical data flow diagram, the five process bubbles can be drawn. Again, they should run left to right and top to bottom in layout on your page. Do not forget to include the process numbers within the bubbles and ensure that the processes are numbered correctly (e.g. a level 0 DFD should have process numbers all ending in 0). Once the processes are included in the logical diagram, they need to be linked together. So you need to go back to table 5.5 and look at the data flows that occur among the processes. Essentially, it is a question of asking what data is needed for the stage to occur and what data does the stage generate for subsequent stages. These flows among processes can then be drawn onto the diagram.

The diagrams prepared to this point represent how the system would function in normal operations, assuming no errors or abnormalities occur. An example of this could be activities 5 or 23, where documents are being reconciled or data checked. The assumption is that the documents and data will agree and there are no errors. If, for example, accounts receivable discover that the purchase order and shipping notice do not agree, they would need to go back through the process to work out why. This is an example of a routine that is performed when the system does not function as is normally expected: an **error routine**. This flow backwards is not shown in the level 0 DFDs. That is, you *cannot* have flows from a higher numbered process to a lower numbered process. (If a process is working as expected, why else would you send an item back to an earlier stage?) If an error routine needs to be documented, then it can be done in a separate DFD. *System documentation convention dictates that error routines and abnormal procedures are not shown on the main level 0 DFD.* All that is needed on the main level 0 DFD is a flow from the entity and the process affected by the error routine, labelled 'Error routine'. Figure 5.19 shows the complete logical DFD for the shipping goods process. Make sure you have attempted to draw your own physical DFD before looking at figure 5.19.

Figure 5.20 (page 236) contains a summary of the steps to follow when preparing a logical DFD.

> **Error routine** *A routine that is performed when the system does not function as is normally expected.*

## *Drawing a systems flowchart*

For the demonstration of drawing a systems flowchart, again the shipping goods process will be used. By now you should be familiar with the details of the system. Also refer to the structured narrative table in figure 5.5. This description draws on the examples and concepts of Lehman[26] and Smith and Smith.[27]

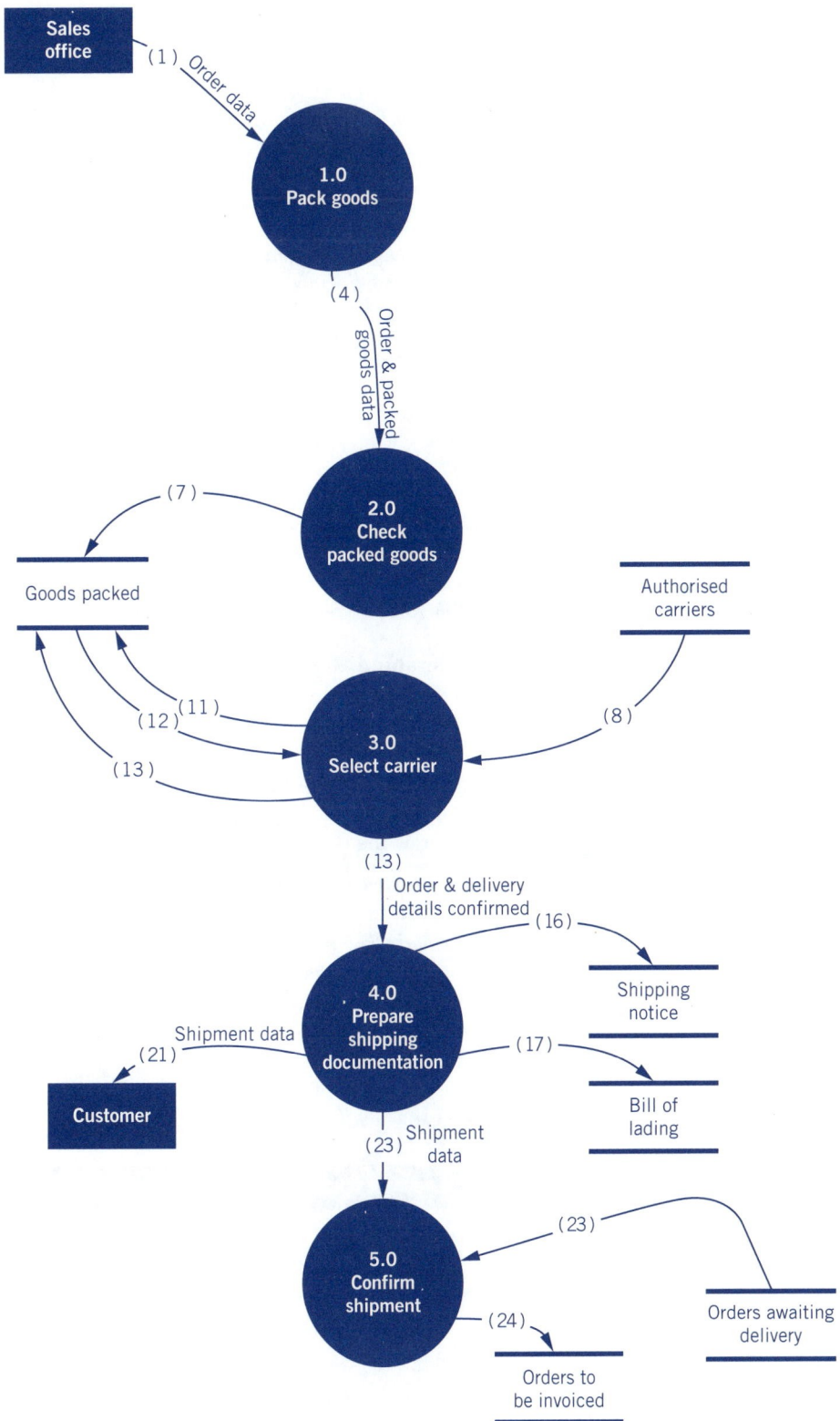

**FIGURE 5.19** Completed logical data flow diagram

1. Identify the external entities (those that do not perform information-processing activities). Draw and label a rectangle for each external entity.
2. From the table with the division, entities and activities (sends or receives and processes performed), eliminate any entities that just send or receive items and any activities that are just send or receive.
3. Group the remaining information-processing activities based on the underlying process they perform. A common method is to group processes that occur at the same time.
4. Number and label the underlying process performed by the group of activities. Draw a bubble for each group of activities.
5. Identify any data flows between the external entities and processes. Draw in these flows and label the data flow arrows.
6. Identify the data flows between the processes. Draw in these data flows between processes and label the arrows with a logical description of the data that is being sent or received.
7. Identify any data stores that are accessed to get data or to store data as part of the process. These may be paper-based or electronic. Draw these data stores in and link them to the process that accesses them by including data flow arrows.
8. Ensure your logical DFD balances with your physical data flow diagram and context diagram.

**FIGURE 5.20** Drawing a logical data flow diagram

### Understand the system

The first stage in drawing a flowchart is to be familiar with the system that is going to be depicted. You can gain this familiarity in several ways, but at the early stages of drawing flowcharts one of the best approaches is to break the system up based on the entities, processes and inputs and outputs. List these entities and processes in a structured narrative table based on the order in which the processes occur. You may want to redraw the table now for yourself or refer to table 5.5 for a refresher.

### Represent the entities

The next step is to represent the entities that are involved in the case within the flowchart. This is similar to the creation of the swim lanes in the process map but for one critical difference: in the process map the entities were listed down the left-hand side of the diagram, but in the systems flowchart they are listed across the top. So while the lanes of the process map run horizontally, the lanes on the system flowchart will run vertically. Divide your page up now, based on the internal entities we have previously identified (warehouse officer, distribution clerk, computer and accounts receivable). You should end up with something similar to figure 5.21.

| Warehouse officer | Distribution clerk | Computer | Accounts receivable |
|---|---|---|---|
| | | | |

**FIGURE 5.21** Representing the entities within a flowchart

## Complete each entity's activities

The next step is to fill in the columns for each of the entities. This is done using the flowchart symbols introduced in table 5.3. Before starting to draw, take some time to recall some of the symbols used in flowcharting.

Within each column of the flowchart we need to depict the inputs, outputs and the activities performed. The task is then to represent what happens using the flowchart symbols. See whether you can fill in the columns of your flowchart with the correct symbols and flows. A few simple rules to keep in mind as you do this are contained in figure 5.22, which shows a list of rules and pointers for flowcharting.

1. Avoid flows that cross over multiple entities. Use the on-page connectors for such situations. This keeps the document relatively simple and easy to read. Another way to avoid lines crossing over multiple entities is to list the entities in the order that they appear in the process when you label your flowchart columns.
2. Make sure that if a document enters the system, you also show where it ends up. For example, once a document is received by an entity, is it forwarded on to another entity? Filed away? Sent out to an external entity? Ensuring completeness of document flows in this way makes the flowchart easier to follow because there are no questions or ambiguities about what happens to the documents that enter or are generated in the system.
3. Where a document is copied, number each individual copy, so their individual flow through the system can be traced.
4. Documents moving from entity to entity should be shown in each column — that is, you should be able to see the source and destination of the document.
5. The filing of documents does not require a manual process symbol. You can simply show the flow of the document into the file symbol, with this making it clear that filing has taken place.
6. Processes should have an input and an output. For example, a manual process should have an input (e.g. a source document) and an output (perhaps a new document and the original document).
7. Only document normal processing operations of the system. Where an error routine or abnormal processing takes place, this can be indicated with an annotation and shown separately on a different flowchart.
8. Where necessary, use annotations to explain or clarify any ambiguities in the flowchart.
9. Manual data stores can only be accessed by people and can only have paper documents entering and exiting them.
10. Electronic data stores can only be accessed by the computer. For each inflow or outflow from an electronic data store there needs to be a related computer process, for example, retrieving data or capturing data.
11. The columns in the flowchart should correspond to the internal entities shown in your physical DFD.
12. Ensure that symbol labels add meaning. For example, don't just label the paper document symbol with the Word document. This is obvious from the symbol. The label should say what document it is. A similar rule applies to labelling computer processes and manual processes.
13. Manual processes can only be performed by people.
14. Computer processes can only be performed by computers.

**FIGURE 5.22** Rules and pointers for flowchart preparation and presentation

Also, as you draw flowcharts keep in mind the conventions discussed in looking at how to read a flowchart. The important things to recall are: (1) the organisational divisions are across the top of the flowchart, (2) the flowchart symbols are used to depict what happens in the system, and (3) the flowchart should generally flow from left to right and top to bottom.

Once you have attempted the flowchart, compare it with figure 5.23. You may have some slight differences in how you have labelled processes and ordered the columns, but your attempt should be comparable. If it is different, you may wish to review the case and the rules discussed above, and consult your lecturer or tutor.

**LEARNING OBJECTIVE 8**
*Compare and contrast different forms of systems documentation.*

# COMPARING THE DIFFERENT DOCUMENTATION TECHNIQUES

Having gone through the process of reading and preparing process maps, DFDs and systems flowcharts, it is useful to revise some of the key concepts covered by thinking about the relationships, similarities and differences among the different types of documentation.

The process map details how a process is performed within an organisation, what entities are involved in the process and what each entity does within the process. The process map gives an overall view of the organisation's process design and allows the interactions among entities across the organisation to be seen. This process perspective can also be obtained from the systems flowchart, which also shows the entities and the tasks performed by the different entities in a process. However, there is a slight difference in the information about the process that can be obtained from these two diagrams. One example of this difference is that the process map does not show what is actually involved in performing the activities that make up a process. For example, a process rectangle on the process map may be labelled 'Check goods for shipment' but we do not know how this check is actually carried out. In comparison, the flowchart shows the activity being performed and what the entity performing the task uses to complete this activity. This is where the extra detail of the systems flowchart can be useful. It can show whether it is a paper document, electronic data transfer or some other form that is part of this activity, how the information is stored (e.g. in paper or electronic form) and whether the process is manually or electronically performed. So the process map in conjunction with the systems flowchart shows what is being done, who does it, as well as what is being used as part of the process. The two in combination provide a very comprehensive picture of a business process.

In contrast, the DFDs have less detail. Recall that the context diagram tells us nothing about what happens within the system of interest. Rather, it merely shows the external entities that interact with the system. The context diagram can be expanded into the physical and logical DFDs. The physical DFD shows the entities involved in a process and the flows among the entities, but no details about what the entities are actually doing. Compare this with the process map and systems flowchart, which not only identify the entities but also give an insight into what activities they are performing. Conversely, the logical DFD shows what processes are performed within a system but not who performs the processes. That is similar to having a process map without labelling the swim lanes. This is because preparing a logical DFD requires grouping the entities. After the grouping process, there can be several activities grouped together

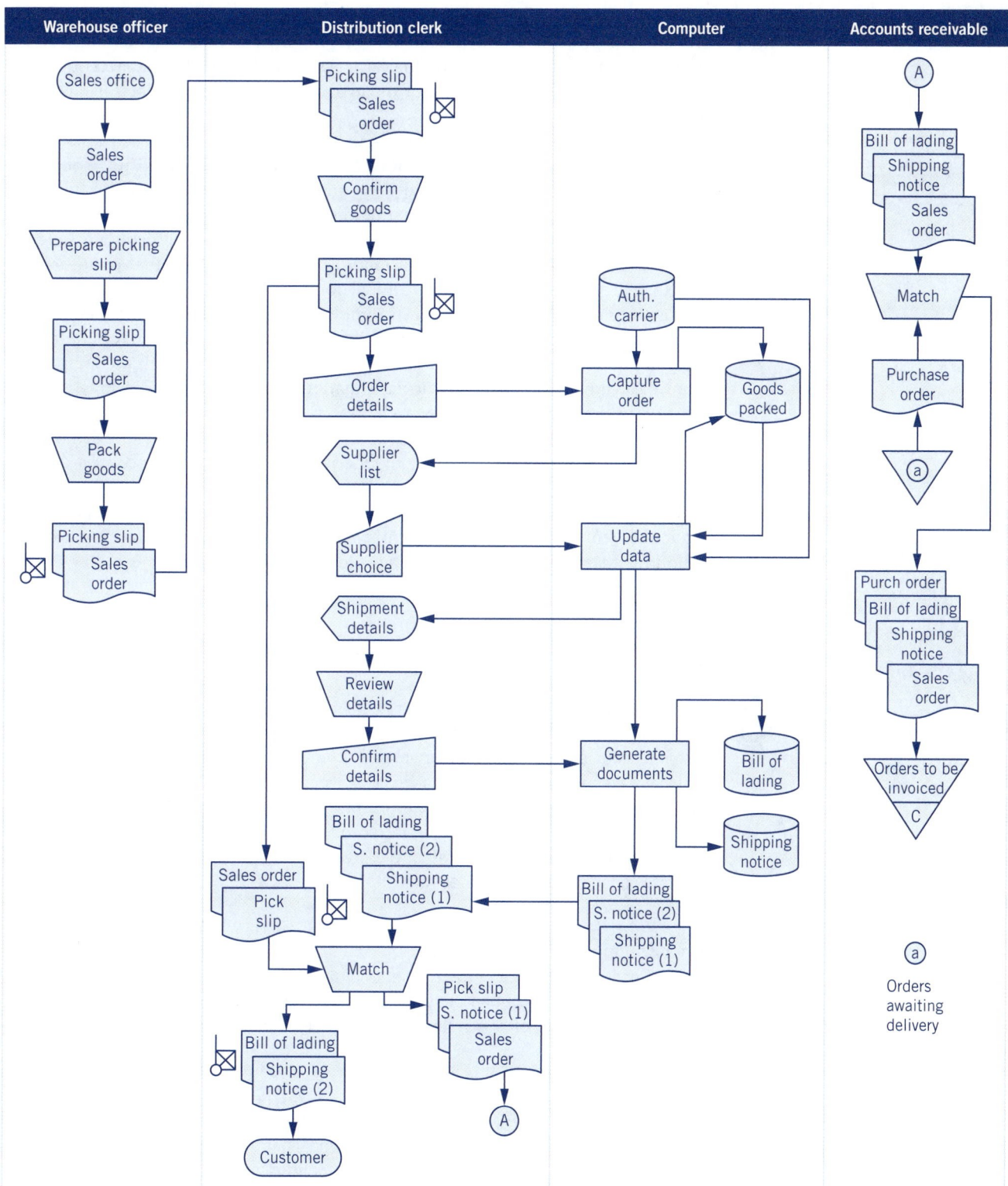

**FIGURE 5.23** Completed systems flowchart

involving different entities and this cannot be represented in the diagram. That is, the process map presents an ungrouped view of the process; activities that are logically grouped together in preparing the logical DFD are individually separated out in the process map, thus allowing detail of the activities and the entities performing these activities to be shown.

From this discussion, you can start to see the relative strengths and weaknesses of each form of documentation. The information each type provides depends on the questions asked about a system's operation, so it becomes necessary to prepare the full set of documentation. The discussion so far should not be seen as an indication of one form of documentation's superiority to another. For example, when designing a system a logical DFD may be useful for understanding the process stages that occur and the data that they need. The specifics required for a flowchart can be captured later in the development effort. Alternatively, to understand the interaction between entities, again for systems design and improvement purposes, a physical DFD may be sufficient. Accordingly, all forms of documentation are equally important, with the appropriate form of documentation for a particular situation dependent on the demands of the situation or the questions that need to be resolved.

Failure to prepare a full set of documentation leads to a loss of valuable detail about a system's operations. Imagine trying to redesign a system with just a context diagram and physical DFD; it would be practically impossible with no idea of what the activities are within the system. Hopefully, you can start to appreciate the complementary nature of the different forms of systems documentation and their importance to an organisation for system design, re-engineering, auditing and monitoring.

## › › SUMMARY › › ›

**LEARNING OBJECTIVE 1**

**Why is systems documentation important to the organisation and the accounting function?**

Systems documentation plays an essential role in the organisation, serving as the organisational memory of how the systems are designed and operate. Systems documentation is the business's roadmap for how systems operate and plays a critical role in the process of systems development. In addition, for the accountant, systems documentation is a means of understanding the audit trail within the organisation as well as the design of business processes and the way data moves through these processes.

**LEARNING OBJECTIVE 2**

**What are some of the uses of systems documentation in the organisation?**

Systems documentation can have a number of uses in the organisation, including helping in the planning and execution of systems development and redesign, and preserving the organisational memory of how systems were designed and how they operate.

**LEARNING OBJECTIVE 3**

**How can the accountant and the auditor be exposed to systems documentation?**

The accountant will be exposed to systems documentation in a range of ways, including through systems development, auditing and internal control based work. As the accountant possesses knowledge of both the necessary accounting processes and controls they will often play an important role in reviewing existing systems and in the design of new systems. This will often involve working with systems documentation. Audit work, both internal and external, places an emphasis on understanding how a process is designed and operated and assessing aspects such as control design and operation. This will require an understanding of how a system operates, which can be acquired by referring to systems documentation. Additionally, flowcharts and other documentation can be used by the auditor as a way of recording their understanding of how a system operates.

LEARNING OBJECTIVE

### What legislative reform has impacted on systems documentation?

In Australia, with the mandatory and legally binding status given to the auditing standards, financial statement auditors are now required to adhere to the prescribed standards. These standards include requirements that the auditor understand how an organisation and its processes operate and indicate a range of documentation techniques that can help in this regard. In addition, the Sarbanes–Oxley legislation in the United States places requirements on management and auditors regarding their control systems. Some of these will necessitate the preparation and maintenance of systems documentation by Australian companies trading on US stock exchanges.

LEARNING OBJECTIVE

### How are different forms of systems documentation read and interpreted?

The different forms of systems documentation provide a different perspective on a system. The structured narrative provides a text-based description of the operations of a system. The context diagram provides an overview of the external entities that interact with the system of interest. This can be expanded to depict the internal entities that make up the system of interest (physical DFD) and the activities within the system of interest (logical DFD). The process map shows the entities and provides a summary of the major stages/activities that operate within a system. The flowchart goes into more detail, showing the entities and the activities and also providing an insight into how the activities are performed (e.g. manual or automated). In each diagram, the emphasis is on mapping the movement of data through the system, whether it be between internal entities or between stages within the process.

LEARNING OBJECTIVE

### What is a balanced set of systems documentation?

A balanced set of systems documentation requires that the external entities and the data flows to the external entities are consistent across the context diagram, physical DFD and logical DFD. The diagrams are looking at the same system, albeit each from a different perspective, so there is no reason why the external entities should differ between the diagrams.

LEARNING OBJECTIVE

### How are different forms of documentation prepared?

The steps provided in the discussion in the chapter outline how to prepare the various forms of systems documentation.

LEARNING OBJECTIVE 8

### How do the different forms of documentation compare?

The different forms of systems documentation provide alternative perspectives on the system of interest. No format of documentation is necessarily superior to the other; rather, the document technique that is to be used will depend on the problem or question being asked. Each type of documentation tells a slightly different story on the operations of the process, and the three documentation approaches (process maps, DFDs and systems flowcharts) complement each other. There is no one perfect approach; all three approaches should be used.

balanced data flow diagrams, p. 220
context diagram, p. 195
data flow diagrams (DFDs), p. 195
decomposing, p. 209
entity, p. 200
error routine, p. 234
external entity, p. 201
internal entity, p. 201
level 0 data flow diagram, p. 212

level 1 data flow diagram, p. 212
logical data flow diagram, p. 195
physical data flow diagram, p. 195
process map, p. 195
stepwise refinement *see decomposing*
structured narration, p. 201
system of interest, p. 195
systems flowchart, p. 195

## DISCUSSION QUESTIONS

5.1 Why does an organisation need to prepare systems documentation? What purpose does systems documentation serve for an organisation? (LO1)

5.2 Explain two reasons accountants need to be familiar with systems documentation techniques. (LO3)

5.3 Describe the information that can be obtained from each of these forms of systems documentation:
(a) Process map
(b) Context diagram
(c) Physical DFD
(d) Logical DFD
(e) Systems flowchart
(LO2, LO3, LO4)

5.4 Discuss the purpose of drawing lower-level DFDs. Why go beyond a level 0 logical DFD? (LO3)

5.5 What is the major difference between a process map and a systems flowchart? (LO2, LO5)

5.6 Explain the differences between the logical DFD, physical DFD and context diagram. (LO5)

5.7 How are error routines handled in DFDs? (LO7)

5.8 Explain the difference between an internal and external entity. (LO5)

5.9 Explain what is meant by balancing a set of DFDs. (LO6)

5.10 What are the two things that you would look for to determine if a set of DFDs are balanced? (LO6)

5.11 Explain what is meant by decomposing a logical DFD. (LO5)

5.12 Explain the difference between a level 0 and a level 1 logical DFD. (LO5)

5.13 Explain why there can only be one physical DFD but many possible representations of a process map. (LO5, LO7)

5.14 Explain the situations where a narration would be used when preparing a systems flowchart. (LO5)

## SELF-TEST ACTIVITIES

5.1 Figure 5.24 is an example of:
(a) a logical DFD.
(b) a physical DFD.

(c) a context diagram.

(d) a process map.

(e) a systems flowchart.

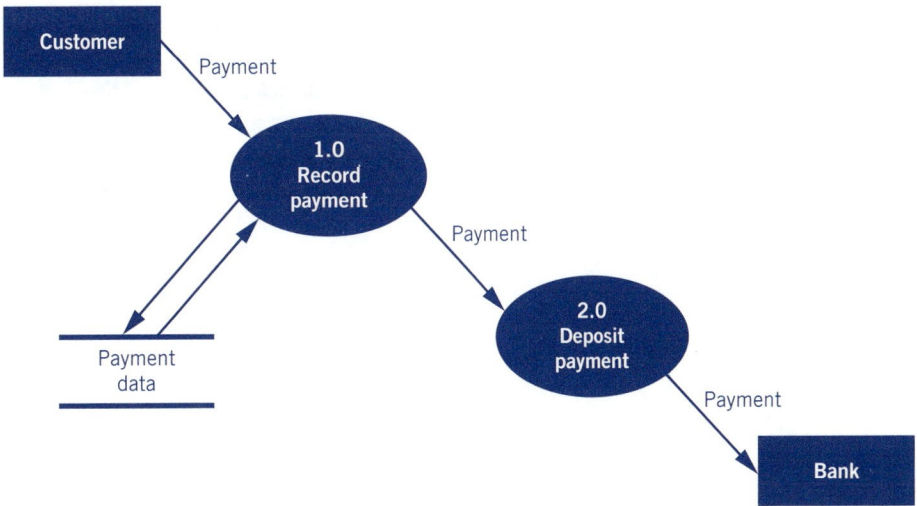

**FIGURE 5.24** Diagram for self-test activity 5.1

5.2 A logical DFD shows:

(a) the groups of entities logically involved in a business process.

(b) how a process is performed.

(c) the logical grouping of activities in a business process.

(d) the methods for performing activities in a process.

(e) none of the above.

5.3 A systems flowchart:

(a) must always have a data store if there are paper documents involved.

(b) must always contain on-page connectors.

(c) includes physical as well as electronic flows.

(d) requires more than one entity.

(e) must be balanced.

5.4 A balanced set of DFDs (logical, physical and context) (i) must have the same external entities, (ii) must have the same number of bubbles in the logical and physical DFDs, (iii) cannot contain only one external entity, (iv) must have the same number of flows to and from external entities, (v) require that the number of flows in the system is the same in the logical and physical DFDs.

(a) i and ii

(b) iii and v

(c) i and iv

(d) ii and v

(e) iv and v

5.5 An external entity in a DFD:

(a) can perform information processing.

(b) only provides inputs to the system.

(c) only receives outputs from the system.

(d) cannot perform data processing activities.

(e) is an entity that is outside the organisation.

5.6 Which of the following narratives best describes the flowchart illustrated in figure 5.25?

(a) A process generates a document that is manually keyed into a computer. Results are stored on tape and three copies of a document generated. One copy is sent to department A, another copy sent to another department and the third copy filed away in numerical order.

(b) A manual process generates a document that is scanned into an offline device and sent electronically to a computer where a process is performed and results stored on disk. Three copies of a document are prepared, with one filed numerically, one sent to another department and the third sent to another place on the flowchart.

(c) A manual process generates a document that is entered online into a computer. The input is then computer-processed, with the results stored on disk. Three copies of a document are prepared, with one filed alphabetically, one sent to another department and the third sent to another place on the flowchart.

(d) A computer process generates a document that is keyed into a computer. Once the form is keyed a process is performed and results stored on disk. Three copies of a document are prepared, with one filed numerically, one sent to another department and the third sent to another place on the flowchart.

(e) A manual process generates a document that is keyed into a computer. A process is performed on the keyed in data and the results stored on disk. Three copies of a document are prepared, with one filed numerically, one sent to another department and the third sent to another place on the flowchart.

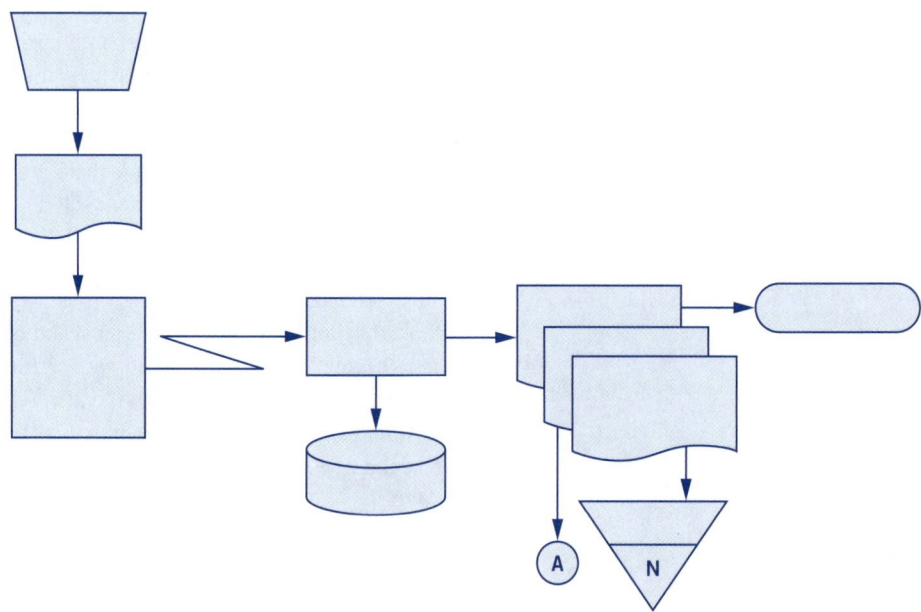

**FIGURE 5.25** Diagram for self-test activity 5.6

## PROBLEMS

5.1 After graduating with Honours from your AIS course you obtain employment with an internationally respected consulting firm. One of the first clients that you work on is undergoing re-engineering of its business processes. The IT manager, who only just scraped through his IT course, pulls you aside one day with a puzzled look on his face. Quietly, he asks you the following: 'Why do we need to do all these different systems documents? Let's just draw a simple context diagram and leave it at that. The sooner we get this system in place the better as far as I am concerned ... my boss wants this system redesign done as soon as possible.' Concerned by this question, you sit down with the IT manager and proceed to set him in the right direction, clarifying his concerns about the role of systems documentation within an organisation.

As part of this discussion you need to explain to him the relationships among the process map, DFD and systems flowchart, as well as the differences among them. You also explain why it is needed to prepare all these forms of documentation. 'That is great,' replies the IT manager when you finish your explanation. 'Could you please put that in writing for me, so I can show it to my boss?' You agree to this and set about writing a brief report for the IT manager.

**Required**

Write the report that you would submit to the IT manager. You should include a discussion of the following points:

- The purpose of preparing systems documentation and the role it plays in the organisation.
- The relationships among the process map, systems flowchart and DFDs.
- Why it is necessary to prepare the different documents and it is not possible just to rely on one form of documentation.

5.2 Summise Inc. offers a hire service to customers, with customers hiring electronic photographic equipment for personal and professional uses. The hiring process is described below.

The client sends in a hire request form which is received by the hire consultant. The hire consultant enters the customer name into the computer and the computer retrieves the customer address from the customer data file and checks the accounts receivable data to ensure no outstanding invoices are owed by the customer. This data is displayed on the computer screen. The item numbers for the products that the customer wishes to hire are keyed in, with the computer retrieving the product description from the equipment data file. The complete order details are displayed on the computer screen and the hire consultant checks that the details match those on the request form. If they agree then the 'confirm order' button is clicked and the data saved in the 'hire orders' data file. The paper hire request form is filed by customer name.

When the computer gets the confirmation of the order from the hire consultant it emails a copy of the hire order form to the inventory control assistant. The order is printed out and the assistant gets the goods listed and packs them securely for sending to the customer. Once packed the assistant goes to the computer and enters the hire order form number, with the computer retrieving the full details from the 'hire orders' data file. The assistant then enters their name and the date the goods were packed. The computer then saves these full details in the invoice file and prints a copy of the invoice and the customer insurance policy. The invoice is attached to the goods and they are sent to the customer at 4 pm each day. At 6 pm each day, once the trading hours for the business are complete, the computer then accesses the invoice data file and takes the data for all invoices created on that day and updates the sales data, accounts receivable data and the inventory availability data. The paper copy of the hire order form is signed by the assistant who packed the goods and filed by date in the inventory on loan file.

**Required**

For the process described:

(a) Prepare the structured narrative
(b) Prepare a process map
(c) Prepare a context diagram
(d) Prepare a physical DFD
(e) Prepare a logical DFD
(f) Prepare a systems flowchart

5.3 Figure 5.26 contains a context diagram and a logical DFD. However, these diagrams contain several errors. Identify the errors contained in each of the diagrams and explain why they are errors.

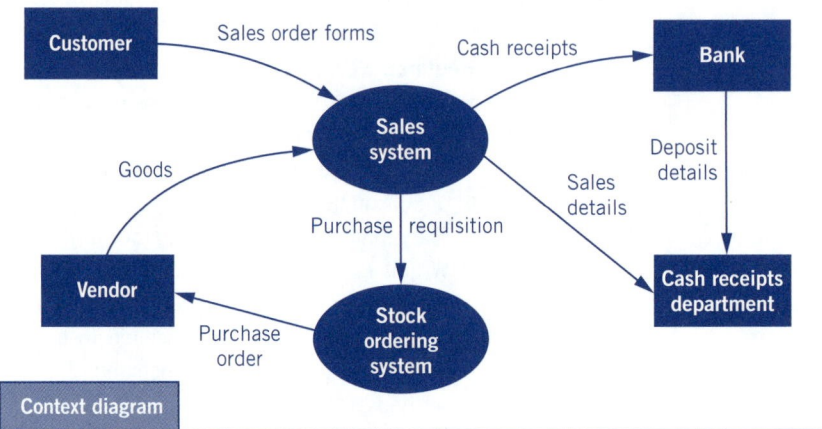

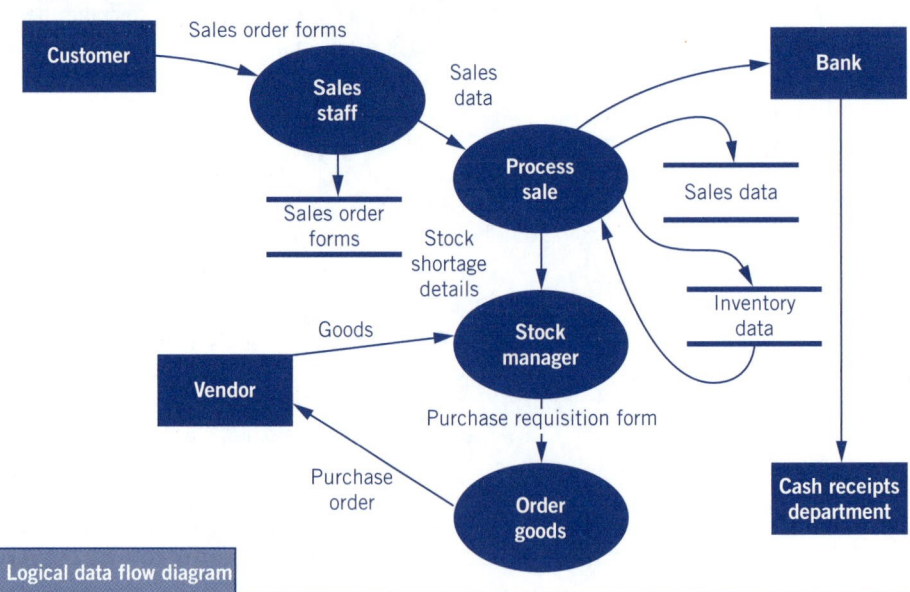

**FIGURE 5.26** Diagrams for problem 5.2

5.4 Semantics Limited is a manufacturer of revolutionary glass windows that are fog and dirt resistant and always provide a clear view wherever they are installed. The accounts receivable process for Semantics is described below.

At the end of month the chief billing manager enters an authorisation code into the computer, allowing the invoice generation program to be run. A confirmation and billing job number is displayed on the screen, with this written down on a 'billing run record' form by the manager. Once the code is entered the manager places the billing run record form in his locked desk drawer and leaves the computer to create customer invoices over night.

In preparing the invoices the computer scans the open invoices file for details of any invoices that were issued to a customer over the previous month. It also searches the cash receipts data for all cash receipts received from customers, as well as the refunds and credits granted file for any other items that may impact on the customer's owing balance. The customer master data is also accessed for the opening account balance and any discount terms that the customer may be entitled to. This data is then used to prepare an invoice for each customer who had a transaction of any sort during the preceding month. The new balance owing is transferred to the customer master data. The invoices are then printed out and the computer displays a summary of the invoices generated – the total number of invoices and the total value of the invoices (based on amount owing) at the end of the month. The next morning, when the manager arrives in their office, they retrieve the 'billing run record' form and record the details of the batch on the form. The invoices and the record form are then forwarded to the billing assistant, who reconciles the number of invoices to the total on the record form before sending the invoices to the customer. The billing run record form, with the completed batch details for the month's invoices, is sent to the accounts manager.

**Required**

For the process described above:

(a) Prepare the structured narrative

(b) Prepare a process map

(c) Prepare a context diagram

(d) Prepare a physical DFD

(e) Prepare a logical DFD

(f) Prepare a systems flowchart

## SELF-TEST ANSWERS

5.1 a, 5.2 e, 5.3 c, 5.4 c, 5.5 d, 5.6 b

## END NOTES

1. Auditing and Assurance Standards Board 2009, Auditing Standard ASA 200 *Overall Objective of the Independent Auditor and the Conduct of an Audit in Accordance with Australian Auditing Standards*, paragraph 3, www.auasb.gov.au.

2. Auditing and Assurance Standards Board 2009, Auditing Standard ASA 315 *Identifying and Assessing the Risks of Material Misstatement through Understanding the Entity and Its Environment*, paragraph 18, www.auasb.gov.au.

3. Auditing and Assurance Standards Board 2006, Auditing Standard ASA 315 *Understanding the Entity and its Environment and Assessing the Risks of Material Misstatement*, paragraph 144.

4. Booth, R 1995, 'To be or not to be: model that process', *Management Accounting*, vol. 73, no. 4, p. 20.

5. Auditing and Assurance Standards Board 2009, Auditing Standard ASA 300 *Planning an Audit of a Financial Report,* www.auasb.gov.au.

6. New Zealand Institute of Chartered Accountants 2003, Auditing Standard 302 *Knowledge of the audit environment*, www.nzica.com; New Zealand Institute of Chartered Accountants 2007. Exposure draft international standard on auditing (New Zealand) 315

*Identifying and assessing the risks of material misstatement through understanding the entity and its environment*, www.nzica.com.

7. Bradford, M, Richtermeyer, SB & Roberts, DF 2007, 'System diagramming techniques: an analysis of methods used in accounting education and practice', *Journal of Information Systems*, vol. 21, no. 1, pp. 173–212.

8. House of Representatives of the United States of America 2002, *Sarbanes–Oxley Act of 2002*.

9. Ivancevich, DC & Sawyer, RS 2004, 'Flowcharting basics for internal auditors', *Internal Auditing*, vol. 19, no. 5, pp. 26–31; Reed, RM, Pence, DK & Doviyanski, A 2006, 'Mending the holes in SOX: the control matrix as an internal audit tool', *Internal Auditing,* vol. 21, no. 1, pp. 18–22; Bradford, Richtermeyer & Roberts 2007.

10. PricewaterhouseCoopers 2005, *Sustainable from the start*, www.pwc.com.

11. PricewaterhouseCoopers 2005.

12. Jones, RA & Lancaster, KAS 2001, 'Process mapping and scripting in the accounting information systems (AIS) curriculum', *Accounting Education*, vol. 10, no. 3, pp. 263–78.

13. Bradford, Richtermeyer & Roberts 2007.

14. Table constructed from results in Bradford, Richtermeyer & Roberts 2007, p. 184.

15. Based on Auditing and Assurance Standards Board 2009; Stimpson, J 2007, 'Audit tools adapt to changes', *The Practical Accountant*, vol. 40, no. 8, pp. 40–42; Reed, Pence & Doviyanski 2006; Stimpson, J 2006, 'Technology's impact on auditing', *The Practical Accountant*, vol. 39, no. 12, pp. 38–40; Ivancevich & Sawyer 2004; House of Representatives of the United States of America 2002.

16. Fulscher, J & Powell, SG 1999, 'Anatomy of a process mapping workshop', *Business Process Management Journal*, vol. 5, no. 3, pp. 208–237; Jones, RA & Lancaster, KAS 2001, 'Process mapping and scripting in the accounting information systems (AIS) curriculum', *Accounting Education*, vol. 10, no. 3, pp. 263–78; Bradford, Richtermeyer & Roberts 2007; Jones & Lancaster 2001; Fulscher, J & Powell, SG 1999, 'Anatomy of a process mapping workshop', *Business Process Management Journal*, vol. 5, no. 3, pp. 208–37.

17. Jones & Lancaster 2001, p. 266.

18. Damelio, R 1996, 'The basics of process mapping', *Quality Resources*, New York, cited in Jones & Lancaster 2001, p. 267.

19. Smith, KT & Smith, LM 2003, 'Tools and techniques for documenting accounting systems', *Internal Auditing,* vol. 18, no. 5 Sept/Oct, pp. 38–45.

20. Smith & Smith 2003.

21. Jones, RA., Tsay, JJ & Griggs, K 2005–06, 'An empirical investigation of the task specific relative strengths of selected accounting and information systems diagramming techniques', *The Journal of Computer Information Systems,* vol. 46, no. 2, pp. 99–114; Carnaghan, C 2006, 'Business process modeling approaches in the context of process level audit risk assessment: an analysis and comparison', *International Journal of Accounting Information Systems,* vol. 7 (2006), pp. 170–204.

22. Smith & Smith 2003.

23. Hunt, VD 1996, *Process mapping: how to re-engineer your business process*, New York, John Wiley & Sons, Inc., pp. 174–7.

24. McCarthy, WE 1982, 'The REA Accounting Model: a generalized framework for accounting systems in a shared data environment', *The Accounting Review*, July, pp. 554–77.

25. Burns, M 2007, 'A better way to flowchart', *CA Magazine*, vol. 140, no. 5 (Jun/Jul), p. 16.

26. Lehman, MW 2000, 'Flowcharting made simple', *Journal of Accountancy,* vol. 190, no. 4, pp. 77–88.

27. Smith & Smith 2003.

# 6

# Enterprise information systems

## Learning objectives

After studying this chapter, you should be able to:

**(1)** understand the different categories of enterprise information systems available on the software market and the characteristics, advantages and disadvantages of each

**(2)** explain why organisations are motivated to implement or upgrade enterprise resource planning (ERP) systems

**(3)** outline the key business processes that ERP systems support

**(4)** describe the modules in an ERP system

**(5)** discuss the considerations for evaluating, purchasing and implementing an ERP system.

# Introduction

Enterprise information systems are software applications used by organisations to capture transactions and produce reports that are used for planning, decision making and statutory reporting. Enterprise information systems have been developed for businesses of all sizes, levels of complexity and information needs.

This chapter has three parts. In the first part, the different categories of enterprise information systems are outlined and their inherent characteristics explained. An understanding of software categories allows organisations to select the enterprise information systems software that best meets their requirements. The second part of this chapter provides a detailed look at enterprise resource planning systems or ERP systems. ERP systems are one of the software categories used in larger, more complex organisations. The third part of this chapter discusses specific purchasing, implementation, benefits and evaluation considerations relating to these systems.

**Business processes** *Any set of interlocking activities that work together, across the organisation, to achieve some predetermined organisational goal, which is typically defined around satisfying customer needs.*

**Software applications** *Computer programs that are written in programming languages or code that are used by organisations to capture their transactions and produce reports that are used for planning, decision making and statutory reporting.*

# THE ENTERPRISE INFORMATION SYSTEMS MARKET

There are many different types of software systems on the market designed to support different functions within organisations as well as enabling functions that span organisations. Software systems automate **business processes**, link businesses processes within an organisation and can link different organisations together. This part of the chapter outlines a framework for categorising software. This framework can be used by organisations for selecting software that best fits their needs to achieve a competitive advantage.

## The software framework

Organisations come in all sizes. Small organisations often have few employees and usually concentrate on a small number of specialised activities. They typically make up one part of a larger interconnection of organisations that together provide an ultimate product or service. An example of such an organisation is one that designs and builds windscreen wipers for car manufacturers. Another example is an organisation that manufactures the glass for the windscreen and windows of a range of cars.

Large organisations are sometimes formed as successful medium-sized organisations grow or acquire smaller organisations. These organisations derive their success from economies of scale and perform a diverse range of activities. For example, a large car manufacturer such as Ford, General Motors or Toyota will assemble vehicles for global markets by sometimes acquiring and combining different businesses and manufacturing processes of many smaller specialised suppliers. Large computer manufacturers such as Dell and IBM assemble computers for global markets in a similar way.

Different sized organisations are likely to have different information and business process requirements. Small organisations with specialised activities and a limited number of products or services often have simpler information needs than large organisations. Larger organisations, such as a car or a computer manufacturer, will have to coordinate business and manufacturing processes with other organisations that supply specialised parts. Regardless of size, organisations need **software applications** to seamlessly communicate internally and with external suppliers and customers for successful operations. Software vendors are under increasing pressure to provide new functionality as part of their suite of software offerings. Systems that merely provide old functions in new ways such as to automate business processes are no longer sufficient. Increasing competition among software vendors means that they need to innovate to survive and prosper.

There are several approaches to categorising the software market, but this chapter utilises the Smith David, McCarthy & Sommer[1] framework because of its simple yet comprehensive coverage. Organisations that are purchasing software can use the framework to identify how available systems software applications differ. **Software vendors** can use the framework to observe industry and market trends in order to develop future strategies that target specific markets or create niche markets that they can participate in. Software vendors cannot provide for the needs of every organisation, but by solving old problems, improving business processes or providing new features and ways of conducting business, they can achieve a competitive advantage. These vendors need to focus on a wide variety of needs that exist within their chosen customer market.

As shown in figure 6.1, enterprise information systems can be organised into three general categories: single-entry systems, inwardly organised systems and outwardly organised systems.

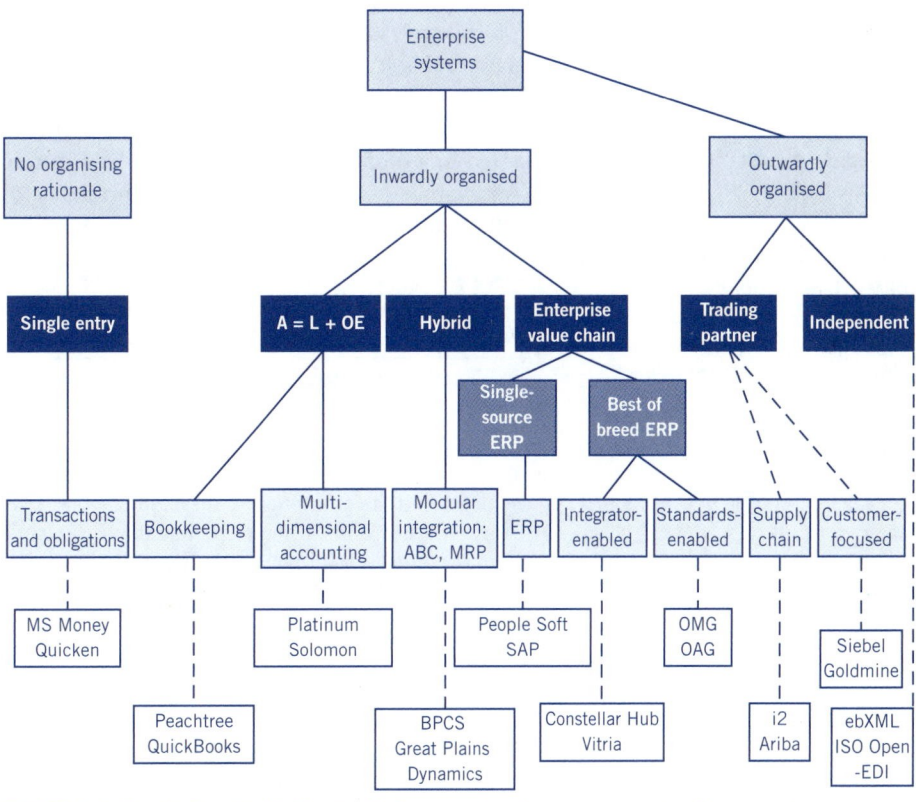

**FIGURE 6.1** Smith David, McCarthy & Sommer's software categories framework

*Transactions* Any business-related exchange, such as the sale of products to customers or payment to suppliers.

*Obligations* Requirements for a business to undertake or complete exchanges, such as paying amounts owing to suppliers.

**Inwardly organised systems**
*Software that focuses on recording and monitoring all exchanges that occur within an organisation.*

**Outwardly organised systems**
*Software that focuses on recording and monitoring all exchanges that occur among organisations.*

The framework suggests that software with no organisational rationale should be known as single-entry enterprise information systems. Single-entry systems merely record **transactions** and **obligations** as they occur. **Inwardly organised systems** focus on recording and monitoring business and manufacturing processes within organisations. These systems include simple bookkeeping systems to advanced accounting systems and enterprise resource planning systems that capture all the internal activities of an organisation. Finally, **outwardly organised systems** support not only the organisation's internal activities, but extend the capture of data to suppliers and customers that the organisation deals with. Outwardly organised systems are able to capture the activities between organisations using supply chain management and customer relationship management systems.

The following sections describe each of the categories of enterprise information systems. For each system, the discussion focuses on the key features, the type of organisation it is most likely to suit, and advantages and disadvantages.

## Single-entry systems

**Single-entry systems** are enterprise information systems that operate without any structure that can help small, simple organisations on a daily basis to record transactions and obligations in conjunction with manual business processes. These systems are designed for individual users and small businesses in which the owner is the key decision maker. Individuals, sole traders, small groups of consultants and small retailers will find these systems useful for recording cash inflows from services provided and products sold, and cash outflows from expenses incurred in obtaining service revenue or purchasing inventory for sale. An example of such a system is Intuit's Quicken.

In general, single-entry systems record cash transactions through a link to the organisation's bank account that downloads customer payment details, make customer payments, and assist with bank account reconciliation. These systems also have the capability to capture and schedule transactions electronically. The transactions are stored in a **database** that is managed by a **database management system or DBMS** (see chapter 3). The DBMS provides limited calculations for reporting purposes.

Table 6.1 outlines the advantages and disadvantages of single-entry systems.

*Single-entry systems* Software that merely records transactions and obligations.

*Database* A shared computerised structure that captures, stores and relates data.

*Database management system (DBMS)* A group of programs that manipulate the database and provide the interface between the database and the user as well as other application programs.

**TABLE 6.1** Advantages and disadvantages of single-entry systems

| Advantages | Disadvantages |
|---|---|
| • Require little accounting knowledge to understand and use. | • Cannot provide classification principles to guide the recognition of transactions (e.g. most will not allow for accruals such as receivables, payables and depreciation). |
| • Users find them intuitive as they can enter transactions in the same way that they occur between the business and its customers | • Transactions are normally recorded and stored chronologically. |
| • Provide easy web browser access and links with email. | • As transaction volumes increase, the transactional database finds it increasingly difficult to classify and store transactions for easy extraction and reporting. |
| • Cater for and satisfy banking requirements and produce limited tax reports. | • Lack of classifications in the software limits the financial reporting capability for external information users and statutory reporting. |
| • Allows electronic banking to schedule and pay bills. | • Ignores non-financial or operating information. |
| • Contain calculators for personal and small business mortgages, insurances, other loans and leases. | • Will not normally have the phone and consultant support of more comprehensive systems. |
| • Can perform financial management and investment processes and track investment performance. | |

**Bookkeeping systems** *Systems that perform accounting functions that include cash receipts and payments, accruals such as accounts receivable and accounts payable, to provide reports on the performance of the organisation.*

**Streamlining** *The act of making business processes within organisations efficient, effective and seamless in their execution.*

## Bookkeeping systems

**Bookkeeping systems** are also known as assets (A) = liabilities (L) + owners' equity (OE) systems because they make use of accrual accounting concepts. They summarise data to fit the chart of accounts in general ledgers based on the classic double-entry accounting equation of assets = liabilities + owners' equity. Bookkeeping systems are the first of three categories of inwardly organised systems, hybrid systems being the second and ERP systems the third.

Bookkeeping systems are generally used by small businesses to monitor their financial performance for reporting and tax purposes. These systems are focused on **streamlining** the financial functions within an organisation without consideration for operating and manufacturing functions that often generate non-financial information. Examples of such systems include Intuit's QuickBooks, MYOB, Simply Accounting and Peachtree.

Table 6.2 outlines the advantages and disadvantages of bookkeeping systems.

**TABLE 6.2** Advantages and disadvantages of bookkeeping systems

| Advantages | Disadvantages |
|---|---|
| • Streamline the financial functions in small businesses, permitting easy financial reporting and taxation calculations. | • Inappropriate when the business requirements extend beyond the scope and activities of a small business. |
| • Easy to install — many packages come with a standard preformatted chart of accounts in common with most business formats that can be used almost immediately by the purchaser. | • Do not normally have manufacturing models that some businesses would like to integrate with their financial systems. |
| • Both accountants and non-accountants can use the systems. | • Bookkeeping reports are pre-programmed, with limited reporting flexibility. |
| • Can provide support for business processes such as order entry or cash receipts. | • Bookkeeping systems with pre-established general ledgers and charts of accounts can be a weakness for a unique business that may not fit the structure required by the system. |
| • Can capture business activities in real-time and transaction processing allows immediate or end-of-day processing options. | • Although available, technical support from the vendor is likely to be more limited than in more sophisticated systems. |
| • Have inbuilt accounting controls that verify the accuracy of transactions. | |
| • Authorise a number of users to operate simultaneously with limited network capabilities. | |
| • Likely to be some document and phone support by the software provider. | |

## Hybrid systems

**Hybrid systems** *Systems that integrate the operations of an organisation with the financial functions in the organisation.*

**Hybrid systems** are an extension of bookkeeping systems. They use independent software to integrate operations and financial functions within an organisation. These systems emerged from the range of software that was independently developed in other functional areas within organisations such as manufacturing systems, inventory management systems, warehouse management systems and customer information systems.

Why did hybrid systems come about? As a result of wanting to capture information outside of financial-based transactions that represent activities within the business.

For example, manufacturing businesses are often structured so that the outputs of a particular manufacturing area are direct inputs into another. Some manufacturers have a requirement to capture data based on the movement of work back and forth between manufacturing areas. This led to the development of materials requirements planning (MRP) software that provided a means for plant managers to plan production and raw materials requirements for each part of the manufacturing process based on sales forecast information from the business's sales department.

MRP software paved the way for hybrid systems because these systems were a culmination of bookkeeping systems being integrated with MRP software used in manufacturing. The hybrid systems were a way to integrate the sales department, finance department and manufacturing department through system software. For example, the Epicor Software Corporation's Vantage manufacturing software can be integrated with a bookkeeping system.

The main advantage of a hybrid system is its ability to integrate an organisation's operations with its financial functions. These systems can facilitate communication and decision making among operational and financial divisions in an organisation. The main disadvantage of a hybrid system is the effort required to integrate specialised systems with financial systems. That is, true integration between different software requires time and resources. Hybrid systems only integrate certain parts of the organisation such as manufacturing with financial functions. There are still requirements to integrate other organisational areas such as human resources, payroll or fleet management. Hybrid systems lack a standardised approach and structure for a fully integrated organisational system. As a result, there is still some duplication of tasks, errors and processing that keep operating costs above a minimum standard.

This disadvantage highlights the requirement for a fully integrated enterprise information system that can holistically capture all of an organisation's activities and transactions.

## ERP systems

**ERP systems** are designed to capture a wide range of information about all business transactions and processes related to the typical four major areas in an organisation: sales and marketing, finance, manufacturing and human resources. These systems link the typical major functions of an organisation, and the organisation's suppliers and customers in the value chain. That is, the systems link:

- sales and marketing: the division of the organisation that sells the products and services
- accounting and finance: the division of the organisation that manages the business's financial assets and maintains its financial records
- manufacturing: the division of the organisation that purchases raw material to be converted into products and services that provide customer value
- human resources: the division of the organisation that attracts, develops and maintains the business's labour resources and employee records
- suppliers: the businesses that provide direct and indirect raw materials into the manufacturing division of the organisation
- customers: the people that purchase products and services from the organisation because they value those products and services.

ERP systems are developed based on Porter's[2] view that organisations are part of a chain of suppliers and customers. Customer demand pulls resources into organisations via suppliers upstream. The customer demand-pull is part of the downstream management of an organisation's **enterprise value chain**, or the series of activities that links sales and marketing with manufacturing, accounting and finance, and human resources. The customers' demands downstream create sales and marketing information that require systems that can capture, calculate and coordinate with distribution, warehouse retrieval and production in the organisation. At the same time, the organisation must have production systems that can coordinate upstream with suppliers for raw material purchasing, acquisition and control. Figure 6.2 illustrates the relationship between ERP functions in the context of a typical enterprise value chain.

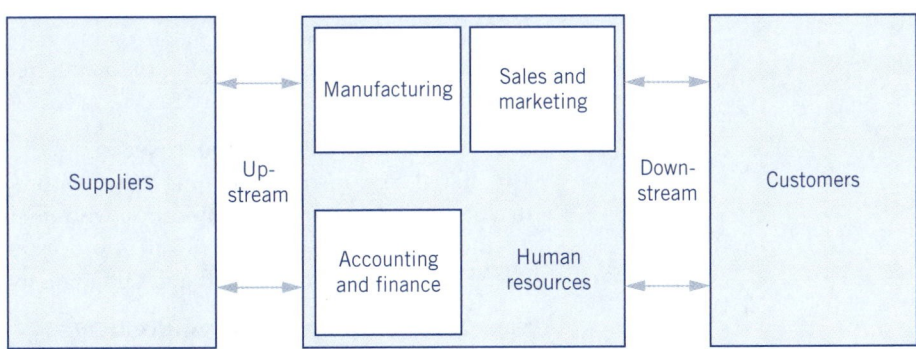

**FIGURE 6.2** Enterprise value chain

A detailed discussion of ERP systems is contained in the second part of this chapter.

## AIS FOCUS 6.1

### ERP vendors

There are many ERP systems commercially available though a large number of software vendors. Table 6.3 lists the major ERP vendors and the type of customer they provide for. Note, however, that software vendors are consolidating at a rapid pace and any list of ERP vendors is frequently changing. The table lists market segments and, alphabetically within each market, the vendors that are generally considered to be leaders in providing ERP solutions. The two dominant vendors for large enterprises are Oracle and SAP, whose ERP system commands the largest percentage of the top 500 global companies.

**TABLE 6.3** Major ERP vendors

| Company Name | Market[a] |
|---|---|
| Oracle[b] | Large |
| SAP | Large |
| Lawson | Large, Small Medium Enterprises |
| Infor[c] | Large, Small Medium Enterprises, Small |
| Microsoft Dynamics[d] | Small Medium Enterprise, Small |
| Sage Group | Small Medium Enterprise, Small |

[a] Large = > US$1b revenue. Small Medium Enterprises = US$30m to US$1b revenues.
Small = < US$30m revenue.
[b] Includes Peoplesoft Inc. and J.D. Edwards & Company.
[c] Includes SSA Global Technologies and Extensity.
[d] Includes XP (Axapta), GP (Great Plains), NAV (Navision), and SL (Solomon).

# Using the software framework

Based on the key differences between the software categories within the software framework as discussed in the previous section, organisations, small and large, can use the software framework to select appropriate systems for their needs. Needs are usually determined by business size, complexity and information requirements.

## *Software selection*

Using the software framework, the following steps can be taken to select software for an organisation.

### Step 1: Define business processes

This initial step involves defining business processes, transactions and interactions that are undertaken by an organisation with its suppliers and customers. For example, a typical restaurant will have business processes for ordering ingredients from suppliers, hiring and rostering staff and taking reservations from customers.

### Step 2: Develop business requirements

The development of **business requirements** is based on an organisation's business processes. Business requirements are defined as the end result and functionality that is required to successfully complete a business process. For example, the business requirement for a restaurant ordering ingredients from suppliers is the ability to capture many specialist ingredient suppliers. For the restaurant to roster staff, a rostering capability should be built into the business requirement. Similarly, a means of recording reservations should be incorporated into the business requirement for taking customer reservations.

### Step 3: Determine the software systems requirements

Software **systems requirements** are the software applications that are required to fulfil the business requirements. This step determines whether a system is required or available to meet the business requirements. In our restaurant example, rostering and reservations software systems are available for allocating staff to shifts and booking in customers for meals. However, either or both systems may not be essential. For example, if the restaurant has a small number of permanent staff, rostering may be a simple manual process and a decision to acquire a rostering software system may not be justified. Similarly, the restaurant may just purchase a bookings system that allows online bookings, with easy manual additions, cancellations and modifications.

### Step 4: Select software

**Software selection** using the software framework requires a particular software category to be chosen that will meet all the systems requirements defined in step 3. For example, assume that the restaurant requires software applications that can track sales and receipts and inventory and services, take customer bookings and provide email and internet. This suggests that an inwardly organised bookkeeping system and an online booking system may satisfy business requirements.

### Step 5: Select vendor

The final step is to determine the vendor that will provide the software applications for the business. Given that an inwardly organised bookkeeping system would satisfy the financial aspect of the restaurant's business requirements for reporting income

*Business requirements* The set of entities, outcomes and functionality required to successfully allow the business process to be performed.

*Systems requirements* The software applications that are required to fulfil the business requirements.

*Software selection* The act of selecting software to satisfy systems requirements.

**Vendor selection** *The act of choosing a vendor that will provide the software to satisfy systems requirements.*

(income statement) and financial position (balance sheet), packages such as Intuit's QuickBooks or MYOB may be sufficient. To provide customers with online booking systems functionality, the restaurant may want to subscribe to ebookaplace.com. However, it should be noted that **vendor selection** for ERP systems can be a complex commercial process. To meet the many requirements of a large organisation, the organisation is required to obtain responses from potential vendors as to how they might provide for the many systems requirements. Details of the vendor selection process for ERP systems are beyond the scope of this text.

## Interpreting the software categories

Before the detailed discussion of ERP systems in the next part of the chapter, the interpretation of the software categories described above should be clarified.

Firstly, the framework does not imply that any category is superior to another. The best software solution is contingent upon the business environment in which it will be used. This highlights the importance of the first two steps in the software selection process, which requires defining the business process and determining the business requirements.

Secondly, moving to the right along the framework in figure 6.1 does not imply newer or older innovations. Each category contains the software vendors that provide the newest and most innovative software for their particular category. These vendors participate in a fast-paced, evolving market and many will have products and services that reside across a number of categories. Vendors may also move between categories as they grow, mature and find their niches.

Finally, divisions among the categories are not absolute. Applications could be in more than one category. Vendors are increasingly offering optional features that take their offering from one category to another. For example, Intuit sells its QuickBooks package to small businesses but offers QuickBooks PRO to larger businesses that require integration with their manufacturing divisions, or internet functionality that allows for e-commerce. These requirements go beyond the financial accounting functionality that QuickBooks provides. Software applications, therefore, fall along a continuum.

**LEARNING OBJECTIVE 2**

*Explain why organisations are motivated to implement or upgrade enterprise resource planning (ERP) systems.*

## ERP SYSTEMS

As indicated above, ERP systems are software systems designed to capture a wide range of information about all key business processes within an organisation and between an organisation and its suppliers and customers. More formally, ERP systems attempt to integrate all departments and functions across a business into a single enterprise-wide information system that can service all those departments' particular needs. Figure 6.3 overleaf shows the interrelationships within an organisation that the ERP system integrates.

Figure 6.3 shows that customer orders trigger the shipping area of a business. The shipping area draws on inventory within the organisation, which in turn triggers manufacturing to produce further stocks of products for inventory. Product manufacturing in turn forces the business to purchase and receive raw materials from suppliers if required. At the same time, customer orders are recorded in the accounts receivable area of the business, while purchases are recorded with accounts payable in the accounting and finance division. To ensure that there is staff to perform the business processes and activities, human resources manages salaries, wages and other functions across the organisation. In summary, ERP systems support key business processes that involve the major functions in an organisation. These processes include:

1. revenue, sales or order to cash
2. payment, purchases or purchase to pay
3. production, manufacturing or conversion
4. human resources and payroll
5. general ledger and financial reporting.

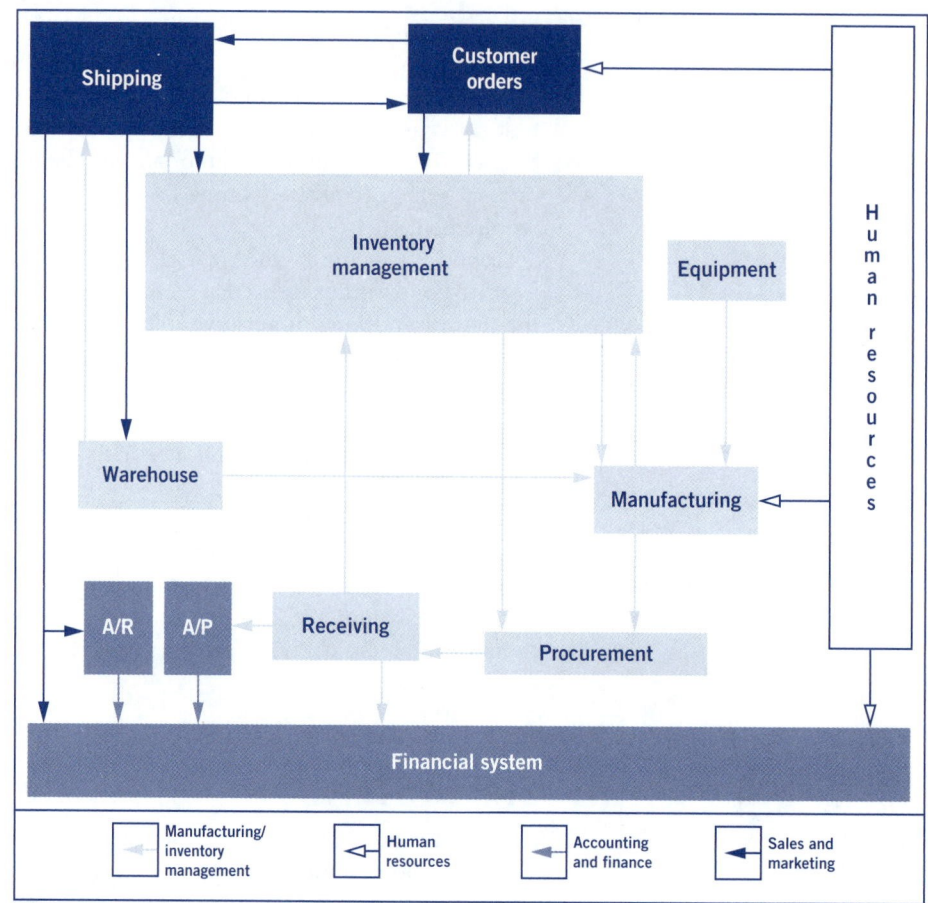

**FIGURE 6.3** ERP system functionality[3]

Each of these key business processes brings together different functions or divisions in the organisation. For example, the revenue process brings together the sales and marketing department with accounts receivable in the accounting department (which records the sales), manufacturing (which produces the product or service to sell) and human resources (which provides the sales, finance and manufacturing staff for the revenue process to be executed). Figure 6.4 illustrates the relationship between the key business processes and the role of ERP systems. The support ERP systems provide for the key business processes are further explained later in the chapter.

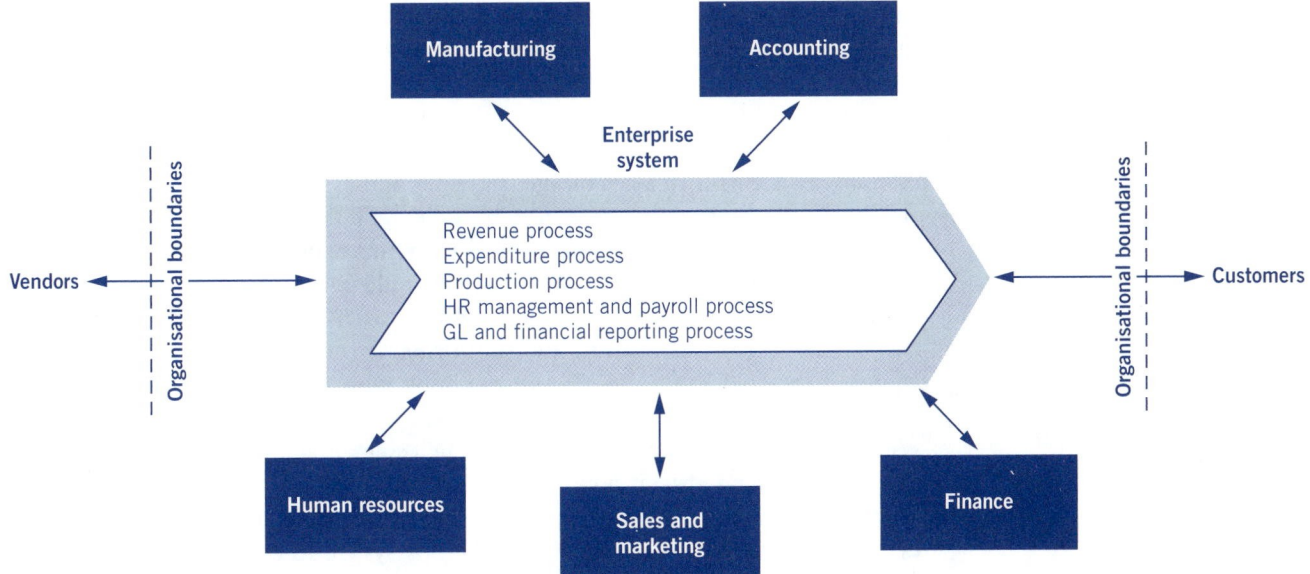

**FIGURE 6.4** Key business processes and ERP systems

## Evolution

The idea of an ERP system began on the factory floor as early as the 1960s. During this time, simple systems were developed as a means for factory and plant managers to plan raw material purchasing and production based on sales forecast information from sales and marketing managers. Inventory and MRP software provided some link between manufacturing and the finance and management areas of the business.

The stimulus for the development of ERP systems was brought about by the harder economic times in the late 1980s and 1990s. To stay competitive and profitable, companies had to provide customers with products and services faster and cheaper than their competition could. Organisations believed that the key was to have an integrated information system that would efficiently and seamlessly integrate their sales and marketing, operations and financial functions. The objectives were to have production schedules meet sales orders precisely without over- or under-estimation; eliminate the obsolescence in production; eliminate warehouse expenses; and ensure information and performance reporting was timely and accurate for planning, controlling and decision making.

Until recently, most businesses had non-integrated information systems that could only support the activities of individual business functional areas, each with its own hardware, software and processing methods. The problems with these non-integrated systems were duplication of effort and poor information timeliness. As a result, there was also poor decision making that led to higher costs and customer dissatisfaction.

Greater power of computers, developments in telecommunications, and local and wide area **networks** have allowed software development to support the greater visions of integrated ERP systems. At the same time, businesses began to view themselves as a set of **cross-functional business processes**. Rather than viewing manufacturing or finance or human resources as separate independent functions without any cause

**Networks** *Connected computers and computer equipment in buildings around the world that enable electronic communications.*

**Cross-functional business processes** *Business processes that require inputs from separate functions in the organisation including manufacturing, finance, sales and marketing.*

and effect, organisations began viewing processes from a complete product or service perspective. For example, the final product of a motor car requires the coordination of purchasing and obtaining the parts, assembling the car in a factory plant, shipping the car to a dealership, and selling the car to a customer.

ERP systems grew from disparate manufacturing and financial systems into centralised systems with a central database that houses all the operational and financial information for the business. As a result, manufacturing, inventory, distribution, logistics, marketing, sales and financial information can be integrated into one central location that can be accessed by all employees in the business.

The development of **client–server hardware architecture** also allows the database to run on a variety of **computer platforms**. This flexible and open architectural approach means that integration and communication are easily achieved. Businesses can also use outwardly organised software systems such as supply chain management systems and customer relationship management systems and integrate these with their ERP systems (these systems are discussed later in the chapter). Hardware items such as barcode scanners, personal digital assistants, mobile phones and other global information systems can also be attached to the ERP system to capture data, transactions and information in the centralised database.

## Enterprise systems value chain

Figure 6.5 takes the enterprise systems value chain in figure 6.2 and shows the specific manufacturing or value chain activities that occur within the four major functions that provide support for these activities. As you can see, the value chain shows how a business purchases raw materials, receives raw materials, produces and delivers its product, markets and sells the product, then installs the product and provides service to customers. The sales and marketing, manufacturing, accounting and finance, and human resources functions/divisions support this value chain process.

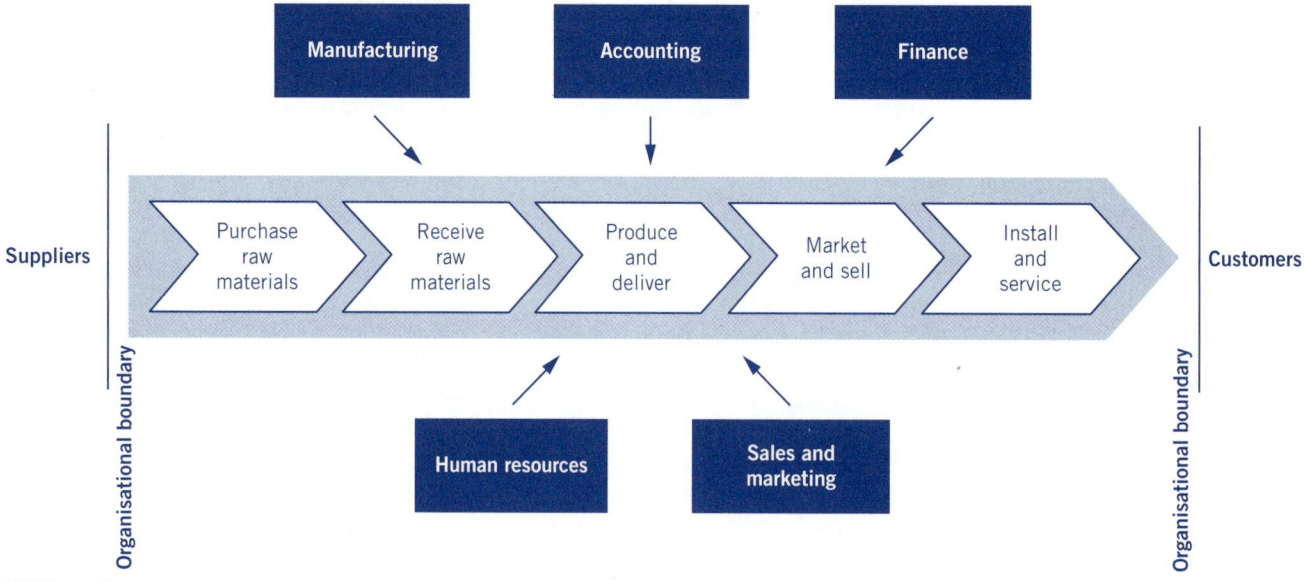

**FIGURE 6.5** Value chain activities and key supporting functions

ERP systems can assist in the value chain process by reducing the cost or improving the quality of performance of the value chain activities performed in the process. For example, ERP systems can be applied to optimise the cost and quality of raw materials by providing information to assist in the selection of the right material at the right cost from the right vendor.

An ERP system can also be applied to the production/inventory process to balance costs and timeliness of manufacturing. In the first case, the optimisation allows the manufacture of a product that is consistent with quality objectives at minimum cost. In the second case, it allows a balance between product availability and cost.

ERP systems can also assist in creating value within the activities that are part of the value chain. These activities are sequential and interdependent, and need to be closely coordinated to be most effective in value creation.

ERP systems can provide the necessary interconnections between an organisation's major functions through the sharing and communication of information and the coordination of activities. For example, customers are satisfied when the activities related to marketing the product, receiving the order, scheduling the production, delivery, installation and after-sales service are coordinated.

To illustrate the value creating benefits of ERP systems, the following sections explain what it would be like for businesses without ERP systems, and how ERP systems address some of these issues.

## The problem

Figure 6.6 overleaf shows the customer ordering process at ABC Ltd, a fictitious business that manufactures and sells electronic gadgets. As you can see, Michael is the customer service representative and requires access to information from a variety of sources to inform customers when they can expect to receive their order and how much that order will cost.

Firstly, Michael needs to know if this is an existing customer and if the customer is within its credit limits (flow 1). To access this information, Michael needs to consult a list of existing customers (and hope that the list is up to date). He then needs to check the customer's credit rating (flow 2) — and hope that that is up to date.

Secondly, Michael needs to tell the customer whether the item they want to buy is available or, if it is not available, when it may be (flow 3). With no automated link, he needs to contact the warehouse or examine computer printouts of inventory balances and again hope that the information is up to date; otherwise, he could be promising his customer an item that has either been committed or is not available. If the item is not available, Michael should also consult the current factory production schedule to see when the item will be available (flow 4).

Thirdly, if we assume that the item is available to ship to the customer, what price should be charged for the order? Michael could consult a price list near his phone but it may be out of date. As the marketing department may determine prices dynamically based on customer status, market conditions, quantity purchased and so on, Michael may be required to contact the marketing department (flow 5).

Do you think that Michael would want to keep the customer on the phone throughout this process? Do you think this is good customer service? What should ABC Ltd do?

**FIGURE 6.6** ABC Ltd customer ordering process

## The solution

The solution to Michael having to contact numerous areas of the business and risk relying on outdated information, as you have probably gathered, is to integrate the information Michael needs into a central system that he can access. This can be done using an ERP system. The ERP system would certainly streamline the customer order process. It would be effective because Michael would have the information he needs at hand, in real time, meaning he could provide the customer with an almost immediate order confirmation or otherwise. The process would also be more efficient because

Michael would not have to consult various lists and reconcile those lists with duplicate information. More importantly, Michael would not have to interrupt the work of his colleagues in the other divisions of the business.

With an ERP system, the customer order process would proceed as follows:

- The input of the customer's name or details gives Michael access to customer data (flow 1).
- Upon entering the item requested, the system establishes whether the item is available or when it will be available (i.e. whether is it is being manufactured or scheduled to be manufactured) (flows 3 and 4).
- The system automatically determines the price based on the customer details and the marketing inputs (flows 5 and 2).
- The system schedules picking or manufacture and calculates an estimated delivery date (flow 3).

As a result, Michael does not keep the customer on the phone for an extended period or take up the time of his colleagues in other areas of the organisation. With an ERP system, all of the above steps are completed in a matter of seconds. The example illustrates that the use of the ERP system minimises duplication of tasks, errors in processing, costs and customer dissatisfaction.

# SUPPORTING KEY BUSINESS PROCESSES

As outlined previously in this chapter, most organisations have five key business processes that ERP systems need to support:

1. revenue, sales or order to cash
2. payment, purchases or purchase to pay
3. production, manufacturing or conversion
4. human resources and payroll
5. general ledger and financial reporting.

The activities, transactions and decision making involved in each of these key business processes are discussed in chapters 9 to 13 in this book. At this point, it is important to explain how an ERP system can support the key business processes. Using the revenue process and the expenditure process as examples, this section outlines how an ERP system captures data in these processes, and facilitates operations and decision making.

Figure 6.7 overleaf depicts a simplified revenue process. Figure 6.8 (p. 265) depicts a simplified expenditure process. These are referred to in the following discussion.

## *Data capture*

**Data capture** *The collection of the four dimension of any business activity (who, what, where and when) so that the organisation can aggregate and summarise data in various forms to answer the questions that a decision maker is asking.*

In essence, the ERP system captures all the necessary activities so that someone who was not a party to the activities can reconstruct every aspect. **Data capture** involves the system looking for four dimensions in the business activity:

1. Who was involved in the activity.
2. What resources were exchanged in the activity.
3. Where the activity took place, including where the resources reside before and after the activity.
4. When the activity was completed, including any future exchanges of resources because of the activity.

By collecting these dimensions of any business activity, the organisation can aggregate and summarise data in various forms to answer the questions that a decision maker may ask. The system will also have programmed procedures to generate routine accounting reports periodically and automatically.

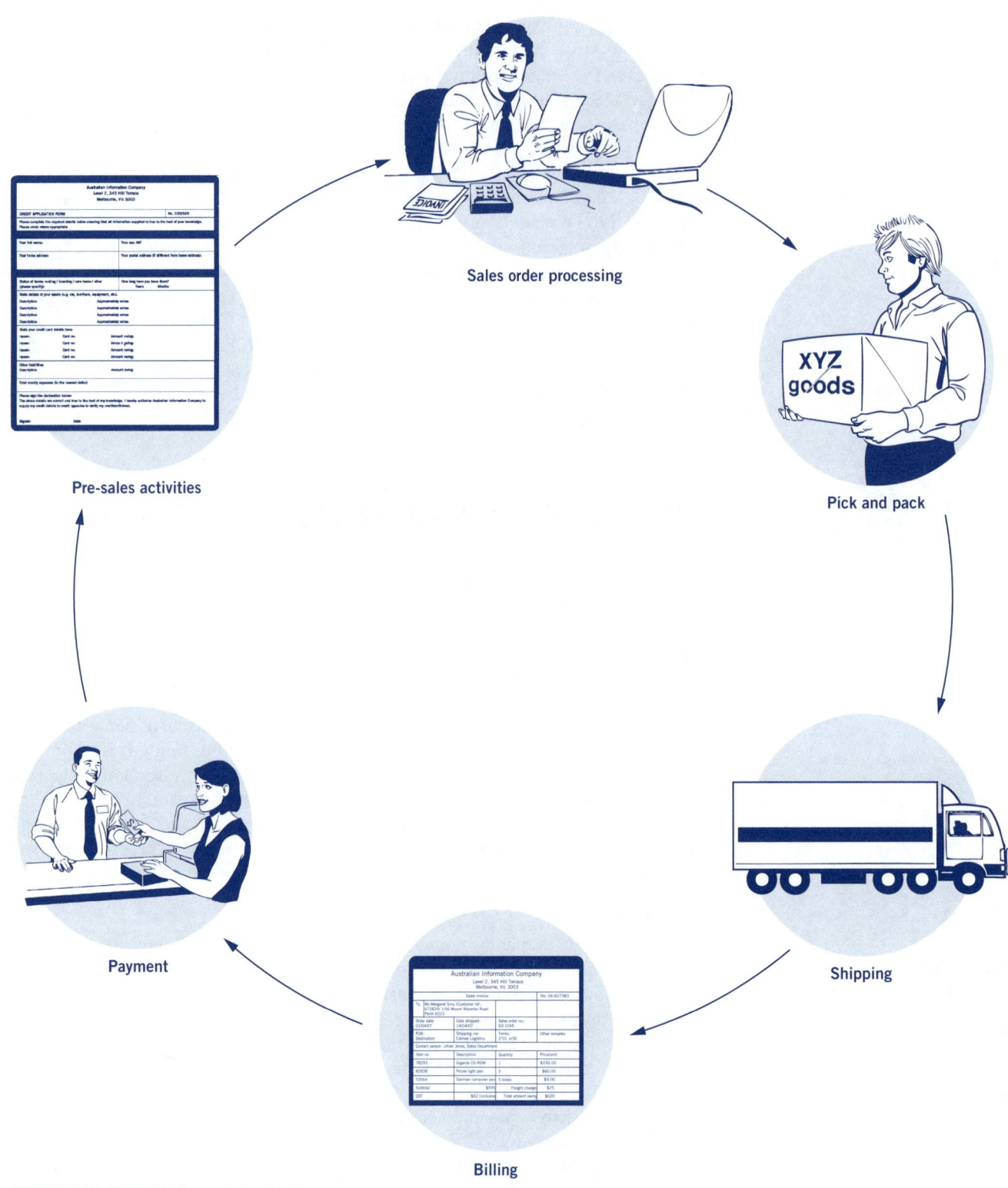

**FIGURE 6.7** Simplified revenue process

Referring to figure 6.7, in the pre-sales activities, data can be captured on responses to customer enquiries about, for example, product features and product functions. When sales order processing is undertaken, customer orders are captured and recorded. The ERP system then links customer, inventory, purchasing and supplier data to determine whether the customer can pay the bill and whether there is inventory available or manufacturing in progress to deliver the product to the customer. As the product is picked and packed for shipment, the system captures and records each action and produces the documents to show that the product has been picked and packed. After shipping, the ERP system calculates and records the cost of goods sold and the inventory reduction. In the billing process, the system prepares the customer invoice and records sales and accounts receivable data in the general ledger. This step links together sales, customer and inventory data. When payment is received, the ERP system records the cash, and updates the cash and accounts receivable amounts in the general ledger.

In figure 6.8, requirements determination includes the preparation of a purchase requisition to request the purchase of products from a supplier. The ERP system generates the purchase requisition, either after authorisation from a manager or automatically in the case of inventories of particular products dropping below a predetermined level. The system can also check if purchases are authorised.

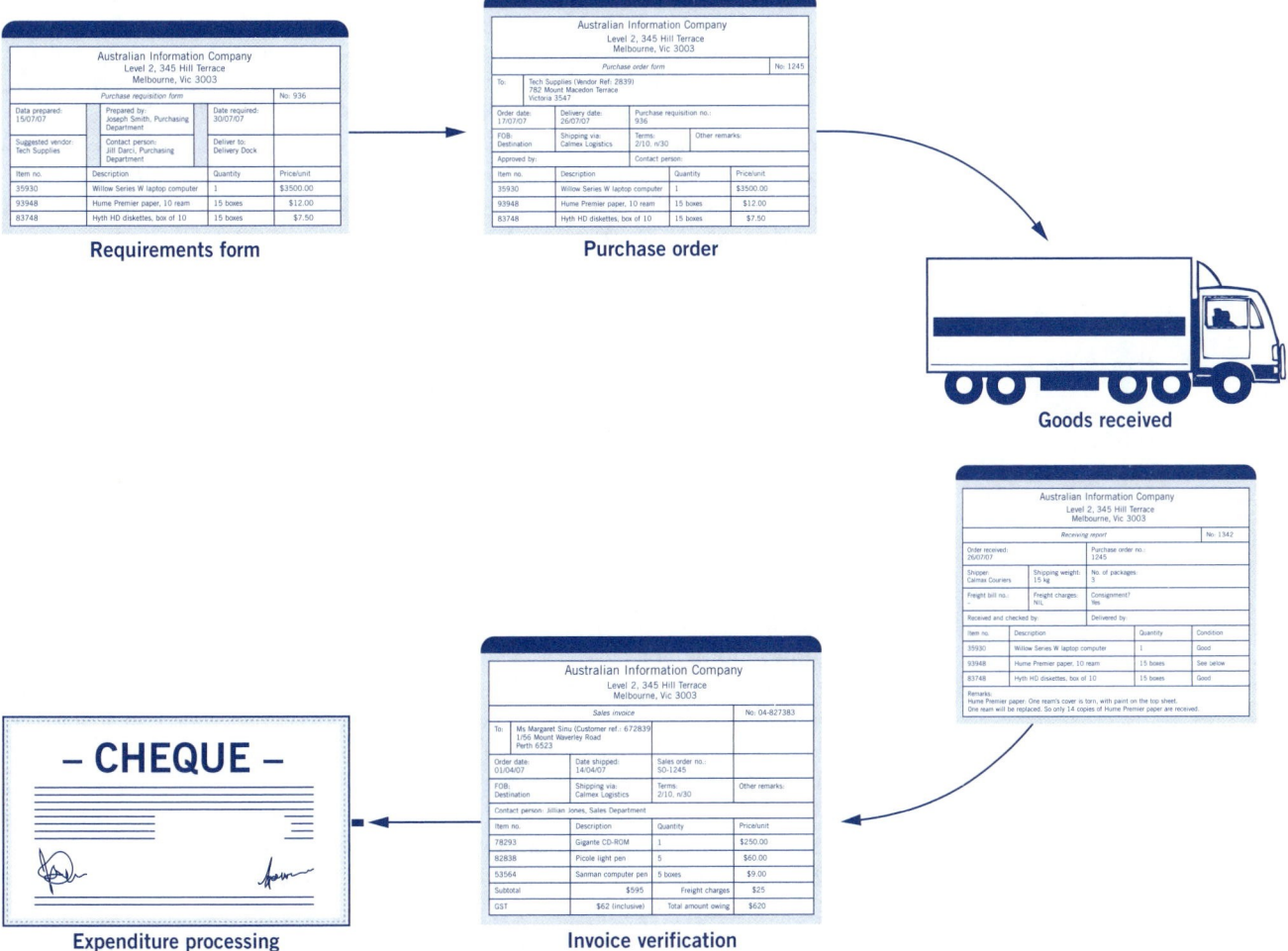

**FIGURE 6.8** Simplified expenditure process

Purchase order processing involves preparing and recording the purchase orders and accounts payable. The ERP system can assist the business in identifying appropriate suppliers for a required purchase based on product specification, budgets and quantities. Once the product is received, the system can compare the purchase order with the product receipt and invoice for any discrepancies. System notifications are sent to the relevant person if the documentation does not match. If all goes well, the system records the data in inventory, records the cash disbursement and updates the accounts payable.

## Operations facilitation

**Business event data** Data that contain financial or non-financial reference information that records and tracks the status of business activities prior to completion.

**Master data** Data that contain completed transactional information, such as a sales transaction. The sales, accounts receivables and customer tables are updated to reflect the sales transaction.

There are two types of data in ERP systems that reside in one location in a centralised database: **business event data** and **master data**. Business event data normally contains reference information about an activity, such as whether a customer order has been shipped. Therefore, business event data records and tracks the status of activities prior to their completion. As a result, business event data references a number of tables that store both non-financial and financial information. Once again, staff from departments other than sales and marketing can view the real-time status of the sale. Master data normally contains completed transactional information, such as a sales transaction. The sales, accounts receivables and customer tables are updated to reflect the sales transaction. At any time, staff from departments other than sales and marketing can view whether the operation has been completed.

Business event data and master data enable organisations to implement general and application controls that contribute to the effectiveness, efficiency and security of the business. For example, in the revenue process in figure 6.7, the existence of a customer record that records the customer's credit limit provides basic authorisation for a sales event to proceed if it is within the dollar limit approved for that customer. Similarly, in the expenditure process in figure 6.8, there may be dollar limits placed on the totals of purchase orders to mitigate the risk of spending large dollar amounts without authorisation.

In summary and in relation to a revenue process, business event data and master data are data related to the customer and the salesperson (who), the products ordered (what), the delivery location (where), and the date of sale and promised delivery date (when).

## Decision making

Business event data and master data can also be used for management decision making. For example, in the revenue process in figure 6.7, a salesperson might look at sales orders that have not yet been shipped to find out why shipping has not yet occurred, or an inventory manager might look at inventory data to identify the items with low stock balances and the popular sales items. In the expenditure process in figure 6.8, the inventory manager might look at the same inventory data to calculate items that need to be purchased.

Business event data and master data from an ERP system can also be used for more complex decision making. For example, in the revenue process in figure 6.7, the marketing manager might want a list of customers who have not made a purchase in the past three months. To obtain this information, the manager would need combined information from sales and customer tables. In the expenditure process in figure 6.8, a warehouse manager may want to examine the schedule of purchase deliveries to determine staffing and warehouse requirements. This information comes from combining information from purchases and supplier tables.

There are countless other decision-making questions that managers and employees in a business may ask. With its centralised database of business event data and master data the ERP system can be queried to extract information that can assist managers and employees in business process management and decision making.

## AIS FOCUS 6.2

### Business process management

Business process management (BPM) involves modelling, automating, managing and optimising business processes in an organisation to achieve the maximum return from customer satisfaction at minimum cost.

The most important element of BPM is the modelling and documentation of business processes. Modelling and documentation allows the organisation to identify areas and gaps in processes that can be improved. The tools of BPM use a process engine that can model and document manual and automated tasks. Using the process engine, tools can call on ERP systems for information in relation to a process. Flexible interfaces allow users to develop their query and analysis. It keeps an audit trail of all process modelling and documentation. It also keeps a record of improvements and optimisations that are made.

BPM vendors include PegaSystems, Lombardi and TIBCO.

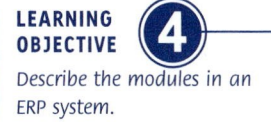

**LEARNING OBJECTIVE 4**

*Describe the modules in an ERP system.*

## ERP SYSTEM MODULES

The typical modules in ERP systems are sales and distribution (revenue process), materials management (expenditure and production processes), financial accounting (general ledger and financial reporting process), controlling and profitability analysis (decision making) and human resources (human resources management and payroll process). As you can see, the modules provide the necessary support for the five key business processes and functions in any business. Most ERP systems contain similar modules and have similar functionality. The modules and functionality mimic the key business processes that occur in reality in organisations. The key business processes are discussed in chapters 9 to 13. The modules are briefly explained below.

### Sales and distribution

The sales and distribution module contains functions related to the revenue or sales order to cash process. It provides the ability to capture and record customer orders, check the customer's ability to pay, execute customer orders, ship products to customers and bill customers. It also contains a process that records each step during picking and packing so that the system can provide the latest status on a customer's order. The module is linked to the materials management module to check product availability, and the financial accounting module to post the sales transactions to the general ledger.

### Materials management

The materials management module contains functions related to the payment or purchase to pay process, including the management of products while they are in stock. The module contains the processes for purchase requisitions and purchase orders. It connects with the financial accounting module when purchases are made from suppliers, and the sales and distribution module when customer orders are processed. When products arrive from suppliers, it compares what is received with what was ordered, then adjusts the records of stock on hand. The master data for accounts payable and cash disbursements are updated when all the source documents (purchase order, product receipt and invoice) are verified.

### Financial accounting

The financial accounting module is connected to all of the other ERP system modules and processes the monetary transactions in the ERP system. The financial accounting module has an accounts receivable function, accounts payable function and an inventory management function. This module is designed to capture the financial transactions in the business to produce the statement of financial position, income statement and statement of cash flows for statutory reporting. Performance reports for internal decision making are generated in the controlling and profitability analysis module.

### Controlling and profitability analysis

The controlling and profitability analysis module handles the analysis of sales, costs and budgets that are used in internal performance reporting. These are the three areas that managers most often ask questions and need to make decisions about to improve the performance of the business. This module can also handle cost accounting and activity-based accounting as well as a host of other accounting functions.

### Human resources

The human resources module contains functions that relate to the recruitment, management and administration of personnel; payroll processing; and personnel training and travel. It captures employee details, changes in those details and the distribution of pay to those employees. When employees undertake training or travel for work purposes, it also captures this information.

## Outwardly organised ERP system modules

ERP systems support key internal business processes and financial transactions with suppliers and customers. These systems are also increasingly reaching out toward the non-financial activities associated with suppliers and customers. For example, while an ERP system can record a purchase of raw materials from suppliers, outwardly organised modules can also suggest ways of improving the sourcing of raw materials. While an ERP system can record the sale of a product to a customer, outwardly organised modules can also suggest ways of improving the revenue process or the customer's buying experience. There are two modules that extend the internal capabilities of ERP systems to suppliers and customers by offering mechanisms to improve supply chain management and customer relationship management respectively. These are **supply chain management (SCM)** and **customer relationship management (CRM)** modules.

### Supply chain management

Supply chain management (SCM), is defined by Koch[4] as:

> The combination of art and science that goes into improving the way your company finds the raw components it needs to make a product or service, manufactures that product or service and delivers it to customer.

**Supply chain management (SCM)** *Systems that monitor and assist the management of supplier interactions with the organisation.*

**Customer relationship management (CRM)** *Systems that monitor and help the management of customer interactions with the organisation.*

In general, it covers applications designed for use in purchasing departments by staff for finding the best supply lines and timing the supply lines for direct and indirect materials at minimum cost. The SCM module is applied in two ways:

- advanced planning and scheduling
- e-procurement (electronic procurement).

Advanced planning and scheduling systems capture the process of balancing materials and plant resources to best meet customer demand while taking into account business profitability goals. They do this by precisely sequencing all materials and plant resources at an operational level, so that, daily, weekly or monthly, customer demands are met without a build up of stock. At the heart of these systems are complex mathematical models of supply, production and distribution, which, coupled with optimisation algorithms, produce planning and scheduling solutions for any given customer demand. This module is normally used for direct materials purchasing. Direct materials purchasing refers to the acquisition of raw materials, parts and assemblies necessary to manufacture finished goods. Figure 6.9 is an example of an advanced planning and scheduling problem. The system calculates the production combination that maximises profit with cost, capacity and time constraints.

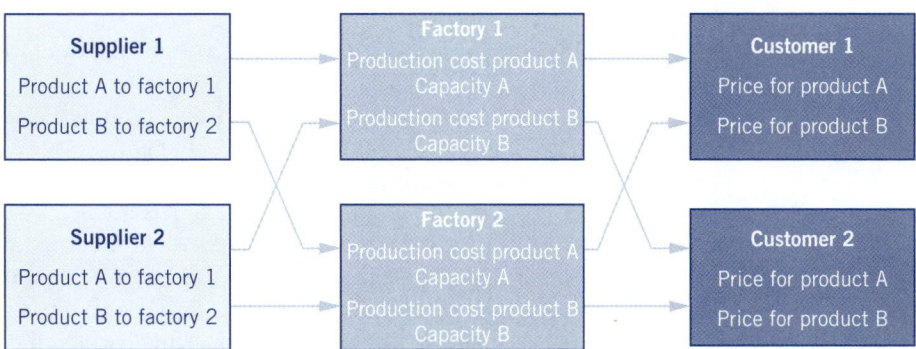

**FIGURE 6.9** An advanced planning and scheduling system problem

Not only can the advanced planning and scheduling system conduct manufacturing planning and scheduling, it can also perform a number of other related functions including:

- distribution planning and scheduling
- fleet management and scheduling
- inventory management and scheduling
- sales and operations planning.

In a similar way to raw materials planning and scheduling, distribution planning and scheduling looks at ways to improve how raw materials are delivered to a business. The algorithms can also help time fleet requirements for manufacturing and sales staff and inventory requirements for sales staff to sell to customers. These algorithms require inputs to perform their calculations. These inputs include:

- capacity
- location
- costs
- revenues.

Capacity inputs state the most the resources of the business can produce. They include maximum outputs of business resources such as factories, equipment, warehouses and employees. Such inputs collectively determine the production capacity of the business.

Location inputs are also important. Linking locations of suppliers with one another as well as that of the business and customer provides the ERP system with the ability to make calculations about production and delivery times from the start until the end of the value chain. The optimisation functions in the advanced planning and scheduling function also require costs and revenues as inputs into the calculations. The function can then translate production materials, lead times and delivery times into costs. The cost inputs can include setups, transportation, carrying, stock-outs and overtime. Revenue inputs include product prices, product mixes and any special promotion pricing that is used by the business.

E-procurement is normally associated with indirect purchasing or procurement. Indirect purchasing involves the selection, purchase and management of a wide range of non-production goods and services from basic office supplies to complex business services such as printing, advertising and temporary labour. There are various ways to procure these indirect materials, but the most common is through the internet on a supplier's website. Businesses often enter into contracts with their indirect materials suppliers, such as office stationery suppliers, to gain access to the supplier's web-based purchasing system, enabling the business to purchase indirect materials for their organisation online.

The main aim of e-procurement systems is to automate communication, transactions and collaboration with indirect supply chain partners. At the same time, such systems can also:

- reduce prices paid through volume discounts and contract terms agreed to between the business and the supplier
- improve contract compliance with numerous indirect suppliers (i.e. the system will allow only certain purchases to be made)
- shorten procurement and fulfilment cycles as a result of direct systems connectivity with the supplier. Purchase orders go directly into the supplier's system and can be processed, picked and shipped without an employee having to re-enter the order. Reductions in duplication and errors shorten the overall cycle
- reduce administration costs through automation
- improve inventory management because the purchasing organisation can order only as required.

## Customer relationship management

Customer relationship management (CRM) is an IT term for the methodologies, strategies, software and other web-based capabilities that help an enterprise organise and manage customer relationships. It is a business-wide strategy designed to reduce costs and increase profitability by solidifying customer loyalty by bringing together information from all data sources within and outside the business to give a holistic view of each customer in real time.

The main aim of the CRM module in the ERP system is to allow customer-facing employees in sales, support and marketing to make quick, informed decisions on cross-selling and up-selling opportunities to target marketing strategies. The CRM module was developed because businesses wanted to gather and have access to information about their customers' buying histories, preferences, complaints and other data so that they could better meet what customers wanted. Businesses found that the costs of attracting new customers were very high (e.g. mailing, calling and visiting), while the costs of retention were much lower. The cost to retain customers was usually associated with their demands being met.

The first wave of CRM emerged in the mid-1990s. It consisted of a single-function client-server CRM solution designed for technical support, sales force, call centres and marketing departments. The second wave of CRM came from the need for a single view of the customer in terms of all contact points the customer had with the business. Integrated full-range client-server CRM solutions gave the full-customer (360-degree) view. This was followed by a raft of CRM solutions providers in the market, although as time went on, these providers started acquiring each other and CRM solutions became more and more integrated. Subsequently, a third wave of CRM arrived in the late 1990s that saw the internet and related architecture creating the need to capture customer interactions online. This gave birth to electronic CRM or e-CRM. We are currently in the fourth wave of CRM. CRM providers are being acquired by ERP systems providers, and the CRM module is being integrated within ERP systems.

There are various functions of the CRM module. Their basis is sales functionality. This facility manages all customer contact and gives sales employees the ability to see customer history. The marketing functionality facilitates the initiation and management of promotions and campaigns. Businesses that use these systems can see which customers have been offered which particular promotions. Management of loyalty programs often uses this functionality.

The emergence of customer contact centres or call centres also sparked the growth in CRM. Call centres were developed to provide a variety of functions including help desk and online support. As these centres collected customer information, they became an avenue for sales and marketing as well. Call centres tracked the issues relating to each customer from initiation to completion and, as more calls were recorded, they could provide a story about the main concerns and wants of a customer. However, as internet use began to grow, CRM entered the e-CRM domain.

E-CRM is concerned with internet interaction management. It gives the organisation the ability to track the products that are purchased and to understand which website content and designs most appeal to the customer. The end result is the ability to provide customised web pages for customers that are conducive to encouraging browsing, purchasing and retention.

CRM modules also have business intelligence functionality. This feature allows the business to use analytical tools on the collected information about customer purchasing patterns to help predict future buying behaviour. Most CRM modules offer a comprehensive toolkit to allow **data analysis** and forecasting to be performed.

CRM modules also provide mobile business functionality. As the term suggests, this function permits sales, support and service personnel from the business to access critical customer and company information while out of the office. Some advanced versions allow field staff not only to send and retrieve data but also to interact with colleagues and customers without having to be in the office.

*__Data analysis__ The act of determining the type of data and the relationships that exist between the data of an organisation.*

## AIS FOCUS 6.3

### Enterprise application integration

While ERP systems combine the key internal and external business processes into one system, there may be occasions that a business may want functionality that is not part of an ERP suite. The business may also prefer to have another software application because it may not be included in the ERP system suite, or because it works better for the business than the equivalent module provided by the ERP system. For example, a

*continued*

business may want an online booking system such as ebookaplace.com that is not part of their ERP system. Enterprise application integration (EAI) allows the business to combine an outside software application with their ERP system.

EAI is a methodology that combines processes, software, standards and hardware to link together two or more systems and allow them to operate as one. EAI systems are characterised by data standards (e.g. **electronic data interchange (EDI), eXtensible Markup Language (XML)**) and platforms (e.g. NT, UNIX). Companies that offer EAI services and products include IBM, Microsoft, and Vitria Technology.

# ERP SYSTEM CONSIDERATIONS

Now that we have discussed ERP systems in detail, we turn to a number of important considerations associated with purchasing and implementing ERP systems. We outline the benefits that ERP systems should provide for an organisation if the correct ERP system is purchased and implementation is successful.

## Single-source and best-of-breed options

ERP systems within organisations can be either single-source or best-of-breed. A **single-source ERP system** is one where all the systems or modules contained within the system are provided by a single software vendor. For example, suppose the following systems or modules were required by a business: sales and distribution, materials management, production planning, quality management, plant maintenance, human resources, financial accounting, asset management, and a project system. One vendor, such as SAP, would provide a single-source ERP system with these components.

A **best-of-breed ERP system** allows the organisation to choose multiple ERP vendors with the best functionality to provide each of the individual components. The best functionality usually means that the organisation would choose the component from the ERP systems vendor that best suits its business processes. For example, an organisation may have financial accounting and human resources modules from Oracle, but a manufacturing module from QAD or SAP.

The decision to go with a single-source or best-of-breed system relies on a number of critical considerations. In general, a single-source or integrated ERP package allows for decreased integration costs and relatively easy implementation. If processes in one area of the organisation change, the required change in integration among modules and components is set and further changes to information flow would not be needed because the system is already working together.

Best-of-breed systems allow the organisation to pick components that work best. It is argued that this maximises the productivity and output of the organisation, but this must be balanced against the cost of integrating the best-of-breed components.

A comparison of single-source and best-of-breed solutions can be considered in terms of:
- functionality
- supply and support
- look and feel
- users and training
- code tables.

## Functionality

Functionality refers to the features, operations and capabilities that the software provides. Single-source or integrated solutions usually fit best in organisations that span a broad range of functions where horizontal structures are required. Best-of-breed solutions are usually sought by organisations that are highly vertically integrated and require special features for their operations and business processes.

## Supply and support

Single-source systems are supplied and supported by a single vendor, which allows easy upgrades, supply and support. As a result of having a single supplier, upgrades are easily synchronised. Support refers to the technical backup provided to the purchaser of the software in the form of personal or telephone assistance. There is only one number to call for every aspect of the single-source ERP system. In contrast, best-of-breed systems require multi-vendor support and upgrades require planning and coordination. Further, upgrades are unsynchronised and organisations normally run different versions of the various ERP systems modules from different vendors.

## Look and feel

Best-of-breed ERP systems will have a different look and feel for each of the modules that are provided by different vendors. However, there have been many instances where a standardised presentation layer is overlaid across the organisation to provide a standard operating environment. Single-source systems have no such issues and have a consistent look and feel throughout the suite.

## Users and training

Single-source system users are usually used and trained in groups for the complete suite of software, while the user groups for a best-of-breed system are segregated by the application systems. Best-of-breed users normally specialise in their own applications with separate training organised for each of the components.

A single-source system will have the tables in the database shared across the suite and organisation. There will only be one location where data are stored. Best-of-breed solutions will have multiple tables in many formats, replicated across applications. Integration allows the multiple tables to be updated automatically.

# ERP implementations

Implementing an ERP system is a major investment, requiring significant amounts of time and money. System costs range between $400 000 and $300 million. On average, systems would cost around $15 million and require anywhere between three months and three years to implement.

Organisations that purchase an ERP system must purchase new networks, servers and computers (hardware) that are capable of running the complex ERP software. The software itself is a database (refer to chapters 3 and 4) that must be installed in the hardware purchased. Often, organisations are unfamiliar with the installation, and consultants are hired, together with staff from the ERP vendor, to install the system. Once installation is completed, the team of consultants (both independent and from the software vendor) must work with the organisation to implement the newly acquired system.

Implementation requires proper planning because of the time required and the disruption that is likely to occur to normal business operations. Before use, the consulting team and the organisation must transfer data from existing or **legacy systems** to the ERP database. The transfer will involve data analysis of existing structures and relationships, with a resulting **conversion process** that will allow easy transfer to the new database. Data are usually cleansed and tested to ensure that the process is successful and no valuable information is lost.

Once the testing and transfer are complete, significant effort and resources are dedicated to training the organisation's employees to use the system. Often, the initiation of the new system is accompanied by opportunities to rework operations and business processes. The most common reason for such rework is that the new system offers means to streamline prior ways of performing tasks and activities. As a result of new operations and business processes, roles and responsibilities within the organisation change. These changes generally cause disruption to normal business.

In short, an organisation should not take the decision to purchase and implement an ERP system lightly. The costs incurred are large and the implications for the organisation significant.

## ERP evaluation criteria

So far, this discussion has suggested that the decision to purchase an ERP system requires careful consideration of single-source versus best-of-breed systems and implementation issues. The decision also depends heavily on the organisation's industry, strategy, culture and operations. By design, ERP packages are likely to require users to follow a way of doing business, and some of the organisation's operations, or segments of its operations, may not be a good match with the software. Because there are significant risks associated with ERP systems, questions relating to an organisation's industry, strategy, culture and operations should be asked before the decision is made, including:

- What are the risks to the organisation's culture and operations?
- What are the implications of spending on an ERP system if the organisation is a low-cost provider?
- If an organisation prides itself on creativity and differentiation in its unique business processes, what is the impact of the rigid and consistent practices in ERP systems?
- If an organisation competes using a differentiating strategy, how does implementing an ERP system that is the same or similar to its competitors affect its competitive advantage?

It has also been suggested that the benefits of an ERP system are arguable and difficult to quantify. There are great potential savings from eliminating redundant effort and duplicated data. Sales are likely to increase as ERP systems help the movement of goods and services, exceeding customer expectations. At the same time, there can be cuts in personnel dealing with administration, suppliers, distributors and customers. However, these benefits are often only realised over time.

There have been many reports indicating that only a low percentage of businesses experience a smooth rollout of their new ERP system with immediate benefits. Others experience an assortment of delays, cost overruns, adoption and performance problems. These problems often owe to the people rather than the system itself. The software will not cure fundamental business problems unless business processes are analysed and problems solved with its help. What is most important is the time taken to plan and implement the system and educate and train employees to use the system with senior management support.

Nevertheless, criteria are required to choose a particular ERP system. The following criteria are suggested for comparing different ERP vendors.

- Functional fit: does an ERP provider provide the features and functions that are suitable to the organisation or does the organisation have to find a best-of-breed solution from a number of providers?
- Tight integration: do the systems and modules integrate in such a way that transactions can be completed with minimal duplication and updating? Does the system pick up the links among all the planned systems and modules?
- Flexibility: does the system give the organisation choice on its entry and calculation methods, such as automated entry, or a variety of depreciation methods?
- Scalability: does the system allow the organisation to grow, expand its product or service range, purchase new assets, and record larger volumes of supplier and customer data?
- User friendliness: is the graphical user interface of the ERP system intuitive, attractive and efficient to work with?
- Implementation time: is the implementation time reasonable and is it incorporated into the calculation of return on investment? Does implementation require many resources either inside or outside the organisation?
- Database technology: is the technology available, easy and cheap to upgrade and integrate, or is it restricted to particular vendors?
- Security: does the system offer adequate security for divisions such as human resources or production development?
- Configuration: if the system does not exactly match the organisation's requirements, can users configure it intuitively and easily without major technical support? Are upgrades affected by the configuration?
- Customisation: is it needed for the system to function in the organisation? Can the ERP vendors customise the software to suit the unique requirements of any part of the business? Are upgrades affected by the customisation?
- Local support: does the system provide it in local languages during business hours and after hours for telephone help? How quick is the response time?
- Reference sites: does the ERP vendor provide online help? How quick is the response time?
- Total cost: how much will it cost (from planning to operation including all resources) to implement the ERP system?

It is clear that if a business was to consider an ERP system, many considerations must be taken into account. Decisions about single-source versus best-of-breed systems, total cost of implementation and ERP system benefits all rely on careful and critical evaluation. In this section, the importance of understanding the data transformation, integration ability and configurability of the ERP systems is also considered. **Data transformation** is the process of converting data in one format to another for the purpose of transformation or integration. **Integration ability** is the ability for the data to be transformed into a form to match a new database destination. **Configurability** is the ability to transform data and define new relationships and structures that are required for an organisation.

**Data transformation** *The process of converting data in one format to another for the purpose of transformation or integration.*

**Integration ability** *The ability for the data to be transformed into a form to match a new database destination.*

**Configurability** *The ability to transform data and define new relationships and structures that are required for an organisation.*

## ERP benefits

If a decision on an ERP system is reached and implementation goes well, the business can gain many benefits. ERP systems allow easier global integration by reducing the barriers of currency, exchange rates, language and culture. ERP systems not only integrate people and data, but also eliminate the requirement to update and repair many separate computer systems. An ERP system allows management to manage operations, not just monitor them. Without an ERP system, getting an answer to a process question of 'How are we doing?' requires obtaining data from each business unit and putting them together for a comprehensive, integrated picture. The ERP system already has all the data, allowing the manager to focus on 'What are we going to do better?' This improves management of the organisation as a whole and makes the business more responsive when change is required.

The benefits of ERP systems can be divided into two groups, **quantifiable benefits** and **intangible benefits**. Quantifiable benefits can be stated in actual dollar amounts, while intangible benefits are felt by an organisation but cannot be so stated.

The quantifiable benefits of implementing ERP systems are normally calculated using the return on investment (ROI) measure.

$$\frac{\text{Net income}}{\text{Sales}} \times \frac{\text{Sales}}{\text{Assets}} = \frac{\text{Net income}}{\text{Assets}} = \text{ROI}$$

The return on investment measure can be specified by two contributing calculations: net income on sales and sales on assets. This suggests that the quantifiable benefits should increase net income by increasing sales and/or decreasing costs. As a result, organisations that implement ERP systems should develop measures to capture increases in sales and reductions in the major costs incurred. The improvements that are claimed by the ERP system implementation should be shown in increases in sales or reductions in the major cost drivers such as labour.

## *Quantifiable benefits*

In this section, the quantifiable benefits are outlined based on comprehensive and recent studies of ERP systems benefits. The AIS focus 'Benefits from ERP systems' discusses this author's own case study of quantifiable benefits of ERP systems. It shows that the elements of a single case study are consistent with the comprehensive results of recent surveys.

According to Hamilton[5] and Shang and Seddon[6], typical quantifiable effects include:
- reductions in inventory, materials, labour and overhead costs
- improvements in customer service and sales.

ERP systems improve planning and scheduling practices, enabling inventory reductions and consequent ongoing savings in carrying costs. Better planning, scheduling and manufacturing practices also minimise rush jobs and parts shortages, so less time and money should be lost to expediting jobs (including paying overtime), material handling, extra setups, disruptions, labour costs associated with reworking and tracking split lots or jobs that have been set aside. Production supervisors have greater awareness of required work and can adjust capacity or loads to meet schedules. Supervisors have more time for managing, directing and training people rather than gathering information. Production personnel have more time to develop better methods to improve quality and throughput. Improved purchasing and ordering practices lead to better supplier negotiations for raw material prices.

Better customer service and increased sales can be achieved through improved coordination of sales and production. Better management of customer contacts comes in the form of making and meeting delivery promises, and in shorter order-to-ship lead times, leading to higher customer satisfaction and repeat orders. In custom product environments, configurations are quickly identified and priced, often by sales personnel or even the customer rather than by production or technical staff.

**Quantifiable benefits** *Benefits that can be stated in actual dollar amounts.*

**Intangible benefits** *Benefits that are felt by an organisation but cannot be stated in actual dollar amounts.*

Gains are also made in accounting. Creating invoices quickly and accurately directly from the shipment transaction means that customers can receive their statements in good time, improving the organisation's collection procedures.

## AIS FOCUS 6.4

### Benefits from ERP systems

XYZ Brewery Ltd had recognised limitations to its legacy systems, which:
- were largely transaction processing systems
- supported mainly manual processes like accounts payable
- contained information that was sometimes of poor quality
- did not contain information required for operating the business effectively
- ran on disparate systems that were difficult to maintain and unsupported by vendors.

There were several tangible benefits realised from the implementation of an ERP system. Firstly, there were reductions in cost through reducing overall staff after realigning jobs. This was achieved through the optimisation of warehouse space and picking operations (advanced warehousing) and advanced transport planning. At the same time, there were small increases in the number of staff and analysts that were required to provide and exploit the information available in the ERP system. For example, additional staff were required to set up item descriptions on the ERP system.

Secondly, controls in business processes were enhanced by the implementation. Procurement was now centralised and spending limits and approvals could be controlled effectively. Pricing decisions could now be controlled at the point of sale and dispatch of goods could be held if the customer has invoices outstanding, by linking accounts payable with creditor information into the dispatch area. The data visibility across the business provided quantifiable business benefits compared with previous processes.

Thirdly, the ERP system supported electronic information exchange about stock allocations, orders and order status between different geographic regions and to and from suppliers and customers. The quantifiable benefits were in reduced data re-entry, data errors and rework.

Finally, the new ERP system integrated information from many of the company's business functions, from production to sales and marketing, and provided significant intangible benefits. These were felt by employees and management but could not be quantified. Firstly, there were process improvements across the company, such as in payments and receivables, which used the centralised general ledger in the ERP system. Secondly, the ability to aggregate and present high-quality, integrated information provided a significant contribution to management knowledge about business operations and supported sound decision making in general. Thirdly, the users found the interface convenient and generally user friendly.

### Intangible benefits

Hamilton[7] and Shang and Seddon[8] also showed that ERP system users claim significant intangible effects in the areas of accounting, product and process design, production, sales and management information systems functions. For example, users suggest that the ERP system provides a framework for working effectively together and devising a consistent plan for action, which cannot be quantified.

With a common database, accounting no longer requires duplicate files and redundant data entry. Customer invoices can be based on actual shipment. As manufacturing transactions are recorded, the financial equivalents can be automatically generated for updating the ledger complete with an audit trail. Detailed transaction activity can be easily accessed online by anyone in the organisation for answering account enquiries. Because manufacturing transactions automatically update the general ledger, time-consuming manual journal entries are eliminated. While these benefits can be argued to result ultimately in cost reductions in lower labour costs, what are the drivers and contribution of faster access, processing, correct customer invoices, real-time information, information access or happier staff to those lower labour costs?

The product structure database in ERP systems offers engineering much greater control over products and process design. Planned changes can be phased in and emergency changes can be communicated immediately. Analytical tools can diagnose the impact of changes in materials and resources, and focus attention on the key components affecting cumulative lead time. However, how do improvements in lead time contribute to sales increases or cost reductions? Many organisations know that they do but cannot provide the quantifiable link.

The ERP system also helps establish realistic schedules for production and communicates consistent priorities, so that staff in the organisation know the most important jobs to work on at all times. Visibility of future requirements helps production to prepare for capacity problems and suppliers to anticipate and meet needs. It eliminates many crisis situations, so that people have more time for planning and quality management. Again, visibility of future requirements can ensure that the right products can always be delivered to the customer so that stock-outs or stock obsolescence are avoided, but how much does this contribute to sales growth or cost reductions?

The ERP system offers advantages to the **management information systems** function. Information can be provided for decision making in product and service development, manufacture and operations, financial reporting, and performance evaluation and control. The connections with sales and cost reductions are, again, hard to quantify.

## Benefits from outwardly organised ERP system modules

The advanced planning and scheduling ERP system module has significant quantifiable benefits. Users have claimed improvements in overall productivity. This comes from improved delivery of raw materials, capacity use and forecast accuracy by linking the production process with the sales and marketing process. It has also come from lower supply chain costs, as inventory can be lower with improved planning and scheduling. Fulfilment cycle time is reduced as a result of knowing what customers demand in advance and pre-ordering raw materials to produce those items that will be needed.

The benefits of CRM are wide and varied. Most businesses that invest in these modules are able to respond faster to customer enquiries. They notice increased efficiency through the automation of the sales and service process. Most importantly, the information provides a deeper understanding of their customers and which are their most profitable customers, and this provides increased marketing and selling opportunities. These systems also enable the businesses to record and analyse customer feedback, leading to new and improved products and services. The indirect outcome of all these benefits is, of course, increased customer retention.

---

*Management information system*
*A system that provides information for decision making. Within the system are structures, relationships, databases and procedures.*

**LEARNING OBJECTIVE 1**

*What are the characteristics of the different categories of enterprise information systems? What are the advantages and disadvantages of each in relation to accounting and managerial decision making?*

Single-entry systems are for individual users or very small businesses with up to a handful of employees where the owner is the key participant. These systems record transactions and obligations in conjunction with manual business processes. Inwardly organised systems include bookkeeping systems, hybrid systems and ERP systems. Bookkeeping systems are basic systems that are organised by accrual accounting concepts. They summarise data to fit the categorisation of general ledgers and charts of accounts based on the classic double-entry accounting equation. Hybrid systems extend the bookkeeping systems using independent software to integrate operations and financial functions within small to medium-sized organisations. ERP systems are designed to capture a wide range of transactions and information about all key business activities including finance, human resources, sales and marketing and manufacturing in large complex organisations.

Based on the key differences between the software categories, organisations, small and large, can use the software framework to select appropriate systems for their needs. Needs are usually determined by business size, complexity and information requirements.

**LEARNING OBJECTIVE 2**

*Why would organisations be motivated to implement or upgrade enterprise resource planning (ERP) systems?*

The idea of an ERP system began on the factory floor as early as the 1960s. During this time, simple systems were developed as a means for factory and plant managers to plan raw material purchasing and production based on sales forecast information from sales and marketing managers. Inventory and MRP software provided some link between manufacturing and the finance and management areas of the business. The stimulus for ERP systems was brought by the harder economic times in the late 1980s and 1990s. To stay competitive and profitable, companies had to provide customers with products and services faster and cheaper than their competition could. Businesses believed that the key was to have an integrated information system that would efficiently and seamlessly coordinate their sales and marketing, operations and financial functions. Without ERP systems, non-integrated systems resulted in duplication of effort and poor information timeliness. This led to poor decision making, higher costs and customer dissatisfaction.

The enterprise systems value chain shows how a business purchases raw materials, receives raw materials, produces and delivers its product, markets and sells the product, then installs the product and provides service to customers. The sales and marketing, manufacturing, accounting and finance, and human resources functions/divisions support this value chain process. ERP systems can assist in the value chain process by reducing the cost or improving the quality of performance of the value chain activities performed in the process.

**LEARNING OBJECTIVE 3**

*What key organisational processes do ERP systems support?*

Most businesses have five key business processes that ERP systems need to support:
1. revenue, sales or order to cash
2. payment, purchases or purchase to pay
3. production, manufacturing or conversion
4. human resources and payroll
5. general ledger and financial reporting.

The activities, transactions and decision making involved in each of these key business processes are discussed in detail in chapters 9 to 13 of this book. ERP systems support those key business processes through data capture, coordinating and facilitating operations, and decision making.

LEARNING OBJECTIVE 4

### What are the key modules in an ERP system?

The typical modules in an ERP system include sales and distribution, materials management, financial accounting, human resources and controlling and profitability analysis. Most ERP systems have similar modules and similar functionality. The modules and functionality support the five key business processes that are typically a part of every business. The sales and distribution module provides the ability to capture and record customer orders, check the customer's ability to pay, execute customer orders, ship products to customers and bill customers. The materials management module contains functions related to the payment or purchase to pay process. The financial accounting module processes all the transactions in the business. The human resources module contains functions that relate to the recruitment, management and administration of personnel, payroll processing, and personnel training and travel. The controlling and profitability analysis module handles analysis of sales, costs and budgets. These areas are analysed because they are most often the areas where managers ask questions about the performance of the business in order to make decisions to improve performance.

Outwardly organised systems support business processes and non-financial activities outside the organisation. These systems extend the capability of ERP systems and include SCM and CRM software for financial and non-financial information exchange between organisations. The SCM module covers applications designed for use in purchasing departments by staff for finding the best suppliers and timing the supplies for sourcing direct and indirect materials at minimum cost. The CRM module allows customer-facing employees in sales, support and marketing to make quick, informed decisions on cross-selling and up-selling opportunities to target marketing strategies.

LEARNING OBJECTIVE 5

### What are the considerations for evaluating, purchasing and implementing an ERP system?

ERP systems can be either single source or best of breed. They differ in terms of:
- functionality
- supply and support
- look and feel
- users and training
- code tables.

Organisations that purchase an ERP system must purchase new networks, servers and computers (hardware) that are capable of running the complex ERP software. Implementation requires proper planning because of the time required and the disruption that is likely to occur to normal business operations. The consulting team and the organisation must transfer existing data from existing or legacy systems to the ERP database and this involves data analysis of existing structures and relationships, with a resulting conversion process that will allow easy transfer with the new database. Once the testing and transfer are complete, significant effort and resources are dedicated to training the organisation's employees to use the system. Often, the initiation of the new system is accompanied by opportunities to rework operations and business processes.

Because there are significant risks associated with ERP systems, questions relating to an organisation's industry, strategy, culture and operations should be asked before the decision to implement is made.

The following criteria are suggested for comparing different ERP vendors: functional fit, tight integration, flexibility, scalability, user friendliness, implementation time, database technology, security, configuration, customisation, local support, reference sites and total cost.

## KEY TERMS

best-of-breed ERP systems, p. 272
bookkeeping systems, p. 253
business event data, p. 266
business processes, p. 250
business requirements, p. 256
client–server hardware architecture, p. 260
computer platforms, p. 260
configurability, p. 275
conversion process, p. 274
cross-functional business processes, p. 259
customer relationship management (CRM), p. 268
data analysis, p. 271
data capture, p. 263
data transformation, p. 275
database, p. 252
database management system (DBMS), p. 252
electronic data interchange (EDI), p. 272
enterprise value chain, p. 254

ERP systems, p. 254
eXtensible Markup Language (XML), p. 272
hybrid systems, p. 253
intangible benefits, p. 276
integration ability, p. 275
inwardly organised systems, p. 251
legacy systems, p. 274
management information system, p. 278
master data, p. 266
networks, p. 259
obligations, p. 251
outwardly organised systems, p. 251
quantifiable benefits, p. 276
single-entry systems, p. 252
single-source ERP system, p. 272
software applications, p. 250
software selection, p. 256
streamlining, p. 253
supply chain management (SCM), p. 268
systems requirements, p. 256
transactions, p. 251
vendor selection, p. 257

## DISCUSSION QUESTIONS

6.1 Explain why a software framework is required from the perspective of an organisation and a software vendor. (LO1)

6.2 What are the different enterprise information systems categories? Provide a brief description and explain the key differences. (LO1)

6.3 Outline the main disadvantages associated with single-entry systems and how they are overcome in the bookkeeping categorisation. (LO1)

6.4 'Hybrid systems don't quite match the seamless integration and power of enterprise resource planning (ERP) systems.' Explain the key differences between the two categories and suggest, with reasons, which system an organisation may purchase. (LO1)

6.5 Describe how you would use the software framework for software selection. (LO1)

6.6 What typical functions of an organisation and the value chain does an ERP system link? (LO1)

6.7 What key business processes does an ERP system support? (LO3)

6.8 Explain how an ERP system supports key business processes? (LO3)

6.9 Describe the typical modules in ERP systems. (LO4)

6.10 Explain how an ERP system integrates the activities within an organisation. (LO2, LO3)

6.11 What factors would organisations consider in making a choice between single-source and best-of-breed ERP systems? (LO5)

6.12 Briefly explain the benefits of an ERP system. (LO2, LO5)

6.13 A low proportion of businesses experience smooth rollout with a new ERP system. Suggest what businesses can learn and do to minimise the problems faced and to achieve immediate benefits? (LO5)

6.14 How does a supply chain management (SCM) system help improve manufacturing and product delivery to customers? (LO4, LO5)

6.15 Explain how the functionalities in customer relationship management (CRM) systems allow customer-facing employees in sales and marketing to develop competitive positioning strategies. (LO4, LO5)

## SELF-TEST ACTIVITIES

6.1 Organisations that are purchasing software can use the software framework to:
   (a) focus on the categories relevant to their business.
   (b) identify the main differences among the systems currently available.
   (c) choose the appropriate software category for their business.
   (d) all of the above.

6.2 Small service organisations should consider:
   (a) bookkeeping systems.
   (b) hybrid systems.
   (c) enterprise value chain systems.
   (d) none of the above.

6.3 The four major functions that are linked by an ERP system are:
   (a) sales or marketing, manufacturing, accounting or finance, and human resources.
   (b) sales or marketing, manufacturing, customer and accounting or finance.
   (c) customer, sales or marketing, accounting or finance, and human resources.
   (d) customer, sales or marketing, production, accounting or finance.

6.4 ERP systems form a basis to develop outwardly organised systems to link organisations together. Other modules could include:
   (a) SCM systems.
   (b) CRM systems.
   (c) e-procurement systems.
   (d) all of the above.

6.5 Which of the following statements is true?
   (a) Developing business requirements follows systems requirements.
   (b) A system is required for every business requirement.
   (c) Determining business processes should be the first step in software selection.
   (d) Software selection should be undertaken after the vendor has been selected.

6.6 The cost of implementing an ERP system in an organisation includes:
   (a) software.
   (b) training.
   (c) process rework.
   (d) all of the above.

6.7 ERP systems should be evaluated on:
   (a) price.
   (b) the risks to the organisation, culture and operation.
   (c) benefits.
   (d) all of the above.

6.8 Which inputs are required by an SCM system?
   (a) Resource capacities and customer histories
   (b) Resource capacities and warehouse locations
   (c) Operational costs and business intelligence information
   (d) None of the above

6.9 Goals of ERP systems include all of the following except:
   (a) improved customer service.
   (b) improvements of legacy systems.
   (c) increased production.
   (d) reduced production time.

6.10 Which statement about ERP implementations is the least accurate?
   (a) For the ERP to be successful, process re-engineering must occur.
   (b) ERP fails because some important business process is not supported.
   (c) When a business is diversified, little is gained from ERP implementation.
   (d) The phased-in approach is most suited to diversified businesses.

6.11 The four Ws of capturing data do not include:
   (a) who.
   (b) what.
   (c) why.
   (d) when.

6.12 Which statement is true?
   (a) ERP system costs include hardware, software and implementation.
   (b) ERP systems are scalable.
   (c) Performance problems are usually technical rather than process related.
   (d) The better ERP systems can handle any problems a business can have.

6.13 Which of the following is not an advantage of single-source ERP systems?
   (a) Features and functionality for highly specialised operations and business processes.
   (b) Decreased integration costs.
   (c) Relatively easy implementation.
   (d) A consistent look and feel interface across the modules.

6.14 Which of the following is a quantifiable benefit of ERP systems?
   (a) Sales growth from access to real-time information.
   (b) Cost reductions from more productive and happier organisation staff.
   (c) Reductions in inventory, materials, labour and overhead costs.
   (d) Improved decision making from real-time information.

6.15 Which of the following statements about the software framework is false?
   (a) The framework does not imply that any category is superior to another.
   (b) Moving to the right along the framework does not imply new or older innovations.
   (c) The divisions among categories are not absolute and applications can be in more than one category.
   (d) Using the framework will lead to the correct software selection decision.

## PROBLEMS

6.1 Fine Food Restaurant is an organisation that provides lunch and dinner for its customers. The restaurant seats up to 85 customers, employs four chefs, eight waiters and four cleaners. The restaurant owners are thinking about expanding their business by opening a similar restaurant on the other side of town. Suggest the category of enterprise information system software that best suits their requirements. You should state any assumptions, follow the software selection process and provide the necessary explanations to back up your recommendation.

6.2 'As far as possible, organisations should purchase systems that are as far towards the right of the framework as possible. It means that the software purchased will be the best and newest available for their business.' Do you agree? Provide reasons.

6.3 Top Quality Fence Manufacturers manufacture iron, steel and wooden materials that are used in fencing. Their operations produce small items from nails to large poles and pickets used in fences. At the present, they are in the market for an ERP system.

(a) Confirm with the management of Top Quality Fence Manufacturers that they require an ERP system. Use the software selection process to support your confirmation.

(b) What evaluation criteria should be used by the company to compare the offerings from different ERP vendors? Provide explanations.

6.4 Sporty Car Maker runs a legacy file system. It has heard of ERP systems and their benefits. Some of these benefits revolve around ERP systems' using databases that are managed by DBMS. As a consultant to Sporty Car Maker, you are asked to address the following:

(a) Explain how the DBMS in an ERP system functions.

(b) How does the database structure in the ERP system overcome the major limitations of the legacy file system?

6.5 Network Books runs eight bookstores around Australia. It sells books from fiction to nonfiction, to academic and technical titles. Network Books has decided on an ERP system but to operate efficiently and effectively it requires a client–server system. Explain the importance of this for ERP systems. How does the system architecture extract the best from an ERP system?

6.6 Fabulous Furniture is a large manufacturing company with an ERP system that sells a variety of furniture to many customers. Its customers often purchase separate pieces of furniture over several visits. The company is having difficulty in recalling which customers have purchased which styles of furniture on their previous visits. What systems might Fabulous Furniture consider to resolve this issue? Explain how your recommendation will overcome the company's customer purchasing problem.

6.7 Imagine that you are conducting a case study research project for your accounting information systems class in a small business that is local. Assume that the business is a local but large fitness centre. During the project you get to meet the owner. You tell the owner that you are using Sage Accpac ERP in your class. The owner asks if they should be using Sage Accpac ERP or some other ERP system in the business. What would be your response? What questions would you ask or what information would you need to answer that question?

6.8 Choose a familiar website, such as Amazon, ebookaplace.com or dvdorchard.com. Describe the sales or order to cash process from the customer's perspective as illustrated by that website.

## FURTHER READINGS

Burns, M 2009, *How to select and implement an ERP system*, ERP white paper, www.180systems.com.

Grabot, B, Mayere, A & Bazet, T (eds) 2008, *ERP systems and organisational change: a socio-technical insight*, Springer Series in Advanced Manufacturing, Springer-Verlag, London Limited.

Gunasekaran, A 2008, *Techniques and tools for the design and implementation of enterprise information systems*, IGI Publishing, Hershey, PA.

Gupta, JND, Sharma, SK & Rashid, MA (eds) 2008, *Handbook of research on enterprise systems*, IGO Global Publishing, PA.

## SELF-TEST ANSWERS

6.1 d, 6.2 a, 6.3 a, 6.4 d, 6.5 c, 6.6 d, 6.7 d, 6.8 b, 6.9 b, 6.10 c, 6.11 c, 6.12 a, 6.13 a, 6.14 c, 6.15 d

## END NOTES

1. Smith David, J, McCarthy, WE & Sommer, BS 2003, 'Agility: the key to survival of the fittest in the software market', *Communications of the ACM*, vol. 46, no. 5, pp. 65–9.
2. Smith David, J 2009, *Personal communication*, Arizona State University.
3. Porter, ME 1985, *Competition advantage: creating and sustaining superior performance*, Free Press, New York.
4. Koch, C 2002, *The ABCs of supply chain management*, CIO Supply Chain Resource Center.
5. Hamilton, S 2003, *Maximizing your ERP system — a practical guide for managers*, McGraw-Hill, New York.
6. Shang, S & Seddon, PB 2003, *Realising benefits from enterprise systems*, Working Paper, University of Melbourne.
7. Hamilton 2003.
8. Shang & Seddon 2003.

# Internal controls I

## Learning objectives

After studying this chapter, you should be able to:

1. describe the concept and discuss the evolution of corporate governance

2. describe what constitutes corporate governance

3. explain the role and objectives of information technology (IT) governance

4. describe an IT governance framework

5. define internal control

6. describe the components of an internal control framework

7. link financial reporting risks to financial statement assertions

8. relate internal control to the COBIT and COSO frameworks

9. explain the enterprise risk model (ERM) and its components and compare it with COSO.

# Introduction

Have you ever set yourself a goal or target that you desperately wanted to achieve? Aimed at achieving a certain grade in an end-of-semester exam? Wanted to save enough money for a new CD player on the market? If you have, then you have been through the process of setting yourself an objective. No doubt, as you strove towards attaining that objective, you kept a check on how you were going. If your goal was to save a certain number of dollars, you would have probably checked your bank statement regularly. If you wanted an Honours grade on your end-of-year exam, you presumably would have studied regularly to keep up to date with class material. For every goal you want to achieve there are steps or measures that need to be put in place to attain it.

It is the same story for any business. A business sets goals and then goes about trying to achieve them. Setting goals and trying to achieve them are the role of a sound corporate governance structure. The corporate governance structure includes the internal control system. There are a range of alternatives for how corporate governance and internal control structures are designed. This chapter presents some of the concepts about the structure and operation of such systems. These structures and systems allow a business to check whether it is achieving its goals and objectives, part of which will include making sure that the right things are being done within the organisation.

This chapter introduces you to the role of internal controls and how they fit within the overall management and governance of the organisation. The chapter will take you through the concepts of corporate governance and IT governance, introduce you to some well-known IT governance standards and explain how these standards fit within a framework of sound corporate governance. The topic of internal controls is introduced with the COSO and ERM frameworks. As part of this coverage, a definition of internal controls will be elaborated upon, with its components explored in detail, providing you with the basis to look at the specific application of controls in the next chapter.

**LEARNING OBJECTIVE**  **1**

Describe the concept and discuss the evolution of corporate governance.

**Corporate governance** *The way companies are managed to create value, enforce accountability and control, and manage risks.*

# CORPORATE GOVERNANCE

Everything that happens in an organisation with regard to goal setting, risk management, performance measurement and management relates to the concept of **corporate governance**. Put simply, corporate governance relates to how organisations are managed. In turn, the management of organisations is central to the topic of internal controls, as will become evident when we look later in the chapter at the example of the corporate governance principles of the Australian Securities Exchange below.

## What is corporate governance?

Corporate governance, as the name implies, refers to the way that organisations are managed and governed. More formally, it is defined by the Organisation for Economic Co-operation and Development (OECD) as:

> the set of relationships between a company's management, its board, its shareholders and other stakeholders . . . [it] provides the structure through which the objectives of the company are set, and the means of attaining those objectives and monitoring performance are determined.[1]

The Australian Securities Exchange defines corporate governance as including:

> the mechanisms by which companies, and those in control, are held to account ... [influencing] how the objectives of the company are set and achieved, how risk is monitored and assessed, and how performance is optimised.[2]

The objectives of a corporate governance system are described by Bushman and Smith[3] as:

1. to ensure that minority shareholders receive reliable information about the value of firms and that a company's managers and large shareholders do not cheat them out of the value of their investments
2. to motivate managers to maximise firm value instead of pursuing personal objectives.

The Australian Securities Exchange more generally describes the purpose of corporate governance as being a means to 'encourage companies to create value, through entrepreneurialism, innovation, development and exploration, and provide accountability and control systems commensurate with the risks involved'.[4]

From these definitions and objectives we see that corporate governance is about the many relationships in which an organisation is involved and how these relationships are managed. Note that the relationships that impact on an organisation's management are both within and external to the organisation. For example, the OECD definition refers to the organisation's relationship with external stakeholders that, if we were to use the example of a mining company, could include those in surrounding areas who may be impacted by potential noise, waste or pollution levels. Corporate governance is about how such relationships are managed by the organisation.

The reality for an organisation is that if these relationships are not managed properly the chances of business success are significantly reduced. For example, potential stakeholders that fall under the broad scope of the corporate governance definition include suppliers/creditors, customers/debtors, shareholders, debt providers and employees. This complex web of stakeholders that the organisation interacts requires the organisation to have a means of managing the interactions with stakeholders to facilitate the attainment of business objectives. This is what corporate governance is all about — putting in place policies and structures that allow for the various relationships of the organisation to be successfully managed, in order that the organisation can work towards the attainment of its goals and objectives. This will include issues relating to the management of relationships with external parties, as well as those relating to the internal operations of the organisation, including executive remuneration, risk management and levels of disclosure.

While the definition presented above may suggest that corporate governance is only relevant at the level of the individual organisation, in fact this could not be further from the truth. While it is important that individual organisations have appropriate corporate governance mechanisms in place (these will be discussed later in this chapter) it also needs to be recognised that the impacts of these mechanisms extend to the wider economy. This is evident from examining the OECD's documentation on corporate governance, with reference to the importance of corporate governance in the wider economy, including areas such as investor confidence, the ability to attract investment funds and the overall functioning of financial markets. In a speech to the Securities Institute and the Institute of Chartered Accountants in 2002, John Howard, the then prime minister of Australia, described corporate governance as a fundamental part of competitive capitalism. Mr Howard referred to the ideas of business disclosure of information to the marketplace in a timely manner, the development, enforcement and monitoring of the application of accounting standards, and executive remuneration levels as being critical components of any system of corporate governance.[5]

The question you may be asking, though, is how does the concept of corporate governance relate to accounting and accounting information systems? As mentioned above, corporate governance mechanisms relate to how an organisation achieves its goals and monitors and rewards organisational performance. At an overall level, a key part of the planning and monitoring of organisational performance will rely on accounting, with the accounting statements prepared by an organisation being one of the major ways it communicates details of its performance to relevant stakeholders — predominantly investors — allowing them to evaluate performance and make investment decisions. In this sense, accounting reports are a key mechanism of corporate governance and the attainment of accountability.

Looking deeper than this, the idea of a business achieving its goals and objectives was mentioned in the corporate governance definition, with the corporate governance structure providing the means through which objectives are set and monitored. These objectives will come from the organisation's board, which is vested with the responsibilities associated with the successful management of the company. These objectives will flow through to the lower levels of the organisation where they will be implemented. This means that the operation of the business processes will be impacted by the goals and objectives that the organisation adopts. For example, if the board decides to pursue a cost-based strategy, differentiating itself from competitors by its low-cost and efficient production methods, it will impact on the way the production business process is designed, as well as the data that is gathered across the process in order to measure performance. From this example we can see how the decisions and policies that are made as part of a corporate governance structure will impact on lower operational levels of the organisation. The monitoring of how these high-level decisions and policies are enacted is where internal control systems play a role. This will be discussed further later in this chapter.

## Brief history of corporate governance

The late 1980s in Australia will be remembered for a series of corporate failures. One prominent example in Victoria was the collapse of Pyramid Building Society. At around the same time, in the late 1980s and early 1990s, the United Kingdom experienced a period of heightened attention on the topic of corporate governance. This attention came about as a result of a number of cases of seemingly unexpected company failures and cases of fraud, as well as concerns about governance matters such as the role of the auditor and the ever common issue of executive remuneration.[6]

These events served to heighten the focus on corporate accountability and governance in the United Kingdom and culminated in the release of *The report of the committee on the financial aspects of corporate governance*[7] (this report is also known as *The Cadbury report*, after the committee chairman Adrian Cadbury). The committee was chartered to investigate financial reporting, accountability and issues of corporate governance, and produced a series of recommendations. This and similar subsequent reports have aimed primarily at financial reporting and auditing controls, including those that relate to the maintenance of proper accounting records and ensuring the reliability of information within the information system.[8] However, the impact of the recommendations had consequences for accounting information systems because the information system is central to the preparation of financial reports.

In the early 2000s, the United States witnessed some stunning corporate collapses: Enron, the resources giant, floundered amid allegations of fraudulent financial reporting and an ill-informed board of directors.[9] There were also issues of concern with the structure of the board of directors and senior management and their relationship with the external auditor, with the latter being clouded by issues revolving around a lack of independence.[10] Australia has also witnessed its own share of dramatic corporate failures. Once a national icon founded upon the traditions of a proud family, the blue and gold insignia of Ansett Airlines was removed permanently from our skies because of insolvency. Add to that retail giant Harris Scarfe, which collapsed following debts of $160 million in 2001 and was subsequently reopened by new owners after being restructured,[11] insurance company HIH and phone company One.Tel, and you have a longer-than-wanted list of failures in the corporate environment. In even more recent times, the global economic crisis has brought about some large corporate concerns for several organisations once considered insurmountable, with General Motors being just one example. The issue that has emerged from this crisis is how organisations deal with financial risk, with attention on organisational risk management and decision-making processes, as well as the potential need for wider regulatory framework reform.[12] Organisational risk management refers to the way an organisation identifies and manages the various risks that it faces in its operations. Risks can come from a range of sources, including financial activities, the internal environment and the influence of external factors such as regulation. The concept of risk management will be discussed further later in this chapter.

Company failures of any sort are undesirable, often leading to unemployment and financial hardship for those affiliated with the formerly solvent organisation, the loss of capital by investors, or large social impacts for the community in which the organisation operated. As a result, the reactions to large corporate collapses have been strong and traditionally focused on why the collapse occurred, including finger pointing at the way that the organisation was managed and how the various risks and threats were addressed — in other words, corporate governance.

Following the Enron collapse in the United States, and confronted with large public pressure for increased accountability for large corporations, in July 2002 then US President George W. Bush signed the Sarbanes–Oxley Act into existence. It aims at tightening corporate governance procedures within a company, representing 'government's way of putting legal teeth into the basic precepts of *good corporate governance and ethical business practices*'.[13] The legislation has implications for internal controls because section 404 requires the company to report to its shareholders on the design and effectiveness of its internal controls and requires that these reports be audited by an internal auditor. It also places the overall responsibility for internal controls on the CEO, with section 302 requiring CEOs to sign that they are responsible for the disclosure controls and procedures within a company.[14]

In 2003, the Australian Securities Exchange created a corporate governance document that provided guidelines for listed companies. The document was consistent with the principles expressed in the OECD guidelines and contained ten principles for companies to follow when setting up their corporate governance structure. This document was subsequently revised and re-released in 2007, with the second edition containing eight principles for corporate governance. These principles are discussed in the following section.

The management of corporations came under increased scrutiny due to the global financial crisis, which saw some companies face increased financial pressure and failure, and the global market suffer estimated losses in excess of $5 trillion.[15] The crisis highlighted that self-regulation was not necessarily working. It also led to a need for government bailouts since many victims were 'innocent bystanders' (e.g. employees, people with superannuation funds tied to company profits and investors concerned about the security of bank deposits). The crisis also raised issues of regulatory oversight of the financial system and the need for increased awareness of general governance issues.

While Australia was largely shielded from the brunt of the crisis, in 2008 ABC Learning was placed into receivership. ABC Learning was one of Australia's largest childcare chains, employing more than 16 000 staff across more than 1000 centres and tending to the needs of more than 100 000 children.[16] It's collapse led to the federal government outlaying more than $50 million to cover staff redundancies and employee entitlements of former ABC Learning staff. It is estimated that the company also has unsecured creditors of approximately $1.5 billion, as well as significant amounts owed to major banks.[17] The failure of ABC Learning has been linked by some sources to ad hoc and flawed accounting processes as well as ethical and corporate governance issues.[18] At the time of writing, a public investigation was being carried out into the collapse, with mention of possible legal action against the company's board, auditors and other related parties.[19] As we shall see in the discussion in this chapter, a company's board and auditors play key roles in corporate governance and the application of corporate governance principles.

**LEARNING OBJECTIVE 2**
*Describe what constitutes corporate governance.*

# CORPORATE GOVERNANCE IN AUSTRALIA

In a report published by the ASX Corporate Governance Council in March 2003, corporate governance is defined as:

> the system by which companies are directed and managed. It influences how the objectives of the company are set and achieved, how risk is monitored and assessed, and how performance is optimised. Good corporate governance structures encourage companies to create value (through entrepreneurism, innovation, development and exploration) and provide accountability and control systems commensurate with the risks involved.[20]

The original policy document from the ASX Corporate Governance Council identified ten factors that can lead to strong corporate governance.[21] These were revised in the second edition of the corporate governance guidelines in 2007. The current eight principles for corporate governance are:[22]

1. *Lay solid foundations for management and oversight.* This principle looks at how the organisation is structured, particularly focusing on the board and management. Typical areas of attention will be how the board and management are evaluated as well as the distribution of authority between the board members and the rest of the organisation. In particular, this section should specify the board's responsibility for the design and implementation of internal controls.

2. *Structure the board to add value.* This principle is concerned with ensuring that there are an appropriate number of directors, with appropriate skill and position. An area of interest in this principle is also the mix between executive and non-executive/independent directors. Executive directors are those directors that are also full-time employees of the company, while non-executive directors sit on the board but are not involved in the operations of the company in any other way. The ASX defines an independent director as 'a non-executive director who is not

a member of management and who is free of any business or other relationship that could materially interfere with — or could reasonably be perceived to materially interfere with — the independent exercise of their judgement'.[23] The argument for the presence of non-executive directors on a board is that non-executive directors provide an independent perspective for board decisions and corporate governance issues. This principle also requires that members of the board have access to all the information they require in order to carry out their responsibilities.

3. *Promote ethical and responsible decision making.* This section emphasises the need for the organisation to have clearly specified codes of conduct for employees and management. These can relate to legal obligations as well as standards for dealing with various organisational stakeholders. An example could be an organisation not allowing employees to trade in the shares of the company.

4. *Safeguard integrity in financial reporting.* This principle covers the measures that an organisation should consider as a means of ensuring that the financial reports provide a 'truthful and factual presentation of the company's financial position'.[24] Some measures that would be considered here include the use of an audit committee to interact with the external auditor (this is discussed later in the chapter).

5. *Make timely and balanced disclosure.* This principle addresses the means by which information is communicated to investors, with concerns about the timeliness and the factuality of information that is released.

6. *Respect the rights of shareholders.* Companies, a specific legal form of an organisation, have a separation of ownership and control. This places owners (or shareholders) in a position where they rely on the company's management to provide information about the company, including financial performance. Accordingly, shareholders should receive timely communications from the company and have an opportunity to participate in the general meetings held by the company. A trend among companies in this area is the increased use of a website for the presentation of information and announcements.

## AIS FOCUS 7.1

## Availability of information to shareholders

If you look at most major company websites they will typically have a section for investors, which will contain past annual reports and announcements to the market. Similarly, the Australian Securities Exchange has a facility that allows users to search for details and announcements by listed companies. The United States is also embarking on a project to make all company announcements from US companies electronically available through an internet-based database that uses eXtensible business reporting language (XBRL) as a means of tagging data, and allowing users to access, search and analyse data in a more user friendly and time efficient manner. The SEC, America's securities exchange regulator, sites the benefits as including greater accessibility and reliability of data for investors.[25]

7. *Recognise and manage risk.* Risks can operate in two ways: they can provide benefits (upside) or lead to losses or negative consequences (downside). This principle requires the board to review the risks that the organisation faces and devise appropriate risk management policies and procedures. A major part of this risk management process is the establishment and monitoring of the internal control system[26] (discussed later in this chapter).

8. *Remunerate fairly and responsibly.* The organisation should be able to demonstrate a clear link between company performance and executive remuneration. The area of executive compensation is commonly a target for criticism in times of economic or company downturn, leading to questions about why a particular amount is being paid to an individual. There is a need to recruit and retain the appropriate experience; however, sound governance also requires that remuneration is commensurate with performance.

Figure 7.1 contains an article from *The Sunday Telegraph* that highlights the attention some of the aspects of corporate governance have received from the popular press. Read the article and try to relate the issues it raises back to the ASX's eight principles of corporate governance.

Figure 7.2 overleaf contains an article from the *Sydney Morning Herald* that focuses on the issue of executive remuneration. Read the article and consider the following questions. How does this article relate to the corporate governance principles? Which specific principles does the article relate to? How? What are some ideas that could be implemented by a company to reduce the criticism it may receive for the amount it pays its executives?

**FIGURE 7.1** Executive excess — how calls to stop ever-increasing corporate salaries are falling on deaf ears

### As earnings fall, who really pays the price for our million dollar bosses?

Australia is living through a period of historically high executive salaries, but shareholders are asking why poor performance should be rewarded.

Like politicians, high-profile executives can rarely expect to enjoy a fat pay rise without drawing some heat.

Australians are almost as uncomfortable with corporate tall poppies as they are with elected officials.

So, when even the politicians start having a go at a chief executive's salary package, you know there must be trouble.

Telstra boss Sol Trujillo found himself in that position last week when Treasurer Peter Costello questioned his $2.58 million 'performance bonus' — a situation made more uncomfortable given that the Government remains his majority shareholder.

And Trujillo wasn't the only corporate high-flyer attracting negative attention.

Costello also hit out at building-products maker James Hardie for its board's decision to award themselves a $1.1 million pay rise, despite failing to resolve the issue of compensation to asbestos victims.

The Treasurer said it was symptomatic of a 'bad culture' within the company.

The irony is Costello's comments came in the same month his fellow federal politicians secured their own lucrative remuneration deal.

In a rare moment of bipartisan accord, the Coalition and Labor parties agreed to reverse their 2004 decision to cut back on the notoriously generous parliamentary superannuation scheme.

*(continued)*

**FIGURE 7.1** *(continued)*

MPs who arrived after 2004 will now be entitled to a 15 per cent employer contribution to their superannuation, and they will receive a redundancy payout of about $35 000 if they're voted out.

Ordinary workers receive an employer contribution of only nine per cent to superannuation.

For all that, politicians' salaries still fall well short of pay packets at the top end of the corporate world — as they never tire of telling us.

So is there a 'bad culture', a culture of greed, in Australia's boardrooms?

The issue resurfaces with almost predictable regularity — often at this time of year, when publicly listed companies are obliged to report their annual results and executive remuneration.

Back in 2003, a forum conducted by the St James Ethics Centre found overwhelming public antipathy towards executive pay.

Telstra chief executive Sol Trujillo earned a $2.58 million bonus after a year in which both the share price and profits went backwards.[27]

**Cap salaries of chief executives: unions**

THE ACTU will press the Federal Government to cap chief executive salaries at no more than 10 times the average wage inside their companies and to allow company shareholders to sue executives for poor performance.

It will release an analysis today showing remuneration packages for chief executives at Australia's top 50 companies listed on the sharemarket rose more than five-fold in the 15 years to 2005. It found the average chief executive's pay package had risen from 18 times average earnings in 1990 to 63 times average earnings, or $3.4 million, in 2005.

In a statement issued last night the ACTU secretary, Jeff Lawrence, said 'outrageous' executive salaries and bonus payments had encouraged a culture of excessive risk-taking and short-term thinking in the upper echelons of the corporate world. This culture had been one of the major causes of the global financial crisis.

He said unions would debate the issue at this week's ACTU Congress and develop industrial strategies to back its proposed legal changes for curbing executive pay.

'Year after year of virtually unlimited increases in CEO pay packets mean that executive remuneration is now out of all proportion with the work performed,' he said. 'Ordinary workers fail to see how the rise in executive pay and bonuses over the past decade can be justified when their own wages have risen much more slowly at 4.2 per cent a year.

'The union proposal would return executive pay to a more realistic level and link rewards and bonuses to the genuine growth and productivity of the enterprise rather than the smoke and mirrors guesswork used by many company boards.'

The Federal Government has asked the Productivity Commission to examine executive remuneration and ways of better aligning the interests of executives with those of shareholders and the community.[28]

**Questions to consider**

1. How does this article relate to the corporate governance principles?
2. Identify and explain the principles that this article could relate to.
3. What are some ideas that could be implemented by a company to reduce the criticism it may receive for the amount it pays its executives?

**FIGURE 7.2** Responsible remuneration — union and government responses

LEARNING
OBJECTIVE

*Explain the role and objectives
of information technology (IT)
governance.*

# IT GOVERNANCE

As is evident from the previous discussion on corporate governance, the responsibilities of those vested with management and control in the organisation are varied. The corporate governance roles that derive from the ASX principles include many dimensions, such as the responsibility for the management of operations and processes in the organisation, and dealing with risk and internal controls. These aspects will be discussed later in this chapter and in more detail in chapter 8. Governance principles also place some responsibility on organisations for how they manage and use information technology within the organisation. The issue of information technology (IT) governance is an important one, since IT investment will typically be of significant value and, as we saw in chapter 2, IT is increasingly being incorporated into organisations, whether in simple ways (e.g. establishing websites and basic e-commerce and electronic communication systems) or more advanced organisation-wide ways (e.g. implementing enterprise resource planning systems and integrating systems with those of customers and suppliers). Given the increasing importance of IT in organisations, the governance and management of IT has implications for many of the areas we examine in this text, including business process design, internal control design, and systems operation and development. Accordingly, this section will now introduce IT governance, including some of the IT governance frameworks and standards that have been prepared to assist organisations with their IT management.

## What is IT governance?

Within the responsibilities of corporate governance is the issue of IT governance. As for other areas of corporate governance, IT governance is a function of the board of directors and the high-level executives within the organisation. It centres on making sure the organisation is using information technology in a manner that is consistent with the overall organisational strategy.[29] IT governance has become an increasingly popular area for attention as organisations face increased scrutiny from shareholders and other stakeholders about how they are inducing accountability within the organisation.[30] Accountability refers to how decisions are allocated to individuals, how they are made and how they are followed up. The increasing importance of IT governance also reflects the growing role that IT plays and concerns about information management within organisations.[31] The governance issues surrounding IT relate to decisions about how IT is to be implemented and used in the organisation as well as the methods used to promote the use of IT consistent with the organisation's intentions. Simply put, IT governance is concerned with whether IT is being used within the organisation in the manner intended.

The IT Governance Institute cites four main objectives of IT governance:[32]

1. ensuring that the IT being used or adopted within an organisation is consistent with the organisation's goals and meets expectations
2. using IT to make the most of existing business opportunities and benefits
3. ensuring the organisation's IT resources are used responsibly
4. ensuring the organisation has appropriate management strategies and techniques in place for dealing with IT-related risks.

Within these four objectives are five specific areas that need to be considered by those with the responsibility of managing IT.[33] These five areas are:

- *Adding value* — ensuring that the IT within the organisation is performing as expected and contributing to the organisation in areas such as productivity, profitability (e.g. cost per transaction performed), customer satisfaction and ease of use. Measures in this area can include accounting-based metrics, such as return on investment and cost savings, as well as more qualitative measures. This can be a subjective area to gauge.

- *Managing risk* — making sure that the organisation's IT resources are protected and able to provide reliable and continuous operations, and that adequate disaster recovery plans are in place in the event of an IT problem. This will also include the establishment and operation of suitable internal controls within and related to the information system.
- *Matching IT to strategy* — consideration needs to be given to what the business currently does, where it intends to go in the future, and the role that IT can play in supporting these goals. Consistency between the direction that the business is heading and the direction that the business's IT is heading is critical to the alignment of IT and strategy. Failure to adopt this top-down perspective will lead to potential inconsistencies between strategy, process design and systems design. The consequence may be that the organisation says one thing (strategy), does another (process design) and captures a different set of data (IT). As discussed in previous chapters, the increasing role that information technology now plays within organisations, representing the means of implementing strategy and supporting business processes, makes managing IT and ensuring IT supports organisational strategy critical for organisations.[34]
- *Measuring performance* — systems are required to measure the performance of IT within the organisation. Recent support has been for the application of methods that include the balanced scorecard, since this addresses a broad range of performance aspects and is not driven solely by financial metrics. Schrage,[35] for example, describes how IT can be used to facilitate the prompt availability of financial information to company executives, enabling them to fulfill their corporate governance obligations. The example given is a secure web page where information was made available to board members, with Schrage arguing that this is part of information technology realising its role in assisting corporate governance within the organisation, since the system was able to make information available to those who need it, thus allowing them to gain feedback on system performance.
- *Managing resources* — ensuring that the resources associated with IT are used appropriately. Resources can include both people and technical infrastructure. Therefore, managing resources can include aspects related to technology (e.g. acquisition, maintenance, retirement) as well as to people (e.g. training and development, and recruitment). Managing resources effectively is seen as a key to realising the full benefits from these resources.

IT governance involves being clear on who is involved in IT decisions, who makes the final decision and how the decision makers are accountable for their decision outcomes.[36] IT governance encompasses areas including principles, infrastructure, architecture, and investment and prioritisation.[37] These are briefly described below and will also be investigated more thoroughly in chapter 14.

## IT principles

This aspect refers to how IT is going to be used in the organisation and will be a general statement or specification about how IT will be positioned and the role it will play in the organisation as it embarks on meeting customer needs.

## IT infrastructure

IT infrastructure, as the name implies, is the basis that the firm's information system rests upon. Organisational decisions about IT infrastructure will include what type of processing is required, the location of the processing and the integration of processing. Decisions will also include how IT is to be used across the organisation. For example, if a coordinated and integrated approach is preferable to a segmented and functional-based approach, ERP systems and centralised data management and storage may be appropriate.

### IT architecture

Having specified the infrastructure, specific decisions need to be made about what will happen in the system, how data will be used, the processing conventions to be applied, the communication standards that need to be followed, and any impact on organisational management structure, roles and responsibilities that will come about from the new IT.

### IT investment and prioritisation

This dimension refers to the means used by the organisation to evaluate alternative IT investment proposals and decide upon which project to pursue. This can include evaluations of anticipated performance, costs, benefits and financial performance. Means of evaluating IT investment proposals is in chapter 14 when we look at systems development. For now, be aware that there will need to be procedures in place for evaluating and making decisions on IT investments.

**LEARNING OBJECTIVE 4**

*Describe an IT governance framework.*

## IT GOVERNANCE FRAMEWORKS AND STANDARDS

IT governance is also associated with various activities across the lifecycle of technology within the organisation,[38] from considering potential IT applications to the implementation and use of IT within the organisation. The different stages of IT within an organisation are specified in Control Objectives for Information and Related Information Technology (COBIT) 4.1,[39] an internationally recognised framework for IT governance that has been widely adopted across organisations of various sizes, from small to medium and large.[40] The COBIT framework (discussed in more detail later in this chapter and in chapter 8) outlines the major IT stages[41] as follows:

1. *Plan and organise.* This first stage addresses the overall awareness and management of IT within the organisation. Typical questions at this stage include:
   - How well do current IT resources map to the organisational strategy?
   - Are existing IT resources being used effectively?
   - How clearly are the IT objectives understood throughout the organisation?
   - Do current IT systems match the current needs of the organisation?

   In this first stage, the emphasis is on how the existing IT resources within the organisation are being managed and applied. The above questions illustrate that the goal is to gain an overall understanding and awareness of existing IT resources, such that if there are problems or opportunities (e.g. the emergence of a new technology that could be applied by the organisation) the organisation is positioned to be able to respond. Being aware of the current organisational use of IT and opportunities that may exist for future IT developments and planning for the future IT needs of the organisation are the focus of this first stage. An example for organisations in recent years has been the opportunity that has emerged through the development of e-commerce. This presented organisations based around a traditional architecture with the need to consider how, if at all, the new technology could be applied.

2. *Acquire and implement.* At this second stage, the concern is with how various IT solutions are to be acquired by the organisation and how well they map to existing organisational processes. Critical issues at this stage are an awareness of the business requirements, what the potential IT solutions are able to provide, and how the requirements and potential solutions map to each other. Also of concern will be the selection and implementation processes that will provide reasonable assurance that any adopted system will meet the business needs, can be put in place on time, will work as intended once implemented and will communicate with existing systems. An example could be an organisation moving to a web-based interface as part of a push towards e-commerce. The concern would be how well this interface will interact with existing systems; for example, will it capture the right data in the right format for the existing back-end systems? Will it record all transactions? Will it adequately authenticate the identity of customers who make purchases? This stage builds from the first stage and involves investment in IT resources that can be used within the organisation. This stage is significant for the organisation in many regards. In recent times, investment in IT has escalated for several reasons, including increased adoption of ERP systems.[42] This makes the following of processes for decisions about investment important, as links between IT investment and performance are increasingly evaluated and returns from IT are scrutinised.

3. *Deliver and support.* At this stage, systems delivery will be the primary focus, with concerns for the implementation of the system, its integration with business processes and activities, and how the new system is to be used by the users within the organisation. In addition, once the new system is in place, does it handle data appropriately in order to meet any concerns or requirements regarding issues of confidentiality, security and privacy? For example, Australian organisations need to be aware of the *Privacy Act 1988* (Cwlth) and its requirements in relation to the capture, storage, use and destruction of data gathered. Concern at this stage will also be for whether the costs of the IT services being used are appropriate. This stage involves keeping IT resources operating and ensuring that they continue to be used appropriately and remain aligned with organisational strategy. This can include issues of how the updating of software and hardware across the organisation is scheduled and managed, as well as specifying the processes to be followed for such activities.

4. *Monitor and evaluate.* This final stage places emphasis on how the system is operating within the organisation, requiring those in management and governance positions to have available information about the system and its operation. It will necessitate a set of performance measures that can be used as benchmarks or targets as well as measures of actual performance. As a simple example, if the target for the new sales system was to be able to process three online transactions per minute, how does the actual transaction processing rate compare to this target? If the target is not being met, what factors have led to this situation? The issue from an IT governance perspective is to make sure that adequate monitoring systems are in place to detect problems in systems performance before it is too late, and to constantly evaluate the extent to which the IT resources are aligned with and supporting the organisation's goals. Staying informed about IT usage within the organisation, evaluating actual IT benefits or outcomes against initial expectations, and looking for future opportunities based on feedback from current performance are all part of this stage. As noted by the International Federation of Accountants, 'IT monitoring is fundamental to IT governance and part of management's stewardship

responsibility to make certain that what was agreed to be done is being done and is being done in line with directions and policies set by the board.'[43]

The analysis across these stages allows management to understand the use of IT within the business, identify and manage the risks associated with IT and work towards the attainment of expected benefits from the organisation's IT investment. As will be seen later in this chapter, this approach is also consistent with the perspective adopted by COBIT 4.1,[44] which provides a control framework for IT within an organisation.

Empirical evidence of the actual management of IT and its link to corporate governance in Australia is available from Musson and Jordan,[45] who surveyed and interviewed directors of Australian companies about the risks of IT and how directors perceived these risks. The results generally showed that the responsibility for dealing with specific risks of IT in the business — especially e-commerce — was that of management, with the board setting the landscape within which this would occur. The board's role thus became one of monitoring the activities of the specific IT managers in the organisation and receiving feedback on their progress. The results also indicated that many organisations had failed to update their risk management policies to deal with the unique risks and issues that are a part of IT governance. Emphasising the strategic imperative of IT investments and the impact on the way an organisation does its business, it was also a common finding that IT investments had changed or would change a business's strategy. The issue of the board and IT governance was also discussed by Damianides,[46] who discusses similar trends to those found by Musson and Jordan,[47] including that of top executives being reluctant to comment on issues of IT governance.

Given the impact of legislative change and the increased pressure on organisations to be accountable for corporate governance issues, as is evident through legislation like the US Sarbanes–Oxley Act, it would be expected that the trends outlined above would alter. As is noted by the IT Governance Institute,[48] in order to be Sarbanes–Oxley compliant an organisation must be able to show that the IT controls it has in place are consistent with the methodology discussed in the COSO framework (discussed later in the chapter). Specifically, management must be able to demonstrate the existence of control strengths in the areas of the control environment, risk assessment, control activities, information and communication, and monitoring activities. Each of these components is discussed in the following sections of this chapter.

The role of IT within the organisation is ever increasing, including its prevalence in the execution of day-to-day business processes as well as being an integral part of an organisation's financial reporting process. Whether through small accounting packages or organisation-wide ERP systems, IT is prevalent and not going to disappear. This makes an awareness of the risks and documentation of the operation of the systems, the controls necessary in an IT environment and more generally maintaining the alignment between IT usage and corporate strategy all critical issues in the board's overall responsibilities in the area of corporate governance.

## Australian IT governance

In the area of IT governance, Australia can be seen as a leader, with Standards Australia having prepared AS8015-2005 *Corporate Governance of Information and Communication Technology*. The standard specifies six main responsibilities for directors to fulfil in the area of IT governance. These are examined in the AIS focus below. The model used in the Australian standard is also reproduced in figure 7.3. It summarises the domain of IT governance and the factors impacting IT governance.

The model, as shown in figure 7.3, indicates two factors to consider in managing IT: the business pressures facing the organisation and the business's IT needs. Examples of business pressures could include changes in technology that impact on the way business is carried out (e.g. the emergence of e-commerce), economic and social pressures (e.g. the move towards electronic communications) and regulatory pressures (e.g. legislation at a state and federal level that impacts how systems are put in place and operate). These pressures will be considered in light of business needs, which are geared around the specified organisational strategy and how the strategy is implemented in order for the organisation to be able to distinguish itself from its rivals and gain a competitive advantage. You will probably notice a strong similarity between the content and emphasis of the Australian standard and the principles discussed above — they both present the same message for an organisation. That is, IT must be managed across the lifecycle of its use in the organisation, and, in order to do this, controls and plans are needed from the point of initial investigation into a potential IT investment to the maintenance and operation of the system once it is in place. While the emphasis across the lifecycle will change, there still needs to be a governance process in place to monitor and control IT and work towards its alignment with business objectives.

The model also shows that direction and guidance for the organisation comes through the policies and plans that are communicated through the organisation, with these informing the IT proposals that are prepared at the lower levels of the organisation and submitted for approval. The board will evaluate the various proposals and select one for implementation and, once implemented, will be concerned with how the system is performing. This is represented by the flow from the business process box to the monitor box in figure 7.3.

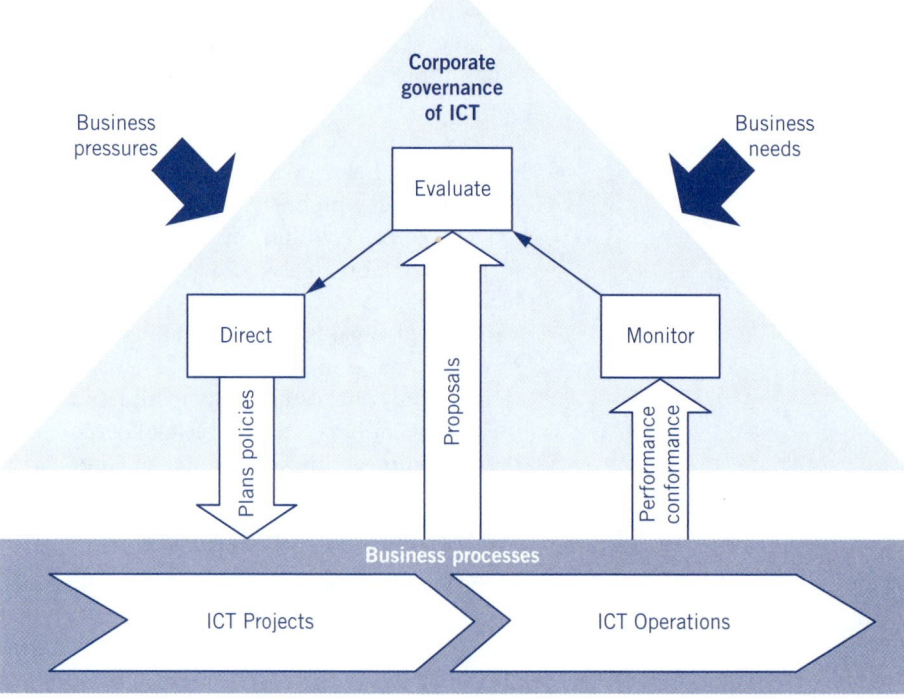

**FIGURE 7.3** AS8015 model for IT governance
*Source:* Standards Australia 2005, AS8015-2005.[49]

## Australia leading the way in IT governance standards

The area of IT governance has gained increased attention in recent years as pushes from various stakeholders have focused attention on corporate governance. While there have traditionally been concerns with general corporate governance issues, including remuneration, transparency and controls, a new area for attention has been that of IT governance.

In 2003, Standards Australia released a standard for corporate governance and, in 2005, followed up with a standard on IT governance. The IT governance standard identifies six principles that encapsulate the domain of IT governance:[50]

1. Put in place well understood responsibilities for ICT [information and communication technology] throughout the organisation.
2. Plan for ICT to support the current and future needs of the organisation to be consistent with overall organisational objectives.
3. Ensure ICT acquisitions are based on analysis and match up with organisational needs and that such investments offer both long and short term benefits.
4. Ensure ICT performs well, with performance including the satisfaction of business needs, responding to changing business needs and being a reliable support for organisational activities whenever required.
5. Ensure ICT conforms with any external obligations (for example, in Australia, data protection and the Privacy Act and financial reporting obligations under the Corporations Act) as well as any internal policies that may exist in the organisation.
6. Ensure ICT use respects human factors, particularly the meeting of the needs of the different system stakeholders.

Following these policy guidelines has implications for the way the organisation goes about identifying IT projects, selects from competing projects, manages the implementation and operation of projects, and aligns IT to overarching business needs.

Australia's leadership in this area was recognised on the international stage when, in 2008, several Australians were selected to be part of an international project to harmonise IT governance standards and develop an international standard.[51]

**LEARNING OBJECTIVE 5**

*Define internal control.*

## INTERNAL CONTROL

In this section we will look at internal control. Up until this point we have discussed corporate and IT governance and the general opinion that the organisation needs to monitor and control its operation, whether it be in relation to financial reporting, business process performance or IT use and implementation. In order to do this the organisation needs to adopt an internal control system. The make-up and operation of such systems are discussed in the following section.

### What is internal control?

Internal control is an essential part of an organisation's corporate governance structure and helps the organisation to meet its objectives. Internal control is about putting in place systems and procedures that help the organisation achieve its objectives. Internal control systems can be seen as fitting in as a part of corporate governance since their primary role is to manage the different risks that the organisation faces and work towards the attainment of organisational goals. One of the most widely accepted and adopted definitions of **internal control** is that provided by the Committee Of Sponsoring Organisations (COSO) Treadway Committee report. The COSO Treadway Committee report was prepared in 1991, following an earlier report into fraudulent financial reporting in the United States, and recommended the establishment of a set of general principles that would promote greater corporate governance in US corporations.[52]

From the Treadway Committee report came the following definition:

> Internal control is a process, effected by an entity's board of directors, management and other personnel, designed to provide reasonable assurance regarding the achievement of objectives in the following categories:
> - effectiveness and efficiency of operations
> - reliability of financial reporting
> - compliance with applicable laws and regulations.[53]

Australian Auditing Standard ASA 315 *Understanding the Identifying and Assessing the Risks of Material Misstatement through Understanding the Entity and its Environment*[54] defines internal control as:

> The process designed, implemented and maintained by those charged with governance, management and other personnel to provide reasonable assurance about the achievement of an entity's objectives with regard to reliability of financial reporting, effectiveness and efficiency of operations, and compliance with applicable laws and regulations.

There are a few key terms within these definitions that should be noted. These are described below.

## Reasonable assurance

First, internal control systems are designed to provide 'reasonable assurance' that an organisation meets its objectives. Notice how both the definitions are carefully worded to emphasise that internal controls do not guarantee attainment of objectives. Both the COSO and ASA 315 definitions state that internal controls can 'provide reasonable assurance'. This is an important point to keep in mind. The reason internal controls do not guarantee attainment of organisational goals becomes clearer in progressing through this and the subsequent chapters. For the moment, however, remember that internal control systems help an organisation attain its objectives. They *do not* guarantee that objectives will be met.

## Management

Second, notice the different people mentioned as being involved in internal controls. The COSO definition explicitly mentions the board of directors, management and other personnel. Similarly, the ASA definition is broad in its coverage, incorporating 'those charged with governance, management, and other personnel'.[55] Everyone within the organisation will be affected by internal controls, but the impact will be felt in different ways. Those vested with governance and management responsibilities in the organisation will typically be involved in the implementation and design of controls while those at lower levels will typically be expected to perform their activities according to internal control specifications. As an example, from your previous accounting studies you would be aware that cash at bank is reconciled to the bank statement on a regular basis, in order to check the accuracy of bank and ledger records. The instruction on how reconciliations are to be performed, who performs them and their frequency is determined by those who manage the cash function. The performance of the reconciliation process will be carried out by lower levels in the organisation according to the management requirements. Additionally, how well internal controls operate within the organisation will be affected dramatically by the people within the organisation — especially management. This idea is further elaborated as the chapter progresses.

## Control objectives

Third, in understanding internal controls, the relationship to keep in mind is the link between the organisation's objectives and the organisation's control system. In analysing the objectives, the Australian Auditing Standard definition[#] tells us that there are three to be aware of:

- reliability of financial reporting
- effectiveness and efficiency of operations
- compliance with applicable laws and regulations.

These objectives can be seen as the generic aims of all organisations. They relate to the internal control system, as will be explained in this chapter and chapter 8. Because of their importance, it is useful to have an explanation of what each of these objectives refers to and how they affect the organisation.

### Effectiveness and efficiency of operations

The objective of effectiveness and efficiency of operations encompasses the typical objectives of an organisation, such as profitable operations and protecting its resources from theft and misappropriation. Controls will be established to help the business operate profitably as well as to safeguard the resources of the organisation. The distinction between effectiveness and efficiency is an important one to be aware of. Effectiveness is how well a system is performing relative to a pre-specified goal or objective. That is, it focuses on whether the system is performing the function it was put in place to achieve. Efficiency, on the other hand, is how well the system is operating based on the resources required for its operation.

An example of a measure of efficiency could be a ratio of inputs required to operate a system to the outputs generated by the system. For example, the number of transactions processed per hour of machine time or the data entry time per sales transaction recorded. An example of effectiveness for a system could be the number of transactions successfully processed.

As an example of a measure of effectiveness, for a transaction cycle like the sales cycle to be effective it needs to meet its pre-defined purpose — typically that of processing sales transactions. This effectiveness could be measured by a ratio of transactions processed successfully to total number of transactions. This ratio is an indicator of how effective the system is at handling transactions. If we were concerned about efficiency of the sales system we might look at a measure of inputs to outputs, for example, how many minutes are used per transaction.

### Reliability of financial reporting

Throughout its life, an organisation will prepare financial reports. Under the *Corporations Act 2001* (Cwlth), an Australian public company that is a disclosing entity must prepare and lodge half-yearly and annual reports with the Australian Securities Exchange, while reporting entities must prepare general purpose financial reports annually. The reports

---

[#] It should be noted that the terminology of the objectives under the Australian Auditing Standard and COSO definitions are consistent in intent, even if worded slightly differently. The Australian Auditing Standard terminology will be used in this discussion.

that are required to be lodged are specified in the Corporations Act — the statement of comprehensive income (income statement), statement of financial position (balance sheet), statement of cash flows, statement of changes in equity and the accompanying notes to the financial statements — should be reliable and accurate, based on the qualitative characteristics of accounting information referred to in the AASB's *Framework*.[56] A sound internal control system will assist in meeting the goal of preparing reliable financial reports.* This is an area that has faced increased attention in the environment of corporate failures; for example, a common question being asked is how is it that a firm reported profits yet was insolvent? Or how is it that the problems in the financial report (e.g. including false sales to bolster revenue, including incorrect classifications of items) were left undetected? As we shall see when we look in more detail at internal controls in chapter 8, the structure and design of the internal control system can contribute to the attainment of reliable and accurate financial information. One thing to keep in mind in relation to reliable financial reporting is that, while this is one area of focus and one area of potential risks for an organisation, organisational risks extend beyond the financial, for example, management of quality and processes within the organisation. The reliability of financial reports and the risk of material misstatements will be of primary concern for auditors of an organisation (discussed further below), but there are other aspects that the controls address that are beyond the pure financial emphasis of the auditor.

### Compliance with applicable laws and regulations

Organisations will also be faced with legislative requirements that must be satisfied. Consider the example of a manufacturing company that may only be allowed to discharge a certain amount of pollution into the air each year. To comply with the legal limits of pollution, the organisation needs a system to monitor its current discharge levels. This is an example of a type of internal control system. Alternatively, the manufacturing company may pump used water back into a local stream. Legal requirements may exist for the required quality and chemical content levels of the water. To help make sure the organisation complies with such legal requirements, it can establish an internal control system to monitor water quality. More generally, as mentioned above, Australian companies will be subject to the reporting requirements specified in the Corporations Act, including how often reports need to be prepared, what reports must be prepared and the content of the reports. Interpretation of this legislation incorporates the accounting standards set by the Australian Accounting Standards Board, which outline the format and content of the financial statements.[57] Financial reporting by companies is scrutinised by the Australian Securities and Investments Commission, which is vested with the power of policing the Corporations Act and can investigate financial reporting practices by companies. As such, companies will seek to ensure that measures are in place within the organisation to monitor activities and reporting and give reasonable assurance that such activities and reports comply with applicable legislation and regulations.

**LEARNING OBJECTIVE 6**
*Describe the components of an internal control framework.*

## WHAT MAKES UP AN INTERNAL CONTROL SYSTEM?

For the three control objectives mentioned in the Australian Auditing Standard and COSO definitions to be achieved, there are five key control components that must exist: the control environment, risk assessment, control activities, information and

---

* In order to be reliable the information contained within the financial reports must be accurate, complete and understandable. This makes accuracy a necessary condition for reports to be able to be relied upon. Refer to the AASB *Framework* for further clarification of these qualities.

communication, and monitoring. Each of these is now discussed in more detail. This discussion will give you the foundation to apply control concepts in chapter 8 and appreciate their operation in the transaction cycle chapters (9–13).

## Control environment

**Control environment** *The attitude, emphasis and awareness of an organisation's management towards internal control and its operation within the organisation.*

The **control environment** is defined in ASA 315 as encompassing 'the governance and management functions and the attitudes, awareness, and actions of those charged with governance and management concerning the entity's internal control and its importance in the entity. The control environment sets the tone of an organisation, influencing the control consciousness of its people.'[58]

As referred to in the definition, the control environment is the basis for all internal control practices within the organisation and impacts on how well the internal control structure operates. The control environment reinforces the concept that leadership comes from the top, and the example set and decisions made by those in positions of authority within an organisation will have an impact on the behaviour of those at lower levels. Some examples of how this influence can be seen are senior management's attitudes towards ethics and ethical behaviour, acting with integrity, philosophy and style, and commitment to competence.[59]

Specific components of the control environment to be aware of, as mentioned in ASA 315 include:

- *The communication and policing of ethical behaviour in the organisation.* An organisation that does not strive to enforce ethical conduct among its staff will face problems regardless of how well the control system is designed. As we shall see later in this chapter, controls can be subverted or manipulated, with these possibilities increased in instances where the ethical tone of the organisation is poor. This aspect of the control environment is linked to the corporate governance objective of ethical and responsible decision making mentioned above.
- *Commitment to competence.* This refers to the awareness by management that different tasks and responsibilities in the organisation will have different pre-requisite skills and knowledge. As such, the organisation should have policies and procedures in place for gaining reasonable assurance that those within the organisation have the necessary skills and knowledge to perform their jobs at a competent level.
- *Management philosophy and operating style.* This component looks at how management addresses the issues and risks that the organisation faces in its day-to-day activities. A sound control environment is one where managers are aware of the risks and are constantly evaluating the extent of their potential impact on financial reporting, compliance with legislation and operating performance. This aspect includes both management's attitude towards such risks (e.g. do they ignore them or do they constantly assess them?) as well as how management responds (e.g. having identified a particular risk do they ignore it or do they put in place a measure to counter it?).
- *Organisational structure.* This refers to the way the organisation is designed in order to facilitate the planning, execution, control and review of business activities. As was mentioned in chapter 2, organisational structures can vary. These structures are typically implemented as a way of managing the risks and information flows within the organisation.
- *Distribution of responsibility.* This section looks at how responsibility is distributed in the organisation, including who has the power to authorise events and the reporting and accountability relationships in place to monitor and review the execution of events in the organisation.

- *Recruitment policies.* This important section is concerned with the policies and procedures followed by the organisation in managing its people. This will include the processes for hiring staff, the mechanisms in place to monitor staff performance and the means in place for employee removal and dispute resolution.

If the control environment is weak, the other components of the internal control system are probably less reliable. For example, if management has no regard for risks or their management, it is unlikely that the subsequent components of the internal control system (i.e. risk assessment, control activities, information and communication, and monitoring, addressed below) will be considered or implemented.

## Risk assessment

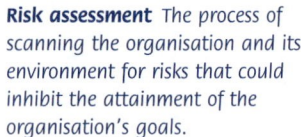

**Risk assessment** *The process of scanning the organisation and its environment for risks that could inhibit the attainment of the organisation's goals.*

**Risk assessment** is all about an organisation being aware of the various risks it faces that could inhibit the successful attainment of its objectives. How does an organisation assess risks? From an accounting information perspective, the concern will be the risks that could lead to a material misstatement in the financial statements and therefore impact on the attainment of reliable financial reporting. Risks could be as particular as data entry errors at the transactional level to, at a higher level, the impact of a major customer moving to another supplier, which could bring inventory valuation into question. Other risks may impact on the operation of the business processes and operations, and on the organisation's broader ability to achieve its objectives. For example, the possibility of things going wrong in a business process (e.g. errors in manufacturing) to higher-level risks that may present themselves as a result of the organisation's strategy and structure, for example, a high reliance on IT and links with others in the supply chain.

Regardless of their source (i.e. financial reporting or other parts of the organisation), the various risks need to be considered and evaluated by those responsible for the implementation of the internal control system. The typical approach advocated for assessing risks, as outlined in the appendix to ASA 315, is to adopt a risk-based approach that asks four questions:[60]

1. What is the risk?
2. What is the overall significance of the risk?
3. What is the chance of the risk eventuating?
4. What can/should be done to deal with the risk?

As an example, consider the aviation industry and its vulnerability to fluctuations in fuel prices in the AIS focus below. The process of identifying risks and linking financial reporting risks to financial statement assertions are explained later in the chapter.

## AIS FOCUS 7.3

### Fuel prices and financials

Changes in fuel prices will impact on airlines in several ways, for example, the increased cost of inputs (fuel for planes) and lower profitability per flight. Fuel is obviously an essential input into the aviation industry and as such the airlines are confronted with the challenge of managing the risk of fuel price increases. A common technique used by many airlines is to hedge the oil price. Qantas, for example, has a hedge system in place where it agrees to fuel prices at the start of each calendar year. With the price agreed and fixed, Qantas is not exposed to the impact of fuel price rises in the current year. However, this is not a perfect system for the airline. It was reported that Qantas' negotiated price of US$72 per barrel ended in 2008 and most of the airline's fuel purchases are subject to current market rates, reported to be around US$130 per barrel.

Applying the risk model we can analyse the process as follows:

- Risk — fuel price increase and impact on profitability of flights and cost of inputs.
- Significance — high: impacts on key business activity and cost of essential key inputs; fuel prices determined externally.
- Likelihood — high: fuel market volatile and subject to fluctuations.
- Action — hedge fuel prices (as had been done to fix the price at US$72 per barrel); change fleet structure to more efficient aircraft (Qantas planned to speed up the retirement of some of its less efficient aircraft and reallocate planes to different routes to manage fuel consumption).

The actions implemented will be considered in light of the cost–benefit that they provide for the organisation. For example, the cost to the airline of placing a smaller, more fuel efficient plane on a route (reduced capacity on the flight) would presumably be less than the benefits that are gained (lower fuel cost per flight, higher fuel efficiency).[61]

## Control activities

**Control activities** The responses by management to the risks identified as part of the risk management stage.

**Control activities** or control procedures (as used in the US auditing standards) are management's response to the risks identified in the risk assessment stage. More formally, they are defined in ASA 315 as 'the policies and procedures that help ensure that management directives are carried out'.[62] Management policies and procedures are put in place in response to the risks identified in the risk assessment stage. Accordingly, there should be a strong link between risks and control activities.

Management will look at the objectives of the organisation and the risks identified as threats to achieving those objectives, and devise ways of reducing the threat of those risks. Various strategies can be employed to negate the risks, including top-level reviews, direct management, information processing, performance indicators, physical controls and segregation of duties.[63] These specific strategies are discussed in more detail in the next chapter in examining some of the types of control activities.

For example, if management identified the threat of inventory being stolen (and hence recorded amounts would be different to actual amounts on hand, and assets would not be protected), then it might respond by suggesting physical controls such as the use of a locked store room and periodic reconciliations of stock on hand to inventory records, as well as separation of duties. Although we are not concerned here with why these controls would meet the specific threat, appreciate that at this point in time management proposes potential solutions to the threats identified.

## Information and communication

Information and communication are essential to the satisfactory functioning of any organisation. Imagine what it would be like if you were the sales manager of a large retail firm and were asked to provide the sales budget for the next quarter without the use of any information — no sales figures or trends, no economic indicators, nothing.

What would you use as the basis of your forecast, apart from a bit of luck and a whole lot of guessing? Clearly, this is not the way for an organisation to operate. Within the organisation, people need enough information to be able to perform their duties. Information and communication are, therefore, centred on making sure that information is with the right people at the right time. To achieve this, it is first necessary to identify what data are needed, then capture them and convert them to a form that is useful for those within the organisation. The information then needs to be accessible, so that employees can use it in carrying out their daily jobs and responsibilities.

Information and communication will also encompass the design of the information system, which includes the 'infrastructure (physical and hardware components), software, people, procedures, and data'.[64] The information system, from an accounting perspective, needs to have in place methods to identify and record transactions, summarise transactions for reporting purposes, measure transactions, record transactions in the correct period and produce reports that allow for appropriate decisions to be made by management in their role as controllers of the activities of the organisation. This will also include the techniques used to communicate the different responsibilities of people within the organisation, for example, job descriptions, and policy and procedure manuals.[65] Notice how an important part of the design of the information system is communication of responsibilities, which leads to the concept of 'accountability' — a key part of the control process. For accountability to be effective, however, there needs to be information flowing up and down through the organisation. More importantly, that information needs to be acted upon. Even if an information system prepares a report showing that some of the organisation's accounts receivable are several months overdue, that report is of little use if no-one ever acts upon it or even reads it! Information must be available and must also be communicated to the relevant people for appropriate action.

## Monitoring

Once an internal control system is established within the organisation the temptation may be to step back and let the organisation take care of itself. This would be a both foolhardy and ignorant approach. For an internal control system to remain effective in helping the organisation to achieve its objectives, it must be monitored continually and corrected as needed.[66] **Monitoring** of an internal control system needs to occur regularly, because over time the objectives of the organisation could alter or the risks confronting the organisation may change. Monitoring is a key activity that aims to ensure that the controls in place relate to current risks faced by the organisation. For example, the emergence of the online environment has increased the risk of fraud through identity theft and fake or stolen credit card details. This has meant that organisations now need to ensure that their controls relating to authenticating customer identity are up to date to deal with this risk. Control activities used in the past may not adequately deal with the new risks presented in today's business environment. This emphasises the need to continually monitor the internal control system and its performance. Failure to do so ignores that the organisation, its objectives and its environment change over time.

Monitoring can take place in several ways within the organisation and can be performed by both internal and external parties. Those within the organisation involved in monitoring activities may include top management, internal auditors and employees, while the external parties could include external auditors and regulatory bodies. These parties will review the control system periodically and ensure that it still fits the organisation's goals and objectives and satisfactorily addresses any risks that may exist. The role of the internal auditor, top management and the external auditor in this monitoring process are discussed briefly in the following paragraphs.

## Internal auditors

Internal auditors are a group of staff within an organisation who are typically independent of all other functions and departments. Their major function is to examine, evaluate and monitor the effectiveness and sufficiency of the internal control system of the organisation,[67] with this responsibility often delegated to them by top-level management. The internal auditors will report back to management on their findings and recommend any improvements to the control system. While the specific duties of the internal audit group will typically be determined by management, some of these duties could include:[68]

- examining financial and operating information, which may include checking individual transactions and the financial reporting process
- reviewing the economy, effectiveness and efficiency of the organisation's operations
- reviewing the adequacy of compliance with external laws and regulations.

## External auditor

The role of the external auditor is typically related to the financial reporting process that a company faces. In Australia, the Corporations Act dictates what type of companies must have a financial statement audit performed. The audit will provide reasonable assurance that:

- transactions that occurred have been recorded and reported
- assets and liabilities in the financial statements exist and transactions reported actually occurred
- assets listed are owned by the organisation and liabilities owed are reported
- amounts on the financial statements have been calculated in accordance with accounting standards
- the statements are correctly classified with appropriate disclosures in the notes, as required by the accounting standards.[69]

As part of these duties, the external auditor will assess the adequacy of the internal control system. Auditors will also communicate with management, providing comments and feedback on the internal control system and notifying them of any deficiencies in the internal control system that were detected.[70] In the United States, as a result of the Sarbanes–Oxley Act, auditors are required to audit declarations by the CEO about the nature and adequacy of internal control within the organisation.

## Senior management

Senior management within an organisation plays a critical role in the design and effectiveness of the organisation's control system. It all starts at the top, with the board of directors responsible for setting the pattern that will run throughout the entire organisation. Recall from the discussion of the control environment earlier in this chapter a quote from the Australian Auditing Standards that referred to 'the attitudes, awareness, and actions of those charged with governance and management concerning the entity's internal control and its importance in the entity'. The implication is that top management can have an enormous impact on the effectiveness or otherwise of internal controls within the organisation. Senior management that puts in place structures for control, emphasises the importance of control to its middle and lower level management, and acts upon the results of the control system sends the message to all within the organisation that ethical behaviour and adherence to the control system are important. Alternatively, a top management that engages in unscrupulous activities and does not consider controls to be important will send exactly the opposite signal to all other employees in the organisation.

Some of the ways that senior management can signal its commitment to a rigorous control system include establishing an internal audit function and supporting its independent operation in the organisation, establishing an audit committee from the board of directors, and having a board structure that consists of both internal and external directors.

As was discussed in the corporate governance in Australia discussion, a company's board of directors can consist of both executive and non-executive directors. Executive directors are full-time employees of the company, who will typically be involved in management of the ordinary operations of the business. By comparison, non-executive directors are not employed by the company on a full-time basis and will usually be external appointments to the board. The benefit of the presence of non-executive directors is that they are usually able to offer independent and unbiased perspectives to the running of the board.[71] From a corporate governance perspective, they are seen as more effective for monitoring and responding to management performance.

Audit committees are established by firms to monitor the organisation's financial performance and as a point of liaison between the company and the internal and external auditors.[72] The audit committee will be made up of a selection of the company's directors and acts as a representative group for the company's shareholders, since a financial statement audit is performed for these shareholders. Important aspects to consider when designing an effective audit committee are that it is independent and able to discuss openly any sensitive issues that may arise, is able to nominate an auditor and arrive at a suitable fee, monitors the perception of auditor independence and provides a forum for sensitive control-related issues to be discussed.[73] As part of reinforcing the independence of the audit committee, it is thought that most of its members should be non-executive directors.[74] Increasingly, the audit committee is being viewed as a key part of an organisation's corporate governance structure and Australian companies are required to disclose in their annual reports whether they have an audit committee in place. As an historical reference, certain companies were mandated by the Australian Securities Exchange to establish an audit committee for the financial year commencing after 1 January 2003.[75]

The control objectives mentioned in the Australian Auditing Standard and COSO definitions of internal control, along with the internal control system components just discussed need to be applied across the entire organisation — from the sales department to the accounting department and the manufacturing department. This gives us the three-dimensional framework for internal controls contained in figure 7.4.

Figure 7.4, reproduced from the American auditing standards,[76] shows an organisation's set of objectives in the top panel of the cube. For these objectives to have a reasonable chance of being attained the organisation will establish the components of internal control that are depicted in the front panel of the cube. The operation of these controls will span all three categories of organisational objectives. There is a direct relationship between the organisational objectives and the components required to achieve these objectives.[77] Additionally, as is reflected by the right-hand panel of the cube, the objectives and control components will span all functions or units of the organisation.

The COSO framework for internal control, introduced previously, provides a general framework that has received endorsement from US, with the Securities and Exchange Commission (SEC) requiring the use of an internal control framework that has been extensively developed and publicly distributed. In making this mandate, the SEC mentioned the COSO framework as one such example.[78]

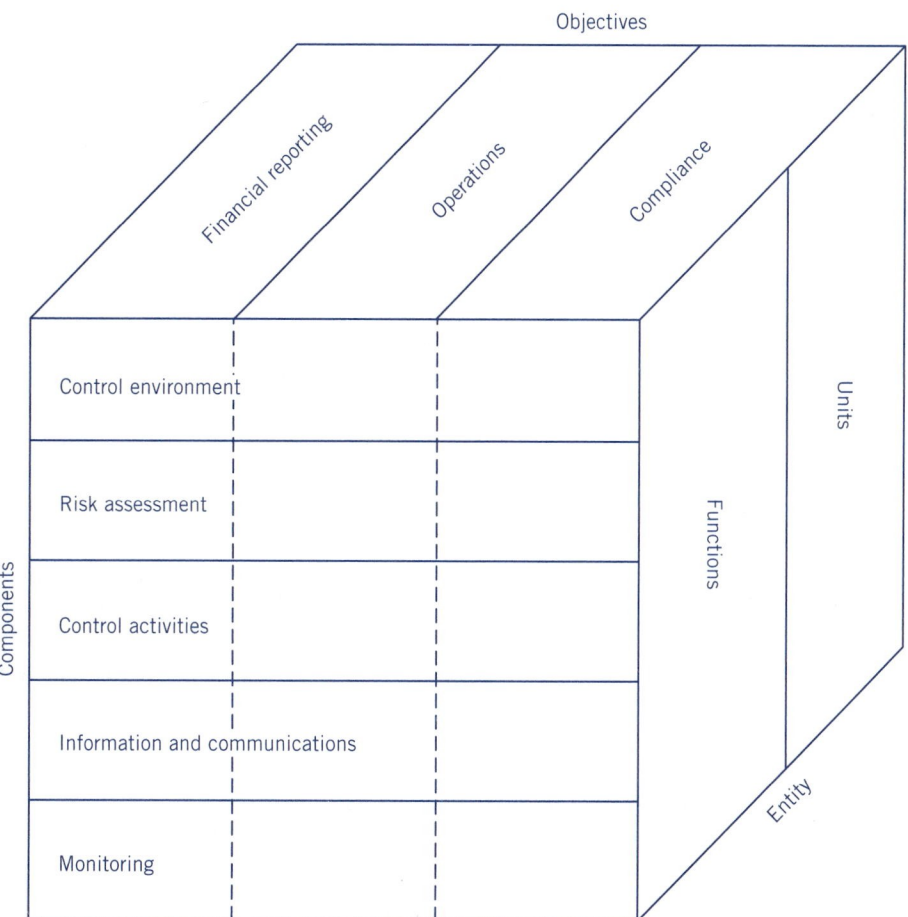

**FIGURE 7.4** The relationship between control objectives and control components

**LEARNING OBJECTIVE**

*Link financial reporting risks to financial statement assertions.*

# IDENTIFYING RISKS

A useful technique to identify risks is to look at the organisation's financial statements. Cast your eyes over the different items that appear in the reports and ask yourself this question: what could go wrong that could affect this item? This question could be answered by considering what could go wrong in calculating and presenting the item in the statement of financial position (e.g. What could lead to a misstatement of the inventory or accounts receivable?) or by considering the actual asset or liability (e.g. What could go wrong with the physical inventory items? What risk is our property, plant and equipment exposed to? What threats face our computing facilities?). You could also look at sales item on the income statement or statement of comprehensive income and identify events that could lead to a drop in sales revenue (e.g. loss of market share, increased competition, poor quality products) or being falsely reported (e.g. inaccurate data about sales being entered, false sales being entered). For assets such as inventory, risks would include physical threats (e.g. theft or wastage and spoilage) or fraudulent recording.

## Linking risks to financial statement assertions

The process of risk assessment requires a good understanding of the business, its operations, its business processes and the environment in which it operates. A set of financial statements represent, as the name suggests, statements of financial facts for the organisation at balance date. In other words they assert that these facts were the case at balance date. As such, the financial statements contain a set of assertions, made by the preparer, about what has happened during the reporting period and the financial position of the organisation at the end of the reporting period. An assertion is a statement or declaration made by someone. In the case of preparing financial statements, managers are asserting that the transactions in the statement of comprehensive income (or income statement) occurred and that the statement of financial position represents the organisation's actual financial position. As an example, preparing the statement of comprehensive income and including the total sales revenue figure is an assertion by management that the sales actually occurred, and have been reported accurately, correctly classified and allocated to the correct accounting period. The organisation will have policies and procedures in place in order to work towards these assertions being satisfied (discussed in the next section). The risks that sales may be false, may relate to a different accounting period or may have been inaccurately reported are the type of financial reporting risks that internal controls aim to address. If we were to consider the risks of what could go wrong in the financial statements that could lead to them being materially misstated, we may come up with the list in table 7.1, depending on whether we are looking at the different transactions or events that the organisation engages in or the presentation of the material in the financial statements.

**TABLE 7.1** Financial reporting risks

**TRANSACTIONS — different transactions and events are impacted by:**

| Assertion | Explanation | Risk | Example of risk | Control focus |
|---|---|---|---|---|
| Occurrence | All transactions included in the financial statements have occurred. | Transactions may be entered that have not occurred. | Sales entered that have not occurred. | Processes to verify that transactions have taken place before being recorded. |
| Completeness | All transactions and events that should have been recorded have been recorded. | Transactions may have been omitted (not included in the statements). | Sales occurring but not recorded. | Process to check for missing transactions or events |
| Accuracy | Data relating to transactions and events have been correctly recorded. | Data entry errors may misrepresent the effect of the event and materially misstate the financial statements. | Entering data incorrectly; (e.g. wrong dollar amount, wrong quantity). | Processes in place to check data as it enters the accounting system. |
| Cut-off | All transactions and events have been reported in the correct reporting period. | Transactions may have been recorded in the wrong period. | Sales from next period pushed into this period; current period expenses pushed into the next period. | Processes in place to provide reasonable assurance that transactions have been correctly included in the current reporting period. |

| Classification | All transactions and events have been recorded in the correct accounts. | Misclassified items could materially distort the financial statements. | An expense that is classified as an asset improvement would overstate assets and understate expenses. | Processes to monitor the classification of transaction and events and provide reasonable assurance as to the correct application of AASB classification requirements. |
|---|---|---|---|---|

**ACCOUNT BALANCES — all account balances should demonstrate:**

| | | | | |
|---|---|---|---|---|
| Existence | The assets, liabilities and owners' equity reported on the statement of financial position actually exist. | Inclusion of assets that do not exist in order to improve the appearance of the statement of financial position. | An asset that does not exist is recorded to improve the overall financial position of the entity (e.g. non-existent accounts receivables). | Processes in place to confirm asset existence before including them in the accounting information system. |
| Rights and obligations | The assets are controlled by the business and the liabilities are the obligations of the entity. | Including assets or liabilities in the statement of financial position even if the rights and obligations do not attach to the organisation. | Asset items may be included that the organisation does not have control over (e.g. goods on consignment) which would lead to assets being erroneously included in the financial statements. | Processes in place to ensure that the rights and obligations attached to assets and liabilities exist and relate to the organisation before they are incorporated into the accounting information system. |
| Completeness | All asset, liability and owners' equity items that relate to the entity and should have been recorded actually have been recorded. | Not all assets, liabilities and equity items have been included in the financial statements. | Liabilities may be omitted from the statement of financial position in order to improve the apparent financial position of the entity. | Processes in place to identify potential completeness issues. |
| Valuation and allocation | Assets, liabilities and owners' equity are correctly valued. | Incorrect valuation and allocation procedures have been applied to the assets, liabilities and equity items. | Some items may not be valued correctly (e.g. inventory may not have been valued at lower of cost or NRV). Alternatively, items may not have been allocated correctly (e.g. revaluation of amounts). | Processes in place to provide reasonable assurance that the correct valuation and allocation procedures have been applied. |

Table 7.1 takes what are known as the audit assertions[79] — the statements that are represented by management when financial statements are prepared — and explains what they mean and the risks for each assertion not being met in the financial reporting process. You will encounter these when you study auditing and assurance services in your later studies, but their inclusion here is to highlight to you, from a financial reporting perspective, what the financial statements purport (i.e. the assertions), the risks of these assertions not being met and the role of internal controls in addressing these risks.

The risks of an assertion not being satisfied should be identified by the organisation and be addressed by control activities (discussed in the next section and in more detail in chapter 8). This is one way of thinking about the risks within the accounting information system. For example, if we look at the first assertion — occurrence — we can consider the risk that transactions and events could have been recorded but have not actually taken place (i.e. the risk of fake transactions being recorded). This has an obvious impact on our financial reports and their reliability and accuracy.

Of course, one thing to keep in mind is that not all of a business's risks will relate to the financial statements. Table 7.1 focuses on the risks from a financial reporting perspective, with the financial statements being the major output of the accounting information system. However, risks extend beyond the financial statements and encompass the entire organisation. Risks can result from a range of factors, including the nature of the business and the industry it operates in (e.g. refer to the earlier example of fuel prices for Qantas).

From the assertions listed in table 7.1, we can appreciate that, as a general rule, the potential threats to consider when analysing the items in the financial statements are:
- the potential for an asset, liability or owners' equity item to be recorded when it does not exist or not recorded when it does exist (*existence*)
- the potential for a revenue or an expense item to be recorded when it has not occurred or not to be recorded when it has occurred (*occurrence*)
- the potential for assets, liabilities, owners' equity, revenues and expenses to be recorded at the wrong amount (*valuation/measurement*)
- the potential for some transactions to be only partly recorded or to be omitted (*completeness*).

Other risks to consider could include:
- the risk of network disruption and how that impacts on the business's ability to operate in an e-commerce environment
- the risk of key suppliers or customers shifting to other organisations
- the risk of organisational data being damaged/destroyed
- the risk of the organisation facing changes in the external environment that impact on its operations (e.g. changes in legislation or the regulatory environment)
- the risk of loss of market share due to faulty or low-quality good being produced
- the risk of new competitors taking market position
- the risk of unauthorised access to IT facilities or online systems.

For example, an organisation may have in place a strategy of being a low-cost producer, allowing it to attract a particular customer group. In order to achieve this strategy it has established an alliance with a particular overseas supplier who has agreed to provide inputs at a low price. If this arrangement was to be impacted, for example, by a change in import regulations or import taxes, the organisation's ability to produce cheaply and, consequently, achieve its strategic objectives, could be jeopardised. Thus, when considering risks, it is important to think in terms of what could go wrong throughout the organisation should such impacts eventuate. While, as accountants looking at the accounting information system our emphasis will be on the accounting aspects as evidenced by our examination of the assertions, internal controls cover the entire organisation and relate to financial as well as non-financial risks that the organisation faces. As noted in ASA 315, 'business risk is broader than the risk of material misstatement ... most business risks will eventually have financial consequences and, therefore, an effect on the financial report. However ... not all business risks give rise to the risks of material misstatement.'[80]

Two points to take from the auditing position on risk are, firstly, that the auditing standards focus on risk from a financial perspective (i.e. the risks that could lead to material misstatement) and, secondly, that the concept of risk is broader than this, and can include risks that come from, for example, poor quality control, compliance with regulatory requirements, or inefficient or ineffective operations. An example of a risk that does not impact the financial statements could be the impact of increased environmental awareness resulting in pressure from environmental lobby groups. While the risks that such groups may present will not necessarily impact on the financial statements, other impacts (e.g. increased threats to the business's position in society or the rise of increased regulation and loss of political control) will be considered as part of risk assessment.

**LEARNING OBJECTIVE**  *Relate internal control to the COBIT and COSO frameworks.*

## COSO AND COBIT

COBIT is a specific framework that has been developed for the control of information technology within the organisation. As was previously mentioned, COBIT spans the lifecycle of IT and offers control objectives and guidance that relate to the stages of planning for IT acquisition, acquiring IT resources, operating IT resources, and monitoring and assessing IT resources within the organisation. At each of these stages, control issues need to be considered by the organisation. The control issues that are present at each stage can be mapped against the Committee of Sponsoring Organisations (COSO) Treadway Committee Report framework. This is shown below in table 7.2 overleaf.[81] The stages that IT goes through within the organisation, based on the COBIT model, run across the table, while the COSO elements of internal control run down the table. The intersecting cells provide examples of the links between the two frameworks, that is, what can be done at each stage, from an IT perspective, to address the five stages of the COSO model.

This is a brief example of the IT-related issues and how these issues, which are part of the COBIT framework, are able to fit within, and support, COSO. The specific details of some of the cell entries in the table will be addressed in the next chapter. For the moment, you should appreciate that COSO provides an internal control system framework and that the need for controls can be mapped against the lifecycle of IT within the organisation. The message from this would seem to be that IT is an important part of the organisation and its ability to achieve its objectives and as a result it will be subject to control policies and procedures that aim to align the IT with the needs of the organisation. These policies and procedures for IT and controls will originate from the top level management of the organisation; that is, those vested with the responsibility for corporate governance. This is the common thread that links corporate governance, IT governance and internal control systems.

COBIT[82] is a widely applied framework for internal control that is often used by organisations as an addition to the COSO framework and a source of IT specific control objectives.[83] Released by the IT Governance Institute, it provides a structure within which an organisation can assess its controls and identify the need for controls at the various stages of the IT lifecycle, which were discussed in the previous section on IT governance. The framework breaks controls up based on the stages of IT within the organisation and the stages followed within a business process. This latter aspect is covered in the next chapter.

**TABLE 7.2** COSO and COBIT

| COBIT | Planning | Acquiring | Delivering | Monitoring |
|---|---|---|---|---|
| **COSO**<br>**Control environment** | Understand the relationships between IT, the organisation, business processes and strategy. Having procedures for the recruitment and keeping of qualified IT staff | Acquisition of IT that is consistent with organisational aims. Training or informing users about new acquisitions. Use of a structured software development lifecycle methodology. | Provide training opportunities to users about system operations and usage. | Define and communicate IT governance principles. Manage internal controls. |
| **Risk assessment** | Evaluate the risks associated with current and future use of IT. | Evaluate potential vendors against a pre-defined criteria (e.g. reputation, reliability). Make or buy decision. | Where outsourcing occurs, establish procedure to monitor the outsource provider. | Identify potential control breaches. Evaluation of IT controls. Loss of staff — monitor for a dependence on particular staff members and ensure their knowledge is documented/captured. |
| **Control activities** | Budget for future and current IT costs and the overall organisational IT investment. Assessment of current position relative to strategy. | Timeline and project management strategies for the acquisition and implementation of IT. Specifying user privileges and rights in new technology. Test new IT prior to full implementation or integration. | Manage security for IT resources, including access, user rights, data security. Backup or disaster recovery procedures. | Tracking of control breaches. Following up on control breaches. |
| **Information and communication** | Compile a report on the aims or objectives of management to the rest of the organisation and alternative IT strategies. | Solicit user input into requirements and design preferences. System documentation prepared and reviewed. | Record and monitor error-events (e.g. invalid logins, firewall breaches). User complaints or feedback. | Management reporting to board on IT performance, usage, compliance, progress. |
| **Monitoring** | Manage projects and have clearly defined approaches for identifying and evaluating IT in the organisation. | Progress and timeliness — set deliverables, feedback reports, accountability. Review implementation process. | System performance measures available (e.g. downtime, transactions processed, errors recorded, complaints). | Balanced scorecard performance measures. Monitor IT staff performance and identify needs for new staff. |

**LEARNING OBJECTIVE 9**

*Explain the enterprise risk model (ERM) and its components, and compare it with COSO.*

# ERM — EXPANDING COSO

The COSO framework that we looked at in the preceding discussion was updated in 2004 by a framework that is referred to as an **enterprise risk model (ERM)**, with the benefit being that it 'expands on internal control, providing a more robust and extensive focus on the broader subject of enterprise risk management'.[84] Enterprise risk management, similarly to internal controls as discussed previously, starts from those vested with governance responsibilities and calls on them to identify the events that could impact on the organisation to manage the risks attached to these events and to provide overall reasonable assurance of the attainment of organisational objectives.[85]

Under the ERM, the objectives of the organisation are:

- strategic — the high-level, overarching goals that the organisation has in place
- operations — resource effectiveness and efficiency
- reporting — reliable financial reporting
- compliance — meeting the relevant laws and regulations.

The model highlights the different nature of the objectives within the organisation, as well as the different nature of the risks that an organisation may face. For example, the risks that could impact on strategic goals would be different to the risks that could lead to financial reporting that is not reliable. The risks of not meeting strategic and operational objectives can come from the people and policies within the organisation, as well as from events beyond the organisation's control, for example, legislative, environmental and customer demand changes.[86]

Remember that under the COSO framework, the internal control structure has five components. The ERM expands these to eight:

1. Internal environment — similar to the control environment, emphasises the way the organisation determines its preferred level of risk.
2. Objective setting — putting in place goals or objectives for the organisation that are consistent with the initial risk preferences of the organisation.
3. Event identification — the events that occur both within and outside the organisation that could impact on the ability of the organisation's ability to achieve its specified objectives.
4. Risk assessment — for the risks, their likelihood, magnitude and impact. These assessments will inform decisions about how the risk should be handled.
5. Risk response — based on the assessment, determines an appropriate response to the risk. Options include avoiding the risk (i.e. do not carry out the risky event or activity), accepting the risk (do nothing about the risk), reducing the risk (reduce the chance of the negative event occurring — e.g. to reduce the risk of bad debts review all credit limits and conduct customer credit checks — or sharing the risk by underwriting or taking out insurance, for example.
6. Control activities — the policies and procedures implemented within the organisation to carry out the risk responses. As an example, if the event of sales on credit was identified as producing the risk of bad debts, the organisation could respond by reducing the risk through background credit checks on customers. The conduct of the credit check is the control activity carried out in response to the event identification and risk assessment and response.
7. Information and communication — is the same as under COSO.
8. Monitoring — is the same as under COSO.

It should be evident that there is considerable overlap between the ERM perspective and that of COSO, with the five internal control components under COSO fully integrated into the ERM perspective. The ERM documentation emphasises this integration of COSO into ERM, with the extension being the breaking out of the control environment and risk assessment of COSO into finer elements that emphasise the link between organisational strategy, risk preferences and risk management. As in COSO, where there is a relationship between the organisational objectives and the control system components, so too will there be a relationship between the objectives and the ERM components. The cubic relationship in COSO, shown in figure 7.4, is the same for the ERM model, with the only difference being four objectives in ERM versus three in COSO and eight components in ERM compared to five in COSO. The underlying message, however, is the same: there needs to be a relationship between the organisational goals and the identification and management of the risks that could impede the attainment of these goals.

## AIS FOCUS 7.4

### Corporate governance, financial reporting ... what else?

The corporate governance and internal control frameworks discussed in this chapter relate predominantly to regulatory requirements imposed on organisations. For example, the Corporations Act mandates reporting requirements for companies and the Australian Securities Exchange publishes corporate governance polices to which listed companies adhere. Following these requirements is a matter of conformance — making sure organisations meet regulatory requirements to which they are subject. Compliance with financial reporting requirements, for example, is monitored through regular financial statement audits and the supervisory role of ASIC.

However, mere compliance is not sufficient for organisations, with the notion of corporate social responsibility (CSR) gaining prominence. CSR is a broader perspective than that of simply following legislative requirements, and includes the concept of 'business practices based on ethical values, with respect for people, communities, and the environment'.[87] This broader emphasis brings into play the relationships the organisation has with its many stakeholders — customers, suppliers, employees and the community in which it operates.

Recognising the broad range of stakeholders an organisation interacts with means that a wider range of potential risks need to be considered. The obligations of the organisation are not limited just to shareholders through financial reporting. Under CSR principles, the obligations are extended. While the CSR perspective looks at economic performance, it also addresses how the organisation benefits employees, the community in which it operates and broader society.

A particular area where CSR has gained prominence is the interaction between organisations and the environment, with environmental lobby groups and the increased political awareness of environmental issues leading to consideration of the sustainability of operations into the mid- to long-term, rather than just emphasis on the current period's profit. Mining companies are just one example of organisations that have faced such pressures, with increasing focus on their impact on the communities in which they operate, especially in instances where they operate in under-developed countries that may not have the resources or structures in place to effectively monitor the organisation. With this trend has come scrutiny from corporate watchdogs that have the potential to generate negative publicity for organisations who do not act in what is deemed to be a socially responsible manner.[88]

As a result, organisations are increasingly putting in place policies to deal with this broader array of risks. An example is Rio Tinto, who on its website has extensive disclosures on how it acts to respect the human rights of those in the communities where it operates, as well as the identification of its various stakeholders and the strategies in place for managing these relationships.[89] This makes the concept of risk far wider than the consideration of financial consequences, shifting the focus beyond financial statements when assessing organisational operations.

›› SUMMARY ›››

LEARNING OBJECTIVE  **What is corporate governance and how has it evolved?**
Corporate governance is the way a company is managed to create value, enforce account-ability, and control and manage risks. Corporate governance principles influence the design and operation of the organisation. An internal control system will be established as part of corporate governance responsibilities

Corporate governance has long been a concern worldwide. In recent years, as we have witnessed some major corporate collapses, attention has increasingly been placed on how organisations are being managed. The OECD has released guidelines on corporate governance, arguing for its importance to the capitalist markets. In Australia, corporate governance has been addressed by the ASX, through the release of the ASX corporate gover-nance guidelines.

LEARNING OBJECTIVE  **What constitutes corporate governance?**
Corporate governance has been addressed by many organisations over time. In Australia, the ASX has issued a document containing principles of corporate governance that apply to Australian companies, and include such concepts as assessing and monitoring risk, remunerating responsibly, providing an ethical environment and promoting independence of the board of directors.

LEARNING OBJECTIVE  **What is IT governance and what are its role and objectives?**
IT governance is concerned with the way the organisation uses IT. It takes a lifecycle perspective for IT, considering the issues from initial ideas about a system through to its implementation and operation, and aims to ensure that IT resources are aligned with organ-isational goals and used effectively within the organisation. IT governance is a process of accountability for the way that IT is adopted and applied in the organisation. It aims to ensure a consistency between the organisation's aims and objectives and the way in which IT is applied within the organisation.

LEARNING OBJECTIVE  **What is an IT governance framework?**
There are various IT governance frameworks available. COBIT 4.1, one commonly referenced framework, identifies control issues across the four stages of the technology lifecycle. In Australia, there is also an IT governance standard, which addresses the process of man-aging IT within the organisation.

LEARNING OBJECTIVE  **What is internal control?**
Internal control is concerned with the measures an organisation employs to help attain the objectives of efficient operations, reliable reporting and compliance with relevant laws.

**LEARNING OBJECTIVE**

*What are the components of an internal control system?*
The five control components are the control environment, risk assessment, control activities, information and communication, and monitoring.

**LEARNING OBJECTIVE**

*What is the link between financial reporting risks and financial statement assertions?*
Financial reporting risks are those risks that present themselves as part of the financial reporting process and that could lead to the financial statements being materially misstated. A financial statement assertion is a declaration about what the financial statements represent. Potentially, financial reporting risks can lead to assertions not being valid. Internal controls are put in place to reduce the risk of financial reporting errors and provide reasonable assurance that the assertions are met.

**LEARNING OBJECTIVE**

*How does internal control relate to the COBIT and COSO frameworks?*
COBIT is a specific framework that has been developed for the control of information technology within the organisation. COBIT spans the lifecycle of IT and offers control objectives and guidance that relate to the stages of planning for IT acquisition, acquiring IT resources, operating IT resources, and monitoring and assessing IT resources within the organisation. At each of these stages, control issues need to be considered by the organisation. The control issues that are present at each stage can be mapped against the COSO framework. COSO provides an internal control system framework and that the need for controls can be mapped against the lifecycle of IT within the organisation.

**LEARNING OBJECTIVE**

*What is the ERM model and how does it compare with COSO?*
The ERM model takes the COSO internal control model and expands it to include four business objectives and eight components. The objectives in ERM highlight the top-down nature of organisational objectives, from strategy to the lower levels of the organisation, while the eight components draw out the different nature of the risks that an organisation confronts and strategies for dealing with these risks. COSO is explicitly integrated into the ERM model: the five components of the COSO internal control system appear as part of ERM model. Where the COSO model had three objectives for the organisation, the ERM model has four. Both models highlight the need for the organisation to evaluate the risks that could impinge on the organisation's ability to attain its objectives, with the ERM approach taking a broader enterprise wide perspective in doing so.

## KEY TERMS

| | |
|---|---|
| control activities, p. 307 | internal control, p. 302 |
| control environment, p. 305 | monitoring, p. 308 |
| corporate governance, p. 287 | risk assessment, p. 306 |
| enterprise risk model (ERM), p. 317 | |

## DISCUSSION QUESTIONS

7.1 What is the relationship between corporate governance and internal control systems? (LO1, LO5, LO6)

7.2 What is IT governance? (LO3)

7.3 List some examples of how IT governance relates across the lifecycle of IT within the organisation. (LO3)

7.4 The article in figure 7.5 appeared in *The Age*. Read the article and answer the following questions. (LO5, LO6, LO7)

(a) What risks are faced by consumers and credit card vendors in an e-commerce environment?

(b) How does this example relate to the components of the COSO internal control system, particularly risk assessment and monitoring?

**Goods for a song — paid for by others**

A website is selling what it describes as the cheapest electronics goods — and telling would-be customers clearly that the reason the goods are so cheap is because they are bought with other people's credit cards.

Cheapest Eletronix has, as its main draw right now, the newest Toshiba plasma, HDTV, Flat Panel, 50″ which it is selling for only $US1890. The website says the model costs $US11999 at any other reseller.

The reason is not far — the site has a link titled 'Why so cheap?' which leads to a page that says, in part:

'Basically all the products are ordered on the internet, on e-commerce websites, by credit card (somebody else's credit card). That means we pay nothing for them, neither us nor the credit card holders. So, who pays the bills? The bilionaries [*sic*] credit card companies like Visa, Mastercard, American Express, because the credit card holders can easily proove [*sic*] they didn't buy those items.'

Reader Andrew Tune of Network Box, a virus and spam protection company in Melbourne, who spotted the site, said the perpetrators could be making money in one of two ways — either by actually sending the goods to the people who ordered them or merely taking the money and not bothering to send the goods.

The domain cheapesteletronix.com is registered to one Darick Stuff. He did not respond to an email query asking where the company was located and where the credit cards were obtained.

Tune has in the past brought banking scams to public notice.[90]

**FIGURE 7.5** Goods for a song

7.5 Explain the relationships presented in the Standards Australia IT governance standard. (LO3, LO4)

7.6 Describe the relationship between the risk assessment and control activities components of the COSO framework. (LO5, LO6)

7.7 Compare the structure of the COSO and ERM frameworks. (LO9)

7.8 Summarise each component of the COSO internal control system. (LO5, LO6)

7.9 Explain why it is necessary for organisations to monitor and review their internal control system. (LO5, LO6)

7.10 Summarise the principles of corporate governance set forward by the ASX. (LO1, LO2)

7.11 List and briefly describe three examples of financial statement risks that could come from within the organisation. (LO7)

## SELF-TEST ACTIVITIES

7.1 Corporate governance is:

(a) an internal control tool.

(b) a factor influencing internal control.

(c) a substitute for internal control.

(d) part of the control environment.

7.2 An internal control system includes the control environment component. This is best described as:
(a) the overall attitude of awareness and actions of management to internal control.
(b) the environment in which the business operates that it wishes to control to negate any business risks.
(c) management's response to the risks that an organisation faces.
(d) the provision of sufficient information to enable employees to effectively operate in their roles.
(e) the monitoring of performance to ensure that the organisation's control system is still relevant and up to date.

7.3 IT governance is concerned with:
(a) ensuring that the correct IT investment is always made.
(b) controlling the use of IT within the organisation.
(c) mandating selection procedures for new IT investments.
(d) policies and procedures helping to align the use of IT and strategy.

7.4 In which component of the internal control system would you see a concern with hiring and recruitment policies?
(a) Control environment
(b) Risk assessment
(c) Control activities
(d) Information and communication
(e) Monitoring

7.5 In which component of the internal control system would you see a concern with reviewing the existing control system operation?
(a) Control environment
(b) Risk assessment
(c) Control activities
(d) Information and communication
(e) Monitoring

7.6 Which financial statement assertion is threatened when the organisation has recorded sales that didn't take place?
(a) Occurrence
(b) Completeness
(c) Accuracy
(d) Classification

7.7 The assertion of cut-off would be at risk when:
(a) the accounting information system accepts a value that is incorrect (e.g. 122 instead of 22).
(b) the accounting information system accepts a fictitious sale.
(c) the accounting information system includes a sale for the next financial year in this year's revenue figure.
(d) a revenue item is classified as an expense when entering the transaction.

7.8 Which of the following components is part of the ERM and not part of the COSO framework?
(a) Event identification
(b) Information and communication
(c) Monitoring
(d) Control activities

7.9 Which of the following statements regarding risks for a business is false?
   (a) Risks can come from both internal and external factors.
   (b) Risks faced by an organisation will always have consequences for the financial statements.
   (c) Management needs to be aware of and evaluate the risks that the organisation faces.
   (d) The risks identified will have varying probabilities of eventuating.

## PROBLEMS

7.1 While out at a consulting engagement, one of your graduate staff members comes to you with the following question, 'I'm confused. Since I first studied AIS at uni, I have never really understood this concept of control ... I mean what is the relationship among the control environment, organisational objectives and the internal control system?'

Prepare a one-page answer in response to the graduate's concerns. You should include a description of what an internal control is, the relationship between internal control components, organisational objectives and the different divisions of the organisation, and a description of the control environment, general controls and application controls and how they relate to one another.

7.2 Conduct a web search for some examples of internal controls that have failed to operate effectively. For the cases you have identified, answer the following questions:
   (a) What factors led to the failure of these controls?
   (b) Could the failure have been avoided? If so, how?

7.3 Describe the circumstances that led to a heightened focus on corporate governance in Australia and the United Kingdom.

7.4 Explain the relationship between corporate governance and accounting information systems.

7.5 Describe the purpose of IT governance.

7.6 Read the article from the *Sunday Telegraph* (figure 7.1, pages 293–4) and answer the following questions:
   (a) What corporate governance issues does the article address?
   (b) Which of the ASX's eight corporate governance principles are relevant to the discussion in the article? Explain why you have chosen the principles.
   (c) What role do Australian Auditing Standards play in corporate governance?
   (d) Given the attention on executive salaries, the article discusses the concept of a 'salary cap' for senior management. What are the arguments for and against this idea?

7.7 The IT Governance Institute mentions five areas that need to be addressed by IT governance.[91] List each of these areas and provide examples of some of the factors that would be considered for each area.

7.8 Describe the role and purpose of COBIT 4.1.

7.9 Explain the relationship between COBIT 4.1 and COSO.

7.10 Summarise the impacts of the Sarbanes–Oxley Act on internal control obligations for companies.

7.11 For each of the following companies, find the latest annual report on the company's website and summarise the corporate governance policy for risk assessment and integrity in financial reporting.
   (a) Qantas (www.qantas.com.au).
   (b) Woolworths (www.woolworthslimited.com.au).

## FURTHER READING

Beavers, JT 2003, 'Are boards control-literate?', *Internal Auditor*, vol. 60, no. 5, p. 85.

Committee of Sponsoring Organisations of the Treadway Commission 2004. *Enterprise risk management integrated framework — executive summary*, www.coso.org/documents/COSO_ERM_ExecutiveSummary.pdf.

Institute of Criminology, Conference paper presented at *Corporate Fraud Strategy: Assessing the Emergence of Identity Fraud*, Sydney 25–26 July 2002, 'Speeches and papers by AIC staff', www.aic.gov.au.

IT Governance Institute 2007, *COBIT 4.1*, www.itgi.org.

Richtel, M 2002, 'Credit companies are growing wary of online betting', *The New York Times*, 21 January, p. C1.

Smith, RG 2002, 'Examining the legislative and regulatory controls of identity fraud in Australia', *Marcus Evans Conference, Corporate fraud strategy: assessing the emergence of identity fraud*, Sydney, 25 July.

Standards Australia 2005, AS 8015–2005 *Corporate governance of information and communication technology*, www.standards.org.au.

## SELF-TEST ANSWERS

7.1 b, 7.2 a, 7.3 d, 7.4 a, 7.5 e, 7.6 a, 7.7 c, 7.8 a, 7.9 b

## END NOTES

1. Organisation for Economic Co-operation and Development 2004, *OECD principles of corporate governance*, Paris, p. 11.
2. ASX Corporate Governance Council 2007, *Corporate governance principles and recommendations,* 2nd edition, Australian Securities Exchange Limited, Sydney.
3. Bushman, RM & Smith, AJ 2003, 'Transparency, financial accounting information and corporate governance', *Federal Reserve Bank of New York Economic Policy Review,* April, pp. 65–87.
4. ASX Corporate Governance Council 2007, p. 3.
5. Howard, J 2002, *Address to the Securities Institute and Institute of Chartered Accountants of Australia Luncheon*, 6 August, www.australianpolitics.com/news.
6. The Committee on the Financial Aspects of Corporate Governance and Gee and Co. Ltd 1992, 2.1–2.2, www.ecgi.org.
7. The Committee on the Financial Aspects of Corporate Governance and Gee and Co. Ltd 1992.
8. Financial Reporting Council 2005, *Internal control — revised guidance for directors on the combined code*, October, p. 3, www.frc.org.uk.
9. Beavers, JT 2003, 'Are boards control-literate?', *Internal Auditor*, vol. 60, no. 5, p. 84.
10. Kirkpatrick, G 2009 'The corporate governance lessons from the financial crisis', *Financial Market Trends,* vol. 2009, no. 1, pp. 1–30.
11. Gluyas, R 2006, 'Accountants criticised', *The Australian*, 20 October.
12. Paletta, D 2009, 'Timothy Geithner calls for tougher standards on risk', *The Australian*, www.theaustralian.news.com.au, 27 March.
13. Deloitte & Touche LLP 2003a, *Moving forward — a guide to improving corporate governance through effective internal control: a response to Sarbanes–Oxley*, January, Deloitte & Touche USA, p. 6.
14. Deloitte & Touche LLP 2003a, p. 3.
15. *Perth Now* 2009, 'Two thirds of banks losses yet to be declared: IMF', 22 April, www.perthnow.com.au.
16. AAP 2008, 'ABC Learning in receivership', 6 November, www.news.ninemsn.com.au.
17. Kruger, C 2009, 'Mission Australia to buy ABC Centres', *Brisbane Times*, 9 December, www.brisbanetimes.com.au.

18. CPA Australia 2010, ABC *Learning case study*, www.cpaaustralia.com.au; Walsh, L 2010, 'Groves set to explain ABC collapse to court', *The Courier-Mail*, 15 February, www.news.com.au; Walsh, L 2009, 'Lawyers piece together puzzle of Groves' chosen creditors', *The Courier-Mail*, 13 December, www.news.com.au.

19. Kruger, C 2009.

20. ASX Corporate Governance Council 2003, *Principles of good corporate governance and best practice recommendations*, March, Australian Stock Exchange Limited, Sydney, p. 3.

21. ASX Corporate Governance Council 2003, pp. 11–61.

22. ASX Corporate Governance Council 2007, pp. 13–37.

23. ASX Corporate Governance Council 2007, p. 16.

24. ASX Corporate Governance Council 2007, p. 25.

25. Associated Press 2008, 'All SEC financial data to be interactive', *The Age*, 20 August, www.theage.com.au.

26. ASX Corporate Governance Council 2007, p. 33.

27. Dickins, J 2006, 'Executive excess: how calls to stop ever-increasing corporate salaries are falling on deaf ears', *The Sunday Telegraph*, 1 October, pp. 44–5.

28. Davis, M 2009, 'Cap salaries of chief executives: unions', 1 June, *The Sydney Morning Herald*, www.smh.com.au.

29. Lainhart, JW 2000, 'Why IT governance is a top management issue', *The Journal of Corporate Accounting & Finance*, vol. 11, no. 5, pp. 33–40.

30. Brown, AE & Grant, GG 2005, 'Framing the frameworks: a review of IT governance research', *Communications of the Association for Information Systems,* vol. 15(2005), pp. 696–712.

31. Gosling, R 2006, 'Corporate governance: the ties that bind — how IT knits together corporate necessities', *New Zealand Management*, May, p. 70; Musson, D & Jordan, E 2005, 'The broken link: corporate governance and information technology', *Australian Accounting Review*, vol. 15, no. 3, pp. 11–19; Lainhart 2000.

32. IT Governance Institute 2003, *Board briefing on IT governance*, 2nd edn, IT Governance Institute, Illinois, p. 11.

33. IT Governance Institute 2003, pp. 20–31.

34. IT Governance Institute 2007, *COBIT 4.1*, www.itgi.org; IT Governance Institute 2003.

35. Schrage, M 2006, 'Visibility for the Board', *CIO*, vol. 19, no. 1, p. 1.

36. Brown, AE & Grant, GG 2005.

37. Weill, P & Woodham, R 2002, 'Don't just lead, govern: implementing effective IT governance', *MIT Sloan Working Paper No. 4237-02,* April, www.ssrn.com.

38. IT Governance Institute 2007; Lainhart 2000.

39. IT Governance Institute 2007.

40. Ridley, GJ. Young, J, Carroll, P 2008, 'Studies to evaluate COBIT's contribution to organisations: opportunities from the literature, 2003–06', *Australian Accounting Review,* vol. 18, no. 4, pp. 334–42.

41. Ridley, GJ, Young, J, Carroll, P 2008.

42. Weill, P & Woodham, R 2002.

43. International Federation of Accountants 2002, *International technology guideline 6: IT monitoring*, International Federation of Accountants, New York, p. 1.

44. IT Governance Institute 2007.

45. Musson & Jordan 2005.

46. Damianades, M 2004, 'How does SOX change IT?', *The Journal of Corporate Accounting & Finance*, vol. 15, no. 6, pp. 35–41.

47. Musson & Jordan 2005.

48. IT Governance Institute 2006, *IT control objectives for Sarbanes–Oxley: the role of IT in the design and implementation of internal control over financial reporting*, 2nd edn, IT Governance Institute, Illinois.

49. Standards Australia 2005a, *AS 8015–2005: Corporate governance of information and communication technology*, www.standards.org.au.

50. Standards Australia 2005a.
51. Standards Australia 2008, 'Australia to lead international working group on corporate governance of IT', 20 November; Standards Australia 2005b, 'Australian world-first ICT governance standard' 3 March; Standards Australia 2005a.
52. Root, SJ 1998, *Beyond COSO: internal control to enhance corporate governance*, John Wiley & Sons, Inc., New York.
53. The Committee of Sponsoring Organizations of the Treadway Commissions (COSO) 'COSO definition of internal control', www.coso.org/key.htm.
54. Auditing and Assurance Standards Board 2009a, Auditing Standard ASA 315 *Identifying and Assessing the Risks of Material Misstatement through Understanding the Entity and Its Environment*, paragraph 4, www.auasb.gov.au.
55. Auditing and Assurance Standards Board 2009a, paragraph 4.
56. Australian Accounting Standards Board 2007, *Framework for the preparation and presentation of financial statements*, paragraphs 24–46, www.aasb.gov.au.
57. Australian Accounting Standards Board 2009, AASB 101 *Presentation of financial statements*, www.aasb.gov.au.
58. Auditing and Assurance Standards Board 2009a, paragraph A69.
59. Hubbard, LD 2003, 'Understanding internal controls', *Internal Auditor*, vol. 60, no. 5, pp. 3–25.
60. Auditing and Assurance Standards Board 2009a, Appendix 1, paragraph 3.
61. Rochfort, S, 2008, 'Qantas grounds jets over soaring fuel bill', *The Age*, 13 November, www.theage.com.au.
62. Auditing and Assurance Standards Board 2009a, paragraph A88.
63. Auditing and Assurance Standards Board 2009a; Deloitte & Touche LLP 2003b, *The growing company's guide to COSO*, June, Deloitte & Touche LLP, New York, pp. 6–7.
64. Auditing and Assurance Standards Board, 2009a, Appendix 1, paragraph 5.
65. Auditing and Assurance Standards Board, 2009a, Appendix 1, paragraphs 5–8.
66. Ernst & Young LLP 2002, *Preparing for internal control reporting: a guide for management's assessment under section 404 of the Sarbanes–Oxley Act*, Ernst & Young, New York.
67. Auditing and Assurance Standards Board 2009b, Auditing Standard ASA 610 *Using the Work of Internal Auditors*, www.auasb.gove.au.
68. Auditing and Assurance Standards Board 2009b.
69. The Institute of Chartered Accountants in Australia 2007, 'Understanding financial statement audits — a guide for financial statement users', *Chartered accountants auditing and assurance handbook 2007*, John Wiley & Sons, Brisbane, p. 4.
70. Auditing and Assurance Standards Board 2009c, ASA 265 *Communicating Deficiencies in Internal Control to Those Charged with Governance and Management*, www.auasb.gov.au.
71. Lipton, P & Herzberg, A 1995, *Understanding company law*, 6th edn, LBC Information Services, Sydney, p. 308.
72. Lipton & Herzberg, 1995, p. 309.
73. Gay, G & Simnett R 2000, *Auditing and assurance: services in Australia*, McGraw-Hill, Sydney, pp. 89–90.
74. Lipton & Herzberg, 1995, p. 308.
75. ASX Corporate Governance Council, 2003, p. 7.
76. AICPA 2001, *Statement on auditing standards 94: the effect of information technology on the auditor's consideration of internal control in a financial statement audit*, May, AICPA, New York (AICPA 2001 SAS 94.8), p. 6.
77. AICPA 2001.
78. IT Governance Institute 2006, p. 22.
79. Auditing and Assurance Standards Board 2009c, Auditing Standard ASA 500 *Audit Evidence*, paragraphs 19–23, www.auasb.gov.au.
80. Auditing and Assurance Standards Board 2009a, paragraph A30–A31.

**326** ‹‹‹‹‹ **PART 2** ‹‹‹ SYSTEMS CHARACTERISTICS AND CONSIDERATIONS ‹‹‹

81. Table based on IT Governance Institute 2006, pp. 54–8; see also IT Governance Institute 2007.
82. IT Governance Institute 2005, *COBIT 4.0*, IT Governance Institute, Illinois; IT Governance Institute 2007.
83. IT Governance Institute 2006, p. 55.
84. Committee of Sponsoring Organisations of the Treadway Commission 2004. *Enterprise risk management integrated framework — executive summary*, p. v, www.coso.org/documents/COSO_ERM_ExecutiveSummary.pdf.
85. Committee of Sponsoring Organisations of the Treadway Commission 2004, p. 2.
86. Committee of Sponsoring Organisations of the Treadway Commission 2004.
87. Bhimani, A & Soonawalla, K 2005, 'From conformance to performance: the corporate responsibilities continuum' *Journal of Accounting and Public Policy*, vol. 24 (2005), p. 169.
88. PavelCastka, P, Bamber, CJ, Bamber, DJ & Sharp, JM 2004, 'Integrating corporate social responsibility (CSR) into ISO management systems — in search of a feasible CSR management system framework', *The TQM Magazine*, vol. 16, no. 3, pp. 216–24.
89. Rio Tinto 2009a, 'Engagement', www.riotinto.com; Rio Tinto 2009b, 'Human rights', www.riotinto.com; Kapelus, P 2002, 'Mining, corporate social responsibility and the "community": the case of Rio Tinto, Richards Bay Minerals and the Mbonambi', *Journal of Business Ethics*, vol. 39(2002), pp. 275–96.
90. Varghese, S 2003, 'Goods for a song — paid for by others', *The Age*, 13 November, www.theage.com.au.
91. IT Governance Institute 2003.

# Internal controls II

## Learning objectives

After studying this chapter, you should be able to:

**(1)** relate control activities to the accounting process

**(2)** classify internal controls as general or application, and based on function and business process stage

**(3)** link controls to the stages of data processing and COSO and COBIT

**(4)** describe the aims of a computerised accounting information system

**(5)** define and provide examples of general controls

**(6)** define and provide examples of application controls

**(7)** describe the operation and components of a disaster recovery plan

**(8)** analyse the execution of control activities

**(9)** understand different techniques for documenting a control system

**(10)** evaluate the effectiveness and limitations of a control system.

# Introduction

Recall from chapter 7 the concept of the internal control system fitting within the wider corporate governance framework of the organisation. The internal control system, with its objectives of reliable financial reporting, efficient and effective operations and compliance with laws and regulations, requires the consideration of the control environment, risks, control activities, information and communication, and monitoring. This framework was introduced as the COSO framework.

In this chapter we focus on the control environment and control activities components of the COSO model, introducing some examples of the types of control activities and the various classification schemes that can be applied to internal controls. We also discuss in more detail how controls relate to the operation of business processes and the accounting function. Recall from chapter 2 that business processes are a series of activities interlocked to achieve a specific objective. What emerges from the discussion of business processes and the description of internal control systems is the reality that business processes will not necessarily operate as expected. As a result, businesses need to have in place means of dealing with the risk of errors or irregularities in their processes. This is where control activities play a role, aiming to prevent, detect or correct such errors or irregularities. The material covered in this chapter is oriented towards for-profit organisations, with the examples typically set in this context. However, other organisations, for example, charities and community-based organisations, have an equal need for internal controls, as they also face risks that inhibit the attainment of their objectives. As such, the material we cover in this chapter applies broadly to different types of organisations.

**LEARNING OBJECTIVE 1**

*Relate control activities to the accounting process.*

# CONTROL ACTIVITIES, BUSINESS PROCESSES AND ACCOUNTING

In conceptualising accounting, business processes and internal controls it is useful to think of the financial reporting process and the possibility of errors occurring in that process. While the scope of internal controls extends beyond the domain of the financial reporting process, commencing from the accounting process and branching out will allow you to start from a basis you are familiar with.

Financial statements make a series of assertions about the events that have taken place and the balances that are presented. These assertions were introduced in chapter 7. Applying internal controls involves looking at the assertions and asking a series of questions, these being:

1. What does the assertion require?
2. What are the sources of risk that could lead to the assertion not being met?
3. How prevalent are the risk sources?
4. What measures can be put in place to reduce the probability of the risk materialising?

These questions will sound familiar — representing the risk assessment concept introduced in chapter 7. For example, the assertion of completeness requires that all transactions be recorded, and the assertion of existence requires that all assets reported actually exist. The assertions lead to the identification of the source of risks that could compromise the assertions. For example, completeness is threatened if not all sales transactions are recorded. The other important consideration is that not all risks are financially based. There will be some risks, for example, unauthorised access to computing facilities that, even if they eventuate, will not necessarily directly impact on the financial statements.

Once an organisation has identified a source of risk its next step is to evaluate the extent of the risk. For example, let's assume the simple example of a sales process requiring that a sales order form be filled in, with this form stored until the end of the day. At the end of the day the form is entered into the computer and the sales and accounts receivable balances are updated.

If we now think about the risks involved in this process, or what could go wrong, perhaps surprisingly, given the somewhat simple nature of the process, there are several areas for potential errors. These include:

1. incorrect details being recorded on the sales order form
2. the sales order form being lost/damaged
3. the sales order form data being entered incorrectly, for example, the quantity of 10 being input as 100
4. accounts receivable and sales data being updated incorrectly, for example, the computer posting data to the wrong location or recording transactions twice, or an error in handling the data being encountered
5. the computer system not being available
6. unauthorised people accessing the computer and entering transactions, either incorrectly due to lack of knowledge of the process, or falsely for motives of fraud or personal gain.

From our small business process example we have asked what could go wrong and come up with six potential threats to the recording and processing of the sales order form. Let us now think about how these errors relate to the financial statement assertions. Let's assume that two sales order forms have been filled in correctly but one has been lost and the other was entered incorrectly into the computer. This means that there is one sale that will not be recorded. As a result we immediately have a concern about the sales figure that will be contained in the financial statements since it will not include all sales made. We would also have a concern about the valuation of accounts receivable and inventory, since accounts receivable would be understated (a credit sale has not been recorded) and inventory would be overstated (inventory that has been sold has not been removed from the records). With the incorrectly entered form, let's assume that the quantity sold was keyed in as 78 instead of 67 units. As a result of this error, the sales figure will be higher than it should be (accuracy of sales figure is threatened), accounts receivable will be higher than it should be (the valuation of the asset will be incorrect) and inventory will be lower than it should be (again, the valuation of asset will be incorrect).

From these two examples, we can see how an error in a business process can impact the financial statements. However, it is not only financial statement errors that internal controls are concerned with. As accountants and auditors you will likely primarily be exposed to the financial statement perspective, but you should also be aware of the environment in which the financial statements are generated and think also in terms of the risks that do not directly impact on the financial statements; for example, someone gaining unauthorised access to the physical computing resources of the organisation or the installation of unlicensed software on the computer system. Regardless of the nature of the risk, the approach in progressing through this chapter should be to constantly ask the four questions on page 329 about the assertions.

After identifying risks, management will decide on appropriate policies and procedures to address the risks. These policies and procedures are called control activities, and will be communicated to the organisation for implementation.

# TYPES OF CONTROL ACTIVITIES

From the COSO framework introduced in chapter 7 we saw that one of the components of the internal control system was control activities. In this section, we take a look at some examples of control activities and the different ways in which they operate. As a starting point we look at the classification provided by Australian Auditing Standards. Financial statement auditors use the auditing standards as a basis for planning and carrying out external financial statement audits with the aim of detecting any material misstatements in the financial statements. The auditor's concern, therefore, is primarily with the financial accuracy of the statements. However, note that, while the auditing perspective provides us with a basis for our controls, for an accountant working with an accounting information system within an organisation, the concern extends beyond financial to non-financial risks and controls. Australian Auditing Standard ASA 315 *Identifying and Assessing the Risks of Material Misstatement through Understanding the Entity and its Environment*[1] classifies controls into four types:

1. performance reviews
2. information processing controls
3. physical controls
4. segregation of duties.

This perspective on control activities focuses on the risk areas/activities within the organisation and emphasises a functionalist perspective — what happens within the organisation and how the controls operate. These control areas should be remembered, since for each one we will see different examples of specific control activities.

**Performance reviews** are those activities that involve some form of review or analysis of performance. The classic accounting example is the comparison of actual and budgeted figures and the conduct of variance analysis to determine the source of the variance. Other types of performance reviews could include comparing two sets of data to see if they match (e.g. a bank reconciliation, which compares bank records to business records to ensure parity between the two).

**Information processing controls** are those that are put in place within the organisation to work towards the accuracy, completeness and authorisation of transactions. **Accuracy** is the aim of making sure that all data that enters the system is correct and reflects the actual events that are being recorded. **Completeness** refers to the aim of ensuring that all events that occur are recorded within the system. **Authorisation** is concerned with whether or not the events that occur are appropriately approved before being executed. Information processing controls can be classified as either general or application controls.

**General controls** are those policies and procedures that 'relate to many applications and support the effective functioning of application controls by helping to ensure the continued proper operation of information systems'.[2] General controls operate across the organisation and relate to the overall environment in which different information systems are located. Note from the definition that general controls do not relate to a specific application or process and, as a result, will not directly affect the operation of the different information systems that may exist within the organisation. General controls may provide a suitable environment in which separation of duties and restricted access to resources can be applied, but they do not help to control the actual operation of the different computer systems that the organisation uses. As such, general controls provide the environment within which application controls operate.

---

**Performance reviews** *Activities that involve some form of review or analysis of performance.*

**Information processing controls** *Controls put in place within the organisation to work towards the accuracy, completeness and authorisation of transactions.*

**Accuracy** *The aim of making sure that all data that enters the system is correct and reflects the actual events that are being recorded.*

**Completeness** *The aim of ensuring that all events that occur are recorded within the system.*

**Authorisation** *Ensuring users have correctly defined access to information within a system and that transactions are executed and recorded by people with the appropriate authority.*

**General controls** *Controls that relate to the overall computerised information system environment.*

**Application controls** 'apply to the processing of individual applications' or processes.[3] As stated in the previous version of ASA 315, 'these controls help to provide reasonable assurance that all transactions have occurred, are authorised, and are completely and accurately recorded and processed'.[4] As this definition indicates, application controls are designed around the control objectives of a specific business process or system (e.g. the sales process, ordering process, manufacturing process, cash receipts process and so on) and relate to processing within individual applications. That is, application controls are specific to a particular business process in that they will be implemented to address the risks and threats unique to that process. Application controls operate within the scope of general controls. In a computerised environment, application controls will typically be classified as input, processing or output. We will look at further examples of these as we progress through this chapter and in chapters 9 to 13 when we examine the different business processes or transaction cycles within the organisation.

As the name suggests, **physical controls** refer to those controls that are put in place to physically protect the resources of the organisation. These will be discussed in more detail later in the chapter.

**Segregation of duties** refers to the concept that certain key functions should not be performed by the same person. The typical reference point within a business process is whether the record keeping (person who records a transaction), execution (person who performs a transaction), custody (person in possession of the assets involved in a transaction) and reconciliation (person reconciling transaction data) should be separated. Segregation of duties also applies across the IT systems within the organisation. These concepts will be discussed further later in the chapter.

These alternative classifications of controls are by no means in conflict. Rather, they represent the numerous perspectives that can be taken when analysing internal controls.

Controls may also be classified based on how they deal with risk and where in the information processing activities they operate. These include classifications of preventive/detective/corrective controls and input/processing/output controls.

## Preventive, detective and corrective controls

Control activities can be broadly classified as preventive, detective or corrective. This classification views control activities based on how they deal with the risks that confront the organisation — do they stop the risk from materialising, detect when a risk has materialised or remedy the situation after the risk has come to fruition? The obvious preference is for preventive controls — those that stop all risks from occurring. However, this is not always possible. That is, some risks will not be anticipated and, as a result, no preventive strategies will have been put in place. Further, it may not be possible to prevent or detect some risks, leaving corrective controls (i.e. fixing the problem after it has occurred) as the only option. An example would be recovering from a new computer virus.

For some risks, even if we anticipate their occurrence, we may not put in place control activities to address them. This is based on the cost–benefit concept, which requires that the benefit obtained from a control activity (i.e. the expected value of the loss) should exceed the cost of putting the control activity in place. An example of the cost–benefit concept can be seen from shopping at the supermarket. One risk that the supermarket wants to address is that of inaccurate prices being charged to customers. To deal with this, barcode scanners are used to record sales data and registers automatically calculate the amount owed by the customer. But what if the scanner gets an item wrong? Or what if an item is scanned but not recorded by the register? This could be dealt with by having a second person scanning the groceries and comparing the original total to the second total. If the totals agree the supermarket can be confident that all goods have been recorded in the sale and recorded at the correct amount. However, supermarkets do not perform this secondary process; they are happy to rely on the items being scanned by one person. Why? Firstly, the probability of an item scanning incorrectly would be assessed as low. As a result, the expected amount to be saved by implementing the control would be minimal, at best. Secondly, the cost of implementing this control would be significant; register numbers would have to be doubled to handle the increased scanning requirements and still process customers through the checkout promptly. This would require additional technology and labour. In addition, customer dissatisfaction from slower sales processing could lead to loss of business. In this case, the benefits of the control do not exceed the costs.

## Preventive controls

**Preventive controls** Controls designed to stop errors or irregularities occurring.

**Preventive controls** are designed to stop errors or irregularities occurring. As a simple example, an employee may try to enter an employee number in the system as 'A1234'. If organisational practice is that all employee numbers have six digits and contain no alphabetic characters, allowing the input of 'A1234' will cause problems because it is an invalid and nonexistent identification number. A properly designed input control (discussed later in the chapter) will detect this anomaly in the input and alert the person performing the data entry, prompting them to correct the input, or at the very least not allow the input to be accepted. This is an example of a control *preventing* errors from entering the system. Similarly, a password is a preventive control because it stops unauthorised users from gaining access to a system. An example that you may be familiar with from your use of the internet is the use of required fields — fields that must be filled in before you can progress to the next screen when creating an online account or making an online booking. Required fields are preventive because they stop the progress of the transaction until all the required data has been provided and therefore prevent incomplete data being gathered.

Alternatively, think of the example of a firewall that protects a computer or network. New viruses are constantly being developed, leaving virus protection developers in a constant race to protect computer users. Installing a firewall is an example of a preventive control — it provides a shield around the computer or network that stops unauthorised users or programs from gaining access to the network. That is, it stops known threats from occurring.

## Detective controls

**Detective controls** Designed to alert those involved in the system when an error or anomaly occurs.

Unlike preventive controls, **detective controls** will not prevent errors from occurring. Rather, the function of a detective control is to alert those involved in the system when an error or anomaly occurs. So, as the name would suggest, it *detects* errors or anomalies. An example is the use of a virus scan program to check for computer viruses. Running a virus scan analyses the computer or network and identifies viruses that may have penetrated the firewall. Once these are identified their existence will be reported. In this case, the threat (a new virus) was not stopped (it entered the network) but was detected within the system, allowing for follow-up action (e.g. quarantine of the file, repair of the file or deletion of the file).

## Corrective controls

**Corrective controls** are designed to correct an error or irregularity after it has occurred. Examples include the organisation's disaster recovery plan, which aims to restore the business to an operating position after the occurrence of a disaster, and the use of virus protection software to remove a virus that has corrupted computer programs within the organisation. In some cases, even if the organisation has a firewall in place (preventive control) and carries out regular system scans (detective control) virus attacks may still occur. For example, if the virus definitions on a scan program are not up to date, a virus will not be known until it has caused damage to data or network operation. The only way to recover from the attack is to correct the situation, typically by restoring the system using recovery disks and backups. Note that a corrective control comes into effect *after* the error or irregularity has occurred.

This classification scheme of preventive, detective and corrective controls can be applied to both general and application controls.

## Input, processing and output controls

Another classification refers to where the control activity fits in the information processing stages of gathering, using and transforming data. The type of controls we see at input, processing and output within a business process will relate specifically to the operation of that business process and be designed based on the particular risks present within the process. Therefore, they are application controls. You will see examples of these in the transaction cycle chapters.

**Input controls** are designed to operate as data enters the system. These controls will typically aim to provide reasonable assurance about the accuracy, validity and completeness of data being entered. **Processing controls** are put in place to work towards the correct handling of data within the information processing stages. An example of the types of issues that processing controls will address include making sure that data is correctly updated in the various data stores, and making sure that all sales are posted to accounts receivable at the right amounts. **Output controls** are concerned with the various outputs generated by the process, and are focused on issues such as who can request outputs, how outputs are prepared and making sure all outputs are accounted for.

# COSO, COBIT AND CONTROL ACTIVITIES

The COSO framework for internal control introduced in chapter 7 provides a general framework that has received endorsement from US authorities, with the Securities and Exchange Commission or SEC requiring the use of an internal control framework that has been extensively developed and publicly distributed. In making this mandate, the SEC mentioned the COSO framework as one such example.[5]

COBIT 4.0 and its follow up version COBIT 4.1[6] are widely applied frameworks for internal control that are often used by organisations as an addition to the COSO framework and a source of IT specific control objectives.[7] Released by the IT Governance Institute, they provide a structure within which an organisation can assess its controls and identify the need for controls at the various stages of the IT lifecycle. The frameworks classify application control goals based on the stages a process goes through when it handles an event or transaction. These stages relate to source document authorisation, input, processing and output.

Table 8.1[8] uses the stages identified in COBIT 4.0[9] as a basis. These steps can be seen as comparable to the input–process–output model of a system, discussed in earlier chapters. In each of these stages there are certain key aims. For example, when authorising a transaction, relevant documentation needs to be prepared, the documents need to be approved, and the documents need to be collected and stored. For each of these activities there are control issues that need to be addressed. These are analogous to the risks that we mentioned earlier. For example, when inputting data into the system a control issue or risk is that of inaccurate or invalid data being entered. The control issues are addressed by specific control activities, listed in the final column of the table. Note that this list is by no means exhaustive.

**TABLE 8.1** Control issues at various data processing stages

| | Aim | Control issues | Example of controls |
|---|---|---|---|
| **TRANSACTION AUTHORISATION** | Document preparation | Is data gathered accurately? | Pre-formatted documents. Review of documents. |
| | Authorisation to prepare documents | Was the preparer authorised to prepare the document? Are prepared documents reviewed? | Job descriptions defining responsibility. Segregation of preparation and approval responsibilities. Review of prepared documents. Restricted access to blank source documents. |
| | Document collection | Are source documents complete? Accurate? Are all source documents accounted for? Are source documents moved through the process in a timely manner for input into the system? | Pre-numbered documents. Sequence checks. Batch totals. Cancelling source documents after completion of transaction. |
| | Document storage | Are documents kept to allow preservation of an audit trail? Are documents kept for required legal time frame? | Maintenance of secure storage systems. |
| **DATA INPUT** | Authorised entry | Is the person entering the data authorised to? | Job descriptions defining responsibility. System access controls. Login procedures. Defined user privileges. Time-out after inactivity. Separation of duties. Data entry and data file maintenance or update. |

*(continued)*

**TABLE 8.1** *(continued)*

| | Aim | Control issues | Example of controls |
|---|---|---|---|
| | Checking for accuracy, completeness and authorisation | Does the system check for accuracy? Does the system check for completeness? Does the system check for validity? When is the data gathered and entered? | Edit checks. Reasonableness. Range checks. Limit checks. Logic checks on entered data. Redundant data check. Completeness checks. Required fields. Batch totals. Reconciliation of transactions entered and transactions processed. Capture data at its point of origin. Turnaround documents. Use of a standard chart of accounts. |
| **DATA PROCESSING** | Integrity | Is processed data verified as being correct? Are checks in place to ensure data updates have occurred correctly? | Run-to-run totals. Batch totals. Comparison of source documents to updated data files. Sequence checks. Processing error logs. |
| **DATA OUTPUT** | Storage | How long is output stored for? Where is output stored? What privacy and security issues impact on the treatment of outputs? | Defined policies for the storage of outputs. Defined policies for the distribution of documents. |
| | Access | Who can access the outputs? | Printing to secure locations for sensitive material. Defined user privileges for accessing or printing outputs. Defined job descriptions or role responsibilities that specify required outputs. |
| | Checking | Are the outputs accurate? Is an adequate audit trail maintained? Are procedures in place for any detected errors? | Reconciliation of outputs to source data. Reconciliation of subsidiary and control accounts. |
| **EXTERNAL DATA** | Reliability | Is the data accurate? Is the data valid? Is the data complete? | Confirmation of details with third parties. Within firm authorisation (e.g. credit checks for sales orders received by fax). Checking that the third party (supplier or customer or creditor) is known to us. Use of existing customer or supplier or credit data to confirm existence. Use of turnaround documents. |

LEARNING
OBJECTIVE  4
Describe the aims of a computerised
accounting information system.

# AIMS OF A COMPUTERISED ACCOUNTING INFORMATION SYSTEM

Any computerised system should aim to ensure transactions are properly authorised, recorded and processed in their entirety in a timely manner.

## Proper authorisation

The aim of proper authorisation is to ensure that transactions are executed by those people with the appropriate authority, and that any modifications to the data in the system are performed by the appropriate people. As an example, a retail company policy may state that all credit sales up to the value of $1000 can be approved by regular sales staff, but for credit sales exceeding the value of $1000, the authorisation of the supervising accounts receivable manager must be obtained. The aim of the system in this scenario would be to ensure that, if a credit transaction valued at more than $1000 occurs, it must have the appropriate approval from the manager. That is, the transaction must be authorised. Authorisation in a computerised information system can be established through user privileges and access rights and by placing restrictions on what different users are able to do within the system. In a manual paper-based system, such a control could work by requiring that sales invoices for credit sales over $1000 are manually approved and signed by the supervising accounts receivable manager before being cleared for shipment.

Authorising a transaction implicitly says that the transaction is valid. When referring to a transaction as valid we mean the transaction actually occurred and the parties involved in the transaction actually exist. Part of the authorisation process will thus be concerned with verifying the bona fide nature of the transaction or event.

## Proper recording

Proper recording of transactions is essentially about accuracy. Accuracy is concerned with making sure that all data that enter the system are in the correct format and of the right type, and that the data gathered accurately reflect the reality of the underlying transaction or event. For each authorised transaction or event the organisation will be concerned with making sure that these events are accurately recorded. As an example, if the data field for staff numbers on a database is preformatted to contain only six numerals then it should not be possible to enter a staff number that contains alphanumeric characters or numbers with five or seven digits. It would also be required that staff numbers entered are valid; that is, that an employee within the organisation actually has the staff number. Ways of doing this are discussed later in this section. Accuracy, as a general principle, can include paper and automated aspects of capturing and recording data. Focusing specifically on the entry of data into the computer, **input accuracy** is the aim of ensuring that all data entered into the system are correct.

**Input accuracy** The aim of ensuring all data entered into the system are correct.

The accuracy objective is very closely linked to the assertions of accuracy and valuation from chapter 7. That is, if the data is not gathered and recorded correctly, the financial statements generated cannot be an accurate reflection of the events that have transpired.

## Completeness

**Input completeness** The aim of ensuring all transaction events and all required data relating to those events are captured within the system.

Completeness can refer to both inputs to the system and transactions handled by the system. **Input completeness** is the aim of ensuring all transaction events and all required data relating to those events are captured within the system. For example, if a sales order form requires a salesperson ID number to be entered, a system should not allow the transaction to progress until the ID number is entered. Note that input completeness operates at two levels. First, to ensure that all details for an individual transaction are captured. This is completeness at the level of the individual transaction. Second, more generally, it must also be ensured that all transactions are captured. This is completeness at the business process level: ensuring all activities within the process are recorded. For example, a sales process that omits data on some of the transactions is undesirable, because reports and information generated about that process would be inaccurate on account of not being based on all of the transactions that occurred. The completeness objective is closely linked to the assertion of completeness, which, from a financial statement perspective, requires that all transactions and accounts that should have been recorded have actually been recorded.

## Timeliness

The goal of **timeliness** works towards ensuring that data are captured, processed, stored and made accessible in the most time-effective manner to enable the production of useful information for system users. Timeliness for an information system does not necessarily mean that all transactions must be processed immediately, rather that they should be processed to suit the needs of the organisation. Options for the processing of data include batch processing, online real-time transaction processing, and online gathering delayed processing.

**Batch processing** operates by accumulating transactions in a group or batch and then processing the group of transactions together. Batch processing can have several advantages for an organisation, including efficiency in processing transactions and fewer system demands during regular operations. However, it also means that data are not immediately updated after each transaction. Taking a retail firm as an example, this would mean sales accumulate and would be processed together at the end of the day. Any queries made during the day about stock levels for items of inventory would not take into consideration sales that had occurred since the last batch process run. Thus, the information would be slightly inaccurate. For some organisations this delay in processing is not necessarily a problem. However, moving from a retail store to an airline booking system, it can be seen that batch processing is not always ideal. This leads to the second processing option: **online real-time data processing**. As the name suggests, this processes data from transactions as they occur. Environments where this approach is needed are where immediate up-to-date information is required for decision making and effective business operations. An example could be an airline. Think of the booking process that it goes through with its passengers and the type of information that it requires when handling a booking. It is obviously infeasible for an airline to say to a customer 'We think we have a seat available on that flight'. The customer needs to know this information when they make the booking. This requires an information system that is immediately updated for the effect of each transaction. Imagine the problems airlines would have if they operated under a batch processing environment — the potential issues of double booking seats could cause nightmares for the airline, not to mention the passenger who has to share a seat with someone!

A compromise between online real-time processing and batch processing is **online data gathering and batch processing**. It has aspects of both systems in its design. As transactions occur they are immediately stored by the system — this is the online component. However, related data files are not updated until the end of the day or the end of some designated interval at which time all transactions that have occurred and been stored will be processed in the system. An example could be a sales system where the details of sales are captured electronically as they occur. This sales data will then be stored until the close of business. At the close of business, all of the sales that have occurred throughout the day will appear in the file and be processed through the system — updating the accounts receivable data, customer data, inventory data and so on. So while data are gathered in real time, they are processed in batches.

Within the framework for analysing and classifying controls, we now turn our attention to some specific examples of control activities. The discussion will cover the operation of the control as well as, where appropriate, flowcharts for how the control would look in a systems flowchart and a classification as preventive/detective/corrective or input/processing/output.

**LEARNING OBJECTIVE 5**

*Define and provide examples of general controls.*

# GENERAL CONTROLS

General controls are those that relate across all the information systems in an organisation. They include areas of physical controls, segregation of duties, user access, systems development procedures, user awareness of risks and data storage procedures. Each of these will be discussed in the remainder of this section.

## Physical controls

Physical controls are concerned with restricting access to the physical resources of the organisation. At the most obvious level, the concern would be who has physical access to the organisation's computing resources. Especially for organisations that have large data processing centres that handle all of the transactions and information processing requirements of the organisation, the risk of unauthorised people accessing and damaging (accidental or otherwise) the physical infrastructure is one the organisation will not be prepared to take. As a result, organisations will employ a range of physical controls to restrict physical access, including:

- *Locked computing premises.* Locking facilities and restricting the distribution of keys to the facility works in two ways. Firstly, the locked premises mean that unless you have a key you are unable to gain access. Secondly, if the distribution of keys is controlled it is possible to narrow down the people who may have entered the premises at a particular time. Locking premises is primarily a preventive control — it stops unauthorised access to the premises.
- *Discrete premises that do not attract attention.* Discrete premises can be a consideration when choosing the location for data processing and technology headquarters. Organisations that do not advertise the location of their information technology centres are theoretically less exposed to targeted attacks on the organisation's physical resources.
- *Swipe card access.* Controlling physical entry to buildings and office facilities through the use of swipe card access means only those with a swipe card will be able to gain access. Swipe card technology also allows for the recording of data about who enter the premises and at what time.
- *Biometric access controls.* A limitation of swipe cards is that the person with the card may not necessarily be the person who is meant to have the card, since swipe cards may be lost, stolen or loaned. A way to overcome this is through the use of biometric controls, such as fingerprint swipes or retina scans. The benefit of this technology is that biometric identification, unlike swipe cards or passwords, ensures that the person gaining access is actually authorised to do so.[10]

- *Onsite security.* The presence of onsite security, such as a manned front desk, can be an effective means of restricting unauthorised people from accessing a building.
- *Security cameras to record access to the premises.* The presence of security cameras can act as both a preventive and a detective access control. From a preventive perspective, if people know cameras are there they are less likely to attempt unauthorised access. Additionally, if the cameras are present they can provide a means of detecting unauthorised access.

An example of a physical control would be a locked storeroom for inventory items, or restricted access to the computer processing centre. In addition, physical controls over key source documents are an important consideration. Probably the best example in this category is the storage of blank cheques. A sound physical control would see cheques stored in a locked location with access limited to a small number of people. Further, a person with access to the blank cheques should not have the power to authorise (sign and approve) cheques, since this creates the risk of cheque misappropriation. Physical controls over cash and inventory are also important. A biannual KPMG survey[11] on fraud consistently identifies the theft of cash and inventory as the most common methods of fraud committed by employees in non-financial sector organisations (see table 8.2). While the percentages may have fallen between surveys, the figures do highlight the risk attached to different asset types. Cash, for instance, is liquid and hard to trace, while inventory is generally easily convertible to cash. In the 2008 survey, theft of cash was estimated by KPMG as accounting for 28 per cent of the total number of frauds and worth an estimated $21.4 million or 44 per cent of the total dollar value of all frauds reported.[12]

**TABLE 8.2** Costs of fraud using assets

| Sector | Financial sector organisations | | | | Non-financial sector organisations | | | |
|---|---|---|---|---|---|---|---|---|
| Level | Management | | Non-management | | Management | | Non-management | |
| Year | 2006 | 2008 | 2006 | 2008 | 2006 | 2008 | 2006 | 2008 |
| Cash | 35% | 14% | 19%* | 30% | 11%# | 11% | 31%** | 17% |
| Inventory | n/a | n/a | n/a | n/a | 21% | 12% | 20% | 9% |

*Includes cash receipts (1%) and cash (18%)
**Includes cash receipts (2%) and cash (29%)
#Includes cash receipts (1%) and cash (10%)
Figures represent the percentage of the total cost of fraud. For example, 35% represents 35% of the total cost of fraud for the survey period.

*Source:* KPMG 2006, 2009.

## Segregation of duties

When we look at the operation of the different transaction cycles in chapters 9–13 we will see that the recording, execution, custody, authorisation and reconciliation functions should be performed by different individuals. When looking at IT systems, separation of duties is equally important. Within the IT function, separation of duties should exist between the users of IT, the maintainers of the IT systems, system designers, system testers and those with access to the data within the systems. The rationale behind this is that combining any of these roles creates a conflict for the individual, places the organisation's resources at risk and enables an individual to carry out fraud without being detected. For example, if the person designing and testing a new application also has access to the organisation's data resources there is the possibility that the live data could be used in the testing process. This exposes the data to the risk of damage or corruption if the testing does not work as expected. Alternatively, if users are also involved in the design of programs there is the risk that, because of their intimate knowledge of how the program was developed, they will be able to work around any controls that may have been built into the program.

## User access

The area of user controls predominantly relates to the logical access of users to the systems within the organisation. The primary example in this area is the use of passwords to restrict system access to authorised users[13] by allocating users a unique identification code that only they are aware of, as well as one of the most common access control methods in operation.[14] Organisations requiring users to have passwords need to consider the following aspects of password operation.

### What format is the password?

Increased sophistication in the development of algorithms and programs designed to break passwords means that password strength becomes an important issue. The strength of the password is related to its length and format. For example, a password that is set as 'CAT' would be much easier to crack than a password that has been set as 'C@9at12#'. Increasingly, online sites that require passwords will provide indicators of password strength, with many advocating a mix of alphanumeric characters, upper and lower case characters and symbols.

A step beyond this is to have the system automatically generate a password for the user, which will ensure that password format protocols are adhered to on a consistent basis. The trade-off with this option is that system generated passwords may be more difficult for users to remember, leading to the tendency to write passwords down and the security risks that presents.[15]

### What is the life of the password?

Increased security comes from passwords that are required to be changed on a regular basis, since the more the password is changed the more the risk of them becoming known is reduced. As a result, some systems will require users to change their password on a regular basis (e.g. every four weeks). While this has the benefit of being dynamic because it changes regularly, it can obviously lead to confusion for the user, with the regularly changing password leading to the user forgetting or confusing their password. Other factors linked to difficult-to-remember passwords include the composition of the password and the selection method of the password (did the user choose it or was it assigned to them?).[16]

### Is the password unique?

A user may have access to several different systems or modules within a system. If each of these requires a password, the potential exists for the user to have to remember numerous passwords. Again, this may lead to confusion for the user in trying to remember their various access codes.[17] The temptation for users may be to use the same password for various systems. For example, you may use the same password for your email, eBay, Amazon and YouTube accounts. Ives, Walsh and Schneider (2004)[18] cite research that found that a typical internet user may have access to as many as 15 different accounts, each requiring a user identification and password. With so many accounts, it makes sense to use the same password to reduce the potential for a forgotten password. However, the risk is that if your password for one account is discovered it can obviously be used to access multiple accounts. As such, the potential consequences of the password breach are magnified.

### What happens if a login is unsuccessful?

If a user forgets their password they will not be able to access their account. A system should be configured to log unsuccessful login attempts. Keeping a log of unsuccessful login attempts can be useful for following up on potential attacks. Analysis may reveal that attempts happen at a particular time or through a particular user name. This could prompt further investigation. In addition, some systems may freeze an account after a number of consecutive failed login attempts.[19] Typically, after three unsuccessful login attempts, an account may be frozen. This control works to stop systematic attempts at determining a user's password. Once an account is frozen the fact should be logged and the user required to apply for a password reset.

### Security of the password

Given that most system users will have multiple passwords, the tendency is for these to be written down. From a control perspective, the writing down of passwords should raise questions about where the document containing the passwords is then stored.[20] For example, storing the passwords in a notebook that is locked in a desk drawer or filing cabinet is preferable to recording them on a Post-it Note affixed to the computer screen where anyone can access them.

A survey conducted by chartered accounting firm Ernst & Young[21] reported that the most common IT internal control issue faced by organisations related to security and user access (see figure 8.1). This would encompass the issues of user verification and password design and implementation. Issues to be considered and addressed include the format of the password, the life of the password, the process for creating and removing user accounts and user training about issues of security and password policy. Other issues that are commonly present include those related to the protection of the IT infrastructure (e.g. physical protection of IT equipment, protection of network resources), data protection (protection from destruction, unauthorised access and unauthorised modification) and change controls (relating to how IT change is managed and carried out within the organisation).

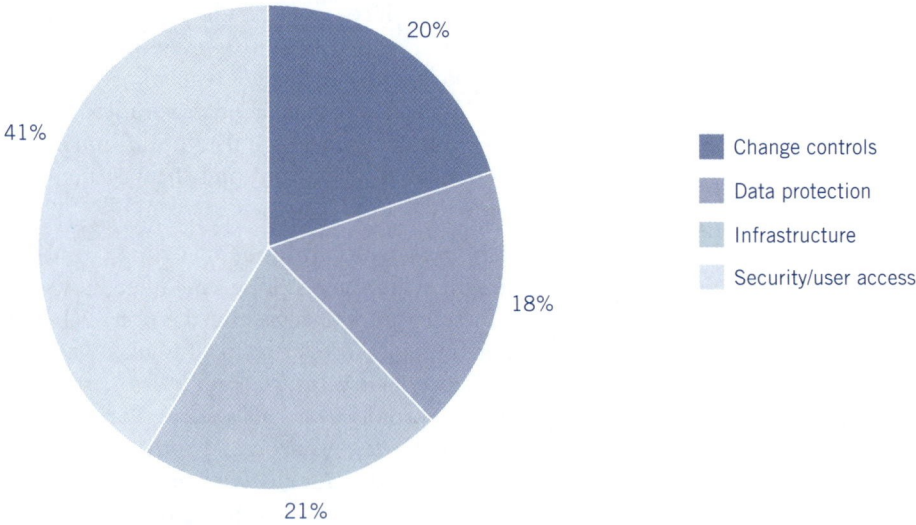

**FIGURE 8.1** IT control issues faced by organisations
*Source:* Ernst & Young 2005.

## System development procedures

A number of different information systems can exist in the organisation that will require maintenance and development at various points in time. It is important to have in place set policies and procedures to be followed in the design and implementation of new software or systems. This should include designated procedures and stages as part of the systems development process as well as restrictions on who is able to initiate and execute the development and installation of new programs within the information system. Within an organisational network you will see this represented, at a simple level, by different user privileges granted across the organisation. For example, the system administrator will have the ability to install software whereas a normal user will not have such rights. Restricting users' ability to install and modify software can be seen as a preventive control since it provides reasonable assurance that untested or incompatible software and software that has not been appropriately reviewed or licensed will not be placed on the system. This issue has emerged in the United States with CADE, a new system being developed by the Internal Revenue Service. It was reported that potentially 'administrators to the CADE system could access, modify and delete information without being detected, that contractors could make changes to system configurations without approval and that backup tapes from offsite storage facilities were not adequately tested to ensure that data would be restored without errors or losses'.[22]

## User awareness of risks

Another organisational control strategy is to ensure that organisations make their employees aware of the various information system risks. This can include briefing sessions about password policies, and procedures for adding to or modifying the operation of systems. Making the users of a system aware of the security threats and issues and motivating them to follow organisational policy is an approach advocated by several researchers.[23]

## Data storage procedures

Data is the lifeblood of the modern organisation, flowing through the business processes and supporting the decision making within the organisation. In addition, an organisation's data represents a potential source of competitive advantage through the details it contains about operations, customers and suppliers. As a result, the data within the organisation, despite not appearing on the statement of financial position, can be regarded as one of the most valuable resources an organisation possesses. In recent years, the risks to organisations' data resources have increased due to a range of threats, both internal and external.[24] The KPMG 2008 fraud survey identified that of fraud committed by non-management staff in the non-financial sector 17 per cent was achieved through the unauthorised manipulation of computer data.[25] Such trends prompt concern about the security of data held by organisations, both public and private, with this being reflected in a range of ways, including US President Obama calling for a review on cybersecurity, including how data are stored and protected by technology.[26]

The external threat to data comes from outsiders attempting to gain access to data held by the organisation through unauthorised access. Common examples of this in recent times have been attempts to hack into banking systems for data such as credit card numbers. It was recently reported that executives in the United States had been the recipients of documents purporting to be subpoenas that contained malicious software that installed itself on the executives' computers and allowed for passwords and other sensitive data to potentially be compromised.[27] The threat to data from within the organisation can come from a variety of sources. One of these is the way that data is shared throughout the organisation while another is through the protocols for transferring data, be it internally or externally. Recently the Australian Taxation Office (ATO) lost the details of more than 3000 trustees, which had been burnt onto a CD, after the CD went missing while being moved between locations. The data on the CD was unencrypted so potentially anyone in possession of the CD could access the data it contained.[28] A similar incident occurred in the United Kingdom when the details of 25 million taxpayers, stored on two discs, were lost in transit by a courier. The data was copied, against security protocols, and intended to be sent to an authorised recipient.[29] Not only do these incidents illustrate the placing of data at risk, the privacy of the individuals whose data on the CDs was also potentially compromised, exposing them to an increased risk of identity theft.

Being clear on what data is needed by different parts of the organisation and setting up access rights accordingly is also an important control step. In addition, where data is of a sensitive nature, logs that record when the data is accessed and who accesses the data can be an important resource. An example of this was reported in an article describing how the ATO had dismissed a number of employees for 'inappropriate access to taxpayer files.[30] It was also mentioned that the ATO, as well as other government departments, maintain audit logs that record access to personal data, with these logs being monitored and systematically reviewed to detect potential cases of unauthorised access.

Another dimension that raises control concerns related to data and technology resources is increased portability. For example, data can now be stored on DVDs, CDs, flash devices and portable hard drives. In addition, laptops and other portable computing devices mean that technology is now incredibly mobile. This poses added risks for the organisation since the theft of data by those within the organisation can potentially occur in an undetected manner due to the discrete nature of modern data storage devices. As an example, it was reported that a laptop belonging to the United Kingdom's Ministry of Defence was stolen, with the laptop containing the banking details of 3500 people, as well as profiles on Defence force applicants and recruits.[31]

Accordingly, control procedures relating to the access, duplication and sending of data are an important aspect of general control policies. Examples of such control policies could include, but are not limited to:

- restricting user privileges — who can read data only versus who can also copy data
- encryption of stored data
- encryption of data being sent between locations
- access logs for the access and alteration of data
- firewalls to protect data and systems from unauthorised external access
- regular updates of virus definitions
- regular system scans
- scanning of attachments before opening/downloading
- policies on attachments that will be accepted by the email system
- password/biometric identification in start-up routines for computing devices
- physical locking of portable computing devices when left unattended.

Backup policies are also important as backups may be the only means of recovery in the event of destruction or corruption of data. The frequency of backups is an organisational decision, based on the extent of data and the extent to which data change on a day-to-day basis. However, important aspects to keep in mind when developing a backup policy are:

- multiple backups should be kept
- storing backups offsite
- keeping multiple versions of backups.
- deciding what and how frequently to backup.

Several organisations now offer services such as offsite storage and backup facilities, making use of internet technology as a way of transferring backup data to remote locations and adding that extra degree of security should something go wrong at a main site.

Scheduling of backups is also of consideration. Traditionally, systems that operated in a batch processing environment would perform scheduled backups of an evening when the system was not performing routine transactions. Of course, once the first transaction of the new day occurs the backup is out of date. In this instance the backup mitigates the loss but does not eliminate it. Movement has been made towards real-time backups, whereby as transactions occur data is updated onsite as well as at the backup site. This approach effectively synchronises the business's main site with the backup site, with processing occurring at both locations and a backup existing that is as recent as the last transaction. The potential downside to this approach is that it obviously places a demand on communications between the two sites and will be more costly to maintain.[32]

**LEARNING OBJECTIVE 6**

*Define and provide examples of application controls.*

# APPLICATION CONTROLS

Application controls are those built around the operation of a particular process and typically relate to the key system stages of input, processing and output. Accordingly, this section looks at each of these stages and considers some examples.

## Input controls

### *Standardised forms*

The use of *standardised forms* can help ensure completeness. The design of the form that users interact with when entering data into a system is also an important consideration. There is benefit in designing the screen to resemble closely its paper-based equivalent in the real world. This makes it easier for users to navigate the screen and ensure completeness in their input. Proper form design can also ensure accuracy, since the form will specify the data that is required, the expected length of the data (e.g. six boxes for a six-digit customer ID) as well as any specific instructions for the data provider. Standardised forms can be seen as a preventive control (they work towards ensuring all relevant data is provided by specifying what must be completed, reducing the chance of incomplete forms) and a detective control (a visual inspection of a completed form will quickly detect if any key components have not been filled in or have been filled in inaccurately).

### *Prenumbering documents*

Prenumbering important documents, such as invoices, purchase orders, cheques and so on, can be a simple but effective way of helping ensure the objective of completeness. When documents are prenumbered, any missing or unaccounted-for documents can easily be identified simply by looking for a gap in the sequence. For example, an organisation may prenumber its purchase order forms. If an examination of the purchase records shows that issued purchase orders on record go from form number 10 011 to 10 013, with no record of 10 012, then potentially a purchase order has gone missing.

This missing document could be explained by honest misplacement, fraudulent use by an employee or simple cancellation. However, if documents were not prenumbered, this missing document would never have been identified. By prenumbering the source documents, a control is built that helps identify any omitted or unrecorded transactions (the assertion of completeness) and also provides a control over the source documents.

Where the source documents are potentially valuable, for example cheques, it is also useful to keep a record of cancelled source documents. Cancelled source documents are those that are removed from circulation by the organisation. For example, document number 10 012, which may have been previously identified as missing, could have been cancelled by the organisation because of an error while filling out the form or cancellation of the order before sending the purchase order. If a record is maintained of cancelled source documents, then reconciling gaps in the sequence of source documents also becomes easier.

Prenumbering documents can also be a useful control to address concern about transactions being classified in the correct reporting period. As an organisation approaches the end of the financial year it can note the last number of key source documents, for example, sales invoices, and set up procedures to make sure that documents after that number are allocated to the next period. The use of prenumbering and classification filters and ranges within accounting software can work towards this goal. For example, if we know that the first source document issued in the period was number 299 and that the last one issued at the end of the period was 542 then, combining knowledge of these numbers with the beginning and end dates for the financial period, we can filter and sort the documents to check that all documents before 299 have been recorded in the previous period and all documents after 542 have been recorded in subsequent periods. The ability to filter transactions in this way is present within various accounting packages, as well as through the downloading of data into a spreadsheet and manually sorting the data.

## Sequence checks

In a computer-based information system, prenumbering can be further enforced through the use of sequence checks. If transactions are entered directly into the system, with no paper documentation, then the document number can be assigned automatically. This will ensure no missing numbers in sequence checks for transactions and reduces the risk of incomplete data (i.e. transactions not being entered). It could also be argued that sequence checks contribute towards ensuring the correct valuation of assets since, for example, if a sale is not recorded the associated increase in accounts receivable will not be recorded.

## Turnaround documents

Turnaround documents are documents that originate as the output of one system and become the input for another system. There are literally hundreds of examples of turnaround documents that you would have been exposed to. If you have ever flown with a major airline you will have unwittingly been exposed to turnaround documents. Think about what happens when you travel by air. You arrive at the airport and check your baggage in at the baggage counter. While there you will also present the relevant identification, including a passport if travelling overseas. The attendant will check your baggage in and allocate you to a seat, and then issue you with a boarding pass. The boarding pass contains details of your flight, departure gate, boarding time, seat allocation and any other relevant details. When you then proceed to the boarding gate you present your boarding pass, which is scanned through a machine. What is the benefit of using this document at the boarding point? Airlines need to keep lists of who actually boards aircraft, because an aircraft will not take off if a passenger has checked in luggage but not boarded the flight. This presents the issue of how to best capture the data about which passengers have boarded the flight. One option could be to have boarding staff rekey data into the system as passengers present their boarding pass. However, this is not the most efficient way — the data have already been captured elsewhere, so why rekey them? Instead, the airline magnetises boarding passes that it issues, enabling a computer to read the data that were stored when the passenger checked in. This has several benefits. The obvious benefit is that staff do not have to rekey passenger data, meaning that boarding can be completed in less time. Second, the risk of error is reduced since there is no opportunity for human error when rekeying the data. The data are accessed electronically from the boarding pass, so the risk of inconsistent data (mismatches between what was captured when the passenger checked in and when the passenger boards the plane) are reduced. This increases the chances of **input validity**.

**Input validity** *The aim of ensuring that data entered into the system are in the correct format and valid.*

The boarding pass is a specific example of a turnaround document. Another example of a turnaround document is a remittance advice. When you receive a bill or a credit card statement you will often notice that is has a detachable slip attached at the bottom. This slip is designed to be returned to the organisation that originally sent you the bill, accompanied with the payment. Take a closer look at the remittance slip and you will notice that a lot of the data are already filled in, for example customer number, amount owed and due date. Why prepare remittance slips? When returned with the payment to the organisation, these slips allow payments to be linked to customers, so the organisation knows which customer the cash receipts come from. Additionally, the details of the cash receipt are on the remittance slip and just have to be entered in by the relevant person. The benefit is that there is no reliance on the customer to fill in the slip, reducing the possibility of errors and helping ensure valid and complete inputs are entering the system.

Use of turnaround documents helps achieve completeness of data entry, with all required data contained in the turnaround document. Turnaround documents that contain values or monetary amounts also help contribute towards the correct valuation and measurement of transactions (assertion of accuracy).

## Data entry routines

A computerised information system can also have built-in programs that ensure inputs are valid and in the correct format. Examples of such routines are field checks, validity checks, completeness checks, limit checks, range checks, reasonableness checks and redundant data checks.

*Validity checks* take a given input for a field and ensure that it is an acceptable value. For example, if a customer number is being entered when recording a sale, the program may take the customer number that is input and check it against a master list of customers contained in the customer table of the database. If the customer number appears on the master list then the input is valid and the input stage can proceed. However, if the customer number does not appear on the list then an invalid customer number has been entered. Obviously, this is not acceptable, so the system will alert the user to this error and refuse the input. This removes the potential for invalid or nonexistent customer numbers entering the system, helping attain existence and occurrence. Statistics from KPMG's 2008 fraud survey indicate that false invoicing accounted for 45 per cent of the cost of all management fraud in the non-financial sector and 1 per cent of the cost of employee fraud in the non-financial sector,[33] making the issue of being able to validate transactions an important one for organisations. In a relational database environment a control of this nature can be established using primary and foreign keys and through the enforcement of referential integrity. This is discussed in chapters 3 and 4 on databases. Validity checks can contribute towards data accuracy, that is, ensuring data are entered correct (e.g. does the customer exist in our customer table?).

An example of how a validity check may appear in a systems flowchart (which shows the internal entities and the activities that they perform) is shown in figure 8.2. In this example, the customer number is being entered and the customer details are then being retrieved and displayed on the screen for the next stage in the process. Notice that this control requires access to the customer data in order to confirm the customer exists on the customer list.

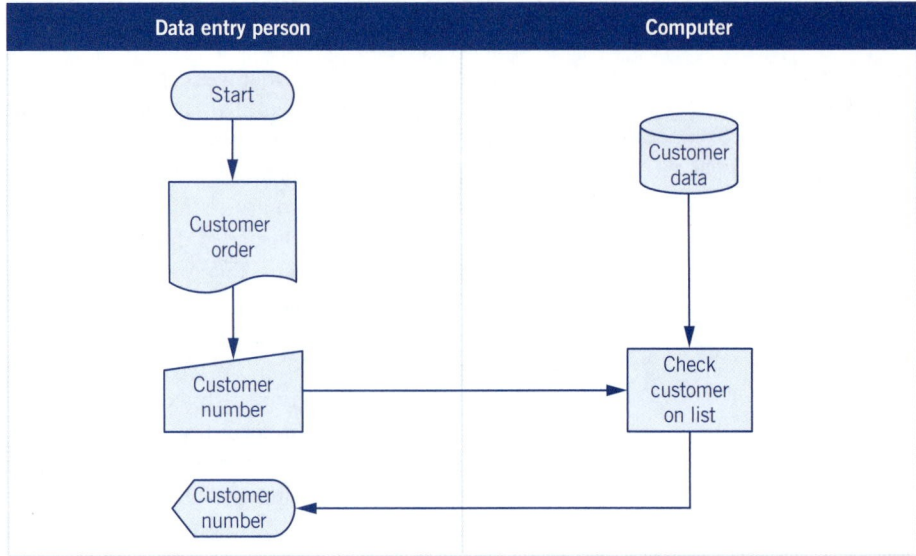

**FIGURE 8.2** Checking customer exists in customer table

An example of a validity check in QuickBooks, one of the popular computerised accounting packages in use in Australia, occurs when entering journal entries. If you try to enter a journal entry with debits and credits that don't balance, an error message appears alerting you that the entry is invalid since the debits and credits do not equal. This is shown in figure 8.3.

*Completeness checks* ensure that all required data are entered. If a user is entering a sale into the sales system and the sales screen has 10 different fields that need to be completed, then it needs to be ensured that the user completes all 10 fields. Failure to do so will lead to incomplete data about the transactions being entered. A completeness check will ensure that all required data are entered before the user can advance to later screens or move to a new sale. A practical example of such a check can be found in a lot of website store fronts and web-based forms. If you have ever completed an online form or made an online purchase, you will have probably noticed that some of the fields are marked to designate them as required fields. If you try to proceed without putting data into the required fields, the site will return an error message and not allow you to go any further until the required fields are completed. This is a way of trying to enforce input completeness for online forms and will contribute to the goal of completeness. Again, this control could contribute to the accuracy of the data that has been recorded; if necessary data about a transaction is not recorded then the details about the transaction cannot be deemed to be accurate.

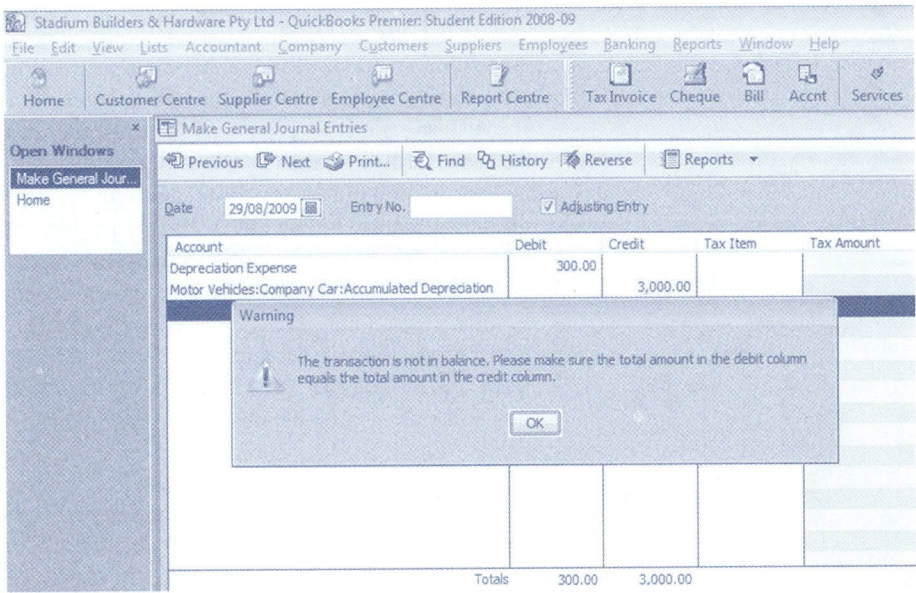

**FIGURE 8.3** Input control for journal entries
*Source:* QuickBooks Student Edition 2008–09.

*Limit checks* will check values input into a field to make sure they fit within a predetermined upper limit. For example, there may be a firm policy that orders a maximum of 50 reams of paper at any one time. A limit check will detect any amount greater than 50 entered in the quantity field and reject it. The application of limit checks is a technique for attaining the correct valuation or measurement of transactions.

*Range checks* function in a manner similar to limit checks, with the exception that the checks apply to both upper and lower limits. Returning to the paper ordering example, if store policy is that anywhere between 30 and 50 reams of paper can be ordered at one time, then the range check will detect any amount outside these upper and lower limits. Similarly to limit checks, range checks help reasonably assure the correct valuation or measurement of transactions.

*Reasonableness checks* operate to check that numeric input for a field is within a reasonable numeric range. For example, if a field requires you to enter your number of hours worked for a week and you key in 400 instead of 40, a reasonableness check should identify this value as outside reasonable values for weekly hours and prompt you to correct the value. Once again, this check will contribute towards the aims that relate to the valuation and measurement of transactions.

If data are being entered for a critical event or important transaction, then a control that can be used to help ensure correctness of inputs is a *redundant data check*. This control operates by having the data entered twice and then checking the two sets of inputs and making sure that they are identical. Ideally, different people will perform the two inputs, making the system's comparison of inputs more meaningful. Obviously, this control has the disadvantage of being costly to implement, since data are required to be entered twice. Accordingly, a key factor in determining whether to implement this control will be the cost–benefit principle. If the cost of having the data entered twice exceeds the benefits, then this control would not be applied.

## Automated form completion

A step forward from the validity checks mentioned above is to automate part of the data entry routine. For example, when entering customer details to record a sale, once the customer number is entered the computer can automatically fill in other customer-related data fields (such as customer name, address, phone number and so on). This is done by looking up the customer number in the customer data table and retrieving all related data. The benefit of this control is that it makes data entry more efficient, since less time is spent keying in details. In addition, by reducing the amount of data entry the chances of data entry errors are reduced (i.e. as long as the customer number is correct all related data items will be correct). Of course, this assumes that the customer details in the database are up to date. An example is shown in the screenshot from QuickBooks in figure 8.4. Once a customer name is selected from the drop-down list, all related details will be completed.

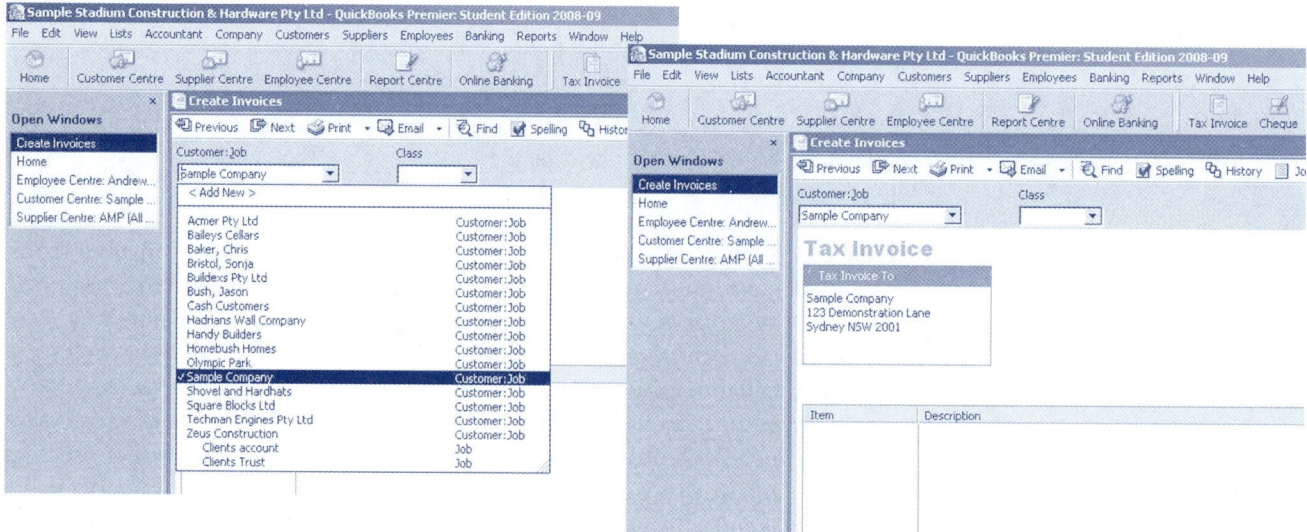

**FIGURE 8.4** Automated data entry

The input controls mentioned above aim to provide reasonable assurance about the accuracy and validity of data that is entered into the system. Data entry errors that make it through the input stage can have costly consequences, as AIS focus 8.1 demonstrates.

 **AIS FOCUS 8.1**

## A million dollar data entry error

Data entry inaccuracies can have severe consequences for an organisation, as Westpac, a bank that operates in Australia and New Zealand, found out when entering the details of a finance arrangement with one of its customers. News reports suggest that the bank's customer was arranging a loan worth NZ$10 000[34] Unfortunately, once approved, the loan was subject to a data entry error that saw the value of the loan entered as $10 000 000.[35] This erroneous amount was transferred to the customer's account.

The mistake is reported to have been the result of a data entry error where the decimal point was misplaced when keying in the value of the loan. The consequences for the bank were large, with a great amount of publicity attracted, while the staff member involved in entering the loan amount was reportedly managed out of the organisation.[36]

A similar incident is also reported to have seen NZ$4.3 million dollars almost transferred to an account when the amount should only have been NZ$43 000. A computer firm manager expected $43 000 to be deposited into the business bank account as a result of customer payments. In a fax from the bank to the customer, the amount specified was NZ$4.3 million. Thankfully for the bank, the error was only in the fax of details sent to the customer not in the amount transferred.[37] The bank stated that it had 'controls, including a verification process ... in place to ensure accuracy'.[38]

## Transaction authorisation procedures

Obviously, an organisation does not want all types of users to enter all types of transactions into the system. For example, it is probably not wanted that a member of the sales staff should handle payroll transactions and someone from manufacturing should enter sales transactions. One way this can be controlled is through the correct setting of user privileges when the system is established. For example, by requiring staff to log on with unique usernames and passwords, user privileges and access rights can be established that restrict the functions they are able to perform in the system. This control can help to prevent unauthorised transactions entering the system. Risks presented by unauthorised transactions can be quite large, for example, the National Australia Bank announced a loss of $360 million as a result of unauthorised foreign currency transactions executed by staff.[39] The issue of authorisation and access rights has become important for organisations with the increased emergence of ERP systems. Because of the integrated nature of an ERP system, along with the 'interconnectivity and automation of processes',[40] correctly authorising employees' access and privileges is an ongoing, time-consuming and complex process.

Authorisation procedures can also help in the attainment of the objectives of existence and occurrence, particularly if a separate person provides the authorisation. They can also include the review of event data before the execution of the event. An example of this could be seeking management approval for an abnormally large sales request from a customer, where the customer is new or unknown or where the transaction is outside the amount the staff member is authorised to execute. A frequent example of the authorisation control in action is in retail transactions. Often there will be a negotiation over the sales price, with the sales attendant being asked about discounts on the marked price for an item. When entering the negotiated price into the system, management authorisation will typically be required to confirm that the discount given was appropriate and approved.

## Batch totals

**Batch total** A total that is added to a batch of documents and is used to make sure that all documents in the batch have been correctly processed. A batch total is usually a summation of a data item with some meaning (e.g. a total of the individual invoice amounts for a batch of invoices). See also hash total.

**Batch totals** are another effective input control. In a batch environment, transactions are accumulated and, at some set interval, processed. In a sales system, for example, invoices may be accumulated until the end of the day and then processed upon the completion of the day's trading hours. A concern in this environment is making sure that all of the invoices are recorded in the system at the end of the day (completeness). This can be helped by the use of batch totals. For example, the sales staff may accumulate their invoices and at the end of the day count how many invoices they have.

This batch of invoices, together with a batch header form detailing who prepared the batch and the number of documents in the batch, could then be sent to the data entry staff, where they will be entered in the system. Staff in data entry should check to ensure that they receive the number of documents indicated in the batch header form, and that all these documents are entered. This is an example of a document count batch total. It operates to make sure no documents go missing, but it has limitations. While the data entry staff may enter all the invoices, they may key in details different from those on the invoices, for example they may key in sales of $100 instead of $1000. This will not be detected by the batch totals based on the number of documents.

An alternative method to help with both completeness and valuation or measurement could be to use total sales dollars for all invoices in the batch. The batch process would operate as described above, but instead would be calculated based on the sales value of the invoices. This overcomes the limitation of the document count approach.

If the batch total is not meaningful in any way, and just a check device, meaningless items can also be used (e.g. the total of all customer numbers in a batch). These sorts of hash totals are typically used as a processing control, and discussed in the next section.

An example of a batch total is shown in the systems flowchart in figure 8.5. In this example a batch of sales invoices has been gathered and a batch total manually calculated. The invoices are then entered into the computer, which displays a batch total on the screen. The total is compared to the manually compared total. If the two totals agree then, as a minimum, we can be confident that all invoices have been entered into the system.

## Independent reviews

An **independent review** is a useful monitoring technique that involves the work of one person being reviewed by a different person to ensure completeness, accuracy and correctness, and potentially make information more valuable. If the same person performs the work and checks the work for errors, the review is of little value. Consider if students were able to mark their own exam papers — there would be a chance that errors will not be detected or proper marking procedures will not be followed. For example, data about banking transactions may be processed into a bank reconciliation report, which can be reviewed by an independent person who can compare it against cash receipts and payments listings and bank statements to verify the reliability of the bank reconciliation process.

## Processing controls

Processing controls aim to ensure data within the system is correctly and accurately processed. An example is sales data entered throughout the day being transferred to accounts receivable to update the account balances. Controls relate to how the computer handles the data in transferring it from one file to another, and assurance is needed that (1) all sales have been transferred to accounts receivable and (2) all sales have been correctly transferred to accounts receivable. This example is illustrated in the following discussion.

### Run-to-run totals

In a computer processing environment, data will be gathered, used in a process and stored at a destination. The idea is that the total of the data before the process of updating the data files should match the total of the data after the update has been performed. If we think of the sales/accounts receivable discussed in the batch total example, the closing balance of accounts receivable (after the sales have been transferred) should equal the opening balance (before transfers) plus sales (ignoring

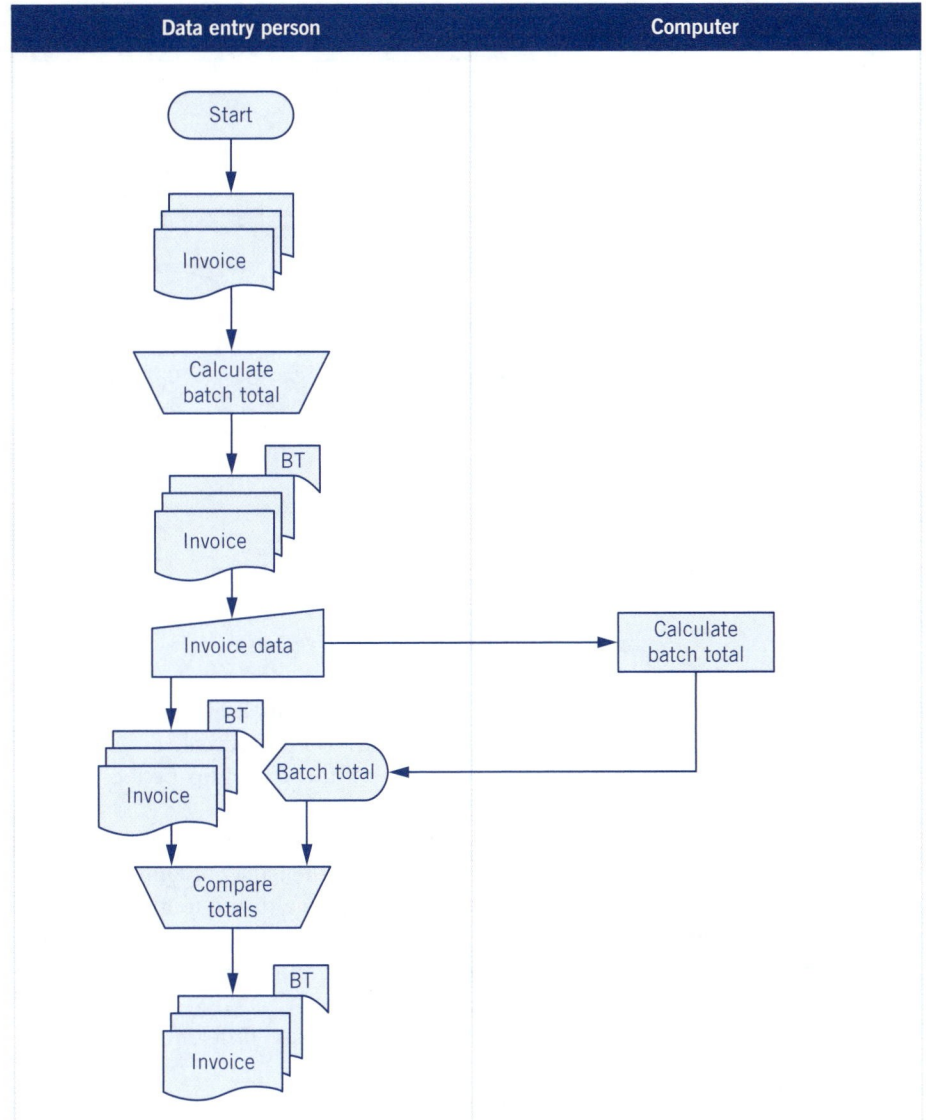

**FIGURE 8.5** Reconciling batch totals

any payments from customers). With this logical relationship between the opening and closing data we are able to build in checks to ensure that updates have been correctly performed. If, after the computer performs the update, the closing accounts receivable balance is less than the check total we calculated prior to the update (opening balance plus sales) the possibility exists that (1) not all sales have been transferred to accounts receivable or (2) all sales have been transferred but they have been transferred at the wrong amount or to the wrong account. Figure 8.6 overleaf illustrates this process. As sales orders are entered into the system they are added to the opening accounts receivable balance to determine the correct balance after the data update has taken place. The accounts receivable file is then updated with the details of the sales and a closing balance is calculated. This closing balance is compared to the one calculated in the data processing activity. If the two totals (pre- and post-processing) agree, the data has been correctly transferred to the accounts receivable file.

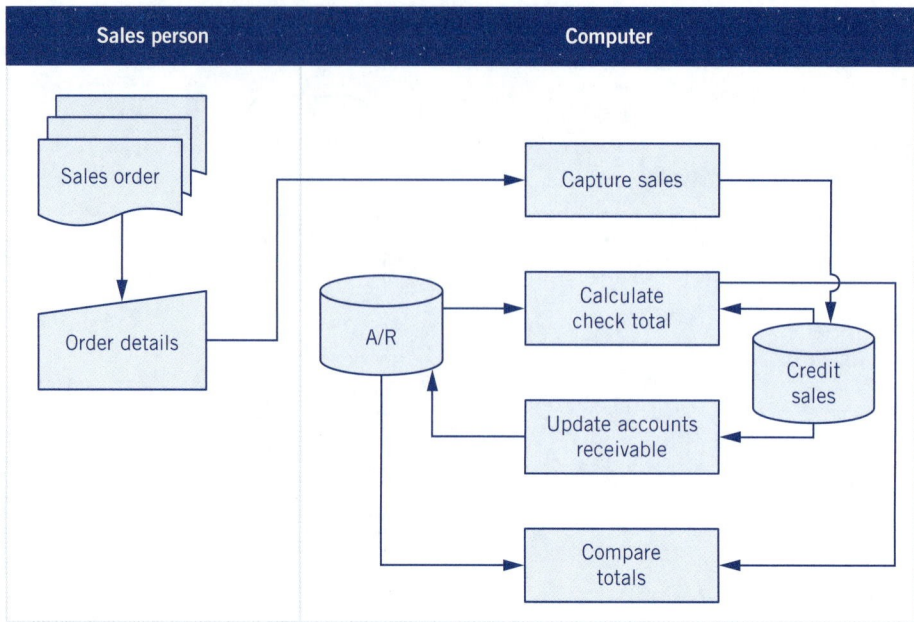

**FIGURE 8.6** Run-to-run totals

An alternative conceptualisation is to think of a typical manual accounting system:

1. Enter transactions into journal.
2. At the end of the reporting period the journals will be posted to the ledger accounts.
3. Take a total of the debits and credits before posting the amounts.
4. Post amounts to the ledger accounts.
5. Compare the change in the totals for debits and credits on the trial balance with the total of the debits and credits for the journal entries. These two amounts should be identical since all that has been done is to add the journal entries to the ledger accounts.
6. If these amounts are different, a problem or error has occurred during data processing.

Run-to-run totals aim to check that processing of data has taken place correctly, no errors have been introduced and no data has been lost. Notice how this control does not *prevent* the error from happening. Rather, it *detects* that there has been an error in processing and alerts the user to the problem.

Run-to-run totals will typically relate to the accurate processing and update of data and, as such, can apply to the correct valuation of accounts (e.g. accounts receivable), accuracy of items (have the amounts been correctly recorded?) and completeness of transactions (have all transactions affecting an account been included?). For example, if there are 10 sales and only nine are transferred to accounts receivable this will be detected by the run-to-run total.

Other examples of detective controls include performing reconciliations, the use of batch totals and independent reviews of people's work.

## Reconciliations

You will recall from introductory financial accounting units that the purpose of a bank reconciliation is to check business records against those of the bank, enabling any inconsistencies between the two to be identified. This reconciliation process is a valuable part of an organisation's internal control activities, providing it with a way to protect its cash resources. Another example is reconciliations of control and subsidiary ledger accounts. Reconciliations allow the comparison of two sets of information that should theoretically be the same to identify any inconsistencies. Reconciliations are more powerful if the two sets of information are prepared by two different people and an independent third person performs the review. For example, the accounts receivable control account may be maintained by the general ledger division, the subsidiary ledger by the accounts receivable department, and the reconciliation of the two may be performed by the finance manager. There is little value in reconciling two sets of information prepared by the same person — as the person preparing the information has the opportunity to cover up any discrepancies.

### Batch totals

Batch totals as explained previously can also be used as a control for data processing, since if data is being shifted from one file to another the data should not change. As such, the total of the data (be it number of records or dollar values) should be the same before and after the processing occurs.

### Sequence checks

Sequence checks as discussed previously can also be used during the processing of data. At the processing stage, these checks can operate to ensure that no data have gone missing during processing activities. An example could be in the transferral of cheque payments from the cash payments journal to the ledger accounts. If, in the journal, we are able to identify a sequence of cheques numbered 1 through to 5 but the ledger contains cheques 1, 2, 3 and 5, the gap in the sequence tells us that somewhere in processing the cheque data an entry has been lost.

### Run-to-run totals

Run-to-run totals will help identify whether any transaction data have gone missing between when they were first gathered and after their processing, while accuracy is attained by checking totals to ensure that they are the same before and after the processing of data.

### Hash totals

Hash totals are batch totals based around meaningless figures, for example, the sum of all customer numbers in a batch. Use of hash totals can help to detect any errors that may have entered the data during processing (e.g. if a hash total is taken before and after processing), as well as attain completeness in updates and processing.

## Output controls

Output controls are built around protecting the outputs of the system. These controls protect access to outputs as well as the format and content of outputs. Examples of output controls include access privileges and the ability to generate reports, page numbering of reports and end-of-report footers.

Within any information system there will generally be users with different responsibilities and duties. For the principle of segregation of duties to operate effectively, these different users should have their access privileges clearly defined based on the requirements of their job, which will be contained in their job descriptions. As an example, for reasons of confidentiality it is not desirable for all employees to be able to access payroll data and reports on annual salary levels and bonuses. Only those in the human resources department should be able to access such details. Alternatively, the salesperson should not be able to update inventory records and the inventory manager should not be able to modify or create sales records. These concerns can be overcome by correctly establishing user privileges that relate to the data the user can add, delete or modify, as well as the reports, queries, outputs and information the user can access. In the integrated environment of an ERP system, the correct definition of user access privileges is especially important.[41]

Another concern about outputs, apart from who can access them, includes the physical control over them once they are generated. Confidential or privileged information should not be printed on a printer accessible by all staff; such output should be printed to a secure location where only those authorised to access the information have access to the site. For example, employee appraisal forms would probably be best printed to a secure printer in the HR manager's office rather than to a general printer that all staff access for their print needs. Once reports or information have been generated, it needs to be ensured that there is an entire set of information. So for a multipage output that is printed, a simple but extremely effective control to ensure completeness of the output received is to preformat footers to provide page numbering, for example, 'Page # of ##'. With this page numbering system, pages collected can be identified as well as the number that there should be in total. So if there are six pages and the footer says there should be seven, it is easy to see that this is not the complete report. Along similar lines, preformatting reports to contain a simple message such as 'END OF REPORT' at the completion of the report is another way to ensure that you have the final page. This, combined with page numbering, can be an effective way of ensuring that any missing pages of output are quickly identified.

## Database queries

Database queries can also be a powerful tool for detecting irregularities or anomalies.[42] For example, if a company suspects that an employee is posing as a vendor, submitting fake invoices and receiving payment for these invoices, a quick crosscheck of employee addresses and vendor addresses could detect this. Alternatively, if it is suspected that accounts staff are keeping cash paid by accounts receivable customers and reducing accounts receivable through a sales return or credit note entry, a query of sales returns by customers and sales staff could be useful to detect irregular levels of returns, which could then prompt further investigation.

## AIS FOCUS 8.2

## Controls in practice

As the internet has increased its presence over the past decade, several organisations have been confronted with control issues that were previously unheard of in the business environment. One area where there are numerous examples of this is in the use of credit cards for online transactions. A growing concern for organisations is the use of credit cards for online gambling.

In the United States there is increasing concern about the legality of internet gambling, with it being legal in some states and not in others. In addition to the issue of legality, some major credit card providers are now refusing to process transactions that are related to internet gambling. VISA, MasterCard and American Express are examples of major credit providers forbidding the use of their credit lines for internet gambling.

This means that while the online casino provider may accept a customer's credit details, process the transaction and provide the customer with money for online gambling, when it comes to collecting that money from the credit card company or bank, the online casinos are being met with refusals. Court judgements in some US states have ruled that gambling debts accrued on credit are not enforceable.

This has raised a new issue for credit card providers, with some offshore credit processors potentially being willing to process the transactions for the online casinos but using fake codes, so that they do not appear as gambling-related items when the credit card company receives the transaction details.

Given this scenario, and the possibility of faking transactions to disguise gambling-related debts, what internal controls could the credit card companies implement to prevent, detect and correct the use of fake transaction details?[43]

**LEARNING OBJECTIVE**  **7**

*Describe the operation and components of a disaster recovery plan.*

**Disaster recovery plan** *The strategy that the organisation will put into action, in the event of a disaster that disrupts normal operations, to resume operations as soon as possible and recover data that relate to its processes.*

# DISASTER RECOVERY PLANS

Another crucial aspect to an organisation's control system is its ability to recover from any accidents or disasters that may occur and to minimise the damage to the organisation and its resources. This aspect of the control system is encompassed in the **disaster recovery plan**, which is the strategy that the organisation will put into action in the event of a disaster that disrupts normal operations, to resume operations as soon as possible and recover data that relate to its processes.

The obvious example of a disaster is the terrorist attacks of 11 September 2001 against the World Trade Center in New York. As the Twin Towers collapsed, businesses were suddenly confronted with the prospect of immense losses, both in terms of assets and knowledge lost and downtime in operations. PricewaterhouseCoopers estimates that '14 600 businesses in and around the World Trade Center were impacted by the disaster' and that '652 companies were temporarily or permanently displaced by the destruction'.[44] Even for organisations not directly affected by the collapse of the Twin Towers, there was still the problem of power outages and disrupted utility services to deal with in trying to keep their operations running.

It can be argued that most Australian businesses are inadequately prepared for any form of major disaster.[45] Internationally, the trend appears to be the same, with AT&T finding that 25 per cent of large companies (those with more than 100 employees) do not have disaster recovery plans.[46] As organisations increasingly place their operations online, the pressure to keep the web interface continuously operating escalates. For an online company, the web server's going down or the IT infrastructure's failing effectively closes the shop. A closed shop means no revenue. Over an extended period of time this can spell disaster for an organisation.

As a result of the threats of disaster — whether they be as a result of terrorism, or natural disasters such as fire, floods, cyclones or earthquakes — organisations must consider how they can deal with such threats. Their reaction to the threat of disaster can be preventive or corrective. The main aim for an organisation in the event of a disaster that disrupts business operations is to limit the time the business is out of operation and minimise the extent of loss to existing business resources — particularly information — so that the business can recommence operating as quickly as possible. The way an organisation does this is outlined in the disaster recovery plan, which will include provisions for temporary sites and the restoration of business networks, staffing and preserving business relationships.

## Temporary sites

In the event of a business's place of operation being destroyed it needs to be able to resume operation in a new location as soon as possible. This is the role of the temporary site, and for a business there are several approaches that can be chosen from, including the establishment of hot sites, cold sites and autonomic infrastructure. An organisation that can ill afford downtime due to disaster may consider the establishment of a **hot site**. This is a separate facility located away from the organisation's usual premises and contains offices and the necessary equipment (such as IT, telecommunications and data) to get the business back up and running in the minimal amount of time after a disaster occurs. Essentially, it is a standby site ready to be called into immediate action should the organisation require it. Many different hot-site subscription services are available, with organisations able to sign up with, for example, HP, which has 44 such sites around the world for lease, or IBM, for the provision of a hot site.[47]

An alternative to the hot site is a **cold site**. Unlike a hot site, a cold site does not have the necessary equipment and data in place for the organisation to immediately continue operations. Rather, it is an available office with basic telephone and electricity supplies ready for use should they be required. However, the organisation using the cold site still has to arrange for the necessary data, technology and other resources that are required to resume business operations.

## Staffing

Staffing issues in the event of a disaster can be divided into two categories, these being the evacuation of staff who are present at the location of the disaster and access to staff after the disaster. In the event of a disaster, obviously staff need to be familiar with the appropriate evacuation procedures. After a disaster, organisations need to be able to contact key employees who are part of the recovery plan, to ensure that the disruption to the business is minimal. Accordingly, plans should be set out for how key staff members such as the CEO and division managers can be contacted. After all, even the best-planned disaster recovery procedure is useless if nobody is present to implement it.

If the recovery plan requires the action of staff, it is critical to ensure that they know what their role is and how they fit in to the overall plan. This is where regular drills to 'practise' the recovery plan are important. Additionally, if part of the plan involves switching to a remote site in another city, town, state or country, the organisation should ensure that the people who are to operate that remote site are aware of what they are required to do and ready to put the plan into action at a moment's notice. There is little point having a fully equipped hot site ready to run in the event of a disaster and not having people who can staff the site and keep it going.

Staff responsibilities and roles in the disaster recovery process should be clearly documented, as should lines of responsibility and reporting relationships.

<aside>
**Hot site** A separate facility located away from the organisation's usual premises that contains offices and the necessary equipment (such as IT, telecommunications and data) to get the business back up and running in a minimal amount of time after a disaster occurs.

**Cold site** An available office with basic telephone and electricity supplies ready for use should they be required.
</aside>

## Restore business relationships

The reality for a business operating in today's environment is that it will typically be involved in networks or arrangements with other organisations or individuals. Such networks or arrangements can include extranets that link the organisation to its customers and suppliers, as well as other arrangements or deals that may be in place with external organisations. This scenario makes it essential that the organisation consults with such partners and related bodies when developing a disaster recovery plan.[48] It is easy just to think in terms of the business that you are involved in when designing a recovery plan, but the relationships this business has with other parties will also be affected and, to keep the business's operations running, it could be essential to plan to keep these relationships operating in the event of a disaster.

However, merely having a hot or cold site arranged should disaster strike is not enough. Once organisations have considered their needs and developed suitable arrangements for a disaster recovery plan, they should then ensure that the plan can be put into operation. Much as you used to have fire drills back when you were a student at school, an organisation should conduct disaster recovery drills. This will involve a mock execution of the disaster recovery plan to ensure that those responsible can perform their required tasks and that the plan actually works. Just as dangerous as not having a disaster recovery plan is the organisation having a plan but not testing that it actually works. Of the 83 per cent of Australian companies that report having a disaster recovery plan, about 50 per cent had never tested it.[49] In the United States, 19 per cent of companies with more than 100 employees that were surveyed by AT&T had not tested their disaster recovery plan in the past five years.[50] The risk in this case is that if something goes wrong, staff will not know how to react, since they have never experienced a drill of the plan. Alternatively, an untested plan left alone for a long time could very quickly become out of date or ignore changes in the organisation or technology.

## AIS FOCUS 8.3

### Sydney disaster recovery plan

In March and April 2009 the Sydney city central business district experienced some major blackouts that saw parts of the city without power for around two hours.[51] The impact of this on business and citizens was extensive, ranging from traffic congestion to business downtime and people being stranded in lifts. While this incident was not the result of what would be considered a disaster, it did highlight the need for contingency plans. For business, issues such as alternative power supplies came to the fore, with computers and networks obviously requiring power in order to operate. The loss of power meant that the Harbour Tunnel and Eastern Distributor — two of Sydney's major roadways — had to be temporarily closed.[52] It also highlighted those organisations that had adequate backup procedures in place. Examples of those with contingency plans in place included hospitals, reported to have been required to switch to backup generator systems in order to maintain operating facilities.[53]

The loss of power was attributed, in one instance, to repair work being carried out on the power network infrastructure. In this situation, where maintenance is scheduled,

*continued*

the state opposition leader argued that businesses 'should be warned and advised to have backup facilities available'.[54] The incident also highlighted the need to consider all alternatives when it was discovered that speakers placed throughout the city as a means of communicating important information and instructions in the event of a disaster were not able to operate since they had no alternative power supply.[55]

The situation highlighted the dependence on power supplies in order to operate as well as the need to consider alternative supply sources — such as generators — in the event that power supplies are disrupted.

**LEARNING OBJECTIVE**  **8**

*Analyse the execution of control activities.*

# EXECUTION OF INTERNAL CONTROL

The execution of the internal control activities is also an important consideration.[56] From the preceding discussion you should have the idea that control activities can be performed manually (e.g. a person reconciling the bank statement to cash records or signing off for a transaction to occur) or through the computer (e.g. edit checks when entering data or run-to-run totals when processing data). The consideration of control execution — be it manual or computerised — is important, since there are different characteristics of manual and computerised controls that can impact on their effectiveness within the organisation.

Manual controls, by definition, are performed by people. The main disadvantage is that they are prone to human error and inconsistent application. For example, if a control is that transactions must be approved by a manager before they can occur, there is the risk that the manager may be inconsistent in granting approval, be it because of fatigue, human error or favouring certain customers. However, a benefit of manual controls is that they offer the ability to handle one-off, irregular or infrequent events that cannot necessarily be prescribed by an algorithm that forms the basis of computer programs. For less frequent or irregular transactions manual controls may be the more suitable option.

In comparison, computer-based controls offer the benefits of consistent application, timely execution and a greater degree of difficulty in working around or avoiding the control. Controls that are programmed into the computer and are exercised by the computer will provide an assurance of consistent application — the computer follows the same steps and rules each time the control needs to be applied. In addition, controls that require any degree of computation are best performed by computers because of their relative efficiency and accuracy in executing calculations. In addition, the data that can be gathered by the computer in executing control activities can provide for further analysis and follow up by the organisation if required. Computer-based controls are also more difficult to work around. The most obvious way of avoiding computer-based controls is to manipulate the programmed instructions that the computer follows; however, few people in an organisation would possess the necessary knowledge to do this. Computer-based controls, however, are extremely dependent on a sound control environment and general controls. For example, if general controls are soundly structured (e.g. the separation of duties within the IT environment, particularly systems development and programming from users), the probability of program manipulation and alteration is reduced. However, if separation is not present there is the risk of program and data manipulation by staff in the operation of the computer systems. As a consequence, when designing computer-based controls it is necessary to consider how well the general controls are applied throughout the organisation.

**LEARNING OBJECTIVE 9**

*Understand different techniques for documenting a control system.*

# DOCUMENTING CONTROLS

Once a set of controls is established within an organisation, there is a need to document how these controls operate. Remember the emphasis in chapter 5 on the importance of systems documentation for creating a record of a system's operation? It is the same principle for internal control systems. Additionally, the Sarbanes–Oxley Act that was introduced in the United States has made it mandatory for documentation of internal controls to be prepared by the organisation and audited by the external auditor. There are several ways that an internal control system can be documented. At an overall level there is the control matrix, which tells us the control objectives of a control system, how they would ideally be attained, and whether they actually exist within a system. Australian Auditing Standards provide guidance on some of the forms of documentation that may be used to document internal control systems within an organisation, with suggestions including narrative descriptions, questionnaires, checklists and flowcharts. Research by Bierstaker[57] found that auditors typically use narratives to document a system, followed by questionnaires, flowcharts and then internal control matrices. A follow up study by Bierstaker and Wright in 2004, following legislative changes and auditing standard changes in the United States, supported this result and found that questionnaires, flowcharts and matrices had declined in popularity.[58] Combinations of questionnaires and narratives and questionnaires, flowcharts and narrative were also found to be popular. Deloitte & Touche LLP[59] also suggests a flowchart-style approach to documenting internal controls at the individual risk level. This approach will be discussed shortly.

## Narrative descriptions

A narrative description of internal controls is probably the simplest method for documenting internal controls. This approach involves a written description of the system's operation and how the controls are carried out within the system. Typically, when carrying out an evaluation of an organisation's internal controls, auditors will use the narrative in conjunction with an additional documentation technique, such as flowcharts or checklists. The benefit of this approach is the flexibility available to the preparer of the documentation; however, this comes at the cost of structure and consistency in format.[60]

## Questionnaires and checklists

Questionnaires and checklists are another common and easy to use approach for documenting an organisation's internal control system. Figure 8.7 overleaf contains an example of a checklist, based on one devised by Ernst & Young LLP.[61] The first column contains a list of the controls one would expect to see in the nominated environment — in this case the information systems environment. These controls would have been identified from a list of commonly used controls or, alternatively, arrived at after viewing the list of threats that was developed during the stage of risk assessment, which was discussed earlier. The second and third columns allow for an indication to be made as to whether the listed controls exist within the system of interest, while the final column allows for comments to be made about the control, for example why it is missing or how well it operates or any defects in its implementation that are observed.

| CONTROL CHECKLIST AREA: INFORMATION SYSTEMS | | | |
| --- | --- | --- | --- |
| Control | Yes | No | Comment |
| Are access security software and operating systems software used to control access to:<br>• data<br>• functions of programs? | | | |
| Is physical security over the IT assets reasonable given the nature of the business? | | | |
| Are critical computer data backed up daily? | | | |
| Is the backup of critical computer data stored off-site? | | | |
| Are there controls over employees' remote access to the system? | | | |
| Is there a monitoring of IT processing activities by designated staff, who periodically report to higher management on IT security? | | | |
| Is there a log for security violations? | | | |
| Is the log of security breaches periodically reviewed and acted upon? | | | |
| Is IT security periodically audited? | | | |
| Is there protection to prevent the unwanted corruption and destruction of and unauthorised access to data records? | | | |
| Is data processing's access to non data-processing assets restricted (e.g. blank cheques that are used in cheque runs.)? | | | |

**FIGURE 8.7** A general control checklist for the information systems function

The checklist approach for documenting controls would be expected to take place periodically within the organisation, with a staff member — typically a member of the internal audit division — walking through the organisation and examining what controls are present or absent. A checklist approach is also commonly employed by external auditors when evaluating the adequacy of internal controls for an information system before the completion of a financial statement audit. The benefit of this approach is that it is a highly structured means of documenting controls; however, the disadvantage is that it can lead to a one-size-fits-all approach to documentation as well as to the possibility that controls not listed on the checklist but in place within the organisation may go undocumented.[62]

# Flowcharts

Systems flowcharts as introduced in chapter 5 illustrate a system and its inputs, processes and outputs. This includes the documents that are part of the system, the processes involved in the system, as well as the entities involved in the system. The benefit of the systems flowchart as a source of control documentation is that it contains these different aspects about a system. Because of the detail in the diagram, who does what tasks can be identified, allowing assessment to be made whether separation of duties is adequately used. It is also possible to see the activities that occur, allowing the identification of controls operating within the system. Additionally, by analysing a systems flowchart, any control weaknesses that may exist can be identified.

The systems flowchart provides an overall view of the operation of a system, for example the credit sales system. However, it provides only a general view of where controls are in operation and little detail about the actual operation of such controls. Complementing the systems flowchart is a control flowchart. The control flowchart is suggested by Deloitte & Touche LLP as a way of documenting the operation of individual internal controls.[63] Deloitte & Touche LLP also suggests that any good documentation of internal control should identify seven key aspects: (1) the risk that the control is addressing, (2) how the control addresses the risk, (3) details of monitoring for the control's effectiveness, (4) how the performance of the control is assessed, (5) any problems identified in the operation of the control, (6) improvements for the control's effectiveness and (7) a signoff date from the control's evaluation.[64] An example of this approach is contained in figure 8.8.[65]

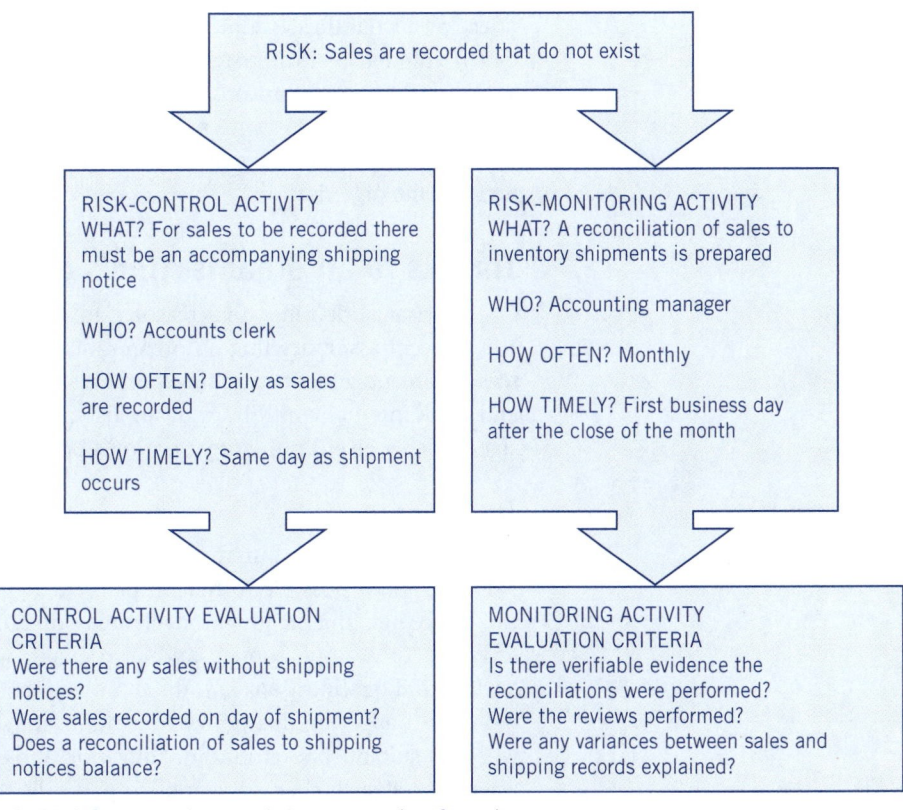

**FIGURE 8.8** Internal control documentation for sales

## Control matrix

A matrix is any grid that combines multiple perspectives or attempts to integrate multiple perspectives. Control documentation benefits from a matrix approach given that there are many perspectives to controls. We may be interested in the risks within a process and the controls in place to address that risk, in which case a matrix linking the two could be prepared. Alternatively, we may be interested in the execution of the various controls within a process, in which case a matrix of controls and characteristics can be prepared. This leads to the possibility of numerous matrix possibilities for documenting controls.[66] While research has acknowledged that control matrices can be time consuming to prepare,[67] the benefits in terms of the perspective they provide on a system can be useful to those within the organisation. Accordingly, preparation of a control matrix was proposed in the COSO report and provides a way of linking the operation of the control activities to the control objectives of an information system.

# THE LIMITATIONS OF CONTROLS

Looking at the concept of internal controls from chapter 7, the emphasis was on the part of the COSO definition that contained the words 'reasonable assurance' and the part of the Australian auditing standards definition that contained the words 'the achievement of an entity's objectives'. Both of these quotes, while insignificant in size, have significant implications for the effectiveness of the internal control system. Effectively, what these simple quotes do is provide a qualification on the effectiveness of any internal control system. The impact of the words 'reasonable assurance' and 'assist' is that even if an organisation has an internal control system in place, problems can still occur. An internal control system is *not* a rock-solid guarantee that the organisation's objectives will be attained or that errors and illegal activity will not occur in the organisation.

## Threats to an organisation's objectives

CPA Australia identifies five reasons an internal control system does not provide 100 per cent assurance that an organisation's objectives will be achieved.[68] These five reasons are judgement error, unexpected transactions, collusion, management override and weak internal controls. You can also add to this list the possibility of conflicting signals being given in the organisation's operations.[69]

### *Judgement error*

Decisions that require human judgement are always prone to human error. The reality is that it is not possible to be 100 per cent right 100 per cent of the time. Any control procedure that requires an element of human judgement is, therefore, prone to error. For example, organisational policy may be to hire employees with suitable background qualifications and three professional referees and a strong character background. In applying this policy to hiring staff, someone must make a judgement on what is a suitable background qualification and exactly what constitutes a strong character. Even if such checks are applied perfectly, there is still the chance that the applicant has set up favourable referees to paint an overly favourable picture.

## Unexpected transactions

Control systems are usually designed around the typical transactions a business undertakes and the typical errors or threats that apply to those transactions and the environments in which they occur. However, the designers of a control system are not clairvoyants — they cannot predict every possible outcome and every future event. Therefore, there will be events or transactions that were unanticipated when the control system was put in place. A sound control environment accompanied by a strong emphasis on ethical and responsible behaviour can assist employees in carrying out these unexpected transactions, as can regularly reviewing the controls and their appropriateness to the business environment.

## Collusion

Collusion is the situation where two or more people conspire to jointly commit a fraud against the organisation. Recall the emphasis on the importance of segregation of duties as a way of restricting fraudulent behaviour. The idea mentioned was that *authorisation* for a transaction that affects an asset should be given by someone different from the person who has physical *custody* of the asset, and these two individuals should be different from the individual who has *record keeping* responsibilities for the asset. In a large organisation this is relatively easy to implement, because there will be many staff members. This makes division of responsibilities in such a way reasonably practical. Unfortunately, it is by no means a foolproof approach. While separation of duties makes it more difficult for an employee to defraud the organisation, it does not make it impossible. If the employees responsible for custody, authorisation and record keeping decide to collude, or work together, to defraud the organisation, then there is little the organisation could have done to prevent it. From an organisation's perspective, the logic is that the more people who have to be involved in a fraud, the greater the chance of one of them slipping up and exposing the fraudulent activity.

Despite the theoretical effectiveness of segregation of duties, it does have one inherent limitation if one tries to apply it to environments other than that of a large firm — simply put, as organisation size decreases, application of segregation of duties becomes increasingly difficult, to the point of almost being an impossibility. From a practical point of view, they simply may not have sufficient staff members to properly enforce adequate separation of duties, with the cost of increasing staff to make it a practical alternative outweighing the expected benefits. In such an environment the organisation must rely on what are best termed 'social controls' to promote the 'right behaviour'. An example of such a social control is the fear of being caught committing fraud and the shame that is attached with it. Alternatively, a strong managerial presence and close relationship with and monitoring of the employees can deter employees from committing such acts.

## Management override

When first introducing controls the idea was mentioned that an organisation's management plays a critical role in the development of an internal control system. This, however, also exposes a weakness in the internal control structure — that controls are only effective in so far as management is ethical and responsible in promoting 'good' behaviour throughout the organisation. Looking at a sales scenario, sales staff might be only allowed to authorise credit sales up to $1000, and for sales greater than this amount the approval of a manager must be obtained. While this control will work at stopping inappropriate approval of sales at the lower level, management has the power to override the control and approve large-value sales. So if management show care and due process in checking sales before they are approved, the control is effective. However, if a manager merely 'rubber stamps' large-value sales, then the control is ineffective in its operation. Within the organisation, any person who has the authority to override a control's operation represents a potential threat to the control system's effectiveness.

## Weak internal controls

Put simply, and possibly quite obviously, a threat to internal control represents controls that are poorly designed or weak in their application. Controls that purport to achieve an aim but do not, or that are designed with inadequacies, obviously present a limitation to an internal control system's ability to achieve its objectives. Often, in designing a control system, it will be the simple things that are overlooked. For example, an organisation wants to ensure that it pays its bills once and only once — after all, you do not want to pay for something twice! A simple control to achieve this aim is the cancellation of invoices once they have been paid.[70] This can be performed by stamping the word 'PAID' across the invoice, or drawing a line through it. This relatively simple control can be extremely effective in preventing duplicate payments.

## Conflicting signals

A final threat to an internal control system's operation is the possibility that different signals are being sent by management to employees. On the one hand, management may give the message that honest and ethical behaviour is the priority of the organisation, yet it may design performance measurement schemes that contradict this message. Take the example of a salesperson who is employed to sell a product. This employee is paid a basic retainer, which makes up about 10 per cent of his or her salary. The remaining income is derived from sales commissions, based on the value of sales he or she is able to generate in each calendar month.

Given this compensation scheme, what type of incentive does such a system create for that salesperson? The obvious temptation, if business is low in a particular month, is to record a few fictitious sales towards the end of the bonus calculation period, to ensure that a bonus is received. From the organisation's perspective this is obviously undesirable, since transactions are being recorded that have not occurred, and potentially these could be to nonexistent customers. This is a breach of the principles of existence and occurrence. The salesperson has merely responded to the pressures imposed by management's compensation policies, and in the process has violated the ideas of honest and ethical behaviour as well as the reliability of the data that enter the information system. The organisation has implicitly created the incentive for the sales staff to commit fraud by logging false sales. So in designing policies and procedures, management should consider whether it is parsimonious with the overall environment that it is trying to promote.

From this discussion it begins to be clear how internal controls are only able to provide *reasonable assurance* that an organisation's goals are being attained. The control environment, particularly management's attitude and philosophy style, can play a big part in limiting the threat of many of the factors discussed in the preceding paragraphs, but it is by no means a total guarantee that the control system is infallible.

## Identity fraud

Identity fraud is the threat that has emerged over recent times and developed into an industry that costs Australia alone almost two billion dollars.[71] According to Macquarie Bank, it is also the 'world's fastest growing form of fraud, growing at more than 50 per cent annually in Australia'.[72] Identity theft is the problem of individuals pretending to be someone else, thus 'stealing' their identity, and engaging in transactions under the stolen identity. The problem has become a very real one for organisations — especially with the continual growth in the usage of the Internet and, more generally, developments in modern technology.[73] KPMG report that identity fraud accounts for 3% of reported fraud in 2008[74] and was worth $1231207 (based on the 166 fraud cases they had in their sample). In one recent case involving Shane Woewodin, a well-known Australian Rules footballer, thieves racked up thousands of dollars of debts on Woewodin's credit card. The thieves got hold of Woewodin's credit card details and used them in a series of transactions.[75]

Identity fraud is a real threat when people are just a number in a system, as is the case with credit card numbers, and when no authentication such as signatures or photo ID is required, as is the case for online credit transactions. This has led to much thought on the topic of control options for preventing identity theft. One technique is that of iris recognition technology. This functions in a similar way to a password in a conventional system, but instead of the user entering a password to gain access to a system or building, they would have their eye scanned, with iris scans unique and reliable as a form of identification. This form of biometric identification can also be applied through the use of fingerprints or retina scans. Moor reports that several law enforcement agencies are calling for the introduction of a national fingerprint or eye scan database in an attempt to combat identity fraud.[76]

A more traditional technique for combating identity fraud was also proposed by the Australian Federal government in 2006. The national Document Verification Service (DVS) will operate as a series of networked databases that will allow the cross-checking of documents such as passports, drivers licences and birth certificates.[77] This network is intended to be made available to banks, government departments and other regulatory bodies.

## Threats to internal controls

In addition to the factors identified by CPA Australia, Rogers et al[78] identify eight factors that can pose as threats to internal controls. These factors are management incompetence, employee turnover, external factors, fraud, complexity of transactions, complexity of organisational structure, regulatory environments and information technology. A selection of these factors is briefly discussed in the following section.

### *Management incompetence*

Since management has the overall responsibility for the establishment of internal controls and is significant in the effectiveness of the overall control environment, any incompetence at the top can flow down and impact on the remainder of the organisation. Alternatively, a panel of skilled board members may not have the expertise to deal with some matters that may confront an organisation. One possible way to circumvent this risk is to encourage the use of independent consultants for advice on business problems for which the board does not have adequate skills or expertise.

### External factors

As was discussed earlier, there are external factors beyond our control that can have dramatic impacts on an organisation. Natural disasters, fires and so on can all affect a business despite the best laid internal control system. While the act itself may not be preventable, the adequacy of an organisation's disaster recovery plan will determine their ability to recover and return to normal operations.

### Fraud

The risk of those within the organisation working around internal controls for their own gain is something that an organisation needs to be aware of. Where management has authority to work around controls or approve events, this use of authority is a risk. At lower levels, this risk can come about through collusion between employees. This scenario may be the result of employee incentive schemes that unwittingly promote fraudulent behaviour.

### Regulatory environment

Changes in the regulatory environment can impact on the way that organisations operate. An example of this can be seen with the introduction of the Sarbanes–Oxley Act in the United States, with its introduction in some situations requiring changes in the way internal controls were implemented and documented within organisations. While it is US legislation, its effect is felt by any company that is monitored by the SEC in the United States, making its impact wide reaching.[79] Being unaware of changes in the regulatory environment exposes an organisation to risk. This risk, however, can be reduced through the use of appropriate outside expertise and professional advice.

### Information technology

Information technology is in a constant state of flux. Threats from viruses and email attacks mean that organisations face new strains of threats to their information technology resources. An example of this type of threat occurred recently when one of Australia's largest banks, the National Australia Bank, had its website attacked by a series of *denial-of-service* attacks, causing the bank's website to fail. See AIS focus 8.5 for a brief discussion of an information technology threat and issues that have received attention in Australia.

## AIS FOCUS 8.5

## Denial-of-service attacks

A denial-of-service attack occurs when an organisation's web server is inundated with hits and requests from external sources, with the traffic of such a magnitude that the web server is unable to handle the traffic and fails.

One recently publicised example of this is the National Australia Bank. The bank's website experienced a denial-of-service attack that caused its web servers to fail. This event had an impact on NAB customers wanting to carry out Internet banking and other online activities through the bank's website.[80]

A denial-of-service attack is just one of many forms of external threats to an organisation's online activities, with other threats including fake emails to customers asking for banking and other such personal details (phishing). The Australian Securities and Investments Commission reports a 25 per cent increase in phishing over the last two years.[81] The ever-changing technology available to perpetrators means that methods of phishing execution are also ever changing and becoming increasingly sophisticated.[82]

## ›› SUMMARY ›››

LEARNING OBJECTIVE

### How do control activities relate to the accounting process?

The accounting process aims to capture data about business transactions and processes and store data, so financial statements can be prepared for various user groups. In this process, data inputs must be gathered and entered into the system and data needs to be updated and moved between different locations, creating the risk of errors. The accounting process, therefore, relies on control activities that operate to prevent, detect or correct any errors or irregularities and help achieve reliable and accurate reporting.

LEARNING OBJECTIVE

### How can internal controls be classified as general or application and based on function and business process stage and how can these be distinguished?

There is a range of ways that internal controls can be classified. The classification of general and application controls sees the classification based on the role controls play as part of the broader information system versus specific to business processes. Application controls relate to specific business processes and typically relate to control over the input, processing and outputs within that process. General controls relate across the compu-terised information system and provide the foundation on which application controls operate.

Internal controls can be applied to the different stages that data goes through in the organisation: input, processing and output. The input/processing/output classification relates to the stage in the data processing cycle that application controls operate. Taking a functional perspective, a preventive/detective/corrective classification looks at whether the control activities avoid, alert or correct problems within a system.

LEARNING OBJECTIVE

### How do controls link to the stages of data processing and COSO and COBIT?

Data processing within the organisation goes through several stages, including data collec-tion, input, processing, output and storage. In each of these stages there are risks that are addressed by the application of control activities. The table presented in the chapter com-bines these aspects, showing the different stages and examples of typical control risks and control activities. The COBIT framework provides an IT control framework for organisations to apply across the stages of IT use within the organisation.

## KEY TERMS

accuracy, p. 331
application controls, p. 332
authorisation, p. 331
batch processing, p. 338
batch total, p. 351
cold site, p. 358
completeness, p. 331
corrective controls, p. 334
detective control, p. 333
disaster recovery plan, p. 357
general controls, p. 331
hot site, p. 358
independent reviews, p. 352
information processing controls, p. 331

input accuracy, p. 337
input completeness, p. 337
input controls, p. 334
input validity, p. 347
online data gathering and batch
    processing, p. 338
online real-time data processing, p. 338
output controls, p. 334
performance reviews, p. 331
physical controls, p. 332
preventive controls, p. 333
processing controls, p. 334
segregation of duties, p. 332
timeliness, p. 338

## DISCUSSION QUESTIONS

8.1 Define the following:
   (a) General control
   (b) Application control (LO2)

8.2 You work for a business that has just established a new data processing centre. In a conversation with one of the directors over lunch one day, you get onto the topic of controls and the design of controls for the new centre. Proudly, the director boasts, 'We have the most hi-tech biometric controls in place. No unauthorised access to the centre is possible. The programmers are able to get on with their day-to-day duties of developing programs and managing the organisation's data resources.'
   You are slightly concerned by this statement and immediately think back to appropriate controls for implementation in the information systems environment — one of which is segregation of duties.
   (a) What are the faults in the director's statement?
   (b) Can the organisation rely on biometric controls alone?
   (c) How can separation of duties be applied in the information systems area?
   (d) What are the critical functions that should be separated?
   (e) What are the risks if these functions are not separated? (LO5)

8.3 (a) What is a turnaround document?
   (b) Provide five examples of turnaround documents. Discuss how turnaround documents help to achieve the aims of input accuracy and input completeness. (LO6)

8.4 Explain situations where manually performed control activities are particularly suitable. (LO8)

8.5 Describe the advantages of computer-executed control activities. (LO8)

8.6 Explain, using an example, why computer-executed controls rely on a sound set of general controls. (LO8)

## SELF-TEST ACTIVITIES

8.1 Examples of preventive controls to prevent incorrect data entry into a sales system include (i) validity checks, (ii) range checks, (iii) completeness checks, (iv) run-to-run total checks, (v) redundant data checks.

(a) i, ii, iii and iv

(b) ii, iii, iv and v

(c) i, iii, iv and v

(d) i, ii, iv and v

(e) i, ii, iii and v

8.2 The use of biometric identification techniques on an entrance to the computer processing centre is an example of a:

(a) preventive control.

(b) detective control.

(c) corrective control.

(d) application control.

(e) access control.

8.3 An organisation is concerned about the possibility of sales to false and nonexistent customers being entered into its sales system by sales staff. The best control to *prevent* this problem would be:

(a) calling a random sample of customers to ensure they exist.

(b) having sales staff maintain a customer master file.

(c) having a customer master file maintained independent of sales.

(d) having a policy of making only in-store sales (e.g. having no phone or web-based orders).

(e) proper screening of sales staff before hiring them.

8.4 Select the best pair of terms to complete the following statement: The threat of collusion among employees can be reduced by the application of (i)_____, which entails (ii)_____.

(a) (i) organisational policies, (ii) having clearly defined job descriptions

(b) (i) organisational policies, (ii) specifying procedures for the authorisation, custody and record keeping relating to assets

(c) (i) separation of duties (ii) keeping employees separate from one another

(d) (i) general controls (ii) having a clear set of organisational policies, such as job notation and forced annual leave

(e) (i) separation of duties, (ii) keeping authorisation, custody and record keeping separate

## PROBLEMS

8.1 Classify the following control activities as general or application and explain your reasoning,

(a) Employees have a password to gain access to the system.

(b) When sales are entered the system retrieves customer details based on the customer number.

(c) A check is performed to identify if all cheques can be accounted for.

(d) Systems development is subject to signoff by the CIO before it can take place.

(e) Virus definitions are updated daily.

(f) The Sales Manager must approve all discounts for items sold below their sticker price.

8.2 A sales system for a small retail store is described in the following paragraph. Once you have read the paragraph, identify any risks within the system, the potential consequences of these risks, and controls that could be implemented to combat these risks.

**The sales system**

As a sale occurs, customer details including customer number and address, as well as the items purchased, are written on a blank invoice form. Item descriptions, quantity sold and unit price are also filled in, with the sales staff having some discretion in setting the unit price for situations such as bulk purchases or repeat customers. These invoice forms are collected at the end of the day and keyed in to the computer, with an invoice number assigned to invoices as they are keyed in. This number is recorded on the store copy of the invoice. Any new customers are added to the customer master list as their sales are entered and any details not gathered on the invoice are left blank. Data are stored on a central server and this server is backed up monthly. The system is also connected up to the organisation's suppliers and used to order goods.

8.3 Explain, using an example, how batch totals can achieve the dual aims of input accuracy and input completeness.

8.4 Conduct a web search for some examples of internal controls that have failed to operate effectively. For the cases you have identified, answer the following questions.
   (a) What factors led to the failure of these controls?
   (b) Could the failure have been avoided? If so, how?

8.5 Turn 'Em Out is a fashion company that sells clothes to retail stores and individual customers, provided that they are registered as a customer. This eliminates the need for off-the-street sales. The organisation recently received a purchase order. The steps that are subsequently followed are:
   (1) Customer service representative prepares a sales order (three copies).
   (2) Send the sales order to the accounts department and sales department.
   (3) The accounts department and sales department will enter the order into the system.
   (4) The computer will capture the data and store it in a temporary file, updating the inventory, sales and accounts receivable files at the end of the day.
   (5) Print a picking slip and invoice and send it to the warehouse.
   (6) Pick the goods.
   (7) Attach picking slip and invoice to the goods.
   (8) Send goods to the customer.

   Analyse the process by breaking it up into the stages of authorisation, input, processing, output, and external data stages, as was discussed in reference to COBIT in the chapter. For each stage state the aims, control issues and controls that could be used by Turn 'Em Out.

8.6 The payments department at Slick Sales has issued a cheque for an invoice it has received from Office Supplies Ltd. The payables clerk has three documents, (1) a receipted purchase order (figure 8.9), (2) a receiving report (figure 8.10), and (3) an invoice (figure 8.11). The clerk has prepared the accompanying cheque and had it signed, ready for sending (figure 8.12).

**Required**
   (a) Explain how the purchase order, receiving report and invoice play an important role in the authorisation of payments to accounts payable.
   (b) Analyse the documents shown and determine if the clerk should have prepared the cheque and if it should be sent off to the supplier. Justify your conclusion.
   (c) What controls should be in place during and subsequent to cheque preparation?
   (d) Discuss the use and function of the remittance advice that is contained as a part of the tax invoice.

## PURCHASE ORDER

### Slick Sales
**45 Westend Road**
**Melbourne**
ABN: 57 999 888 777

No. **64971**

**SENT**
05 MAY 10

TO:

Office Supplies Ltd
5 Broadway Road
East Melbourne

**Date Ordered:** 5/5/2006

Purchase Req No.: 54937

| Product No. | Description | Price | Quantity | Total |
|---|---|---|---|---|
| 101-A1 | A4 Copy Paper 500 sheets | 5.50 | 10 | 55.00 |
| 202-C4 | Printer cartridge – Laserjet | 68.00 | 5 | 340.00 |
| 054-B2 | Electronic stapler | 75.00 | 2 | 150.00 |
| 391-J8 | Paper files – pack of 100 | 35.50 | 4 | 142.00 |
| 452-P3 | Binder – A4 2 ring large | 6.75 | 2 | 13.50 |
| | | | **TOTAL** | 700.50 |

Prepared By: *Sam*
Sam Toms

Approved By: *Tim Lees*
Tim Lees

**FIGURE 8.9** Purchase order

## RECEIVING REPORT

### Slick Sales

No. **68431**

Purchase Order No: 64971

Entered By: Louise Hanninton

Goods Received From: Office Supplies Ltd

Receipt Date: 12/5/10

| Product No. | Description | Quantity | Comments |
|---|---|---|---|
| 101-A1 | A4 Copy Paper 500 sheets | 10 | Condition OK |
| 202-C4 | Printer cartridge – Laserjet | 5 | Box damaged, item OK |
| 054-B2 | Electronic stapler | 2 | Condition OK |
| 391-J8 | Paper files – pack of 100 | 4 | Condition OK |
| 452-P3 | Binder – A4 2 ring large | 2 | Condition OK |

Report Prepared By: *Julie Mantini*
Julie Mantini

Goods Received By: *Ross Scambly*
Ross Scambly

**FIGURE 8.10** Receiving report

## TAX INVOICE

**Office Supplies Ltd**

5 Broadway Road

East Melbourne

ABN: 10 567 893 111

No. **159473**

**To:** Slick Sales
45 Westend Road
Melbourne

**Acct No.:** S1149
**Terms:** 2/10, n/35
**Payment Due: 29/06/10**

**Invoice Date:** 25/5/2010    **Purchase Order No.:** 54937

| Product No. | Description | Price | Quantity | Total |
|---|---|---|---|---|
| 101-A1 | A4 Copy Paper 500 sheets | 5.50 | 10 | 55.00 |
| 202-C4 | Printer cartridge – Laserjet | 68.00 | 5 | 340.00 |
| 054-B2 | Electronic stapler | 75.00 | 3 | 225.00 |
| 391-J8 | Paper files – pack of 100 | 35.50 | 4 | 142.00 |
| 452-P3 | Binder – A4 2 ring large | 6.75 | 2 | 13.50 |
| | | | SUB TOTAL | 775.50 |
| | | | + GST | 77.55 |
| | | | TOTAL | **853.05** |

**PLEASE QUOTE YOUR ACCOUNT NUMBER WHEN ENQUIRING ABOUT INVOICE DETAILS**

- - - ✂ - - - - - - - - - - - - - - - - - - - - - - - - - - - - - - - - -

### *REMITTANCE ADVICE*
Please return with payment

**Account Number:** S1149

**Account Name:** Slick Sales

**Amount Owing: 853.05**

**Due Date: 29/06/10**

**Invoice No:** 159473

| OFFICE USE ONLY |
|---|

Date Received: - - - - - - - - - - - - - -    Date Entered: - - - - - - - - - - - - - - - - - - - -

Received By: - - - - - - - - - - - - - -    Entered By: - - - - - - - - - - - - - - - - - - - -

Amount Received:    Cheque Number:

**FIGURE 8.11** Tax invoice

---

| Cheque 101 | | **TRIMOND BANKING GROUP** 349 Victoria Avenue Melbourne East | Date 30-05-10 |
|---|---|---|---|
| **Payee:** Office Supplies Ltd | | | |
| **For:** Office Supplies Invoice 159473 | Pay Office Supplies Ltd    Or bearer The sum of Eight hundred and fifty-three dollars and five cents | | $853.05 |
| **Date:** 30-05-10 | Slick Sales | | |
| **Amount:** 853.05 | II 648 317 101II | | |

**FIGURE 8.12** Cheque

8.7 The following purchase order (figure 8.13) was sent by Giddy Up Pty Ltd to Stable Supplies Ltd. The second copy of the purchase order (figure 8.14) from Giddy Up was sent to the receiving department and was stamped and signed when the goods were received.

**Required**

(a) Identify the control features of both documents.

(b) Discuss the functioning of the control features in both documents.

(c) What controls could have been present when the purchase requisition details (not shown) were entered into the computer and the purchase order generated?

## PURCHASE ORDER
### Giddy Up Pty Ltd
**1 Winning Post Lane**
**Flemington**
ABN: 11 111 111 111

SUPPLIER COPY

No. 64971

**To:**

Stable Supplies
4 Fetlock Road
Caulfield

**Order Date:** 1/11/2010          **Purchase Req No.:** 61111

| Product No. | Description | Price | Quantity | Total |
|---|---|---|---|---|
| A-187 | Barrier blanket | 150.00 | 5 | 750.00 |
| A-199 | Riding crop | 45.00 | 4 | 180.00 |
| C-297 | Racing saddle – light | 300.00 | 1 | 300.00 |
| G-851 | Norton bit | 80.00 | 3 | 240.00 |
| | | | **TOTAL** | 1470.00 |

**Prepared By:** *Mary Bethany*

**Approved By:** *Kym Dilaney*

**FIGURE 8.13** Purchase order sent to vendor

# PURCHASE ORDER

**Giddy Up Pty Ltd**
**1 Winning Post Lane**
**Flemington**
ABN: 11 111 111 111

**RECEIVING DEPT COPY**

**No. 64971**

**To:**

Stable Supplies
4 Fetlock Road
Caulfield

**Received 07 NOV 10**

**Order Date:** 1/11/2010     **Purchase Req No.:** 61111

| Product No. | Description | Price | Quantity | Total |
|---|---|---|---|---|
| A-187 | Barrier blanket | | | |
| A-199 | Riding crop | | | |
| C-297 | Racing saddle – light | | | |
| G-851 | Norton bit | | | |
| | | | **TOTAL** | |

**Prepared By:** *Mary Bethany*

**Approved By:** *Kym Dilaney*

**FIGURE 8.14** Copy of purchase order routed to receiving department

8.8 For each of the following risks suggest a control that could be used to reduce it.
   (a) Entering negative values for order quantity in a sales order
   (b) Selling to a customer with an overdue account
   (c) Ordering from a nonexistent supplier
   (d) Paying for goods that have not been received
   (e) Entering an alphanumeric customer ID when the business policy is for numeric customer IDs
   (f) Misappropriation of goods by receiving staff, who also maintain inventory records
   (g) Ordering too much of a product

8.9 An accounts payable process is documented in the flowchart contained in figure 8.15. Using this flowchart as a reference:
   (a) Write a brief narrative that describes the operation of the process.
   (b) Identify any risks that are present in the system.
   (c) Identify any controls that are present in the case and explain their operation and the risks that they address.
   (d) Identify any risks that do not have relevant control activities and discuss the internal control activity that would be appropriate to address the risk.

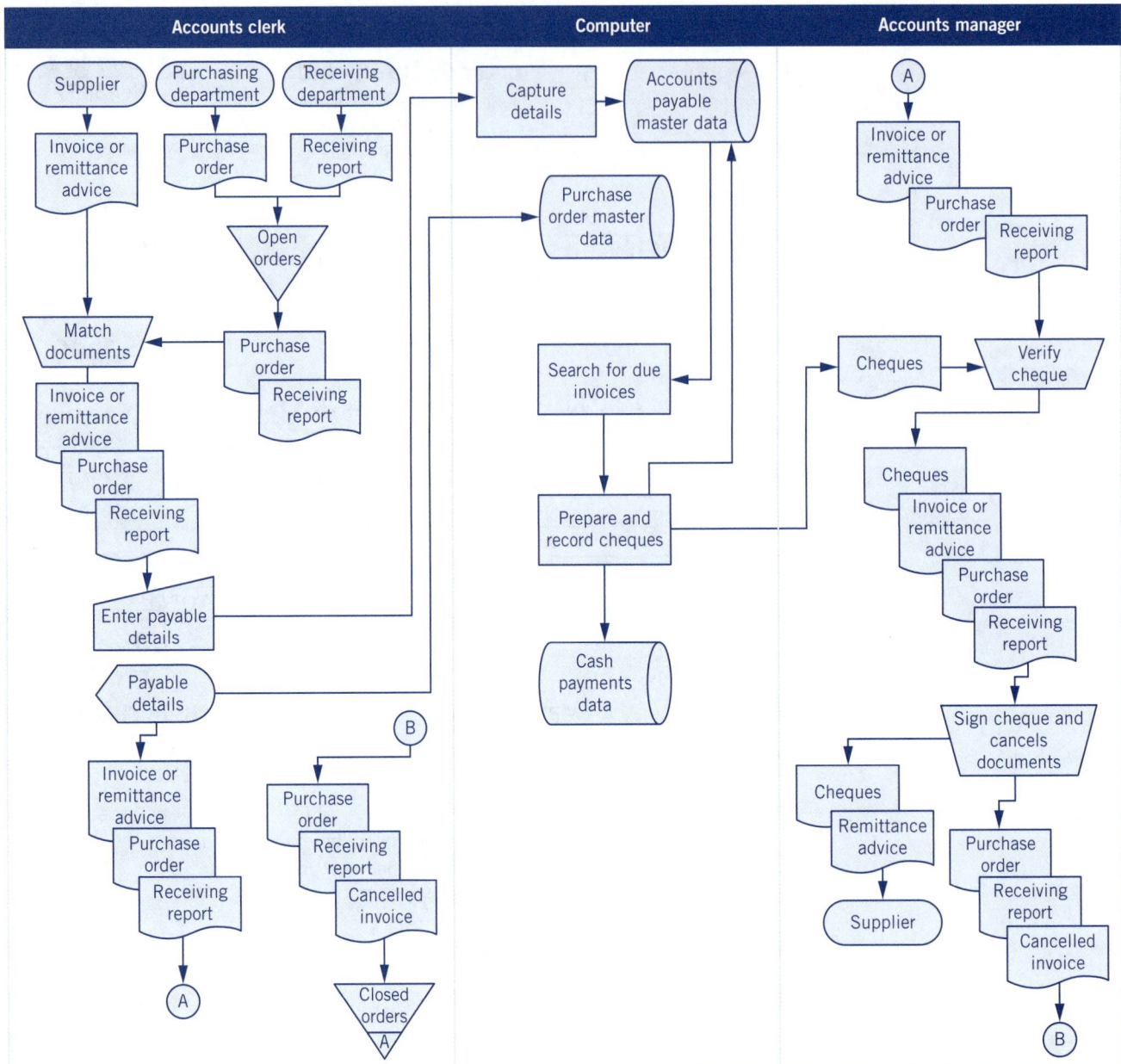

**FIGURE 8.15** Flowchart of the accounts payable process

8.10 The sales and warehouse of Truly Legit, a retail company, operates as follows and is currently under review:

Truly Legit is implementing a new credit sales approval system. Based on an analysis of their existing sales data for credit sales in the financial year just ended the following data has been obtained.

| Transaction value | Total value | Number of transactions | % of sales |
|---|---|---|---|
| $1–$500 | $357 950 | 1431 | 27.9 |
| $501–$1000 | $455 845 | 585 | 35.6 |
| $1001–$2500 | $287 675 | 145 | 22.5 |
| >$2500 | $180 000 | 60 | 14.0 |
| TOTAL | $1 281 470 | 2221 | 100.0 |

The current system has a standard sales process whereby the sales person provides the approval and authorisation for goods to be released by signing a sales order, a copy of which goes to the warehouse and serves the dual purpose of a picking ticket and shipping authorisation. The documents are prepared on computer by the salesperson, printed out and sent via internal mail at the end of the day to the warehouse. If a new customer comes in off the street, then the sales person adds them to the system immediately and gives them the default credit limit of $750. Customer credit limits are not checked unless the customer name appears on a credit warning list, which is produced by the accounts receivable division at the start of each month. All sales follow this process.

The stages of the COSO framework, as they apply to Truly Legit, are:

- *control environment:* The board of directors is constantly receiving feedback from the various functional divisions about their performance and meeting of targets. Additionally, the board places great emphasis on corporate governance and has held numerous organisation-wide workshops and training sessions for middle-level management to reinforce the importance of proper governance and control. The board also has an audit committee, who monitor internal control functionality, which is comprised wholly of non-executive directors.
- *risk assessment:* Management is concerned about the following risks in the sales process.

| Risk |
|---|
| • Sales to customers who have exceeded their credit limit |
| • Large transactions taking place without proper approval |
| • Fraudulent sales of low value entering the system |
| • Goods being shipped without proper authorisation |
| • Sales orders going missing between sales person and warehouse |
| • Customers' records containing nonexistent customers |

- *control activities*
- *information and communication*
- *monitoring.*

**Required**
(a) Using the COSO framework, derive control activities that could be implemented within the sales process to overcome the risks involved.
(b) For each control activity that you identified in (a), identify the information and communication necessary as well as how monitoring can occur to assess the process performance

8.11 Refer to AIS focus 8.3 on the Sydney power supply and answer the following questions.
   (a) What issues about disaster recovery plans does this case highlight? Explain.
   (b) Comment on the adequacy of the backup plans for the city of Sydney. What evidence is there of strengths and weaknesses in the design of the program?
   (c) What could some of the consequences be from a loss of power?
   (d) How well do you think the Sydney disaster plan matches to the ideas presented in the chapter? Explain your answer.

8.12 Refer to AIS focus 8.1 'A million dollar data entry error' and answer the following questions.
   (a) Explain how the data entry errors referred to in the case could have happened
   (b) Identify a control that could have been put in place to prevent the errors described. Explain how the control would have solved the problem.
   (c) Explain a control that could have been put in place to detect the errors mentioned in the case. Explain how they could have solved the problem.
   (d) Describe other internal controls that you would expect to see in the case described.

8.13 Below is a description of a business process.

> The computer system requires all users to log on with a user identification (their first initial and the first six letters of their surname), and a password that is assigned to users when they join the firm (that is unable to be changed). The users have access to the internet and several have installed Windows Live Messenger and other chat programs on their machines.
>
> The main task of John, one of the staff members, is to perform data entry. Each day he receives a bundle of orders from the customer assistant, with John's job being to enter the details into the system. John first enters the customer name, address and contact number then clicks on the 'Next' button to enter the items and quantities ordered by the customer. If the customer name is not provided the computer will prompt John to go back and fill in the details before proceeding to the next screen. In addition, the computer will only accept numeric values for the quantities ordered. Once all orders are entered John clicks the 'Done' button and the computer displays the number of orders entered on the screen. John usually ignores this, because by the time orders have been entered it is usually lunch time.

**Required**
(a) Identify four risks in the process.
(b) Suggest an internal control for each risk (the control may be mentioned in the case or missing and you think it should be applied).
(c) Indicate whether the control is present or missing in the case.
(d) Classify the control as general or application.
(e) Identify the control goal that the control addresses.
(f) Classify the control as manual or computerised.
Use the template matrix shown below to document your answer.

| Risk | Control | Present? | General/ Application | Goal | Manual/ Computerised |
|------|---------|----------|----------------------|------|----------------------|
|  |  |  |  |  |  |
|  |  |  |  |  |  |
|  |  |  |  |  |  |
|  |  |  |  |  |  |

8.14 Explain why pre-numbering source documents is a necessary but not sufficient condition for completeness to be satisfied.

8.15 Explain how edit checks can help to achieve the assertion of accuracy.

8.16 Organisations are often subject to legal requirements, with controls put in place to meet these. An example is the Privacy Act, which places restrictions on how data is to be gathered, used and stored. It also addresses security of data and procedures for protecting access to data.

**Required**

(a) Explain why protecting data is an increasing challenge for organisations.

(b) Suggest organisational control activities that could be implemented to protect data.

8.17 Read the article by Fiona Smith[83] in figure 8.16 and answer the following questions.

**FIGURE 8.16** Make no mistake, this will save money

Human error in business isn't as unpredictable and unavoidable as it may seem.

One day last July, Talsico International — a company specialising in reducing human errors — received an urgent call from one of the world's largest pharmaceutical groups. The group was in dire straits. One of its plants in the US was threatened with deregistration because of repeated errors in paperwork. The staff at the plant were diligent, but couldn't seem to stop themselves from making mistakes when filling out the forms after performing clearance procedures.

A clearance procedure is the meticulous cleaning of an area after workers finish making one drug and are about to start manufacturing another, says Filomenia Sousa, CEO of Talsico, an Australian-based consultancy. 'A small contaminant could kill, or make you very sick, and the cost of someone suing could run into millions and millions of dollars,' Sousa says. There were no problems with the cleaning, it was simply a matter of the paperwork, and the Food and Drug Authority (FDA) had issued two warnings. 'The FDA doesn't care if it is a paperwork error, or a process error ... if you fail three times, they can close you down,' Sousa says.

Sousa says the implication for the pharmaceutical company — which she declined to name — were enormous. The plant was risking millions of dollars in losses, a disastrous blow to the company reputation and, at that site, 3000 jobs were on the line. Almost in desperation, they called our office in the US,' she says.

Sousa got on a plane and flew to the site and, when she took a look at the paperwork, was immediately able to identify a number of places where staff were likely to make mistakes. 'They were absolutely amazed, they thought it was some sort of black magic,' she says. 'There was nothing magical about it at all. The reason these poor operators were making these paperwork errors was because the design of the forms was really not good for the human brain. So, when they were tired or flustered — which often happened during clearances — they made errors.' The paperwork was changed and, within two weeks, they had a 73 per cent decrease in errors. Previously, they had made an error every time they did a clearance procedure, which was once every three or four days.

Human error is one of those risks in business that can seem unpredictable and — to an extent — unavoidable. According to Talsico, 70 to 96 per cent of mistakes made in business are due to human error. And mistakes are happening all the time. 'In manufacturing industries I have worked with, the majority of documents would have some errors that need to be corrected,' Sousa says.

Human error has been blamed for everything from damaging client relationships, product recalls, multi-million-dollar losses on products, plane crashes, the

*(continued)*

Chernobyl nuclear accident and the loss of the Mars space probe. 'But to be honest, those spectacular errors that happen once very few months are not the biggest cost,' Sousa says. The biggest cost comes from the ones that are made day in day out in an organisation. They can end up costing millions of dollars a year. In fact, for large organisations, it would be billions of dollars. One of the pharmaceutical companies we work with estimated that every time an error was made, in paperwork or process, investigating that error — just investigating it — cost $5000.'

What Talsico does is to examine the way things are done to find weaknesses, using an understanding of the way the brain processes information. They types of errors are categorised, so that the reasons can be understood and dealt with. By doing this, the consultancy claims to cut documentation errors by a minimum of 73 per cent and waste and rework by 60 per cent. Sometimes the answer is as simple as designing a system to stop factory workers from ever so slightly over-filling detergent bottles, errors that were costing one manufacturer more than $1 million a year. It is also as effective as redesigning a pure oxygen tap behind hospital beds so that it cannot be confused with the adjacent tap for clean air. The medical workers were connecting to the wrong taps at least once a week and patient safety was threatened. The hospital was already subject to an expensive lawsuit from one patient. 'The cost to fix that was less than $15 per patient. It was nothing,' says Sousa.

The savings that can be made by reducing error rates can be enormous. 'In one of the companies we work with, in just one department of one branch of the organisation, by reducing some of the errors they were having, we saved $360 000 a year,' Sousa says. Another pharmaceutical company, by reducing errors and subsequent product waste, saved $2.6 million a year, Sousa says.

It is surprising then that there aren't more companies specialising in this field. Sousa says she can't think of one other such consultancy. Launched in Australia 12 years ago (Sousa is one of the founders), Talsico now works with 1200 companies, up to 900 of them overseas. Clients in this country include: Qantas, BHP Billiton, Arnotts, Colgate-Palmolive, AstraZeneca, Mt Isa Mines and the Australian Nuclear Science and Technology Organisation.

Sousa, a geneticist and former computer systems engineer, says that some of the measures taken by organisations to prevent mistakes actually do the opposite. One of them is to respond to mistakes by retraining or punishing. This assumes that people who make mistakes either don't know any better, or don't care. However, a study of 1000 people in the US by Talsico over the course of a year discovered only 6 per cent of the errors were due to people not knowing what to do. As for not caring, most people want to do a good job, says Sousa.

'And if you want to create an environment where people are punished for errors — particularly if it is done subconsciously — it is not that they'll make fewer errors, but that they will hide the errors they make.' Another false measure taken by employers is to have a rigorous checking process, but this can actually encourage people to take less responsibility for the accuracy of their own work, says Sousa. Sousa has seen mistakes being made on medical labels after the text and layout had been checked by seven different people. Each of them had thought: "Well, I'll do a quick check and if I miss something one of the others will get it," says Sousa. A wrong label could mean a product recall costing millions of dollars. A better system is to give each person sole responsibility for a small part of the task. 'They will then give it their full attention,' Sousa says.

**Required**

(a) What does the article suggest is the main source of errors in a business?

(b) What are the implications of this article for the design and use of source documents in an organisation?

(c) Explain, using this article as a reference, why it is preferable to deal with errors at the input stage, rather than rely on detection or corrective controls that operate later in the data processing stages.

(d) Suggest three ways that organisations could make source documents less prone to errors.

(e) What does the article suggest about the role of checking procedures? Do you agree with the assertion? Explain your answer.

(f) What do you think are some of the potential impacts of this article on the design and implementation of an internal control system?

## SELF-TEST ANSWERS

8.1 e, 8.2 e, 8.3 c, 8.4 d

## END NOTES

1. Auditing and Assurance Standards Board 2009, Auditing Standard ASA 315 *Identifying and Assessing the Risks of Material Misstatement through Understanding the Entity and Its Environment*, paragraph 9, www.auasb.gov.au.

2. Auditing and Assurance Standards Board 2009, paragraph 9.

3. Auditing and Assurance Standards Board 2009, paragraph 9.

4. Auditing and Assurance Standards Board 2006, Auditing Standard ASA 315 *Understanding the Entity and Its Environment and Assessing the Risks of Material Misstatement*, Appendix 2(o), p. 60, www.auasb.gov.au.

5. IT Governance Institute 2006, *IT control objectives for Sarbanes–Oxley: the role of IT in the design and implementation of internal control over financial reporting*, 2nd edn, IT Governance Institute, Illinois, p. 22.

6. IT Governance Institute 2005, *COBIT 4.0*, IT Governance Institute, Illinois; IT Governance Institute 2007, *COBIT 4.1*, www.itgi.org.

7. IT Governance Institute 2006, p. 55.

8. Based on COBIT 4.0 (IT Governance Control Institute 2005, pp. 16–17).

9. IT Governance Institute 2005, pp. 16–17.

10. Jain, AK, Ross, A & Prabhakar, S 2004, 'An introduction to biometric recognition', *IEEE Transactions on Circuits and Systems for Video Technology, Special Issue on Image- and Video-Based Biometrics*, vol. 14, no. 1, www.citer.wvu.edu/members/publications/files/RossBioIntro_CSVT2004.pdf.

11. KPMG Australia 2009, *Fraud Survey 2008*, pp. 9–12, www.kpmg.com.au; KPMG Australia 2006, *Fraud Survey 2006*, pp. 11–13, www.kpmg.com.au/Portals/0/FraudSurvey%2006%20WP(web).pdf.

12. KPMG Australia 2009.

13. Ives, B, Walsh, K & Schneider, H 2004, 'The domino effect of password reuse', *Communications of the ACM*, vol. 47, no. 4, pp. 75–8.

14. Zviran, M & Haga, W 1999, 'Password security: an empirical study', *Journal of Management Information Systems*, vol. 15, no. 4, pp. 161–85.

15. Adams, A & Sasse, MA 1999, 'Users are not the enemy', *Communications of the ACM*, vol. 42, no. 12, pp. 41–6.

16. Zviran, M & Haga, W 1999.

17. Gaw, S & Felten, E 2006, 'Password management strategies for online accounts', *Symposium on Usable Privacy and Security (SOUPS) 2006*, July 12–14, Pittsburgh, PA, USA.

18. Ives, B, Walsh, K & Schneider, H 2004.

19. Ives, B, Walsh, K & Schneider, H 2004; Zviran, M & Haga, W 1999.

20. Zviran, M & Haga, W 1999.

21. Ernst & Young 2005, *Emerging trends in internal controls: fourth survey and industry insights*, p. 25, www.sarbanes-oxley.be/aabs_emerging_trends_survey4.pdf.

22. Abrams, J 2008, 'Treasury office faults IRS computer security', *The Age*, 8 April, www.news.theage.com.au.

23. West, R 2008, 'The psychology of security', *Communications of the ACM*, vol. 51, no. 4, pp. 34–41.

24. Neumann, PG 1999, 'Risks of insiders', *Communications of the ACM*, vol. 42, no. 12, p. 160.

25. KPMG Australia 2009.

26. Elliot, P 2009, 'Obama orders review of cyber security', *The Age*, 10 February, www.news.theage.com.au.

27. Chapman, G 2008, 'Hackers harpoon US executives with phony email subpoenas', *The Age*, 6 May, www.news.theage.com.au.

28. Sharma, M 2008, 'Lost CD with tax details missing: ATO', *AustralianIT*, 30 October 2008, www.australianit.news.com.au.

29. Reuters 2007, 'UK govt apologises for losing data', *The Age*, 21 November, www.theage. com.au; May, J 2007, 'UK Chancellor's job on line after data on millions lost', *The Age*, 22 November, www.theage.com.au.

30. Woodhead, B 2006, 'Tax office sacks "spies"', *Australian IT*, 29 August, www.australianit.news.com.au.

31. AFP 2008, 'UK suffers new personal data loss', *The Age*, 19 January, www.theage.com.au.

32. Choy, M, Leong, HV & Wong, MH 2000, 'Disaster recovery techniques for database systems', *Communications of the ACM*, vol. 43, no. 11, pp. 272–80.

33. KPMG Australia 2009.

34. Brisbane Times 2009s, '$10m instead of $10 000: couple on run after bank bungle', *Brisbane Times*, 21 May, www.brisbanetimes.com.au.

35. Ritchie, K 2009, 'NZ couple flees after $8m bank error', *ABC News*, 21 May, www.abc.net.au.

36. McLean, T 2009, 'Kiwi banker ditched over dropped decimal', *Brisbane Times*, 20 July, www.brisbanetimes.com.au.

37. Brisbane Times 2009b, 'Forget Lotto, just bank at Westpac NZ for a jackpot', *Brisbane Times*, 28 June, www.brisbanetimes.com.au.

38. Brisbane Times 2009b.

39. Boreham, T 2004, 'New NAB boss to restore "pride"', *The Australian*, 3 February, p. 1; Gluyas, R 2004, 'Late-night call puts Scotsman in top job', *The Australian*, 3 February, p. 1.

40. Lightle, SS & Vallario, CW 2003, 'Segregation of duties in ERP', *Internal Auditing*, vol. 60, no. 5, pp. 27–31.

41. Lightle & Vallario 2003, pp. 27–31.

42. Lehman, MW 1999, 'Searching for unusual transactions', *The Internal Auditor*, vol. 56, no. 6, pp. 27–9.

43. Based on Richtel, M 2002, 'Credit companies are growing wary of online betting', *The New York Times*, 21 January, p. C1.

44. PricewaterhouseCoopers 2002, 'Disaster recovery and business continuity planning, post 9/11', *The Secure Solution*, April, PricewaterhouseCoopers, www.pwcglobal.com.

45. Timson, L 2003, 'Flirting with disaster', *The Sydney Morning Herald*, 14 October, www.smh.com.au.

46. AT&T 2002, 'Survey finds many businesses still unprepared for disasters', 27 August, www.att.com.

47. Timson, 2003.

48. PricewaterhouseCoopers, 2002.

49. Timson, 2003.

50. AT&T, 2002.

51. AAP 2009, 'Major cable fault causes second Sydney blackout in a week', 4 April, www.news.com.au.

52. Lester, T 2009, 'The blackout blessing', 1 April, www.news.ninemsn.com.au.

53. Walters, A 2009, 'St Vincent's hospital hit in Sydney's latest power cut', *The Sunday Telegraph*, 12 April 2009, www.dailytelegraph.com.au.

54. AAP 2009, 'Sydney's power supply an embarrassment, says Barry O'Farrell', *The Australian*, 28 April, www.theaustralian.com.au.
55. Walters, A 2009, 'Third blackout in two weeks for Sydney', *The Daily Telegraph*, 13 April, www.dailytelegraph.com.au; Walters, A 2009.
56. Auditing and Assurance Standards Board 2009.
57. Bierstaker, JL 1999, 'Internal control documentation: which format is preferred?', *The Auditor's Report*, vol. 22, no. 2, pp. 12–13.
58. Bierstaker, JL & Wright, A 2004, 'Does the adoption of a business risk audit approach change internal control documentation and testing changes?', *International Journal of Auditing*, vol. 8, pp. 67–78.
59. Deloitte & Touche LLP 2003a, *Moving forward — a guide to improving corporate governance through effective internal control: a response to Sarbanes–Oxley*, January, Deloitte & Touche USA, p. 6.
60. Bierstaker, JL & Wright, A 2004.
61. Ernst & Young LLP 2003, *Evaluating internal controls: considerations for evaluating internal control at the entity level*, Ernst & Young, New York.
62. Bierstaker, JL & Wright, A 2004.
63. Deloitte & Touche LLP 2003a.
64. Deloitte & Touche LLP 2003b, *The growing company's guide to COSO*, June, Deloitte & Touche LLP, New York, pp. 6–7.
65. Adapted from Deloitte & Touche LLP 2003b, p. 9. Reproduced with permission.
66. Ernst & Young LLP 2003.
67. Bierstaker, JL & Wright, A 2004.
68. Campbell, S & Hartcher J 2003, *Internal controls for small business*, CPA Australia, Melbourne, p. 12.
69. Deloitte & Touche LLP 2003b.
70. Campbell & Hartcher 2003.
71. Graycar, A 2002, 'Identity fraud — perspective', *Australian Institute of Criminology*, 17 April.
72. AAP 2003, 'Iris recognition helps to prevent ID fraud', *Sydney Morning Herald*, 27 February, www.smh.com.au.
73. Graycar 2002.
74. KPMG Australia 2009, p. 16.
75. Healey, K 2004, 'Thieves target Brownlow hero', *The Mercury*, 11 January, www.themercury.news. com.au.
76. Moor, K 2002, 'National ID plan to combat fraud', *Herald Sun*, 11 June, www.heraldsun.news.com.au.
77. Attorney-General's Department, 'Protecting identity security', www.crimeprevention.gov. au.
78. Rogers, V, Marsh, TA & Ethridge, JR 2004, 'Internal controls: winning the battles against risks', *Internal Auditing*, vol. 19, no. 4, pp. 28–34.
79. International Federation of Accountants 2006, *Internal controls — a review of current developments*, International Federation of Accountants, New York.
80. Moses, A & AAP 2006, 'Saboteurs attack NAB bank online', *The Age*, 20 October.
81. ASIC 2006a, '06-192 "Phishing" scams more common and sophisticated — ASIC warning', *ASIC Media and Information Releases*, www.asic.gov.au.
82. ASIC 2006b, '06-055 Don't take the bait: ASIC renews phishing warning', *ASIC Media and Information Releases*, www.asic.gov.au.
83. Smith, F 2007, 'Make no mistake, this will save money', *Australian Financial Review*, 3 April, p. 59.

# PART 3

# Systems in action

Part 3 of the text examines the application of the concepts introduced in part 2 to specific examples of business cycles or processes that operate within a wide range of businesses. These examples of transaction cycles that occur within a business are central to the business being able to attain its objectives. Each cycle operates through a series of activities aimed at achieving a particular goal or solving a particular problem within the organisation. Each chapter outlines the particular business process and the appropriate systems documentation.

Figure P3.1 overleaf introduces the business processes described in detail in the following five chapters; it depicts the interrelationships between these processes, and the interactions between the processes and external entities. The following discussion examines the process interrelationships and related risks.

The revenue cycle (**chapter 9**) commences when a customer indicates they want to purchase a product, and ends after the product has been delivered and payment received. The level of activity within the revenue cycle drives the activity levels for all the other business processes. During the sales phase described in chapter 9, a customer may request a product which is manufactured in house, but is currently out of stock. Under these circumstances the revenue cycle would send a request to the production cycle (**chapter 11**) for the product to be manufactured. Marketing staff may also send supply forecasts to the production cycle for use in production planning. Production planning staff would incorporate these data into their planning phase, as described in chapter 11.

Once production planning has been finalised the availability details for any requested goods should be sent back to the revenue cycle for use when communicating with the customer. This relationship between the revenue and production cycles is important for a number of reasons. If the goods requests or sales forecasts sent to production are incorrect then production planning will be flawed, leading to inefficiencies and wastage. If production does not correctly advise revenue of product due dates in a timely manner there is a risk that customers will be given incorrect information, leading to customer dissatisfaction and the potential for reputation damage and associated drops in demand for the organisation's products.

Once the revenue cycle is complete details of sales commissions due are sent to the HR management and payroll cycle (**chapter 12**) for payment. Failure to correctly advise the details of sales commission earned will result in under or overpayment of sales staff entitlements, which not only creates inefficiencies, but also has the potential to alienate or de-motivate sales staff.

The production cycle commences when a new product has been designed, and ends when all scheduled production has been successfully completed and the associated costs recorded. Activity levels within the production cycle act as one of the drivers for expenditure cycle activity levels. In particular, the production cycle sends requests for raw materials to the expenditure cycle (**chapter 10**) for use when ordering goods from suppliers. If production staff miscalculate the raw material requirements, or make errors when advising purchasing of their requirements, there is a risk that the raw materials purchased during the expenditure cycle will be unnecessary or unsuitable, resulting in inefficiencies and cost overruns. The expenditure cycle commences when a section of the organisation reports a need for goods or services to be provided, and ends when the goods or services have been received and paid for. The expenditure cycle needs to advise details of the requested raw materials' availability back to the production cycle. If the expenditure cycle does not correctly advise the production cycle of availability dates for the requested raw materials there is a risk that production schedules may be unable to be executed as planned, leading to inefficiencies and wastage.

Once the production cycle has been completed details of the hours worked by production staff are sent to the HR management and payroll cycle for payment as described in chapter 12. Failure to correctly advise production labour details will result in under or overpayment of production staff entitlements, which not only creates inefficiencies, it also has the potential to alienate or de-motivate production staff.

After the transaction cycles have been successfully completed details are sent to the general ledger and financial reporting cycle **(chapter 13)** to enable updating of the general ledger and subsequent financial reporting. The revenue cycle provides details of invoices raised by the billing system and payments received from customers; the production cycle sends details of all production costs incurred; the payroll cycle sends details of salaries and wages paid; and the expenditure cycle forwards details of payments established and made. These data are validated, consolidated, adjusted and used for reporting and analysis of the organisation's performance. Any errors made here can have serious consequences; reporting incorrect values can result in poor internal decision making, issues with capital markets and the possibility of regulatory prosecution if corporate laws are breached.

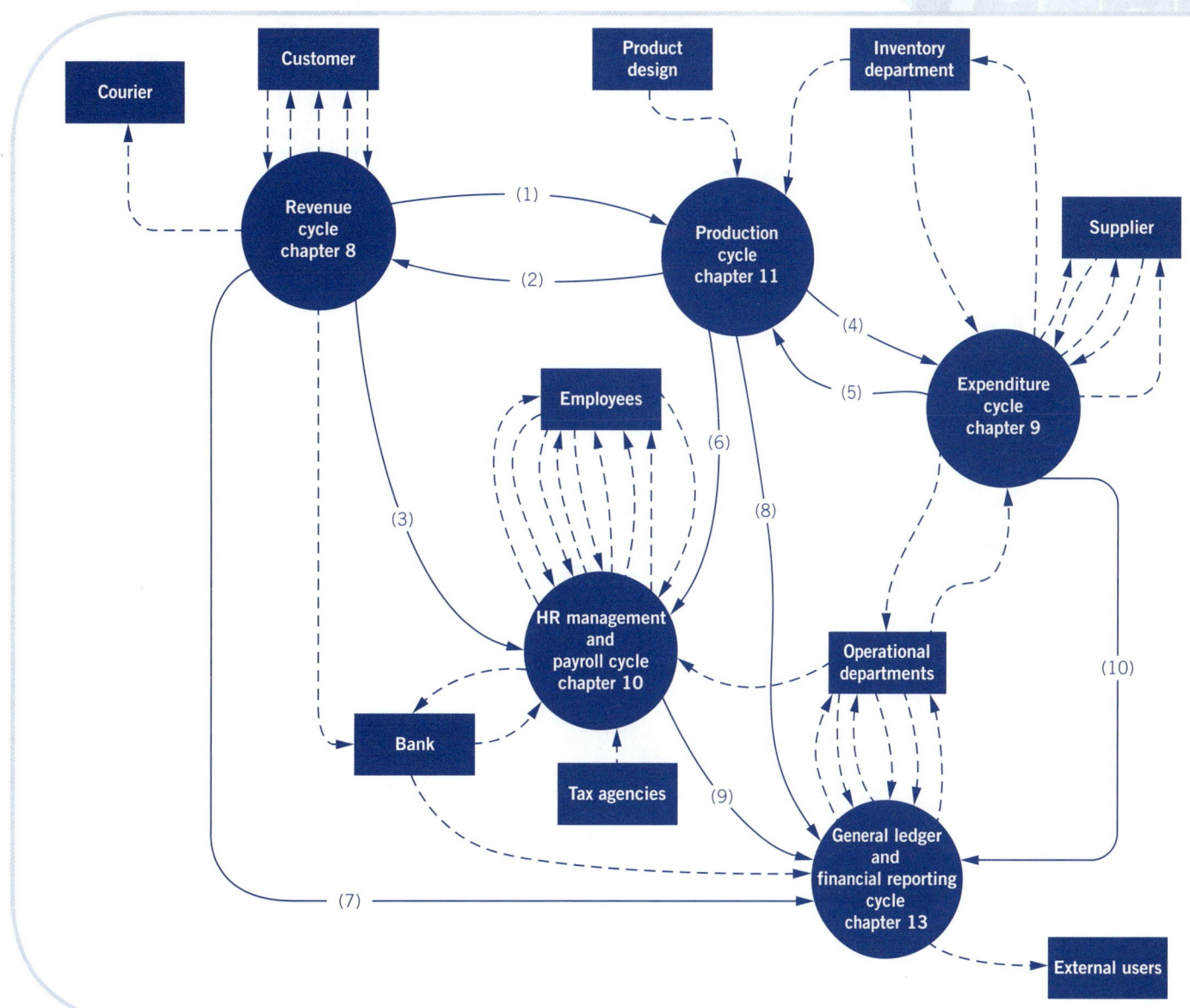

**FIGURE P3.1** Integrated process perspective

Table P3.1 *details the data flows between the transaction cycles.*

**TABLE P3.1** Data flows between the transaction cycles

| Flow # | Initiating cycle | Receiving cycle | Flow description |
|---|---|---|---|
| 1 | Revenue | Production | Sales and marketing staff send sales forecasts and requests for currently unavailable products to production planning staff for use during production planning. |
| 2 | Production | Revenue | Production planning staff provide details of the requested goods planned availability to sales and marketing staff for use when planning their future activities, and communicating with customers. |
| 3 | Revenue | HR management & payroll | Sales management send details of sales commissions earned to payroll staff for use when calculating salary and wages payable. |
| 4 | Production | Expenditure | Production planning staff send requests for raw materials required for production to purchasing staff for use when ordering goods from suppliers. |
| 5 | Expenditure | Production | Purchasing staff send details of the requested raw materials planned availability to production planning staff for use in production planning. |
| 6 | Production | HR management & payroll | Production operations staff send details of production labour timesheets to payroll staff for use when calculating salary and wages payable |
| 7 | Revenue | General ledger & financial reporting | Accounts receivable staff send details of invoices raised by the billing system and payments received from customers to the finance staff to enable updating of the general ledger and the subsequent financial reporting. |

| Flow # | Initiating cycle | Receiving cycle | Flow description |
|---|---|---|---|
| 8 | Production | General ledger & financial reporting | Production operations staff send details of production costs incurred to the finance staff to enable updating of the general ledger and the subsequent financial reporting. |
| 9 | HR management & payroll | General ledger & financial reporting | Payroll staff send details of salaries and wages paid to the finance staff to enable updating of the general ledger and the subsequent financial reporting. |
| 10 | Expenditure | General ledger & financial reporting | Accounts payable staff send details of payments established and made to finance staff to enable updating of the general ledger and the subsequent financial reporting. |

# Transaction cycle — the revenue cycle

## Learning objectives

After studying this chapter, you should be able to:

1. describe the key objectives and strategic implications of the revenue cycle

2. identify common technologies underpinning the revenue cycle

3. describe revenue cycle data and key revenue business decisions

4. identify and document the primary activities in the revenue cycle and the data produced by these activities

5. analyse risks and develop control plans pertinent to the primary activities in the revenue cycle

6. develop metrics to monitor revenue cycle performance.

# Introduction

Revenue related activities are some of the most essential conducted by an organisation. The revenue cycle commences when a customer indicates they wish to purchase a good or service, and ends when payment has been received. During the process, sales need to be properly authorised and correctly recorded. Goods must be packed and shipped to customers in a timely and correct manner. Customers need to be billed the right amount, at the right time, for the goods and/or services supplied. Finally, payments received from customers need to be quickly and accurately receipted and banked.

This chapter commences with an overview of the revenue cycle, and then considers the strategic implications of that process. Technologies that underpin the cycle are discussed, and then the data produced and consumed during the cycle activities are identified. Typical business decisions are examined, along with some of the primary considerations related to those decisions. A revenue cycle is fully documented using dataflow diagrams (DFDs) and flowcharts, along with a set of tables containing additional details to aid in understanding the process activities, and the related risks and controls of the activities. Finally, issues relating to measuring performance of the revenue cycle are discussed, and examples of performance metrics suitable for measuring revenue cycle performance are provided.

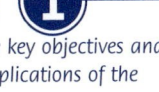

**LEARNING OBJECTIVE 1**

*Describe the key objectives and strategic implications of the revenue cycle.*

## REVENUE CYCLE OVERVIEW AND KEY OBJECTIVES

For an organisation to prosper it is essential that the revenue cycle is well managed and controlled. Marketing, sales and finance are the organisational units that have primary responsibility for the revenue cycle. Sales are the primary driver of all organisational activity, and the most intensive customer contact point. Sales are easily lost if consumers are confronted with an inadequate sales process or improper billing practices. Losses are likely if deliveries are not accurate, timely and well controlled. An inadequate revenue cycle, or failure to collect revenues, can lead to declining sales, cash flow difficulties and, in the worst cases, potential insolvency or cessation of the business. The organisational units most involved in the revenue cycle are shown in figure 9.1 overleaf.

The revenue cycle is conventionally divided into two major elements. The front end of the cycle is client facing and is where the sales transaction takes place. The objective of the sales phase is to effectively conduct, record and monitor sales of goods and services, and arrange the prompt supply of goods and services. Essentially, staff involved in the sales phase need to make sure that the organisation provides the right product at the right time and place. To achieve this objective, customer orders must be properly recorded and controlled, sales should only be made to creditworthy customers and delivered goods must meet the customer's needs.

Following directly on from sales is the accounts receivable phase, where the objective is to ensure payments for goods and services are correctly received, recorded and banked. This part of the cycle is sometimes referred to as 'back-office' or 'back-end' processing. The activities in this latter part of the cycle are often carried out by staff who do not have the same direct contact with customers as the front-end, or client-facing, staff who process sales. In order to maintain good client relationships the linkages between the front-end (client-facing) and back-end revenue systems must be well defined. The accounts receivable phase needs to make sure that customers are billed the right amounts for the right products, and that those amounts are collected at the right time. This involves ensuring that customer invoices and receipts are prepared and recorded in an accurate and timely manner, that cash receipts are protected from fraud and misuse, that receivables balances are kept to a minimum level and that the organisation collects amounts owing to it on a timely basis. A description of documentation commonly used in the revenue cycle is contained in table 9.1.

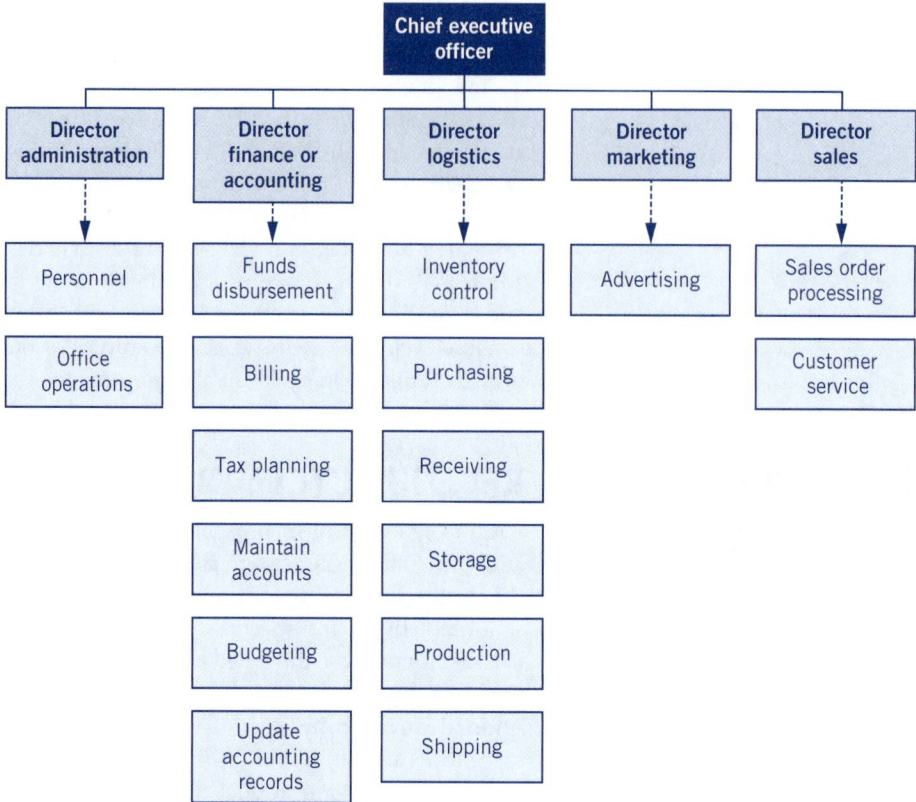

**FIGURE 9.1** Organisational units in the revenue cycle

*Note:* The dashed lines with the arrows show the business activities that each unit is responsible for.

**TABLE 9.1** List of source documents in a revenue cycle

| Documents | Description |
| --- | --- |
| Customer order | Allows the customers to order goods from the organisation. This form can be in the form of a customer's purchase order prepared by the customer or a customer order form prepared by a salesperson in the sales unit. |
| Order acknowledgement | A copy of the customer order that is sent to the customer in acknowledgement of the customer's order. The order acknowledgement is often prepared by the salesperson who receives the customer's order form (or purchase order form). |
| Credit application | A form that is prepared for a new customer applying for credit. The form shows the customer's financial position and the customer's ability to repay any debts owing. |

| Documents | Description |
| --- | --- |
| Sales order | A formal document that is prepared using the customer order form. Multiple copies of the document are also prepared to initiate shipment and receive payments from customers. The sales order form is prepared by a salesperson in the sales unit. |
| Goods packing slip | A document that is generated by the shipping clerk in the logistics unit and attached with the goods sent to the customer. |
| Bill of lading | A document that is prepared for the common carriers that transport the goods to the customer. The shipping clerk in the logistics unit prepares this document. |
| Shipping notice | A document that advises the customer what goods, in what quantity, have been shipped. The shipping clerk in the logistics unit generates this document. Sometimes a copy of the sales order form acts as the shipping notice. |
| Sales invoice | This document is sent to the customer in respect of the goods that he or she has purchased and shows the amount of sales. The billing clerk in the finance or accounting unit prepares this document. |
| Remittance advice | A document that shows the cash receipts from a customer. This document may be prepared by the finance or accounting unit and attached as a stub with the sales invoice. The customer then returns this stub with the necessary payment to the finance or accounting unit. The customer may also send a remittance advice informing the finance or accounting unit of the nature of the payment. |
| Customer service log | A document that is used by customer service personnel in the marketing unit to record customer enquiries and the necessary actions (if any) undertaken to address the customer's queries or concerns. |

## Strategic implications of the revenue cycle

The revenue cycle is strategically important; the level of sales achieved drives all other activity levels within the organisation. In order to survive and prosper an organisation must not only remain profitable (i.e. revenues must exceed expenses), it also must be able to achieve positive cash flows. A sound, well-controlled revenue cycle can provide a competitive advantage by providing superior customer service levels, which in turn translate to opportunities to sustain higher product pricing. An alternative form of competitive advantage is the potential to control costs that is afforded by ensuring that the revenue cycle is efficient and effective. This translates into an opportunity to price goods and services at a level that undercuts less efficient competitors and increases market share.

Ideally, both these competitive advantages would be realised simultaneously, with an efficient and effective revenue cycle ensuring superior levels of customer services at a low cost; however, in reality these goals often prove to be incompatible. The revenue cycle generally offers consumers greater value either by offering lower prices, or by providing benefits and service that justify a higher price. As discussed in chapter 2, the most important organisational issue is successful alignment of processes, including the revenue cycle, with the organisation's strategy, which should overarch and guide all business process design. A well-aligned revenue cycle will be congruent with the organisational strategy, and compatible with organisational goals, mission and culture. AIS focus 9.1 overleaf illustrates the benefits of aligning business strategy with the revenue cycle.

# AIS FOCUS 9.1

## Verbatim

Verbatim is a well established data storage business based in the Asia–Pacific, including Australia. Verbatim is experiencing continual growth; recently it opened offices in India and China. Paul Johnson, General Manager for Verbatim Asia–Pacific, comments, 'Our previous mainframe computer system was large, old, and woefully inadequate for a marketing and distribution company as big as ours'.

Verbatim's business strategy requires timely provision of information to their network of distributors and resellers; global expansion meant that a 24-hour virtual store of this information was necessary. Verbatim had to take advantage of the information sharing opportunities provided by the internet. It chose a data warehouse and customer relationship management (CRM) solution that was SQL supportive, enabled internet linkages and integrated well with its existing ERP system. In order to improve productivity Verbatim also took the opportunity to standardise business systems and processes across its operating regions. 'Someone working in Australia could go to work in India, without having to be retrained or use the system differently,' says Johnson.

The standardisation of systems and processes improved both the quality and the consistency of information across the enterprise. Verbatim had experienced problems with differences in the way numbers were recorded, and how performance results were measured, meaning that results came out differently from region to region. The new data warehouse gave Verbatim the ability to make direct comparisons; it was also able to make sure everyone was doing things in a similar way, and that the way that information was entered into the system was standardised.

Verbatim found that by expanding its ERP to include CRM and providing a data warehouse it experienced greater productivity and standardisation across the enterprise. The new consistency of information generated more accurate reports and analysis for the business, which in turn led to better decision making. In many areas efficiency gains of 30 per cent were achieved. Verbatim believe that the potential returns from better communication and analysis over the years to come will be immeasurable.[1]

# TECHNOLOGIES UNDERPINNING THE REVENUE CYCLE

There are a number of technologies suitable to support activities within the revenue cycle, acting to improve the overall functioning of the process. A range of data management tools are available to help improve the ability to capture and analyse revenue data. Transparency and management of cash and cash flow can also be improved by use of appropriate technologies.

**Enterprise resource planning (ERP) systems** assist with enabling and integrating the revenue cycle. The revenue cycle links into many areas within the organisation; an ERP system not only improves the integration of enterprise-wide data but also provides tighter linkages between relevant modules such as marketing, sales, production, shipping, billing, accounts receivable and general ledger.

*Enterprise resource planning (ERP) system* An integrated suite of software that records and manages many different types of business transactions within a single integrated database. Examples include SAP and Oracle.

The revenue cycle can benefit greatly from technologies that provide an efficient means of data exchange. It is more efficient, timely and cost effective to transact electronically. Much of the 'paperwork' generated by the revenue cycle (e.g. invoices, shipping documents) originates in-house and is sent outwards to customers. The ability to transact online not only speeds up the revenue transaction cycle, it can also act to outsource some of the transactional work, and therefore costs, to the customer. Technologies such as **electronic data interchange (EDI)** (to produce specifically tailored systems for large repeat customers) and **eXtensible Markup Language (XML)** (for online sales sites) help provide efficient data exchange.

Paper documentation sent into the organisation as part of the revenue cycle (typically remittance advices and customer purchase orders) can be handled more efficiently using digital imaging. Scanning documents speeds up processing by providing broader immediate access to incoming documentation.

Improvements in the revenue cycle can be made by undertaking data mining or trend analysis in order to improve understanding of markets and product performance. Providing some form of revenue data warehouse is necessary in order to undertake these activities. Revenue data warehouses typically store summarised historical revenue data arranged along product or segment lines, allowing data mining to take place.

**Customer relationship management (CRM)** technologies can support revenue cycle activities by improving understanding of customers and their interactions with the organisation. CRM technologies typically store historical revenue data arranged by customer, in contrast to data warehouses, which tend to store data arranged by market segments or chronology.

Online payment facilities such as BPAY provide a simple and cost effective way for organisations to receive payments. In addition to providing more timely payments, using customer self-service systems, such as BPAY, helps cut data entry costs and reduces error rates. The use of online banking facilities improves transparency and **reconciliation** of transactions; also there is less cash handling which improves security and cash flows.

Tracking and recording inventory forms a large part of the sales process. The efficiency and accuracy of inventory related activities can be improved by the use of barcode scanners. An example of a barcode is shown in figure 9.2.

**FIGURE 9.2** Example printed bar code

Barcode scanning not only reduces error levels by automating data input, it improves timeliness as scanned data is immediately uploaded and available for use. AIS focus 9.2 gives an example of how technology can be used to improve the sales process.

## Caffe Primo Chain

Caffe Primo of Adelaide, South Australia, is a group of 20+ cafe/restaurants that specialises in providing good quality meals at value prices. When making plans to expand his restaurant chain in metropolitan Adelaide and regional South Australia, owner Dino Vettesse knew exactly what type of Point of Sale Management system he had to have. 'It absolutely had to be easy to install and learn. We have a lot of casual staff in this industry, and they need to be able to pick up a new system and become productive very quickly.'

It also had to provide timely management controls and key performance measurements. 'Only hard facts let you run a smooth operation. We need to know accurately what's selling and not selling, how one week compares to the next, especially when we make menu changes, and I needed a system that would give me the reports that would make the facts I need jump out at me from the paper or the screen.'

When asked about the support provided, Vettesse responded 'It's very good. The system has never been down for more than a couple of hours since the first day we had it. If we do have a problem, we get on the phone to the helpdesk and we're fixed in no time.'

'We've been running the [Redcat point of sale] system for a number of years now,' Vettesse says, 'and we think it's a great system. We could never go back to our old system. The chefs and the floor staff love it!'[2]

---

**LEARNING OBJECTIVE**

*Describe revenue cycle data and key revenue business decisions.*

# DATA AND DECISIONS IN THE REVENUE CYCLE

A range of data are both produced and consumed by activities within the revenue cycle. The actual data stores are documented in detail later in this chapter; this current section describes the general purpose and types of data that the revenue cycle requires. The business decisions made during the life of the revenue cycle are also described here.

## Data and the revenue cycle

Revenue cycle activities require access to customer data, which contains details of all existing customers, in order to identify authorised customers. Customer data is ideally produced by a dedicated customer management section of the organisation, which has responsibility for identifying and authorising new and existing customers but is not involved in revenue cycle activities. This customer management section would also be responsible for assigning and reviewing customer credit limits. The revenue cycle uses customer data in several different activities; for example, customer credit data helps to decide if a customer is creditworthy, customer address data is used to arrange shipment and invoicing of goods, data relating to customer demographics and order characteristics is often collected during revenue cycle activities for use in future marketing programs.

An important data source for the revenue cycle is inventory data, which is a record of each item stocked or regularly ordered. Inventory data is primarily created by activities within the expenditure cycle; however, the revenue cycle also updates inventory data by recording decreases in stock levels created by shipment of goods. Inventory data related to existing stock levels is also accessed by the sales process when deciding whether there is sufficient inventory for a potential sale to occur.

Accounts receivable data is both created and updated by activities within the revenue cycle; invoices created by billing activities are recorded in accounts receivable, as are details of payments received during the accounts receivable process. More detailed information about customer payments is recorded in the cash receipts data. The most detailed data produced by the revenue cycle is sales data, which contains all details of each sale made by the organisation, and the status of the sale. An additional common data record is accounts receivable adjustments data, where any bad or doubtful debts and sales returns are recorded. This data is useful when undertaking analysis of revenue cycle performance, in addition to forming part of financial reports.

## Revenue cycle business decisions

Process business decisions are made at different levels during the life of the revenue cycle. When the cycle is originally designed, or subsequently reviewed, a number of strategy-level decisions need to be made. These decisions are typically made by senior management within the organisation, and create the policy framework within which the cycle operates. To be effective, strategy-level business process decisions should be congruent with the overarching business strategy. Strategy-level decisions would include creation of policies for areas such as:

- price setting — requires construction of pricing algorithms, consideration of competitor price points, and an understanding of the degree of market tolerance
- sales return and warranty policies — involves predicting potential volume of returns, incorporating any relevant legislation, identifying any product characteristics that make returns more or less acceptable
- provision of customer credit facilities — requires consideration of the options available, and the costs, benefits and risks of each of these for the organisation
- cash collection policies and procedures — needs knowledge of average payment times, industry standards, customer credit policies, legal requirements.

In addition to these strategy-level decisions, there are a range of operational level decisions that will be made every time the revenue cycle is enacted. These operational decisions are typically made by less senior staff and relate only to a specific instance of the cycle. Typical operational decisions include:

- responding to customer inquiries such as a request to purchase goods, or to return goods for credit — requires consideration of the customer's purchase history and their accounts receivable history, in addition to knowing the options available under the applicable policy
- responding to a request to extend credit to a particular customer — requires consideration of the customer's prior history and likely sales volume
- calculation of inventory availability — requires knowledge of current levels of stock on hand, stock on order, stock promised to customers and supplier lead times
- selecting goods delivery method — requires understanding of policy alternatives available combined with the costs and risks of the specific transaction being considered
- determining correct cash receipt allocations for a customer payment — requires access to details of invoices outstanding, and any remittance advice data supplied by the customer.

# REVENUE CYCLE DOCUMENTATION

The revenue cycle is documented in the following section as a series of diagrams with increasing amounts of details. An overview of these revenue cycle diagrams is contained in figure 9.3 overleaf.

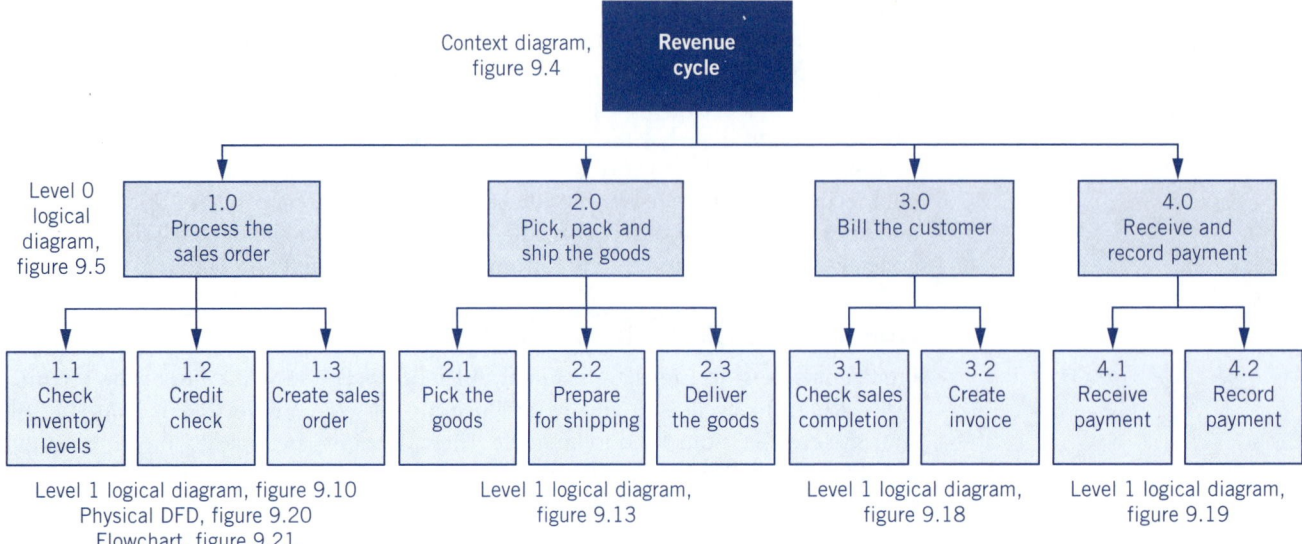

**FIGURE 9.3** Revenue diagrams overview

## Revenue cycle context

The context diagram of a typical revenue cycle is depicted in figure 9.4. The revenue cycle involves direct interaction with entities outside the organisation such as customers, couriers and banks. Within the organisation, the revenue cycle interacts with the production, HR management and payroll, and general ledger and financial cycles as shown in figure P3.1 (page 389). Details of the logical data flows depicted in the revenue context diagram are contained in table 9.2 (page 402).

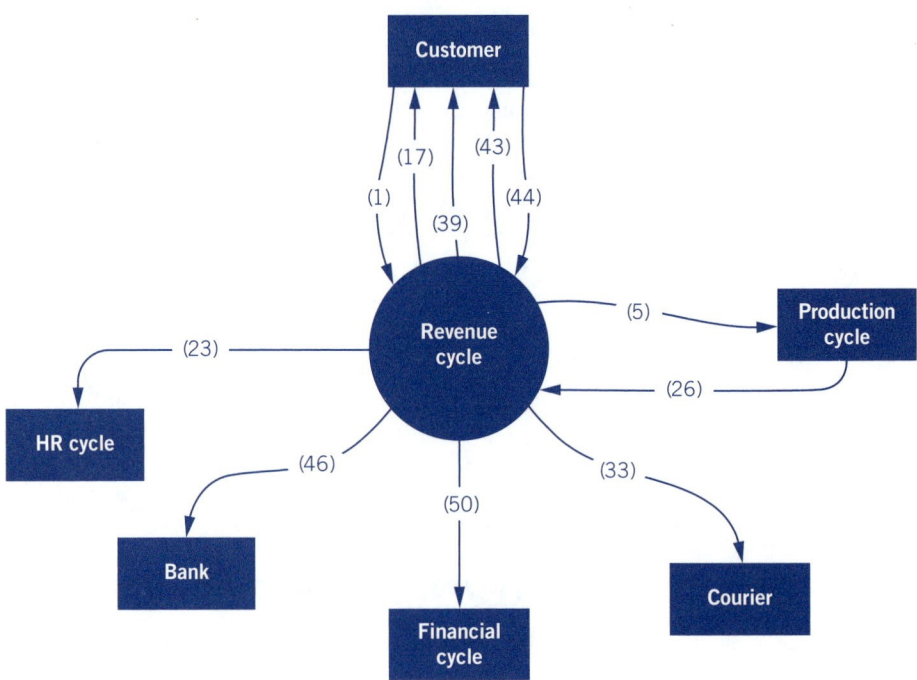

**FIGURE 9.4** Revenue cycle context diagram

# Revenue cycle logical data flows

Figure 9.5 depicts a level 0 logical DFD. This diagram shows the entire revenue cycle, in greater detail than that depicted in the context diagram.

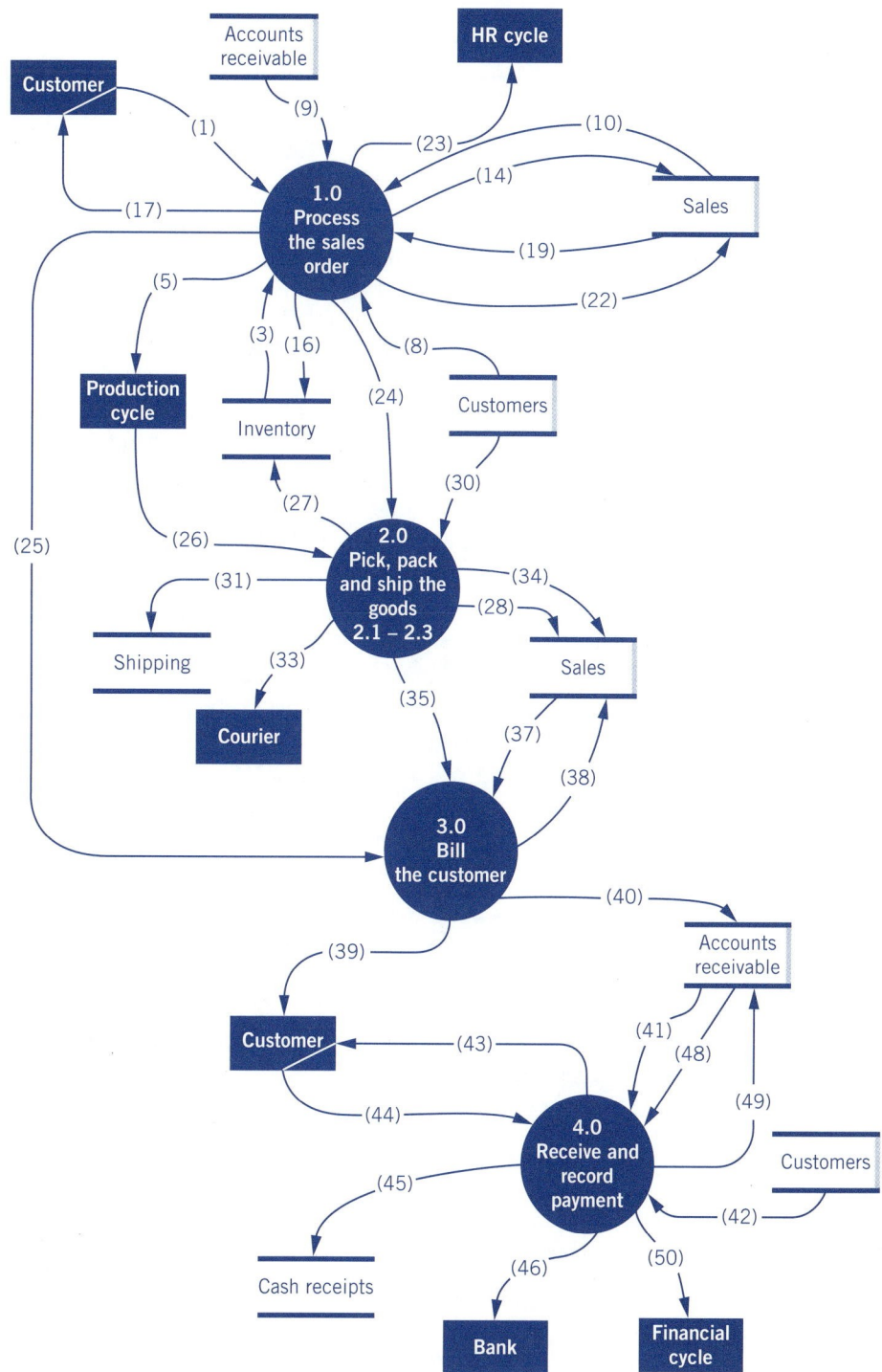

**FIGURE 9.5** Revenue cycle level 0 logical diagram

The logical DFD is an exploded version of the context diagram, with the bubble described as 'revenue cycle' in the context diagram broken down into four processes. The logical diagram at level 0 helps to analyse and understand the revenue cycle in its entirety. It depicts the chronology of the cycle, the data stores and external entities involved in each of the processes, and the interactions between these processes, entities and data stores. The logical level 0 diagram in figure 9.5 is itself broken down to describe even lower levels of detail in figures 9.10, 9.13, 9.16 and 9.19 later in this chapter. Details of the logical data flows depicted in this diagram are contained in table 9.2.

## Description of logical data flows in the revenue cycle

A logical DFD contains only those data flows relating to inputs and outputs of the activities contained within each of the processes, as opposed to the details of all interactions between entities which are depicted in a physical DFD. As a result, the number of flows in a logical DFD is always less than those that would be shown in a physical DFD for the same process. To illustrate this, compare figures 9.10 and 9.20, which both show exactly the same process; however, figure 9.10 is a logical description whereas figure 9.20 is a physical depiction. To ensure completeness, all the data flows relating to the revenue cycle appear in table 9.2.

**TABLE 9.2** Description of logical data flows in the revenue cycle

| Flow # | Typical data source | Typical data destination | Data description | Explanation of the logical data flow |
|---|---|---|---|---|
| **Process 1.0 Process the sales order** | | | | |
| 1 | Customer | Sales clerk | Details of the goods the customer wants to purchase | The customer contacts the sales clerk to request the goods. |
| 2 | This flow takes places physically between the sales clerk and the computer; it happens within the 1.0 bubble in the logical diagram. | | | |
| 3 | Inventory data store | Sales clerk | The level of stock on hand for requested products | The level of stock for any products the customer wishes to buy is checked. This ensures that the customer is not promised goods that cannot be delivered, or alternatively that a sale is erroneously rejected. |
| 4 | This flow takes places physically between the sales clerk and the computer; it happens within the 1.0 bubble in the logical diagram. | | | |
| 5 | Sales clerk | Production cycle | Details of goods required to be produced | If the company manufactures its products in-house, and there is insufficient finished goods inventory available to fill the sales order, the sales clerk will notify the production cycle of the demand for the goods. |
| 6 | Inventory check | Credit check | Trigger for next process | After the inventory check has been completed the credit check process can commence (not necessary in a level 0 diagram). |
| 7 | This flow takes places physically between the sales clerk and the computer; it happens within the 1.0 bubble in the logical diagram. | | | |

| Flow # | Typical data source | Typical data destination | Data description | Explanation of the logical data flow |
|---|---|---|---|---|
| 8 | Customer data store | Sales clerk | The customer's credit limit | The sales clerk should ensure that the customer is creditworthy before the sale is processed. If no credit limit exists, or the credit is insufficient to cover the requested purchase, the sale should not proceed. |
| 9 | Accounts receivable data store | Sales clerk | Current accounts receivable balance for the customer | The sales clerk can determine whether there is sufficient credit available by comparing the current amount of credit currently being used to the credit limit for the customer. If the remaining credit is insufficient to cover the requested purchase, the sale should not proceed. |
| 10 | Sales order data store | Sales clerk | Recent sales to the customer | The sales event data will contain detail of any recent sales that may not yet have been updated into the accounts receivable data store. The value of any recent sales should be deducted from the remaining credit available for the customer; if the requested purchase exceeds this amount the sale should not proceed. |
| 11 | This flow takes places physically between the sales clerk and the computer; it happens within the 1.0 bubble in the logical diagram. | | | |
| 12 | Credit check | Sales order creation | Trigger for next process | After the credit check is complete the create sales order process can commence (not necessary in a level 0 diagram). |
| 13 | This flow takes places physically between the sales clerk and the computer; it happens within the 1.0 bubble in the logical diagram. | | | |
| 14 | Sales order clerk/ customer | Sales order data store | Sales order details | This data flow represents the action of updating of the sales order data with the newly created sales order. Only orders that have inventory available and a sufficient customer credit limit will be created. |
| 15 | This flow takes places physically between the sales clerk and the computer; it happens within the 1.0 bubble in the logical diagram. | | | |
| 16 | Sales order data store | Inventory data store | Details of inventory items in sales order | The items listed on the sales order are used to update the inventory data. The inventory item status is typically marked as 'promised' for any items included on the sales order, and the goods available balance is reduced by the quantity of these items. |
| 17 | Sales clerk | Customer | Sales order confirmation | The sales clerk should advise the customer whether or not the sale will proceed. |
| 18 | This flow takes places physically between the sales manager clerk and the computer; it happens within the 1.0 bubble in the logical diagram. | | | |
| 19 | Sales order data store | Sales manager | Commissions payable | Identification of sales on which commissions are payable, and calculation of commission amounts that are going to be paid. |
| 20; 21 | These flows take place physically between the sales manager clerk and the computer; they happen within the 1.0 bubble in the logical diagram | | | |

*(continued)*

**TABLE 9.2** *(continued)*

| Flow # | Typical data source | Typical data destination | Data description | Explanation of the logical data flow |
|---|---|---|---|---|
| 22 | Sales manager | Sales order data store | Approved sales order details | Once the sales manager has approved the commission amounts proposed, the sales order record is updated to indicate a commission payment has been approved for the sale. |
| 23 | Sales manager | HR cycle | Approved sales order details | This flow would take place where sales people have a commission component included in their salary. |
| 24 | Sales clerk | Picking clerk | Sales order details | This flow alerts the picking clerk in the warehouse that a sales order has been processed, and advises which goods need to be packed for the sales order. |
| 25 | Sales clerk | Billing clerk | Sales order details | When a sales order is created, the billing section needs to receive notification that the sale has occurred. |
| **Process 2.0 Pick, pack and ship the goods** | | | | |
| 26 | Production cycle | Warehouse staff | Finished goods available notification | When the production cycle has completed the manufacture of the goods requested, warehouse staff are advised of goods availability. |
| 27 | Picking clerk | Inventory data store | Sales order status | The inventory status for the relevant items is updated to 'picked'. |
| 28 | Picking clerk | Sales order data store | Sales order status | The sales order status is updated to 'picked'. |
| 29 | Picking the goods | Delivering the goods | Trigger for next process | After the goods are picked the delivery process can commence (not necessary in a level 0 diagram). |
| 30 | Customer data store | Shipping clerk | Customer delivery details | The customer delivery details are combined with the picking ticket and used to produce a shipping label. |
| 31 | Shipping clerk | Shipping data store | Shipment details | Shipment details are stored in the shipping data store. |
| 32 | Preparing for shipping | Delivering the goods | Trigger for next process | After the goods have been packed and labelled the delivery process can commence (not necessary in a level 0 diagram). |
| 33 | Shipping clerk | Courier driver | Delivery details | The goods and shipping details are given to the courier for delivery to the customer. |
| 34 | Shipping clerk | Sales order data store | Sales order status | The sales order status is updated to 'shipped'. |
| 35 | Shipping clerk | Billing clerk | Sales order and shipment details | The data flow advises the billing clerk that a sales order has been completed and goods despatched, and requests that an invoice be raised. |
| **Process 3.0 Bill the customer** | | | | |
| 36 | Checking completed sales | Creating the invoice | Trigger for next process | Once the billing clerk has checked that goods have been despatched in accordance with the sales order, the invoice can be created (not necessary in a level 0 diagram). |

| Flow # | Typical data source | Typical data destination | Data description | Explanation of the logical data flow |
|---|---|---|---|---|
| 37 | Sales data store | Billing clerk | Sales details | Details of the unbilled sale are extracted from the sales data store and used to create the invoice. |
| 38 | Billing clerk | Sales data store | Sales order status | The sales order status is updated to 'billed'. |
| 39 | Billing clerk | Customer | Invoice details | The invoice details are sent to the customer, either electronically or on paper. |
| 40 | Billing clerk | Accounts receivable data store | Invoice details | The invoice details are posted to the customer's account in the accounts receivable data store. |
| **Process 4.0 Receive and record payment** | | | | |
| 41 | Accounts receivable data store | Accounts receivable clerk | Invoice and cash receipts details | Details of unpaid invoices and payments receipted since the last statement was issued are extracted from the accounts receivable data store for use in preparing the customer's statement. |
| 42 | Customer data store | Accounts receivable clerk | Customer details | Customer details such as name and address are added to the accounts receivable data for use in preparing the customer's statement. |
| 43 | Accounts receivable clerk | Customer | Statement details | The statement of account is sent to the customer, either electronically or on paper. |
| 44 | Customer | Cashier | Payment details | The customer sends payment and an accompanying remittance advice to the cashier. |
| 45 | Cashier | Cash receipts data store | Cash receipt details | The cashier receipts the payment and the data is saved into the cash receipts data store. |
| 46 | Cashier | Bank | Cash receipt details | Cheques and related cash receipts data are taken to the bank to be deposited into the company bank account. |
| 47 | Receiving payment | Recording payment | Trigger for next process | Once the payment has been receipted and banked, the payment can be recorded against the customer's accounts receivable account (not necessary in a level 0 diagram). |
| 48 | Accounts receivable clerk | Accounts receivable data store | Unpaid invoice details | The accounts receivable clerk extracts details of unpaid invoices to help determine how to allocate the payment received to the customer's accounts receivable account. |
| 49 | Accounts receivable data store | Accounts receivable clerk | Cash receipt details | The payment received is allocated to unpaid invoices to the customer's account in the accounts receivable. Invoices for which payment has now been received are updated with a status of 'paid'. |
| 50 | Accounts receivable clerk | Financial cycle | Invoice and cash receipt details | The data relating to the invoices raised and payments received which is contained in the accounts receivable data store is transferred to the financial cycle, where it is used to update general ledger accounts. |

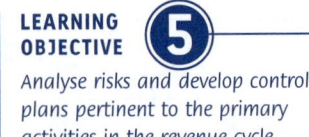

# REVENUE CYCLE ACTIVITIES AND RELATED RISKS AND CONTROLS

The activities within the revenue cycle and the associated risks and controls are now described under the four revenue process headings. Following the activity descriptions for each of the processes is the level 1 DFD for the process and a table summarising the activities, risks and controls within the process.

## Process the sales order — activities, risks and controls

Process 1.0, process the sales order, comprises the following activities.

### Check inventory levels

The revenue cycle starts when a customer contacts the organisation wanting to purchase some goods. This request could be made electronically, either as an email or an online order placed through a website, or on paper as a letter or form (purchase order) completed by the customer and posted or faxed to the organisation. In the case of traditional retail sales the customer usually selects the goods they require from an open display and presents them directly to the cashier with their payment.[#] After a customer makes their request for goods, the level of stock for the products the customer wishes to buy is checked; this ensures that the customer is not promised goods that cannot be delivered, or that a potential sale is erroneously rejected when stock is actually available. Figure 9.6 contains an example of an inventory query screen.

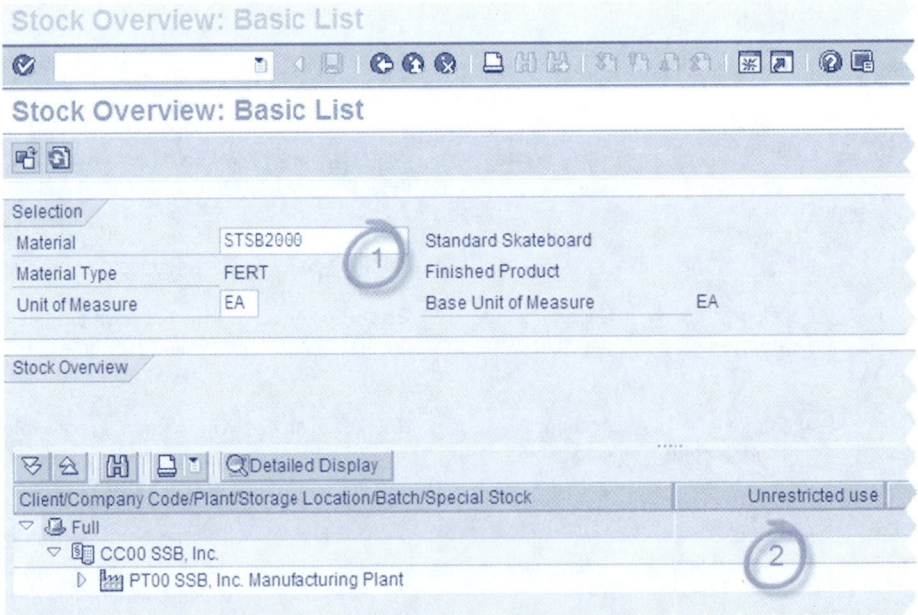

**FIGURE 9.6** Inventory query screen
*Source:* © Copyright SAP AG 2008.

---

[#] In order to display the depth and complexity of the revenue process this very simple retail sales process is not documented in this chapter. The process documented assumes that a customer places an order for goods which need to be packed and despatched, and that the customer is billed and makes payment subsequent to delivery.

If the company manufactures its products in-house, and there is insufficient finished goods inventory available to fill the sales order, the production cycle would need to be notified of the demand for the unavailable goods so they can be manufactured. A common risk is the potential for individuals to create fictitious sales. Controls to reduce this risk include requesting a signed purchase order form from the customer prior to accepting a sale, and confirming customer accounts regularly by sending statements of account. One risk of the revenue cycle is promising goods to a customer that are not available to be shipped; in order to avoid this risk an inventory check should always be performed before accepting a sale. An additional related risk is that of poor decision making, which could result in deciding to allow an order to proceed when goods are not available, or rejecting an order when goods are available. To reduce the risk of poor decisions it is important to maintain accurate and timely perpetual inventory records and periodically conduct physical inventory checks. Accurate timely data will support more accurate decision making. The controls suggested act to ensure that the stock levels recorded and used for decision making are accurate and timely.

### Credit check

The sales clerk should also ensure that the customer is creditworthy before the sale is processed. A credit check requires three separate pieces of information. The first piece of information identifies if a credit limit has been established for the customer. Figure 9.7 shows an example of a credit application form. If no credit limit exists the sale should not proceed. The second piece of information is whether there is sufficient credit available; this information is obtained by comparing the amount of credit currently used (i.e. the amount the customer currently owes the organisation) to the credit limit for the customer. If the remaining credit is not enough to cover the requested purchase, the sale should not proceed. The final piece of information is the detail of any recent sales that may not yet have been updated into the customer's accounts receivable account. The value of any recent sales should be deducted from the remaining credit available for the customer; if the requested purchase exceeds this amount the sale should not proceed. The credit check is undertaken to ensure that the organisation does not sell goods to a customer who won't or can't pay for the goods and is an important control. There is a risk of poor decision making attached to this activity, either by accepting an uncreditworthy customer, or incorrectly rejecting a creditworthy customer. To reduce this risk it is important to independently maintain customer accounts and credit limits. The ability to add a new customer and change or assign a credit limit should not be devolved to staff in the sales area; this helps avoid situations where credit limits are established based on desired sales targets, rather than on the fiscal soundness of the customer. To remove the risk of non-payment altogether the organisation may wish to consider the use of a pre-billing system. **Pre-billing systems** require payment before the goods are despatched and are almost universal in online sales environments. Pre-billing systems are in contrast to **post-billing systems** where the customer is billed for the goods after the goods are dispatched. Additional useful controls for the risk of selling to uncreditworthy customers include producing regular **exception reporting** listing any sales rejected, and regularly monitoring accounts receivable balances and the age of all receivables. These controls also provide a post-hoc analysis of the effectiveness of customer credit decision making.

# Australian Information Company

**Level 2, 345 Hill Terrace**
**Melbourne, Vic 3003**

| *Credit application form* | No: 1002919 |
|---|---|

Please complete the required details below ensuring that all information supplied is true to the best of your knowledge. Please circle where appropriate.

### Personal details

| | |
|---|---|
| Your full name: | Your sex: M/F |
| Your home address: | Your postal address (if different from home address): |

### Credit history

| | |
|---|---|
| Status of home: renting / boarding / own home / other (please specify): | How long have you been there?<br>Years          Months |

State details of your assets (e.g. car, furniture, equipment etc)
Description:                                        Approximate value:
Description:                                        Approximate value:
Description:                                        Approximate value:
Description:                                        Approximate value:

State your credit card details here:
Issuer:                          Card no.:                          Amount owing:
Issuer:                          Card no.:                          Amount owing:
Issuer:                          Card no.:                          Amount owing:
Issuer:                          Card no.:                          Amount owing:

Other liabilities:

Description:                                        Amount owing:

Total monthly expenses (to the nearest dollar):

Please sign the declaration below:
The above details are correct and true to the best of my knowledge. I hereby authorise Australian Information Company to supply my credit details to credit agencies to verify my creditworthiness.

Signed:                                        Date:

**FIGURE 9.7** Sample credit application form

## Create sales order

After the sales request has been checked and the inventory and credit levels confirmed the sales order can be processed. Any time delay between deciding to accept the sales order and inputting the data related to that sales order increases the potential for a sale to be lost or forgotten. A risk of failure to process a valid sales request exists here. To reduce this risk it is important to enter sales data physically close to where the order request was received and to enter all sales data in a timely manner. A sales order can be produced either manually or by computer; a computerised environment would be used in all but the smallest of businesses. The creation of the sales order is accomplished by inputting all the details relating to the customer and the products, then generating a sequentially numbered sales order. Only orders that have inventory available and a sufficient customer credit limit should be created. The sales order should ideally be created as soon as each sales transaction is processed, but it could also occur as a **batch process** at regular predetermined intervals. The sales order is a document that is internal to the organisation, it may never be necessary for it to be produced in paper form; its primary purpose is to notify two different areas of the new sale. Generating a new sales order notifies the warehouse that goods need to be packed and despatched to the customer, and notifies the accounts area that a sale has been accepted. An example sales order is shown in figure 9.8. The sales order forms the basis for subsequent billing of the customer. The actual billing of the customer can occur prior to goods despatch, but more often occurs after (or simultaneously with) the customer receiving the goods. In addition to triggering these workflows, the items listed on the sales order are used to update the inventory data. The inventory item status is typically marked as 'promised' for any items included on the sales order, and the goods available balance is reduced by the quantity of these items. This ensures that future inventory balance checks take account of items promised to a customer, but not yet picked or shipped, helping to ensure that decisions relating to stock availability are accurately supported.

**Batch process** *A type of transaction processing where transactions are saved up until there are a number ready to be processed (a batch), then processed together. Batch processing is typically used to improve controls over data entry and provide efficiency gains. Batch processing is most useful where timeliness is not an issue as there is always some delay in processing transaction batches.*

---

### Australian Information Company
**Level 2, 345 Hill Terrace**
**Melbourne, Vic 3003**

| *Sales order form* | | | No: SO-1245 |
|---|---|---|---|
| To: | Ms Margaret Sinu (Customer ref.: 672839) 1/56 Mount Waverley Road Perth 6523 | | |
| Entered by: Mike Myers, Sales Department | | Approved by: Zincal Sion, Sales Manager | |
| Order date: 01/04/10 | Customer order no.: Int-029389 | | |
| Delivery speed: Normal | Shipping via: Calmex Logistics | Payment method: Invoice customer | |
| Remarks: NIL | | | |
| Item no. | Description | | Quantity |
| 78293 | Gigante CD-ROM | | 1 |
| 82838 | Picole light pen | | 5 |
| 53564 | Sanman computer pen | | 5 boxes |

**FIGURE 9.8** Sample sales order form

The customer should be advised whether or not the sale will proceed; this acknowledgement can take the form of a copy of the sales order sent to the customer in either electronic or paper form, as shown in figure 9.9. If the sale is not able to proceed due to inventory being unavailable, the customer should be advised of possible product alternatives if any are available, or offered the opportunity to have the product placed on **back order** for later delivery. If the order is not proceeding due to a credit limit problem, the customer should be advised of the reason and given a contact if they wish to discuss this further. Note that the sales clerk should not be able to update the credit limit for a customer. If a credit limit is to be renegotiated this would normally be undertaken by a separate customer finance approval division. The risks related to this activity include an incorrect decision outcome being advised to the customer, or a customer not being advised of the outcome at all. Controls to reduce these risks include automating the sales order creation process using a pre-devised workflow, or exception reporting identifying any customer orders received but not acknowledged within a reasonable timeframe.

**Back order** *An order used where a customer has asked to purchase goods which the organisation does not currently have available. A back order records the customer request for the goods, with the intention of supplying the goods at a later date once they become available.*

## Australian Information Company
### Level 2, 345 Hill Terrace
### Melbourne, Vic 3003

| *Order acknowledgement form* | No: C12-2004 |
|---|---|

| To: | Ms Margaret Sinu (Customer ref.: 672839) 1/56 Mount Waverley Road Perth 6523 |
|---|---|

| Date order received: 01/04/10 | Entered by: Mike Myers, Sales Department |
|---|---|

*Order summary*
*Please carefully check the order details below and contact the sales department if any details shownare incorrect.*

| Item no. | Description | Quantity | Price/unit |
|---|---|---|---|
| 78293 | Gigante CD-ROM | 1 | $250.00 |
| 82838 | Picole light pen | 5 | $60.00 |
| 53564 | Sanman computer pen | 5 boxes | $9.00 |

**FIGURE 9.9** Sample order acknowledgement form

Once the sales order has been created it is also possible to identify sales on which commissions are payable, and calculate commission amounts payable. This activity takes place only where sales staff have a commission component included in their salary. Details of sales used for commission purposes should be prepared, or at least approved, by someone other than the sales staff involved. Note this activity may alternatively be conducted as part of the HR management and payroll cycle depending on the organisation's policy regarding commission payments. There are several alternatives for paying sales commissions: some organisations withhold payment of sales commissions until the goods have been delivered, others wait until goods have been paid for, and still other organisations impose a quota system with sales commission being calculated monthly or quarterly based on meeting sales targets. There is a risk that an incorrect sales amount will be advised, resulting in under/overpayment of commissions to sales staff. Automatic calculation of commissions payable based on sales order data, and requiring independent authorisation before commissions can be paid are controls that reduce this risk.

## Process the sales order — DFD

The level 1 DFD in figure 9.10 contains a lower level of detail about the first process represented in the level 0 logical DFD in figure 9.5. In the same way in which the level 0 logical diagram explodes out the 'revenue cycle' bubble in the context diagram, the level 1 diagram explodes out the 'process the sales order' bubble.

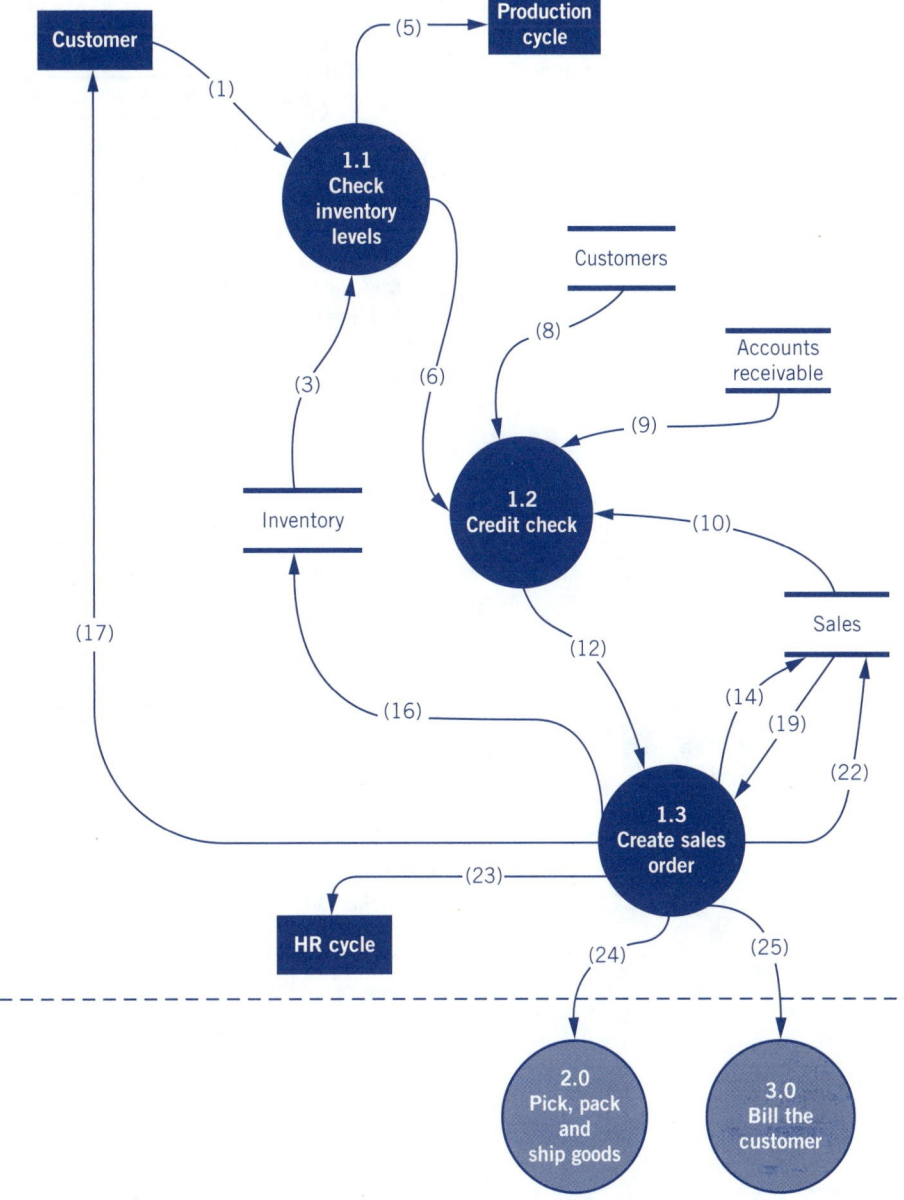

**FIGURE 9.10** Revenue cycle level 1 logical diagram — process 1.0 Process the sales order

## Summary description of activities in processing the sales order

Table 9.3 summarises the activities, risks and controls when processing a sales order, as depicted in figure 9.10. Table 9.2 (page 402) explains the logical data flows depicted in figure 9.10. Exploring the diagram in conjunction with the material contained in the tables will assist in improving your understanding of the process depicted.

**TABLE 9.3** Activities in processing the sales order

| Activity # | Activity | Usually conducted by | Activity description | Typical risks encountered | Common controls |
|---|---|---|---|---|---|
| 1.1 | Check inventory levels | Sales clerk | Decide if sufficient stock is available to proceed with the order by comparing the goods available to the goods requested by the customer. | Selling goods that are not available to be shipped | Performing inventory checks |
| | | | | Poor decision making — allowing an order to proceed when goods are not available, or rejecting an order when goods are available | Maintaining accurate and timely perpetual inventory records, periodically conducting physical inventory checks. Exception reporting for management of any sales rejected |
| 1.2 | Credit check | Sales clerk/ sales manager | Decide if customer is creditworthy and whether the sale should proceed by determining currently available credit capacity. | Selling goods to a customer who won't/ can't pay for the goods | Performing credit checks. Independent maintenance of customer accounts and credit limits, pre-billing systems. |
| | | | | Poor decision making, accepting an uncreditworthy customer, or rejecting a creditworthy customer | Exception reporting for management of any sales rejected. Regular monitoring of accounts receivable balances and age |
| 1.3 | Create sales order | Sales clerk/ sales manager | Input data, create the sales order and update sales data. Once order is created advise the customer of the sales order outcome. May also advise HR of any commissions payable. Need to advise warehouse picking clerk of goods required, and advise billing that the sales order has been created. | Creating fictitious sales | Signed purchase order form from customer, confirming customer accounts regularly via statements of account |
| | | | | Failure to process valid sales request received from customer | Entering data physically close to where order request is received; entering data in a timely manner |
| | | | | Incorrect decision outcome advised | Automation via pre-devised workflow |
| | | | | Customer not advised of outcome | Exception reporting of customer orders not acknowledged within a reasonable timeframe |
| | | | | Incorrect sales advised, resulting in under/ overpayment of commissions to sales staff | Automation using sales order data Obtaining approval from sales manager before commissions are paid |
| | | | | Incorrect goods included on picking ticket | Automation using sales order data |
| | | | | Warehouse not advised of the picking ticket details | Automation using sales order data Exception reporting of sales orders with no picking tickets generated |

## Pick, pack and ship the goods — activities, risks and controls

Process 2.0, pick, pack and ship the goods, comprises the following activities.

### *Pick the goods*

When the warehouse receives a new sales order they need to pick and pack the requested goods. Some organisations create a new document from the sales order data called a picking ticket. Creating picking tickets is typically fully automated, often as a batch job, with picking tickets being created and printed out in a warehouse on a daily basis. Figure 9.11 contains an example of a screen displaying sales orders due to be picked and packed. A picking ticket identifies the sales order number but not necessarily the customer details, and lists all the items required to be assembled to fill the order. For larger warehouses the picking ticket may include references to the rows or bays in which the required stock is held. Very large warehouses employ automated stock picking, where the electronic details from the sales order trigger a robot arm to select and group the required items.

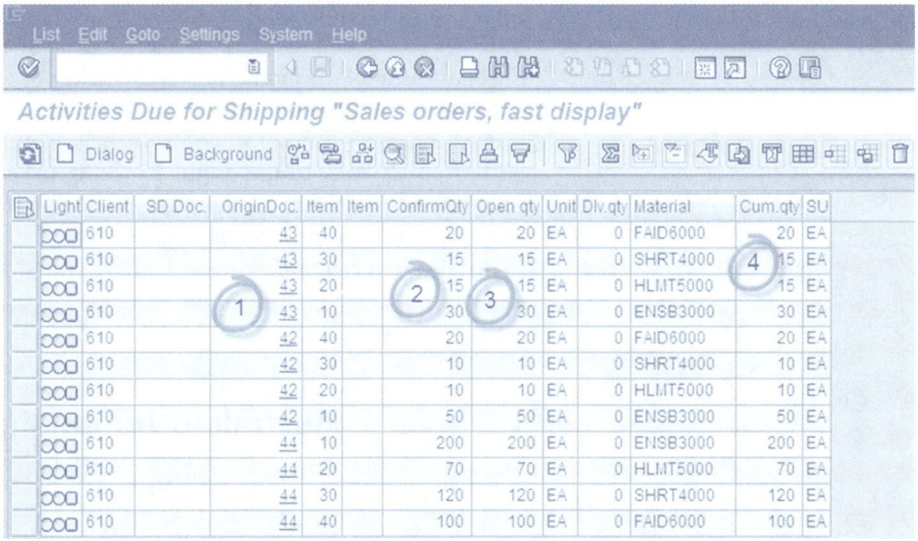


| Light | Client | SD Doc. | OriginDoc. | Item | Item | ConfirmQty | Open qty | Unit | Dlv.qty | Material | Cum.qty | SU |
|---|---|---|---|---|---|---|---|---|---|---|---|---|
| OOO | 610 | | 43 | 40 | | 20 | 20 | EA | 0 | FAID6000 | 20 | EA |
| OOO | 610 | | 43 | 30 | | 15 | 15 | EA | 0 | SHRT4000 | 15 | EA |
| OOO | 610 | | 43 | 20 | | 15 | 15 | EA | 0 | HLMT5000 | 15 | EA |
| OOO | 610 | | 43 | 10 | | 30 | 30 | EA | 0 | ENSB3000 | 30 | EA |
| OOO | 610 | | 42 | 40 | | 20 | 20 | EA | 0 | FAID6000 | 20 | EA |
| OOO | 610 | | 42 | 30 | | 10 | 10 | EA | 0 | SHRT4000 | 10 | EA |
| OOO | 610 | | 42 | 20 | | 10 | 10 | EA | 0 | HLMT5000 | 10 | EA |
| OOO | 610 | | 42 | 10 | | 50 | 50 | EA | 0 | ENSB3000 | 50 | EA |
| OOO | 610 | | 44 | 10 | | 200 | 200 | EA | 0 | ENSB3000 | 200 | EA |
| OOO | 610 | | 44 | 20 | | 70 | 70 | EA | 0 | HLMT5000 | 70 | EA |
| OOO | 610 | | 44 | 30 | | 120 | 120 | EA | 0 | SHRT4000 | 120 | EA |
| OOO | 610 | | 44 | 40 | | 100 | 100 | EA | 0 | FAID6000 | 100 | EA |

**FIGURE 9.11** Sales orders due to be picked and packed screen
*Source:* © Copyright SAP AG 2008.

Once the required items have been assembled the order should be checked, and the sales order or picking ticket updated to indicate that the picking activity has been successfully completed. This acts to trigger the next set of activities: packing and despatching the order to the customer, and ensuring that the inventory status for the relevant items is updated to 'picked'. Recording the current status of inventory is vital; if the status is not updated as each activity is completed, data related to inventory availability will be unreliable and the inventory availability check discussed earlier will be invalid. A risk related to picking goods is that of having the incorrect goods included on the picking ticket. Automatic generation of the picking ticket data directly based on the sales order data will act to reduce this risk. In addition to receiving incorrect picking tickets, the warehouse may not be advised in a timely and correct manner of the new picking ticket details. Automatically creating the picking ticket using sales order data and exception reporting identifying any sales orders with no picking tickets generated would help detect and reduce this risk. When picking the goods there is risk that incorrect goods will be selected. In order to reduce this risk, checking picked goods against the picking ticket by an independent staff member before the goods are packed is often required. In any activity involving inventory movement there is always a risk of theft of the inventory. Common controls include restricting warehouse access and conducting random periodic physical stocktakes to verify stock levels. The risk of theft is directly related to the desirability and portability of the inventory items carried — the controls in place should reflect these dimensions. For example, appropriate controls would be different for a warehouse full of grand pianos, compared to a warehouse full of laptop computers.

### Prepare for shipping

Once the goods have been assembled and checked they need to be packed for despatch. In larger organisations a shipping area generally receives the goods and the picking ticket from the warehouse and packs them to be sent to the customer. An example packing slip is shown in figure 9.12. Ideally, checking and packing the goods would be performed by a staff member not responsible for picking the goods, as this provides an opportunity for an independent check of the goods prior to despatch. In smaller organisations one division or person may be responsible for the entire span of activities involving picking, packing and despatching the goods. In these organisations the controls in place should reflect the risks posed by the lack of segregation of duties. Risks related to packing include goods being packed incorrectly (i.e. the wrong goods packed together). Common controls include enforcing an independent check of the packed goods back to the original picking ticket or automation in the form of barcode scanners to check the goods. Barcode scanning systems used to handle inventory movement act not only to improve data accuracy, they also improve data timeliness as inventory movement is tracked and captured real time, and the status of inventory items can be updated immediately.

## Australian Information Company
### Level 2, 345 Hill Terrace
### Melbourne, Vic 3003

| To: | Ms Margaret Sinu (Customer ref.: 672839)<br>1/56 Mount Waverley Road<br>Perth 6523 | |
|---|---|---|
| Packing slip no.:<br>P04-1292 | Delivery date:<br>15/04/10 | Sales order no.:<br>SO-1245 |
| Item no. | Description | Quantity |
| 78293 | Gigante CD-ROM | 1 |
| 82838 | Picole light pen | 5 |
| 53564 | Sanman computer pen | 5 boxes |
| Remarks: | | |

**FIGURE 9.12** Sample goods packing slip

**Deliver the goods**

When despatching the goods to the customer a shipping label containing the details necessary for the goods to be delivered is required. This could be a handwritten form taken from a book supplied by the courier company, or a computer generated label based on the data contained in the sales order. Customer delivery details are combined with the picking ticket/sales order data and used to produce a shipping label. Note that often customers will have different shipping and billing addresses so the customer data used to create the sales order will not necessarily be appropriate for shipping purposes. Goods may be despatched using an employee of the firm, or an external courier company may be contracted to perform deliveries. In either case there should be a final check conducted before the goods and shipping label are handed over to the delivery driver. Once the goods are handed to the delivery driver the status of the sales order should be updated to 'shipped' to indicate that the goods are on their way. Updating the status of sales orders is important as it allows accurate information to be provided in response to customer enquiries. If a customer queries an order delivery timing, the **status code** will show the current status of the order, so a customer can be accurately advised whether the order has been picked, packed and shipped, and the likely delivery date.

To reduce the risk of goods being labelled incorrectly it is important to firmly attach shipping labels to the goods immediately after packing them and possibly include an independent three-way check of the goods to the picking ticket and the shipping label prior to despatch. Other risks related to the despatch of goods include slow delivery or non-shipment of the goods. To reduce these risks an exception report that identifies goods picked for a sales order but not shipped within a reasonable timeframe is helpful. Common controls to reduce risks related to the theft of goods include requiring an independent shipping authorisation check and restricting access to packed goods waiting to be collected for delivery. The actual delivery of the goods involves several risks: the goods may be delivered incorrectly, or may be stolen along the way. The level of risk encountered differs depending on whether the delivery is undertaken by a company employee or a contract delivery service. The controls in place should reflect the degree and type of risk involved, and should include separately and clearly packaging and labelling each order, and requiring the delivery driver to provide a valid customer signature for any delivery made.

*Status code A code on transactions that are moving through an iteration of a process indicating which stage of the process the transaction is at. As an example, a sales transaction may be first 'created', then 'picked', then 'packed' then 'shipped' then 'paid'. When each of these relevant activities has been completed the status of the transaction is changed to reflect the new status.*

## *Pick, pack and ship the goods — DFD*

The level 1 DFD in figure 9.13 overleaf contains a lower level of details about the second process represented in the level 0 logical DFD in figure 9.5. This process takes place after the sales order has been approved and created in the preceding process, and prior to the customer being billed in process 3.0.

## *Summary description of activities in picking, packing and shipping the goods*

Table 9.4 (page 417) summarises the activities, risks and controls when preparing and despatching the goods, as depicted in figure 9.13. Table 9.2 (page 402) explains the logical data flows depicted in figure 9.13. Exploring the diagram in conjunction with the material contained in the tables will assist in improving your understanding of the process depicted.

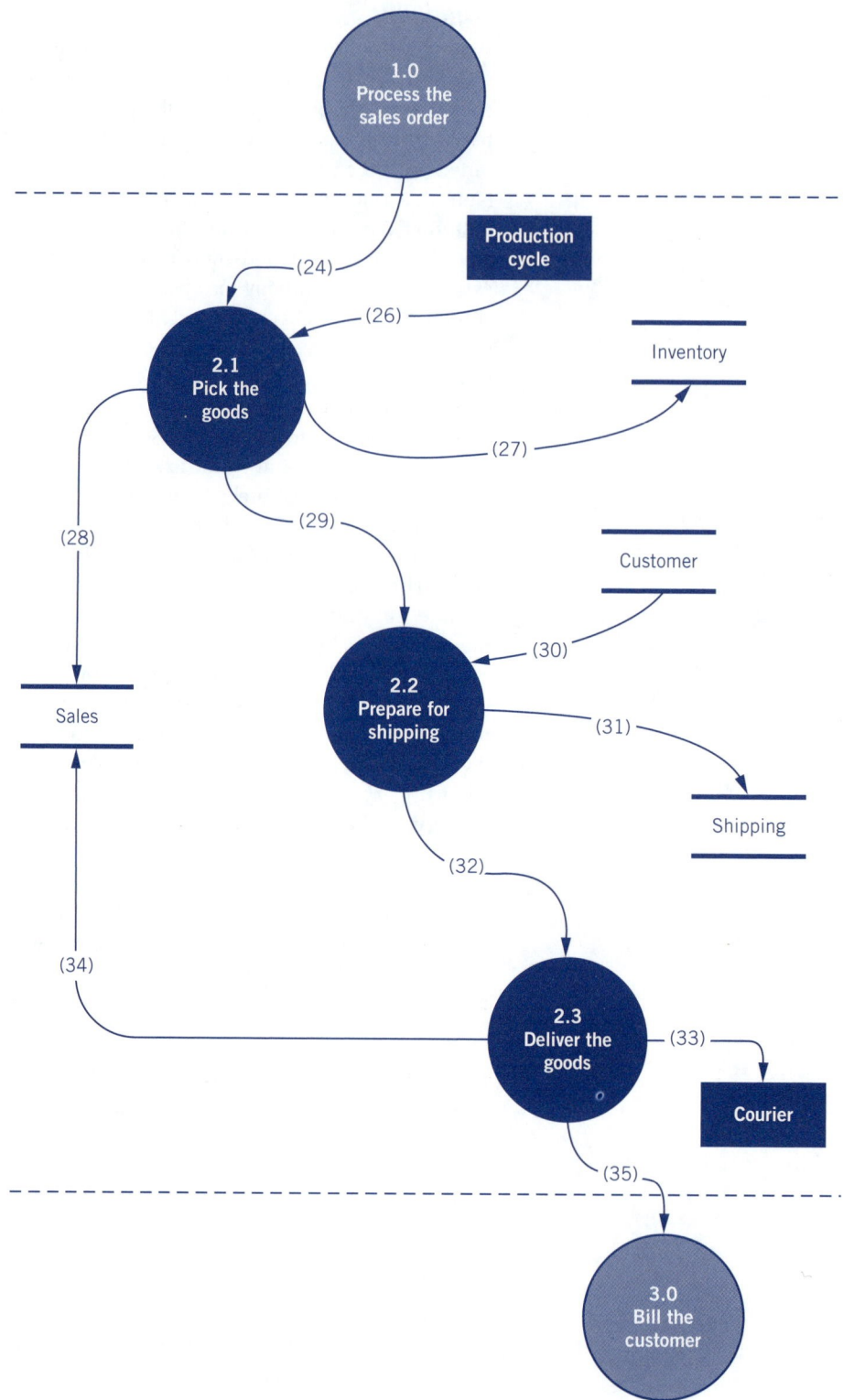

**FIGURE 9.13** Revenue cycle level 1 logical diagram — process 2.0 Pick, pack and ship the goods

**TABLE 9.4** Activities in picking, packing and shipping the goods

| Activity # | Activity | Usually conducted by: | Activity description | Typical risks encountered | Common controls |
|---|---|---|---|---|---|
| 2.1 | Pick the goods | Picking clerk | When the picking clerk receives a picking ticket they go into the warehouse and pick up the goods required for the sales order. | Picking the wrong goods | Checking goods to picking ticket by an independent staff member |
| | | | | Theft of inventory | Restricting warehouse access Conducting random periodic physical stocktakes |
| 2.2 | Prepare for shipping | Shipping clerk | The shipping clerk receives the goods and the picking ticket from the warehouse and packs them. A shipping label is created and after undergoing a final check, the goods and shipping label are handed over to the delivery driver. | Goods packed incorrectly | Independent checking of packed goods to picking ticket Using barcode scanners to check goods |
| | | | | Goods labelled incorrectly | Firmly attaching shipping label to goods after packing Independent checking of goods to picking ticket and shipping label |
| | | | | Slow/non-shipment of goods | Exception reporting of goods picked but not shipped within a reasonable timeframe |
| | | | | Theft of goods | Independent shipping authorisation check Restricted access to packed goods waiting to be delivered |
| 2.3 | Deliver the goods | Delivery staff/ courier | The goods are delivered to the customer. | Goods delivered incorrectly | Separately and clearly packaging and labelling each order |
| | | | | Theft of goods | Requiring delivery driver to provide valid customer signature for each delivery made |

## Bill the customer — activities, risks and controls

Process 3.0, bill the customer, comprises the following activities.

### Check sales completion

Once the sales order has been completed and the goods despatched an invoice can be raised. Before commencing the billing activities it is important to check that there is a matching shipping label for each sales order. Only after the sale has been recorded and goods shipped it is permitted to bill the customer for the goods. Figure 9.14 overleaf shows a screen indicating sales orders due to be billed.

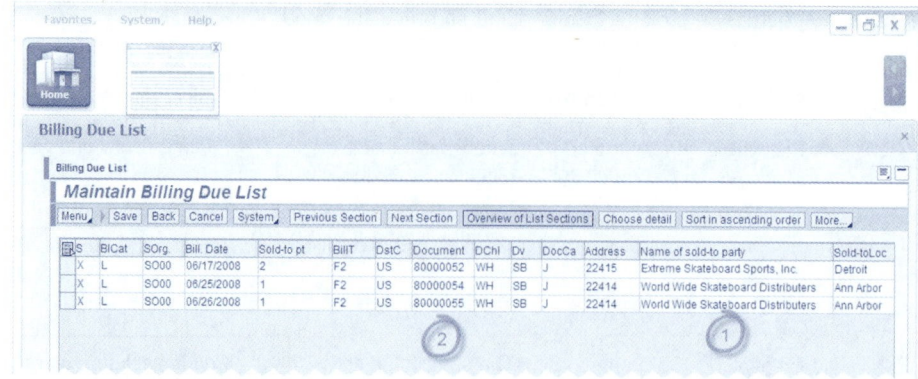

**FIGURE 9.14** Sales orders to be billed screen

*Source:* © Copyright SAP AG 2008.

### Create invoice

The billing system creates an invoice (an example is shown in figure 9.15) for each valid sale, based on data from the sales order and the customer data. Ideally, this activity would be fully automated and run as a batch job once a day, or as appropriate based on volume. At this stage the sales order status should be updated to 'billed'. Figures 9.16 and 9.17 contain example screens displaying sales order status; figure 9.16 displays a billed but unpaid sales order, figure 9.17 shows a paid sales order. Changing the status code in this way helps prevent a sales order being billed twice. The newly created invoice details are posted to the customer's account in the accounts receivable data store in order to record the amounts owing by the customer.

# Australian Information Company
### Level 2, 345 Hill Terrace
### Melbourne, Vic 3003

| *Sales invoice* | | | No: 04-827383 |
|---|---|---|---|
| To: | Ms Marg Sinu (Customer ref.: 672839) 1/56 Wave Road Perth 6523 | | |
| Order date: 01/04/10 | Date shipped: 14/04/10 | Sales order no.: SO-1245 | |
| FOB: Destination | Shipping via: Calmex Logistics | Terms: 2/10, n/30 | Other remarks: |
| Contact person: Jillian Jones, Sales Department | | | |
| Item no. | Description | Quantity | Price/unit |
| 78293 | Gigante CD-ROM | 1 | $250.00 |
| 82838 | Picole light pen | 5 | $60.00 |
| 53564 | Sanman computer pen | 5 boxes | $9.00 |
| Subtotal | $595 | Freight charges | $25 |
| GST | $62 (inclusive) | Total amount owing | $620 |

**FIGURE 9.15** Sample sales invoice

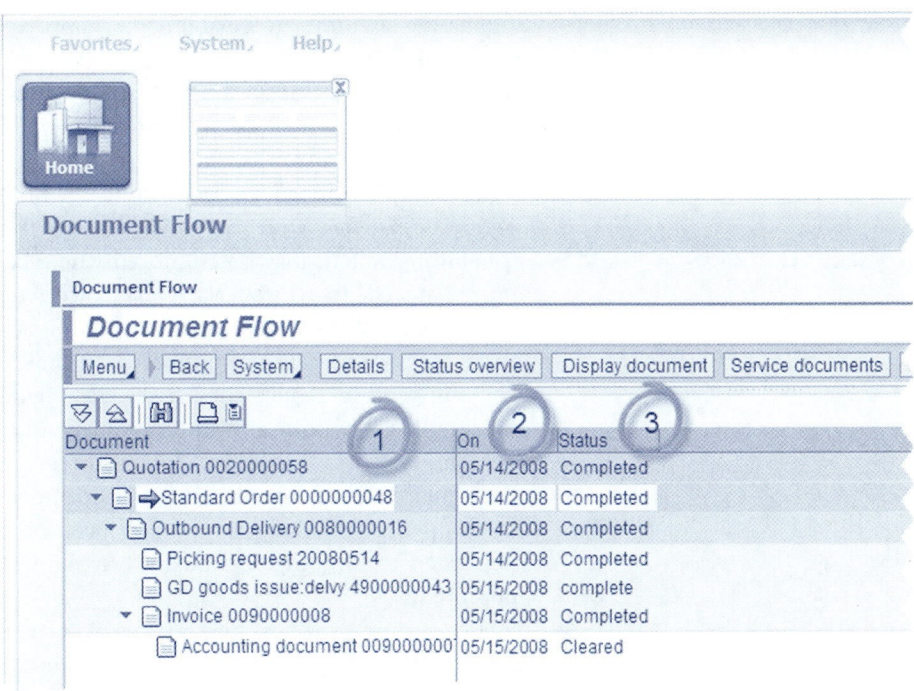

**FIGURE 9.16** Billed but unpaid sales order screen
*Source:* © Copyright SAP AG 2008.

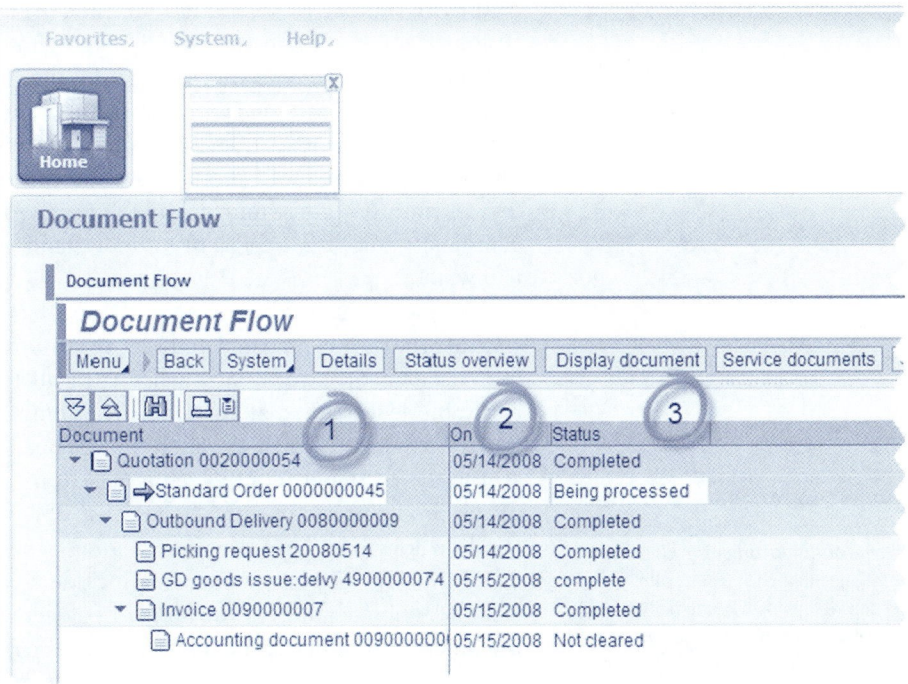

**FIGURE 9.17** Paid sales order screen
*Source:* © Copyright SAP AG 2008.

Updating accounts receivable may happen in real time as the transaction is invoiced, but more commonly occurs as a batch job usually run at the end of each day. If invoices are not posted regularly the amounts showing as owing in accounts receivable accounts will be understated, invalidating the credit check control discussed earlier. Details of invoices raised also need to be sent to the customer, either electronically or on paper. Depending on billing and credit policies this invoice may be despatched with the goods or after the goods are delivered. Alternatively, a pre-billing system may be employed where payment is required before the goods are despatched, in which case the invoice would be created much earlier in the revenue cycle. Risks relating to these billing activities include failing to bill a customer for a valid sale, or billing a customer erroneously when no goods have been shipped. To reduce these risks the organisation should separate the billing and shipping functions and impose independent checks to ensure that goods have been shipped prior to billing the customer. Pre-numbering shipping documents and regularly reviewing any shipping documents not invoiced will help to detect any shipped goods that have not yet been billed, as will regular reconciliation of sales orders to shipping documents. Alternatively, using a pre-billing system may be appropriate.

When creating invoices there is a risk of error, including both over-billing and under-billing. Common controls include using independent pricing data and/or fixed price lists and populating invoice prices directly from those price lists. This reduces the potential for staff to deviate from corporate pricing policies, either accidentally or deliberately. In common with most risks there are two underlying areas of problem: risks related to human error, and risks related to deliberate fraudulent activity. When creating and assessing control plans, it is important to consider and control for both areas. In addition to using fixed price lists, it is important to confirm customer account balances regularly. Note, however, that this is a control for over-billing; it is not likely to detect under-billing. That is, it is unlikely that a customer would inform you if you undercharge them; however, it is almost certain that they would be quick to let you know if you overcharge them. An important consideration here is the need to think about individual controls in terms of the contexts in which they operate. A control may provide differing forms of assurance under different circumstances, and it is important to understand exactly where and how a control plan will work.

Customer balances owing should be regularly confirmed by means of an account statement, which is prepared and sent to customers with amounts outstanding. A customer statement is really just a listing of all transactions recorded in the accounts receivable ledger for that customer. The transaction types contained in a customer statement relate to invoices raised and payments received. This statement is usually sent to the customer monthly, either electronically or on paper, and contains details of the preceding month's receipts, a list of invoices that are unpaid and their age (i.e. how long they have been outstanding), the current balance payable and the due date for payment. Many statements include a remittance advice for the customer to tear off, annotate and return with their payment. This is an example of a **turnaround document**. Although generation of these customer statements is almost always automated it is important to check the statements prior to despatch. Statements for small amounts (usually less than $10) or statements intended for customers who are already in a debt recovery process should not be sent. Ideally, these types of edit

**Turnaround document** *A document that is printed with a separate section designed to be detached, completed and returned to the issuing organisation. Examples include a tear-off section on a delivery docket which is signed and returned to a courier.*

checks should be automated and embedded into the statement generation program; however, if they are not, a manual visual check is helpful.

## Bill the customer — DFD

The level 1 DFD in figure 9.18 contains a lower level of details about the third process represented in the level 0 logical DFD in figure 9.5. This process takes place after the goods have been despatched to the customer in the preceding process and before payment is received in the following process.

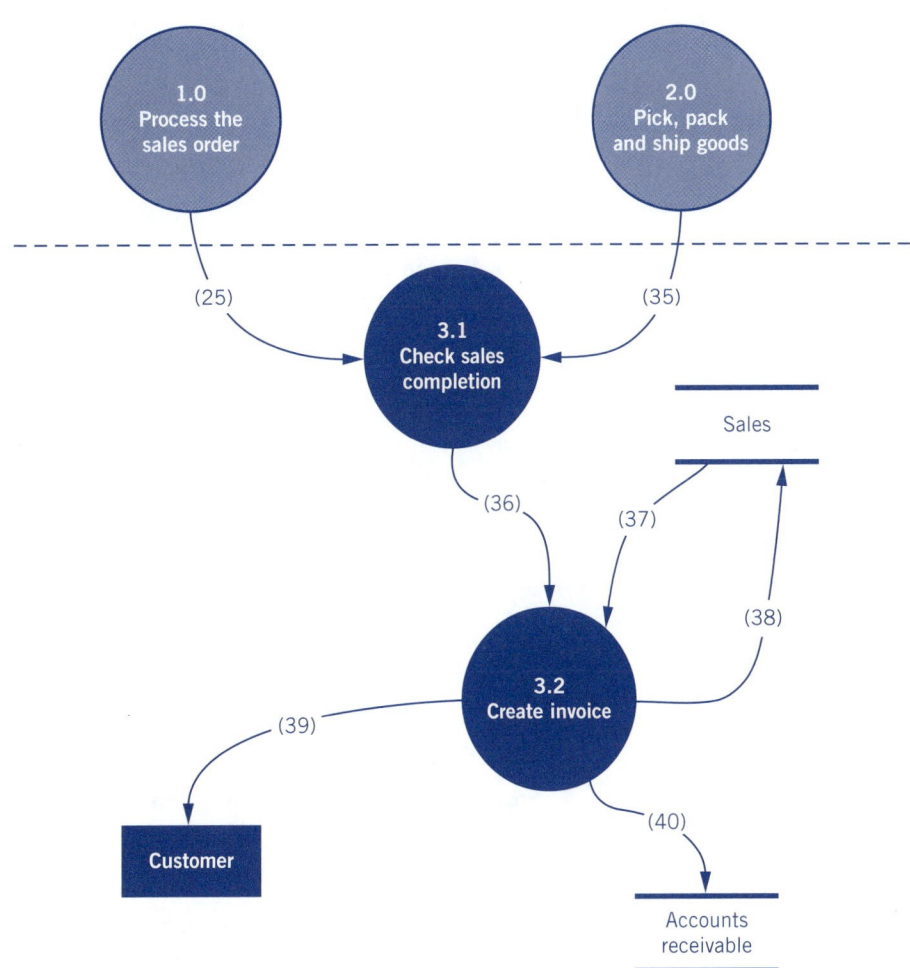

**FIGURE 9.18** Revenue cycle level 1 logical diagram — process 3.0 Bill the customer

## Summary description of activities in billing the customer

Table 9.5 overleaf summarises the activities, risks and controls involved when billing the customer, as depicted in figure 9.18. Table 9.2 (page 402) explains the logical data flows depicted in figure 9.18. Exploring the diagram in conjunction with the material contained in the tables will assist in improving your understanding of the process depicted.

**Table 9.5** Activities in billing the customer

| Activity # | Activity | Usually conducted by: | Activity description | Typical risks encountered | Common controls |
|---|---|---|---|---|---|
| 3.1 | Check sales completion | Billing clerk | The billing clerk checks that they have a matching shipping label for each sales order. | Failure to bill customers | Separation of billing and shipping functions |
| | | | | Billing customers when no goods have been shipped | Pre-numbering shipping documents and reviewing any shipping documents not invoiced, use of a pre-billing system (vs. a post-billing system) |
| | | | | | Reconciliation of sales order to shipping documents |
| 3.2 | Create invoice | Billing clerk | An invoice is created for each valid sale. Details of the invoice are sent to the customer, and the invoice data is recorded in the customer's accounts receivable account. | Invoice errors — both over-billing and under-billing | Using independent pricing data and/or fixed price lists |
| | | | | | Populating price data with data from those price lists |
| | | | | | Confirming customer accounts regularly — note this is a control for over-billing only, it will not detect under-billing |

## Receive and record payment — activities, risks and controls

Process 4.0, receive and record payment, comprises the following activities.

### Receive payment

In response to the statement, a customer usually sends payment and an accompanying remittance advice to the organisation. A major risk here is that of late, slow or non-payment of accounts. Prompt invoicing of customers acts to reduce this risk, as does setting suitable payment terms. The regular and consistent follow-up of overdue accounts and the prompt removal of credit facilities for any non-payers are also important. Ideally, a cashier would be responsible for receiving payments from customers, issuing receipts for those payments, and depositing the payments into the company bank account. This cashier should not be assigned any other duties relating to billing or sales activities in order to reduce the risk of fraud and error. The cashier receipts all payments and the data is recorded as a cash receipt. These cash receipts data are often used to generate automatically a bank deposit slip. Many organisations also have a mailroom where checks are received and recorded prior to being sent to the cashier for processing. Creating an independent record of details of all cheques received in the mailroom is a helpful independent check of the bank deposit records, and can help with detection of lapping and similar frauds by use of one-for-one checking against deposit slips and cheques. The cheques and deposit slips are taken to the bank to be deposited into the company bank account. Note that for electronic payments this step is not necessary. Accepting and banking cash and cheque payments carries a risk of theft or misappropriation of the cash and/or cheques. Common controls to reduce this risk include minimising the number of cash handling points and the numbers of people handling cash. It is also important to enter cash receipts close to where they are received; allowing undocumented cash to sit around is likely to lead to a higher level of opportunistic theft.

Once payments have been receipted the physical security of cash and cheques can be improved by the use of bank lockboxes or company safes, and by banking regularly and not allowing large amounts of cash to build up on the organisation's premises. Cheques received should be immediately stamped or written on (called **cheque endorsement**) and separated from the accompanying remittance advices. This separation allows the cheque to be receipted and deposited by the cashier, and the payment to be allocated promptly and independently by accounts receivable staff. Having two separate input points for the cash receipts data supports later reconciliation by an independent person. In addition to these controls a regular bank reconciliation should be conducted by an individual who has no direct responsibility for any other revenue or expenditure activities.

### Record payment

If a payment is made electronically the cashier will need to download and reconcile the online banking transactions and use this data to populate the cash receipts records. If online banking is used it is important to limit access to the online bank accounts, and prepare regular customer receipts and statements. Once a payment has been receipted it can be recorded against the customer's accounts receivable account. The accounts receivable clerk must examine details of all unpaid invoices and the customer-completed remittance advice in order to determine how to allocate the payment received.

Receipt allocation is the process of allocating the total payment received against one or more of the unpaid invoices in the customer's accounts receivable account. Those invoices that have a payment allocated against them need to be updated with a status of 'paid' (this is also known as an invoice being 'closed'). There is a risk that payments received will be incorrectly recorded against the customer accounts. To control this potential problem it is important to create **batch totals** or **hash totals** of cash receipts and reconcile all inputs to accounts receivable. The use of regular customer statements is also important; however, these will only detect any amounts under-receipted — any amounts over-receipted may not be detected using this control as discussed earlier in relation to under- and over-billing. Data generated by billing and accounts receivable activities is transferred through to the financial cycle, where it is used to update general ledger accounts and create reports as described in chapter 13.

## *Receive and record payment — DFD*

The level 1 DFD in figure 9.19 overleaf contains a lower level of details about the final process represented in the level 0 logical DFD in figure 9.5. This process takes place after the customer has been billed in the preceding process.

**Cheque endorsement** *Stamped or writing on a cheque to stop the cheque being diverted to a different bank account than that intended. An endorsement often is written as, for example, 'Not Negotiable — pay only to Smith & Co'.*

**Batch total** *A total that is added to a batch of documents and is used to make sure that all documents in the batch have been correctly processed. A batch total is usually a summation of a data item with some meaning (e.g. a total of the individual invoice amounts for a batch of invoices). See also hash total.*

**Hash total** *A total that is similar to a batch total but the number that is added has no meaning by itself (e.g. a hash total of customer numbers). See also batch total.*

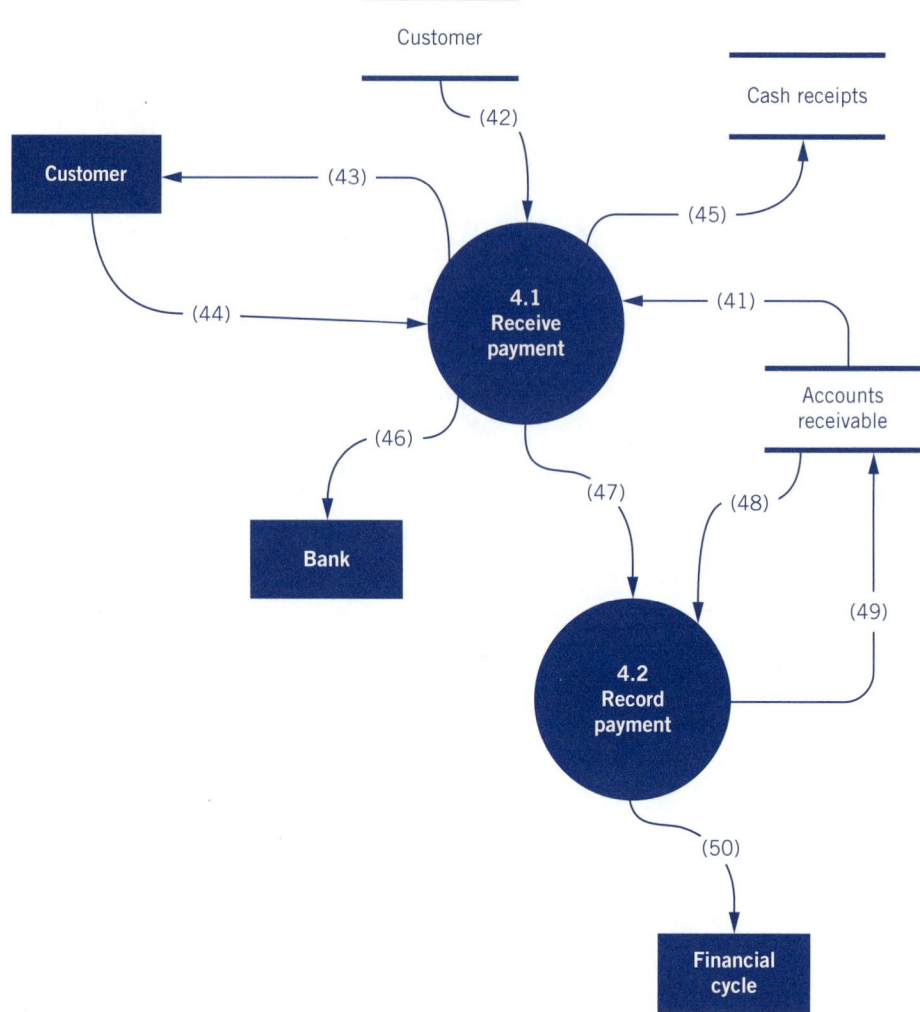

**FIGURE 9.19** Revenue cycle level 1 logical diagram — process 4.0 Receive and record payment

## *Summary description of activities in receiving and recording payment*

Table 9.6 summarises the activities, risks and controls when receiving and recording payment, as depicted in figure 9.19. Table 9.2 (page 402) explains the logical data flows depicted in figure 9.19. Exploring the diagram in conjunction with the material contained in the tables will assist in improving your understanding of the process depicted.

**TABLE 9.6** Activities in receiving and recording payment

| Activity # | Activity | Usually conducted by: | Activity description | Typical risks encountered | Common controls |
|---|---|---|---|---|---|
| 4.1 | Receive payment | Accounts receivable clerk/cashier | The accounts receivable clerk prepares a customer account statement which is sent to the customer. | Late/slow/non-payment of accounts | Prompt invoicing, and setting suitable payment terms |

| Activity # | Activity | Usually conducted by: | Activity description | Typical risks encountered | Common controls |
|---|---|---|---|---|---|
| | | | The cashier receives payments from customers, issues receipts, and deposits the payment into the company bank account. If a payment is made electronically the cashier will download and reconcile the online amounts. | | Regularly and consistently follow up of overdue accounts<br>Removing credit facilities for any non-payers |
| | | | | Theft of cash and/or cheques | Minimising the cash handling points and the numbers of people handling cash<br>Entering cash receipts close to where received<br>Using lockboxes or safes and bank regularly<br>Immediate/prompt cheque endorsement and immediate separation of remittance advice and cheques<br>One-for-one checking of deposit slip and cheques<br>Regular bank reconciliations by an independent person<br>Limiting access to online banking<br>Preparing regular customer statements |
| 4.2 | Record payment | Accounts receivable clerk | The accounts receivable clerk enters the details of cash received into the customer's accounts receivable account | Incorrect recording of customer accounts | Creating batch or hash totals of cash receipts and reconciling inputs to accounts receivable<br>Issuing regular customer statements, incorporating use of turnaround documents |

## Physical DFD — process the sales order

The physical DFD depicted in figure 9.20 overleaf shows an example of how a sales order may be processed. The physical diagram draws the process from a different perspective to the logical DFD of this process contained in figure 9.10, as it shows who is involved in the activities of the process, rather then when those activities occur. This process of processing a sales order involves the sales clerk and the sales manager, who both interact with a central computer. The sales clerk also interacts with the customer during this process. Outputs from this process are sent through to the production and HR cycles, and also to the picking clerk and billing clerk for use in subsequent parts of the revenue cycle.

Details of the physical data flows in figure 9.20 are contained in table 9.7. As this diagram is drawn from a different perspective to the logical DFD, it contains far more detail about the interactions between each of the entities involved in process the sales order.

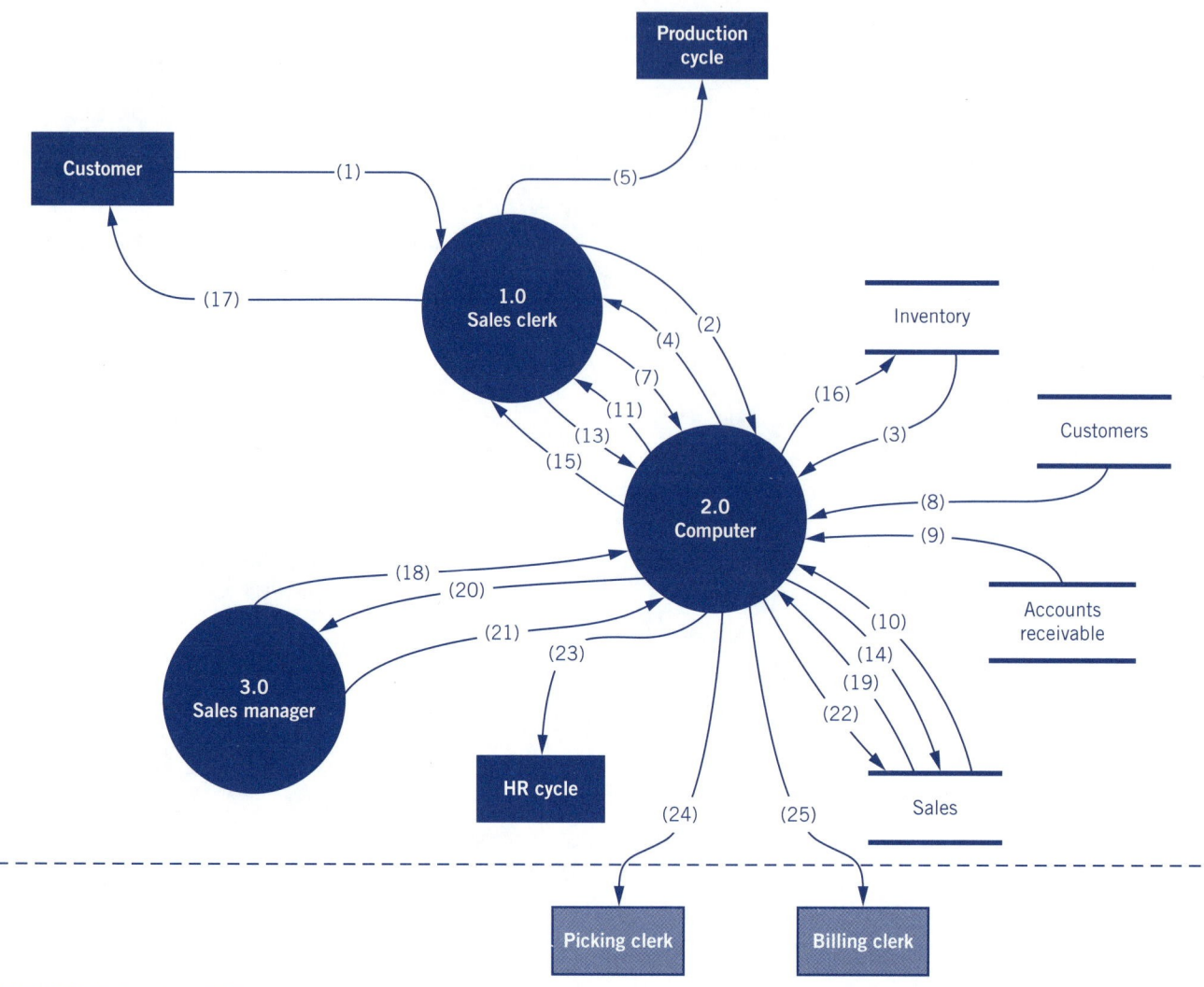

**FIGURE 9.20** Physical DFD — process the sales order

**TABLE 9.7** Description of data flows in physical DFD and flowchart in processing the sales order

| Flow # | Data source | Data destination | Explanation of the physical data flows |
| --- | --- | --- | --- |
| 1 | Customer | Sales clerk | The customer posts a paper purchase order to the sales clerk containing details of the goods the customer wants to purchase. |
| 2 | Sales clerk | Computer | The sales clerk inputs a request for stock levels of requested products into the computer. |
| 3 | Inventory data store | Computer | The required stock levels are extracted from the inventory data store. |
| 4 | Computer | Sales clerk | The requested stock levels are displayed to the sales clerk. |
| 5 | Sales clerk | Production cycle | The sales clerk sends details of goods required to be produced to the production cycle. |

| Flow # | Data source | Data destination | Explanation of the physical data flows |
|---|---|---|---|
| 6 | Sales clerk | Sales clerk | When the inventory check is complete the credit check can commence (not depicted in a physical DFD). |
| 7 | Inventory check | Computer | The sales clerk inputs a request for a credit check on the customer into the computer. |
| 8 | Customer data store | Computer | The computer extracts the customer's credit limit from the customer data store. |
| 9 | Accounts receivable data store | Computer | The computer extracts the current accounts receivable balance for the customer from the customer data store. |
| 10 | Sales data store | Computer | The computer extracts details of any recent sales that have not yet been posted to accounts receivable for the customer from the sales data store. |
| 11 | Computer | Sales clerk | The computer displays the result of the credit check for the customer to the sales clerk. |
| 12 | Sales clerk | Sales clerk | Once the credit check is complete the sales order can be created (not depicted in a physical DFD). |
| 13 | Sales clerk | Computer | The sales clerk inputs a request to create the sales invoice into the computer. |
| 14 | Computer | Sales data store | The computer stores details of the sales order in the sales data store. |
| 15 | Computer | Sales clerk | The computer displays the completed sales order to the sales clerk. |
| 16 | Computer | Inventory data store | The computer marks the relevant inventory item status as 'promised' in the inventory data store. |
| 17 | Sales clerk | Customer | The sales clerk advises the customer whether the sale will proceed. |
| 18 | Sales manager | Computer | The sales manager requests the computer to create a report of sales commissions payable. |
| 19 | Computer | Sales data store | The computer extracts details of sale on which commission is payable from the sales data store. |
| 20 | Computer | Sales manager | The computer displays sales commission payable to the sales manager. |
| 21 | Sales manager | Computer | The sales manager inputs and authorisation to pay the sales commissions. |
| 22 | Computer | Sales data store | The status of the relevant sales are up dated to 'commission approved'. |
| 23 | Computer | HR cycle | The computer transfers details of commissions payable to the HR cycle. |
| 24 | Computer | Picking clerk | The computer sends details of the sales order to the picking clerk. |
| 25 | Computer | Billing clerk | The computer sends details of the sales order to the billing clerk. |

## System flowchart — process the sales order

The DFD in figure 9.20 shows an example of how a sales order may be physically processed. The logical DFD in figure 9.16 shows that same process from a logical perspective. The flowchart contained in figure 9.21 shows that same process from yet another perspective. The system flowchart in figure 9.21 is the most detailed picture of the process, and includes both logical and physical perspectives. The detail contained in the system flowchart is useful when considering process redesign, and when analysing the control environment of the process depicted. Details of the flows shown in the flowchart in figure 9.21 are documented in table 9.7.

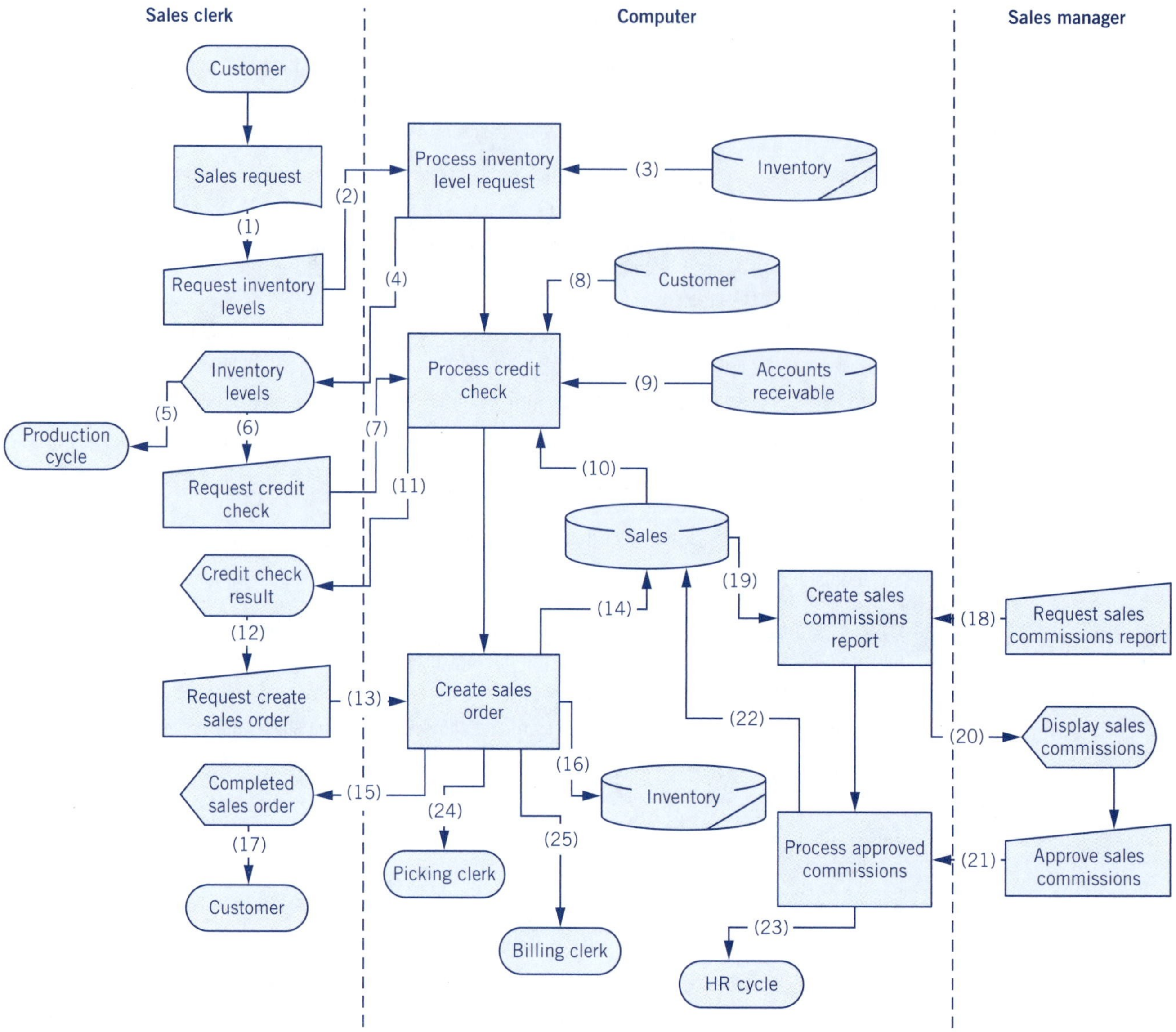

**Sales clerk** | **Computer** | **Sales manager**

**FIGURE 9.21** Systems flowchart — process the sales order

# MEASURING REVENUE CYCLE PERFORMANCE

Cycle performance should be measured relative to how well the process outcomes achieve the overall objectives of that cycle. At the start of this chapter the objectives of the revenue cycle were described as being to effectively conduct, record and monitor sales of goods and services; to arrange the prompt supply of goods and services; and to ensure payments for goods and services are correctly received, recorded and banked.

To monitor performance against these objectives a range of **metrics** needs to be employed, along with some realistic targets. Figure 9.22 contains an example of the analytical data available for performance evaluation of the supply of goods and services to customers.

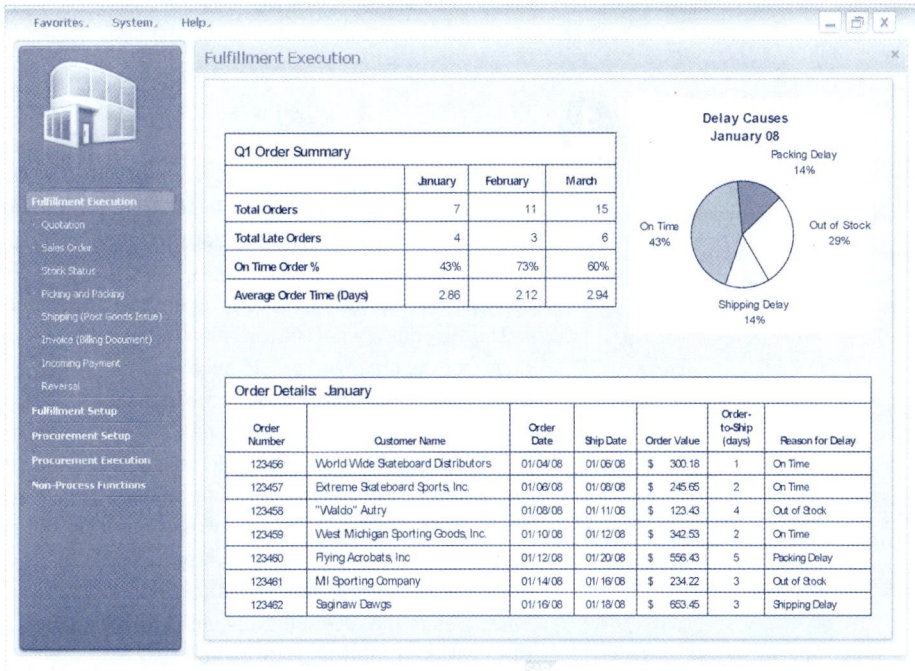

**FIGURE 9.22** Fulfillment analytics
*Source:* © Copyright SAP AG 2008.

Examples of suitable metrics or key performance indicators (KPIs) for the revenue cycle objectives are contained in table 9.8.

**TABLE 9.8** Example KPIs mapped to cycle objectives

| Objective | Example KPI |
|---|---|
| To effectively conduct, record and monitor sales of goods and services | • Number of data entry errors detected<br>• Customer complaints/satisfaction<br>• Credit requests<br>• Number of credit memos raised due to billing errors<br>• % sales invoiced on day of shipping |
| To arrange the prompt supply of goods and services | • Cycle time to fill and deliver orders<br>• % of sales on back order<br>• Sales returns |
| To ensure payments for goods and services are correctly received, recorded and banked. | • Aged accounts receivable reporting<br>• Number of bad debts written off<br>• Average payment times |

**LEARNING OBJECTIVE 1**

### What are the key objectives and strategic implications of the revenue cycle?

The revenue cycle is divided into two major processes: sales and accounts receivable. The sales process is client facing as it is where the sales transaction takes place. The objective of the sales process is to effectively conduct, record and monitor sales of goods and services, and arrange the prompt supply of goods and services. Following directly on from sales is the accounts receivable process, where the objective is to ensure payments for goods and services are correctly received, recorded and banked.

The revenue cycle is strategically important as the level of sales activity is a primary driver for the organisation. To survive long term an organisation must not only remain profitable (i.e. revenues must exceed expenses), it also must be able to achieve positive cash flows. A sound, well-controlled revenue cycle can provide a competitive advantage by providing superior customer service levels, which in turn translate to opportunities to sustain higher product price levels. An alternative form of competitive advantage is the potential to control costs that is afforded by ensuring that the revenue cycle is efficient and effective. This translates into an opportunity to price goods and services at a level that potentially undercuts less efficient competitors and increase market share. It is important to align the objectives of the revenue cycle with the overall organisation strategy that overarches all the businesses within the organisation.

**LEARNING OBJECTIVE 2**

### Which technologies underpin the activities of the revenue cycle?

Activities within the revenue cycle benefit from underpinning technologies that improve the ability to capture and analyse revenue data, and manage cash and cash flows. Enterprise resource planning (ERP) systems assist with enabling and integrating activities across the enterprise, and technologies to support efficient data exchange such as EDI and XML help provide efficient exchanges of revenue data. Management of outgoing inventory forms a significant component of the revenue cycle; the conduct of inventory-related activities can be improved by the use of barcode scanners and readers, whereas scanning incoming documents will support faster transaction processing. A revenue data warehouse would support data mining to improve understanding of markets and product performance. The opportunity to improve understanding of individual customers is afforded by customer relationship management (CRM) systems, which present a customer-centric view of process activities and outcomes. Online payment and banking facilities provide a cost effective way for organisations to receive and monitor payments. Use of these facilities cuts costs and reduces error rates.

**LEARNING OBJECTIVE 3**

### What data and business decisions are involved in the revenue cycle?

The revenue cycle uses or produces data including customer, inventory, accounts receivable and sales data. Process business decisions are made at both strategic and operational levels. Strategy-level decisions include the creation of policies such as price setting, sales return and warranty policies, provision of customer credit facilities, and cash collection policies and procedures. Typical operational decisions include responding to customer inquiries such as a request to purchase goods, or to return goods for credit or a request to extend credit to a particular customer, calculation of inventory availability, selecting a goods delivery method and determining the correct cash receipt allocations for a customer payment.

**LEARNING OBJECTIVE 4**

### What are the primary activities in the revenue cycle; and what data is produced by these activities?

Contextually the revenue cycle involves direct interaction with entities outside the organisation such as customers, couriers and banks. Within the organisation, the revenue cycle interacts with the production, HR management and payroll, and general ledger and financial cycles. Primary activities in the revenue cycle include processing the sales order, despatching goods to the customer, billing the customer and receiving and recording payments.

A range of data types are accessed by activities within the revenue cycle including customer data, inventory data, accounts receivable data, cash receipts data, sales data and accounts receivable adjustments data. Revenue data is used to support decision making related to the revenue cycle, and for evaluating process performance and reporting financial results for the organisation.

LEARNING OBJECTIVE *What risks relate to the revenue cycle activities, and how might we control for these risks?*

Activities within the revenue cycle create exposure to a range of known risks. Risks related to customer accounts include failing to bill customers, or not billing customers correctly, data entry errors, late/slow/non-payment of customer accounts, slow processing of sales orders, raising inappropriate credit memos, and bad or doubtful debt recording errors.

Risks related to the inventory management aspect of the revenue cycle activities include making errors when picking and packing goods for despatch, theft of inventory, incorrectly recording goods movements, despatching incorrect goods to customers, and slow shipment of goods.

To reduce risk exposure, the control environment must include controls that minimise human error, as well as prevent fraudulent behaviour. Controls need to be created over both manual and automated activities, and some degree of control redundancy should be embedded in the control environment. Important controls in the revenue cycle include performing credit checks, maintaining perpetual inventory records, appropriate segregations of duties, exception reporting, regular monitoring of customer outstandings, regularly issuing statements to customers and performing regular bank reconciliations.

LEARNING OBJECTIVE *How can we best monitor revenue cycle performance?*

Cycle performance should be measured relative to the desired outcomes of the process. To monitor cycle performance a wide range of metrics needs to be employed, along with some realistic targets. Examples of suitable performance metrics for a revenue cycle include numbers of data entry errors, customer satisfaction levels, cycle times at both process and activity levels, volume of back orders and sales returns, accounts receivable ageing, number of bad debts written off and average payment times achieved.

## KEY TERMS

back order, p. 410
batch process, p. 409
batch total, p. 423
cheque endorsement, p. 423
customer relationship management (CRM), p. 397
electronic data interchange (EDI), p. 397
enterprise resource planning (ERP) system, p. 396
exception report, p. 407

eXtensible Markup Language (XML), p. 397
hash total, p. 423
metric, p. 428
post-billing system, p. 407
pre-billing system, p. 407
reconciliation, p. 397
status code, p. 415
turnaround document, p. 420

# DISCUSSION QUESTIONS

9.1 Brisbane Ltd has always had a strategy of product differentiation; that is, providing high quality products and extracting a price premium from the market. During the recent economic downturn, Brisbane Ltd has seen its customer base diminish and has decided to move strategically to a cost leadership strategy, that is, to try to sell more products at a lower price.

(a) What are the implications of this strategy change for the revenue cycle? (LO1).

(b) What changes would you expect to see in the revenue cycle? (LO4).

(c) What are the implications of this strategy change in terms of the usefulness of historical sales data for decision making? (LO3).

9.2 Melbourne Ltd has decided to introduce electronic payment facilities to allow customers to pay for goods online.

(a) What controls would you expect to see introduced to ensure the safety of the online banking data? (LO5)

(b) Which activities in the cash receipting and accounts receivable process would be affected? (LO2, LO4)

(c) What changes would you expect to see in these activities? (LO4)

(d) What metrics could you use to measure the success of this initiative post implementation? (LO6)

9.3 Sydney Ltd has just realised that it has a problem with revenue data as its sales order system does not record goods requested by a customer that are unable to be supplied due to inventory shortages.

(a) What decisions made during the revenue cycle would be affected by this data problem? (LO3, LO4)

(b) How would those decisions be affected? How would this data problem affect the performance of the revenue cycle? (LO3, LO4, LO6)

(c) How would this data problem affect other processes at Sydney Ltd? (LO1, LO3, LO4, LO6)

9.4 Perth Ltd has a reconciliation problem. The amount of cash receipted and banked by the cashier does not seem to match to the amount recorded in the accounts receivable customer records from the customer remittance advices. Perth Ltd seems to have good controls — it separated the receipting and recording of cash, and it regularly conducts a reconciliation.

(a) Which internal controls might be missing? (LO5)

(b) What documentation would you examine in order to investigate this problem? (LO4)

9.5 Darwin Ltd has a new CEO who is keen on improving process efficiency. She has reviewed the process documentation for the revenue cycle and has asked you to remove the inventory check from the sales order process as it appears to be totally inefficient.

(a) Should you agree to remove the inventory check? Why or why not? (LO1, LO3, LO5)

(b) If you would not agree to remove the inventory check, how would you explain this decision to the CEO? (LO1, LO5)

(c) If you do agree to remove the inventory check how would you justify this change to the picking and packing manager? (LO1, LO5)

(d) If you remove the inventory check will you need to measure the process performance differently? (LO1, LO6)

# SELF-TEST ACTIVITIES

9.1 Which of the following drives the activity levels of a business?
- (a) The level of sales
- (b) The number of customers
- (c) The number of different products sold
- (d) The business strategy

9.2 A well aligned revenue cycle is congruent with the:
- (a) organisational strategy.
- (b) organisational goals.
- (c) organisational culture.
- (d) All of the above.

9.3 Use of barcode scanning technology could *not* help to:
- (a) reduce data errors.
- (b) improve data timeliness.
- (c) improve customer payment times.
- (d) speed up data collection.

9.4 Correctly calculating the amount of inventory on hand does *not* require knowledge of:
- (a) stock on hand.
- (b) stock on order.
- (c) stock shipped to customers.
- (d) supplier lead times.

9.5 The revenue cycle interacts internally with:
- (a) the production cycle.
- (b) the HR management and payroll cycle.
- (c) the financial cycle.
- (d) all of the above.

9.6 Primary risks of the revenue cycle include:
- (a) customers not paying for goods.
- (b) slow dispatch of goods.
- (c) theft of inventory.
- (d) all of the above.

9.7 A credit check should be performed:
- (a) for new customers.
- (b) for new products.
- (c) for slow-paying customers.
- (d) for all sales.

9.8 It is not necessary to check shipping label details when:
- (a) the customer buys products frequently from you.
- (b) the same person who picks the goods also packs and labels them.
- (c) the delivery driver is going to check this anyway.
- (d) you should always check the shipping label details.

9.9 Not reconciling invoices raised by the billing system to shipping documents increases the risk of:
- (a) not shipping goods to customers.
- (a) shipping the wrong goods to customers.
- (c) not billing the customer.
- (d) picking the wrong goods.

9.10 Sending customers a regular statement of account helps to detect:
- (a) under-billing only.
- (b) over-billing only.
- (c) neither (a) nor (b).
- (d) both (a) and (b).

9.11 Monitoring the number of bad debts written off is useful to determine:
- (a) how accurately sales of goods and services are recorded.
- (b) how promptly goods and services are delivered.
- (c) how well payments are recorded.
- (d) how well the credit check control is working.

## PROBLEMS

The case narrative below (AB Hi-Fi) will be used to complete problems 9.1–9.13. Make sure you read and understand the activities and the case thoroughly before you commence work on the problems.

**AB Hi-Fi revenue cycle**

AB Hi-Fi is a multi-store retail business that sells products such as DVDs, CDs, mp3 players, game consoles and TVs. In addition to these retail sales, AB Hi-Fi also sells music, games and DVDs via its website. The narrative of the revenue cycle relating to online sales at AB Hi-Fi follows.

**Process 1.0 Process the sales order**

Customers browse the AB Hi-Fi online store looking for products to purchase from the product catalogue. When they have located an item they wish to purchase they click on a 'buy this item' link located underneath the item required. The computer displays a screen showing the product ID number and asks the customer to enter the quantity of the item required. The customer keys in the quantity required. The computer then displays a screen asking the customer if they want to continue shopping. Once the customer indicates that they do not want to continue shopping the computer calculates and displays an order confirmation screen containing the product ID number, product price, quantity and total cost per item for each different item ordered, the shipping amount (AB has a standard shipping rate within Australia of $10 per delivery), and a total for all items and shipping costs. The screen asks the customer to input their credit card and delivery details to complete the order. The customer inputs the delivery details (name and address) and credit card details (card number and expiry date) into the order confirmation screen. The computer assigns the next sales order number to the transaction, then displays a screen for the customer which provides the sales order number and confirms that the order has been completed. The computer records the sales order details in the sales event data store. At 11 pm every evening the computer extracts details of the day's sales and updates the inventory levels. The computer prints a picking ticket (barcoded sales order number, items and quantities) on the warehouse printer and produces an electronic credit card check file listing all the credit card details (customer name, credit card number and expiry date) from the previous day's sales.

**Process 2.0 Pick, pack and ship the goods**

At 8 am every morning the warehouse clerk collects the picking tickets from the warehouse printer and picks the required goods from the shelf. If any of the goods are not available the warehouse clerk puts back any goods they have already picked for the order and places the picking ticket in a folder on their desk labelled 'awaiting goods'. If all the goods are available the warehouse clerk takes the goods and the picking ticket to the shipping department. The shipping clerk scans the sales order number from the picking ticket, and the computer displays the order on the screen. The shipping clerk manually checks each item picked against the original sales order, and the picking ticket. The shipping clerk also checks the name on the sales order against the names highlighted on the credit card status report. If the name on the order matches a name on the credit card status report, the goods and the picking ticket are sent back to the warehouse with a note attached indicating they cannot be shipped due to non-payment. Once they are satisfied that the credit card payment is not invalid, and that the correct items are being shipped, the shipping clerk checks a box on the sales order to indicate that shipping is complete. The computer updates the sales order and inventory data. The computer also prints a delivery slip for the order on a printer in the shipping department. The shipping clerk attaches the delivery slip to the goods and places them on the loading dock. Every day at 3 pm a carrier picks up the goods from the loading dock and delivers them to the customer.

### Process 3.0 Bill the customer

The computer sends the electronic credit card check file that was produced at 11 pm to the bank's computer for verification. At 1 pm every day the bank sends an electronic report via email to the accounts receivable clerk indicating the status of each of the credit card orders (valid/invalid). The accounts receivable clerk prints out two copies of the credit card status report. The accounts receivable clerk files one copy of the credit card status report and uses a highlighter pen to mark out on the second copy the name of any customers whose credit card was reported as invalid. The accounts receivable clerk takes the highlighted report to the shipping clerk who is responsible for checking that these customers do not receive any goods.

### Process 4.0 Receive and record payment

Immediately after the bank sends the electronic status report the funds for all valid credit card orders are transferred into the company's bank account. The accounts receivable clerk receives an email from the bank advising them of the total amount of the funds transferred. The accounts receivable clerk compares the total in the email to the total in the credit card status report. If these totals agree the amount is input into the computer and the cash receipt data store is updated. If the totals do not match the problem is referred to the accounts receivable manager for resolution.

9.1 Prepare a context diagram for the revenue cycle at AB Hi-Fi.

9.2 Prepare a level 0 logical DFD for the revenue cycle at AB Hi-Fi.

9.3 Prepare a level 1 logical DFD for:
    (a) Process 1.0 at AB Hi-Fi
    (b) Process 2.0 at AB Hi-Fi
    (c) Process 3.0 at AB Hi-Fi
    (d) Process 4.0 at AB Hi-Fi.

9.4 Prepare a physical DFD for:
    (a) Process 1.0 at AB Hi-Fi
    (b) Process 2.0 at AB Hi-Fi
    (c) Process 3.0 at AB Hi-Fi
    (d) Process 4.0 at AB Hi-Fi.

9.5 Prepare a systems flowchart for:
  (a) Process 1.0 at AB Hi-Fi
  (b) Process 2.0 at AB Hi-Fi
  (c) Process 3.0 at AB Hi-Fi
  (d) Process 4.0 at AB Hi-Fi.
9.6 Table 9.3 (page 412) identifies eleven risks typically encountered when processing a sales order.

**Required**
  (a) Analyse the degree of exposure to each of these risks for the sales process at AB Hi-Fi.
  (b) Determine how many of the common controls described in table 9.3 are present in the sales process at AB Hi-Fi.
  (c) Prepare a short report suitable for senior management to explain how risky you think the sales process is, and how comprehensive the current internal controls are.
  (d) Prepare a recommendation describing any changes you would like to make to the sales process at AB Hi-Fi in order to reduce the level of risk.

9.7 Table 9.4 (page 417) identifies eight risks typically encountered when despatching a sales order.

**Required**
  (a) Analyse the degree of exposure to each of these risks for the goods despatch process at AB Hi-Fi.
  (b) Determine how many of the common controls described in table 9.4 are present in the goods despatch process at AB Hi-Fi.
  (c) Prepare a short report suitable for senior management to explain how risky you think the goods despatch process is, and how comprehensive the current internal controls are.
  (d) Prepare a recommendation describing any changes you would like to make to the goods despatch process at AB Hi-Fi in order to reduce the level of risk.

9.8 Table 9.5 (page 422) identifies three risks typically encountered when billing a sale.

**Required**
  (a) Analyse the degree of exposure to each of these risks for the billing process at AB Hi-Fi.
  (b) Determine how many of the common controls described in table 9.5 are present in the billing process at AB Hi-Fi.
  (c) Prepare a short report suitable for senior management to explain how risky you think the billing process is, and how comprehensive the current internal controls are.
  (d) Prepare a recommendation describing any changes you would like to make to the billing process at AB Hi-Fi in order to reduce the level of risk.

9.9 Table 9.6 (page 424) identifies three risks typically encountered when receiving and recording payments.

**Required**
  (a) Analyse the degree of exposure to each of these risks for the receiving payments process at AB Hi-Fi.
  (b) Determine how many of the common controls described in table 9.6 are present in the receiving payments process at AB Hi-Fi.

(c) Prepare a short report suitable for senior management to explain how risky you think the receiving payments process is, and how comprehensive the current internal controls are.

(d) Prepare a recommendation describing any changes you would like to make to the receiving payments process at AB Hi-Fi in order to reduce the level of risk.

9.10 AB Hi-Fi has adopted a cost leadership strategy. Its overall plan is to undercut competitors on pricing and so gain market share. (a) How well does its current revenue cycle align with this business strategy? (b) Are there any opportunities to improve the degree of alignment between the revenue cycle and the business strategy? Explain what you would change and how this would improve the strategic alignment.

9.11 (a) Identify and describe the technologies that AB Hi-Fi uses in its revenue cycle activities. (b) For each of those technologies you identified in part (a), how well does AB Hi-Fi use the technology? Could you suggest a way to improve the business benefit obtained by use of any of these existing technologies? (c) Are there other suitable technologies available that AB Hi-Fi could be using for the revenue cycle activities? What additional technologies could AB Hi-Fi implement? What business benefit would these additional technologies provide?

9.12 During process 2.0 Pick, pack and ship the goods at AB Hi-Fi, a shipping clerk has to decide whether to complete the shipment of goods to a customer. Take a moment to review this section of the narrative before you complete the following questions.

**Required**

(a) What data does the shipping clerk draw on when making the decision?

(b) Where do the data you identified in part (a) come from?

(c) Are these data reliable, that is, is there any possibility that there could be errors in the data?

(d) Are these data sufficient to make the decision, or can you identify additional data that the clerk should consider when making the decision?

(e) What would be the consequences of an incorrect decision?

9.13 Explain how you would measure performance of the revenue cycle at AB Hi-Fi; specifically:

(a) What metrics would you would use to measure performance?

(b) For each metric, explain where you would obtain the data required for that metric.

(c) For each metric, explain why it is a good metric to help measure how well the revenue cycle is meeting its objectives.

The case narrative below (AB Hi-Fi) will be used to complete problems 9.14–9.20. Make sure you read and understand the activities and the case thoroughly before you commence work on the problems.

**AB Hi-Fi record payments process**

AB Hi-Fi is a multi store retail business that sells products such as DVDs, CDs, mp3 players, game consoles and TVs. In addition to these retail sales, AB Hi-Fi also sells music, games and DVDs via its website. The narrative of the recording payments process for AB Hi-Fi follows.

*(continued)*

In addition to prepaid online sales and retail cash sales, AB Hi-Fi offers a credit facility to selected larger customers. These customers receive invoices when they purchase goods, and are sent a statement at the end of each month. Payments made by these customers are received by the cashier. Every morning the accounts receivable clerk receives a report of customer receipts from the cashier. The customer receipts report contains the customer number and name, the amount received from each customer and the total of the customer receipts. The accounts receivable clerk logs on to the computer and opens a new cash receipts batch. The accounts receivable clerk enters the first customer number from the customer receipts report. The computer displays details of the open (unpaid) invoices for that customer. The accounts receivable clerk selects the invoices that have been paid by clicking on a check box. The computer calculates a total for the customer based on the invoices checked. Once the accounts receivable clerk has checked that they have selected the correct invoices and that the customer total matches the total received by the cashier from that customer, they authorise the receipt allocation. The computer records the cash receipt total and changes the status of the selected invoices from 'open' to 'closed' (paid). The accounts receivable clerk does this for every customer receipt on the report. Once all the customer receipts have been entered, the accounts receivable clerk updates the computer to record the cash receipts batch as complete. The computer automatically prints out a report that contains details of the cash receipts batch. The accounts receivable clerk attaches the cash receipts batch report to the customer receipts report and files them away.

9.14 Prepare a context diagram for the recording payments process at AB Hi-Fi.

9.15 Prepare a level 0 logical DFD for the recording payments process at AB Hi-Fi.

9.16 Prepare a physical DFD for the recording payments process at AB Hi-Fi.

9.17 Prepare a systems flowchart for the recording payments process at AB Hi-Fi.

9.18 Table 9.5 (page 422) identifies three risks typically encountered when receiving and processing a payment.

**Required**

(a) Analyse the degree of exposure to each of these risks for the record payments process at AB Hi-Fi.

(b) Determine how many of the common controls described in table 9.5 are present in the recording payments process at AB Hi-Fi.

(c) Prepare a short report suitable for senior management to explain how risky you think the recording payments process is, and how comprehensive the current internal controls are.

(d) Prepare a recommendation describing any changes you would like to make to the recording payments process at AB Hi-Fi in order to reduce the level of risk.

9.19 During the recording payments process at AB Hi-Fi the accounts receivable clerk has to decide which open invoices to allocate the cash receipts amount against. Take a moment to review this section of the narrative before you complete the following questions.

**Required**

(a) What data does the accounts receivable clerk draw on when making the decision?

(b) Where does the data you identified in part (a) come from?

(c) Is this data reliable, that is, is there any possibility that there could be errors in the data?

(d) Is this data sufficient to make the decision, or can you identify additional data that the clerk should consider when making the decision?

(e) What would be the consequences of an incorrect decision?

9.20 Consider how you would measure performance of the recording payments process at AB Hi-Fi; specifically:

(a) What metrics would you use to measure performance?

(b) For each metric, explain where you would obtain the data required.

(c) For each metric, explain why it is a good metric to help measure how well the revenue cycle is meeting its objectives.

## FURTHER READING

Brown, SA 1996, *What customers value most: how to achieve business transformation by focusing on processes that touch your customers: satisfied customers, increased revenue, improved profitability,* John Wiley & Sons Inc.

Davenport, TH, Harris, JG, Jones, GL, Lemon, KN, Norton, D & McCallister, MB 2007, 'The dark side of customer analytics', *Harvard Business Review*, May, vol. 85, no. 5, pp. 37–48.

Goldstein, D, Johnson, E, Herrmann, A & Heitmann, M 2008, 'Nudge your customers toward better choices', *Harvard Business Review*, November, vol. 86, no. 12, pp. 99–105.

## SELF-TEST ANSWERS

9.1 a, 9.2 a, 9.3 c, 9.4 c, 9.5 d, 9.6 d, 9.7 d, 9.8 d, 9.9 c, 9.10 b, 9.11 d

## END NOTES

1. Sage Business Solutions 2009, 'Verbatim success story', www.sagebusiness.com.au.
2. PossumIT 2009, 'Café chain uses robust POS solution to improve productivity and customer satisfaction', www.possumit.com.au.

# 10

# Transaction cycle — the expenditure cycle

## Learning objectives

After studying this chapter, you should be able to:

1. describe the key objectives and strategic implications of the expenditure cycle

2. identify common technologies underpinning the expenditure cycle

3. describe expenditure cycle data and key expenditure business decisions

4. identify and document the primary activities in the expenditure cycle and the data produced by these activities

5. analyse risks and develop control plans pertinent to the primary activities in the expenditure cycle

6. develop metrics to monitor expenditure cycle performance.

# Introduction

Expenditure related activities are strategically and operationally important for all organisations. The expenditure cycle commences when a section of the organisation signals a need for goods or services to be provided, and ends when the goods or services have been paid for. During the cycle, demand for requested goods or services needs to be correctly established and any resulting purchase orders need to be accurate and appropriately authorised. Delivered goods must be received in a timely fashion and both the quality and quantity of goods delivered needs to be checked before acceptance. Payments made to suppliers must be both timely and accurate.

This chapter commences with an overview of the expenditure cycle, and then considers the strategic implications of that cycle. Technologies that underpin the cycle are discussed, and then the data produced and consumed during the cycle activities are identified. Typical business process decisions are examined, along with some of the primary considerations related to those decisions. An expenditure cycle is fully documented using data flow diagrams (DFDs) and flowcharts, along with a set of tables containing additional details to aid in understanding the process activities, and the related risks and controls of the activities. Finally issues relating to measuring performance of the expenditure cycle are discussed, and examples of performance metrics suitable for measuring expenditure cycle performance are provided.

**LEARNING OBJECTIVE 1**

*Describe the key objectives and strategic implications of the expenditure cycle.*

# EXPENDITURE CYCLE OVERVIEW AND KEY OBJECTIVES

In order to achieve overall business objectives and remain profitable, the expenditure cycle needs to be well designed and tightly controlled. Poorly controlled expenditure can lead to cash flow and liquidity problems. An additional consideration for the expenditure cycle is the need to balance the supply and demand for products within the organisation. The revenue cycle sales phase discussed in chapter 9 determines the demand for the goods and services provided by the company. The primary responsibility of the expenditure cycle purchasing phase is to ensure the supply of goods balances this demand. The organisational units most involved in the expenditure cycle are shown in figure 10.1 overleaf.

Similarly to the revenue cycle described in chapter 9, the expenditure cycle is generally thought of as two separate elements. The first of these is purchasing. This phase interacts extensively with external suppliers of goods and services; the overall objective is to procure the right goods at the right amount, and to receive those goods at the right time. In order to achieve this outcome, initiated purchases need to be properly approved and authorised; goods and services need to be obtained from authorised or pre-vetted suppliers; all purchase commitments and obligations need to be recorded accurately; and accepted goods and services must meet quality and delivery specifications. Errors in the purchasing phase can lead to a situation where goods are not available to meet customer needs if demand is underestimated, or the organisation incurs unnecessary inventory holding costs if demand is overestimated.

Following the purchasing phase is the accounts payable phase, where the objective is to pay the right people the right amount at the right time. The activities in this phase are typically conducted by back-office staff that will not necessarily have had previous contact with the suppliers of the goods. In order to ensure ongoing good relationships with suppliers and minimise the risk of improper payments, it is essential that all relevant information relating to the purchasing phase is shared with the accounts payable phase. Additionally, the quality of the goods received, although not a data point conventionally thought of as related to accounting, is a vital indicator when deciding whether a payment should be made to a supplier. The accounts payable phase needs to ensure that payments are made by authorised employees only, and that those payments are both accurate and timely, while ensuring that they maximise favourable **settlement terms**. In order to ensure the integrity of financial reporting and financial statements all accounts payable liabilities must be recorded accurately and promptly. A description of documentation commonly used in the expenditure cycle is contained in table 10.1.

**Settlement terms** *Payment terms negotiated with a supplier.*

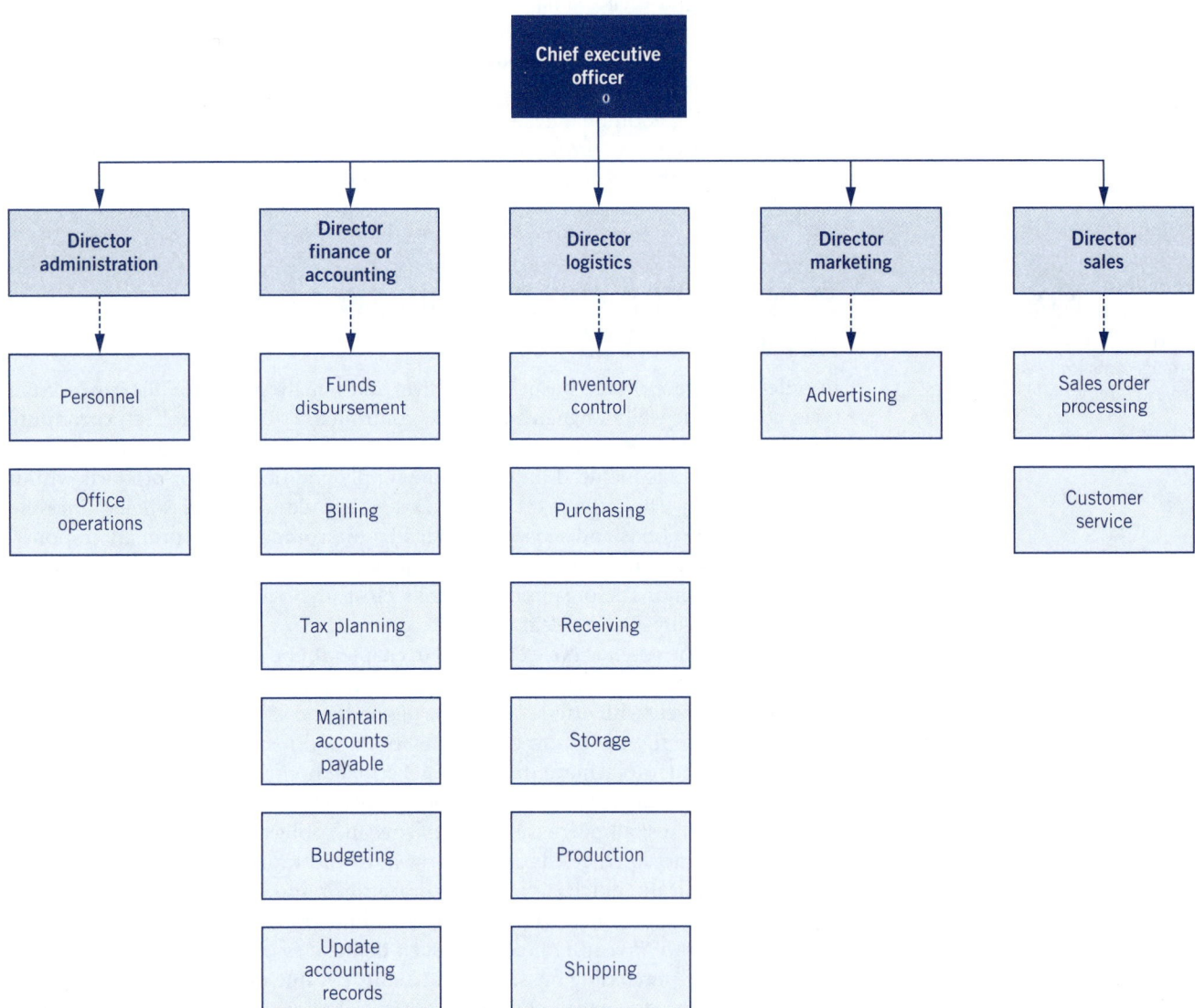

**FIGURE 10.1** Organisational units in the expenditure cycle
*Note:* The dashed lines with the arrows show the business activities that each unit is responsible for.

**TABLE 10.1** List of source documents in the expenditure cycle

| Documents | Description |
| --- | --- |
| Purchase requisition | Allows the requisitioning department to place an order for goods or services. The requisitioning department or the inventory control section prepares the purchase requisition form. The purchase requisition document is shared only within the organisation. |
| Purchase order | Acts as evidence of purchase as well as a binding contract between the firm and the vendor. The purchase order is prepared by the purchasing department. The purchase order document is shared both within the organisation and externally. |
| Vendor list | List of authorised vendors that offer quality goods and services at reasonable prices. The vendor list is kept as part of the organisational database and is viewed and edited by the business processes in the expenditure cycle. |
| Purchase invoice | Details the amounts due and payment terms and conditions. This document is prepared by the vendor. |
| Goods packing slip | Generated by the vendor and attached with the goods sent to the purchasing organisation. |
| Receiving report | Provides details of each delivery such as vendor details, shipping weight, corresponding purchase order number and description of delivered goods. The receiving department generates this report. |
| Remittance advice | Used to notify the payee of the items being paid for. This document may be an invoice or a stub attached to the payer's cheque or other forms of notification. The remittance advice can be prepared by both the accounting/finance unit and the vendor (in the case of a stub that the vendor prepares). |

## Strategic implications of the expenditure cycle

The expenditure cycle is strategically important to an organisation, particularly in terms of the degree of alignment with the overall business strategy. A sound, well-controlled expenditure cycle can provide a competitive advantage by providing high-quality products and services, which in turn translates to an opportunity for higher product pricing. An alternative form of competitive advantage is the potential to control costs that is afforded by ensuring that the expenditure cycle is efficient and effective. This translates into an opportunity to provide goods and services at a level that undercuts less efficient competitors and increases market share. An organisation seeking to maintain or improve market share by using a cost leadership strategy (i.e. pricing its product low enough to attract additional sales) will behave in a fundamentally different way to that of an organisation seeking to differentiate its product in that same market. A key strategic alignment area within the purchasing process relates to the selection and approval of suppliers of goods and services. A cost leadership strategy would indicate that suppliers who can provide goods of suitable quality at a lower price should be selected, whereas a differentiated strategy would be better served by selecting suppliers with high quality products and good service standards. Failure to correctly align this activity set with the overall strategy can invalidate strategic intent.

In terms of the purchasing phase, failure to correctly manage purchasing can lead to systemic problems: an unreliable supply of goods and services has the potential to negatively impact the revenue, production and inventory management processes. Buying too much, too little or the wrong items creates inventory problems and can lead to increased costs or a decline in revenues. The accounts payable phase involves cash leaving the business and, as a result, has a high potential exposure for fraud.

Accounts payable fraud often involves fictitious suppliers and false invoices, which requires collusion, inside knowledge and access; whereas, cash payments frauds are often less sophisticated and becoming easier and more common with computer duplication technology. Arranging and making payments creates an exposure to potentially costly errors and mistakes; whereas, poor payment practices can damage cash flow and/or supplier relationships.

**LEARNING OBJECTIVE** ②

Identify common technologies underpinning the expenditure cycle.

# TECHNOLOGIES UNDERPINNING THE EXPENDITURE CYCLE

There are a number of technologies suitable to support activities within the expenditure cycle, and improve the overall functioning of the process. A range of inventory management tools are available to help improve the ability to balance supply and demand for goods and services. Transparency and management of cash payments and cash flows can also be improved by the use of appropriate technologies.

**Enterprise resource planning (ERP) systems** assist with enabling and integrating the activities within the expenditure cycle. The expenditure cycle links into many areas within the organisation, and an ERP system can not only improve the integration of enterprise-wide data but also provide tighter linkages between relevant modules such as sales, production, accounts payable, **cash budgeting** and general ledger. In essence, an ERP system acts to provide tighter connections between demand and supply functions within the organisation.

The expenditure cycle can benefit greatly from technologies that provide an efficient means of data exchange with suppliers of goods and services. Some of the 'paperwork' associated with the expenditure cycle (e.g. purchase orders, purchase requisitions) originates in-house and is sent outwards to customers, and the remainder is generated externally by suppliers (e.g. price quotes, invoices, delivery dockets). Use of technologies such as **electronic data interchange (EDI)** can provide accurate, timely and cost-effective data sharing.

The expenditure cycle involves many activities related to the physical handling and movement of goods. Where volumes are sufficiently high to warrant the use of printed barcodes or radio frequency identification (**RFID**) tags, hand-held scanning devices can cut stock handling and recording costs and improve the accuracy and timeliness of inventory and expenditure data.

Specialised **supply chain** management software (SCM) can be used to improve both the planning (identifying demand for products) and execution (receiving orders, routing goods) of the supply chain by providing detailed supply chain analytics. SCM can be incorporated as an integrated module within an existing ERP system, or acquired and operated independently using a best-of-breed supplier such as Manhattan Associates or i2 Technologies.

The ability to make electronic payments provides a fast and comparatively inexpensive way for organisations to settle their accounts with suppliers. When using electronic payment facilities such as those provided by the major banks it is important to consider the timing and cash flow implications. A payment made electronically will take funds from a company bank account immediately, whereas a payment made via cheque may take up to 10 working days before any funds are withdrawn from the company account. In addition to these payment timing issues, it is vital to consider and appropriately design access security over online payment facilities.

**Enterprise resource planning (ERP) system** *An integrated suite of software that records and manages many different types of business transactions within a single integrated database. Examples include SAP and Oracle.*

**Cash budget** *A budget showing forecast levels of future cash flows into and out of the organisation.*

**Electronic data interchange (EDI)** *A bespoke link that enables exchange of data between two separate computer systems. It is used when transaction flow and volume is large and transaction syntax is predictable.*

**RFID** *A small plastic tag attached to an item that contains data about that item and is able to be scanned using an RFID reader.*

**Supply chain** *An integration of suppliers and customers with the aim of producing and distributing goods and services by quantity, location and time to minimise costs and satisfy required service levels. Specialised software in this area is known as supply chain management software (SCM).*

# AIS FOCUS 10.1

## Getting behind the scenes — managing your supply chain

Australia's retail sector is an enormous industry generating a turnover of $292 billion and employing over 1.2 million people. Underpinning the sector is its suppliers who provide businesses sustenance to service their client base, generate revenue, and with some efficiency, make a profit.

The importance of a retailer's supply chain cannot be understated. A team of Accenture, INSEAD and Stanford University researchers has drawn statistical correlation between companies' financial success and the depth and sophistication of their supply chains. (D'Avanzo, R et al. 2003, 'The link between supply chain and financial performance', *Van Wassenhove Supply Chain Management Review*) According to the research, companies with best practice supply chain management demonstrated a higher than industry average growth rate. Maintaining an efficient supply chain goes well beyond keeping overheads to a minimum. In a fiercely competitive retail market, customers have little tolerance for out of stock items and long waits for products. With fewer loyal shoppers today, it only takes one bad experience to send them and their money to the competition. More than ever, customers cannot be taken for granted and it is critical to meet their demands through efficiencies in supply chain management.

Operating in a consumer-driven market and matching supply to demand is one of the key focuses of supply chain management. The challenge for most retailers is servicing customer demands while not overstocking products that are not in demand.

The proliferation of information and communications technologies (ICTs) has played an integral role in increasing retail supply chain efficiencies. Bar code, radio frequency identification devices (RFIDs) and remote sensors have all improved our ability to replenish stock, accurately measure movements from end to end, assess a product's success or failure and collaborate with our suppliers so that consumer demands are met with as little wastage as possible. Technology alone will not be enough to achieve these goals. Best practice supply chain management involves going beyond a company's four walls.

Technologies facilitate these means to an end, but to achieve complete integration it is important all partners in the supply chain are speaking the same language. The adoption of open global standards in data integration has ensured companies can easily exchange information and conduct business without unnecessary communication obstacles or bottlenecks.

An exemplary case of best practice supply chain management is European clothing manufacturer/retailer Zara. Zara's store managers constantly send customer feedback to in-house designers using hand held devices to inform them in real time of what is happening on the shop floor. Designers are quickly able to ascertain which merchandise is moving and what should be culled resulting in tighter linkages between supply and demand and more efficient inventory management due to fewer unsellable products being left on the shop floor or in the stock room. This together with a range of other supply chain innovations during the manufacturing process enable Zara to deliver new styles to their stores in three to six weeks, as opposed to the industry standard of five months.[1]

*Source:* Australian Retailers Association www.retail.org.au.

# DATA AND DECISIONS IN THE EXPENDITURE CYCLE

A range of data are both produced and consumed by activities within the expenditure cycle. The actual data stores are documented in detail later in this chapter. This section describes the general purpose and types of data that the expenditure cycle requires. The business decisions made during the life of the expenditure cycle are also discussed here.

## Data and the expenditure cycle

Expenditure cycle activities require access to data related to inventory to help identify existing stock levels. In order to correctly identify how much to purchase it is important to be familiar with both the current demand for the goods (which comes from the sales process) and how much inventory is currently available for sale. Expenditure cycle activities ultimately result in an increase in the amount of inventory on hand. Inventory data should ideally be updated regularly by expenditure activities to indicate the current **status code** of goods that have been ordered but not yet received. Inventory data typically includes many non-financial indicators such as quality of the goods received. There are also a number of dates of significance when analysing inventory and supplier performance, such as date ordered, date confirmed, date expected and date delivered.

> *Status code A code on transactions that are moving through an iteration of a process indicating which stage of the process the transaction is at. As an example, a sales transaction may be first 'created', then 'picked', then 'packed', then 'shipped', then 'paid'. When each of these activities has been completed, the status of the transaction is changed to reflect the new status.*

In addition to inventory data, the expenditure cycle requires access to data about suppliers, including both basic name and address details and information about preferred suppliers, including past performance. In terms of the data produced by expenditure activities, an organisation may store detailed data related to both informal product requests and formal product requisitions. A third type of data created is purchase order data, which records details of all open (incomplete) purchase orders, including the current status of each of the items on the order. Goods receiving activities also produce goods received data, which lists items received from suppliers and typically updates the inventory status of those goods. Goods received data are also used to verify invoice validity during the accounts payable phase.

Accounts payable data are both created and updated by activities within the expenditure cycle; invoices received from suppliers are recorded in accounts payable, as are details of payments made during the accounts payable phase. More detailed information about payments made is recorded in the cash payments data store.

## Expenditure cycle business decisions

When the expenditure cycle is originally designed, or subsequently reviewed, a number of strategic level decisions need to be made. These decisions are typically made by senior management within the organisation, and create the policy framework within which the cycle operates. To be effective, strategy-level business process decisions should be congruent with the overarching business strategy. Strategy-level decisions would include creation of policies such as:

- whether the organisation should consolidate purchases across units to obtain optimal prices — involves a trade-off between the flexibility afforded by decentralisation and the potential for economic gains provided by centralised purchasing.
- how IT can be used to improve both the efficiency and the accuracy of the inbound logistics function — the introduction of new technologies such as SCM may require considerable expense and incur high risks. Dependent on product volumes and

values of inventory items it may be difficult to cost justify a large technology implementation of this nature.

- identifying where inventories and supplies should be held — options include onsite warehousing in either a centralised or decentralised format. An alternative solution is to set up a **just-in-time (JIT) supply chain** under which goods are delivered only when they are required.

In addition to these strategy-level decisions, there are a range of operational level decisions that will be made every time the expenditure cycle is enacted. These operational decisions are typically made by middle management or operational staff and relate only to a specific instance of the process. Figure 10.2 shows some example performance analytics used for decision making during the purchasing phase.

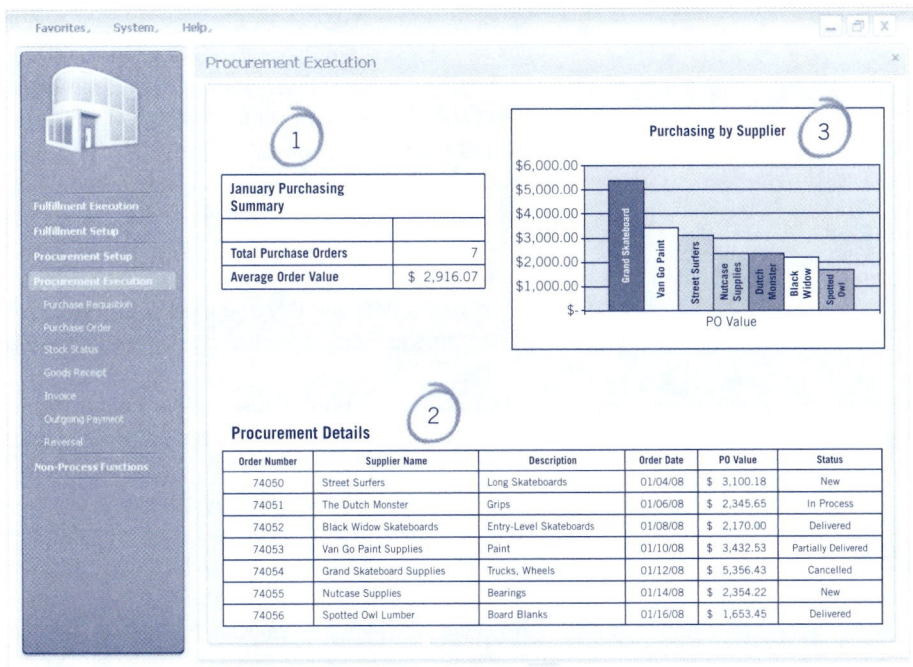

**FIGURE 10.2** Procurement analysis

*Source:* © Copyright SAP AG 2008.

Typical operational decisions include:

- determining the optimal level of inventory and supplies to carry — requires knowledge of previous sales and/or some form of analysis of likely future sales, along with supplier data such as the lead time to supply ordered goods. Also need to know current stock levels including numbers of the stock on hand, stock already promised to customers and stock ordered but not yet delivered.
- deciding which suppliers provide the best quality and service at the best prices — often requires a trade-off between price, quality and service. The weighting attached to each of these dimensions should be determined by reference to the overall business strategy and to the type of product being procured.
- identifying if sufficient cash is available to take advantage of any discounts suppliers have offered — requires knowledge of cash flow budgets and cash level predictions.

- determining how payment can be made to suppliers in order to maximise cash flow — payment should be made when due and not before. Paying too early unnecessarily inhibits cash flows; paying too late may alienate a supplier.

## AIS FOCUS 10.2

### City's sustainable purchasing to help the environment

The City of Armadale is taking a sensible approach to reducing its own greenhouse gas emissions by buying more environmentally sustainable products and services.

The City has a new Sustainable Purchasing Action Plan to guide its acquisition of 'greener' products, as a practical way of achieving its corporate greenhouse gas reduction goals. Armadale Chief Executive Officer, Ray Tame, said it was important for the City to set an example in the community by adopting realistic, environmentally friendly initiatives. 'One thing we can do is consider the environment as we make each purchase,' Mr Tame said. 'All things being equal we will choose the most environmentally friendly option when acquiring goods and services. The action plan guides the City and its staff in making purchasing decisions. In doing so we can show local businesses and individuals that it is feasible and beneficial to "go green".'

One of the City's initial sustainable purchasing success stories has been its use of Green Power in a number of buildings. This has led to a saving of 2500 tonnes of greenhouse gases over an 18-month period. Buying energy efficient computer screens for its main administration building has saved 330 tonnes in greenhouse gases in a similar time. The City recognises that it cannot compromise the delivery of services, but believes it can always make further inroads into its greenhouse goals, according to Mr Tame. 'The City of Armadale is part of the Cities for Climate Protection program and works with other local councils as the South East Regional Energy Group to promote efficient energy and water use and waste reduction in our community,' he said.

'Sustainable purchasing is another way we can lead the way at a corporate level. We see a number of key areas where there are opportunities to apply greenhouse criteria to purchases, including electrical products such as photocopiers, printers, whitegoods and IT equipment, resources and raw materials, paper-based products, other stationery, chemicals, plastics, food and drink products and contracts and services. Ultimately we want to see other businesses in our region supporting this initiative.'[2]

**LEARNING OBJECTIVE 4**

*Identify and document the primary activities in the expenditure cycle and the data produced by these activities.*

## EXPENDITURE CYCLE DOCUMENTATION

The expenditure cycle is documented in the following section as a series of diagrams with increasing amounts of details. An overview of these expenditure cycle diagrams is contained in figure 10.3.

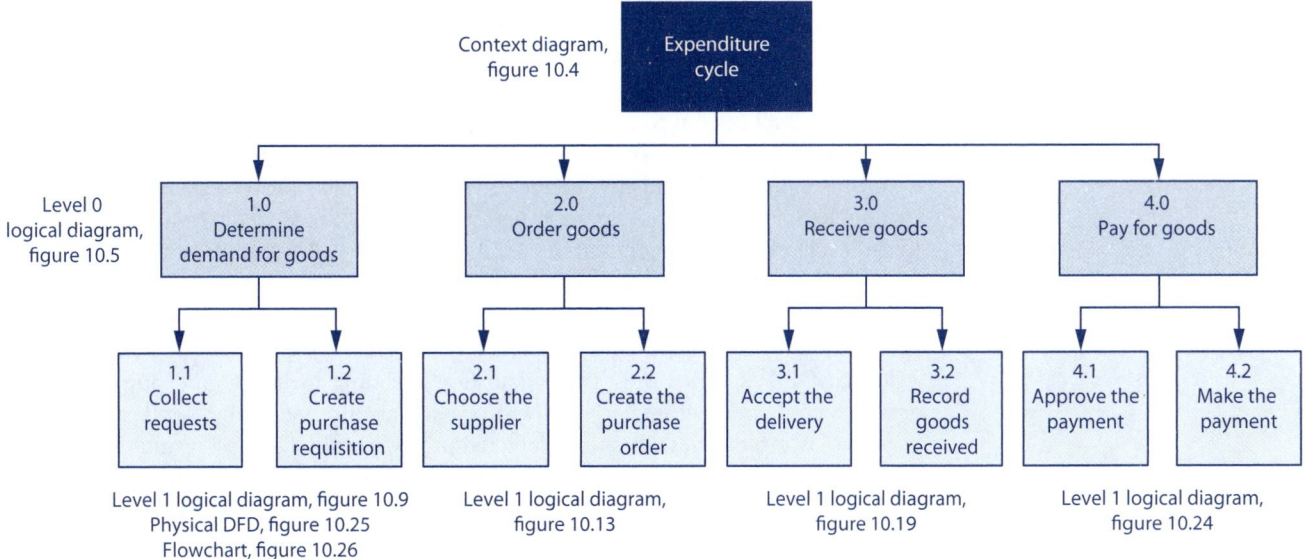

FIGURE 10.3 Expenditure diagrams overview

## Expenditure cycle context

The context diagram of a typical expenditure cycle is depicted in figure 10.4. The expenditure cycle involves direct interaction with suppliers located outside the organisation. Within the organisation, the expenditure cycle interacts with the production cycle, the inventory department and a range of miscellaneous departments, and the financial cycle as shown in figure P3.1 (page 389). Details of the logical data flows depicted in the expenditure context diagram are contained in table 10.2 (page 450).

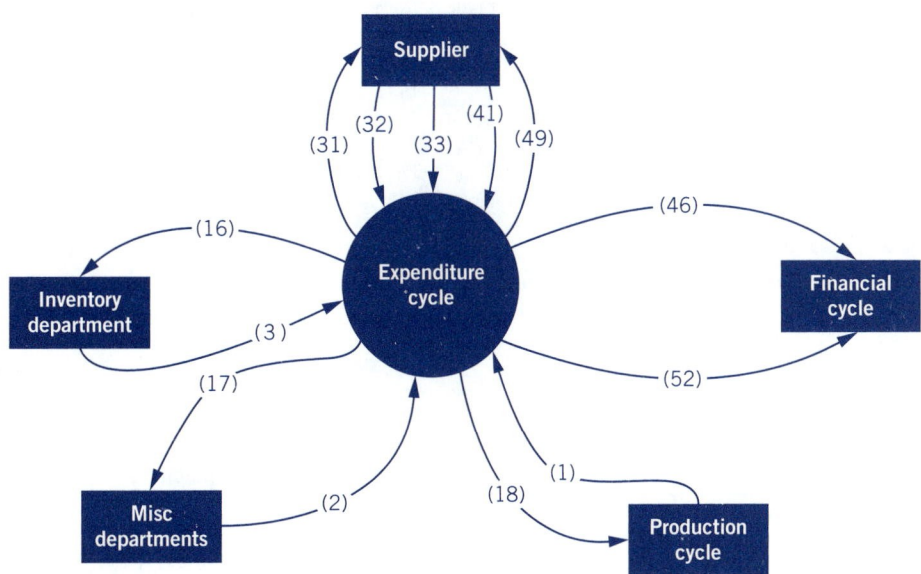

FIGURE 10.4 Expenditure cycle context diagram

# Expenditure cycle logical data flows

Figure 10.5 (page 454) depicts a level 0 logical DFD. This diagram shows the entire expenditure cycle in greater detail than that depicted in the context diagram. The logical DFD is an exploded version of the context diagram, with the bubble described as 'expenditure cycle' in the context diagram broken down into four processes. The logical diagram at level 0 helps to analyse and understand the expenditure cycle in its entirety. It depicts the chronology of the cycle, the data stores and external entities involved in each of the processes, and the interactions between these processes, entities and data stores. The logical level 0 diagram in figure 10.5 is itself broken down to describe even lower levels of detail in figures 10.9, 10.13, 10.19 and 10.24. Details of the logical data flows depicted in this diagram are contained in table 10.2.

## *Description of logical data flows in the expenditure cycle*

A logical DFD contains only those data flows relating to inputs and outputs of the activities contained within each of the processes, as opposed to the details of all interactions between entities which are depicted in a physical DFD. As a result, the number of flows in a logical DFD is always less than those that would be shown in a physical DFD for the same process. To illustrate this, compare figures 10.9 and 10.25, which show exactly the same process; however, figure 10.9 is a logical description whereas figure 10.25 is a physical description. To ensure completeness all the data flows relating to the expenditure cycle appear in table 10.2.

**TABLE 10.2** Description of logical data flows in the expenditure cycle

| Flow # | Typical data source | Typical data destination | Data description | Explanation of the logical data flow |
|---|---|---|---|---|
| **Process 1.0 Determine demand for goods** | | | | |
| 1 | Production cycle | Purchase requisition clerk | Purchase request | The production cycle requires raw materials in order to produce the finished goods; this data flow would occur when additional raw materials are required. |
| 2 | Miscellaneous departments | Purchase requisition clerk | Purchase request | These requests relate to the purchase of non-inventory or consumable items such as stationery. |
| 3 | Inventory department | Purchase requisition clerk | Purchase request | These requests relate to inventory items (i.e. items that are purchased with the intention of reselling to customers). |
| 4 | Purchase requisition clerk | Purchase request file | Purchase request | Requests are sometimes accumulated over a period of time before an order is placed. |
| 5 | Purchase request file | Purchase requisition clerk | Purchase request | This data flow is showing the accumulated requests being removed from the file and actioned. |
| 6 | Collect requests | Create purchase requisition | Trigger for next process | After purchase requests are collected and accumulated a purchase requisition can be created (not necessary in a level 0 diagram). |
| 7 | This flow takes places physically between the purchase requisition clerk and the computer; it happens within the 1.0 bubble in the logical diagram. | | | |

| Flow # | Typical data source | Typical data destination | Data description | Explanation of the logical data flow |
|---|---|---|---|---|
| 8 | Inventory data store | Purchase requisition clerk | Inventory levels | Before a purchase requisition is created the purchase requisition clerk should check existing stock records to determine whether the requested item is currently held in inventory, and how many of the item are currently in stock. |
| 9 | Sales data store | Purchase requisition clerk | Prior sales history | The purchase requisition clerk may check the previous sales history for items requested as part of the finished goods inventory. |
| 10, 11 | These flows take place physically between the purchase requisition clerk and the computer; they happen within the 1.0 bubble in the logical diagram. | | | |
| 12 | Purchase requisitions data store | Computer | Number of last purchase requisition raised | In order to allocate a sequential number the system needs to know the last number allocated so it can increment that number by one. |
| 13 | Computer | Purchase requisition data store | Purchase requisition details | Once the purchase requisition has been created a record is written in the data store recording all the details of the requisition. |
| 14 | Computer | Inventory details | Purchase requisition details | The amount of inventory included in the purchase requisition is recorded in the inventory data store with a status of 'requisitioned'. |
| 15 | This flow takes places physically between the purchase requisition clerk and the computer; it happens within the 1.0 bubble in the logical diagram. | | | |
| 16 | Purchase Requisition clerk | Inventory department | Purchase requisition details | Details of the purchase requisition raised are communicated back to the department that originally requested the goods. |
| 17 | Purchase Requisition clerk | Miscellaneous departments | Purchase requisition details | Details of the purchase requisition raised are communicated back to the department that originally requested the goods. |
| 18 | Purchase Requisition clerk | Production cycle | Purchase requisition details | Details of the purchase requisition raised are communicated back to the department that originally requested the goods. |
| 19 | Purchase Requisition clerk | Purchase order clerk | Purchase requisition details | Details of the purchase requisition are sent to the purchase clerk so that a purchase order can be created. |
| **Process 2.0 Order goods** | | | | |
| 20 | Supplier data store | Purchase order clerk | Supplier details | Where authorised suppliers exist the purchase order clerk would obtain data relating to those suppliers to help decide who to purchase from. |
| 21 | Choose supplier | Create the purchase order | Trigger for next process | Once the supplier has been chosen the purchase order can be created (not necessary in a level 0 diagram). |
| 22 | Purchase requisition data store | Purchase order clerk | Purchase requisition details | Purchase requisition data such as product details and quantity required are retrieved and used to create the purchase order. |

*(continued)*

**TABLE 10.2** *(continued)*

| Flow # | Typical data source | Typical data destination | Data description | Explanation of the logical data flow |
|---|---|---|---|---|
| 23 | Supplier data store | Purchase order clerk | Supplier details | Supplier details such as name and address are retrieved for use in the purchase order. |
| 24 | Inventory data store | Purchase order clerk | Inventory details | Inventory details such as the stock numbers and usual order quantities (i.e. each, dozen, pallet) are retrieved for use in the purchase order. |
| 25 | Purchase order data store | Purchase order clerk | Purchase order details | In order to allocate a sequential number the system needs to know the last number allocated so it can increment that number by one. |
| 26 | Purchase order clerk | Purchase order data store | Purchase order details | Details of the newly created purchase order are written into the purchase order data store. |
| 27 | Purchase order clerk | Purchase requisition data store | Purchase order details | The status of the purchase requisition is updated to 'ordered'. |
| 28 | Purchase order clerk | Inventory data store | Purchase order details | The status of the inventory items is updated to 'ordered'. |
| 29 | Purchase order clerk | Warehouse staff | Purchase order details | Details of the purchase order are forwarded to allow warehouse staff to anticipate receiving the goods |
| 30 | Purchase order clerk | Accounts payable | Purchase order details | Details of the purchase order are forwarded to the accounts payable clerk to allow them to anticipate paying for the goods once they have been received. |
| 31 | Purchase order clerk | Supplier | Purchase order details | Details of the purchase order are forwarded to the supplier to confirm the order and ensure that they correctly supply the goods required. |
| 32 | Supplier | Purchase order clerk | Order acknowledgement details | An order acknowledgement should be received from the supplier detailing the acceptance of the order and the likely delivery date. |
| **Process 3.0 Receive goods** | | | | |
| 33 | Supplier | Goods receiving clerk | Delivery details | The supplier sends the goods along with some delivery documentation. The documentation should contain details of the goods despatched (type, quantities, number of cartons) and the purchase order number that the goods relate to. |
| 34 | Accept delivery | Record goods received | Trigger for next process | Once the goods have been accepted they can be checked and the goods receipt recorded (not necessary in a level 0 diagram). |
| 35 | Goods received clerk | Purchase order data store | Purchase order details | Purchase order details are extracted for use in recording goods received. |
| 36 | Goods receiving clerk | Goods received data store | Goods received details | Details of the goods received (date, product details, supplier details and related purchase order details) are written into the goods received data store. |

| Flow # | Typical data source | Typical data destination | Data description | Explanation of the logical data flow |
|---|---|---|---|---|
| 37 | Goods receiving clerk | Supplier data store | Goods received details | Details of the goods received including quality of goods and delivery timeliness data are written into the supplier data store. |
| 38 | Goods receiving clerk | Purchase order data store | Goods received details | The purchase order status is updated to 'goods received'. |
| 39 | Goods receiving clerk | Inventory data store | Goods received details | The inventory status for the relevant product is updated to 'goods received'. |
| 40 | Goods receiving clerk | Accounts payable | Goods received details | Details of the receipt of the goods are sent to the accounts payable section to facilitate processing of payment to the supplier. |
| **Process 4.0 Pay for goods** | | | | |
| 41 | Supplier | Accounts payable clerk | Invoice details | An invoice, which is a request for payment for the goods supplied, is received from the supplier. |
| 42 | Purchase order data store | Accounts payable clerk | Purchase order details | Details of the purchase order are extracted and used to check that the details of the invoice are correct. |
| 43 | Goods received data store | Accounts payable clerk | Goods received details | Details of the goods received order are extracted and used to check that the details of the invoice are correct. Processing should only continue if the details of the purchase order, goods received and invoice all agree. |
| 44 | Supplier data store | Accounts payable clerk | Supplier details | Details of the supplier (name, address, and payment terms) are extracted for use in making the payment. |
| 45 | Accounts payable clerk | Accounts payable data store | Payment details | Details of the approved payment (due date, amount, supplier and invoice details) are written into the accounts payable data store. |
| 46 | Accounts payable clerk | Financial cycle | Payment details | The data relating to payments approved which is contained in the accounts payable data store is transferred to the financial cycle, where it is used to update general ledger accounts. |
| 47 | Approve payment | Make payment | Trigger for next process | Once the payment has been approved the payment can be made (not necessary in a level 0 diagram). |
| 48 | Accounts payable data store | Accounts payable clerk | Payment details | On the due date established in the previous process a payment is generated. |
| 49 | Accounts payable clerk | Supplier | Payment details | The payment is sent to the supplier. |
| 50 | Accounts payable clerk | Accounts payable data store | Payment details | Summarised details of the payment made are written to the accounts payable data store. |
| 51 | Accounts payable clerk | Cash payment data store | Payment details | Full details of the payment made are written to the cash payments data store. |
| 52 | Accounts payable clerk | Financial cycle | Cash payment details | The data relating to the payment made which is contained in the accounts payable data store is transferred to the financial cycle, where it is used to update general ledger accounts. |

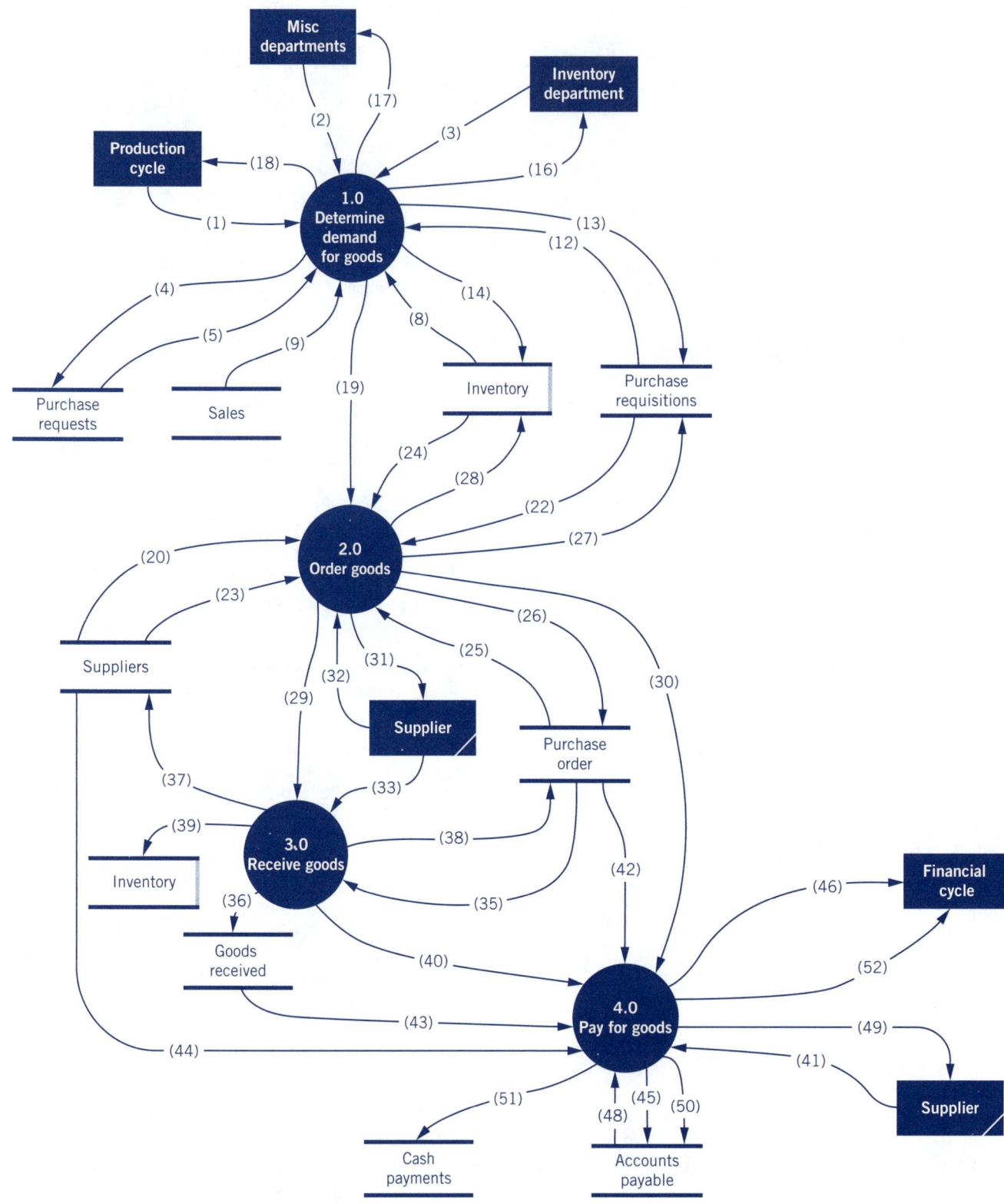

**FIGURE 10.5** Expenditure cycle level 0 logical diagram

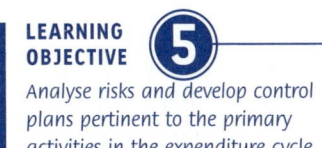
# EXPENDITURE CYCLE ACTIVITIES AND RELATED RISKS AND CONTROLS

The activities within the expenditure cycle and the associated risks and controls are described under the four expenditure process headings below. Following the activity descriptions for each of the processes is the level 1 DFD for the process and a table summarising the activities, risks and controls within the process.

## Determine demand for goods — activities, risks and controls

Process 1.0, determine demand for goods, comprises the following activities.

### Collect requests

The expenditure cycle commences when a request is received to purchase goods or services. These requests come from a number of places within the organisation, including the warehouse which may request items required for inventory. Inventory items are purchased with the intention of reselling to customers and are also known as finished goods inventory. Inventory purchase requests may be paper or electronic, and could be triggered by reaching an **automatic reorder point** in the inventory system. Automatic reorder points are based on predefined minimum inventory levels recorded for individual items; when the stock on hand drops down to this level a purchase requisition is automatically generated.

The production cycle may request the purchase of raw materials required for production. This request would occur when additional or different raw materials are required, and may be either electronic or paper. Raw material requests from production may be automatically generated by production control software, or created manually by production staff. The trigger for an automated request would be a reorder point embedded in the production system that operates in a similar manner to the inventory reorder described above and produces a request to purchase raw materials identified as being required for production of goods.

Other requests commonly received relate to the purchase of non-inventory or consumable items used in the day-to-day running of the business such as stationery. These requests could be paper or electronic, and may be triggered by some internal stocktaking process for items such as stationery, or could be ad hoc for other, less predictable consumables such as travel or catering. Due to the heightened risk of fraud or errors related to ad hoc requests, they should be carefully scrutinised to ensure that requests are valid and approved before processing.

Purchasing staff may elect to hold requests for processing until an economically viable order quantity is reached. The purpose of accumulating requests is so that economies of scale can be gained. This accumulation should take place where there is a potential to achieve a better price outcome by buying in bulk, or where transaction costs can be lowered by a smaller number of larger orders. Requests would not be accumulated where time is critical for the items being purchased. If accumulation is practised then requests will need to be filed temporarily until sufficient quantities of requests accumulate. It is important to establish a mechanism to ensure any requests held in this way are not forgotten. The trigger for actioning accumulated requests could be temporal, such as a particular day of the month, or could be triggered by the receipt of a similar purchase request.

**Automatic reorder points** *An inventory order point based on predefined minimum inventory levels recorded for individual items. When the stock on hand drops down to this level a purchase requisition is automatically generated.*

### Create purchase requisition

After purchase requests have been received and, if necessary, accumulated, a purchase requisition can be created. An example of a purchase requisition is shown in figure 10.6. Note that this responsibility may be devolved and undertaken within the initiating department, rather than being centralised within the purchasing function as documented here. A purchase requisition is a document that is used internally only; it is simply a request from one section of the organisation to another asking for goods to be ordered. Before the purchase requisition is created, existing stock records should be checked to determine whether the item requested is currently held in inventory, and how many of the item are currently in stock. This control is particularly important if purchase requests are made manually, as there is a possibility that the person raising the request may not have checked stock records prior to requesting the goods. This inventory check would not be necessary where the purchase request was generated automatically by an automatic reorder function.

## Australian Information Company
### Level 2, 345 Hill Terrace
### Melbourne, Vic 3003

| Purchase requisition form | | | No: 936 |
|---|---|---|---|
| Data prepared: 15/07/10 | Prepared by: Joseph Smith, Purchasing Department | Date required: 30/07/10 | |
| Suggested vendor: Tech Supplies | Contact person: Jill Darci, Purchasing Department | Deliver to: Delivery Dock | |
| Item no. | Description | Quantity | Price/unit |
| 35930 | Willow Series W laptop computer | 1 | $3500.00 |
| 93948 | Hume Premier paper, 10 ream | 15 boxes | $12.00 |
| 83748 | Hyth HD diskettes, box of 10 | 15 boxes | $7.50 |

**FIGURE 10.6** Sample purchase requisition form

The sales history for items requested may also be checked; prior sales history is useful to determine sales volume and patterns, which helps decide whether the request seems reasonable. If there are multiple requests received from different divisions, prior sales data can also help to determine the optimal economic ordering quantity.

Purchasing requisition staff should obtain approval from a more senior staff member before creating a purchase requisition. Purchase requisitions can be created either electronically or manually. An example of an electronic purchase requisition screen is shown in figure 10.7. A manual purchase requisition would be created by filling in a form (similar to the one in figure 10.6), having it authorised, and sending a copy to the purchasing office. For an electronic version, a new record is written in the purchase requisition data store recording all the details of the requisition. Documents such as purchase requisitions are often pre-numbered so that the organisation is able to ensure that all documents are processed. Pre-numbered documents are issued with a sequential number to allow clearer identification and better tracking of each document issued. In order to allocate a sequential number electronically the system needs to know the last number allocated, so it can increment that number (usually by one) to assign a number to the new purchase requisition.

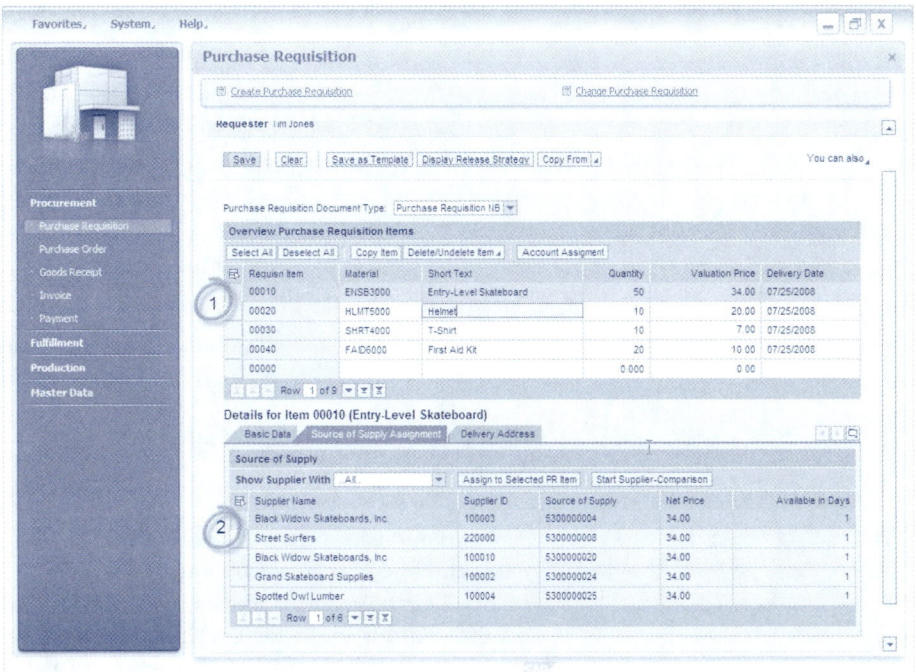

**FIGURE 10.7** Purchase requisition screen
*Source:* © Copyright SAP AG 2008.

Once the purchase requisition has been created the inventory record should be updated to show details of the goods on the purchase requisition. The amount of inventory included in the purchase requisition is recorded in the inventory data store with a status of 'requisitioned'. This is particularly important when predetermined reorder points are used, as failure to record this status could result in an item being repeatedly requested, creating overstock problems.

The purchase requisition details should be communicated to the department that originally requested the goods, to advise them that the goods have been requisitioned. This may happen electronically, in which case an automated message would be generated directly from the computer once the purchase requisition has been created.

The purchase requisition also needs to be sent to purchasing staff so a purchase order can be raised for the goods requisitioned. This may happen electronically, in which case a message would be generated directly from the computer, or manually, where a copy of the completed purchase requisition form is sent via an internal mail system or delivered by hand. An example of a purchase requisition history screen is contained in figure 10.8 overleaf.

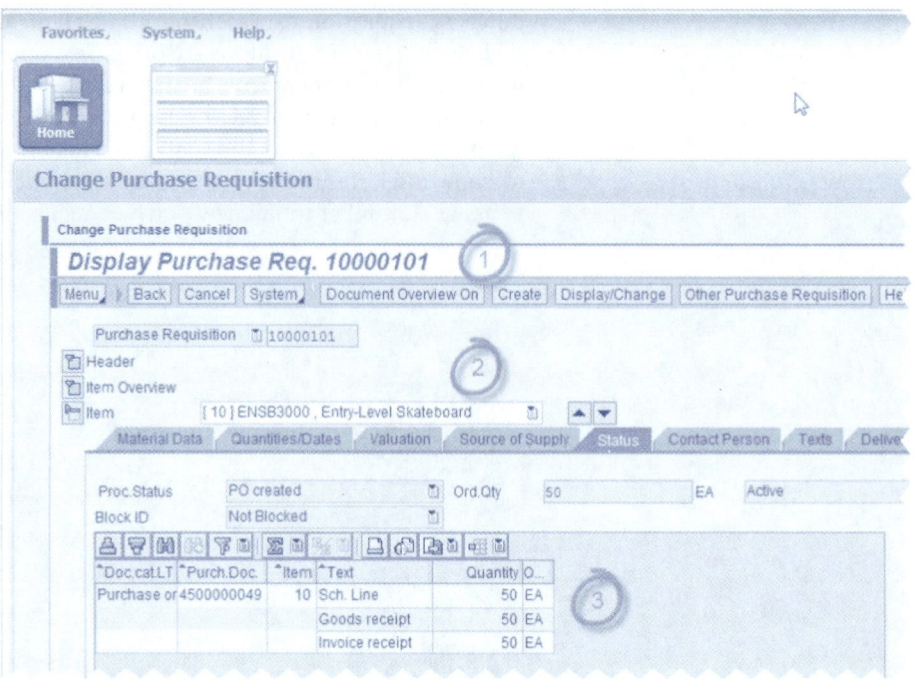

**FIGURE 10.8** Purchase requisition history
*Source:* © Copyright SAP AG 2008.

The major risks related to creating a purchase requisition are requesting unnecessary items and under or overestimating requirements. Although the requisition is only used internally as a precursor to creating a purchase order it is important not to rely solely on the controls embedded within the purchase order process. That is, it is important to independently review and approve all requisitions generated. In particular, validity checks should be carried out for requests related to expensive or unusual items. Note that adequate controls are necessary in the sales process to achieve accurate and complete sales and inventory records and accurately determine demand. If there are flaws in the sales and/or inventory data, demand will be incorrectly calculated and erroneous purchase requisitions may be raised. **Exception reporting** and monitoring of stock outs and/or obsolete goods will help reduce this risk.

**Exception report** *A report type that is designed specifically to identify exceptions for particular transactions. An example is a report identifying any sales orders which have been shipped but not billed, or a report identifying all customers who have overdue accounts receivable accounts.*

## Determine demand for goods — DFD

The level 1 DFD in figure 10.9 contains a lower level of detail about the first process represented in the level 0 logical DFD in figure 10.5. In the same way in which the level 0 logical diagram explodes out the 'expenditure cycle' bubble in the context diagram, the level 1 diagram explodes out the 'determine demand for goods' bubble.

## Summary description of activities in determining demand for goods

Table 10.3 summaries the activities, risks and controls when determining the demand for goods, as depicted in figure 10.9. Table 10.2 (page 450) explains the logical data flows depicted in figure 10.9. Exploring the diagram in conjunction with the material contained in the tables will assist with improving your understanding of the process depicted.

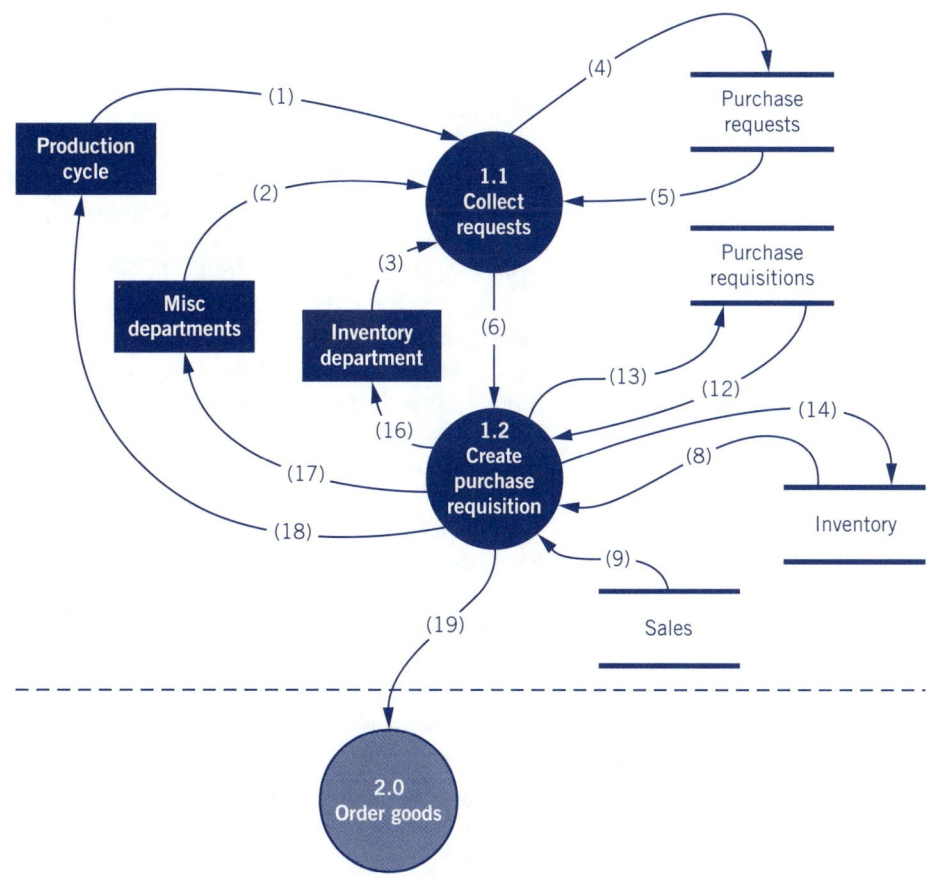

**FIGURE 10.9** Expenditure cycle level 1 logical diagram — process 1.0 Determine demand for goods

**TABLE 10.3** Activities in determining demand for goods

| Activity # | Activity | Usually conducted by | Activity description | Typical risks encountered | Common controls |
|---|---|---|---|---|---|
| 1.1 | Collect requests | Purchase requisition clerk | The purchase requisition clerk receives requests for consumables and inventory items from a number of different departments within the organisation.<br><br>The purchase requisition clerk should obtain approval from a more senior staff member before creating the purchase requisition. | Under/over estimating requirements | Exception reporting and monitoring of stock outs and/or obsolete goods<br><br>Separating review and approval of requisitions generated |
| 1.2 | Create purchase requisition | Purchase requisition clerk | Once the request is ready to be actioned a purchase requisition is created. | Requesting unnecessary items | As above plus validity checks on large dollar or unusual items |

## Order goods — activities, risks and controls

Process 2.0, order goods, comprises the following activities.

### Choose the supplier

When the purchasing department receives a completed and authorised purchase requisition, the first task is to decide who to order the requisitioned goods from. Some organisations will have a list of pre-approved or authorised suppliers to choose from for various products. This list should ideally be created and maintained by someone who has no direct responsibility for placing purchase orders, to reduce the risk of collusion and fraud. Where an authorised supplier list exists, purchasing staff should access and assess the supplier data to help decide who to purchase from. During the search for a suitable supplier many organisations require purchasing staff to obtain price quotes from a given number of suppliers (often three supplier quotes are required) in order to establish that they are not paying too much for the goods. In addition to this competitive tendering process, the risk of paying too much for goods can also be controlled by using pre-negotiated prices, and by using only pre-approved suppliers. Expenditure budgets are also an important control; purchasing staff procure goods on behalf of other departments, so a regular review of budget variances or one-by-one checking of expenditure transactions should assist in identifying any significant overspends. In addition to paying too much, there is a risk that poor quality goods will be purchased. Common inventory quality controls include using only pre-approved suppliers, conducting ongoing monitoring of supplier performance and undertaking inventory quality checks. Policies relating to the timely termination of supply contracts or removal of substandard suppliers from approved lists should also be in place; compliance with these policies should be audited regularly.

Supplier performance is not solely financial: supplier data files should also contain non-financial information related to delivery and service standards such as on-time delivery history, service request response times and after-sales contacts. If no supplier list exists, purchasing staff will need to search the market and determine a suitable supplier. Supplier suitability parameters will differ based on the product requested. As an example, procuring reams of photocopy paper requires a totally different analysis to purchasing a motor vehicle or a computer component. The choice of suitable suppliers is vital for the organisation: inferior quality goods or late deliveries can cause loss of sales or delays in production. The risk of purchasing from unauthorised suppliers can be reduced by ensuring appropriate approval is received for all purchase orders, enforcing independent maintenance of supplier data and using pre-approved suppliers. A common risk in this area is that of purchasing staff receiving kickbacks or secret commissions or inducements from suppliers. To control for these risks the organisation should create and enforce policies relating to acceptance of corporate gifts and require disclosure of any contracts where a conflict of interest exists, or the transaction is not conducted at arm's length. Using personnel policies such as job rotation and enforced annual leave help ensure that an individual does not maintain sole power over a supplier relationship. Supplier audits may also be considered, particularly if product quality appears to be an issue.

Controls and restrictions on corporate credit cards where used are also important. Corporate cards are often used for ad hoc purchasing. Where they are used, an organisation may wish to restrict purchases to certain dollar limits, or to certain organisations. Most organisations that issue corporate credit cards insist that the cardholder retains all receipts, regularly reconciles, or acquits, the charges on their card against those receipts, and forwards the **reconciliation** for independent audit and approval.

*Reconciliation An activity where two different sets of data that purport to represent one transaction or set of events are compared to see if they agree. A common example is a bank reconciliation, which reconciles the organisation's accounting records of cash inflows and outflows with the bank's record (i.e. a bank statement).*

### Create the purchase order

After a suitable supplier has been identified, and the choice of supplier authorised, the purchase order can be created. A purchase order can be either paper or electronic. A paper purchase order example is shown in figure 10.10. Figure 10.11 shows an example of a screen used to input an electronic purchase order. The purchase order is distributed to a number of departments within the organisation, and externally to the supplier. A purchase order creates a commitment to buy and pay for the goods, so the ability to create a purchase order, and any stocks of blank purchase order forms, should be closely controlled. The purchase order is created based on purchase requisition data such as the product details and quantity required. Supplier details such as name and address, and inventory details such as the stock numbers and usual order quantities (e.g. each, dozen, pallet) are also used when creating a purchase order. Purchase orders should always be pre-numbered so that the organisation is able to ensure that all documents have been processed and track every document issued. In order to allocate a sequential number the system needs to know the last purchase order number allocated, so it can increment that number, usually by one.

## Australian Information Company
### Level 2, 345 Hill Terrace
### Melbourne, Vic 3003

| Purchase order form | | | No: 1245 | |
|---|---|---|---|---|

| To: | Tech Supplies (Vendor Ref: 2839) <br> 782 Mount Macedon Terrace <br> Victoria 3547 | | | |
|---|---|---|---|---|

| Order date: <br> 17/07/10 | Delivery date: <br> 26/07/10 | Purchase requisition no.: <br> 936 | | |
|---|---|---|---|---|
| FOB: <br> Destination | Shipping via: <br> Calmex Logistics | Terms: <br> 2/10, n/30 | Other remarks: | |
| Approved by: | | Contact person: | | |

| Item no. | Description | Quantity | Price/unit |
|---|---|---|---|
| 35930 | Willow Series W laptop computer | 1 | $3500.00 |
| 93948 | Hume Premier paper, 10 ream | 15 boxes | $12.00 |
| 83748 | Hyth HD diskettes, box of 10 | 15 boxes | $7.50 |

**FIGURE 10.10** Sample purchase order form

The details of the newly created purchase order are written into the purchase order data store and the status of the purchase requisition should be updated to 'ordered'. This helps to ensure that the purchase requisition staff are aware that the goods requested have been ordered so that they can factor this into any subsequent requisition calculations. At the same time the status of the inventory items ordered should be updated to 'ordered'. This status update allows accurate forecasting of future stock levels. Details of the purchase order should be forwarded to the warehouse to allow staff to anticipate receiving the goods. The copy of the purchase order sent to the warehouse may be a 'blind' copy (called a **blind purchase order**) with the quantity ordered obscured. Obscuring quantities ordered forces goods receiving staff to count goods when completing a receiving report, rather than simply being able to tick off a list. The details of the purchase order should also be forwarded to the accounts payable staff to allow them to pay for the goods once they have been received. Finally, details of the purchase order are forwarded to the supplier to confirm the order and ensure that they correctly supply the goods required. An example of a purchase order history screen is contained in figure 10.12. An order acknowledgement should be received from the supplier detailing the acceptance of the order and the likely delivery date. This confirms that the supplier has the goods available and is able to deliver them in accordance with the terms and conditions contained in the purchase order.

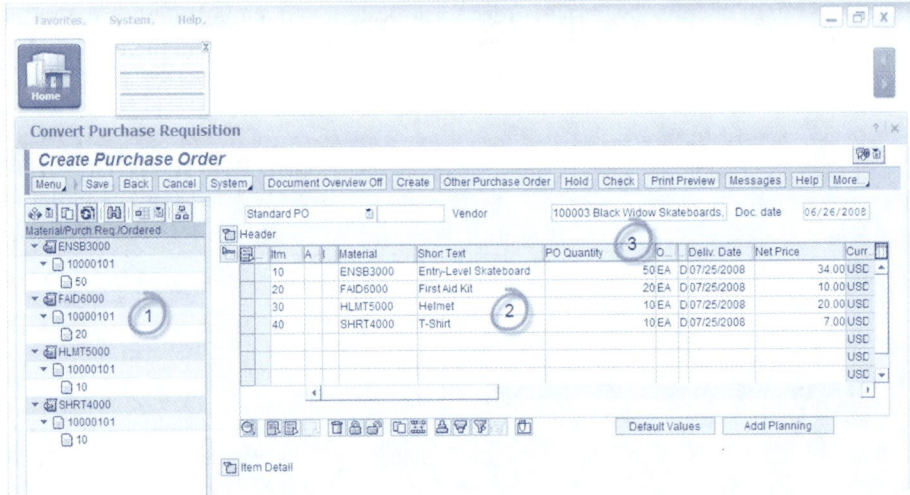

**FIGURE 10.11** Purchase order screen

*Source:* © Copyright SAP AG 2008.

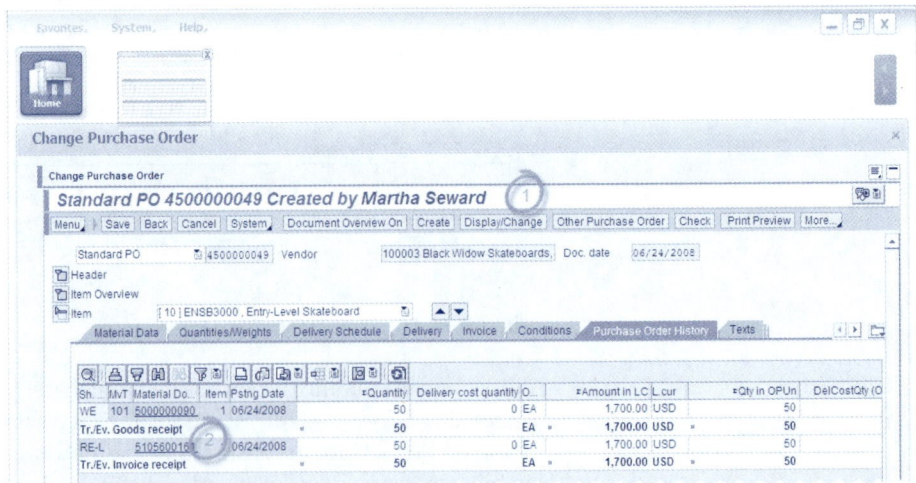

**FIGURE 10.12** Purchase order history screen

*Source:* © Copyright SAP AG 2008.

## Order goods — DFD

The level 1 DFD in figure 10.13 contains a lower level of details about the second process represented in the level 0 logical DFD in figure 10.5. This process takes place after the demand for goods has been determined in the preceding process and before the goods are received in the following process.

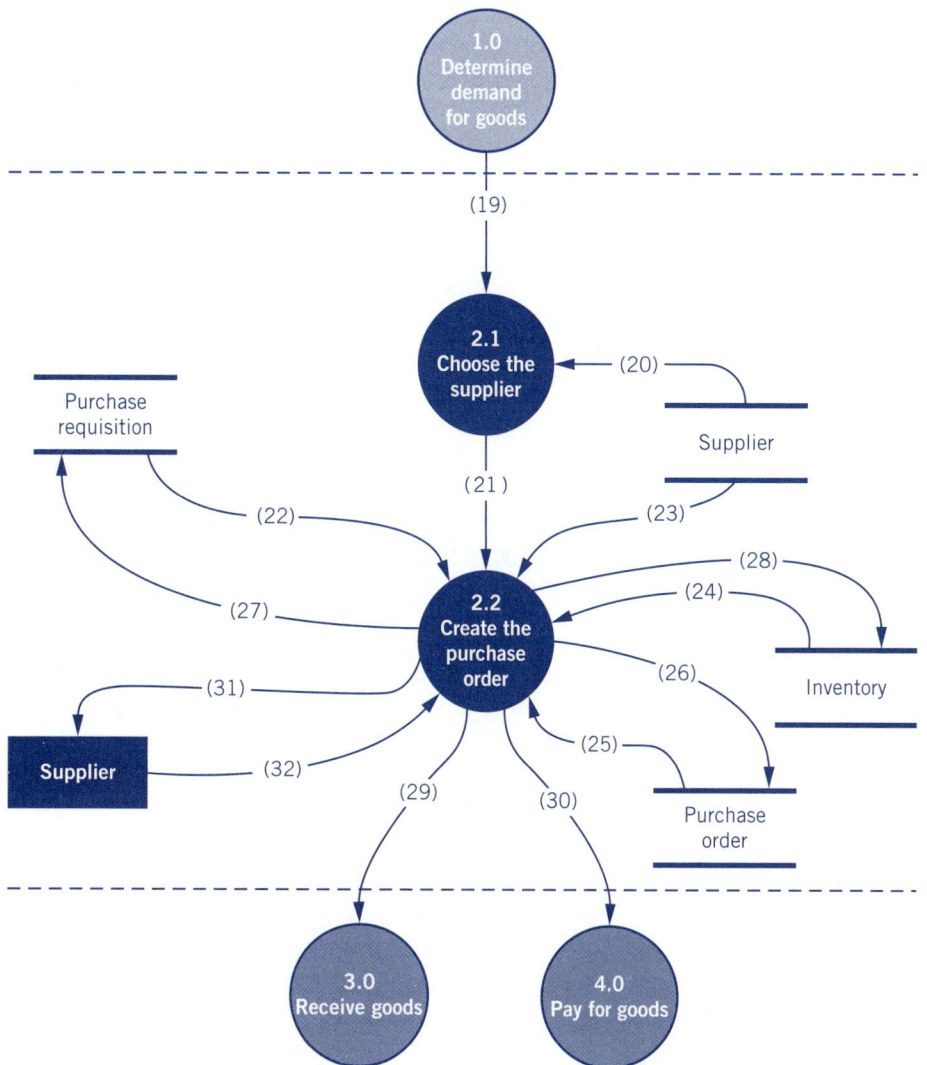

**FIGURE 10.13** Expenditure cycle level 1 logical diagram — process 2.0 Order goods

## Summary description of activities in ordering the goods

Table 10.4 overleaf summarises the activities, risks and controls when ordering goods, as depicted in figure 10.13. Table 10.2 (page 450) explains the logical data flows depicted in figure 10.13. Exploring the diagram in conjunction with the material contained in the tables will assist in improving your understanding of the process depicted.

**TABLE 10.4** Activities in ordering goods

| Activity # | Activity | Usually conducted by: | Activity description | Typical risks encountered | Common controls |
|---|---|---|---|---|---|
| 2.1 | Choose the supplier | Purchase clerk | The purchase clerk decides who to order the requisitioned goods from. | Purchasing from unauthorised suppliers | Approval of purchase orders<br>Independent maintenance of supplier data<br>Restrictions on corporate credit card use<br>Using pre-approved suppliers |
| | | | | Paying too much | Price lists<br>Using pre-approved suppliers<br>Competitive tendering<br>Budgets |
| 2.2 | Create the purchase order | Purchase clerk | Once a supplier has been selected the purchase clerk creates a purchase order. | Buying poor quality goods | Using pre-approved suppliers<br>Ongoing monitoring of supplier performance<br>Inventory quality checks |
| | | | | Kickbacks | Corporate gift policies<br>Job rotation<br>Enforced annual leave<br>Supplier audits<br>Disclosure requirements (conflict of interest, not at arm's length) |

## Receive goods — activities, risks and controls

Process 3.0, receive goods, comprises the following activities.

### Accept the delivery

The supplier sends the goods ordered accompanied by some delivery documentation. An example of a goods delivery slip is show in figure 10.14.

| Tech Supplies Packing Slip | | 782 Mount Macedon Terrace Victoria 3547 |
|---|---|---|
| **To:** | Australian Information Company<br>Level 2, 345 Hill Terrace<br>Melbourne, Vic 3003 | |
| Packing slip no.: P03-0939 | Delivery date: 26/07/10 | Purchase order no.: AIC-1245 |
| Item no. | Description | Quantity |
| 35930 | Willow Series W laptop computer | 1 |
| 93948 | Hume Premier paper, 10 ream | 15 boxes |
| 83748 | Hyth HD diskettes, box of 10 | 15 boxes |
| Remarks: | | |

**FIGURE 10.14** Sample goods packing slip

The delivery documentation should contain details of the goods despatched (type, quantities, number of cartons) and the purchase order number that the goods relate to. Delivery may be made by the supplier's employees, or by a third party courier company. The most important control consideration here is the need to check the goods thoroughly before accepting the delivery. That is, the goods must be checked prior to signing any delivery documentation and before the delivery driver departs. There are two important checks to be carried out. Firstly, goods receiving staff should check that there was a purchase order placed for the goods. Receiving staff need to verify that the purchase order number is valid, that the goods and supplier listed on the purchase order approximate those on the delivery documentation, and that the goods listed on that purchase order have not been received already (to check against the possibility of incorrect or double deliveries). Secondly, once it has been established that a valid purchase order exists, goods receiving staff should carefully check the goods to ensure they are not damaged, and that the quantity of goods delivered is correct.

The types of counts and checks conducted will vary depending on the volume and value of goods received. Receiving a small number of high value items would require careful checking of the quality of the item, and that the item is exactly as indicated on the purchase order. Receiving a large number of low value items might require scrutinising the cartons for any obvious damage, and then counting the number of cartons. For large volume deliveries there is always a decision to be made as to whether it is cost effective to actually open cartons and count individual goods. A more detailed count should take place where individual item values are high, or if there is some doubt as to the correctness of the volume claims made on the carton labels. If counting is being conducted manually it is necessary to introduce some controls against the risk of errors when counting goods received. These controls could include providing some incentives for accuracy to motivate receiving staff appropriately, or conducting a double check of the count (but only where this is cost effective). As mentioned above, many organisations use a blind copy of the purchase order for goods receipts; this copy of the purchase order does not contain any quantities for the items ordered, forcing receiving staff to physically count the goods.

The activities of checking purchase order details and counting the goods may be conducted using a handheld scanner. This is a highly effective practice; use of handheld scanners not only improves efficiency, it also increases data quality and timeliness. In order to use a handheld scanner both the goods and the delivery advice must contain a printed barcode, as shown in the example in figure 10.15.

**FIGURE 10.15** Example printed barcode

When using a scanner, receiving staff scan the barcode printed on the delivery docket to obtain information about the related purchase order. Information is retrieved from the purchase order data store using the scanned data to locate the relevant purchase order. Once the purchase order has been verified the goods are scanned to record their individual receipt. It is important to note that although data accuracy is improved by removing the need to manually record goods received, 100 per cent accuracy is not guaranteed. For example, a carton may not be scanned, or it may be scanned twice. Further, there is no guarantee that the contents of a carton match the barcode unless the carton is opened and the goods are visually checked.

An alternative form of scanning device reads an RFID tag. An example is shown in figure 10.16. The primary advantage of an RFID tag is that it can be scanned from a greater distance than a barcode, and it can have new data about the item added to it, uniquely identifying the item and its current location and status. Large-scale scanning of items containing RFID tags can be automated by building a scanner-equipped gateway through which parcels are moved and scanned automatically. This method of scanning reduces the need to manually locate and scan each item individually, reducing both labour costs and errors.

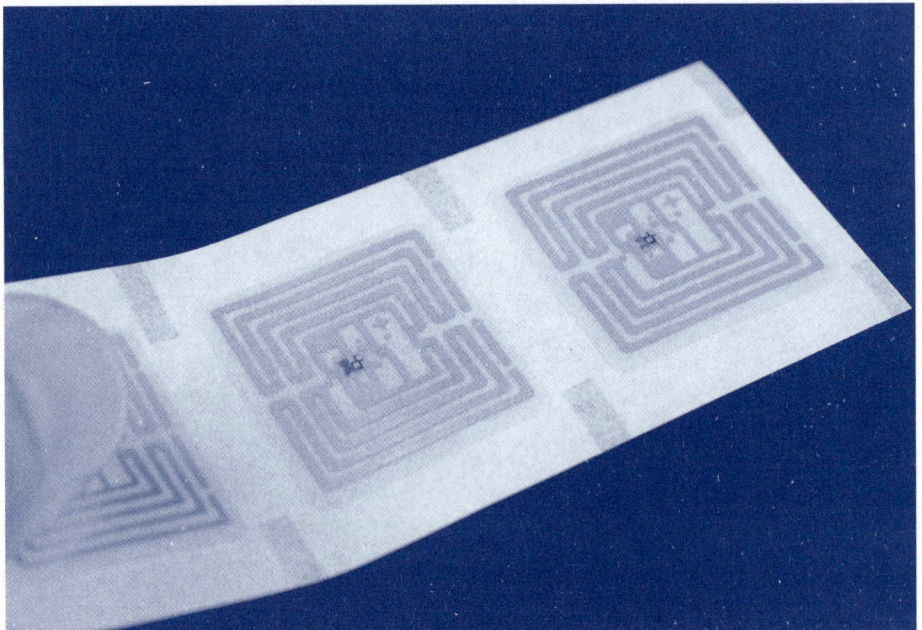

**FIGURE 10.16** Example RFID tag

Once all the receiving checks have taken place goods receiving staff should sign the delivery docket to indicate that the delivery has been accepted. Most delivery documentation consists of two copies. One copy should be retained by the receiver, the other copy should be signed and returned to the delivery driver. To reduce the risk of theft of inventory, goods should be relocated immediately into a secure storage place once the delivery has been checked and accepted. Additional controls to guard against this risk include implementing physical controls, limiting access to the warehouse and conducting periodic inventory counts. Segregation of duties is also important; in particular, goods should be received by a staff member who is not able to order or request goods to be purchased, or to subsequently arrange the despatch of those goods. For organisations that operate at multiple locations, it is important to ensure that any internal transfers of inventory are correctly documented. Failure to document internal transfers will lead to inaccurate inventory records at both locations, and increase the risk of inventory theft.

### Record goods received

Goods-receiving staff need to record the details of the goods received. This may take place manually by writing the quantities of goods on a copy of the purchase order to create a receiving report. An example of a manual receiving report is shown in figure 10.17. Figure 10.18 overleaf displays an example of electronic goods receipting. Alternatively, the goods received data collection may be computerised, in which case the receiving staff would enter data into the computer either by typing it in or using a barcode or RFID scanner as described above. For either method it is important to accurately identify any variance between the goods ordered and the goods received. If goods receiving is computerised the use of data input edit checks to identify variances at input stage, or automatic generation of any exception reports should be considered. The details of the goods received (date, product details, supplier details and related purchase order details) are written into the goods received data store and the status of the related purchase order should be updated to 'goods received'. The inventory status for the relevant product should also be updated to 'goods received' to ensure accuracy of inventory records. Details of the goods received data often include the quality of the goods and the delivery timeliness. This data is usually written into the supplier data store in order to be able to maintain control over the quality of suppliers selected for future purchases. Details of the receipt of the goods should also be sent to the accounts payable section to facilitate processing of the payment to the supplier.

## Australian Information Company
### Level 2, 345 Hill Terrace
### Melbourne, Vic 3003

| *Receiving report* | | | | No: 1342 |
|---|---|---|---|---|

| Order received: 26/07/10 | | | Purchase order no.: 1245 | |
|---|---|---|---|---|

| Shipper: Calmax Couriers | | Shipping weight: 15 kg | No. of packages: 3 | |
|---|---|---|---|---|

| Freight bill no.: – | | Freight charges: NIL | Consignment? Yes | |
|---|---|---|---|---|

| Received and checked by: | | | Delivered by: | |
|---|---|---|---|---|

| Item no. | Description | | Quantity | Condition |
|---|---|---|---|---|
| 35930 | Willow Series W laptop computer | | 1 | Good |
| 93948 | Hume Premier paper, 10 ream | | 15 boxes | See below |
| 83748 | Hyth HD diskettes, box of 10 | | 15 boxes | Good |

Remarks:
Hume Premier paper: One ream's cover is torn, with paint on the top sheet. One ream will be replaced. So only 14 copies of Hume Premier paper are received.

**FIGURE 10.17** Sample receiving report

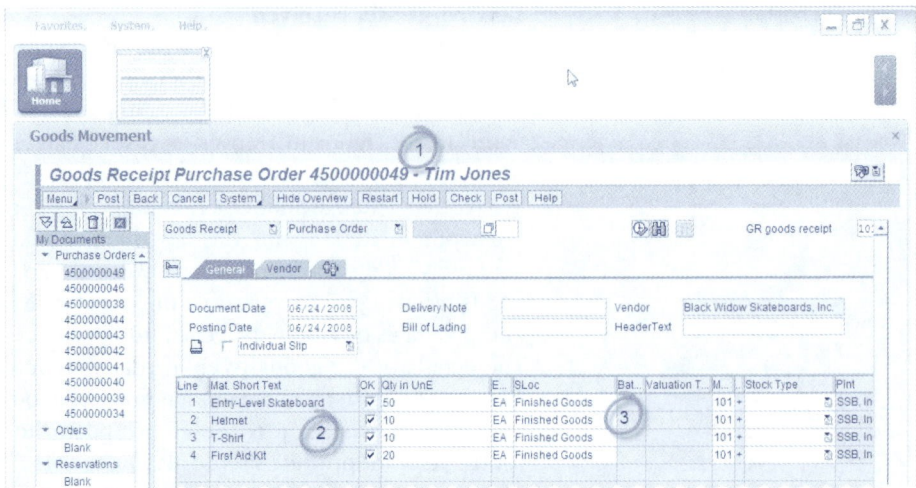

**FIGURE 10.18** Goods receipt screen

*Source:* © Copyright SAP AG 2008.

## Receive goods — DFD

The level 1 DFD in figure 10.19 contains a lower level of details about the third process represented in the level 0 logical DFD in figure 10.5. This process takes place after the goods have been ordered from the supplier in the preceding process and before payment is made in the following process.

## Summary description of activities in receiving the goods

Table 10.5 summarises the activities, risks and controls when receiving goods, as depicted in figure 10.19. Table 10.2 (page 450) explains the logical data flows depicted in figure 10.19. Exploring the diagram in conjunction with the material contained in the tables will assist in improving your understanding of the process depicted.

**TABLE 10.5** Activities in receiving goods

| Activity # | Activity | Usually conducted by: | Activity description | Typical risks encountered | Common controls |
|---|---|---|---|---|---|
| 3.1 | Accept the delivery | Goods receiving clerk | The goods receiving clerk decides if the goods can be accepted by referring to the purchase order. The goods receiving clerk should carefully check the goods to ensure they are not damaged, and that the quantity of goods being delivered is correct. The goods receiving clerk signs the delivery docket to indicate that the delivery has been accepted. | Receiving unordered goods | Checking the existence of a purchase order before accepting the delivery |
| | | | | Errors in counting goods received | Providing incentives for accuracy |
| | | | | | Double checking the count (only where cost effective to do so) |
| | | | | | Using blind purchase orders |
| | | | | | Using barcodes/RFIDs |
| | | | | Theft of inventory | Physical access controls |
| | | | | | Periodic inventory counts |
| | | | | | Correct documentation for all transfers of inventory |
| | | | | | Segregation of duties |

| Activity # | Activity | Usually conducted by: | Activity description | Typical risks encountered | Common controls |
|---|---|---|---|---|---|
| 3.2 | Record goods received | Goods receiving clerk | The goods receiving clerk records the details of the goods received | Data entry errors | Use of barcodes or RFIDs<br><br>Exception reporting<br><br>Identifying variances between goods ordered and goods received<br><br>Data input edit checks identifying variances at input stage |

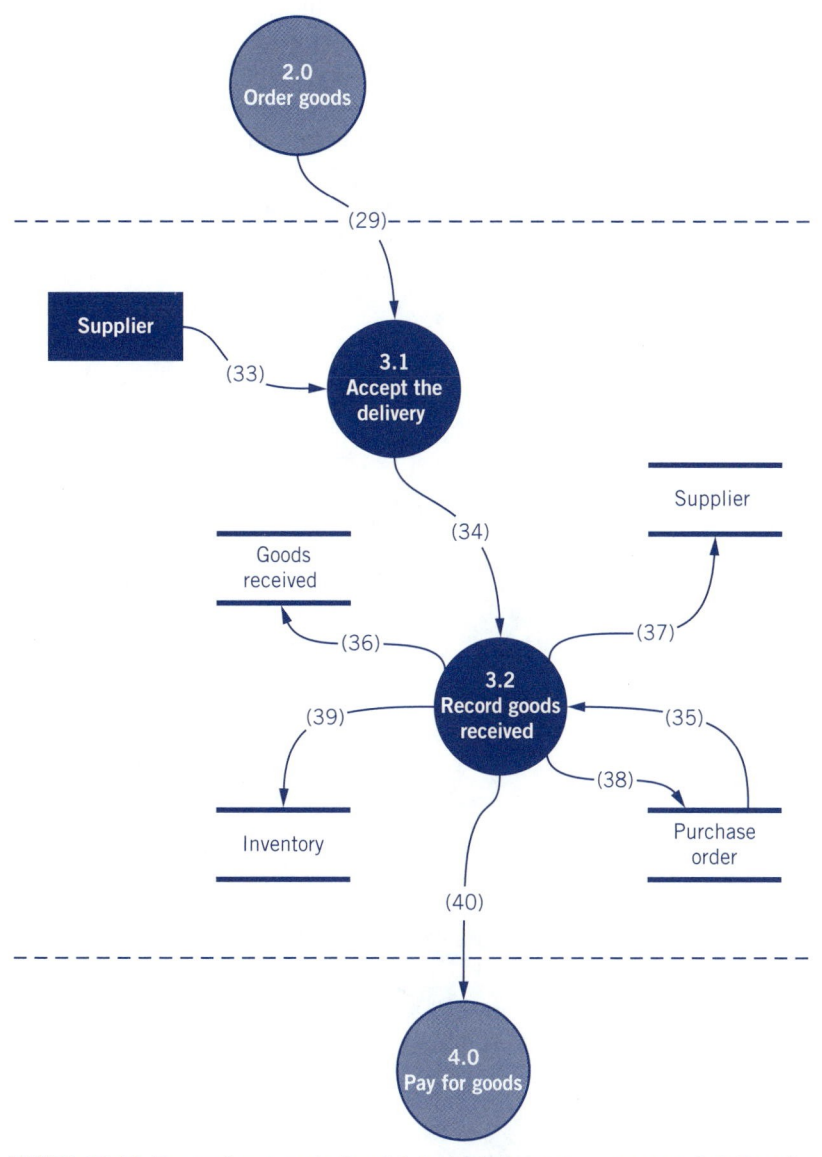

**FIGURE 10.19** Expenditure cycle level 1 logical diagram — process 3.0 Receive goods

# Pay for goods — activities, risks and controls

Process 4.0, pay for goods, comprises the following activities.

### Approve the payment

An invoice, which is a request for payment for goods or services supplied, is received from the supplier. The invoice may be delivered with goods, or sent at a later date. Invoices can be either paper or electronic. Accounts payable staff should check the invoice for accuracy and compare it to the purchase order and goods received data to make sure that what was ordered was delivered, and that the goods received match what has been invoiced. This three-way match can be conducted manually or be computerised. In a manual three-way check, accounts payable staff would physically match and compare the three pieces of paper. If the details match, the copies are usually stapled together and stamped 'matched', or 'approved' prior to any additional processing. For computerised matching, the details of the supplier invoice are input, and then details of the related purchase order and the goods receipt are extracted and used to check that the details of the invoice are correct. Figure 10.20 shows an example of an invoice input screen. Payment processing will only continue if the details of the purchase order, goods received and invoice all agree. This three-way check helps reduce the risk of paying for goods not received, or good that were not ordered. Another common control in this area is to formulate and monitor detailed expenditure budgets.

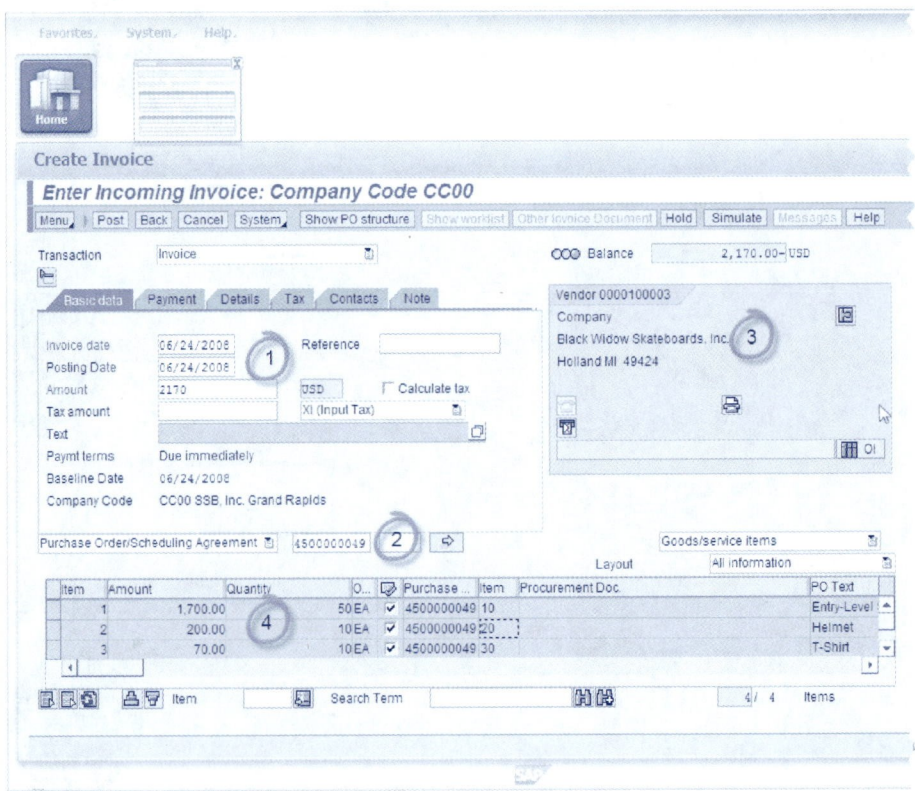

**FIGURE 10.20** Invoice input screen

*Source:* © Copyright SAP AG 2008.

Larger organisations may wish to consider the use of invoice-less trading or evaluated receipt settlement techniques. These techniques ignore the supplier invoice when establishing a payment, relying instead only on the data contained in the purchase order and the goods received report. If invoice-less trading is being used it is vital that purchase order pricing is accurate, as any resulting payment will be based solely on the price data held in the original purchase order. Under invoice-less trading, when goods received data is entered and matched against a purchase order a supplier payment is generated automatically. This reduces the risk of paying for goods not received, as it is not possible to pay a supplier unless the goods receipt has been recorded. This technique increases payables efficiency as it reduces the labour costs incurred to process and match invoices to the purchase order and goods received documentation. Risks related to errors in supplier invoices are eliminated by the use of invoice-less trading, but, alternatively, an organisation may wish to check the mathematical accuracy or double check all matched supplier invoices prior to payment.

A significant risk in the area of accounts payable is the potential to pay invoices twice. Common techniques to control for this risk include allowing payments to be made using original source documents only, or physically stamping or otherwise marking paid invoices to avoid double processing. Most computerised accounts payable software restricts the processing of duplicate transaction numbers for a given supplier. In order for this computerised control to work effectively it is important to ensure that duplicate supplier accounts are not created for a single supplier. It is also important to control the ability to change or add supplier data; that is, staff responsible for processing payments should not be allowed to add new suppliers or change existing suppliers.

Once accounts payable staff have determined that an invoice should be paid the payment due data is recorded. Figure 10.21 overleaf contains an example input screen for establishing a payment. This includes establishing the due date for payment of the invoice, which should be based on payment terms originally negotiated with the supplier. Existing supplier details (name, address and payment terms) are extracted for use in establishing the payment. Payments being made electronically will also require additional supplier data relating to the supplier's bank account or electronic payment details. A common risk relating to payment is that of generating an incorrect payable. This risk is particularly relevant where large volumes of data are keyed into computerised systems from suppliers' invoices. Controls to reduce this risk include processing invoice inputs in batches and verifying the associated batch totals, and using preformatted data entry screens and data entry input masks where possible. Exception reports identifying unusual or large payments are also helpful for reducing this risk.

Accounts payable staff need to decide whether to take advantage of any payment discounts offered when establishing the due date for payment. This decision may be made based on a corporate policy, or it could be left up to the discretion of the individual. A discount should only be taken where cash flow is sufficient to support the early payment, and the discount offered is a reasonable inducement. The risk of failing to take available purchase discounts can be reduced by automatically calculating payables dates based on supplier terms and a computerised calendar function.

Details of the approved payment (due date, amount, supplier and invoice details) are written into the accounts payable data store and subsequently transferred to the financial cycle where they are used to update general ledger asset and liability accounts. Note that if an organisation is using commitment accounting (where liabilities are recognised when goods are ordered, rather than when goods are received) the details of payments due for purchase orders raised would be transferred earlier in the process, that is, immediately after the purchase order is created.

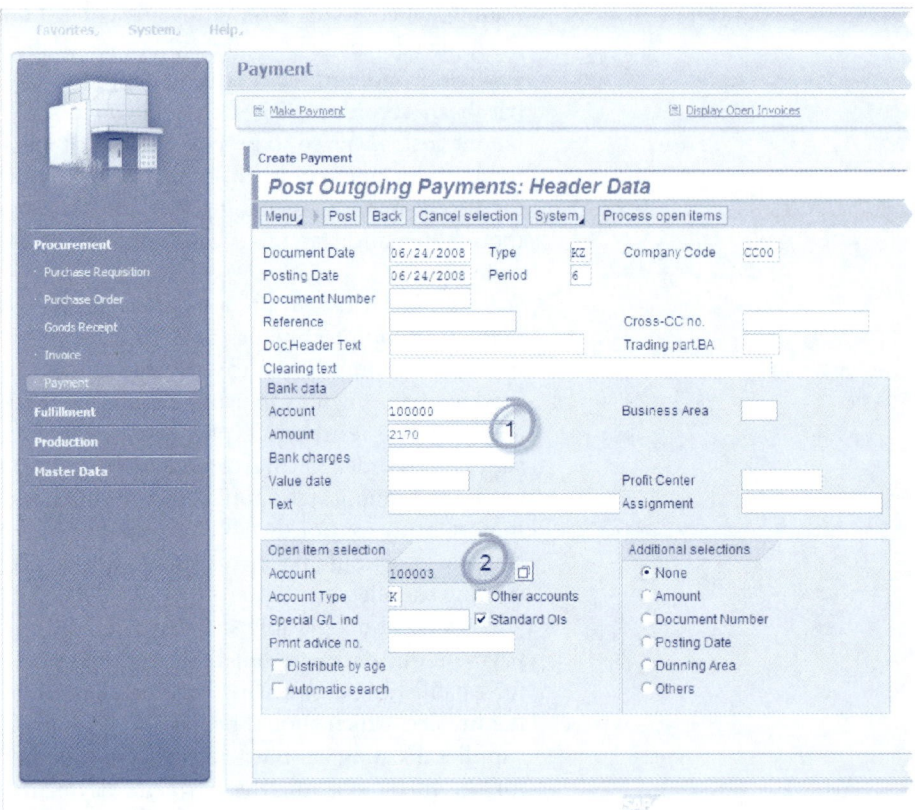

**FIGURE 10.21** Vendor payment screen
*Source:* © Copyright SAP AG 2008.

Not all payments processed have a related purchase order; common examples are recurrent payment such as rent or loan payments. Many organisations also allow employees to pay for small expenses directly and subsequently reimburse them. The controls over these payments need to be stronger and better enforced than those of payments for which there is a purchase order. Payments with no purchase order have sidestepped all the controls in place over the ordering and receiving of goods. Typically a payment request for which there is no purchase order would need to be independently checked and authorised by a staff member with sufficient seniority and financial delegation before the payment can be processed. Vouchers of the kind shown in figure 10.22 are commonly used to document these payments. Another common control technique used is to monitor the proportion of payments being processed without a related purchase order. If this proportion is increasing it may indicate a weakness or inefficiency in the purchase order process that should be addressed.

## Australian Information Company
### Level 2, 345 Hill Terrace
### Melbourne, Vic 3003

| *Disbursement voucher* | | | | | No: 1458 |
|---|---|---|---|---|---|
| Remit to: | Tech Supplies (Vendor Ref: 2839) 782 Mount Macedon Terrace Victoria 3547 | | | | |
| Order processed: 26/07/10 | | | Prepared by: Dianne Gillian | | |
| Vendor invoice number | Date | Amount | Returns and allowances | Discount | Net amount |
| 67289 | 30/07/10 | 3792.50 | NIL | 379.25 | 3413.25 |
| | | | | | |
| | | | | | |

**FIGURE 10.22** Sample disbursement voucher

### Make the payment

On the due date the payment should be automatically processed. An example is shown in figure 10.23 overleaf. A payment may relate to a single invoice or to a number of invoices if multiple invoices have been received and approved since the last payment made to the supplier. Payment can be made in a number of ways. A payment may be generated by printing cheques based on data in a batch file created automatically by the computer, or by creating a hand-written cheque if the volume of payments is small. If payment is being made electronically the computer may automatically generate a file to be sent to the bank for processing, or accounts payable staff may log on to an online banking website and process the payments individually. **Online banking** is an internet-based banking facility that allows organisations to manage and view their bank accounts online and conduct transactions such as transfers from those accounts.

Whichever form of payment is adopted the payment needs to be sent to the supplier. This may be in the form of a cheque that is posted to the supplier, or an electronic payment that is transferred though an online banking system. Both forms of payment should include a remittance advice that explains the accompanying payment. A remittance advice would usually list which invoices are being paid, the individual amounts of those invoices and the total payment remitted. Generating and transmitting payments carries a risk of misappropriation of the cash, cheques or electronic funds transfers (EFTs). Common controls when cheques are issued include restricting access to blank cheque stationery and requiring dual signatories. For larger volume cheque printing, many firms also use a cheque signing machine to control and log all cheques released. Controls over EFTs include the use of secure logins and passwords, requiring two people to authorise payment transfers,

*Online banking An internet-based banking facility that allows organisations to manage and view their bank accounts online and conduct transactions such as transfers from those accounts.*

and severely restricting access to online banking functionality. Segregation of duties and performing regular bank reconciliations is vital to control payment-related risks. People responsible for making payments ideally would not also be responsible for establishing payments, or for arranging to purchase goods. Bank reconciliations should be performed by an employee who has no other revenue or expenditure responsibilities if at all possible.

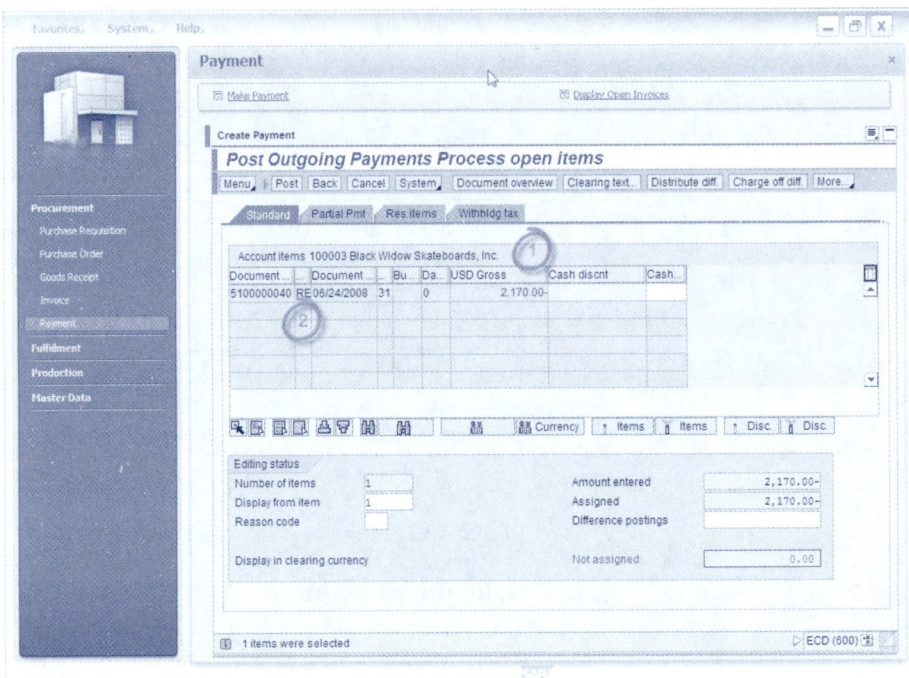

**FIGURE 10.23** Vendor payment processing screen
*Source:* © Copyright SAP AG 2008.

Once the payment has been successfully processed, summarised details of the payment made should be written to the relevant supplier record in the accounts payable data store, and the full details of the payment should be recorded in a separate cash payments data store. The data contained in the accounts payable data store is transferred to the financial cycle where it is used to update general ledger accounts as discussed in chapter 13.

## Pay for goods — DFD

The level 1 DFD in figure 10.24 contains a lower level of details about the final process represented in the level 0 logical DFD in figure 10.5. This process takes place after the goods have been received in the preceding process.

## Summary description of activities in paying for goods

Table 10.6 summarises the activities when receiving and recording payment, as depicted in figure 10.24. Table 10.2 (page 450) explains the logical data flows depicted in figure 10.24. Exploring the diagram in conjunction with the material contained in the tables will assist in improving your understanding of the process depicted.

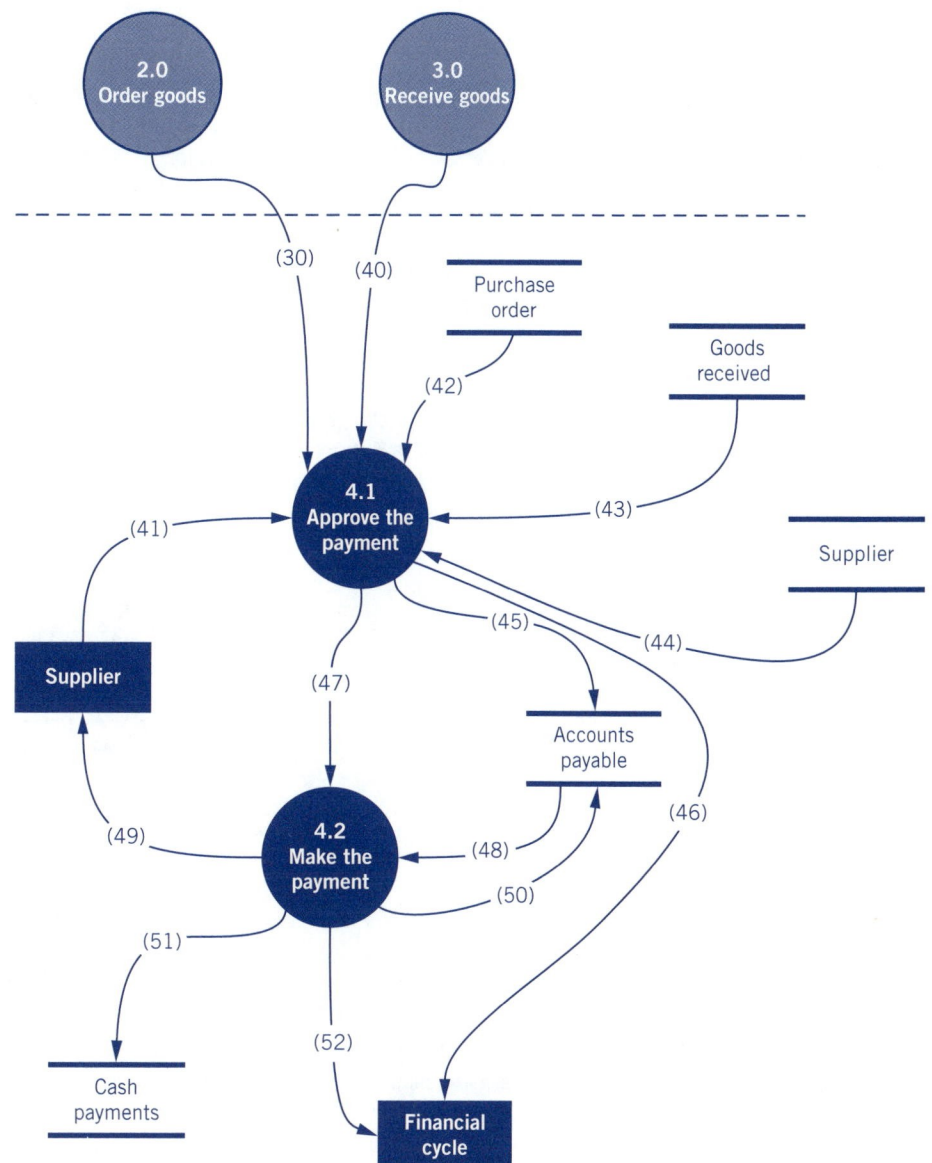

**FIGURE 10.24** Expenditure cycle level 1 logical diagram — process 4.0 Pay for goods

## Physical DFD — determine demand for goods

The physical DFD depicted in figure 10.25 shows an example of how demand for goods may be processed. The physical diagram draws the process from a different perspective to the logical DFD of this process contained in figure 10.9, as it shows who is involved in the activities of the process, rather than when those activities occur. This process of determining demand for goods involves the purchase requisition clerk who interacts with a central computer and one or more internal departments who request goods. Outputs from this process are sent through to the department that originally requested the goods, and also to the purchase order clerk for use in subsequent parts of the expenditure cycle.

**TABLE 10.6** Activities in paying for goods

| Activity # | Activity | Usually conducted by: | Activity description | Typical risks encountered | Common controls |
|---|---|---|---|---|---|
| 4.1 | Approve the payment | Accounts payable clerk | The accounts payable clerk checks the invoice for accuracy and compares it to the purchase order and goods received data to make sure that what was ordered was delivered, and that the data matches what has been invoiced. Once the accounts payable clerk has determined that the invoice should be paid the payment is created. | Failing to notice errors in supplier invoices | Mathematical accuracy check<br>Verification — double checking invoices<br>Independent validation of supplier invoices, invoice-less trading (i.e. payment based on purchase order details on receipt of goods, rather than payment based on invoice details) |
| | | | | Paying for goods not received | Matching invoice to receiving report<br>Budgets<br>Invoice-less trading |
| | | | | Failing to take available purchase discounts | Automated calculation of payables<br>dates |
| | | | | Paying an invoice twice | Paying on original source documents only<br>Stamping or otherwise marking paid invoices<br>Restricting processing of duplicate transaction numbers<br>Controlling access to the supplier master file, and not allowing duplicate suppliers |
| 4.2 | Make the payment | Accounts payable clerk | On the due date the payment should be automatically processed. | Recording or posting errors in accounts payable records | Use of preformatted screens and data entry input masks where possible<br>Exception reports identifying unusual or large payments<br>Preparing and sending remittance advices |
| | | | | Misappropriation of cash, cheques, EFTs | Restricting access to cheque blanks<br>Using dual signatories/logins<br>Using a cheque signing machine<br>Segregation of duties<br>Performing regular bank reconciliations<br>Exception reporting |

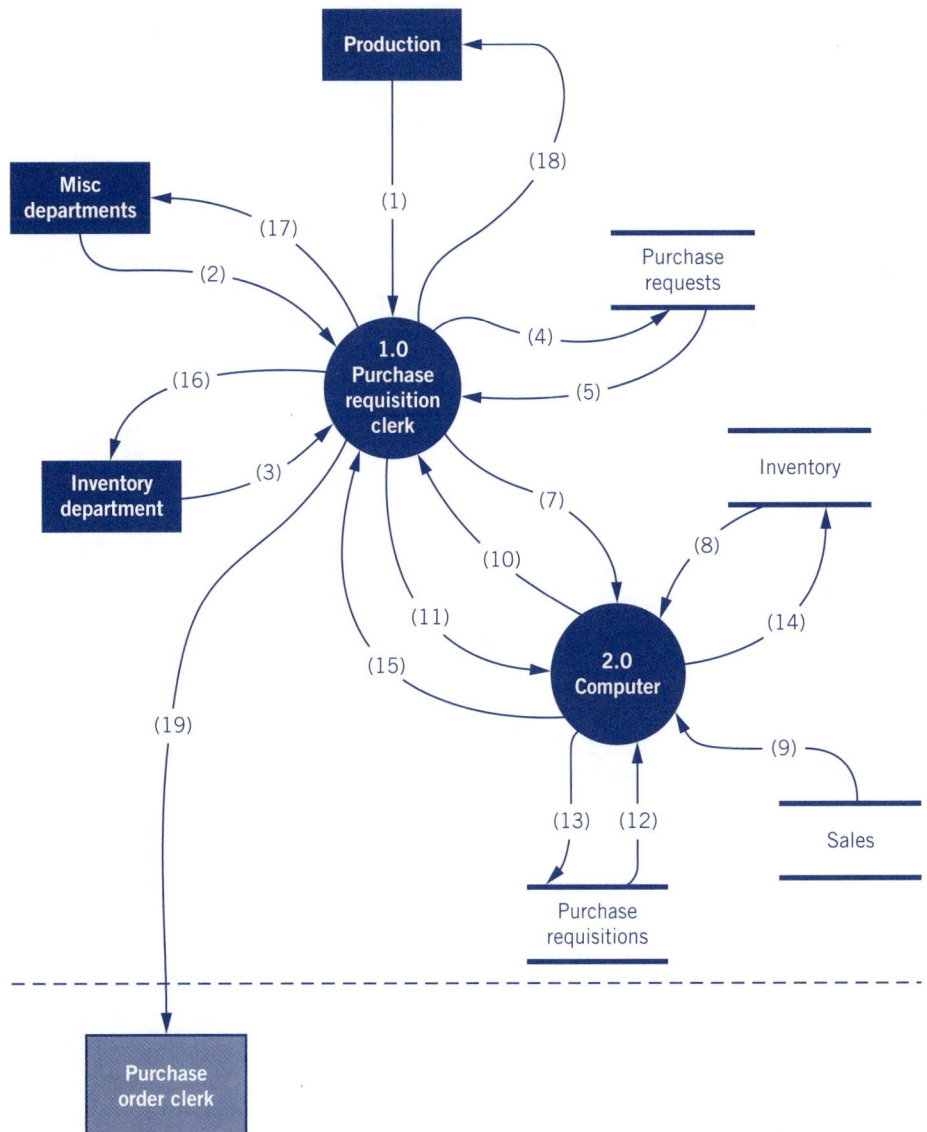

**FIGURE 10.25** Physical DFD — determine demand for goods

Details of the physical data flows in figure 10.25 are contained in table 10.7. As this diagram is drawn from a different perspective to the logical DFD it contains far more detail about the interactions between each of the entities involved in processing the sales order.

## System flowchart — determine demand for goods

The DFD in figure 10.25 shows an example of how demand for goods may be physically determined. The logical DFD in figure 10.9 shows that same process from a logical perspective. The flowchart contained in figure 10.26 overleaf shows that same process from yet another perspective. The system flowchart in figure 10.26 is the most detailed picture of the process, and includes both logical and physical perspectives. The detail contained in the system flowchart is useful when considering process redesign, and when analysing the control environment of the process depicted. Details of the flows shown in the flowchart in figure 10.26 are documented in table 10.7 (page 479).

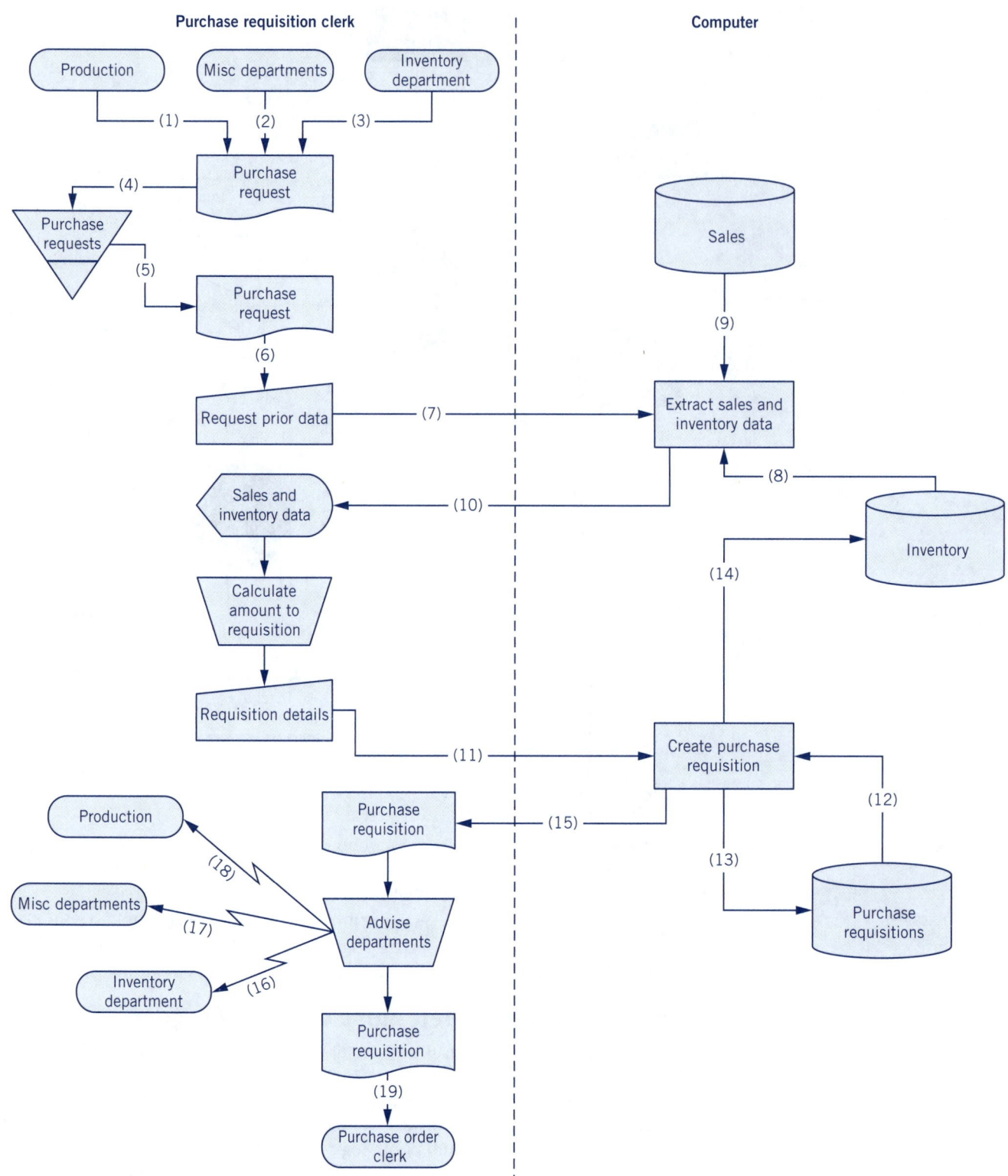

**FIGURE 10.26** Systems flowchart — determine demand for goods

**TABLE 10.7** Description of data flows in physical DFD and flowchart — determine demand for goods

| Flow # | Data source | Data destination | Explanation of the physical data flows |
|---|---|---|---|
| 1 | Production department | Purchase requisition clerk | Requests to purchase raw materials required for production of goods. These requests may be automatically generated by production cycle control software, or created manually by production staff. |
| 2 | Miscellaneous departments | Purchase requisition clerk | Requests to purchase consumable items used in the day-to-day running of the business, for example, stationery items. This type of request is often ad hoc and created manually by various departments. |
| 3 | Inventory department | Purchase requisition clerk | Requests to purchase items required for inventory; these are items that the business purchases with the intention of holding them temporarily and making them available for sale to customers. These requests may be triggered automatically by reaching a reorder point predefined in the inventory software, or they may be created manually by inventory management staff. |
| 4 | Purchase requisition clerk | Purchase requests | When requests are received by the purchase requisition clerk they may elect to hold them for processing until an economically viable order quantity is reached. If this happens the requests will be filed temporarily until sufficient requests are received. |
| 5 | Purchase requests | Purchase requisition clerk | Requests to purchase items are retrieved from the file for processing once sufficient quantities have been requested. |
| 6 | Purchase requisition clerk | Purchase requisition clerk | After a request is received a purchase requisition can be processed (not depicted in a physical DFD). |
| 7 | Purchase requisition clerk | Computer | The purchase requisition clerk requests previous sales and inventory data. |
| 8 | Inventory data store | Computer | The computer extracts the current inventory data for the requested product. |
| 9 | Sales data store | Computer | The computer extracts the previous sales data for the requested product. |
| 10 | Computer | Purchase requisition clerk | The computer displays the sales and inventory data to the purchase requisition clerk. The clerk uses this data, along with the data on the purchase request, to determine what quantity of goods should be ordered. |
| 11 | Purchase requisition clerk | Computer | The purchase requisition clerk requests the computer to create a purchase requisition. |
| 12 | Purchase requisition data store | Computer | The computer extracts the number of the previous purchase requisition processed. This number is incremented (usually by one) to assign a number to the new purchase requisition. |
| 13 | Computer | Purchase requisition data store | The computer stores the details of the new purchase requisition in the purchase requisition data store. |
| 14 | Computer | Inventory data store | The computer updates the inventory record to include details of the goods in the purchase requisition. |

*(continued)*

**TABLE 10.7** *(continued)*

| Flow # | Data source | Data destination | Explanation of the physical data flows |
|--------|-------------|------------------|----------------------------------------|
| 15 | Computer | Purchase requisition clerk | The computer prints out the new purchase requisition. This document may also be electronic rather than paper based. |
| 16 | Purchase requisition clerk | Inventory department | The purchase requisition clerk advises the department that the goods they requested have been requisitioned. This may also happen electronically, in which case a message would be generated directly from the computer. |
| 17 | Purchase requisition clerk | Miscellaneous departments | The purchase requisition clerk advises the department that the goods they requested have been requisitioned. This may also happen electronically, in which case a message would be generated directly from the computer. |
| 18 | Purchase requisition clerk | Production department | The purchase requisition clerk advises the department that the goods they requested have been requisitioned. This may also happen electronically, in which case a message would be generated directly from the computer. |
| 19 | Purchase requisition clerk | Purchase order clerk | The purchase requisition is sent to the purchase order clerk so a purchase order can be raised for the goods requisitioned. This may also happen electronically, in which case a message would be generated directly from the computer |

**LEARNING OBJECTIVE 6**

*Develop metrics to monitor expenditure cycle performance.*

**Metric** *A specific measure used for a particular purpose. An example of a metric is the number of bad debts the organisation has, which could be used to monitor accounts receivable or sales performance.*

# MEASURING EXPENDITURE CYCLE PERFORMANCE

Process performance should be measured relative to how well the process outcomes achieve the overall objectives of that cycle. At the start of this chapter the objectives of the expenditure cycle were described as being to correctly establish demand for requested goods and services and produce purchase orders that are accurate and appropriately authorised. Goods must be received in a timely fashion and both the quality and quantity of goods delivered must be checked before acceptance. Payments made to suppliers must be both timely and accurate.

To monitor performance against these objectives a range of **metrics** needs to be employed, along with some realistic targets. Examples of suitable metrics or key performance indicators (KPIs) for the expenditure cycle objectives are contained in table 10.8.

**TABLE 10.8** Example KPIs mapped to cycle objectives

| Objective | Example KPI |
|-----------|-------------|
| To correctly establish demand for requested goods and services | • Number of invalid requests received<br>• Number of requester complaints |
| To produce purchase orders that are accurate and appropriately authorised | • Number of purchases from approved suppliers<br>• Number of supplier complaints<br>• Number of accounts payable adjustments |
| To ensure goods are received in a timely fashion and both the quality and quantity of goods delivered are checked before acceptance | • Number of quality complaints<br>• Number of requester complaints<br>• Number of returns to suppliers |

| Objective | Example KPI |
|---|---|
| To ensure payments made to suppliers are both timely and accurate | • $ cash losses<br>• $ or # unauthorised payments<br>• Financial delegations compliance<br>• Discounts claimed/overlooked<br>• Average payment time<br>• Number of supplier complaints<br>• $ overpayments |

## ›› SUMMARY ››› 

LEARNING OBJECTIVE

### What are the key objectives and strategic implications of the expenditure cycle?

The expenditure cycle consists of two phases. The first is purchasing, where the organisation interacts extensively with external suppliers of goods and services. The objective of purchasing is to procure the right goods for the right amount, and to receive those goods at the right time. In order to achieve this outcome, purchases need to be properly approved and authorised; goods and services need to be obtained from authorised suppliers; all purchase commitments and obligations need to be recorded accurately; and accepted goods and services must meet quality and delivery specifications. Following the purchasing phase is the accounts payable phase, where the objective is to pay the right people the right amount at the right time. The accounts payable phase ensures that payments are both accurate and timely, while ensuring that they maximise favourable settlement terms. In order to ensure the integrity of financial reporting all accounts payable liabilities must be recorded accurately and promptly.

The expenditure cycle is strategically important to an organisation, particularly in terms of the degree of alignment with overall business strategy. The expenditure cycle can provide a competitive advantage by providing high quality products and services, or by acting to contain costs. In terms of the purchasing phase failure to correctly manage purchasing can lead to systemic problems: an unreliable supply of goods and services has the potential to negatively impact revenue, production and inventory management processes. Buying too much, too little or the wrong items creates inventory problems and can lead to increased costs or a decline in revenues. Arranging and making payments creates an exposure to potentially costly errors and mistakes, whereas poor payment practices can damage cash flow and/or supplier relationships.

LEARNING OBJECTIVE

### Which technologies underpin the activities of the expenditure cycle?

There are a number of technologies suitable to support activities within the expenditure cycle. A range of inventory management tools are available to help improve the ability to balance out supply and demand for goods and services. Transparency and management of cash payments and cash flows can also be improved by use of appropriate technologies. Enterprise resource planning (ERP) systems act to provide tighter connections between demand and supply functions within the organisation, which are essential for correct purchasing practices. Use of technologies such as electronic data interchange (EDI) can provide accurate, timely, cost-effective data sharing and barcodes or radio frequency identification (RFID) tags cut handling costs and improve data quality. Specialised supply chain management software (SCM) can be used to improve both planning and execution of the supply chain. The ability to make electronic payments provides a fast and comparatively inexpensive way for organisations to settle their accounts with suppliers.

LEARNING
OBJECTIVE

**What data and business decisions are involved in the expenditure cycle?**

The expenditure cycle uses or produces data including inventory, supplier, product, purchase order, goods received and accounts payable data. Business process decisions are made at both strategic and operational levels. Strategy-level decisions include whether the organisation should consolidate purchases across units to obtain optimal prices, how IT can be used to improve both the efficiency and accuracy of the inbound logistics function, and identifying where inventories and supplies should be held. Typical operational decisions include determining the optimal level of inventory and supplies to carry, deciding which suppliers to purchase from, identifying if sufficient cash is available to take advantage of supplier discounts and determining how payment can be made in order to maximise cash flow.

LEARNING
OBJECTIVE

**What are the primary activities in the expenditure cycle and what data are produced by these activities?**

Contextually, the expenditure cycle involves direct interaction with supplier entities outside the organisation. Within the organisation, the expenditure cycle interacts with the production cycle, inventory department and a range of miscellaneous departments, along with the financial cycle. Primary activities in the expenditure cycle include determining the demand for goods, ordering goods from suppliers, receiving goods and paying for goods received.

A range of data types are accessed and updated by activities within the expenditure cycle, including inventory data and supplier data. Expenditure activities create purchase requests, purchase requisitions, purchase orders, and accounts payable and cash payments data. Expenditure data are used to support decision making related to the expenditure cycle, and also for evaluating process performance and reporting financial results for the organisation.

LEARNING
OBJECTIVE

**What risks relate to the expenditure cycle activities, and how might we control for these risks?**

Activities within the expenditure cycle create exposure to a range of known risks. Risks related to determining demand for goods include under or overestimating requirements, and requesting unnecessary items. Risks related to ordering goods include using unauthorised suppliers, paying too much for goods, buying poor quality goods and kickbacks or collusion between suppliers and purchasing staff. Risks related to receiving goods include receiving unordered goods, errors in counting goods, theft of inventory and data entry errors. Risks related to paying for goods include failing to notice errors in supplier invoices, paying for goods not received, failing to take available discounts, paying an invoice twice, incorrectly recording accounts and misappropriation of cash or electronic funds transfers.

To reduce risk exposure the control environment must include controls that minimise human error, as well as prevent fraudulent behaviour. In the case of expenditure cycle, controls over inventory and cash or EFTs are of primary importance. Significant controls in the expenditure cycle include obtaining approvals for purchase requisitions and purchase orders, regular monitoring of supplier performance, appropriate segregation of duties, physical security over goods, exception reporting and regular bank reconciliations.

LEARNING
OBJECTIVE **6**

**How can we best monitor expenditure cycle performance?**

Process performance should be measured relative to the desired outcomes of the process. To monitor cycle performance a wide range of metrics needs to be employed, along with some realistic targets. Examples of suitable performance metrics for an expenditure cycle include numbers of data entry errors, product quality levels, cycle times to procure goods, volume of returned goods, number of discounts claimed and average payment times achieved.

## KEY TERMS

| | |
|---|---|
| automatic reorder point, p. 455 | just-in-time (JIT) supply chain, p. 447 |
| blind purchase order, p. 462 | metric, p. 480 |
| cash budget, p. 444 | online banking, p. 473 |
| enterprise resource planning (ERP) | reconciliation, p. 460 |
| system, p. 444 | RFID, p. 444 |
| electronic data interchange (EDI), | settlement terms, p. 442 |
| p. 444 | status code, p. 446 |
| exception report, p. 458 | supply chain, p. 444 |

## DISCUSSION QUESTIONS

10.1 Martin Ltd has always had a strategy of product differentiation; that is, providing high-quality products and extracting a price premium from the market. During the recent economic downturn Martin Ltd saw its customer base diminish, and decided to move strategically to a cost leadership strategy, that is, to try to sell more products at a lower price.

(a) What are the implications of this strategy change for the expenditure cycle? (LO1).

(b) What changes would you expect to see in the expenditure cycle? (LO4).

(c) What are the implications of this strategy change in terms of the usefulness of historic sales data for decision making related to demand predictions? (LO3).

10.2 Johnson Ltd has decided to use online banking electronic payment facilities to pay suppliers for goods.

(a) What controls would you expect to see introduced to ensure the safety of the online banking data? (LO5)

(b) Which activities in the accounts payable process would be affected? (LO2, 4)

(c) What changes would you expect to see in these activities? (LO4)

(d) What metrics could you use to measure the success of this initiative post implementation? (LO6)

10.3 Nguyen Ltd has just realised that it has a problem with its expenditure data as its goods received records do not easily identify whether a supplier has delivered the ordered goods on the due date.

(a) What decisions made during the expenditure cycle would be affected by this data problem? (LO3, 4)

(b) How would those decisions be affected? How would this data problem affect the performance of the expenditure cycle? (LO3, LO4, LO6)

(c) How would this data problem affect other processes at Nguyen Ltd? (LO1, LO3, LO4, LO6)

10.4 Wilson Ltd has a reconciliation problem. The amount of new goods booked into inventory records by the warehouse staff does not always seem to match with the amount of goods recorded as received by the goods receiving staff. Wilson Ltd seems to have good controls, it has separated the receiving and warehousing of goods, and it regularly conducts ad hoc duplicate counts of inventory items received.

(a) Which internal controls might be missing? (LO5)

(b) What could you do in order to investigate this problem? (LO4)

10.5 Anderson Ltd has a new CEO who is keen on improving process cycle times. She has reviewed the process documentation for the expenditure cycle and is asking you to stop accumulating purchase requests before determining the demand for goods as it appears to be slowing the process down.

(a) Should you agree to stop accumulating the purchase requests? Why or why not? (LO1, LO3, LO5)

(b) If you would not agree to stop accumulating purchase requests, how would you explain this decision to the CEO? (LO1, LO5)

(c) If you would agree to stop accumulating purchase requests how would you justify this change to the purchasing manager? (LO1, LO5)

(d) If you stop accumulating purchase requests would you need to measure the cycle performance differently? (LO1, LO6)

## SELF-TEST ACTIVITIES

10.1 Which of the following helps to determine demand for products?

(a) The level of previous sales

(b) The forecast for future sales

(c) The business strategy

(d) All of the above

10.2 When choosing a supplier you should consider the:

(a) product price only.

(b) product quality only.

(c) supplier service levels only.

(d) business strategy.

10.3 An organisation has committed to purchase goods from a supplier when:

(a) purchasing staff obtain a quote for the goods.

(b) a purchase request is created.

(c) a purchase order is created.

(d) a purchase requisition is created.

10.4 Supply chain management software (SCM) is not useful for:

(a) identifying product demand.

(b) making payments to suppliers.

(c) receiving goods.

(d) routing goods.

10.5 The expenditure cycle could receive purchasing requests from:

(a) the production cycle.

(b) the inventory department.

(c) miscellaneous departments.

(d) all of the above.

10.6 If an organisation does not use authorised or approved suppliers there is a risk that:

(a) it may pay too much for the goods they buy.

(b) it may buy poor quality goods.

(c) frauds such as kickbacks may occur.

(d) all of the above.

10.7 Goods should be counted and checked on receipt when:

(a) the number of goods is small enough to count them easily.

(b) the cartons look damaged.

(c) the delivery docket has a barcode on it.

(d) all goods deliveries should be checked and counted.

10.8 You should take a supplier discount for early payment when:
   (a) the goods have been delivered.
   (b) the invoice has been received.
   (c) you have enough cash available to pay the invoice early.
   (d) the supplier asks you to pay early.

10.9 Not checking that goods have been received within a reasonable period of time for all purchase orders placed increases the risk of:
   (a) running out of stocks of the goods.
   (a) not paying for the goods.
   (c) incorrect inventory records.
   (d) receiving the wrong goods.

10.10 Using a barcode scanner to record goods received reduces the risk of:
   (a) counting the goods incorrectly.
   (b) forgetting to record the goods received.
   (c) neither (a) nor (b).
   (d) both (a) and (b).

## PROBLEMS

The case narrative below (AB Hi-Fi) will be used to complete problems 10.1–10.13. Make sure you read and understand the activities and the case thoroughly before you commence work on the problems.

**AB Hi-Fi expenditure cycle**

AB Hi-Fi is a multi-store retail business that sells products such as DVDs, CDs, mp3 players, game consoles and TVs. AB Hi-Fi has a central warehouse that is located in Melbourne. All products purchased by the business are delivered to this central warehouse. The narrative of the AB Hi-Fi expenditure cycle follows.

**Process 1.0 Determine demand for goods**

Purchase clerks at AB Hi-Fi monitor stock levels via the computer. The computer has predefined reorder points and reorder quantities for each inventory item. When stock levels for a particular item drop down to this reorder point a purchase requisition is automatically generated by the computer and forwarded via email to the purchase clerk responsible for these items. The purchase clerk is responsible for reviewing sales trends for this item, and deciding whether to reorder the goods listed on the purchase requisition. The purchase clerk can cancel the order if they feel that the goods are not worth reordering, amend the purchase requisition if they think that the quantity is too high or too low, or accept the requisition without change. Once the purchase clerk has made a decision about the purchase requisition they log on to the computer and open the purchase requisition. They make any changes required to the quantities and products on the purchase requisition, and then mark the requisition as complete by ticking on a check box.

   The completed purchase requisition is then sent via email to the purchasing manager for review. The purchasing manager logs onto the computer and opens the purchase requisition. The purchasing manager is offered a choice of two tick boxes for each open purchase requisition. If the manager selects the 'reject' box the purchase requisition is cancelled and no further action is taken. If the purchasing manager selects the 'accept' box an email is sent to the purchase clerk informing them that the purchase requisition has been approved.

*(continued)*

### Process 2.0 Order goods

When the purchase clerk receives the approved purchase requisition email they log on to the computer and request a list of approved suppliers for each of the items on the approved requisition. The purchase clerk sends an electronic copy of the purchase requisition via email to each of the approved suppliers, requesting quotes for product and delivery costs, and an estimated delivery date.

When all the quotes have been received the purchase clerk decides which supplier to place the order with. The purchase clerk logs on to the computer and opens the relevant purchase requisition. They select the option to create a purchase order by ticking on a check box. The computer requests input of a valid supplier number then uses the supplier data and the purchase requisition data to produce a purchase order. The purchase order is sent via email to the supplier, the purchase clerk and the warehouse clerk responsible for these products.

### Process 3.0 Receive goods

As part of their trading agreement with AB Hi-Fi all suppliers are required to provide a delivery docket that lists the items they are delivering, the number of cartons being delivered and the purchase order number the delivery relates to. On arrival at the warehouse the delivery driver hands the warehouse clerk two copies of the delivery docket. If there is no purchase order number included on the delivery docket, the warehouse clerk will refuse to take delivery of the items. The warehouse clerk enters the purchase order number from the delivery docket into the computer. The computer extracts the purchase order status from the purchase order data store. If the purchase order number is invalid, or the status of the purchase order is 'closed', the computer will display an error message, and the warehouse clerk will refuse to take delivery of the items. If the purchase order number is valid, the computer will display a message indicating that it is OK to accept a delivery for this purchase order, and asking if the warehouse clerk would like to print a goods received report for the purchase order. The warehouse clerk requests the computer to print the goods received report. The computer retrieves a list of the items ordered from the purchase order data store, and the supplier details from the supplier data store. The computer prints the goods received report on a printer in the office of the warehouse clerk.

The warehouse clerk counts the number of cartons, and verifies the count against the delivery docket. Once the warehouse clerk has checked that the number of cartons delivered matches the number of cartons on the delivery docket the warehouse clerk signs the first copy of the delivery docket and gives the signed delivery docket to the delivery driver.

The warehouse clerk opens the cartons and checks and counts the items delivered, and writes the quantity of each item on the printed goods received report. Some orders are quite large, so individual boxes are not always opened and counted; in this case, the warehouse clerk relies on the external label stuck to the outside of the carton. Once all the items are counted and checked the warehouse clerk dates and signs the goods received report. The warehouse clerk staples the completed goods received report to the second copy of the delivery docket then puts the completed goods received reports in a tray on the desk of the goods receiving clerk.

Each morning the goods receiving clerk retrieves the previous day's completed goods received reports from the tray on their desk. The goods receiving clerk inputs the purchase order number from the goods received report into the computer. The computer retrieves and displays the purchase order data, without the item quantities. The goods receiving clerk works through line by line and inputs the quantities received for each item from the goods received report. Once the goods receiving clerk has accounted for all the items on the goods received report they tick a box on the computer screen to indicate that the goods received report input is complete. The computer will update the purchase order and inventory data stores with the goods received information and then display a message confirming the completion. The goods receiving clerk dates and signs the goods received report, and then sends the completed input goods received report to the accounts payable clerk. The goods receiving clerk processes each completed goods received report in the tray in the same way. The accounts payable clerk receives the completed input goods receiving report from the warehouse clerk. The goods receiving report is filed in an awaiting invoice folder.

### Process 4.0 Pay for goods

As part of their trading agreement with AB Hi-Fi all suppliers are required to provide the related purchase order number on their invoice. When the accounts payable clerk receives an invoice from a supplier they enter the purchase order number from the invoice into the computer. The computer extracts the purchase order status from the purchase order data store. If the purchase order number is invalid, or the status of the purchase order is 'paid', the computer will display an error message. If the purchase order number is valid and unpaid the computer will display a message indicating that it is OK to make a payment against this purchase order, and asking if the accounts payable clerk would like to print the purchase order. The accounts payable clerk requests the computer to print the purchase order. The computer retrieves details of the items ordered from the purchase order data store and the supplier details from the supplier data store. The computer prints the purchase order on a printer in the office of the accounts payable clerk.

The accounts payable clerk retrieves the relevant goods receiving report from the awaiting invoice folder. The accounts payable clerk attaches the goods receiving report to the purchase order report and the invoice, then checks to identify if there are any quantity discrepancies between the three documents. If any quantity discrepancies are identified the accounts payable clerk sends the reports to the warehouse supervisor. If no quantity discrepancies are identified the accounts payable clerk inputs the purchase order number into the computer and requests a payment screen. The computer displays a payment screen containing the purchase order details. The accounts payable clerk enters the invoice data (item quantity and price). The computer extracts the purchase order price from the purchase order data store and compares the invoice price with the purchase order price. If there is a price variation of more than 5 per cent the computer displays a price variation message and routes the payment data to the accounts payable supervisor for approval. If the invoice price is within 5 per cent of the purchase order price the computer displays a payment accepted message. The computer calculates the payment due date based on details held in the supplier data store, records the invoice in the accounts payable data store, and updates the purchase order and general ledger data stores. The accounts payable clerk files the goods receiving report, purchase order and invoice documents in an awaiting payment folder.

At the end of each week the computer extracts details of payments due from the accounts payable data store and produces a payments file which is forwarded electronically to AB Hi-Fi's bank. The bank transfers money from AB Hi-Fi's bank account to the relevant suppliers in accordance with the details in the payments file. After the payments file has been successfully transferred to the bank the computer prints a report of payments made on the central printer, then updates the accounts payable and general ledger data stores. The accounts payable clerk collects the printed report of payments made

*(continued)*

and retrieves the appropriate documentation from the awaiting payment folder. The accounts payable clerk matches documents in the awaiting payment folder with the payments listed on the payments made report. Matched sets of documents are attached to the payments made report, then filed in a paid folder.

10.1 Prepare a context diagram for the expenditure cycle at AB Hi-Fi.

10.2 Prepare a level 0 logical DFD for the expenditure cycle at AB Hi-Fi.

10.3 Prepare a level 1 logical DFD for:
   (a) process 1.0 at AB Hi-Fi
   (b) process 2.0 at AB Hi-Fi
   (c) process 3.0 at AB Hi-Fi
   (d) process 4.0 at AB Hi-Fi.

10.4 Prepare a physical DFD for:
   (a) process 1.0 at AB Hi-Fi
   (b) process 2.0 at AB Hi-Fi
   (c) process 3.0 at AB Hi-Fi
   (d) process 4.0 at AB Hi-Fi.

10.5 Prepare a systems flowchart for:
   (a) process 1.0 at AB Hi-Fi
   (b) process 2.0 at AB Hi-Fi
   (c) process 3.0 at AB Hi-Fi
   (d) process 4.0 at AB Hi-Fi.

10.6 Table 10.3 (page 459) identifies two risks typically encountered when determining demand.

**Required**
   (a) Analyse the degree of exposure to each of these risks for the determine demand process at AB Hi-Fi.
   (b) Determine how many of the common controls described in table 10.3 are present in the determine demand process at AB Hi-Fi.
   (c) Prepare a short report suitable for senior management to explain how risky you think the determine demand process is, and how comprehensive the current internal controls are.
   (d) Prepare a recommendation describing any changes you would like to make to the determine demand process at AB Hi-Fi in order to reduce the level of risk.

10.7 Table 10.4 (page 464) identifies four risks typically encountered when ordering goods.

**Required**
   (a) Analyse the degree of exposure to each of these risks for the order goods process at AB Hi-Fi.
   (b) Determine how many of the common controls described in table 10.4 are present in the order goods process at AB Hi-Fi.
   (c) Prepare a short report suitable for senior management to explain how risky you think the order goods process is, and how comprehensive the current internal controls are.
   (d) Prepare a recommendation describing any changes you would like to make to the order goods process at AB Hi-Fi in order to reduce the level of risk.

**10.8** Table 10.5 (page 468) identifies four risks typically encountered when receiving goods.

**Required**

(a) Analyse the degree of exposure to each of these risks for the receive goods process at AB Hi-Fi.

(b) Determine how many of the common controls described in table 10.5 are present in the receive goods process at AB Hi-Fi.

(c) Prepare a short report suitable for senior management to explain how risky you think the receive goods process is, and how comprehensive the current internal controls are.

(d) Prepare a recommendation describing any changes you would like to make to the receive goods process at AB Hi-Fi in order to reduce the level of risk.

**10.9** Table 10.6 (page 476) identifies six risks typically encountered when paying for goods.

**Required**

(a) Analyse the degree of exposure to each of these risks for the pay for goods process at AB Hi-Fi.

(b) Determine how many of the common controls described in table 10.6 are present in the pay for goods process at AB Hi-Fi.

(c) Prepare a short report suitable for senior management to explain how risky you think the pay for goods process is, and how comprehensive the current internal controls are.

(d) Prepare a recommendation describing any changes you would like to make to the pay for goods process at AB Hi-Fi in order to reduce the level of risk.

**10.10** (a) AB Hi-Fi has adopted a cost leadership strategy; the overall plan is to undercut competitors on pricing and so gain market share. How well does the current expenditure process align with this business strategy? (b) Are there any opportunities to improve the degree of alignment between the expenditure process and the business strategy? Explain what you would change and how this would improve the strategic alignment.

**10.11** (a) Identify and describe the technologies that AB Hi-Fi uses in its expenditure process activities. (b) For each of those technologies you identified in part (a), how well does AB Hi-Fi use the technology? Could you suggest a way to improve the business benefit obtained by use of any of these technologies? (c) Are there other suitable technologies available that AB Hi-Fi could be using for the expenditure process activities? What additional technologies could AB Hi-Fi implement? What business benefit would these additional technologies provide?

**10.12** During process 2.0 Order goods at AB Hi-Fi a purchase clerk has to decide which supplier to purchase the requisitioned goods from. Take a moment to review this section of the narrative before you complete the following questions.

**Required**

(a) What data does the purchase clerk draw on when making the decision?

(b) Where do the data you identified in part (a) come from?

(c) Are these data reliable; that is, is there any possibility that there could be errors in the data?

(d) Are these data sufficient to make the decision, or can you identify additional data that the clerk should consider when making the decision?

(e) What would be the consequences of an incorrect decision?

10.13 Explain how you would measure performance of the expenditure cycle at AB Hi-Fi; specifically:

(a) What metrics would you would use to measure performance?

(b) For each metric, explain where you would obtain the data.

(c) For each metric, explain why it is a good metric to help measure how well the expenditure cycle is meeting its objectives.

## SELF-TEST ANSWERS

10.1 b, 10.2 d, 10.3 c, 10.4 b, 10.5 d, 10.6 d, 10.7 d, 10.8 c, 10.9 a, 10.10 d

## FURTHER READING

Coyle, JJ, Langley, CJ, Gibson, B, Novack, RA, Bardi, EJ 2008, *Supply chain management: a logistics perspective,* 8th edn, Cengage Learning Australia.

Kaplan, RS & Norton, DP 2008. 'Protect strategic expenditures', *Harvard Business Review,* vol. 86, no. 12, p. 28.

Porter, ME 1998, *Competitive advantage: creating and sustaining superior performance,* New York: Free Press; London: Collier Macmillan,

## END NOTES

1. Retail Times 2008, 'Getting behind the scenes — managing your supply chain', Australian Retailers Association, 21 December, www.retailtimes.com.au.

2. City of Armadale 2008, 'City's sustainable purchasing to help the environment', 3 April, www.armadale.wa.gov.au.

# 11

# Transaction cycle — the production cycle

## Learning objectives

After studying this chapter, you should be able to:

**(1)** describe the key objectives and strategic implications of the production cycle

**(2)** identify common technologies underpinning the production cycle

**(3)** describe production cycle data and key production business decisions

**(4)** identify and document the primary activities in the production cycle and the data produced by these activities

**(5)** analyse risks and develop control plans pertinent to the primary activities in the production cycle

**(6)** develop metrics to monitor production cycle performance.

# Introduction

Production activities are conducted by organisations that choose to manufacture some or all of their products for sale, as opposed to purchasing them ready-made (as discussed in chapter 10). The production cycle commences when a new product has been designed, and ends when all production costs have been recorded. During the production cycle all production activities and schedules must be authorised and approved, inventory items including raw materials, work in progress and finished goods need to be kept secure and used appropriately, and all production runs need to be scheduled, conducted, recorded and costed accurately.

This chapter commences with an overview of the production cycle, and then considers the strategic implications of that cycle. Technologies that underpin the cycle are discussed, and then the data produced and consumed during the cycle activities are identified. Typical process business decisions are examined, along with some of the primary considerations related to those decisions. A production cycle is fully documented using data flow diagrams and flowcharts, along with a set of tables containing additional details to aid in understanding the process activities, and the related risks and controls of the activities. Finally, issues relating to measuring performance of the production cycle are discussed, and examples of performance metrics suitable for measuring production cycle performance are provided.

## PRODUCTION CYCLE OVERVIEW AND KEY OBJECTIVES

In order to meet business objectives and contain costs, the production cycle needs to be well managed. Poor production controls can lead to imbalances between supply and demand for products within the organisation. Additionally, the balance between the demand and supply of raw materials must be managed to ensure production efficiencies are realised. The revenue cycle discussed in chapter 9 drives the demand for the goods and services provided by the company. The primary responsibility of the production cycle is to ensure that sufficient goods are manufactured in time to meet this demand. Errors in the production cycle can lead to goods not being available to meet customer needs if the volume of production is underestimated, or the organisation may incur unnecessary inventory holding costs if production requirements are overestimated. In addition to balancing the quantities of **finished goods** required, within the production cycle, the flows of **raw materials** required to support scheduled production need to be effectively managed to ensure raw materials are available as and when required. Failure to stock sufficient raw materials can lead to costly production interruptions and delays. Conversely, oversupply of raw materials can lead to increased materials handling and storage costs. The organisational units most involved in the production cycle are shown in figure 11.1.

The production cycle is conventionally divided into two major elements. The front-end of the cycle is where production requirements are determined for new products and the overall production schedule is planned. The objective of this planning phase is to effectively plan production at both a product and schedule level. Staff involved in this phase need to understand both the individual product-level requirements necessary to produce each product, and the overall goals and constraints relating to future production scheduling.

**Finished goods** *Goods available for sale to customers, that is, the final results of the manufacturing process.*

**Raw materials** *Items used in the manufacturing of products, for example, timber, paint and nails.*

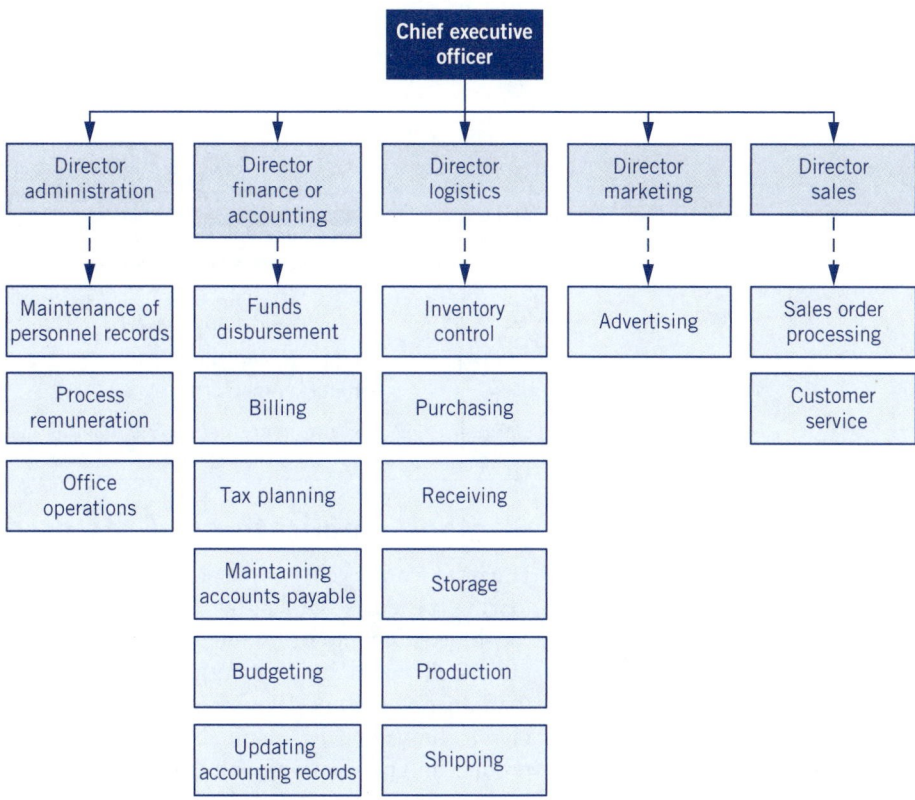

**FIGURE 11.1** Organisational units in the production cycle

*Note:* The dashed lines with the arrows show the business activities that each unit is responsible for.

Following directly on from planning is the execution phase, where the objective is to ensure that the planned production activities are carried out accurately and effectively, and that all production records are correctly updated. Staff involved in this phase need to understand the requirements and the nature of the plans devised, and have the ability to manage the execution plans. Failing to accurately execute production plans can lead to under/oversupply issues for both finished goods and raw materials inventories. Failure to correctly analyse and record production costs can lead to incorrect product pricing and potential decreases in profitability. A description of documentation commonly used in the production cycle is contained in table 11.1.

**TABLE 11.1** List of source documents in a production cycle

| Documents | Description |
|---|---|
| Purchase order | Acts as evidence of purchase as well as a binding contract between the firm and the vendor. The purchase order is prepared by the purchasing department. |
| Bill of material | A document that details the raw material and work-in-process that is required to produce the finished good. |
| Work order | A document that allows the store to release the raw materials and work-in-process so that the production process can start. The work order typically contains the items and quantities of the items required for production. |
| Material requisition | A document that serves to authorise the store to release the raw materials and work-in-process inventory to the production department. |

*(continued)*

**TABLE 11.1** *(continued)*

| Documents | Description |
|---|---|
| Vendor list | List of authorised vendors that offer quality goods and services at reasonable prices. |
| Inventory | This document reflects the nature and quantity of raw materials, work-in-process and finished goods in the store. |
| Production schedule | This document details when the raw materials will be used, when the work-in-process goods will be stored and finally when the finished goods will be available at the end of the production process. The production schedule also details the machines and employees who will be involved in each stage of production. |
| Timesheet | Displays the details of job hours and pay rates relating to a job or for a particular time period. |
| Work-in-process | This document details the manufacturing costs (labour, material and overhead costs) related to the manufacture of a finished good. |

## Strategic implications of the production cycle

The production cycle is strategically important. An organisation that chooses to manufacture products itself rather than purchase them as finished goods must have the capability to manufacture the goods at a lower cost than those same goods could be purchased externally. If an organisation cannot manufacture goods at a lower cost than the potential purchase price of those same goods there is no competitive advantage to be gained by manufacturing the goods in-house. Maintaining control over product and production costing is particularly vital, as incorrect cost allocations could lead to a situation where uneconomically viable production occurs to the overall detriment of the business.

A sound, well controlled production cycle can provide a competitive advantage by providing high-quality, lower cost products, which in turn can translate into an opportunity for higher product pricing or greater market share through price leadership. An alternative form of competitive advantage is the ability to manufacture a unique product range in-house. This translates into an opportunity to provide goods and services not available elsewhere and capture market share.

In terms of the planning phase, failure to correctly manage product and production planning can lead to systemic problems: an unreliable supply of goods and services has the potential to negatively impact the revenue and inventory management processes. Buying too much, too little or the wrong raw materials, and producing too many or too few individual products can create inventory problems resulting in increased costs or a decline in revenues. The product costing phase involves accurately determining product cost in order to support product sales pricing decisions made during the revenue cycle. Failure to correctly record or apply production costs can lead to errors in product pricing, which can flow on to create cash flow and liquidity problems.

**LEARNING OBJECTIVE** ② *Identify common technologies underpinning the production cycle.*

## TECHNOLOGIES UNDERPINNING THE PRODUCTION CYCLE

There are a number of technologies suitable to support activities within the production cycle, and improve the overall functioning of the cycle. A range of product and production planning tools are available to help improve the ability to correctly forecast product demand. Materials handling and production execution can also be improved by using appropriate technologies.

**Enterprise resource planning (ERP) systems** assist with enabling and integrating the production cycle. The production cycle is an entirely internal process, and acts to connect the revenue and expenditure cycles. An ERP system not only improves integration of enterprise-wide data but also provides tighter linkages between relevant modules such as product design, product development, product manufacturing, inventory management and the general ledger.

The production cycle involves many activities related to the tracking and recording of inventory items. The efficiency and accuracy of these inventory related activities can be improved by the use of scanners. **Barcode scanners** or radio frequency identification (**RFID**) tags not only reduce error levels by automating data input, they also improve timeliness as scanned data is immediately uploaded and available for use.

Specialised production planning software known as **manufacturing resource planning (MRP) systems** can improve production planning by identifying demand for products and calculating the resulting raw material, equipment and labour requirements to meet the scheduled production levels.

Execution of production plans can be improved by using a **computer aided manufacturing (CAM) system**, which links into the machinery used during production and acts to automate the production requirements. This degree of automation can improve throughput for a machine and ensure consistency of manufacture. As an example, CAM is used widely in the car manufacturing industry, where standard production line techniques are employed. Computerised control of manufacturing allows a predetermined sequence of activities to be repeated multiple times using a range of different equipment without any downtime while ensuring that each product produced by the equipment is identical. **Flexible manufacturing systems (FMSs)** may also be using during production to provide improved response to any changes encountered during scheduled production runs. An example of how these various manufacturing systems may be integrated is shown in figure 11.2.

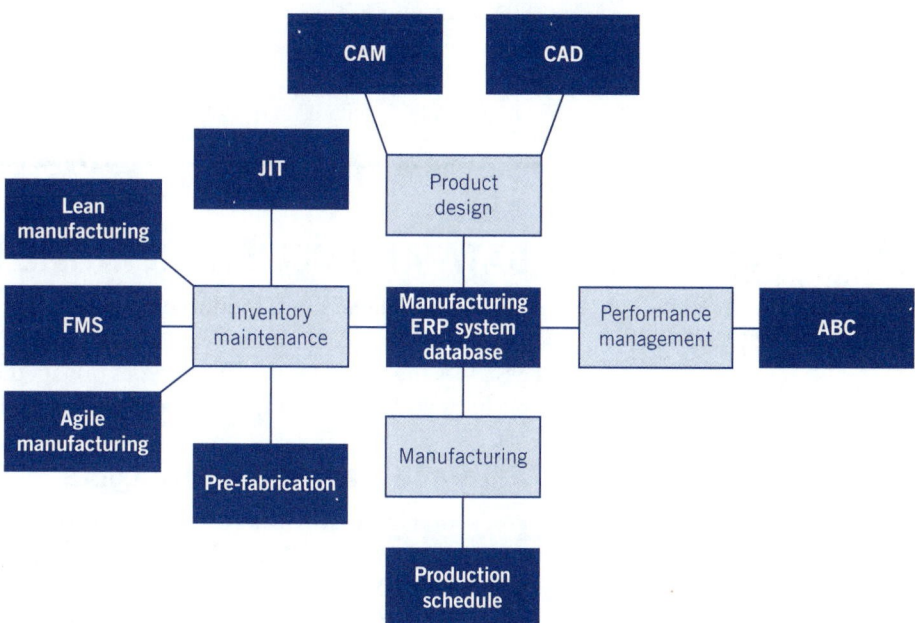

**FIGURE 11.2** Manufacturing ERP systems

## AIS FOCUS 11.1

### Simba: custom made success

The Australian textile industry has been dying a slow death since the early 1990s, when a squeeze was put on prices and margins through falling tariffs and the fact that third world countries started specialising in manufacturing. Local companies came under tremendous price pressure from overseas competitors, and many simply could not compete.

For Simba Textiles, Australia's smallest towel manufacturer, the changing global industry brought about positive change and marked the beginning of a new path for the company. 'We had a choice: compete with the importers on price, which would mean somehow increasing our own economies of scale, or separate ourselves from them through niche products,' said Hiten Somaia, Director, Simba.

In the middle of the tech-crash in late 2000, Somaia pitched an idea that would result in one of the few, remarkable successes in the dot com arena. Simba, in conjunction with Sun iForce Partner SolNet, built www.mysimbatowel.com — a site where customers can design and order an individual towel.

The success of the system relies on automating the workflow, from customers ordering the towels, through the production cycle, to accounts and shipping. The new web-based system eliminates many of the fixed costs associated with production, enabling Simba to capture this niche effectively.

Already, Simba has more than 300 registered users in Australia, more than 700 in North America and over 50 users in Europe. These users, typically promotional companies, on-sell the Simba services to corporate clients, amateur sporting clubs, schools and any other organisations seeking customised textile products.

'It is refreshing to see SME companies such as Simba using new technologies to transform their business,' said Paul O'Connor, Director Partner Sales, Sun Microsystems. 'With the SME market so buoyant right now, Sun partners are in an ideal position to help them grow their business in positive and rewarding ways. SolNet's long term relationship with Sun pays dividends when it is able to offer its customers the latest Sun ONE software solutions with confidence and technical expertise.'[1]

---

**LEARNING OBJECTIVE 3**

*Describe production cycle data and key production business decisions.*

# DATA AND DECISIONS IN THE PRODUCTION CYCLE

A range of data are both produced and consumed by activities within the production cycle. The actual data stores are documented in detail later in this chapter. This section describes the general purpose and types of data that the production cycle requires. The business decisions made during the life of the production cycle are also discussed here.

## Data and the production cycle

Production cycle activities require access to data related to products as well as data related to production schedules. Data relating to design specifications for new products are created by product designers, and used in the production cycle for creating the new product's production sequencing data. The product production sequence describes the manufacturing steps and timings necessary to produce the product,

**Bill of materials** A list of the items required to make a product.

along with details of the manufacturing machinery and equipment required to produce the product. In addition to the production sequence data for the new product, a **bill of materials** must be created for each product based on data obtained from the raw material inventory and the product specification. A bill of materials contains details of the raw materials required to manufacture that product.

The most important data created during the production planning process is the production schedule data. The production schedule data contains details of which products are to be produced, and the volumes of each product required. The production schedule identifies all planned future production outputs, and is the key to balancing supply and demand for finished goods inventories. Figure 11.3 contains an example of this production data. In addition, production schedule data determines the levels of raw materials, labour and equipment required to execute the planned production.

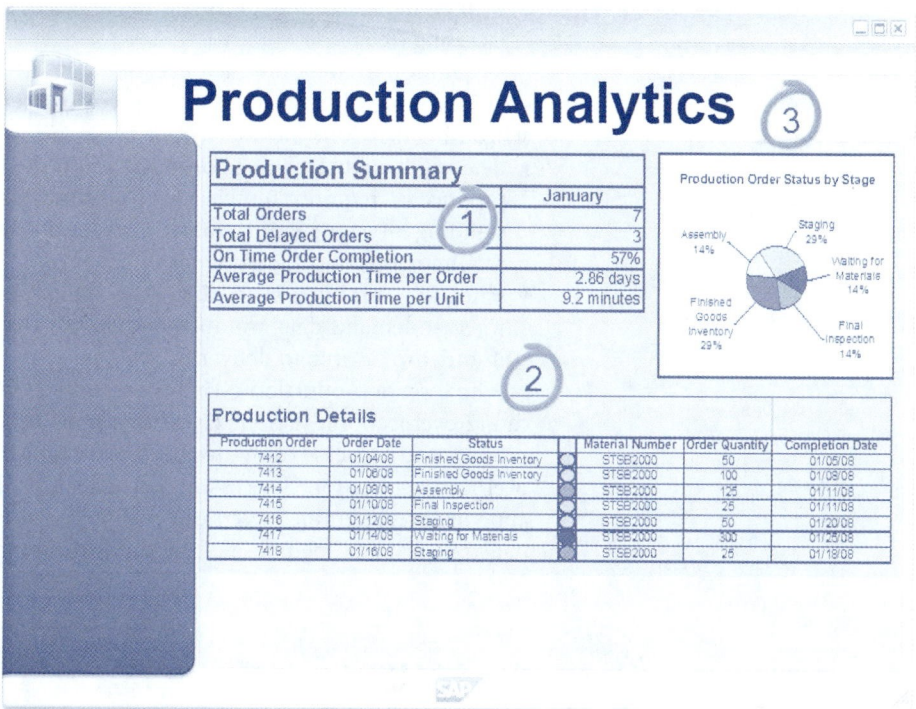

**FIGURE 11.3** Production analytics
*Source:* © Copyright SAP AG 2008.

The production execution phase uses production schedule, bill of materials, inventory and labour data when checking and assembling required resources prior to starting production. Effective production outcomes rely on this data to ensure that the scheduled production can be undertaken successfully. During the actual production process, inventory data records move from the raw materials inventory data store into **work in progress** inventory while production is underway and finally into finished goods inventory once production has been completed.

**Work in progress** Inventory while it is in the process of being manufactured. Also known as work in process.

During the production execution phase, cost details relating to labour and overheads are created and written into the relevant data stores. The final set of activities in the product costing process draws on all the data produced during production planning and execution to create data used by the revenue and financial cycles for monitoring and managing production activities.

## Production cycle business decisions

Process business decisions are made at different levels during the production cycle. When a new product is designed a number of decisions need to be made relating to that product. In addition to these product-level decisions, production planning decisions relating to numbers and types of goods to be produced are made during the execution stage.

Product level decisions include determining:

- material requirements — requires knowledge of specified raw materials requested and which raw materials are currently available
- labour requirements — involves understanding skills required to manufacture the product as well as amount of labour required
- equipment requirements — requires knowledge of the manufacturing steps required for the product and the equipment currently available to make the product, along with an understanding of the timing and sequencing of each of the required manufacturing steps.

In addition to these product-level decisions, there are a range of production-related decisions that will be made every time production is scheduled. Typical production scheduling decisions include:

- determining what types of products to produce and how many of each product to produce — requires knowledge of demand for the product, along with an understanding of any manufacturing constraints relating to potentially incompatible requirements for different types of products
- scheduling production to align with demand — requires the ability to deal with forecast demand data and integrate it with the lead times for production processes in order to be able to deliver finished goods at the required time.

A final set of production cycle business decisions related to product costing are allocating overhead and labour costs to various products, which requires knowledge of product and process costing techniques along with an understanding of the available overhead application choices and consequences. This decision making would involve applying predetermined overhead costing algorithms, typically created during the initial strategic planning phase of the production cycle.

## AIS FOCUS 11.2

### Best strategic sustainability outcomes

Vinidex, one of Australia's leading thermoplastic pipe systems manufacturers was awarded the 'Best Strategic Sustainability Outcomes' category in a $5 million 'Profiting from Cleaner Production' Industry Partnership Program sponsored by the Department of Environment and Conservation (NSW).

The Vinidex Smithfield manufacturing site in NSW was recognised for their achievement in reducing greenhouse gases through cleaner production and energy efficiency, thus reducing operating costs as well as protecting the environment.

The Vinidex company culture embraces continuous improvement, including environmental performance. As a major consumer of electricity, we are actively involved in introducing energy-saving initiatives to achieve savings in production as well as benefiting the environment.

Vinidex introduced key performance indicators directly related to production output measuring energy consumption per tonne of product. New technology was the key to improvement so Vinidex embarked on several upgrading projects to significantly reduce energy consumption.

- *Moulding machines upgrade:* Old injection moulding machines were replaced by new state-of-the-art units, which use less energy to mould fittings and improve the output consistency.
- *Lighting upgrade:* Light-sensitive switches were installed on all outdoor lights so they automatically turn off during daylight. Throughout indoor areas, existing globes were replaced by metal halide lights. Energy consumption per tonne have been reduced by 20 per cent over the 2003–04 period — a reduction of approximately 5000 tonnes of $CO_2$ emissions, which is equivalent to 1050 cars off the road each year!
- *Develop energy efficient products:* Through better product design, Vinidex have pioneered a new PVC pipe calling it 'Supermain', which requires 25 per cent less raw materials, uses less energy to make as well as having superior physical characteristics.
- *Recycling & waste management programs:* By reusing and recycling PVC, Vinidex had reduced landfill waste by 85 tonnes in 2003. Working with external waste management firms, recyclable waste at Vinidex is segregated, collected and sent off site for recycling, saving a total of 12 tonnes of cardboard and 13 tonnes of metal scrap from landfill.[2]

**LEARNING OBJECTIVE 4**

*Identify and document the primary activities in the production cycle and the data produced by these activities.*

# PRODUCTION CYCLE DOCUMENTATION

The production cycle is documented in the following section as a series of diagrams with increasing amounts of detail. An overview of these production cycle diagrams is contained in figure 11.4.

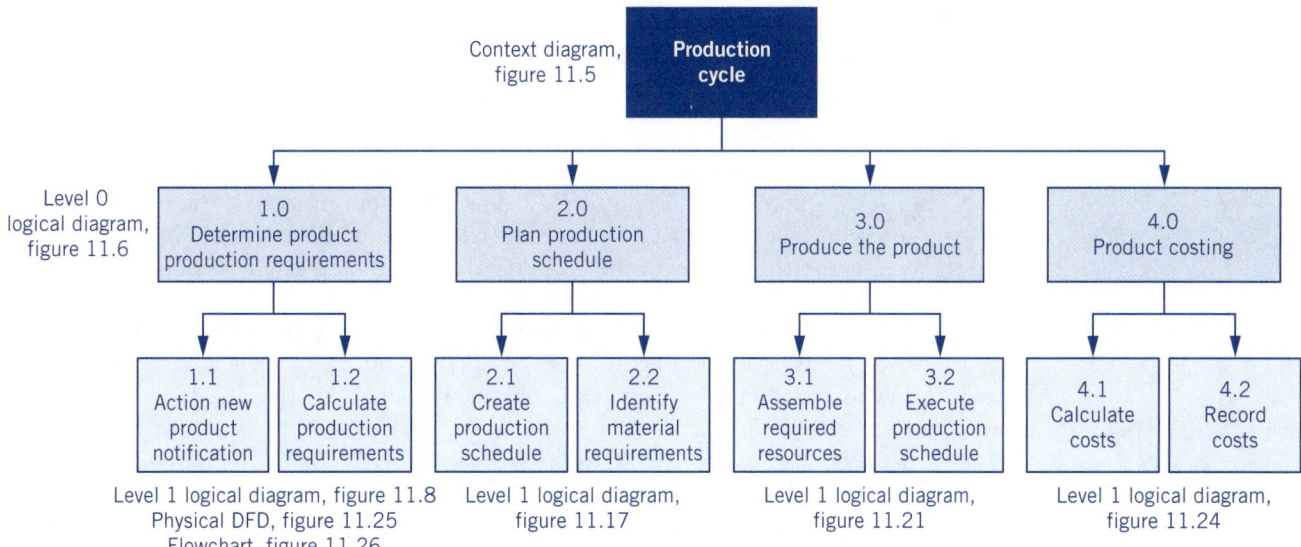

**FIGURE 11.4** Production diagrams overview

## Production cycle context

The context diagram of a typical production cycle is depicted in figure 11.5 overleaf. The production cycle does not interact with any entities outside the organisation; instead, it interacts internally with the product design and inventory departments. The production cycle also interacts with the revenue, human resources, expenditure and financial cycles within the organisation as shown in figure P3.1 (page 389). Details of the logical data flows depicted in the production context diagram are contained in table 11.2 (pages 502).

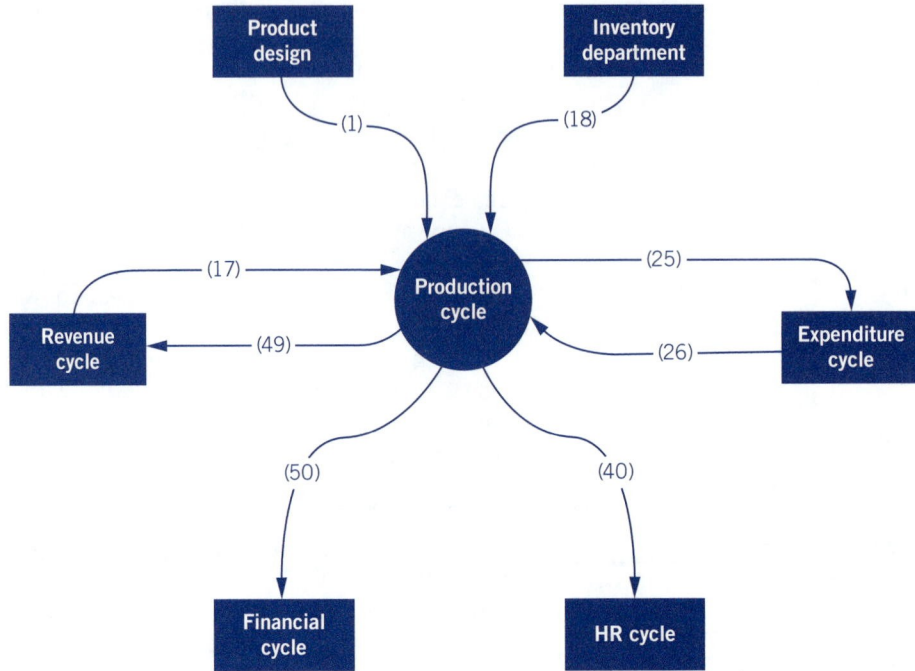

**FIGURE 11.5** Production cycle context diagram

## Production cycle logical data flows

Figure 11.6 depicts a level 0 logical DFD. This diagram shows the entire production cycle in greater detail than that depicted in the context diagram. The logical DFD is an exploded version of the context diagram, with the bubble described as 'production cycle' in the context diagram broken down into four processes. The logical diagram at level 0 helps us to analyse and understand the production cycle in its entirety. It depicts the chronology of the cycle, the data stores and external entities involved in each of the processes, and the interactions between these processes, entities and data stores. The logical level 0 diagram in figure 11.6 is itself broken down to describe even lower levels of detail in figures 11.8, 11.17, 11.21 and 11.24. Details of the logical data flows depicted in this diagram are contained in table 11.2 (page 502).

### Description of logical data flows in the production cycle

A logical DFD contains only those data flows relating to inputs and outputs of the activities contained within each of the processes, as opposed to the details of all inter-actions between entities which are depicted in a physical DFD. As a result, the number of flows in a logical DFD is always less than those that would be shown on a physical DFD for the same process. To illustrate this, compare figures 11.8 and 11.25, which show exactly the same process; however, figure 11.8 is a logical description whereas figure 11.25 is a physical description. To ensure completeness all the data flows relating to the production cycle appear in table 11.2 on page 502.

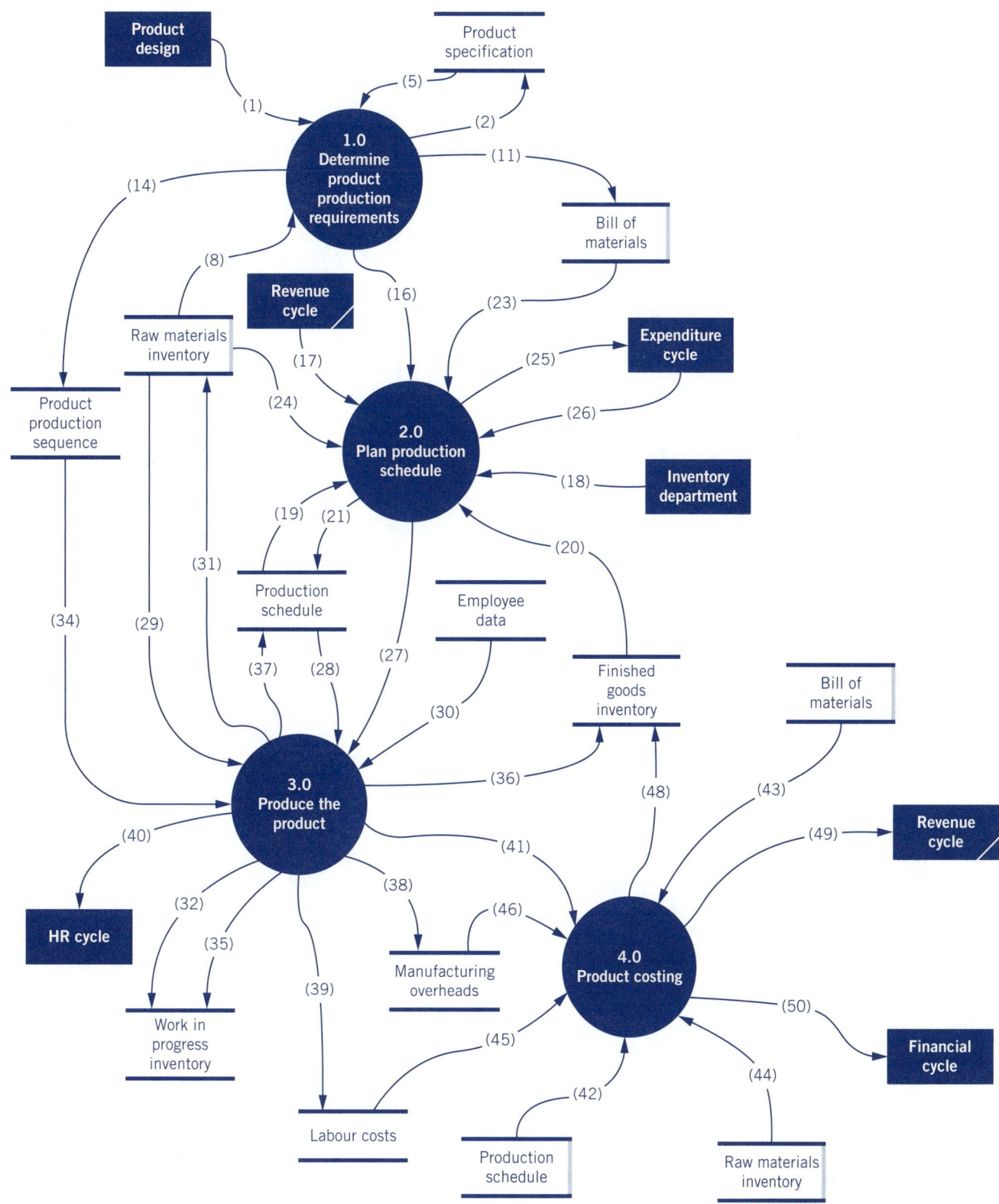

**FIGURE 11.6** Production cycle level 0 logical diagram

**TABLE 11.2** Description of logical data flows in the production cycle

| Flow # | Typical data source | Typical data destination | Data description | Explanation of the logical data flow |
|---|---|---|---|---|
| **Process 1.0 Determine product production requirements** | | | | |
| 1 | Product designers | Computer | Newly designed product details | Once the design team have finalised a new product specification they forward details of the product to the product planning staff. |
| 2 | Computer | Product specifications data store | New product details | Details of the product design are stored in the product specification data store. |
| 3; 4 | These flows take place physically between production planning staff and the computer; they happen within the 1.0 bubble in the logical diagram. | | | |
| 5 | Product specifications data store | Product planning staff | New product details | The product planning staff retrieve details of the new product so they can plan the production requirements. |
| 6 | Action new product notification | Calculate production requirements | Trigger for next process | Once the new product has been retrieved and examined the associated production requirements can be calculated (not shown in a level 0 diagram). |
| 7 | This flow takes place physically between production planning staff and the computer; it happens within the 1.0 bubble in the logical diagram. | | | |
| 8 | Raw materials inventory | Product planning staff | Inventory details | Product planning staff use the data from the product specification to determine whether raw materials are available for the newly designed product. If a raw material is required that is not currently held in inventory a request is sent to inventory management to arrange supply of the new materials. |
| 9; 10 | These flows take place physically between production planning staff and the computer; they happen within the 1.0 bubble in the logical diagram. | | | |
| 11 | Product planning staff | Bill of materials data store | Product component details | Product planning staff use data from the product specification and the raw materials inventory data to create a detailed list of all the materials required to produce the new product. |
| 12; 13 | These flows take place physically between production planning staff and the computer; they happen within the 1.0 bubble in the logical diagram. | | | |
| 14 | Product planning staff | Product production sequence data store | Product production sequence details | Product planning staff use data from the product specification to create a detailed list describing how to manufacture the new product. |
| 15 | This flow takes place physically between production planning staff and the computer; it happens within the 1.0 bubble in the logical diagram. | | | |
| 16 | Product planning staff | Production planning staff | Product production details | Once the product production details have been determined and documented the new product can be added into production scheduling. |

| Flow # | Typical data source | Typical data destination | Data description | Explanation of the logical data flow |
|---|---|---|---|---|
| **Process 2.0 Plan production schedule** | | | | |
| 17 | Sales forecasts | Production planning staff | Details of forecasted sales | The calculated product demand (forecasted sales) of finished goods is received from the revenue cycle. |
| 18 | Inventory department | Production planning staff | Requests for finished goods | Product demand may also be received from predetermined automatic reorder points in the inventory management system. |
| 19 | Production schedule data store | Production planning staff | Scheduled production details | The current production schedule is obtained and used to identify what quantity of goods has already been scheduled for future production. |
| 20 | Finished goods inventory data store | Production planning staff | Details of current finished goods inventory | The current level of finished goods on hand is obtained in order to accurately calculate quantities required to be manufactured. |
| 21 | Production planning staff | Production schedule data store | Updated scheduled production details | Once the quantity and types of goods required to be manufactured has been determined the production schedule is updated. |
| 22 | Create production schedule | Identify materials requirements | Trigger for next process | Once the production schedule has been updated the materials required to produce these products can be identified (not shown in a level 0 diagram). |
| 23 | Bill of materials data store | Production planning staff | Details of bill of materials | The details of all raw materials required are obtained from the bill of materials for each product included on the production schedule. These data are used to calculate the total production material requirements. |
| 24 | Raw materials inventory data store | Production planning staff | Details of raw materials available | The raw materials inventory is queried to see what materials will be available for planned production run. |
| 25 | Production planning staff | Expenditure cycle (purchasing) | Details of raw materials required for scheduled production | Production planning staff create and send a purchase requisition for any additional required raw materials. |
| 26 | Expenditure cycle (purchasing) | Production planning staff | Details of raw materials ordered for scheduled production | Purchasing staff involved in the expenditure cycle advise the expected delivery date for the raw materials requested. |
| 27 | Plan production schedule | Produce the product | Updated scheduled production details | Once the production schedule is finalised and raw materials requirements have been identified the production schedule is complete. |
| **Process 3.0 Produce the product** | | | | |
| 28 | Production schedule data store | Production operations staff | Finalised scheduled production details | The data relevant to the production schedule for the day is extracted. |

*(continued)*

**TABLE 11.2** (continued)

| Flow # | Typical data source | Typical data destination | Data description | Explanation of the logical data flow |
|---|---|---|---|---|
| 29 | Raw materials inventory data store | Production operations staff | Details of raw materials available for scheduled production | Production operations staff query details of stocks of raw materials available for the planned day's production. |
| 30 | Employee data store | Production operations staff | Details of labour available for scheduled production | Production operations staff query the employee data store to ensure that sufficient labour is available for the planned day's production. |
| 31 | Production operations staff | Raw materials inventory data store | Details of raw materials moved into the production environment | The raw materials inventory is updated to record the reduction in raw material stock levels caused by moving raw materials into the work in progress inventory. |
| 32 | Production operations staff | Work in progress inventory data store | Details of raw materials moved into the production environment | The work in progress inventory is updated to record the increase in stock levels caused by moving raw materials into the work in progress inventory. |
| 33 | Assemble required resources | Execute production schedule | Trigger for next process | Once all resources are checked and assembled the production run can commence (not shown in a level 0 diagram). |
| 34 | Product production sequence data store | Production operations staff | Details of the production sequence for each product to be produced | The production sequence for each of the products included in the day's production schedule is extracted for use in the day's production. |
| 35 | Production operations staff | Work in progress inventory data store | Details of the products produced | After the scheduled production has been completed the work in progress inventory is updated (reduced) to reflect items moved to finished goods inventory. |
| 36 | Production operations staff | Finished goods inventory data store | Details of the products produced | The finished goods inventory is updated (increased) to reflect the new products now available as a result of the production run. |
| 37 | Production operations staff | Production schedule data store | Details of the days production results | The production schedule is updated to record completion of the production run. |
| 38 | Production operations staff | Manufacturing overheads data store | Details of manufacturing overhead costs | Any overhead costs incurred during production are recorded in the manufacturing overheads data store. |
| 39 | Production operations staff | Labour costs data store | Details of labour costs | Labour costs incurred during production are recorded in the labour costs data store. |
| 40 | Production operations staff | Human resources cycle | Employee labour details | Details of the hours worked and duties performed by each employee during production are sent to the human resources cycle to facilitate payroll calculations. |

| Flow # | Typical data source | Typical data destination | Data description | Explanation of the logical data flow |
|---|---|---|---|---|
| 41 | Production operations staff | Product costing staff | Details of the day's production costs | Once production is complete product costing can commence. |
| **Process 4.0 Product costing** | | | | |
| 42 | Production schedule data store | Product costing staff | Details of the products produced | Details of the quantity and type of products produced are obtained from the production schedule data store. |
| 43 | Bill of materials data store | Product costing staff | Details of the materials required for each product | Details of the raw materials used for each type of product manufactured as shown in the production schedule are obtained from the relevant bill of materials. |
| 44 | Raw materials inventory data store | Product costing staff | Details of raw material costs | Details of raw material costs for each product manufactured, based on the data recorded in the bill of materials for that product, are obtained from the raw materials inventory records. |
| 45 | Labour costs data store | Product costing staff | Details of labour costs | Details of direct labour costs incurred during production are obtained from the labour costs data store. |
| 46 | Manufacturing overheads data store | Product costing staff | Details of manufacturing overheads applied | Details of manufacturing overheads allocated are obtained from the manufacturing overheads data store. |
| 47 | Calculate costs | Record costs | Trigger for next process | Once details of all relevant production costs have been retrieved and checked, the cost of production can be recorded (not shown in a level 0 diagram). |
| 48 | Product costing staff | Finished goods inventory | Details of costs of finished goods produced | The calculated manufacturing cost for each individual product type is stored in the finished goods inventory data store. |
| 49 | Product costing staff | Revenue cycle | Details of costs of finished goods produced | The revenue cycle is notified of costs relating to individual products. This data is used to determine the selling price for the manufactured products. |
| 50 | Product costing staff | Financial cycle | Details of costs of finished goods produced | Summarised details of the production costs are sent through to the financial cycle to enable cost reporting and variance analysis. |

**LEARNING OBJECTIVE 5**

*Analyse risks and develop control plans pertinent to the primary activities in the production cycle.*

# PRODUCTION CYCLE ACTIVITIES AND RELATED RISKS AND CONTROLS

The activities within the production cycle and the associated risks and controls are described under the four production process headings below. Following the activity descriptions for each of the processes is the level 1 DFD for the process and a table summarising the activities, risks and controls within the process.

## Determine product production requirements — activities, risks and controls

Process 1.0, determine product production requirements, comprises the following activities.

### Action new product notification

The production cycle starts when a new product has been developed. Product development is undertaken by specialised research and development staff. (The product development process is not documented as part of the production cycle.) The production cycle is triggered by advice that a new product design has been finalised. This would typically be electronic, in the form of an output from computer aided design software (CAD), but could also take the form of a memo, or an email, or even a cross-departmental meeting at which new products are launched and discussed. The first thing that product planning staff need to do is examine the product details so they can plan the production requirements for the new product. Product planning staff need to be able to identify exactly what materials and equipment are required to make the product, so a detailed product specification must be obtained from the design staff. Details of the product design are stored in the product specification data store. The primary risk attached to actioning new product notifications is failing to action a product. This risk can be diminished by use of controls such as automatically transferring new product details into the production planning workflow, and **exception reporting** identifying any new designs created but not actioned within a reasonable period of time. The frequency of new products will determine the importance of controls in this area. A company which routinely has large numbers of new products will also have a higher risk of some of these products not moving into production, so controls would need to be tighter; a company that has very few new products would not find it as necessary to formalise controls in this area.

### Calculate production requirements

Once the existence of a new product has been recognised and recorded, the production requirements can be calculated. This activity involves performing detailed planning for the new product to identify and record the materials required to manufacture the product, and the operational steps involved in manufacturing the product. Product planning staff retrieve details of the new product so they can plan the production requirements. Product-level plans are used at a later stage in the process; they form a major data source for production planning.

Product planning staff use the data from the detailed product specification to determine whether the raw materials required are currently stocked and available. Ideally the product specification will contain sufficiently detailed information about the raw materials. Product planning staff read the specification and compare the materials described to available inventory materials in order to determine if anything new is required. Raw material details would be obtained from the raw materials inventory data store. It is vital that the staff member performing this job has a good knowledge of the inventory items and can competently read and comprehend the product specifications. Raw material specifications need to be precise in order to avoid a situation where an unsuitable inventory items is chosen or a new inventory item is requested unnecessarily. If a raw material is required that is not currently held in inventory a request needs to be sent to inventory staff to arrange supply of the new material. The entire process of calculating production requirements can be automated, requiring design staff to access raw materials inventory directly and specify the product requirements as part of the design process. The process documented in this chapter shows the request for a new raw material being sent to a specialised inventory management section; however, this request could also go directly to the purchasing process in the form of a purchase requisition. If the request was sent directly to the purchasing process it would need to be sent at a later stage, once volumes of the material required had been determined during production planning. The process as documented allows for a situation where new inventory items are independently sourced, approved and added to the inventory catalogue, allowing for purchase requests for these items to be processed as required at a later date. Providing advance notice of new material requirements allows the activity of material sourcing to be conducted separately from material purchasing. It also acts to reduce the risk of delays in the process, which may occur if the need for a new raw material is not advised until production planning is underway.

Product planning staff use data from the product specification and the raw materials inventory data to create a bill of materials for the product. Each product manufactured will have its own unique bill of materials, a detailed list of all the raw materials required to produce one unit of the product. Figure 11.7 shows an example of an input screen used when creating a bill of materials. Details of the materials required to make the product are stored in the bill of materials data store. The bill of materials is vital to production planning; use of an inaccurate bill of materials will result in production delays and errors. To reduce the risk of poor bill of materials design any new or changed bill of materials should be checked and approved by production management, or by staff involved in the initial product design.

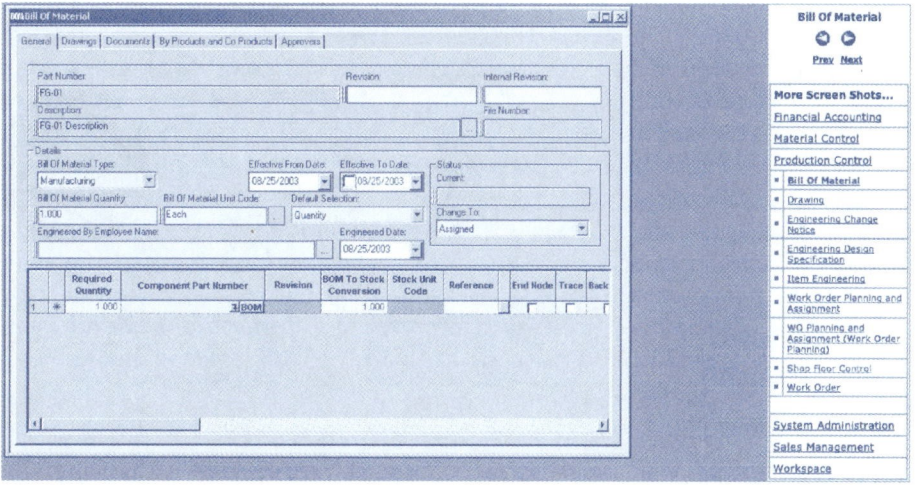

**FIGURE 11.7** Bill of material screen

Product planning staff also use data from the product specification to create a detailed description of how to manufacture the new product. This detailed list is known as the production sequence for the product and includes details of the individual steps required to manufacture the product, the equipment used when making the product, and timings for the production of the new product. The primary risk encountered is the possibility of errors in the production sequence. This risk can be minimised by requiring that the product production sequence be checked and approved by production management, or by staff involved in the initial product design.

Once the product's bill of materials and production sequence have been determined, approved and documented the new product can be added into production scheduling.

## Determine product production requirements — DFD

The level 1 DFD in figure 11.8 contains a lower level of detail about the first process represented in the level 0 logical DFD in figure 11.6. In the same way in which the level 0 logical diagram explodes out the 'production cycle' bubble in the context diagram, the level 1 diagram explodes out the 'determine product production requirements' bubble.

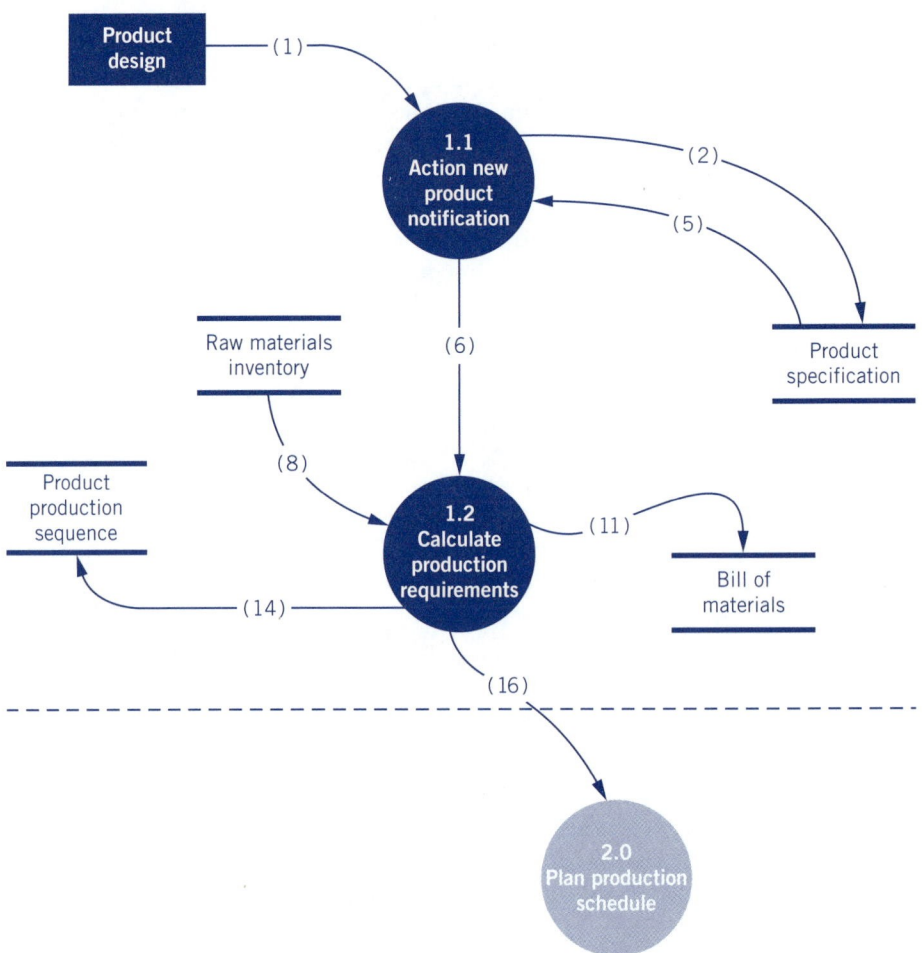

**FIGURE 11.8** Production cycle level 1 logical diagram — process 1.0 Determine product production requirements

## Summary description of activities in determining product production requirements

Table 11.3 summarises the activities, risks and controls when determining production requirements, as depicted in figure 11.8. Table 11.2 explains the logical data flows depicted in figure 11.8. Exploring the diagram in conjunction with the material contained in the tables will assist in improving your understanding of the process depicted.

**TABLE 11.3** Activities in determining product production requirements

| Activity # | Activity | Usually conducted by: | Activity description | Typical risks encountered | Common controls |
|---|---|---|---|---|---|
| 1.1 | Action new product notification | Product planning staff | After receiving advice that a new product design has been finalised, product planning staff need to retrieve and examine the product details so they can plan the production requirements for the new product. | Failure to action new product | Automated follow-up activities Exception reporting of any new designs not actioned within a reasonable period of time |
| 1.2 | Calculate production requirements | Product planning staff | Performing detailed planning for the new product to ascertain all the individual materials required to manufacture the product, and all the mechanical steps involved in manufacturing the product. | Poor bill of materials design | Approval of bill of materials by production management |
| | | | | Errors in manufacturing sequence | Approval of sequencing by production management |

## Plan production schedule — activities, risks and controls

Process 2.0, plan production schedule, comprises the following activities.

### Create production schedule

Creating a production schedule involves calculating future demand for products to determine how many of each product need to be produced. Once the overall demand has been forecast the production planners need to work within the constraints of resource availability (machinery, labour and raw materials) to produce a viable schedule and meet the forecast demand. An example of a production schedule is shown in figure 11.9 overleaf.

Forecasted demand for products can be received from the revenue cycle, where it is calculated based on previous sales history. This document is often called a work order. An example input screen for a work order is shown in figure 11.10 overleaf. Note that adequate controls are necessary in the sales process to achieve accurate and complete sales records and accurately determine demand. If there are flaws in the sales data then production demand will also be incorrectly calculated.

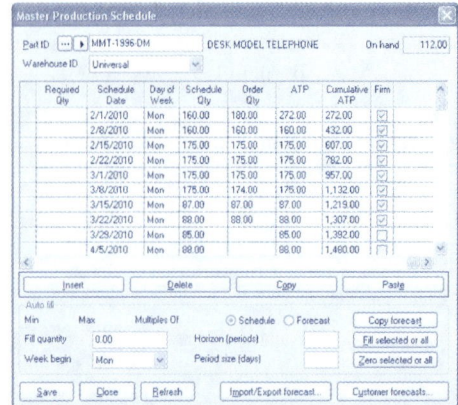

**FIGURE 11.9** Production schedule screen
*Source:* Infor ERP Visual.

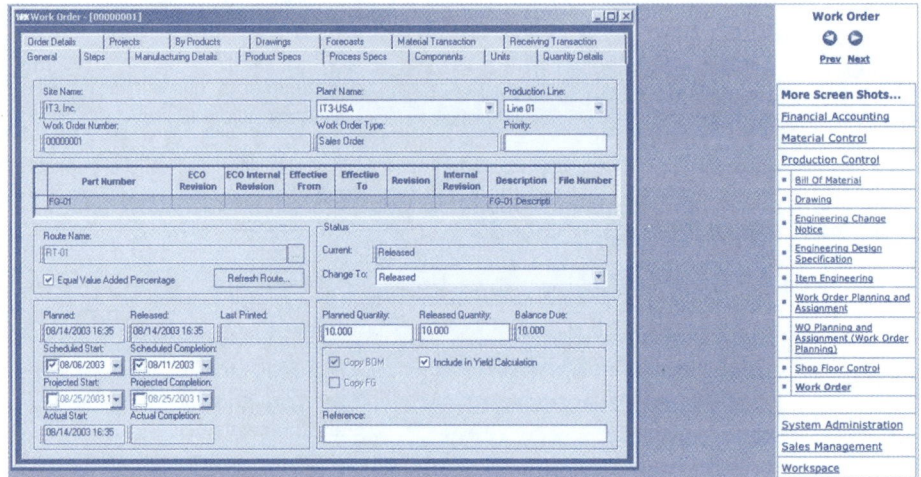

**FIGURE 11.10** Work order screen

**Automatic reorder points** An inventory order point based on predefined minimum inventory levels recorded for individual items. When the stock on hand drops down to this level a purchase requisition is automatically generated.

Product demand may also be received from predetermined **automatic reorder points** in the inventory management system. Automated reorder points for goods that need to be manufactured are similar to those for goods that are purchased from a third party as discussed in chapter 10; however, the timing of the trigger point needs to take production capabilities and lead times into consideration. The primary risk is under or overestimating product demand. This risk can be controlled by requiring separate checking and authorisation of demand forecasts, or by automating product demand calculations. Precision in demand forecasting is vital; however, the risk of incorrect forecasts can be reduced by the use of a flexible manufacturing system (FMS). Use of an FMS will allow production systems to react more rapidly if production requirements vary, acting as a natural buffer to protect against demand forecast inaccuracies. An organisation that has an inflexible manufacturing system would need to ensure higher levels of precision in the planning process as the time required to detect and correct inaccurate production plans may be quite lengthy.

After the demand forecast has been finalised the current production schedule should be used to identify what quantity of goods has already been scheduled for future production. Figure 11.11 shows an example of data relating to future production and demand.

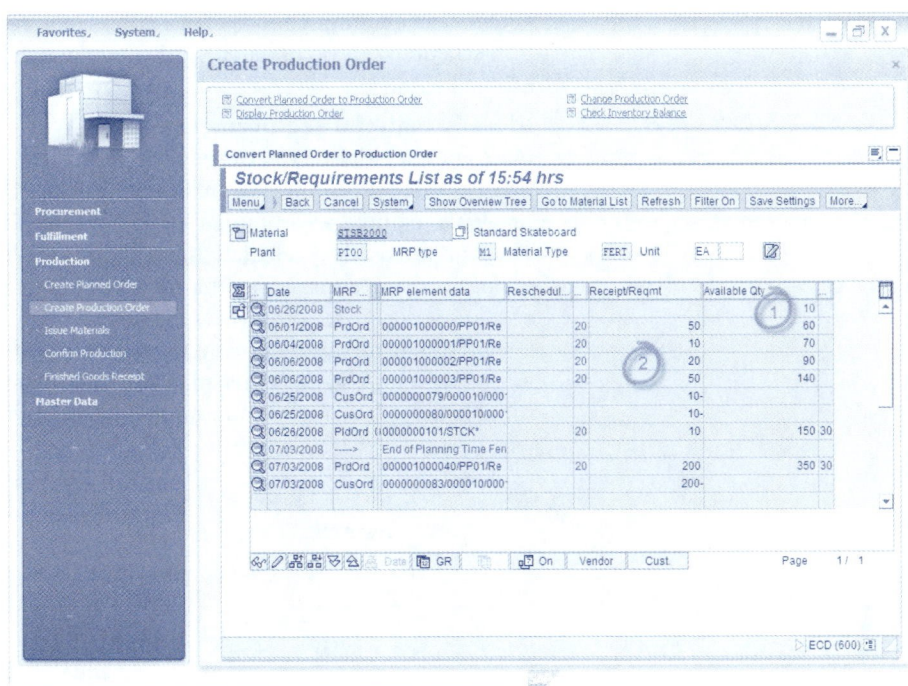

**FIGURE 11.11** Stock requirements list screen
*Source:* © Copyright SAP AG 2008.

Overall production schedules are typically planned on a regular basis, often a month or more in advance, and are eventually broken down into a series of daily production runs or batches. To ensure appropriate numbers of products are being produced it is important to incorporate any and all future planned production into the production planning process. In addition to any planned production, the current level of finished goods on hand must be incorporated into production planning in order to accurately calculate quantities required to be manufactured. An example of this planning calculation is shown in figure 11.12. This example assumes planning in late May for production in July.

| Product description | Chrome widgets | Black widgets |
|---|---|---|
| Product # | WC23452 | WB23489 |
| Forecast sales — June | 23 000 | 12 000 |
| Forecasted sales — July | 20 000 | 18 000 |
| **Total required** | 43 000 | 30 000 |
| Production planned — June | 20 000 | 15 000 |
| Current stock on hand | 4 000 | 2 000 |
| **Total available** | 24 000 | 17 000 |
| **Minimum production level required for July** | 19 000 | 13 000 |

**FIGURE 11.12** Production planning calculation example

Once the quantities and types of goods required have been determined the production schedule can be updated, and the materials required to produce these products can be identified.

### Identify material requirements

Once the quantity of each product required has been determined the raw materials needed to provision the production plan must be identified. The details of all the raw materials required are obtained by reference to the bill of materials for each product. The data are used to calculate the total production material requirements, by multiplying all the materials listed on the bill of materials for each product by the number of that product to be produced.

Once the materials required have been calculated the raw materials inventory needs to be queried to see whether materials will be available for the planned production run. Figure 11.13 contains an example raw materials inventory report.

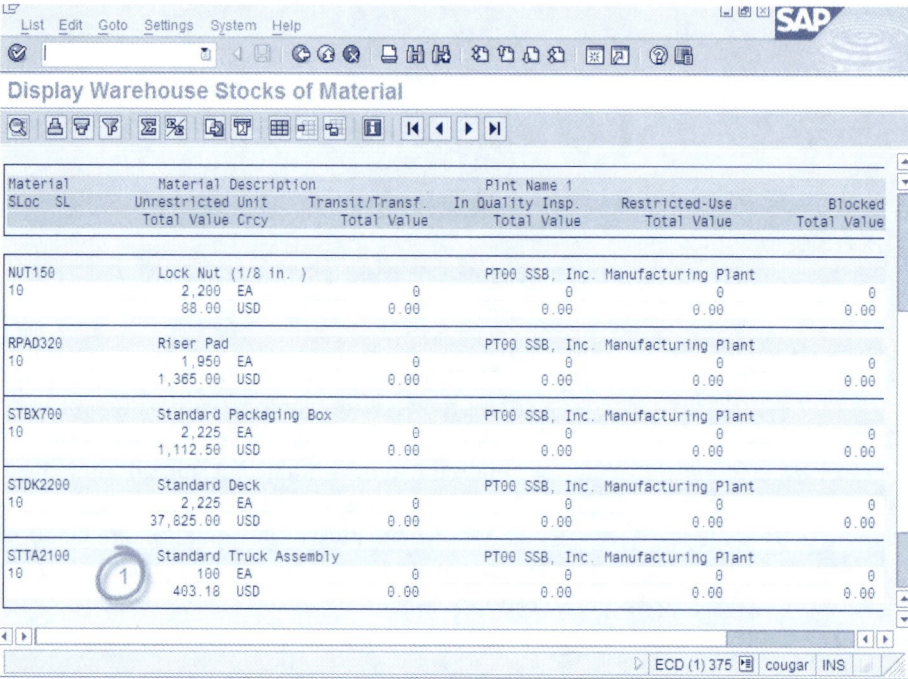

**FIGURE 11.13** Inventory report for raw materials
*Source:* © Copyright SAP AG 2008.

A **purchase requisition** is an internal document used to indicate an approved request for goods or services. The purchase requisition is used to support the purchase order.

Note that the raw materials inventory data should include materials on hand, already allocated to production, and on order. This inventory level calculation should be done well in advance and on a daily basis if production schedules are planned on a daily basis; overall monthly planning is of no use if the production line is forced to sit idle for days or even weeks awaiting delivery of an essential raw material. If additional inventory of raw materials is identified as being required to meet production scheduling, production planning staff would create and send a **purchase requisition** for these raw materials. An example of this is shown in figure 11.14. This purchase requisition could be created manually but more likely would be automatically generated by the production planning software once the production schedule is finalised. An example of a materials requisition input screen is shown in figure 11.15. The required quantities may be adjusted upwards to allow for economic order quantities. As an example, it may be necessary to order paint in multiples of 100 litres, or nails by the 10 000.

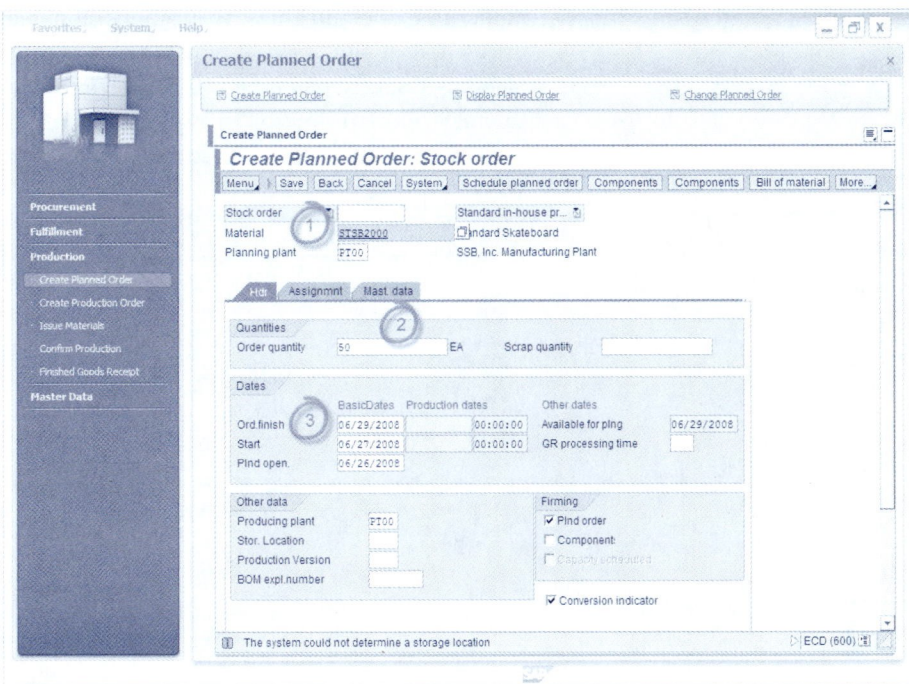

**FIGURE 11.14** Planned order creation screen
*Source:* © Copyright SAP AG 2008.

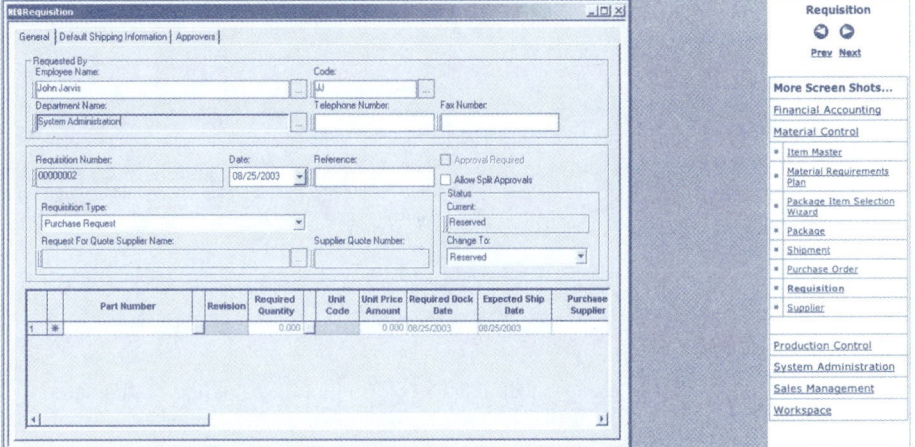

**FIGURE 11.15** Materials requisition screen

Purchasing staff involved in the expenditure cycle need to advise production planning staff of the expected delivery date for the raw materials requested. Production planning staff should check to ensure that sufficient quantities of all raw materials will be available in time to meet the production schedule. Once the production schedule is finalised and raw materials requirements have been identified, the production schedule is complete. Figure 11.16 overleaf contains an example of a production schedule status screen.

The major risk in this activity is under or overestimating materials requirements. Common controls to reduce this risk include requiring independent approval and authorisation of purchase requisitions and materials requirements, and automatic calculation of raw material requirements such as that provided when using a manufacturing resource planning (MRP) system discussed earlier. An additional risk relates to under or overutilisation of available resources, which can be reduced by use of specialised production planning software such as computer aided manufacturing (CAM) systems, also discussed earlier in this chapter.

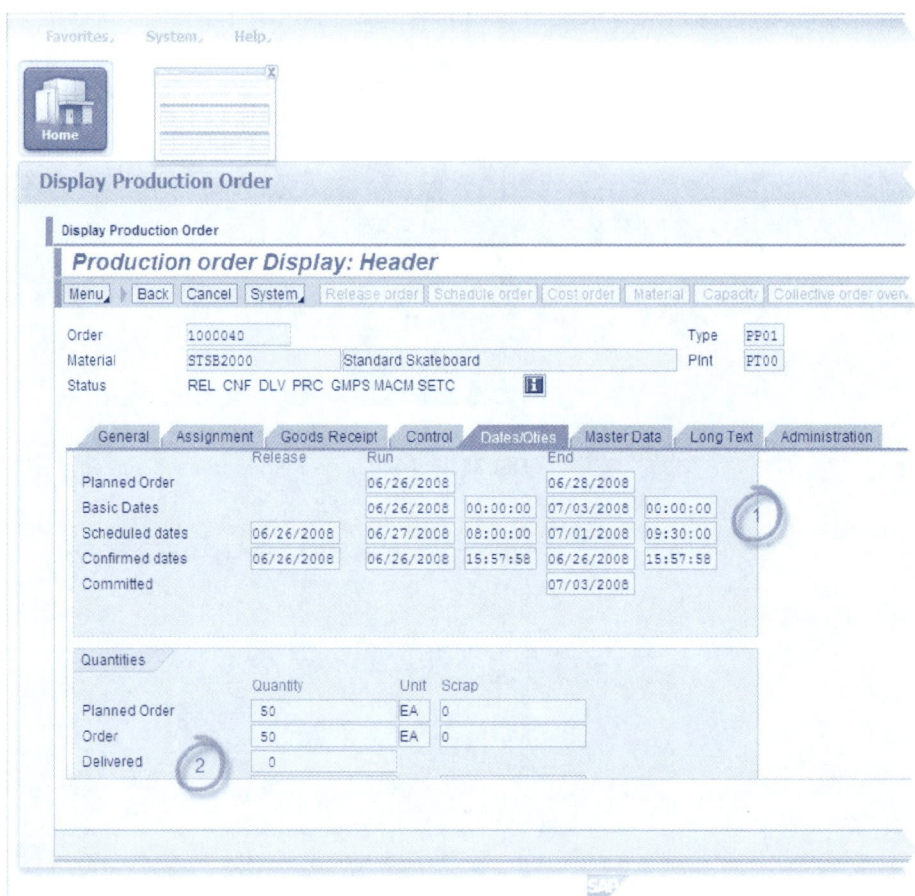

**FIGURE 11.16** Production schedule status screen

Note that adequate controls are necessary in the inventory management and purchasing processes to ensure timely and accurate raw materials inventory data. If there are flaws in the inventory data then materials requirements will also be incorrectly calculated.

## Plan production schedule — DFD

The level 1 DFD in figure 11.17 contains a lower level of detail about the second process represented in the level 0 logical DFD in figure 11.6. This process takes place after the new product production requirements have been created in the preceding process and prior to products being produced in the following process.

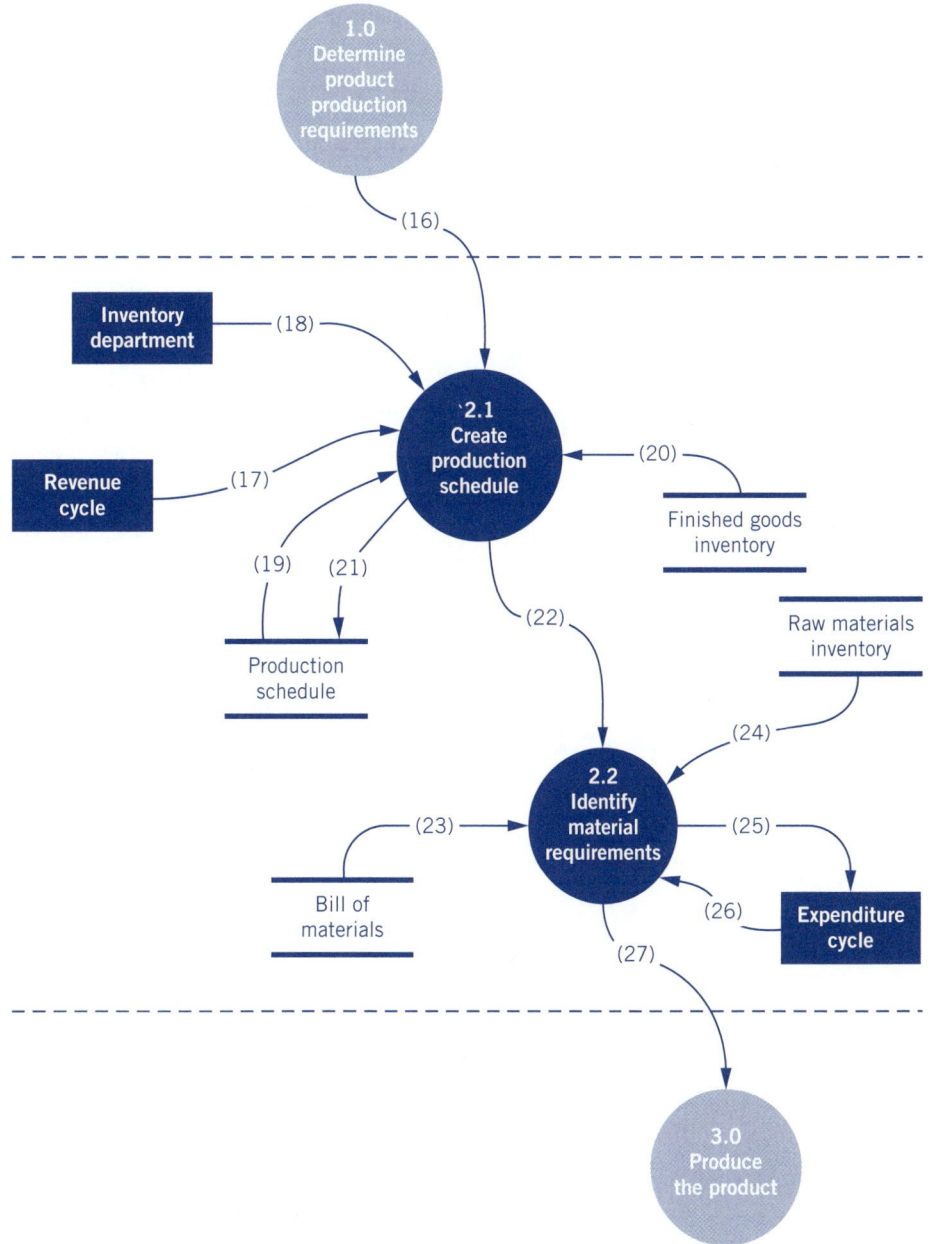

**FIGURE 11.17** Production cycle level 1 logical diagram — process 2.0 Plan production schedule

## *Summary description of activities in planning the production schedule*

Table 11.4 overleaf summarises the activities, risks and controls when planning the production schedule, as depicted in figure 11.17. Table 11.2 (page 502) explains the logical data flows depicted in figure 11.17. Exploring the diagram in conjunction with the material contained in the tables will assist in improving your understanding of the process depicted.

**TABLE 11.4** Activities in planning the production schedule

| Activity # | Activity | Usually conducted by: | Activity description | Typical risks encountered | Common controls |
|---|---|---|---|---|---|
| 2.1 | Create production schedule | Production planning staff | The schedule of production for a future time period is determined. This production schedule involves calculating demand for products to determine how many of each product to produce. Planners need to work within the constraints of resource availability (machinery, labour and raw materials) to produce a viable schedule. | Under/overestimating product demand<br><br><br><br><br><br>Underutilisation of available resources | Separate approval of production schedules<br>Automation of product demand calculations<br>Flexible manufacturing systems (FMSs) to enable agility and flexibility<br>Using accurate and timely sales forecasts<br>Using specialised production planning software such as computer aided manufacturing (CAM) systems |
| 2.2 | Identify material requirements | Production planning staff | Once the numbers of each product to be produced have been determined the raw materials available to support this production plan must be identified and obtained. | Under/overestimate materials requirements | Approval and authorisation of material requisitions<br>Automation of raw material requirements<br>Timely and accurate raw materials inventory data<br>Using manufacturing resource planning (MRP) systems |

## Produce the product — activities, risks and controls

Process 3.0, produce the product, comprises the following activities.

### Assemble required resources

The daily production schedule needs to be extracted and checked each morning. This extraction should ideally be automated and triggered by the production date stored in the production schedule data. At the start of the day, before production starts, production operations staff should check that all resources detailed on the production schedule for the day's production run are available and ready for use.

The first thing that production operations staff need to check is whether there are sufficient raw materials available for the planned day's production. If there are not enough raw materials available to support the planned production, production management should be consulted to amend the day's production schedule.

The raw material required should be obtained from the warehouse. This transfer of goods must be accompanied by some form of paperwork, authorising the release of the materials to production staff. An example of this is shown in figure 11.18. This paperwork is known as a material requisition. After the raw materials are issued the raw materials inventory should be updated to record the reduction in stock levels caused by moving the raw materials. The work in progress inventory also needs to be updated to record the increase in stock levels caused by issuing the raw materials. This transfer would ideally be automated, either by use of barcodes and RFIDs on the stock items, or it could be triggered by the processing and input of the material requisition. Any movement of inventory carries a risk of theft of the inventory items; this risk can be reduced by restricting access to inventory and production areas, documenting all transfers and movements of inventory items in a timely manner, and conducting periodic stock counts of inventory.

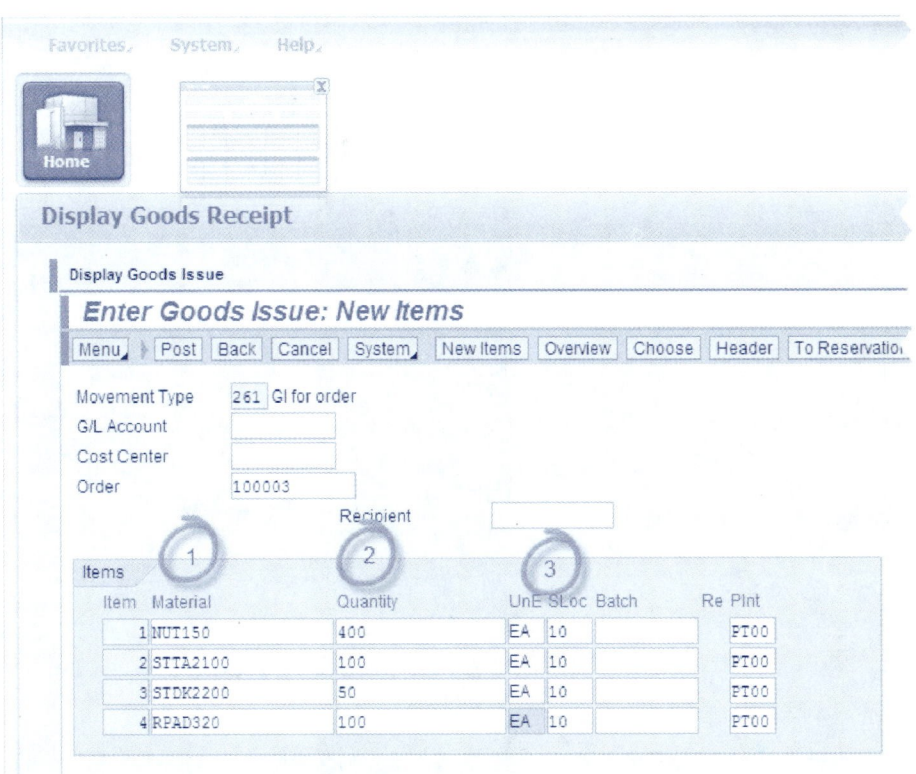

**FIGURE 11.18** Material requisition screen
*Source:* © Copyright SAP AG 2008.

Production operations staff also need to check whether sufficient labour is available for the planned day's production. This might be as simple as a headcount where production operations are small, or it may be necessary to check staff time records to determine who is required to work that day and whether they are present at work. If there is not sufficient labour available to support the planned production run, production management should be consulted to determine whether to amend the day's production schedule. Alternatively it might be possible to recruit additional short-term labour. Once all the required resources have been checked and assembled, the production run can commence.

## Execute production schedule

The production run is undertaken based on information contained in the production schedule. The production schedule details which products are to be produced, how many of each product is required, the resources required to produce these products, and the production sequence for each product. Figure 11.19 overleaf shows an example production schedule. The process of actually producing and manufacturing products is beyond the scope of this book; however, references have been included in the further reading section at the end of this chapter for those interested in learning more about manufacturing systems. The primary risk related to the production run is disruption of production through, for example, a machine failure. In order to reduce this risk the following controls are suggested: arranging access to an alternative power supply such as a generator, establishing a well-documented disaster recovery plan and ensuring staff are trained in the use and maintenance of production equipment.

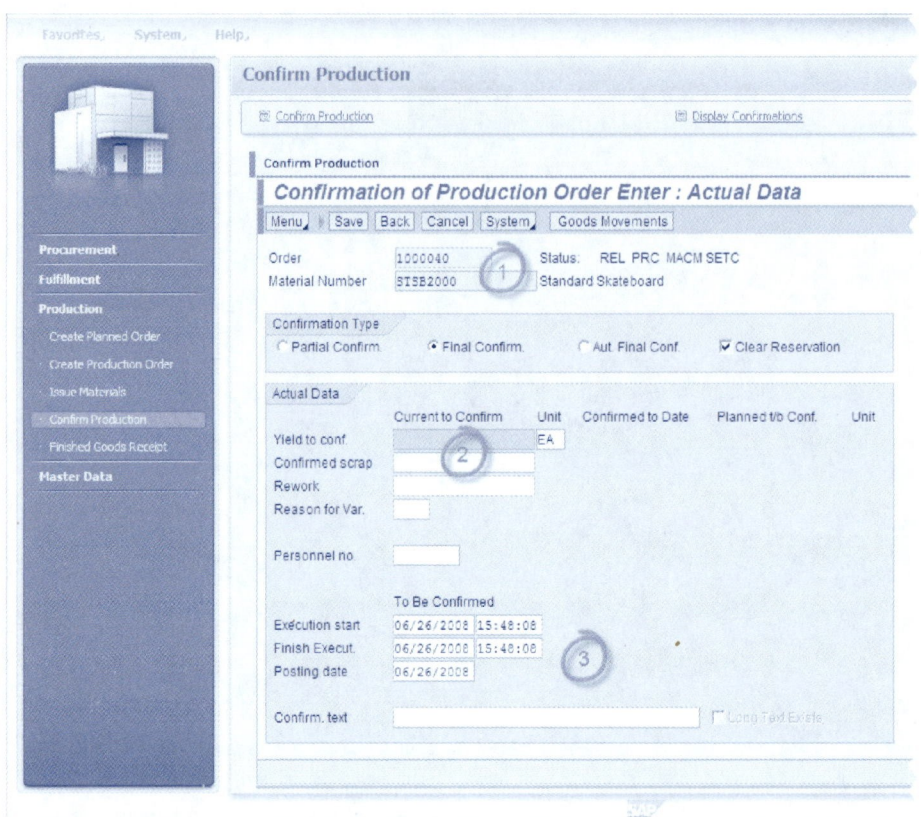

**FIGURE 11.19** Production schedule screen
*Source:* © Copyright SAP AG 2008.

After the scheduled production has been completed the work in progress inventory should be reduced to reflect items moved into the finished goods inventory. Figure 11.20 shows an example of this. The finished goods inventory is correspondingly increased to reflect the new products' availability as a result of the production run. The production schedule also needs to be updated to record the successful completion of the production run.

Any overhead costs incurred during production are recorded in the manufacturing overheads data store. Manufacturing overheads includes costs for elec-tricity used to operate the production equipment, depreciation on the production equipment and buildings, and any miscellaneous factory supplies such as oil or cleaning products. Personnel related costs other than labour costs for those people directly involved in the production process (e.g. cleaners, security guards, maintenance staff) are also part of manufacturing overheads. Direct labour costs incurred are recorded in the labour costs data store, and details of the hours worked and duties performed by each employee are also sent to the human resources cycle to facilitate payroll calculations. Once production is complete, product costing can commence.

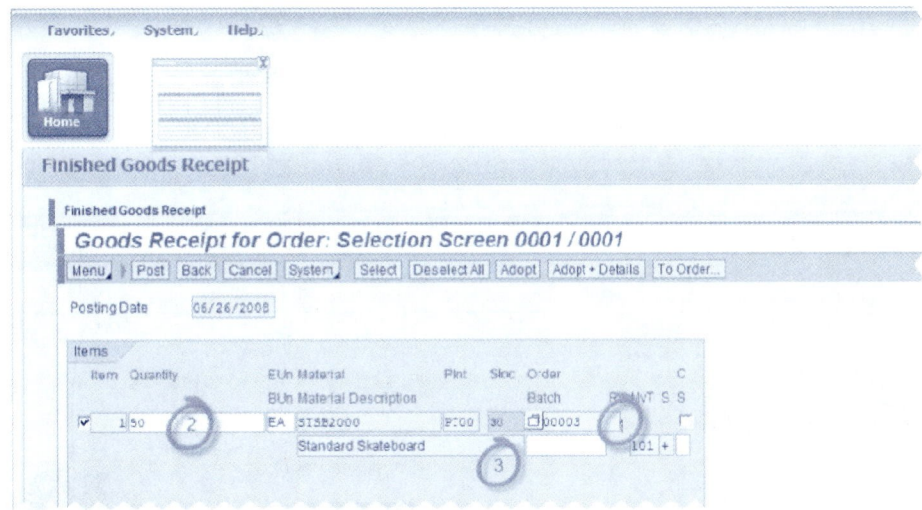

**FIGURE 11.20** Goods receipt for production order screen
*Source:* © Copyright SAP AG 2008.

### Produce the product — DFD

The level 1 DFD in figure 11.21 overleaf contains a lower level of detail about the third process represented in the level 0 logical DFD in figure 11.6. This process takes place after the production schedule planning has occurred in the preceding process and before product costing is undertaken in the following process.

### Summary description of activities in producing the product

Table 11.5 summarises the activities when producing the product, as depicted in figure 11.21. Table 11.2 (page 502) explains the logical data flows depicted in figure 11.21. Exploring the diagram in conjunction with the material contained in the tables will assist in improving your understanding of the process depicted.

**TABLE 11.5** Activities in producing the product

| Activity # | Activity | Usually conducted by: | Activity description | Typical risks encountered | Common controls |
|---|---|---|---|---|---|
| 3.1 | Assemble required resources | Production operations staff | The production operations staff check that all resources detailed on the production schedule for the day's production run are available and ready for use. If any required resource is not available, the operations staff should consult with planning staff and production management to determine how to amend the day's production schedule. | Theft of inventory items | Restricting access to production areas<br>Documenting all transfers and movements of inventory items<br>Periodic stock counts of inventory |
| 3.2 | Execute production schedule | Production operations staff | The production run is undertaken using the information contained in the production schedule relating to the number of each type of product required to be manufactured, the resources required for these products, and the production sequence for each product. | Disruption of production (e.g. machine failure) | Providing access to an alternative power supply such as a generator<br>Having a well documented disaster recovery plan<br>Appropriate staff training |

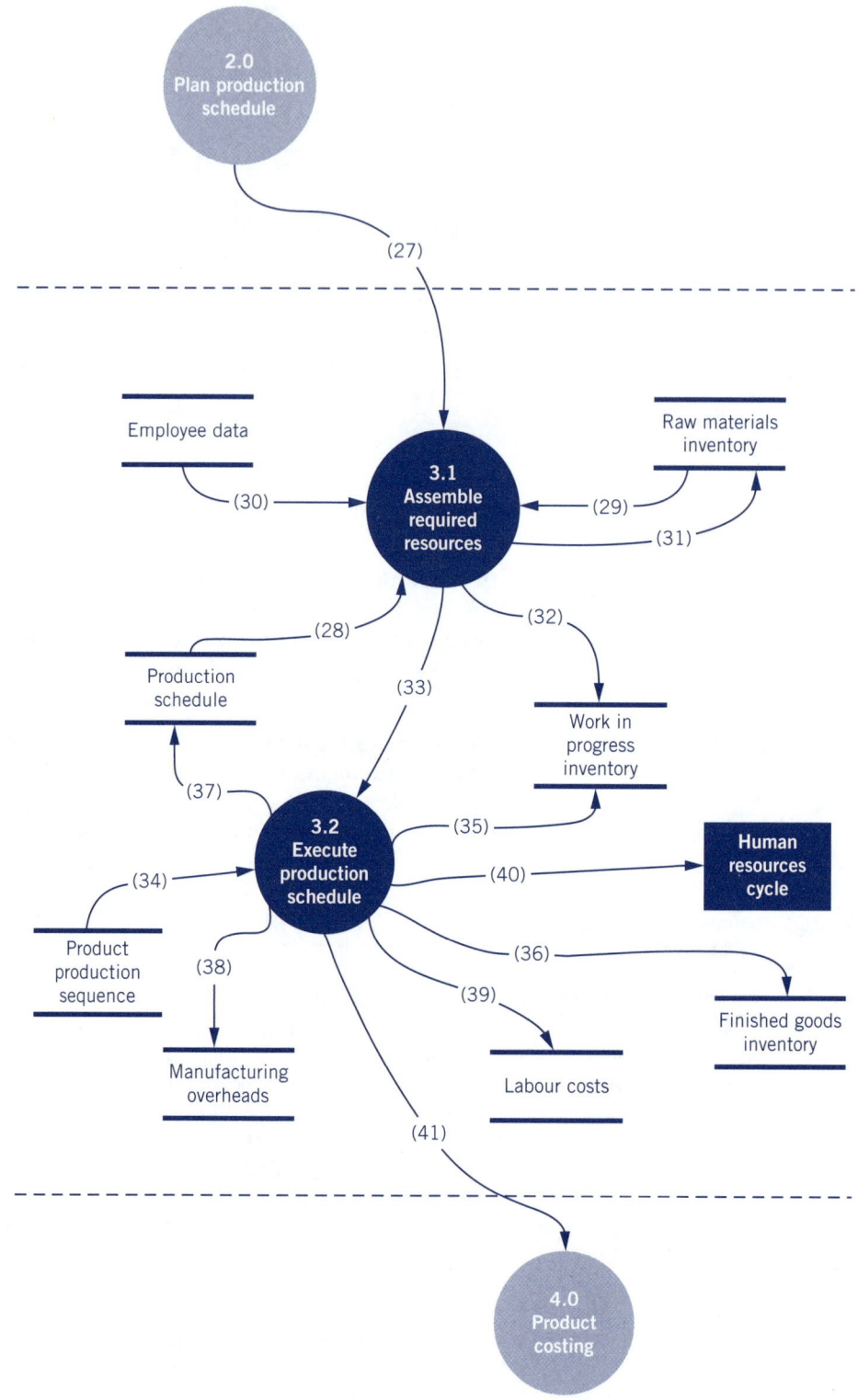

**FIGURE 11.21** Production cycle level 1 logical diagram — process 3.0 Produce the product

# Product costing — activities, risks and controls

Process 4.0, product costing, comprises the following activities.

### Calculate costs

How costs are assigned to products has an impact on the measurement of an individual product's profitability and on the pricing of that item. To allow product costing to be undertaken, details of all the costs incurred during the production cycle are accumulated, including costs relating to labour, raw materials and manufacturing overheads. This data is used to calculate total production costs incurred and apply those costs to individual products. The algorithms used to apply costs are vital. These algorithms must capture as closely as possible the true cost of manufacturing the product. If product costs are misstated, poor decision making is inevitable. Costs related to direct labour and raw materials are easy to allocate correctly via the use of product or job numbers assigned as the costs are incurred. The allocation of manufacturing overheads can be performed using a number of different methods. One way of allocating manufacturing overhead costs is to apply costs based on the proportion of direct labour allocated to the product; another way is to allocate costs based on machine time devoted to producing that product. An example of traditional cost accounting is shown in figure 11.22.

An alternative to this form of cost allocation is activity based costing, where production is broken down into a sequence of activities and the costs of performing each of those activities forms the basis of cost allocation. An example of activity based costing is shown in figure 11.23 overleaf. The further reading section at the end of this chapter suggests a reading on activity based costing.

| Overhead costs | $3 000 000 | | |
| --- | --- | --- | --- |
| Number of labour hours | 100 000 | | |
| Rate per hour | $30 | | |
| | **Product A** | **Product B** | **Product C** |
| Parts | 50 | 100 | 150 |
| Labour hours | 10 | 20 | 30 |
| Materials cost | $700 | $1 300 | $2 100 |
| Labour costs ($20 per hour) | $200 | $400 | $600 |
| Overhead costs ($30 per hour) | $300 | $600 | $900 |
| Total costs | $1 200 | $2 300 | $3 500 |

**FIGURE 11.22** Traditional cost accounting

Once the cost allocation method has been decided, the details of the quantity and type of products produced are obtained from the production schedule data store and used in conjunction with the raw material costs, the direct labour costs and the manufacturing overheads allocated for each product. Once details of all relevant production costs have been retrieved and checked, the cost of production can be recorded.

| | Assembly Activity 1 | Assembly Activity 2 | Assembly Activity 3 |
|---|---|---|---|
| Overhead costs | $80 000 | $120 000 | $100 000 |
| Number of labour hours or parts | 20 000 hours | 50 000 parts | 30 000 parts |
| Rate | $10 per part | | $20 per hour |
| | Product A | Product B | Product C |
| Parts | 50 | 100 | 150 |
| Labour hours | 10 | 20 | 30 |
| Materials cost | $700 | $1 300 | $2 100 |
| Labour costs ($20 per hour) | $200 | $400 | $600 |
| Overhead costs ($10 per part) | $500 | $1 000 | $1 500 |
| Overhead costs ($20 per hour) | $200 | $400 | $600 |
| Total costs | $1 600 | $3 100 | $4 800 |

**FIGURE 11.23** Activity based costing

## Record costs

After costs for both process and product have been established they are recorded in the finished goods inventory. The calculated total manufacturing cost for each individual product type is stored in the finished goods inventory data store. Details of production costings are sent to the revenue cycle to enable product pricing to be determined, and to the financial cycle to support financial reporting. Production costs are also used for cost analysis and manufacturing variance reporting. Manufacturing variances are obtained by comparing the actual costs and volumes of materials, labour and overhead incurred during production with the standard costs for those items. Standard costs and volumes of labour and manufacturing overheads are obtained from the product's production sequence; the standard costs and volumes of materials required are obtained from the bill of materials for that product. Some of the more common variances analysed include:

- direct material variances (differences between what the output actually cost and what it should have cost, in terms of material). This variance can be divided into two sub-variances: direct material price variances (differences between what the actual quantity of material used did cost and what it should have cost) and direct material usage variances (differences between how much material should have been used for the number of units actually produced and how much material was used)

- direct labour variances (differences between what the output should have cost and what it did cost in terms of labour). This variance can be divided into two sub-variances: direct labour rate variances (differences between what the actual number of hours worked should have cost and what it did cost) and direct labour efficiency variances (differences between how many hours should have been worked for the number of units actually produced and how many hours were worked).

The primary risk in this cost recording activity relates to inaccurate calculation or recording of cost data. Controls that are useful to reduce this risk include the use of bar code or RFID technology to support accurate and timely tracking and recording of inventory movements, and accurate and timely recording of labour related data. In addition, the formation and use of appropriate overhead allocation algorithms, and independent review and approval of overhead cost allocations are helpful to reduce risks around incorrect cost allocations.

### Product costing — DFD

The level 1 DFD in figure 11.24 overleaf contains a lower level of detail about the final process represented in the level 0 logical DFD in figure 11.6. This process takes place after the product has been produced in the preceding process.

### Summary description of activities in product costing

Table 11.6 summarises the activities, risks and controls when costing products, as depicted in figure 11.24. Table 11.2 (page 502) explains the logical data flows depicted in figure 11.24. Exploring the diagram in conjunction with the material contained in the tables will assist in improving your understanding of the process depicted.

## Physical DFD — determine product production requirements

The physical DFD depicted in figure 11.25 shows an example of how production requirements may be determined for a new product. The physical diagram draws the process from a different perspective to the logical DFD of this process contained in figure 11.8, as it shows who is involved in the activities of the process, rather than when those activities occur. The process of determining product production requirements involves product planning staff interacting with a central computer and product designers. Outputs from this process are sent through to the production planning staff for use in subsequent parts of the production cycle.

Details of the physical data flows in figure 11.25 are contained in table 11.7. As this diagram is drawn from a different perspective than the logical DFD it contains far more detail about the interactions between each of the entities involved in determining the product production requirements.

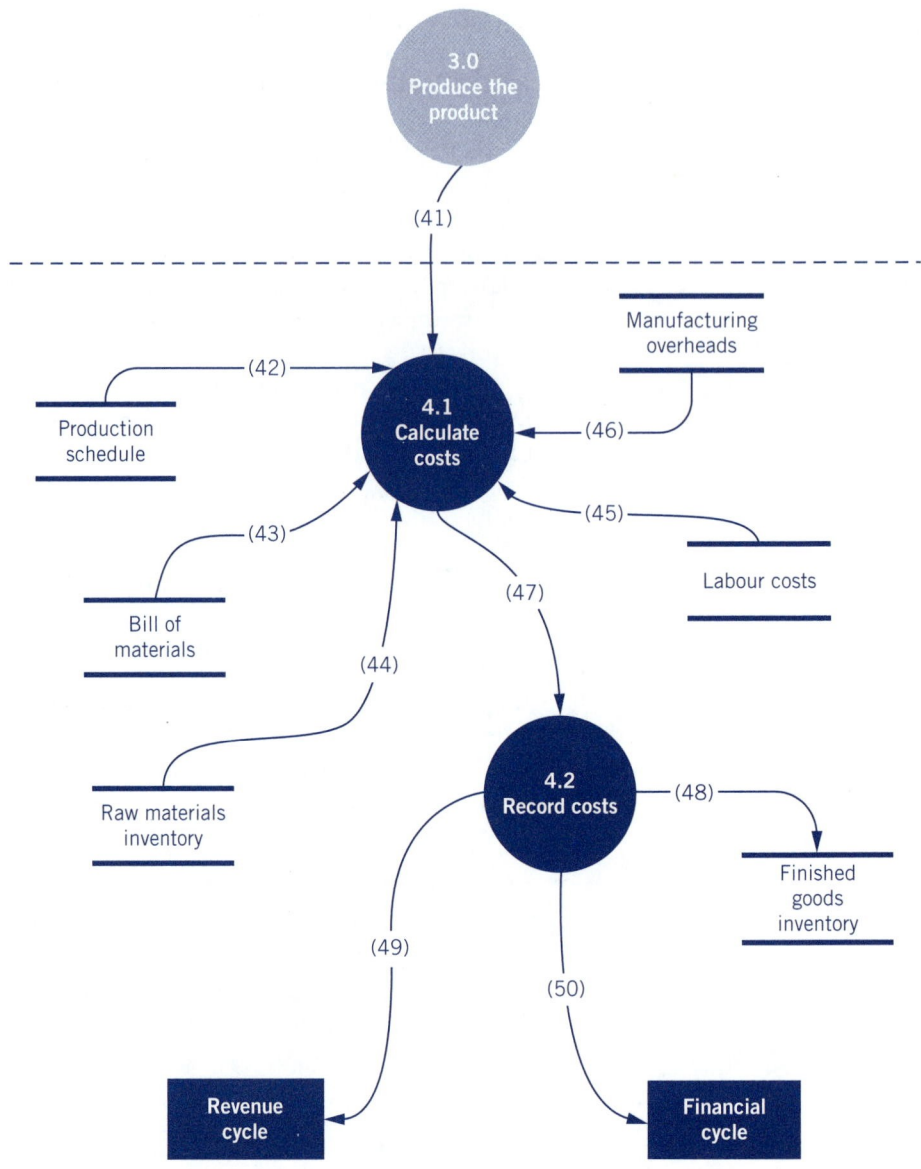

**FIGURE 11.24** Production cycle level 1 logical diagram — process 4.0 Product costing

**TABLE 11.6** Activities in product costing

| Activity # | Activity | Usually conducted by: | Activity description | Typical risks encountered | Common controls |
|---|---|---|---|---|---|
| 4.1 | Calculate costs | Cost clerk | Details of all the costs incurred during the production process are accumulated, including costs relating to labour, raw materials and manufacturing overheads. This data is used to calculate total costs incurred, and individual product level costs. | Inaccurate calculation/recording of cost data | Using barcode or RFID technology to accurately track inventory movements<br>Accurate and timely recording of labour related data<br>Independent review and approval of overhead allocations<br>Using appropriate overhead allocation algorithms |

| Activity # | Activity | Usually conducted by: | Activity description | Typical risks encountered | Common controls |
|---|---|---|---|---|---|
| 4.2 | Record costs | Cost clerk | Once costs for both process and product have been established they are recorded in the finished goods inventory. Details of production costings are sent to the revenue cycle, and to the financial cycle to support manufacturing variance analysis and reporting. | Inaccurate calculation/recording of cost data | Using barcode or RFID technology to accurately track inventory movements<br>Accurate and timely recording of labour related data<br>Independent review and approval of overhead allocations<br>Using appropriate overhead allocation algorithms |

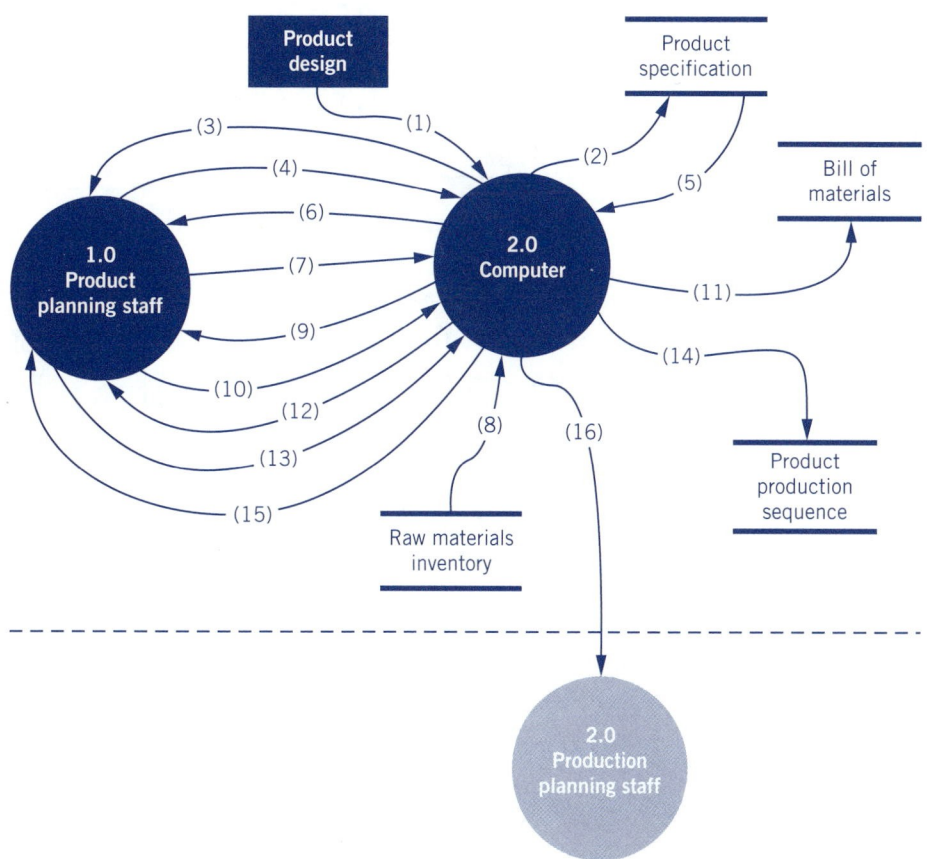

**FIGURE 11.25** Physical DFD — determine product production requirements

## System flowchart — determine product production requirements

The DFD in figure 11.25 shows an example of how the production requirements may be physically determined for a new product; the logical DFD in figure 11.8 shows that same process from a logical perspective. The flowchart in figure 11.26 overleaf shows that same process from yet another perspective. The system flowchart is the most detailed picture of the process, and includes both logical and physical perspectives.

The detail contained in the system flowchart is useful when considering process redesign, and when analysing the control environment of the process depicted. Details of the flows shown in the flowchart in figure 11.26 are documented in table 11.7 (page 527).

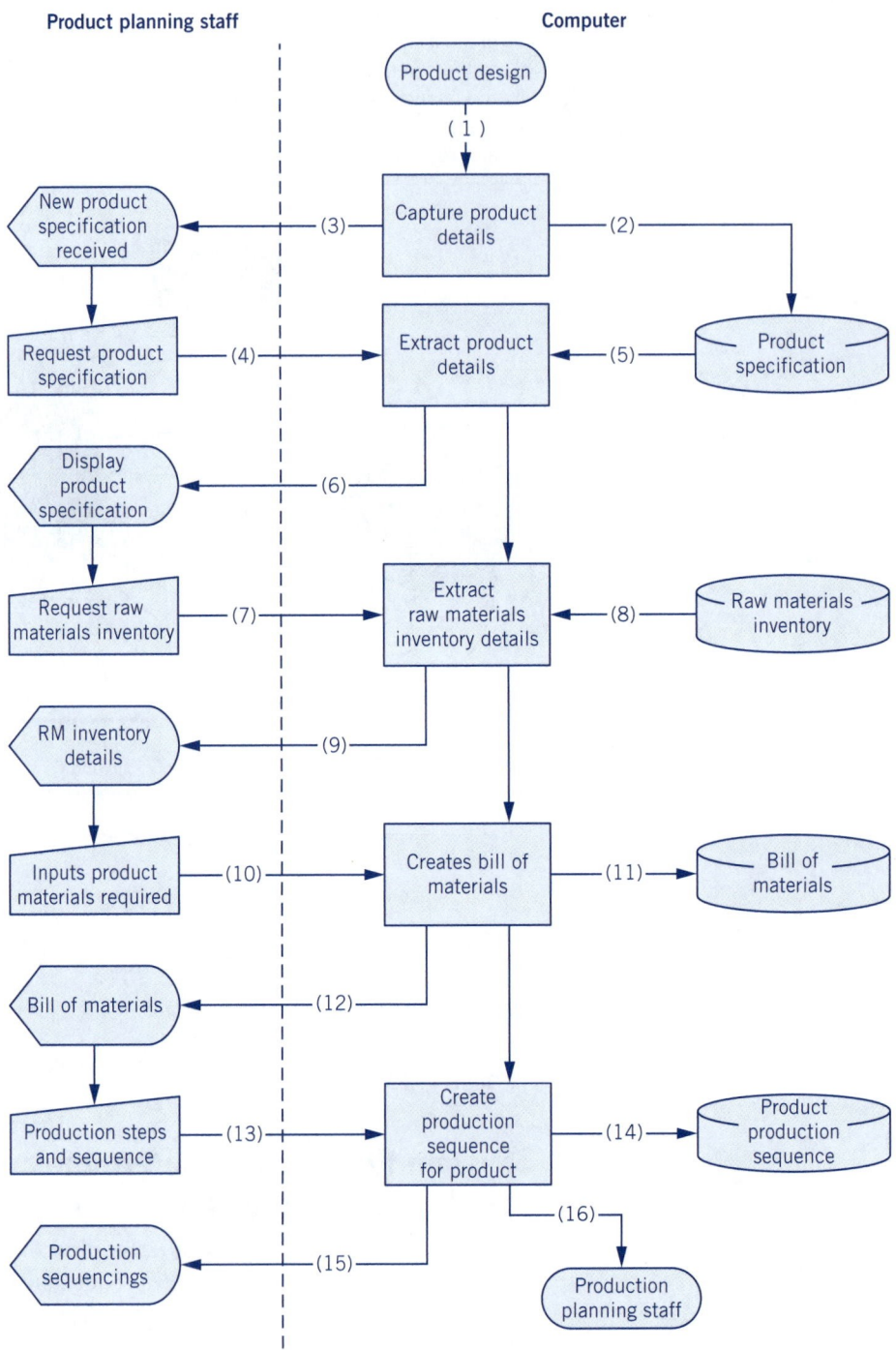

**FIGURE 11.26** Systems flowchart — determine product production requirements

**TABLE 11.7** Description of data flows in physical DFD and flowchart — determine product production requirements

| Flow # | Data source | Data destination | Explanation of the physical data flows |
|---|---|---|---|
| 1 | Product designers | Computer | Once the physical design of a new product is completed, the product design details are sent to the computer. This diagram depicts the product details as being sent electronically, as an output from specialised design software known as computer aided design (CAD). |
| 2 | Computer | Product specification data store | The details of the product design are stored as a specification for the new product in the product specifications data store. |
| 3 | Computer | Product planning staff | Product planning staff are advised that a new product specification has been received from product design. |
| 4 | Product planning staff | Computer | Product planning staff request details of the new product specifications as part of their planning cycle. |
| 5 | Product specification data store | Computer | The computer extracts the details of the new product specifications from the product specification data store. |
| 6 | Computer | Product planning staff | The computer displays the product specification to the product planning staff. |
| 7 | Product planning staff | Computer | Product planning staff request details of currently available raw materials inventory to determine whether all materials required in the product specification are available. |
| 8 | Raw materials inventory data store | Computer | The computer extracts the raw materials inventory details from the raw materials inventory data store. |
| 9 | Computer | Product planning staff | The computer displays the raw material inventory details to product planning staff. |
| 10 | Product planning staff | Computer | Product planning staff identify and input a list of the raw materials required to create the product based on data from the raw materials inventory and the product specification. |
| 11 | Computer | Bill of materials data store | Details of the materials required to make the product are stored in the bill of materials data store. |
| 12 | Computer | Product planning staff | The bill of materials for the product is displayed to product planning staff. |
| 13 | Product planning staff | Computer | Details of the production steps and associated sequencing required to manufacture the product are determined and input by the product planning staff. |
| 14 | Computer | Product production sequence data store | Details of the production steps and sequencing are stored in the product production sequence data store. |
| 15 | Computer | Product planning staff | Details of the production sequence are displayed to product planning staff. |
| 16 | Computer | Production planning staff | Production planning staff are advised that a bill of materials and a production sequence has been finalised for the new product. |

**LEARNING OBJECTIVE 6**

*Develop metrics to monitor production cycle performance.*

**Metric** *A specific measure used for a particular purpose. An example of a metric is the number of bad debts the organisation has, which could be used to monitor accounts receivable or sales performance.*

# MEASURING PRODUCTION CYCLE PERFORMANCE

Process performance should be measured relative to how well the process outcomes achieve the overall objectives of that cycle. At the start of this chapter the objectives of the production cycle were described as being to effectively conduct, record and monitor production, and to accurately record the costs of production related to products.

To monitor performance against these objectives a range of metrics needs to be employed, along with some realistic targets. Examples of suitable **metrics** or key performance indicators (KPIs) for the production cycle objectives are contained in table 11.8.

**TABLE 11.8** Example KPIs mapped to production cycle objectives

| Objective | Example KPI |
|---|---|
| To ensure all production activities and schedules are authorised and approved. | • Number of product production sequence errors detected<br>• Number of changes made to production schedules<br>• Level of inspection and testing costs incurred |
| To secure and appropriately use inventory items including raw materials, work in progress and finished goods | • Inventory costs per product<br>• Number of stock outs of raw materials |
| To ensure all production runs are accurately scheduled, conducted, recorded and costed. | • Number of quality complaints<br>• Number of requester complaints<br>• Amount of rework required<br>• Number of product defects<br>• Production cycle times<br>• Production cost budget overruns<br>• Changes in standard costs<br>• Variations in manufacturing variances |

## ›› SUMMARY ›››

**LEARNING OBJECTIVE 1**

*What are the key objectives and strategic implications of the production cycle?*
Production activities are conducted by organisations choosing to manufacture some or all of their products for sale. The primary responsibility of the production cycle is to ensure that sufficient goods are manufactured in time to balance sales demand. The production cycle is conventionally divided into two major phases: production planning and production execution. The objective of the planning phase is to effectively plan production at both a product and schedule level. The objective of the production execution phase is to ensure that all planned production activities are carried out accurately and effectively, and that production records are correctly updated.

The production cycle is strategically important: if an organisation cannot manufacture goods at a lower cost than the potential purchase price of those same goods there is no competitive advantage to be gained by manufacturing goods in-house. A sound, well-controlled production cycle can provide a competitive advantage by providing high-quality, lower cost products, which in turn can translate into an opportunity for either higher product pricing or greater market share through price leadership. An alternative form of competitive advantage provided by in-house manufacturing is the ability to manufacture a unique product range.

**LEARNING OBJECTIVE**

*Which technologies underpin the activities of the production cycle?*

A range of product and production planning tools are available to improve the accuracy of product demand forecasts. Materials handling and production execution can also be improved by use of appropriate technologies. Enterprise resource planning (ERP) systems assist with integration of production cycle data. Use of barcodes or RFIDs reduces data error levels for activities related to inventory items and improves data timeliness. Specialised production planning software known as manufacturing resource planning (MRP) systems can improve production planning. Execution of those production plans can be improved by use of a computer aided manufacturing (CAM) system, which automates the production requirements. Flexible manufacturing systems (FMSs) may also be using during production to provide improved response to any changes encountered during scheduled production runs.

**LEARNING OBJECTIVE**

*What data and business decisions are involved in the production cycle?*

The production cycle uses or produces data including product and production schedule data. Business process decisions are made at both product and production levels. Typical product-level decisions include determining the material, labour and equipment requirements for each product. Typical production scheduling decisions include determining what types of products to produce and how many of each product to produce, and scheduling production to align with demand. A final set of production process business decisions related to product costing involve allocating overhead and labour costs to various products.

**LEARNING OBJECTIVE**

*What are the primary activities in the production cycle and what data is produced by these activities?*

Contextually, the production cycle does not involve any interaction with entities outside the organisation. Within the organisation, the production cycle interacts with the revenue, expenditure, human resources and financial cycles, and the product design and inventory departments. Primary activities in the production cycle include determining the product production requirements, planning the production schedule, producing the products and product costing.

A range of data types are accessed by activities within the production cycle, including product specification data, inventory data, bill of materials data, and overhead and labour cost data. Production data is used to support decision making related to production planning and execution, and for evaluating production cycle performance.

**LEARNING OBJECTIVE**

*What risks relate to the production cycle activities and how might we control for these risks?*

Activities within the production cycle create exposure to a range of known risks. Risks related to determining product production requirements include failure to action a new product, poor design of the bill of materials and errors when determining the product manufacturing sequence. Risks related to planning the production schedule include incorrectly estimating product demand, underutilisation of available resources and incorrect calculations of materials requirements. Risks of producing the product relate to either theft of inventory items or disruptions of production. When costing products there is a risk that costs will be incorrectly calculated or recorded.

Production cycle controls need to be created over both manual and automated activities, and some degree of control redundancy should be embedded in the control environment. Important controls in the production cycle include automation of production planning and execution, obtaining approvals for bills of material and production schedules, variance and budget analysis, timely and accurate perpetual inventory records, appropriate segregations of duties and exception reporting.

**How can we best monitor production cycle performance?**

Process performance should be measured relative to the desired outcomes of the process. To monitor cycle performance, a wide range of metrics needs to be employed along with some realistic targets. Examples of suitable performance metrics for a production cycle include cycle timings, level of stock outs, number of quality complaints and rework, and inventory costs.

## KEY TERMS

automatic reorder points, p. 510

barcode scanner, p. 495

bill of materials, p. 497

computer aided manufacturing (CAM) system, p. 495

enterprise resource planning (ERP) system, p. 495

exception report, p. 506

finished goods, p. 492

flexible manufacturing systems (FMS), p. 495

manufacturing resource planning (MRP) system, p. 495

metric, p. 528

purchase requisition, p. 512

raw materials, p. 492

RFID, p. 495

work in progress, p. 497

## DISCUSSION QUESTIONS

11.1 Focus Ltd has always had a strategy of product differentiation; that is, providing high-quality products and extracting a price premium from the market. During the recent economic downturn, Focus Ltd has seen its customer base diminish and has decided to move strategically to a cost leadership strategy; that is, to sell more product at a lower price.

(a) What are the implications of this strategy change for the production cycle? (LO1)

(b) What changes would you expect to see in the production cycle? (LO4)

(c) What are the implications of this strategy change in terms of the usefulness of historical sales data for production decision making? (LO3)

11.2 Progressive Ltd has decided to introduce integrated computer aided design/computer aided manufacture (CAD/CAM) software to automate the design and planning of new products.

(a) What controls would you expect to see introduced to ensure the accuracy of future production planning? (LO5)

(b) Which activities in the production planning process would be affected? (LO2, LO4)

(c) What changes would you expect to see in these activities? (LO4)

(d) What metrics could you use to measure the success of this initiative post implementation? (LO6)

11.3 Prepared Ltd has just realised that it has a problem with its inventory data as its inventory management system does not record lead times required to procure raw materials.

(a) What decisions made during the production cycle would be affected by this data problem? (LO3, LO4)

(b) How would those decisions be affected? How would this data problem affect the performance of the production cycle? (LO3, LO4, LO6)

(c) How would this data problem affect other processes at Prepared Ltd? (LO1, LO3, LO4, LO6)

11.4 Agree Ltd has a cost allocation problem. The total direct labour costs allocated to products produced in the previous month does not seem to match the total amount recorded in the labour costs data store. Agree Ltd seems to have good controls; it allocates labour costs of production regularly, and reconciles labour charges at the end of each month.

(a) Which internal controls might be missing? (LO5)

(b) What documentation would you examine in order to investigate this problem? (LO4)

11.5 Better Ltd has a new CEO who is keen on improving process efficiency. She has reviewed the process documentation for the production cycle and has asked you to replace the current system of bar code scanning and recording with a less onerous system. Currently all inventory movements that occur during the production cycle are recorded, as well as when inventory is received from, or returned to, the warehouse. The new proposal is that inventory will only be scanned when it comes out of the warehouse as a raw material or goes back into the warehouse as a finished good.

(a) Should you agree to this change? Why or why not? (LO1, LO3, LO5)

(b) If you would not agree to change the inventory scanning procedures, how would you explain this decision to the CEO? (LO1, LO5)

(c) If you would agree to remove the inventory scanning how would you justify this change to the production manager? (LO1, LO5)

(d) If you remove these inventory scans would you need to measure the cycle performance differently? (LO1, LO6)

## SELF-TEST ACTIVITIES

11.1 A firm should manufacture its own products in-house when:

(a) it has designed a new product.

(b) it is faster to manufacture in-house.

(c) the number of products being sold increases.

(d) it is less expensive to manufacture in-house than to purchase the goods.

11.2 Production planning involves balancing the supply and demand for:

(a) raw materials.

(b) finished goods.

(c) both (a) and (b).

(d) neither (a) nor (b).

11.3 Computer aided manufacturing (CAM) systems cannot help to:

(a) automate production machinery.

(b) improve machine throughput.

(c) design new products.

(d) improve manufacturing consistency.

11.4 Planning a production schedule involves knowledge of:

(a) product demand.

(b) manufacturing constraints.

(c) stock on hand.

(d) all of the above.

11.5 The production cycle interacts externally with:

(a) no other entities; production is internal only.

(b) customers.

(c) suppliers.

(d) the bank.

11.6 Primary risks of the production cycle include:
    (a) producing too many/too few products.
    (b) slow production cycles.
    (c) bad product design.
    (d) all of the above.

11.7 A bill of materials is produced:
    (a) for each day's production schedule.
    (b) for each product.
    (c) for each piece of machinery used.
    (d) for each production staff member.

11.8 It is necessary to adjust production schedules when:
    (a) product demand changes.
    (b) raw materials are readily available.
    (c) excess labour is a problem.
    (d) one product is cheaper to manufacture than the others.

11.9 Not using appropriate overhead costing algorithms increases the risk of:
    (a) losing control of total production costs.
    (b) incorrectly pricing products for sale.
    (c) making errors in production planning.
    (d) producing the wrong goods.

11.10 The production cycle generates cost data related to:
    (a) labour costs.
    (b) material costs.
    (c) manufacturing overheads.
    (d) all of the above.

## PROBLEMS

The case narrative below (AB Hi-Fi) will be used to complete problems 11.1–11.13. Make sure you read and understand the activities and the case thoroughly before you commence work on the problems.

### AB Hi-Fi production cycle

AB Hi-Fi is a multi-store retail business that sells products such as DVDs, CDs, mp3 players, game consoles and TVs. In addition to retail stores, AB Hi-Fi also sells music, games and DVDs via its website. AB Hi-Fi manufactures all its personalised packaging and marketing materials in-house as it believes this gives greater product flexibility and creates cost saving opportunities. The narrative of the production cycle for AB Hi-Fi follows.

#### Process 1.0 Determine product production requirements

When product designers create and save a new product specification, the computer automatically generates and sends a message to the product planning clerk to advise them of the new product. The product planning clerk inputs the new product number into the computer and requests the computer to print a copy of the relevant product specification. After the product planning clerk collects the copy of the product specification they read it carefully to ensure they understand the nature and details of the new product. If any part of the product specification is unclear they liaise with the product designers to ensure that they understand the specification before continuing with the product planning. The product planning clerk keys in a request for details of current stocks of raw material inventory items. The computer extracts and displays a list of the items, including the inventory item's number, a description of the material, and the amount of material currently in stock. The product planning clerk compares the list of materials inventory with the details of the raw materials required for the product in the product specifications. If a raw material is required that is not currently held in inventory the product planning clerk sends a copy of the product specification to the inventory management department along with a request for them to investigate supply of the material. The product planning clerk cannot create a bill of materials until all required raw materials are held in inventory, so if all materials are not available they file the printed copy of the product specification in a folder marked 'awaiting materials'. If all the raw materials are available the product planning clerk inputs the product number into the computer and requests the creation of a bill of materials for the product. The computer checks that a bill of materials does not already exist for that product number, and then displays a bill of materials input screen. The product planning clerk inputs the inventory number for each raw material required into the bill of materials, along with the quantity of each of the materials required to produce a single unit of the product. When all the raw materials and quantities have been input the product planning clerk saves the bill of materials. The product planning clerk then examines the product specification and identifies the equipment and production steps required to manufacture the product, along with the logical sequencing of the steps. Once this has been determined the product planning clerk inputs the production sequence data into the central computer and sends it to the production manager for approval. The product planning clerk is notified of production sequence approvals by the computer. Once the product production sequence has been approved the production planning clerk updates the status code of the product specification to 'product planning complete'.

### Process 2.0 Plan production schedule

On the last day of every month the sales forecasting team inputs details of the forecasted demand for all packaging and marketing products for the next six months into the computer. The production schedule for AB Hi-Fi is master planned on a six monthly basis and finalised in the first week of every month for the following month's production. At 10 am on the first working day of the month the production planning clerk requests a printed copy of the product demand forecast. The computer extracts and prints the report, which lists each of the products required, the number of each product required, and the priority assigned to manufacturing each product. The production planning clerk retrieves a copy of the six monthly master production schedule from their filing cabinet, then requests a list of products currently held in the finished goods inventory. The computer creates and prints a report listing current finished goods inventory items. The production planning clerk manually estimates the finished goods levels for the end of current month by adding together the current inventory level and the volume on the master production plan for each product. After the predicted total on hand for the month-end has been determined the production planning clerk compares this to the forecasted demand to identify which products will be under or overproduced. The production planning clerk uses this information, along with their knowledge of the various production machinery constraints and the priorities assigned by sales forecasting staff, to determine the day-by-day monthly production schedule. The production planning clerk inputs the data to create the production planning schedule. After the monthly production planning schedule has been created the computer automatically updates the master planning schedule and prints a revised copy of this master schedule for the production planning clerk to file. The computer automatically extracts the bill of materials data for each product on the day-to-day monthly production schedule,

*(continued)*

and then calculates the total raw material required for that month's production along with the dates those materials are required. The computer compares the raw materials requirements to the raw materials available and calculates the purchasing requirements. The computer automatically generates a purchase requisition for the raw materials required and sends it to the purchasing clerk.

### Process 3.0 Produce the product

Every morning at 5 am the computer retrieves the detailed production schedule for that day, and then verifies that the required raw materials and labour are available. If there is insufficient labour or materials for the scheduled production a message is generated to advise the production operations clerk. If sufficient labour and materials are available the computer prints two copies of the daily production schedule on the printer in the production operations office. When the production operations clerk arrives at work at 7.30 am they check the printed report, then they sign one copy and send it to the production manager. The production operations clerk inputs an approval code into the computer to indicate that the day's production can commence. The computer updates the day's production schedule status to 'in progress', prints out an inventory movement docket, and then transfers data from the raw materials inventory to the work in progress inventory data store. The inventory movement docket is used by production staff to obtain the raw materials required from the inventory warehouse. The production operations clerk requests a printed copy of the production sequence for each product scheduled for the day, attaches the production sequence reports to the second copy of the day's production schedule, then gives the attached reports and the inventory movement docket to production staff. Production staff verbally advise the production operations clerk when the day's production has been completed, and give them the production timesheets for the day. This usually happens around 4 pm. The production operations clerk inputs an approval code into the computer to indicate that the day's production is finished. The computer updates the day's production schedule status to 'complete', and then prints out an inventory movement docket to allow the finished goods to be moved into the inventory warehouse. The computer calculates the overhead costs of production for the day based on a predefined algorithm, then records these overhead costs in the manufacturing overheads data store. Before the production operations clerk leaves for the day they input details from the staff timesheets into the computer. The computer calculates and records the direct labour costs of production in the labour costs data store, and forwards details of the hours worked for each employee to the payroll clerk.

### Process 4.0 Product costing

Every night at 10 pm the computer extracts all the relevant details for that day's production, including costs of raw materials, direct labour and manufacturing overheads. The total cost of manufacturing per product is calculated. This cost figure is saved against the relevant products in the finished goods inventory data store. A report listing the total production costs per product is generated and forwarded to the revenue section to assist with product pricing, and production cost totals are transferred through to the appropriate general ledger accounts.

11.1 Prepare a context diagram for the production cycle at AB Hi-Fi.
11.2 Prepare a level 0 logical DFD for the production cycle at AB Hi-Fi.
11.3 Prepare a level 1 logical DFD for:
    (a) process 1.0 at AB Hi-Fi
    (b) process 2.0 at AB Hi-Fi

(c) process 3.0 at AB Hi-Fi

(d) process 4.0 at AB Hi-Fi.

11.4 Prepare a physical DFD for:

(a) process 1.0 at AB Hi-Fi

(b) process 2.0 at AB Hi-Fi

(c) process 3.0 at AB Hi-Fi

(d) process 4.0 at AB Hi-Fi.

11.5 Prepare a systems flowchart for:

(a) process 1.0 at AB Hi-Fi

(b) process 2.0 at AB Hi-Fi

(c) process 3.0 at AB Hi-Fi

(d) process 4.0 at AB Hi-Fi.

11.6 Table 11.3 (page 509) identifies three risks typically encountered when determining product production requirements.

**Required**

(a) Analyse the degree of exposure to each of these risks for the determine product production requirements process at AB Hi-Fi.

(b) Determine how many of the common controls described in table 11.3 are present in the determine product production requirements process at AB Hi-Fi.

(c) Prepare a short report suitable for senior management to explain how risky you think the determine product production requirements process is, and how comprehensive the current internal controls are.

(d) Prepare a recommendation describing any changes you would like to make to the determine product production requirements process at AB Hi-Fi in order to reduce the level of risk.

11.7 Table 11.4 (page 516) identifies three risks typically encountered when planning the production schedule.

**Required**

(a) Analyse the degree of exposure to each of these risks in the plan production schedule process at AB Hi-Fi.

(b) Determine how many of the common controls described in table 11.4 are present in the plan production schedule process at AB Hi-Fi.

(c) Prepare a short report suitable for senior management to explain how risky you think the plan production schedule process is, and how comprehensive the current internal controls are.

(d) Prepare a recommendation describing any changes you would like to make to the plan production process at AB Hi-Fi in order to reduce the level of risk.

11.8 Table 11.5 (page 519) identifies two risks typically encountered when producing products.

**Required**

(a) Analyse the degree of exposure to each of these risks for the produce the product process at AB Hi-Fi.

(b) Determine how many of the common controls described in table 11.5 are present in the produce the product process at AB Hi-Fi.

(c) Prepare a short report suitable for senior management to explain how risky you think the produce the product process is, and how comprehensive the current internal controls are.

(d) Prepare a recommendation describing any changes you would like to make to the produce the product process at AB Hi-Fi in order to reduce the level of risk.

11.9 Table 11.6 (page 524) identifies a risk typically encountered when costing products.

**Required**

(a) Analyse the degree of exposure to each of these risks for the costing products process at AB Hi-Fi.

(b) Determine how many of the common controls described in table 11.6 are present in the costing products process at AB Hi-Fi.

(c) Prepare a short report suitable for senior management to explain how risky you think the costing products process is, and how comprehensive the current internal controls are.

(d) Prepare a recommendation describing any changes you would like to make to the costing products process at AB Hi-Fi in order to reduce the level of risk.

11.10 (a) AB Hi-Fi has adopted a differentiation strategy. Its overall plan is to establish highly distinctive brand awareness and so gain market share through customer loyalty. How well does the current production cycle align with this business strategy?

(b) Are there any opportunities to improve the degree of alignment between the production cycle and the business strategy? Explain what you would change and how this would improve the strategic alignment.

11.11 (a) Identify and describe the technologies that AB Hi-Fi uses in its production cycle activities. (b) For each of these technologies you identified in part (a), how well does AB Hi-Fi use the technology? Could you suggest a way to improve the business benefit obtained by use of any of these technologies? (c) Are there other suitable technologies available that AB Hi-Fi could be using for the production cycle activities? What business benefit would these additional technologies provide?

11.12 During process 2.0 plan production schedule at AB Hi-Fi a production planning clerk decides how many of each product should be produced during the upcoming month. Take a moment to review this section of the narrative before you complete the following questions.

**Required**

(a) What data does the production planning clerk draw on when making their decision?

(b) Where do the data you identified in part (a) come from?

(c) Are these data reliable; that is, is there any possibility that there could be errors in the data?

(d) Are these data sufficient to make the decision, or can you identify additional data that the clerk should consider when making the decision?

(e) What would be the consequences of an incorrect decision?

11.13 Explain how you would measure performance of the production cycle at AB Hi-Fi; specifically:

(a) What metrics would you would use to measure performance?

(b) For each metric, explain where you would obtain the data required.

(c) For each metric, explain why it is a good metric to help measure how well the production cycle is meeting its objectives.

## SELF–TEST ANSWERS

11.1 d, 11.2 c, 11.3 c, 11.4 d, 11.5 a, 11.6 d, 11.7 b, 11.8 a, 11.9 b, 11.10 d

## FURTHER READING

Groover, M 2007, *Automation, production systems and computer-integrated manufacturing*, 3rd edn, Prentice Hall

Kaplan, RS & Anderson, SR 2007, *Time-driven activity-based costing*, Harvard Business Press.

Nunes, P, Mulani, N, Brandazza, G, Taggart, J & Cummings, C 2008, 'Can knockoffs knock out your business?', *Harvard Business Review*, vol. 86, no. 10, pp. 41–50.

## END NOTES

1. Sun Microsystems Australia 2009, 'Simba: custom made', www.au.sun/com.
2. Vinidex Pty Ltd 2008, 'An environmental success story', www.vinidex.com.au.

# 12

# Transaction cycle — the HR management and payroll cycle

## Learning objectives

After studying this chapter, you should be able to:

**1** describe the key objectives and strategic implications of the HR management and payroll cycle

**2** identify common technologies underpinning the HR management and payroll cycle

**3** describe HR management and payroll data and key HR management and payroll business decisions

**4** identify and document the primary activities in the HR management and payroll cycle and the data produced by these activities

**5** analyse risks and develop control plans pertinent to the primary activities in the HR management and payroll cycle

**6** develop metrics to monitor HR management and payroll cycle performance.

# Introduction

Human resource (HR) management and payroll are activities that relate to hiring employees, maintaining personnel records, paying employees and generating reports for internal purposes as well as external users such as taxation authorities and employee deductions. One of the essential aspects of this cycle is ensuring that the authorisation of any personnel details or pay rate changes is done by HR management. Once required changes are made, the payroll department can prepare the payroll and payslips for individual employees at the right amounts.

This chapter begins with an overview of the HR management and payroll cycle, and then considers the strategic implications of that cycle. Technologies that underpin the cycle are discussed, and then the data produced and consumed during the cycle activities are identified. Typical process decisions are examined, along with some of the primary considerations related to those decisions. A HR management and payroll cycle is fully documented using data flow diagrams and flowcharts, along with a set of tables containing additional details to aid in understanding the process activities, and the related risks and controls of the activities. Finally issues relating to measuring performance of the HR management and payroll cycle are discussed, and examples of performance metrics suitable for measuring HR management and payroll cycle performance are provided.

**Timesheet** *A document that records an employee's hours worked, is submitted to the departmental supervisor for approval and is used in calculating payroll.*

## HR MANAGEMENT AND PAYROLL CYCLE OVERVIEW AND KEY OBJECTIVES

In order to achieve overall business objectives, the HR management and payroll cycle needs to be well designed and tightly controlled. Poorly controlled HR management and payroll can lead to employees being paid for time they did not work or fictitious employees being paid. An additional consideration for the HR management and payroll cycle is that it is a special form of the expenditure cycle — the organisation is paying for human capital. Many organisations use an external body such as a chartered accounting firm or a payroll outsourcing business to calculate the total amount to be paid to senior managers in the organisation in order to keep information about senior management salaries confidential from employees within an organisation.

The primary responsibility of the HR management and payroll cycle is to ensure that human capital is paid for accurately and on time. The organisational units most involved in the HR management and payroll cycle are shown in figure 12.1 overleaf.

Similarly to the expenditure cycle described in chapter 10, the HR management and payroll cycle is generally thought of as two separate phases. The first of these is HR management. This phase interacts extensively with management of the organisation. The HR manager ensures correct pay rates and any changes to pay rates are recorded for each employee. The production manager may be required to supply or authorise hours worked for an employee as claimed on the employee's **timesheet**. Employee labour time details are forwarded from the production cycle as discussed in chapter 11. In addition, the sales manager may be required to authorise commission if sales staff have a commission component included in their salary. The details of sales and commissions should be prepared, or approved, by a sales manager and forwarded from the revenue cycle to the HR management process as discussed in chapter 9. In summary, in order to ensure employees are paid correctly, pay rates, deductions, changes in pay rates and deductions, and hours worked need to be properly approved and authorised — from HR management (for employee details and pay rates), production management (for employee labour time details) and, if the employee is a salesperson paid on commission, sales management (for commission components of sales transactions).

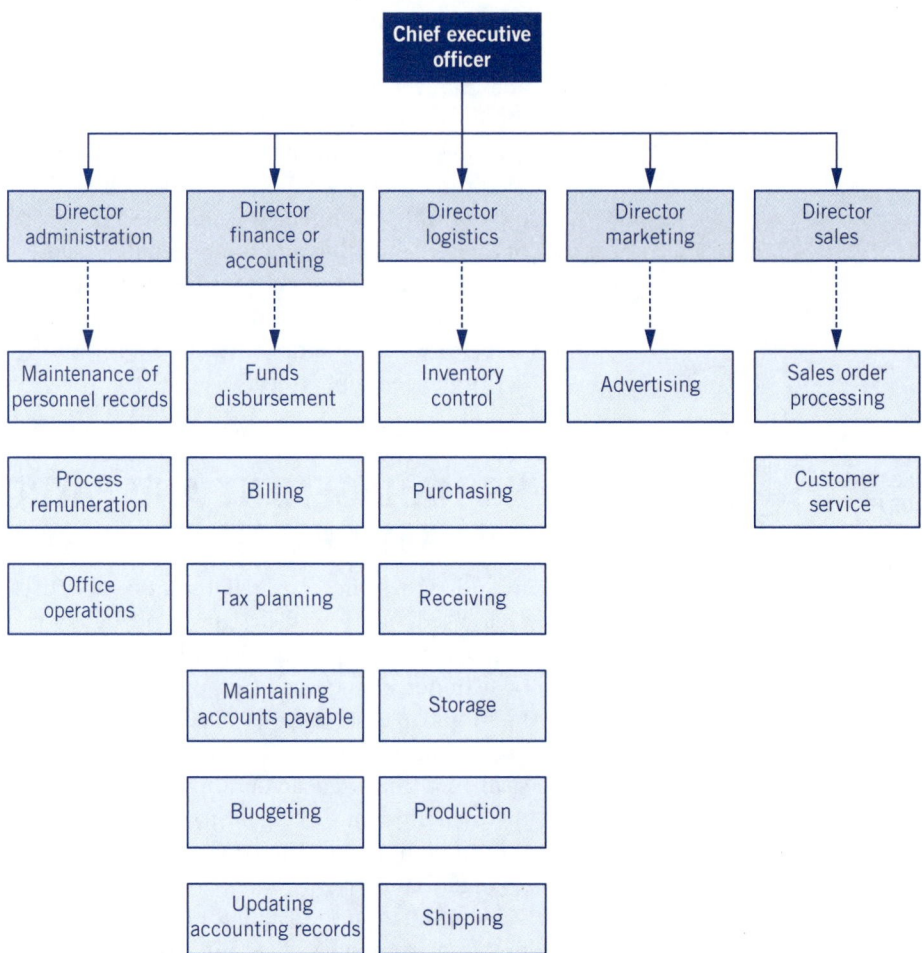

**FIGURE 12.1** Organisational units in the HR management and payroll cycle

*Note:* The dashed lines with the arrows show the business activities that each unit is responsible for.

Following the HR management phase is the payroll phase, where the objective is to pay the right people the right amount at the right time. The activities in this phase are typically conducted by payroll staff; it is important that these staff are not involved in the authorisation of the details they are processing. Once payroll staff finish calculating the amounts of the **payroll**, the information is provided to the cash disbursements area to handle the actual payments to employees. This segregation of the recording of the payroll and the distribution of the cash needs is needed to ensure that payments are accurate, timely and made to authorised employees only. Further, to ensure the accuracy and integrity of the financial statements, all accounts payable liabilities relating

**Payroll** *A formal pay document that lists the hours worked by an employee, the rates of pay, taxes withheld, deductions and the amounts deposited in the employees' bank accounts.*

to payroll such as taxes and deductions must be recorded accurately and promptly. A description of documentation commonly used in the HR management and payroll cycle is contained in table 12.1.

**TABLE 12.1** List of source documents in a HR management and payroll cycle

| Documents | Description |
|---|---|
| Employee personal details | Stores personal information of employees such as their name, age, sex, address and contact details. |
| Employee employment details | Stores employment related information of an employee such as employment start date, pay, employment award scheme and long service leave entitlements. |
| Selection criteria | Details the job description and selection criteria relating to a particular job. |
| Job application | Organisations save job applications that are received in order to fill a present position or review for a future position. |
| Termination letter | States the terms (date, payout etc.) of termination of employment. |
| Employee performance review | Employers use this form to review an employee's job performance. |
| Timesheet | Displays the details of job hours and pay rates relating to a job or for a particular time period. |
| Payroll | This formal pay document lists the hours worked by an employee, the rates of pay, tax withheld and the amounts deposited in the employee's bank. |

## Strategic implications of the HR management and payroll cycle

The HR management and payroll cycle is strategically important to an organisation, particularly in terms of the degree of alignment with the overall business strategy. A sound, well controlled HR payroll process can provide a competitive advantage by paying employees accurately and in a timely manner.

In particular, the payroll phase of the cycle involves cash leaving the business as payments to employees, taxation authorities and for other employee deductions. As a result, the process has a high potential of exposure to fraud. Fraud in HR management and payroll often involves fictitious employees and false employee time cards which requires collusion and inside knowledge and access.

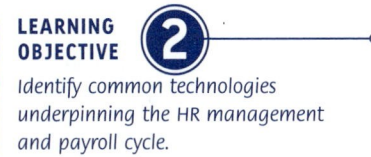

**LEARNING OBJECTIVE 2**

*Identify common technologies underpinning the HR management and payroll cycle.*

# TECHNOLOGIES UNDERPINNING THE HR MANAGEMENT AND PAYROLL CYCLE

There are a number of technologies suitable to support activities within the HR management and payroll cycle, and improve the overall functioning of the cycle. A range of tools are available for the automated collection of time worked. A traditional time clock card requires an employee to place a time card in a time clock when arriving and leaving the workplace. Alternatively, time card records can be completed on paper or electronically. There is also scanning technology that can be used to scan barcodes on an employee's workstation/machine, which link to the organisation's time and cost systems. Transparency and management of cash payments and cash flows can also be improved by use of appropriate technologies such as a direct debit payroll.

**Enterprise resource planning (ERP) systems** assist with enabling and integrating the HR management and payroll cycle. The HR management and payroll cycle links into many areas within the organisation. An ERP can not only improve the integration of enterprise-wide data but can also provide tighter linkages between relevant modules such as sales, production, accounts payable, cash budgeting and the general ledger. In essence, an ERP system acts to provide tighter connections between demand and supply functions within the organisation. For example, to ensure sales employees are paid for the sales they make, once the sales are made the commission amount can be calculated easily if the sales amount and employee details are transmitted to the payroll system. Also, if hours worked are recorded in the production module, this data can flow seamlessly through to the payroll calculation process.

The HR management and payroll cycle can benefit greatly from technologies that provide an efficient means of data exchange with banks and employees. In the case of the HR management phase some of the 'paperwork' associated with the process (e.g. employee details, employee change details and deductions) that originates from the employee and is used to maintain personnel records can be handled through electronic forms with appropriately designed security.

The ability to make electronic payments directly into employees' bank accounts via **direct debit form** provides a fast and comparatively inexpensive way for organisations to pay their employees. When using electronic payment facilities such as those provided by the major banks it is important to consider the timing and cash flow implications. A payment made electronically will take funds from a company bank account immediately, whereas a payment made via cheque may take up to 10 working days before any funds are withdrawn from the company account. In addition to these payment timing issues, it is vital to consider and appropriately design access security over online payment facilities.

## Online HR management systems

Many organisations are matching global trends in the usability of ERPs by introducing employee self-service (ESS) human resource systems. These companies recognise the benefits, and low risk, of allowing employees instant direct access to their personal details. The big players in such systems include SAP and PeopleSoft. Companies that have adopted these systems use them to integrate electronic HR processes, including payroll, leave entitlements and superannuation, providing better data transparency and employee empowerment. The subsequent return on investment for the company is substantial. Transaction costs can be halved and administrative costs reduced by 40 per cent. ESS systems reduce double handling and manual data input, and can speed up HR processes by 10 times.[1]

## AIS FOCUS 12.1

### SAP Business Suite

SAP Business Suite software supports end-to-end business processes in a range of areas. Organisations can configure the processes to meet their specific needs. The areas include finance, manufacturing, procurement, product development, marketing, sales, service, human resources, supply chain management and IT management. The human resources offering allows organisations to manage all aspects of the workforce and control costs through automated HR processes.[2]

**LEARNING OBJECTIVE 3**

Describe HR management and payroll cycle data and key HR management and payroll business decisions.

# DATA AND DECISIONS IN THE HR MANAGEMENT AND PAYROLL CYCLE

A range of data are both produced and consumed by activities within the HR management and payroll cycle. The actual data stores are documented in detail later in this chapter; this current section describes the general purpose and types of data that the HR management and payroll cycle requires. The business decisions made during the life of the HR management and payroll cycle are also described here.

## Data and the HR management and payroll cycle

HR management and payroll cycle activities require access to employee master data to assist in identifying the employees to be paid. Paying an employee will generally occur weekly, every two weeks or monthly. In addition to the employee master files, which contain names, rates, pay periods and deductions such as medical insurance and union dues, the payroll process may also require the current period's working hours for those employees paid by the hour. This data will flow from the production cycle via employee labour hours as described in chapter 11. Data on commissions to be paid will flow from the revenue cycle.

Accounts payable data are both created and updated by activities within the HR management and payroll cycle, including the amounts to pay to employees, taxation authorities and deductions such as medical and union dues. These additional payments may be made at different times of the month to when employees are paid.

## HR management and payroll cycle business decisions

When the HR management and payroll cycle is originally designed, or subsequently reviewed, a number of strategic decisions need to be made. These decisions are typically made by senior management within the organisation, and create the framework within which the policy operates. To be effective, strategy-level process decisions should be congruent with the overarching business strategy. Strategy-level decisions would include the creation of policies such as:

- rates at which differing employees are paid
- pay periods employees will be paid on

- how IT can be used to improve both the efficiency and accuracy of payments to employees.

In addition to these strategy-level decisions, there are a range of operational decisions that will be made every time the HR management and payroll cycle is enacted. These operational decisions are typically made by middle management or operational staff and relate only to a specific instance of the cycle.

**LEARNING OBJECTIVE 4**

*Identify and document the primary activities in the HR management and payroll cycle and the data produced by these activities.*

# HR MANAGEMENT AND PAYROLL CYCLE DOCUMENTATION

The HR management and payroll cycle is documented in the following section as a series of diagrams with increasing amounts of details. An overview of these HR management and payroll cycle diagrams is contained in figure 12.2.

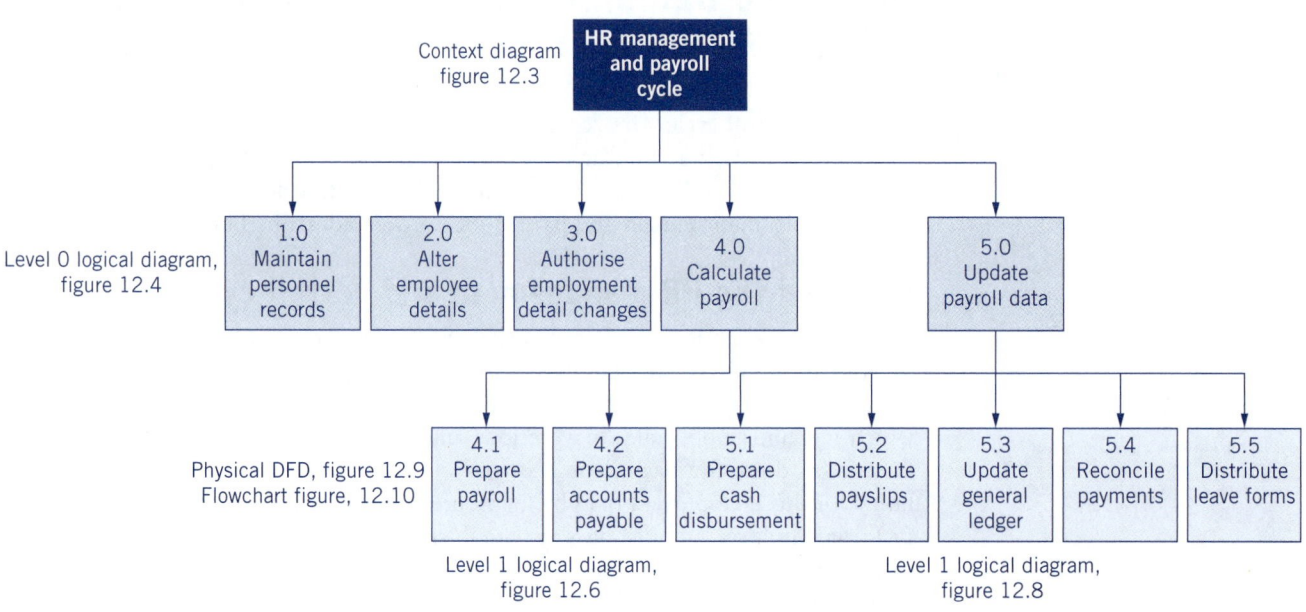

**FIGURE 12.2** HR management and payroll diagrams overview

## HR management and payroll cycle context

The context diagram of a typical HR management and payroll cycle is depicted in figure 12.3. The HR management and payroll cycle involves direct interaction with employees. Within the organisation, the HR management and payroll cycle interacts with the production cycle which may provide timesheet data detailing employee labour hours. The data produced within the HR management and payroll cycle is sent to the general ledger and financial reporting cycle as shown in figure P3.1 (page 389). Details of the logical data flows depicted in the HR management and payroll context diagram are contained in table 12.2.

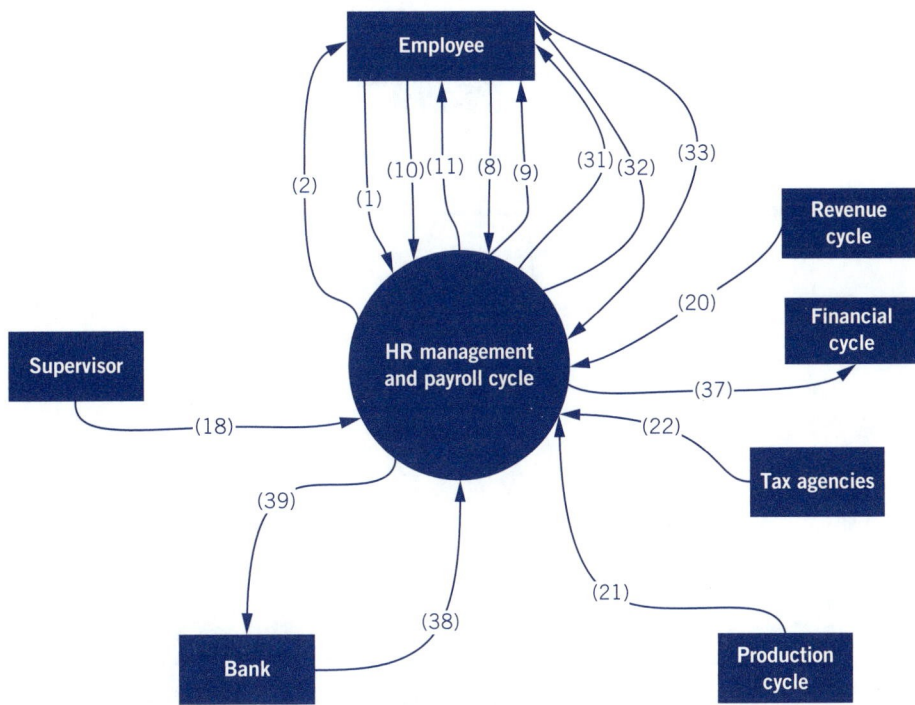

**FIGURE 12.3** HR management and payroll cycle context diagram

## HR management and payroll cycle logical data flows

Figure 12.4 (overleaf) depicts a level 0 logical DFD. This diagram shows the entire HR management and payroll cycle, in greater detail than that depicted in the context diagram. The logical DFD is an exploded version of the context diagram, with the bubble described as 'HR management and payroll cycle' in the context diagram broken down into five processes. The logical diagram at level 0 helps to analyse and understand the HR management and payroll cycle in its entirety. It depicts the chronology of the cycle, the data stores and external entities involved in each of the processes, and the interactions between these processes, entities and data stores. The logical level 0 diagram in figure 12.4 is itself broken down to describe even lower levels of detail in figures 12.6 and 12.8 later in this chapter. Details of the logical data flows depicted in this diagram are contained in table 12.2 (page 547).

### *Description of logical data flows in the HR management and payroll cycle*

A logical DFD contains only those data flows relating to inputs and outputs of the activities contained within each of the processes, as opposed to the details of all interactions between entities which are depicted in a physical DFD. As a result the number of flows in a logical DFD is always less than those that would be shown on a physical DFD for the same process. To illustrate this, compare figures 12.4 and 12.9, which both show exactly the same process; however, figure 12.4 is a logical description whereas figure 12.9 is a physical description. In order to maintain consistency of documentation, the larger number of flows contained in the physical DFD shown in figure 12.9 are numbered sequentially in table 12.5. The numbering of the subset of data flows for process 1.0 depicted in the logical diagram contained in figure 12.4 and documented in table 12.2 are therefore not sequential.

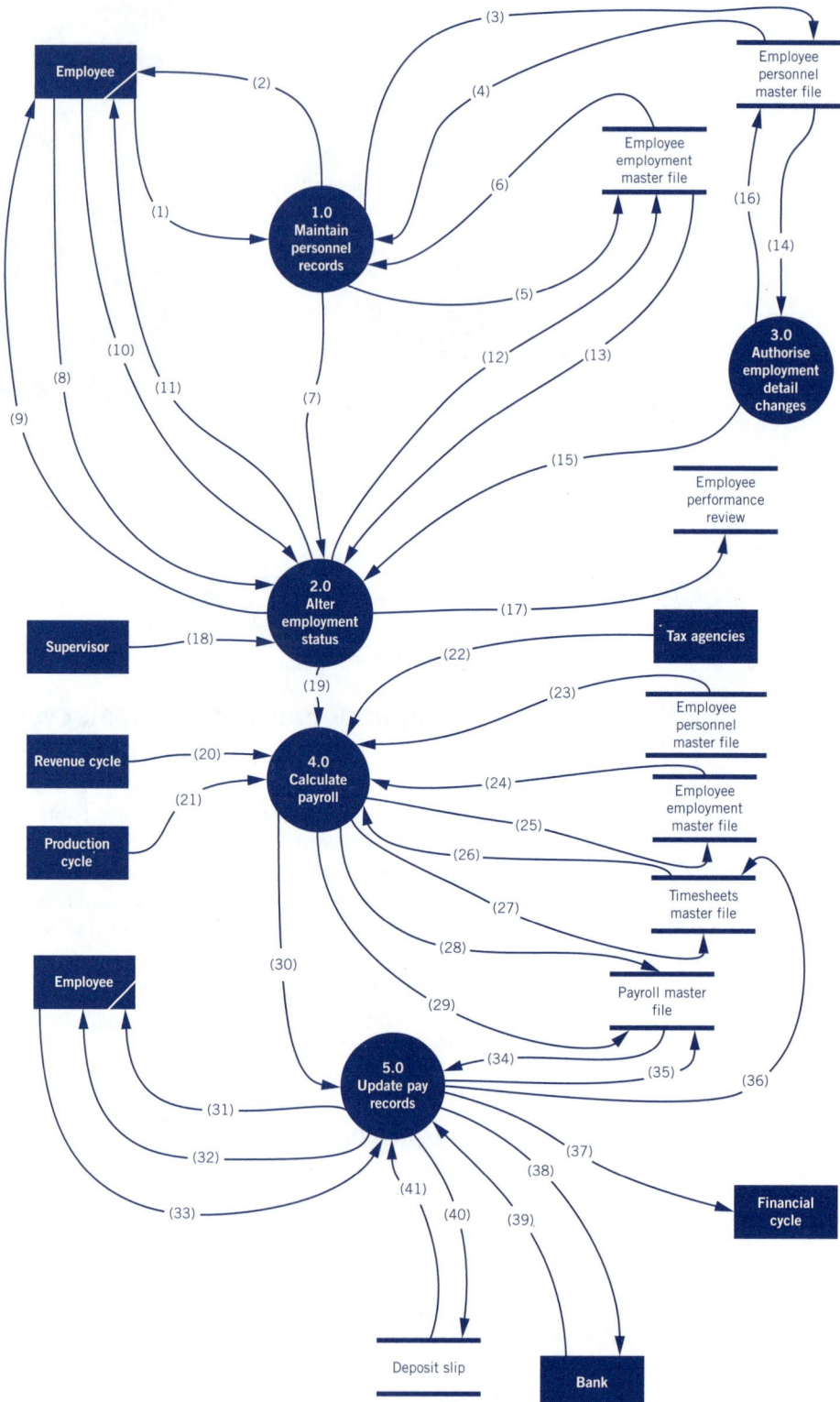

**FIGURE 12.4** HR management and payroll cycle level 0 logical diagram

**TABLE 12.2** Description of logical data flows in the HR management and payroll cycle

| Flow # | Typical data source | Typical data destination | Data description | Explanation of the logical data flow |
|---|---|---|---|---|
| **Process 1.0 Maintain personnel records** | | | | |
| 1 | Employee | Maintain personnel records | Employee details amended data | The HR production and payroll cycle requires that employees can amend their details such as their address or the types and amounts of deductions they want removed from their salary such as a medical insurance deduction. This data flow enables this information to be collected electronically or on paper; however, evidence would need to be kept that the employee has provided authorisation for these details to be changed. Usually an employee details amendment form would be used and filed. |
| 2 | Maintain personnel records process | Employee | Employee details amended acknowledgement | Once an employee has requested that details of their records such as address or deductions be changed, they would be sent an acknowledgement either electronically or on paper that the amendments have been made. |
| 3 | Maintain personnel records process | Employee personnel master file | Employee details | The employee personnel master file stores the personal information relating to employees such as name, age, sex, address and other contact details. This activity updates details in this master file. |
| 4 | Employee personnel master file | Maintain personnel records process | Employee details amended acknowledgement | This data flow retrieves the detail currently in the master file and enables the updating of this information. |
| 5 | Maintain personnel records process | Employee employment master file | Employee details | The employee employment master file stores the employment related information such as the employment start day, pay rate and leave applications. This activity updates the details in this master file. |
| 6 | Employee employment master file | Maintain personnel records process | Employee details amended acknowledgement | This data flow retrieves the detail currently in the master file and enables the updating of this information |
| 7 | Maintain personnel records process | Alter employment status | Employee details | This data flow relates to an employee starting or terminating with the organisation. If the employee is terminating with the organisation data will also come from the maintain personnel records activity. |
| 8 | Employee | Alter employment status | New employee details | This activity collects new employee details. |
| 9 | Alter employment status | Employee | Employee details acknowledgement | This activity acknowledges the set up of the employee and their details in the employee data store either electronically or on paper. |
| **Process 2.0 Alter employment status** | | | | |
| 10 | Employee | Alter employment status | Terminated employee details | This activity collects details on the termination of an employee. |

*(continued)*

**TABLE 12.2** *(continued)*

| Flow # | Typical data source | Typical data destination | Data description | Explanation of the logical data flow |
|---|---|---|---|---|
| 11 | Alter employment status | Employee | Employee details acknowledgement | This activity acknowledges the termination of an employee. |
| 12 | Alter employment status | Employee employment master file | Employee details | Once the personnel record has been created a record is written in the data store recording all the details of the new employee or terminated employee back to the employee personnel master file. |
| 13 | Employee employment master file | Alter employment status | Employee details | The updating of the records for new and terminated employees is submitted to the alter employment status process. |
| 17 | Alter employment status | Employee performance review data store | Employee performance review details | Details of the employee performance review are submitted to file. |
| 18 | Supervisor | Alter employment status | Employee performance review details | Details of the employee performance review are submitted to the alter employment status activity. |
| 19 | Alter employment status | Calculate payroll | Employee details | Details of any changes to the employee records are communicated to the payroll process so that the current pay can be calculated using the changed details. |
| **Process 3.0 Authorise employment detail changes** | | | | |
| 14 | Employee personnel master file | Authorise employment detail changes | Employee details | There may be details in the personnel record that need to be approved to be updated such as pay increases. This data is authorised by HR management. |
| 15 | Authorise employment detail changes | Alter employment status | Employee details | The updating of the records of employees in relation to new pay rates or conditions. These would be transmitted from general management to HR management to action or be instigated directly by HR management. |
| 16 | Authorise employment detail changes | Employee personnel master file | Employee details | The updated details that have been authorised are saved back to the employee personnel master file. |
| **Process 4.0 Calculate payroll** | | | | |
| 20 | Revenue cycle | Calculate payroll | Commission details | This flow would take place where sales people have a commission component included in their salary. |
| 21 | Production cycle | Calculate payroll | Timesheet details | For hourly paid employees the authorised timesheets from the production supervisor will be sent through for employees that have worked in the current pay period. |
| 22 | Tax agencies | Calculate payroll | Taxation details | Taxation details, rates and rules used in calculating the payroll are input to the system |

| Flow # | Typical data source | Typical data destination | Data description | Explanation of the logical data flow |
|---|---|---|---|---|
| 23 | Employee personnel master file data store | Calculate payroll | Employee details | Employee details such as name and address are retrieved for use on the payroll payslips. |
| 24 | Employee employment master file data store | Calculate payroll | Employee details | Employee details such as contract type, rate and leave records are retrieved for use on the payroll payslips. |
| 25 | Calculate payroll | Employee employment master file data store | Employee details | Details of the newly utilised leave days used are written into the employee employment master file data store. |
| 26 | Timesheets master file | Calculate payroll | Purchase requisition details | Timesheet details are retrieved from the data store to be used in the calculation of the payroll. |
| 27 | Calculate payroll | Timesheets master file | Timesheet details | Timesheet details are saved in the data store. |
| 28 | Calculate payroll | Payroll master file | Payroll details | The amount to be paid to each employee as well as the amounts of deductions to be paid for each employee are calculated. |
| 29 | Calculate payroll | Update pay records | Payroll details | Details of the payroll and approved leave forms are used to complete the employee payslips and deductions payments. |
| 30 | This flow takes place physically between payroll staff and accounts payable staff; it happens within the 4.0 bubble in the logical diagram. | | | |
| 42 | This flow takes place physically between payroll staff and accounts payable staff; it happens within the 4.0 bubble in the logical diagram | | | |
| **Process 5.0 Update pay records** | | | | |
| 31 | Update pay records | Employee | Payslip details | Details of the payslip are forwarded to the employee so they can see the gross pay calculation, less taxes and deductions resulting in the net pay they will be paid for the period. The gross pay may be a salary or an hourly rate multiplied by the number of hours worked in the pay period. Details of previous pays may also be included on the payslip. |
| 32 | Update pay records | Employee | Approved leave form details | Details of approved leave form details are sent to the employee. |
| 33 | Employee | Update pay records | Employee leave form details | Details of the employee leave forms are used to update the employee's employment master file. |
| 34 | Payroll master file | Update pay records | Payroll payment details | Details of the payment of the payroll are retrieved to be updated when the payroll is paid. |
| 35 | Update pay records | Payroll master file | Payroll payment details | Details of the payment of the payroll are updated on the payroll master file |

*(continued)*

**TABLE 12.2** *(continued)*

| Flow # | Typical data source | Typical data destination | Data description | Explanation of the logical data flow |
|---|---|---|---|---|
| 36 | Update pay records | Timesheets master file | Leave details | The leave details used in the current period are updated to the payroll master file. |
| 37 | Update pay records | Financial cycle | Payroll details | The payroll details are supplied to the general ledger and financial reporting cycle. |
| 38 | Update pay records | Bank | Payroll details | Amounts to be paid to employee bank accounts (if using direct debit) and deduction accounts are updated. Or if a payroll imprest account is being used, the amount of the payroll is transferred into the payroll imprest account and amounts to be paid to employee bank accounts and deduction accounts are made from this account. |
| 39 | Bank | Update pay records | Deposit details | Deposit details are confirmed. |
| 40 | Update pay records | Deposit slip data store | Deposit details | Details of the deposit slip for the payroll are written into the deposit slip data store. |
| 41 | Deposit slip data store | Update pay records | Deposit details | The deposit details are used to update the payroll master file when the payroll is paid. |
| 43 | This flow takes place physically between cash disbursements staff and the paymaster — the payslips are given the paymaster to distribute; it happens within the 5.0 bubble in the logical diagram. | | | |
| 44 | This flow takes place physically between cash disbursements staff in charge of the reconciliations and the general ledger — the general ledger is updated when payments are made; it happens within the 5.0 bubble in the logical diagram. | | | |
| 45 | This flow takes place physically between payroll staff and the general ledger — the general ledger is updated when the payroll is paid; it happens within the 5.0 bubble in the logical diagram. | | | |

**LEARNING OBJECTIVE 5**

*Analyse risks and develop control plans pertinent to the primary activities in the HR management and payroll cycle.*

**Employee personnel master file** *A file that stores personal information of employees such as their name, age, sex, addresses and other contact details.*

**Employee employment master file** *A file that stores employment related information of an employee such as employment start date, pay rate, employment award scheme and long service leave entitlements.*

**Employee details amendment form** *A form that allows the employees to change their personal and employment details.*

# HR MANAGEMENT AND PAYROLL CYCLE ACTIVITIES AND RELATED RISKS AND CONTROLS

The activities within the HR management and payroll cycle and the associated risks and controls are described below.

## Maintain personnel records — activities

This is process 1.0 in the HR management and payroll cycle. An employee's personal details such as name, age, sex, addresses and other contact details are recorded in the **employee personnel master file**. An employee's employment related information such as employment start date and pay rate are recorded in the **employee employment master file**. The cycle requires that employees can amend their details such as address or the types and amounts of deductions they want taken from their salary such as a medical insurance deduction. Amendments can be electronic or on paper; however, evidence would be required that the employee has provided authorisation for these details to be changed. Usually an **employee details amendment form** would be used and filed. Figure 12.5 shows an example of an employee details amendment form.

## Australian Information Company
### Level 2, 345 Hill Terrace
### Melbourne, Vic 3003

| EMPLOYEE DETAILS AMENDMENT FORM | | | No.: 100/06 |
|---|---|---|---|
| EMPLOYEE PERSONAL DETAILS | | | |
| Date: 20/08/10 | Employee name: Smith Jones | Employee department: Purchasing department | Employee no.: 1018292 |
| HOME ADDRESS | | | |
| Address: | 181 Hilly Billy Street | | |
| City or suburb: | Melbourne | State: | VIC |
| Postcode: | 3005 | Country: | Australia |
| Is the above your mailing address? (if not indicate your mailing address overleaf) | (YES) | | NO |
| CONTACT | | | |
| Home no.: | (03) 8998 8998 | Office no.: | (03) 4334 4334 |
| Mobile no.: | 0459 999 999 | Other: | n/a |
| OTHER | | | |
| Birth date: | 15/08/1968 | Sex: | Female |
| Educational level: | BCom. | Citizenship status: | Citizen |
| EMPLOYEE EMPLOYMENT DETAILS | | | |
| EMPLOYMENT HISTORY | | | |
| Job history (Note this cannot be amended. Contact the personnel officer.) | | | |
| Date joined organisation: | 12/01/2005 | Pay level | HE1 CLASS 2 |

**FIGURE 12.5** Employee details amendment form

## Alter employment status — activities

Process 2.0 in the HR management and payroll cycle collects details and acknowledges a new employee starting or the termination of an employee. Once the personnel

*Employee performance review* Employers use this form to review an employee's job performance.

record has been created a record is written in the data store recording all the details of the new employee or terminated employee back to the employee personal master file. The updating of the records for new and terminated employees is acknowledged back to the employee via the alter employment status process. Details of the **employee performance review** are submitted to file in this process. Details of any changes to the employee records are communicated to the payroll process so that the current pay can be calculated using the changed details.

## Authorise employment detail changes — activities

Process 3.0 in the HR management and payroll cycle involves the authorisation of employment detail changes. There may be details in the personnel record that need to be approved to be updated such as pay increases, new pay rates and other condition changes. These changes in terms and conditions are authorised by HR management directly or transmitted from general management to HR management to enact. These authorised employment detail changes are saved back to the employee personnel master file.

## Calculate payroll — activities, risks and controls

Process 4.0, calculate payroll, comprises the following activities.

### Prepare payroll

The payroll clerk prepares the payroll based on the information in the employment master files and the timesheets master file. These files have been updated previously by authorised individuals: the employment master files by HR management and timesheet data by production management. The objective of this process is to pay employees at the correct rate for the correct number of hours worked. To achieve this purpose, there are controls on the employee master files to ensure that data in these files cannot be overridden.

### Prepare accounts payable

Accounts payable staff check the payroll for accuracy and then establish the due dates for payment. The checking for accuracy by accounts payable staff of the work of the payroll clerk provides a control over the payroll clerk's work. The employee salary will more than likely be paid on a different day than payroll taxes due and employee deductions payments (e.g. medical insurance, union fees). To ensure the correct amounts are paid on the correct dates, accounts payable staff check the information provided by the payroll clerk.

### *Calculate payroll — DFD*

The level 1 DFD in figure 12.6 contains a lower level of detail about the fourth process represented in the level 0 logical DFD in figure 12.4. In the same way in which the level 0 logical diagram explodes out the 'HR management and payroll cycle' bubble in the context diagram, the level 1 diagram explodes out the 'calculate payroll' bubble. This process takes place after the employment detail changes have been authorised in the preceding process and before the pay records are updated in the following process.

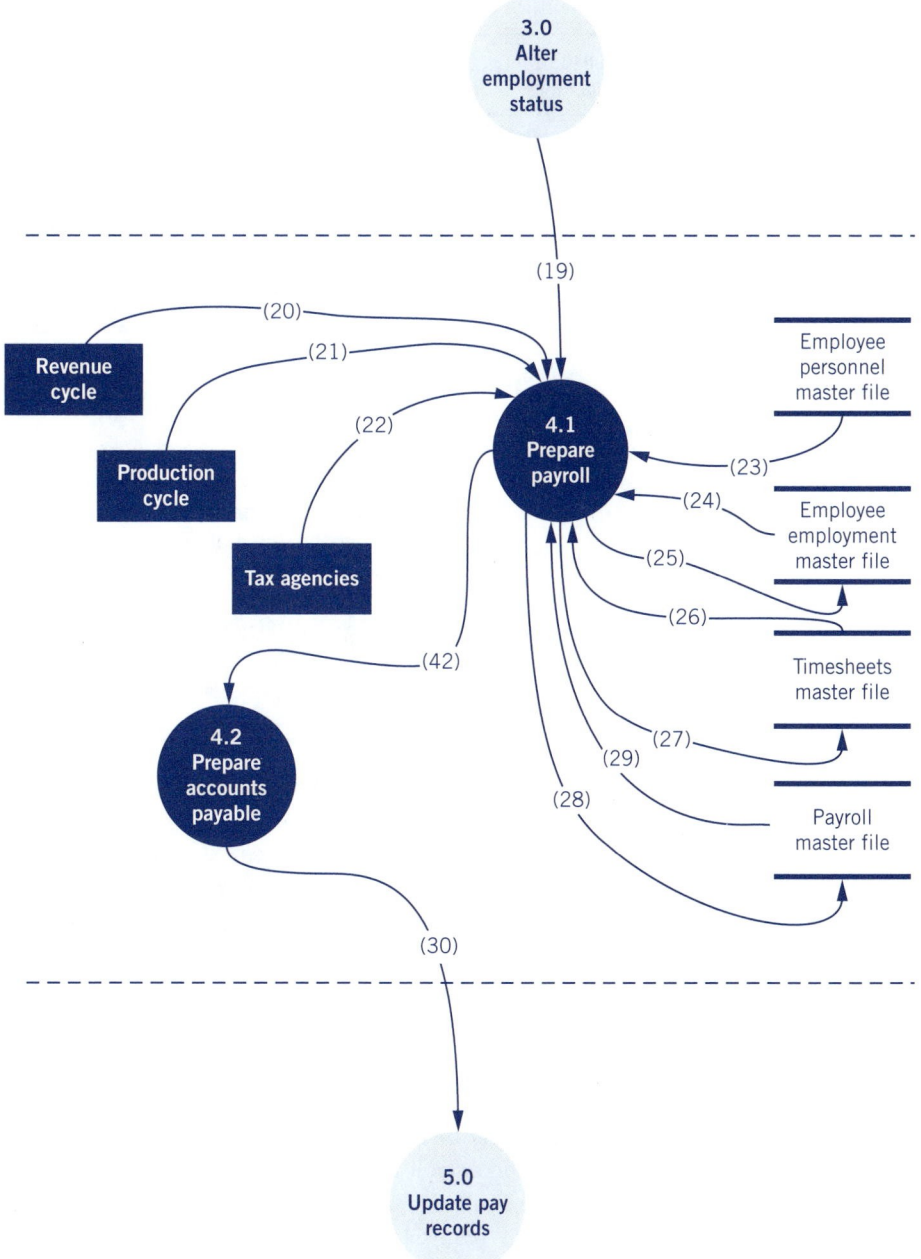

**FIGURE 12.6** HR management and payroll cycle level 1 logical diagram — process 4.0 Calculate payroll

## Summary description of activities in calculating payroll

Table 12.3 overleaf summarises the activities when calculating payroll, as depicted in figure 12.6. Table 12.2 (page 547) explains the logical data flows depicted in figure 12.6. Exploring the diagram in conjunction with the material contained in these tables will assist with improving your understanding of the process depicted.

**TABLE 12.3** Activities in calculating payroll

| Activity # | Activity | Usually conducted by: | Activity description | Typical risks encountered | Common controls |
|---|---|---|---|---|---|
| 4.1 | Prepare payroll | Payroll clerk | The payroll is prepared based on the information in the employment master files and the timesheets master file. These files have been updated previously by authorised individuals: the employment master files by the HR management staff and the timesheets master files by the production supervisor. | Not paying the employees at the correct rate for the correct number of hours worked | Controls so that master files cannot be overridden |
| 4.2 | Prepare accounts payable | Accounts payable | Accounts payable staff check the payroll for accuracy and then establish the due dates for payment. Payments to employees may be made on different dates than those to taxation authorities and for employee deductions. | That the correct amounts are not paid on the correct dates | Accounts payable staff checking the work of the payroll clerk |

## Update pay records — activities, risks and controls

Process 5.0, update pay records, comprises the following activities.

### Prepare cash disbursements

On the due date, payments should be automatically processed. Cheques would be hand written or printed based on a batch file generated from the payroll, or direct debit transactions would be actioned by the bank to pay employees and other payroll expenses. Ensuring the security of cheques and that each cheque equals the payroll amount is vital. A **payroll imprest account** is a control whereby the total amount of the payroll is paid into a special bank account. All employee payments and payroll expenses are made out of this account. The imprest account should have a zero balance once all expenses are paid.

*Payroll imprest account* A special bank account used as a control to ensure the correct payroll amounts are paid.

### Distribute payslips

The payroll clerk distributes **payslips** to employees. A risk is that pay slips are prepared for fictitious employees.

A control to manage this risk is to have a paymaster or other person in HR management that is not involved with the pay calculations or authorising any pay change details distribute the payslips. It is also important to ensure that payslips are physically handed to employees. An example of a payslip is shown in figure 12.7.

*Payslip* A document given to an employee as evidence of them being paid for the pay period that contains their personal details, gross pay calculation, taxes and deductions, net pay, leave entitlements and previous pay details.

### Update general ledger

Totals of the payroll and expenses accrued and then paid are updated in the general ledger. It is vital that the payroll liability is stated correctly in the financial statements. To ensure this, the system should automatically record payroll amounts, accruals, reductions in accruals and expenses to update the general ledger once payments are made.

# Australian Information Company
Level 2, 345 Hill Terrace
Melbourne, Vic 3003

| EMPLOYEE PAY SLIP | | | | No: 10-828279 |
|---|---|---|---|---|
| | | | | Employee no.: 81729 |
| Department: Administration | | | | |
| Date | Description | Rate (per hour) | Hours worked | Total pay ($) |
| 12/01/10 | Project 1 | 56 | 7 | 392 |
| 15/01/10 | Project 1 | 56 | 4 | 224 |
| 16/01/10 | Project 1 | 56 | 8 | 448 |
| Total pay before tax for period ending 16/01/10 | | | | 1064 |
| Tax withheld | | | | 345 |
| Total pay deposited into bank account | | | | 699 |
| | | | | |
| Prepared by: James Holland, pay officer | | Date entered: 12/01/10 | | Pay period: 3-10 |

**FIGURE 12.7** Sample pay slip

### Reconcile payments

The cash disbursements clerk ensures the amounts to be paid have been deposited in an imprest account and the correct amounts of the employee salary and payroll expenses are paid. This ensures no fraud has occurred by checking that the calculated amount to be paid is the actual amount disbursed. Having the cash disbursements clerk perform this duty ensures that the work of the payroll clerk is checked. Also in this process, the payroll clerk ensures all leave applications are updated. A control over leave balances is having a calculated leave balance based on leave taken.

## Update pay records — DFD

The level 1 DFD in figure 12.8 overleaf contains a lower level of detail about the fifth process represented in the level 0 logical DFD in figure 12.4. This process takes place after the payroll has been calculated in the preceding process and prior to the payroll being paid.

## Summary description of activities in updating pay records

Table 12.4 (page 557) summarises the activities involved when updating pay records, as depicted in figure 12.8. Table 12.2 (page 547) explains the logical data flows depicted in figure 12.8. Exploring the diagram in conjunction with the material contained in the tables will assist in improving your understanding of the process depicted.

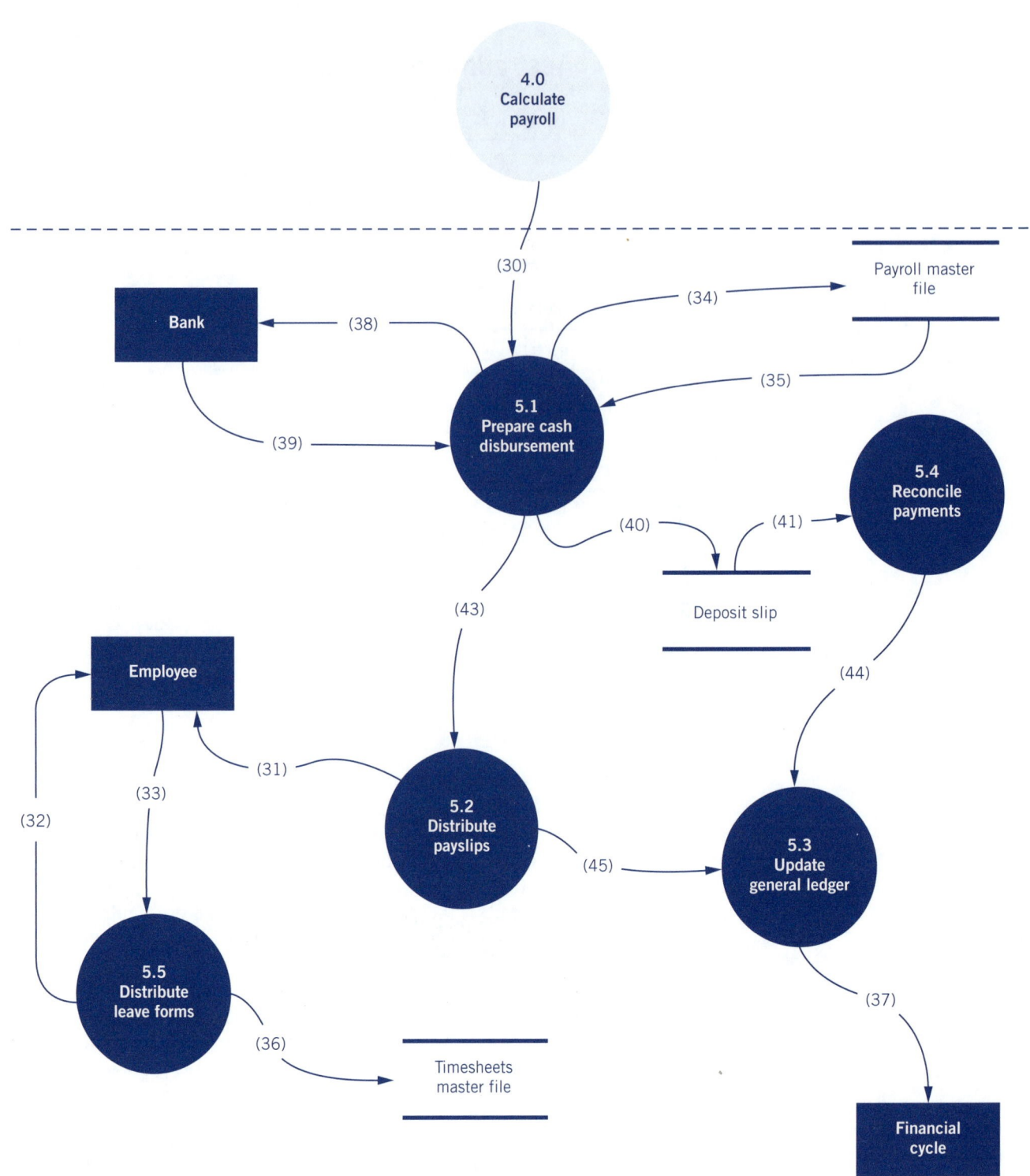

**FIGURE 12.8** HR management and payroll cycle level 1 logical diagram — process 5.0 Update pay records

**TABLE 12.4** Description of typical activities in update pay records

| Activity # | Activity | Usually conducted by: | Activity description | Typical risks encountered | Common controls |
|---|---|---|---|---|---|
| 5.1 | Prepare cash disbursements | Cash disbursements | On the due date the payment should be automatically processed. Cheques could be printed based on a batch file generated from the payroll, or they may be hand written. Alternatively a direct debit is actioned by the bank to pay employees and other payroll expenses. | Ensuring the security of the cheques and that each cheque equals the payroll amount | Using a payroll imprest account whereby the total amount of the payroll is paid into a special bank account. All employee cheques and payroll expenses come out of this account. The check is that imprest account should come to zero once all expenses are paid. |
| 5.2 | Distribute payslips | Payroll clerk | The payslips are distributed to the employee. | Payslips are prepared for fictitious employees | Having a paymaster or a person in HR management that is not involved with pay calculations or authorising any pay change details distribute the payslips Ensuring that each employee is physically handed their payslip |
| 5.3 | Update general ledger | Computer | Totals of the payroll and expenses yet to be paid are accrued and then paid and updated in the general ledger. | Ensuring the payroll liability is stated correctly in the financial statements | Ensuring when the payroll is calculated the amounts are accrued automatically and when they are paid these accruals are reduced to show the actual payroll expenses |
| 5.4 | Reconcile payments | Cash disbursements clerk | Ensuring that the amount to be paid has been deposited in an imprest account and the correct amounts of the employee salary and payroll expenses yet to be paid. | That fraud may occur | Ensuring the amount calculated to be paid for the payroll is the actual amount that was paid |
| 5.5 | Distribute leave forms | Payroll clerk | Ensuring all leave applications are updated. | That leave balances do not reflect leave taken | Having a calculated leave balance based on leave taken |

## Physical DFD — HR management and payroll

The physical DFD depicted in figure 12.9 overleaf shows how the HR management and payroll cycle may be processed. The physical diagram draws the cycle from a different perspective to the logical DFD of this process contained in figure 12.4, as it shows who is involved in the activities of the cycle, rather than when those activities occur. This HR management and payroll cycle involves the HR management clerk who interacts with a central computer and inputs changes in pay details into the computer. Outputs from this process are used by the payroll department to calculate the payroll and authorise the payment of various payroll expenses.

Details of the physical data flows in figure 12.9 are contained in table 12.5 (page 561). As this diagram is drawn from a different perspective to the logical DFD it contains far more detail about the interactions between each of the entities involved in the HR and payroll cycle.

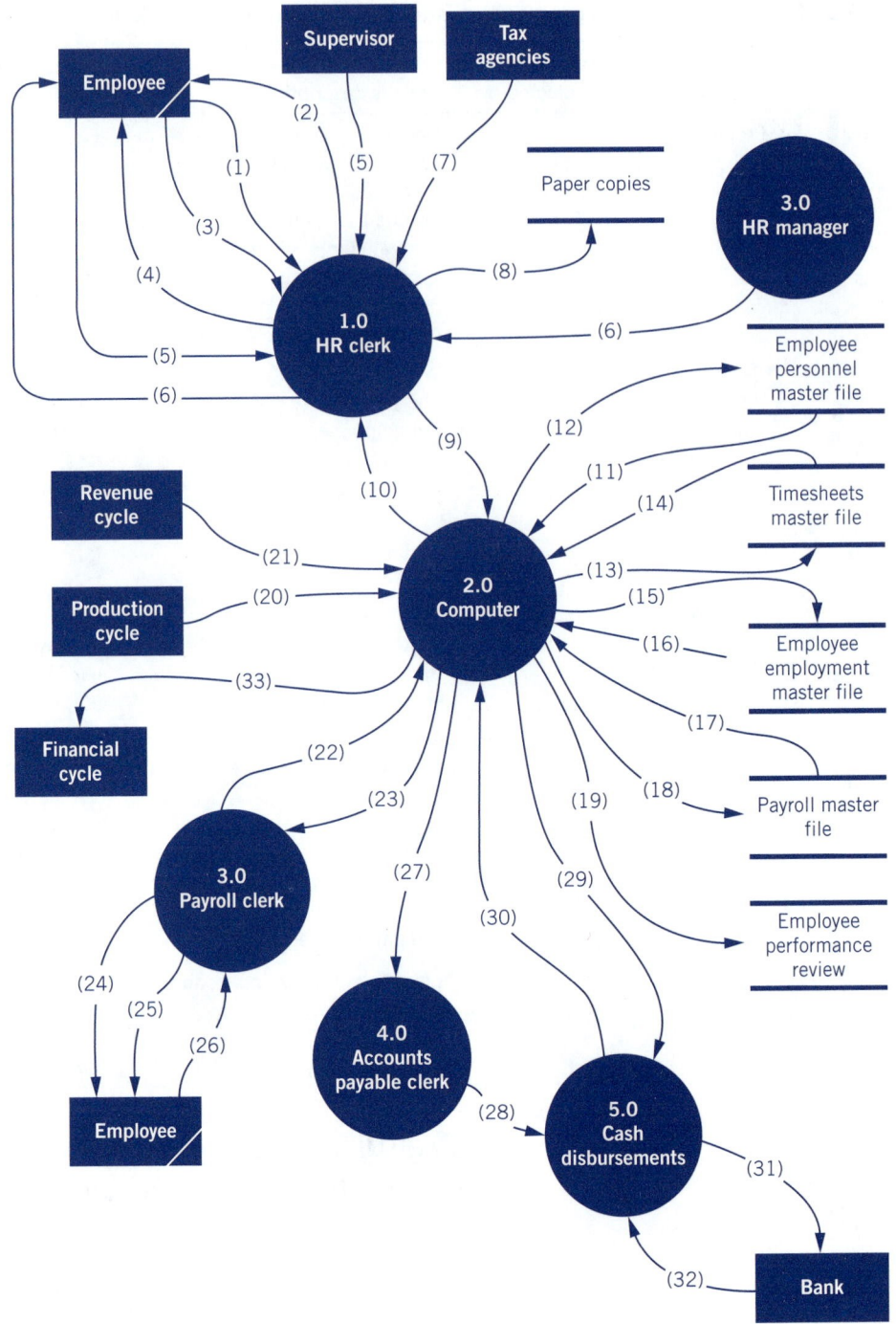

**FIGURE 12.9** Physical DFD — HR management and payroll

## System flowchart — HR management and payroll

The physical DFD in figure 12.9 shows how the HR management and payroll cycle may be processed; the logical DFD in figure 12.4 shows that same process from a logical perspective. The flowchart in figure 12.10 shows that same process from yet another perspective. The system flowchart is the most detailed picture of the process, and includes both logical and physical perspectives. The detail contained in the system flowchart is useful when considering process redesign, and when analysing the control environment of the process depicted. Details of the flows shown in the flowchart in figure 12.10 are documented in table 12.5.

**FIGURE 12.10** Systems flowchart — HR management and payroll

*(continued)*

**FIGURE 12.10** *(continued)*

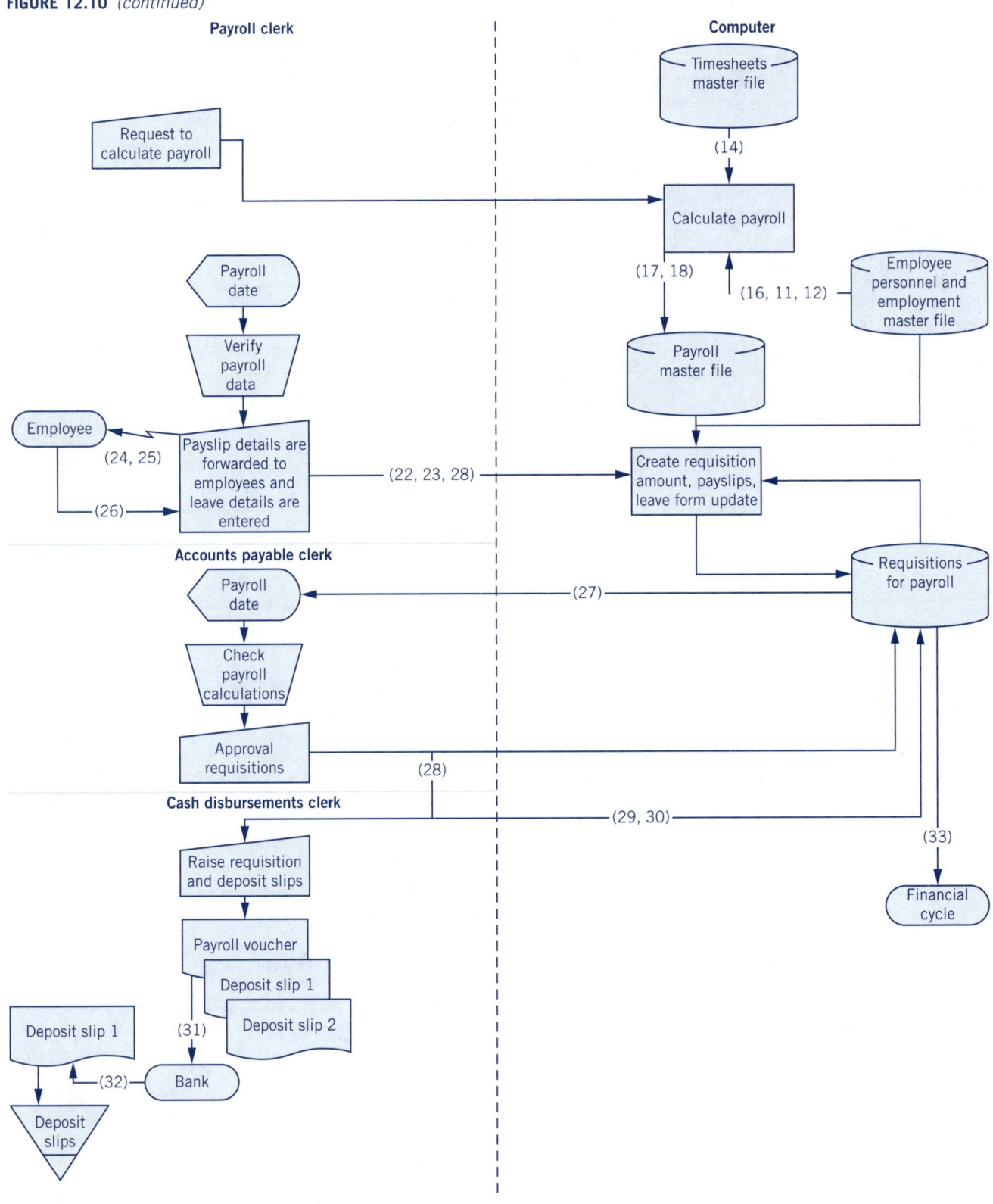

**TABLE 12.5** Description of data flows in physical DFD and flowchart — HR management and payroll

| Flow # | Data source | Data destination | Explanation of the physical data flows |
|---|---|---|---|
| 1 | Employee | HR clerk | Initial employee information to be set up in the employment files. |
| 2 | HR clerk | Employee | Acknowledgement of employee details. |
| 3 | Employee | HR clerk | Request to amend employee details by the employee. |
| 4 | HR clerk | Employee | Request to amend details acknowledged. |
| 5 | Supervisor | HR clerk | Employee performance review. |
| 6 | HR manager | HR clerk | Authorisation to enter new rates, terms for employees. |
| 7 | Tax agencies | HR clerk | New tax rates or tax details to be entered into the system. |
| 8 | HR clerk | Paper copies file | Paper copies evidence the data that has been input. |
| 9 | HR clerk | Computer | HR clerk entering in the computer the new or changed employee details, employee performance review reports, tax rates and employee changes based on the authorisation of HR management. |
| 10 | Computer | HR clerk | The HR clerk receives acknowledgement that the changed employee details, employee performance review reports, tax rates and employee changes have been entered into the computer. |
| 11 | Employee personnel master file | Computer | The computer downloads the current details of the employee personnel master file. |
| 12 | Computer | Employee personnel master file | The computer updates the employee personnel master file for details of the new or changed employee details. |
| 13 | Computer | Timesheets master file | The computer updates the timesheet details for the employees for the current work period and stores it in the data store. |
| 14 | Timesheets master file | Computer | The computer downloads the current the timesheet details to use in the payroll calculation. |
| 15 | Computer | Employee employment master file | The computer updates the employee employment master file for new terms of employment, leave, etc. |
| 16 | Employee employment master file | Computer | The computer downloads the current details of the employee personnel master file. |
| 17 | Payroll master file | Computer | The computer downloads all the information relating to the employee details in the employee personnel master file, and timesheet data for the current period from the timesheets master file. |

*(continued)*

**TABLE 12.5** *(continued)*

| Flow # | Data source | Data destination | Explanation of the physical data flows |
|---|---|---|---|
| 18 | Computer | Payroll master file | The payroll master file has been calculated and is written back to the payroll master file so the amount each employee is to be paid and the personnel details such as name, address or bank account number are prepared for the payslip details. |
| 19 | Employee performance review | Computer | The computer updates and stores details of the employee performance review. |
| 20 | Production cycle | Computer | The production manager inputs details of the hours worked by employees that work on an hourly basis. |
| 21 | Revenue cycle | Computer | The revenue manager inputs details of the sales commissions due to employees that work on a commission basis. |
| 22 | Payroll clerk | Computer | Details of leave forms are entered and updated in the employee employment master file and the timesheet master file and affect the payroll master file if the leave days affect that current pay period. |
| 23 | Computer | Payroll clerk | Details of the payroll are sent to the payroll clerk so that they can print payslips for the employees. |
| 24 | Payroll clerk | Employee | Payslips are printed and sent to employees. This may also happen electronically, in which case a message would be generated directly from the computer and sent to employees. |
| 25 | Payroll clerk | Employee | Leave form acknowledgement is provided to the employee. |
| 26 | Employee | Payroll | Leave form details are provided to the payroll clerk. |
| 27 | Computer | Accounts payable clerk | Details of the amount of the payroll are sent to the accounts payable clerk so they can check the payroll and send to cash disbursements the amount of the disbursement that should occur. |
| 28 | Accounts payable clerk | Cash disbursements | The amount of the cash disbursements needed are paid into the payroll imprest account to satisfy the payroll disbursements to employees and for other expenses. |
| 29 | Computer | Cash disbursements | The computer sends to cash disbursements the amount of the payroll that has been calculated. |
| 30 | Cash disbursements | Computer | The amount that has been transferred and the date of the transfer to the payroll imprest account. |
| 31 | Cash disbursements | Bank | The cash disbursements department sends to the bank the amount of cash to be disbursed. |
| 32 | Bank | Cash disbursement | Verification of the cash disbursements. |
| 33 | Computer | Financial cycle | The amounts of disbursements and the accruals for the payroll expenses for the pay period. |

# MEASURING HR MANAGEMENT AND PAYROLL CYCLE PERFORMANCE

Process performance should be measured relative to how well the process outcomes achieve the overall objectives of that cycle. At the start of this chapter the objectives of the HR management and payroll cycle were described as being to ensure that human capital is paid for accurately and on time and that all payments are appropriately authorised.

To monitor performance against these objectives a range of metrics needs to be employed, along with some realistic targets. Examples of suitable metrics or key performance indicators (KPI) for the HR management and payroll cycle objectives are contained in table 12.6 below.

**TABLE 12.6** Example KPI mapped to cycle objectives

| Objective | Example KPI |
|---|---|
| To calculate payroll and pay employees and employee expenses that are timely and accurate. | • Dollar cash losses due to fraud in the payroll cycle<br>• Dollar overpayments of wages to employees<br>• Number of employee complaints |

## ›› SUMMARY ›››

**LEARNING OBJECTIVE 1**

*What are the key objectives and strategic implications of the HR management and payroll cycle?*

The HR management and payroll cycle consists of two phases. The first is HR management, where the organisation interacts extensively with employees, management and production. The objective of this phase is to ensure that the correct employee details are used and the correct hours worked are input for an employee. In order to achieve this outcome, these inputs need to be properly approved and authorised.

Following after the HR management phase is the payroll phase, where the objective is to pay the right employees and payroll expenses the right amount at the right time. The accounts payable process ensures that payments are both accurate and timely. In order to ensure the integrity of financial reporting all accounts payable liabilities must be recorded accurately and promptly.

**LEARNING OBJECTIVE 2**

*Which technologies underpin the activities of the HR management and payroll cycle?*

There are a number of technologies suitable to support activities within the HR management and payroll cycle. Transparency and management of cash payments and cash flows can also be improved by use of appropriate technologies. Enterprise resource planning (ERP) systems act to provide tighter connections between the ways employees are paid within the organisation, which is essential for correct payroll practices. Barcodes on employee workstations and jobs improve data quality as employees do not have to input the job they are working on and in what location. The ability to make electronic payments provides a fast and comparatively inexpensive way for organisations to settle their payroll expenses with employees, tax authorities and other payroll expenses.

**LEARNING OBJECTIVE 3**

*What data and business decisions are involved in the HR management and payroll cycle?*

Process decisions are made at both strategic and operational levels. Strategy-level decisions include pay periods, pay types and rates. Typical operational decisions include determining that sufficient cash is available and taking advantage of the best times to pay the payroll.

**What are the primary activities in the HR management and payroll cycle and what data are produced by these activities?**

The primary activities involved in the HR management and payroll cycle are the authorisation of payroll details and changes to payroll details for employees. The main activity of the payroll process is calculating the amounts due to employees and disbursing those amounts. This includes the amounts paid to employees as well as for taxation and employee deductions.

A range of data types are accessed and updated by activities within the HR management and payroll cycle, including employee personnel details, employment terms, employee performance reviews, timesheets and pay-to-date for the pay year. The payroll data is sent to the financial cycle for inclusion in the financial reports for the organisation.

  **What risks relate to the HR management and payroll cycle activities, and how might we control for these risks?**

One of the main risks is ensuring that only employees that are working for the organisation are paid for the hours that they work. Significant controls in the cycle are those on the establishment of new employee records to make sure they are for valid employees. Also, any change to those records needs to be authorised. Controls on timesheet data for employees also need to occur to ensure that the employees actually work the hours recorded. Lastly, there needs to be controls on the calculation of employee pays to ensure employees are paid the correct amounts.

To reduce risk exposure, the control environment must include controls that minimise human error, as well as those that prevent fraudulent behaviour. In the case of the HR management and payroll cycle, controls over personnel data, timesheet data, and cash and EFT payments are of primary importance. An appropriate segregation of duties between HR management and payroll needs to occur as well as physical controls over cash and regular bank reconciliations.

  **How can we best monitor HR management and payroll cycle performance?**

Process performance should be measured relative to the desired outcomes of the process. To monitor cycle performance, a wide range of metrics needs to be employed, along with some realistic targets. Examples of suitable performance metrics for the HR management and payroll cycle include numbers of data entry errors.

## KEY TERMS

direct debit form, p. 542
employee details amendment form,
  p. 550
employee employment master file, p. 550
employee performance review, p. 552
employee personnel master file, p. 550

enterprise resource planning (ERP)
  system, p 542
payroll, p. 540
payroll imprest account, p. 554
payslip, p. 554
timesheet, p. 539

## DISCUSSION QUESTIONS

12.1  Would the HR management and payroll cycle differ between a manufacturing firm and a service-oriented firm?

12.2  Discuss the following statement:

'Controls in a HR management and payroll cycle can be easily enforced through a HR management system. Hence, there is no need to closely monitor the controls with the HR management and payroll cycle.'

12.3 Are these documents necessary in a HR management and payroll cycle? Comment by looking at the purpose of the following documents:
(a) Employee details amendment form
(b) Timesheets
(c) Payslips

12.4 Discuss the controls that will be appropriate in the following instances.
(a) An employee submits a duplicate timesheet inadvertently.
(b) An employee spends 15 hours extra on a job than what has been budgeted for. The employee claims the hours as part of a forthcoming project.
(c) The payroll clerk receives timesheet information, checks that the number of hours allocated for a job are not exceeded and arranges for payment of salaries.

12.5 Zahir has been promoted and assumes the position of a manager of the logistics department at Kiyer Limited. Zahir wants to streamline the human resource procedures at Kiyer. He advises employees to lodge their timesheets ahead of time for all jobs that they are allocated to. Zahir ensures that each employee receives the job time summary for each of their jobs. Discuss the pros and cons of such an approach.

12.6 Gundawana Continental Café is a new café located in Surrey Hills. The café has recently hired three employees. The manager of the café has asked you how she should divide up the various jobs so as to maintain good internal control practices. Discuss your approach.

## SELF-TEST ACTIVITIES

12.1 Which of the following personnel is responsible for authorising timesheet changes?
(a) Personnel officer
(b) Manager or supervisor of an employee
(c) Payroll clerk

12.2 What logical process does the HR management and payroll cycle not perform?
(a) Receiving employee amendment forms from employees.
(b) Receiving request for new employees from the requisition department.
(c) Providing goods in lieu of salaries payable to employees.
(d) Budgeting each project so that amounts spent within an organisation on salaries are accounted for.

12.3 Which of the following statements is incorrect about roles and responsibilities of the employees involved in the HR management and payroll cycle?
(a) The HR clerk automatically alters the rates of pay for employees to keep in line with inflation.
(b) The approval of the supervisor or manager is sought before employee personal and employment related information is updated.
(c) The pay officer must reconcile the timesheets, job time summary and deposit slip from the bank.
(d) The HR manager provides maintenance of the HR management system.

12.4 Which of the following procedures, noted by an auditor during a preliminary survey of the payroll function, indicates inadequate control?
(a) All changes to payroll data are documented by the personnel officer on approved change forms.
(b) Prior to distribution, payroll amounts are verified against the timesheets and job time summary records.

(c) All unclaimed hours for a job are provided as bonuses for employees immediately following a job.

(d) The approval of a supervisor or manager needs to be sought before employee records are updated.

12.5 An accountant has been engaged to review a company's payroll procedures. For which of the following would the accountant advise the company of internal control inadequacies if the HR clerk was assigned the responsibility for that procedure?

(a) Allocating salary adjustments to employees.

(b) Reviewing and approving changes to an employee's personal details.

(c) Preparing selection criteria in consultation with a selection committee and the department manager.

(d) Reconciling timesheets with job time summaries to account for any discrepancies.

## PROBLEMS

The case narrative below (AB Hi-Fi) will be used to complete problems 12.1–12.10. Make sure you read and understand the activities and the case thoroughly before you commence work on the problems.

---

### AB Hi-Fi HR and payroll cycle

AB Hi-Fi is a multi-store retail business that sells products such as DVDs, CDs, mp3 players, game consoles and TVs. In addition to retail stores, AB Hi-Fi also sells music, games and DVDs via its website. AB Hi-Fi manufactures all its personalised packaging and marketing materials in-house as it believes this gives greater product flexibility and creates cost saving opportunities. The narrative of the HR management and payroll cycle for AB Hi-Fi follows.

### Process 1.0 Maintain personnel records

Each area of AB Hi-Fi hires its own employees. These employees are generally full-time (F/T), contracted (C/T) or casual staff. Job advertisements for casual employees in JB Hi-Fi's production, warehouse and shipping areas are first posted in the local newspapers and on websites. Causal employees perform a range of duties including packing, ensuring that the production line flows smoothly, assembling different parts for shipment, and ensuring the required adjustments are made to the production line so that all personalised packaging and marketing materials are available in line with the demand for goods. Potential employees apply for the job via the manager of the department that they are intending to work for (i.e. production manager, warehouse manager or shipping manager). The department manager of the department personally interviews each potential applicant and handpicks the successful candidate. The employee is generally paid an hourly rate based on their qualifications and experience. The department manager advises the HR clerk the starting pay rate and any future adjustments.

### Process 2.0 Alter employee details

Each day, the employee fills in a pay claim (through a timesheet) based on what time they start and finish each day. At the end of each week, all the timesheets for the week are accumulated and passed to the departmental manager. The departmental manager peruses the timesheets and signs the timesheets as authorisation.

### Process 3.0 Calculate payroll

The timesheets are then forwarded to the HR department for processing. The payroll is calculated by the HR department. Before a pay is deposited into the employee's

---

bank account by electronic funds transfer, the approval of the departmental manager in which the employee is employed is sought. This allows the departmental manager to make any necessary adjustments to pay.

**Process 4.0 Update payroll data**

The bank deposits clerk, upon approval of the departmental manager, deposits the pay of the employee into the employee's bank account. General ledger is advised of the amounts of the payroll disbursement.

12.1 Prepare a context diagram for the HR and payroll cycle at AB Hi-Fi.

12.2 Prepare a level 0 logical DFD for the HR and payroll cycle at AB Hi-Fi.

12.3 Prepare a physical DFD for the HR and payroll cycle at AB Hi-Fi.

12.4 Prepare a systems flowchart for the HR and payroll cycle at AB Hi-Fi.

12.5 Table 12.3 (page 554) identifies two risks typically encountered when calculating the payroll.

**Required**

(a) Analyse the degree of exposure to each of these risks for the payroll process at AB Hi-Fi.

(b) Determine how many of the common controls described in table 12.3 are present in the payroll process at AB Hi-Fi.

(c) Prepare a short report suitable for senior management to explain how risky you think the payroll process is, and how comprehensive the current internal controls are.

(d) Prepare a recommendation describing any changes you would like to make to the payroll process at AB Hi-Fi in order to reduce the level of risk.

12.6 Table 12.4 (page 557) identifies five risks typically encountered when updating the pay records.

**Required**

(a) Analyse the degree of exposure to each of these risks for the update pay records process at AB Hi-Fi.

(b) Determine how many of the common controls described in table 12.4 are present in the update pay records process at AB Hi-Fi.

(c) Prepare a short report suitable for senior management to explain how risky you think the update pay records process is, and how comprehensive the current internal controls are.

(d) Prepare a recommendation describing any changes you would like to make to the update pay records process at AB Hi-Fi in order to reduce their level of risk.

12.7 (a) AB Hi-Fi has adopted a HR strategy; its overall plan is to hire the best and most flexible employees. How well does their current HR and payroll cycle align with this business strategy? (b) Are there any opportunities to improve the degree of alignment between the HR and payroll cycle and the business strategy? Explain what you would change and how this would improve the strategic alignment.

12.8 (a) Identify and describe the technologies that AB Hi-Fi uses in its HR and payroll cycle activities (b) For each of those technologies you identified in part (a) how well does AB Hi-Fi use the technology? Could you suggest a way to improve the business benefit obtained by use of any of these existing technologies? (c) Are there other suitable technologies available that AB Hi-Fi could be using for the HR and payroll cycle activities? What additional technologies could AB Hi-Fi implement? What business benefit would these additional technologies provide?

**12.9** During process 3.0 Calculate payroll at AB Hi-Fi, before the salary is deposited into the employees' bank accounts by electronic funds transfer, the approval of the departmental manager is sought. This allows the departmental manager to make any necessary adjustments to pay.

**Required**
(a) What data does the departmental manager draw on when making the decision?
(b) Where do the data you identified in part (a) come from?
(c) Are these data reliable; that is, is there any possibility that there could be errors in the data?
(d) Are these data sufficient to make the decision, or can you identify additional data that the departmental manager should consider when making the decision?
(e) What would be the consequences of an incorrect decision?

**12.10** Explain how you would measure performance of the HR and payroll cycle at AB Hi-Fi, specifically:
(a) What metrics would you would use to measure performance?
(b) For each metric, explain where you would obtain the data required for that metric.
(c) For each metric, explain why it is a good metric to help measure how well the HR management and payroll cycle is meeting its objectives.

**12.11** Read the narrative below and answer the following questions.

The University of Agricultural Sciences is an open university in Perth, Western Australia. Each department within the university hires its own casual employees. The following narration relates to the practice within the Department of Business Systems (DBS).

DBS has 12 full-time staff members teaching in a range of courses at undergraduate and postgraduate levels. Each unit typically consists of the lecturer-in-charge (LIC), an associate lecturer (who lecturers and provides administrative support to the lecturer-in-charge), other lecturers who lecture in parts of the unit, and casual tutors. Each unit is organised into large group lecturers and small group tutorials. Students attend a two-hour lecture per week and a one-hour tutorial per week. Tutorials reinforce the material covered in lectures through the review of a series of short answer questions. The lecturer-in-charge notifies DBS's administration clerk well before the start of the teaching semester for the requirements for casual tutors. Job advertisements for casual tutors appear in the local newspapers as well as on noticeboards around the university. Potential applicants for the position of casual tutor (CT) are then short-listed and asked to attend an interview with the LIC. The LIC appoints CTs at different pay rates depending on the applicants' teaching experience and qualifications. At times, an applicant may be appointed at a higher pay rate if the LIC feels that the applicant can help other CTs with their tutoring. Once the applicant accepts the offer for a position of a CT, the LIC sends the name and address of the CT to the pay officer (PO). The PO then prepares a casual academic contract and sends the contract to the LIC to sign. The signed contract is then forwarded back to the pay officer (PO) who prepares the payroll information for the new CT. Where the qualification of the CT has changed, the LIC sends an email to the PO who notes the change in the contract of the CT. CTs are paid fortnightly once they submit a timesheet to the PO. The timesheet lists the number of hours worked and must be initialled by the CT. Also a declaration that the number of hours worked by the CT as listed in the timesheet is correct needs to be signed by the CT and attached with each timesheet submitted to the PO. The payslips advising the CTs of their pay are forwarded by the PO to the LIC. The LIC keeps these payslips in case the CT wants to query his or her pay.

**Required**

(a) Based on the narrative above, what are the weaknesses in the system of internal control?

(b) What enquiries should be made with respect to clarifying the existence of possible additional weaknesses in the system of internal control?

(c) Draw a flowchart of the business activities at DBS.

## SELF-TEST ANSWERS

12.1 b, 12.2 c, 12.3 d, 12.4 d, 12.5 b

## FURTHER READING

Jones, P & Burger, J 2009, *Configuring SAP ERP, financials and controls*, 1st edn, John Wiley & Sons Inc.

## END NOTES

1. Hawking, P & Stein, A 2003, 'B2E portal maturity: an employee self-service case study', *AuSWeb 2003 the ninth Australian world wide web conference 2003*, pp. 5–9 July, www.auswe.scu.edu.au.

2. SAP 2009, 'SAP Business Suite features and functions', www.sap.com/australia.

# 13

# Transaction cycle — the general ledger and financial reporting cycle

## Learning objectives

After studying this chapter, you should be able to:

**1** describe the key objectives and strategic implications of the general ledger and financial reporting cycle

**2** identify common technologies underpinning the general ledger and financial reporting cycle

**3** describe general ledger and financial reporting cycle data and key general ledger and financial reporting business decisions

**4** identify and document the primary activities in the general ledger and financial reporting cycle and the data produced by these activities

**5** analyse risks and develop control plans pertinent to the primary activities in the general ledger and financial reporting cycle

**6** develop metrics to monitor general ledger and financial reporting cycle performance.

# Introduction

General ledger and financial reporting activities are critical to ongoing business success. The general ledger and financial reporting cycle commences when budgets are created and ends when reports have been generated and distributed. During this cycle all data needs to be validated and correctly input and transferred. Adjusting journal entries must be prepared accurately and independently authorised. Reports must be well designed and contain relevant and accurate data.

This chapter commences with an overview of the general ledger and financial reporting cycle, and then considers the strategic implications of that cycle. Technologies that underpin the cycle are discussed, and then the data produced and consumed during the cycle activities are identified. Typical process business decisions are examined, along with some of the primary considerations related to those decisions. A general ledger and financial reporting cycle is fully documented using data flow diagrams and flowcharts, along with a set of tables containing additional details to aid in understanding the process activities, and the related risks and controls of the activities. Finally, issues relating to measuring performance of the general ledger and financial reporting cycle are discussed, and examples of performance metrics suitable for measuring general ledger and financial reporting cycle performance are provided.

**LEARNING OBJECTIVE 1**

*Describe the key objectives and strategic implications of the general ledger and financial reporting cycle.*

# GENERAL LEDGER AND FINANCIAL REPORTING CYCLE OVERVIEW AND KEY OBJECTIVES

The general ledger and financial reporting cycle summarises, adjusts and reports on data from all the previous operational cycles. During the general ledger and financial reporting cycle, budgets are created and agreed upon, and transactional level data is accumulated, summarised, adjusted and, finally, reported to internal and external users. Most decision making by managers within the organisation is based on data supplied by the financial reporting cycle, investors rely on these reports when making investments decisions, and reports are also supplied to external regulators for assessing compliance with relevant corporate legislation. Assuring the timeliness, validity, accuracy and completeness of reported data is critical to organisational success. The organisational units most involved in the general ledger and financial reporting cycle are shown in figure 13.1 overleaf.

The first part of the financial reporting and general ledger cycle involves creating an operational budget for the organisation. Budgets are usually created on an annual basis and updated monthly, or more frequently if required. The purpose of budgeting is to facilitate organisational planning and control. Creating budgets requires careful estimation of future activity levels and the associated potential costs and revenues; finalised budgets are then used as a control measure to help ascertain and monitor required organisational and individual performance levels. In order to motivate desirable behaviour by managers within the organisation, budgets should be framed so that activity targets are achievable but challenging.

When reporting and monitoring using variance analysis (budget estimates compared to actual results), it is important to identify the root cause of any variances observed. As an example, an unfavourable variance between budgeted and actual data may be the result of poor performance, or it is possible that budget estimates were set at an unrealistic or unachievable level. It is necessary to identify which of these circumstances apply, as differing remedial actions are appropriate. An incorrect budget estimate should be corrected, and analysis should be undertaken to determine how the estimation error occurred in order to prevent recurrence. If the budget is realistic but poor performance is the underlying cause of the variance, the poor performance should be addressed via performance management of the individual or division involved.

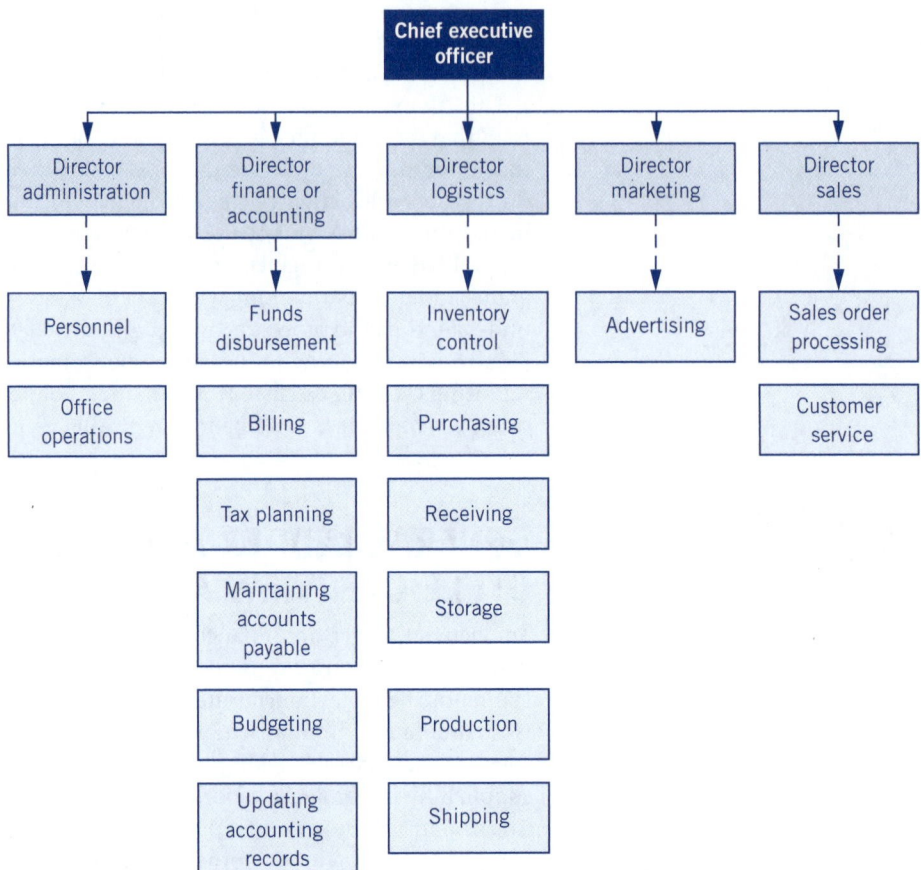

**FIGURE 13.1** Organisational units in the general ledger and financial reporting cycle
*Note:* The dashed lines with the arrows show the business activities that each unit is responsible for.

Once budgets have been finalised, the ongoing work of extracting transactional data generated during the operational transaction cycles (revenue, expenditure, production and payroll) and transferring a summarised version of these transaction streams into the relevant general ledger accounts takes place. This initial set of activities creates a trial balance of the accounts. An example of a trial balance is shown in figure 13.2. It is important to note that this extraction activity does not provide any assurance that the original transactions were recorded accurately. If an operational process has a control weakness that results in inaccurate data being recorded at a transactional level this same flawed data will be transferred into the general ledger accounts.

At periodic intervals, a bank reconciliation is performed in order to independently verify the balances of the cash-based general ledger accounts. After this reconciliation is successfully completed, adjusting journal entries are prepared and input. These adjusting journals create an adjusted trial balance, where the values contained in the accounts comply with the requirements for recognising revenues and expenses contained in the accounting standards. Once the adjusted trial balance has been finalised, financial reporting can take place.

| Account description | Debit | Credit |
| --- | --- | --- |
| Assets | — | — |
| Office supplies | $720 000 | — |
| Furniture | $893 929 | — |
| Property, plant and equipment | $1 020 021 | — |
| Liabilities | — | — |
| Short-term loan | | $500 000 |
| Debentures | | $1 200 000 |
| Overdraft | | $500 000 |
| Owners' equity | — | — |
| Capital | | $1 000 000 |
| Drawings | $510 000 | |
| Loss | $56 050 | |
| Balance | $3 200 000 | $3 200 000 |

**FIGURE 13.2** Sample trial balance

Typically, we divide reports into two major categories: management reports, which are used within the organisation, and general purpose financial statements, which are distributed externally. Management reports tend to be far more detailed in terms of content, and are not intended for sharing outside the organisation. General purpose financial statements are constructed in accordance with the requirements of the relevant accounting standards and contain far less detailed information, but are freely available to a wider range of users.

The objective of the general ledger and financial reporting cycle is to synthesise and report data that accurately represents business transactions and activities. In order to achieve this objective, budgets must be accurately and completely determined and recorded, and transactions extracted and posted must be complete and accurate. In addition, any adjustments that are required must be made prior to financial reporting taking place. Any financial report that is based on accrual accounting assumptions can only be relied upon if it is generated using correctly adjusted data.

An exception is where an operational report (e.g. a simple transaction listing) is required by management — basic reports can be generated at any time after a transaction is recorded, it is not necessary to wait until end-of-period adjustments have been completed. These types of detailed reports usually extract and report data directly from more detailed subsidiary ledgers (e.g. accounts receivable, cash sales) rather than the summarised general ledger. A description of documentation flowing through the general ledger and financial reporting cycle is contained in figure 13.3 overleaf.

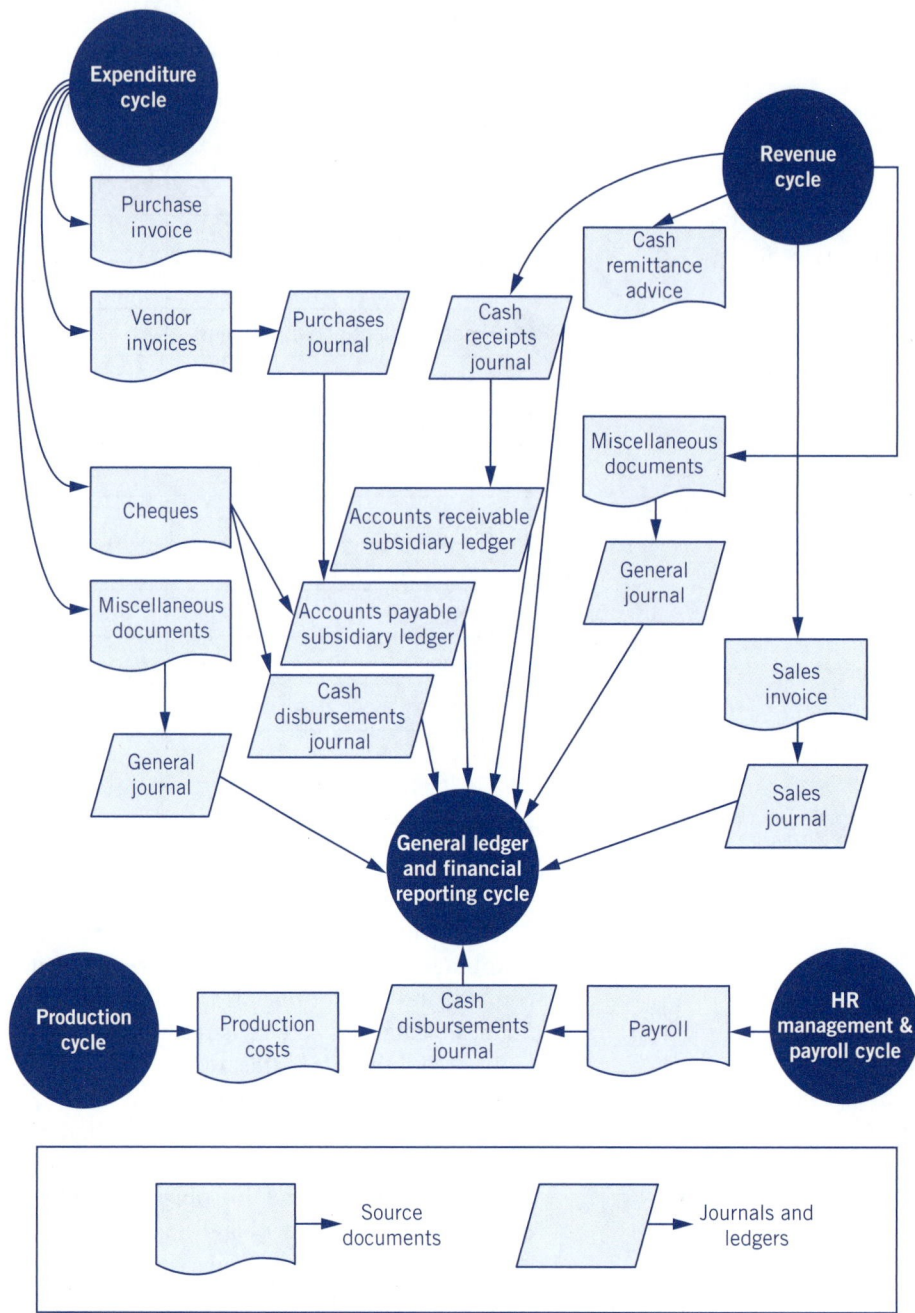

**FIGURE 13.3** Documentation flowing through the general ledger

## Strategic implications of the general ledger and financial reporting cycle

The strategic implications of the general ledger and financial reporting cycle revolve around two main areas. The first is to do with the need for good decision making within the organisation. If management rely upon reported data that is invalid, or not timely, accurate or complete, inevitably decision-making performance will be compromised.

An additional issue is the design of reports. Too much data can lead to an inability for the reader to comprehend the contents. Poorly arranged data can be misleading, and a seemingly simple issue like selecting the appropriate font size or column heading has implications in terms of the understandability of the report. While there is no perfect solution to report design issues, it is important for designers of financial reports to consider report aesthetics, in addition to data content, when designing reports. Poor reports lead to poor decision making, which can lead to eventual business failure; high-quality decision making requires good data and comprehensible reports. The second area is equally serious. External reports are distributed to corporate regulators, analysts and investors, among others. Errors in financial reporting can lead to problems such as incorrect market pricing of company shares, inequitable increases in the cost of capital, inability to access capital markets and the potential for prosecution if corporate laws are breached.

# TECHNOLOGIES UNDERPINNING THE GENERAL LEDGER AND FINANCIAL REPORTING CYCLE

There are a number of technologies suitable to support activities within the general ledger and financial reporting cycle, and improve the overall functioning of the cycle. A range of data management tools are available to help improve the ability to transfer, analyse and report financial data.

**Enterprise resource planning (ERP) systems** assist with integrating the general ledger into the operational cycles that precede general ledger and financial reporting processes in the overall business transaction cycle. The general ledger links back into most areas within the organisation, so an ERP system acts to improves enterprise data integration and facilitate stronger controls over the extraction and posting of data from subsidiary ledgers.

A robust, user-friendly report generating tool such as Cognos or Crystal Reports is essential for the production of both ad hoc and standard financial reports. These business intelligence tools typically provide a simplified user interface to allow interrogation of the underlying data and data dictionary, and the creation of reports using a drag-and-drop-style interface. The deployment of these user-friendly tools is particularly useful in an environment where end users of financial systems take responsibility for designing and producing their own financial reports.

Access to **online banking** is helpful in terms of being able to monitor and reconcile cash transactions more easily. Access to online banking can also be helpful for organisations that wish to automate bank **reconciliations**. The ability to download files in electronic format directly from a bank website presents an opportunity to compare bank statement and cash transaction files electronically, improving both the timeliness and accuracy of bank reconciliations.

**eXtensible Business Reporting Language (XBRL)** is a data standard used when generating financial reports. The importance of this standard is that it allows semantics, or meaning, to be embedded within strings of financial data, allowing more in-depth analysis to be conducted by users or recipients of the data. This meaning is conveyed by inserting embedded tags that identify where separate pieces of data start and end within strings of data. Corporate regulators worldwide are gradually moving towards mandating XBRL data for corporate filings and reporting. Detailed information about the use of XBRL is available at www.xbrl.org/au. The Standard Business Reporting website (www.sbr.gov.au) has additional information on Australian business reporting trends and standards. An example of how XBRL is used to add meaning to text data is shown in figure 13.4 overleaf.

**Enterprise resource planning (ERP) system** *An integrated suite of software that records and manages many different types of business transactions within a single integrated database. Examples include SAP and Oracle.*

**Online banking** *An internet-based banking facility that allows organisations to manage and view their bank accounts online and conduct transactions such as transfers from those accounts.*

**Reconciliation** *An activity where two different sets of data that purport to represent one transaction or set of events are compared to see if they agree. A common example is a bank reconciliation, which reconciles the organisation's accounting records of cash inflows and outflows with the bank's record (i.e. a bank statement).*

**eXtensible Business Reporting Language (XBRL)** *A data standard used when generating financial reports.*

```
Text String: 24072009PAR034523897456200
Text string with XBRL tags inserted:
<date>24072009<customer_id>PAR0345<invoice_#>23897<invoice_
total$>456200.
```

**FIGURE 13.4** XBRL example

## AIS FOCUS 13.1

### Tagged economy — XBRL — emerging opportunity

XBRL is a language for the electronic communication of business and financial data which is revolutionizing business reporting around the world. It provides major benefits in the preparation, analysis and communication of business information. It offers cost savings, greater efficiency and improved accuracy and reliability to all those involved in supplying or using financial data. In the next 5 years, all worldwide electronic business reporting and exchange of financial information between machines, applications and people will be made using XBRL. It is set to become the standard for business reporting. The idea behind XBRL, eXtensible Business Reporting Language, is simple. Instead of treating financial information as a block of text — as in a standard internet page or a printed document — it provides an identifying tag for each individual item of data. This is computer readable. Companies can use XBRL to save costs and streamline their processes for collecting and reporting financial information. Consumers of financial data, including investors, analysts, financial institutions and regulators, can receive, find, compare and analyse data much more rapidly and efficiently if it is in XBRL format.

XBRL is NOT a proprietary technology. XBRL is freely licensed and available to the public. XBRL is XML-based and therefore is expected to be widely available in software applications.

#### XBRL and business
All types of organizations can use XBRL to save costs and improve efficiency in handling business and financial information. Because XBRL is extensible and flexible, it can be adapted to a wide variety of different requirements. All participants in the financial information supply chain can benefit, whether they are preparers, transmitters or users of business data.

#### Data collection and reporting
By using XBRL, companies and other producers of financial data and business reports can automate the processes of data collection. For example, data from different company divisions with different accounting systems can be assembled quickly, cheaply and efficiently if the sources of information have been upgraded to using XBRL. Once data is gathered in XBRL, different types of reports using varying subsets of the data can be produced with minimum effort. A company finance division, for example, could quickly and reliably generate internal management reports, financial statements for publication, tax and other regulatory filings, as well as credit reports for lenders.

Not only can data handling be automated, removing time-consuming, error-prone processes, but the data can be checked by software for accuracy. Small businesses can benefit alongside large ones by standardizing and simplifying their assembly and filing of information to the authorities.

**Data consumption and analysis**

Users of data which is received electronically in XBRL can automate its handling, cutting out time consuming and costly collation and re-entry of information. Software can also immediately validate the data, highlighting errors and gaps which can immediately be addressed. It can also help in analyzing, selecting, and processing the data for re-use. Human effort can switch to higher, more value-added aspects of analysis, review, reporting and decision-making. In this way, investment analysts can save effort, greatly simplify the selection and comparison of data, and deepen their company analysis. Lenders can save costs and speed up their dealings with borrowers. Regulators and government departments can assemble, validate and review data much more efficiently and usefully.

With XBRL, software developers can build tools that can be installed into a wide variety of systems, without the need to customize the interface to the company. Installation may require custom configuration based on how a company will want to deploy its internal control systems, however, that would likely be at a much lower cost. Additionally, because XBRL is an external standard that supports financial reporting based on US generally accepted accounting principles (GAAP) and International Financial Reporting Standards (IFRS), companies will have the ability to respond to rapid changes in regulatory reporting requirements.

The ability to consolidate acquisitions and integrate business systems has historically been challenging due to differences in data and account structures. XBRL has the potential to significantly reduce the time and effort required to integrate new acquisitions if both companies are using the standard. Integration would simply be a matter of consistently classifying the already tagged information. There would be little need for a large information gathering and consolidation effort that exists with acquisitions today.[1]

**LEARNING OBJECTIVE 3**

*Describe general ledger and financial reporting data and key general ledger and financial reporting business decisions.*

# DATA AND DECISIONS IN THE GENERAL LEDGER AND FINANCIAL REPORTING CYCLE

A range of data are both produced and consumed by activities within the general ledger and financial reporting cycle. The actual data stores are documented in detail later in this chapter. This section describes the general purpose and types of data that the general ledger and financial reporting cycle requires. The business decisions made during the life of the general ledger and financial reporting cycle are also discussed here.

## Data and the general ledger and financial reporting cycle

Budget data is often initially created based on prior year data, then manually adjusted and entered into the financial system by finance personnel and operational managers. Budget data is held in the general ledger chart of accounts, and is used in reporting, largely as a target or benchmark level against which actual results are compared.

The general ledger and financial reporting cycle initially extracts existing transactional data from subsidiary ledgers. These subsidiary ledgers include the accounts receivable ledger (which contains details of customer invoices raised and payments received) and the accounts payable ledger (which contains details of supplier invoices received and payments approved and made). The payroll data store provides details of salary and wage transactions. The raw materials, labour and overheads data stores from the production cycle provide details of production costs incurred. The general ledger uses all this transactional data to create summarised transactions in the accounts within the general ledger. These general ledger accounts are conventionally referred to as the chart of accounts for the organisation.

A typical general ledger account code will contain a string of indicators representing items such as the transaction type (e.g. revenue, expense, equity), the division or section of the organisation the transaction relates to, and the nature of the transaction. As an example, a general ledger code of 41235602132801 may represent:

- 4    = Expenditure
- 12   = Office supplies
- 356  = Paper
- 02   = Victorian branch
- 13   = Melbourne
- 28   = Finance department
- 01   = CFO division.

Any transaction coded with this number would be accumulated and stored in the same general ledger account. This coding structure would permit data extraction and reporting based on any of the indicators included. For this example, it would be possible to report all paper purchased, or all expenditure, or all office supplies expenditure, or all costs for the division, department or branch, or any combination of these items. Given this code structure, however, it would not be possible to report on purchases of coloured paper separately from white paper, nor would it be possible to report on the purpose for which the paper was used, that is, the job number or activity undertaken using the paper. An example showing chart of account categories is contained in figure 13.5.

| Account code | Account category |
|---|---|
| 100–199 | Current assets |
| 200–299 | Noncurrent assets |
| 300–399 | Liabilities |
| 400–499 | Noncurrent liabilities |
| 500–599 | Owners' equity |
| 600–699 | Revenues |
| 700–799 | Cost of sales |
| 800–899 | Operating expenses |
| 900–999 | Non-operating expenses |

**FIGURE 13.5** Major account categories

The chart of accounts establishes the basis upon which reports can be generated; a fully flexible chart of accounts would include an indicator for every possible dimension that the transaction may conceivably need to be reported on. In practice, however, there is a trade off — the more digits a general ledger account number contains, the more likely data processing errors become. General ledger account codes are added to every transaction prior to it being processed into the subsidiary ledger during the operational cycles. The purpose of the general ledger is to extract these transactions and their associated account numbers, then summarise and transfer the data into the general ledger. A well-designed chart of accounts will support diverse reporting requirements while maintaining an acceptably low data entry error rate. Adoption of any alternative costing or reporting requirements, such as activity based costing, will increase the number of tags, or indicators, needed to code transactions accurately into the general ledger accounts.

The only new data created by the general ledger and financial reporting cycle are general journal entries. Although small in volume, these adjusting journals can have a huge financial impact on the financial results subsequently reported. General journal data is typically stored in a separate journal voucher data store, as well as in the relevant general ledger accounts.

Data produced by the general ledger and financial reporting cycle are used by all levels of management within the organisation, and by investors, analysts and regulators external to the organisation. Access to financial data usually occurs by means of paper or electronic reports for users within the organisation. External reporting has traditionally been paper based only, with recent augmentation by electronic reporting.

## AIS FOCUS 13.2

### School settled with Greentree for good

Organisational needs often change over five years. Software packages often can't handle an organisation's changing needs. But five years after Lutheran Education Queensland (LEQ) installed Greentree, accountant Julie Rogers is still a proponent of the accounting package.

'By putting them into transaction analysis codes you're classing them like a sub code but you can report on everything relating to one business manager. It's a more efficient way of reporting,' she says. 'And from the data-entry side of things, there's less room for error because you use a drop-down to pick the person the expense relates to.'

Because the organisation is non-profit, they are audited every year and must fulfil strict requirements. One example is that LEQ's data and payments must be entered into Excel first and reconciled within each spreadsheet, before being input again into an accounting package.

But now LEQ can upload its accounts receivables, invoices, expense claims, journals and other data from the spreadsheets straight into Greentree, without having to key each line again.

'We used to have to manually enter everything; now we just attach the relative sheet and functions, and upload it. Using this function has probably saved about a quarter of the time it used to take. Some of the spreadsheets can contain a hundred invoices, so you can imagine how long it used to take to enter 100 invoices manually. It's been a real lifesaver for us.'

*continued*

Greentree's integration with Excel has also been useful for reporting, and it's one of the things Rogers most likes about the package. 'Once you understand what you're doing, you can create any sort of report,' she says. 'You build a tree in Greentree and then export it to Excel, whereas in a standard package you're stuck with the same old Profit & Loss, Balance Sheet and Trial Balance.'

LEQ is considering implementing Greentree's customer relationship management module for its booking management. In the third quarter of the year, in particular, LEQ can run a conference a day, training new teachers. All of these conference bookings are done via LEQ's website. Rogers says the intention is that the bookings will link in with the website, and will then be uploaded to accounts receivable invoices. It will eliminate the need for an Excel spreadsheet and save hours of input time. Another way Greentree has saved LEQ time and money is by enabling emailed supplier remittances and customer invoices. 'We can now pay everything by direct credit, and send a remittance to tell them it's in their bank.' Rogers says Greentree has been easy to use and easy to learn. 'We just love the fact you can manipulate it and get out of it what you want.'[2]

*Source:* blueStar Business Solutions, www.bluestar.net.au.

## General ledger and financial reporting cycle business decisions

Process business decisions are made from several different perspectives during the general ledger and financial reporting cycle. Budget decisions relating to the initial establishment of budget levels and the subsequent monitoring and adjustment of budgets require a good understanding of both the operational pragmatics of the organisation and the financial performance aspirations of senior management. Typical budget decisions include:

- budget level — budgets can be set at a range of levels. Many organisations budget down to a level known as 'line item' where budgets are set for each different type of revenue and expense for each division as contained in the chart of accounts. An alternative is to set higher level budgets where items such as office expenses or production costs may be aggregated. Although more aggregate budgets are easier to plan, their usefulness during monitoring of performance is limited due to the lack of information they provide.
- budget breakdown — budgets can be established with an annual total, or they can be broken down into months. The degree of granularity at which the budget is set determines how useful the budget targets will be during performance monitoring. If an annual budget is set, month-by-month monitoring could be misleading when variances are considered. An additional consideration is the behaviour of the item being budgeted; not all revenue and expenses divide evenly into 12 over a fiscal year. Using an expenditure example, an insurance policy may be paid annually, in which case a month-by-month budget would show that cost only in the month in which it is expected the policy would be renewed. The example in figure 13.6 contains two report extracts illustrating this issue. In the annual budget report a total favourable variance of $24 600 is shown for the year to date, whereas the more detailed month-by-month analysis reveals that a mixture of favourable and unfavourable variances are actually occurring.

- budget targets — setting budget targets requires balance between what is desired in terms of performance and what is thought to be possible. A good budget target will require some 'stretch' to achieve but not be so high as to be seen as unobtainable. Most budget targets are set during discussion between managers, and often budget decisions end up being the result of a compromise.

**Annual budget example**

**Budget vs. actual report 30 September 2011**

|  | Budget | Actual | Variance |  |
|---|---|---|---|---|
| Insurance | 15 000 | 0 | 15 000 | (F) |
| Electricity | 8 000 | 4 800 | 3 200 | (F) |
| Consumables | 12 000 | 5 600 | 6 400 | (F) |
| Total | 35 000 | 10 400 | 24 600 | (F) |

**Month-by-month budget example**

**Budget vs. actual report 30 September 2011**

|  | July | | | August | | | September | | |
|---|---|---|---|---|---|---|---|---|---|
|  | Budget | Actual | Variance | Budget | Actual | Variance | Budget | Actual | Variance |
| Insurance | 0 | 0 | 0 | 0 | 0 | 0 | 0 | 0 | 0 |
| Electricity | 0 | 0 | 0 | 2 000 | 2 900 | (900) | 0 | 0 | 0 |
| Consumables | 1 000 | 950 | 50 | 1 000 | 1 020 | (20) | 1 000 | 1 240 | (240) |
| Total | 1 000 | 950 | 50 | 3 000 | 3 920 | (920) | 1 000 | 1 240 | (240) |

**FIGURE 13.6** Example budget analysis — annual vs. month-by-month

Decisions relating to the creation of general journal adjustments take place during the cycle, and the data and reports produced by this cycle underpin subsequent decision making within the organisation. Decisions relating to general journal entries would include consideration of:
- accounting standards — requires knowledge of relevant standards and understanding of their applicability to the business
- accounting policies and procedures — requires knowledge of these procedures and understanding of their use and intention
- timing differences for a given accounting period — requires understanding of how accruals and liabilities are affected by events such as arbitrary period-end dates and transaction cycle cut-off dates
- the need to incorporate data from external sources such as bank statements that are not already captured during the operational cycles.

In addition to these journal adjustment decisions, reports produced by this cycle are used to support decision makers within the organisation. Common examples of these reports include:
- profitability analysis for the organisation or a division
- analysis of performance for an individual or division (variance analysis)
- analysis of profitability potential to guide future investment decisions
- cost management analysis for decision making.

**LEARNING OBJECTIVE 4**

*Identify and document the primary activities in the general ledger and financial reporting cycle and the data produced by these activities.*

# GENERAL LEDGER AND FINANCIAL REPORTING CYCLE DOCUMENTATION

The general ledger and financial reporting cycle is documented in the following section as a series of diagrams with increasing amounts of details. An overview of these general ledger and financial reporting cycle diagrams is contained in figure 13.7.

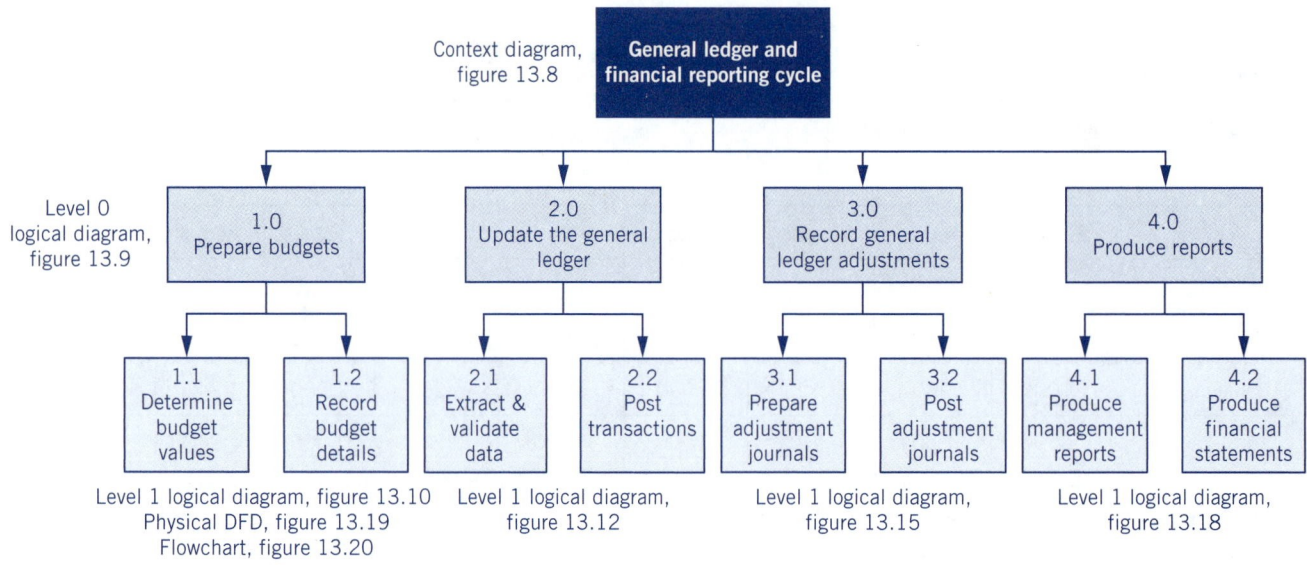

**FIGURE 13.7** General ledger and financial reporting diagrams overview

## General ledger and financial reporting cycle context

The context diagram of a typical general ledger and financial reporting cycle is depicted in figure 13.8. The general ledger and financial reporting cycle involves direct interaction with entities outside the organisation that read and use the general purpose financial statements produced by this cycle, and with the bank to obtain data related to bank account transactions. Within the organisation, the general ledger and financial reporting cycle interacts with the production, human resource and payroll, expenditure and revenue cycles as shown in figure P3.1 (page 389), along with managers of operational departments. Details of the logical data flows depicted in the general ledger and financial reporting context diagram are contained in table 13.1 (page 585).

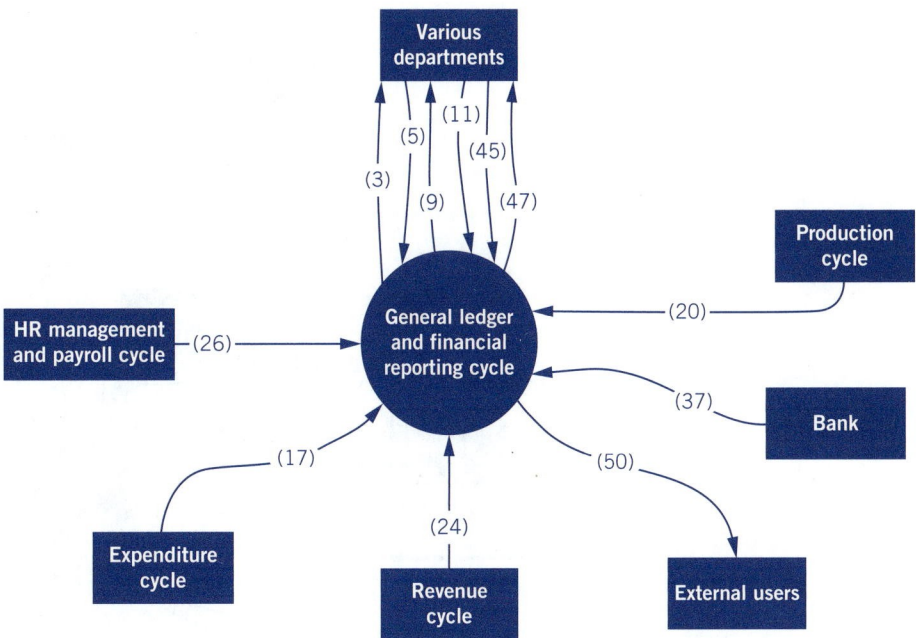

**FIGURE 13.8** General ledger and financial reporting cycle context diagram

## General ledger and financial reporting cycle logical data flows

Figure 13.9 depicts a level 0 logical DFD. This diagram shows the entire general ledger and financial reporting cycle in greater detail than that depicted in the context diagram. The logical DFD is an exploded version of the context diagram, with the bubble described as 'general ledger and financial reporting cycle' in the context diagram broken down into four processes. The logical diagram at level 0 helps us to analyse and understand the general ledger and financial reporting cycle in its entirety. It depicts the chronology of the cycle, the data stores and external entities involved in each of the processes and the interactions between these processes, entities and data stores. The logical level 0 diagram in figure 13.9 is itself broken down to describe even lower levels of detail in figures 13.10, 13.12, 13.15 and 13.18 later in this chapter. Details of the logical data flows depicted in this diagram are contained in table 13.1 (page 585).

### *Description of logical data flows in the general ledger and financial reporting cycle*

A logical DFD contains only those data flows relating to inputs and outputs of the activities contained within each of the processes, as opposed to the details of all interactions between entities as depicted in a physical DFD. As a result, the number of flows in a logical DFD is always less than those that would be shown in a physical DFD for the same process. To illustrate this, compare figures 13.9 and 13.19, which both show exactly the same process; however, figure 13.9 is a logical description whereas figure 13.19 is a physical description. In order to maintain consistency of documentation references, the larger number of flows contained in the physical DFD of process 1.0 shown in figure 13.19 are numbered sequentially in table 13.6. The numbering of the subset of data flows for process 1.0 depicted in the logical diagram contained in figure 13.10 and documented in table 13.1 are therefore not sequential.

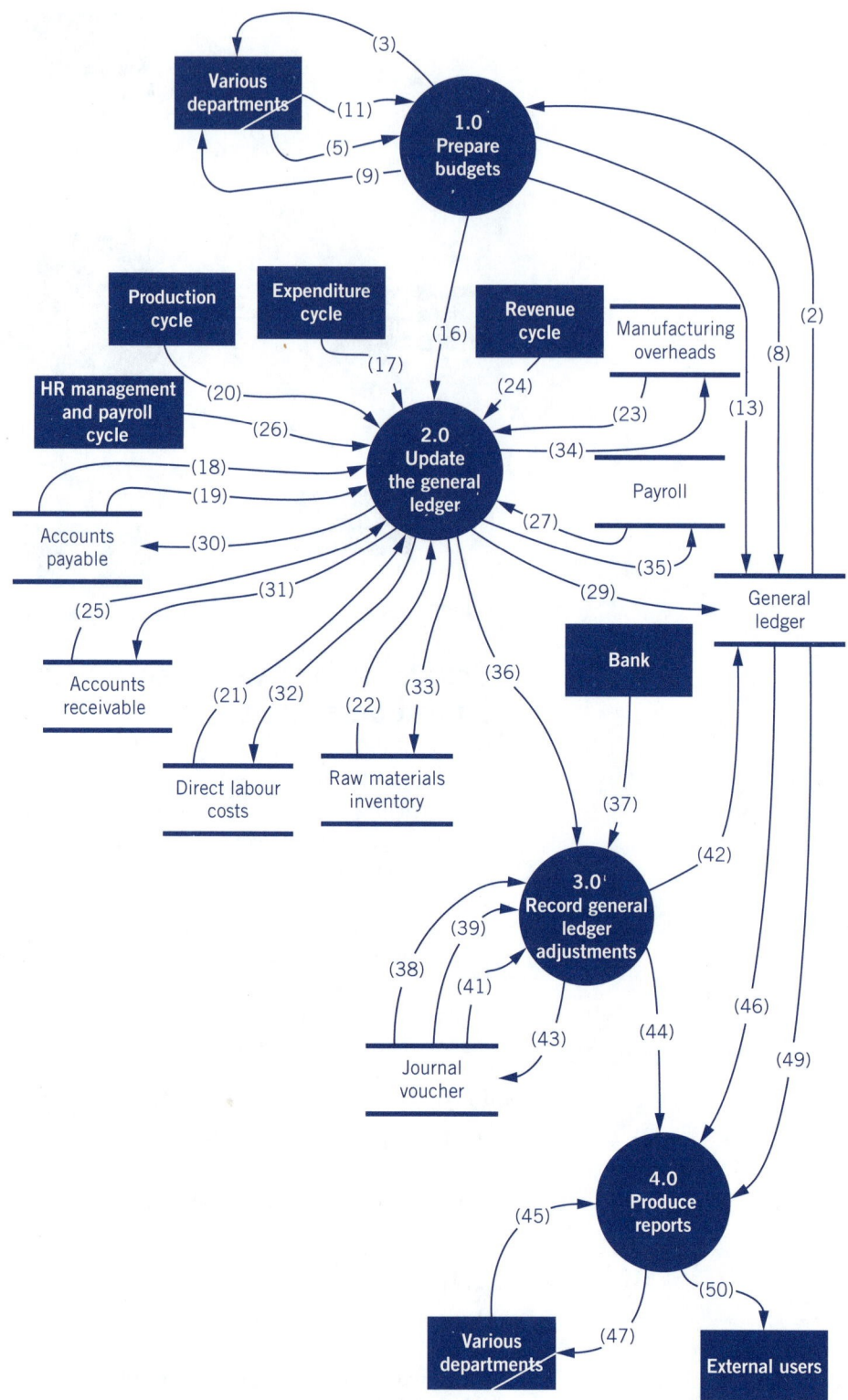

**FIGURE 13.9** General ledger and financial reporting cycle level 0 logical diagram

**TABLE 13.1** Description of logical data flows in the general ledger and financial reporting cycle

| Flow # | Typical data source | Typical data destination | Data description | Explanation of the logical data flow |
|---|---|---|---|---|
| **Process 1.0 Prepare budgets** | | | | |
| 1 | This flow takes place physically between the budget clerk and the computer; it happens within the 1.0 bubble in the logical diagram. | | | |
| 2 | Prior transaction history | Budget clerk | Details of prior totals for revenue and expenditure items | The computer extracts historical totals for each of the revenue and expenditure accounts in the general ledger. |
| 3 | Prior transaction history | Operational departments | Prior revenue and expenditure items embedded in a proforma budget worksheet | The revenue and expenditure totals have been loaded into a worksheet and are distributed to the relevant operational departments. |
| 4 | This flow takes place physically between the budget clerk and the computer; it happens within the 1.0 bubble in the logical diagram. | | | |
| 5 | Operational departments | Budget manager | Details of adjusted budget estimates | The operational managers responsible for the various departments consider the proforma worksheets and adjust budget items if necessary. |
| 6 | Operational departments | Budget manager | Trigger for next process | Once budget values have been adjusted the budget details are ready to be input in to the computer (not necessary in a level 0 diagram). |
| 7 | This flow takes place physically between the budget clerk and the computer; it happens within the 1.0 bubble in the logical diagram. | | | |
| 8 | Operational departments | General ledger data store | Details of approved adjusted budget estimates | Once budgets have been checked and approved the budget data is recorded against the appropriate general ledger accounts. |
| 9 | General ledger data store | Operational departments | Details of approved adjusted budget estimates | Department managers are advised of finalised approved budget details. |
| 10 | This flow takes place physically between the budget clerk and the computer; it happens within the 1.0 bubble in the logical diagram. | | | |
| 11 | Operational departments | Budget clerk/ manager | Approval of finalised budgets | Operational managers positively confirm their acceptance of the finalised budget amounts. |
| 12 | This flow takes place physically between the budget clerk and the computer; it happens within the 1.0 bubble in the logical diagram. | | | |
| 13 | Operational departments | General ledger data store | Details of approved final budget estimates | Once final budgets have been accepted and approved, the status of the budget data is updated to 'approved'. |
| 14 | This flow takes place physically between the computer and the budget manager; it happens within the 1.0 bubble in the logical diagram. | | | |

*(continued)*

**TABLE 13.1** (continued)

| Flow # | Typical data source | Typical data destination | Data description | Explanation of the logical data flow |
|---|---|---|---|---|
| 15 | This flow takes place physically between the budget clerk and the computer; it happens within the 1.0 bubble in the logical diagram. | | | |
| 16 | Prepare budgets | Update general ledger | Final budget estimates | Once the budget has been finalised for the year, ongoing revenue and expenditure transactions can be recorded against the relevant general ledger accounts. |

**Process 2.0 Update the general ledger**

| Flow # | Typical data source | Typical data destination | Data description | Explanation of the logical data flow |
|---|---|---|---|---|
| 17 | Expenditure cycle | Computer | Subsidiary ledger processing completed | During the expenditure cycle described in chapter 10, transactions related to payments established and made are posted through to the accounts payable data store. Once this processing is complete, a notification is sent to the financial cycle to advise that posting to the general ledger accounts can commence. |
| 18 | Accounts payable data store | Computer | Details of payments approved and scheduled | Details of payments approved and scheduled to be paid are extracted from the accounts payable data store. |
| 19 | Accounts payable data store | Computer | Details of payment made | Details of payments made are extracted from the accounts payable data store and validated. |
| 20 | Production cycle | Computer | Subsidiary ledger processing completed | During the production cycle described in chapter 11 transactions related to production costs are posted through to the relevant data stores. Once this processing is complete, a notification is sent to the financial cycle to advise that posting to the general ledger accounts can commence. |
| 21 | Direct labour costs data store | Computer | Details of direct labour costs | Details of direct labour costs of production incurred are extracted from the direct labour costs data store and validated. |
| 22 | Raw materials inventory data store | Computer | Details of raw material costs | Details of raw material costs incurred are extracted from the raw materials data store and validated. |
| 23 | Manufacturing overheads data store | Computer | Details of manufacturing overheads incurred | Details of manufacturing overhead costs incurred are extracted from the manufacturing overheads data store and validated. |
| 24 | Revenue cycle | Computer | Subsidiary ledger processing completed | During the revenue cycle described in chapter 9 transactions related to invoices raised and payments received are posted through to the accounts receivable data store. Once this processing is complete, a notification is sent to the financial cycle to advise that posting to the general ledger accounts can commence. |
| 25 | Accounts receivable data store | Computer | Details of invoices raised and cash payments received | Details of invoices raised and cash payments received are extracted from the accounts receivable data store and validated. |

| Flow # | Typical data source | Typical data destination | Data description | Explanation of the logical data flow |
|---|---|---|---|---|
| 26 | HR management and payroll cycle | Computer | Subsidiary ledger processing completed | During the HR management and payroll cycle described in chapter 12 transactions related to payroll costs are posted through to the relevant data stores. Once this processing is complete, a notification is sent to the financial cycle to advise that posting to the general ledger accounts can commence. |
| 27 | Payroll master file | Computer | Salary and wage payment details | Details of salary and wages payments made are extracted from the payroll data store and validated |
| 28 | Extract and validate data | Post transactions | Trigger for next process | After all transaction data have been extracted and validated the summarised totals can be posted to the relevant general ledger accounts in the general ledger data store (not necessary in a level 0 diagram). |
| 29 | Transactional processes | General ledger data store | Summarised validated transaction totals. | The transaction totals extracted and validated in the preceding process are posted into the appropriate general ledger accounts. |
| 30 | Computer | Accounts payable data store | Details of transactions posted to the general ledger | Once the accounts payable transactions have been posted to the general ledger their status code in the subsidiary ledger is updated to 'posted'. |
| 31 | Computer | Accounts receivable data store | Details of transactions posted to the general ledger | Once the accounts receivable transactions have been posted to the general ledger their status code in the subsidiary ledger is updated to 'posted'. |
| 32 | Computer | Direct labour costs data store | Details of transactions posted to the general ledger | Once the direct labour cost transactions have been posted to the general ledger their status code in the subsidiary ledger is updated to 'posted'. |
| 33 | Computer | Raw materials inventory data store | Details of transactions posted to the general ledger | Once the raw materials transactions have been posted to the general ledger their status code in the subsidiary ledger is updated to 'posted'. |
| 34 | Computer | Manufacturing overheads data store | Details of transactions posted to the general ledger | Once the manufacturing overhead transactions have been posted to the general ledger their status code in the subsidiary ledger is updated to 'posted'. |
| 35 | Computer | Payroll data store | Details of transactions posted to the general ledger | Once the payroll transactions have been posted to the general ledger their status code in the subsidiary ledger is updated to 'posted'. |
| 36 | Update general ledger | Record general ledger adjustments | Summarised transaction data | Once all transactions have been posted to the general ledger any accounting adjustments necessary can be processed. |
| **Process 3.0 Record general ledger adjustments** | | | | |
| 37 | Bank | Accounting staff | Bank statement transaction details | The bank supplies details of transactions from the bank accounts on a regular basis. |

*(continued)*

**TABLE 13.1** *(continued)*

| Flow # | Typical data source | Typical data destination | Data description | Explanation of the logical data flow |
|---|---|---|---|---|
| 38 | Accounting staff | Journal voucher data store | Details of general journal entries | Accounting staff prepare and input details of the general journal entries required. |
| 39 | Senior accounting staff | Journal voucher data store | Approval for general journal entry | Details of the proposed general journal entries are sent to senior accounting staff for approval. |
| 40 | Prepare adjustment journals | Post adjustment journals | Trigger for next process | After journal entries have been approved the relevant general ledger accounts in the general ledger data store can be updated (not necessary in a level 0 diagram). |
| 41 | Computer | Journal voucher data store | Details of approved general journal entries | Periodically, the computer extracts details of all the approved, but not yet processed, journal entries from the journal voucher data store. |
| 42 | Computer | General ledger data store | Details of approved general journal entries | Approved general journal entries are posted to the relevant general edger accounts. |
| 43 | Computer | Journal voucher data store | Posted general journal entries | The status of the general journal voucher is updated to 'processed'. |
| 44 | Record general ledger adjustments | Produce reports | Posted general journal entries | Once the adjusting entries have been approved and posted, reports can be generated. |
| **Process 4.0 Produce reports** | | | | |
| 45 | Operational departments | Accounting staff | Ad hoc report requests | Operational department managers submit requests for reports on an ad hoc basis. |
| 46 | General ledger data store | Computer | General ledger data | The computer extracts the data required to populate the requested reports from the general ledger data store. |
| 47 | Computer | Operational departments | Requested report data | Once an ad hoc report has been generated it is sent to the department that requested it. |
| 48 | Produce management reports | Produce financial statements | Trigger for next process | Once the management reports have been generated and examined the general purpose financial statements can be produced (not necessary in a level 0 diagram). |
| 49 | General ledger data store | Computer | General ledger data | At regular predetermined intervals the computer extracts the data required to populate the general purpose financial statements from the general ledger data store. |
| 50 | Computer | External users/senior management | Financial statements data | Once the general purpose financial statements have been generated they are distributed to external users and to senior management. |

**LEARNING OBJECTIVE**

*Analyse risks and develop control plans pertinent to the primary activities in the general ledger and financial reporting cycle.*

# GENERAL LEDGER AND FINANCIAL REPORTING CYCLE ACTIVITIES AND RELATED RISKS AND CONTROLS

The activities within the general ledger and financial reporting cycle and the associated risks and controls are described under the four general ledger and financial reporting cycle headings below. Following the activity descriptions for each of the processes is the level 1 DFD for the process and a table summarising the activities, risks and controls within the process.

## Prepare budgets — activities, risks and controls

Process 1.0, prepare budgets, comprises the following activities.

### Determine budget values

The general ledger and financial reporting cycle begins with the creation of an operational budget. Note that differing phases of the general ledger and financial reporting cycle run concurrently; for example, while budgeting is taking place the finance staff will still be recording general ledger adjustments and the transaction cycles will still be processing and generating data. This sequencing is identical to that experienced in other cycles. For example, in the revenue cycle the sales phase runs continuously, as does the shipping and billing phases; however, to improve understandability we document each cycle as a linear procedure, with activities happening in sequence. The cycle documentation is drawn to represent one single cycle from start to finish; however, multiple transaction cycles will always run simultaneously.

Budgets are planning estimates of future revenue and expenditure items, and are an important management tool. Budgets are used for planning and for comparison against actual performance for monitoring and control purposes. There are several common methods used to construct a budget. Budgets may be incrementally calculated by referencing historical transactions and indexing by some estimated percentage amount, or by analysing proposed activity levels for the future period and then calculating estimated revenue and expenditure based on those predicted activity levels. Another alternative is zero-based budgeting where prior results are not used as a starting point for future estimates at all; rather, all budget values are based on future estimates only. Zero-based budgeting requires that each estimate be individually justified by management, and is not concerned whether the total budget is increasing or decreasing.

In addition to the operational budgets described above, organisations generally prepare a capital expenditure budget where a central pool of funding is allocated to major works and projects. Capital expenditure budgets are generally allocated by a competitive application process, with project proposals ranked and funded on the basis of potential to return value to the business.

Where prior transactional data is used to form the operational budget the computer would extract totals for each of the revenue and expenditure accounts in the general ledger to establish a starting point for determining future budget estimates. Once the revenue and expenditure totals have been extracted they need to be distributed to the relevant operational departments, either electronically in a form similar to an Excel spreadsheet, or on paper. Proforma budgets are usually prepared on a month-by-month basis for the upcoming fiscal year. The operational managers responsible for the various departments would consider the proforma worksheets and adjust budget items if necessary. These adjustments are often required due to local knowledge of changes in operating conditions that make prior estimates imperfect predictors of future outcomes.

The primary risk when determining budget values is under or overestimating revenue and expenditure amounts. Common controls to reduce this risk include requiring independent approval of budget estimates, and the preparation of estimates by operational managers. Budgets are often aggregated to show department budget totals and independent approval should be obtained for overall budget totals. The existence of tight linkages between budget values and performance monitoring is an important control; that is, if managers are aware that their performance is being monitored and measured against budget estimates they are more likely to provide thoughtful input into the budget estimates, and to attempt to meet their budget targets.

### Record budget details

Once budgets have been checked and approved, the budget totals can be input into the central computer to establish the budget levels for future periods against the appropriate general ledger accounts.

Operational managers need to be aware of final budget details, as these form their performance targets for future periods. This is particularly important where managers may not have determined the final budget estimates; these managers need a chance to consider budget estimates before the budget is finalised. The finalisation of budgets is an interactive process involving both senior management and operational staff. Operational managers should positively confirm their acceptance of the finalised budget amounts. As these amounts will be used to monitor and manage their future performance, it is important to establish the commitment and buy-in by managers to the budgeted amounts. Once final budgets have been accepted and approved by senior management the ongoing revenue and expenditure transactions can be recorded against the relevant general ledger accounts for those time periods.

The primary risk related to recording budgets is data entry errors. This risk is particularly relevant where budgets are created and revised using Excel spreadsheets or similar, and manually keyed into the computer, a practice that is quite common. Controls to reduce this risk include adding edit or reasonability checks on input, for example producing a warning message if budget estimate varies by more than a fixed percentage from last year's budget. The use of batch totals is also helpful, especially where budgets are being entered at line item level. A final common control is requiring independent approval of final budget inputs by senior management.

## *Prepare budgets — DFD*

The level 1 DFD in figure 13.10 contains a lower level of detail about the first process represented in the level 0 logical DFD in figure 13.9, prepare budgets. In the same way in which the level 0 logical diagram explodes out the 'general ledger and financial reporting cycle' bubble in the context diagram, the level 1 diagram explodes out the 'prepare budgets' bubble.

## *Summary description of activities in preparing a budget*

Table 13.2 summarises the activities, risks and controls when preparing a budget, as depicted in figure 13.10. Table 13.1 (page 585) explains the logical data flows depicted in figure 13.10. Exploring the diagram in conjunction with the material contained in the tables will assist in improving your understanding of the process depicted.

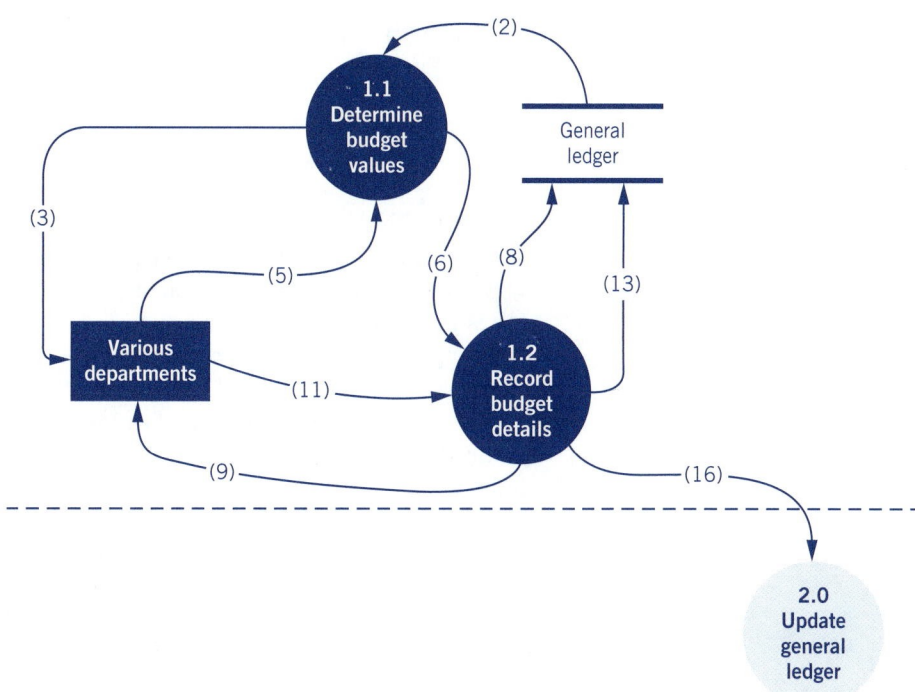

**FIGURE 13.10** General ledger and financial reporting cycle level 1 logical diagram — process 1.0 Prepare budgets

**TABLE 13.2** Activities in preparing a budget

| Activity # | Activity | Usually conducted by: | Activity description | Typical risks encountered | Common controls |
|---|---|---|---|---|---|
| 1.1 | Determine budget values | Budget staff, department managers | Determine budgets for revenue and expenditure items for the following period. This may be calculated by referencing historical transactions and indexing by some estimated percentage amount, or by analysing proposed activity levels for the future period and then calculating estimated revenue and expenditure based on predicted activity levels. | Under/overestimating revenue and expenditure | Independent approval of budget estimates<br><br>Preparation of estimates by operational managers<br><br>Aggregation of department budgets totals and independent approval of overall budget totals<br><br>Tight linkages between budget values and performance monitoring systems |
| 1.2 | Record budget details | Budget clerk/various departments | The approved budget totals are input into the central computer to establish the budget levels for future periods. | Data entry errors | Edit checks on input<br><br>Reasonability checks<br><br>Using batch totals<br><br>Independent approval of final budget inputs |

## Update the general ledger — activities, risks and controls

Process 2.0, update the general ledger, comprises the following activities.

### Extract and validate data

Once processing in the subsidiary ledgers has been successfully completed the revenue, expenditure, production, and HR management and payroll cycles send notifications to the financial cycle. The summarised details from all the subsidiary transaction systems created by these other cycles are then extracted for posting into the general ledger. This is typically an automated batch job usually run at the end of the business day in preparation for the next business day.

During the expenditure cycle described in chapter 10, transactions related to payments established and made are posted to the accounts payable data store. Once this processing is complete, a notification is sent to the financial cycle to advise that posting to the general ledger accounts can commence. Details of payments approved and scheduled to be paid are extracted from the accounts payable data store. This flow usually occurs on a daily basis, so only the totals for the preceding day would be extracted. A more detailed listing of these transactions is retained for each supplier in the accounts payable data store. Details of payments made are extracted from the accounts payable data store and validated. This flow usually occurs on a daily basis, so only the totals for the preceding day would be extracted. A more detailed, but still summarised, listing of these transactions is retained for each supplier in the accounts payable data store. A complete detail of each individual payment transaction is held in the cash payments data store.

During the production cycle described in chapter 11, transactions related to production costs are posted to the relevant data stores. Once this processing is complete, a notification is sent to the financial cycle to advise that posting to the general ledger accounts can commence. Details of direct labour costs of production incurred are extracted from the direct labour costs data store and validated. This flow usually occurs on a daily basis, so only the totals for the preceding day would be extracted. A detailed listing of these transactions is retained in the labour costs data store. Details of raw material costs incurred are extracted from the raw materials data store and validated. This flow usually occurs on a daily basis, so only the totals for the preceding day would be extracted. A detailed listing of these transactions is retained in the raw materials inventory data store. Details of manufacturing overhead costs incurred are extracted from the manufacturing overheads data store and validated. This flow usually occurs on a daily basis, so only the totals for the preceding day would be extracted. A detailed listing of these transactions is retained in the manufacturing overheads data store.

During the revenue cycle described in chapter 9, transactions related to invoices raised and payments received are posted to the accounts receivable data store. Once this processing is complete, a notification is sent to the financial cycle to advise that posting to the general ledger accounts can commence. Details of invoices raised and cash payments received are extracted from the accounts receivable data store and validated. This flow usually occurs on a daily basis, so only the totals for the preceding day would be extracted. A more detailed, but still summarised, listing of these transactions by customer is retained in the accounts receivable data store. A complete detail of each individual transaction is held in the sales data store (invoices raised) and the cash receipts data store (payments received). Figure 13.11 contains an example of how data may appear in each of these journals. Note the data becomes progressively more summarised as it moves though the relevant journals.

## Sales data

| Date | Invoice # | Sales Rep id | Customer # | Amount | |
|---|---|---|---|---|---|
| 23/9/10 | 154723897 | MLB005 | PAR569 | 1 659 | |
| 23/9/10 | 154723898 | SYD002 | CON002 | 54 566 | |
| 23/9/10 | 154723899 | MLB001 | OEL021 | 2 568 948 | |
| 23/9/10 | 154723900 | MLB001 | SMI045 | 597 821 | |
| 23/9/10 | 154723901 | SYD011 | JON045 | 86 429 | |
| 23/9/10 | 154723902 | SYD005 | DOW345 | 1 549 730 | |
| 23/9/10 | 154723903 | SYD008 | DAV498 | 16 897 | |
| 23/9/10 | 154723904 | MEL006 | LYO345 | 159 397 054 | |
| 23/9/10 | 154723905 | MEL015 | LEE945 | 1 230 | |
| 23/9/10 | 154723906 | SYD003 | ZHU564 | 36 710 | |
| 23/9/10 | 154723907 | SYD004 | BRO983 | 3 215 667 | |
| 23/9/10 | Total sales | | | | 167 526 711 |

## Accounts receivable data

| | Sales Ref # | Customer # | Amount | | |
|---|---|---|---|---|---|
| | 154723907 | BRO983 | 3 215 667 | | |
| | 154723898 | CON002 | 54 566 | | |
| | 154723903 | DAV498 | 16 897 | | |
| | 154723902 | DOW345 | 1 549 730 | | |
| | 154723901 | JON045 | 86 429 | | |
| | 154723905 | LEE945 | 1 230 | | |
| | 154723904 | LYO345 | 159 397 054 | | |
| | 154723899 | OEL021 | 2 568 948 | | |
| | 154723897 | PAR569 | 1 659 | | |
| | 154723900 | SMI045 | 597 821 | | |
| | 154723906 | ZHU564 | 36 710 | | |
| | Total sales | | | 167 526 711 | |

## General ledger data

| | | Amount | Amount | |
|---|---|---|---|---|
| | Accounts receivable | 167 526 711 | | |
| | Sales | | 167 526 711 | |

**FIGURE 13.11** Example revenue data posting

During the HR management and payroll cycle described in chapter 12, transactions related to payroll costs are posted through to the relevant data stores. Once this processing is complete, a notification is sent to the financial cycle to advise that posting to the general ledger accounts can commence.

Details of salary and wages payments made are extracted from the payroll data store and validated. This flow usually occurs on a weekly, fortnightly or monthly basis, so only the totals for the preceding payroll runs would be extracted. A more detailed listing of these transactions is retained for each employee in the payroll data store.

After all transaction data has been extracted and validated the summarised totals can be posted to the relevant general ledger accounts in the general ledger data store.

The primary risks related to extracting and validating data are incomplete and inaccurate data. Common controls used to reduce this risk include the use of batch totals (e.g. to check sales totals) and hash totals (e.g. to check customer numbers). In addition, most accounting systems use ledger control accounts that detail the total posted from each subsidiary ledger and compare those totals back to the relevant subsidiary ledgers. Generating automated system **exception reports** that identify any problems encountered during extraction and validation should form part of the daily processing routines for financial systems.

### Post transactions

The verified summarised transaction data is posted to the relevant general ledger accounts. This is also automated and run immediately following validation of the data in the previous activity. Once transactions have been successfully posted to the relevant accounts the transactions contained in the subsidiary ledger data stores are updated with a **status code** to indicate that they have been posted to the general ledger accounts.

Once all transactions have been posted to the general ledger any accounting adjustments necessary can be processed. The main risk related to posting transactions to the general ledger is inaccurate updating; use of batch and hash totals act to reduce this risk, as does performing regular control account reconciliations to assist with detecting any errors.

## Update the general ledger — DFD

The level 1 DFD in figure 13.12 contains a lower level of detail about the second process represented in the level 0 logical DFD in figure 13.9. This process takes place after the budget has been prepared in the preceding process and prior to the accounting adjustments made in the following process.

## Summary description of activities in updating the general ledger

Table 13.3 summarises the activities, risks and controls when updating the general ledger, as depicted in figure 13.12. Table 13.1 (page 585) explains the logical data flows depicted in figure 13.12. Exploring the diagram in conjunction with the material contained in the tables will assist in improving your understanding of the process depicted.

**Exception report** *A report type that is designed specifically to identify exceptions for particular transactions. An example is a report identifying any sales orders which have been shipped but not billed, or a report identifying all customers who have overdue accounts receivable accounts.*

**Status code** *A code on transactions that are moving through an iteration of a process indicating which stage of the process the transaction is at. As an example, a sales transaction may be first 'created', then 'picked', then 'packed', then 'shipped', then 'paid'. When each of these activities has been completed, the status of the transaction is changed to reflect the new status.*

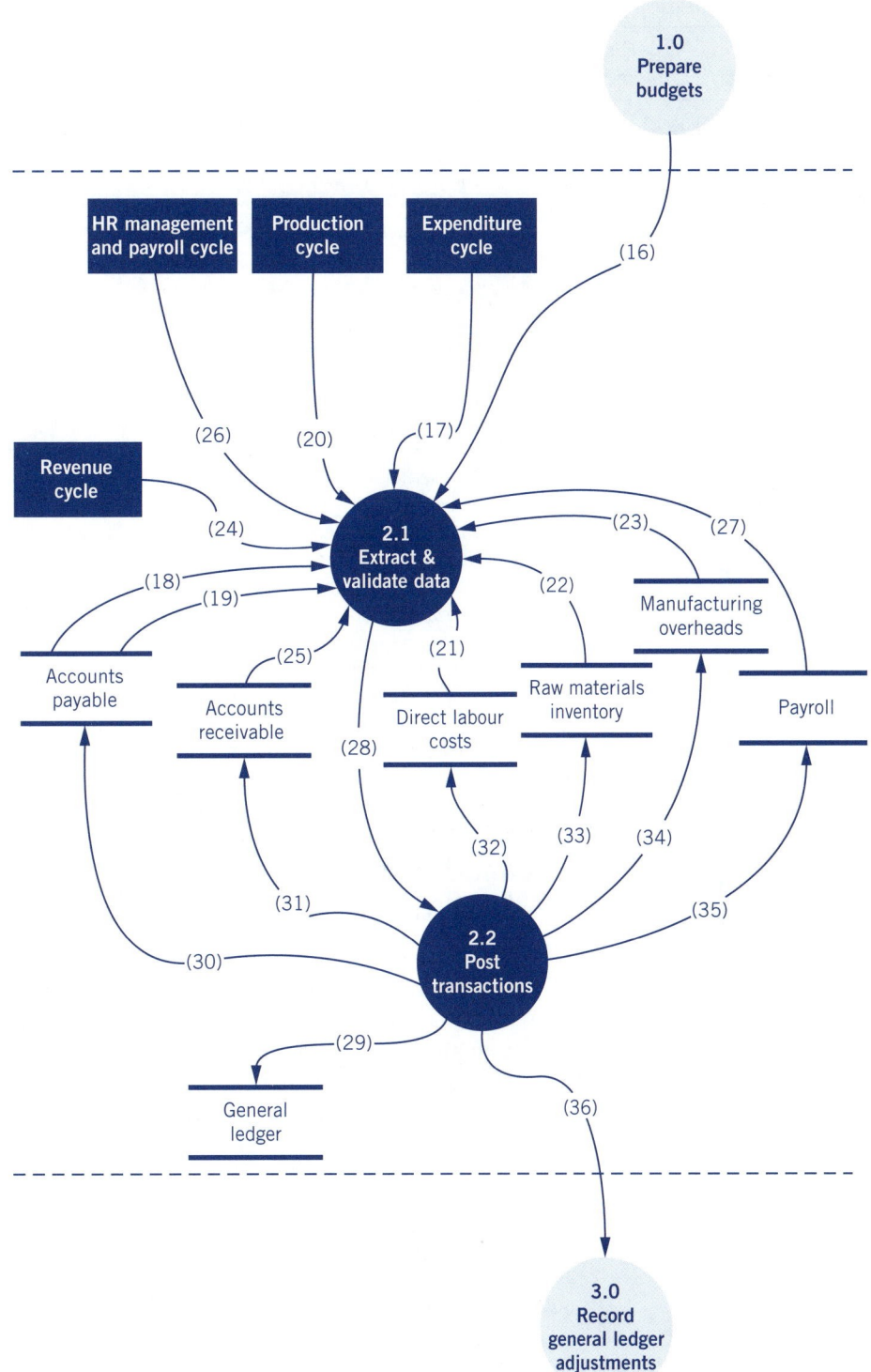

**FIGURE 13.12** General ledger and financial reporting cycle level 1 logical diagram — process 2.0 Update the general ledger

**TABLE 13.3** Activities in updating the general ledger

| Activity # | Activity | Usually conducted by: | Activity description | Typical risks encountered | Common controls |
|---|---|---|---|---|---|
| 2.1 | Extract and validate data | Computer | Once processing in the subsidiary ledgers has been successfully completed the revenue, expenditure, production, and HR management and payroll cycles send a notification to the financial cycle. The summarised details from all the subsidiary transaction systems created by these other cycles are then able to be extracted for posting into the general ledger. | Incomplete data | Batch totals and hash totals. Using ledger control accounts that detail totals posted from each ledger and allow comparison of those totals |
| | | | | Inaccurate data | Automated system exception reports that identify any problems encountered during extraction and validation |
| 2.2 | Post transactions | Computer | The verified summarised transaction data is posted to the relevant general ledger accounts. Once transactions have been successfully posted to the relevant accounts the transactions contained in the subsidiary ledger data stores are updated with a status code to indicate that they have been posted to the general ledger accounts. | Inaccurate updating | Batch totals and hash totals. Regular control account reconciliations |

## Record general ledger adjustments — activities, risks and controls

Process 3.0, record general ledger adjustments, comprises the following activities.

### Prepare adjustment journals

At regular intervals a bank reconciliation is completed. The bank supplies details of transactions from the bank accounts on a regular basis, usually daily, weekly or monthly depending on the volume of transactions processed. This data consists of all the deposits and withdrawals processed to the bank accounts, along with details of any bank fees or charges and periodical payments processed by the bank against the bank account. The bank transaction data could be supplied on paper, in the form of a bank statement, or online via a download from the bank's internet banking facilities.

General journal entries are prepared for any accounting adjustments required. An example of a journal voucher is shown in figure 13.13. Figure 13.14 shows a typical screen used to input the journal data. These adjustments typically recognise end-of-period accruals and also capture transactions such as bank fees or interest charges not captured by transaction processing cycles. All journal entries should be approved by senior accounting staff to ensure conformance with accounting standards and organisational policies. Accounting staff prepare and input details of the general journal entries required. General journal data is stored in the journal voucher data store. General journal entries are usually numbered sequentially and cross-referenced to supporting working papers to enable easy identification and tracking. Details of the proposed general journal entries should be sent to senior accounting staff for approval. After journal entries have been approved the relevant general ledger accounts in the general ledger data store can be updated.

| Australian Information Company | | | | |
| --- | --- | --- | --- | --- |
| Level 2, 345 Hill Terrace | | | | |
| Melbourne, Vic 3003 | | | | |
| *Journal voucher* | | | | No.: 72890 |
| Received from: Margaret Duns | Date entered 1/05/10 | Prepared by: Jacob Jones | Approved by: Tim Chen | Posted by: XXX |
| Account code | Account title | | Debit amounts | Credit amounts |
| 101 | Cash | | 100 | |
| 149 | Accounts receivable — control | | | 100 |
| Remarks: | | | | |

**FIGURE 13.13** Sample journal voucher

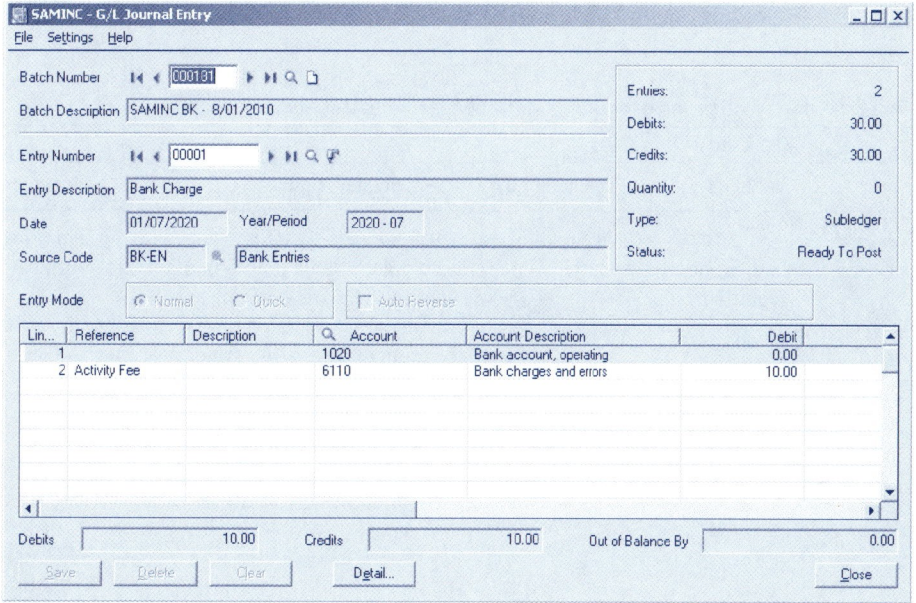

**FIGURE 13.14** Sample general journal

The primary risk when preparing adjusting journals is errors in journal entries. Common controls to reduce this risk include obtaining independent approval of journal entries by senior accounting staff and attaching full working papers to support journal entry calculations. Organisations should also document any assumptions and algorithms relied on when calculating journal amounts and mandate the provision of source documents where available.

### Post adjustment journals
Periodically, the computer extracts details of all the approved, but not yet processed, journal entries from the journal voucher data store. The approved general journal

entries are posted to the relevant general ledger accounts and the status of the general journal voucher is updated to 'processed'. The main risk when posting adjusting journals is data entry errors; use of batch totals (to ensure correct amounts entered) and hash totals (to ensure correct general ledger accounts selected) act to reduce this risk, as does one-for-one checking of general journal entry inputs. Once the adjusting entries have been approved and posted, reports can be generated.

## Record general ledger adjustments — DFD

The level 1 DFD in figure 13.15 contains a lower level of details about the third process represented in the level 0 logical DFD in figure 13.9. This process takes place after the transactional data has been posted to the general ledger accounts in the preceding process and before reports are generated in the following process.

## Description of activities in recording general ledger adjustments

Table 13.4 summarises the activities, risks and controls when recording general ledger adjustments, as depicted in figure 13.15. Table 13.1 (page 585) explains the logical data flows depicted in figure 13.15. Exploring the diagram in conjunction with the material contained in the tables will assist in improving your understanding of the process depicted.

**TABLE 13.4** Activities in recording general ledger adjustments

| Activity # | Activity | Usually conducted by: | Activity description | Typical risks encountered | Common controls |
|---|---|---|---|---|---|
| 3.1 | Prepare adjustment journals | Accounting staff | A bank reconciliation is completed and general journal entries are prepared for any accounting adjustments required. These adjustments typically recognise end-of-period accruals and capture transactions such as bank fees or interest charges not captured by the transaction processing systems. | Errors in journal entries | Independent approval of journal entries by senior accounting staff<br><br>Attaching full working papers to support journal entry calculations<br><br>Documenting any assumptions and algorithms relied on when calculating journal amounts<br><br>Mandating the provision of source documents where available |
| 3.2 | Post adjustment journals | Accounting staff | The approved journals are posted to the relevant general ledger accounts. | Data entry errors | Batch totals (to ensure correct amounts entered) and hash totals (to ensure correct general ledger accounts selected)<br><br>One-for-one checking of general journal entry inputs |

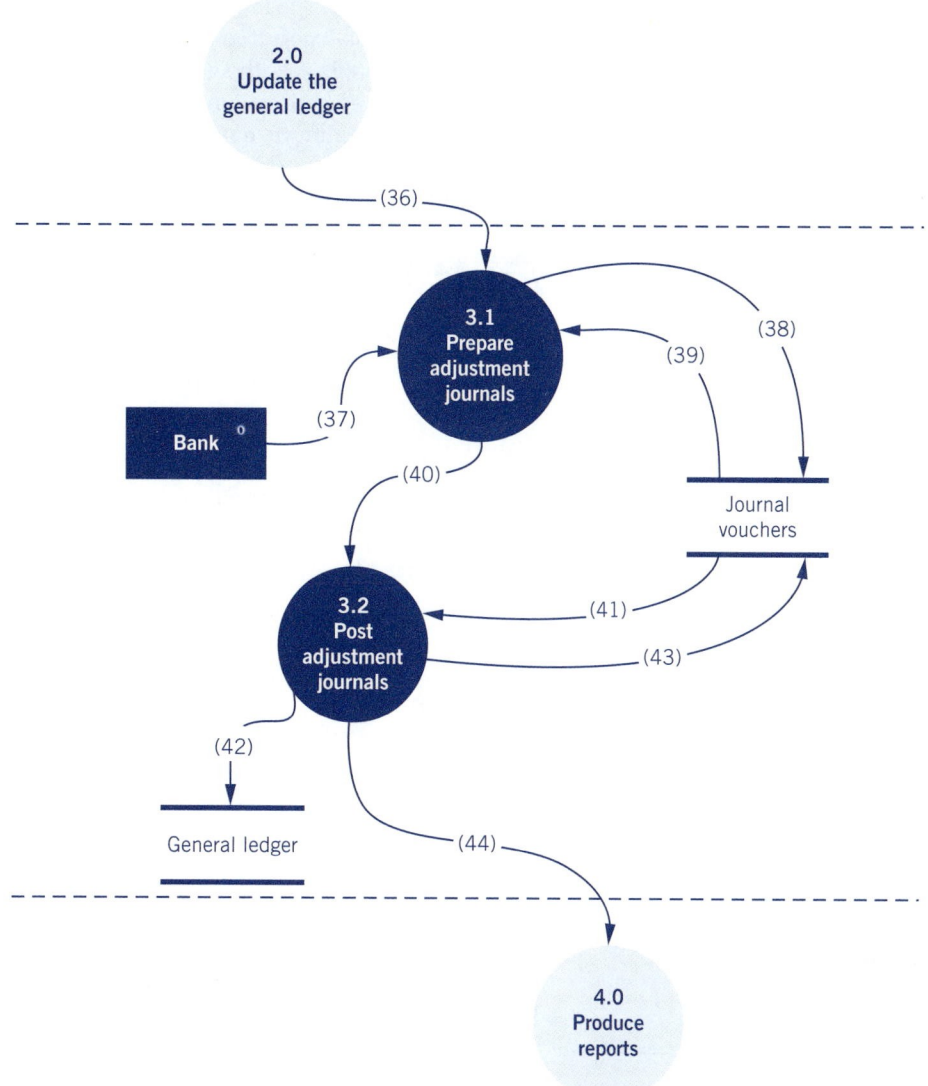

**FIGURE 13.15** General ledger and financial reporting cycle level 1 logical diagram — process 3.0 Record general ledger adjustments

## Produce reports — activities, risks and controls

Process 4.0, produce reports, comprises the following activities.

### Produce management reports

There are two main triggers to produce management reports. Most organisations have a standard set of reports that are produced at the end of each accounting period; these are triggered and created automatically by the computer, and distributed based on a predetermined list to department staff. The second trigger for reporting is in response to an ad hoc request from a department. These reports are typically one-off reports, and are often requested to support a particular decision.

Both types of reports are created based on a report specification template that outlines the column headings, totals required and layout for the required report.

This report template is then populated with the transaction data that fits the requested report parameters. Report data parameters typically include the start and finish dates of the transactions required, the general ledger account numbers to be reported on, and the divisions, or operational units, to be included in the report. Additional criteria can also be added to limit the data to that required; for example, reported sales data may be constrained to a particular geographic region, store or sales person. An example of a management report is shown in figure 13.16.

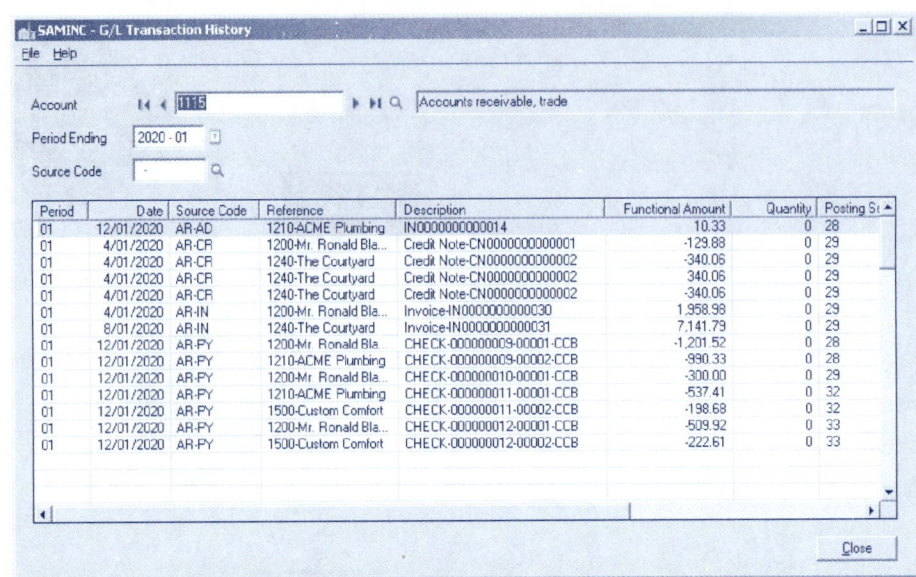

**FIGURE 13.16** Sample general ledger report

Reports may be specified, tested and generated by accounting staff or operational managers and staff may have the capability to independently create their own ad hoc reports. Most accounting systems contain basic reporting functionality supporting one-off special-purpose reports along with a standard suite of reports that can be automatically generated and distributed on a regular basis.

The computer extracts the data required to populate the requested reports from the general ledger data store. Once a report has been generated it is sent to the system user who requested it. This can be done either electronically (email or on screen) or printed. The primary risk related to producing management reports is using incorrect report parameters or reporting incorrect data. To reduce this risk it is important to limit report generation functionality to appropriately trained staff, and require independent authorisation for any new report prior to circulation of that report.

Due to the detailed nature of management reporting there is also a risk of unauthorised distribution of financial data as, unlike the general purpose financial statements, these reports are not intended for use or distribution outside the organisation. Controls to reduce this risk include applying secure privacy settings on electronic reports limiting ability to print/redistribute reported data and using a document management system for reports containing sensitive data. In addition, security profiles allowing read-only access to financial data need to be granted and maintained at an individual staff member level.

Once the management reports have been generated and examined, the general purpose financial statements can be produced.

## Produce financial reports

General purpose financial statements are produced at predetermined intervals and are constructed in accordance with the relevant accounting standards. Accounting standards are used to create the business rules and specifications underlying the financial data and report parameters. When a trigger date occurs, the reports are automatically produced and distributed, either electronically or on paper. At these regular predetermined intervals the computer extracts the data required to populate the general purpose financial statements from the general ledger data store. Note that any adjustments required should have already been made to the underlying data; reporting outputs may require formatting or similiar presentation manipulation but the data contents should remain unchanged. Once the general purpose financial statements have been generated they are distributed to external users and to senior management, either electronically or on paper. Electronic distribution of general purpose financial statements can be made either in a static form such as a PDF file or dynamically via the use of XBRL. Examples of general purpose financial statements produced by BHP Billiton are shown in figure 13.17.[3]

**FIGURE 13.17** BHP Billiton general purpose financial statements

**BHP Billiton Limited (Single Parent Entity)**
**Income statement**
**For the year ended 30 June 2009**

| | Notes | 2009 US$M | 2008 US$M |
|---|---|---|---|
| Revenue | 2 | 8 211 | 8 861 |
| Other income | 3 | 14 | – |
| Expenses, excluding net finance costs | 4 | (1 513) | (4 763) |
| Financial income | 4 | 1 664 | 804 |
| Financial expense | 4 | (676) | (1 891) |
| Profit before taxation | | 7 700 | 3 011 |
| Income tax credit | 6 | 430 | 68 |
| Profit after taxation | | 8 130 | 3 079 |
| Profit is attributable to: | | | |
| Equity holders of BHP Billiton Limited (Single Parent Entity) | | 8 130 | 3 079 |

*(Revenue cycle — Revenue, Other income)*
*(Expenditure cycle — Expenses, excluding net finance costs)*

**BHP Billiton Limited (Single Parent Entity)**
**Balance sheet**
**As at 30 June 2009**

| | Notes | 2009 US$M | 2008 US$M |
|---|---|---|---|
| ASSETS | | | |
| Current assets | | | |
| Cash and cash equivalents | 7 | – | 9 |

*(continued)*

**FIGURE 13.17** *(continued)*

| | Notes | 2009 US$M | 2008 US$M |
|---|---|---|---|
| Receivables | 8 | 23 449 | 23 668 |
| Other | 9 | – | 7 |
| Total current assets | | 23 449 | 23 684 |
| Non-current assets | | | |
| Receivables | 10 | 3 272 | 3 183 |
| Other financial assets (at cost) | 11 | 15 649 | 14 506 |
| Property, plant and equipment | 12 | 1 | 1 |
| Deferred tax assets | 13 | 454 | 332 |
| Other | 14 | – | 183 |
| Total non-current assets | | 19 376 | 18 205 |
| Total assets | | 42 825 | 41 889 |
| LIABILITIES | | | |
| Current liabilities | 15 | | |
| Payables (a) | 16 | 22 511 | 27 707 |
| Provisions | 17 | 322 | 267 |
| Current tax payable | | 1 413 | 1 000 |
| Total current liabilities | | 24 246 | 28 974 |
| Non-current liabilities | | | |
| Payables (a) | 18 | 1 924 | 2 040 |
| Provisions | 19 | 689 | 234 |
| Total non-current liabilities | | 2 613 | 2 274 |
| Total liabilities | | 26 859 | 31 248 |
| NET ASSETS | | 15 966 | 10 641 |
| EQUITY | | | |
| Share capital | 20 | 938 | 938 |
| Reserves | 21 | 329 | 681 |
| Retained earnings | 22 | 14 699 | 9 022 |
| Total equity | | 15 966 | 10 641 |

Revenue cycle — accounts receivable

Expenditure cycle — accounts payable

**BHP Billiton Limited (Single Parent Entity)**
**Cash flow statement**
**For the year ended 30 June 2009**

| | Notes | 2009 US$M | 2008 US$M |
|---|---|---|---|
| Operating activities | | | |
| Profit before taxation | | 7 700 | 3 011 |
| Adjustments for: | | | |
| Employee share awards expense | | 131 | 62 |

| | Notes | 2009 US$M | 2008 US$M |
|---|---|---|---|
| Loss on cancellation of BHP Billiton Plc shares | | – | 4 008 |
| Dividend income | | (7 956) | (8 595) |
| Net finance costs | | (988) | 1 087 |
| Impairment of investment in controlled entities | | 58 | – |
| Debt forgiven — related entity | | 28 | – |
| Loss on sale of related entity | | 28 | – |
| Exceptional item — Newcastle closure | | 508 | – |
| Changes in assets and liabilities | | | |
| Receivables | | (29) | (28) |
| Other assets | | 190 | (190) |
| Payables | | (26) | (40) |
| Provisions | | (45) | 81 |
| Cash generated from operations | | (401) | (604) |
| Dividends received | | 7 956 | 8 595 |
| Interest received | | 646 | 796 |
| Interest paid | | (640) | (970) |
| Income tax paid | | (2 208) | (2 178) |
| Net operating cash flows | | 5 353 | 5 639 |
| Investing activities | | | |
| Purchases of, or increased investment in, subsidiaries, net of their cash | | (1 201) | (1 422) |
| Net investing cash flows | | (1 201) | (1 422) |
| Financing activities | | | |
| Proceeds from ordinary share issues | | 27 | 24 |
| Purchase of shares by Employee Share Ownership Plan Trusts | | (132) | (230) |
| Share buy back — BHP Billiton Plc | | – | (3 115) |
| Dividends paid | | (2 754) | (1 881) |
| Net financing (to)/from related entities | | (1 302) | 188 |
| Net financing cash flows | | (4 161) | (5 014) |
| Net decrease in cash and cash equivalents | | (9) | (797) |
| Cash and cash equivalents, net of overdrafts, at beginning of period | | 8 | 809 |
| Effect of foreign currency exchange rate changes on cash and cash equivalents | | (1) | (4) |
| Cash and cash equivalents at end of year | 7 | (2) | 8 |

The main risk attached to producing financial reports is reporting incorrect data. Oversight by senior accounting staff and internal audit and regular checks for compliance with accounting standards and policies will act to reduce this risk.

## *Produce reports — DFD*

The level 1 DFD in figure 13.18 contains a lower level of details about the final process represented in the level 0 logical DFD in figure 13.18. This process takes place after the general ledger accounts have been adjusted in the preceding process.

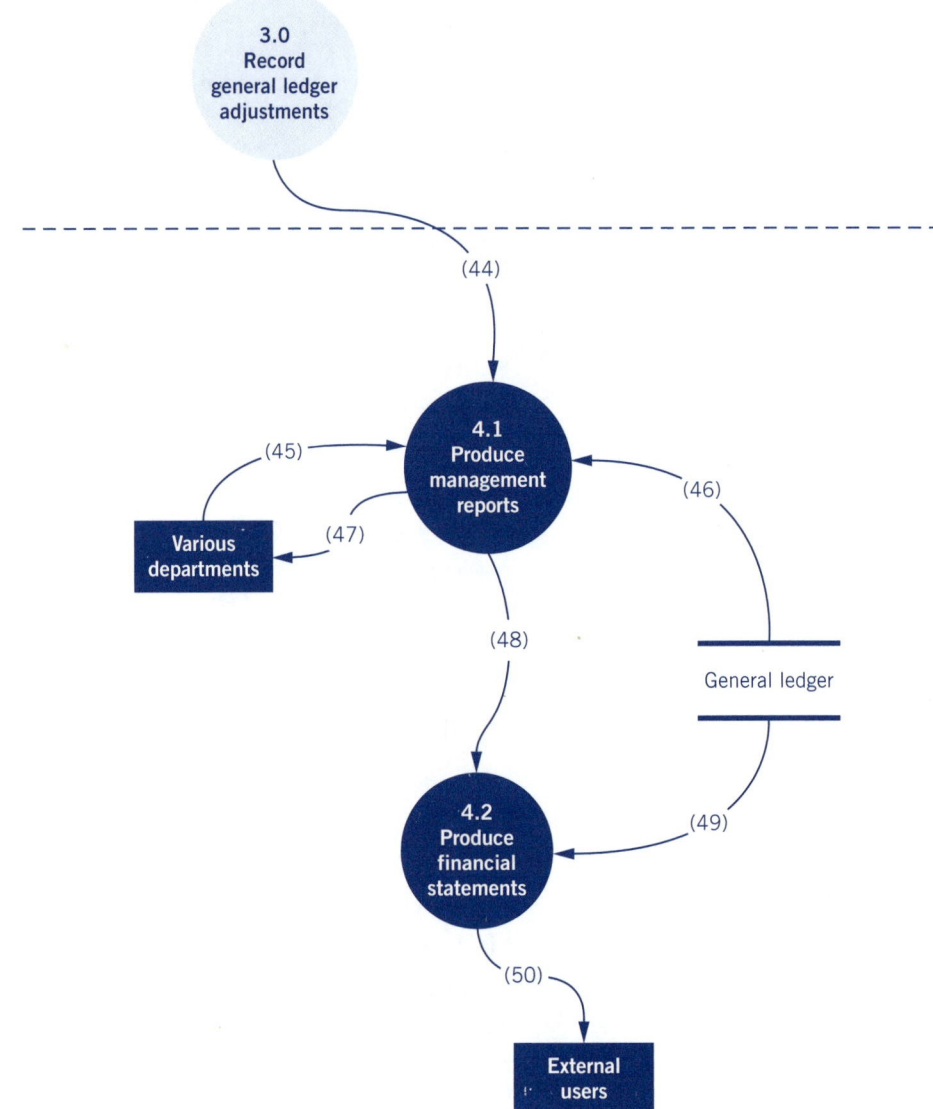

**FIGURE 13.18** General ledger and financial reporting cycle level 1 logical diagram — process 4.0 Produce reports

## Summary description of activities in producing reports

Table 13.5 summarises the activities, risks and controls when producing reports, as depicted in figure 13.18. Table 13.1 (page 585) explains the logical data flows depicted in figure 13.18. Exploring the diagram in conjunction with the material contained in the tables will assist in improving your understanding of the process depicted.

**TABLE 13.5** Activities in producing reports

| Activity # | Activity | Usually conducted by: | Activity description | Typical risks encountered | Common controls |
|---|---|---|---|---|---|
| 4.1 | Produce management reports | Accounting staff/ department staff/ computer | Reports are created based on a report specification template that outlines the column headings, totals required and layout for the required report. This report template is then populated with the transaction data that fits the requested report parameters. | Incorrect report parameters/ incorrect data reported | Limiting report generation functionality to appropriately trained staff<br><br>Requiring independent authorisation for any new report |
| | | | | Unauthorised distribution of financial data (unlike the general purpose financial statements these reports are not intended for use or distribution outside the organisation) | Secure privacy settings on electronic reports limiting ability to print/redistribute reported data<br><br>Secure document management for reports containing sensitive data<br><br>Security profiles allowing read-only access to financial data maintained at an individual staff member level |
| 4.2 | Produce financial statements | Accounting staff/ computer | General purpose financial statements are produced at predetermined intervals and are constructed in accordance with relevant accounting standards. Accounting standards are used to create the business rules and specifications underlying the financial data and report parameters. | Incorrect data reported | Oversight by senior accounting staff and internal audit<br><br>Regular checks for compliance with accounting standards and policies |

## Physical DFD — prepare budgets

The physical DFD depicted in figure 13.19 shows an example of how a budget may be prepared. The physical diagram draws the process from a different perspective to the logical DFD of this process contained in figure 13.10, as it shows who is involved in the activities of the process, rather than when those activities occur. This process of preparing budgets involves the budget clerk and the budget manager, who interact with a central computer and with each other, and with various operational departments. Outputs from this process are recorded in the general ledger data store for use in monitoring and managing future performance.

Details of the physical data flows in figure 13.19 are contained in table 13.6. As this diagram is drawn from a different perspective than the logical DFD it contains far more detail about the interactions between each of the entities involved in preparing the budget.

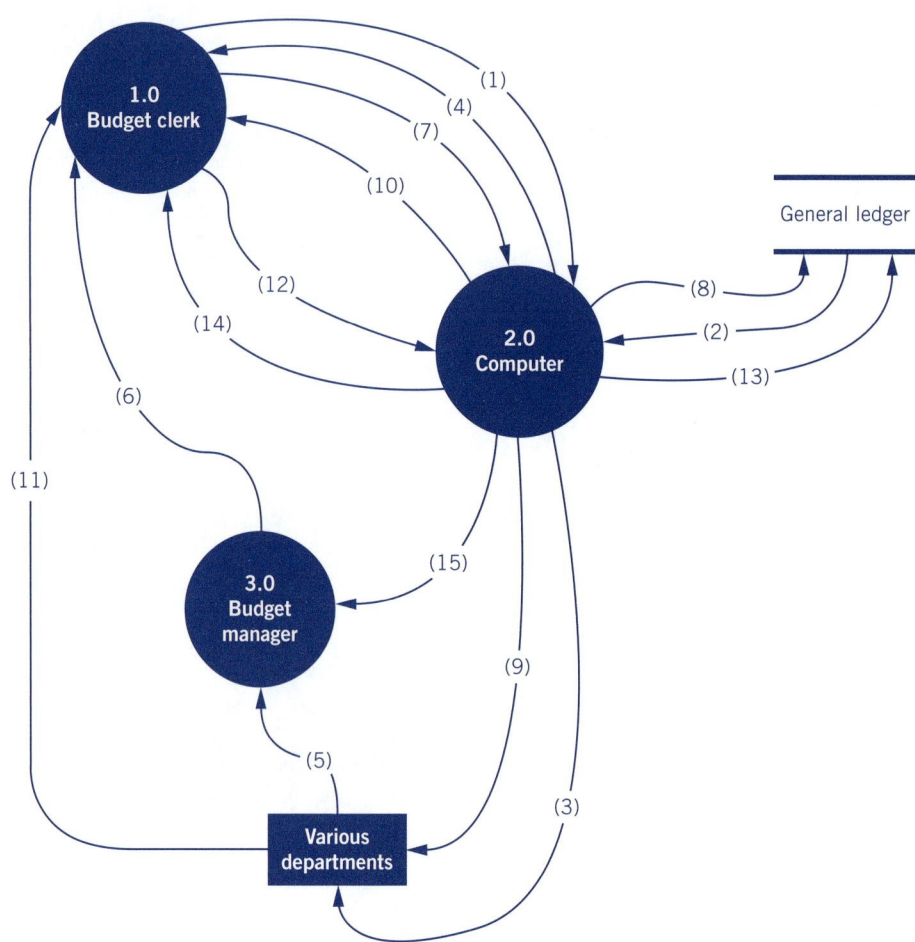

**FIGURE 13.19** Physical DFD — prepare budgets

## System flowchart — prepare budgets

The DFD in figure 13.19 shows an example of how a budget may be prepared; the logical DFD in figure 13.10 shows that same process from a logical perspective. The flowchart in figure 13.20 shows that same process from yet another perspective. The system flowchart is the most detailed picture of the process, and includes both logical and physical perspectives. The detail contained in the system flowchart is useful when considering process redesign, and when analysing the control environment of the process depicted. Details of the flows shown in the flowchart in figure 13.20 are documented in table 13.6 (page 608).

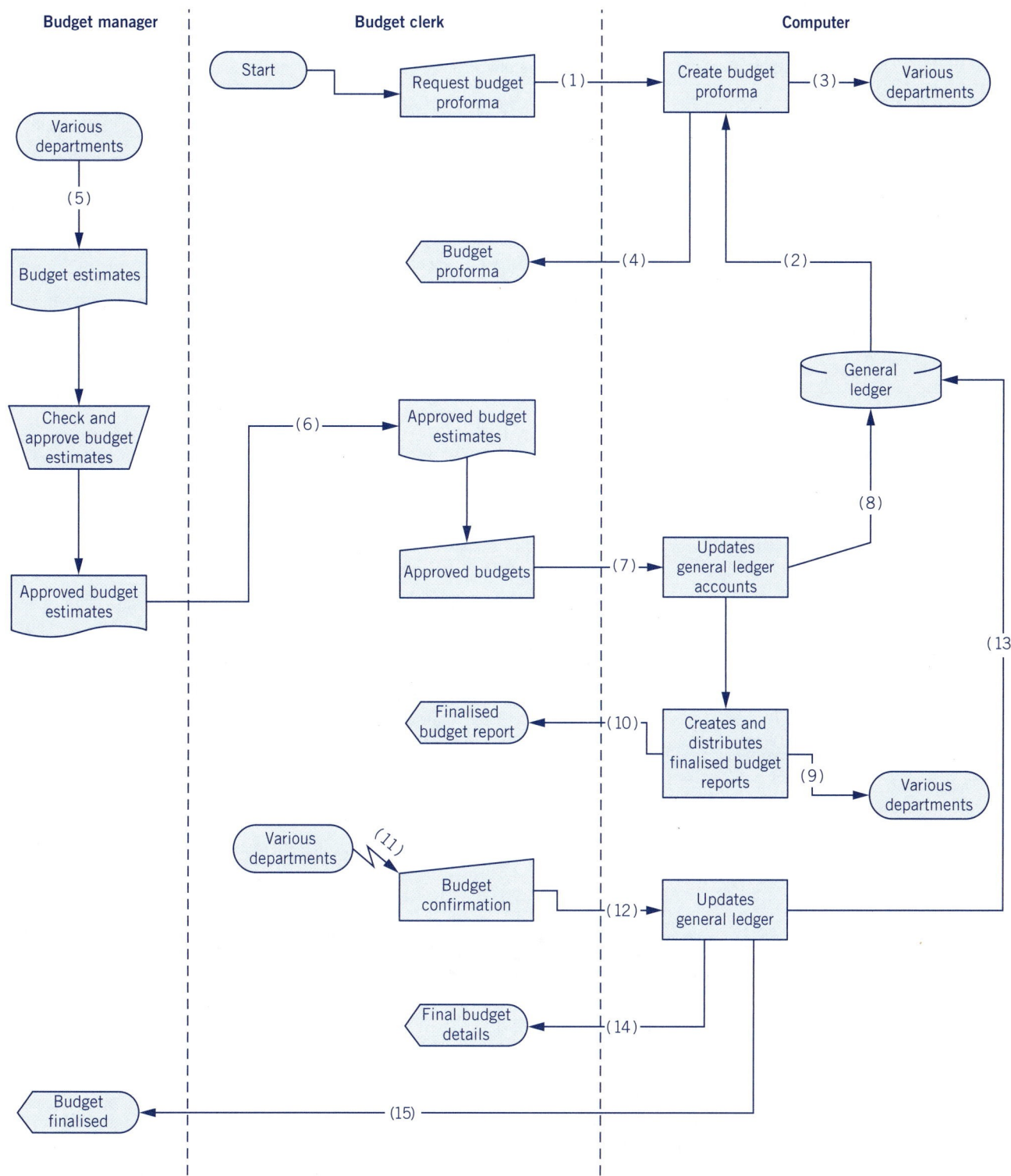

**FIGURE 13.20** Systems flowchart — prepare budgets

**TABLE 13.6** Description of data flows in physical DFD and flowchart — prepare budgets

| Flow # | Data source | Data destination | Explanation of the physical data flows |
| --- | --- | --- | --- |
| 1 | Budget clerk | Computer | The budget clerk requests the computer create a proforma budget worksheet. The process documented assumes budget preparation is based on the previous year's results. |
| 2 | General ledger data store | Computer | The computer extracts historic general ledger data and creates a budget proforma worksheet. |
| 3 | Computer | Department managers | The computer distributes the budget proforma worksheet to the various department managers along with a request for them to consider and update the budget estimates in light of their expectations for the coming year. |
| 4 | Computer | Budget clerk | The computer sends a copy of the budget proforma worksheet to the budget clerk. |
| 5 | Department managers | Budget manager | Department managers prepare and forward budget estimates for the following year to the budget manager for approval. |
| 6 | Budget manager | Budget clerk | The budget manager checks and approves the budgets then forwards them to the budget clerk. |
| 7 | Budget clerk | Computer | The budget clerk inputs the approved budget amounts. |
| 8 | Computer | General ledger data store | The computer updates the relevant general ledger accounts with the new budget estimates. |
| 9 | Computer | Department managers | The computer creates finalised budget reports and distributes them to the relevant departments. |
| 10 | Computer | Budget clerk | The computer sends a copy of the finalised budget reports to the budget clerk. |
| 11 | Department managers | Budget clerk | The relevant department managers confirm their acceptance of the final budget details to the budget clerk. |
| 12 | Budget clerk | Computer | Once all budget details have been confirmed the budget clerk advises the computer that the budget has been finalised. |
| 13 | Computer | General ledger data store | The computer updates all the relevant general ledger accounts with the final approved budget amounts. |
| 14 | Computer | Budget clerk | The computer displays the final budget details to the budget clerk. |
| 15 | Computer | Budget manager | The computer advises the budget manager that the budget has been finalised. |

**LEARNING OBJECTIVE**  **6**

*Develop metrics to monitor general ledger and financial reporting cycle performance.*

# MEASURING GENERAL LEDGER AND FINANCIAL REPORTING CYCLE PERFORMANCE

Process performance should be measured relative to how well the process outcomes achieve the overall objectives of that cycle. At the start of this chapter the objectives of the general ledger and financial reporting cycle were described as being to effectively accumulate, summarise and transfer transactional data, to adjust that transactional data in accordance with relevant accounting standards and policies in an accurate and timely manner, and to ensure all reports generated are timely, accurate, valid and complete.

To monitor performance against these objectives a range of metrics needs to be employed, along with some realistic targets. Examples of suitable **metrics** or key performance indicators (KPIs) for the general ledger and financial reporting cycle objectives are contained in table 13.7.

**Metric** *A specific measure used for a particular purpose. An example of a metric is the number of bad debts the organisation has, which could be used to monitor accounts receivable or sales performance.*

**TABLE 13.7** Example KPIs mapped to general ledger and financial reporting cycle objectives

| Objective | Example KPI |
|---|---|
| To accurately and completely determine and record budget estimates | • Number of budget variances reported<br>• Cycle time to create budgets<br>• Operational manager complaints received regarding budget errors |
| To validate and correctly transfer all relevant transactional data | • Number of data errors detected<br>• Reconciled balances in subsidiary ledger control accounts<br>• Number of uncleared transactions in suspense accounts |
| To ensure all adjusting journal entries are accurately prepared and independently authorised | • Number of erroneous adjustments detected<br>• Level of unadjusted balances in asset and liability accounts<br>• Degree of compliance with accounting policy |
| To ensure all reports generated are well designed and contain relevant and accurate data | • Number of complaints received from report users<br>• Number of data errors identified in reports |

## ›› SUMMARY ›››

LEARNING OBJECTIVE **1**

### What are the key objectives and strategic implications of the general ledger and financial reporting cycle?

The first part of the financial reporting and general ledger cycle involves creating budgets for the upcoming period, then extracting transactional data generated by the operational cycles. A summarised version of these transaction streams is transferred into the relevant general ledger accounts to create a trial balance. Once a bank reconciliation has been successfully completed, adjusting journal entries are prepared and input to create an adjusted trial balance. After the adjusted trial balance has been finalised, reporting can take place.

The objective of the general ledger and financial reporting cycle is to synthesise and report data that accurately represent business transactions and activities. To achieve this, budgets must be accurate, and all transactions extracted and posted must be complete and accurate. The strategic implications of the general ledger and financial reporting cycle revolve around two main areas. The first is to do with the need for good decision making within the organisation. Poor reports lead to poor decision making, which can lead to eventual business failure; high-quality decision making requires good data and comprehensible reports. Second, the strategic implications of producing external reports are equally serious. As external reports are widely distributed, any errors in financial reporting can lead to serious corporate problems.

LEARNING OBJECTIVE **2**

### Which technologies underpin the activities of the general ledger and financial reporting cycle?

A range of data management tools are available to help improve the ability to transfer, analyse and report financial data within the general ledger and financial reporting cycle, including enterprise resource planning (ERP) systems, which integrate the general ledger with the operational cycles that precede it and facilitate stronger controls over the extraction and posting of data from the subsidiary ledgers. Access to online banking is helpful when preparing bank reconciliations, improving the timeliness and accuracy of this important reconciliation. Business intelligence tools can support interrogation of the underlying data and data dictionary, and the creation of reports. eXtensible Business Reporting Language (XBRL) allows semantics, or meaning, to be embedded within strings of financial data, allowing more in-depth analysis to be conducted by users and recipients of financial data.

LEARNING OBJECTIVE

## What data and business decisions are involved in the general ledger and financial reporting cycle?

Process business decisions are made from several different perspectives during the general ledger and financial reporting cycle. Budget-related decisions include what level to budget at, how far to break budget amounts down to and how high (or low) to set budget targets. Decisions relating to general journal entries would include consideration of accounting standards, accounting policies and procedures, timing differences and the need to incorporate data from external sources such as bank statements.

In addition to these journal adjustment decisions, the reports produced by this cycle are used to inform decision makers within the organisation. Common examples of such reports include profitability analysis for the organisation or a division, analysis of performance for an individual or a division, analysis of profitability potential to guide future investment decisions and cost management analysis for decision making.

LEARNING OBJECTIVE

## What are the primary activities in the general ledger and financial reporting cycle and what data is produced by these activities?

Contextually, the general ledger and financial reporting cycle involves direct interaction with entities outside the organisation that use the general purpose financial statements produced, and with the bank to obtain details of bank account transactions. Within the organisation, the general ledger and financial reporting cycle interacts with the production, HR management and payroll, expenditure and revenue cycles, along with managers of operational departments, initially to create budgets and later when conducting variance analysis relating to operational performance. Primary activities within the cycle include preparing budgets, updating the general ledger accounts, recording general ledger adjustments and producing reports.

A range of data types are accessed by activities within the general ledger and financial reporting cycle, including those contained in the accounts payable, accounts receivable, production costs and payroll costs data stores. General ledger data stores are used to provide and store budget data. The general ledger and financial reporting cycle activities generate the journal voucher and general ledger data. The general ledger and financial reporting data is used to support decision making within the organisation and to create all external general purpose financial statements.

LEARNING OBJECTIVE

## What risks relate to the general ledger and financial reporting cycle activities and how might we control for these risks?

Activities within the general ledger and financial reporting cycle create exposure to a range of known risks. Risks related to preparing budgets include under or overestimating future revenues and expenditures, and data entry errors. Risks related to updating the general ledger include using incomplete or inaccurate transactional data, or inaccurately updating that data. Risks related to adjusting the general ledger include creating erroneous journal entries, and data entry errors. When producing reports there are risks that incorrect parameters of report data may be selected, or that reports may be distributed to unauthorised users.

Common controls in the general ledger and financial reporting cycle include independent authorisation of all data inputs and regular reconciliations of key general ledger accounts.

LEARNING OBJECTIVE

## How can we best monitor general ledger and financial reporting cycle performance?

Process performance should be measured relative to the desired outcomes of the process. To monitor process performance a wide range of metrics needs to be employed along with some realistic targets. Examples of suitable performance metrics for the general ledger and financial reporting cycle include variance analysis, the number of data errors detected, evidence of reconciled balances in subsidiary ledger control accounts, the number of uncleared transactions in suspense accounts and the level of unadjusted balances in asset and liability accounts. Success in reporting could be measured by the degree of compliance with accounting policies, the number of complaints received from report users and the number of data errors identified in reports.

## KEY TERMS

enterprise resource planning (ERP) system, p. 575
exception report, p. 594
eXtensible Business Reporting Language (XBRL), p. 575
online banking, p. 575
metric, p. 608
reconciliation, p. 575
status code, p. 594

## DISCUSSION QUESTIONS

13.1 Monash Ltd has always had a strategy of product differentiation; that is, providing high-quality products and extracting a price premium from the market. During the recent economic downturn, Monash Ltd has seen its customer base diminish, and has decided to move strategically to a cost leadership strategy, that is, to try to sell more products at a lower price.
  (a) What are the implications of this strategy change for the financial reporting cycle? (LO1)
  (b) What changes would you expect to see in the financial reporting cycle? (LO4)
  (c) What are the implications of this strategy change in terms of the usefulness of historic transactional data for decision making? (LO3)

13.2 Flinders Ltd has decided to devolve responsibility for creating new financial reports from the central IT division to the operational and central finance areas.
  (a) What controls would you expect to see introduced to ensure that any new reports generated contain reliable data? (LO5)
  (b) Which activities in the Produce reports process would be affected? (LO2, LO4)
  (c) What changes would you expect to see in these activities? (LO4)
  (d) What metrics could you use to measure the success of this initiative post implementation? (LO6)

13.3 Griffith Ltd has just realised that it has a problem with its general ledger data. It posts daily transactional data from subsidiary systems to the general ledger at 10 pm each evening. The resulting general ledger month-end reporting data is made available at 9 am on the first day of the month. Griffith Ltd is a global organisation with operations in every possible time zone worldwide.
  (a) What decisions made during the general ledger and financial reporting cycle would potentially be affected by this data problem? (LO3, LO4)
  (b) How would those decisions be affected? How would this data problem affect the reported results of the organisation? (LO3, LO4, LO6)
  (c) How would this data problem affect other processes at Griffith Ltd? (LO1, LO3, LO4, LO6)

13.4 Curtin Ltd has a reconciliation problem. The bank reconciliation clerk is unable to reconcile the cash at bank value recorded in the general ledger account with the cash at bank balance disclosed on the bank statements. Curtin Ltd seems to have good controls; it has separated all cash handling and recording functions from the bank reconciliation function, and it prepares a bank reconciliation on a weekly basis.

(a) Which internal controls might be missing? (LO5)

(b) What documentation would you examine in order to investigate this problem? (LO4)

13.5 Macquarie Ltd has a new CEO who is keen on improving process efficiency. She has reviewed the process documentation for the prepare budgets process and has asked you to remove the requirement for operational managers to confirm their acceptance of the finalised budget amounts, as it appears to be totally inefficient.

(a) Should you agree to remove this budget confirmation activity? Why or why not? (LO1, LO3, LO5)

(b) If you would not agree to remove the budget confirmation activity, how would you explain this decision to the CEO? (LO1, LO5)

(c) If you would agree to remove the budget confirmation activity how would you justify this change to the various department operational managers? (LO1, LO5)

(d) If you remove the budget confirmation activity would you need to measure process performance differently? (LO1, LO6)

## SELF–TEST ACTIVITIES

13.1 The general ledger and financial reporting cycle:

(a) creates, adjusts and reports data.

(b) summarises, adjusts and reports data.

(c) creates, summarises and adjusts data.

(d) creates, summarises, adjusts and reports data.

13.2 Preparing a budget involves estimating the level of future:

(a) activities.

(b) revenues.

(c) expenditures.

(d) all of the above.

13.3 Adjusting entries are used to:

(a) manipulate profit levels.

(b) reduce reported variances.

(c) improve report readability.

(d) bring raw transaction data into line with accounting standards.

13.4 Management reports are often more detailed than general purpose financial statements because:

(a) accounting standards prohibit reporting of details.

(b) managers need lots of data to make decisions; more data = better decisions.

(c) these reports are not available externally so data security and confidentiality are not an issue.

(d) we need lots of data diversity in these reports to satisfy different managers' demands.

13.5 The general ledger and financial reporting cycle interacts internally with:

(a) the production, expenditure, and HR management and payroll cycles.

(b) the revenue and expenditure cycles.

(c) the production, expenditure, revenue, and HR management and payroll cycles.

(d) the revenue, expenditure and production cycles.

13.6 Primary risks of the general ledger and financial reporting cycle include:

(a) erroneous budget estimates.

(b) inappropriate journal entry adjustments.

(c) data entry errors.

(d) all of the above.

13.7 A bank reconciliation should be performed:

(a) regularly.

(b) if there is a problem in the cash account balance.

(c) by the finance manager.

(d) if you don't use online banking facilities.

13.8 It is not useful to base your budget on prior year results when:

(a) operational managers want to prepare their own estimates.

(b) predictable change in the business environment will affect the coming year's operations.

(c) unpredictable change in the business environment will affect the coming year's operations.

(d) you had low budget variances reported in the prior year.

13.9 Keeping detailed supporting documentation for all adjusting journal entries helps to:

(a) pass an audit.

(a) ensure that all accounting standards have been considered.

(c) provide an audit trail to enable identification and tracking of adjustments made.

(d) prepare better management reports.

13.10 Risks encountered when extracting and validating transactional data typically include:

(a) incomplete data.

(b) inaccurate data.

(c) neither (a) nor (b).

(d) both (a) and (b).

13.11 Variance analysis reporting is used to monitor:

(a) whether adjusting journal entries were accurate.

(b) organisational and/or process performance.

(c) compliance with accounting standards.

(d) future activity levels.

## PROBLEMS

The case narrative below (AB Hi-Fi) will be used to complete problems 13.1–13.13. Make sure you read and understand the activities and the case thoroughly before you commence work on the problems.

### AB Hi-Fi general ledger and financial reporting cycle

AB Hi-Fi is a multi-store retail business that sells products such as DVDs, CDs, mp3 players, game consoles and TVs. In addition to retail stores, AB Hi-Fi also sells music, games and DVDs via its website. AB Hi-Fi has a small central finance and accounts unit that is responsible for oversight of all accounting matters. The finance and accounts unit consists of a full-time finance clerk, a seasonal budget clerk who works full time from May to July, and a part-time accountant who works three days per week. The narrative of the AB Hi-Fi general ledger and financial reporting cycle follows.

*(continued)*

**Process 1.0 Prepare budgets**

AB Hi-Fi creates its budgets in May of each year for the upcoming fiscal year (1 July to 30 June). The budget for AB Hi-Fi is set at store level, with each store manager responsible for contributing to the budget process. In addition to the store budgets, which focus on expected sales revenue and associated costs, expenditure budgets are created for corporate service units such as the production division, information technology, warehousing and human resources.

The budget process starts on 1 May every year. On this date the computer automatically extracts the current year's budget and actual totals for every revenue and expenditure account code in the general ledger data store. The computer calculates the forecasted actual totals for the current year by taking the value of the transactions for the year to date (i.e. 1 July to 30 April) and increasing this total by 17 per cent to allow for the remainder of the year. The computer then creates a proforma budget for each of the stores and corporate service units. The proforma budget is based on the current year budget; it also includes the forecast actual year total, and the estimated annual variance for each account. Once the proforma budgets have been created the computer distributes an electronic copy to the nominated manager for each division, and prints copies on the budget clerk's printer. The budget clerk files the proforma budgets in a folder named 'pro-forma budgets 20xx–xx'.

When a manager receives their proforma budget they open and view the data, then make any adjustments they feel are necessary. Any adjustment must have an accompanying note explaining why the adjustment was considered necessary. Typical notes would include 'I adjusted my sales revenue up by 5 per cent as this region is experiencing population growth' or 'The cost of raw materials is increasing so I have increased costs overall by 2 per cent'. Once the manager has finished making adjustments they tick a box on the proforma to indicate their adjustments are final, then close and save the proforma budget. Immediately after an adjusted proforma budget is finalised and saved the central computer prints a copy of the adjusted budget and the relevant notes on the printer in the budget clerk's office. The budget clerk compares the adjusted version to the proforma version to identify changes made. They then read through the adjustment explanations and highlight anything that they think looks unusual for follow up. For store budgets, the budget clerk also calculates the estimated gross profit percentage to make sure it meets acceptable guidelines, highlighting any store budget that will not meet the required gross profit target. The budget clerk attaches the copy of the original proforma budget to the adjusted version and the explanatory notes, and then files them in a folder called 'adjusted budgets awaiting approval'.

Every Friday during May and June, the budget clerk and the senior management team meet to consider the adjusted proforma budgets received during that week. During the meeting, the budget clerk records any amendments requested by senior management in a notepad. After the meeting, the budget clerk requests the computer to open the first proforma budget discussed at the meeting and checks their notes to see if any amendments were requested. If an amendment is necessary, the clerk types the new amounts into the proforma budget. Once all the numbers look correct, the clerk ticks a box on the proforma to indicate the budget is complete, then saves and closes the amended final budget. The computer transfers each budget amount into the relevant general ledger revenue and expenditure accounts. The clerk processes each amended proforma budget in the same manner. Once all the budget amendments have been completed, the budget clerk requests a print of the final budgets. The computer prints two copies of each final budget on the budget clerk's printer. The budget clerk attaches one copy of the final budget to the related proforma budget then files them in a folder named 'final budgets 20xx–xx'. The budget clerk sends the second copy of the final budget to the relevant manager, along with a memo explaining what has been amended and why. If no amendments were made, the budget clerk sends just the printed copy of the final budget to the manager.

### Process 2.0 Update the general ledger

Every night at 10 pm the computer receives details of production cost totals for the preceding day from the production cycle. The computer debits the relevant totals to the raw materials, direct labour and manufacturing overhead general ledger accounts, and credits the total of all the production costs to the production cost control general ledger account. Once this processing is completed the computer updates the status of the transactions held in the production data stores to 'posted'.

After every payroll run the computer receives details of salary and wages costs for the preceding pay period from the payroll cycle. The computer debits the amounts to the relevant salary expense accounts, and credits the total amount to the cash at bank general ledger account. Once this processing is completed the computer updates the status of the transactions held in the payroll data store to 'posted'.

At 1 am every morning the computer automatically extracts the details of any supplier invoices approved for payment during the preceding day from the accounts payable data store and then calculates a batch total. The batch total of the invoices is credited to the accounts payable general ledger account, and offsetting debits are created in each of the relevant general ledger expenditure accounts. Once this processing is completed the computer updates the status of the transactions held in the accounts payable data store to 'posted'. Immediately after processing the invoices the computer extracts the total of payments made during the day from the accounts payable data store and calculates a batch total. The batch total of payments made is credited to the cash at bank general ledger account and debited to the accounts payable general ledger account, then the original cash payment transaction status is updated to 'posted'. Once all accounts payable processing has been completed the computer runs a balance check to ensure that the balance of the accounts payable general ledger account agrees with the total of all the supplier balances owing in the accounts payable data store. If these totals do not agree an email is sent to the IT help desk requesting follow up.

At 5 am every morning the computer automatically extracts the details of any customer invoices raised during the preceding day from the accounts receivable data store, and then calculates a batch total. The batch total of the invoices is debited to the accounts receivable general ledger account, and offsetting credits are posted to each of the relevant general ledger revenue accounts. Once this processing is completed the computer updates the status of the original transactions held in the accounts receivable data store to 'posted'. Immediately after this process has been completed the computer runs a balance check to ensure that the totals contained in the accounts receivable general ledger account agree with the total of all the customer balances owing contained in the accounts receivable data store. If these totals do not agree an email is sent to the IT help desk requesting follow up.

At 1 pm every day an electronic payment notification is received from the bank that contains details of all credit card payments received from online orders for the previous day. The computer calculates the total transferred, then credits this total to the online sales general ledger account and debits the same total to the cash at bank general ledger account.

Throughout the day, whenever a cash receipts batch is successfully processed the computer extracts the batch total details then credits this total to the accounts receivable general ledger account. The total is debited to the cash at bank general ledger account and the status of the cash receipts batch is updated to 'posted'.

*(continued)*

### Process 3.0 Record general ledger adjustments

Throughout the month the finance clerk receives requests from stores and divisions for general journal entries to correct and adjust financial records. A typical example would be where a transaction has been incorrectly coded, and it is necessary to reverse the original transaction and post a correct transaction to ensure the financial reports are accurate. Another common request would relate to stock or labour transfers between stores, where a transfer price has been agreed upon. The finance clerk checks the general ledger account numbers on the journal request for accuracy, and then enters the journal into the computer. The computer checks that the journal transaction balances (i.e. debits = credits) then updates the relevant general ledger accounts.

Every Monday, the finance clerk manually prepares a bank reconciliation for the main trading account of AB Hi-Fi. Once the bank reconciliation is balanced the finance clerk prepares journal entries to record any bank initiated transactions such as bank fees or periodical payments. The finance clerk inputs the amounts from each journal entry as a separate batch into the computer. The computer checks that the journal transaction balances, and then updates the relevant general ledger accounts. After all the journal transactions have been input successfully the finance clerk checks that the balance displayed for the cash at bank general ledger account agrees with the balance calculated during the bank reconciliation. Once the finance clerk is sure that the cash at bank balance in the general ledger is correct they sign and date the bank reconciliation documentation, attach the related journal entries and then file the paperwork in date order in a file called 'bank reconciliations'.

On the fourth day of every month, the month-end processing begins. Note that accruals for standard items such as accounts receivable and payable are automatically created during routine processing. At 7 am the computer automatically initiates processing of preset depreciation charges by debiting depreciation expenses accounts and crediting the relevant asset accounts. The computer also adjusts the doubtful debts provision based on a predefined algorithm, and makes any necessary reversals for previous months' journal entries.

On the next working day, the finance clerk manually adjusts the general ledger balances to record any payroll liabilities. The finance clerk calculates the value of any salary and wages owing, then writes up an adjusting journal to debit the relevant salary and wage expense general ledger accounts and credit the salary and wages payable general ledger account. The finance clerk inputs the journal entry into the computer and ticks a box on the journal entry screen to indicate that the journal must be automatically reversed during the next accounting period. The computer checks that the journal balances, and then posts the transactions to the nominated general ledger accounts.

### Process 4.0 Produce reports

AB Hi-Fi has a suite of standard month-end reports that are automatically generated and distributed. These reports include a profit and loss account, and a budget vs. actual variance report for each store and corporate service unit. On the seventh day of every month, the computer extracts data from all the relevant general ledger accounts, generates the standard reports and prints them on a central printer. A staff member from the IT help desk collects the reports, writes the relevant manager's name on the back of each one, and then puts them into unlocked mailboxes for distribution to the managers.

During the month, requests are often received from managers for additional reports. These requests are sent to the finance clerk who decides whether a new report needs to be created, or if there is an existing report that would present the data required. The finance clerk always checks the supplementary report folder to see whether there is a previous report that might suit, but most requests need a new report. For new reports, the finance clerk sends the report request to the IT help desk for action. Once the report has been created a copy is sent to the requesting manager, and also to the finance clerk. The finance clerk files copies of all new reports in a folder called 'supplementary reports'.

AB Hi-Fi produces quarterly financial statements that are distributed to senior management and the board of directors. After board acceptance and audit sign off these financial statements form the basis of the company's tax returns and the corporate reports required to be lodged with ASIC. On the tenth day of every new quarter (i.e. October, January, April, July) the computer extracts data from all the relevant general ledger accounts, generates the financial statements and prints them on a central printer. A staff member from the IT help desk collects the reports, addresses them, and puts them into unlocked mailboxes for distribution to senior management. Copies of the reports for board members are posted to their supplied address.

**Required**

13.1 Prepare a context diagram for the general ledger and financial reporting cycle at AB Hi-Fi.

13.2 Prepare a level 0 logical DFD for the general ledger and financial reporting cycle at AB Hi-Fi.

13.3 Prepare a level 1 logical DFD for:
   (a) process 1.0 at AB Hi-Fi.
   (b) process 2.0 at AB Hi-Fi.
   (c) process 3.0 at AB Hi-Fi.
   (d) process 4.0 at AB Hi-Fi.

13.4 Prepare a physical DFD for:
   (a) process 1.0 at AB Hi-Fi.
   (b) process 2.0 at AB Hi-Fi.
   (c) process 3.0 at AB Hi-Fi.
   (d) process 4.0 at AB Hi-Fi.

13.5 Prepare a systems flowchart for:
   (a) process 1.0 at AB Hi-Fi.
   (b) process 2.0 at AB Hi-Fi.
   (c) process 3.0 at AB Hi-Fi.
   (d) process 4.0 at AB Hi-Fi.

13.6 Table 13.2 (page 591) identifies two risks typically encountered when preparing a budget.

**Required**

   (a) Analyse the degree of exposure to each of these risks for the prepare budgets process at AB Hi-Fi.
   (b) Determine how many of the common controls described in table 13.2 are present in the prepare budgets process at AB Hi-Fi.
   (c) Prepare a short report suitable for senior management to explain how risky you think the prepare budgets process is, and how comprehensive the current internal controls are.
   (d) Prepare a recommendation describing any changes you would like to make to the prepare budgets process at AB Hi-Fi in order to reduce the level of risk.

13.7 Table 13.3 (page 596) identifies three risks typically encountered when updating the general ledger.

**Required**

(a) Analyse the degree of exposure to each of these risks for the update the general ledger process at AB Hi-Fi.

(b) Determine how many of the common controls described in table 13.3 are present in the update general ledger process at AB Hi-Fi.

(c) Prepare a short report suitable for senior management to explain how risky you think the update the general ledger process is, and how comprehensive the current internal controls are.

(d) Prepare a recommendation describing any changes you would like to make to the update the general ledger process at AB Hi-Fi in order to reduce the level of risk.

13.8 Table 13.4 (page 598) identifies two risks typically encountered when adjusting the general ledger.

**Required**

(a) Analyse the degree of exposure to each of these risks for the adjust the general ledger process at AB Hi-Fi.

(b) Determine how many of the common controls described in table 13.4 are present in the adjust the general ledger process at AB Hi-Fi.

(c) Prepare a short report suitable for senior management to explain how risky you think the adjust the general ledger process is, and how comprehensive the current internal controls are.

(d) Prepare a recommendation describing any changes you would like to make to the adjust the general ledger process at AB Hi-Fi in order to reduce the level of risk.

13.9 Table 13.5 (page 605) identifies three risks typically encountered when producing reports.

**Required**

(a) Analyse the degree of exposure to each of these risks for the produce reports process at AB Hi-Fi.

(b) Determine how many of the common controls described in table 13.5 are present in the produce reports process at AB Hi-Fi.

(c) Prepare a short report suitable for senior management to explain how risky you think the produce reports process is, and how comprehensive the current internal controls are.

(d) Prepare a recommendation describing any changes you would like to make to the produce reports process at AB Hi-Fi in order to reduce the level of risk.

13.10 (a) AB Hi-Fi has adopted a cost leadership strategy. Its overall plan is to undercut competitors on pricing and so gain market share. How well does its current prepare budgets process align with this business strategy? (b) Are there any opportunities to improve the degree of alignment between the prepare budgets process and the business strategy? Explain what you would change and how this would improve the strategic alignment.

13.11 (a) Identify and describe the technologies that AB Hi-Fi uses in its general ledger and financial reporting cycle activities. (b) For each of those technologies you identified in part (a), how well does AB Hi-Fi use the technology? Could you suggest a way to improve the business benefit obtained by use of any of these technologies? (c) Are there other suitable technologies available that AB Hi-Fi could be using for the general ledger and financial reporting cycle activities? What business benefit would these additional technologies provide?

**13.12** During process 1.0 Prepare budgets at AB Hi-Fi a budget clerk has to decide whether an adjusted budget submitted by a manager looks reasonable. Take a moment to review this section of the narrative before you complete the following questions.

**Required**

(a) What data do the budget clerk draw on when making the decision?

(b) Where do the data you identified in part (a) come from?

(c) Are these data reliable; that is, is there any possibility that there could be errors in the data?

(d) Are these data sufficient to make the decision, or can you identify additional data that the clerk should consider when making the decision?

(e) What would be the consequences of an incorrect decision?

**13.13** Explain how you would measure performance of the general ledger and financial reporting cycle at AB Hi-Fi, specifically:

(a) What metrics would you would use to measure performance?

(b) For each metric, explain where you would obtain the data required.

(c) For each metric, explain why it is a good metric to help measure how well the general ledger and financial reporting cycle is meeting its objectives.

## SELF-TEST ANSWERS

13.1 d, 13.2 d, 13.3 d, 13.4 c, 13.5 c, 13.6 d, 13.7 a, 13.8 c, 13.9 c, 13.10 d, 13.11 b

## FURTHER READING

Collier, PC 2009, *Accounting for managers: interpreting accounting information for decision-making,* 3rd edn, John Wiley & Sons, Inc.

Lee, YW 2006, *Journey to data quality,* Cambridge, Mass: MIT Press.

## END NOTES

1. Nasscom Emerge Blog 2007, 'Tagged economy — XBRL — emerging opportunity', 26 December, www.blog.nasscom.in/emerge/.

2. blueStar Business Solutions 2009, 'School settled with Greentree for good', www.bluestar.net.au/customers/profiles/lutheran-education.php.

3. BHP Billiton Limited 2009, *(Single parent entity) financial statements*, pp. 2, 4, 5, www.bhpbilliton.com.

# PART 4

# Systems issues

The issues considered in this part of the text are the macro type issues that apply across the organisation and its collection of business processes. These include system development, auditing and ethics. In this final section, with the knowledge you have acquired about systems concepts and process examples, you are able to take a step back and place the operation of the processes in the broader context of the organisation. Issues that emerge as part of doing this include questions about how the organisation can manage change within its business process. The reality is that the environment and the needs of the organisation will change over time, necessitating systems development. In addition, issues of how the technology is used and the risk of inappropriate use of technology emerge, raising ethical considerations in the operation of our processes. The role of monitoring process operation also becomes important, with internal audit filling this capacity.

# 14

# Systems development

## Learning objectives

After studying this chapter, you should be able to:

**1** explain how business size and complexity may influence the choice of systems development strategy for an organisation

**2** describe the stages of the systems development lifecycle and discuss the importance of organisational strategy as the basis for systems development

**3** describe the software development options available to smaller businesses and outline the systems selection processes for decision making

**4** describe alternative approaches to systems development

**5** describe typical systems development problems and propose solutions for their resolution

**6** identify and describe some common systems development tools.

# Introduction

Systems development is an important part of the organisation. Information technology (IT) represents the way that an organisation recognises the need for a new system, goes through the process of meeting the need and implements the system within the organisation. Systems development is a project for an organisation, the outcome of which is intended to be a better system that allows the organisation to function more effectively. Organisations face the need for systems development for various reasons, including:

- An existing system has reached the end of its usefulness and is in need of replacement because of outdated technology or slow processing time.
- A new strategic opportunity has been identified that will allow the business to improve its strategic position (for example, linking the system with a customer or supplier to increase efficiency of transactions and strengthen relationships).
- The business is just starting out and has no systems in place.

Whatever the reason for the systems development, organisations need an approach that they can employ in their systems development activity. This chapter emphasises the traditional approach, that of the systems development lifecycle. The chapter introduces the stages of the systems development lifecycle, the process of prototyping, application service providers and some common problems in systems development. Many textbooks have been written on systems development as a stand-alone topic. This chapter is intended as an overview to the area, to promote thinking about systems development within the organisation. The chapter particularly highlights the different roles an accountant will need to employ within the systems development process, for example, as a user of the final system or as an auditor of the system. The references at the end of the chapter are a useful source for further discussion.

In recent years, the management of systems development within the organisation has been a critical issue as businesses have upgraded systems, implemented new systems or looked for add-on systems, such as CRM (customer relationship management). The adoption of an enterprise resource planning (ERP) system is an example of an organisation-wide systems development effort. As you would recall from chapter 6, such efforts require careful management and consideration. This chapter aims to introduce some of these considerations in the systems development effort of an organisation.

**LEARNING OBJECTIVE**

*Explain how business size and complexity may influence the choice of systems development strategy for an organisation.*

## BUSINESS SIZE AND COMPLEXITY

Table 14.1 overleaf splits Australian and New Zealand business into three broad classifications (large, medium and small) based on size (number of employees) and turnover, and indicates appropriate levels of sophistication of accounting systems. The classifications are arbitrary and the specification of systems are generalisations: in some cases a firm with $10 million turnover and 50 employees may find that a simple package meets all its needs, while another organisation of similar size may consider that the additional cost and complexity of an ERP system is justified by the unique features of its business.

Choosing an accounting system is not a one-size-fits-all exercise. The complex, time-consuming and expensive process described in the next section, while absolutely essential for the successful implementation of an ERP system, goes well beyond the needs of medium and small businesses. A simpler methodology for system selection for these businesses is described later in the chapter.

**TABLE 14.1** Australian and New Zealand business size classifications

|  | Small | Medium | Large |
|---|---|---|---|
| Number of employees | 1–20 | 21–200 | 201+ |
| Annual turnover | <$5m | $5m–$50m | >$50m |
| Accounting system | Simple | Mid-range | ERP |

# SYSTEMS DEVELOPMENT LIFECYCLE

The systems development lifecycle has parallels in any other lifecycle that you can think of. It represents the stages that are followed in the design, implementation and maintenance of an information system within an organisation. As the subsequent sections reveal, the systems development lifecycle offers a structured, well-controlled and well-documented approach to systems development. This control and this structure can be important for managing large systems development projects, and can also be a way of ensuring that available resources for the systems development effort are maximised. The systems development lifecycle is the most popular and traditional method of systems development. Alternative methods of systems development — prototyping, object-oriented analysis and agile/adaptive methods — will be covered later in the chapter.

The systems development lifecycle consists of five stages: (1) investigation, (2) analysis, (3) design, (4) implementation and (5) maintenance and review. In the investigation and analysis stages, the problems facing the organisation are investigated in light of the current system and its operations. Alternative responses for the problem will be evaluated based on their feasibility. After selecting the most feasible option, the design for that option will commence, with this consisting of both logical and physical design perspectives. After the design is complete, the system will be physically implemented and, once implemented, will require regular maintenance and review. As figure 14.1 shows, the cycle begins with investigation, then analysis, design, implementation, and lastly maintenance and review. Once the maintenance and review part of the lifecycle can no longer successfully maintain the system the cycle will start again with investigation.

As the following sections describe, each of these stages has predefined inputs and outputs. The outputs of each stage provide the inputs into subsequent stages, thus building a control into the systems development effort, because latter stages cannot commence until there has been a signing-off on the earlier stages. As a result of this built-in control over stage commencement, a degree of accountability is built into the systems development lifecycle. Participants involved in a system's development require their superiors to sign off on their work before proceeding to later tasks. This can be seen as a strength of the lifecycle and is a characteristic of its controlled and structured approach. The internal auditor needs to be involved in each stage of systems development to ensure that adequate internal controls are built into the new system as it is designed. However, as the example of Very Limited in figure 14.2 illustrates, the limitation of the traditional approach to systems development is the time involved.

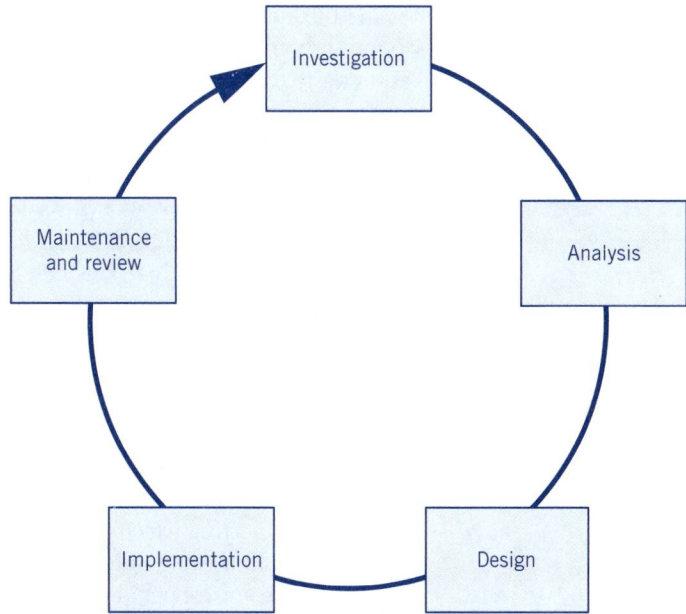

**FIGURE 14.1** Systems development lifecycle

June, the accountant for Very Limited, just wants the new system. She is concerned with all the time the systems development people are taking. She books a meeting to discuss why they aren't just designing the new system. Sue from the IT development team explains that there are several steps they need to take. To figure out the requirements of the new system they must analyse the old system; that is, before they can establish what the new system should do they first need to establish what the old system actually does. These steps are part of the systems development lifecycle. Sue explains that each step has inputs and outputs and by following these steps June and the other system users in the organisation will get the system they need. June explains that it is also important for users to understand each of the steps in the lifecycle and the inputs and outputs of each step, so they know what they need to contribute. Proposing a solution without investigating the problem, scope and current system may cause problems later. The worst case could be that the solution (new system) does not fix the problems and doesn't even do what the old system used to do. So, even though the systems development is taking time, the time spent is valuable in getting the right result.

**FIGURE 14.2** Very Limited example

The following sections discuss the stages in the systems development lifecycle.

## Investigation

The investigation phase of the systems development lifecycle is concerned with identifying any problems or opportunities with the current systems and the feasibility of responding to these problems and opportunities. Notice how the trigger for a systems development effort can be either a problem or a perceived opportunity. The point in emphasising this is that systems development is not triggered solely by the advent of a problem in the existing systems, for example, the processing speed is inadequate and the process throughput time is slowed down as a result. A perceived opportunity for the business can be another trigger for a systems development project. Perceived opportunity means a way that the organisation can use its existing resources or acquire resources that would enable it to build on its existing strategy and increase its competitive advantage within its industry.

An example of an opportunity can be seen in the process used by supermarkets in their checkouts. Before the advent of computers supermarkets manually processed items through the checkout, with sales staff keying prices into manual registers that kept a total of all purchases. As computers and database technologies emerged and became widely accessible to business these manual registers were computerised, with staff entering product codes, which were then taken by the register and looked up in the database of products to find a price for the items being purchased. This made the checkout process quicker.

A further advance came with barcode scanning technology, allowing the quicker capture of data about products being purchased. Instead of product codes having to be keyed manually into the register, barcodes from products could be electronically read by the scanners, enabling an even faster and more accurate checkout process. Similarly, connecting electronic scales to the point-of-sale terminal allowed the checkout operator, using only the product look up (PLU) code or a name, to have the system look up a price per kilogram for fruit and vegetables. These simple examples of technology evolution show how businesses are able to benefit from new technologies and develop new systems around the technology. Extending the technology even further, in the United States, Ireland and Australia self-service checkouts have been successfully introduced into supermarkets, while a possible future advance involves RFID tags attached to all products and the trolley being equipped with a reading device that will calculate the amount due as each item is loaded in. Therefore, systems development is not just about identifying the problems with the existing systems. It is also about being aware of new technologies and how they can be used to bring the organisation advantage.

However, the critical point to keep in mind when considering new opportunities for technology within the organisation is the issue of **organisational fit**. Organisational fit refers to how well the technology is aligned with the overall organisational strategy and strategic priorities. This is an important point to bear in mind because it emphasises the idea that technology should be used to tackle problems and opportunities that originate within the business. The relationship does not work in reverse, that is, not all new technologies are blindly adopted even if there is no real application for them or they conflict with overall organisational strategy and mission. Therefore, consider new technologies in light of the underlying business environment — new technologies are not necessary for all businesses. It is the matching of the technology to the opportunity that is important, not just blind adoption of technology because it is seen as the cool thing to do.

*Organisational fit* How well the technology is aligned with the overall organisational strategy and strategic priorities.

## Problem identification

Problem identification will usually involve those working on the system development and a user representative group. The user representative group will consist of a cross-section of employees from different parts of the organisation who are able to provide feedback, on behalf of their colleagues, about a system's operation. As an accountant you may be required to be a member of such a user representative group. Therefore, it is important to understand the goals of the problem identification phase and how you can contribute to the system development. Problems with existing systems can be identified in several ways. One way is through user and stakeholder feedback, which can take the form of formal and informal comments that have been received from those involved in a system's operation. For example, telephone operators at a booking centre may alert those in charge to a slow system that takes an excessive amount of time to process ticketing requests from customers who are waiting on the other end of the line. As another example, customers may complain to an organisation about a system that bills them incorrectly. This feedback will typically be provided ad hoc as problems or issues emerge in the systems operation.

Alternatively, a periodic review of system operations can identify systems opportunities and problems. A current example of an event that may trigger systems development is the introduction of the Sarbanes–Oxley Act in the United States. Many companies faced issues of legislative compliance after the introduction of the Act, prompting them to review their existing system's internal controls and potentially design a new system that is compliant. Other factors to consider when investigating any problems or opportunities with a system include system speed, system adequacy, system support, new changes and general triggers. Each of these is discussed briefly in the following.

- *Is the speed of the system adequate for its current role?* As organisations grow, so too will the amount of data that they handle and store. This can place increased demands on existing systems and may provide a trigger for systems development. In the supermarket example mentioned above, the speed of transaction completion at the checkout was a major motivation behind the series of developments mentioned. In each case, the changes increased the speed at which the system could capture and process data about sales. Other examples can include new data access and storage techniques that allow for faster systems.
- *Does the system adequately handle the events that occur in a process?* Information systems are put in place to support the operations of the organisation. The design and operation of the system should be driven by the organisation's needs. To this end, as the organisation changes, so too will the requirements of the information system. Growth in customer numbers may mean that old systems become slow and inadequate for the fast processing of customer requests. The introduction of a store credit system may mean that systems based on a cash-only basis need to be modified or redeveloped. In both of these examples, the need for systems development has been driven by the system's inability to handle existing and new business events. From an organisation's perspective, it can be useful to identify the key events that occur within a business process and then assess how well the information system handles these events. This can be a powerful way to identify any problems in the current system.
- *Is the system able to generate the required information to support management decision making?* The system's role within the organisation should be to gather data from business events and allow for the summarising of these data into meaningful and useful information that supports management decision making. Feedback from managers that they need a new type of information or a new report or have other new requirements can be a trigger for systems development activities.
- *Are there predicted circumstances that may require a change to the current system?* Several examples of systems development have been triggered by anticipated future events. Two are the 'year 2000' problem and the introduction of the goods and services tax (GST). The year 2000 problem — the possibility that older systems would not be able to recognise the 2000 date because of a two-digit year rather than a four-digit year in systems data — prompted many organisations to undergo major systems development efforts. The possible threat of systems failure when 2000 arrived was

potentially catastrophic, prompting many organisations operating old mainframe systems to upgrade their systems through major systems development projects, many of which included the adoption of ERP systems.

In Australia, the change in the tax legislation that saw the introduction of the GST on 1 July 2000 (in New Zealand the change was much earlier, in 1986, with a GST rate change in 1989) prompted many systems development efforts. Many organisations were forced to review the operation of their existing information systems and, where necessary, change them or upgrade them so that they could handle the new taxation environment, which brought with it new requirements for data gathering and statutory reporting. Many commercial producers of accounting packages recognised this need by producing GST-compliant accounting software.

- *Has there been an event that would trigger concerns about the current system?* Events within the organisation may also act as a trigger for systems development, including the failure of existing systems (e.g. a processing system that crashes frequently), the occurrence of organisational fraud owing to inadequate information controls, or rapid growth that has made the old systems inadequate for the new operating environment. One example is the advent of the e-commerce environment. Organisations that make the decision to support the avenue of e-business face associated issues of ensuring that existing systems support this environment and, where necessary, development occurs to support the e-commerce operations. This could include the development of web interfaces and environments that support the integration of the new e-commerce environment with the existing systems environment.

Other ways of identifying avenues for potential systems development can include surveying existing users regularly, observing the system in action by watching users and interviewing key users of a system. These provide first-hand information on the operation of the system and, as is discussed later in the chapter, can also provide the users with the perception that they are involved in, and an important part of, systems development within the organisation.

Once the information has been gathered, a report detailing the problems and opportunities will be prepared, which will form the basis of the investigation of alternative ways to solve the problems or exploit the opportunities.

## Alternatives

Once the problems with or opportunities of the existing system have been identified, the organisation must develop ideas for how these problems or opportunities can be met. The first step in doing this is to define what the systems development project will cover. This is the critical issue of defining the **systems development scope**. For example, is the scope of the system a sales order or a sales order and inventory system? Several problems may have been identified but not all of these may be high priority. Defining the scope of the system helps in clarifying what the systems development effort is aiming to achieve and reduces the risk of heading off on tangents that do not solve the identified problems. From an accounting perspective of the system, the scope defines the systems development effort and what it aims to achieve; anything outside this scope is not attempted by the systems development effort. As a result, it is important to ensure that the scope covers the identified problem, as the scope cannot be varied once the project is underway.

*Systems development scope Defining what problems the systems development project will cover.*

## Feasibility

Feasibility will determine whether something will actually occur. The **feasibility analysis** involves the evaluation of the alternatives identified to determine whether they are legitimate options for the business to consider at later stages of the development.

*Feasibility analysis Involves the evaluation of the alternatives identified to determine whether they are legitimate options for the business to consider at later stages of the development.*

Feasibility will be assessed on five dimensions: financial, legal, schedule, technical and strategic feasibility.

## Financial feasibility

**Financial feasibility** is based around the economic costs and benefits of a system. In assessing the financial feasibility of a system, the costs involved in adopting the new system will be systematically compared with the financial benefits of the new system. Costs can include items such as consultants' fees, the purchase of new hardware, software and equipment, and the costs associated with training staff in the operations of the new system. Financial benefits of a new system can include the cost savings that may arise, for example, reduced wages if a system automates a previously manual process, along with any increases in sales or revenue that may arise. Note, however, that it is typically far more difficult to estimate the benefits of a system in financial terms. This problem arises from the difficulty in directly attributing any changes in organisational performance to a new system. For example, if a new system is introduced and sales increase, does all of the increase owe to the new system? Additionally, benefits typically require evaluation. In contrast, costs are usually easily identified and able to be determined to a relatively precise degree. As a result, if one were to rely on financial feasibility alone most projects would face rejection at this early stage.

Another factor to consider when assessing the financial feasibility of a system is the concept of the **total cost of ownership**. This refers to a need to consider not just the initial costs of installing a system but also the ongoing costs following the implementation of a system. Compaq estimates that only 4 per cent of executives realise that these post-implementation costs represent the largest component of IT costs, often representing up to 80 per cent of total costs for a system.[1] These costs are driven by three areas: people, processes and technology.[2] People refers to making sure that the users of the system are adequately skilled to use the system as it was intended to be used. Process costs relate to the configuration of the system to meet the processes of the organisation, and can include the cost of removing old processes and reconfiguring them to match the newly adopted technology. Technology costs refer to the costs of acquiring the necessary technology to implement the proposed solution.

The costs and benefits of each alternative will be assessed through a financial feasibility report, which will summarise the financial perspective over several years, incorporating both initial and ongoing costs associated with a system. Advanced techniques may also use a discounted cash flows model, allowing the time value of money to be taken into account. This can also allow the assessment of investment alternatives based on their net present value, or the use of concepts such as internal rate of return. These concepts are beyond the scope of this text and can be found in any good introductory finance textbook.

## Legal feasibility

**Legal feasibility** is concerned with how the proposed system would operate given the legal environment faced by the organisation. The legal environment refers to the laws and regulations an organisation is required to comply with. This can include reporting obligations, for example, companies have reporting obligations imposed on them under the Federal *Corporations Act 2001* of Australia or the *Companies Act 1993* in New Zealand, as well as the legality of the systems operation techniques. Examples of reporting requirements could be a company that is considering the adoption of a new system but is not able to prepare reports according to (generally accepted accounting principles (GAAP) and International Financial Reporting Standards (IFRSs). The preparation of these reports is a major part of the company's reporting obligations and to

**Financial feasibility** *Assessment of the costs involved in adopting a new system, systematically compared with the financial benefits of a new system.*

**Total cost of ownership** *The need to consider not just the initial costs of installing a system but also the ongoing costs following the implementation of a system.*

**Legal feasibility** *How the proposed system would operate given the legal environment faced by the organisation.*

meet these obligations the system should be able to comply with GAAP. Therefore, a system that could not meet GAAP requirements may be rejected on the legal feasibility criteria.

The other aspect to the legality of a system is the legality of its operations. Examples here could include the way the system gathers, stores and uses data. Issues to consider include the legality of data-gathering techniques, for example, refer to the discussion of the Privacy Act for example.

### Schedule feasibility

**Schedule feasibility** refers to the ability of the proposed solution to be implemented within the period of time that is specified by the organisation. A project that takes two years to implement for a problem that the organisation wants solved in three months will fail the test of schedule feasibility. The assessment of schedule feasibility requires the assessment of the expected project time and a comparison of the expected time with the time available. Estimating schedule feasibility requires a thorough understanding of the tasks that need to be performed and an estimate of their time for completion. Some tools that can be used to assist in estimating schedule feasibility, as well as for controlling projects once they are undertaken, include **programmed evaluation review technique (PERT) charts** and **Gantt charts**. These tools are discussed later in this chapter.

### Technical feasibility

**Technical feasibility** involves the assessment of how well the organisation's existing technology infrastructure meets the requirements of the proposed alternative. If the current resources are unable to meet the requirements of the new system, an assessment of what new technology is required may also be performed. This stage involves the consideration of different design options for the proposed alternative and weighing them up against the organisation's existing technical resources and the resources that are available for purchase.

### Strategic feasibility

**Strategic feasibility** refers to how well the proposed systems development alternative fits with the organisation's existing operating environment and strategy. You should recall the importance of being clear about an organisation's strategy and business process design as mentioned earlier in this chapter and in chapter 2. One of the issues that needs to be considered is how well the proposed system alternative meets this strategic position. For example, a firm that has built up a position as a quality differentiator, offering customers a highly personalised and quality-driven service, would not be keen to adopt a system that was built around the principles of a cost leadership strategy. Why? Because the system would conflict with the strategy. On the one hand, the organisation would have a strategy and set of business processes designed to serve the quality differentiator position, while, on the other, the organisation would be adopting a system that functioned in support of a contrasting strategy. This situation can only create confusion for the organisation and its customers, and has been a common problem in the adoption of ERP systems in organisations, because they discovered that the business processes embodied within the ERP systems did not fit with the pre-existing organisational strategy. The result was that the business strategy was undermined when ERP systems were adopted.

Once the project's feasibility in each of the five areas has been evaluated and documented, a decision must be made on whether to proceed with the systems development. This decision will be made on the overall feasibility of the system alternatives based on the consideration of the five dimensions discussed in this section. The overall feasibility will be summarised and forwarded to the organisation's systems development steering committee, discussed in the next section, which has the task of selecting an alternative.

## *Decide on feasibility*

*Systems development steering committee* Responsible for determining whether the systems development project should proceed; members typically occupy positions of power throughout the organisation.

The task of selecting the most feasible alternative rests with the **systems development steering committee**, which represents a key part of the systems development process. The members of the systems development steering committee typically occupy positions of power throughout the organisation. The systems development steering committee is responsible for determining whether the systems development project should proceed. Since the steering committee decides on the project's approval, the members should have the power to allocate resources throughout the organisation, because once a project is approved it requires financial and other resources for its successful completion. The job of the steering committee is to select the alternative that it views as the most viable. Once selected, the committee will sign off on the selected option, with this forming the basis of the design stage. The steering committee also performs a critical role throughout the lifecycle of the project, receiving reports at the end of each major phase and signing the phase off so that the next phase can commence.

# Analysis

The analysis stage of the systems development lifecycle has two key parts. The first is to understand what the current system does and how it operates. The second part is to specify what the new system will need to do. The understanding of the current system is called the systems analysis, while the specification of what the new system needs to do is called the requirements analysis.[3] The requirements identified will be suggested by the needs of the end-users of the system. As a user of an information system, accounting personnel will be required to identify their needs.

## *Requirements analysis and specification*

Systems analysis requires a thorough understanding of the current system, its operations and design. There are several ways that this understanding can be gained. One method is to analyse the systems documentation, which can include the process map, logical dataflow diagram, physical dataflow diagram, systems flowchart and any other documentation that may exist within the organisation (see chapter 5 for a general discussion of systems documentation and chapters 9–13 for examples of systems documentation for specific business processes). If no such documentation exists, it can be useful to generate it before progressing, because it provides a way of understanding how the current system operates. Understanding the system requires an appreciation of the logical processes that occur in the system, the physical entities that are involved in the processes, the documentation and data flows that occur in the system and the interaction across the organisation that takes place: this is the impact of organisational structure and design on the operation of the system and the flows across the organisation that occur.[4] As mentioned in chapter 2 on business processes, documentation techniques allow these various aspects of a system to be shown. This analysis can help identify what the current system does, as well as how the system needs to be changed. If using existing documentation it is important to ensure that this remains accurate, since procedures are often changed over time without the documentation being updated to reflect the changes. In many cases, the accountant or internal auditor will have used logical and physical data flow diagrams and systems flowcharts to document their systems; these can be used as a basis of the systems documentation. With their understanding of the techniques in producing data flow diagrams and flowcharts, the accountant can also evaluate any documents produced by the systems development team to verify their understanding of the existing system or potential new system.

Requirements analysis then necessitates going from an understanding of what the current systems does to what the new system needs to do. Essentially, this is about understanding what the system is required to do and how the different users use and interact with the system.[5] It is also about how the existing system can be improved, making a thorough understanding of the operations of the current system an important starting point. There are several ways that this information can be obtained. As a starting point, it is useful to speak to the key users of the system to understand how they use the system in their roles and what features they regularly use or seldom use. Different users in an organisation can include those involved in direct data entry, managers who use reports or output from the system and any other stakeholders who may have a role in using the system. This can present the analyst with challenges, because different users or stakeholders of a system can have different views on requirements. Additionally, what the stakeholders see as a requirement is often linked to the context of the organisation that they are involved in, thus making requirements analysis a technical task (what the system needs to do) and a social task (the impact of organisational structure and individual roles). This can present the analyst with unique challenges.[6]

There are several techniques for gathering requirements information, including questionnaires, observation, interviews and prototyping. When a questionnaire is used, a survey is given to the different users, asking them about the features of the system and what they use and do not use in a system. For example, a survey to managers may ask them which of the reporting features they regularly use and which they do not. This helps to gain an understanding of the important features required in a system. Questionnaires can be designed so they are open-ended, in which case the user can write responses and elaborate on answers, or contain closed questions, which limit the nature of the responses that the user can give. Another option is for the system analyst to observe the process in action or be a part of the business process and a part of its operation. This will provide them with first-hand experience of the operations of the process, the types of problems that may occur and what different users need. Another alternative is to generate a prototype, based on the earlier investigation specifications, and involve users in the evaluation of the different features of the prototype. Prototyping for systems development is discussed in more detail later in the chapter.

Having gained an understanding of the current system, spoken to users about its operation and elicited suggestions for change, a list of requirements that the systems development needs to fulfil is generated. This is a description of what the new system will need to do in the organisation. From the accounting information systems perspective, some of the issues that may be evaluated at this point include:

- Do we need batch or online processing of transaction data to support the business process?
- What information do the different users require to perform their functions?
- What is needed for the business process to integrate successfully with other systems and business processes within the organisation?

Care needs to be taken when analysing requirements that the scope of the systems development effort is realistic. Users, when asked, may offer suggestions that are beyond the scope of the current systems development effort. Alternatively, they may make suggestions for things that do not add much improvement to the system.

Eliciting the needs of the various users and determining what the new system is required to do is used to provide some structure when designing the new system. It also helps in relating the objectives of the systems development back to the original scope of the problem and the overarching business context and strategy. It is also important to keep in mind the things that are important to the business and make sure that the systems development and, in particular, the requirements specification, are consistent with the original scope of the project. Having done this, a design needs to be arrived at for a system to achieve these aims. This is referred to as the design phase, and is discussed in the next section.

Once the analysis phase is complete the documentation is reviewed by the steering committee to ensure the analysis and the scope of the project to see how they fit in with the company's plans. The steering committee could decide at this point that the project should not commence.

## Design

Once a systems development project has been deemed feasible and signed off by the steering committee, the task is to design the system. System design can take two perspectives: the **logical perspective** and the **physical perspective**. The logical perspective of systems design is concerned with a design that is independent of the actual technology required for its implementation. The physical design requires the specification of the technical aspects. The logical design, also referred to as the conceptual design, describes what the system will do; the physical design describes how it will actually be done.

This is much the same concept as for the logical and physical data flow diagrams shown in chapters 9–13. To use an analogy, the logical design is like drawing a floor plan for a house — it contains the key features such as the number of rooms, location of the bathroom and so on, while the physical design is how the house will actually be built, for example, will it be made of bricks or timber, will the windows be single or double glazed?

In this phase, the internal auditor needs to be involved as internal controls need to be built into a system at the time it is designed, not later. Building in internal controls later is a costly and inefficient process compared to building them in at the time the systems development occurs.

### *Determine outputs*

Following the investigation and analysis stages of the systems development lifecycle we would be familiar with the different user requirements. In particular, we would be aware of the types of outputs users require from a system to complete their daily tasks. The understanding of these outputs is crucial to the design of the system. Typical systems design theory recommends starting from the systems outputs as the basis for designing the system. At first this may seem a little back-to-front; however, if you think about it the proposition is not so nonsensical. By starting with the required outputs of the system we are determining what we need to get from the system. It is only by understanding what we want from a system that we are able to clarify what inputs the system will require and how the input data must be processed. By starting from the outputs we can work backwards to identify the necessary inputs. This flow back from outputs helps to ensure that the new system is able to do what the users require it to do and generate the necessary information.

**Logical perspective** *An approach that is concerned with a design that is independent of the actual technology required for its implementation.*

**Physical perspective** *Requires the specification of the technical aspects of how a design will be achieved.*

## Determine inputs

Once it is clear what outputs are required from the system, it is possible to work backwards and determine what inputs are required to generate the specified outputs. As part of designing the inputs, reports are deconstructed, breaking them down into the different pieces of data that go into their generation. In determining the inputs into a system, the designers need to understand the processes that the system will operate as a part of and the different data that are generated within that process. One way to gain an understanding of that is to examine processes based on where data come from, the form they come in and how they are used within the system. This can include looking at existing source documents within the system, any electronic data that may be received from other sources, as well as how forms are used by participants working with the system.

An example of working backwards from outputs to inputs is shown in figure 14.3, which shows the process of working backwards from a report, in this case a monthly sales report by customer, to the inputs required to generate the report.

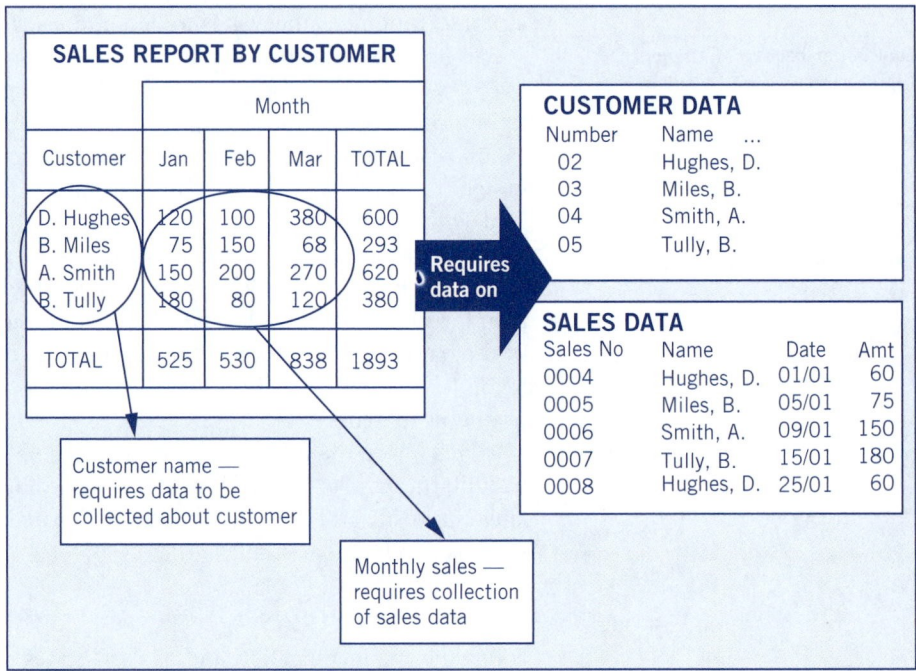

**FIGURE 14.3** From reports to inputs

Once the inputs have been clarified the next step is to design the storage mechanism, with this typically leading to database design and the generation of entity-relationship diagrams, discussed in chapters 3 and 4. Documenting the analysis of inputs into a system can also be useful for understanding what inputs are prepared, how they are used and where they end up. The inputs that are going to be input into the system must be considered in how the accuracy of them will be tested. It is important to ensure that your input is validated and accurate. This can help identify any redundant documents that may exist. Clarke provides, as a basis for this analysis, a form identification sheet, which would be used to record the different input forms within a system.[7] An example is provided in figure 14.4.[8]

| FORM IDENTIFICATION SHEET | | | | |
|---|---|---|---|---|
| **Prepared by:**<br>**Date:** | | | | |
| **Form name:** _____ | | **Form number:** _____ | | |
| **Purpose of form:** | | | | |
| **Form generated by: (describe event and person)** | | | | |
| **Form used by: (describe role in process)** | | | | |
| **Frequency of form use:** | >daily / | Daily / | Weekly / Monthly / | <once a month |
| **Period form is retained for:** | | | | |
| **Storage location:** | | | | |
| **Time from generation to storage:** | | | | |
| **Controls over form: (e.g. is it prenumbered...)** | | | | |

**FIGURE 14.4** Form identification sheet

## Logical design

As mentioned, the logical design describes how the new system will operate. Based on the information gathered as part of the requirements analysis, a system will be designed that incorporates the features or alterations that were identified as important to users. This could include changes in the operation of the system as well as changes in the business processes that interact with the system. A key part of the logical design phase is to arrive at a model of how the new system should operate. Some of the techniques that are used in doing this include the mapping of business processes that are mentioned in chapter 2.

The business process map can be used to illustrate any changes in activities or functions as a result of the new system design, as well as clarifying how the system will interact with others involved in a business process. Similarly, data flow diagrams (both logical and physical) can be used to show how the different data flows will be handled by the new system. Note that these documents are technology independent, that is, they do not specify the technology that will be used in the new system. This is the key feature of the logical design: it specifies what the system will do, not how it will do it. What processing occurs needs to be considered in light of internal controls as well. For instance, if all the inputs to the system are to be validated for accuracy, what processes are going to occur within the system to do this and how can we ensure the accuracy of these processes. For example, how can we put in checks to ensure the correct customer account has been increased by the correct amount?

The preparation of mapping business processes for the new system can also be useful in gaining an understanding of how the new system is different from the old. Particularly with regard to the logical activities that occur within a business process, preparing logical data flow diagrams for the new and existing system and comparing them can be a useful way of understanding what changes have been made and how the new design addresses the requirements identified as part of the analysis stage of the systems development project.[9] Internal controls are needed to be designed into the system at this point and the auditor of the system needs to be involved at this point.

Another part of the logical design can involve the conceptual design of any databases that may exist within the system. This will involve the preparation of entity-relationship diagrams, which is discussed in chapters 3 and 4. Again, however, note that these diagrams show what the database design will be and not the actual technical aspects of the database. That is, they represent a logical perspective of the system, not a physical perspective.

### Technical design

Once the logical design is arrived at, the challenge for the designers is to find the technology that can allow for the successful implementation of the logical design. This can include specifying the nature of the hardware and technical resources that are required for the system to successfully operate (e.g. server capabilities, network requirements, telecommunications transfer rates and so on). The technical design also involves consideration of the user interface, which is what the users see and work with on the computer screen. There are various options for the design of this, with the key principle being user friendliness. The area of design concerned with the user interface is referred to as human computer interaction, because it is through the interface that the user interacts with the computer.

## Design approval

As the design phase is now complete, in addition to having the designer's superiors sign off, it is also essential to obtain user approval before progressing further. All user input and output screens and printed report designs should be approved and signed off by user management, internal auditors and preferably also by the actual users of these items, as their more intimate knowledge may pick up otherwise unrecognised changes. Possibly, a prototype could be developed at this point to assist users in envisaging how the screens will look and how the system will operate (prototypes are discussed later in this chapter). It is imperative that designers and users concur that this design meets all requirements, as at this stage the cost in both time and money of making any changes is far less than it will be later on in the project lifecycle. Once the design has been signed off, no further design changes should be permitted, as continual change and rework will inevitably cause significant cost increases and delays to the entire project. Any proposed changes can be incorporated as maintenance tasks after implementation.

### Selecting vendors

Once the design of the new system has been finalised, the organisation must determine from where it is going to source the required hardware and software. One alternative that may be pursued is the tendering of the implementation to an outside organisation.

**Request for proposal (RFP)**
*A document that outlines the specifications for the new system, with these documents being sent out to potential vendors.*

This is initiated through a **request for proposal (RFP)**. This is a document that outlines the specifications for the new system, with these documents being sent out to potential vendors. The RFP provides vendors with details about the company, the current system and the problem that they are addressing by undergoing the systems development. It will then proceed to detail the requirements of the new system and the general design of the new system. The typical contents of an RFP are contained in figure 14.5. A possible way of laying out an RFP is shown in figure 14.6.[10]

**FIGURE 14.5** Contents of the RFP

1. **Description of the organisation**
   (a) Operations
   (b) Current system
   (c) Problems with the current system

2. **Outline**
   (a) Timeline for project
   (b) Proposal requirements
   (c) Cost responsibility

3. **Requirements for the new system**
   (a) Hardware
       i. Requirements
       ii. Features
       iii. Criteria
   (b) Software
       i. Requirements
       ii. Features
       iii. Criteria
   (c) Service and maintenance
       i. Requirements

4. **Conclusion**
   The intention is for the vendors to return the document with a tender containing details of how they are able to meet the different design specifications contained in the RFP. The organisation will then rank the tenders and select the one that best meets its criteria. In selecting the vendor from those who reply to the RFP, the organisation will consider several different factors. These are discussed in AIS focus 14.1.

**FIGURE 14.6** A sample layout of an RFP for a restaurant looking at a new sales system

| Recommended System (Name and Description) | | | |
|---|---|---|---|
| How many of your clients currently use this system? | | | |
| | Yes/No | Quantity | Explanation/Comments |
| Is the processor part of one of the terminals? | | | |
| Can terminals be read (polled) remotely by using telephone lines? | | | |
| Can terminals be read from remote terminals? | | | |
| Can terminals be programmed from remote terminals? | | | |
| Can the system use PCs to poll transactional data? | | | |

*(continued)*

**FIGURE 14.6** *(continued)*

|  | Yes/No | Quantity | Explanation/Comments |
|---|---|---|---|
| Do you supply the PC? |  |  |  |
| Can you recommend what brand and model of PC to purchase? |  |  |  |
| How many cash drawers can be connected to one terminal? |  |  |  |
| To which accounting system does your system interface? |  |  |  |
| Can your system be connected to a credit-card chip reader? |  |  |  |
| Does your system have the ability to enter and store daily sales forecasts? |  |  |  |
| Does your system compare forecasted numbers with actual counts during each period? |  |  |  |

*Note*: The respondent would fill in the details and return the document to the organisation.

## AIS FOCUS 14.1

### Selecting a vendor based on RFPs

Kasavana and Smith David (1992) detail nine steps for selecting vendors.[11] These steps are summarised as follows:

1. *Assign responsibility:* someone needs to be in charge of managing the selection process. This can include coordinating the time line for the project and initiating the investigation and analysis phases.
2. *Describe your needs:* in the simplest terms, describe what you expect the system to do. This involves understanding the business process in question, how it operates and the different input and output documents that are a part of the system.
3. *Prepare the RFP:* convert identified needs into an RFP. This should tell potential vendors about the organisation, its aims, what it wants now and what it expects in the future. Standardised response formats can greatly assist in comparing different vendor responses.
4. *Rank RFP replies:* criteria used for ranking replies from vendors are typically multidimensional, and include ability to meet specifications, the reputation of the vendor, the financial costs involved, and the usability of the proposed solution, among other factors. The organisation needs to determine the important factors and the weights for each factor. This leads to a weighted score for each proposal.
5. *Demonstrations from approved vendors:* a shortlist of vendors who have replied, based on their weighted scores, will be invited to demonstrate their product. This can involve coming on-site and responding to scenarios that are context specific,

for example, showing how the product meets requirements such as performance, ability to handle unique firm transactions, ability to meet firm's unique needs. This is essentially an elaboration, in person, of what the vendor specified in its RFP reply.

6. *Presentation evaluations:* evaluate vendor presentations and shortlist a group of acceptable presentations.

7. *Second round vendor visits:* for the second group of shortlisted vendors, visit their sites and deal with any concerns that may be lingering from stage 5.

8. *View clients of shortlisted vendors:* see how other clients of the shortlisted vendors have found the vendor. Ask about service quality, reliability, quality of product and so on. Do not just follow the customer list the vendor gives you — ask around for yourself and find out what their clients have to say about the vendor.

9. *Select a vendor:* negotiate the terms of the agreement and begin the process of implementation.

The steering committee is also involved at the end of the design phase ensuring that all the design sign-offs have occurred relating to the design from the users, designers, designers' superiors and management. The steering committee also gives final approval relating to the vendor that has been chosen by the design team from the requests for proposals. Once final approval is given the project will continue to the implementation phase.

## Implementation

The implementation stage of the systems development lifecycle involves getting the system up and running within the organisation. This requires the activities of building the physical environment required for the new system to operate in (e.g. the network infrastructure) as well as the data storage facilities (databases). When building the databases, the logical schema developed through the entity-relationship diagrams will be the basis for the physical implementation. Any required programming must also be completed, with this involving both writing and testing code before its implementation. If the system does not require the preparation of source code, with the system instead being already developed, that system must also be installed and tested. The auditor also needs to be involved in the testing of the internal controls that were designed in the design phase. After these installation activities, thorough testing will occur and the conversion plan for switching from the old system to the new system will be prepared and executed. After this, the critical issue of user training will be tackled.

### Network and database

If the new system requires the installation of new network or database facilities, they will be the starting point of the implementation phase. The technical specifics for the network and database come from the specifications that were developed in the analysis and design stages. This implementation stage represents the flow-through from the logical design to a set of specifications to a physical implementation of the network and database. Many of the tasks at this stage will be performed by technicians and network administrators. If an external vendor has been selected through an RFP process, then it may handle this stage of the implementation. Further discussion of the technical intricacies of this stage are beyond the scope of this text.

## Programs

The programs for the new system can come in two forms: existing programs requiring modification (customisation) or in-house-developed programs. Depending on the options chosen, the tasks required will vary.

### Modified existing programs

Most existing systems in organisations were designed for a wide range of users with no specific organisational context in mind, while some others were designed for a specific user and then generalised for sale to a wider market. A way around the problem of the system not meeting specific user needs of the adopting organisation is to redesign the modules of the program and customise them to meet these needs. This can be done by arrangement with the vendor of the program. While offering the benefit of a well-developed product that is customised to meet individual needs, this approach introduces several risks, which should be evaluated seriously. These include the possibility of introducing bugs as the code is altered, the reluctance of the vendor to support the product once it has been modified and the potential extra costs involved in modification.

In recent years, as organisations increasingly turned towards ERP systems as a way of better managing their organisations, the issue of customisation has been topical. Theoretically, ERP systems should be adopted as they are, that is, off the shelf, because their design represents 'best practice', otherwise known as the best way of doing things. However, there will be situations where the ERP system does not match the strategy of the organisation. This can require the modification of the ERP system to meet the organisation's unique aspects. In theory this makes sense but the reality is that it can significantly increase the cost and risk of ERP implementation within an organisation.

### In-house-developed programs

Programming is the conversion of system processes that were specified in the design phase into instructions that the computer can understand and execute. The development and coding of in-house-developed programs requires the involvement of programmers and other technical specialists in coming up with a set of code that meets the requirements of the organisation. Often, the programming completed at this stage will be based on a simple prototype that was developed as part of the design phase. Prototyping is discussed in more detail later in this chapter. Issues for programmers to consider when developing programs include how well the program will interact with any existing systems, as well as the reliability of the program: does it do what it is meant to do and with minimal error? Considerable effort will be devoted as part of the programming stage to debugging and testing. Testing will be planned and documented on a test plan, with any exception outcomes noted and subject to investigation.[12] At the lowest level there is stub level testing then unit level and, lastly, system level testing.[13]

Testing at the stub level involves looking at the different components of a program and making sure that they each function properly. In the example of an accounting program, it may involve looking at the cash receipts, cash payments, accounts receivable, accounts payable, sales and inventory modules individually, ensuring that they function as expected.

When moving to testing at the unit level, the concern becomes how the different modules work when combined. Again, using the accounting program example, the concern would be how well the cash receipts, cash payments, accounts receivable, accounts payable, sales and inventory modules work together. For example, when a sale is recorded in the sales module, are the accounts receivable and inventory modules updated correctly? When cash is received from debtors, do the data entered into the cash receipts module help the updating of records by the accounts receivable module?

At the highest level is system testing, which is concerned with how the developed program integrates with any existing programs. Again, with reference to the accounting program, there may be interest in the newly developed accounting system's ability to share data with pre-existing programs related to manufacturing and warehousing. This stage of system testing will involve a range of stakeholders, including designers, users and auditors. The sample data that are used as a part of the testing phase may also be incorrect, for example, a customer number that is meant to be numeric (e.g. 312968) may be entered in an alphanumeric form (e.g. C31296). Entering incorrect data and ensuring that the system detects the errors are just as important as ensuring that correct inputs are handled properly.

To test a system, a 'test deck' of transactions is created, including all possible errors and invalid transactions. Testing should be done by users working with the development team rather than solely by developers. The expected results from processing this group of transactions are calculated manually. The test results are compared with the expected results and if there are discrepancies the cause of the error is found and corrected. Testing is cyclic: test, compare, correct and test again until no further errors are found. The test deck should be kept for reuse, for example, for any subsequent modification to the system.

## Testing

The final stage of testing will be aimed at making sure the new and the old systems are able to operate with the same results. At this stage of testing, a set of sample data may be input into the system, with interest in ensuring that it is processed and stored correctly and accurate outputs are generated. This stage of testing can be described as full system testing with test data and will involve operators inputting test data, with attention paid to how well operators are able to correctly use the system. Finally, testing with live data may occur. This will involve taking existing data that has been processed by the old system and running it through the new system. This will allow for a comparison of the outputs from the old and new systems.

In this situation, if the results differ and no errors can be located in the new system, it may pay to check that the old system is working correctly. It is not unknown for this process to uncover that the old system had been making unnoticed errors for years!

## Implementation approach

There are three implementation approaches that an organisation may consider when switching over from its old to its new system: direct, parallel or phased-in conversion.

As the name would suggest, the **direct conversion** method involves switching off the old system today and switching on the new system tomorrow. It is an immediate switch from the old to the new. This can have an advantage of lower costs in the implementation, when compared with the parallel approach, if the new system functions as expected. However, the direct approach can also expose the business to several risks. One example is that if there is a problem with the new system that has gone undetected until the switch-over, and it causes the new system to fail, then the organisation is left without an information system. Therefore, a back-up plan of being able to switch back to the old system if, after a certain period of time (e.g. 24 hours), the new system fails to operate.

**Parallel conversion** involves running the new system and the old system together for a period of time, that is, operating them in parallel. This overcomes the risk of the

**Direct conversion** *Involves switching off an old system and immediately switching on a new system.*

**Parallel conversion** *Involves running the new system and the old system together for a period of time, or operating them in parallel.*

direct switch-over previously discussed: the impact of a problem with the new system on the organisation is kept to a minimum because the old system is still operating. Of course, the downside of the parallel approach is that for some time the two systems need to be kept running, which can add to costs. Also, in many cases this may not be practicable. For example, if checkout terminals in a supermarket are connected to the new system they cannot physically also send data to the old system.

The **phased-in conversion** involves a gradual implementation of the system throughout the organisation. Under this approach, the new system will be introduced in a small part of the organisation and gradually phased in throughout the entire organisation. This is, in a sense, a compromise between the direct and parallel methods because it allows the system to be implemented and operational while at the same time reducing exposure should it fail. This approach is practical if there are separate business units; for example, a state branch office may be selected as the pilot for the rest of the country. There is an additional safeguard here as the organisation can have a 'plan B' whereby, if the new system fails, the pilot branch's data may be processed in another state branch until the problems are rectified.

## Preparation for conversion

There are a two other main issues for an organisation to consider in preparing for the conversion of the old to the new system: the preparation of the users of the system and reviewing the system documentation, ensuring that users are able to follow the documentation and procedures correctly.

### Users

Preparing the users to use the new system has consistently been identified in information systems research as one of the critical factors in the success of projects. The users adopting the new system are critical to the new system achieving its intended objectives. Organisational facets such as structure, management style and change approaches can be important in this area.[14] To this end, organisations can pursue various strategies to improve the prospects of user acceptance. User involvement in systems development is an important way of giving the users a sense of control.[15] Historically, many within an organisation have been resistant to the introduction of new technology in the workplace because it represents a threat to the way things have been done in the past and they may feel that their jobs are threatened. A new system also challenges worker competency: a user who is proficient with the existing system may suddenly be faced with the prospect of not knowing how to use the new system. This can be damaging to the individual's self-esteem. A way around this is to give users the perception that they are actively involved in the determination of the implementation schedules. A way of doing this is by providing the users with an instrumental voice, which is the chance for users to have their say and express their concerns.[16] This will occur before decisions are made. For example, in the implementation stage, rather than management mandating training courses across a range of areas, an instrumental voice would suggest the need for employees to suggest courses that may be relevant for them to improve their skills at using the new system.

As part of user training in the way the new system operates, Wastell suggests the use of transitional objects.[17] As Wastell observes:

> ISD [Information systems development] is a process of organizational change in which IT systems are designed and deployed to enable more effective operational practices. To bring this about, the prevailing business paradigm must be questioned with goals, processes and roles considered in the light of new technological potentialities. Both IS professionals and

users must engage in an intensive learning experience, the former to develop a thorough understanding of the business domain, the latter to reflect on current practices and to acquire an understanding of the potential of IT to transform how work is done. Through this process of communication and discovery, design work is progressively accomplished, ultimately resulting (if all goes well) in a technically sound system that satisfies the users and meets the business requirement . . . an effective learning process is thus critical to the success of ISD.[18]

The role of users in the systems development process, with their function as both learners and possessors of knowledge, is critical to the success of the development efforts.[19] Users of the system possess a great deal of knowledge about how the existing system operates, including its problems and strengths. This knowledge is vital to improving a system and can be gained from users early on in the systems development process, typically as a part of the investigation and analysis stages of the systems development lifecycle. This is the main reason that accountants and internal auditors need to be involved at this stage of the lifecycle, and highlights the importance of them understanding why different information is being requested from them.

Once systems are complete and ready for implementation, users may have to be retrained in the use of the new system. Users are learners in this process, seeing how the new system operates and being introduced to new features, processes and support material. The people who could fill the role of trainer include system designers or analysts who possess a deep knowledge of the systems design and operations, professional in-house trainers or, where the system is purchased from a third-party vendor, the vendor's own training staff. This latter option is common in organisations adopting ERP systems, with vendors such as Oracle offering education programs for management, end-users and project teams implementing an ERP system.[20]

Focusing on the end-user group, Oracle sees the benefits of its end-user training programs as follows: 'With the right set of skills, you can give . . . [end-users] the confidence, knowledge, and competency to achieve long-term success. As a result, you'll see faster acceptance of the solution and new application-related processes, and you'll be able to establish a higher level of capability and performance. Put simply — the more skilled your end-users, the more value you'll get from your PeopleSoft [Oracle] solution'.[21] Another leader in the ERP market, SAP, has developed a tutorial and simulation environment to assist in the training of end-users.[22]

The impact on the user of having to learn a new system should not be underestimated, making the role of change agents and project leaders critical in getting and maintaining support for the system. It should also be recognised that training has to be targeted to the needs of the different users. Not all users need to know how all of the system works. To train all users in all aspects of the system wastes time and ignores the typical distribution of responsibilities within the organisation. Therefore, a training program for different groups (e.g. sales, accounting and purchasing) at different times is important. The goal of training is for end-users to have the skills to perform their jobs. They do not have to know every working of the system in intimate detail.[23]

### Documentation

The importance of mapping business processes is introduced in chapter 2, where the role of data flow diagrams and systems flowcharts in providing a graphical representation of a system's operation is discussed. These documentation formats play an important role in systems development, representing invaluable planning and design tools at the various stages of the systems development lifecycle. Other forms of documentation are also important. The internal controls chapters (chapters 7 and 8) discuss the role that job descriptions can play in outlining individual responsibilities and accountabilities within the organisation. Some of these may alter as a result of the systems development effort in conjunction with the internal auditors input, which makes it important for organisations to review existing documentation in light of the new system, identifying any changes that may have been missed and ensuring that the revised documentation captures them.

Other important pieces of documentation at this juncture of the development lifecycle are user manuals and support materials. User documentation may come in various formats (e.g. paper-based, online or on CD). It must be usable, understandable and accurate, enabling users to follow the material.

It is critical that documentation is developed progressively during the development of the system and not left until the end. All too often developers move on to other jobs inside or outside the organisation before documentation is completed and there is no-one who really understands the inner workings of the system available to prepare and finalise documentation.

## Maintenance and review

Once the system is implemented and operating smoothly and users are trained in its operations, the main tasks of the development team become those of maintenance and review. The maintenance and review activity can be a significant part of the cost of system development (up to 80 per cent). Naturally, when there are changes in maintenance activities, the internal auditor or accountant needs to be involved to ensure adequate internal controls have been redesigned into the improvement or modification.

The maintenance phase has the general aim of keeping the new system running and supporting users in their interactions with the system. This helps contribute to the end goal of enabling the system to reach the benefits identified in the investigation and analysis stages of the system's development. Typical maintenance activities that will be required are system improvements, system modifications and bug correction.[24]

**System improvement** activity involves adding new features or functions to the system, thus increasing its potential usefulness. Ideas for system improvements may emerge as users operate the new system in day-to-day operations and identify small points that could be added or modified to improve the usability of the system. An example of system enhancement could include adding a new function to a menu.

**System modification** is, as the name suggests, a change to the system. Rather than adding to the existing features, as is the case with system improvement, it takes an existing feature and alters it. An example of a potential reason for system modification is the introduction of a new law that affects the operation of the organisation (e.g. a requirement to collect a new tax, such as GST).

The final type of maintenance is **bug correction**, which involves fixing any errors in the system. These errors are the result of programming mistakes and are more of a threat when organisations develop their own system in-house or attempt to customise an existing package. A critical part of the maintenance task is to log any problems that occur with the system, enabling the appropriate people to be informed so the problems can be fixed. Therefore, a log should be available to record any bugs that users encounter while using the system. The log may be generated electronically — for example, as a program experiences an error condition, an error is automatically logged to an electronic file that technical staff periodically review or an audit alarm bell is activated — or manually recorded by users as they encounter bugs in their daily duties.

If the scope of the improvement, modification or correction is large, the maintenance effort may provide the trigger for a new systems development project to be launched. This emphasises the iterative nature of the systems development lifecycle: development

*System improvement Involves adding new features or functions to the system, thus increasing its potential usefulness.*

*System modification Involves taking an existing feature and altering or changing it.*

*Bug correction Involves fixing any errors in the system as a result of programming mistakes.*

is an ongoing feature within the organisation and does not stop once the system is implemented and the development team has signed off.

Whether the maintenance task is adequately performed relies on the maintenance team being aware of the problems or issues confronting users of the system. To this end, a maintenance system that gains user feedback and provides a forum for users to log their requests or problems is essential. Traditionally, this would have been carried out through the use of a maintenance request form (see figure 14.7[25]). These requests will be logged in a maintenance request log, maintained by the IT department. Many organisations now have online facilities where users can log their requests through a webpage. This also allows the tracking of the requests by users.

| **FORM 001 — MAINTENANCE REQUEST FORM** | |
| --- | --- |
| This form is to be completed by users encountering problems in the system's operation, signed by the supervisor and lodged with the IT department. | |
| System/application: | Request date: |
| Originating department: | |
| Request lodged by: | |
| Problem: | |
| Details of problem: | |
| Priority: | |
| Approved by: | Date: |

**FIGURE 14.7** Sample maintenance request form

The **review** stage completes the systems development lifecycle and is concerned with carrying out an ex-post analysis of how well the systems development project has worked. Aspects that may be considered as part of the review can include the project team's performance and the new system's performance. When reviewing the performance of the project team, factors such as good performers, bad performers and the relevant skills contributed by team members may be considered, as well as ability to meet deadlines. The review should not be conducted immediately after implementation, but should allow for a suitable settling down period for users to become familiar and comfortable with the new system and for any teething trouble-shooting to be completed.

System review is concerned with how well the new system is performing. In carrying out the system review, the initial costs and benefits developed at the early stages of the systems development lifecycle should be referred to, with these providing the rubric for evaluating how well the new system has met expectations.

**LEARNING OBJECTIVE 3**

*Describe the software development options available to smaller businesses and outline the systems selection processes for decision making.*

# SOFTWARE SELECTION FOR SMEs

While the reasons for acquiring new accounting software for small to medium-sized enterprises (SMEs) are as described in the introduction to this chapter, and the same as for larger enterprises, the software will almost certainly be a pre-developed program and the selection process is therefore usually simpler.

## Pre-developed programs

Using pre-developed programs means that the business is adopting a package that already exists: the code has already been written and the program is typically ready to run. An example of this approach is purchasing a program such as Microsoft Word or the MYOB accounting package. The program comes on a set of CDs that need to be installed on the user's machine and it is ready to be used. Acquiring software with this approach can provide several advantages for an organisation; the major advantage is avoiding the costs of programming and development. The organisation also receives a well developed and hopefully error-free product. For fairly mainstream requirements, such as word-processing applications or simple accounting packages, using pre-developed programs makes economic sense. It is important for both simple and mid-range accounting systems that the built-in internal controls are evaluated by the organisation's accountant or auditor.

## Types of accounting packages

While enterprise resource planning (ERP) systems are discussed in detail in chapter 6, we will examine the key features of two other levels of accounting software here — mid-range and simple systems. We will also introduce software-as-a-service providers — companies that provide software applications that can be leased to customers.

### Mid-range accounting packages

Mid-range accounting packages may be purchased direct from the developer or a value-added reseller; for example, a CPA firm or consultant who provides installation assistance, training and ongoing support. These packages are usually developed as a series of interlocking modules including most or all of the following features: general ledger, sales, point-of-sale, receivables, inventory, purchases, payables, payroll and a report writer. It is generally possible to purchase only those single modules actually required by the nature of the business. Mid-range systems also have the benefit of a flexible chart of accounts, which facilitates producing reports for the consolidated entire organisation, by state or store, or alternatively by product groups.

Most systems are built on top of sophisticated database software, such as SQL. Users are normally able to access the database directly, to answer ad hoc queries or perform unique analyses, and are able to produce reports not already coded by the software.

Mid-range products provide a large number of optional 'switches' enabling users to select from a broad range of options for each feature, and can accommodate a large number of simultaneous users depending on the licence purchased.

### Simple accounting packages

Simpler accounting packages may be purchased direct from the developer or an office supplies or big box retailer. They are normally purchased 'as is', without modifications or unique features. Such simple packages usually carry a relatively inflexible chart of available accounts, compared to mid-range modules, and users are generally unable to directly access the underlying database to conduct more unique processes. Compared to mid-range packages, users are generally restricted to fewer options for each feature, and such programs generally operate at a capacity of around five simultaneous users. Generic accounting packages of this nature are significantly cheaper, with the entire package similar to the cost of a single module in a mid-range product.

## Software-as-a-service

A common choice faced by organisations as part of the systems development effort is whether they should buy the required software, develop it themselves or customise an existing package to suit their needs. In the modern environment of technology where the internet is omnipresent, a fourth option has emerged: the use of a **software-as-a-service provider (SP)**, previously known as an *application service provider* (some vendors use the alternative term *on-demand computing*). SPs are companies that provide software applications that can be leased by a range of clients. The leased program is typically made available to the customers through the use of internet and portal technology.[26] SP services have arrived as a derivative of the traditional outsourcing function, representing a way for small and mid-sized organisations to gain access to the systems and technologies — such as ERP systems and CRM technology — that are traditionally only available to larger organisations.[27] Motivations for using an SP might include a desire to reduce the total cost of ownership, a desire to focus on core competencies, a more predictable expenditure pattern for IT, better efficiency and meeting the technology used by competitors. Technological reasons for using an SP can include a lack of adequate skills within the organisation, a quicker implementation time, a shift of risk of ownership and the ability to have best technology in place.[28]

SPs can offer organisations several advantages that would not necessarily be available under conventional acquisition methods, including cost savings, lower initial investment, better performance and the ability to focus on dealing with key strategy and competency issues rather than peripheral technology-based issues. Cost savings from the use of SPs come from the economies of scale that the SP has in providing the required software. The SP can provide for many users and is therefore able to develop and maintain the software at a cheaper cost per user than if firms were to develop the software themselves. Organisations using SPs are potentially also able to benefit from a lower total cost of ownership. For organisations using the services of an SP, it can also present a way of benefiting from the use of applications without needing to make a large initial investment. This leads to the service being implemented within the organisation more quickly and also allows the organisation to place its emphasis on its competencies, rather than worrying about IT and peripheral issues associated with IT. SPs thus allow an organisation to focus its attention on what it does best. The SP can also provide the subscribing organisation with its bank of support services, technical advice and training, thus ensuring qualified technical support, the cost of which is not the responsibility of the organisation but rather that of the SP.

SPs also present some disadvantages that an organisation should take into consideration. These include the degree of customisation, the reliability of the SP, speed and infrastructure.

The degree of customisation of applications provided through an SP may not be as high as that experienced for applications that have been developed in-house. This may mean that applications provided through an SP do all of the general tasks required by an organisation but not specific tasks unique to it. A further issue to consider in using an SP is its reliability, which can be broken up into two main areas for the subscribing customer: quality of service and long-term stability. The issue of reliability of service is fairly obvious as a consideration: is the SP able to provide the quality and level of support that is required? Requirements regarding the level of service that is required from the SP will normally be specified in the **service level agreement**, a document specifying what responsibilities the SP has and how they are to be fulfilled. Typically, this document will specify responsibilities in periods of normal operation, as well as what is to happen in the event of maintenance, service and disaster.

**Software-as-a-service provider (SP)** *Companies that provide software applications that can be leased by a range of clients.*

**Service level agreement** *Document specifying what responsibilities the software-as-a-service provider has and how these are to be fulfilled.*

The long-term stability aspect of reliability acknowledges that for the subscribing organisation, a fair reliance is being placed on the SP to be able to provide the services in the mid to long term. This presupposes that the SP is able to keep operating in the mid to long term. As a result, organisations should consider factors such as the financial stability of the SP before committing to a particular one, because an SP that collapses can leave an organisation without valuable services, which can be disruptive, if not disastrous. One way of minimising this risk is for the client to require that the service level agreement provides for a copy of the software code to be deposited in *escrow* (i.e. in trust with a third party). If the SP fails for any reason then the code is made available to the client to use on their own system. This requires first that the escrow copy is kept current and second that the code and associated documentation is sufficiently user-friendly for it to be successfully installed by the client company.

A final issue for organisations to consider when evaluating an SP is the security of services offered. Security in this sense refers to how safe the data are that reside with the SP, especially if they are related to key strategic activities or areas of operation. Because SPs potentially can be providing the same set of services to many different organisations at once, the concern about the security of proprietary data is a very real one.[29]

Software-as-a-service is not a new concept. SPs represent a different avenue for businesses to go down, allowing them to focus on their core competencies and strategically important activities. However, use of an SP is no different from any other systems project, requiring careful planning and investigation. At their best, 'SPs offer the ability for a company to focus on its core competencies, reduce value chain activity costs and enhance overall competitive advantage'.[30] At their worst, however, they can cause disruption to an organisation's operations and result in significant downtime and costs.

## System selection process

The selection process for SMEs considering a systems change is similar to that undertaken by larger enterprises. However, there are a number of issues unique to SMEs that need to be considered before a change is made. These considerations are discussed in the selection process detailed in this section.

### 1. Identify the company's needs

Before implementing any changes to the current system, it is important the enterprise adequately identifies the need for such a change. SMEs often operate with relatively small budgets and tight margins, making any unnecessary or mistaken expenditure an expensive liability.

Firstly, the enterprise should identify all the problems with the current system, even relatively minor ones. Inefficiencies can have a relatively significant effect on the operation of a smaller business. Seek opinions from all users of the system. What additional features would make them able to do their job more efficiently? If the organisation uses the services of an external accountant, discuss what systems will best facilitate transfer of data to the accountant. Similarly, if the organisation makes or receives electronic payments then this is the time to discuss what systems will best facilitate transfer of data to and from the bank.

Then, consider what position the business is expected to be in, in five years' time. It is pointless to buy a system adequate for now if the business will outgrow it inside five years. Finally, examine direct competitors and their systems. Do they have a system that is giving them a competitive advantage?

It is important to document the requirements of the organisation. List the modules required (for example, general ledger, sales order entry, e-commerce, receivables, inventory), and for each module list the required features. It may also be helpful to categorise them as (a) essential, (b) highly desirable or (c) would be nice but could do without it.

## 2. Survey the market

Start with a list of every software product that may be a candidate. Sources of such information may include personal knowledge from employees or consultants, advertisements, reviews in computer publications or on the internet, and possibly other organisations in the industry.

For each product on the list, set up a spreadsheet to record the cost and identify the features included. Consider issues such as vendor stability and support, the software provider's upgrade policy, and the availability of third-party assistance for implementation, training and ongoing support. List the cost and benefits of each of these issues for each package.

## 3. Identify the shortlist

Evaluate each of the candidate products carefully and eliminate any that don't have all the essential features from step 1. Also eliminate any where the technology required is beyond the current resources of the organisation.

If there are still more than four or five candidates, eliminate those that provide fewest of features listed under (b) and (c) in step 1 or where there are any reservations about support issues.

## 4. Arrange a demonstration

If the organisation is considering a mid-range accounting package the vendor will usually be happy to demonstrate the software and make a sales presentation. At the demonstration, ensure that the vendor carefully considers the needs identified in step 1 and how the proposed solution will meet them, rather than attempting to change the way the business operates to fit the demands of the system. Prepare a list of questions for the vendor and ask them for website references to contact.

## 5. Decision and implementation

Finally, eliminate any candidates where the demonstration was not convincing, or where processes in the package don't seem easy to use. Follow up the references provided by the vendors, and make sure to ask about any problems that they incurred. Be cautious: remember that the vendor will have provided references for successful implementations not disasters.

If, at the end of this stage, there are still several candidates, reconsider the needs identified in step 1. While the final decision should not be made on cost alone, it can be a deciding factor if there are two similar candidates still in the running. Estimate the complete cost of the system, including hardware or software acquisition, consulting fees, and conversion, implementation and training costs.

The implementation, testing and review activities of software in smaller businesses are the same as those described in the previous section, but may require adaptation to suit the scale of the business.

# ALTERNATIVE SYSTEMS DEVELOPMENT APPROACHES

While there are many benefits from following the steps of the traditional systems development lifecycle due to its structured, well-controlled and well-documented approach to systems development, there are also a number of alternatives to the traditional systems development lifecycle. These methods are usually used in certain circumstances and they do employ aspects of the traditional systems development lifecycle. These methods are outlined below for completeness.

## Prototyping

The systems development lifecycle represents a very structured and methodical way of undertaking development projects. However, it is often criticised for its lack of user involvement. Potentially, users are only involved in the early stages and late stages of the lifecycle, with little scope for user involvement during mid-stages, such as design. This has led to support for the **prototyping approach** to systems development. This actively involves the users in the development of systems by continually seeking their feedback on and evaluation of progressive designs for a system.

**Prototyping approach** *Involves the progressive building of models and allowing users to experience these models and provide feedback on their operation and suitability.*

The prototyping approach centres on the concept of building models and allowing users to experience these models and provide feedback on their operation and suitability. This can be advantageous in situations where the users know what they want but are unable to clearly communicate it to designers, or where users think they know what they want but are not sure. Providing feedback on design and features allows the prototype to be altered to meet users' needs. The revised prototype will then be presented to users for further evaluation and feedback. The prototyping process is described as an iterative process: the model of the system goes back and forth between user and designer until an agreed version is arrived at.

Prototyping can be used as a stand-alone systems development technique but can also be used in conjunction with the stages of the systems development lifecycle previously described. The advantage of prototyping is that it allows the users to be involved in a more hands-on manner with the systems development efforts and can help to achieve a usable and accepted system when implementation occurs. Prototyping is also an ideal approach where the systems development effort is small and focused on a key group of users.

## Object oriented analysis methods

**Object oriented analysis methods** *An alternative approach to systems development used when designing systems using objects.*

**Object oriented analysis methods** are used when designing systems using objects. Objects, as briefly discussed in chapter 3, are things that combine data and programs together. Object oriented analysis methods are generally used when the object oriented model is used. That is, as objects are members of classes of objects and there are object hierarchies, this technique is used to model object oriented systems. Object oriented analysis methods follow a series of steps such as analysis, design, planning, and the analysis and design tasks that interact with prototypes that are tested and implemented. These stages of analysis, design, planning, prototype and testing are repeated.

## Agile/adaptive methods

**Agile/adaptive methods** *An alternative approach to systems development that involves short, team-based efforts whereby a small amount of functionality is built designed and tested.*

**Agile/adaptive methods** involve short, team-based efforts whereby a small amount of functionality is built designed and tested at a time. These methods aim to reduce the risks of the long systems development lifecycle by using shorter, smaller steps. The overall project, as it is attempted in small pieces, may be fluid to changes in requirements. This is because the process between the developer and the user of the system continues as the system is developed. Iterative, spiral cycles over time build up the system. An overall scope, objective and original requirements, as determined in a traditional systems development lifecycle investigation phase, are never determined under these methods. As a result, the project can never be measured against these elements. This is considered an area of risk. However, a positive of these development methods is that if the needs of the organisation change the agile methods are able to adapt and respond to user feedback. So the changing needs of the organisation may be able to be accommodated with these methods. Agile methods promote an 'agile manifesto' that lists the principles that are followed by these methods. This manifesto is contained in figure 14.8.

**Principles behind the Agile Manifesto**

*We follow these principles:*
- Our highest priority is to satisfy the customer through early and continuous delivery of valuable software.
- Welcome changing requirements, even late in development. Agile processes harness change for the customer's competitive advantage.
- Deliver working software frequently, from a couple of weeks to a couple of months, with a preference to the shorter timescale.
- Business people and developers must work together daily throughout the project.
- Build projects around motivated individuals. Give them the environment and support they need, and trust them to get the job done.
- The most efficient and effective method of conveying information to and within a development team is face-to-face conversation.
- Working software is the primary measure of progress.
- Agile processes promote sustainable development. The sponsors, developers, and users should be able to maintain a constant pace indefinitely.
- Continuous attention to technical excellence and good design enhances agility.
- Simplicity — the art of maximizing the amount of work not done — is essential.
- The best architectures, requirements, and designs emerge from self-organizing teams.
- At regular intervals, the team reflects on how to become more effective, then tunes and adjusts its behavior accordingly.[31]

**FIGURE 14.8** Principles behind agile approaches to systems development

There are a variety of other methods that use concepts from these alternative methods to ensure that developers develop what users require, including extreme programming, scrum, joint application methods and rapid application development. These methods are not detailed in this book; however, the further readings section of this chapter contains useful references. While alternative system development methods focus on ensuring that users get the system they require, the disadvantages include a lack of linkage between what is being achieved at the team level and an overall vision of the system development. As a result, the traditional systems development lifecycle has survived over time as the most popular method for systems development. The COSO and COBIT frameworks outlined in chapter 7 recommend structured systems analysis using the systems development lifecycle with a clearly set out scope and requirements. However, agile/adaptive methods are gaining popularity, particularly as they enable changes when priorities within an organisation change, and many of these methods incorporate aspects of the systems development lifecycle.

**LEARNING OBJECTIVE 5**

*Describe typical systems development problems and propose solutions for their resolution.*

# TYPICAL PROBLEMS OF SYSTEMS DEVELOPMENT

Systems development projects can present organisations with myriad challenges and issues that must be dealt with for the project to have any chance of being successfully completed. Many of these centre on the areas of cost, scope and time.[32] Some problems include the great potential for conflict, escalation of commitment, project goal issues, technical skills, interpersonal skills and a lack of scope. Each of these is now briefly discussed, highlighting how they inhibit the success of systems development projects.

## Conflict

Conflict is disagreement between individuals, groups or organisations. While conflict is widely viewed as positive for an organisation, because it promotes diversity of opinion and open discussion of ideas, it can also have devastating effects on the organisation. The systems development process, by virtue of it uniting a wide range of stakeholders, is an environment that is ripe for conflict. Users often feel that designers are not listening to their requests, while designers think users do not know what they want and can never be satisfied.[33] These two stakeholders, users and designers, approach the systems development project from very different perspectives, with one often not totally understanding the other. Jealousy and hostility can result.

## Escalation of commitment

Escalation of commitment has been extensively researched in the management accounting area and refers to an increased level of commitment towards a project that has previously been chosen and that is not progressing as expected and that should be abandoned or redirected.[34] In systems development projects, the reality is that very few will be completed on time, even less on time and under cost, and some just will not be completed at all because they were doomed to fail from the start. Despite such poor outcomes, organisations may spend significant money on a systems development project that is not progressing as planned, in the desperate hope of righting the wrongs of the past and getting the project back on track. The reality is that this is like rearranging the deckchairs on the *Titanic*.

The question that needs to be answered is why does such commitment allow the continued support of what would appear to be doomed projects? Keil et al. suggest several theories for why this escalation occurs, including self-justification theory, prospect theory and agency theory.[35]

*Self-justification theory* states that a person makes a decision to justify a previous decision and to save face. For example, rather than terminate a systems development project that is over budget, off schedule and destined for failure, the theory posits that the manager will invest more resources in the project in the hope of turning it around. This behaviour is particularly prevalent where the manager was involved in the earlier decision to go ahead with the project.

*Prospect theory* explains escalation of commitment through the way a decision to proceed or terminate a project is framed for the decision maker. It works on the premise that people will be willing to take a risk if the outcome is guaranteed to be negative. In the case of systems development, this can be seen as the definite loss of the initial investment if the decision to withdraw from the project immediately is made versus the possible larger loss or success that could eventuate from continuing with the project. This explains the idea of throwing 'good money after bad' and ignoring sunk costs: a management accounting term for costs that have already been incurred and are irrelevant to the decision to proceed with the project.

*Agency theory* refers to the problem of the person in charge of the systems development project having an information asymmetry over the higher levels within the organisation. Because of the technical nature of many systems developments efforts, it is possible for those involved to make statements about progress that are difficult for others to prove or disprove. This is especially the case for programmers and other technical specialists, whose technically specific knowledge places them in an almost unmonitorable position. In such a situation, because individuals are motivated by self interest, the inclination is to protect one's own reputation and position. As such, people may be reluctant to report bad news about the progress of the project, so the firm continues to support a project that is not progressing as expected. Another example of the agency problem in systems development is the inability to monitor those who work in technically specific areas. For example, if you are in charge of supervising a project and have no programming experience, how do you monitor the performance and progress of the programmers? Without the requisite knowledge and skills such monitoring becomes problematic. Many tasks that require specific skills and are highly specialised may exist in a systems development project, making the monitoring of progress difficult.

## Project goal issues

Typical problems with project goals can include goals that do not have the universal support of those involved and goals that are too broad in scope. The systems development effort needs to occur within the boundaries of what the system is required to do, its goals and objectives and the importance of the system within the organisation. Having a clear concept of the boundaries of the scope of the project is important when it is first conceived, as well as during its progression through its various stages.[36] The goals of the systems development project will ultimately drive the information requirements that are fulfilled in the development stages. Consequently, a project that is not clear on what it is meant to achieve may deal with the wrong issues and lack consensus on what the real issues to be dealt with should be. This becomes an issue for the systems steering committee which is required to sign off on scope, analysis and requirements stages of the project.

## Technical skills

The systems development project requires a mix of technical, people and process skills. Process skills refer to the knowledge about how the business operates, what is done and who does it. People skills refer to the ability to manage different groups of people, assimilate differences of opinion and manage conflict towards a workable solution that benefits the project as a whole (conflict was discussed in an earlier section as an aspect of systems development). Technical skills refer to the ability to perform the tasks required in developing and implementing the system within the organisation. Organisations undergoing systems development need to assess the capabilities that they have within the organisation. There may be instances where the proposed systems development is beyond the skills and expertise of the staff within the organisation, in which case they should look towards help from outside the organisation, such as consultants or those with the relevant expertise. Acknowledging a deficiency in skills and making it up early can be important in the progress of a systems development project.

As an example, an IT department that has previous experience in maintaining a business's systems is probably not adequately skilled to run a systems development effort, because other required skills such as interacting with different stakeholders to determine user requirements, project management skills and so on will most probably not be present.

## Interpersonal skills

Interpersonal skills are essential in any systems development effort. These skills come to the forefront as systems development efforts can involve people from a wide range of backgrounds and levels throughout an organisation working together on the one project. The perspective of the IT personnel or the programmer may be very different from that of the end-user of the system. This makes an ability to work with others, acknowledge different viewpoints and collaborate towards the attainment of a mutually acceptable solution important.

**Computer-aided software engineering (CASE) systems** *Software packages that can help in the various stages of systems development, but particularly in the design of source code and user documentation.*

# SYSTEMS DEVELOPMENT MANAGEMENT TOOLS

Many tools can be used in managing the systems development project within an organisation. An awareness of these tools is important. Many failed information systems development projects are identified as such because the project ran out of control, both financially and time-wise. Tools that assist in the planning and control of systems development projects force those involved to have a thorough understanding of the steps involved in completing the project and can provide a basis for accountability in systems development projects, while also providing structure and an overall picture for larger projects. Some of the commonly mentioned tools are Gantt charts, and critical path analysis/PERT charts for project planning and controlling, critical path analysis/PERT charts and **computer-aided software engineering (CASE) systems** for analysis and design.

## Gantt charts

A Gantt chart is a graphical way of planning and controlling the progress of a systems development project. The Gantt chart depicts the timeframe for the project along the x-axis and the activities that are part of the project along the y-axis. Horizontal bars for each activity depict how long it is planned to take and how long it actually has taken. As figure 14.9 shows, the Gantt chart identifies the major activities that occur within the project and the timeframe for each activity. In the figure, the investigation activity took less time than expected while the analysis activity took longer than expected. The overall project was completed after the budgeted completion date.

The level of detail in the Gantt chart is up to the preparer: the chart could equally have looked at activities within the investigation stage or the analysis stage. The degree of detail is determined by user needs. However, one thing to note about the chart is that it does not identify dependencies between activities; that is, we do not know how the different activities in our chart relate to and affect each other in very much detail. As can be seen, this is overcome through the preparation of a PERT chart/critical path analysis.

## Critical path analysis/PERT charts

PERT charts are also known as critical path charts. These charts also provide a way of controlling projects.[37] A PERT chart is constructed through the identification of all the activities that must take place for the project to be successfully completed. Time allocations are also given to each activity, with activities also being sequenced

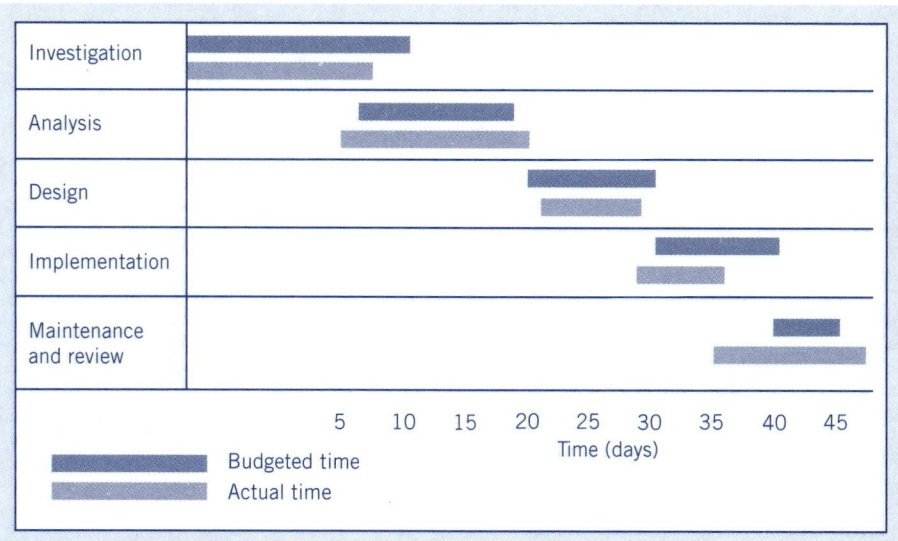

**FIGURE 14.9** A Gantt chart

based on necessary prerequisite and subsequent activities. This is an important feature of the PERT chart technique, because it recognises the relationship between different activities and allows for the scheduling of concurrent activities.

The steps in preparing a PERT chart are as follows:

1. Identify activities that need to occur.
2. Assign time estimates to each activity.
3. Identify relationships among activities (particularly precedent activities).
4. Illustrate the relationship.
5. Calculate earliest start time and latest finish time.
6. Identify any slack.

Each of these steps is demonstrated in the following discussion.

Take a fictitious example of a project that contains 11 stages (A–K). Each stage has a set amount of time allocated for its completion as well as an identified precedent activity (see table 14.2 overleaf). The table represents the culmination of the first three steps. First, the individual activities would have been identified, then an estimate of the time required to complete each activity would have been calculated. Third, the relationship of each activity with other activities was identified by specifying necessary precedent activities. Based on these three columns on the table, the diagram shown in figure 14.10 can be constructed. This is done by starting with the earliest activity from node 1 (a node is a circle on the PERT chart) and mapping out the sequence of activities based on the relationships that were identified previously and listed in the table. For example, the table tells us that activities B and C cannot be completed until activity A is finished. Also, activity A has no prerequisite activity. This makes activity A the first activity to be completed, with B and C following the completion of activity A.

The arrows on the critical path diagram in figure 14.10 overleaf indicate the activities taking place and the nodes indicate the combination of precedent activities to proceed to the next activity. For example, it can be seen that activity A is the first completed, taking two days. This is shown on the path with the notation A, 2. Once A is completed activities B and C can be completed, and so on.

**TABLE 14.2** Project activities, precedents and times

| Activity | Immediate precedent | Time taken | Earliest start | Latest finish | Earliest finish | Slack |
|---|---|---|---|---|---|---|
| A | — | 2 | 0 | 2 | 2 | 0 |
| B | A | 3 | 2 | 26 | 5 | 21 |
| C | A | 5 | 2 | 5 | 5 | 0 |
| D | C | 5 | 5 | 10 | 10 | 0 |
| E | D | 10 | 10 | 20 | 20 | 0 |
| F | E, B | 5 | 20 | 25 | 25 | 0 |
| G | F | 4 | 25 | 29 | 29 | 0 |
| H | G | 2 | 29 | 31 | 31 | 0 |
| I | B | 5 | 5 | 31 | 10 | 21 |
| J | H, I | 7 | 31 | 38 | 38 | 0 |
| K | J | 3 | 38 | 41 | 41 | 0 |

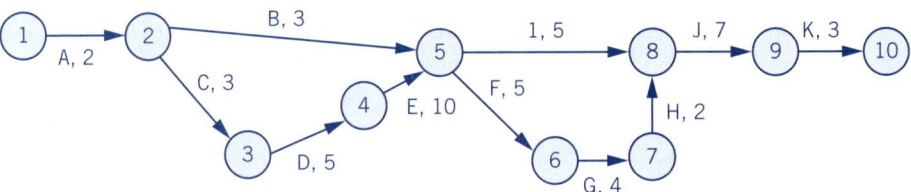

**FIGURE 14.10** Critical path diagram

In the figure, there are four possible paths from node 1 to node 10, these being as follows:
- A – B – I – J – K, taking 20 days.
- A – C – D – E – F – G – H – J – K, taking 41 days.
- A – C – D – E – I – J – K, taking 35 days.
- A – B – F – G – H – J – K, taking 26 days.

The path that takes the longest time to complete is referred to as the **critical path**. In the example, this would be the path A – C – D – E – F – G – H, which takes 41 days to complete. From a project management perspective, any activity that is on the critical path that is delayed will delay the finish of the project — there is no room for **slack**. This refers to the amount of time available for delays before disruption to the critical path, and thence the completion of the project, occurs.

In table 14.2, you may have also noticed the earliest start time, earliest finish time, latest finish time and slack columns. The earliest start time is calculated by working *forwards* in the diagram. For example, the earliest possible time for activity D to commence is day 5, calculated by adding the budgeted time for activities A and C together, since these must precede the commencement of D. The earliest finish time is calculated based on the budgeted time for the activity and all preceding activities (the earliest finish time for D is 2 + 3 + 5, while the earliest finish time for B is 2 + 3).

The latest start time is the latest possible time at which a task can commence without delaying the project, that is, extending the time allowed along the critical path. The latest start time is used in calculating the amount of slack or spare time available for disruptions. Disruptions can happen for several reasons. For example, when building a house, delays may occur due to inclement weather or a tradesperson not being available at a certain time. When installing a system, delays may also occur for many reasons, with some examples being hardware needing to be shipped in from overseas, complications in wiring a network that were not anticipated, consultant expertise not being available until a certain time. If the activities on the critical path are delayed, then the time required to complete the project will increase. However, activities not on the critical path can have slack time built into them, meaning that delays in their performance will not affect the overall timely completion of the project.

As an example, if activity I is delayed and takes ten days instead of five to complete, there will be no disruption to the overall project. Why? (Make sure you can work out the logic based on the diagram.) This is because activity I is not on the critical path. I is a prerequisite activity for J but so too is H. The earliest possible time H can be completed is on day 31. As a result, activity I does not have to be completed until day 31 at the latest to avoid disrupting the project. The latest finish time is calculated by working backwards through the diagram. The time for the critical path is used as the starting point, and the time for the immediately previous activity is subtracted. For example, the critical path time was identified as being 41 days. Therefore, the latest finish time for J is 38 days (41 – 3), 31 days for I and H (41 – 3 – 7) and 26 days for B (41 – 3 – 7 – 5).

The difference between the earliest finish time and the latest finish time is the amount of slack that is available. Notice in the table how all activities on the critical path have zero slack available. Also observe how the slack available for activity I is dependent on how well activity B is performed. If A and B are performed to schedule, then activity I has 21 days of slack, since it does not have to be completed until day 31 but is ready to start on day 5. However, if activity B takes eight days instead of the scheduled three, then the slack available for I without disrupting the critical path is reduced to 16 days from 21. This is referred to as **dependent slack**: activity I's slack is dependent on how well activity B is performed. Contrary to this, the slack available to B is independent of any preceding activities because its preceding activity (A) is on the critical path. This is referred to as **independent slack**.

As you can see, the planning and control options offered by the PERT diagram can be significant because it allows coordination of activities in a sequence that minimises project time. This can then facilitate the support of activities on the critical path, because they directly affect the critical path, as well as allowing for spare time, or slack, for activities that are not on the critical path.

There are various commercial project management software packages that will calculate and illustrate critical paths. Obviously, as the number of activities increases and the degree of interconnectedness increases, so too does the number of paths that can be taken between the start and finish. This can make identification of the critical path complex and the software packages a viable option.

## CASE

CASE systems are software packages that can help in the various stages of systems development, but particularly in the design of source code and user documentation. McNurlin and Sprague (1998) describe CASE software as consisting of, among other

**Dependent slack** *The slack available at a step in the process when it is dependent on the timing of an earlier step.*

**Independent slack** *The slack available at a step in the process that is independent of any previous steps.*

things, a planning facility and a code generator.[38] The planning facility is where the designs, such as entity-relationship diagrams, are specified. These allow for the identification of the relationships among different parts of the software that is being developed. The code generator will then generate code based on the specifications and requirements that have been entered. The CASE tools are designed to support those developing systems, offering help in generating the necessary code, and supporting the production of user documentation. A detailed discussion of CASE technology is beyond the scope of this text.

## ›› SUMMARY ›››

**LEARNING OBJECTIVE 1**

**How does business size and complexity influence the choice of systems development strategy for an organisation?**

Choosing an accounting system is not a one-size-fits-all exercise. Organisations may be classified by their size and turnover, with corresponding accounting packages varying in sophistication, but a larger entity may still find that a simple package fulfils all its needs, while a smaller business may be able to justify the expense of a complex ERP system due to the unique features of their operations. In most cases, however, the complex, time-consuming and expensive process of evaluating the need for an ERP is unnecessary for SMEs, and a simpler methodology may be followed in this case.

**LEARNING OBJECTIVE 2**

**What are the stages of the systems development lifecycle and what is the importance of organisational strategy as the basis for systems development?**

There are five stages to the systems development lifecycle, with these being investigation, analysis, design, implementation and, finally, maintenance and review. Investigation is aimed at identifying any problems with the current system. Analysis develops potential solutions to the identified problems and evaluates them based on their feasibility. The design stage prepares a logical and physical design for the newly proposed system and will culminate in the preparation of an RFP. The returned vendor proposals will be assessed by the organisation and a final vendor selected. This leads to the implementation stage, which relies heavily on the role of user training and education. Implementation can occur using a direct, parallel or phased approach. Once implemented, a system will be monitored for any errors or problems in its operations, as well as being improved with new features.

Organisational strategy needs to be the basis for evaluating systems development project ideas. A system that does not meet an organisation's strategic priorities can distract it from doing the things it does best and will weaken the distinctive nature of the organisation. The notion of organisational fit between what the system does and what the organisation aims to do is important.

**LEARNING OBJECTIVE 3**

**What are the software development options available to smaller businesses, and what is the systems selection process for decision making?**

SMEs usually decide to work with pre-developed programs, rather than undertaking to develop and test a unique product in-house. Pre-developed accounting packages come in two forms — mid-range packages, which are modular and allow a reasonably significant number of options for each feature, and simple packages, which allow fewer options but are much cheaper. Organisations looking to change their software systems should consider the following selection process: identify the company's needs, survey the market, identify a shortlist, arrange a demonstration, and decide and implement.

Service providers could also be used as they are a means for businesses to acquire access to a system or program through an independent provider. The programs are typically delivered through web-based means and offer benefits in economies of scale and lower upfront investment. Issues to consider with SPs are reliability, the level of service and the strategic nature of any data or processes connected with the SP.

LEARNING OBJECTIVE 4

### What are the features of alternative approaches to systems development?

Prototyping is a development approach that makes strong use of the users in evaluating models of the proposed system. This allows for a user-friendly system and for high consultation between user and designer, helping reduce potential resistance to a system once it is introduced. Object oriented analysis methods are generally used when object oriented systems are being developed. Agile/adaptive methods use small spiral cycles to develop systems; users and developers work in conjunction under these approaches. Alternative approaches lack overall systems objectives and outputs for the new system to be measured against, but are gaining popularity due to their flexibility.

LEARNING OBJECTIVE 5

### What are some typical systems development problems and some solutions for their resolution?

Typical problems encountered in systems development projects include the potential for conflict that arises when stakeholders from different perspectives try to agree on what is needed. The problem of escalation of commitment can also emerge once a project has commenced, which can lead to good money being thrown after bad. Project goal issues can also emerge, largely as a result of poorly defined goals, goals that lack support from those involved or goals that lack clarity and scope in their definition. The range of technical skills and interpersonal skills required to successfully complete a systems development project can also present many challenges for an organisation.

LEARNING OBJECTIVE 6

### What are some common systems development tools?

Common systems development tools include Gantt charts, PERT charts and CASE tools. Gantt charts and PERT charts provide graphical techniques for monitoring the progress of a project and for scheduling activities that need to occur. CASE tools provide computerised tools that assist in activities such as code generation and systems documentation.

## KEY TERMS

agile/adaptive methods, p. 650
bug correction, p. 644
computer-aided software engineering (CASE) systems, p. 654
dependent slack, p. 657
direct conversion, p. 641
feasibility analysis, p. 628
financial feasibility, p. 629
Gantt charts, p. 630
independent slack, p. 657
legal feasibility, p. 629
logical perspective, p. 633
object oriented analysis methods, p. 650
organisational fit, p. 626
parallel conversion, p. 641
phased-in conversion, p. 642

physical perspective, p. 633
programmed evaluation review technique (PERT) charts, p. 630
prototyping approach, p. 650
request for proposal, p. 637
schedule feasibility, p. 630
service level agreement, p. 647
software-as-a-service provider (SP), p. 647
strategic feasibility, p. 630
system improvement, p. 644
system modification, p. 644
systems development scope, p. 628
systems development steering committee, p. 631
technical feasibility, p. 630
total cost of ownership, p. 629

## DISCUSSION QUESTIONS

14.1 Explain the relationship between strategy and systems development. (LO1)

14.2 Describe the key activities that occur in the investigation stage of the systems development lifecycle. (LO2)

14.3 Describe the key activities that occur in the analysis stage of the systems development lifecycle. (LO2)

14.4 Describe the key activities that occur in the design stage of the systems development lifecycle. (LO2)

14.5 Describe the key activities that occur in the implementation stage of the systems development lifecycle. (LO2)

14.6 Describe the key activities that occur in the maintenance stage of the systems development lifecycle. (LO2)

14.7 Discuss the advantages and disadvantages of a phased-in and direct switch-over implementation strategy. (LO2)

14.8 What is the role of the steering committee in a systems development project? (LO2)

14.9 What is the role of a feasibility analysis within systems development projects? (LO2)

14.10 Describe each type of feasibility that is considered as part of a feasibility analysis. (LO2)

14.11 Critically evaluate how much end-users are actively involved in the systems development lifecycle approach to systems development. (LO2)

14.12 What are some of the advantages of using an SP? (LO3)

14.13 What are some of the disadvantages of using an SP? (LO3)

14.14 Describe alternative methods to the systems development lifecycle. (LO4)

14.15 Critically evaluate the usefulness of prototyping as a systems development approach. (LO4)

14.16 Summarise the five typical problems associated with systems development. (LO5)

14.17 For each of the typical systems development problems identified in the chapter, suggest a solution that could potentially overcome the problem. (LO5)

14.18 Describe how a PERT chart and a Gantt chart can be used to manage and control systems development projects. (LO6)

14.19 Critically evaluate the usefulness of Gantt and PERT charts in managing systems development projects. (LO6)

14.20 Describe how CASE tools can be used to manage and control systems development projects. (LO6)

## SELF-TEST ACTIVITIES

14.1 The systems development lifecycle commences with the stage of:
   (a) implementation.
   (b) investigation.
   (c) analysis.
   (d) design.

14.2 The RFP:
   (a) details the requests of users to be included in the system.
   (b) lists the requirements identified in the requirements investigation stage.
   (c) details requirements for potential vendors to follow.
   (d) offers guidance about the existing systems operations and the required changes.

14.3 Prototyping has the advantage of:
- (a) providing a structured development process.
- (b) providing thorough documentation.
- (c) strongly involving users in the development process.
- (d) ensuring users and technicians agree on design features.

14.4 SPs are an attractive option because:
- (a) all SPs are reliable.
- (b) businesses avoid having to invest large amounts in applications.
- (c) they give the organisation control over application development.
- (d) they provide applications that service the business's specific requirements.

14.5 Which of the following is *not* a level of testing?
- (a) Stub level testing
- (b) Unit level testing
- (c) System level testing
- (d) Enterprise level testing

Answer the following questions based on the Gantt chart contained in figure 14.11.

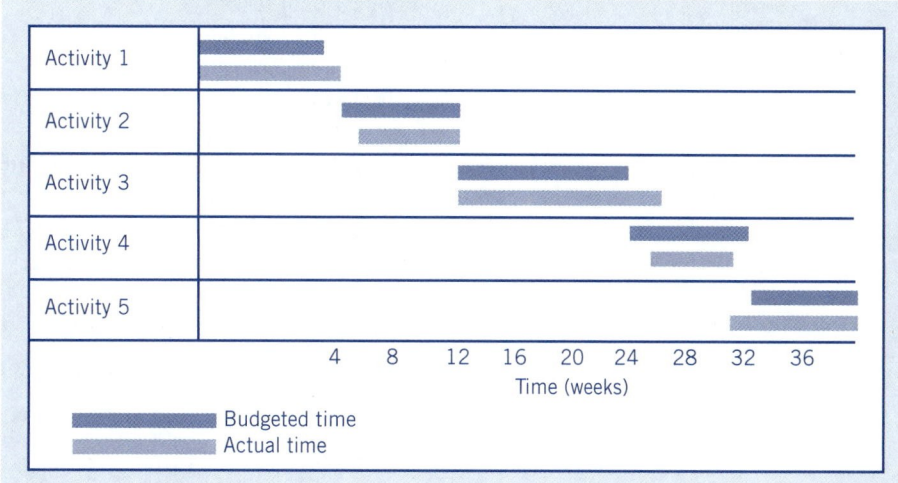

**FIGURE 14.11** Gantt chart

14.6 After the completion of activity 3, the project is progressing:
- (a) ahead of schedule.
- (b) behind schedule.
- (c) on schedule.
- (d) cannot be determined based on information available.

14.7 Activity 2 was completed:
- (a) on time.
- (b) ahead of time.
- (c) behind time.
- (d) cannot be determined from the information available.

14.8 The time taken to complete activity 2:
- (a) was more than expected.
- (b) was less than expected.
- (c) was as expected.
- (d) cannot be determined from the information available.

Answer the following questions based on the PERT chart contained in figure 14.12.

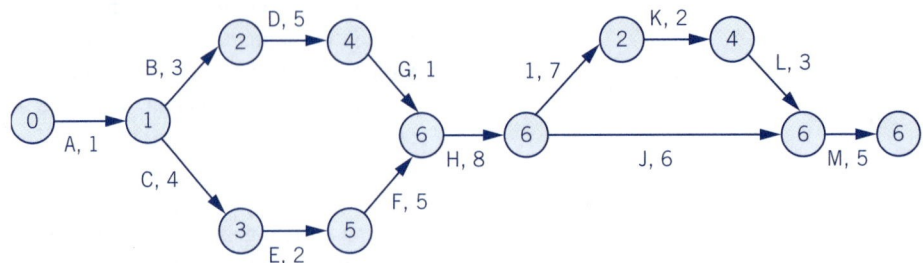

**FIGURE 14.12** PERT chart

14.9 The critical path for the project is:
   (a) A–B–D–G–H–I–K–L–M.
   (b) A–B–D–G–H–J–M.
   (c) A–C–E–F–H–I–K–L–M.
   (d) A–C–E–F–H–J–M.

14.10 The critical path takes:
   (a) 29 days to complete.
   (b) 31 days to complete.
   (c) 35 days to complete.
   (d) 37 days to complete.

14.11 If activity C is delayed by two days, the critical path is:
   (a) not affected.
   (b) increased by two days.
   (c) possibly increased, depending on slack in subsequent activities.
   (d) unable to be determined.

14.12 The amount of slack in activity D is:
   (a) no days.
   (b) one day.
   (c) two days.
   (d) three days.

## PROBLEMS

14.1 Encosta Memories is a small family photography business. The business has a good reputation for high-quality photos and enjoys long-standing arrangements with many schools for the provision of school photos. Encosta Memories has traditionally used a small accounting package to manage its operations, with Make Your Business Profitable 'MYBP' being the package currently in use. Recently, however, a few of the staff in the administration team have complained that MYBP has become slow in processing transactions. The computer that runs the program is also fast approaching its capacity, having not been updated for several years and now also handling some of the business's digital imaging requirements.

As a result of the strained system, Encosta Memories is considering the possibility of an upgrade. However, it is concerned that should it go ahead with an upgrade, it would have to employ a programmer to develop its new system, as well as a full-time IT specialist to keep the system running. It is also unsure of what needs to be done in managing the systems development process.

One of the things particularly troubling Mr De Lago, the part owner of Encosta Memories, is the possibility of investing capital now and having to do so again in a couple of years' time as technology changes. However, he does not mind spending a large sum now if the system is a long-term answer, since, as De Lago himself said, 'Once the system is acquired then the business can get back to normal and do what it does best — take photos — without having to spend money on IT.'

In light of the details you have about Encosta Memories, prepare a discussion in relation to the following questions.

(a) How correct is De Lago's statement that: 'Once the system is acquired then the business can get back to normal and do what it does best — take photos — without having to spend money on IT'? Explain your reasoning.

(b) Explain how it may not be necessary for Encosta Memories to employ a programmer to design a new system.

(c) How could Encosta Memories limit the costs of maintaining the system once it is in place within the organisation?

(d) Identify the key user requirements that would need to be fulfilled by the new system.

(e) Would you recommend that Encosta Memories make or buy the new system?

(f) Describe the process that Encosta Memories could use for selecting a vendor for the new system.

(g) What are some of the possible consequences for Encosta Memories of relying on a single vendor for the system?

(h) What typical systems development problems may Encosta Memories face in developing the new system? Suggest strategies for each potential problem.

14.2 A software development project has been identified as having six stages, these being (i) design the logical plan for the software operation, (ii) select a programming language, (iii) write source code, (iv) test the source code, (v) integrate software with existing applications, and (vi) train users. The time estimates for each of these activities are contained in table 14.3, as well as actual time taken (where available, since the project is only partly complete).

**TABLE 14.3** Project activities, budgeted time and actual time

| Activity | Budgeted time (days) | Actual time (days) |
|---|---|---|
| Design the logical plan for the software operation | 8 | 7 |
| Select a programming language | 2 | 2 |
| Write source code | 15 | 25 |
| Test the source code | 24 | Not available |
| Integrate software with existing applications | 4 | Not available |
| Train users | 7 | Not available |

**Required**

(a) Using the data in the table, construct a Gantt chart.

(b) Comment on the ability of the project to meet its schedule: if all remaining activities are completed according to budgeted times, will the project be completed on time?

(c) What activities are over schedule?

(d) Recognising that you are under pressure to meet the budgeted deadline for this software implementation, since it forms a part of an organisation-wide strategic initiative that will propel the company into the future, your boss suggests that you may want to revise your plans for testing and training, to ensure that the original 60-day schedule is met. One suggestion is to cut back on testing at the unit and system level and just focus on testing at the stub level. What is your response to this suggestion? Is it a good idea? Why? In your response be sure to distinguish between the different levels of testing and the aims of each level of testing.

14.3 The data contained in table 14.4 refer to a project that contains 13 activities. Based on the details of the activity, precedent activities and time estimates you are required to:

(a) Construct a PERT diagram.

(b) Identify all possible paths through the diagram, including how long each path takes.

(c) Identify the critical path and how long it takes.

(d) Calculate, for each activity:

  (i) earliest start time

  (ii) latest finish time

  (iii) earliest finish time

  (iv) slack time.

(e) For the activities identified as containing slack, is the slack dependent or independent? Explain your classification.

(f) What is the effect on the critical path if the following events occur independent of each other?

  (i) Activity B takes four days instead of seven.

  (ii) Activity J experiences three days of unplanned delays.

  (iii) Activity M is able to be completed in two days.

**TABLE 14.4** Project activities, precedents and times

| Activity | Immediate precedent | Time taken | Earliest start | Latest finish | Earliest finish | Slack |
|---|---|---|---|---|---|---|
| A | — | 3 | | | | |
| B | A | 7 | | | | |
| C | B | 6 | | | | |
| D | — | 4 | | | | |
| E | C, D | 2 | | | | |
| F | E | 4 | | | | |
| G | — | 8 | | | | |
| H | G | 1 | | | | |
| I | F, H | 5 | | | | |
| J | I | 10 | | | | |
| K | F | 2 | | | | |
| L | K | 9 | | | | |
| M | J, L | 4 | | | | |

## FURTHER READING

Satzinger, JW, Jackson, RB & Burd, SD 2009, *Systems analysis and design in a changing world*, 5th edn, Cengage Learning.

Shelly, GB, Rosenblatt, HJ 2010, *Systems analysis and design*, 8th edn, Cengage Learning.

## SELF-TEST ANSWERS

14.1 d, 14.2 c, 14.3 c, 14.4 b, 14.5 d, 14.6 b, 14.7 a, 14.8 b, 14.9 c, 14.10 d, 14.11 b, 14.12 c

## END NOTES

1. Compaq n.d., 'TCO models and approaches', www.hp.com.
2. Compaq n.d.
3. Hawryszkiewycz, I 2001, Introduction to systems analysis and design, Pearson Education Australia, Sydney.
4. De Michelis, G, Dubois, E, Jarke, M, Matthes, F, Mylopoulos, J, Schmidt, JW, Woo, C & Yu, E 1998, 'A three-faceted view of information systems', *Communications of the ACM*, vol. 41, no. 12, pp. 64–70.
5. Donzelli, P & Bresciani, P 2004, 'Improving Requirements Engineering by Quality Modelling – A quality based requirements engineering framework', *Journal of Research and Practice in Information Technology*, vol. 36, no. 4, pp. 277–94.
6. Donzelli & Bresciani 2004.
7. Clarke, RT & associates 1987, *Systems life cycle guide*, Prentice Hall, Englewood Cliffs, NJ.
8. Based on Clarke, RT & associates 1987.
9. Hawryszkiewycz 2001.
10. Kasavana, ML & Smith David, J 1992, 'Scripted computer demonstrations — how to standardize vendor's presentations', *The Cornell HRA Quarterly*, June, p. 78. Reproduced with permission.
11. Kasavana & Smith David 1992, pp. 75–83. Reproduced with permission.
12. Dennis, A & Wixom, BH 2000, *Systems analysis and design — an applied approach*, John Wiley & Sons, New York.
13. Whitten, JL, Bentley, LD & Dittman, KC 2001, *Systems analysis and design methods*, 5th edn, international edn, McGraw-Hill Higher Education, New York.
14. De Michelis et al. 1998.
15. Baronas, A-MK & Louis, MR 1988, 'Restoring a sense of control during implementation: how user involvement leads to system acceptance', *MIS Quarterly*, vol. 12, no. 1, pp. 111–23.
16. Hunton, JE & Beeler, JD 1997, 'Effects of user participation in systems development: a longitudinal field experiment', *MIS Quarterly*, vol. 21, no. 4, pp. 359–88.
17. Wastell, DG 1999, 'Learning dysfunctions in information systems development: overcoming the social defenses with transitional objects', *MIS Quarterly*, vol. 23, no. 4, pp. 581–600.
18. Wastell 1999, p. 582.
19. Wastell 1999.
20. Oracle 2005, 'Education services can help maximize the value of your Peoplesoft investment', www.peoplesoft.com.
21. Oracle 2005.
22. SAP 2005, 'SAP education: end user and performance solutions', www.sap.com; SAP 2002, 'Knowledge is power, knowledge is productivity', www.sap.com.
23. Dennis, A & Haley Wixom, B 2000, *Systems analysis and design: an applied approach*, John Wiley & Sons, New York.
24. Clarke & associates 1987.
25. Based on Clarke & associates 1987, p. E-22.
26. Smith, AD & Rupp, WT 2002, 'Application service providers (ASP): moving downstream to enhance competitive advantage', *Information Management and Computer Security*,

vol. 10, nos 2/3, pp. 64–72; Smith David, J, McCarthy, WE & Sommer, BS 2001, 'Agility: the key to survival of the fittest in the software market', unpublished paper.

27. Sofiane Tebboune, DE 2003, 'Application service provision: origins and development', *Business Process Management Journal*, vol. 9, no. 6, pp. 722–34.

28. Sofiane Tebboune 2003, p. 726.

29. Sofiane Tebboune 2003, p. 727.

30. Smith & Rupp 2002, p. 67.

31. Manifesto for agile software development 2001, 'Principles behind the agile manifesto', www.agilemanifesto.org.

32. Schwalbe, K 2002, 'Chapter 1: Introduction to project management', in *Information technology project management*, 2nd edn, Course Technology, Thomson Learning.

33. Barki, H & Hartwick, J 2001, 'Interpersonal conflict and its management in information system development', *MIS Quarterly*, vol. 25, no. 2, pp. 195–228.

34. Keil, M, Mann, J & Rai, A 2000, 'Why software projects escalate: An empirical analysis and test of four theoretical models', *MIS Quarterly*, vol. 24, no. 4, pp. 631–64.

35. Keil, et. al. 2000, pp. 631–64.

36. Schwalbe 2002.

37. Bourke, R 1992, *Project management: planning and control*, 2nd edn, John Wiley & Sons, Chichester, UK, chapter 5, pp. 103–38.

38. McNurlin, BC & Sprague, RH 1998, *Information systems management in practice*, 4th edn, Prentice Hall, Upper Saddle River, NJ.

**666** ‹‹‹‹‹ **PART 4** ‹‹‹ SYSTEMS ISSUES ‹‹‹

# 15

# Auditing of accounting information systems

## Learning objectives

After studying this chapter, you should be able to:

1. explain a financial (statutory) audit

2. explain the influence on the auditor of auditing standards and best practice

3. explain an information systems audit

4. identify the internal control frameworks and computer auditing tools and techniques (CATTs) available to an auditor

5. describe the steps to be taken in planning the audit

6. describe how audit fieldwork is carried out and analysed

7. describe the processes of completion, review, monitoring and reporting

8. describe other types of AIS audits.

# Introduction

An **audit** may traditionally be defined as 'an **examination** of financial statements by an **independent** expert, with a view to forming an opinion as to their accuracy and reliability, and reporting thereon'. Critical words in the definition are 'independent' and 'examination'. Independent means that the auditor is not otherwise a participant in the system under review, and is able to state an adverse opinion freely as he or she has no financial or other interest in the outcome. Examination includes a careful study and evaluation of the financial statements, the underlying records traced back to the source documents, and the system(s) used to prepare these statements. The examination will include an assessment of the risks associated with the system of misstatements or losses occurring caused by inadvertent errors or fraudulent or malicious actions and of the system of controls in place to mitigate these risks. While the auditor's opinion is subjective, it will be the result of a judgement informed by the evidence gathered during the audit examination, and the skill and experience of the auditor.

There are at least six different types of audit relating to an accounting information system (AIS). These are:

- *a financial audit.* This is a component of the statutory audit process discussed in the next section.
- *an information systems audit.* This is primarily to ensure that the system has adequate internal controls, and that they are working effectively. This topic is discussed later in this chapter.
- *an IT governance audit.* This is a review by an independent expert of governance and control systems in order to ascertain whether risks (including information security risks) are minimised. This topic is discussed at the end of this chapter.
- *a management audit.* This is a review of system performance, operational effectiveness and efficiency. Both human and physical elements may be included, and performance criteria may include (but are not limited to) timeliness, completeness and cost. Further discussion of this topic is outside the scope of this text.
- *an audit of systems under development.* This aims to ensure that appropriate controls are incorporated in new systems. This topic is discussed at the end of this chapter.
- *special purpose audits.* These may be commissioned by management for a variety of reasons. This topic is discussed at the end of this chapter.

**Audit** *An examination of financial statements by an independent expert, with a view to forming an opinion as to their accuracy and reliability, and reporting thereon.*

**Examination** *Includes a careful study and evaluation by the auditor of the financial statements, the underlying records traced back to the source documents, and the system(s) used to prepare these statements.*

**Independent** *A situation where an auditor is not otherwise a participant in the system under review, and is able to state an adverse opinion freely as he or she has no financial or other interest in the outcome.*

**LEARNING OBJECTIVE 1**

*Explain a financial (statutory) audit.*

# FINANCIAL (STATUTORY) AUDIT

A financial AIS audit is not an end in itself, but is a vital component of the audit of an entity. Because IT technology changes at a rapid and ever increasing speed, specialised AIS audit staff are needed with the required knowledge and skills to audit an AIS. The complexity of current AISs and this need for cutting-edge skills has created the need for AIS auditors to continually update their skills to maintain their understanding of new systems as they are introduced. It would be impracticable for all audit staff in accounting firms to acquire and maintain this level of specialised skills, which in turn has led to the development of AIS auditing as a specialised career path with its own postgraduate qualifications.

## Requirement for a statutory audit

All publicly listed companies in Australia and New Zealand are required by statute to be audited by an appropriately qualified and certified chartered accountant. In practice,

**Attest service** *An independent accountant expressing a written opinion about the reliability of a written assertion prepared by another party.*

almost all of them are audited by one of the four large international audit firms, generally referred to as the 'Big 4', Deloitte, Ernst & Young, PriceWaterhouseCoopers and KPMG. The auditor is required to state whether or not in their opinion the accounts give a 'true and fair view' of the company's activities for the period under review and whether or not the accounts have been prepared in accordance with generally accepted accounting principles (GAAP). The process of the auditor forming an opinion and reporting on it is technically termed an **attest service**, which may be defined as an independent accountant expressing a written opinion about the reliability of a written assertion prepared by another party. Similar audit requirements apply to all levels of federal, state and local government organisations, larger private companies, major charities, sporting, religious and cultural organisations and the like. As you have learned in chapter 13, the external accounts are prepared from summarised data in the general ledger system, and this in turn is derived from summarising the data generated by the transaction cycles examined in chapters 9–13. All of this data has been captured, processed and stored by the AIS; therefore, it follows that if the auditors are to form an opinion that the final accounts truly and fairly summarise the underlying transactions then they must have confidence in the integrity of the AIS. The way in which the auditors go about obtaining that confidence in the integrity of the AIS is the focus of the remainder of this chapter. Note that while the financial audit is the main focus of this chapter, other types of AIS audits will be discussed at the end of the chapter.

## External and internal auditors

The auditors described above are known as external or independent auditors. In the course of their review of the client organisation's financial statements the external auditor will examine the client's systems over a brief period once or twice a year. Many larger organisations also have internal auditors who, as their name implies, are employed by the organisation and are in a position to monitor the system on an ongoing basis. One of the principal functions of the internal audit unit is to monitor the effectiveness of the AIS and the controls associated with it. The Institute of Internal Auditors expects its members 'to evaluate and improve the effectiveness of risk management, control and governance processes'[1] of their employers. Ideally, the internal audit unit should report directly to the board of directors or to the board audit committee, but in many cases it reports to the chief financial officer (CFO). Inevitably an internal audit unit reporting to a CFO will be perceived as having less independence than one reporting to a higher level. In the private sector, internal auditors have no statutory authority; instead, they work as directed by the level of management to whom they report and in accordance with 'best practice'. In the public sector, authority is granted to internal auditors by the legislation governing the organisation. Depending on an assessment of the independence and competence of the internal audit unit, the external auditor may decide to perform fewer tests personally, and rely, to some degree, on testing performed by the internal audit unit.

## Auditors reporting responsibilities: directors and audit committees

Traditionally, while nominally responsible to the shareholders of a public company, the external auditors were appointed by, had their fees set by and effectively reported to the board of directors. The Australian Securities Exchange (ASX) has issued a set of corporate governance principles. These are 'aspirational statements' intended to encourage companies to follow best practice in their governance processes and to make meaningful disclosures of these processes. While the governance principles are not prescriptive they operate on an 'if not, why not' basis, requiring non-complying companies to state their reasons for not complying and explain what steps they are taking to achieve the objectives.

Principle 4 Safeguard integrity in financial reporting requires companies to put in place a structure designed to ensure truthful and factual presentation of the company's financial position.[2] Recommendations 4.1 and 4.2 require the board of directors to establish an audit committee consisting of at least three non-executive directors with an independent chair. The audit committee should review the integrity of the company's financial reporting and oversee the independence of the external auditors and report to the board thereon. The report should contain all matters relevant to the committee's role and responsibilities, including:

- assessment of the management processes supporting external reporting
- procedures for the selection and appointment of the external auditor and for the rotation of external audit engagement partners
- recommendations for the appointment or, if necessary, the removal of the external auditor
- assessment of the performance and independence of the external auditors
- assessment of the performance and objectivity of the internal audit function.

The Listing Rules of the ASX help to ensure that companies provide adequate disclosures to various stakeholders, and include requirements for continuous disclosure, changes in capital and new issues, restricted securities and trading halts, suspension and removal. Listing Rule 12.7 specifically requires that a company in the S&P All Ordinaries Index[3] has an audit committee. The New Zealand Stock Exchange's Good Corporate Governance guide similarly advocates the use of audit committees. The 2002 US **Sarbanes–Oxley Act** (SOX) similarly required the establishment of an audit committee. The significant difference is that the Australian and New Zealand approach encourages companies to follow best practice while the US legislated for mandatory compliance. Despite the varied approaches, the existence of an independent audit committee is recognised internationally as an important feature of good corporate governance.

**Sarbanes–Oxley Act** *A US Act that requires generally higher standards of financial reporting. The Act is binding on subsidiaries of US companies.*

**LEARNING OBJECTIVE 2**

*Explain the influence on the auditor of auditing standards and best practice.*

# INFLUENCES ON THE AUDITOR

There are a number of influences on the auditor in performing an AIS audit. These are discussed in the sections below.

## Auditing standards

Accounting and auditing standards have for many years been promulgated by professional accounting organisations in various jurisdictions. We introduced auditing standards in chapter 5 and quoted several extracts showing how they relate to the audit process.

The **Auditing and Assurance Standards Board (AUASB)** issued 35 **Australian Auditing Standards (ASAs)** in 2006. The ASAs are legally enforceable legislative instruments under the *Legislative Instruments Act 2003*. As a statutory body, the AUASB was granted powers — by section 227B of the *ASIC Act 2001* — to make auditing standards under section 336 of the *Corporations Act 2001*, to formulate auditing and

**Auditing and Assurance Standards Board (AUASB)** *An independent statutory body and the national auditing and assurance standards setter that develops high-quality standards and related guidance for auditors and providers of other assurance services.*

assurance standards for other purposes and to formulate guidance on auditing and assurance-related matters.[4]

The AUASB uses International Standards on Auditing (ISAs) issued by the **International Auditing and Assurance Standards Board (IAASB)** as the basis to develop ASAs. The entire suite of International Standards on Auditing (ISAs) was redrafted and, in some cases, substantively revised as part of the Clarity format project, initiated by the IAASB to improve the consistent application of ISAs worldwide.[5] All of the ASAs have been correspondingly redrafted and came into force for reporting periods commencing on or after 1 January 2010.

## Best practice

While compliance with statutes and accounting standards is mandatory for members of the standard issuer, AIS auditors often need other sources of guidance, and may turn to best practice as a source. Best practice may be defined as being what a skilled experienced auditor familiar with the issue at hand would do. It is the distilled wisdom of the auditor community and emerges from discovery of what works best through trialling a variety of techniques and choosing the best. It responds to environmental change more quickly than regulatory processes can. Sources of best practice include:

- ISO 27002 (2005) is an information security standard published by the International Organization for Standardization (ISO). It is an internationally accepted standard of good practice for information security management. ISO 27002 is currently undergoing revision; the review team met in Beijing in May 2009 and hoped to release the update in 2011.[6]
- individual accounting firms' procedure and training manuals
- materials and procedures developed by the vendors of various enterprise systems and general accounting systems.

## Sarbanes–Oxley Act requirements

In chapter 5 we showed how the Sarbanes-Oxley Act has put pressure on entities to ensure that their systems are properly documented. It was mentioned that, as United States legislation, the Act has no legal force in Australia or New Zealand, except that compliance is required for all Australian and New Zealand companies dual-listed on a US stock exchange. In addition, it is binding on subsidiaries of US companies such as the Ford Motor Company or Coca-Cola. The Act also exerts an indirect influence as an exemplar of best practice.

The statute also has strong moral force in that the 'Big 4' chartered accounting firms are all US based, so their worldwide policies and procedures incorporate requirements of the Act. As mentioned, significant requirements (mainly in section 404 of the Act or Securities and Exchange Commission rules made under it) include the mandatory appointment of an audit committee and an:

> internal control report [that] must include: a statement of management's responsibility for establishing and maintaining adequate internal control over financial reporting for the company; management's assessment of the effectiveness of the company's internal control over financial reporting ... and a statement that ... [the auditor] has issued an attestation report on management's assessment of the company's internal control over financial reporting.[7]

Thus, the directors and senior management are specifically charged with the responsibility for the financial statements and the processes (including internal control) that were used in their preparation. This responsibility includes certifying that they believe the financial reporting process to be adequate, and the auditors are required to issue an opinion on the management assertion, in addition to their own opinion on the effectiveness of the company's internal control procedures.

Other significant SOX requirements designed to ensure the independence[8] of auditors include:

- prohibiting the audit firm from carrying out non-audit services including information system consulting, design and implementation
- requiring audit committee approval of the audit firm performing services such as internal audit and setting up the internal control procedures
- requiring audit committee approval for any other non-audit services provided by the auditor and full disclosure of fees paid for such services
- requiring mandatory rotation of lead audit partners after five years and a time-out of five years before becoming eligible to resume the audit
- requiring, for a staff member of the audit firm taking up employment with the client, a time-out of one year after leaving; otherwise the audit firm will not be considered independent.

To carry out the tasks described above, SOX created the Public Company Accounting Oversight Board (PCAOB), a body responsible for the oversight of the auditors of public companies, with a view to ensuring that the audit is independent and the audited accounts true and fair.[9]

In 2007 the PCAOB issued *Auditing Standard No. 5: An Audit of Internal Control Over Financial Reporting That Is Integrated with An Audit of Financial Statements.* The standard includes the important assertion of the nexus between internal control providing reasonable assurance of reliability (section 2) and an explanation of the auditor's objective in undertaking an audit (section 3):

2. Effective internal control over financial reporting provides reasonable assurance regarding the reliability of financial reporting and the preparation of financial statements for external purposes.[10]

3. The auditor's objective in an audit of internal control over financial reporting is to express an opinion on the effectiveness of the company's internal control over financial reporting. Because a company's internal control cannot be considered effective if one or more material weaknesses exist, to form a basis for expressing an opinion, the auditor must plan and perform the audit to obtain competent evidence that is sufficient to obtain reasonable assurance about whether material weaknesses exist as of the date specified in management's assessment.[11]

Auditing Standard No. 5 also defines internal control over financial reporting as:

A process designed to provide reasonable assurance regarding the reliability of financial reporting and the preparation of financial statements for external purposes in accordance with generally accepted accounting principles. A company's internal control over financial reporting includes those policies and procedures that (1) pertain to the maintenance of records that, in reasonable detail, accurately and fairly reflect the transactions and dispositions of the assets of the company; (2) provide reasonable assurance that transactions are recorded as necessary to permit preparation of financial statements in accordance with generally accepted accounting principles, and that receipts and expenditures of the company are being made only in accordance with authorizations of management and directors of the company; and (3) provide reasonable assurance regarding prevention or timely detection of unauthorized acquisition, use, or disposition of the company's assets that could have a material effect on the financial statements.[12]

Other definitions are also outlined, including that of a control deficiency, which occurs 'when the design or operation of a control does not allow management or employees in the normal course of performing their assigned functions, to prevent or detect misstatement on a timely basis'.

## AIS FOCUS 15.1

### Help on the way

*A variety of new software can help end the feeling you're drowning in a sea of rules designed to prevent financial fraud.*

OpenPages Inc. rolled out a software application called SOX Express in 2003, just as Sarbanes–Oxley took effect. It was designed to help businesses comply with the new law.

While the industry spawned by Sarbanes–Oxley might be expected to be levelling off today, when most public companies have updated their financial reporting procedures to meet the law's stringent requirements, the compliance business is continuing to grow.

Sarbanes–Oxley is no longer driving all the growth, however. Some of the new business has been sparked by antifraud measures enacted in other countries where multinational corporations do business, from Canada to Japan to the European Union. Other drivers are new government regulations in areas like privacy, or in sectors like energy or drug discovery. And small and mid-size private businesses, which aren't subject to Sarbanes–Oxley, have been moving to upgrade their own financial controls at the urging of executives and directors.

The emerging broader market is known in the research and consulting field by the acronym GRC, or 'governance, risk management, and compliance'.

'Companies have gotten over the initial shock of Sarbanes–Oxley,' said John Hagerty, a vice president at AMR Research in Boston. 'They're now looking at the regulations as something they have to live with. So if they have to live with it, they might as well be prepared.'

Between 2003 and 2005, almost all OpenPages' revenue came from SOX Express. It then introduced a software suite called OpenPages Governance Platform, including the financial controls program it developed for Sarbanes–Oxley and new applications for operational risk management, general compliance, and information technology governance.

It gives customers a standardised way to capture and document their critical processes (such as payroll or accounts receivable) that can affect financial reporting across multiple divisions. And it also enables businesses to automate their work flow.

Accounting firms report that small and mid-size businesses and nonprofit institutions are seeking to bring their financial controls up to Sarbanes–Oxley standards, even if they don't make financial reports to the US Securities and Exchange Commission. In many cases, the pressure is coming from outside parties like banks, which are requiring more detailed documentation when small businesses apply for loans.

'There's a big demand for services, and it's filtering down to companies with $20 million to $200 million in annual sales,' one said. 'Their boards of directors want to put good governance in place partly because they're concerned about their own responsibilities and their exposure to lawsuits.'[13]

# INFORMATION SYSTEMS AUDITS

An information systems audit is commissioned by management to seek assurance that the system has adequate internal controls included, and that they are working effectively. The first step in the audit is to assess the risks the system faces. These risks may be classified as:

- Inherent risk — the risk of material misstatement, without regard to the effects of controls. For example, there is an inherent risk that at the end of a financial year, sales that did not occur until after balance date may be included (to boost company profit or individual commissions).
- Control risk — the risk of material misstatement resulting from the internal controls in place failing to detect a fraudulent or erroneous transaction, such as the next-year sales described in the previous paragraph.
- Detection risk — the risk that internal and/or external auditors will not detect a material misstatement.

The next step is to evaluate the risks facing the system, and prioritise them with a view to devoting the greatest amount of audit resources in the areas at most risk.

## OVERVIEW OF THE AIS AUDIT

The primary purpose of a financial AIS audit is to give the auditor confidence that the system has properly recorded and processed the organisation's transactions, and therefore that the financial statements produced by the system may be relied on to represent a summary of the underlying transactions that have occurred. The primary purpose of an information systems audit is to assure management that the system's internal controls are adequate. While the purposes differ, the audit processes are similar; therefore, the discussion in the following sections applies to both types of audit.

### An historical perspective

Scott's Plumbing Supplies is a well-established firm selling bathroom and kitchen fittings and general plumbing supplies. It offers credit accounts to regular customers, mainly builders and plumbers. When the business was founded, all transactions were recorded manually, using a system little different to that first described by Pacioli.[14] Sales orders were recorded using a six-copy pre-numbered form that included a customer's purchase order field. The order form was either signed by the customer or was authorised by a written purchase order sent by the customer. The first order copy went to the customer, the second, third and fourth to the warehouse, the fifth to the invoicing section and the last copy remained in the book and was kept in the sales department. Warehouse staff picked the order, authorised by the order document, and made any required changes for items out of stock. The second and third copies of the form were sent to the customer with the goods, which were delivered using the company's own trucks; the customer kept the second form and signed and returned the third, which was filed in the warehouse. The fourth copy was sent to the invoicing section where it was matched to the fifth copy. The invoicing section prepared a two-part invoice using data from the sales order form and a price list, using the order number as the invoice number. The invoice top copy went to the customer and the second copy was used to post the sales journal, and then filed. The sales journal was subsequently used to post the item to the customer's account in the debtors' ledger.

The audit process carried out to establish the reliability of the system entailed reconciling figures on source documents (for example, sales orders with customer invoices) then reconciling invoices with totals on output documents (for example, customer statements) with a view to confirming that transactions were being processed correctly and that all transactions were included. This was referred to as following an audit trail. Scott's process described above left a clear **audit trail**. The auditor could look at any customer's account balance in the debtors' ledger and trace each debit back to the individual invoice and to the signed sales order copy. Similarly, he or she could examine any sales order and trace it forward through the system to a charge to a customer. Sequence checks could be used to ensure that all order forms resulted in invoices being issued, or that missing documents were accounted for as either having been cancelled or still in progress.

As technology became available, Scott's replaced hand-written records with typed invoices and posted the debtors' ledger using an accounting machine but there was little change to the underlying process or the documentation, so the audit trail remained intact. Even when Scott's introduced its first computer system in the mid 1970s little changed. The hand-written sales order forms were retained; the invoicing section wrote the customer number and the item unit price on the sales order form; and the data was then keyed into the computer system. The computer system calculated extended prices, subtotals, taxes and final totals and printed the invoice. At the end of each day it also printed a listing of all invoices prepared that day, and a cumulative electronic file of invoice data. At the end of the month, this file of invoice data was used to prepare customer statements.

Originally, Scott's auditors treated computer systems as a 'black box' and attempted to audit 'around the computer', without finding a need to understand what the computer was doing. Scott's first computer system described above left a clear audit trail from sales order forms to invoices and daily listings to customer statements and its auditors were confident in their ability to audit 'around the computer'.

However, in some cases such a procedure is no longer possible and, instead, auditors must audit 'through the computer'; that is, they audit the processes undertaken by the computer. One reason for this change is that with a contemporary point-of-sale system there are often no longer any source documents to be found so there is no independent audit trail.

## Auditing today

Let's now look at Scott's today. The business now has several branches across the metropolitan area and delivers using outside carriers and couriers. Sales staff 'on the road' may enter customer orders into Scott's 'state of the art' point-of-sale system using a laptop, or customers may place orders by phone or email in which case a branch salesperson enters the order. In either case the system prints or electronically displays appropriate documents or screens authorising the picking and despatch of the order to a building site, and subsequently invoices the customer. The invoicing process involves pricing using a base price, applicable volume or special customer discount, seasonal promotion, or damaged and obsolete stock price.

The entire process is entered and possibly edited by the salesperson, the only external evidence of the transaction is a possible signature of an unknown person on a building site, either written on a document or possibly recorded from a tablet into a computer system, and probably held by a third-party carrier or courier company. Clearly, no visible audit trail exists to examine and so in such a case it is impossible to audit around the computer. The auditor can only confirm the integrity of the computer processes involved.

So, how does an auditor go about confirming this integrity? One advantage of using computer systems is their predictability; they do not have the same lapses in performance, nor do they make the occasional mistakes that humans are prone to. Computers follow rules embedded in programs. If a computer correctly processes a particular transaction in a certain manner then the auditor can confidently predict that similar transactions will be treated in an identical manner. Therefore, the auditor needs to create a sample of test transactions and process them through the system to ensure that they are processed correctly. This is known as auditing 'through the computer'.

An AIS audit broadly comprises five distinct phases:
- planning the audit
- field work
- analysis
- completion, review and reporting
- monitoring and review.

We will study each of these phases in following sections but first we will look at the tools available to a 21st century auditor.

# AUDIT TOOLS

Audit tools fall into two categories: internal control frameworks and computer auditing tools and techniques, generally known as CATTs.

## Internal control frameworks

We discussed both the COSO and COBIT frameworks in detail in chapter 7. These are both more applicable to management in its tasks of planning and implementing internal control than they are to auditors. However, where organisations have implemented either or both of these frameworks the auditor is able to evaluate the controls in place against the framework and it provides a reference point from which a company and its auditor can negotiate an agreement as to what are the control objectives and which controls are appropriate to meet those objectives.

### COSO

In its 2009 publication *Guidance on monitoring internal control systems,* COSO poses the question 'How does monitoring benefit the governance process?' and responds 'Unmonitored controls tend to deteriorate over time. Monitoring . . . is implemented to help ensure that internal control continues to operate effectively'.[15] Therefore, the auditor must confirm that management are actively monitoring the internal control system and that deficiencies identified are rectified.

### COBIT

COBIT claims that it appeals to auditors 'to substantiate their opinions and/or provide advice to management on internal controls'.[16]

COBIT also stresses the importance of monitoring:

> Establishing an effective internal control programme for IT requires a well-defined monitoring process. This process includes the monitoring and reporting of control exceptions, results of self-assessments and third-party reviews.
>
> Monitoring is to provide assurance regarding effective and efficient operations and compliance with applicable laws and regulations.
>
> Control . . . is achieved by:
> - monitoring and reporting on the effectiveness of the internal controls over IT
> - reporting control exceptions to management for action.[17]

# AIS FOCUS 15.2

## COBIT *and* IT *governance case studies*

COBIT has been adopted worldwide. In this AIS focus, we introduce four adopters, including two major Australian organisations, and describe some of the advantages they identified.

1. A large Australian Government service organisation adopted COBIT to develop a customised audit plan for an audit of mainframe capacity planning. The plan contained control objectives, audit objectives and testing strategies. The plan was approved by management and used to successfully complete the audit. The findings and recommendations of the audit were accepted by management and resultant action was put in place. The organisation believes that without COBIT, the quality of the audit would not have been as high.

2. A major Australian university adopted COBIT and found it to be a useful tool to improve practices and approaches to teaching tasks and responsibilities. The COBIT implementation arose in conjunction with an audit review of the university's strategic planning, based on the balanced scorecard methodology. Since COBIT is compliant with the balanced scorecard, it fit well with the university's internal strategy.

   Together, information systems management and the internal audit function led the adoption of COBIT as the university's official IT governance methodology. The next strategic step was to implement COBIT at the operational level. The drive for implementation by information systems management greatly accelerated the implementation and acceptance rate of the framework.

   The internal audit function observed in relation to the adoption of COBIT:

   • COBIT was a high resource commitment for internal audit who invested significant staff time in the implementation, and had an ongoing commitment post-implementation.

   • Some staff members initially were concerned with the term 'performance indicators'. They thought it caused more pressure in already pressured jobs. By renaming these 'measures of success', concerns were alleviated.

   • COBIT is a robust framework that is well-thought out for diverse environments. It is best learned and appreciated during the implementation process.

3. A large United Arab Emirates integrated and government-owned energy company implemented COBIT as a result of its IT services having difficulty adapting to the company's rapid growth, IT projects not being properly prioritised and IT value being increasingly questioned. A significant issue contributing to the problems was that many IT processes were not standardised and, thus, not repeatable, which contributed to the inefficiency of IT service delivery. The IT department faced significant challenges in trying to meet the expectations of the business.

   The main goal of the COBIT implementation was to improve the efficiency of delivery of IT services through improving existing processes or designing and implementing new processes. The goal has been accomplished.

*continued*

4. A leading US health insurance company adopted COBIT, in part, because it was aware that COBIT could be leveraged to meet Sarbanes–Oxley compliance requirements. External factors caused the company to modify its approach from a risk-based to a compliance-based focus. The approach to adopting COBIT was termed 'COBIT Lite' and was to concentrate on financially significant applications. The implementation was performed by employees who also had other responsibilities, so they focused on reasonable and prudent controls for the environment.

The company identified numerous benefits from implementing the COBIT framework, including formalising and documenting controls, policies and procedures. For the most part, the required controls were in place before COBIT was implemented; however, there was little documentation and procedures were informal.

Many areas achieved benefits from the implementation of COBIT, including being able to identify and address minor exceptions before they became significant issues. The team also found that it could use COBIT as a common language between various process areas and with internal auditors.

The company listed several lessons learned, including:
- the audit/compliance perspective is different from the perspective of implementing a framework with a focus on governance, risk management and IT control
- it is best to build controls into a process, as it makes the controls easier to sustain and self-testing more efficient and effective
- enterprise-wide change must occur in implementing a governance framework such as COBIT, and senior-level support and communication is essential, as often the most difficult part of a program is overcoming resistance to change.[18]

## Computer auditing tools and techniques

Computer auditing tools and techniques (**CATTs**) may be defined as the tools and techniques used to directly examine the internal logic of an application as well as the tools and techniques used to indirectly draw inferences upon the application's logic by examining the data processed by the application.[19] The first two techniques listed in this section are used to directly examine the internal logic and the other two examine it indirectly.

### Testing using test data

The auditor needs to create a sample of test transactions and process them through the system to ensure that they are processed correctly. This will ensure the auditor can have faith in the integrity of the program and systems, and in the information contained within them.

The predicted results of the test transactions should be manually calculated in advance and compared to the test results processed by the system, and any differences thoroughly investigated. Testing should start with the simplest calculations and proceed from there, and should be made at both the individual transaction level and the various summary total levels:
- In a sales system, these tests may start with simple transactions such as: Does quantity *times* unit price *equal* extended price?
- In a multi-item transaction, it could include: Does *sum of* extended price *equal* subtotal?
- The auditor should check that GST and any other applicable taxes are correctly applied: Does the subtotal *plus* tax *equal* invoice total?

Further queries might include:

- Does *sum* of invoice total *equal* daily summary total?
- Is the resulting daily sales journal entry arithmetically correct and posted to appropriate general ledger codes?
- Does the customer's previous balance *plus* this invoice *equal* the current balance?

These test transactions should include every possible permutation of valid and invalid transactions that could be entered into the system. This is to test that the system will provide an appropriate response to every invalid input, and follow through every programmed logic step in response to acceptable input. For example, if testing customer validation and credit-checking procedures, the test data should include an invalid customer number and a normal valid customer number, a transaction for a customer within their credit limit, one already over their credit limit and another that would, if processed, exceed the credit limit. All error and warning messages received from the system should be carefully recorded. Similarly, testing the inventory system's response to a sale of inventory should include a sale of an available item, one where the sale should trigger the inventory replenishment supplier purchase order generation process, one where the item is already on a supplier purchase order (to check that a duplicate purchase order is not created) and one where there is insufficient stock available to supply the order (to test the back order process).

Testing of the payables process should include the following questions: Does the system require a three-way match of purchase order to receiving report and vendor invoice to authorise a disbursement? If, when checking vendor invoices back to purchase order, a 'tolerance' is built in, is it reasonable? (If the purchase order used the last purchase price and the vendor has increased prices by 5 per cent since then, that is probably reasonable, and building in a 5 per cent tolerance will save a lot of manual intervention to approve payment of a supplier invoice. However, allowing a 20 per cent tolerance may be excessive.) Are all disbursements approved by two individuals entering approval codes? If so, is this responsibility taken seriously or is it simply performed mechanically by the signatories? (This procedure is clearly harder to check, particularly if individuals know that they are being observed by an auditor, when they are more likely to 'follow the book'.)

Test results should be fully documented and retained as part of the audit working papers.

The **test data** (usually known as a '**test deck**', a name referring to the deck of punched cards originally used) should be retained for reuse after any modification to the system. When a modification has taken place the entire system should be tested, not just the area modified. This is to ensure that no inadvertent or fraudulent changes have been made to other areas.

Running test data through the system imposes several limitations on the auditors. For a start, if the testing is performed using client staff, it will lessen the degree of independence. The testing may be done on the 'live' system (i.e. when the system is in normal operating mode) or on a 'dead' system (e.g. after normal working hours). Testing may also be carried out on a copy of the production system, supplied by the client to the auditors for that purpose. There is a small risk that if there have been any fraudulent modifications made to the production system it may be restored to the original state before performing a 'dead' system test or making a copy of the system for the auditors. If the testing has been performed on the 'live' system, which is the more desirable situation, then after the testing is complete all the test transactions should be reversed to remove them from the system. If it was done on a 'dead' system, then the files would be simply rolled back to their previous status and the changes discarded.

## Integrated test facility (ITF)

*Embedded audit software* Software written by or for the auditor and embedded into the client's computer system.

*Integrated test facility (ITF)* A simple version of embedded audit software that populates a client's system with 'dummy' records.

A superior but more complex and expensive approach is to use **embedded audit software**. That is software written by or for the auditor and embedded into the client's computer system. The simpler version is an **integrated test facility (ITF)**. In this case, the auditors have reserved a range of customer numbers, inventory numbers, supplier numbers and so on for test purposes and populated each of these groups with 'dummy' records. They then run transactions using these records, merged in with the client's normal transaction processing. The principal advantage is that the auditors may be assured that the test transactions are being processed in an identical manner to normal transactions, and it does not require the use of client staff. The principal disadvantage is the risk that adding these transactions to normal processing may mean that they are included in summary totals, resulting in incorrect totals appearing in client reports.

## Embedded audit software

*Systems control and review file (SCARF)* A sophisticated example of embedded audit software that involves continuous review of all transactions passing through the client's system.

A more sophisticated example of embedded audit software is continuous auditing using a **systems control and review file (SCARF)**. This method involves continuous review of all transactions passing through the client's system. It is used to draw auditor attention to 'outliers' in transactions that are noteworthy by virtue of their size or because in some other way they differ significantly from the norm. The auditor sets a series of parameters to identify such transactions warranting further investigation, for example in a payroll system all new or changed salary or wage payments over $10 000 per month. The software will write all details of the transaction to the SCARF file, including the date and time, snapshots of before and after images of records updated, the user ID of the person entering the transaction and the workstation ID of the terminal used. The auditor can then examine the transaction, comparing it to the underlying records (in this case a payroll change authorisation form) to ensure that the transaction has been correctly entered and has the required authorisation approval signatures. This type of software often incorporates an off/on switch. Because examining all transactions passing through the system may add to processing overhead the client may pressure the auditor to only switch it on for limited periods. Doing so obviously restricts its usefulness.

## Generalised audit software

*Generalised audit software* Software designed to read and process data, typically from large databases, to perform a wide range of audit tasks.

**Generalised audit software** (GAS) is software designed to read and process data, typically from large databases, to perform a wide range of audit tasks. While the first two CATTs described previously are used dynamically to test the system in action and embedded audit software examines transactions dynamically to identify those warranting further investigation, GAS is used statically after the event to identify transactions or balances of interest to the auditor. This software is very flexible and can read and extract data from a wide range of software running on all types of hardware platforms. It can be used either to interrogate the client's files on their own system or to copy the client data from the source to the auditor's own system for further analysis and processing. Typically, this processing will involve selecting records for further investigation by the auditor. This may be a selection of random samples of records using stratified statistical techniques, or a targeted selection of records of particular interest or containing potential problems. Statistical sampling techniques are outside the scope of this book. Records of particular interest will typically include 'outliers' that do not conform to the normal pattern by virtue of size or frequency; or where there is an unexpected volume of transactions for a particular customer or of a specific amount; or where there are abnormal clusters of transactions in a particular range.

In a sales system these may be, for sales invoices and credit notes or credit adjustments, the largest and smallest percentile by dollar value and/or number of transactions; in accounts receivable, the largest percentile by dollar value and age of debt; and in inventory, the largest percentile by dollar value and slow stock turnover, and also items with negative quantity on hand or negative value. Examples of clustered transactions are abnormally large numbers of credit notes in the range \$450–\$500 or abnormally large numbers of capital expenditure items in the range \$45 000–\$50 000.

So, why are these records of particular interest to the auditor? The answer is that auditors' naturally suspicious natures and their previous experience have taught them that abnormal transactions may have perfectly innocent explanations but also may be indicators of fraud or non-compliance with corporate policies. High-value transactions are always of interest because a fraudulent high-value transaction can cause greater loss than a fraudulent low-value transaction. Overdue receivable items may be difficult or impossible to collect and therefore adequate provision for potential loss should be made, and some of the slow-moving inventory may be unsaleable and should be written down in value to allow for this. Credit notes and adjustments may be raised fraudulently to conceal the theft of cash or theft of goods originally invoiced to fictitious customers. In the first clustered transactions example it may be the case that a (dishonest) accounts receivable clerk has authority to authorise credit notes up to a \$500 limit. The second case may be where a plant manager has authority to acquire capital expenditure items up to a \$50 000 limit and has conspired with vendors to invoice larger items in several parts to avoid compliance with more rigorous approval procedures required for larger expenditures.

GAS may also be used to test for compliance with Benford's Law, which demonstrates the counterintuitive fact that the first digits of most naturally occurring numbers fit into a non-uniform pattern. Instinctively we may believe that there is an equal 10 per cent probability of any number starting with 1, 5 or 9. Benford's Law[20] shows there is a 30% probability that the first digit will be 1, and the probability decreases logarithmically until there is only a 5 per cent probability that the first digit will be 9. As most people are unaware of this phenomenon anyone creating a fraudulent list of, for example, vendor invoices, is likely to instinctively create numbers with the first digits randomly allocated.

In the United States in 1993 in State of Arizona v. Nelson (CV92-18841), the accused (a manager in the State Treasurer's office) was found guilty of trying to defraud the state of nearly \$2 million by making fraudulent payments to a bogus vendor.[21] The first digits of the fake invoices were mostly 7, 8 or 9. A routine test for compliance with Benford's Law first drew the auditor's attention to the problem.

GAS software can carry out normal arithmetical calculations on the entire data population or selected samples, analyse the data statistically and produce reports in any required format.

Issues that may arise in using this type of software include whether the software can run on the live production database, or whether instead data are copied by client staff to a test file for the auditor's use. This latter method means that the testing is slightly less independent as the copy process could be corrupted, for example, by dishonest data processing staff applying a filter to remove fraudulent transactions from the test file before passing it to the auditor.

Many generalised audit software programs incorporate artificial intelligence and expert systems characteristics, specifically the ability to 'learn' from previous experience. Over time, characteristics of the database may change: such software will be able to identify what are now the unusual transactions without specific direction.

Examples of generalised audit software include Audit Command Language (ACL), the market leader, Interactive Data Extraction and Analysis (IDEA), and various proprietary software created and used by the 'Big 4' chartered accounting firms such as KPMG's System 2190. Two other examples of GASs are Activedata for Excel and TopCAATs, both of which are third-party add-ins for Microsoft Excel. While less sophisticated than the others mentioned these are both powerful tools available at a far lower cost.

## THE RISK–BASED APPROACH TO AN AUDIT

The risk-based approach depicted in figure 15.1 provides a useful framework for designing the audit process and ensuring that all known weaknesses and exposures are taken into account.

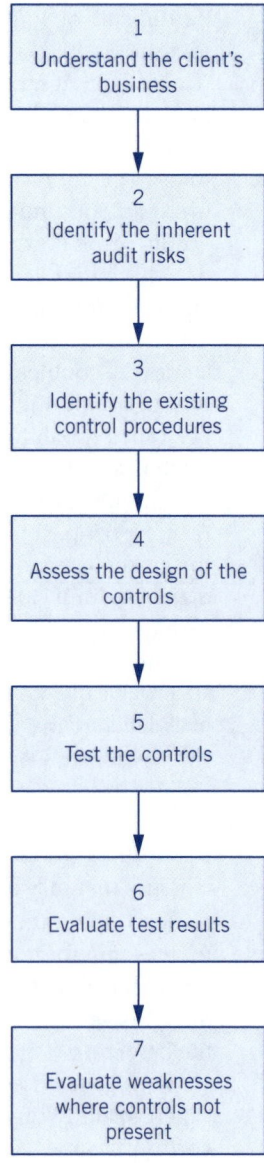

**FIGURE 15.1** The risk-based approach to an audit

Steps 2 through 6 require the auditor to carefully consider each inherent risk (i.e. what could go wrong) then identify the control procedure(s) in place to mitigate that risk, decide whether or not those procedure(s) are appropriate, test the control(s) in operation and, lastly, determine whether or not the control(s) successfully addressed the risk.

# PLANNING THE AUDIT

**LEARNING OBJECTIVE** **5**

*Describe the steps to be taken in planning the audit.*

Planning includes all of the preparatory steps taken in advance of carrying out the fieldwork in an audit. Good planning is an essential part of the audit process. The first step is deciding on the scope of the audit, what is to be edited and what is the principal focus of the audit. If the AIS audit is a part of the statutory audit process then the scope is determined by the auditor. For any other type of audit, the scope is agreed between the auditor and those instructing the auditor.

Planning is an iterative process, the plan and the audit program may be modified as needed as the audit progresses. For example, if test results reveal an unsatisfactory level of control in one area, the auditors may decide that it is necessary to carry out further testing not only in that area, but also in other areas.

## Studying the client and industry

The next step in the planning phase is for the auditor to familiarise him or herself with the client's entire business and the industry in which it operates. This step is required to provide the auditor with an understanding of any accounting practices or transactions unique to that industry. For example, to minimise unused capacity, hotels and airlines offer different rates for the same room or seat by making a limited number of rooms or seats available for sale at lower rates with more restrictive conditions. Such a detailed understanding will help the auditor in deciding whether a particular transaction is within a normal range or unusual, and if it requires further investigation.

This study will also allow the auditor to assess the control environment and the attitudes and capability of senior management. If the auditors believe that there is a strong control environment and capable senior management acting with integrity they will be more inclined to accept management assertions about controls in place. From this study they may also form an opinion as to whether there are circumstances that increase the **inherent risk**, which is the potential for fraudulent activity or serious and material errors in financial statements. Such factors may include, and are not limited to, directors and senior management integrity, directors and senior management skill and experience, external pressures arising from market expectations, general economic conditions or those specific to the client's industry, worsening foreign exchange rates and severe unusual climate conditions.

*Inherent risk The potential for fraudulent activity or serious and material errors in financial statements.*

## Studying the client's system

The auditor next needs to study each of the system(s) under audit including system documentation, broken down into the various business cycles and their component subsystems, for example the revenue cycle and its component sales, billing and accounts receivable subsystems and the expenditure cycle and its component purchasing, payables, payroll and inventory management subsystems. This will involve, for each component subsystem, studying all available process maps, dataflow diagrams and systems flowcharts, and any written descriptive material. In addition, the auditor will need to obtain samples of the inputs and outputs of the system. The auditor should also observe the system in use and interview a range of users at all levels, from managers to sales staff, to understand how the system operates in practice.

Often procedures have been modified officially or unofficially, and the documented system may differ from the actual system in place. At this time the auditor may consider the use of an **internal control questionnaire (ICQ)**. This is a standard form used by the audit firm, and is a checklist of questions for each business process. For example, in a retail environment the cash sales process ICQ might include: Is a register receipt issued for every sale? Does the register produce a daily or shift sales total? Is the register assigned to a single staff member or multiple users? Who reconciles the cash collected to the sales total? Who prepares the banking? Who performs the bank reconciliation? How are significant cash shortfalls treated? Analysing the answers will help the auditor form a conclusion as to the strength of the system. Some examples of ICQ questions are given in figures 15.2, 15.3 and 15.4.[22]

**FIGURE 15.2** Excerpts from an internal control questionnaire — control environment

| CLIENT *Allied Industries Limited* Completed by: *LRG* Date: *12/3/11* | | BALANCE DATE *30/6/11* Reviewed by: *DRS* Date: *29/4/11* | |
|---|---|---|---|
| Internal control questionnaire component: Control environment | | | |
| Question | | Yes, No, N/A | Comments |
| *Integrity and ethical values* | | | |
| 1. | Does management set the 'tone at the top' by demonstrating a commitment to integrity and ethics through both its words and deeds? | Yes | *Management is conscious of setting an example. Entity does not have a formal code of conduct.* |
| 2. | Have appropriate entity policies regarding acceptable business practices, conflicts of interest, and codes of conduct been established and adequately communicated? | Yes | *Expectations of employees included in a policy manual distributed to all employees.* |
| 3. | Have incentives and temptations that might lead to unethical behaviour been reduced or eliminated? | Yes | *Profit-sharing plan monitored by audit committee.* |
| *Board of directors and audit committee* | | | |
| 1. | Are there regular meetings of the board and are minutes prepared on a timely basis? | Yes | *Board has nine inside members, three of whom serve on the audit committee. Considering adding three outside members to the board who would comprise the audit committee.* |
| 2. | Do board members have sufficient knowledge, experience and time to serve effectively? | Yes | |
| 3. | Is there an audit committee composed of outside directors? | No | |
| *Management's philosophy and operating style* | | | |
| 1. | Are business risks carefully considered and adequately monitored? | Yes | *Management is conservative about business risks.* |
| 2. | Is management's selection of accounting principles and development of accounting estimates consistent with objective and fair reporting? | Yes | |
| 3. | Has management demonstrated a willingness to adjust the financial statements for material misstatements? | Yes | *Management has readily accepted all proposed adjustments in previous audits.* |
| *Human resource policies and practices* | | | |
| 1. | Do existing personnel policies and procedures result in the recruitment or development of competent and trustworthy people needed to support an effective internal control structure? | Yes | Formal job descriptions are provided for all positions. |

FIGURE 15.2 *(continued)*

| Question | | Yes, No, N/A | Comments |
|---|---|---|---|
| 2. | Do personnel understand the duties and procedures applicable to their jobs? | Yes | |
| 3. | Is the turnover of personnel in key positions at an acceptable level? | * Yes | Normal 'turnover'. |

FIGURE 15.3 Excerpts from an internal control questionnaire — computer information system (CIS) general controls

| CLIENT *Allied Industries Limited*<br>Completed by: *LRG*   Date: *12/3/11* | | | BALANCE DATE *30/6/11*<br>Reviewed by: *DRS*   Date: *29/4/11* |
|---|---|---|---|
| **Internal control questionnaire component: CIS general controls** | | | |
| Question | | Yes, No, N/A | Comments |
| *Organisational controls* | | | |
| 1. Are the following duties segregated within the CIS department?<br>   (a) Systems design<br>   (b) Computer programming<br>   (c) Computer operations<br>   (d) Data entry<br>   (e) Custody of systems documentation, programs and files<br>   (f) Data control | | <br>Yes<br>Yes<br>Yes<br>Yes<br>Yes<br>Yes | <br><br><br><br><br>*Good segregation in CIS department.* |
| 2. Are the following duties performed only outside the CIS department?<br>   (a) Initiation and authorisation of transactions<br>   (b) Authorisation of changes in systems, programs and master files<br>   (c) Preparation of source documents<br>   (d) Correction of errors in source documents<br>   (e) Custody of assets | | <br>Yes<br>Yes<br>Yes<br>Yes<br>Yes | |
| *Systems development and documentation controls* | | | |
| 1. Is there adequate participation by users and internal auditors in new systems development? | | Yes | *Wide consultation.* |
| 2. Is proper authorisation, testing and documentation required for systems and program changes? | | Yes | *Strong controls in this area.* |
| 3. Is access to systems software restricted to authorised personnel? | | Yes | |
| 4. Are there adequate controls over data files (both master and transaction files) during conversion to prevent unauthorised changes? | | Yes | |
| **Access controls** | | | |
| 1. Is access to computer facilities restricted to authorised personnel? | | No | *Facilities in unlocked area of main office.* |
| 2. Does the librarian restrict access to data files and programs to authorised personnel? | | Yes | |
| 3. Are computer-processing activities reviewed by management? | | No | *More review by management needed.* |

*(continued)*

**FIGURE 15.3** *(continued)*

| Question | Yes, No, N/A | Comments |
|---|---|---|
| *Data and procedural controls* | | |
| 1. Is there a disaster contingency plan to ensure continuity of operations? | Yes | |
| 2. Is there off-site storage of backup files and programs? | Yes | |
| 3. Are sufficient generations of programs, master files and transaction files maintained to facilitate recovery and reconstruction of CIS processing? | Yes | |
| 4. Are there adequate safeguards against fire, water damage, power failure, power fluctuations, theft, loss, and intentional and unintentional destruction? | Yes | |

| CLIENT *Allied Industries Limited*<br>Completed by: *LRG*   Date: *13/3/11* | | BALANCE DATE *30/6/11*<br>Reviewed by: *DRS*   Date: *29/4/11* |
|---|---|---|
| **Internal control questionnaire component: CIS general controls** | | |
| Question | Yes, No, N/A | Comments |
| *Cash payments transactions* | | |
| 1. Is there an approved payment voucher with supporting documents for each cheque prepared? | Yes | |
| 2. Are prenumbered cheques used and accounted for? | Yes | |
| 3. Are unused cheques stored in a secure area? | Yes | *Safe in treasurer's office.* |
| 4. Are only authorised personnel permitted to sign cheques? | Yes | *Only treasurer and assistant treasurer can sign.* |
| 5. Do cheque signers verify agreement of details of cheque and payment voucher before signing? | Yes | |
| 6. Are vouchers and supporting documents cancelled after payment? | Yes | *Vouchers and all supporting documents are stamped 'Paid'.* |
| 7. Is there segregation of duties for:<br>(a) approving payment vouchers and signing cheques?<br>(b) signing cheques and recording cheques? | Yes<br>Yes | |
| 8. Are there periodic independent reconciliations of cheque accounts? | Yes | *Performed by assistant controller.* |
| 9. Is there an independent check of agreement of daily summary of cheques issued with entry to cash payments? | No | *Comparison is now made by assistant treasurer; will recommend it be made by assistant controller.* |

**FIGURE 15.4** Excerpts from an internal control questionnaire — cash payments

## Developing the audit program

The next step is to expand the scope to a more detailed audit program. This will include an estimate the number and seniority of the staff needed and the time required to complete the audit.

At this stage the auditor must assess the risks of misstatements or losses occurring. In the sales system possible risks are that a sale transaction may not be invoiced or an item may be priced incorrectly. The auditor then uses the knowledge obtained from studying the client's system and any ICQs to identify the controls in place to mitigate these risks. Controls addressing the second risk are using the inventory master file to obtain prices and requiring a supervisor to enter a code to authorise additional discounts. A useful way to record risks and controls is to create a risk–control matrix. This is a table with risks recorded in the first column and controls recorded across the matrix. Where a control is identified as addressing a particular risk a tick is placed in the cell where the risk and control intersect. In most cases the relationship between risks and controls is many-to-many; each risk is addressed by more than one control and each control addresses more than one risk. Studying the risk–control matrix may highlight areas where controls appear to be weak or non-existent and suggest that the auditor includes those areas in the schedule of items for testing.

The audit program is essentially a checklist of all the tests and other procedures that the auditor intends to carry out in order to form a judgement as to the reliability and integrity of the AIS. The auditor will form this judgement after evaluating the results of performing this test program.

The audit program will be carefully documented and retained for use in future periods, thus promoting consistency from year to year.

The audit program should include substantive tests designed to verify the integrity of each of the application systems (see page 687). In addition, it should cover all aspects of the environment in which the system operates. Environmental controls are discussed in detail on page 692.

### Master audit programs

**Master audit program (MAP)** A standardised program that has a large number of 'switches' that may be set to customise the program for the particular client system.

Most audit firms use a **master audit program (MAP)**. This is a standardised program that has a large number of 'switches' that may be set to customise the program for the particular client system; for example, the parts of the program relating to the inventory system may be deactivated if the client is a service organisation such as an educational institution. Advantages of a MAP include shortening the preparation time and reducing the likelihood of omitting significant desirable test procedures, providing guidance for less experienced audit team members and ensuring a consistent approach by the audit firm to all clients. Possible disadvantages include encouraging a 'by the book' attitude and curbing the urge to follow up on ideas outside the scope of the MAP.

**LEARNING OBJECTIVE 6**
Describe how audit fieldwork is carried out and analysed.

## FIELDWORK (PERFORMING THE AUDIT)

Fieldwork involves carrying out the tests identified in the planning stage described in the previous section, either onsite or in the auditor's own offices. All instances of test failures should be fully documented and recorded in a list of unresolved problems for later discussion with the client. Testing procedures and the use of CATTs for performing substantive tests to verify program integrity was discussed in detail in the audit tools section earlier in this chapter. It is also necessary to perform verification or confirmation testing.

### Verification or confirmation testing

Verification or confirmation testing involves performing a series of tests for the auditor to be able to satisfy themselves that the numbers in the accounts accurately represent the underlying reality. This method will include such tests as, for inventory for example, obtaining assurance that the inventory recorded in the computer system physically exists and is properly valued. To do this, the auditor will carry out both an observation of the company's stocktake procedures and a physical inspection of a sample of inventory items to confirm that there are in fact $X$ units of product $Y$ in stock, and the unit value recorded of $Z$ is appropriate. Testing receivables will involve confirming that, for each receivable recorded in the computer system, the listed customer $A$ exists and that the amount claimed is indeed owed by $A$ to the client. This test may entail, where possible, looking at external evidence that customer $A$ (1) ordered the items claimed to be supplied, and (2) received them. Such evidence may be in the form of a purchase order and a delivery docket each signed by or on behalf of $A$. It is also important to verify that the sales transaction is recorded in the correct accounting period as many frauds involve booking up sales at the end of an accounting period to either increase revenue (and hence profits) in line with market expectations, or to maximise bonuses and commission payments to dishonest employees. Such sales may either be genuine sales but taking place in a future period, or nonexistent transactions reversed in the new financial year. One test may involve looking for an abnormal number of credits issued in the first month of a financial year.

Testing payables will also incorporate procedures to ensure that all liabilities of the client have been taken up in the accounts. The 'cut-off' procedure at the end of the financial year must be designed to ensure that all invoices received in the first few weeks of a new year, but pertaining to transactions incurred in the previous year, are properly recorded. It may also be necessary to adjust inventory records where a vendor despatched and invoiced goods in the 'old' year but they were in transit at year-end and received in the 'new' year. Again, management seeking to inflate profits may postpone recording vendor invoices until the new year. Expense items are more likely to be subject to this fraud than physical inventory as there may be no record of services having been performed by suppliers. One test may include looking for abnormally high expenses in the first month of a financial year.

Again, instances of verification failures should be fully documented and recorded in the list of unresolved problems.

The selection of items for testing was discussed in the generalised audit software section earlier in this chapter.

Fieldwork also always involves spending time at the client's site, observing procedures and conducting interviews with managers and staff at all levels involved in the AIS. As part of the process the auditor will make copies of input documents and printouts created by the system under review.

## Analysis

Analysis involves a careful study of the test outcomes, the interview notes and the documentation accrued from fieldwork. While fieldwork and analysis are depicted as two sequential steps they are often iterative; insights gained from analysis may demonstrate a need for further fieldwork. An important analysis process is evaluating the system's internal control.

### *Evaluating the system's internal control*

We described internal controls in chapters 7 and 8. The evaluation activities may be divided into three broad areas: an assessment of the client's overall control environment; are the controls appropriate and adequate for the system under review; and are the controls working as intended? This final question is important, as in many cases controls may not be working as intended. For example, a segregation of duties control may have been implemented in a small business where clerk $A$ enters customer receipts into the computer system and prepares the banking, and clerk $B$ performs the bank reconciliation. On the face of it, this control gives reasonable assurance that a theft of cash by $A$ would be detected by $B$. However, this control is circumvented by $A$ and $B$ agreeing between themselves, either innocently or fraudulently, that $A$ will do both tasks.

In studying the system, the auditor will have learned of the internal controls designed into the system. The next stage is to test that they are in fact operating as intended. Internal controls can be subdivided into management controls and programmed application controls. Assume that the sales system has a management control over credit granting policy requiring that all decisions are documented in writing and that sets the authorisation limit, and also has an application control that is designed to prevent any sale being processed which would take the customer over limit.

The management control states that a new customer may be granted credit up to $2000 by a credit department clerk on receiving a 'no known problems' report from an external credit bureau. Higher credit limits require two written references in addition to the external credit check, and the application must also be countersigned by the credit manager.

The management control may be tested by inspecting the documentation for a random sample of new customers and ensuring that all the specified documents and required signatures are in place. The programmed application control may be tested by obtaining a list of customer balances and credit limits. If the policy is enforced there will be no over-limit customers.

Application control may be divided into the following five categories:
- data entry and input controls
- processing controls
- output controls
- database controls
- e-commerce controls.

We will examine each of these categories in turn.

### Data entry and input controls

Data entry and input controls are in place to ensure that all data captured is correct, complete, entered only once and properly authorised by staff designated able to do so. Audit checks for the last item (authorisation) may involve inspecting a sample of documents for authorisation signatures. The traditional input control was batch verification. Given that most twenty-first century systems are real-time systems, batch control has little application. However, where it is applicable — for example, treating a bank deposit total of cheques or direct credit payments received as a batch and reconciling the deposit total to the total input — batch control is a useful control.

Data entry controls include verification against master files: when a data entry operator keys in a customer number or product number, the customer or inventory details are displayed. The clerk can check that the correct items are selected, and otherwise back-up a step if an incorrect customer or product was selected. An error message will be displayed if there is no record with that number.

Limit or reasonableness checks are programmed checks that may detect errors where the number is almost certainly wrong. For example, in a single transaction a delicatessen may sell 500 g of ham but is highly unlikely to sell 500 kg, and a factory worker may be paid $20 an hour but is unlikely to be paid $2000.

Check digits are a control where a calculation is performed on some digits; the result is another digit. For example, the first five digits of a six-digit number are multiplied by various predetermined numbers, the results are added, the sum is then divided by 11 and the remainder should equal the sixth digit. This is a useful control when entering long numbers not originating from the organisation entering them; for example, bank account numbers and tax file numbers both incorporate check digits. Check digits will detect 99 per cent of errors such as digit transposition. The check digit algorithm is made known to software developers, so that they can incorporate it in their software. As a result, attempts to enter an invalid bank account number into a banking system or tax file number into a payroll system will generate an error message.

Sequence numbers can also be used: if every transaction is allocated a sequence number on input, then a sequence check can be run after processing and any missing transactions identified and investigated.

### Processing controls

Processing controls are in place to ensure that transactions are processed completely and accurately. The main processing control technique is the use of run-to-run controls. These are to ensure that correct versions of master files are updated, and for every record updated (both at record level and master file total level) the previous balance *plus* current transaction *equals* new balance.

### Output controls

Output controls are in place to ensure that outputs are produced completely and accurately and distributed to the appropriate recipients in a timely manner. If there are no input errors and the system is processing transactions correctly, then there should be no output errors. That said, in any system involving fallible humans, errors occur and some of these may be detected by physical inspection of the output.

Other significant controls include maintaining security over pre-printed cheque forms and the like, ensuring that all outputs are delivered to users in a timely fashion, and that appropriate confidentiality is kept over sensitive items, including shredding or other secure disposal of any additional copies of sensitive material. Refer also to the discussion of output controls in chapter 8.

### E-commerce controls

E-commerce controls are in place to ensure all e-commerce activities have effective internal controls. Given the complexity of the systems involved, the rate of change in technology, the prevalence of 'hacking' and the widely publicised concerns over internet security this is an area that requires more coverage than is possible in a general-purpose textbook. As a minimum, the system should have a reliable and available security system, require authentication of transactions, provide for the secure transmission of credit card data, provide a safe secure environment for the transfer of cash to and from the entity, and maintain adequate evidence of transactions. Because there are significant risks in allowing unknown persons access to an organisation's computer system via its website, all possible precautions should be taken. To minimise the risks, a company selling goods or services over the internet should, in conjunction with its bank, set up a secure website page for the transmission of credit card data direct to the bank. The online sales system should pass the customer to that page when the customer clicks the 'Order' button. The bank will return the customer back to the sales system along with an approval number after it has received the credit card data and verified that the card is valid and the transaction is accepted. The client should not under any circumstances store customer credit card data on its own website as it could be liable if it negligently allowed the data to be stolen by third parties.

To endeavour to ensure that customers are who they declare themselves to be, the company can require that new customers fill in a customer registration page, and the registration process emails the customer, who then has to reply to finalise the registration. Additional security can be added by requiring the customer to use a traceable email account and excluding customers using free email addresses from providers such as hotmail.com or yahoo.com.

General internet environmental controls are listed in the section on environmental controls later in this chapter.

## Application-specific internal control summary

Deciding whether the controls are appropriate and adequate for the system under review is a matter for auditor skill and judgement. Testing that they are working as intended can be verified using test data. Only after evaluating the effectiveness of the internal controls will the auditor be in a position to apply skill and judgement in determining the nature, level and number of substantive tests needed to satisfy him- or herself that the system is performing satisfactorily.

AIS Focus 15.3 examines some of the internal control issues confronting the banking technology industry.

**AIS FOCUS 15.3**

## Securing the future of IT

*Regulation and privacy-conscious consumers up the security ante for banks*

Perhaps nowhere in the banking technology space is change occurring more rapidly than in the area of information security.

### Identity and access management

Identity and access management (IAM) is becoming increasingly important, particularly within the banking industry because of regulatory compliance requirements. Sarbanes–Oxley has led many organisations to deploy IAM to allow better accountability and control over their financial systems. They also have looked to these solutions to centralise management and reporting, and provide more-consistent access control to systems and applications across the enterprise.

### Security comes out of the shadows

No longer are product managers of online banking services concerned that raising security as an issue will dampen acceptance of the electronic channel. An increasingly security-aware user community, highly publicised incidents of disclosure of personal information and regulatory pressure have combined to catalyse a fundamental change — users are comforted by well-integrated security measures.

### Standards-based security assessments

Today, many organisations are interested in demonstrating due diligence in the security realm. Instead of one-time exhaustive testing, they embrace ongoing, periodic independent assessments and audits that are standards-based ...

### Tech to watch: SOA

The promise of reduced development costs and faster time to market through code reuse makes deployment of service-oriented architecture (SOA) technology inevitable in the banking industry. Securing SOA environments is going to be a long-term challenge, and it is important to create a governance structure up front. There are big issues that need to be resolved, including data confidentiality when data is communicated among services and stored within a service, how services authenticate one another, and whether it is important to track various services' changes to transactions as they flow through a system that has no defined beginning or end.[23]

## Evaluating the system's general infrastructure controls

### Logical access controls

An audit program should involve testing access controls: Are passwords required for all logins? Are these sufficiently complex? Are they changed periodically? Are users logged out automatically after (say) 30 minutes inactivity? Are user IDs locked after (say) three unsuccessful logon attempts? Is an access control log maintained and if so is it examined regularly? In reviewing access control logs, items of interest may include unsuccessful attempts to gain access to areas of the system that a user was not authorised to access or repeated unsuccessful logon attempts. Does the system extract and report separately suspicious events promptly, for example attempts to break password or logons outside normal hours? Is the list of these events promptly reviewed and appropriate follow-up initiated? Are terminated employees' accounts disabled promptly?

### Database controls

Database controls could take the form of access controls when the database administrator grants users access to various files. Restricting access to those who need it to perform their work is an important part of enabling adequate segregation of duties. As the database administrator has access to the entire system he or she should not carry out any transaction processing. As part of the audit trail are database administrator activities recorded in a log file? If so, is that file regularly reviewed by an independent third party?

Performing regular file dumps and setting up checkpoints to enable data recovery in the event of a system crash are essential controls.

Ensuring that there is an adequate audit trail is essential. An audit trail should contain, for every transaction processed, the date and time, details of the transaction and the before and after images of records updated, as well as the user ID of the person entering the transaction and the work station ID of the terminal used.

If the transaction is initiated over the internet then the URL of the other party should be recorded.

### Physical environmental controls

There are a number of issues about which the auditor should seek to obtain management assurances. These include:

- Is the physical environment secure? Risks include theft, vandalism, sabotage.
- Is there an adequate fire prevention/detection/extinguishing system in place?
- Are there all possible actions to prevent flood damage in place?
- Is there an adequate air conditioning to protect equipment at all times?
- Is there an adequate uninterruptible power supply (UPS) to permit 'graceful degradation' of the system? (i.e. completing processing and saving of all current transactions, and setting up checkpoints to facilitate restoration of data).

The auditor should also review contingency plans: does the client have an adequate, regularly updated disaster recovery plan? Does this include insurance cover at current replacement cost? Are the actions proposed in this plan tested regularly?

Environmental controls should also ensure adequate backup procedures are in place, including off-site storage of backups of critical data. The auditor should also ask whether the capability of restoring the system from backup files is tested regularly.

Other questions the auditor should ask include:

- Is all software properly licensed?
- Are appropriate information system security policies, procedures and equipment in place? This measure is particularly important if the client conducts business over

the internet. These controls should include, but are not limited to, current anti-virus software, encryption, physical and logical firewalls, invasion detection software, protection against denial-of-service attacks and so on.

### Storage controls

Control over storage media has two aims, to ensure that stored data is kept safe from accidental or deliberate destruction, and to prevent unauthorised disclosure of data, particularly when it is of a private or confidential nature. Controls include restricting access to data as discussed in the logical access controls subsection, and controls to ensure that all discarded storage media are erased before disposal.

Questions should also be asked concerning portable equipment: are there adequate physical security controls over hardware, particularly laptops? If sensitive data is stored or used on laptop hard drives, is it encrypted to avoid misuse of the data should the laptop be lost or stolen? (This is not a trivial issue; the New Zealand Inland Revenue Department recently revealed that it had 'lost' more than 100 laptops over a period of one year, and concerns have been raised that these may contain sensitive taxpayer data, although the department claims that this is not the case.[24] Similar concerns apply to USB memory sticks, which are more frequently carried around and are easier to mislay than laptops. A UK police officer in the West Midlands is recently reported to have lost an unencrypted memory stick containing top-secret information on terror suspects.[25]

### Change controls

The nature of computing is that changes occur often. Changes may be planned, for example implementing an updated version of a software product, or unplanned, for example responding to a crisis situation when a program has crashed. The auditor should ensure that there are proper protocols for making changes (even in emergency situations). These include authorisation, documentation, ensuring that security is not compromised and whenever possible leaving an escape route where a change can be wound back to revert to the pre-change state if unforeseen problems occur.

**LEARNING OBJECTIVE** **7**

*Describe the process of completion, review, monitoring and reporting.*

## COMPLETION, REVIEW, MONITORING AND REPORTING

On completion of the audit, the auditors are required to complete a review process, usually undertaken by senior supervisors, and to attest to the accuracy of the data audited in a reporting procedure. These tasks are discussed further in the following sections.

### Analytical review

*__Analytical review__ A process that involves analysing transactions in a database and identifying relationships.*

Auditors will normally wish to perform an **analytical review**. This is a process involving analysing transactions in a database and identifying relationships. These relationships may be within the same client database for the current year, or the same client in earlier time periods, or comparing this client with industry norms. Having identified what is 'normal', the auditor may then examine, for example, the database of sales transactions and look for items that do not conform to the general trend. If the client company has a normal gross profit rate of 20 per cent of sales, then transactions with a gross profit rate of less than 10 per cent could be regarded as exceptional and pulled out for investigation. Of course, adequate explanations may be forthcoming: they could have been loss leaders, discounted during sales, or damaged or obsolete stock, but equally they could have been mispriced accidentally or deliberately as part of a fraud scheme. The analytical review is designed to highlight any transactions that may be unusual, based on more over-arching cross-transactional criteria than previously used in the testing procedures.

## Completion and review

Where the AIS audit forms part of the normal external audit, the completion procedures and the reporting process described in the following section are part of the wider audit completion process, and are an adaptation of the process described here. These processes can be divided into two sections: those involving the client and those internal to the auditors.

The list of unresolved problems generated by the testing program will usually be worked through with the client: some may turn out to be trivial and possibly a consequence of auditors not appreciating what was being done in the system, and others may be minor and included for subsequent action in a management letter written at the conclusion of the audit. Some may be major and of sufficient magnitude to impact on the auditor's overall conclusions about the integrity of the AIS processes.

Because of the hierarchical nature of audit teams, the internal part of the completion process is usually a review of work done by team members, carried out by their immediate supervisor. Thus, senior auditors review the work of their juniors; managers review seniors; and the partner in charge reviews managers. These reviews are designed to demonstrate that all the tasks as set out in the audit program have been completed with an appropriate level of professional care and skill, that all items on the list of unresolved problems have been dealt with as far as possible, and that the results of all audit activities have been fully documented and any judgements (particularly adverse findings) can be fully justified.

## Monitoring, reviewing and closure

This phase includes ensuring that any dummy data created during the audit is removed from the client's active system and that all the audit files are properly closed. It also includes preparing detailed notes ready for the next audit. The reviewing activities largely comprise ensuring that management have, in fact, made the changes to the system that they had earlier promised to do. The monitoring activities ensure that the changes are in place and working as designed.

## Reporting

The last step in the review process is to report to those to whom the terms of engagement have specified. In the case of the external audit, the report is nominally addressed to the shareholders but is, in practice, presented first to the directors. The auditor is required to state whether or not, in their opinion, the accounts give a **true and fair view** of the company's activities for the period under review, and whether or not the accounts have been prepared in accordance with **generally accepted accounting principles (GAAP)**. In any other case, this report will typically be submitted to either the board of directors or its audit committee. Presumably, such a report will be commissioned with a view to finding and correcting any weaknesses, particularly those actually giving rise to material misstatements and errors, or with the potential to do so. Therefore, the report should be prepared at a level of detail to enable appropriate corrective action to be taken. In either case, the report will normally go through several revisions before final submission, particularly if the findings are adverse or the recommended future changes to procedures are considered by the client to be unduly onerous. There may be a need for judgement to be exercised to negotiate a compromise between what should be included in the auditor's view and what is acceptable to and likely to be acted on by the client. In addition to the formal audit report, the auditor normally also prepares a management letter detailing errors requiring adjustment found in the course of the audit and required improvements to controls. These items may be addressed progressively during the audit process and the final report may be issued contingent on management undertaking to rectify the situation.

**LEARNING OBJECTIVE 8**
*Describe other types of AIS audits.*

# OTHER TYPES OF AIS AUDITS

Other types of AIS audits include IT governance audits, audits of systems under development and special purpose audits. Each of these is discussed briefly below.

## IT governance audit

We discussed IT governance in detail in chapter 7. We drew particular attention to five specific areas that need to be considered by those with responsibility for managing IT. These are:

1. adding value
2. managing risk
3. matching IT to strategy
4. measuring performance
5. managing resources.

While governance is ultimately the responsibility of the board, in operational terms most of these tasks are normally delegated to 'information security managers who develop, implement and operate information security control systems for ICT governance. IT auditors review ICT governance/control systems in order to ascertain whether risks (including information security risks) are minimised. These may sound similar but are fundamentally different roles: information security managers have executive responsibilities for securing the organisation's information assets against hackers, malware and other threats while auditors review, advise, report and persuade. The common ground is minimisation of risks'.[26] The underlying reason for an IT governance audit is for the board to obtain an independent expert opinion as to how well (or otherwise) they are doing in carrying out the above list of tasks, where they are falling short, and constructive advice as to how to remedy the problems.

## Audit of systems under development

A strong case can be made for auditors to be involved in the design and development of new systems. The auditor will need to be assured that all possible risks arising from the use of the new system have been identified, and that appropriate controls will be included to mitigate these risks. It is critical that controls are incorporated in the design phase, at which stage the cost of their inclusion is minimal compared with the costs involved in subsequently modifying the system when it is operating. In addition, there may be large but unquantifiable costs resulting from exposure to the risks posed by missing controls. The auditor will also either be involved in testing the new system, or at the very least be required to review the test plans to ensure that all possible risk factors are included and tested for, and also to review test results to confirm that all controls are in place and working as intended.

In addition, auditors may be appointed by senior management to audit the entire project development, to provide management with an independent opinion of the project progress in contrast to the possibly 'rose-tinted' views of project team leadership. Such an audit will involve most or all of:

- ensuring that the project and its funding have been approved by senior management, and that management are committed to and supportive of the project
- ensuring that the project team's leaders are qualified to undertake the implementation of the project
- reviewing user requirements documentation, and being assured that the projected system will meet these requirements
- monitoring actual progress against projected completion dates for milestones
- monitoring project expenditures against budget, and seeking explanations for significant overspending
- reviewing documentation and verifying that all required documents, including user manuals have been prepared and are kept current as the system is modified during development
- ensuring that all necessary approvals have been granted.

## Special purpose audits

Special purpose audits may be commissioned by management to:

- investigate proven or suspected fraud by employees or others (e.g. customers or vendors) with access to the client's system
- investigate intrusion (hacking) into a system. Attempted intrusion may be to introduce viruses or Trojan horses, sabotage the system or steal data
- obtain an independent opinion of the system's possible vulnerability to such events.

In such cases there is no uniform approach; the auditor's approach will be dictated firstly by the terms of the engagement and secondly by the particular circumstances of the client. Required skill sets will include a strong knowledge of IT generally and IT security specifically, particularly relating to the type of system(s) used by the client. Additional skills needed may vary from those of a fraud squad detective to a criminal hacker.

## › › SUMMARY › › ›

**1** *What is a financial (statutory) audit?*
A financial (statutory) audit is an independent examination and evaluation of the financial statements and the system(s) used to prepare these statements. Ultimately, in the case of a public company, the report is addressed to the shareholders, but, in practice, it is originally presented to the board of directors via the audit committee. An audit of the AIS is a vital component of the statutory audit required by law.

**2** *What is the influence on the auditor of auditing standards and best practice?*
Auditors have a professional obligation to comply with auditing standards issued by their professional body. They also aim to comply with what is generally regarded as best practice.

**3** *What is an information systems audit?*
An information systems audit is undertaken to assure management that a system has adequate internal controls working effectively. Typically the report is addressed to the chief executive.

**LEARNING OBJECTIVE**
### What are the internal control frameworks and computer auditing tools and techniques (CATTs) available to an auditor?

The COSO and COBIT frameworks are more applicable to management in implementing internal controls, but, where available, the auditor can evaluate the controls in place against these frameworks. Computer auditing tools and techniques (CATTs) include the use of test data, the use of an integrated test facility, the use of embedded audit software and the use of generalised audit software.

**LEARNING OBJECTIVE**
### What are the steps to be taken planning the audit?

Planning includes all of the preparatory steps taken in advance of performing fieldwork (including detailed testing). It includes studying the client's entire business and the industry in which it operates, and studying the client's accounting system and each of its subsystems.

**LEARNING OBJECTIVE**
### How is audit fieldwork carried out and analysed?

Fieldwork includes observing the system operating, interviewing a range of client staff and detailed testing of the system. The evaluation activities may be divided into three broad areas: an assessment of the client's overall control environment, deciding whether the controls are appropriate and adequate for the system under review, and confirming that the controls are working as intended. A series of testing procedures assists in this assessment.

**LEARNING OBJECTIVE**
### What is the process of completion, review, monitoring and reporting?

The most significant activity is reporting to the client, including any suggestions for modification to the system that the auditor considers desirable. Monitoring is checking that any actions that the client has promised to perform have, in fact, been completed. Reviewing comprises closing down the audit and preparing for the next one.

**LEARNING OBJECTIVE**
### What are other types of AIS audits?

Other types of AIS audits include IT governance audits, audits of systems under development and special purpose audits.

## KEY TERMS

analytical review, p. 693
attest service, p. 669
audit, p. 668
audit trail, p. 675
Auditing and Assurance Standards Board (AUASB), p. 670
Australian Auditing Standards (ASAs), p. 671
embedded audit software, p. 680
examination, p. 668
CATTs, p. 678
generalised audit software, p. 680
generally accepted accounting principles (GAAP), p. 694

independent, p. 668
inherent risk, p. 683
integrated test facility (ITF), p. 680
internal control questionnaire (ICQ), p. 684
International Accounting and Assurance Standards Board (IAASB), p. 671
master audit program (MAP), p. 687
Sarbanes–Oxley Act, p. 670
systems control and review file (SCARF), p. 680
test data, p. 679
test deck, p. 679
true and fair view, p. 694

## DISCUSSION QUESTIONS

15.1 Explain how an accounting information systems audit is related to the statutory audit required of a publicly listed company. (LO1)

15.2 What is 'best practice'? With reference to an accounting information systems audit, why do auditors aim to comply with best practice? (LO2)

15.3 'Neither Australia nor New Zealand is subject to US legislation, so the Sarbanes–Oxley Act does not concern us.' Discuss this comment. (LO2)

15.4 The Sarbanes–Oxley Act requires the appointment of an audit committee. Who does this comprise and what is its function? (LO2)

15.5 List and briefly describe the steps required to perform an information systems audit. (LO3)

15.6 Why do auditors use generalised audit software? (LO4)

15.7 Explain why it is no longer always possible to follow an audit trail in a sales system processing transactions online in real time. (LO4)

15.8 Explain the use of an integrated test facility (ITF). (LO4)

15.9 Airline and hotel pricing practices are discussed in the chapter (page 683). What other unique industry-specific accounting practices are you aware of? (LO5)

15.10 Why do auditors concern themselves with the attitudes of senior management? (LO5)

15.11 What do you consider to be the principal advantage of using an internal control questionnaire? (LO5)

15.12 Explain the use of a systems control and review file (SCARF). (LO5)

15.13 Why is check digit verification a more useful control when the number does not originate from the organisation entering it, than it is for locally generated numbers? (LO6)

15.14 Why is control strengthened if the database administrator is not allowed to perform any transaction processing? (LO6)

15.15 If there are no problems with the system, why should staff spend time and effort restoring the system from backup files? (LO6)

15.16 Why is it more desirable to run test data through the 'live' system than the 'dead' system? (LO6)

15.17 What is the prime purpose of maintaining a list of unresolved problems during the testing phase of an audit? (LO6)

15.18 Explain why many accounting firms use a 'master audit program'. (LO5)

15.19 During fieldwork auditors conduct interviews with client staff at many levels. Why do they not simply interview the person in charge of the relevant section? (LO6)

15.20 Why is there often tension between the auditor and the client over what is to be included in the final report and accompanying management letter? (LO7)

15.21 Explain why it is necessary for the auditor to conduct post-audit monitoring. (LO7)

15.22 List and briefly describe the other types of AIS audits discussed in the chapter. (LO8)

## SELF-TEST ACTIVITIES

15.1 Which of the following is *not* an advantage of using a master audit program?

   (a) It will typically shorten the audit program preparation time.

   (b) It will curb the urge to follow up on ideas outside the scope of the MAP.

   (c) It will provide guidance for less-experienced audit team members.

   (d) It will lessen the likelihood of omitting significant desirable test procedures.

15.2 Which of the following is *not* a feature of using a generalised audit software package?
   (a) It can be used to produce reports in any required format.
   (b) It can be used to generate a random sample of records using statistical techniques.
   (c) It must be run on a copy of the production database.
   (d) It may incorporate artificial intelligence and expert systems characteristics.

15.3 Which of the following is *not* likely to increase the inherent risk?
   (a) Directors and senior management inexperience
   (b) Worsening general economic conditions
   (c) Improving foreign exchange rates
   (d) External pressures arising from market expectations

15.4 In a company with fewer than 200 employees, client personnel procedures require that for all new employees earning over $60 000 per annum the new employee authorisation form is approved by the personnel manager in writing. As an auditor, how would you test the operation of this control?
   (a) Inspecting the new employee authorisation forms for all of those employees
   (b) Interviewing the personnel manager
   (c) Obtaining from the computer system a printout of all new employees and inspecting it
   (d) Inspecting the new employee authorisation forms for a sample of those employees

15.5 Which of the following are classed as application controls?
   (a) e-Commerce controls
   (b) Processing controls
   (c) Database controls
   (d) All of the above are classed as application controls.

15.6 Which of the following is *not* an access control?
   (a) Disabling terminated employees' accounts promptly
   (b) Storing backup files off-site
   (c) Logging inactive users out automatically
   (d) Reviewing the access control log

15.7 Which of the following is *not* a test to detect schemes to fraudulently increase profit?
   (a) Looking for an abnormal number of credits issued in the last month of a financial year
   (b) Over-valuing or double-counting inventory
   (c) Checking for vendor invoices covering transactions occurring in the 'old year' not brought to account until the 'new year'
   (d) Failing to write off inventory which has been discarded, stolen or scrapped

15.8 An analytical review may involve identifying relationships:
   (a) by comparing this client's data for the current year with industry norms.
   (b) within the same client database for the current year.
   (c) by comparing this client's data for the current year with this client's data in prior time periods.
   (d) all of the above.

15.9 Sarbanes–Oxley Act requirements include:
   (a) a prohibition on the audit firm carrying out non-audit services.
   (b) mandatory rotation of lead audit partners.
   (c) an internal control report including a statement of management's responsibility for establishing and maintaining adequate internal control.
   (d) all of the above.

## PROBLEMS

**15.1** The chapter gives a list of possible questions that might be found in an internal control questionnaire (ICQ) for a retail cash sales process. Prepare a list of the ten most important questions that you would expect to find in an ICQ for the:

(a) credit sales process

(b) inventory acquisition process

(c) payroll process (assume that the client makes all deductions required by law in the country and state or territory in which your institution is located and also makes voluntary superannuation deductions for employees desiring this).

**15.2** Traditionally, auditors followed a paper 'audit trail' from source documents to final accounts and vice versa. With the advent of computerised business systems, auditors modified their approach to 'audit around the computer' by comparing source documents before processing with output reports after processing, and treating the computer as a mysterious 'black box' in the middle. In the twenty-first century this approach is no longer possible. In many cases there are no source documents, and data and files are only available in machine-readable form and not on paper documents.

Explain, with reference to the revenue cycle, how auditors have adapted the audit process to use the computer as an aid in performing an audit.

**15.3** The Blue Chip Bank is a major trading bank with branches and ATMs throughout Australia and New Zealand. Blue Chip issues its customers debit cards, termed BlueCards, for them to use in ATMs and for EFTPOS transactions.

Within Blue Chip's credit card department there is a card control subunit that deals with a range of problems. These include:

- reviewing ATM transaction logs and identifying and investigating potentially suspicious transactions
- handling cards returned by postal services marked 'Gone No Address'
- resetting PINs for customers with poor memories.

The bank automatically mails out new cards to customers every two years. The returned card process involves making every possible attempt to contact the customer, using mobile phone numbers, employers and so on. If these prove ineffective and the account is not in current use, it is declared 'dormant' and deactivated.

Michael Brook, the head of the card control subunit, was recently arrested and charged with fraud. Brook found a returned card for which he was unable to locate the customer. The account was not in current use but had a large balance, so he reset the PIN, increased the daily withdrawal limit from the default $400 to the maximum of $2000 and used the card at ATMs to withdraw all the cash from the account. Brook's fraud was not discovered by the bank or its auditors but was reported by his wife, incensed on discovering that he was spending the stolen money on other women.

As the new head of internal audit for Blue Chip Bank, identify the control weaknesses that Brook exploited and explain the changes in procedure that you recommend to prevent a repetition.

**15.4** You are a member of the team of a 'Big 4' audit firm that is auditing Boomerang, a retail clothing chain with stores in major shopping malls throughout Australia and New Zealand. You have been assigned the task of testing the supplier invoice data entry and approval process for non-inventory items. Details of the system are:

- All accounting is done at the group head office and suppliers are instructed to mail their invoices there directly.

- Orders for non-inventory items are issued by store staff. The person ordering enters the first three letters of the vendor name. The system displays a list of all vendors starting with those letters, together with their corresponding short codes, and the person ordering selects the required vendor.
- Required order details are entered as shown in the table below:
  The system carries out the following edit checks.
  - Vendor short code corresponds to existing vendor (existence check)
  - Quantity and unit price numeric (format check)
  - Total purchase order value < $500 (limit check)
  - There are uncommitted funds in budget for selected expense code (authorisation check)
- Orders are automatically added to the open order file at group head office.
- When the items are received the store updates the order file to set the received status to Yes.
- The system also provides for standing orders for regular transactions. These are automatically generated each month and the received status is not checked for these.
- When entering a vendor invoice the accounts payable clerk selects the vendor as previously described.
- The system displays all outstanding orders for that vendor. The clerk selects the required order. The system displays all order details on file as shown in the table below, except for Unit Price and Received fields.
- The clerk enters the following data from the invoice: invoice date, invoice number, due date and unit price (for each item). The system checks the price entered against the file price. If the price entered is less than the file price, or exceeds the file price by 5 per cent or less, the system updates the file price. If it exceeds the file price by more than 5 per cent, the system routes the transaction to the purchasing manager who must enter an override code before the transaction will be accepted into the system.
- For normal invoices, if the received status is not Yes, the transaction will be rejected. The clerk will have to contact the store and if necessary the store will update the order file.
- The system calculates and displays the invoice price, including GST and any other applicable taxes. The clerk checks the invoice total against the calculated total. If these differ the clerk has to investigate the difference, otherwise the clerk accepts the transaction, which authorises the system to pay the vendor on the due date.

**Required**

Make up test data for 10 simulated orders that a branch may make and 10 simulated vendor invoices to test that the system is acting correctly as described, using the data in the tables below and opposite.

**Vendor table**

| Vendor code | Vendor name |
| --- | --- |
| COF305 | Coffee Supplies |
| CON249 | Consolidated Plastics |
| CON077 | Control Systems |
| CON021 | Convergent Technology |

**Store table**

| Code | Store |
| --- | --- |
| 1038 | Cairns |
| 2013 | Canberra |
| 3067 | Carnegie |
| 5790 | Chatswood |
| 6702 | Christchurch |
| 4690 | Coolangatta |

**General ledger codes table**

| GL code | Expense |
| --- | --- |
| 7893 | Plastic carrier bags |
| 7832 | Tape |
| 7822 | Tissue paper |
| 5034 | Staff refreshments |
| 5697 | Telephone rental |
| 5618 | Local call charges |
| 5847 | Security alarm monitoring |

**Purchase order file structure**

| Field | Comments |
| --- | --- |
| Order Number | System generated |
| Order Type | Values N(ormal) or S(tanding) |
| Order Date | System supplied |
| Store | System supplied |
| Quantity | Repeating group |
| Unit of Measure | e.g. dozen, 100, 1000 |
| Description | |
| Unit Price | |
| Received | Values Yes / No / NA (for standing orders) |
| Vendor Code | |
| Gl Code | |

15.5 You are a manager in the team of a 'Big 4' audit firm that is auditing Boomerang, a retail clothing chain with stores in major shopping malls throughout Australia and New Zealand. You have been assigned the responsibility for confirmation of the client's valuation of the inventory held at its distribution centre.

The structure of the client's inventory master file is:

| **Item number** |
| --- |
| Description |
| Size |
| Colour |
| Quantity on hand |
| Weighted average cost |
| Last cost |
| Vendor code |
| Economic order quantity |
| Reorder point |
| Quantity issued for year |
| Quantity purchased for year |

The client has had stock count sheets prepared in duplicate with the first four fields above filled in and a blank space for quantity on hand to be written in. Client staff are about to count the inventory and complete the stock sheets. The second copies were given to you.

**Required**

How do you plan to go about substantiating the client's inventory valuation, assuming that you have a comprehensive generalised accounting software package available?

## FURTHER READING

Cascarino, RE 2007, *Auditor's guide to information systems auditing*, John Wiley & Sons, Inc., Hoboken NJ.

Champlain, JJ 2003, *Auditing information systems*, John Wiley & Sons, Inc., Hoboken.

Gray, I & Manson, S 2005, *The audit process*, Thomson Learning, London.

Hall, JA & Singleton T 2005, *Information technology auditing and assurance,* 2nd edn, South-Western, Mason, Ohio.

Weber, R 1999, *Information systems control and audit*, Prentice Hall, New Jersey.

## SELF-TEST ANSWERS

15.1 b, 15.2 c, 15.3 c, 15.4 a, 15.5 d, 15.6 b, 15.7 a, 15.8 d, 15.9 d

## END NOTES

1. The Institute of Internal Auditors (IIA) Research Foundation 2009, *International Professional Practices Framework (IPPF),* www.theiia.org.
2. ASX Corporate Governance Council 2007, *Corporate governance principles and recommendations,* 2nd edition, Australian Securities Exchange Limited, Sydney, p. 25.
3. A list of the 500 largest companies listed on the Australian Stock Exchange measured by market capitalisation, www.http://www2.standardandpoors.com/spf/pdf/index/SP_Australian_Indices_Methodology_Web.pdf.
4. CPA Australia 2009, 'About Australian Auditing Standards', www.cpaaustralia.com.au.
5. Australian Auditing and Assurance Standards Board (AUASB) 2008, 'News', www.auasb.gov.au.

6. International Standards Organisation 2005, *ISO 27002:2005 Code of practice for information security management*, www.iso.org.
7. US Securities and Exchange Commission 2003, 'Final rule: management's reports on internal control over financial reporting and certification of disclosure in exchange act periodic reports' Release no. 33-8238, 5 June, www.sec.gov.
8. It is generally believed that the Enron auditor, Arthur Andersen, allowed the Enron audit partners and senior staff to become too close to Enron executives, compromising their independence and, in turn, leading to the issue of unqualified reports, and allowing the fraud to grow exponentially and continue for longer than may otherwise have been the case.
9. Public Company Accounting Oversight Board (PCAOB) 2009, 'Our mission', www.pcaobus.org.
10. Public Company Accounting Oversight Board (PCAOB) 2007, Auditing Standard No. 5: An audit of internal control over financial reporting that is integrated with an audit of financial statements, 27 July, p. 397.
11. PCAOB 2007, p. 397.
12. PCAOB 2007, p. 427.
13. Extracts based on Weisman, R 2007, 'Help on the way — a variety of new software can help end the feeling you're drowning in a sea of rules designed to prevent financial fraud', *The Boston Globe*, 23 April. Reproduced with permission.
14. Fra Luca Pacioli was an Italian mathematician who is widely regarded as the 'Father of Accounting'. His 1494 mathematics textbook included a detailed description of the double-entry bookkeeping system used by Venetian merchants, which is the foundation stone of all modern accounting systems.
15. Committee of Sponsoring Organisations (COSO) 2009, *Guidance on monitoring internal control systems*, www.coso.org, p. 2.
16. IT Governance Institute 2007, COBIT 4.1, p. 25, www.itgi.org.
17. IT Governance Institute 2007, pp. 156–7.
18. IT Governance Institute 2009, www.itgi.org.
19. Hall, JA & Singleton, T 2005, *Information technology auditing and assurance*, 2nd edn, South-Western, Mason, Ohio.
20. Benford was a physicist who observed this characteristic and tested it across a wide range of different types of data. Nigrini first applied it to accounting data.
21. Nigrini, MJ 1999, 'I've got your number', *Journal of Accountancy*, May, www.journalofaccountancy.com.
22. Leung, P, Coram, P & Cooper, BJ 2007, *Modern auditing and assurance services*, 4th edn, John Wiley & Sons, Brisbane, pp. 296–8. Reproduced with permission.
23. CMP Media LLC 2007, 'Securing the future of IT — regulation and privacy-conscious consumers up the security ante for banks'. Reproduced with permission.
24. New Zealand *TVOne News,* 19 April 2007.
25. *Daily Mail* 2008, 'Police lose memory stick with top secret terrorist information', 15 September, www.dailymail.co.uk.
26. Hinson, G 2009, 'How does IT audit fit with governance, risk management and information security?' IT audit FAQ, www.isect.com.

# 16

# Ethics, fraud and computer crime

## Learning objectives

After studying this chapter, you should be able to:

**1** describe the nature of ethics and morals

**2** describe and apply the ethical decision-making model

**3** consider some areas in which ethical problems may emerge for businesses that use accounting information systems (AIS)

**4** describe some of the different perspectives of computer crime

**5** describe the impact of fraud on Australian and New Zealand business

**6** consider potential ways to reduce the risk of computer crime.

# Introduction

This chapter introduces you to two important concepts related to the study of accounting information systems (AIS): ethics, and computer crime and fraud. Different ethical perspectives can be applied to any ethical problem. There are various methods for achieving ethical behaviour within an organisation, including providing an example from the top and the existence of some sort of professional affiliation or code of conduct.

The use of an AIS in an organisation gives rise to several ethical issues that this chapter examines, including stakeholders' rights to privacy and how the data gathered within the AIS are going to be used.

From the discussion of ethics the chapter moves on to the area of computer crime and fraud. Examples of computer crime include phishing, spam and viruses. Fraud is another potential threat to an organisation. The chapter examines some types of fraud as well as techniques an organisation can use for dealing with fraud.

**LEARNING OBJECTIVE 1**

*Describe the nature of ethics and morals.*

**Ethics** *The term given to the implicit rules that guide us in our everyday behaviour, thoughts and actions.*

# ETHICS AND MORALS

**Ethics** is the term given to the implicit rules that guide us in our everyday behaviour, thoughts and actions. Ethics concern what a person sees as being right and wrong. Of course, seldom will two people view the same ethical situation in the same way. People view things differently based on cultural background, their upbringing and life experiences, to name but three factors. As a result, when viewing an ethical dilemma, you should be conscious that your way is not necessarily the 'right' way for other people.

We all have our own personal set of ethics, initially defined during our formative years, but they may be modified by the various pressures that we face in later life. Our code of ethics will have come from a large range of influences, including our parents and wider family, our schooling, in some cases a church, and in many cases our sports coaches. From an early age sport is a major influence in the lives of most young Australians and New Zealanders. Ethical issues abound in sport since there is usually a tension between doing all that you can to ensure a win for your team and observing the rules and 'playing fair'. The cricketing practice of 'walking' is a good example. Traditionally, when cricket was an amateur sport, players observed the gentlemanly code of 'walking' — honourably admitting you were out without waiting for the umpire's decision. In fact, 50 years ago the phrase 'it's not cricket', meaning 'it's unfair', was in common use. In the professional era, this practice has largely been replaced by the attitude 'leave it to the umpire', and rationalising this attitude by a belief that while umpires do make occasional mistakes these will even out over a season, to the benefit of both teams equally. Nonetheless, some players such as former Australian vice-captain Adam Gilchrist staunchly advocate the practice of 'walking' as an ethical issue, and the matter is still the subject of heated debate whenever it surfaces in the game.

**Morals** *How a person approaches and responds to an ethical issue.*

**Morals** are how a person approaches and responds to an ethical issue. There can be a difference between what a person thinks is right and what a person actually does. The classic example is organisational whistleblowing, which is discussed later in the chapter. Most employees recognise immoral or unethical behaviour if they see it happening, but not all of them will report it.

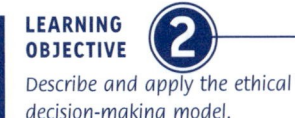
# Ethical decision making

A framework is needed in which to apply ethical principles. This section discusses the different stages of ethical decision making and how ethical perspectives can be applied to ethical decision-making scenarios. The stages to go through when making an ethical decision are:

1. Identify the facts.
2. Define the issue(s).
3. Identify the principles that can be applied.
4. Identify possible actions and the stakeholders affected by these actions.
5. Compare steps 3 and 4.
6. Select a course of action.
7. Implement the selected course of action.

## 1. What are the facts?

The first step is to identify the main facts of the case you are dealing with. This can include the identification of stakeholders who are involved in the decision, actions leading up to the decision and any other information relevant to making an informed decision.

## 2. Define the issue

Based on the facts of the case identified in step 1, what is the ethical issue you are dealing with? Note that a case could have more than one ethical issue involved.

## 3. What principles can be used to solve the issue?

Having identified the ethical issue, principles or sources of authority for solving the ethical issue must be sought. The decision maker will identify the different sources of authority and principles that are relevant to resolution of the ethical issue identified in step 2.

## 4. What are the alternative courses of action and the stakeholders affected by these actions?

The next step is to identify all the possible alternatives. At this point the best alternative is not being selected. Rather, the aim of this stage is to be aware of what possibilities exist for resolving the ethical problem. Do not be restrictive at this point: all possible courses of action should be listed. Also of interest is how the different courses of action affect the different stakeholders identified in stage 1 of the decision-making process. Therefore, each alternative needs to be evaluated from the perspective of the different stakeholders. Does the alternative produce a desirable outcome for the stakeholder? Why?

## 5. How do the principles match up with the alternative actions?

At the fifth stage, the interest lies in matching up the courses of action with the ethical principles. The fundamental question at this point is whether the alternatives are consistent with the principles identified in step 4.

## 6. Select the most appropriate action

With the alternatives to the ethical principle mapped, the best alternative needs to be selected. Is the concern the alternative that has the best course of action or that produces the best result? Will the best outcome be pursued regardless of the actions required to achieve it? Again, the answers here will depend on the ethical perspective of the individual.

### 7. Implement the decision

Having evaluated the alternatives, mapped them against ethical principles and selected the most desirable option, the chosen option now needs to be implemented. Afterwards, the person and organisation may be interested in any feedback from the decision. For example, if the decision was to restructure the production line and replace all workers with machines, was there negative feedback in the print media? Does this affect the likelihood of repeating the decision in the future?

**LEARNING OBJECTIVE 3**

*Consider some areas in which ethical problems may emerge for businesses that use accounting information systems (AIS).*

# ETHICAL ISSUES FOR BUSINESSES WITH AN AIS

Think of some of the recent events you may have experienced as a customer — for example visiting the doctor or consulting an accountant — that require you to divulge personal information. Implicit in this is the expectation that the doctor or accountant will use the information ethically (and in fact, the codes of ethics of their respective professional associations require them to maintain confidentiality). For example, you would not expect your family doctor to discuss details of your ailments and problems at the next dinner party the doctor attends. Likewise, you would expect your accountant to keep details of your financial position and wealth to themselves and not discuss it with other clients. In each of these cases there is an expectation that the professional acquiring the information from the client will use it only for the purpose for which it has been gathered. Commercial enterprises face similar ethical expectations when dealing with their customers. From an organisation's perspective, the issue of ethics is one that never disappears. As we move increasingly to an electronic business environment, the issue becomes even more prevalent.

## Customer protection and privacy

Privacy and trust are two big issues for those people and organisations that interact with an organisation. Many people place great value on their privacy. Consider, for example, the controversy when in 1986 the Australian government proposed the introduction of the 'Australia Card': a national identity card that would see each Australian allotted a unique number that would be used in all dealings. Such cards are used throughout the world for a variety of purposes including greater government efficiency, reducing social security fraud and improving border control. Their effectiveness in achieving these aims is debatable. The primary argument for the Australia Card was a reduction in tax evasion and avoidance, along with the benefit of rationalised record keeping.[1] The Australia Card proposal raised many public concerns about the individual's right to privacy. Potentially, such a system would allow a massive pooling of data about an individual. Data on the card's owner can also be stored in a smart card chip. Provisions were in place to protect the use of the data associated with each person's unique number but some questioned their effectiveness.[2] Social unease included the concern that Australia could, given the correct combination of political and social factors, become an authoritarian state with the ability to extensively track individuals. Additionally, concerns emerged that 'merged data' — the data pooled from several databases — could be misinterpreted, and that data may not be secure. The Australia Card was never introduced, the proposal being twice rejected by the Senate.

Similar issues have arisen in New Zealand, and data sharing between government agencies is restricted to specific cases where the social benefit outweighs the privacy concerns. For example, taxation and work and income data are compared to identify people fraudulently claiming an unemployment benefit while working.

Privacy issues centre on the questions of:

- What happens to my personal information once I give it to you?
- Who can access my personal information?
- How secure is my personal information?

Consider Blockbuster Video in the United States.[3] Blockbuster Video maintains an extensive database of borrowers and the videos that they hire. Profiling these data enables Blockbuster to categorise its customers based on the types of movies that they hire. This gives Blockbuster a profile of its customers that has many third-party marketers desperate for a piece of the action. Here, a set of simple transaction data can be sorted and filtered to yield insightful perspectives on customers that would be worth money to the organisation. Blockbuster customers, however, may be outraged to have their watching habits disclosed, potentially receiving unsolicited and even offensive marketing materials from unrelated companies. This is a quandary for those in the area of AIS: as technology develops, making data gathering and analysis easier and more sophisticated, the issue of what is best for the company versus what is best for the customers presents itself. This is discussed further in the section on managers.

Another example is that of Lotus Development Corporation, which planned to release a CD-ROM containing the names, addresses, demographic information and purchase behaviour of 120 million consumers.[4] The proposal caused unrest and was eventually scrapped due to privacy issues.

A final example of privacy of information can be gleaned from an incident involving Telstra, the major telecommunications provider in Australia. Some years ago, the *Herald-Sun* reported that Telstra had inadvertently published hundreds of silent (unlisted) numbers in its paper and internet-based telephone directories.[5] Outsourcing of directory production was attributed as the cause of the error. The concern surrounding this error, according to the article, centred on the fact that many professionals — for example teachers, doctors or psychiatrists — have silent home numbers for professional reasons.

An AIS captures, verifies, stores, sorts and reports data relating to an organisation's activities. Electronic AIS allow organisations to gather much more information about people than was possible in the more traditional environment. Indeed, the details of any interaction with the AIS can be captured and this information can then be used in many ways.

The person interacting with the AIS is not necessarily aware of what information is being captured or how it will be used. This raises some ethical concerns for those who design and use information systems. The organisation has both ethical and legal responsibilities to respect people's right to privacy and this affects how the organisation can capture and use information.

Consider organisations' use of websites. Businesses are increasingly turning to the internet to advertise and sell their products. E-commerce offers efficient transactions, customer convenience (the ability to shop whenever and from wherever they like) and the potential to reach to a broader marketplace. A business can also capture extensive information about visitors to its website. When users visit a website they leave behind electronic footprints, which enable the site owner to identify what site they came from, what they did while on the site and where they went after viewing the site. Based on these data, viewers can be profiled and advertising targeted to meet user interests, needs and preferences.

A second issue stemming from e-commerce is what happens to the data about consumers after they have been gathered. Organisations can undertake **data mining** and **customer profiling**, often without the user being aware of it: there is often no explicit seeking of consent to the gathering and use of the data collected. Consumer advocates see this as an invasion of privacy that can lead to a lack of trust on the part of the consumer. This lack of trust has big implications for the future development of e-commerce. Additionally, the customer profiling may not necessarily generate an accurate picture of the customer.

One company that has been particularly successful in offering products that assist organisations in monitoring and responding to usage of their websites is DoubleClick.[6] DoubleClick makes extensive use of **cookies**: small files stored on a computer's hard drive that keep a record of websites viewed, viewing preferences, user profiles and so on. Developed ostensibly to allow websites to display in the most user-friendly format, based on the operating system used, browser type and so on, cookies can also help organisations to gather data about the people that access their websites. For example, a cookie can:

- ensure the browser does not display ads the user has already seen
- ensure ads are shown in a particular sequence
- track whether a user has visited the site before
- track the previous and next sites the user visits.

This information can, for example, allow advertisers to measure the effectiveness of their ads by tracking which ones are bringing users to their website to purchase or register.[7] Through the tracking of IP addresses, as well as gathering the details of users as they log on and purchase from internet-based store interfaces, companies are able to build up relatively comprehensive profiles of a customer, including interests, purchasing patterns and viewing patterns on the internet.[8] This information can then be used to target online advertisements and banner displays that appear when the user accesses a particular page. Through these technologies, DoubleClick offers a way for organisations to target online advertising to specific customers, thus increasing the relevance of banner advertising and adding to revenue through increased sales.

It is clear that this practice raises some ethical issues, particularly privacy issues, which directly affect the customers of an organisation. If a consumer makes a purchase through an online store or accesses a website, are they aware that information is being gathered about them, and a profile being developed that could be used in future marketing efforts? If not, then is it right for the organisation to gather this information? These are very real issues for information systems professionals that extend to the AIS domain, especially as the development of electronic commerce sees the AIS playing a major role in supporting online consumer activities. The controversy surrounding DoubleClick's plan to merge its extensive customer information, gathered by cookies, with a database maintained by a marketing firm brought privacy and the use of information to the forefront of the e-commerce debate.[9] The central issues in the debate were the potential use of customer data for purposes other than those they had originally been gathered for, and the ability to profile customers based on those data. Such was the concern at one stage that class legal action was initiated against DoubleClick, alleging breaches of various American statutes. The suit was eventually dismissed.[10]

Before moving on to look at security of data, read AIS focus 16.1, which describes how microchips have been implanted in animals to allow lost animals to be tracked and returned to their owners. It even describes how people have been 'microchipped', allowing identification for entry into nightclubs, purchasing drinks and aiding in the

**Data mining** *A data analysis technique where large amounts of data are taken and analysed for potential patterns and relationships that may exist.*

**Customer profiling** *A process where data on a customer's website viewing habits are used to build a profile of their interests, needs and preferences, which can then be used for targeted advertising.*

**Cookies** *Small files stored on a computer's hard drive that keep a record of websites viewed, viewing preferences and user profiles.*

care of sufferers of diseases such as Alzheimer's. This raises some interesting issues for privacy. Microchipping allows movements to be tracked with extreme accuracy — even to the point of knowing the order aisles are walked down in the supermarket. The AIS focus article also describes 'wearable' chips. In New Zealand, short-term prisoners are required to wear a 'chipped' ankle bracelet when they are released on a home detention scheme. This practice permits authorities to monitor their presence in an approved place, normally their home or workplace. Prisoners are willing to accept this as a condition of being released from jail.

## AIS FOCUS 16.1

### Chipping away our privacy

We laughed a few years ago when an American family announced they all wanted to be microchipped.

Hey, if Rover could have a rice-grain-sized computer injected under his skin by the vet, why couldn't mum, dad and the kids?

Well, laugh no more. Chip implants seem to be catching on. And the day mightn't be far away when you'll be having yourself computerised.

Indeed the day mightn't be far away when it becomes compulsory, to help in the fight against terrorism.

America's powerful Food and Drug Administration has just approved the use of this technology in hospitals.

By implanting microchips in their patients, doctors and nurses will be able to immediately identify the patient just by running a scanner over them.

And, at the same time, they'll receive a readout of the person's recent medical history. Now, no doubt, there are great benefits in this for some people.

Sufferers of Alzheimer's disease who can't remember their names, for instance, could be scanned and identified easily if found wandering.

And the chips might also be useful for people suffering cancer, who often have to go through quite complex chemotherapy and other treatment regimes.

A chip under the skin should make it easier to keep track of their various medicines and procedures, making mix-ups less likely.

But you have to wonder how long it will be before an implanting craze spreads beyond the hospital — and what it will mean for individual privacy.

Recently, for instance, nightclubbers in Spain had chips implanted in their left arms.

Getting this hardware upgrade meant they no longer had to queue to get into the club: they just walked past a scanner at the entrance and straight to the bar. And the bionic barflies' chip implants mean they can also buy a drink in a blink.

No precious imbibing time wasted pulling out cash and waiting round for change. The bartender simply scans their chip and the drinks are automatically added to the bill.

In a more serious application, the US company that makes the implants, Applied Digital Solutions, is hoping gun owners will go for an insert in the hand.

That way personalised smart guns could be developed: weapons that would only fire if the gun's owner was the one pulling the trigger.

The system would work via a scanner in the gun interrogating the chip in the shooter's hand.

If the gun finds the wrong person is holding it, it simply doesn't fire.

Police officers and security guards could be fitted with the system.

That way, no one could steal their weapons and use them against them.

The big catch with having a chip implanted in your body is that you can't just take it out when you leave work or the nightclub.

And so you are effectively walking around with a permanent ID tag on you.

Anyone with a scanner could point it at you and identify you.

Shops fitted with scanners, for instance, could track your comings and goings, and that way work out better ways to sell you more stuff.

So far, no one has suggested kids be chipped, but a school in Japan has recently introduced a wearable, rather than implantable, version of the chip.

These allow the teachers to better keep an eye on the children and work out who is and isn't at school.

Legoland in Denmark has wearable chips too.

They say they're to prevent kids getting lost, but critics claim they're used by Lego to track the children and sell them more stuff.

But the biggest question is, will a computer chip in the arm become compulsory for all of us?

If the implants turn out to be safe, and society has begun to accept them for some purposes, having everyone chipped would certainly have benefits.

The entire population would essentially have super-ID cards implanted in them 24 hours a day.

Today it may sound like a far-fetched sci-fi plot.

But so did the idea of compulsory fingerprinting and face scanning a few years ago.

Yet, that now happens to anyone who wants to visit America — in the name of the fight against terrorism.

Compulsory chip implants would just be another step in the same direction.[11]

For businesses, information about the habits of people could prove extremely profitable. However, with this approach come the ethical issues of privacy and freedom. Your opinion on these issues will very much depend on how you perceive the threat to privacy from technology. For the customers, incidences where personal data are disclosed do the most damage to their image of a company. This can occur by accident or through unauthorised 'hacking' into the system (discussed later). Either way, it is these indirect costs related to loss of customer trust that will affect an organisation in the largest way, crippling market share and confidence.[12]

## Security

Data and the programs that maintain or use data must be kept secure. One reason, as discussed, is to respect the privacy rights of individuals. Measures need to be in place to ensure that data cannot be accessed by unauthorised personnel or copied or used for illegitimate purposes. Well-defined user access rights and user activity logs can be ways of working towards such aims.

Another aspect to consider is the protection of the quality of the data, that is, to make sure that the data are accurate. Customers generally have the right to view data that an organisation holds about them to make sure that they are correct, and to demand that any errors be corrected.

## Consent

Information about users of an AIS can be gathered:

- without the consent of the individual (though this may be illegal and/or unethical)
- with the informed consent of the individual
- with the implied consent of the individual.

There is a big difference among these three scenarios. A common concern is whether it is ethical to gather data about someone without his or her knowledge or consent. Some would say that such acts are tantamount to electronic espionage and constitute a violation of a person's basic right to privacy. Gathering information without the person's consent would appear to be prohibited under the Australian *Privacy Act 1988* (Cwlth). *Implied consent* refers to the individual consenting to the information gathering through their subsequent actions. For example, if you complete a page on a website that asks for your personal details and you click the 'next' button to proceed to the next screen, your actions imply that you agree to forward this information on to the website owner. At no stage were you asked for an express statement of consent. An express statement of consent would occur where the information is entered into the fields on the screen and then, as you click on the 'next' button, a box appears asking if you wish to proceed and informing you that if you do proceed your details will be gathered by the website owner.

There is a big difference between express and implied consent. Some may argue that by agreeing to use a website and entering information you are giving consent for that information to be gathered. Others would argue that the only form of true consent is that which is expressly obtained from the subject of the information.

## Privacy laws and standards

There are laws that govern privacy in both Australia and New Zealand. One such example is the Australian Privacy Act, which is a piece of federal legislation enacted in order to create standards for the gathering, collection and use of personal information. Section 14 of the Privacy Act outlines 11 principles of information privacy. Principle 1 states:

1. Personal information shall not be collected ... for inclusion in a record or in a generally available publication unless:
   (a) the information is collected for a purpose that is a lawful purpose directly related to a function or activity of the collector; and
   (b) the collection of the information is necessary for or directly related to that purpose.
2. Personal information shall not be collected by a collector by unlawful or unfair means.

The privacy principles are summarised in figure 16.1 overleaf.

The New Zealand *Privacy Act 1993* contains similar provisions. The principles apply to federal government agencies as well as to organisations, which are defined to include individuals, body corporates, partnerships, other unincorporated associations and trusts.[13]

Of course, consumers may waive their right to privacy. Application forms and 'conditions of offer' generally outline the conditions under which the data are collected, and who may be granted access to it. Loyalty cards, for example, where cardholders earn points that may be credited towards rewards, special offers or discounts warn potential members that their data will be used for various purposes.

| Principle | Description | Explanation |
|---|---|---|
| 1 | Collection of information | Information can only be collected in lawful ways and for lawful purposes and the information gathered must relate to the lawful purpose. |
| 2 | Solicitation | The person gathering information shall inform the subject of the purpose of the gathering of information, whether it is required by law and who the information may be legally forwarded to. |
| 3 | Solicitation | The person gathering information should gather it in a non-intrusive manner and ensure that the information is complete and up to date. |
| 4 | Storage | Information shall be stored in such a manner that it is protected from loss, damage, unauthorised access or general misuse. |
| 5 | Record keeping | Records shall be kept detailing the nature, purpose and types of personal information being stored, including storage time and access rights. |
| 6 | Access | An individual who is the subject of information records is, subject to legal limitations, allowed to view the information that is kept about them and to require that any inaccuracy be corrected. |
| 7 | Alteration | Record keepers shall ensure that personal records are kept accurate, relevant, up to date and not misleading. |
| 8 | Accuracy in use | Where information is being used, the record keeper shall ensure the information being used is accurate for that purpose. |
| 9 | Relevant use | Information that is kept shall only be used for the purpose that it was gathered. |
| 10 | Usage | Relevant use must be followed unless there are extreme grounds for not doing so, such as subject consent for non-relevant use, life-threatening circumstances, law enforcement or legal obligation. |
| 11 | Disclosure | The information shall not be disclosed to a third party unless such disclosure was made known to the subject at the time the information was solicited, the subject consented to disclosure, or grounds such as those referred to in principle 10 exist. |

**FIGURE 16.1** Information privacy principles from the *Privacy Act 1988* (Cwlth) s. 14

This warning, from FlyBuys, is typical of this kind of notification:

Personal information including your electronic addresses will be used for two primary purposes. First, it will be used to ensure the proper functioning of the FlyBuys program. Secondly, and subject to the restrictions set out in paragraph 3.3, it will be used by FlyBuys and the participating retailers for marketing, planning, product development, research, FlyBuys account administration and fraud and crime prevention and investigation.[14]

New Zealand supermarket chain Progressive Enterprises Ltd (PEL) (owner of Foodtown and Woolworths) offers similar information regarding the personal details collected in processing applications for their Onecard loyalty program:

> We may hold personal information submitted to us by you through your use of the Site. You have the right to access and correct your personal information under the Privacy Act 1993.[15]

The Internet Industry Association (IIA) is a registered company in Australia and acts as a regulatory body for organisations involved in the internet within Australia. The IIA believes that industry must adhere to ethical privacy practices to create consumer confidence and enable the long-term success of e-commerce.[16] It also supports the adoption of an information-gathering approach based on informed consent, rather than the surreptitious gathering of information about users. The IIA has set out to create standards for industry members to protect users of the internet, particularly children, bring Australian standards into line with European standards, and provide a general industry best practice when dealing with issues of electronic privacy. The code applies to IIA members, with membership of the IIA an option for businesses that provide internet services from Australia, operate an internet-related business or possess a direct or indirect interest in the internet.[17]

The IIA's privacy principles correlate quite strongly with the sections of the Privacy Act discussed previously, so the IIA code is only summarily described here (figure 16.2).[18]

| Principle | Description |
| --- | --- |
| 1 | Collection of information |
| 2 | Use of information |
| 3 | Data quality |
| 4 | Data security |
| 5 | Openness |
| 6 | Access and correction |
| 7 | Identifiers |
| 8 | Anonymity |
| 9 | Transborder data flows |
| 10 | Sensitive information |

**FIGURE 16.2** IIA code of practice privacy principles

## Access to technology

An additional issue for customers is their ability to access technology, particularly as organisations move towards the e-commerce environment. Access to computer technology can vary depending on socioeconomic conditions and geographic location. The International Telecommunications Union ranked both Australia and New Zealand in the top 20 countries in the world for internet access in 2008, at 72 and 70 users per 100 of the population.[19] These numbers are well behind Holland, the four Scandinavian countries, the United Kingdom and Korea, all of which have 80 users or more per 100 of the population. Comparable figures for broadband access in 2008 were Australia 24 and New Zealand 22 users per 100 of the population.[20] Both were in the top 30 countries but well behind those previously listed, all of which, except the United Kingdom, have 32 users or more per 100 of the population.

However, despite the wide adoption of the technology by Australian households, there are factors that still restrict access to internet technology. These factors are identified by Curtin as:[21]

- *Age*. Research indicates that young people are more likely to have internet access.
- *Family structure*. The traditional nuclear family structure of two parents and children is the most likely to have internet access, followed by couples without children and single-parent households.
- *Income*. There is a clear delineation between those with and without home internet access based on the level of income, with wealthier people more likely to have access.
- *Education*. Higher education tends to be associated with internet access.
- *Geography*. There is a consistent gap between city and country residents having access to a computer and also to the internet. Farms in particular have a lower internet access rate.

Other issues for those in rural areas include the degree of choice they have in an internet service provider, and higher costs for, and technical difficulties in, providing access. Similar problems beset rural areas in New Zealand; however, the government there has funded the connection of broadband into every rural school as outlined by the then Agriculture Minister, Jim Anderton:

> Rural and remote schools are seeing the benefits of PROJECT PROBE, one of a number of ongoing initiatives designed to encourage broadband uptake — including the subsequent Digital Strategy and Broadband Challenge. The project identified about 900 schools where high-speed internet was not available and has enabled every school in New Zealand to have access to broadband. Rather than just connecting the schools, it has brought broadband into rural communities.[22]

As businesses move towards an e-commerce environment, with 74 per cent of Australian businesses using the internet as a part of their business processes[23] and 59 per cent of users using the internet for e-commerce or banking-related activities (for example, checking account balances, transferring funds and paying bills online),[24] issues of *equitable access* and *costs* could become a concern. Curtin concludes that the internet in Australia, 'has built upon, and may exacerbate, inequalities that already exist in Australian society ... a range of social, economic and technical barriers will have to be addressed'.[25]

Clearly this access issue concerned government. In June 2007, then Communications Minister Helen Coonan announced the Australia Connected initiative, aiming to provide fast affordable broadband to 99 per cent of the population by June 2009.[26]

The change of government caused that plan to be replaced and in December that year her successor, Stephen Conroy, promised a national high-speed broadband fibre-to-the-node network serving 98 per cent of the population.[27] In April 2009, the government announced that the National Broadband Network would be built and operated by a new company to be jointly owned by the government and the private sector specifically established by the Australian Government to carry out this project, and committed to invest up to $43 billion over 8 years.[28] In July 2009, the government announced the start of the first stage of the rollout of the National Broadband Network by calling for tenders for laying fibre-optic cable in Tasmania.[29]

## Managers

Managers working with an AIS have a duty to ensure that the system is being used appropriately. They need to ensure that their systems and organisations comply with federal and state laws relating to privacy and the usage of information. This includes monitoring the creation of, access to and use and alteration of information. Managers also need to ensure compliance with internal privacy policies and practices. Top management sets the tone and example for ethical practice, which then carries through the rest of the organisation. Managers that set the example of ethical use of information and the ethical gathering of information promote similar behaviour from their colleagues. Setting an example is thus an important part of promoting ethical behaviour in the organisation.[30]

As end-user computing has placed more power in the users' hands and the use of organisation-wide databases has increased, managing AIS resources properly has become an increasingly important issue. Information systems managers in particular have responsibilities for ensuring that the data and programs within the organisation are adequately protected. Straub and Collins identify three main issues confronting managers:[31]

- the creation of workable systems that do not breach intellectual property rights (e.g. ensuring that all software is properly licensed)
- gaining information from external sources (such as external databases) without breaching copyright
- gaining and distributing information on individuals without breaching their right to privacy.

The establishment of *internal controls* can be a useful step in achieving these aims. Controls that could be relevant in meeting legislative requirements, as well as promoting the ethical use of data, include password-restricted access, user logs for sensitive information, and thorough audit trails. Internal controls were discussed in chapters 7 and 8.

Passwords are a way of restricting access to authorised users and can also prevent white-collar crime, which is discussed later in the chapter.[32] Further to having passwords in place, policies on the format and changing of passwords should exist, requiring 'strong' passwords, (i.e. having a minimum length and being a combination of upper and lower case letters, digits and symbols and not names or other dictionary words), and promoting regular changing of passwords. Logs should also be kept for unsuccessful access attempts. While some of these may be legitimate errors by authorised users, others could suggest attempts to gain unauthorised access. Such logs should be reviewed regularly by a security officer or other appropriate manager, and possible attempts to gain unauthorised access investigated. Control matrices should also be established that restrict what information different users are able to view, and logs should be maintained on who views what information. The classic example is the restriction on who can access payroll information within the organisation. Obviously, as a matter of respect to employees and their privacy, only a select group of people should be privy to this information. For obvious reasons only authorised payroll department staff should be able to change pay rates. Undetected unauthorised changes could result in an employee being overpaid for an infinite period. Unauthorised attempts to access or change payroll data should be logged and followed up, to create an audit trail and promote ethical use of confidential data.

Many organisations have also responded to concerns about privacy by creating a new position within the organisation called the chief privacy officer (CPO).[33] The position of CPO will typically involve responsibility for drafting organisation privacy policies, enforcing the policies and guidelines, and creating an organisational awareness of the issues associated with privacy. They can also act as a mediator between legislators and the organisation, attempting to convince them of their good corporate practices. Recall the DoubleClick case discussed previously in this chapter and how there were some concerns about perceptions of reduced individual privacy through the data that DoubleClick gathered. Jules Polonetsky was appointed as the CPO of DoubleClick. Polonetsky describes his role as ensuring that people are aware of DoubleClick policies and that DoubleClick follows the policies that it tells people it does.[34]

Some of the ways that the CPO can have an impact on an organisation include creating privacy manuals, developing an organisational awareness of privacy issues, developing procedures for handling information and the establishment of policies and procedures that must be followed before sharing data with third parties. However, the reality is that many managers involved with the AIS and making decisions related to it are bound as members of the company. What they as individuals think is the right thing to do may be different from what the corporate reality demands. This is a unique position in which managers will often find themselves when confronted with ethical problems. Several theories have been proposed to help managers work through such scenarios. Each of these theories is described briefly, based on a paper by Smith and Hasnas.[35]

- *Stockholder theory*. This compels managers to act in the best interest of the owners of the company: the stockholders. This implies an emphasis on maximising profit and the corporation acting within the confines of applicable laws and regulations.
- *Stakeholder theory*. The focus shifts beyond the owners, taking under its wing all those parties that play a role in the company's success or who are affected by the company's operations. This includes shareholders but can also include suppliers, customers, employees, residents of the local community and other such interested parties.
- *Social contract theory*. This takes a broader view of the corporation, placing it within a wider society. The corporation gains its authority to operate through society's sanction; however, this is theoretically only forthcoming if the actions of the corporation benefit society as a whole. The sanction for operations is not automatic and can be withdrawn if society is disadvantaged by the corporation or the corporation deceives society.

These three theories have been suggested as perspectives that managers can take when confronted with ethical issues. Think back to Blockbuster Video's plan to sell its database of customer contact details and movie-watching preferences. An analysis of the proposal under each of these perspectives would have provided different issues for resolution and potentially different courses of action.[36]

Organisations such as credit providers also have the responsibility of ensuring that all information is correct. Failure in this regard can have severe consequences for the customer, especially if a credit report is released that says the customer is a risk when he or she is not. While there are also statutory provisions relating to obligations in this area, there is also an ethical obligation to ensure that data about the customer are accurately recorded and properly maintained.

## Employees

Some of the ethical issues that confront employees within an organisation centre on privacy and the use of organisational resources. The organisation is challenged with encouraging ethical conduct by employees and treating employees ethically.

Is it ethical for employees to use organisational resources for non-work purposes and is it ethical for organisations to monitor such usage? Research by Healy and Iles reveals that 72 per cent of organisations allow their employees unrestricted use of the internet for both work and personal activities and that 24 per cent of employees use work internet facilities for entertainment purposes.[37] On the other hand, organisations may be concerned about the misuse of work resources and staff time. Many organisations arrive at a compromise, allowing an amount of time for personal use of IT facilities such as email and internet browsing. Many take steps to limit or eliminate non-work usage. Many employers ban staff from using social networking sites such as Facebook or auction sites like eBay and Trademe as distractions and time-wasters. There is, however, a fine line between ensuring the productive and efficient use of resources and intruding on an employee's privacy.

Many organisations set up firewalls to restrict employee internet browsing to work-related sites. Alternatively, the organisation can maintain a log that tracks individual usage of the internet, including user identification details, the sites visited and the time spent on sites. Some employees would argue that such monitoring of internet usage is an invasion of privacy and a sign of a lack of trust on the part of the organisation. Another alternative is the screening of employee emails, with organisations arguing that it is motivated by the need to address concerns over employee productivity and potential misbehaviour.

Another step that many organisations take in order to help ensure that staff use IT resources ethically is the prescription of a code of conduct. Healy and Iles observed that in response to the corporate use of the internet, client–server technologies and end-user computing, organisations have broadened the scope of their codes of conduct that govern how IT resources are to be used. Some of the ethical issues are:[38]

- confidentiality of information
- ownership and control of information
- non-work related use of resources (particularly the internet) at work
- avoiding sites displaying objectionable material — for example, pornography
- surveillance of employees' use of technology
- business's objectives in connection with codes of conduct.

Of course a code of conduct covers many ethics areas other than IT-related issues. Examples include:

- unapproved personal use of business assets like vehicles or equipment
- conflicts of interest where an employee (or their spouse or other close relative) may have a financial interest in a supplier
- acceptance (or giving) of gifts
- obtaining a personal benefit from a business transaction, for example paying suppliers with a personal credit card to earn frequent flier points then claiming the amount back, or using frequent flier points earned from business travel for personal travel (while these may not seem harmful they may prevent a cash discount being given or influence the employee to use a higher-cost airline or take a circuitous route to maximise their points)
- substance abuse
- sexual harassment
- falsification of qualifications on a résumé (A senior New Zealand public servant was recently dismissed after it was discovered that she had falsely claimed to have a PhD from a leading British university.)
- taking sick leave without just cause.

Data from the United Kingdom suggest the use of a code of conduct is common across most industries as well as across organisations of varying size.[39] Of course, the prescription of a code of conduct is only effective if it is actually monitored and enforced. For example, simply stating in a code of conduct that IT resources are not to be used for non-work related purposes is not sufficient. The organisation also needs to have mechanisms to detect non-work use and must be seen as enforcing these policies with appropriate sanctions when breaches are detected. This can be a challenge for many organisations, especially large ones.

Additionally, these policies need to relate to the key issues associated with employee use of the IT resources. One policy would be that employees are not to use personal data gathered and stored by the AIS in a manner that is inconsistent with its original purpose. Surprisingly, only one-third of UK companies that had an IT use policy included clauses relating to the use of data within the system.[40]

One factor that has been found to promote ethical behaviour among employees is that of **organisational self-esteem**. This refers to how well a person identifies and fits with the firm, its beliefs, culture, philosophy and operating style. An employee will form ideas about how well they fit in with the organisation and how competent and valuable they are to the organisation. Hsu and Kuo cite examples of research that has found employees with a high level of organisational self-esteem are more likely to act ethically.[41]

**Deindividuation** is another factor identified as influencing how employees act. Deindividuation refers to how anonymous a person perceives their actions to be. A high level of deindividuation would be expected for employees who use systems that do not require unique logons or user identification, since their actions are not able to be traced. The greater the degree of identification and tracing within a system the lower the degree of deindividuation and the higher the likelihood that employees will act ethically.[42]

Employees who become aware of unethical behaviour within the organisation face a dilemma whether to report the behaviour. Reporting unethical behaviour is known as **whistleblowing**. It raises some interesting issues. As children we were all taught not to be a 'tell-tale' and a complaint to a teacher about trivial offending would result in the complainant being ostracised by his or her classmates. With school misbehaviour a continuum from name-calling and hair-pulling at one end, to serious physical or sexual assault at the other, a child may be uncertain as to where the need to protect the victim overrides loyalty to the offenders and a reluctance to get involved. In just the same way, an employee may be torn between protecting the organisation and self-protection. While the person reporting the unethical behaviour is often doing so because they believe that what is happening is wrong and someone higher up in the organisation should be made aware of it so they can act on it, they are often confronted with several obstacles. As Cohan says, 'subordinates who may want to "blow the whistle" may be thwarted by an intimidating corporate culture, or simply because of the hierarchical structure that effectively forecloses adverse information from getting to senior management'.[43] An example of these obstructions to whistleblowing activities can be seen in a case study of the demise of Enron, where it is documented that, 'Enron had a corporate climate in which anyone who tried to challenge questionable practices of Enron's former chief financial officer ... faced the prospect of being reassigned or losing a bonus'.[44] Employees in such an environment can be intimidated into keeping silent about any unethical behaviour that may be occurring, for fear of demotion, pay cuts, job loss or reprisal and alienation by colleagues.

**Organisational self-esteem** How well a person identifies and fits with the firm, its beliefs, culture, philosophy and operating style.

**Deindividuation** How anonymous a person perceives their actions to be.

**Whistleblowing** The reporting, by an employee or member of an organisation, of the unethical behaviour of a colleague.

Consider an employee who suspects that spare parts from an engine company's storeroom are being stolen by the inventory manager and sold to customers for a cheaper price than the company would normally charge for such parts. If the staff member were to report this to the manager above the inventory manager, there is a very real prospect that this report could be lost or watered down, thus never being investigated fully. Management's inclination, largely as a result of the traditionally hierarchical structure employed in medium-to-large corporations, is to report good news to their superiors and suppress or water down any bad news. This can occur for several reasons, including fear on the part of the manager of negative reactions that might affect career progress and employment stability, as well as impression management: wanting to look good in the eyes of a superior. This can lead to the ignorance or dilution of whistleblowing actions and potentially create an environment where whistleblowing is actively discouraged. These corporate cultures create great challenges for employees contemplating whistleblowing.

Despite these challenges, whistleblowing does take place. In 2002, three women overcame their reluctance to 'blow the whistle' and reported unethical or potentially dangerous behaviour to their superiors: Enron vice-president Sherron Watkins wrote to chairman Kenneth Lay warning him that the company's methods of accounting were improper; Cynthia Cooper exploded the bubble that was WorldCom when she informed its board that the company had covered up $3.8 billion in losses through phoney bookkeeping; and FBI staff attorney Coleen Rowley wrote a memo to the FBI Director about how the bureau brushed off her pleas that an identified 11 September co-conspirator needed to be investigated.[45] These three women's actions in 2002 resulted in *Time Magazine* declaring 2002 the 'Year of the Whistle-Blower', honouring the women as *Time's* Persons of the Year.

Other whistleblowers have been immortalised in the popular media: the movie *Erin Brockovich*, directed by Steven Soderbergh and starring Julia Roberts, was based on the real-life story of the title character's fight against the West Coast energy giant PG&E over the company's systematic cover-up of the industrial poisoning of the town of Hinkley's water supply.

We discussed earlier how organisations can establish a code of conduct to promote the ethical use of IT resources by staff. While this approach is an extremely common technique for encouraging ethical behaviour, it is interesting to note that employees do not see this as an effective way of influencing how they use the IT resources of the business. This reaction by employees could be related to how well the policies are actually enforced within the organisation. Simply having a policy that sits in the filing cabinet and is never acted upon will obviously not have a strong influence on employee behaviour and the ethical use of IT resources.

## Information systems staff

Information systems staff have several ethical responsibilities, including ensuring the security and privacy of data held by the organisation. There have been cases recently where organisations have sold old computers and storage devices without properly removing data stored on them.[46] The purchaser of the computer and hardware received a lot more than they bargained for and, in the process, people's private details were at risk of disclosure beyond their intended source. IT staff who are responsible for maintaining and upgrading IT resources must ensure that devices being disposed of — either by sale or rubbish dump — are properly cleaned of all data or destroyed, leaving them in an unreadable state.

Apart from the actual data, the programs that maintain or use organisational data need to be protected from improper or unethical use. Many programs developed within an organisation will represent proprietary knowledge and may contain business rules that are a source of competitive advantage. Organisations need to take measures to ensure this intellectual property (IP) is safely kept within the organisation and does not fall into the hands of competitors.

Information systems staff should also take responsibility for the organisation's adherence to licensing agreements and the protection of IP that is contained within the various software packages used in the organisation. This can include making sure software is only installed on authorised machines and that the number of installations matches the number of site licences held, as well as protecting both the programs and the data that reside within them from unauthorised copying.

## Ethical issues surrounding bribes, gifts and rewards

In many cultures it is the norm for either minor central or local government officials either directly or through a 'middleman' to be paid a 'fee' to expedite the passage of bureaucratic regulations and requirements. Such transactions may be necessary to secure, for example, the issuing of an import licence or a building permit, or to influence the choice of supplier. The most notorious case of this type was the 1976 payment of $US1 million by Lockheed, a US aircraft manufacturer, to a member of the Dutch royal family who was also an Air Force general. Most recently, the Australian Wheat Board (AWB) was embroiled in a scandal involving the payment of 'kick-backs' to Saddam Hussein's government in Iraq, through 'trucking and transport' fees paid to a nonexistent transportation company. Clearly, demanding or receiving a bribe in such circumstances in Australia or New Zealand is unethical, and possibly also criminal. However, while making payments of this nature may not appeal to Australian and New Zealand businesses, in some environments it may be necessary to do so in order to carry out business.

Both Australia and New Zealand enjoy a reputation for being perceived as not corrupt, as evidenced by the Transparency International Corruption Perceptions Index which placed New Zealand second least and Australia ninth least corrupt of 180 countries in 2008.[47] Instances of corruption are isolated and punished severely. In July 2009, both a Queensland Government minister[48] and a former New Zealand cabinet minister[49] were convicted and jailed on corruption charges.

Is it ethical for the purchasing manager of a company to accept a gift from a supplier?

This is not an easy question to answer definitively. In some cultures, to decline to accept a gift may be interpreted as a profound insult to the offeror.

Most people would respond 'no problem' to a purchasing manager receiving a ballpoint pen or a wall calendar with the supplier's name on it. We would probably express concern about their accepting an all-expenses-paid overseas holiday or a new car, however. So where do we draw the line? A bottle of wine at Christmas? What about a carton? A pallet? If offered a gift in this situation, ask yourself these questions:

- *Is this intended as a reward for past transactions or is it intended as a bribe to ensure that the relationship continues in the future?* If the former then it is probably acceptable; if not, think carefully and if the value is significant then discuss the situation with your manager. Many organisations have a code of conduct which specifies a maximum monetary value for gifts that an employee may receive.

- *If I accept, am I going to feel obligated to direct orders to this supplier even if their prices or quality are not competitive?* If there is any possibility that your impartiality might be compromised, then you should not accept.
- *Is this part of the culture of the offeror? Are all clients receiving it or just me?* For example, in the advertising industry it is normal business practice for agencies to throw lavish Christmas parties and invite large contingents from all the major clients, who attend en masse. However, both the agency and the client are aware that if the account is up for tender in January, the party is forgotten: the decision is based solely on the presentation of their bid for the following year.

# COMPUTER CRIME AND FRAUD

Some examples of computer crime and fraud are described in this section but the list is by no means an exhaustive one. The section concludes with some strategies for reducing the exposure to computer crime and fraud, with many of these relating back to the ethics material that was covered earlier in the chapter.

**LEARNING OBJECTIVE** ④
*Describe some of the different perspectives of computer crime.*

## What is computer crime?

We all have our own concept of computer crime and, if asked, could probably arrive at some cogent definition. Take a moment to jot down a few points on what you think constitutes computer crime. No doubt you thought of concepts such as fraud and theft: for example credit card fraud, hacking into systems and manipulating payroll systems. Computer crime can appear in many guises. For example, each of the following could be classified as computer crime:

- sending a virus to crash a computer system
- using a computer to acquire funds illegally
- using illegally obtained data files for self gain
- intercepting a message sent by a third party.

It is, therefore, difficult to define computer crime concisely. Generally, crimes committed through a computer or where a computer is the target would fall under the banner of computer crime.

### Spam

**Spam** *The sending of unsolicited emails or junk email.*

**Spam** is the sending of unsolicited emails or junk email. Spam is a problem for several reasons. From a user's perspective, the spam mail can clog up valuable space in an email account. Spam is also a common technique for spreading viruses: it can contain attachments that, when executed, are damaging to a system. The content of spam is also sometimes offensive to those receiving it, for example invitations to purchase drugs and links to adult-oriented sites. The content can also trick the unwary into being defrauded, for example by falling for a 'Nigerian' fraud scam where the victim is recruited to help the fraudster claim a (nonexistent) amount from a dormant bank account in exchange for a share of the proceeds. The victim is then lured into making a series of progressively larger payments to meet so-called upfront fees.

Spam is also potentially dangerous to organisations through the damage it can cause to their reputation and image. Typically, the creators of spam send their messages through the servers of well-known organisations.[50] The receiver of the email will often be tricked by this technique, believing it to be a bona fide email from that organisation.

Organisations can also suffer from spam through the effects it has on their email server and the computer system generally.[51] Large volumes of spam can slow down a server, while spam emails that contain viruses can damage an organisation's computer resources.

As a result, spam is an issue of importance to the organisation and the individual. The internet security company Symantec estimates that 80 per cent of all email sent is spam.[52] The *Spam Act 2003* (Cwlth) was introduced on 11 April 2004 in Australia to regulate the use of email. Under the Spam Act, the Australian Communications Authority (ACA) is vested with the responsibility of policing spam. The Spam Act also applies to SMS text messages on mobile phones. Because of the international nature of email and consequently spam, Australia has also entered into various agreements with other nations, in a bid to cooperatively deal with the problem. These include:[53]

- the bilateral memorandum of understanding between Australia and Korea
- memorandum of understanding among Australia, the United Kingdom and the United States
- Australia–Thailand joint statement on telecommunications and IT.

## Phishing and identity fraud

**Phishing** A technique of online deception that has users go to a fraudulent website and leave personal details, which are then used for identity theft and deception.

**Phishing** is a technique of online deception that has users go to a fraudulent website and leave personal details. The information is then used for identity theft and deception. In the United States more than US$2.4 billion has been stolen from users on the internet, with 17 per cent of the theft attributed to identity theft, which includes phishing schemes.[54] Banks are a common target, with the perpetrators setting up sites that resemble the URL of the genuine site.[55] For example, if a bank had the URL www.bank1.com.au, the site created by the phishers might be www.bank1.org.au. At first glance, especially to an uninitiated user, these site addresses seem to be the same, so the user unwittingly clicks on the address ending in org.au: the phisher's site. The fraudulent site will resemble the bank's genuine site, so no suspicion is raised. Any details submitted by the user will be sent to the creators of the phishing site. The fraud perpetrators (phishers) send an email purporting to be from bank1, advising that to tighten security customers must re-register their details and instructing them to click on a link in the email, which directs the customer to the phishing site where the customer is instructed to enter their username and password. Having obtained that data the phishers strip as much cash from the account as they can before the customer notices and sounds the alarm.

This is a real threat for organisations. Websites are relatively easy to create and domain names are easy to acquire. This leaves organisations vulnerable to phishing scams that damage customer trust in the organisation and e-commerce, as well as denting the organisation's image. Organisations can overcome some of the risks involved through information about IT usage and policies and ensuring that customers are aware of the policies. For example, one policy could be that the organisation will never request personal details by email or will not communicate at all with users by email. Users aware of this policy would, it is hoped, be alerted to attempts at phishing.

Naturally, this relies both on the organisation having clear communication policies in place, and on the organisation's customers being aware of such policies.

The very fact that phishing continues unabated suggests that warnings from banks and other financial organisations have not proved effective and that enough naïve bank customers are responding to make this fraud worthwhile to its perpetrators.

## Hacking

**Hacking** *Gaining unauthorised access to a system.*

**Hacking** is gaining unauthorised access to a system. There are many examples of hackers gaining access to high-profile systems, for example NASA's system. Hacking is a threat, particularly for large and prominent organisations that, by virtue of their position, become targets for hackers. The increased use of the internet, combined with the higher levels of IT sophistication in adolescents, has made hacking an increased threat.[56]

Recognising hacking as a risk to their system, many organisations are now hiring hackers to test the vulnerability of their systems. The term given to this activity is 'penetration testing', which, while familiar to the large banks, is a new concept for other organisations just venturing into the world of telecommunications.[57]

The hacking issue is seen as being particularly real as businesses head towards integrated environments, with interorganisational network connections becoming increasingly common. In this integrated environment, companies must ensure that their suppliers, partners and other third parties are meeting security benchmarks. A company's security is only as strong as the weakest link in its network.[58]

The challenge for organisations is to take reasonable measures to protect their systems from unauthorised access. In Australia, guidance can be sought on how to do this from Standard Australia's *AS/NZS ISO/IEC 27001:2005: Information technology — Security techniques — Information security management systems — Requirements.* This standard provides a benchmark for assessing exposure to hacking. Certification of compliance with the Australian standards is available for organisations. A list of officially certified organisations is available through the website of Standards Australia: SAI Global.[59] Information about comparable standards for information protection is available from this site.

Alternative ways of gaining confidence in a website and its data transmission were also developed by Dun & Bradstreet and KPMG, who have designed digital certification products,[60] while WebTrust and Verisign also offer online protection for organisations and their e-commerce customers.

The distinction that needs to be drawn in this section is that of ethical and unethical hacking.[61] Ethical hackers are employed by organisations to test systems for exposures and security weaknesses, with the hacker generally working to instructions from the organisation. Unethical hacking is the sort that generally makes the headlines in the newspapers: it is unauthorised and illegal access to a system.

## Identity theft

**Identity theft** *The fraudulent theft and use of another person's personal information to obtain illegal benefit.*

**Identity theft** is discussed in chapter 8 in the context of internal controls. An example reported recently involved a virus that steals the identity details of users of the various banking websites (see AIS focus 16.2). In this example, viruses, called 'trojans' or 'malware', are planted on the user's computer and triggered when certain conditions are met or certain events occur. In this case, the user is directed to what appears to be a legitimate new service, which instead loads the malicious software onto their computer.

The trojan then monitors their keystrokes, and may even specifically target internet banking login data. The user is potentially exposed to fraudulent use of their financial resources, with the fraudsters now possessing details that can gain access to their online accounts. Additionally, such instances have a negative impact on any specific banks identified, with corporate image and reputation, as well as the image of online banking in general, taking some damage.

## PM 'heart attack' email dupes bank customers

Hackers may have captured the login details of around 2500 banking customers by circulating a trojan email claiming Australia's then Prime Minister had suffered a heart attack, according to a security company.

Entitled 'John Howard, the current Prime Minister of Australia has survived a heart attack', the email claimed Howard suffered the heart attack while staying at his official residence in Sydney and is fighting for his life in hospital.

The email then provided a link purporting to be an online news report. Users that clicked the link however were directed to a standard 404 error page which downloads a trojan to their computer.

Joel Camissar, Websense country manager for Australia and New Zealand, said the trojan monitored infected users' internet activity. This included logging keystrokes, he said — which could include banking login details.

Websense, which had been tracking the scam, has identified one of the servers used in the hacking attempts and recorded compromised IP addresses, as well as other data stored by the server, according to Camissar.

He said 2500 users around the world had been infected by the trojan, with around 30 per cent — or 750 people — from Australia. Customers of banks across Europe and the United States may have had their passwords captured, said Camissar, adding that customers of Australia's Commonwealth and Westpac banks may specifically have had their account details captured.

Both banks denied the trojan infected their systems. A spokesperson for Westpac said its systems have not been compromised and the bank was unaware of any fraud losses as a result. A Commonwealth Bank spokesperson said its website had not been infected by the trojan.

However, as Camissar explained, the website is not the issue: 'The Commonwealth Bank website hasn't been compromised but the trojan horse monitors user sites visited and sends back the [bank site] username and password to the server computer'.

Websense was working with law enforcement authorities to find the scammers, said Camissar.[62]

### Money laundering

The move towards a cashless society has come with the development of e-commerce. Credit cards and bank-issued debit cards (also known as EFTPOS cards or ATM cards) have become common forms of paying for online transactions. With this has come the risk of identity theft and credit card fraud, through techniques such as phishing and hacking, which have been discussed. Partly in response to these concerns, electronic cash has developed as a means of funding electronic transactions. It is similar in concept to physical cash: the customer buys electronic tokens, which function as cash in the electronic world. These tokens can then be electronically exchanged for goods and services provided by a vendor, who can then convert the tokens back in to cash. These can offer a form of security to e-customers because they do not have to divulge details of credit cards over the internet. Instead, the e-tokens can be purchased for cash and used in place of the credit card when executing transactions. However, there have been concerns raised by the federal government about improper uses of e-cash technology, with a paper issued by the Science, Technology, Environment and Resources Group raising the prospect of e-cash being used as a tool for money laundering and tax evasion.[63] Electronic cash has not to date attracted significant volumes of patronage.

## What is fraud?

**Fraud** is an act of deception committed by someone against another entity, usually with the intent of either causing damage to the victim or bringing benefit to the perpetrator. White-collar crime can be described as deliberately misusing one's employer's resources or assets for personal enrichment.

Christensen and Byington identify 12 ways that white-collar crime can be committed: fraud or conspiracy, bribery, kickbacks, price-fixing, embezzlement, violations of securities laws (such as insider trading), illegal political contributions, tax issues, bid-rigging, forgery, corporate theft, and fraudulent financial reporting.[64]

As the list demonstrates, white-collar crime can occur in many different forms. Similarly, fraud can occur within an organisation in many different ways. Table 16.1, while by no means an exhaustive list, is an indicator of some of the ways that fraud can occur.[65]

**TABLE 16.1** Examples of fraud

| Fraud type | Business process affected | Example |
|---|---|---|
| Asset theft | Expenditure cycle | Paying fictitious vendors. |
| | Expenditure cycle | Fraudulent use of corporate credit card. |
| | Expenditure cycle | Recipient knowingly withdrawing funds credited to their bank account in error, and failing to refund them on demand. |
| Asset theft | Revenue cycle | Misappropriation of incoming cash — e.g. lapping[a] — will affect accounts receivable and cash and potentially related accounts such as discounts. |
| | Revenue cycle | Goods invoiced to fictitious customers. |
| | Revenue cycle | Unjustified credit notes issued to customers. |
| | Revenue cycle | Goods returned by customers are not recorded. |
| Perquisites | Expenditure cycle | Personal items paid for by company. |
| Artificial revenue inflation | Revenue cycle | Creating fictitious invoices. Inappropriate cut-offs or recognition criteria applied to sales. |

| Fraud type | Business process affected | Example |
|---|---|---|
| Asset valuation | Revenue cycle | Recognising asset revaluations as revenue. Creating non-existent debtors. Kiting.[b] Valuation of inventory at wrong amount. Capitalising inappropriate expenses. Misclassifying work-in-process as finished goods. |
| Payroll | Expenditure cycle | Paying nonexistent employees. Siphoning money from employees' pay. |
| Expense manipulation | Expenditure cycle | Capitalising expenses that should be recognised immediately as expenses.[c] |

a. Lapping is using cash payments from one customer to cover up theft of a previous customer's payment. The thief steals cash paid by *X*, the next day records a payment from *Y* and credits *X*, the following day records a payment from *Z* and credits *Y*, etc.

b. Kiting refers to the practice of inflating cash balances by exploiting the delay between a cheque being written and being cleared. A cheque may be written from account *A* and deposited in account *B*. It will be recognised immediately as a deposit in account *B* but not as a withdrawal in account *A* until it has cleared through the bank. This will inflate the overall cash balance. Electronic cheque clearing by banks has reduced the clearance cycle time, hence this type of fraud has become less effective.

c. This type of fraud was a major contributor to the WorldCom collapse.

There are several possible ways to act fraudulently in the world of information systems. Consider some of the following:

- The payroll manager who places a nonexistent staff member on the payroll and collects his or her salary in addition to his or her own
- The programmer who adjusts a payroll program so that one cent from every pay every week goes to an account he or she has created
- The hacker who gains credit card numbers with the intent of using them for personal gain
- The person who creates a website purporting to be that of a large organisation and gains private customer details (including bank account details) through the site.

Fraud is a real problem for organisations and, as was alluded to in chapter 8 on internal controls, the growth of e-commerce has heightened consumer and organisational awareness of the very real risk that fraud presents. Various discussions of fraud refer to the notion of a 'fraud triangle', which says that for fraud to occur three things are necessary: a reason, pressure and an opportunity.[66]

- The *reason* is the way that individuals justify their fraudulent activity. For example, the bank teller who takes some cash home on a Friday night and bets it on a 'sure thing' at the races on Saturday may justify these activities on the basis that no one will get hurt and, if the horse wins, the original amount of money can be returned and no one will know the difference. In effect the teller was only borrowing, albeit unethically.
- The *pressure* for fraud can come from various sources, including the individual's personal life and work environment. For our bank teller, for example, pressure at home, with mortgage payments rapidly approaching and credit cards nearing their credit limit, may provide the financial pressure for the teller's actions. Another

example could be the corporate accountant who is under pressure to achieve target results, so as not to disappoint the sharemarket. Consequently, he or she creates fictitious sales to boost revenue and bolsters the value of inventory and assets with some judicious revaluations. These are two examples of pressures that led to fraud: the first personal and the second job-related pressure.

- The *opportunity* refers to the individual's perceived ability to carry out the fraud and conceal the fraudulent activity. In the bank teller case, the opportunity was available because the teller could take the money on Friday night and return it on Monday and no one would be any the wiser. After all, sure things do not lose ... do they?

Research studies have found that the incidence of fraud tends to be related to the ethical environment of the organisation.[67] This makes ethics and the promulgation of ethical values and practices vitally important to the organisation. They can be promoted through, for example, codes of conduct and professional registration. Codes of conduct or ethical standards provide guidelines for acceptable behaviour. For example, ethical guidelines exist to guide auditors when making client acceptance decisions, when determining the level of non-audit service fees and on what gifts from the client can be accepted. Similarly, both the Australian and New Zealand Computer Associations have a code of conduct for their members to follow. It is important, however, that such codes have the ability to impose significant and enforceable sanctions against any failure to comply by members, while mere voluntary membership of professional organisations can also reduce the efficacy of such codes.

Membership of a profession carries benefits; for example, professions are typically in possession of a base of knowledge that is valued in society (as with doctors or accountants), their professional authority is recognised in the wider community that they serve, and they have a professional culture and ethical codes that govern their actions.[68] Codes of ethics can be both formal and informal, and enforced by the self and by the professional body. For example, the professional accounting bodies hold disciplinary meetings for allegations of breaches of the codes of conduct. For professionals who consider themselves a part of the professional group, such as a CA or CPA or a doctor, the prospect of being disciplined and potentially excluded from the group and prevented from earning their livelihood is generally a strong enough means of ensuring behaviour in accordance with the professional code of ethics.

Organisations can therefore help induce ethical behaviour by having employees who are members of professional bodies that enforce a professional and ethical code of conduct, or by creating and enforcing their own ethical code of conduct, to which the employee signs up when joining the organisation.

## Sales fraud or e-commerce fraud

Some hypothetical examples of sales fraud or e-commerce fraud are discussed in this section. In the exercises at the end of this chapter you have the opportunity to develop some control plans that could be applied to reduce the risk of these occurring.

### Example 1: Paying nonexistent suppliers or false invoices

John MacIntosh, a payment clerk for Deep Water, creates a company called ABC Enterprises. ABC Enterprises then proceeds to issue invoices to Deep Water, where John is responsible for approving and paying them. Several invoices, valued at several thousands of dollars, are processed and paid by Deep Water, with the money going to MacIntosh.

### Example 2: Credit fraud

Susan Falmer purchases items online using credit card numbers that she has obtained illegally through a phishing scheme she established a few years ago. She purchases the items on credit and then sells them to customers over the internet at prices much less than retail. Because the credit card details were stolen, Susan never incurs any of the debts. The company selling the goods to Susan never incurs any debt because credit transactions are guaranteed by credit card companies. Of course, in the long run all credit card users bear the cost of Susan's fraud because card companies factor fraud losses into their charges.

### Example 3: Nonexistent sales

The end of the financial year is fast approaching and GHI Ltd is slightly below its budgeted forecast sales, which were released to the stockmarket with mid-year earnings figures. Recognising the poor signal that lower than expected earnings would send to the market, the chief financial officer of GHI Ltd instructs the financial accountant to push forward some sales, recognising them in the current period, even though the inventory is yet to be shipped. For GHI this has several benefits: it increases its sales figures, and its asset base also increases through the higher accounts receivable. The accountant responds by calling up some pending sales orders on the system and altering their status, thus recognising them as sales. The following year, however, will show reduced sales as a result, and the chief financial officer may be under more pressure to anticipate even more sales transactions.

### Example 4: Nonexistent customers

Brad is the accounts receivable manager at Tee Up Ltd, a seller of golf-related accessories. A keen golfer himself, Brad would like to use the products of Tee Up but is unable to afford them. To overcome this difficulty Brad creates fictitious customers on the accounts receivable master list, with addresses that correspond to those of his close friends. As Brad orders goods through these customers the goods are shipped to the addresses, where Brad collects the goods. Payment is never received from Brad for the goods. Instead he either records the goods returned by the customer due to damage (damaged returns do not go to inventory but are written off as an expense), writes the account off as a bad debt or clears the accounts receivable amount owing through non-cash entries such as allowances and returns.

### Example 5: Inventory theft

Jenny is a disaffected ex-employee of Magna Corp, a supplier of high-quality expensive audio components. Masquerading as a buyer for The Sound Shop, a large retail chain and Magna customer, Jenny phones an order worth several hundreds of thousands of dollars to Magna and arranges for the order to be delivered the following morning. The Magna driver arrives at The Sound Shop inward goods dock as arranged and thrusts a delivery receipt in front of Gary, the receiving storeman, collects Gary's signature and unloads the shipment. Gary then hunts through his computer system and, not surprisingly, can find no trace of this order. When the Magna truck delivered the order, Jenny's boyfriend Tim was waiting in a van parked outside The Sound Shop's gate, wearing a Magna logo shirt. Tim drives up with a very plausible story: 'Terribly sorry, our driver delivered an order to you in error, it was meant for another customer'. A relieved Gary loads the shipment into Tim's van. Tim and Jenny subsequently sell the items for cash from a shop that they rented for a week for that purpose and vanish without trace. Magna duly invoices The Sound Shop, who repudiate the invoice. After both companies have spent several months investigating the issue, Gary remembers a young man in a van picking up the goods. However, this remains undocumented and Magna deny all knowledge. Ultimately Magna insist 'you received it, your employee Gary signed for it, you must pay for it'.

# FRAUD WORLDWIDE

There are indicators that fraud is increasing both in numbers of instances and value in many countries. Some examples include the conviction of US investment fund CEO Bernard Madoff for running a 'Ponzi' (pyramid) investment scheme that defrauded clients of a total of US$65 billion. This goes down as the largest fraud ever committed, and it is matched in size by Madoff's jail sentence of 150 years. Madoff's victims included Hollywood celebrities and many of his own family and friends. His claim to have his investments continually return abnormally high returns should have alerted investors to be more cautious, but his unsullied reputation over a long period blunted their caution.[69] Another example is from the United Kingdom, where the *Financial Times* quotes KPMG as saying 'A record number of fraud cases (163) reached the courts in the first six months of this year, with the numbers set to rise further in the recession … but the worst is yet to come. It will be a number of years before the impact of the recession fully feeds through into the fraud statistics'.[70]

Credit card fraud is prevalent at the consumer level. Electronic payments software provider ACI Worldwide's 2009 global card fraud survey revealed that 18 per cent of consumers questioned have been victims of credit or debit card fraud in the past five years.

Pete Corrie of Nationwide Building Society, comments 'The number of card payments globally has increased drastically over the past few years and, consequently, the whole industry has seen associated fraud levels go up'.[71]

LEARNING OBJECTIVE 5
Describe the impact of fraud on Australian and New Zealand business.

## Fraud in Australia and New Zealand

International accounting firm KPMG conducts a biennial survey of fraud[72] in Australia and New Zealand, in association with the University of Melbourne and the University of Queensland. In the 2008 survey, responses were received from just over 20 per cent of the 2000 largest organisations in the two countries. This is a high enough response rate to infer that the results found would hold true for all organisations in the two countries. Major findings were:

- Almost half the respondents reported one or more instances of fraud. The average fraud value was over $1.5 million per organisation experiencing fraud[73] and the largest individual fraud was $15 million.[74] Larger organisations experienced both more and larger frauds.[75] Fraud was committed by internal parties, both management (23 per cent by number and 54 per cent by total value) and lower-level staff (48 and 6 per cent), and by external parties (29 and 40 per cent). The value of management individual frauds were over twenty times those of other staff, and double those of external perpetrators.[76]

  Major types of fraud were:
  – theft of cash
  – theft of inventory
  – identity fraud
  – false invoicing.[77]
- Fraud is more likely to be committed by a person within the organisation; the typical fraudster is a 38-year-old male non-management employee, working alone, and with no history of dishonesty.[78]

- The major motivation for fraud in Australia is gambling (44 per cent), followed by greed and desire for a luxury lifestyle (37 per cent).[79] In the only survey result where New Zealand data varied significantly from Australian, gambling dropped to a low level with greed the principal motivation.[80] Surprisingly, substance abuse does not rate.
- Fraud is most likely to be detected by internal control (43 per cent), followed by notification by employee (22 per cent) and notification by external party (23 per cent).[81]
- The average time taken to detect a fraud is almost one year.[82]
- The two most significant factors that allowed the fraud to occur were poor internal controls (26 per cent) and overriding of internal controls (22 per cent).[83] An example of overriding is that a payroll system usually includes a segregation of duties control, where an operations supervisor interviews and appoints a new staff member, and the new employee is then seen by the human resources (HR) department to complete formalities including providing tax and bank account details. This can be overridden by a more senior manager giving the completed form including the above details to HR, and using his position to quash any attempt by HR to insist on seeing the new person.
- In 22 per cent of the frauds reported in the survey, 'red flag' warnings had been noticed but ignored.[84] (We discuss red flags in the next section.)

## AIS FOCUS 16.3

### What would you do?

'What would you do?' (if you woke up with $10 million in your bank account) is a question posed in lottery commercials, which then suggest luxury cars, boats and travel as spending possibilities. Rotorua New Zealand businessman Thomas Hoa (not his real name) faced this question in April 2009, but he had not won Lotto! Thomas had requested an overdraft from his bank, Westpac Banking Corporation, and the bank approved a loan of $100 000.00 but a bank employee left out the decimal point and Thomas found $10 million had been credited to his current account[85] (presumably the equivalent amount was debited to a loan account, but that detail has not been made public).

So what were Thomas's choices?
- Contact the bank and request it to correct the error?
- Wait for the bank to find out for itself?
- Take the money and run?

What would you do in Thomas's shoes?

Thomas chose the third option, started to transfer the money offshore in small parcels and left New Zealand, accompanied by his partner, her daughter from an earlier relationship, and her sister. Knowingly using money credited to a bank account in error is specifically defined as a criminal act in New Zealand, so in leaving the country Thomas became a criminal fugitive. Thomas and his companions were dubbed

*continued*

'the accidental millionaires' by the press, who reported the story, which was subsequently picked up by overseas newspaper and television media. Thomas's destination was scarcely a secret; the sister, who has since returned to New Zealand, reportedly posted a blog of their travel to Hong Kong, Macau and China on Facebook![86]

On discovering the situation the bank froze the funds remaining in Thomas's account and set about tracing and recovering the stolen money. To date, $6.2 million has been recovered,[87] the remaining $3.8 million was apparently moved out of the bank's reach. Efforts by the NZ police to have Chinese authorities actively search for Thomas or the money have to date met with bureaucratic delays. At the date of writing, Thomas remains at liberty with the $3.8 million and the bank employee responsible for the error has been dismissed.[88]

So where are the internal control, ethics and criminal issues in this saga? Clearly there was a failure in Westpac's internal control. The bank has stated that it was a human error not a systems error and is making no further comment, but it appears strange that an amount of this magnitude could be transferred without review from a more senior employee. Thomas has acted both criminally and unethically, and the women's action in (presumably) travelling using the stolen money is unethical and possibly also criminal.

However, the most surprising outcome is the attitude of the general New Zealand public as revealed in blog postings on *TVNZ* and the *The New Zealand Herald* newspaper's websites. More than 20 per cent of posters say they would do likewise[89] if their bank made a similar mistake and many others who disagreed with Thomas's actions were more concerned about never being able to return home than the moral issues. Obviously blog posters are self-selected and may not be telling the truth so polling their responses has little statistical validity, but a widely held belief that it is acceptable behaviour to steal from a bank in this manner is surprising. (Thomas's support level may have been higher had he not earned a black mark for leaving his dog tied up without food or water!) Westpac is not a victim likely to receive much sympathy in some quarters as it and the other three largest banks in New Zealand are Australian-owned, and there is a sentiment that 'Aussie banks rip off Kiwi customers' arising from bank fees and interest rate differentials between the two countries. It also appears that 'the accidental millionaires' may have become folk heroes, plugging into a tradition dating back to Robin Hood in medieval England, Ned Kelly in 18th century Australia, Bonnie and Clyde in 1920s America, and George Wilder in 1950s New Zealand. All of these were fugitives who eluded and mocked authorities for many months or even years, and won public sympathy in doing so.

**LEARNING OBJECTIVE 6**

*Consider potential ways to reduce the risk of computer crime.*

## WHAT CAN ORGANISATIONS DO?

In response to a series of major financial accounting scandals, including Enron, WorldCom, Tyco and Fannie Mae, in 2002 the US government passed the Sarbanes–Oxley Act (SOX) requiring generally higher standards of financial reporting. While this has no direct application in Australia or New Zealand, it is binding on subsidiaries of US companies such as the Ford Motor Company or Coca-Cola. It also has strong moral force in that the 'Big 4' chartered accounting firms are all US based, so their world-wide policies and procedures incorporate SOX requirements. Significant SOX requirements of the Act or SEC (Securities and Exchange Commission) rules made under it include the appointment of an audit committee typically comprising the non-executive or independent members of the board of directors. This committee is charged with oversight of the financial reporting process, appointment of external auditors and negotiating with the auditors on any issues over the selection of accounting policies. This committee normally also has oversight of the internal control procedures, for example, and internal control report that must include:

> ... a statement of management's responsibility for establishing and maintaining adequate internal control over financial reporting for the company; management's assessment of the effectiveness of the company's internal control over financial reporting; ... and a statement that the auditor has issued an attestation report on management's assessment of the company's internal control over financial reporting.[90]

Thus the directors and senior management are specifically charged with the responsibility for the financial statements and the processes, including internal control, which were used in their preparation.

There are several ways that organisations can manage their exposure to computer crime and fraud. The discussion in chapter 8, which looked at internal control systems, is the obvious starting point. Establishing a sound corporate governance structure that pursues a strong control environment and thoroughly designed general and application controls is a good starting point. However, these formal controls are not the only tools available to the organisation. Other mechanisms for reducing the risk of computer crime and fraud are now discussed.

The emphasis for organisations wanting to reduce the threat of fraud appears to be having a strong ethical culture that starts at the top of the organisation, having appropriate reporting and monitoring mechanisms that are followed up on, providing ethical training, and facilitating employee reporting of fraud (or whistleblowing). SOX provides: 'Each audit committee shall establish procedures for the confidential, anonymous submission by employees of the issuer of concerns regarding questionable accounting or auditing matters'.[91]

One informal but effective approach is to know your employees. This means not simply knowing their names when you meet them in the lunchroom for coffee. Rather, it means being aware of who they are, their background and so on. This can help identify potential instances of fraud. For example, seeing the employee who has typically ridden to work on a 20-year-old bicycle drive through the employee car park in a brand new shiny red Porsche would probably lead you to ask the question: How did you get the car? While changes in lifestyle will not typically be as extravagant as the example given, monitoring employees for changes in lifestyle and habits can be an effective red flag for detecting fraud in the organisation.

Similarly, policies that force employees to take annual leave on a regular basis can be an effective means of detecting fraud. Why? An employee carrying out fraudulent activities will not want to leave their job for any period of time for fear that someone else will discover their actions. As discussed, this can be a common technique that is effective for detecting fraud in cash-handling areas of the organisation, where there is a risk of activities such as lapping occurring.

Other potential red flags identified by Singleton et al. are listed in table 16.2.[92] The factors relate to either the employee or the company level.

**TABLE 16.2** Fraud red flags

| Employee red flags | Company red flags |
| --- | --- |
| Financial pressure | Lacking internal controls |
| Vices | No follow-up in internal and external audits |
| Extravagant lifestyle | Falling employee morale |
| Not happy with organisation | Changing lifestyle of employee |
| Internal performance pressure | Unusual expenses |
| Unexplained work hours | Unexplained losses |

The role of the internal and external auditor can be crucial in preventing and detecting fraud and, somewhat ironically, one of the best tools available for both of these parties for detecting fraud is the computer.[93] The range of analytical techniques, searching power and processing tools that a computer can possess make the analysis of a large volume of transactional data relatively simple to accomplish, especially when combined with modern computer-assisted audit techniques.

## ›› SUMMARY ›››

LEARNING OBJECTIVE  **What are ethics and morals?**
Ethics is the term given to the implicit rules that guide us in our everyday behaviour. Morals are how a person approaches and responds to an ethical issue. There can be a difference between what a person thinks is right and what a person actually does.

LEARNING OBJECTIVE  **What is the ethical decision-making model?**
The ethical decision-making model represents a way of working through ethical dilemmas. There are seven stages in the model, these being: (1) identify the facts, (2) define the issues, (3) identify the principles, (4) identify possible actions and those affected, (5) compare steps 3 and 4, (6) select an action or outcome and (7) implement the action chosen in step 6.

LEARNING OBJECTIVE  **What are some areas in which ethical problems may emerge for businesses that use accounting information systems (AIS)?**
The ethical problems related to the area of AIS vary, depending on the perspective from which they are viewed. These include issues from the customer's perspective, which can be the right to privacy, the accuracy of information being gathered and the use of information that is gathered about customers. From an organisation's perspective, some of the ethical issues include how the resources of the AIS are used within the organisation, with a responsibility to ensure that usage matches the purpose for which information was originally gathered. Employees' use of the AIS and the broader set of IT resources is also an issue for organisations. This can include the use of email and the internet. A social issue that is emerging as e-commerce becomes increasingly prevalent is that of access to the technology required to support e-commerce and the potential discrimination and alienation that can emerge.

LEARNING OBJECTIVE  **What are some of the different perspectives of computer crime?**
Computer crime can be broadly defined, potentially including crimes committed through the use of the computer and crimes where computers are the object of the crime. This creates a range of potential actions that could fall within the scope of computer crime.

Spam, phishing, identity theft and hacking are threats faced by the AIS in the increasingly popular world of e-commerce. Spam is the sending of unsolicited emails and exposes the organisation to excessive email traffic and potential viruses and computer attacks. Phishing and identity fraud affect the validity of transactions that individuals and organisations engage in, as individuals pretend to be others through the fraudulent use of websites (phishing) or personal details such as credit card numbers and other identifying traits (identity theft). Hacking is someone gaining unauthorised access to a system. These areas all represent threats to the effective running of the AIS within the organisation.

**LEARNING OBJECTIVE**

### What is the impact of fraud on Australian and New Zealand business?

Almost half of the largest organisations in Australia and New Zealand reported one or more instances of fraud in 2007–08. The average fraud value is over $1.5 million per organisation, with the largest individual frauds amounting to $15 million. Fraud is committed by both internal and external parties, with the most common types of fraud being theft of cash, theft of inventory and false invoicing. The major motivations for fraud are gambling and greed and desire for a luxury lifestyle. Fraud is most likely to be detected by internal control but the average time taken to detect a fraud is one year, and the two most significant factors that allow fraud to occur are poor internal controls and overriding of internal controls.

**LEARNING OBJECTIVE**

### How can organisations reduce the risk of computer crime?

There are varied ways to reduce the risk of computer crime. The establishment of a sound internal control policy can be a good start. Other strategies can include codes of conduct and registration with professional bodies. These can be ways of encouraging ethical behaviour and a shared set of attitudes and beliefs throughout the organisation. Management's possession of knowledge of employees — enabling the identification of changes in lifestyle and the opportunities employees may face to act illegally or unethically — can also be effective.

## KEY TERMS

cookies, p. 710
customer profiling, p. 710
data mining, p. 710
deindividuation, p. 720
ethics, p. 706
fraud, p. 727
hacking, p. 725

identity theft, p. 725
morals, p. 706
organisational self-esteem, p. 720
phishing, p. 724
spam, p. 723
whistleblowing, p. 720

## DISCUSSION QUESTIONS

16.1 Discuss how some of the ethical considerations faced by professional sports players (for example, cricketers 'walking') might translate to other private and work-related situations. Consider the large amounts of money players are paid and the significant public pressure some sportspeople can encounter. (LO1)

16.2 Discuss some of the ways in which a person's privacy is threatened through AIS and e-commerce. (LO3)

16.3 What strategies can firms employ to promote ethical behaviour among staff? (LO3)

16.4 Describe the key differences between express and implied consent when gathering information about someone. (LO3)

16.5 What are some of the organisational concerns with spam? (LO4)

16.6 Can hacking be 'good'? Explain. (LO4)

## SELF-TEST ACTIVITIES

16.1 Deindividuation, if it is not reduced, is likely to lead to:
- (a) ethical behaviour because employees know they are being observed.
- (b) unethical behaviour because employees can collude and overcome observation mechanisms.
- (c) ethical behaviour because employees feel a part of the organisation.
- (d) unethical behaviour because employees feel their actions are anonymous.

16.2 The relevant use principle of the *Privacy Act 1988* (Cwlth) says that:
- (a) information shall only be used for the purpose for which it was gathered.
- (b) information can only be gathered in lawful ways.
- (c) information being used must be accurate.
- (d) information shall not be disclosed unless consent is obtained.

16.3 Which of the factors below were not mentioned as having an influence on access to technology?
- (a) Age
- (b) Geography
- (c) Income
- (d) Religion

16.4 The CPO:
- (a) represents consumers in issues about privacy and data gathering.
- (b) prosecutes organisations charged for breaches of the *Privacy Act 1988* (Cwlth).
- (c) acts as an advocate for all companies accused of violating the *Privacy Act 1988* (Cwlth).
- (d) creates and enforces privacy policies within an organisation.

16.5 Spam is:
- (a) sending unsolicited emails.
- (b) acquiring personal details by means of deception.
- (c) gaining unauthorised access to a system.
- (d) pretending to be someone else in an online transaction.

16.6 Which of the following is not normally a responsibility of the audit committee under the Sarbanes–Oxley Act ?
- (a) Oversight of internal control procedures
- (b) Appointment of external auditors
- (c) Negotiating issues over the selection of accounting policies with the auditors
- (d) Appointment of the chief financial officer (CFO)

16.7 A company discovers that an employee has created a fictitious vendor on the vendor master file and the company has paid a total of $250 000 to this vendor through fake invoices. This is an example of fraud in the:
- (a) revenue cycle.
- (b) inventory management cycle.
- (c) expenditure cycle.
- (d) cash receipts cycle.

16.8 Which of the following is not needed for a fraudulent act?
- (a) A reason
- (b) Pressure
- (c) A system with weak internal controls
- (d) An opportunity

# PROBLEMS

**16.1** For each of Coles, David Jones, Telstra and Bunnings, (or, in New Zealand: Progressive Enterprises (Foodtown), Farmers, Telecom and Placemakers) go to the company's website and answer the following questions:

(a) Does the company have a privacy policy that relates to customers and data gathered from customers?

(b) Does it disclose the use of cookies on its page?

(c) Is there an option for the user to disable cookies?

(d) Does the company disclose how data gathered will be used? Does it expressly rule out the possibility of the data being given to third parties for purposes other than that for which it was originally gathered?

**16.2** SellItNow is an online company that sells hardware products for new houses to both industrial clients and individual consumers. As a result of its very competitive price schemes, SellItNow has developed an extensive customer base, which is reflected in its burgeoning database of customer details, purchasing history and internet usage data. Recognising that these data are potentially valuable to third parties, SellItNow's directors discuss the prospect of selling its customer database to a large insurance company, thus allowing the insurance company to target advertising and mailouts about home and contents insurance packages to new home buyers. The directors are split on the issue — some view this as an exciting way to add value to their customers, through complementary product offerings, while others see it as a gross misuse of information that is not in keeping with the original purpose for which the data were gathered.

You have been engaged by SellItNow as an ethics consultant and requested to advise it on the possibilities that exist to resolve the boardroom debate.

**Required**

Work through the steps of the ethical decision-making model and evaluate what SellItNow should decide and what it should do.

**16.3** Refer to AIS focus 16.1 (page 711), which discussed the use of microchipping technology in humans. Analyse this case and identify the ethical issues involved from the point of view of the individual and society. Is this technology an invasion of individual privacy? Discuss the advantages and disadvantages and potential applications of the system.

**16.4** For each of the examples of fraud mentioned in the chapter (see page 729), discuss:

(a) what fraud is occurring

(b) why this is a problem

(c) some control plans that may help reduce the likelihood of this fraud occurring.

**16.5** You work as the credit manager for Broad Sounds, a music store that supplies recording equipment and performance apparatus to bands and DJs. Your job is to ensure that data on customer credit ratings, credit limits and credit history are maintained accurately and completely, because these records are consulted before the sales staff approve a sale.

Mollie, a new young DJ in the area, has recently purchased a large amount of equipment from your company and has almost used up all of her credit limit. Because she is a new customer to the organisation, Broad Sounds is reluctant to extend her credit limit any further. The DJ contacts you directly and asks you to either increase her credit limit or create a new account for her under her personal name, rather than her business name, so she can purchase a new turntable to develop her business. You are confident of her ability to repay the credit purchases but feel bound by company credit policy, which clearly states how and when credit limits should be increased. When you joined Broad Sounds it was mentioned to you that company policies form part of your terms and conditions of employment. You tell Mollie this and she says, 'Look, OK — do it and I will promote your services at my gigs. Or I can pay you some cash now to make it worth your while.'

   (a) Analyse the scenario above using the ethical decision-making model presented in the chapter.

   (b) What would you do in this situation?

   (c) If the credit manager went ahead with these actions, would it be a case of computer crime?

   (d) Would it be ethical?

16.6 'Ethical behaviour is all about following the law.' Do you agree with this statement? Why?

## FURTHER READING

Albrecht, WS & Albrecht, C 2004, *Fraud examination and prevention*, Thomson South Western, Ohio.

Culnan, MJ 1993, — '"How did they get my name?": an exploratory investigation of consumer attitudes toward secondary information use', *Management Information Systems Quarterly*, vol. 17, no. 3, pp. 341–61.

Internet Industry Association 2001, 'Internet Industry Association privacy code of practice: consultation draft 1.0 — a code for industry co-regulation in the area of privacy', www.iia.net.au.

Smith, HJ & Hasnas, J 1999, 'Ethics and information systems: the corporate domain', *Management Information Systems Quarterly*, vol. 23, no. 1, pp. 109–27.

## SELF-TEST ANSWERS

16.1 d, 16.2 a, 16.3 d, 16.4 d, 16.5 a, 16.6 d, 16.7 d, 16.8 c

## END NOTES

1. Clarke, R 1988, 'Just another piece of plastic for your wallet: the 'Australia Card' scheme', *Computers and Society*, vol. 18, no. 1, pp. 7–21; Clarke, R 1988, 'The Australia Card — Postscript', *Computers and Society*, vol. 18, no. 3, pp. 10–13.

2. For example, Greenleaf, G 1987, 'The Australia Card: towards a national surveillance system', *Law Society Journal* (NSW), vol. 25, no. 9, October 1987.

3. Smith, HJ & Hasnas, J 1999, 'Ethics and information systems: the corporate domain', *Management Information Systems Quarterly*, vol. 23, no. 1, pp. 109–27.

4. Culnan, MJ 1993, "How did they get my name?': an exploratory investigation of consumer attitudes toward secondary information use', *Management Information Systems Quarterly*, vol. 17, no. 3, pp. 341–61.

5. Dickins, J 2002, 'Telstra's not so silent lines', *Herald Sun*, 12 August, p. 3.

6. DoubleClick, www.doubleclick.com.

7. DoubleClick, 'Privacy', www.doubleclick.com.

8. Rodger, W 2000, 'DoubleClick privacy dust-up may draw regulators' eye', *USA Today*, 2 February, p. 03.D.

9. Tobias, Z 2000, 'Putting the ethics in e-business', *Computerworld*, www.computerworld.com.

10. Bloomberg News 2001, 'DoubleClick privacy lawsuit dismissed', *New York Times*, late edn, East Coast, 31 March, p. C.4.

11. Phillips, G 2004, 'Chipping away our privacy', *Herald Sun*, 21 October, p. 21. Reproduced with permission. (Graham Phillips is a science writer and reporter on ABC TV's Catalyst.)

12. Loeb, MP 2004, 'The cost of cybercrime', *Network Magazine*, vol. 19, no. 4, p. 47.
13. *Privacy Act 1988*, s. 6C.
14. 'FlyBuys Policy on Information Privacy', www.flybuys.com.au.
15. Progressive Enterprises Ltd 2009, 'Legal', www.progressive.co.nz
16. Internet Industry Association 2001, 'Internet Industry Association privacy code of practice: consultation draft 1.0 — a code for industry co-regulation in the area of privacy', www.iia.net.au.
17. Internet Industry Association 2001, 3.2 a–c.
18. Internet Industry Association 2001, s. 6.
19. International Telecommunications Union 2008, www.itu.int.
20. International Telecommunications Union 2008.
21. Curtin, J 2001, Current issues brief no. 1 2001–02: a digital divide in rural and regional Australia?, Department of the Parliamentary Library, Information and Research Services, Commonwealth of Australia.
22. Anderton, Jim 2006, 'Address to TUANZ Rural Broadband Symposium', 30 March, www.beehive.govt.nz.
23. Department of Communications, Information Technology and the Arts 2005, *The Current State of Play 2005*, Department of Communications, Information Technology and the Arts, Australian Government, p. 8.
24. Department of Communications, Information Technology and the Arts 2005, p. 13.
25. Curtin 2001, p. 15.
26. Senator The Hon. Helen Coonan 2007, 'Australia connected: fast affordable broadband for all Australians', 18 June, www.minister.dcita.gov.au/coonan.
27. Senator The Hon. Stephen Conroy 2007, 'Government committed to FTTN national network', 7 December, www.minister.dbcde.gov.au.
28. Senator The Hon. Stephen Conroy 2009a, 'New National Broadband Network', 7 April, www.minister.dbcde.gov.au.
29. Senator The Hon. Stephen Conroy 2009b, 'Stage 1 of the National Broadband Network rollout in Tasmania begins', 16 July, www.minister.dbcde.gov.au.
30. Cohan, JA 2002, '"I didn't know" and "I was only doing my job": has corporate governance careered out of control? A case study of Enron's information myopia', *Journal of Business Ethics*, vol. 40, no. 3, p. 287.
31. Straub, DW & Collins, RW 1990, 'Key information liability issues facing managers: software piracy, proprietary databases, and individual rights to privacy', *Management Information Systems Quarterly*, vol. 14, no. 2, pp. 143–56.
32. Corbiun 1998.
33. Mogul, F 2000, 'Rise of the CPO', *Internet World*, vol. 6, no. 21, pp. 35–8.
34. Mogul 2000, p. 36.
35. Smith & Hasnas 1999.
36. Smith & Hasnas 1999.
37. Healy, M & Iles, J 2002, 'The establishment and enforcement of codes', *Journal of Business Ethics*, vol. 39, no. 1/2, p. 122.
38. Healy & Iles 2002, pp. 117–24.
39. Healy & Iles 2002, p. 121.
40. Healy & Iles 2002, p. 122.
41. Hsu, MH & Kuo, FY 2003, 'The effect of organisation based self-esteem and deindividuation in protecting personal information privacy', *Journal of Business Ethics*, vol. 42, no. 4, pp. 305–20.
42. Hsu & Kuo 2003, pp. 305–20.
43. Cohan 2002, p. 276.
44. Cohan 2002, p. 277.
45. Lacayo, Richard and Amanda Ripley, 2002, 'Persons of the Year 2002: Cynthia Cooper, Coleen Rowley and Sherron Watkins', *Time*, 22 December, www.time.com.

46. De Paula, 2004, 'One man's trash is . . . dumpster-diving for disk drives raises eyebrows', *USBanker*, vol. 114, no. 6, p. 12.

47. Transparency International 2008, '2008 corruption perceptions index ("cpi 2008 table")', www.transparency.org.

48. McKenna, M & Elks, S 2009, 'Corrupt ex-minister Gordon Nuttal in jail facing extra charges', *The Australian*, 16 July, www.theaustralian.com.au.

49. *The New Zealand Herald* 2009, 'Guilty verdicts for Taito Phillip Field', 4 August, www.nzherald.co.nz.

50. ACA 2004, 'MR06/2004: Australia joins international anti-spam campaign', media release no. 06, 30 January 2004, www.acma.gov.au.

51. Wilson, E 2003, 'Working to minimize the risks involved in doing business through email', *The Age, Next*, 5 August 2003, p. 6.

52. Quoted by Hendery, S, *NZ Herald*, 8 February, 2007, p. C4.

53. ACMA, Spam: Consumer information, www.acma.gov.au.

54. Wolfe, D 2004, 'In brief: theft target: checking accounts', *American Banker*, vol. 169, no. 115, p. 12.

55. Varghese, S 2004, 'Westpac online customers fazed by pop-ups', *The Age*, 15 September, theage.com.au.

56. Dearne, K 2003a, 'Putting hacking skills to work', *The Australian*, IT Business section, 28 October, p. 4.

57. Dearne, K 2003b, 'Hire a hacker', *The Australian*, IT Business section, 28 October, pp. 1, 4.

58. Dearne 2003b, pp. 1, 4.

59. SAI Global Certification Register, www.saiglobal.com.

60. James, ML 1999, 'Electronic commerce: security issues', Science, Technology, Environment and Resources Group, research paper 12, 1998–99, Parliament of Australia Parliamentary Library, www.aph.gov.au, p. 13.

61. Dearne 2003a, p. 4.

62. Deare, S 2007, 'PM "heart attack" email dupes bank customers', 20 February, www.silicon.com. Reproduced with permission.

63. James 1999.

64. Derived from Christensen, J & Byington JR 2003, 'The computer: An essential fraud detection tool', *The Journal of Corporate Accounting and Finance*, vol. 14, no. 5, pp. 23–7.

65. Developed from Albrecht, WS & Albrecht, C 2004, *Fraud examination and prevention*, Thomson South Western, Ohio; Singleton, T, King, B, Messina, FM & Turpen, RA 2003, 'Pro-ethics activities: do they really reduce fraud?', *The Journal of Corporate Accounting and Finance*, vol. 14, no. 6, pp. 85–94.

66. For example, Albrecht & Albrecht 2004; Singleton & King et al. 2003, pp. 85–94.

67. Singleton & King et al. 2003.

68. Greenwood, E 1957, 'Attributes of a profession', *Social Work*, vol. 2, no. 3, pp. 45–55; Klegon, D 1978, 'The sociology of professions: an emerging perspective', *Sociology of Work and Occupations*, vol. 5, no. 3, pp. 259–83.

69. Foley, S 2009, 'No mercy for Madoff', *The New Zealand Herald*, 1 July, www.nzherald.co.nz.

70. Timmins, N 2009, 'Record total of fraud cases in court — and worse to come', *Financial Times*, 20 July, www.ft.com.

71. www.aciworldwide.com.

72. KPMG Australia, 'KPMG fraud survey 2008', kpmg.com.au.

73. KPMG Australia, p. 6.

74. KPMG Australia, p. 16.

75. KPMG Australia, p. 6.

76. KPMG Australia, p. 17–8.

77. KPMG Australia, p. 16.

**CHAPTER 16** ››››ETHICS, FRAUD AND COMPUTER CRIME ››››› **741**

78. KPMG Australia, p. 26.
79. KPMG Australia, p. 18.
80. KPMG New Zealand, 'Fraud survey 2008: a New Zealand perspective', kpmg.co.nz.
81. KPMG Australia, p. 19.
82. KPMG Australia, p. 20.
83. KPMG Australia, p. 23.
84. KPMG Australia, p. 20.
85. Tiffen, R 2009, '$6m runaways have head start', *The New Zealand Herald*, 22 May, www.nzherald.co.nz.
86. Fisher, D 2009, '$10m fugitive drinking beer, enjoying heat', *The New Zealand Herald*, 24 May, www.nzherald.co.nz.
87. Beck, V & Tiffen, R 2009, 'Bank hits back at millionaire runaways', *The New Zealand Herald*, 24 May, www.nzherald.co.nz.
88. *The New Zealand Herald* 2009, 'Bank worker responsible for $10m blunder sacked', 9 August, www.nzherald.co.nz.
89. *The New Zealand Herald* 2009, 'What would you do if a banking blunder made you a multi-millionaire?', 21 May, www.nzherald.co.nz.
90. US Securities and Exchange Commission, 'Spotlight on Sarbanes Oxley Rulemaking and Reports: Management's Reports on Internal Control Over Financial Reporting and Certification of Disclosure in Exchange Act Periodic Reports', Release no. 33-8238, www.sec.gov.
91. Sarbanes–Oxley Act, s. 302.
92. Singleton & King et al. 2003.
93. Christensen & Byington 2003.

# ›› GLOSSARY ››››

**accounting information system** ›› The application of technology to the capturing, verifying, storing, sorting and reporting of data relating to an organisation's activities   p. 14

**accuracy** ›› The aim of making sure that all data that enters the system is correct and reflects the actual events that are being recorded   p. 331

**agile/adaptive methods** ›› An alternative approach to systems development that involves short, team-based efforts whereby a small amount of functionality is built designed and tested   p. 650

**analytical review** ›› A process that involves analysing transactions in a database and identifying relationships   p. 693

**application controls** ›› Controls that are designed for a specific business process or application   p. 332

**attest service** ›› An independent accountant expressing a written opinion about the reliability of a written assertion prepared by another party   p. 669

**attributes** ›› Characteristics of entities   pp. 122, 146

**audit** ›› An examination of financial statements by an independent expert, with a view to forming an opinion as to their accuracy and reliability, and reporting thereon   p. 668

**audit trail** ›› A traditional method that auditors used to follow a paper 'audit trail' from source documents to final accounts and vice versa   p. 675

**Auditing and Assurance Standards Board (AUASB)** ›› An independent statutory body and the national auditing and assurance standards setter that develops high-quality standards and related guidance for auditors and providers of other assurance services   p. 670

**Australian Auditing Standards (ASAs)** ›› Official, legally binding auditing standards, issued by the Australian Auditing and Assurance Standards Board, which set out audit requirements for listed companies under the Corporations Act   p. 671

**authorisation** ›› Ensuring users have correctly defined access to information within a system and that transactions are executed and recorded by people with the appropriate authority   p. 331

**automatic reorder points** ›› An inventory order point based on predefined minimum inventory levels recorded for individual items. When the stock on hand drops down to this level a purchase requisition is automatically generated   pp. 455, 510

**back order** ›› An order used where a customer has asked to purchase goods which the organisation does not currently have available. A back order records the customer request for the goods, with the intention of supplying the goods at a later date once they become available   p. 410

**back-end application software** ›› Software that is usually loaded onto the server to provide essential background services to clients   p. 181

**balanced data flow diagrams** ›› Diagrams (context diagram, physical DFD and logical DFD) with the same external entities and flows   p. 220

**barcode scanner** ›› A hand-held device used to scan and read a printed barcode   p. 495

**batch process** ›› A type of transaction processing where transactions are saved up until there are a number ready to be processed (a batch), then processed together. Batch processing is typically used to improve controls over data entry and provide efficiency gains. Batch processing is most useful where timeliness is not an issue as there is always some delay in processing transaction batches   p. 409

**batch processing** ›› Data from transactions are accumulated in a group or batch and processed together   p. 338

**batch total** ›› A total that is added to a batch of documents and is used to make sure that all documents in the batch have been correctly processed. A batch total is usually a summation of a data item with some meaning (e.g. a total of the individual invoice amounts for a batch of invoices). See also hash total   pp. 351, 423

**best practice** ›› The best way of performing a particular process   p. 62

**best-of-breed ERP systems** › › Systems provided by vendors that have the best modules for organisation-specific functional requirements. These modules must be integrated to function and coexist with other selected modules   p. 272

**bill of materials** › › A list of the items required to make a product   p. 497

**blind purchase order** › › A copy of the purchase order with quantities concealed, so as to force a count of goods received   p. 462

**bookkeeping systems** › › Systems that perform accounting functions that include cash receipts and payments, accruals such as accounts receivable and accounts payable, to provide reports on the performance of the organisation   p. 253

**bug correction** › › Involves fixing any errors in the system as a result of programming mistakes   p. 644

**business event data** › › Data that contain financial or non-financial reference information that records and tracks the status of business activities prior to completion   p. 266

**business function** › › A specific subset of the organisation that is designed to perform a particular task that contributes to the organisation achieving its objectives   p. 51

**business process** › › Any set of interlocking activities that work together, across the organisation, to achieve some predetermined organisational goal, which is typically defined around satisfying customer needs   pp. 53, 250

**business process design** › › The task of changing the operation of a business process in an organisation   p. 65

**business process re-engineering (BPR)** › › The fundamental rethinking and radical redesign of business processes to achieve dramatic improvements in critical contemporary measures of performance, such as cost, quality, service and speed   p. 66

**business requirements** › › The set of entities, outcomes and functionality required to successfully allow the business process to be performed   p. 256

**cardinality** › › The specific number of allowed entity occurrences associated with a single occurrence of the related entity by assigning a specific value to connectivity   p. 122

**cash budget** › › A budget showing forecast levels of future cash flows into and out of the organisation   p. 444

**CATTs** › › The tools and techniques used to directly examine the internal logic of an application as well as the tools and techniques used to indirectly draw inferences upon the application's logic by examining the data processed by the application   p. 678

**cheque endorsement** › › Stamped or writing on a cheque to stop the cheque being diverted to a different bank account than that intended. An endorsement often is written as, for example, 'Not Negotiable — pay only to Smith & Co'   p. 423

**client** › › A computer that requests services from a server   pp. 114, 180

**client–server hardware architecture** › › Computers that are assigned client and server functions   p. 260

**client–server system** › › A computing model that is based on distributing functions between two types of independent and autonomous processes: servers and clients. A client is a computer that requests services from a server. A server is a computer that has special processing functions that provide requests for clients   pp. 120, 180

**cold site** › › An available office with basic telephone and electricity supplies ready for use should they be required   p. 358

**communications middleware** › › Software that holds different types of software that aid the transmission of data and control of information between the client and server   p. 181

**completeness** › › The aim of ensuring that all events that occur are recorded within the system   p. 331

**composite key** › › A combination of more than one primary key. It indicates an M:N (many-to-many) relationship between the columns   pp. 110, 147

**computer aided manufacturing (CAM) systems** › › Software that is used to automate production machinery, allowing better control and more reliable outputs   p. 495

**computer platforms** › › Operating systems underlying the network of computers within the organisation   p. 260

**computer-aided software engineering (CASE) systems** › › Software packages that can help in the various stages of systems development, but particularly in the design of source code and user documentation   p. 654

**conceptual models** › › Models that focus on a logical view of what is represented in the database   p. 117

**configurability** › › The ability to transform data and define new relationships and structures that are required for an organisation   p. 275

**context diagram** › › A representation of the system of interest and the entities that provide inputs to, or receive outputs from, the system of interest   p. 195

**control activities** › › The responses by management to the risks identified as part of the risk management stage   p. 307

**control environment** › › The attitude, emphasis and awareness of an organisation's management towards internal control and its operation within the organisation   p. 305

**controlled redundancies** › › Redundancies that are allowed for the convenience of structuring data, data manipulation or reporting   pp. 137, 114

**conversion process** › › The process of moving data from legacy systems to a newly implemented system   p. 274

**cookies** › › Small files stored on a computer's hard drive that keep a record of websites viewed, viewing preferences and user profiles   p. 710

**corporate governance** › › The way companies are managed to create value, enforce accountability and control, and manage risks   p. 287

**corrective controls** › › Controls designed to correct an error or irregularity after it has occurred   p. 334

**cross-functional business processes** › › Business processes that require inputs from separate functions in the organisation including manufacturing, finance, sales and marketing   p. 259

**customer profiling** › › A process where data on a customer's website viewing habits are used to build a profile of their interests, needs and preferences, which can then be used for targeted advertising   p. 710

**customer relationship management (CRM)** › › Software designed with the specific purpose of viewing the organisation's data from a customer centric perspective that monitor and help the management of customer interactions with the organisation. Examples include Siebel and SAP   pp. 268, 397

**data** › › Raw facts relating to or describing an event   pp. 9, 107

**data analysis** › › The act of determining the type of data and the relationships that exist between the data of an organisation   p. 271

**data anomalies** › › Inconsistencies or errors that exist in a database because of entry or changes   p. 113

**data capture** › › The collection of the four dimension of any business activity (who, what, where and when) so that the organisation can aggregate and summarise data in various forms to answer the questions that a decision maker is asking   p. 263

**data flow diagrams (DFDs)** › › Graphical representations of the data flows that occur within a system   p. 195

**data integrity** › › Data that provide a consistent and correct representation regardless of where they are sourced from within a file system   p. 113

**data mining** › › A data analysis technique where large amounts of data are taken and analysed for potential patterns and relationships that may exist   p. 710

**data redundancy** › › The situation where exactly the same data are recorded and stored in multiple locations, which can lead to data inconsistency and anomalies   p. 112

**data transformation** › › The process of converting data in one format to another for the purpose of transformation or integration   p. 275

**database** › › A shared computerised structure that captures, stores and relates data   pp. 108, 252

**database administrator** › › A person who controls access by users to the database, maintains the data dictionary and oversees backup and recovery in the DBMS   p. 117

**database management system (DBMS)** › › A group of programs that manipulate the database and provide the interface between the database and the user as well as other application programs   pp. 114, 252

**database models** › › Diagrams of data entities and their relationships   p. 117

**database system** › › A system of hardware, software, people, procedures and data that allow the capture, storage, management and use of data within a database environment   p. 114

**decomposing (stepwise refinement)** › › The process of breaking a logical DFD down to a lower level to extract more detail about a process within the diagram   p. 209

**deindividuation** › › How anonymous a person perceives their actions to be   p. 720

**deletion anomalies** › › Data anomalies that can occur when the deletion of data about an entity inadvertently deletes data about another entity   p. 113

**dependent slack** › › The slack available at a step in the process when it is dependent on the timing of an earlier step   p. 657

**detective controls** › › Designed to alert those involved in the system when an error or anomaly occurs   p. 333

**direct conversion** › › Involves switching off an old system and immediately switching on a new system   p. 641

**direct debit form** › › A bank form containing the bank account numbers of employees and the amounts to pay to them. By an employer submitting this form to the bank, employees will have the amounts they are to be paid debited directly to their bank accounts on the following day   p. 542

**disaster recovery plan** › › The strategy that the organisation will put into action, in the event of a disaster that disrupts normal operations, to resume operations as soon as possible and recover data that relate to its processes   p. 357

**electronic data interchange (EDI)** › › A bespoke link that enables exchange of data between two separate computer systems. It is used when transaction flow and volume is large and transaction syntax is predictable   pp. 272, 397, 444

**embedded audit software** › › Software written by or for the auditor and embedded into the client's computer system   p. 680

**employee details amendment form** › › A form that allows the employees to change their personal and employment details   p. 550

**employee employment master file** › › A file that stores employment related information of an employee such

as employment start date, pay rate, employment award scheme and long service leave entitlements   p. 550

**employee performance review** › › Employers use this form to review an employee's job performance   p. 552

**employee personnel master file** › › A file that stores personal information of employees such as their name, age, sex, addresses and other contact details   p. 550

**enterprise resource planning (ERP) system** › › An integrated suite of software that records and manages many different types of business transactions within a single integrated database. Examples include SAP and Oracle   pp. 396, 444, 495, 542, 575

**enterprise risk model (ERM)** › › A model that expands on internal control, providing a more robust and extensive focus on the broader subject of enterprise risk management   p. 317

**enterprise value chain** › › A series of activities that link sales and marketing with manufacturing, accounting and finance, and human resources within an organisation   p. 254

**entities** › › Representations of real-world things or objects that correspond to a table in a relational database   pp. 122, 146, 200

**entity-relationship model** › › A data model that graphically depicts relationships between entities and attributes   p. 121

**ERP systems** › › Software designed to capture a wide range of information about all key business events including accounting and finance, human resources, sales and marketing, and manufacturing   p. 254

**error routine** › › A routine that is performed when the system does not function as is normally expected   p. 234

**ethics** › › The term given to the implicit rules that guide us in our everyday behaviour, thoughts and actions   p. 706

**examination** › › Includes a careful study and evaluation by the auditor of the financial statements, the underlying records traced back to the source documents, and the system(s) used to prepare these statements   p. 668

**exception report** › › A report type that is designed specifically to identify exceptions for particular transactions. An example is a report identifying any sales orders which have been shipped but not billed, or a report identifying all customers who have overdue accounts receivable accounts   pp. 407, 458, 506, 594

**eXtensible Business Reporting Language (XBRL)** › › A data standard used when generating financial reports   p. 575

**eXtensible Markup Language (XML)** › › A hypertext language which is used to add syntax to strings of data by embedding semantic tags. Useful for transaction processing where the data syntax is predictable and well defined   pp. 272, 397

**external entity** › › Any entity that provides inputs into a process or receives outputs from a process   p. 201

**external environment** › › The factors or pressures outside a system that influence its design and operation   p. 13

**feasibility analysis** › › Involves the evaluation of the alternatives identified to determine whether they are legitimate options for the business to consider at later stages of the development   p. 628

**feedback** › › The method using alerts to ensure that the system is running as normal and that there are no problems or exceptional circumstances   p. 13

**field** › › A characteristic of a record that contains data that have a specific meaning   pp. 109, 146

**file** › › is a collection of records that are related   p. 109

**financial feasibility** › › Assessment of the costs involved in adopting a new system, systematically compared with the financial benefits of a new system   p. 629

**finished goods** › › Goods available for sale to customers, that is, the final results of the manufacturing process   p. 492

**flexible manufacturing systems (FMS)** › › Systems used during production execution that are designed to respond to any changes detected during production; that is, they make production more flexible   p. 495

**foreign key** › › An attribute whose values must match the primary key in another table   pp. 129, 152

**fraud** › › An act of deception committed by someone against another entity, usually with the intent of either causing damage to the victim or bringing benefit to the perpetrator   p. 727

**front-end application software** › › Software that is usually loaded onto the client computers as the means for the users to interact with the server as part of the client process   p. 181

**functional perspective** › › A view of organisational design that emphasises hierarchical reporting roles, narrowly specified worker roles and an emphasis on departments   p. 50

**Gantt charts** › › A graphical way of planning and controlling the progress of a systems development project   p. 630

**general controls** › › Controls that relate to the overall computerised information system environment   p. 331

**generalised audit software** › › Software designed to read and process data, typically from large databases, to perform a wide range of audit tasks   p. 680

**generally accepted accounting principles (GAAP)** › › Accepted conventions, rules and procedures that define accounting practice   p. 694

**hacking** › › Gaining unauthorised access to a system   p. 725

**hardware** › › Physical devices including the computer and network   pp. 114, 181

**hash total** › › A total that is similar to a batch total but the number that is added has no meaning by itself (e.g. a hash total of customer numbers). See also batch total   p. 423

**hot site** › › A separate facility located away from the organisation's usual premises that contains offices and the necessary equipment (such as IT, telecommunications and data) to get the business back up and running in a minimal amount of time after a disaster occurs   p. 358

**hybrid systems** › › Systems that integrate the operation of an organisation with the financial functions in the organisation   p. 253

**identity theft** › › The fraudulent theft and use of another person's personal information to obtain illegal benefit   p. 725

**implementation models** › › Models that show how the data are represented in the database including the structures implemented

**independent** › › A situation where an auditor is not the system under review, otherwise a partici and is able to state an adverse opinion freely as he or she has no financial or other interest in the outcome   p. 668

**independent reviews** › › A control tool where the work of one person is reviewed by another, thus creating accountability   p. 352

**independent slack** › › The slack available at a step in the process that is independent of any previous steps   p. 657

**information** › › Data or facts that are processed in a meaningful form   p. 107

**information overload** › › The situation where an individual has more information than is needed or is able to be processed in a meaningful way when working through a decision   p. 10

**information processing controls** › › Controls put in place within the organisation to work towards the accuracy, completeness and authorisation of transactions   p. 331

**information technology (IT)** › › Technology used to handle information and aid communication   p. 74

**inherent risk** › › The potential for fraudulent activity or serious and material errors in financial statements   p. 683

**input accuracy** › › The aim of ensuring all data entered into the system are correct   p. 337

**input completeness** › › The aim of ensuring all transaction events and all required data relating to those events are captured within the system   p. 337

**input controls** › › Controls with the aim of detecting errors or irregularities at the time data are first entered into the system   p. 334

**input validity** › › The aim of ensuring that data entered into the system are in the correct format and valid   p. 347

**inputs** › › Data and other resources that are the starting point for a system   p. 12

**insertion anomalies** › › Data anomalies that can occur when new data are entered into the customer file and not all occurrences are updated   p. 113

**intangible benefits** › › Benefits that are felt by an organisation but cannot be stated in actual dollar amounts   p. 276

**integrated test facility (ITF)** › › embedded audit software that simulates a client's system with 'dummy' records   A simple version of

**integration ability** › › The ability for the data to be transformed into a form to match a new database destination   p. 275

**internal control** › › The measures an organisation employs to help attain the objectives of efficient operations, reliable reporting and compliance with relevant laws   p. 302

**internal control questionnaire (ICQ)** › › A standard form used by an audit firm to evaluate internal control procedures comprising a checklist of questions for each business process   p. 684

**internal entity** › › An entity that processes or transforms the data within the business process of interest   p. 201

**International Accounting and Assurance Standards Board (IAASB)** › › A committee of the International Federation of Accountants, established to issue standards on auditing and reporting practices to improve the degree of uniformity of auditing practices and related services throughout the world   p. 671

**inwardly organised systems** › › Software that focuses on recording and monitoring all exchanges that occur within an organisation   p. 251

**just-in-time (JIT) supply chain** › › An inventory management strategy where the goal is to time the ordering of goods so they arrive just in time to be used, so as to reduce inventory holding costs   p. 447

**legacy systems** › › Hardware and software formats that exist within an organisation   p. 274

**legal feasibility** › › How the proposed system would operate given the legal environment faced by the organisation   p. 629

**level 0 data flow diagram** › › The highest level logical DFD providing an overarching view of the processes that occur   p. 212

**level 1 data flow diagram** › › The second level logical DFD that takes one of the process bubbles from the level 0 diagram and expands it to provide detail about the activities that occur within the process   p. 212

**logical data flow diagram** › › A diagram that illustrates the processes that take place within a system, the flows among these processes, and how these processes interact with the external entities that provide inputs to, or receive outputs from, the system of interest   p. 195

**logical perspective** › › An approach that is concerned with a design that is independent of the actual technology required for its implementation   p. 633

**logical representation** › › A model that represents data and their relationships independent of hardware and software. This representation can then be used to select a database management system (DBMS)   p. 117

**management information system** › › A system that provides information for decision making. Within the system are structures, relationships, databases and procedures   p. 278

**manufacturing resource planning (MRP) systems** › › Software that is used to calculate demand for products, and identify the raw materials required to produce those products   p. 495

**many-to-many relationships (N:M)** › › A relationship between two entities in which the cardinality of both entities in the relationship is many   pp. 128, 166

**master audit program (MAP)** › › A standardised program that has a large number of 'switches' that may be set to customise the program for the particular client system   p. 684

**master data** › › Data that contain completed transactional information, such as a sales transaction. The sales, accounts receivables and customer tables are updated to reflect the sales transaction   p. 266

**metric** › › A specific measure used for a particular purpose. An example of a metric is the number of bad debts the organisation has, which could be used to monitor accounts receivable or sales performance   pp. 429, 480, 528, 608

**modification anomalies** › › Data anomalies that can occur when a field value is changed and not all occurrences are updated   p. 113

**monitoring** › › Continually checking the control system to ensure that the risks it addresses are still relevant and the controls are operating effectively   p. 308

**morals** › › How a person approaches and responds to an ethical issue   p. 706

**networks** › › Connected computers and computer equipment in buildings around the world that enable electronic communications   p. 259

**normalisation** › › A set of rules and a process of assigning attributes to entities to eliminate repeating

groups and data redundancies, and form tables representing entities that promote structural and data independence   pp. 137, 144

**object oriented analysis methods** › › An alternative approach to systems development used when designing systems using objects   p. 650

**obligations** › › Requirements for a business to undertake or complete exchanges, such as paying amounts owing to suppliers   p. 251

**one-to-many relationship (1:N)** › › A relationship between two entities in which the cardinality of one entity in the relationship is one and the other entity's cardinality is many   pp. 127, 153

**online banking** › › An internet-based banking facility that allows organisations to manage and view their bank accounts online and conduct transactions such as transfers from those accounts   pp. 473, 575

**online data gathering and batch processing** › › Data from transactions are stored immediately but related data files are updated in a batch   p. 338

**online real-time data processing** › › Data from transactions are captured immediately and the associated data file is updated immediately   p. 338

**operating system** › › Computer programs that control hardware to interface with software application programs   p. 114

**organisational design** › › (also called organisational structure or hierarchy) The organisation of a business enterprise through the structure of the relationships, interactions and reporting responsibilities among staff   p. 50

**organisational fit** › › How well the technology is aligned with the overall organisational strategy and strategic priorities   p. 626

**organisational self-esteem** › › How well a person identifies and fits with the firm, its beliefs, culture, philosophy and operating style   p. 50

**output controls** › › Controls designed to protect the outputs of the system   p. 332

**outputs** › › What is obtained from a system, or the result of what the system does   p. 13

**outwardly organised systems** › › Software that focuses on recording and monitoring all exchanges that occur among organisations   p. 251

**parallel conversion** › › Involves running the new system and the old system together for a period of time, or operating them in parallel   p. 641

**partial dependency** › › A dependency based on only part of a composite primary key   p. 151

**payroll** › › A formal pay document that lists the hours worked by an employee, the rates of pay, taxes withheld, deductions and the amounts deposited in the employees' bank accounts   p. 540

**payroll imprest account** › › A special bank account used as a control to ensure the correct payroll amounts are paid   p. 554

**payslip** › › A document given to an employee as evidence of them being paid for the pay period that contains their personal details, gross pay calculation, taxes and deductions, net pay, leave entitlements and previous pay details   p. 554

**performance reviews** › › Activities that involve some form of review or analysis of performance   p. 331

**phased-in conversion** › › Involves a gradual implementation of the system throughout the organisation   p. 642

**phishing** › › A technique of online deception that has users go to a fraudulent website and leave personal details, which are then used for identity theft and deception   p. 724

**physical controls** › › Controls that are put in place to physically protect the resources of the organisation   p. 332

**physical data flow diagram** › › A diagram that provides details of the entities involved in a process and the flows between those entities, as well as their interaction with external entities   p. 195

**physical perspective** › › Requires the specification of the technical aspects of how a design will be achieved   p. 33

**physical representation** › › A model that presents all the database storage details, including all specifications for hardware and software   p. 117

**post-billing system** › › A billing system where the customer is billed for the goods after the goods are despatched   p. 407

**pre-billing system** › › A billing system where the customer is billed for the goods before the goods are

despatched. Payment should also be received before goods are despatched. Very common in online sales environments   p. 407

**preventive controls** › › Controls designed to stop errors or irregularities occurring   p. 333

**primary key** › › An attribute (or column) that uniquely identifies a particular object (or row)   pp. 110, 147

**procedures** › › The instructions and rules that govern the design and use of the software outside programming   p. 115

**process map** › › A simple graphical representation of a business process, detailing the activities that occur, the areas of the business responsible for completing the activities, and any decisions that need to be made as part of the process   p. 195

**processes** › › The sets of activities that are performed on the inputs into the system   p. 12

**processing controls** › › Controls that operate with the aim of detecting any errors or irregularities during the processing of data   p. 334

**programmed evaluation review technique (PERT) charts** › › A chart constructed through the identification of all the activities that must take place for the project to be successfully completed, with time allocations given to each activity, and activities sequenced based on necessary prerequisite and subsequent activities   p. 630

**prototyping approach** › › Involves the progressive building of models and allowing users to experience these models and provide feedback on their operation and suitability   p. 650

**purchase requisition** › › is an internal document used to indicate an approved request for goods or services. The purchase requisition is used to support the purchase order   p. 512

**quantifiable benefits** › › Benefits that can be stated in actual dollar amounts   p. 276

**raw materials** › › Items used in the manufacturing of products, for example, timber, paint and nails   p. 492

**reconciliation** › › An activity where two different sets of data that purport to represent one transaction or set of events are compared to see if they agree. A common example is a bank reconciliation, which reconciles the organisation's accounting records of cash inflows and outflows with the bank's record (i.e. a bank statement) pp. 397, 460, 575

**record** › › A connected set of fields that describe a person, place or thing pp. 109, 146

**relational database** › › A database that stores data in a number of tables pp. 108, 146

**request for proposal** › › (RFP) A document that outlines the specifications for the new system, with these documents being sent out to potential vendors p. 637

**RFID** › › A small plastic tag attached to an item that contains data about that item and is able to be scanned using an RFID reader pp. 444, 495

**risk assessment** › › The process of scanning the organisation and its environment for risks that could inhibit the attainment of the organisation's goals p. 306

**Sarbanes–Oxley Act** › › A US Act that requires generally higher standards of financial reporting. The Act is binding on subsidiaries of US companies p. 670

**schedule feasibility** › › The ability of the proposed solution to be implemented within the period of time that is specified by the organisation p. 630

**scientific management** › › An approach to job design that sees workers repeatedly perform narrowly defined tasks p. 50

**segregation of duties** › › The concept that certain key functions should not be performed by the same person p. 332

**server** › › A computer that has special processing functions that provide requests for clients pp. 114, 180

**service level agreement** › › Document specifying what responsibilities the software-as-a-service provider has and how these are to be fulfilled p. 647

**settlement terms** › › Payment terms negotiated with a supplier p. 442

**single-entry systems** › › Software that merely records transactions and obligations p. 252

**single-source ERP systems** › › Systems provided by a single vendor for an organisation that capture all the organisation's business requirements p. 272

**software** › › Computer programs that are written in programming languages or code and instruct the operations of a computer pp. 114, 181

**software applications** › › Computer programs that are written in programming languages or code that are used by organisations to capture their transactions and produce reports that are used for planning, decision making and statutory reporting p. 250

**software selection** › › The act of selecting software to satisfy systems requirements p. 256

**software-as-a-service provider (SP)** › › Companies that provide software applications that can be leased by a range of clients p. 647

**spam** › › The sending of unsolicited emails or junk email p. 723

**status code** › › A code on transactions that are moving through an iteration of a process indicating which stage of the process the transaction is at. As an example, a sales transaction may be first 'created', then 'picked', then 'packed' then 'shipped' then 'paid'. When each of these relevant activities has been completed the status of the transaction is changed to reflect the new status pp. 415, 446, 594

**strategic feasibility** › › How well the proposed systems development alternative fits in with the organisation's existing operating environment and strategy p. 630

**streamlining** › › The act of making business processes within organisations efficient, effective and seamless in their execution p. 253

**structural independence** › › A data attribute that exists when changes in the database structure do not affect access p. 119

**structured narration** › › A written description of how a process operates p. 201

**structured query language (SQL)** › › A database query language that allows the user to specify what must be done without having to specify how it is to be done p. 117

**supply chain** › › An integration of suppliers and customers with the aim of producing and distributing goods and services by quantity, location and time to minimise costs and satisfy required service levels. Specialised software in this area is known as supply chain management software (SCM) p. 444

**supply chain management (SCM)** › › Systems that monitor and assist the management of supplier interactions with the organisation p. 268

**system** › › Something that takes inputs, applies a set of rules or processes to the inputs and generates outputs   p. 12

**system improvement** › › Involves adding new features or functions to the system, thus increasing its potential usefulness   p. 644

**system modification** › › Involves taking an existing feature and altering or changing it   p. 644

**system of interest** › › The system or process that is the focus of the documentation; it will have a clear boundary or scope   p. 195

**system scope** › › The domain or problem that a system addresses   p. 13

**systems control and review file (SCARF)** › › A sophisticated example of embedded audit software that involves continuous review of all transactions passing through the client's system   p. 680

**systems development scope** › › Defining what problems the systems development project will cover   p. 628

**systems development steering committee** › › Responsible for determining whether the systems development project should proceed; members typically occupy positions of power throughout the organisation   p. 631

**systems flowchart** › › A flowchart that illustrates a system and its inputs, processes and outputs in more detail than a process map or DFD, providing information about the documents and processes performed within the system, as well as who is involved in the system   p. 195

**systems requirements** › › The software applications that are required to fulfil the business requirements   p. 256

**table** › › A collection of columns (attributes) and rows (objects) that describe an entity   pp. 108, 146

**technical feasibility** › › The assessment of how well the organisation's existing technology infrastructure meets the requirements of the proposed alternative   p. 630

**test deck (test data)** › › A name referring to the deck of punched cards originally used by the auditor to test the integrity of the program and systems, and the information contained within them   p. 679

**timeliness** › › The aim of ensuring that information and data are available for users when required   p. 338

**timesheet** › › A document that records an employee's hours worked, is submitted to the departmental supervisor for approval and is used in calculating payroll   p. 539

**total cost of ownership** › › The need to consider not just the initial costs of installing a system but also the ongoing costs following the implementation of a system   p. 629

**Total Quality Management (TQM)** › › A progressive approach to organisational change that works on the principle that a series of small progressive steps is the best way to improve operations   p. 65

**transactions** › › Any business-related exchange, such as the sale of products to customers or payment to suppliers   p. 251

**transitive dependency** › › A dependency that occurs when one attribute is dependent on another, but neither is part of a primary key   p. 151

**true and fair view** › › A legally required and binding statement from an auditor attesting to the accuracy of a company's financial statements for the period under review   p. 694

**turnaround document** › › A document that is printed with a separate section designed to be detached, completed and returned to the issuing organisation. Examples include a tear-off section on a delivery docket which is signed and returned to a courier   p. 420

**vendor selection** › › The act of choosing a vendor that will provide the software to satisfy systems requirements   p. 257

**vendor-managed inventory** › › A system that involves the buyer transferring to the seller the responsibility for determining what, when and how much is purchased   p. 75

**whistleblowing** › › The reporting, by an employee or member of an organisation, of the unethical behaviour of a colleague   p. 720

**work in progress** › › Inventory while it is in the process of being manufactured. Also known as work in process   p. 497

# ›› INDEX ›››